THE LAW OF PROFESSIONAL-CLIENT CONFIDENTIALITY

THE LAW OF PROFESSIONAL–CLIENT CONFIDENTIALITY

REGULATING THE DISCLOSURE OF CONFIDENTIAL PERSONAL INFORMATION

ROSEMARY PATTENDEN

B. Comm, LLB (NSW), D. Phil (Oxon),
Professor of Law, University of East Anglia

For updates see: http://www.uea.ac.uk/law/resources/professional-client_index.htm

OXFORD
UNIVERSITY PRESS

OXFORD
UNIVERSITY PRESS

Great Clarendon Street, Oxford OX2 6DP

Oxford University Press is a department of the University of Oxford.
It furthers the University's objective of excellence in research, scholarship,
and education by publishing worldwide in

Oxford New York

Auckland Bangkok Buenos Aires Cape Town Chennai
Dar es Salaam Delhi Hong Kong Istanbul Karachi Kolkata
Kuala Lumpur Madrid Melbourne Mexico City Mumbai Nairobi
São Paulo Shanghai Taipei Tokyo Toronto

Oxford is a registered trade mark of Oxford University Press
in the UK and in certain other countries

Published in the United States
by Oxford University Press Inc., New York

© R Pattenden 2003

The moral rights of the author have been asserted
Database right Oxford University Press (maker)

First published 2003

Crown copyright material is reproduced under
Class Licence Number C01P0000148 with the permission of the
Controller of HMSO and the Queen's Printer for Scotland

All rights reserved. No part of this publication may be reproduced,
stored in a retrieval system, or transmitted, in any form or by any means,
without the prior permission in writing of Oxford University Press,
or as expressly permitted by law, or under terms agreed with the appropriate
reprographics rights organization. Enquiries concerning reproduction
outside the scope of the above should be sent to the Rights Department,
Oxford University Press, at the address above

You must not circulate this book in any other binding or cover
and you must impose this same condition on any acquirer

British Library Cataloguing in Publication Data

Data available

Library of Congress Cataloging in Publication Data

Data available

ISBN 0–19–826850–5

1 3 5 7 9 10 8 6 4 2

Typeset by Hope Services (Abingdon) Ltd
Printed in Great Britain
on acid-free paper by
Biddles Ltd., Guildford and King's Lynn

FOREWORD

For centuries the law has given some protection to personal information. 'The right of the people to be secure in their persons, houses, papers and effects' was of sufficient concern to be protected (against the state) in the Fourth Amendment to the Constitution of the United States. In the days when information could be widely disseminated only if it was recorded in printed form, protection of the property in the paper often provided protection to the information recorded on it.

Increasingly rapid developments in recent years have made such protection ineffective. Vast amounts of personal information are now easily recorded in digital or paper form, which can just as easily be copied and disseminated. And it is essential that such vast amounts of information be recorded. The means now available to meet the needs of individuals, through professional advice and services, have increased, are increasing, and, it is to be hoped, will continue to increase. But the provision of effective professional services depends on the recording of accurate and detailed personal information. And professional services can be delivered best not through one individual, as was often the case in the past, but through teams of specialists, all of whom must have access to the relevant information. So we all now extend to numerous strangers a degree of trust which many would not, in the past, have extended to any but their nearest relatives, even if to them.

The law must respond to this, and it has done so. There is now a mass of law and other sources of guidance on how such information is to be collected, stored and disclosed—not just statute and case law, but also guidance issued by regulatory bodies and other less formal sources. The solutions to the problems that arise could not be found in black letter law, even if that were remaining stable. In fact, influenced by the increasing regard being paid to human rights, the traditional sources of law are themselves changing and developing. Much work has been done in the past. There are chapters on confidentiality in books on professional negligence, and there are chapters on professional duties in books on confidentiality.

What this book does is of a different order. An exceptional range of source material is made available in a systematic and comprehensible form. Legal problems involving personal information commonly arise at short notice. Decisions have to be made with little time for research. Judges have commonly found themselves provided, either with little or nothing in the way of detailed reasoning, or with too many authorities for them to be able to digest in the short time available. This book contains in one place a very wide and deep discussion of the materials and issues on the subject. It will meet a real need. It is a pleasure to recommend it.

Michael Tugendhat
Royal Courts of Justice

PREFACE

This book, which is about professionals and the confidential personal information that they handle in their work, has had a long gestation period. During that time professional confidentiality has been subjected to attrition by a public sector that has built up an impressive arsenal of powers enabling personal information to be extracted from professionals and exchanged within the public sector without the consent of the source. This is not some conspiracy directed against professionals and their clients but part of a general trend. 'Information' is power: the more the government has the more effectively it thinks it can govern.

Simultaneously the government has pursued a policy of protecting personal information by enacting the Data Protection Act 1998, the Human Rights Act 1998 and a host of minor provisions. Since the Human Rights Act 1998 (which incorporates a right to respect for private life and correspondence) came into force, any interference with professional confidentiality by a public authority must be necessary for a legitimate aim and proportionate. The courts have also actively supported professional–client confidentiality: the House of Lords by conferring on legal professional privilege the attribute of a fundamental right and the Court of Appeal by liberating the breach of confidence action from a relationship of trust thereby providing protection against interception of confidential information. Both courts have advanced the cause of professional–client confidentiality by giving the Human Rights Act 1998 some horizontal effect.

The result of all this has been to make the law of professional–client confidentiality extremely complex; the law of confidentiality has become a multi-layered affair with rich pickings for lawyers. The aim of this book is to create a chart of the territory, locate it in its wider social context and to lay bare the trouble spots and the under-explored regions. The book is ambitious; it contains both academic analysis and black letter law of something that is evolving rapidly. Inevitably the book is flawed. It would be more so had I not been able to draw on advice from colleagues (none of whom share any responsibility for the errors and omissions that remain). I would like to thank Andrew Bainham, David Fox, Alastair Mullis, Gareth Miller, Yvonne Cripps, Ian Smith and Raymond Toney (who undertook research for me while pursuing his own unrelated studies in Oxford) for their thoughts and time. Michael Tugendhat kindly supplied me with the proofs of his book, useful judgments and comment on some issues. I have also greatly benefited from reading the discussions of data protection matters on the data-protection@JISCMAIL.ac.uk e-mail list and access to the Squire and University Libraries, Cambridge.

If this book were to be dedicated to anyone, it would have to be to the purveyors of ready-made meals and to Mrs N who maintained a semblance of order chez Pattenden. Without them my long-suffering family would have long ago mutinied and this book could not have been written.

The law set out in this book and the addendum is that available on 12 April 2003. A webpage containing updates of case law and secondary literature is available on http://www.uea.ac.uk/law/resources/professional-client_index.htm

Rosemary Pattenden
The Norwich Law School
University of East Anglia
1 May 2003

ADDENDUM

Douglas v Hello! Ltd [2003] EWHC 786 (Ch)

Judgment in *Douglas v Hello! Ltd* [2003] EWHC 786 (Ch) was delivered by Lindsay J. too late to include in the main text of this book. This judgment follows an earlier decision by the Court of Appeal (*Douglas v Hello! Ltd* [2001] 2 All ER 289) to lift an interim injunction prohibiting Hello! magazine from publishing unauthorized photographs of the Douglases' wedding and leave the Douglases and the magazine that had paid £1 million for the exclusive rights to the wedding photographs to pursue a claim in damages. Lindsay J. held that Hello!'s publication of the unauthorized photographs (which he found to have been taken with a hip camera by an intruder who had resorted to misrepresentation and subterfuge) constituted a breach of commercial confidence. '[T]he Claimants had here a valuable trade asset, a commodity the value of which depended at least in part upon its content at first being kept secret and then of its being made public in ways controlled by [the Douglases] for the benefit of them and of the third Claimant.' ([2003] EWHC 786 [196]). The award of compensation to the Douglases and to OK! magazine was deferred. The High Court judgment makes numerous contributions to the evolving law of confidentiality.

4.59 *Infringement of privacy: effect of the Human Rights Act 1998*

The Douglases and OK! magazine had a remedy within existing English law. It was therefore unnecessary to decide whether there was a free-standing law of privacy. The judgment refers to *Peck v UK* (Application 44647/98 28 January 2003), a successful application to the ECtHR by a complainant who, prior to the coming into force of the HRA, failed to obtain a remedy under domestic law for a breach of Article 8(1) when closed circuit television footage was disclosed by Brentwood Borough Council to the media. Lindsay J. said that if Parliament takes no action, the courts will be obliged to do something in the next case in which 'neither the law of confidence nor any other domestic law protects an individual who deserves protection'. Like Buxton L.J. in *Home Office v Wainwright* [2001] EWCA Civ. 2081 paras 110–111 and Liberty in its *Response to the Culture, Media and Sport Select Committee inquiry into privacy and media intrusion* (February 2003 available at http://www.liberty-human-rights.org.uk/resources/policy-papers/policy-papers-2003/pdf-documents/privacy-and-the-media.pdf), Lindsay J. would prefer to see a statutory privacy law to a judicially created one since Parliament can consult widely and is not obliged to create law 'bit by bit at the expense of litigants and with inevitable delays and uncertainty': ibid [229]. Query, is a court able to create a new cause of action to bridge the gap between English law and the ECHR or only to extend an existing cause of action? (see main text para **3.06 n27**). The opportunity to settle this may not arise very quickly. Today Peck would have a remedy against the Council under the HRA, s 7(1) and for many actions between private parties, as in *Douglas v Hello!*, an extension of the breach of confidence action will provide a solution.

5.06 *Elements of the action for breach of confidence: the Megarry test*

A commercial confidence with respect to visual appearance shares similarities to an intellectual property right; the big difference is that the former operates by reference to the conscience of the defendant: [2003] EWHC 786 (Ch) [215]. In other words equity does not intervene in aid of a property right but because of the intervention the confidence acquires some of the characteristics of property.

5.08 *Quality of confidentiality: information of a trivial character*

Triviality affects whether equity affords substantive relief in the particular case; it does not affect the existence of the confidence: ibid [193].

5.09 *Quality of confidentiality: information in the public domain*

Partial publicity does not result in wholesale loss of confidentiality: 'disclosure to the public of a chosen part can still leave rights in confidence in an unpublicized remainder': ibid [217] per Lindsay J.

5.17 *Quality of confidentiality: does information remain in the public domain forever?*

The eclipse of the unauthorized photographs by the publication of the much better authorized ones in OK! made it likely that the 'look' of the former had 'passed out of the public mind'. The claimants were therefore entitled to seek a perpetual injunction (or an undertaking in lieu) to prevent reuse of the unauthorized wedding photographs. 'It does not follow from the fact that an item has passed into the public domain that it must be taken to have remained there in such a way that its confidentiality has been irretrievably lost': ibid [278] per Lindsay J.

5.23 *Quality of confidentiality: obviously private information*

Lindsay J. ibid [188] may have agreed with the observation by Gleeson C.J. in *ABC v Lenah Game Meats Pty Ltd* [2001] HCA 63 that information is not private simply because it describes something that happened on private property and for that reason was not readily accessible to public gaze. But he did not think that he could decide whether the photographs had that quality of confidentiality needed to satisfy the first prong of the test laid down by Megarry in *Coco v AN Clark*

(Engineers) Ltd ([1969] RPC 41, 49 and para **5.06** main text) for determining trade secrets by using the Gleeson test for detecting 'private' information viz. whether 'disclosure or observation of information or conduct would be highly offensive to a reasonable person of ordinary sensibility'. According to Lindsay J., 'quality of confidentiality' has 'to do, and to do only, with whether the information is already public property and public knowledge. It is not concerned with whether or not the information is 'private' in the sense that its disclosure would be significantly harmful.' ([2003] EWHC 786 (Ch) [189]).

In this writer's view, it is doubtful whether significant harm from disclosure is essential for personal information to be considered private or to be the object of an obligation of confidentiality (see para **5. 41** main text) though it may affect the relief a court is prepared to give if it is (cp **6.16** below). Lindsay J.'s remarks about confidential quality depending exclusively on the information not already being 'public property and public knowledge' should be read in the light of his finding that the Douglases' appearance on their wedding day was a commercial confidence tantamount to a trade secret [ibid 227]. When (1) there has been no consensual dealing between claimant and defendant (a situation not envisaged in *Coco supra*) and (2) the personal information is not a commercial confidence, as a practical matter the first and second prongs of the Megarry test overlap (para **6.13** main text). For liability the personal information must be outside the public domain *and* be 'obviously confidential' (*Att-Gen v Guardian Newspapers Ltd (No.2)* [1983] 3 All ER 545, 658-9 and para **7.26** main text). Personal information is not 'obviously confidential' unless the defendant knew or should have known of the claimant's reasonable expectation of privacy in that information. (cp *A v B & C plc* [2002] EWCA Civ 337 [11 (ix)] per Lord Woolf, *Campbell v MGN* [2002] EWCA Civ 1373 para 40 per Lord Phillips).

5.43 *Who can bring an action for breach of confidence?*
A commercial confidence in personal information can be shared and enforced by a co-owner where the defendant knew or ought to have known of the co-owner's existence. Likewise the benefit of a commercial confidence can be assigned as a thing in action to a third party who can enforce it: ibid [187(ii)]. There is no suggestion that the benefit of non-commercial personal confidences can be assigned.

5.50 *Post-mortem legal protection of the equitable obligation of confidentiality*
fn 209: If commercially valuable personal information is shared or assigned, the co-owner or assignee can sue in respect of an unauthorized disclosure: ibid [187 (ii)].

5.59 *Effect of information entering the public domain: the general rule*
The right to confidence in personal information is not invariably lost by an intention to publish the information: ibid [210], [228]. Unauthorized publication of a

commercial confidence in advance of the date of intended publication is unconscionable: ibid [204,[213],[217],[224],[227].

6.16 *Reasonable expectation of privacy: the reasonable expectations test*

In the US private facts tort liability depends upon disclosure being highly offensive to the reasonable person (para **4.55** main text). The Court of Appeal has said as much (para **6.16 fn 63** and **6.24** main text). Lindsay J. considered that degree of offensiveness was relevant at the 'remedy or relief stage' (ibid [193]). This must be right when the complaint is about a commercial confidence which is devalued by publication. The Hello! Defendant's liability was therefore unaffected by the judge's conclusion that the publication (although it had offended the Douglases) was not 'highly offensive or offensive at all' (ibid [192]). Query, will substantive relief in cases involving unauthorized disclosure of non-commercial personal confidences depend (especially in cases where the injury is purely mental) upon the offensiveness of the disclosure? In determining offensiveness should the court take into account the manner in which the information was obtained? Since in the first case in which disclosure of personal information was enjoined, namely *Prince Albert v Strange* (1849) 41 ER 1171 (para **5.02** main text), the etchings and catalogue were not of themselves offensive but the probable manner of their obtaining was illicit, the answer to the second question is likely to be 'yes'.

6.24 *Reasonable expectation of privacy: what public figures can reasonably expect to remain confidential (private)*

'To hold that those who have sought *any* publicity lose all protection would be to repeal Article 8's application to very many of those who are likely most to need it' ibid [225] per Lindsay J.

6.26 *Detriment caused by unauthorized disclosure*

The judge found detriment in the distress caused to Mr and Mrs Douglas, 'who also had to re-arrange their plans for approval of the authorized photographs. They incurred expenses that would otherwise have been unnecessary' and they 'may also have suffered financial loss': ibid [199] per Lindsay J.

6.30 *Tort: breach of statutory duty*

fn 160: cp *Douglas v Hello! Ltd* [2003] EWHC 786 (Ch) [180(iii)],[239]

6.49 *Tort: conspiracy and interference with trade, business or economic interest*

Lindsay J. found that on the evidence the Hello! Defendants had no intention to spoil OK! magazine's sales and consequently could not be held liable for the tort of interfering with the OK! Claimants' business interests by unlawful means. It was accepted that contravention of the DPA or publishing in breach of an obligation of confidence were unlawful means [ibid 249].

Addendum

7.20 Client v third party: accessory liability of dishonest third party

Hello! knew that OK! had an exclusive contract to cover the wedding and must have known from its own experience that such a contract would include provisions to preclude intrusion and unauthorized photography: ibid [198]. The text of Hello! magazine had even spoken of the 'elaborate security procedures' adopted by the Douglases. Lindsay J. ruled that a third party such as Hello! is liable for a breach of confidence if that party 'received information with notice that he received it by way of a breach of confidence by the confidant . . . and [this] includes also cases where the third party has deliberately closed his eyes to the obvious': ibid [184].

7.31 Client v third party: defences (other than public interest): bona fide purchaser for value

A defence of *bona fide* purchaser for value is envisaged: ibid [208]. A right of confidence in commercially valuable photograph material may be very similar to an intellectual property right: see **5.06** above.

7.42 Professional v third party

Obtaining or encouraging someone else to obtain confidential personal information by deception is not *per se* a tortious interference with a contractual obligation to provide reasonable security for that information: ibid [241].

8.04 Permanent injunction: unavailability: information in public domain

On the possibility of information regaining the quality of confidentiality necessary to support a breach of confidence action see **5.17** above.

8.07 Permanent injunction: judicial discretion

The triviality of information is something to be considered at the relief stage: ibid [193] and **5.08** above.

8.13 Interim injunctions: media cases

Imminent authorized publication may make it harder to justify unauthorized publication: ibid [186(viii)] cp [204], [210].

8.14 Interim injunctions: 'particular regard' to freedom of expression

Freedom of expression does not take automatic priority over rights of confidence: ibid [186(v)]. If it did, it would be pointless of Article 10(2) to make freedom of expression subject to such a right. A right of confidence that is protected by Article 8 will have greater weight than one that is not: ibid [186(vii)].

8.21 The Woolf guidelines: criticism of the guidelines

In spite of evidence that Hello!'s readership was interested in the unauthorized photographs (ibid [205]) and their publication therefore protected the magazine's circulation (ibid [245]), counsel for the Hello! Defendants did not argue that there was any material public interest either within the general law or within the terms of the PCC's privacy code in publication of the unauthorized photographs: ibid [204].

8.25 *The Woolf guidelines: summary of relevant factors*

(11) imminence of authorized disclosure: cp ibid [186 (viii)].
fn 112: cp *Douglas v Hello* [2003] EWHC 786 (Ch) [205].
fn 113: A private place is a place in respect of which there is a reasonable expectation of privacy: ibid.

8.37 *'Damages' in Equity: breach of confidence*

The refusal of an interim injunction to restrain publication does not prevent post-disclosure recovery of compensation for injury caused by publication: ibid [209].

It does not follow from the presence of all the elements of a successful case in breach of confidence that substantive relief must follow: ibid [193], [202]. Intention to publish personal information is not a reason for refusing relief particularly when the case involves a commercial confidence: ibid [210].

8.42 *Heads of damage: tangible injury*

A claimant who succeeds with a claim for damages for breach of confidence and proves that the conduct also constitutes a contravention of the DPA will be awarded nominal damages for the DPA breach. To recover 'damage' under DPA, 13 the claimant must show that it was caused by the data controller's contravention of the DPA: [239]. Query, why did the judge allow nominal damages for the breach of the DPA when the judge was not satisfied about causation?

Lindsay J. acknowledged detriment to the Douglases in the shape *inter alia* of extra expenses and possible reduction in syndication receipts: ibid [199].

8.54 *Mental distress: policy considerations*

On the restriction of recovery to disclosures that are 'highly offensive' see **6.16** above.

8.58 *Mental distress: assessing damages for mental distress for breach of confidence*
fn 248: *Douglas v Hello* [2003] EWHC 786 (Ch) [202]–[203].

8.66 *Heads of damage: aggravated damages*
fn 273: cp *Douglas v Hello* [2003] EWHC 786 (Ch) [275].

Addendum

8.69 *Heads of damage: exemplary damages*

Lindsay J. assumed (ibid [272]) that equity could award exemplary damages.

9.10 *The PCC and privacy: privacy code*

Surreptitious non-consensual use of a short lens photography in a private place breaches the PCC's privacy code: ibid [205]. Imminent public disclosure may negate public interest in unauthorized publication (see **8.13** above).

11.08 *Nature of the public interest: defence or a limiting principle?*

The public interest is treated as a bar to relief: ibid [193].

18.05 *Introduction*

Digitally processed photographs are 'personal data' within the meaning of DPA, s.1(1): ibid 230.

18.07 *Scope of data protection: forms of data storage*

As regards transitional arrangements see **18.37** below.

18.08 *Personal data: processing the data*

'Processing' includes publishing digitally held personal data as hard copy and on a website: ibid [230], [231] and main text para **18.39**.

18.16 *Fair processing of personal data: significance of the method of obtaining*

fn 92: eg *Douglas v Hello* [2003] EWHC 786 (Ch) [236].

18.20(3) '*Conditions' permitting processing of personal data: problematic points*

The Hello! Defendants had a legitimate interest in publishing photographs of the Douglases wedding: ibid [238] Query, was this because the wedding was the sort of event that their readers expected Hello! to cover? Contrary, however, to Oliver's expectations, Lindsay J. did not adopt a proportionality test. He said that processing that causes any prejudice 'beyond the trivial' to the legitimate rights and interests of the data subject is 'unwarranted'. Para 6 does not require 'some general balance between freedom of expression and rights to privacy or confidence': ibid [238] per Lindsay J. Where there is a public interest in the processing of data by the press, this has to be considered under DPA, s 32. Since the judge was satisfied that the prejudice to the Douglases was 'substantial' this interpretation of para 6 is *obiter*.

The Douglases' contract with OK! magazine to publish the data did not affect their rights under the DPA: ibid [238].

18.37 *Exemptions*

Schedule 8 Parts II and III contain various transitional exemptions for the processing of manual and automated data 'which was already under way immediately before 24 October 1998' (Sch 8, Pt 1, para 1(1)). Lindsay J. thought that '"already underway" . . . suggest[s] a continuous process from the 24th October 1998 as would be the case where, for example, a running bank account was processed both before and after that date': ibid [233]. The fact that *other* photographs of the data subjects were processed before that date was irrelevant: 'photographs even of the same subjects are quite separate items of personal data in a way that, say, operations on a running bank account, where the balance at any time is dependent upon the cumulative effect of earlier transactions, are not' ibid [233].

18.38 *Exemptions: section 32 (journalism, literature, art)*

A reasonable belief by a media data controller that the public will be interested in personal data does not attract the DPA, s 32 exemption; 'that the public would be interested is not to be confused with there being a public interest' ibid [237] per Lindsay J.

Three Rivers District Council v Bank of England (No 5) [2003] EWCA Civ 474

16.17 *Legal advice privilege: what it is and when it arises*

A narrow view was taken of what constitutes the giving of legal advice. If the Court of Appeal was wrong, and Tomlinson J. right, about the scope of legal advice privilege (see **16.22** below), Longmore L.J. said that the Bank could not invoke the privilege because the documents (including those requested by the inquiry) were 'prepared for the dominant purpose of putting relevant factual material before the inquiry in an orderly and attractive fashion, not for the dominant purpose of taking legal advice upon such material': ibid [37] per Longmore L.J.

16.18 *Legal advice privilege: what it is and when it arises*

In an *obiter dictum* Longmore L.J. suggested that receipt by the legal adviser of a communication from the client seeking legal advice was unnecessary for legal advice privilege: ibid [21]. Loss of the communication in transit would therefore not prevent a privilege claim.

16.22 *Scope of litigation and legal advice privilege: derivative materials*

The client cannot claim legal advice privilege for preparatory work done before he communicates with the legal adviser where the preparatory work is by an employee. Tomlinson J., the judge at first instance ([2002] EWHC 2730) was wrong to hold that legal advice privilege applied to documents prepared by the client's employees with the dominant purpose of submission to the client's solicitors, whether or not those documents were actually communicated to the solicitors. There is no precedent for legal advice privilege to extend beyond communications passing between legal adviser and client (whether or not through an intermediary) and evidence of the contents of such communications: ibid [21]. *Wheeler v Le Marchant* (1881) 17 Ch D 675 is authority that documents from a third party to be shown to a solicitor for his advice are not within its scope. Information from an employee (or agent) must be treated in the same way as information from a third party. 'It may . . . be a mere matter of chance whether a solicitor, in a legal advice privilege case, gets his information from an employee or an agent or other third party. It may also be problematical . . . to decide whether any given individual is an employee or an agent and undesirable that the presence or absence of privilege should depend upon the answer' ibid [18] per Longmore L.J. The Court of Appeal's decision does not rule out a claim for legal advice privilege for client's own preparatory work undertaken with the dominant purpose of communicating its contents to the lawyer to obtain legal advice.

16.29 *Scope of litigation and legal advice privilege: death of the client*

The death of the client before the legal adviser receives a communication does not defeat legal advice privilege: ibid [21].

16.39 *Non-adversarial proceedings: litigation privilege*

The Bank accepted that this privilege is restricted to adversarial proceedings and did not extend it to documents prepared for the purposes of a private non-statutory inquiry set up by the Government.

16.46 *Privilege for non-lawyers: the English situation*

The Court of Appeal was conscious of the anomalous nature of legal professional privilege. Privilege has been refused in respect of all professionals save legal advisers. 'In these circumstances it is important that it be confined to its proper limits': ibid [26]. Doubt was expressed about the traditional rationale of legal advice privilege. 'It is by no means clear that, in the absence of contemplated litigation, there is any temptation for the client not to offer a clean breast to his legal adviser': ibid [26] per Longmore L.J. cp main text para 1.52. An alternative rationale is mentioned, namely that legal advice is a fundamental legal right, albeit one that can be overridden by legislation.

'Soft Law' Developments

The Council of Europe has produced a draft additional protocol to the Convention on Human Rights and Biomedicine (1997). This deals with many genetic confidentiality issues including consent, the position of those unable to consent, patient access to results, secure storage and genetic testing of the dead. The draft is available at the www.coe.int website.

Addendum

The NHS Information Authority (NHSIA) has begun a public consultation on a draft strategy for protecting patient confidentiality. This includes a Draft DoH *Confidentiality: A Code of Practice for NHS Staff* (October, 2002), a *Draft National Patient Information-Sharing Charter* (October, 2002) and a proposed confidentiality model, *Caring for Information: Model for the Future* (October, 2002) as well as the results of a survey NSIA, *Share with Care!* (October, 2002) that examines people's views on consent and confidentiality of patient information. Documents can be accessed from http://www.nhsia.nhs.uk/confidentiality/pages/default.asp.

Further updates of the book will be available at http://www.uea.ac.uk/law/resources/professional-client_index.htm. The author welcomes information for inclusion in the web update.

CONTENTS—SUMMARY

Addendum	ix
Tables of Cases	xxix
Table of Statutes	lxiii
Table of Statutory Instruments	lxxix
European Convention on Human Rights	lxxxv
Abbreviations	lxxxvii

PART I. INTRODUCTION

1. Definitions and Rationales	3
2. The Social Context	33
3. The Legal Framework	55

PART II. RESPONDING TO DISCLOSURE

4. Contract and Tort Solutions to Intentional Disclosure	99
5. Equity and Copyright Solutions to Intentional Disclosure	131
6. Dealing with Unintentional Disclosure	175
7. Suing and Tracing Third Parties and Strangers	231
8. Remedies	255
9. Alternatives to Litigation	295

PART III. DEFENCES

10. Compelled Disclosure	311
11. Disclosure in the Public Interest	337
12. Other Lawful Voluntary Disclosure	383
13. Consent	405

PART IV. CONFIDENTIALITY AND PRIVILEGE IN THE LITIGATION PROCESS

14. Investigations and Pre-Trial Disclosures	445
15. Trials, Tribunals and Inquiries	509
16. Grounds for Non-Disclosure	535
17. Protection of Privacy	577

PART V. RELATED MATTERS

18. Data Protection and Freedom of Information	607
19. Disclosure to the Client	641
20. Duty to Warn Third Parties	691
21. The Employed Professional and Partnerships	717
Bibliography	737
Index	761

CONTENTS

Addendum	ix
Tables of Cases	xxix
Table of Statutes	lxiii
Table of Statutory Instruments	lxxix
Convention on Human Rights	lxxxv
Abbreviations	lxxxvii

PART I. INTRODUCTION

1. Definitions and Rationales

A. Use of Terms in the Book	1.02
Personal Information	1.02
Privacy, Confidentiality and Privilege	1.06
Professionals and their Clients	1.23
Third Parties, Interceptors and Strangers	1.33
B. Justifying and Limiting Professional Confidentiality	1.35
Justifying Confidentiality	1.35
Justifying Breaches of Confidentiality	1.54

2. The Social Context

A. Technological, Political and Social Change	2.01
Increased Recording and Storage of Information	2.02
New Technology	2.04
Pressures for Disclosure to Third Parties	2.11
Employed Professionals	2.21
Workplace Pressures	2.25
Public Attitudes to Professional Confidentiality	2.26
Children's Rights	2.29
Public Trust in the Protection of Personal Information	2.30
Attitudes of Professionals to Confidentiality	2.32
B. The Issues Confronting the Law	2.34

3. The Legal Framework

A. Human Rights	3.02
Article 8(1)	3.03
Relevance of Other Convention Articles	3.10
Justified and Unjustified Interference with Convention Rights	3.19
When Convention Rights Collide	3.26
B. Legislating about Confidentiality	3.33
Compulsory Disclosure	3.33
Non-disclosure	3.41
Disclosure to the Subject of the Information	3.45
C. Professional Codes of Ethics	3.46
Purpose of a Code	3.46
Legal Significance of an Ethics Code	3.47
D. Domestic 'Soft Law'	3.48
Public Sector Guidance	3.48
Information Commissioner's Guidance	3.50
E. The International Dimension	3.52
Supranational and International Instruments	3.52

PART II. RESPONDING TO DISCLOSURE

4. Contract and Tort Solutions to Intentional Disclosure

A. Contract	4.02
Contract Basics	4.02
Confidentiality as a Contractual Term	4.04
B. Tort	4.19
Negligence	4.20
Intentional Infliction of Distress	4.29
Defamation	4.34
Injurious Falsehood	4.41
Conspiracy	4.43
Breach of Statutory Duty	4.45
Infringement of Privacy	4.53
Breach of Confidence	4.60

5. Equity and Copyright Solutions to Intentional Disclosure

A. Equity	5.02
Breach of Confidence	5.02
Breach of Fiduciary Duty	5.64
B. Copyright	5.84

6. Dealing with Unintentional Disclosure

A. Interception and Disloyalty 6.02
   Civil Actions: Client v Interceptor 6.02
   Civil Actions: Client v Professional 6.32
   Civil Actions: Professional v Employee 6.38
   Civil Actions: Professional v Interceptor 6.48
   Prosecuting Interceptors and Disloyal Employees in the Criminal Courts 6.54
   Prosecuting a Stranger in the Criminal Courts 6.84
   Committing a Criminal Offence in the Public Interest ... 6.88
B. Accidental Disclosure 6.89
   The Professional's Liability 6.90
   Admissibility of Accidentally Disclosed and Intercepted Materials in Court Proceedings 6.95
   Restraining the Use of Materials by Means of the Action for Breach of Confidence 6.103

7. Suing and Tracing Third Parties and Strangers

A. Tracing 7.02
   Introduction 7.02
   Discovery Proceedings 7.03
B. Actions Against Third Parties and Strangers 7.20
   Breach of Confidence 7.20
   Breach of Fiduciary Duty 7.35
   Tort 7.36
   Copyright 7.44

8. Remedies

A. Prior Restraint 8.02
   Permanent Injunction 8.02
   Interim Injunctions 8.08
   Data Protection Compliance Order 8.26
B. After-the-Event Remedies 8.28
   Monetary Awards 8.28
   Account of Profits 8.71
   Delivery Up and Destruction of Items 8.74
   Constructive Trusts 8.76

9. Alternatives to Litigation

A. Litigation	9.01
Selecting Civil Causes of Action	9.01
Pros and Cons of Civil Litigation	9.02
B. Litigation Alternatives	9.04
The Alternatives	9.04
Media Regulatory Bodies	9.08

PART III. DEFENCES

10. Compelled Disclosure

A. Coercive Statutory Disclosure	10.02
The Targets of Coercive Disclosure	10.02
Confidentiality and Coercive Disclosure	10.04
Legal Professional Privilege and Coercive Disclosure	10.13
Making the Disclosure and Notifying the Client	10.16
Consequences of Non-Disclosure	10.22
Compulsory Disclosure Under Foreign Law	10.23
B. Money Laundering	10.24
Reporting Obligation	10.25
Related Offences	10.32
C. Use of Information Disclosed Under Compulsion	10.34
In a Criminal Prosecution	10.34
For a Collateral Purpose	10.35

11. Disclosure in the Public Interest

A. The Public Interest	11.02
B. Disclosure of Iniquity	11.09
C. Incriminating Physical Evidence	11.39
D. Disclosure Without Iniquity	11.41
E. Genetic Information	11.53
F. HIV Infection	11.58
G. Procedural and Miscellaneous Matters	11.60
H. Interceptors, Strangers and Third Parties	11.72
I. The Public Interest and Privileged Communications	11.77
J. Tort Defences and the Public Interest	11.81
K. Copyright and the Public Interest	11.82

12. Other Lawful Voluntary Disclosure

- A. Disclosure in Client's Best Interests — 12.02
  - The Competent Adult — 12.02
  - The Incompetent Adult — 12.09
  - Children — 12.11
- B. Disclosure With Statutory Authority — 12.14
  - Statutory Provisions Allowing the Disclosure of Confidential Information — 12.14
- C. Disclosure Motivated by Self-Interest — 12.23
  - Breaching Confidentiality Defensively — 12.23
  - Breaching Confidentiality Affirmatively — 12.34

13. Consent

- A. Express Consent — 13.02
  - Forms of Consent — 13.02
  - Duration of Consent — 13.05
  - Capacity to Consent — 13.08
  - Reality of Consent — 13.22
  - Informed Consent — 13.28
- B. Implied Consent — 13.34
  - Disclosure for Primary Purposes — 13.34
  - Disclosure for Secondary Purposes — 13.46
  - Parameters of Express and Implied Consent — 13.59
- C. Waiver — 13.63
  - English Waiver Cases — 13.63
  - Prerequisites of the Defence — 13.67

PART IV. CONFIDENTIALITY AND PRIVILEGE IN THE LITIGATION PROCESS

14. Investigations and Pre-Trial Disclosures

- A. Civil Cases — 14.02
  - Compulsory Pre-Trial Disclosure — 14.02
  - Search Orders — 14.15
  - Criminal Assets Recovery Authority — 14.18
- B. Criminal Cases — 14.19
  - Acquisition of Confidential Information by the Prosecution — 14.19
  - Covert Surveillance — 14.70
  - Acquisition of Confidential Information by the Defence — 14.123

C. Proceedings Abroad	14.133
Civil Litigation	14.133
Criminal Proceedings	14.137

15. Trials, Tribunals and Inquiries

A. Civil and Criminal Trials	15.02
Documentary Evidence	15.02
Oral Evidence	15.13
Lawyer's Duty Not to Mislead the Court	15.31
Public Authority Disclosure of Confidential Information to a Court	15.36
B. Tribunals and Public Inquiries	15.41
Tribunals	15.41
Statutory and Non-Statutory Inquiries Ordered by Ministers	15.49

16. Grounds for Non-Disclosure

A. Statutory Inadmissibility	16.02
Admissibility of Confidential Information	16.02
B. Privilege	16.05
Categories of Privilege	16.05
Legal Professional Privilege	16.08
Public Interest Immunity	16.52

17. Protection of Privacy

A. Control of Documents	17.02
Withholding Information From a Party	17.02
Collateral Use of Documents	17.09
Access to Documentary Evidence by Non-Parties	17.22
B. Restricting Publicity	17.26
Open Justice	17.26
Hearing Evidence in Private	17.30
Anonymity Orders	17.38
Reporting Restrictions	17.44

PART V. RELATED MATTERS

18. Data Protection and Freedom of Information

A. Data Protection Act 1998	18.01
Introduction	18.01

First Data Protection Principle	18.08
Second Data Protection Principle	18.29
Other Data Protection Principles	18.34
Exemptions	18.37
Enforcement of the Data Protection Principles	18.47
B. Freedom of Information	18.51
The Freedom of Information Act 2000	18.51
Requests for Personal Information	18.53

19. Disclosure to the Client

A. Client's Right to See Own Records	19.03
Common Law Rights	19.03
Client's Statutory Rights of Access to Records	19.21
B. Client's Right to Information	19.58
Fiduciary-Professionals	19.58
Disclosure by Professionals Not Owing Fiduciary Duties	19.64
C. Records and Information Relating to Minors	19.72
Access to Records	19.72
Right to Information	19.83
D. Records and Information of Incompetent Adult	19.114
E. Requiring Disclosure to Third Parties	19.116

20. Duty to Warn Third Parties

A. Public Law Duty	20.01
When a Public Law Duty to Warn Might Arise	20.04
Impact of the Human Rights Act 1998	20.05
B. Private Law Duty	20.06
Risk of Bodily Harm	20.07
Child and Elder Abuse	20.23
Risk of HIV Infection	20.28
Genetic Conditions	20.37
Risk of Non-Violent Crime or Fraud	20.40

21. The Employed Professional and Partnerships

A. Disclosure to the Employer	21.02
Employer Access to Confidential Client Information	21.02
B. Disclosure Outside the Workplace	21.17
The Professional's Obligation of Confidentiality to the Employer	21.17
Whistleblowing	21.23

European Convention on Human Rights, Article 10   21.29
C. Employer's Responsibilities for Employee's Disclosures   21.31
     Civil Liability for Breach of Confidence by an Employee   21.31
D. Partnerships   21.37

Bibliography   737
Index   761

TABLES OF CASES

AUSTRALIA

A v Hayden (1984) 156 CLR 532	11.11
A v Hayden (No 2)(1984) 56 ALR 82	11.32
Abbasi v Minister for Immigration and Multicultural Affairs [2001] FCA 1274	13.34
ABC v Lenah Game Meats Pty Ltd [2001] HCA 63	1.12, 5.23, 6.16, 6.17
Apple v Wily [2002] NSWSC, 855	1.27
Att-Gen (NT) v Maurice (1986) 65 ALR 230	16.19
Att-Gen for UK v Heinemann Publishers (1987) 10 NSWLR 86	5.71, 6.41
B and BT v Oei [1999] NSWSC 1082	20.32, 20.35, 20.36
Baker v Campbell (1983) 153 CLR 52	16.11
Bathurst City Council v Saban [1985] 2 NSWLR 704	6.19
Battersby v Tottman (1985) 37 SASR 524	19.68
Bell, *ex p.* Lee, Re (1980) 146 CLR 141	16.23
Benecke v National Bank of Australia (1993) 35 NSWLR 110	16.34
Bennett v Minister of Community Welfare (1992) 66 ALJR 550	8.45
Breen v Williams (1994) 35 NSWLR 522 (CA); (1996) 138 ALR 359 (HC)	5.56, 5.66, 5.83, 5.84, 7.31, 19.03, 19.04, 19.07, 19.08, 19.09, 19.10, 19.12
British Tobacco Australia Services Ltd v Cowell [2002] VSCA 197	16.34
BP Australia Pty Ltd v Nyran Pty Ltd [2002] FCA 1302	16.34
Brown v Brooks 1998 NSW LEXIS 9221 (SC)	11.36
Bunyan v Jordan (1937) 57 CLR 1	4.32
Carson v John Fairfax & Sons Ltd (1993) 178 CLR 44	8.49
Carter v Northmore Hale Davy & Leake (1995) 183 CLR 121	16.11, 16.25
Commissioner for Corporate Affairs v Guardian Investments [1984] VR 1019	10.28
Commonwealth Bank of Australia v Smith (1991) 102 ALR 453	8.45
Controlled Consultants Pty Ltd v Commissioner or Corporate Affairs (1985) 59 ALJR 254	16.06
Corrs Pavey Whiting and Bryne v Collector of Customs (1987) 74 ALR 428	11.05
CS v News Ltd (NSW SC, 10 February 1999, NSW LEXIS 441)	4.51, 8.60, 8.61
Dalleagles Pty Ltd v Australian Securities Commission (1994) 4 WAR 325	16.22
Daly v Sydney Stock Exchange Ltd (1986) 160 CLR 371	5.65
Dawson, Re [1966] 2 NSWLR 211	8.45
DPP v Kane (1997) 140 FLR 468	6.89
Duke Group v Pilmer (1999) 73 SASR 64, 219	5.66
Farrow & Mortgate Services Pty Ltd v Webb (1996) 39 NSWLR 601	16.16, 19.59
Farrow Mortgage Services Pty Ltd v Mendall Properties Pty Ltd [1995] 1 VR 1 19	6.93
Federal Commissioner of Taxation v Coombes (199) 164 ALR 131	16.23
Flanagan v Pioneer Building Society Ltd [2002] QSC 346	6.92
Foster v Mountford & Rigby Ltd (1976) 29 FLR 233	5.11
Franklin v Giddins [1978] 1 Qd R 72	5.06, 5.29, 8.74
Furney, Re [1964] ALR 814	16.23
G v Day [1982] 1 NSWLR 24	4.32, 5.16, 6.17, 7.23
George v Rockett (1990) 179 CLR 104	10.28
Goldberg v Ng (1995) 185 CLR 183	6.96, 16.11, 16.32
Griffis v Griffis (1991) FLC 92–233	5.67

Grofam Pty Ltd v KPMG Peat Marwick [1993] 27 IPR 215 .... 11.32
Grofam Pty Ltd v Maccauley [1994] 121 ALR 22 .... 16.06, 17.02
Health and Life Care Ltd v Pricewaterhouse (1997) 69 SASR 362 .... 16.21
Health Services for Men v D'Souza [1999] NSSC 969 .... 19.08
Hitchcock v TCN Channel Nine Pty Ltd [2000] NSWSC 198 .... 8.25
Hunt v Judge Russell (1995) 63 SASR 402 .... 15.07
Independent Management Resources Pty Ltd v Brown [1987] VR 605 .... 6.41
James v Commonwealth (1939) 62 CLR 339 .... 7.37
Johnson v Buttress (1936) 56 CLR 113 .... 5.80
Kwok v Thang [1999] NSWC 1034 .... 5.16
McGuiness v Att Gen of Victoria (1940) 63 CLR 73 .... 15.53, 16.42
Marron v J Chatham Duant Pty Ltd (Vic SC 13 November 1998) 19.58
Meltend Pty Ltd v Restoration Clinics of Australia Pty Ltd (1997) 145 ALR 391 .... 6.96
Moorgate Tobacco Co Ltd v Philip Morris Ltd (No 2)(1984)
    156 CLR 414 .... 5.43, 5.73, 5.75, 5.78
National Mutual Life Association of Australia Ltd v Godrich (1909) 10 CLR 1 .... 16.43
Paramasivam v Flynn 1998 Aus Fed Ct, Lexis 1161 .... 5.79
R v P [2001] NSWCA 473 .... 12.03
R v Braham [1976] VR 574 .... 16.17
R v Lowe 1996 Vic LEXIS 1330 .... 14.70, 20.09
R v O'Halloran, ex p. Hamer [1913] VLR 116 .... 21.37
R v Ward (1981) 3 A Crim R 171 .... 15.29
R v Young (1999) 46 NSWLR 681 .... 16.47, 16.59, 16.60
Rogers v Whitaker (1992) 175 CLR 479 .... 19.67, 19.68
Secretary, Department of Health and Community Services v JWB (1992) 175 CLR 215 ...... 13.15
Sender v Commonwealth [2002] NSWSC 1109 .... 15.25, 15.32
Slater v Bissett (1986) 85 FLR 118 .... 13.45
Smithkline & French Laboratories (Australia) Ltd v Department of Community Services
    and Health (1999) 99 ALR 679 .... 5.31
Spermolin v John Winter [1962] CLR 2441 .... 4.43
Sutherland Shire Council v Heyman (1985) 157 CLR 424 .... 20.09
Talbot v General Television Corp Pty Ltd [1980] VR 224 .... 6.91
Tuckiar v R (1934) 52 CLR 335 .... 11.38
US Surgical Corp v Hospital Products International Pty Ltd [1982] 2 NSWLR 766 .... 8.36
Waterford v Commonwealth (1987) 163 CLR 54 .... 16.16
Welfare v Birdon Sands Pty Ltd (Aust Fed Ct, 1997) 900 .... 15.11
Wentworth v De Montfort (1988) 15 NSWLR 348 .... 19.05, 19.07
X v Y [1954] VLR 708 .... 4.02, 14.09
Zeus Chemical Products Pty Ltd v Jaybee Design and Marketing Pty Ltd
    NSW 1998 532, (1998) 41 I.P.R. 491 .... 19.07

CANADA

Abramzik v Brenner (1967) 65 DLR (2d) 651 .... 4.30
Att-Gen of Ontario v Gowling & Henderson (1984) 12 DLR (4th) 623 .... 7.27
Att-Gen of Ontario v Holly Big Canoe [2002] Ont CA Lexis 543 .... 16.28
Att-Gen for Quebec and Keable v Att-Gen for Canada [1979] SCR 218 .... 15.53
Axelrod, Re (1994) 119 DLR (4th) 37 .... 19.03
Bell v Smith (1968) 68 DLR (2d) 751 .... 16.28
Bielitski v Obadiak (1922) 65 DLR 627 .... 4.32
Boulianne v Flynn [1970] 3 OR 84 .... 16.28
Brickenden v London Loan & Savings Co [1934] 3 DLR 465 .... 8.45
C v D [1925] 1 DLR 734 .... 20.33
Canadian Aero Service Ltd v O'Malley (1973) 40 DLR (3d) 371 .... 5.75, 5.78

Canson Enterprises Ltd v Boughton (1991) 85 DLR (4th) 129...8.45
Carosella, Re [1997] 1 SCR 80...14.128
Carter v Carter (1974) 6 OR(2d) 603..16.03, 16.59
Cronkwright v Cronkwright (1970) 14 DLR (3d) 168 ....15.15
Dagg v Canada (Minister of Finance) [1997] 2 SCR 403 ....5.23, 6.13
Damien v O'Mulvenny (1981) 34 OR (2d) 448 ....4.44, 4.51
Descoteaux v Mierzwiski [1982] 1 SCR 860; (1982) 70 CCC (2d) 385 ....16.11, 16.16
Eldridge v Att-Gen of British Columbia (1997) 3 BHRC 137 ....4.47
Frenette v Metropolitan Life Insurance Co (1992) 89 DLR (4th) 653........................13.07, 13.59
Gauthier v Soloman (1990) 90 ACWS (3d) 39..16.47
General Accident Assurance Co v Chrusz (1999) 92 ACWS 15134 ....16.21
Godbout v Longueuil (City) [1997] 3 SCR 844 ....1.14
Gordon v Gilroy (1994) 5 E.T.R. (2d) 289 ....16.29
Guertin v Royal Bank of Canada (1983) 1 DLR (4th) 68..5.72
Halls v Mitchell [1928] 2 DLR 97 ....4.38, 4.39, 11.11, 11.71
Hay v University of Alberta Hospital (1990) 69 DLR (4th) 755 ....12.31, 13.34, 14.09
Hay and Institute of Chartered Accountants, Re (1988) 54 DLR (4th) 26 ....19.07, 19.14
Hill v Church of Scientology of Toronto [1995] 2 SCR 1130...1.12
Hollinsworth v BCTV (1998) 83 ACWS (3d) 525.......................................4.36, 5.07, 5.44, 13.61
International Corona Resources Ltd v Lac Minerals Ltd
    (1987) 44 DLR (4th) 592 ....5.70
Investors Syndicate Ltd v Versatile Investments (1983) 42 OR (2d) 397 ....5.75
Jacks v Davis [1980] 6 WWR 11...19.58
Kennedy v Diversified Mining Interests (Can) Ltd [1949] 1 DLR 59..13.40
Kines Estate v Lychuk (1998) 123 ManR (2nd) 151 ....20.18
Klassen v College of Physicians and Surgeons Ontario [2002] ACWSJ Lexis 6966 ....16.14
Kowall v McRae (1980) 108 DLR (3d) 486...16.19
Lac Minerals Ltd v International Corona Ltd (1989) 611 DLR (4th) 14........5.70, 5.74, 5.81, 8.76
Laidlaw v Lear (1898) 30 OR 26 ....7.43
Lavallee, Rackel and Heintz v Canada (Att-Gen) (1998) 160 DLR (5th) 508 (QB).................5.29
Lavallee, Rackel and Heintz v Canada (Att-Gen) (2000) Alta D Crim J 244 (CA) 16.24
Les Editions Vice Versa Inc v Aubry [1998] 1 SCR 591 ....1.14, 6.22
M v Ryan (1997) 143 DLR (4th) 1 ....16.47
MacDonald Estate v Martin [1990] 3 SCR 1235...6.93
McInerney v MacDonald (1990) 66 DLR (4th) 736 (CA)...19.07
McInerney v MacDonald (1992) 93 DLR (4th) 415 (SCC) 5.81, 5.83, 19.12, 19.15
Malette v Shulman (1990) 67 DLR (4th) 321 ....12.08
M(K) v M(H)(1992) 96 DLR (4th) 289..5.81
Montana Band of Indians v Canada (Minister of Indian and Northern Affairs)
    [1989] 1 FC 143 ....1.04
Norberg v Wynrib (1992) 92 DLR (4th) 449 ....8.70
Ott v Fleishman [1993] 5 WWR 721 ....4.08, 6.32, 8.57, 11.05
Peters-Brown v Regina General Hospital (1995) 58 ACWS (3d) 1044 ....4.34, 6.32, 8.43
Pierre v Pacific Press Ltd (1994) DLR (4th) 511 ....8.54
Pittman v Bain (1994) 112 DLR (4th) 257...20.32, 20.36
R v S (RJ) (1985) 19 CCC (3d) 115 ....16.47
R v Cuerrier [1998] 2 SCR 371 ....11.59
R v Dersch (1993) 18 CR (2d) 87..11.35, 11.37
R v Dunbar (1982) 68 CCC (2d) 13...12.27, 16.16, 16.27, 16.32
R v Dyment (1988) 55 DLR (4th) 503...11.35, 11.37
R v Fehr (1983) 6 DLR (4th) 281 ....16.47
R v Gruenke (1991) 67 CCC (3d) 289 ....16.47
R v Jack (1992) 70 CCC (3d) 67 ....11.47, 16.23, 16.29
R v Kotapski (1981) 66 CCC (2d) 78...16.31

R v Law [2002] SCC 10 ....6.19
R v McClure (2001) 151 CCC (3d) 321; [2001] SCC 14........................1.48, 3.10, 16.08, 16.27
R v Murray (2000) 144 CCC (3d) 289 ....11.39, 12.26
R v Neil [2002] SCC 70..5.65, 5.67, 5.77, 5.80, 13.35
R v O'Connor [1995] 4 SCR 411..15.09
R v Pabani (1994) 89 CCC (3d) 437 ....16.07
R v Peddle [2000] NJ No 311 ....16.47
R v Perron (1990) 54 CCC (3d) 108 ....15.29
R v Ross 1993 NSR (2d) LEXIS 182 (CA); 1993 NSR (2d) 1981 (SC) 11.51
R v Stewart (1988) 50 DLR (4d) 1 ....6.70, 6.71
R v Stone (1997) 13 CCC (3d) 158 ....15.29
R v Thawer [1996] OJ No. 989...12.28
SAS, Re (1977) 1 Legal Medical Quarterly 139 ....16.47
Schenberg Industries Ltd v Borowski (1979) 101 DLR (3d) 701....................................8.70
Seaway Trust Co v Markle (1991) 47 CPC (2d) 258..11.27, 20.41
Slavutych v Baker (1975) 55 DLR (3d) 224 ....6.95, 12.37, 16.47
Smith v Jones [1999] 1 SCR 455 (1999) 169 DLR
   (4th) 385..11.05, 11.15, 11.21, 11.66, 11.80, 15.29, 16.11 20.09, 20.17
Solicitor-General of Canada v Royal Commission of Inquiry into Confidentiality of
   Health Records in Ontario [1981] 2 SCR 494...11.64
Spencer v R (1985) 21 DLR (4th) 756 ....10.23
Spillane v Wasserman (1992) 37 ACWS (3d) 412 ....20.31
Stevens and Prime Minister of Canada (1997) 144 DLR (4th) 553 ....6.96
Stewart v Canadian Broadcasting Commission (1997)
   150 DLR (4th) 24 ....5.76, 5.77, 8.45, 8.52
Szarfer v Chodos (1986) 54 OR (2d) 663 ....5.72, 6.81, 8.52
Tanner v Norys [1980] 4 WWR 33...20.09
Tatone v Tatone (1980) 16 CPC 285..13.02
Taylor v McGillivray (1993) 110 DLR (4th) 64 ....5.81
Thorson v Jones (1973) 38 DLR (3d) 312...16.23
Union of Canada Life Insurance v Levesque Securities Inc (1999) 42 OR (3d) 633 ....16.47
Valiquette v Gazette (1991) 8 CCLT (2d) 302, 1996 ACWSJ LEXIS 97344 ....1.14
Wenden v Trikha (1991) 116 AR (2d) 80...20.09, 20.17
Wilson, King & Co v Torabian (1991) ACWSJ LEXIS 38428 ....12.36
Wilson v HM Advocate (2001) SCCR 633 ....15.25
Wujda v Smith (1974) 49 DLR (3d) 476 ....16.28

EIRE

Cook v Carroll [1945] IR 515 ....16.43
Doyle v Commissioner of An Garda Siochana [1978] 1 ILRM 229.............................7.10
Kennedy v Ireland [1987] IR 587 ....6.03, 6.17, 8.62, 8.64

ENGLAND AND WALES

A, Re [2000] 1 FLR 549..12.10
A, Re [2000] 4 All ER 961 ....13.16
A, Re [2001] 1 FLR 1..13.18
A, Re (HC, 16 June 2001)...6.17
A v A [2000] 1 FLR 701 ....15.33, 16.03, 17.16
A v A Health Authority [2002] EWHC 18; [2002] Fam 213 ....13.11
A v B [2000] EMLR 1007 ....5.85, 5.87, 8.10, 8.74, 8.75, 11.83, 15.08
A v B Bank (Bank of England Intervening) [1992] 1 All ER 778 ....10.01, 10.06

A v B plc and C ('Flitcroft')[2002] EWCA Civ 337; [2002]
   3 WLR 542 reversing [2001] 1 WLR 2341 .... 3.28, 3.30, 3.32, 4.59, 5.05, 5.25, 5.29, 6.08,
                                                6.12, 6.14, 6.16, 6.17, 6.19, 6.22, 6.23, 7.17,
                                                7.26, 7.28, 7.41, 7.44, 8.10, 8.11, 8.16, 8.18,
                                                8.24, 8.25, 8.52, 9.03, 9.09, 11.03, 11.05,
                                                11.06, 11.10, 11.72, 11.76, 13.63, 17.42
A v M [2000] 1 FCR 1 ....13.21
A v National Blood Authority [2001] 3 All ER 289 ....17.42
A and B (No 2), Re [1995] 1 FLR 351..14.04
A and B and C and D v Times Newspapers Ltd and Express Newspapers Ltd
   [2002] EWHC 2444...17.31, 17.36
A CC v W [1997] 1 FLR 574..17.20
A Firm of Solicitors, Re [1992] 1 All ER 253 ....19.58, 19.60
A Health Authority v X [2001] EWCA Civ 2014; [2002] 2 All ER 780 (CA);
   affirming [2001] Lloyds' Rep Med 349 ....1.48, 2.16, 10.10, 11.46, 14.04, 15.20,
                                                17.18, 17.20, 17.201.48, 21.161.48
AB v CD (1851) 14 D 177 ....11.44, 13.51
AB v South West Water Services Ltd [1993] 1 All ER 609 ....8.48, 8.69
ABK Ltd v Foxwell [2002] EWHC 9, Ch..7.28
Ablitt v Mills & Reeve, *The Times*, 25 October 1995 ....6.89
Acrow (Automation) Ltd v Rex Chainbelt Inc [1971] 1 WLR 1676.......................6.48
Adams v Attridge (QB, 8 October 1998) 7.09, 8.10, 8.25
Adams v R [1995] 2 Cr App R 295...6.80
Addis v Gramophone Co [1909] AC 488 ....8.46, 8.61
Adenjii v Newham LBC (QB, 16 October 2001) 1.41, 8.37, 8.63
Agip (Africa) Ltd v Jackson [1992] 4 All ER 451; affirming [1990] Ch 265 ....5.27, 12.38
Air Canada v Secretary of State for Trade (No 2)[1983] 1 All ER 910 ....16.61
Airedale NHS Trust v Bland [1993] 1 All ER 821..................................1.38, 19.65
Aitken, Re (HC, 10 September 1999) 6.17
Al Fayed v Commissioner of Police of the Metropolis [2002] EWHC 562 ....6.110
Al-Kandari v J R Brown & Co [1988] 1 All ER 833 ....12.29, 20.12, 20.41
Alfred Crompton Ltd v Customs and Excise Commissioners (No 2)[1973] 2 All ER 1169....16.55
Allcard v Skinner (1887) 36 Ch D 145 ....5.80
Allison v Clayhills (1907) 97 LT 709..5.77
AM & S Europe Ltd v EC Commission [1983] QB 878 ....16.08, 16.13, 16.16
American Cyanamid v Ethicon [1975] 1 All ER 504...8.09, 8.17
Amway Corp. v Eurway International Ltd [1974] RPC 82 ....8.10
Anderson Consulting v CHP Consulting Ltd (Ch, 26 July 1991) 5.64
Annesley v Anglesea (1743) 17 State Trials 1140 ....16.17
Anon, Re (1693) 90 ER 179...16.49
Anton Piller KG v Manufacturing Processes Ltd [1976] Ch 55 ....14.15, 14.17
Appleton v Garrett [1996] PIQRP1 ....8.50
Arab Monetary Fund v Hashim (No 2)[1990] 1 All ER 673 ....7.11, 15.17
Archer v Brown [1984] 2 All ER 267..8.48
Archer v Williams, *The Guardian*, 23 March 2002 ....6.89
Argyll v Argyll [1967] 1 Ch 302; [1965] 1 All ER 611.......4.50, 5.04, 5.27, 5.29, 6.17, 7.31, 17.47
Arklow Investments Ltd v MacLean [2000] 1 WLR 594.......................................5.67
Armagas Ltd v Mudogas SA [1986] 2 All ER 385 ....21.32
Armstrong v UK Application 48521/99, *The Times*, 6 August 2002......................6.17
Arnott, Re (1888) 60 LT 109 ....16.23
Arrows Ltd, Re [1994] 3 All ER 814..15.39
Ashburton v Pape [1913] 2 Ch 469 ....6.09, 6.103, 6.105
Ashcroft v Att-Gen [2002] EWHC 1122 ....6.35, 10.39, 18.08, 18.23
Ashdown v Telegraph Group [2001] 4 All ER 666 ....3.19, 5.84, 6.17, 8.14, 11.82

Tables of Cases

Ashgar v Ahmed (1995) 17 HLR 25 .... 8.50
Ashworth Security Hospital v MGN Ltd [2002] UKHL 29; [2002] 1 WLR 2033;
  [2001] 1 All ER 991 .... 1.50, 3.19, 4.10, 5.43, 6.17, 6.38, 6.47, 7.04, 7.08,
        7.09, 7.10, 7.11, 7.15, 7.16, 7.17, 7.27, 8.02, 8.25, 11.57
Aspinall v MSI Mech Forge Ltd (EAT/891/01, 5 July 2002) 21.24
AT & T Istel Ltd Tully [1993] AC 45 .... 16.06
AT Poeton (Gloucester Plating) Ltd v Horton [2000] ICR 1208 .... 21.20
Att-Gen v Barker [1990] 3 All ER 257 .... 8.02, 8.09, 8.25
Att-Gen for Hong Kong v Nai-Keung (1988) 86 Cr App R 174 .... 6.55
Att-Gen for Hong Kong v Reid [1994] 1 All ER 1 .... 8.77
Att-Gen v Blake [1996] 3 All ER 903 (Ch); [1998] 1 All ER 833 (CA);
  [2000] 3 WLR 625 (HL) 4.10, 4.14, 4.50, 5.08, 5.16, 5.64, 5.68,
        5.74, 5.77, 8.48, 8.77, 8.78, 21.20, 21.21
Att-Gen v Clough [1963] 1 All ER 420 .... 15.44
Att-Gen v Greater Manchester Newspapers Ltd [2001] TLR 688 .... 5.12, 7.24
Att-Gen v Guardian Newspapers Ltd (No 1) [1987] 1 WLR 1248; [1987] 3 All ER 316......... 5.75
Att-Gen v Guardian Newspapers (No 2) [1988] 3 All ER 545 .... 1.35, 3.19, 4.12, 4.14,
        5.03, 5.06, 5.08, 5.11, 5.12, 5.16, 5.23, 5.27, 5.28, 5.29, 5.41, 5.59,
        5.60, 5.61, 5.62, 6.08, 6.14, 6.17, 6.24, 7.23, 7.26, 7.31, 7.32, 7.33,
        8.05, 8.06, 8.07, 8.25, 8.38, 8.72, 8.78, 10.37, 10.38, 11.08, 11.12,
        11.42, 11.60, 11.62, 11.64, 11.65, 11.72, 11.73, 21.17
Att-Gen v Jonathan Cape [1975] 3 All ER 484 .... 1.12, 8.06
Att-Gen v Leveller Magazine [1979] 1 All ER 745 .... 17.44
Att-Gen v Lundin (1982) 75 Cr App R 90 .... 15.14, 15.16, 15.18
Att-Gen v Manchester Corp [1893] 2 Ch 87 .... 8.03
Att-Gen v Mulholland [1963] 1 All ER 767 .... 6.111, 15.16, 15.44, 16.42
Att-Gen v Newspaper Publishing plc [1987] 3 All ER 276 .... 7.24, 8.10
Att-Gen v Observer Ltd [1989] 2 FSR 3 .... 7.23, 7.31, 7.32
Att-Gen v Punch [2002] UKHL 50 .... 7.24
Att-Gen v Times Newspapers Ltd [2001] 1 WLR 885; [2001] EMLR 19 .... 5.12, 5.59, 8.06
Att-Gen's Reference (No 1 of 1991) [1992] 3 All ER 897 .... 6.61
Att-Gen's Reference (No 3 of 1999) [2001] 2 WLR 56 .... 15.12
Att-Gen's Reference (No 7 of 2000) [2001] EWCA Crim 888 .... 10.15
Axa Equity & Life Assurance Plc v National Westminster Bank Plc
  [1998] CLC 1177 .... 7.10, 7.12
B, Re [2002] All ER (D) 167 .... 15.09, 17.02, 17.06
B (A Child) (Sexual Abuse: Expert's Report), Re [2000] 1 FLR 871 .... 1.29
B (A Minor) (Disclosure of Evidence), Re [1993] 1 FLR 191 .... 17.06, 19.101
B (A Minor) v RP [2001] 1 FLR 589 .... 11.52
B (Disclosure to Other Parties), Re [2001] 2 FLR 1017;
  [2002] 2 FCR 32 .... 3.23, 15.09, 17.02, 17.06, 17.08
B (Minors) (Abduction: Disclosure), Re [1995] 1 FLR 774 .... 10.02
B v B [1991] 2 FLR 487 .... 17.02
B v H Bauer Publishing Ltd [2002] EMLR 145 .... 6.07, 8.04
B v NHS Hospital Trust [2002] EWCH 429; [2002] 2 All ER 449 .... 5.47, 17.42
Baker v Kaye (1996) 39 BMLR 12 .... 1.28
Baker, Norman (MP) v Secretary of State for the Home Department (Information
  Tribunal (National Security Appeals), 1 October 2001), [2001] UKHRR 1275....... 3.04, 19.31
Balabel v Air India [1988] Ch 317; [1988] 2 All ER 246 .... 16.17
Balfron Trustees Ltd v Russell, Jones & Walker (HC, 9 July 2001) 21.34
Ball v Druces [2002] EWCA Civ 157 .... 6.93, 6.94, 16.34
Balston Ltd v Headline Filters Ltd [1987] FSR 330 .... 21.20
Bank of Scotland v A Ltd [2001] 3 All ER 58 .... 10.18
Bankers Trust Company v Shapira [1980] WLR 1274 .... 7.08, 14.03

Banque Financiere de la Cite v Westgate insurance [1990] 2 All ER 947 ....20.41
Banque Keyser Ullmann SA v Skandia (UK) Insurance Co Ltd
  [1986] 1 Lloyd's Rep 336..16.35, 16.36
Barazancha v Pannone Napier (CA, 5 February 1998) 13.40
Barclays Bank v Eustice [1995] 4 All ER 511 ....11.77, 16.35, 16.37
Barclays Bank plc v Taylor [1989] 3 All ER 563..10.20, 14.31, 14.32,
                                                                        14.43, 15.06, 15.22, 16.36
Barings Plc v Coopers & Lybrand (2000) 150 NLJ 681 ....17.27
Barlow Clowes Gilt Managers Ltd, Re [1991]
  4 All ER 385 ....10.35, 11.08, 12.14, 13.02, 14.128, 15.40
Barrett v Ministry of Defence, *The Times*, 24 January 1990 ....16.55
Barrymore v NGN Ltd [1997] FSR 600 ....5.04, 5.11, 5.24, 6.17, 6.19, 13.66
Bartlett v Barclays Bank Trust Co Ltd (No 2) [1980] Ch 515 ....8.45
BCCI v Ali [1999] IRLR 508 ....15.26
BCCI v Price Waterhouse [1997] 4 All ER 781 ....10.06, 16.02, 16.04
Beckham v MGN Ltd (QBD, 28 June 2001)...3.30, 5.05
Beddow v Beddow (1878) 9 Ch D 89..8.07
Beer v Ward (1821) Jacob 77 ....16.30
Bell v Alfred Franks & Bartlett co Ltd [1980] 1 All ER 356..13.02
Beloff v Pressdram Ltd [1973] 1 All ER 241 ....6.17, 8.29, 11.83
Bennett v Compass Group UK [2002] EWCA Civ 642..14.08
Bernstein v Skyviews [1977] 2 All ER 902 ....6.51
Birmingham DC v O [1983] 1 All ER 497...12.01
Birmingham Post and Mail Ltd v Birmingham City Council [1993]
  17 BMLR 118...17.29, 17.49, 17.50
Blair v Associated Newspapers Ltd (QBD, 13 November 2000, 2000 WL3116509)...............6.38
Blair v Lister (QB, 2000, WL 33116509) 5.59, 7.10, 8.74
Boardman v Phipps [1967] 2 AC 46 ....8.36, 8.76, 19.04
BOC Ltd v Barlow [2001] All ER (D) 53 ....15.12
Bolam v Friern Hospital Management Committee [1957] 2 All ER 118 ....19.64, 19.65
Bolitho v City and Hackney Health Authority [1997] 4 All ER 771..19.66
Bolkiah v KPMG [1999]
  1 All ER 517............................1.48, 5.28, 5.36, 5.77, 6.39,6.90, 6.92, 6.93, 8.03, 16.08, 16.45
Bonnard v Perryman [1891] 2 Ch 269 ....8.11
Borax Europe Ltd v Cave [2002] EWCA Civ 741..8.06
Bourns Inc v Raychem Corp [1999] 3 All ER 154 (CA); affirming
  [1999] 3 All ER 154 ....16.31, 16.34, 17.14, 17.15, 17.16
Bowden Brothers v Amalgamated Pictorial Ltd [1911] 1 Ch 386..13.05
Bradford Hospitals NHS Trust v Burcher (EAT/958/01, 28 September 2001) 15.44, 16.28
Bradford-Smart v West Sussex CC [2002] EWCA Civ 7; [2002] 1 FCR 425 ....20.21
Brandeis (Brokers) Ltd v Black [2001] 2 All ER (Comm) 980...............................5.65, 5.67
Brannigan v Davison [1996] 3 WLR 859 ....15.23, 15.44
Brassington v Cauldron Wholesale Ltd [1977] IRLR 479...21.24
Breeze v John Stacey [2000] CP Rep 77 ....6.108, 6.110
Brimelow v Casson [1924] 1 Ch 302...11.81
Bristol & West Building Society v Baden, Barnes Groves and Co [2000]
  Lloyd's Rep PN 788...19.61
Bristol & West Building Society v Merrimans [1996] 2 All ER 801 ....5.64
Bristol & West Building Society v Mothew [1996] 4 All ER 698 ....5.65, 5.67, 6.32, 6.90, 13.40
British Coal Corp v Dennis Rye Ltd (No 2)[1988] 3 All ER 816.................................16.20, 16.31
British Gas Trading Ltd v Data Protection Registrar [1997–98]
  Info TLR 393...10.37, 18.09, 18.11, 18.13
British Industrial Plastics Ltd v Ferguson [1940] 1 All ER 479 (HL); [1938]
  4 All ER 504 (CA) 7.21, 7.36, 7.43

Tables of Cases

British Steel Corp v Granada Television Ltd [1981]
  1 All ER 417 ....6.46, 7.09, 7.10, 7.13, 7.42, 11.28, 15.15, 15.16, 16.59
Broad v Pitt (1828) 3 C&P 518 ....15.16, 16.42, 16.49
Broadmoor Special Hospital Authority v R (1999) 52 BMLR 137 ....5.43, 8.02, 10.07
Broome v Cassell & Co Ltd [1972] AC 1027 ....8.49
Brown v Bennett (HC(Ch), 18 December 2001) 16.22
Brown v Foster (1857) 1 H & N 736 ....16.23
Brown v Inland Revenue Commissioners [1964] 3 All ER 119 ....5.27
Brown v Stott [2001] 2 All ER 97 ....3.20, 3.23
BSC v Granada Television Ltd [1981] 1 All ER 417 ....15.15, 15.16, 16.59
Buckoke v Greater London Council [1971] 2 All ER 254 ....6.88
Bullivant v Att-Gen for Victoria [1901] AC 196 ....16.29
Bullock v Corry (1878) 3 QBD 356 ....16.28
Bunn v BBC [1998] 3 All ER 552 ....5.18, 5.59, 8.07, 8.10, 8.18, 10.37, 11.11, 17.09, 17.26
Burris v Azadani [1995] 4 All ER 802 ....8.02
Bursill v Tanner (1885) 16 QBD 1 ....16.23
Butler v Board of Trade [1970] 3 All ER 593 ....6.106, 7.23, 11.37, 16.36, 16.37
Buttes Gas and Oil v Hammer (No 3)[1980] 3 All ER 475 ....16.16, 16.32
C, Re [1994] 1 All ER 819 ....19.114
C, Re (Fam Div, 29 November 2001) 16.02
C (A Child) (HIV Testing), Re [1999] 2 FLR 1004 ....12.11, 19.109
C (A Minor) (Care Proceedings: Disclosure), Re [1997] Fam 76 ....17.18
C (A Minor) (Child Support Agency: Disclosure), Re [1995] 1 FLR 201 ....10.35
C (A Minor) (Evidence: Confidential Information), Re [1991]
  2 FLR 478 ....11.07, 11.49, 11.50, 11.57, 16.59
C (A Minor) (Wardship: Medical Treatment) (No.2), Re [1989]
  2 All ER 791 ....5.26, 5.27, 19.94
C (Adult: Refusal of Medical Treatment), Re [1994] 1 All ER 819 ....13.10
C (Residence: Child's Application for Leave), Re [1995] 1 FLR 927 ....13.14
C v C [1946] 1 All ER 562 ....14.11, 16.62
C v C [2001] 1 FCR 756 ....16.17, 16.23, 16.35
C v S [1999] 2 All ER 343 ....14.05
C (on the application of C) v LB Waltham Forest [2002] EWCH 2007 ....20.05
Caird v Sime (1887) 12 App Cas 236 ....5.11
Calcraft v Guest [1898] 1 QB 759 ....6.96, 6.98, 6.99, 12.37, 14.76, 16.10, 16.28, 16.29
California v Kaufman [1973] RPC 635 ....7.36
Calver v Westwood Veterinary Group [2001] Lloyd's Rep Med 20 ....3.47, 19.66
Cambridge Nutrition Ltd v BBC [1990] 3 All ER 523 ....8.15, 8.61
Camelot v Centaur Communications Ltd [1998] 1 All ER 251;
  [1998] IRLR 80 ....6.46, 7.09, 7.16, 7.19
Campbell v Frisbee [2002] EWCA Civ 1374 reversing [2002] EWHC 328;
  [2002] EMLR 31 ....1.55, 3.25, 3.26, 4.15, 5.05, 8.13, 8.14,
                                                                        8.25, 11.02, 11.10, 11.12, 11.74, 21.20
Campbell v MGN [2002] EWCA Civ 1373 (CA) reversing [2002] EWHC 499;
  [2002] EMLR 30 ....1.21, 1.42, 3.17, 3.54, 4.49, 5.05, 6.13, 6.16, 6.17, 6.19, 6.22,
                   6.24, 6.26, 7.20, 8.13, 8.18, 8.38, 8.44, 8.48, 8.54, 8.56, 8.58, 8.61,
                   8.66, 9.03, 11.03, 11.08, 11.10, 11.67, 18.09, 18.16, 18.19, 18.24, 18.27, 18.39
Campbell v Tameside MBC [1982] 2 All ER 791 ....14.07, 15.07, 16.59, 16.62
Caparo Industries v Dickman [1990] 1 All ER 568 ....4.21, 20.09, 20.13
Capital and Counties plc v Hampshire CC [1997] 2 All ER 865 ....20.09
Capital Corporate Finance Group Ltd v Bankers Trust Co [1995] 1 WLR 172 ....17.27
Cardinal Packaging Ltd v Atkinson (CA, 24 March 2000) 7.36
Carlton Film DIstributors v VDC Ltd [2003] EWHC 616 (Ch) 7.08, 7.10
Carter v Palmer (1842) 8 ER 256; (1841) 8 Cl & Fin 657 ....5.72, 8.77

Cassidy v Ministry of Health [1951] 1 All ER 574..21.31
Cathcart, Re (1870) LR 5 Ch App 703...16.23
Causton v Mann Egerton Ltd [1974] 1 WLR 162......................................13.40, 16.21
CC Bottlers Ltd v Lion Nathan Ltd [1993] 2 NZLR 445..........................16.19, 16.32
Central Manchester Health Care NHS Trust v Michaelangelo Attard
 (18 June 2001, varied 25 August 2001) 17.41
Chandler v Church (1987) 137 NLJ 451..16.35
Channon v Johnstone [2002] EWCA Civ 353; [2002] Lloyd's Rep PN 342 ....8.47
Chant v Brown (1849) 7 Hare 84..16.28
Chantrey Martin (A Firm) v Martin [1953] 2 QB 286; [1953]
 2 All ER 691..14.14, 16.42, 19.06, 19.07
Chapman v Honig [1963] 2 All ER 171..15.22
Chartered Bank of India v Rich (1863) 32 LJQB 300..16.20
Chase v NGN Ltd [2002] EWCH 1101..17.16
Chatterton v Gerson [1981] QB 432..13.24, 13.28
Chatterton v Secretary of State for India [1895] 2 QB 189....................................16.10
Chaudhary v Cowan (1973) British Medical J 181 ....4.37
CHC Software Care Ltd v Hopkins & Wood [1993] FSR 241........................7.06, 7.08
Cheese v Clark (QBD Feb 2, 2003)...8.49
Chester v Afshar [2002] EWCA Civ 724; [2002] 3 All ER 552..................3.28, 19.65
Chief Constable of West Yorkshire Police v S [1998] 2 FLR 973.........................10.02
China National Petroleum v Fenwick Elliott [2002] EWHC 60..............16.10, 16.21
Christofi v Barclays Bank plc [1999] 4 All ER 437..4.10, 4.11
Church of Scientology of California v DHSS [1979] 3 All ER 97..............17.02, 17.14
Church of Scientology of California v Kaufman [1973] 1 RPC 627........................1.21
CIBC v Sayani (1993) 83 BCLR (2d) 167..11.29
Clark Boyce v Mouat [1993] 4 All ER 268..13.28, 19.59
Clarke v Chief Constable of Cleveland Police, *The Times*, 13 May 1999 ....8.50
Clauss v Pir [1988] 1 Ch 267...12.09
Cleveland CC v F [1995] 2 All ER 236..17.45
Clibbery v Allan [2002] EWCA Civ 45; [2002] 1 All ER 865 (CA);
 affirming [2001] 2 FCR 577; [2001] 2 FLR 819 ....3.28, 17.17, 17.22, 17.31,
                                                                 17.32, 17.33, 17.36, 17.44, 17.51
Clough v Tameside & Glossop Health Authority [1998] 2 All ER 971............15.24, 15.25, 16.34
CMI-Centers for Medical Innovation GmbH v Phytopharm plc
 [1999] FSR 235..5.29, 5.39, 8.10, 14.17
CMS Dolphin Ltd v Simonet [2001] 2 BCLC 704...............................5.44, 5.77, 8.48
Cobeldick, *Ex p*. (1883) 12 QBD 149..19.03
Coco v AN Clark (Engineers) Ltd [1968] FSR 415; [1969]
 RPC 41..5.06, 5.25, 5.40, 5.41, 6.03, 6.13, 6.14, 13.01
Collins (Engineers) Ltd v Roberts & Co Ltd [1965] RPC 429 ....5.28
Columbia Picture Industries v Robinson [1986] 1 All ER 779.............................14.17
Company's Application, Re [1989] 2 All ER 248 ....11.07, 11.26, 11.28, 11.61, 11.63, 11.64
Conway v Rimmer [1968] 1 All ER 874..1.55
Corelli v Wall (1906) 22 TLR 532..6.09
Cork v McVicar, *The Times*, 31 October 1984..11.63, 11.65
Cornelius v de Taranto [2001] EWCA Civ 1511; [2002] EMLR 6 (CA);
 affirming [2001] EMLR 12 ....4.35, 4.36, 5.41,
                                                8.41, 8.45, 8.56, 8.57, 8.59, 13.42
Cossey v UK [1991] 2 FLR 492...3.55
Coulthard v Disco Mix Club [1992] 2 All ER 457..5.12
Cowell v Law Society (Ch D, 12 October 2001)..10.02, 16.13
Cranleigh Precision Engineering Ltd v Bryant [1965] 1 WLR 1293.......................5.59
Cream Holdings Ltd v Banerjee [2003] EWCA Civ 103.....................3.26, 8.16, 8.17

Creation Records Ltd v NGN Ltd [1997] EMLR 444 .... 6.06, 6.17, 6.19, 8.10
Crescent Farm (Sidcup) Sports Ltd v Sterling Offices Ltd [1971]
  3 All ER 1192 .... 11.77, 16.35, 16.36
Crest Homes plc v Marks [1987] 2 All ER 1074 .... 17.14, 17.16
Crofter Hand Woven Harris Tweed Co Ltd v Veitch [1942] AC 435 .... 11.81
Crompton (Alfred) Amusement Machines Ltd v Customs and Excise
  Commissioners (No 2) [1972] 2 All ER 353 .... 14.07, 16.16
Cumbria CC v X, *The Times*, 25 June 1990 .... 17.41
Currie v Chief Constable of Surrey [1982] 1 All ER 89 .... 15.41
Curtis v Beany [1911] PD 181 .... 16.29
Customs and Excise Commissioners v AE Hamlin & Co [1983] 3 All ER 654 .... 14.17
D , Re (1997) 45 BMLR 191 .... 17.39
D , Re [2002] All ER D 167 .... 17.06
D (Infants), Re [1970] 1 All ER 1088 .... 15.07
D (Minors) (Adoption Reports: Confidentiality), Re [1995] 4 All ER 385 .... 17.05, 17.06
D (Minors) (Conciliation: Disclosure of Information), Re [1993]
  2 All ER 693 .... 11.23, 16.05, 16.38
D (Minors) (Wardship: Disclosure), Re [1994] 1 FLR 346 .... 14.129, 16.59, 17.18
D & M, Re [2002] EWHC 2820 .... 17.17, 17.18
D v NSPCC [1976] 2 All ER 993 .... 4.32, 7.10, 8.50
D v NSPCC [1978] AC 171;
  [1977] 1 All ER 589 .... 11.64, 15.15, 15.16, 15.18, 16.05, 16.42, 16.55, 16.58, 16.59
D v NSPCC [1997] 1 All ER 589 .... 15.13
Dalgleish v Lothian & Borders Police Board [1991] IRLR 422 .... 5.29
Daniel v Clifford Chance (28 April 1989) 19.58
Data Protection Registrar v Amnesty International [1995] Crim LR 633 .... 6.56
David Lee & Co (Lincoln) Ltd v Coward Chance [1991] 1 All ER 668 .... 3.47, 6.93
Davies v Flackett [1973] RTR 8 .... 6.52
DB Deniz Nakliya TAS v Yugopetrol [1992] 2 All ER 205 .... 14.04
De Freitas v Permanent Secretary of Ministry of Agriculture, Fisheries,
  Lands and Housing [1999] 1 AC 69 .... 3.20
Dean v Allin & Watts (A Firm) [2000] Lloyd's Rep PN 469 .... 13.40
Def American Inc v Phonogram Ltd, *The Times*, 16 August 1994 .... 6.104
Derby v Weldon (No 2), *The Times*, 20 October 1988 .... 17.15, 17.27
Derby & Co Ltd v Weldon (No 7) [1990] 3 All ER 161 .... 16.37
Derby & Co Ltd v Weldon (No 8) [1991] 1 WLR 73 .... 6.105
Derby & Co Ltd v Weldon (No 9), *The Times* 9 November 1990 .... 15.24
Derry v Peak (1889) 14 App Cas 337 .... 6.52
DH, Re [1994] 1 FLR 679; [1994] 2 FCR 3 .... 10.02, 10.12, 10.14, 10.21, 11.11, 11.37,
                                                         12.11, 15.12, 16.39, 16.40, 19.87, 20.03
Dickinson v Rushmer (2002) 152 NLJ 58 .... 12.35
Distillers Co (Biochemicals) Ltd v Times Newspapers Ltd [1975] 1 All ER 41 .... 11.10, 17.14
Dobson v Hastings [1992] 2 All ER 94 .... 17.22
Dobson v North Tyneside Health Authority [1996] 4 All ER 474 .... 5.47
Donoghue v Poplar Housing Association [2001] 4 All ER 604 .... 4.47
Doody v Secretary of State [1993] 3 All ER 92 .... 19.01
Dooley v Law Society (Ch D, 13 December 2001) 17.20, 17.33, 17.44
Dora v Simper (CA, 15 March 1999) 16.38
Douglas v Hello! Ltd [2001] 2 All ER 289; [2002] EWHC 2560 .... 1.12, 3.05, 3.08, 3.22, 3.27,
                                       3.28, 3.30, 4.41, 4.44, 4.59, 4.60, 5.04, 5.24, 5.27, 5.43, 5.82,
                                       6.05, 6.07, 6.08, 6.09, 6.11, 6.12, 6.13, 6.17, 6.19, 6.21, 6.24,
                                       7.26, 8.10, 8.16, 8.17, 8.19, 8.25, 8.37, 8.38, 8.78, 18.11
Douglas v Hello! Ltd (No2) [2003] EWCA Civ 139 .... 18.11
Douihech v Findlay [1990] 3 All ER 118 .... 14.14

DPP v Channel Four Television Co Ltd [1993] 2 All ER 517 ....14.48
DPP v Ray [1973] All ER 131 ....6.74
DPP v Wither [1974] 3 All ER 984 ....6.77
Dranez Anstalt v Hayek [2002] 1 BCLC 693 ....5.77, 21.19
Du Barre v Livette (1790) 1 Peake 108 ....16.42
Dubai Aluminium Co Ltd v Al Alwai [1999] 1 WLR 1964 ....6.50, 16.35
Dubai Aluminium Co Ltd v Salaam [2002] UKHL 48 ....21.39
Dubai Bank Ltd v Galadari [1989] 3 All ER 769 ....16.22
Dubai Bank Ltd v Galadari (No 6), *The Times*, 22 April 1991 ....16.35
Dubai Bank Ltd v Galadari (No 7) [1992] 1 All ER 658 ....14.22
Dunn v British Coal Corporation [1993] ICR 591 ....14.09, 21.04
Dwyer v Collins (1852) 21 LJ Ex 225 ....16.23
E v Cardiff Crown Court, *ex p.* Kellam (1993) 16 BMLR 76 ....14.22, 14.23, 14.28
Eagles v GMC (1995) 311 British Medical J 1240 ....9.07
El Jawhary v Bank of BCCI [1993] BCLC 396 ....12.40
Elliott v Chief Constable of Wiltshire, The Times, 5 December 1996 ....5.18
Elliott v MEM Ltd (CA, 11 March 1993) 17.02
English v Dedham Vale Properties Ltd [1978] 1 WLR 93 ....5.78
English and American Insurance Ltd v Herbert Smith [1988] FSR 232 ....6.98, 6.105
Entick v Carrington (1765) 19 How St Tr 1029 ....6.50, 6.51
Eronat v Tabbah [2002] EWCA Civ 950 ....14.137, 17.16
Erven Warnink Besloten Vennootschap v J Townsend & Sons [1979] 2 All ER 927 ....13.12
Esterhuysen v Lonrho plc, *The Times*, 29 May 1989 ....17.15
Evett v Price (1827) 1 Sim 483, 57 ER 659 ....8.02
Evitt v Price [1964] 3 All ER 119 ....5.65, 5.72
EX, Re [1997] Fam 76 ....17.18
Exchange Telegraph Co Ltd v Central News Ltd [1897] 2 Ch 48 ....5.11
Exchange Telegraph Co Ltd v Gregory & Co [1896] 1 QB 147 ....7.36
Exchange Telegraph Co Ltd v Howard (1906) 22 TLR 375 ....6.09
F (A Minor), Re [1977] 1 All ER 114 ....17.31, 17.45
F v West Berkshire Health Authority [1989] 2 All ER 545 ....13.11, 17.31, 19.114
Faccenda Chicken Ltd v Fowler [1986] 1 All ER 617 ....5.77, 6.19, 6.39, 6.40, 21.19, 21.20
Falmouth v Moss (1822) 147 ER 530 ....15.02
Farley v Skinner [2001] UKHL 49; [2001] 4 All ER 801 ....8.46, 8.47
Farnsworth v Hammersmith and Fulham LBC [2000] IRLR 691 ....1.29
Femis-Bank (Anguilla) Ltd v Lazer [1991] Ch 391; [1991] 3 WLR 80 ....4.43, 11.81
Fielding v Variety Inc [1967] 2 All ER 497 ....4.34
Fine Arts Society Ltd v Union Bank of London Ltd (1886) 17 QBD 705 ....7.42
Finers v Miro [1991] 1 All ER 182 ....12.38
Firm of Solicitors, In the matter of a [2000] 1 Lloyd's Rep 31 ....6.93, 6.94
First American Corp v Clark M Clifford (DC, 16 December 1997) 14.133
Flett v North Tyneside Health Authority [1989] CLY 2968 ....16.59
Fogg v Gaulter and Blane (1960) 110 LJ 718 ....4.17, 5.05, 5.27
Fomento (Sterling Area) Ltd v Selsdon Fountain Pen Co. Ltd [1958] 1 All ER 11 ....13.01
Foucher v France (1998) 25 EHRR 234 ....3.03, 3.21, 14.99
Franchi v Franchi [1967] RPC 149 ....5.11
Francis & Francis (A Firm) v Central Criminal Court [1988]
    3 All ER 775 ....10.17, 10.30, 14.22, 14.25, 14.30, 16.35
Francome v MGN Ltd [1984] 2 All ER 408; [1984]
    1 WLR 892 ....4.50, 6.05, 6.17, 6.20, 6.51, 7.43, 8.10, 8.11, 8.70, 11.03, 11.75, 15.15
Frank Film v Video Information [1981] 2 All ER 76 ....6.82
Frank Truman Export Ltd v Metropolitan Police Commissioner [1977] QB 952 ....6.103
Fraser v Evans [1969] 1 QB 349;[1969] 1 All ER 8 ....5.03, 5.43, 5.86, 8.11, 11.08
Fraser v Thames Television [1983] 2 All ER 101 ....5.86, 13.01

Fyffes Group v Templeman [2000] 2 Lloyd's Rep 643..7.31
G (A Minor), Re [1996] 2 All ER 65 ....3.49, 11.34, 16.53, 16.59, 17.17
G (A Minor) (Parental Responsibility: Education), Re [1994] 2 FLR 964 ....13.20, 13.21
G (Minors) (Celebrities: Publicity), Re [1999] 1 FLR 409 ....17.46
G v G (Ouster: *Ex Parte* Application) [1990] 1 FLR 395...20.04
G v UK [2002] Crim LR 308 ....3.15
Gain v Gain [1961] 1 WLR 1469...16.10
Gamlen Chemical Co (UK) Ltd v Rochem Ltd [1980] All ER 1049 ....19.03
Garner v Garner (1920) 36 TLR 196...16.03, 16.42
Gartside v Outram (1856) 26 LJ Ch (NS) 113..11.07, 11.09
Garvin v Domus Publishing Ltd [1989] 2 All ER 344..15.16
General Mediterranean Holdings v Patel [1999]
    3 All ER 673 ....3.04, 5.03, 12.28, 16.25, 16.26, 16.34
Gillick v West Norfolk and Wisbech Area Health Authority [1985] 3 All ER 402 (HL); [1985]
    1 All ER 533 (CA) 12.11, 13.13, 13.19, 19.87, 19.95, 19.96, 19.99, 19.103, 19.108, 20.25
Gio Personal Investment Services Ltd v Liverpool and London Steamship Protection and
    Indemnity Association Ltd [1999] 1 WLR 984 ....17.27
Gleaves v Deakin [1979] 2 All ER 497 ....6.87
GMC v BBC [1998] 1 WLR 515 ....7.14
Goddard v Nationwide Building Society [1986]
    3 All ER 264 ....5.27, 6.103, 6.105, 6.111, 7.23, 7.31
Gogay v Hertfordshire CC [2000] IRLR 703 ....8.48
Gold v Haringey Health Authority [1987] 2 All ER 888 ....3.47, 19.65
Golden Cross Hire Co Ltd v Lovell [1979] IRLR 267..6.38
Goldsmith v Pressdram [1977] 2 All ER 557 ....6.87
Goldstone v Williams [1899] 1 Ch 47 ....16.20, 16.21, 17.26
Goodson v Richardson (1874) 9 Ch App 221..8.07
Goodwill v British Pregnancy Advisory Service [1996] 2 All ER 161 ....20.09, 20.33, 20.35, 20.36
Gore v Scales (ChD, 14 November 2002) 21.38
Gotha City v Sotheby's [1998] 1 WLR 114...16.32
Governor and Company of the Bank of Scotland v A Ltd [2001] All ER (D) 81 ....10.17
Graham v Delderfield [1992] FSR 313...8.09
Great Atlantic Insurance Co. v Home Insurance Co [1981]
    2 All ER 485...6.96, 13.40, 16.16, 16.19, 16.34
Greenlaw v King (1838) 48 ER 891 ....16.42
Greenough v Gaskell (1833) 39 ER 618 ....1.48, 16.08
Griffith v Davies (1833) 110 ER 876..16.17
Grobbelaar v NGN Ltd [2001] 2 All ER 437 (CA) 11.66
Grobbelaar v Sun Newspapers, *The Times*, 12 August 1999 ....6.95
Groom v Crocker [1938] 2 All ER 394 ....1.28, 4.40, 8.47, 19.62
Guiness Peat Properties Ltd v Fitzroy Robinson Partnership [1987]
    2 All ER 716 ....6.96, 6.109
Gulf Oil (Great Britian) Ltd v Page [1987] 3 All ER 14 ....4.43
Guyer v Walton [2001] STC (SCD) 75 ....3.35, 10.06, 16.13, 16.23, 18.38
H (Child Abduction: Whereabouts Order to Solicitors), Re [2000] 1 FLR 766;
    [2000] 1 FCR 499..1.23, 10.02, 10.12, 10.14, 10.19, 16.16, 16.23
H (A Healthcare Worker) v Associated Newspapers Ltd [2002] EWCA Civ 195;
    [2002] EMLR 23..3.31, 3.32, 5.26, 6.17, 6.19, 7.24, 8.02, 8.03, 8.25, 10.07,
                    10.08, 11.50, 12.08, 17.33, 17.41, 17.42, 17.43, 17.45, 17.46
H v Commissioners of Inland Revenue [2002] EWHC 214 ....14.65
Halewood International v Addleshaw Booth & Co [2000] Lloyd's Rep PN 298............6.93, 6.94
Halford v Sharples [1992] 3 All ER 624 ....16.56
Halifax Mortgage Services v Secretary of State [1998] PNLR 616 ....19.61
Hamlyn v Johnston & Co [1903] 1 KB 81 ....21.39

Handmade Films (Productions) Ltd v Express Newspapers plc [1986] FSR 463	7.14
Harman v Secetary of State for the Home Department [1983] 1 AC 280	17.50
Harmony Shipping Co v Davis [1979] 3 All ER 171	15.22, 15.25
Harmony Shipping Co v Saudi Europe Line [1979] 3 All ER 177	16.30
Harrison v Festus Timothy [1998] 2 CL 1	19.03
Harvest Trucking v Davis [1991] 2 Lloyd's Rep 638	3.47
Hassneh Insurance Co of Israel v Mew [1993] 2 Lloyds Rep 243	15.08
Hawglen Ltd, Re [2001] 1 All ER 376	15.07
Hayes v Dodd [1990] 2 All ER 815	8.47
Health Authority v X [2001] Lloyd's Rep Med 349	15.20
Healys v Mishcon de Reya [2002] EWCH 2480	5.57, 7.42, 21.33
Heather v Leonard Cheshire Foundation [2001] EWHC Admin 429; [2001] ACD 75	3.06, 4.47, 4.48
Hedley Byrne & Co Ltd v Heller & Partners Ltd [1964] AC 465	20.41
Hellenic Mutual War Risks Association v Harrison [1997] 1 Lloyd's Rep 160	13.01
Hellewell v Chief Constable of Derbyshire [1995] 1 WLR 804; 4 All ER 473	1.29, 5.06, 6.06, 6.17, 6.19, 10.37, 11.08, 11.60
Henderson v Merrett Syndicates Ltd [1994] 3 All ER 506	6.32, 9.01
Henley v Henley [1955] 1 All ER 590n	16.07
Herbage v Times Newspapers Ltd, *The Times*, 1 May 1981	8.11
Hession v Health Commissioner for Wales [2001] EWHC Admin 619	15.13, 15.44
Hill v Chief Constable of West Yorkshire [1988] 2 All ER 238	20.09, 20.18
Hilton v Barker Booth & Eastwood [2002] EWCA Civ 723; [2002] Lloyd's Rep P.N. 500	5.67, 5.76, 5.80, 8.45, 13.28, 16.31, 19.58, 19.61
Hipwood v Gloucester Health Authority (1995) 24 BMLR 27	17.02
Hivac v Park Royal Scientific Instruments Ltd [1946] Ch 169	21.17
Hodgson v Imperial Tobacco [1998] 2 All ER 673	17.30
Home and Away Ltd v Commissioners of Customs and Excise VAT and Duties Tribunal, 17 January 2002	15.44
Home Office v Dorset Yacht Co Ltd [1970] 2 All ER 294	20.09
Home Office v Wainwright [2001] EWCA Civ 2081	4.30, 4.33, 6.12, 6.28, 8.31, 8.42, 13.25
Hooper v Rogers [1975] 1 Ch 43	8.03
Hornsby v Clark Kenneth Leventhal [1998] PNLR 635	21.32
Horsfall, *ex p*. (1827) 108 ER 820	19.07
Howard v Beall (1889) 23 QBD 1	14.10
Howard v Gunn (1863) 55 ER 181	19.07
Howard v Secretary of State for Health [2002] EWHC 396	3.18, 15.54, 15.55, 15.56
Howell-Smith v Price (CA, 26 April 1996)	12.03, 12.05, 12.06, 20.27
Howglen Ltd, Re [2001] 1 All ER 376	14.06, 14.10
HRH Prince of Wales v MGN Ltd (QB, 8 November 1993)	4.09
Hubbard v Vosper [1972] 1 All ER 1023	8.07, 8.11, 11.08
Hubble v Peterborough Hospitals NHS Trust (21 March 2001)	19.22, 19.24
Hulton v Jones [1910] AC 20	7.38
Hunter v Canary Wharf Ltd [1997] 2 All ER 426	8.50
Hunter v London Docklands Development Corp [1997] 2 All ER 426	8.48
Hunter v Mann [1974] 2 All ER 414	10.06, 11.11, 15.16
Hurd v Moring (1824) 1 C & P 372	16.23
Hurst v Bryk [2002] 1 AC 185	4.15
Hussein v Chong Fook Kam [1969] 3 All ER 1626	10.28
Hyde Park Residence Ltd v Yelland [2000] 3 WLR 215	5.84, 11.82, 11.83
Idenburg v General Medical Council (2000) 55 BMLR 101	15.46
Imutran Ltd v Uncaged Campaigns Ltd [2001] 2 All ER 385	1.02, 8.06, 8.16, 11.62, 11.63
Indata Equipment Supplies Ltd v ACL Ltd [1998] 1 BCLC 412	5.71, 5.73
Information Commissioner v Islington LBC [2002] EWHC 1036	6.56

Initial Services Ltd v Putterill [1967]
  3 All ER 145 ....1.21, 6.38, 11.04, 11.07, 11.10, 11.41, 11.61, 11.62, 11.63, 21.17, 21.19
Inland Revenue Commissioners v Rossminster Ltd [1980] 1 All ER 80......................14.65, 14.66
Innovations (Mail Order) Ltd v Data Protection Registrar
  (29 September 1993) Data Protection Tribunal 18.11
Interbrew SA v Financial Times Ltd [2002] EWCA Civ 274; [2002]
  2 Lloyd's Rep 229 (CA); 1 Lloyd's Rep 542 (HC).........1.21, 7.10, 7.15, 7.16, 7.17, 7.18, 13.35
Irvine v Talksport Ltd [2002] EWHC 367; [2002] 1 WLR 2355, Ch D 8.57
ITC Film Distributors v Video Exchange Ltd
  [1982] 2 All ER 241 ....6.09, 6.98, 6.105, 15.12
Jackson v Royal Bank of Scotland [2000] CLC 1457 ....6.90
Jackson v Wells (1985) 5 FCR 296..17.02
Jade Engineering (Coventry) Ltd v Antiference Window Systems Ltd [1996] FSR 461 ....7.08, 7.09
Jaggard v Sawyer [1995] 2 All ER 189 ....8.33, 8.34
Janvier v Sweeney [1919] 2 KB 316...4.30
Jeffrey v Black [1978] 1 All ER 555 ....15.46
Jockey Club v BBC [2002] EWHC 1866 [2003] 2 WLR 178 ....3.31, 7.24, 7.33, 11.08, 11.65
John v Express Newspapers Ltd [2000] 3 All ER 257 ....7.14, 7.15, 7.17
John v Joulebine (QB, 26 January 2001)...6.11, 6.24, 7.27, 8.56
John v MGN Ltd [1996] 2 All ER 35 ....8.49
John Reid Enterprises Ltd v Pell [1999] EMLR 675 ....6.17, 7.17, 14.15
Johnson v Agnew [1980] AC 367 ....8.33
Johnson v Bingley [1997] PNLR 392 ....3.47, 19.64
Johnson v Gore Wood & Co [2001] 1 All ER 481 ....4.86
Johnson v Unisys Ltd [2001] 2 All ER 801 ....8.69
Jones v University of Warwick [2003] EWCA Civ 151 ....2.13, 14.117, 15.17
Joyce v Sengupta [1993] 1 All ER 897 ....4.42, 8.48
Kalmneft v Denton Wilde Sapte QB Leeds Mercantile Court MERC
  No1 MC 000410 (2002) 7.10
Kampadia v Lambeth LBC *The Times*, 4 July 2000..13.34
Kapfunde v Abbey National plc [1998] IRLR 583 ....1.30
Kavanagh, Re [1949] 2 All ER 264 ....5.05, 8.51
Kaye v Robertson [1991]
  FSR 62.....................3.08, 4.34, 4.35, 4.41, 4.42, 4.57, 4.59, 460, 5.62, 6.17, 6.22, 8.08, 13.55
Kelly v BBC [2002] 1 All ER 323...5.22, 8.02, 13.21, 17.41
Kelly v Cooper [1993] AC 205 ....5.65, 19.58
Kelly v Kelly 1946 SLT 2 ....14.07
Kennedy v Brown (1863) 13 CBNS 677 ....4.02, 12.35
Kershaw v Whelan [1996] 2 All ER 404 ....16.28, 16.34
Khanna v Lovell White Durrant [1994] 4 All ER 267 ....15.10
Khashoggi v Smith (1980) 124 SJ 14....................................1.09, 6.21, 6.38, 8.07, 13.63
Khodaparast v Farrokh-Shad (CA, 26 February and 28 April 1997) 6.17, 8.37
Khodaparast v Shad [2000] 1 All ER 545..4.42, 8.50
Khorasandjian v Bush [1993] 3 All ER 669...4.33, 8.48
Kingston (Duchess) case (1776) 20 State Tr 335 ....15.13, 16.42
Kitechnology BV v UNCOR GmbH Plastmaschinen [1995] FSR 765 ....5.03
Kitson v Playfair (1896) 1 British Medical J 815; *The Times*, 28 March 1896 ....4.40, 11.25
Koch Shipping Inc v Richards Butler [2002] EWCA Civ 1280 ....6.93, 21.20
Konigsberg, Re [1989] 3 All ER 289...13.01, 16.16, 19.59
Korsner v Royal Pharmaceutical Society of Great Britian (DC, 19 February 1999)................15.43
Kralji v McGrath [1986] 1 All ER 54 ....8.48
Kuddus v Chief Constable of Leicestershire Constabulary [2001] UKHL 29;
  [2001] 3 All ER 193 ....8.69, 8.70
Kuruma v R [1955] 1 All ER 236...11.37, 15.12, 15.46

Kuwait Oil Tanker Co v Al-Bader [2000] 2 All ER (Comm) 271 ....4.44
L (A Minor) (Police Investigation: Privilege), Re [1996]
    2 All ER 78...................10.02, 12.24, 16.13, 16.14, 16.21, 16.39, 16.40, 16.41, 17.18
L (A Minor) (Wardship: Freedom of Publication), Re [1988] 1 All ER 418 ....7.24
L (Care Proceedings: Disclosure to Third Party), Re [2000]
    1 FLR 913...10.10, 17.18, 17.21
Ladbroke (Football) Ltd v William Hill (Football) Ltd [1964] 1 WLR 273............................5.84
Laker Airways Inc v FLS Aerospace Ltd [2000] 1 WLR 113...6.93
Lane v Willis [1972] 1 All ER 430..14.09
Law Society v KPMG Peat Marwick [2000] 4 All ER 540...20.40
Law Society v Y (A Solicitor) (Ch D, 14 February 2000, WL 191148) 14.15
Leeds Teaching Hospitals NHS Trust v A (QB, 4 November 2002) 17.41
Legal Aid Board, *ex p.* Kaim Todner [1998] 3 All ER 541 ....17.28
Leicestershire CC v Farada [1941] 2 All ER 483 ....19.05, 19.09
Lennon v NGN Ltd [1978] FSR 573 ....13.64
Lillicrap v Halder & Son [1993] 1 All ER 724 ....13.34, 16.34
Lilly Icos Ltd v Pfizer Ltd [2002] EWCA Civ 2; [2002] 1 All ER 842....................................17.23
Linguaphone Institute Ltd v Data Protection Registrar (DA/94 31/49/1, 14 July 1995) 18.11
Linstead v East Sussex, Brighton v Hove [2001] PIQR P 25...16.25, 16.26
Lion Laboratories Ltd v Evans [1984]
    2 All ER 417 ....6.17, 8.09, 11.03, 11.08, 11.41, 11.61, 11.65, 11.73, 11.75, 21.19, 21.27
Lister v Hesley Hall Ltd [2001] UKHL 22; [2001] 2 All ER 769..21.33
Lister v Stubbs (1890) 45 Ch D 1...8.77
Lloyd v Mostyn (1842) 152 ER 558 ....6.98, 12.37
Lock International plc v Beswick [1989] 3 All ER 373 ....14.17
London & Leeds Estates Ltd v Paribas Ltd (No 2) [1995] 1 EGLR 102....................15.05, 15.07
London Regional Transport Ltd v Mayor of London [2001] EWCA 1491
    [2003] EMLR 4.....................3.05, 3.18, 4.15, 5.28, 5.33, 11.02, 11.04, 11.08, 11.42, 11.61
London School Board v Northcroft (1889) 2 Hudson's BC (4th) 147...................................19.04
Longstaff v Birtles [2001] EWCA Civ 1219; [2002] 1 WLR 470 ....5.77, 8.36
Lonrho Ltd v Shell Petroleum Ltd [1981] 2 All ER 456 ....4.50
Lonrho plc v Fayed [1991] 3 All ER 303 HL 4.43, 6.49
Lonrho plc v Fayed (No 4) [1994] 1 All ER 870 ....14.07
Lonrho plc v Fayed (No 5)[1994] 1 All ER 188..4.44, 8.48, 8.61, 8.66
Lord Levy v Times Newspapers Ltd (HC, 23 June 2000) 3.22, 6.17, 11.28
Lyell v Kennedy(No 3)(1884) 27 Ch D 1..16.22
Lynch v Knight (1861) 9 (HL) Cas 577...4.35, 8.54
M, Re [2002] EWCA Civ 1199...16.54
M, Re [2002] EWHC 2482 ....17.17
M (A Minor) (Disclosure of Material), Re [1990] 2 FLR 36..16.59
M (Minors: Disclosure of Evidence), Re [1994] 1 FLR 760 ....17.06, 19.63
M (Minors) (Confidential Documents), Re [1987] 1 FLR 46 ....16.59
M and N (Minors),Re [1990] 1 All ER 205 ....3.31, 11.11, 17.32
McCarey v Associated Newspapers Ltd [1964] 3 All ER 947..8.49
McCreery v Massey Plastic Fabrication [2003] EWHC Claim MA091748 (QB) 16.28
McIvor v Southern Health and Social Services Board [1978] 2 All ER 625 ....17.04, 17.27
McKenna v British Aluminium, *The Times*, 16 January 2002 ....3.06
MacKinnon v Donaldson, Luftkin and Jenrette Securities Corp
    [1986] 1 All ER 653...14.04, 14.10
Maclaine Watson & Co Ltd v International Tin Council [1990] 2 AC 418...........................3.53
McLeish v Amoo-Gottfried & Co, *The Times*, 13 October 1993..................................8.47, 8.60
McMaster v Byrne [1952] 1 All ER 1362...5.77, 19.61
McTaggart v McTaggart [1948] 2 All ER 754 ....16.05, 16.07
Mahon v Rahn [1997] 3 All ER 687.............................14.125, 15.22, 17.12, 17.13, 17.14, 17.15

Makanjuola v Commissioner of Police of the Metropolis [1992] 3 All ER 617 .... 16.53
Malik v BCCI [1997] 3 All ER 1 .... 1.21, 4.35, 8.61, 21.17
Malone v Commissioner of Police of the Metropolis (No 2)[1979] 2 All ER 620 .... 6.03, 6.14,
        6.17, 6.51, 6.67, 7.23, 8.39, 11.07, 11.09, 11.41, 11.60, 11.63, 11.75, 13.36
Mammone v Baken (10 February 1989) 6.90
Manda, Re [1993] 1 All ER 733; [1993] 1 FLR 205 .... 17.18, 17.19
Marcel v Commissioner of Police of the Metropolis [1992] 1 All ER 72 (CA); reversing in part
   [1991] 1 All ER 845 .... 5.25, 5.27, 10.36, 14.07, 15.06, 15.36, 15.37, 17.09, 17.10, 17.26
Marks v Beyfus (1890) 25 QBD 494 .... 11.64
Marrinan v Vibart [1963] 1 QB 528 .... 4.44
Marrow v DPP (1993) 14 BMLR 54 .... 15.07, 16.59, 16.60
Masterman-Lister v Jewell & Brutton & Co [2002] EWCA Civ 1889; [2002]
   EWHC 417; [2002] Lloyd's Rep Med 239 .... 12.03, 12.07, 13.10, 19.114
Matron v Rahn [1997] 3 All ER 687 .... 10.01
Matter of ABC Ltd, Re [1984] CILR 130 .... 13.23
MB (Caesarean Section), Re (1997) 2 FLR 436 .... 12.05, 12.06, 13.10, 13.15
Medcalf v Weatherill [2002] UKHL 27; [2002] 3 WLR 172 .... 12.25, 12.29, 15.31
Merchantile Group (Europe) AG v Aiyela [1994] 1 All ER 110 .... 7.11
Mergenthaler Linotype Co Ltd [1926] 43 RPC 381 .... 8.74
Mersey Care NHS Trust v Ackroyd [2002] EWHC 2115 .... 7.09, 7.10, 7.14, 7.17
Metall und Rohstoff AG v Donaldson Lufkin and Jenrette Inc [1990] 1 QB 391 .... 7.37, 8.38
MGN Ltd v Attard (Fam Div, 19 October 2001) 3.22, 3.31, 6.19, 8.25
MGN Ltd v Jackson, *The Times*, 29 March 1994 .... 14.09
Michael O'Mara Books Ltd v Express Newspapers plc [1998] EMLR 383 .... 7.09
Midland Bank Trust Co Ltd v Hett, Stubbs and Kemp (A Firm) [1978] 3 All ER 571 .... 19.62
Miller v Scorey [1996] 3 All ER 18 .... 17.14
Mills v NGN Ltd [2001] EMLR 957 .... 3.30, 5.05, 5.16, 5.23, 8.16, 8.25
Minter v Priest [1930] AC 558 .... 16.16, 16.28
Mole v Mole [1950] 2 All ER 328 .... 16.07
Moody v Cox [1917] 2 Ch 71 .... 19.58
Moore v News of the World Ltd [1972] 1 All ER 915 .... 13.01
Morison v Moat (1851) 68 ER 492 .... 5.03, 5.50, 7.31
Morris v Serious Fraud Office [1993] 1 All ER 788 .... 15.38
Morris v West Hartlepool Steam Navigation Co Ltd [1956] 1 All ER 385 .... 19.64
Mortgage Express Ltd v Bowerman & Partners [1996] 2 All ER 836 .... 19.59, 19.61
Murjani, Re [1996] All ER 65; [1996] 1 BCLC 272 .... 16.15, 17.06
Murphy's Settlement [1998] 3 All ER 1 .... 7.08
N (Forensic Examination: Negligence), Re [1999] Lloyd's Rep Med 257 .... 1.31
Naidoo v Naidu, *The Times*, 1 November 2000 .... 5.80
National Home Loans Corp plc v Giffen, Coach and Archer [1997] 3 All ER 808 .... 19.61
Nationwide Building Society v Balmer Radmore [1999] Lloyd's Rep PN 241 .... 13.40, 19.61
Nationwide Building Society v Various Solicitors (1998) 148 NLJ 241 .... 16.28, 16.35
Nationwide Building Society v Various Solicitors (No 2) [1998]
   All ER (D) 119 .... 6.105, 6.109, 7.29, 11.08, 16.30, 16.35
Nederlandse Reassurantie Groep Holding NV v Bacon & Woodrow
   [1995] 1 All ER 976 .... 16.17, 16.19, 16.34
Nelson v Nelson [1997] 1 All ER 970 .... 5.27, 5.65
Neufang v Aetna Casualty & Surety Co (No 81-08118-CSs Fla Cir Ct,
   Broward Country) 20.20
New Victoria v Ryan [1993] ICR 201 .... 16.16
Newen [1903] 1 Ch 812 .... 13.40
Nicholls v BBC [1999] EMLR 791 .... 6.17, 13.05
Nicholson v Halton General Hospital NHS Trust [1999] PIQR 310 .... 14.09
Nichrotherm Electrical Co Ltd v Percy [1957] RPC 207 .... 5.06, 8.38

Nocton v Lord Ashburton [1914] AC 932...8.36, 9.01
Normanshaw v Normanshaw (1893) 69 LT 468 ....16.42
Norwich Pharmacal Co v Customs and Excise Commissioners [1973]
  2 All ER 943..5.29, 7.04, 7.06, 7.09, 7.10, 7.11, 7.12, 14.03, 16.55
Nottidge v Prince (1860) 66 ER 103 ....5.80
Nottinghamshire Healthcare NHS Trust Ltd v NGN Ltd [2002] EWHC 409;
  [2002] EMLR 33 ....5.86, 8.68, 11.83
NRG v Bacon & Woodrow [1995] 1 All ER 976..13.01, 13.44
NUR v John Wyeth & Brother Ltd [1996] 7 Med LR 300 ....14.09
Nuttall v Nuttall (1964) 108 SJ 605 ....15.13, 15.14, 16.42
NWL Ltd v Woods [1979] 3 All ER 614 ....8.15
O (Disclosure Order), Re [1991] 2 QB 461...16.06
Ocular Sciences Ltd v Aspect Vision Care Ltd [1997] RPC 289 ....8.76, 8.78
Official Solicitor to the Supreme Court v K [1963] 1 All ER 191 ....17.06
Ogle v Chief Constable of Thames Valley [2001] EWCA Civ 598............................8.54
Omega Trust Co Ltd v Wright Son and Peppe [1998] PNLR 337 ....19.61
Ord v Upton [2000] 1 All ER 193..5.50
O'Rourke v Darbishire [1920] AC 581..16.37, 19.13
O'Shea v MGN ltd [2001] EMLR 943..4.34, 7.38
Osman v Ferguson [1993] 4 All ER 344..20.11, 20.13
O'Sullivan v Herdmans Ltd [1987] 3 All ER 129...14.08, 15.02
Oxford v Moss (1979) 68 Cr App R 183 ....6.70
Oxfordshire CC v L [1997] 1 FLR 235...17.18
Oxfordshire CC v M [1994] 2 All ER 269; [1994] Fam 151 ....10.02, 16.39, 16.40
P v P (Removal of Child to New Zealand) [2001] EWCA Civ 166; [2001] Fam 473.........16.40
P v T Ltd [1997] 4 All ER 200 ....7.10
P v Wozencroft [2002] EWHC 1724, [2002] 2 FLR 1118..........................18.11, 19.21, 19.48
Pais v Pais [1970] 3 All ER 491 ....16.07
Palmer v Tees Health Authority [1998] 45 BMLR 88 ....20.15, 20.18
Pamplin v Law Society [2001] EWCH Admin 300 ....17.10
Panayiotou v Sony Music Ltd [1994] Ch 142...15.07
Paragon Finance Plc v Freshfields [1999] 1 WLR 1183...................................16.34, 16.42
Parkhurst v Lowten (1819) 2 Swans 194 ....16.23
Parkins v Sodexho Ltd [2002] IRLR 109 ....21.25
Parmiter v Coupland (1840) 9 LJ Ex 202...4.34
Parry-Jones v Law Society [1969] 1 Ch 1; [1968] 1 All ER 177 ....1.22, 5.27, 10.01,
                          10.02, 10.06, 11.01, 15.13, 16.11, 16.15, 16.42
Pascal v Barclays Bank plc Mayor's and City of London Court May 1999
  LTL 18 May 2001 ....8.48
Pascall v Galinski [1969] 3 All ER 1090 ....16.23
Payne v Payne [2001] 1 FLR 1052 ....19.87
P-B (A Minor) (Child Cases: Hearings in Open Court), Re [1997] 1 All ER 58 ....17.31, 17.46
PCR Ltd v Dow Jones Telerate Ltd [1998] FSR 170..7.22
Pearce v Foster (1885) 15 QBD 114...16.28
Pearce v United Bristol Healthcare NHS Trust (1998) 48 BMLR 118 ....19.66, 19.67
Pearse v Pearse (1846) 63 ER 950...16.11
Peck v UK *The Times* 3 Feb 2002 ....3.03, 3.21, 6.19, 8.25, 8.55, 9.15, 13.67
Peek v Gurney (1893) LR 6 HL 377..6.52
Perharic v Hennessey (CA, 9 June 1997) 8.50, 8.54
Perry v Sidney Phillips & Son [1982] 3 All ER 705..8.47
Persey v Secretary of State for the Environment [2002] EWHC 371 ....3.18
Peter Pan Manufacturing Corp v Corsets Silhouette Ltd [1964] 1 WLR 96 ....8.73
Pfizer Corp v Minister of Health [1965] AC 512 ....4.02, 19.12
Pharaon v BCCI [1998] 4 All ER 455 ....7.24, 11.05, 11.66, 11.72

Tables of Cases

Phelps v Hillingdon LBC [2000] 4 All ER 504; (1997) 147 NLJ 1421 .... 4.23, 20.09, 20.21
Philip v Pennell [1907] 2 Ch 577 .... 5.86, 6.17
Pickering v Liverpool Daily Post [1991] 1 All ER 622 .... 4.50, 4.52, 15.45
Pierson v Secretary of State for the Home Department [1997] 3 All ER 577 .... 16.14
Pilmer v Duke Group Ltd [2001] HCA 31 .... 8.45
Pizzey v Ford Motor Co Ltd [1994] PIQR P15 .... 6.105
Pollard v Photographic Co (1889) 40 Ch D 345 .... 5.06, 6.17
Pratt v BMA [1919] 1 KB 244 .... 4.44
Preston BC v McGrath *The Times* 19 May 2000 .... 10.40
Price v Strange [1978] Ch 337 .... 8.33
Price Waterhouse (A Firm) v BCCI Holdings (Luxembourg) SA
 [1992] BCLC 583 .... 10.06, 11.04, 11.05, 11.08, 11.28, 15.53, 16.19, 16.42
Prince Albert v Strange (1849) 64 ER 293; (1849)
 41 ER 1171 .... 1.42, 5.02, 5.11, 5.41, 5.45, 6.17, 8.74
Princess of Wales v MGN (QB, 8 November 1993) 6.06, 8.10, 8.39
Printers & Finishers v Holloway [1965] RPC 239 .... 5.06, 7.31, 7.37
Proctor v Bayley (1889) 42 Ch D 390 .... 8.39
Prudential Assurance Co v Fountain Page Ltd [1991] 3 All ER 878 .... 17.14, 17.15
Quinn v Leathem [1901] AC 495 .... 4.44
R, Re [2003] EWCA Civ 19 .... 17.18
R (A Child) (Care: Disclosure: Nature of Proceedings), Re [2002] 1 FLR 755 .... 16.02, 16.59
R (A Child) (Care Proceedings: Disclosure), Re [2000] 2 FLR 751 .... 3.40
R (A Minor) (Disclosure of Privileged Material), Re [1993]
 4 All ER 702 .... 10.02, 10.14, 12.13, 13.21, 16.41, 19.98, 20.03
R (Disclosure), Re [1998] 1 FLR 433 .... 11.49, 11.68, 17.19, 17.20
R v A [2001] 2 FLR 1017 .... 3.23
R v A (Complainant's Sexual History) [2001] 3 All ER 1; [2001] UKHL 25; [2002] 1 AC 45 ...... 3.23
R v Allen [2001] UKHL 45 .... 10.15
R v C (1991) 7 BMLR 138 .... 11.03
R v C (1993) 14 Cr App R(S) 562 .... 20.24
R v K [2002] EWCA Crim 2878 .... 14.127
R v K (TD) (1993) 97 Cr App R 342 .... 15.07, 16.59, 16.63, 16.64
R v P (Telephone Intercepts: Admissibility of Evidence) [2001] 2 WLR 463;
 [2001] 2 All ER 58 .... 3.15, 3.19, 14.77, 14.99, 15.12
R v R (Blood Sample: Privilege) [1994] 4 All ER 260 .... 15.27, 15.28, 16.17, 16.22
R v R (Disclosure to Revenue) [1998] 1 FLR 922 .... 17.16
R v Abadom [1983] 1 All ER 364 .... 15.26
R v Absolom, *The Times*, 14 September 1983 .... 6.70
R v Acton Crown Court, *ex p.* Layton [1993] Crim LR 458 .... 14.30
R (on the application of the DPP) v Acton Youth Court [2001] EWHC Admin 402;
 [2001] 1 WLR 1828 .... 16.52
R v Ali [2001] EWCA Crim 863 .... 16.33
R v Allsop (1976) 64 Cr App R29 .... 6.80
R v Arlidge (1995) 145 NLJ 1776 .... 6.61
R v Att-Gen, *ex p.* Rockall [1999] 4 All ER 312 .... 6.76
R v Azmy (1996) 34 BMLR 45 .... 15.08, 16.59
R (on the application of ProLife Alliance) v BBC [2002] EWCA Civ 297;
 [2002] 2 All ER 756 .... 3.19, 6.19, 8.22, 8.25, 9.09
R v BCC, *ex p.* Granada Television Ltd [1995] EMLR 163 .... 5.17, 5.20, 9.18
R v Beck, *ex p.* Daily Telegraph [1993] 2 All ER 177 .... 17.48
R v Bedfordshire Coroner, *ex p.* Local Sunday Newspapers Ltd (2000) 164 JP 283 .... 17.38
R v Bedworth (17 March 1993) *The Times* 18 March 1993 .... 6.62
R v Birmingham City Council, *ex p.* O [1983] 1 All ER 497 .... 3.40
R v Botmeh [2001] EWCA Crim 226; [2002] 1 WLR 531 .... 16.63, 17.07

R (on the application of Pelling) v Bow County Court [2001] EWCA Civ 122 ....3.18, 17.34
R v Bow County Court, *ex p.* Pelling [1999] 4 All ER 751 ....17.33
R v Bow Street Magistrates' Court, *ex p.* Government of the US [1999] 4 All ER 1 ....6.61
R v Bow Street Magistrates' Court, *ex p.* King (DC, 8 October 1997) 14.137
R v Bowden [1999] 4 All ER 43 ....16.33
R v Brentwood BC, *ex p.* Peck [1998] EMLR 697...2.16, 3.44, 9.17
R v Britton [1987] 2 All ER 412..15.14
R v Broadcasting Complaints Commission, *ex p.* Barclay [1997] EMLR 62 ....9.19
R v Broadcasting Complaints Commission, *ex p.* BBC [1993] EMLR 419..............................9.19
R v Broadcasting Standards Commission, *ex p.* BBC [2000]
    3 All ER 989 ....1.06, 1.08, 1.12, 6.19, 9.19, 18.16
R v Brown [1996] 1 All ER 545..6.27, 6.56
R v Brushett [2001] Crim LR 471 ....14.126
R v Cadette [1995] Crim LR 229 ....14.77
R v Central Criminal Court, *ex p.* Adegbesan (1987) 84 Cr App R 219 ....14.31
R v Central Criminal Court, *ex p.* AJ Holdings [1992] Crim LR 669 ....14.31, 14.35
R v Central Criminal Court, *ex p.* Bright [2000] 2 All ER 244..........................14.26, 14.27, 14.34
R v Central Criminal Court, *ex p.* Brown, *The Times*, 7 September 1992 ....14.28
R v Central Criminal Court, *ex p.* Carr, *The Independent*, 5 March 198..................................14.31
R v Central Criminal Court, *ex p.* Propend [1996] 2 Cr App R 26 ....14.19, 14.25
R v Central Independent Television plc [1994] 3 All ER 641..3.31
R v Chesterfield Justices and Chief Constable of Derbyshire, *ex p.* Bramley
    [2000] 1 All ER 411..14.37
R (on the application of A) v Chief Constable of C [2001] 1 WLR 461 [2001]
    2 FCR 431 ....3.40, 3.49, 18.44
R v Chief Constable of North Wales Police, *ex p.* AB [1997]
    4 All ER 691 ....5.18, 5.20, 5.21, 6.20, 10.37, 10.39, 11.71
R v Chief Constable of the West Midlands, *ex p.* Wiley [1994]
    3 All ER 420 ....16.53, 16.55, 16.57, 16.58, 16.61,
R v Chief Registrar of Friendly Societies, *ex p.* New Cross Building Society
    [1984] 2 All ER 27 ....17.34
R v City of London Magistrates' Court, *ex p.* Asif [1996] STC 611 ....14.68
R v City of London Magistrates' Court, *ex p.* Peters [1997] STC 141 ....14.68
R (on the application of Robertson) v City of Wakefield Metropolitan Council
    [2001] EWHC Admin 915; [2002] 2 WLR 889.................1.02, 2.27, 3.41, 3.54, 13.23, 18.05
R v Clowes [1992] 3 All ER 440 ....14.129, 15.07, 16.63
R (on the application of M) v Commissioner of Police for the Metropolis
    [2001] EWHC Admin 553 ....3.11
R v Cottrill [1997] Crim LR 56...6.101, 6.106
R v Cox (1884) 14 QBD 153 ....16.35, 16.36
R v Croydon Health Authority (1997) 40 BMLR 40 ....1.31
R v Crozier (1990) 8 BMLR 128 ....11.11, 11.22, 11.57, 11.63, 11.71, 16.59, 20.15
R v Customs and Excise Commissioners, *ex p.* Popely [1999] STC 1016.........14.20, 14.36, 14.68
R v Davies [2002] EWCA Crim 85...1.29, 15.29, 15.30, 16.21, 16.34
R v Daye [1908] 2 KB 333 ....15.08
R v Department of Health, *ex p.* Source Infomatics Ltd [2000] 1 All ER 786 CA;
    [1999] 4 All ER 185 QB....................1.10, 1.48, 3.54, 5.04, 5.26, 5.29, 5.31, 5.32, 5.33, 5.34,
                                            5.35, 5.38, 5.41, 6.17, 6.19, 6.26, 7.28, 7.31, 7.34, 11.07,
                                            11.44, 11.57, 13.01, 13.28, 13.46, 13.50, 13.51, 18.08
R v Derby Magistrates' Court, *ex p.* B [1995] 4 All ER 526............1.48, 3.13, 6.107, 10.13, 11.27,
                                            11.80, 11.116, 12.24, 12.25, 12.35, 12.39, 15.07, 16.07,
                                            16.08, 16.12, 16.25, 16.27, 16.28, 16.29, 16.30, 16.36
R v Devon County Council, *ex p.* L [1991] 2 FLR 541..11.63, 20.04
R (on the application of Pretty) v DPP [2001] UKHL 61; [2002] 1 AC 800 ....12.08, 20.05

Case	Reference
R v Duff [2002] EWCA Crim 2117	10.25
R v Effick (1994) 99 Cr App R 312	14.89
R v Epsom Justices, *ex p.* Bell [1989] STC 169	14.68
R v Evesham Justices, *ex p.* McDonagh (1988) 87 Cr App R 25	17.39
R (on the application of Wooder) v Feggetter [2002] EWCA Civ 554; [2002] 3 WLR 591	3.05, 19.68
R v Forbes [2001] 1 All ER 686	3.23
R v Galvin [1987] 2 All ER 851	5.11
R v Gayle [1994] Crim LR 679	1.29
R v Ghosh [1982] QB 1053; [1982] 2 All ER 1032	6.68, 6.79
R v Gold [1988] 2 All ER 186	6.74
R (on the application of N) v Governor of HM Prison Dartmoor [2001] EWHC Admin 93	3.40
R v Governor of HM Prison Dartmoor, *ex p.* N (QBD Admin, 13 February 2001)	5.20
R (on the application of Cannan) v Governor of HMP Full Sutton [2003] EWHC 97 Admin	10.14
R v Governor of Pentonville Prison, *ex p.* Osman [1989] 3 All ER 701	16.37
R v Governors of Dunraven School, *ex p.* B [2000] BLGR 494	17.05
R v Griffin (1853) 6 Cox CC 219	15.16
R v Griffiths (1974) 60 Cr App R 14	6.85
R v Grossman (1981) 73 Cr App R 302	14.57, 14.132
R v Hardy [2002] EWCA Crim 3012	14.90
R v Harrison (CA, 10 July 2000)	11.21, 11.25, 14.77, 20.02
R v Hay (1860) 175 ER 933	11.40
R v Home Secretary, *ex p.* Brind [1991] 1 All ER 720	3.55
R v Inland Revenue Commissioners, *ex p.* Banque Internationale a Luxembourg [2000] STC 708	3.19
R v Inland Revenue Commissioners, *ex p.* Davis Frankel & Mead (a firm) *The Times*, 11 July 2000	3.35
R v Inland Revenue Commissioners, *ex p.* Kingston-Smith [1996] STC 1210	14.65
R v Inland Revenue Commissioners, *ex p.* Lorimer [2000] STC 751	16.13
R v Inland Revenue Commissioners, *ex p.* Tamosious [1999] STC 1077	16.16
R v Inland Revenue Commissioners, *ex p.* Taylor (No 2)[1990] 2 All ER 409	10.02
R v Inland Revenue Commissioners, *ex p.* Ulster Bank Ltd [2000] STC 537	3.35, 10.20
R v Inner London Crown Court, *ex p.* Baines & Baines [1987] 77 Cr App R 111	14.19
R v Institute of Chartered Accountants in England and Wales, *ex p.* Brindle [1994] BCC 297	12.31
R (on the application of NTL Group Ltd) v Ipswich CC [2002] EWHC 1585 [2003] QB 131	6.64, 14.31
R v K [2002] EWCA Crim 2878	14.127
R v K (1993) 97 Cr App R 342	16.64
R v Keane [1994] 2 All ER 478	16.63
R v Kennedy (CA, 30 April 1998)	20.01, 20.15, 20.20, 21.15
R v Kennedy [1999] Cr App R 54	11.21
R v Khan [1996] 3 All ER 289	3.14, 3.15, 14.77, 14.79, 15.12
R v King [1983] 1 All ER 929	11.40, 15.24, 15.25, 16.23
R v Lambert [2001] UKHL 37; [2001] 3 All ER 577; [2001] 3 WLR 206	3.05, 3.55
R v Leeds Crown Court, *ex p.* Hill [1991] Crim LR 376	14.10, 14.26
R v Leeds Crown Court, *ex p.* Switalski [1991] Crim LR 559	14.19, 14.30, 14.33
R v Leicester Crown Court, *ex p.* DPP [1987] 3 All ER 654	14.32
R v Lewes CC, *ex p.* Hill (1990) 93 Cr App R 60	14.26, 14.32, 14.57
R v Lewes Crown Court, *ex p.* Weller & Co (DC, 12 May 1999)	14.19, 14.25
R v Lewes Prison (Governor), *ex p.* Doyle [1917] 2 KB 254	17.31
R v Lloyd [1985] 2 All ER 661	6.69, 6.70

England and Wales

R v Local Authority and Police Authority in the Midlands, *ex p.* LM [2000] 1 FLR 612 ....20.05
R v Loveridge [2001] 2 Cr App R 29 ....6.19, 18.16
R v Lyons [2002] UKHL 44..3.53
R v McCreadie [1992] Crim LR 872 ....6.72
R v McLeod [2002] EWCA Crim 989 ....3.15
R v McPherson [1985] Crim LR 508 ....6.80
R v McShane (1977) 66 Cr App R 97 ....6.57
R v Maidstone Crown Court, *ex p.* Wait [1988] Crim LR 384 ....14.19, 14.30
R v Manchester Crown Court, *ex p.* Rogers [1999] 4 All ER 35.....................16.17, 16.23
R v Manchester Crown Court, *ex p.* Taylor (1988) 87 Cr App R 358 ....14.31, 14.43
R v Marlborough Street Magistrates Court, *ex p.* Simpson (1980) 70 Cr App R 291...........14.57
R v Mason [2002] EWCA Crim 385 ....3.14, 14.70, 14.108
R v Medical Council, *ex p.* Toth [2000] 1 WLR 2209...15.48
R v Mid Glamorgan Family Health Services, *ex p.* Martin [1995]
  1 All ER 356...12.03, 19.03, 19.08, 19.16, 19.17
R v Middlesex Guildhall Crown Court, *ex p.* Salinger [1993] 2 All ER 310 ....14.48
R v Molloy [1997] 2 Cr App R 283 ....16.29
R v Myers [1997] 4 All ER 314 ....15.18
R v Natwest Investment Bank (unreported, 23 January 1991) 16.32
R v Naviede (Central Criminal Court, 9 November 1993) 15.07
R v Northampton Crown Court, *ex p.* DPP (1991) 93 Cr App 376 ....14.27
R v Norwich Crown Court , *ex p.* Chethams [1991] COD 271............................14.26
R (on the application of F) v Oxfordshire NHS Trust [2001] EWHC Admin 535 ....17.42
R v P, C & S (CA, 16 May 2000) 3.19
R (on the application of Ford) v PCC [2001] EWHC Admin 683;
  [2002] EMLR 5 ....6.19, 8.25, 9.15
R v PCC, *ex p.* Stewart-Brady [1997] EMLR 185 ....9.15
R v Peterborough Justices, *ex p.* Hicks [1977] 1 WLR 1371 ....11.40
R (on the application of Stevens) v Plymouth City Council [2002] EWCA Civ 388;
  [2002] 1 FLR 1177 ....1.38, 1.45, 5.27, 13.10, 13.11, 15.13, 16.39,
                                17.05, 17.08, 17.43, 19.77, 19.89, 19.92, 19.114
R v Rataou [1988] 2 All ER 321 ....16.27, 16.30
R v Rathbone, *ex p.* Dikko [1985] 2 WLR 375 ....14.134
R v Reading Justices, *ex p.* Berkshire Crown Court [1996] 1
  Cr App R 239 ....14.129, 15.07
R (on the application of Pearson) v DVLA [2002] EWHC 2482 ....5.20
R v Rees (CA, 20 October 2000) 6.56, 18.05
R v Registrar General, *ex p.* Smith [1990] 2 All ER 170.....................................19.89
R (on the application of Wilkinson) v Responsible Medical Officer, Broadmoor
  [2001] EWCA Civ 1545; [2002] 1 WLR 419 ....1.38
R v Robinson [2002] EWCA Crim 2489 ....14.115
R v Roble [1997] Crim LR 449 ....16.33
R (on the application of Panjawani) v Royal Pharmaceutical Society of GB
  [2002] EWHC 1127 ....4.47
R v Rule [1937] 2 KB 375 ....6.87
R v Sang [1979] 2 All ER 1222...6.95
R v Secretary of State for Health, *ex p.* SW (2000) HRLR 702 ....5.21
R v Secretary of State for Health, *ex p.* Wagstaff [2001] 1 WLR 292..............3.18, 17.50
R (on the application of Holding & Barnes plc) v Secretary of State for the
  Enviroment [2001] UKHL 23; [2001] 2 WLR 1389......................................3.55
R v Secretary of State for the Home Department, *ex p.* Daly [2001] UKHL 26;
  [2001] 2 AC 532 ....2.22, 3.04, 3.19, 3.20, 3.55,
                                                                          10.14, 15.44, 16.14, 16.15
R v Secretary of State for the Home Department, *ex p.* Gashi [1999] INLR 276 ....16.39, 16.39

R v Secretary of State for the Home Department, *ex p.* Kingdom of Belgium
(DC, 15 February 2000) 3.19, 10.09, 10.40
R v Secretary of State for the Home Department, *ex p.* Leech [1993] 4 All ER 539 ....3.10, 16.14
R v Secretary of State for the Home Department, *ex p.* Simms [1999] 3 All ER 400..................3.17
R v Secretary of State for the Home Department, *ex p.* Taj (QBD, 20 October 1999) 13.09
R v Secretary of State for the Home Department, *ex p.* The Kingdom of Belgium
(QBD, 15 February 2000) 3.19
R (on the application of Addinell) v Sheffield City Council
[2001] ACD 61, 2000 WL 33148776 ....13.18, 19.76, 19.91
R v Singleton [1995] 1 Cr App R 431 ....11.37, 11.63, 14.28, 14.41, 15.20
R v Smith (1979) 69 Cr App R 378 ....1.29
R v Snaresbrook CC, *ex p.* DPP [1988] 1 All ER 315 ....16.20, 16.20
R v Solicitor [1997] 1 FLR 101 ....17.04
R v Souter [1995] Crim LR 729 ....1.29
R v Southampton Crown Court, *ex p.* J & P [1993] Crim LR 962....................14.25, 14.30, 14.31
R v Southwark Coroner, *ex p.* Hicks [1987] 1 WLR 1642..15.13, 15.13
R v Southwark Crown Court, *ex p.* Bowles [1998] 2 All ER 193................................14.18, 14.53
R v Southwark Crown Court, *ex p.* Sorsky Defries [1996] Crim LR 195 ....14.19
R (on the application of Morgan Grenfell & Co Ltd) v Special Commissioner
[2002] 1 All ER 776, [2001] EWCA Civ 329 ....10.14, 16.12, 16.13
R v Special Commissioner, *ex p.* Morgan Grenfell & Co [2002] UKHL 21, [2002]
2 WLR 1299 (HL)..10.06, 10.14, 16.08, 16.11, 16.13,
16.14, 16.30, 16.35, 16.39, 18.48, 19.07
R v Statutory Visitors to St Lawrence's Hospital, *ex p.* Caterham [1953]
2 All ER 766 ....15.20, 16.59
R v Stratford Justices, *ex p.* Imbert [1999] 2 Cr App R 276 ....14.123
R v Sutherland (Nottingham Crown Court unreported,
29 January 2002) LTL 22/2/2002 ....3.06, 3.11, 3.14, 6.102, 14.115, 14.117, 14.122, 16.18
R v Taylor [1995] Crim LR 253 ....17.38
R (on the application of Bozkurt) v Thames Magistrates' Court [2001]
EWHC Admin 400; [2002] RTR 246 ....16.16
R v Thompson [1984] 3 All ER 565..6.52
R v Tompkins (1977) 67 Cr App R 181 ....6.101, 6.106
R v Turner [1995] 1 WLR 264..11.64
R v Umoh (1986) 84 Cr App R 138 ....14.22, 16.59
R v University of Cambridge, *ex p.* Persaud [2001] ELR 64 (QB); [2001]
EWCA Civ 534; [2001] ELR 480 (CA) 19.35, 19.38, 19.71
R v Ward [1993] 2 All ER 577 ....15.24
R v Wescott [1983] Crim LR 545 ....15.10
R v Westminster City Council, *ex p.* Castelli (1995) 30 BMLR 123 ....17.38, 17.49
R v Wheeler (1991) 92 Cr App R 279 ....6.85
R v Whitely (1991) 93 Cr App R 25 ....6.82
R v Wilson (1982) 4 Cr App R (S) 337 ....6.76
R v Wilson [1996] 3 WLR 125 ....11.22
R v Woodly (1834) 1 M & Rob 390...16.17
R v Wrights [2001] EWCA Crim 1394..14.77
Rakusen v Ellis, Munday and Clarke [1912] 1 Ch 831 ....5.65, 6.92, 21.38
Ramsbotham v Senior (1869) 8 LR Eq 575 ....16.23
Randolph M Fields v Watts, *The Times*, 22 November 1984 ....14.17
Rank Film Distributors Ltd v Video Information Centre [1981]
2 All ER 76 ....17.14
RCA Corp v Reddingtons Rare Records [1974] 1 WLR 1445..7.10
Redrow Homes Ltd v Bretts Brothers Plc [1997] 24 FSR 828 ....7.44, 8.68
Reed v Madon [1989] 2 All ER 431..4.52, 8.57

l

Regal (Hastings) Ltd v Gulliver (Note) [1967] 2 AC 134...8.72
Republic of Haiti v Duvalier [1989] 1 All ER 456 ....14.44
Reynolds v Times Newspapers Ltd [1999] 4 All ER 509 ....4.36, 7.38, 19.38
Rhodes v Bate (1865–66) LR 1 Ch App 252..5.80
Ricci v Chow [1987] 3 All ER 534 ....7.04
Riddick v Thames Board Mills Ltd [1977] 3 All ER 677 ....16.58, 17.14
Rio Tinto Zinc Corp v Westinghouse Electric Corp [1978] 1 All ER 434 ....14.134
Roberts v Jump Knitwear Ltd [1981] FSR 527 ....7.06, 7.07, 7.08
Robertson v Canadian Imperial Bank of Commerce [1995]
    1 All ER 824 ....5.21, 8.54, 10.16, 12.39, 15.06, 15.08, 16.42
Roger Bullivant Ltd v Ellis [1987] IRLR 491..21.19
Rogers v Secretary of State for the Home Department [1972] 2 All ER 1057 ....15.53
Roker International Properties Inc v Couvaras [2001] 2 FLR 976 ....15.02
Rookes v Barnard [1964] AC 1129..8.69, 8.70
R (on the application of Rose) v Secretary of State for Health [2002]
    EWHC 1593, [2002] 2 FLR 962..1.08, 2.26, 19.112
Rouchefoucauld v Boustead (1896) 65 LJ Ch 794..16.16
Royal Brunei Airlines v Tan [1995] 3 All ER 97...7.20, 7.35
Rumping v DPP [1962] 3 All ER 256 ....6.95
Rush & Tompkins Ltd v Greater London Council [1988] 3 All ER 737 ....16.05
Russel v Jackson (1851) 68 ER 558 ....16.42
Russell v Jackson (1851) 9 Hare 387...16.29, 16.42
Russo v Nugent Care Society [2001] EWHC Admin 566; [2002] 1 FLR 1 ....5.48, 19.20
S, Re [2003] EWHC 254 (Fam) 8.04, 17.49, 17.51
S (Hospital Patient: Court's Jurisdiction) (No.1), Re [1995] 1 FLR 1075 ....13.11
S (A Minor) (Adoption Order: Conditions), Re [1994] 3 All ER 36....................................13.14
S CC v B [2000] 3 WLR 53 ....16.13, 16.16, 16.20, 16.21, 16.25, 16.30, 16.39, 16.41, 16.45
SC (A Minor) (Leave to Seek Residence Order), Re [1994] 1 FLR 96 ....13.14
SL, Re [1987] 2 FLR 412 ....15.03, 15.10
S v S (Judgment in Chambers: Disclosure) [1997] 2 FLR 774 ....17.17, 17.18
Saif Ali v Sydney Mitchell & Co [1978] 3 All ER 1033..15.31
Salih v Enfield Health Authority [1991] 2 Med LR 235 ....8.48
Saltman Engineering Co Ltd v Campbell Engineering Co Ltd [1963]
    3 All ER 413n..5.03, 5.08, 8.38, 8.75
Sasea Finance Ltd v KPMG [2000] 1 BCLC 989...20.41
Satnam Investments Ltd v Dunlop Heywood [1999] 3 All ER 652................5.747, 35, 8.77, 8.78
Saunders v Punch Ltd [1998] 1 All ER 234 ....7.14
Savage v Chief Constable of Hampshire [1997] 2 All ER 631 ....16.62
Savoy Hotel plc v British Broadcasting Corp [1983] NLJ 105...6.51
Schering Chemicals v Falkman Ltd [1981]
    2 All ER 321 ....3.31, 4.11, 5.16, 5.38, 5.63, 5.64, 5.70, 7.20, 7.31, 11.12, 12.30, 20.02
Schneider v Leigh [1995] 2 All ER 173...16.28
Science Research Council v Nasse [1979] 3 All ER 673; [1980] AC 1028........14.07, 15.42, 16.52
Scott v Metropolitan Police Commissioner [1974] 3 All ER 1032..................................6.79, 6.80
Scott v Scott [1913] AC 417...17.33
Seager v Copydex Ltd [1967] 2 All ER 415 ....5.38, 5.40, 5.78, 6.91, 7.28, 8.37, 8.73, 12.37
Secretary of State for Defence v Guardian Newspapers Ltd [1984] 1 All ER 453 (CA)....7.13, 7.19
Secretary of State for Defence v Guardian Newspapers Ltd [1984] 3 All ER 601 (HL) 7.14
Sega Enterprises Ltd v Alca Electronics Ltd [1982] FSR 516...7.07
Senat v Senat [1965] P 172 ....15.14
Senior v Holdsworth, *ex p.* Independent Television News Ltd [1975]
    2 All ER 1009 ....15.02, 15.07, 15.08, 15.16, 15.20,
Service Corp International plc v Channel Four [1999] EMLR 83 ....6.19, 8.11
Seyfang v GD Searle & Co [1973] 1 QB 148..14.135

Tables of Cases

Shah v Standard Chartered Bank [1998] 4 All ER 155 ....10.01
Shelfer v City of London Electric Co [1895] 1 Ch 287 ....8.06
Shelley v Paddock [1978] 3 All ER 129 ....8.48
Shelley Films Ltd v Rex Features Ltd [1994] EMLR 134.............................6.06, 6.17, 6.19
Sidaway v Bethlem Royal Hospital [1984] 1 All ER 1018 (CA); [1985]
    1 All ER 643 (HL) 5.27, 5.79, 5.80, 13.28, 19.13, 19.14, 19.15, 19.65, 19.66
Sim v Manchester Action Health (2001) EAT/0085/01 ....21.24
Sim v Stretch [1936] 2 All ER 1237 ....4.34
Simba-Tola v Trustees of Elizabeth Fry Hostel [2001] EWCA Civ 1371....................14.06, 14.07
Skaw v Skeet [1996] 7 Med LR 371 ....14.09
Skjevesland v Geveran Trading Co Ltd [2002] EWCA Civ 1567 ....6.92, 6.93, 15.31
Skyrail Oceanic Ltd v Coleman [1980] IRLR 226 ....6.38
Slipper v BBC [1991] 1 All ER 165 ....7.38
Smith v Director of Serious Fraud Office [1992] 3 All ER 456.......................................14.59
Smith v Tunbridge Wells Health Authority [1994] Med LR 334...................................19.66
Smith New Court Ltd v Scrimgeour Vickers (Asset Management) Ltd [1996] 4 All ER 769....8.42
Smithkline Beecham Biologicals SA v Connaught Laboratories Inc [1999]
    4 All ER 498 ....17.16, 17.27
Société Romanaise de la Chaussure FA v British Shoe Corporation Ltd [1991] FSR 1 ....7.10
Soul v Inland Revenue Commissioners [1963] 1 All ER 68 ....15.41
Southwark and Vauxhall Water Company v Quick [1878] 3 QBD 315 ....16.20
Special Hospital Service Authority v Hyde (1994) 20 BMLR 75 ....7.17
Spector v Ageda [1971] 3 All ER 417 ....19.58
Speed Seal Products Ltd v Paddington [1986] 1 All ER 91 ....5.60
Sphere Drake Insurance plc v Denby, *The Times*, 20 December 1991 ....15.05
Spring v Guardian Assurance [1994] 3 All ER 129 ....19.117
State of Norway's Application (No 2), Re [1989] 1 All ER 701 ....14.135
Steel v Savory [1891] WN 195 ....15.07
Steele v Moule [1999] CLY 326 ....17.02
Stephens v Avery [1988]
    2 All ER 477 ....5.03, 5.04, 5.08, 5.11, 5.24, 5.25, 6.17, 6.19, 6.23, 8.51, 8.52, 13.67, 19.16
Stevenson, Jordan & Harrison Ltd v MacDonald & Evans (1952) 69 RPC 10 ....7.31
Storer v British Gas plc [2000] 2 All ER 440 ....15.45, 15.47
Subpoena (Adoption: Commissioner for Local Administration), Re [1996] 2 FLR 629.........15.07
Sumitomo Corp v Credit Lyonnais Rouse Ltd [2001] EWCA Civ 1152;
    [2002] 1 WLR 479...14.05, 16.22, 16.23
Sunday Times v UK (1979) 2 EHRR 245...3.19, 4.59
Sunderland v Barclays Bank Ltd (1938) 5 LDAB 163 ....12.32, 12.39, 18.38
Surrey CC v Bredero Homes Ltd [1993] 3 All ER 705 ....8.29
Svenska v Sun Alliance [1995] 2 Lloyd's Rep 84 ....16.32
Swindle v Harrison [1997] 4 All ER 705..8.36, 8.45
Swinney v Chief Constable of Northumbria [1996]
    3 All ER 449 ....2.25, 4.23, 4.26, 6.17, 6.90, 9.01, 10.01
Sykes v DPP [1961] 3 All ER 33..10.12
T (Adult: Refusal of Treatment), Re [1992] 4 All ER 649.....................13.22, 13.27, 13.28, 13.57
T v T [1988] Fam 52 ....13.11
T and A (Children) (Risk of Disclosure), Re [2000] 1 FLR 859 ....6.93
Tang Man Sit (dec'd) v Capacious Investments Ltd [1996] 1 All ER 193 ....8.36
Target Holdings Ltd v Redferns [1995] 3 All ER 785 ....8.45
Taylor v SFO [1998] 4 All ER 801 ....17.12, 17.14
TC Coombs & Co v Inland Revenue Commissioners [1991] 3 All ER 623....................3.35
Temperton v Russell [1893] 1 QB 715 ....7.36
Tennant, Lady Anne v Associated Newspapers [1979] FSR 298 ....7.32, 7.44
Terrapin Ltd v Builders' Supply Co Ltd [1960] RPC 128 ....5.29, 12.37

The Bank v A Ltd (HC, 23 June 2000, WL 774924) 10.17, 16.03
Theakston v MGN Ltd [2002] EWHC 137; [2002]
  EMLR 22 .... 5.05, 6.17, 6.19, 6.22, 6.24, 8.16, 11.10, 11.65, 11.73, 13.63, 13.67, 18.39
Thomas v NGN Ltd [2001] EWCA Civ 1233; [2002] EMLR 4 .... 7.40, 7.41
Thomas v Pearce [2000] FSR 718 .... 7.20, 7.21, 7.32
Thompson v Stanhope (1774) 27 ER 476 .... 6.17
Thomson, Re (1855) 52 ER 714 .... 19.07, 19.14
Thornley v ARA Ltd (EAT 669/76, 11 May 1977) 21.17
Three Rivers District Council v Bank of England (No. 3) [2000] 3 All ER 1 .... 10.39
Three Rivers District Council v Bank of England [2000] EWCA Civ 1182,
  [2003] 1 WLR 210 .... 14.06
Three Rivers District Council v Bank of England [2002] EWHC 2730
  (Comm) .... Addendum, 16.22
Three Rivers District Council v Bank of England (No. 5) [2003] EWCA
  Civ 474 .... Addendum
Thurston v Charles (1905) 21 TLR 659 .... 6.51
Times Newspapers Ltd v MGN Ltd [1993] EMLR 442 .... 8.10
Tombridge v Universal Bulb Co Ltd [1951] 2 TLR 289 .... 15.34
Totalise plc v Motley Fool Ltd [2001] EWCA Civ 1897; [2002] 1 WLR 1233 .... 7.11
Tournier v National Provincial and Union Bank [1942] 1 KB 461 .... 3.47, 4.07, 4.08, 4.12,
       4.14, 5.27, 5.29, 11.01, 11.02, 11.07, 11.09, 11.32, 12.02, 12.34, 12.39, 13.23, 16.42
Trustor v Smallbone [2000] 1 All ER 811 .... 17.31
TSB v Robert Irving [2000] 2 All ER 826 .... 16.34
Turner v Royal Bank of Scotland plc [2001] EWCA Civ 64; [2001] 1 All ER
  (Comm) 1057 .... 11.43, 11.52, 13.35, 13.47, 19.117
Tweedle v Atkins (1861) 1 B & S 393, 121 ER 762 .... 4.03
Twinsectra Ltd v Yardley [2002] 2 All ER 377; [2002] UKHL 12;
  [2002] 2 AC 164 .... 7.20, 7.35
Underwood Ltd v Bank of Liverpool & Martins [1924] 1 KB 776 .... 7.42
Unilever plc v Proctor & Gamble [2001] 1 All ER 783 .... 16.05, 16.38
Universal Thermosensors Ltd v Hibben [1992] 3 All ER 257 .... 5.36, 8.04, 14.15, 14.16
USP Strategies plc v London General Holdings Ltd [2002] EWHC 2577 .... 5.84
V (Minors) (Sexual Abuse: Disclosure), Re [1999] 1 FLR 267 .... 10.10, 17.18, 20.05
Valeo Vision SA v Flexible Lamps Ltd [1995] RPC 205 .... 7.22, 7.31
Van Laun, ex p. Chatterton, Re [1907] 2 KB 23 .... 5.27, 5.65
Vel v Owen [1987] Crim LR 496 .... 15.12
Venables v NGN Ltd [2001] 1 All ER 908; [2001] Fam 430 .... 1.03, 1.40, 3.06, 3.30,
             4.59, 4.60, 5.27, 5.43, 5.59, 6.07, 6.08, 6.17, 6.19, 7.20, 7.24, 7.26,
             8.02, 8.03, 8.04, 8.14, 8.25, 9.08, 9.16, 11.23, 16.59, 19.94, 20.05
Ventouris v Mountain [1991] 1 WLR 607 .... 11.77, 12.35, 14.05, 16.22, 16.35
Vernon v Bosley (No 2)[1997] 1 All ER 614 .... 15.33, 16.39, 17.18
W (A Minor) (Medical Treatment), Re [1992] 4 All ER 627 .... 13.16, 13.18, 19.98
W (A Minor) (Wardship: Restrictions on Publication), Re [1992]
  1 All ER 794 .... 3.31, 13.12
W (EEM), Re [1971] Ch 123 .... 12.05, 12.09, 19.114
W (Minors) (Social Worker: Disclosure), Re [1998] 2 All ER 801;
  [1998] 2 FLR 135 .... 16.54, 17.18
W v Egdell [1990] 1 All ER 835 (CA); affirming [1989] 1 All ER 801 .... 1.55, 3.03, 3.47, 4.12,
            4.13, 4.14, 5.05, 5.27, 6.17, 8.37, 8.51, 8.52, 8.56, 11.03, 11.08, 11.11,
            11.12, 11.13, 11.21, 11.22, 11.57, 11.61, 11.62, 11.67, 11.71, 11.78,
            11.79, 11.83, 12.31, 15.28, 16.59, 19.15, 20.01, 20.02, 20.15, 20.18
W v S CC [2001] EWCA Civ 691 .... 20.18, 20.20
W v W (HC, 22 February 2001) 6.17
Wadman v Dick [1998] 3 FCR 9 .... 14.135, 15.16

Wai Yu-tsang v R [1991] 4 All ER 664 ....6.80
Walker v Eli Lilly & Co [1986] ECC 550 ....14.11
Wallace Bogan & Co v Cove [1997] IRLR 453 ....19.07, 21.19
Walsh Automation (Europe) Ltd v Bridgeman [2002] EWHC 1344 ....16.35, 16.37
Warner-Lambert Co v Glaxo Laboratories Ltd [1975] RPC 354 ....17.14
Watson v McEwan [1905] AC 480 ....15.22
Watts v Marrow [1991] 4 All ER 937 ....8.46
Waugh v British Railway Board [1979] 2 All ER 1169 ....6.98, 16.08, 16.21
WEA Records Ltd v Visions Channel 4 Ltd [1983] 2 All ER 589 ....17.05
Webster v James Chapman & Co [1989] 3 All ER 939 ....6.96, 6.105
Weld-Blundell v Stephens [1920] AC 956 (HL); affirming
 [1919] 1 KB 520 ....5.27, 8.42, 11.04, 11.10, 11.11, 11.37, 12.08, 16.36
Welham v DPP [1960] 1 All ER 805 ....6.80
Wentworth v Lloyd (1864) 10 HLC 589 ....16.10, 19.14
Western Home Counties Developments Ltd v Stone, Toms Partners (CA, 19 March 1984) 19.64
Wheatcroft, Re (1877) 6 Ch D 97 ....19.07
Wheatley v Bell [1984] FSR 16 ....7.31
Wheeler v Le Marchant (1881) 17 Ch D 675 ....16.19, 16.21, 16.42, 16.55
White v Jones [1995] 1 All ER 691 ....19.62, 20.41
Wilder Pump & Engineering Co v Melvin Fusfeld [1985] FSR 159 ....16.42
Wilkinson v Downton [1897] 2 QB 57 ....4.30, 4.32, 4.33, 8.42
William Coulson & Sons v James Coulson & Co [1887] 3 TLR 46 ....8.11
Williams v Settle [1960] 1 WLR 1072 ....6.23, 8.67, 8.68
Williams v Summerfield [1972] 2 All ER 1334 ....14.57
Willis v Governor of Her Majesty's Prison, Winchester
 (Ch D, 21 December 1994) 6.101, 6.106
Wilson v Rastall (1792) 4 Tr 753; (1792) 100 ER 1283 ....16.08, 16.42
Wong v Parkside Health NHS Trust [2001] EWCA Civ 1721 ....4.33
Woodward v Hutchins [1977]
 1 WLR 760 ....6.19, 8.10, 8.11, 8.37, 11.10, 11.12, 11.41, 11.61, 13.64, 13.65, 21.27
Wookey v Wookey [1991] Fam 121 ....8.04
Woolgar v Chief Constable of Sussex Police [1999]
 3 All ER 604 ....1.29, 10.20, 11.63, 11.71, 17.10, 17.21
Wright v Pepin [1954] 2 All ER 52 ....13.40
X (A Child) (Injunctions Restraining Publication), Re [2001] 1 FCR 541 ....3.17
X (A Minor), Re [1975] Fam 47 ....4.57
X (A Minor) (Wardship: Injunction), Re [1984] 1 WLR 1422 ....8.02
X, Re [2002] EWCA Civ 525 ....17.06, 17.07
X (Disclosure of Information), Re [2001] 2 FLR 440 ....17.18, 19.18
X AG v Bank, A [1983] 2 All ER 464 ....5.59, 10.23, 12.34, 14.134
X County Council v A [1985] 1 All ER 53 ....3.31
X v Bedfordshire CC [1995] 2 AC 633 [1995] 3 All ER 353, [1995]
 3 WLR 152 ....1.28, 1.30, 4.23, 4.50, 20.04
X v Dempster [1999] 1 FLR 894 ....17.46
X v A Health Authority [2001] Lloyd's Rep Med 349 ....10.10
X v Y [1988] 2 All ER 648 ....1.48, 4.51, 5.04, 5.41, 6.17, 6.19, 7.15, 7.34, 7.36,
 7.37, 8.18, 8.25, 11.12, 11.50, 11.57, 17.34, 20.34
X Ltd v Morgan-Grampian Ltd [1990] 2 All ER 1 ....6.06, 6.46, 7.14, 7.16, 7.17, 7.18
X NHS Trust v A (Fam Div, 31 July 2002) 17.41
Yates v Buckley (CA, 3 November 1997) 14.07
Young v Holloway (1887) 12 PD 167 ....4.08
Young v Robson Rhodes [1999] 3 All ER 524 ....6.93, 6.94
Youssoupoff v Metro-Goldwyn Mayer Pictures Ltd (1934) 50 TLR 581 ....4.34
Yuen Kun Keu v Att-Gen of Hong Kong [1990] 1 WLR 821 ....20.41

Z, Re (Fam Div, 13 October 2000) 17.36
Z (A Minor) (Freedom of Publication), Re [1995] 4 All ER 961 ....5.27, 6.17, 13.20, 19.87, 19.94
Zakay v Zakay [1998] 3 FCR 35 ....14.135

EUROPEAN COURT OF HUMAN RIGHTS

A v UK (1998) 27 EHRR 611 ....20.05
Abdulaziz v UK [1985] ECHR 9214/80 ....8.55
ADT v UK (2001) 31 EHRR 33 ....6.17
Airey v Ireland (1980) 2 EHRR 305 ....3.06
Amann v Switzerland (2000) 30 EHRR 843 ....3.03, 3.19, 8.31
Andersson (Anne-Marie) v Sweden (1998) 25 EHRR 5.52, 10.08
Autronic AG v Switzerland (1990) 12 EHRR 1 ....3.17
Axen v Germany (1984) 6 EHRR 195 ....3.13
B v UK [2001] FCR 221; [2001] 2 FLR 261 ....17.36, 17.50, 17.51
Bergens Tidende v Norway (2003) 31 EHRR 16 ....12.37
Bladet Tromso v Stensas Norway (1999) 29 EHRR 125 ....5.22
Bodil Lindqvist v Kammaraklagen [2002] Celex No 601C0101 ....18.01
Botta v Italy (1998) 26 EHRR 241 ....5.20, 19.20, 20.05
Brennan v UK (2002) 34 EHRR 507 ....3.11
Bugallo v Spain Application 58496/00 18 Feb 2003 ....3.03, 6.14
Camenzind v Switzerland Application 21353/93, partial decision February 27 1995 ....6.19
Campbell v UK (1993) 15 EHRR 137 ....3.03, 3.11, 3.21, 16.09
Chappell v UK (1989) 12 EHRR 1 ....14.15
Costello-Roberts v UK (1993) 19 EHRR 112 ....5.08
Dalban v Romania (2001) 31 EHRR 39 ....8.25
De Geillustreerde Pers v Netherlands (1976) DR 8 ....8.22
De Haes v Belgium (1998) 25 EHRR 1 ....3.18, 16.27
Diennet v France (1995) 21 EHRR 554 ....15.45
Domenichini v Italy (2001) 32 EHRR 4 ....3.03, 3.19, 8.31
Doorson v Netherlands (1996) 22 EHRR 330 ....3.23, 17.38
Dudgeon v UK (1982) 4 EHRR 149 ....3.22, 11.30
E v UK Application 33218/96, 26 November 2002 ....9.06, 20.05
Edward v UK Application 46477/99 (2002) 35 EHRR 19 ....15.53
Edwards v UK (1992) 15 EHRR 417 ....3.14, 16.26
Fitt v UK (2000) 30 EHRR 441 ....16.63
Foxley v UK Application 33274/96 (2000) 8 BHRC 571 ....10.13, 10.15, 11.13
Fressoz v France (2001) 31 EHRR 2 ....3.21, 3.22, 3.29, 6.17, 8.25, 11.83
Funke v France (1993) 16 EHRR 297 ....8.57, 14.119, 16.03, 16.09, 16.27
Gaskin v UK (1989) 12 EHRR 36 ....3.03, 8.55, 8.57, 19.17, 19.20, 19.91, 19.111, 19.112
Gautin v France (1999) 28 EHRR 195 ....15.45
Gaygusuv v Austria (1996) 23 EHRR 364 ....8.69
Ginikawa v UK (1988) 55 DR 251 ....15.46
Goodwin v UK (1996) 22 EHRR 123 ....1.32
Golder v UK (1975) 1 EHRR 524 ....16.45
Grigoriades v Greece (1977) 27 EHRR 464 ....21.30
Guerra v Italy (1998) 26 E HRR 357 ....3.18
Hakansson v Sweden (1990) 13 EHRR 1 ....17.35
Halford v UK (1997) 24 EHRR 523 .....3.03, 4.46, 6.13, 6.14, 6.17, 6.22, 8.55, 8.57, 8.64, 14.89
Handyside v UK (1976) EHRR 737 ....3.17, 3.19
Harman v UK (1984) 3 DR 38 ....17.50
Hentrich v France (1994) 18 EHRR 440 ....3.19
Herczwgfahy v Austria Series A No 244 (1993) 15 EHRR 437 ....3.18
Hewitt and Harman v UK (1991) 67 DR 88 ....14.71

lv

Hilton v UK (1988) 57 DR 108 ....3.03, 4.46
Huvig v France (1990) 12 EHRR 528 ....3.19, 3.21, 14.71
Jabardo v Spain (1994) 11 EHRR 360 ....8.44
Jasper v UK (2000) 30 EHRR 441 ....16.63
Jersild v Denmark (1995) 19 EHRR 1 ....5.22
Jespers v Belgium (1981) 27 DR 61 ....14.125, 16.26
K & T v Finland (1994) 76A DR 140 ....3.21
Khan v UK (2001) 31 EHRR 45 ....3.21
Klass v Germany (1978) 2 EHRR 214 ....3.03, 4.46, 14.71
Konig v Germany (1979) 2 EHRR 170 ....15.46
Kopp v Switzerland (1999) 27 EHRR 91 ....3.21, 8.31, 10.14, 14.40, 14.117
Krone Verlag GmBH v Austria Application 34315/96 (21 March 2002) 3.30, 6.24
Kruslin v France (1990) 12 EHRR 547 ....14.71
L (A Child) v United Kingdom (Disclosure of Expert Evidence) [2000]
   2 FLR 322 ....3.10, 11.13
Lambert v France [1999] EHRLR 123 ....8.57
LCB v UK (1999) 27 EHRR 212 ....20.05
Le Compte Van Leuven & De Meyere v Belgium (1982) 4 EHRR 1 ....15.46
Leander v Sweden (1987) 9 EHRR 433 ....3.03, 3.18, 3.19, 3.22, 17.35, 19.01
Lingens v Austria (1986) 8 EHRR 407 ....6.24
Ludi v Switzerland (1992) 15 EHRR 173 ....6.17
Lundwall v Sweden (1985) 45 DR 121 ....3.19
Lustig-Prean v UK (2000) 31 EHRR 734 ....8.57, 8.66
M v UK Application 39393/98, 24 September 2002 ....19.19
McCann v UK (1995) 21 EHRR 97 ....4.46
McGinley v UK (1998) 27 EHRR 1 ....16.26, 19.111
Malone v UK (1984) 7 EHRR 14 ....3.03, 3.14, 3.19, 3.21, 14.70, 14.88
Marckx v Belgium (1979–80) 2 EHRR 330 ....3.19
Markt Intern and Beermann v Germany (1989) 12 EHRR 161 ....3.19, 3.31
Martin v UK (1996) 21 EHRR CD 113 ....11.07, 11.13, 19.17, 19.68, 19.111
MG v UK Application 39393/98, (24 September 2002) 19.18, 19.103, 19.111, 19.112
MK v Austria (1997) 24 EHRR CD 59 ....3.23
MM v Netherlands, Application 39339/98 18 April 2003 ....3.03
MS v Sweden (1999)
   28 EHRR 313; 1.48, 3.03, 3.08, 3.21, 10.09, 10.20, 11.13, 11.30, 12.33, 16.02
Mukulic v Croatia Application 53176/99 [2002] IFCR 720 ....19.111
Muller v Switzerland (1988) 13 EHRR 212 ....3.19
Murray v UK (1995) 19 EHRR 193 ....3.03, 3.19
Neves v Portugal Application 20683/92 (20 February 1995) 3.30, 3.31, 8.22
Nielson v Denmark (1989) 11 EHRR 175 ....19.112
Niemietz v Germany (1992) 16 EHRR 97 ....1.14, 3.03, 3.11, 3.21, 6.22, 8.62, 10.15, 14.71
Observer and Guardian v UK (1991) 14 EHRR 153 ....8.11
Odiévre v France Application 42326/98 13 Feb 2003 ....19.112
Open Door Counselling Ltd and Dublin Well Woman v Ireland Series A
   No 246 (1993) 15 EHRR 244 ....3.18
Osman v UK (1998) 5 BHRC 293;
   (1998) 29 EHRR 245 ....4.46, 11.23, 20.05, 20.13, 20.16, 20.18
Peck v UK Application 00044647/98, (21 June 2001) 6.19
Peck v UK *The Times* 3 Feb 2003 ....3.03, 3.21, 6.19, 8.25, 8.55, 9.15, 13.67
PG v UK (44787/98) [2002] Crim LR 308 ....1.08, 3.19
R v Austria Application 12592/86 ....14.68
R v Finland (1997) 25 EHRR 371 ....1.48
R v A Local Authority in the Midlands, *ex p.* LM [2000] 1 FCR 736;
   [2000] UKHRR 143 ....10.40, 13.25

Rotaru v Romania Application 2834/95, (2000) 8 BHRC 449 ....1.11, 3.19, 5.20, 6.22, 8.62
Rutili v Minister of the Interior [1975] ECHR 1219 ....3.04
S v Switzerland (1992) 14 EHRR 97 ....3.11
Sahin v Germany [2002] 1 FLR 119..16.40, 19.87
Saunders v UK (1996) 23 EHRR 313 ....10.15, 10.34, 16.03, 16.09, 16.27
Schenk v Switzerland (1988) 13 EHRR 242 ....3.14, 3.15
Scherer v Switzerland (1994) 18 EHRR 276...5.52
Schönenberger & Durmaz v Switzerland(2000) 11 EHRR 202 ....8.55
Sekanina v Austria (1993) 17 EHRR 221 ....8.44
Sheffield v Horsham v UK (1999) 27 EHRR 163 ....3.06
Silver v UK (1983) 5 EHRR 347...3.19
Spencer v UK (1998) 25 EHRR CD 105 ....5.38, 6.07, 8.72, 9.11
Sporrang v Sweden (1982) 5 EHRR 35 ....3.20
Stes Colas Est v France Application 37971/97 (16 April 2002) 1.12
Stjerna v Finland (1997) 24 EHRR 195 ....3.06
Sturesson v Sweden (1990) 13 ECHR 1 ....13.63
TP V UK Application 28945/95 (2002) 34 EHRR 2 ....3.21, 4.21, 19.87, 19.92
TV v Finland Application 21780/93 76A DR 140 ....11.50, 11.59
Tammer v Estonia Application 41205/98, 10 (2001) BHRC 543........3.28, 3.30, 3.31, 8.23, 8.25
Tamosius v UK [2002] STC 1307 ....3.11, 3.19, 3.21, 14.30, 14.65, 14.66, 14.67, 14.68
Tyrer v UK (1976) 2 EHRR 1...3.55
Valenzuela Contreras v Spain (1998) 28 EHRR 483..3.19
Van Mechelen v Netherlands (1998) 25 EHRR 647...3.23
Van Raalte v Netherlands (1997) 24 EHRR 503 ....3.19
Vereniging Weekblad 'Bluf' v Netherlands (1995) 20 EHRR 189..................................3.21, 5.61
Vernon v UK Application 38753/97 (2001) 29 EHRR CD 264 ....3.10, 14.08
Vogt v Germany (1996) 21 EHRR 205 ....3.19, 21.29
Weber v Switzerland (1990) 12 EHRR 508...5.61
Willsher v UK (1997) EHRR CD 188 ....19.114
X v France Series A, No 235-C (1992) 1 EHRR 483 ....5.52
X v Iceland (1976) 5 DR 86 ....1.16
X v Norway (1977) 14 DR 228 ....5.20
X v UK (1977) 2 Digest 452 7366/76 ....17.37
X v UK (1982) 30 DR 239 ....3.21
X, Y & Z v UK (1997) 24 EHRR 143 ....19.111, 19.112
X and Y v Netherlands (1985) 8 EHRR 235 ....3.03, 3.06, 20.05
Z v Austria Application 10392/83 (1998) 56 DR 13 ....3.18
Z v Finland (1998) 25 EHRR 371...........................1.48, 3.03, 3.21, 3.22, 8.55, 10.08, 11.13,
      15.06, 15.19, 17.37, 17.38, 17.39, 17.40, 17.51
Z v Switzerland Application 10343/83, (1983) 35 DR 224 ....3.29
Z v UK (2002) 34 EHRR 3 ....20.05, 20.13

HONG KONG

China Light & Power Company Ltd v Ford [1996] HKC LEXIS 250 ....5.29
Nga v Hospital Authority [2002] 1100 HKCU 1 ....16.22
Robert v Commissioner of Police [2002] 1412 HKCU 1............10.28, 10.30, 10.31, 16.14, 16.23
Rockefeller & Co Inc v Secretary for Justice [2000]
   3 HKC 48 ....6.103, 6.107, 15.18, 16.31, 16.32
Seng Yuet-Fong v HKSAR [1999] 2 HKC 833 ....10.28
Wilkinson v Wilkinson [1994] HKC 58 ....16.38

NEW ZEALAND

Case	Reference
Allied Finance and Investments Ltd v Haddow & Co [1983] NZLR 22	20.41
Aquaculture Corp v New Zealand Green Mussel Co [1990] 3 NZLR 299	8.38, 8.70
Att-Gen for England and Wales v R [2002] 2 NZLR 91	8.04, 13.22, 13.27
Att-Gen for England and Wales v Television New Zealand Ltd and X (1998) 44 IPR 123	4.10
Att-Gen for UK v Wellington Newspapers [1988] 1 NZLR 129	7.33
Auckland District Law Society v B [2002] 1 NZLR 721	16.31
Auckland Medical Aid Trust v Commissioner of Police [1976] 1 NZLR 485	5.85
Bradley v Wignut Films [1993] 1 NZLR 415	4.31, 4.41, 4.53
Commissioner of Police v Ombudsman [1988] 1 NZLR 385	1.02
Cook v Evatt (No 2)[1992] 1 NZLR 676	5.65
Crisford v Haszard [2000] 2 NZLR 729	16.21
Day v Mead [1987] 2 NZLR 443	8.45
DHL International (NZ) Ltd v Richmond Ltd [1993] 3 NZLR 10	5.64
Duncan v Medical Practitioners Disciplinary Committee [1986] 1 NZLR 513	5.81, 11.11, 11.22, 12.31, 13.45, 20.02
Estate Realities v Wignall [1991] 3 NZLR 482	5.65
Euro Banking Corp v Fourth Estate [1993] 1 NZLR 559	5.60
European Pacific Banking Corp v Television NZ Ltd [1995] 3 NZLR 381	16.44
Fahey v Att-Gen [1993] 1 ERNZ 161	16.45
Furniss v Fitchett [1958] NZLR 396	3.47, 4.03, 4.24, 4.25, 4.26, 4.29, 4.36, 5.81, 8.42, 8.48
G v Att-Gen [1994] 1 NZLR 714	4.52, 6.17, 8.42
Haira v Burbery Mortgage Finance & Savings Ltd [1995] 3 NZLR 396	19.59
HJ Van de Wetering v Capital Coast Health Ltd (NZ HC, 19 May 2000) 9	20.09, 20.15
Hobbs v North Shore City Coucil [1992] 1 ERNZ 32	21.29
JD v Ross [1998] NZFLR 951	5.26, 5.64, 8.45, 8.52, 11.67
L v G [2002] DCR 234; 2002 NZDCR LEXIS2	5.35, 6.17, 6.19, 8.50
L v Robinson [2000] 3 NZLR 499	5.81
Legal Services Agency v Att-Gen [2002] 1 NZLR 842	16.20
Long v Att-Gen [2001] 2 NZLR 529	16.59
Lowe v Tararua District Council (27 June 1994)	21.29
M v L [1997] 3 NZLR 424	16.22, 16.44, 16.47, 17.02
McKaskell v Benseman [1989] 3 NZLR 75	5.65, 13.01, 13.44, 19.62
McLean v Arklow Investments Ltd [1998] 3 NZLR 680	5.67, 5.73, 5.75
Moreton v Police [2002] 2 NZLR 236	6.14
Mouat v Clarke Boyce [1992] 2 NZLR 559	4.23, 8.38
MP, Re [1997] NZFLR LEXIS 141	12.31
National Insurance Co Ltd v Whirlybird Holdings Ltd [1994] 2 NZLR 513	6.96
NZ Post Ltd v Prebble [2001] NZAR 360	11.05
P v D [2000] 2 NZLR 591	4.58, 6.17
R v H [2000] 2 NZLR 257	12.12
R v Howse [1983] NZLR 246	16.43
R v Lory [1997] 1 NZLR 44	16.16
R v Rapana [1995] 2 NZLR 381	16.44
R v Secord [1992] 3 NZLR 570	16.44
R v Uljee [1982] 1 NZLR 561	6.98, 6.105
Rosenburg v Jaine [1983] NZLR 1	16.11
Russell McVeigh Mckenzie Bartleet & Co v Auckland District Law Society (HC, M 1539SD/99, 6 July 2000)	11.79
Stevenson v Basham [1922] NZLR 225	4.32
Susan Hosiery Ltd v Minister of National Revenue [1969] 2 Ex CR 27	16.19

Thompson v Commission of Inquiry [1983] NZLR 98 ....14.07, 15.53, 15.54, 15.55
Tucker v News Media Ownership Ltd [1986] 2 NZLR 716 ....4.31, 4.32, 8.25, 13.63, 20.16
X v Att-Gen [1997] 2 NZLR 623 ....8.45, 8.52

NORTHERN IRELAND

C , Re [2002] NI Fam 14 ....19.87
O'Neill v Department of Health and Social Services (No 2)
  [1986] 5 NIJB 60 ....4.60, 7.37, 8.37, 8.38, 8.39, 8.40, 8.51, 8.52

SOUTH AFRICA

Financial Main (Pty) Ltd v Sage Holdings 1993 (2) SA 451 ....1.12
Investigating Directorate v Hyundai Motor Distributors [2000] ZACC 13 ....1.12
Jansen van Vuuren NNO v Kruger 1993(4) SA 842 (A) 11.50

SCOTLAND

AB v CD (1904) 7 Sess Cas (5th Ser) 72 ....4.35
AB v Glasgow and West of Scotland Blood Transfusion Service (1989)
  15 BMLR 91 ....16.59
Brown's Trustees v Hay (1898) 35 SLR 877 ....11.29
Charnos plc v Donnelly (EAT(Scot) 27 July 2000) 14.07, 15.44
Conoco (UK) Ltd v Commercial Law Practice [1997] SLR 372 ....16.23, 16.35
Dickson Minto WS v Bonnier Media Ltd [2002] SLT 776 ....8.16
Grant v Allan 1988 SLT 11 ....6.71
Higgins v Burton 1968 SLT 52 ....14.07
HMA v Kelly (HC Glasgow, 23 March 2001) 11.59, 14.22
Jindal v University of Glasgow (EAT/74/01, 31 May 2001) 15.42
McGrath v McGrath [1999] SLT 90 ....17.06
McLeon v British Railway Board [1997] SLT 434 ....16.59
Orr v McFadyen [2003] SLT 29 ....17.07
Wyatt v Wilson [1994] SLT 1135 ....5.45
X Pte Ltd v CDE [1992] SLR 996 ....4.44

UNITED STATES

Alberts v Devine 479 NE 2d 112 (1984) 5.40, 7.37
Anderson v State of Maryland 427 US 463 (1976) 16.06
Barber v Time, Inc 159 SW 2d 291 ....4.60, 6.24, 8.25
Bartnicki v Vooper 532 US 514, 538 (2001) 3.18
Bellah v Greenson 73 Cal App (3d) 911 (1977) 20.17
Betesh v US 400 F Supp 238 (1974) 1.31
Board of Medical Quality Assurance v Gherardini 93 Cal App 3d 669 (1979) 6.25
Boyd v US 116 US 616, 630 (1885) 1.07
Boynton v Burglass 590 So 2d 635 (1999) 20.14
Bradshaw v Daniel 854 SW 2d 865 (1993) 20.28
Brady v Hopper 570 F Supp 1333 ....20.19
Briscoe v Reader's Digest Ass Inc 483 P 2d 34, 40 (1971); 93 Cal Rptr 866 ....5.20, 8.62
Cabaniss v Hipsley 151 SE 2d 496 (1966) 6.22
Cannell v Medical Surgical Clinic 315 NE 2d 278 (1974) 19.15
Carlisle v Fawcett Pub Inc 20 Cal Rptr 405 (1962) 6.23

Tables of Cases

Carr v Watkins 177 A 25 841 (1962)	4.56
Chizmar v Mackie 896 P 2d 196, 208 (1995)	11.59
Clayman v Bernstein 38 Pa D & C 543 (1940)	4.09
Cox Broadcasting Corp v Cohn 420 US 469 (1975)	5.20
Cutter v Brownbridge 228 Cal. Rptr. 545 (1986)	6.25
Daily Times Democrat v Graham 162 So 2d 474 (1964)	4.53
Diaz v Oakland Tribune 188 Cal Rptr 762 (1983)	6.24
DiMarco v Lynch Homes-Chester County Inc 583A 2d 422, 424–425 (1990)	20.32
Doe v Delie 257 F 35 309 (2001)	21.13
Doe v Prime Health/Kansas City AIDS Litigation Reporter 1641 (1988)	20.29
Doe v Roe 400 NYS 2d 668 (1977)	8.02
Doe v Univision Television Group 717 So 2d 63 (1998)	13.62
Edwards v State Farm Insurance Co and 'John Doe' 833 F 2d 535 (1987)	2.10, 6.14, 13.36
Emmett v Eastern Dispensary and Casualty Hospital 396 F 2d (1967)	19.15
Estate of Behringer v Medical Center at Princeton 592 A 2d 1251 (1991)	6.17, 6.32
Evans v Rite Aid Corp 478 SE 2d 846 (1996)	4.42
Finkel, Estate of 395 NYS 2d 343 (1977)	19.09
Fitch v Voit 624 So 2d 542 (1993)	5.47
Florida Star v BJF 491 US 524 (1989)	6.23
Garcia, Re 78 BR 68 (1987)	19.07
Garcia v Santa Rose Health Care Corp 925 SW 2d 372 (1996)	20.29
Geisberger v Willuhn 390 NE 2d 945 (1979)	5.29
Goebel, Re 703 NE 2d 1045 (1998)	20.12
Golden Spread Council, Inc v Atkins 926 SW 2d 287, 290 (1996)	20.25
Gooden v Tips 651 SW 2d 364 (1983)	20.31
Hague v Williams 181 A 2d 345 (1962)	13.34, 14.09
Hawkins v King County 602 P 2d 360, 365 (1979)	20.17, 20.20
Hill v National Collegiate Athletic Association 865 P 2d 633 (1994)	6.25
Hitt v Stephens 675 NE 2d 275 (1997)	16.29
Hoesl v US 451 F Supp 1170, 1176 (1978)	1.28
Humphers v First Interstate Bank of Oregon 696 P 2d 527 (1985)	4.60, 19.105
Jablonski v US 712 F 2d 391, 398(1983)	20.17
Jaw v Roberts 627 NE 2d 802 (1994)	20.24
Katz v US 389 US 357, 361 (1967)	6.15
Kennedy v Gurley 208 Ala 623 (1923)	4.37
Leverton v Curtis Pub Co 192 F 2d. 974 (1951)	6.19
Lipari v Sears, Roebuck & Co 497 F Supp 185 (1980)	20.17
Little v All Phoenix South Community Health Center 919 P 2d 1368 (1995)	20.17
McDonald v Clinger 84 D 2d 482 (1982)	4.60
Melvin v Reid 112 Cal App 285, 292 (1931)	5.19, 8.62
Meyerhofer v Empire Fire & Marine Insurance Co 497 F 2d (1974) 190	12.31
Miller v Rivard 585 NYS 2d 523, 527 (1992)	20.33
Molien v Kaiser Foundation Hospitals 616 P 2d 813 (1980)	4.38
Moore v Regents of University of California 271 Cal Rptr 146 (1990)	5.83
Morris v Consolidation Coal Co 446 SE 2d 648 (1994)	7.37, 11.35
Mulka v Fain (Conn Sup Ct, 14 April 1994, WL 146793)	11.25
Multimedia WMAZ v Kubach 443 SE 2d 491 (1994)	13.62
Munsell v Ideal Food Stores 494 P 2d 1063, 1075 (1992)	4.56
Myers v Quesenberry 144 Ca App 3d 888 (1983)	20.31
Nader v General Motors Corp 255 NE 2d 765 (1970)	6.27
Nasser v Parker 455 SE 2d 502, 506 (1995)	20.10, 20.14
New York Times Co v National Aeronautics and Space Administration 920 F, 2d 1002, 1009–10 (1990)	18.59
Nix v Whiteside 475 US 157 (1986)	15.32

O'Brien v Cunard Steamship Co 28 NE 266 (1891)..13.34
Ochse, *Ex p.* (1951) 238 P 2d 561 ....15.29
Pate v Threlkel 661 So 2d 278 (1995) 20.38, 20.39
Pavesich v New England Life Assurance Co 50 SE 68 (1905)...4.54
Peck v Counseling Service of Addison County 499 A 2d 422, 424 (1985)............................20.17
People v Belge 372 NYS 2d 798 (1975) 11.40
People v Meredith 631 P 2d 46 (1981) 11.40
Porten v University of San Fransisco 64 Cal App 3d 825 (1976) 4.55, 6.25
Prasesel v Johnson 967 SW 2d 391 (1998) 20.31
Quarles v Sutherland 289 SW 2d 29 (1965) 4.02
Reid v Pierce County 961 P 2d 3 33 (1998) 4.32, 5.47, 5.50, 6.17
Reisner v Regents of the University of California 37 Cal Rptr 2d 518 (1995) 20.30
Richmond Newspapers v Virginia 488 US 555 (1980) 17.35
Safer v Estate of Pack 677 A 2d 1188 (1996) 20.39
Salgo v Leland Stranford Jr v University Board Trustees 317 P 2d 180 (1957).....................13.28
Sanford v State 21 SW 3d 337 (2000) 1.40
Schaffer v Spicer, 215 NW 2d 134 (1974) 4.51
Sec v Willis 787 F Supp 58 (1992) 5.38
Sidis v F-R Publishing Corp 113 F 2d 806, 809 (1940)..4.56, 13.63
Simonsen v Swenson 177 NW 831 (1920) 10.16, 11.49, 20.01
Sokol v Mortimer 225 NE 2d 496 (1967) 12.36
State v Hansen 862 P 2d 117 (1993) 15.35
Swidler and Berlin v US 118 S.Ct 2081 (1998) 4.16, 5.46, 16.29
Tarasoff v Regents of University of California 551 P 2d 334 (1976);
  529 P 2d 553, 554 (1974) 11.23, 18.22, 20.07, 20.08, 20.10, 20.14, 20.15, 20.29
Thapar v Zezulka 994 SW 2d 635 (1999) 20.14
Thompson v County of Alameda 614 P 2d 728 (1980)...20.17
Tylo v Superior Court 64 Cal Rptr 2d 731, 736 (1999) 14.09
Urbaniak v Newtown 226 Cal App 3d 1128, 1143 (1991) 4.33, 5.29, 6.25
Valley Bank of Nevada v Superior Court 15 Cal 3d 652 (1975) 6.25, 15.06
Washington Olwell 394 P 2d 381 (1964) 11.40
Whalen v Roe 429 US 589 (1977)..21.13

OTHER JURISDICTIONS

Decision about the Census Act (1984) 5 HRLJ 94..19.21
Philipe v France Editions Gaz Pal 1966 1 er sem Jur 38 ....8.22
Princess Caroline BGH NJW 1996 128 ....8.22
Police v Georghiades (1983) 2 Cyprus LR 33 ....3.03, 3.15, 6.19, 6.24, 6.95
X v Hospital Z (1998) 8 SC India 293..1.43

TABLE OF STATUTES

Access to Health Records
    Act 1990 ....13.17, 14.04
Access to Justice Act 1999
    s 29 ....9.03
    s 94 ....3.40
Access to Medical Reports Act
    1988.....................1.30, 13.59, 19.116
    s 3 ....19.49
      (1)..19.52
      (2)..19.52
    s 4 ....19.49, 19.52
    s 5 ....19.49
      (1)..19.52
      (2)..19.51
    s 6 ....19.49, 19.51
      (2)..19.52
    s 7(1) 19.39, 19.53, 19.68
      (2)..19.53
      (3)(a) 19.53
    s 8 ....19.52
Accessories and Abettors Act 1861
    s 8 ....6.84
Administration of Justice Act 1960
    s 12 ....17.45
      (1)(a) 17.45
Administration of Justice Act 1985
    s 31 ....10.03
    s 33 ....16.42
Adoption Act 1976
    s 51 ....19.105
    s 51A..19.105
    s 64 ....17.31
Adoption and Children Act 2002 ....19.105
    s 62 ....19.105
      (6)(a) 19.111
    s 101 ....17.45
    s 111 ....19.84
    s 112 ....19.84
Adults with Incapacity Act 2000
    (Scotland) 13.11
Age of Legal Capacity (Scotland)
    Act 1991 ....13.12
Anti-Terrorism, Crime and Security
    Act 2001 ....2.16, 3.35,
        10.11, 10.24, 12.14, 12.18

s 17 ....11.32, 12.18, 12.22
  (2)...12.18
  (3)...12.18
  (7)...12.19
s 18 ....12.19
  (4)...12.19
s 19 ....11.32, 12.22
  (1)...12.19
  (2)...12.19
s 102 ....14.104
  (3)...3.40
    (a)–(b) 14.104
  (5)..14.104
s 104 ....14.104
s 107 ....14.104
s 117 ....11.32
Sch 4 ....3.43, 12.18
Sch 6
  para 1(2)(b)................................14.50
  para 1(3) 14.50
  para 5 ....14.50
  para 6(1) 14.50
Sch 6A
  para 2(5) 14.50
  para 3(1) 14.50
  para 6
    (1)...14.50
    (2)...14.50
Audit Commission Act 1998
  s15(4) 1.03
Bankers' Books Evidence
  Act 1879 ....14.04, 14.10
  s 7 ....14.10, 14.26, 14.132
  s 9 ....14.10
Bankers' Evidence Act 1875
  s 7 ....14.57
Banking Act
  1987 ....16.04
  s 39 ....10.06
    (13)..10.06
  s 43 ....10.22
  s 47(1)..12.14
  s 82 ....10.35
    (1)..................................10.06, 16.04
  s 83 ....6.88

Table of Statutes

Birth and Deaths Registration Act 1953
    s 32 .... 5.51
Broadcasting Act 1990 .... 9.21
    s 166(1) 6.87
Broadcasting Act 1996 .... 9.18
    s 107(1) 1.12, 9.17
    s 111 .... 9.18
    s 114(2) 9.17
    s 115(1) 9.17
        (2) 9.17
    s 119 .... 9.18
        (8) 9.18
        (10) 9.18
    s 120 .... 9.18
Building Societies Act 1986
    s 82(8)(c) 12.14
Care Standards Act 2000
    s 10 .... 15.51
        (3) 15.54
        (4) 15.54
    ss 80–89 .... 2.15
Census Act 1920
    s 8(2)(3) 3.43
Chancery Amendment Act 1858 (21 & 22
    Vict., c27) (Lord Cairns'
    Act) 8.33, 8.34, 8.36, 8.38, 8.39
Charities Act 1993
    s 9(1) 3.34
Child Abduction and Custody Act 1985
    s 24A 10.02, 16.23
Child Care Act 1980
    s 1 .... 20.04
    s 76 .... 9.05
Child Support Act 1991 .... 10.11
    s 15 .... 10.02, 10.11
        (4) 3.37, 10.02
        (6) 3.37, 10.02
        (9)(b) 10.02, 10.22
    s 50 .... 10.35
Children Act 1989 .... 2.29, 10.03, 10.11,
                                 12.24, 13.14, 16.39,
                                 17.22, 17.45, 20.04,
                                                20.25
    s 1 .... 10.14, 15.51, 16.40
    s 2 .... 19.73, 19.84
        (7) 13.20
    s 3 .... 19.73, 19.84
        (5) 13.20
    s 4 .... 13.20, 19.84
    s 7 .... 10.03
    s 8 .... 13.21
        (1) 19.78, 19.79, 19.90
    s 10(8) 13.14
    s 17(1) 20.04

    s 22(4) 19.85
    s 27 .... 3.40, 20.04
    s 42(1) 3.40
    s 47 .... 3.40, 10.22, 20.25
        (9) 10.11, 20.04, 20.25
        (10) 10.11, 20.04
    s 50(3)(c) 10.02
    s 80 .... 3.37
        (5) 3.37
        (7) 3.37
    s 98 .... 16.03
    Sch 2, Pt I, para 4(1) 20.04
    Pt III 20.04
Children and Young Persons Act 1969
    s 9 .... 3.40
Civil Evidence Act 1995 .... 15.07
Civil Procedure Act 1997
    s 1 .... 12.28
    s 7(2) 14.16
        (3) 14.16
        (4) 14.16
        (5) 14.15
        (7) 14.17
    s 7(5)(a) 14.16
    Sch 1, para 4 .... 12.28
Companies Act 1985
    s 4(2) 3.34
        (4) 16.12
    s 83(2) 3.34
    s 84 .... 3.34
    s 432 .... 3.38
    s 434(3) 3.38
    s 436 .... 10.22
    s 446 .... 3.38
    s 447 .... 3.38
        (6) 10.22
    s 448 .... 10.22, 14.69
    s 451 .... 10.22
    s 452(1)(a) 16.12, 16.23
        (1A) 10.04
        (1B) 10.04
    ss 723B–F 3.42
    Sch 14 .... 3.34
    Pt 1 .... 16.12
Companies Act 1989
    s 83(5) 16.12
    s 84(4) 10.04
Competition Act 1998
    s 25 .... 10.02
    s 28 .... 14.69
    s 30 .... 16.12
    s 42(1) 10.23
Computer Misuse Act 1990 .... 6.60, 21.17
    s 1 .... 6.60, 6.62

(1)
    (a) 6.61, 6.62
    (c) 6.62
    (2) 6.62
s 2 .... 6.63
    (4) 6.63
ss 2–2 .... 6.63
s 3(6) 6.82
s 4 .... 6.61
s 17 .... 6.62
    (2) 6.61
Congenital Disabilities (Civil Liability) Act 1976
s 1 .... 14.04
s 31 .... 14.04
Consumer Credit Act 1974
s 162(3) 10.22
Contempt of Court Act 1981
s 2(1) 7.14
s 4(1) 17.26
    (2) 17.12, 17.48
s 10 .... 6.46, 7.10–7.19
s 11 .... 17.44, 17.49, 17.50
s 19 .... 7.14
Contracts (Rights of Third Parties) Act 1999 .... 4.03
Copyright Act 1956
s 5(3) 7.07
s 17(3) 8.68
Copyright, Designs and Patents Act 1988 .... 7.08
s 1 .... 5.84
s 3 .... 5.85
s 4(1)(a) 5.84
s 7 .... 13.01
s 9 .... 5.84, 5.85
s 10(1) 6.82
s 11 .... 5.84, 5.85
    (2) 5.85
s 12 .... 5.84
s 30 .... 11.83
s 45 .... 5.87
    (1) 5.87
s 84 .... 5.51
s 85 .... 5.85
s 86(1) 5.85
s 95(5) 5.51
s 97(1) 7.44
    (2) 7.44, 8.68
s 113 .... 9.01
s 171(3) 11.82
s 230 .... 8.74
s 280 .... 16.42
s 284 .... 16.42

Coroners Act 1988,
s 10(2) 15.13
s 21 .... 15.13
    (5) 15.13
County Court Act 1984
s 52 .... 14.13
    (2) 17.02
s 53 .... 14.05, 14.12
    (2) 17.02
Courts and Legal Services Act 1990 .... 4.02
s 49(4) 10.35
s 63 .... 16.42
Crime and Disorder Act 1998 .... 3.04, 12.14, 12.15, 12.17
ss 6–7 .... 12.15
s 115 .... 2.16, 3.40, 12.14, 12.15, 12.16
    (1) 12.15
Criminal Appeal Act 1995
s 17(4) 10.05
s 25 .... 10.35
Criminal Damage Act 1972
s 1 .... 6.82
s 10(1) 6.82
Criminal Justice Act 1987 .... 6.80
s 1 .... 14.58
    (3) 14.58
s 2 .... 14.58
    (1)(a) 13.01
    (4) 16.12
    (4)–(5) 14.52, 14.60
    (9) 14.52, 14.59, 16.23
    (10) 10.03, 10.04, 14.59
    (13) 14.58
    (14) 14.58
    (15) 14.58
s 12(3) 6.78
Criminal Justice Act 1988 .... 10.24, 10.32, 14.53
s 25 .... 15.07
s 32 .... 6.82
s 36 .... 15.34
s 71(9)(c) 10.32
s 93A 10.18, 10.32, 16.15
    (1) 10.24
    (7) 10.32
s 93B 10.32, 16.15
    (5)
       (a) 10.26
       (b)
          (i) 10.33
          (ii) 10.33
    (7) 10.33
s 93D 10.17, 10.32, 16.03
    (4) 10.17

Criminal Justice Act 1988 (cont.):
- (5) 10.17
- (6) 10.17
- s 93H 14.53
  - (10) 14.53
    - (b) 14.53
- s 93I(5) 14.53
- s 159 .... 17.48

Criminal Justice Act 1991 .... 3.41

Criminal Justice (International Co-operation) Act 1990
- s 4 .... 14.137, 14.138
  - (2) 14.137
- s 7(1) 14.19
- Sch 1 .... 14.137
  - para 4 .... 14.137

Criminal Justice and Police Act 2001 ..... 14.38
- s 50 .... 14.38, 14.51, 14.52, 14.54, 14.60, 14.67, 14.69
  - (3) 14.38
- s 51 .... 14.38
- s 52 .... 14.39
  - (4) 14.39
- s 53(2)(c) 14.38
- s 55(1) 14.51
  - (2) 14.51
    - (b) 14.38
  - (3)(b) 14.38
  - (4) 14.51
  - (10)
    - (b) 14.51
    - (c) 14.51
- s 56 .... 14.35, 14.51
- s 59(3)(b) 14.39
- s 60 .... 14.39
- s 61 .... 14.39
- s 62 .... 14.39
- Sch 1, Pt 1 .... 14.51, 14.52, 14.54, 14.60, 14.105

Criminal Justice and Public Order Act 1994 .... 2.13
- s 34 .... 16.33

Criminal Law Act 1977
- s 1 .... 6.81
- s 4 .... 14.44

Criminal Procedure (Attendance of Witnesses) Act 1965
- s 2 .... 15.04
  - (1) 14.129
  - (2) 15.05, 15.07
    - (c) 15.20
- s 2A 14.131
- s 3 .... 15.04, 15.13
- s 4 .... 15.13

Criminal Procedure and Investigations Act 1996 .... 17.12
- s 3(1) 14.124
  - (2) 14.124
  - (6) 14.127
- s 5(5) 14.124
- s 7(2) 14.124
  - (3) 14.124
  - (5) 14.127
- s 8(3)(c) 14.124
  - (5) 14.127
- s 16 .... 14.127
- s 17 .... 17.12
  - (1) 17.12
  - (2) 17.12
  - (3) 17.12
  - (4) 17.12, 17.13
  - (6) 17.12
- s 21(2) 14.127

Crown Proceedings Act 1947
- s 28(1) 16.52

Data Protection Act 1984
- s 29 .... 19.39

Data Protection Act 1998 .... 1.03, 1.12, 2.28, 3.01, 3.41, 3.51, 4.49, 5.18, 6.18, 6.30, 6.36, 6.59, 6.90, 7.04, 8.13, 9.05, 9.43, 10.16, 11.02, 11.55, 11.72, 12.16, 12.21, 13.02, 13.03, 13.11, 13.30, 13.49, 13.50, 13.54, 13.57, 14.04, 14.105, 18.01, 18.02, 18.03, 18.04, 18.05, 18.06, 18.07, 18.08, 18.09, 18.10, 18.11, 18.14, 19.103, 21.17, 21.22
- Pt II 13.46
- Pt IV 18.57, 19.30
- Pt V 4.49
- s 1 .... 1.03, 6.27, 6.36, 18.04, 18.08, 19.22, 19.37
  - (1) 1.05, 5.51, 6.30, 6.58, 8.26, 18.02, 18.04, 18.08, 18.11
    - (a) 18.06
    - (b) 18.06, 18.08
    - (c) 18.06
    - (e) 18.04, 18.07, 18.46
  - (2) 3.50
- s 2 .... 12.33, 18.23, 18.28, 19.49
  - (a) 6.18
  - (c) 18.23
  - (e)–(f) 6.18
  - (g) 6.18
  - (h) 6.18
- s 3 .... 4.49, 18.28, 18.39
- s 5 .... 6.27, 18.11
- s 6 .... 2.16

Data Protection Act 1998 (*cont.*):
- s 7 ....3.45, 18.39, 18.42, 19.24, 19.35, 19.38, 19.72, 19.89, 19.103, 19.114
  - (1)(a) 19.21, 19.23, 19.73
    - (b)(i) 19.24
    - (ii) 19.24
    - (iii) 19.24
    - (c) 19.24, 19.73
    - (d) 19.24
  - (2) 19.21
  - (3) 19.21
  - (4) 19.32, 19.36, 19.81
    - (a) 19.32
    - (b) 19.32
  - (5) 19.32, 19.33, 19.36
  - (6) 19.33
  - (7) 19.24
  - (8) 19.24
  - (9) 18.41, 19.27
- s 8(2) 3.45, 19.24
  - (3) 19.29
  - (4) 19.29
  - (6) 19.24
  - (7) 19.32
- s 9 ....3.45
- s 9A
  - (2) 19.22
  - (3) 19.22
- s 10 ....18.39
  - (1) 8.26, 18.50, 19.48
  - (2) 19.48
  - (3)(b) 19.48
  - (4) 8.27, 19.48
- s 11 ....3.41
- s 12 ....3.41, 18.39
- s 13 ....3.41, 4.49, 6.36, 8.27, 8.43, 8.48, 10.16, 11.02, 18.41, 18.50, 19.27
  - (1) 4.49, 6.30, 6.36
  - (2) 6.30, 6.36
    - (a) 8.43, 8.48, 19.27
    - (b) 8.48
  - (3) 4.49, 6.36
- s 14 ....3.41, 3.45, 18.05, 19.48
  - (1)–(3) 18.07, 18.39
- s 15 ....19.27
  - (1) 18.50
- s 16(1) 18.03
- s 17(1) 6.30, 18.03
  - (2) 18.03
- s 19(7) 12.21
- s 21 ....18.03
  - (1) 6.58
  - (2) 18.03
  - (3) 18.03
- s 27 ....18.38
  - (5) 19.07, 19.25, 19.26, 19.38
- s 28 ....10.20, 12.21, 14.55, 18.44, 19.30
  - (1)(c) 6.56
  - (2) 18.44, 19.31
  - (4) 18.44, 19.31
  - (5) 19.31
- s 29 ....2.16, 10.20, 12.16, 12.21, 14.45, 18.22, 18.33, 18.44, 18.45, 19.30
  - (3) 18.44, 18.45
- s 30(1) 19.39
- s 31 ....10.20, 18.44, 19.30
  - (2) 18.44
  - (3) 8.13
- s 32 ....8.13, 18.16, 18.39, 19.30
  - (1) 18.39
    - (b) 8.13, 18.39
    - (c) 18.39
  - (3) 9.09
  - (4) 18.41
    - (b) 18.39
- s 33 ....19.30
  - (1) 18.42
    - (a) 18.42
    - (b) 18.42
  - (1)(b) 13.55
  - (2) 18.31, 18.32
  - (4) 13.55
    - (b) 18.42
  - (5)(a) 18.42
- s 33A 18.04, 18.07, 18.46
- s 34(4) 8.27
- s 35(1) 18.33, 18.38, 19.30
  - (2) 18.38, 19.30
    - (a) 18.38
    - (b) 18.38
  - (3) 18.40
- s 35A 19.106
- s 36 ....18.02
- s 37 ....19.38
- s 40 ....18.48, 19.34
  - (1) 19.27
  - (3) 19.48
- s 42 ....3.41, 19.48
  - (1) 18.47
  - (2) 18.48
- s 43(1) 18.48
  - (b) 18.47
  - (3) 18.48
  - (6) 18.48
  - (7) 18.48
- s 44 ....3.35, 8.27, 18.41
  - (5) 8.27, 18.41
  - (6) 8.27

Table of Statutes

Data Protection Act 1998 (*cont.*):
  s 45 ....8.27, 14.69, 18.41
  s 47(3)..18.49
  s 48...18.48
    (1)...8.27, 18.41
  s 49(6)(a) 18.49
  s 51(1)...3.50
    (3)..3.50
  s 52(3)...3.50
  s 55 ....6.56, 6.84, 21.22
    (1).............................6.56, 6.84, 18.33
    (2).............................6.56, 6.88, 21.22
      (d)..6.84, 11.02
    (3)..6.56
    (4)..6.57
    (5)..6.57
    (6)..6.57
  s 56 ....2.12
  s 57 ....13.24
  s 58 ....18.48
  s 59 ....3.43, 18.50
    (1)(b)..1.05
  s 60(1)...6.59
    (2)..........................6.59, 18.03, 18.49
    (4)......................................6.59, 18.49
  s 68 ....18.04, 18.06, 18.25
    (1)(a) 19.22
      (b)...19.22
      (c)...19.22
    (2)..18.04
Sch 12...18.04
  s 69 ....18.04, 19.32
  s108(3)(ff) 21.24
  s123..21.24
Sch 1 ....6.35, 13.46
  para 1(b) 18.25
  para 13..18.35
  para 14..18.36
  para 15..18.35
  Pt I 10.20, 18.30, 19.27
    para 1..18.08
  Pt II 18.10, 18.30
    para 1
      (1)...18.16
      (2)..................................10.20, 18.10
    para 2..18.29
      (1)(a) 10.20
      (3)
        (c)...18.11
        (d)...18.11
    para 3..18.29
      (2)......................................18.17, 18.43
        (b)...10.20
    para 4..18.29

    para 5 ....18.03, 18.11, 18.29
    para 7..19.48
    para 9..6.36
    para 10 ....6.32, 6.37
    paras 11–12 ....6.31
Sch 2 ....18.09, 18.22, 18.38
  para 1 ....13.01, 19.73
  para 2
    (a) 18.19
    (b)..18.19
  para 3 ....10.16, 18.19, 18.201
  para 4..18.19
  para 5
    (a) 18.19
    (b).......................................18.19, 18.21
    (c).......................................18.19, 18.21
    (d).......................................18.19, 18.21
  para 6 ....12.30, 12.34, 13.49,
                          18.19, 18.22, 19.73
    (1)..18.21
    (2)..18.20
  paras 1–4 ....3.41
Sch 3 ....13.44, 18.09,
                                18.22, 18.38
  para 1 ....12.33, 13.03, 18.25, 19.73
  para 2 ....10.16, 18.25
  para 3 ....18.25, 19.73
  para 4..18.25
  para 5 ....5.63, 18.25, 18.26
  para 6..18.25
    (c)..19.73
  para 6(c).............................12.30, 12.34
  para 7..10.16
    (1)(a) 18.25
      (b)......................................18.25, 19.73
      (c)...18.25
  para 8 ....8.25, 10.16,
                              13.49, 18.43
  para 9 ....10.16, 18.25, 18.27
Sch 4,
  para 1 ....18.36
  para 2 ....18.36
  para 3 ....18.36
  para 4..18.36
  para 5 ....18.36
  para 6..18.36
  para 8..18.36
  para 9 ....18.36
Sch 7..19.38
  para 1 ....19.35
  para 8..19.43
    (1)..19.43
    (2)..19.43
    (3)..19.43

Table of Statutes

Data Protection Act 1998 (*cont.*):
   para 9 .... 19.43
   para 10 .... 19.46
   para 11
     (1) 19.46
  Sch 8, para 14 .... 18.07
  Sch 9 .... 14.69
   para 1(2) 14.69
   para 8 .... 14.69
   para 9 .... 14.69
   para 12 .... 14.69
  Sch 11
   para 2 .... 18.04, 19.44
   para 3 .... 19.44
   para 4 .... 19.44
  Sch 16, Pt I 19.54
Defamation Act 1952
  s 3 .... 4.41, 4.42
Defamation Act 1996
  s 1 .... 7.38
Disability Discrimination Act 1995
  s 31B(4), (6)(a) 5.34
   (7) 15.12, 16.07
Disability Rights Commission Act 1995
  s 31B(4)(6)(a) 5.34
  s 31B(7) 15.12, 16.07
Disability Rights Commission Act 1999
  s 4 .... 10.02
   (1)(b) 3.38
   (3) 16.12
    (a) 3.38
   (5) 10.22
  Sch 3, para 22(2)(f) 3.43
Disease of Fish Act 1983 .... 12.18
Divorce Act 1986 (Can)
  s 10(5) 16.43
Drug Trafficking Act 1994 .... 10.24, 10.32
  s 16 .... 10.32
  s 17 .... 10.32
  s 49 .... 10.25
  s 50 .... 10.25, 10.32
   (3)(b),
    (i) 10.33
    (ii) 10.33
   (4) 10.33
  ss 50–52 .... 16.15
  s 51 .... 10.25, 10.32
   (5)(b)(1) 10.33
    (ii) 10.33
   (7) 10.33
  s 52 .... 10.25, 10.30
   (2) 10.30
   (3) 10.29
   (4) 10.26

   (5) 10.27
   (6) 10.26
   (8) 10.30
   (9) 10.30
  s 53 .... 10.17, 16.03
   (4) 10.17
   (5) 10.17
   (6) 10.17
  s 55(4)(b)(ii) 16.12
Education Act 1993 .... 2.24
Education Act 1996
  s 576 .... 19.79, 19.83
Education Act 1997
  s 40 .... 3.37
Electronic Communications Act 1998
  s 115 .... 3.44
Employment Protection Act 1996
  s 49 .... 21.24
Employment Rights Act 1996
  s 43 .... 11.69
  s 43B 21.25
   (2) 21.25
   (3) 21.25
   (4) 21.28
  s 43C 21.25
  s 43D 21.28
  s 43E 21.25
  s 43F 21.25
  s 43G 21.25, 21.26
   (2) 21.26
   (3)(d) 21.26
  s 43H 21.25
   (1) 21.25
    (e) 21.25
   (2) 21.25
  s 43J 21.23
  s 43K(1) 21.24
  s 48(1A) 21.24
   (2) 21.24
  s 100 .... 21.24
  s 103A 21.24
  s 202 .... 15.44
Enduring Power of Attorney Act 1985
  s 3(1) 12.09
European Communities Act 1972 .... 3.54
Evidence Act 1955 (NSW)
  s 126A 16.44
  s 126G–I 16.44
Evidence Act 1958 (Vic)
  Pt II, Div 2A 16.44
Evidence Act 1970 (Nfld)
  s 6 .... 16.43
Evidence Act 1984
  s 78 .... 6.101

Table of Statutes

Evidence Amendment Act (No 2) 1980 (NZ)
- s 31 .... 16.43
- s 32 .... 16.43
- s 35 .... 16.44
- (2) 16.44

Evidence (Proceedings in Other Jurisdictions) Act 1975
- s 2A 14.133
- s 3(1) 14.134
- (a) 14.134
- (b) 14.134

Explosive Substances Act 1883
- s 6 .... 3.38

Family Law Act 1986
- s 33 .... 10.02, 16.23

Family Law Reform Act 1969 .... 13.12
- s 8(1) 13.12, 19.107, 19.111
- (3) 13.12

Family Proceedings Act 1980 (NZ)
- s 18(1)(a) 16.43

Federal Trade Commissions Act 15 USC (1994)
- s 5 .... 18.35

Finance Act 1972
- s 110 .... 3.40
- s 127 .... 3.40

Finance Act 1989
- s 182 .... 3.43, 10.35

Finance Act 2000
- s 149 .... 14.62
- s 150 .... 14.62

Financial Services Act 1986
- s 109(1) 12.14
- s 177(3) 3.382
- s 180 .... 6.88

Financial Services and Markets Act 2000
- s 161 .... 10.02
- (6) 10.11
- s 168 .... 14.56
- s 172 .... 10.02
- s 173 .... 3.38, 10.02
- s 174 .... 10.34
- s 175 .... 10.02
- (4) 16.23
- (5) 10.04
- (d) 10.04
- s 176 .... 14.56
- (1) 10.22
- s 177 .... 10.22
- (2) 10.11
- s 348(4)(b) 1.05
- s 413 .... 16.12

Foreign Tribunals Evidence Act 1856 ..... 15.135

Forgery and Counterfeiting Act 1981 ...... 6.74
- s 8(1)(d) 6.74

Freedom of Information Act 2000 .... 2.26, 3.45, 5.51, 18.01, 18.46, 18.51, 19.23
- Pt VII 3.45
- s 1 .... 18.51
- (3) 18.51
- s 2 .... 18.57
- (1)(b) 18.57
- (2)(b) 18.57
- s 4 .... 18.52
- s 5 .... 18.52
- s 8(1)(c) 18.53
- s 9 .... 18.51
- s 12 .... 18.51
- s 14 .... 18.51
- s 16 .... 18.53
- s 17 .... 18.55
- s 20 .... 18.51
- s 21 .... 18.51
- s 28 .... 18.59
- s 30(1) 18.54
- (2) 18.54
- (3) 18.54
- s 31 .... 18.57
- s 32 .... 18.54
- (3) 18.54
- s 38 .... 18.57
- s 40(1) 3.45
- (2) 18.57
- (3) 18.57
- (4) 18.57
- s 41 .... 18.57
- s 42 .... 3.13, 16.27, 18.57
- (1) 18.59
- s 44 .... 18.57
- s 45 .... 18.51
- s 50 .... 18.55
- s 52 .... 18.55
- s 53 .... 18.55
- s 54 .... 18.55
- s 56(1) 18.55
- s 62(1) 18.60
- s 63(1) 18.60
- s 65 .... 18.60
- s 68 .... 18.53
- s 69 .... 18.53
- s 77 .... 18.51
- (1) 19.24, 19.37
- s 84 .... 18.51
- Sch 1 .... 18.52
- Pt IV 4.47
- Pt VI 9.15

Table of Statutes

Health Act 1999
   s 4 ....5.51
   s 23 ....3.37
   s 24 ....3.43, 5.51, 12.20
      (6) 11.33
Health and Safety Act 1974 ....3.36, 3.37
   s 20 ....3.34, 3.37
      (8) 16.12
      (j) 3.37
      (k) 3.37
   s 27 ....10.02
   s 33 ....3.37
Health and Social Care
   Act 2001 ....2.16, 13.53, 13.54, 18.42
   s 60 ....2.16, 5.29, 18.14, 19.57
      (3)–(4) 13.54
      (6) 13.54
      (9)(a) 5.34
   s 61 ....13.54
   s 64(3) 13.54
Health Commissioner Act 1993
   s 15 ....10.35
Health Records Act 1990 ....19.55
   s 1(1) 19.54
   s 2 ....19.54
   s 3(1)(c) 19.72
      (f) 19.54
   s 4(2) 19.87
      (a) 19.72, 19.96
      (b) 19.99
      (3) 19.55
   s 5(1) 19.55
      (a)(i) 19.54
         (ii) 19.54
      (b) 19.54
      (2) 19.54
      (3) 19.55, 19.97
      (4) 19.54
   s 8 ....19.56
Health Service Commissioners Act 1993
   s 11(2) 15.45
   s 12 ....10.03
      (3) 10.05
   s 15(1)(c) 10.20
      (2) 16.03
Housing Act 1996
   s 30 ....3.34
      (4)(a) 16.12
   s 30(4)(a) 16.12
Human Fertilization and Embryology
   Act 1990 ....3.41
   s 20 ....19.26
   s 31(2) 1.05
      (3) 19.106

   s 33 ....13.08
      (5) 19.106
      (6B) 13.01
      (6D) 13.29
   s 34 ....19.106
   s 35 ....19.106
      (1) 14.04
   s 40 ....14.69
   s 41 ....3.42
Human Fertilization and Embryology
   (Disclosure of Information)
   Act 1992 ....13.08
Human Organ Transplants Act 1989
   s 3 ....3.36
Human Rights Act 1998 ....3.01, 3.02,
      3.04, 3.09, 4.45, 4.59, 5.04, 5.20,
      6.07, 6.21, 6.47, 6.103, 8.11, 8.13,
      8.16, 8.25, 8.30, 8.31, 8.32, 8.44,
      8.55, 8.61, 8.66, 8.69, 10.06, 10.08,
      10.40, 11.13, 11.46, 12.21, 13.54,
      14.07, 14.59, 14.71, 15.06, 16.02,
      16.09, 16.29, 16.48, 18.09, 18.28,
      19.31, 20.05
   s 2 ....3.55, 20.05
   s 3 ....18.37
      (1) 3.04, 3.05, 3.55, 15.18
        (c) 3.04
   s 4 ....3.04
   s 6 ....3.09, 3.12, 3.13, 3.14, 3.51,
      4.45, 5.21, 11.13, 12.07, 14.65, 14.77
      (1) 3.05, 3.12, 6.102,
        14.122, 17.51, 20.05, 21.29
      (3) 3.05
      (b) 4.47, 15.25
      (5) 4.47
      (6) 3.05
   s 7 ....3.09, 4.46, 8.30, 8.31,
      8.44, 8.55, 20.05
      (1) 3.06
      (5) 4.45
   s 8 ....3.14, 8.30, 8.31
      (1) 3.06, 14.122
      (4) 8.44
   s 9 ....3.06, 3.09
   s 11 ....4.45
   s 12 ....3.05, 3.08, 3.17, 6.47,
      7.28, 8.06, 8.11–8.14,
      8.18, 8.59, 8.65, 8.70,
      11.65, 11.73, 18.40
      (1) 3.27, 9.14
      (2) 8.12
        (a) 8.12
        (b) 8.12
      (3) 8.11, 8.15–8.17

Human Rights Act 1998 (*cont.*):
   (4) 3.17, 3.27, 3.47, 6.21,
                 8.10, 8.13, 8.14, 8.18,
                 8.25, 8.70, 9.09, 18.26
     (b) 3.08, 8.13, 8.14
       (i) 7.17
       (a)(i) 8.13
       (ii) 8.13
   s 13(3)...8.16
   s 21 ....3.02
   s 43B(1)(c)..11.51
Immigration Act 1971
   s 28D...14.69
   s 28E..14.69
   s 28F..14.69
Immigration and Asylum Act 1999
   s 93(1)..12.14
      (3)(a) 13.01
       (d) 11.05
Income and Corporation Taxes
   Act 1988,
   s 745 ....10.02
      (3) 16.23
      (4)(c) 16.23
      (5) 10.03
   s 767C..3.35
Information Act 1982 (Aus) 1.02
   s 12(4)(b) 3.08
Inheritance Tax Act 1984
   s 219(4)..16.23
Insolvency Act 1986
   s 236 ....3.34, 15.39, 16.15
   s 291 ....16.15
   s 311(1) 10.03, 16.15
   s 312(2) 10.03
   s 363(3)..14.69
   s 366 ....3.34, 10.02
   s 371 ....10.13
Insurance Companies Act 1982,
   s 43A..10.03
Intelligence Services Act 1994 ....14.78,
                       14.79, 14.85
   s 1(2)..14.78
   s 2(2)(a) 14.79
   s 3(2)..14.78
   s 5 ....14.79
      (2) 14.80
      (2A) 14.80
      (3) 14.79
      (3A) 14.81
      (3B) 14.81
      (4) 14.79
   s 6(2)–(3) 14.79
   s 8(4)..3.40

Interception of Communications
   Act 1985 ....14.88, 14.89
   s 9 ....16.03
International Court Act 2001 s30(2) ...14.137
Judicial Proceedings (Regulations of
   Reports) Act 1926 ....17.47
   s 1 ....17.44
      (1)(a) 17.47
       (b) 17.47
      (2) 17.47
Law of Libel Amendment Act 1888
   s 8 ....6.87
Learning and Skills Act 2000
   s 19(4)(d) 13.01
   s 119(4) 1.05
Libel Act 1843
   s 4 ....6.87
   s 5 ....6.87
   s 6 ....6.87
Limitation Act 1980
   s 2 ....9.01
   s 4A..9.01
   s 5 ....9.01
   s 36(1)...9.01
Local Authority Social Services Act 1970...3.49
   s 7 ....21.10
   s 7C 15.51
Local Government Act 1972
   ss 250(2)–(5) 15.51
   Sch 12A
      para 5..3.42
      para 16..3.42
Local Government Act 1974
   s 29 ....3.40, 9.06
      (1) 10.02
      (4) 15.07, 16.55
      (7) 16.12
   s 32 ....10.35
Local Government Act 2000
   s 62(1)...3.38
Local Government Finance Act 1992
   s 68 ....1.03
      (2) 1.05
   Sch 2, para 17
      (2)(b) 13.08
      (3) 1.03
Magistrates' Courts Act 1980
   s 44 ....6.84
      (1) 6.62
   s 69(4)..17.31
   s 97 ....15.04
      (1) 15.07
Matrimonial Causes Act 1973
   s 48(2)..17.31

Table of Statutes

Medical Act 1983
  s 5A(6) 16.12
  s 35A(1) 3.35
      (4) 3.35
      (6) 3.35
Medical Practice Act 1992 (NSW)
  Sch 2, cl 16 .... 4.51
Medicine Act 1983
  s 35A 18.19
Mental Health Act 1959 .... 12.09
  s 143 .... 15.51
Mental Health Act 1983 .... 17.42, 21.11
  Pt IV 12.10
  s 6(1) 12.10
  s 25B(3) 13.57
  s 29 .... 16.39
  s 63 .... 12.10, 13.11
  s 94 .... 12.09
  s 95 .... 12.09, 19.114
  s 115 .... 3.37, 12.17
Merchant Shipping (Liner Conferences)
  Act 1982 .... 12.18
Misuse of Drugs Act 1971
  s 23(1) 3.37
      (3) 14.51
National Audit Act 1983
  s 8 .... 3.34
National Health Service Act 1977 .... 21.16
  s 2 .... 15.51
  s 84(1) 15.51
  s 98 .... 13.52
  s 124 .... 10.02
National Immigration and Asylum Act 2002
  s 135 .... 3.34
Offences Against the Person Act 1861
  s 16 .... 16.35
Office of Communications Act 2002 .... 9.20
Official Secrets Act 1911 .... 14.54
  s 9 .... 14.54
Official Secrets Act 1920
  s 6 .... 3.38, 14.55
Official Secrets Act 1989 .... 1.12, 14.54
  s 1 .... 3.43, 10.38
  s 4 .... 10.38
      (3)(b) 14.80
Parliamentary Commissioner Act 1967
  s 11 .... 3.43
Partnership Act 1890
  s 9 .... 21.39
  s 10 .... 21.39
Pensions Act 1995
  s 100 .... 10.22
Police Act 1964
  s 51(3) 11.32, 14.44

Police Act 1996
  s 49 .... 15.51
Police Act 1997 .... 14.72, 14.85, 14.93
  Pt V 2.15
  s 51(3) 11.39, 11.40
  s 91 .... 14.73
  s 92 .... 14.72
      (2)(a) 14.72
  s 93(2) 14.75
      (b) 14.72
      (2B) 14.75
      (4) 14.72
      (5) 14.73
  s 97(2)(a) 14.73, 14.81
      (3) 14.73
      (5) 14.75
  s 98 .... 14.73
  ss 98–100 .... 14.81
  s 99 .... 14.73
      (2) 1.03, 1.05
Police and Criminal Evidence
  Act 1984 .... 10.36, 11.17
  s 8 .... 14.19
      (2) 14.35
  s 9 .... 14.25, 14.31, 14.53
      (1) 14.25, 14.57, 14.62
  s 10 .... 3.33, 10.30, 14.22,
              14.25, 14.67, 14.114, 16.12
      (1)(b) 16.20
          (c)(ii) 15.27
      (2) 10.30, 14.22, 14.31, 16.35
  s 11 .... 14.22
      (1) 14.41
      (2) 14.22
  s 12 .... 10.04, 14.22
  s 13 .... 8.13
      (1) 14.22
      (2) 14.22
      (3) 14.22
  s 14 .... 14.21, 14.25
      (4) 14.21
      (5) 14.21
  s 15(3) 14.29
      (6)(b) 14.35
  s 16(8) 14.35
  s 17 .... 14.35
  s 19 .... 14.35
      (4) 14.35
      (6) 14.35, 14.37, 14.51,
                      14.54, 14.56, 14.68
  s 20 .... 14.35
  s 20B(9) 10.04
      (2) 10.04
  s 21(5) 14.35

Table of Statutes

Police and Criminal Evidence Act 1984 (*cont.*):
  s 58 ....14.122
  s 62 ....13.09, 15.28
    (4) 13.09
  s 76 ....11.37
  s 78 ....3.15, 6.95, 14.77,
                  14.118, 15.12, 15.18
  s 116 ....11.17, 14.19, 14.25
    (7) 14.25
  s 117 ....14.34
  Sch 1 ....14.25, 14.53, 14.57
    para 2 ....14.26
    para 3 ....14.28
    para 4 ....14.26
    para 8 ....14.31
    para 11 ....14.31, 14.33
    para 12(b) 14.29, 14.33
    para 14 ....14.29
    para 15 ....14.33
  Sch 5 ....14.19
Prevention of Corruption Act 1906 ....6.75
Prevention of Terrorism (Temporary
  Provisions) Act 1989
  s 17(2) 16.03
Privacy Act 1970 (Man)
  s 2(2) 4.53
Privacy Act 1990 (Nfld)
  s 3(1) 4.53
Proceeds of Crime Act 2002 ....10.24,
        10.27, 10.30, 10.32, 14.18, 14.53
  ss 327–229 ....10.32
  s 328(1) 10.32
  s 329(2)
    (a) 10.33
    (b) 10.33
  s 330 ....10.25
    (1) 10.11
    (6)(a) 10.29
      (b) 10.30
    (7) 10.27
    (8) 10.29
    (10) 10.30
    (11) 10.30
  s 331 ....10.27
  s 333 ....10.17
  s 335 ....10.18
  s 337 ....10.25
    (1) 10.26, 12.14
  s 338(4) 10.26
  s 340(2) 10.25
    (3) 10.32
  s 343 ....14.18
  s 345–251 ....14.18
  s 348 ....14.18

    (4) 14.18
  s 352 ....14.18
    (5) 14.18
  s 354 ....14.18
  s 357(2) 14.18
  ss 357–259 ....14.18
  s 361 ....14.18
    (6) 14.18
  s 363 ....14.50
  ss 363–266 ....14.18
  s 368 ....14.18
  s 370 ....14.50
  ss 370–273 ....14.18
  s 374 ....14.18
  s 378 ....14.18
  s 379 ....14.18
  s 383(1) 14.18
  s 436 ....3.40
  s 437 ....3.43
  s 438 ....3.40
  Sch 9 ....10.25
Prosecution of Offences Act 1985
  s 10 ....6.88
Protection from Harassment
  Act 1997 ....7.40–7.44
  s 3(2) 7.41
Protection from Harassment Act 1997 (*cont.*):
  s 7 ....7.40
    (2) 7.40
    (3) 7.41
Protection of Children Act 1999
  s 3 ....2.15
  ss 5–6 ....2.15
Public Bodies Corrupt Practices
  Act 1889 ....6.75
  s 1(1) 6.75
Public Health (Control of Disease)
  Act 1984 ....3.36, 10.03
Public Interest Disclosure
  Act 1998 ....6.88, 21.18, 21.23, 21.24
Public Records Act 1958 ....5.51
  s 5(2) 18.60
Race Relations Act 1976
  s 50
    (1)(b) 3.38
    (3)(a) 3.38, 16.12
    (4) 10.22
  s 52 ....3.43
Regulation of Investigatory Powers
  Act 2000 ....3.04, 3.33, 3.55, 6.64,
          6.65, 14.31, 14.83, 14.90, 14.93,
            14.105, 14.118, 14.122, 17.11
  Pt II 14.91
  s 1 ....14.86

Regulation of Investigatory Powers
Act 2000 (cont.):
- (1) 6.64
- (3) 4.49, 7.43
- (6) 6.65, 14.91
- (7) 6.66
- (8) 6.66
- s 2 .... 14.89, 14.90
  - (1) 6.64, 6.65
  - (2) 6.28, 6.65, 14.90
  - (7) 6.64
- s 3
  - (1) 14.91
  - (2) 14.91
- s 4
  - (1) 14.92
  - (2) 14.92
  - (4) 14.92
  - (5) 14.92
- s 5
  - (2)(b) 14.93
  - (3) 14.92
  - (4) 14.93
- s 6(1) 14.94
- s 7 .... 14.92, 16.03
- s 8
  - (1) 14.95
  - (2) 14.95
  - (5) 14.95
- s 11
  - (4) 14.95
  - (7) 14.95
- s 12 .... 14.95
  - (7) 14.95
- s 17 .... 14.99
  - (1) 14.99
  - (7) 14.99
- s 18 .... 14.99
  - (4) 14.99
  - (5) 14.99
- s 19 .... 10.38, 14.99
- s 20 .... 14.95
- s 21 .... 14.102
  - (3) 14.102
  - (4) 14.102
  - (6) 14.102
- s 22 .... 14.102, 14.104
  - (2) 3.40, 14.105
- s 25 .... 18.45
- s 26(2) 14.83, 14.84
  - (3) 14.107
  - (5) 14.107
  - (9)(a) 14.83
- s 28 .... 14.119

- (2) 14.121
- s 32 .... 14.110
  - (2) 14.133
  - (3) 14.112
  - (4) 14.113
  - (6) 14.110
- s 38 .... 14.110
- s 39 .... 14.110
- s 42 .... 14.110
  - (3) 14.112
- s 48(1) 14.107, 14.108
  - (2) 14.83
- ss 49–52 .... 14.95
- s 54 .... 14.99
- s 62 .... 14.122
- s 65 .... 14.87
  - (2)(a) 14.87
- s 67(2) 14.87
  - (7) 14.87
  - (8) 14.87
- s 68(4) 14.87
- s 71 .... 14.96
- s 78(1) 14.95
- s 81 .... 14.78, 14.93
Rehabilitation of Offenders
Act 1974 .... 2.15, 5.18, 5.20
- s 4(5) 4.36
Road Traffic Act 1972,
- s 168(2)(b) 10.06
- s 172(2)(b) 10.06
  - (b) 10.06
Road Traffic Act 1988
- s 7A 11.35,
  12.14, 13.09
Security Service Act 1989 .... 14.78
- s 1(2) 14.78
  - (3) 14.78
  - (4) 14.78
- s 2(a) 10.35
- s 4(4) 3.40
Security Service Act 1996
- s 1(1) 14.78
Sex Discrimination Act 1975
- s 58(3)(a) 3.38, 16.12
- s 59(1)(b) 3.38
- s 61 .... 3.43
Sexual Offences (Amendment) Act 1976
- s 4(5A) 13.01
Social Security Administration Act 1992
- s 109B 2.16
- s 122 .... 2.16, 3.40
- s 122A 2.16
- s 123 .... 10.35
- s 179A 2.16

Table of Statutes

Social Security Administration (Fraud)
Act 1997
- s 1 ....2.16
- s 2 ....2.16

Social Security Contributions and Benefit
Act 1992
- s 137 ....2.16

Social Security Fraud Act 2001 ....2.16, 3.04
Solicitors Act 1957 ....16.11
Solicitors Act 1974
- s 22A 14.69
- s 34 ....20.40
- s 35 ....10.03
- s 44B 10.03
- s 46(11) 15.41

Supreme Court Act 1981
- s 33(2) 14.13
  - (b)(iii) 17.02
- s 34 ....14.05, 14.08, 14.09, 14.12, 17.16
  - (2) 14.05, 17.04
    - (b)(iii) 17.02
- s 36(6) 14.133
- s 37(1) 7.02
- s 50 ....8.06, 8.33, 8.38, 8.39, 8.41
- s 51(7) 12.29
- s 72 ....14.17

Tax Credits Act 2002
- Sch 5
  - para 4 ....3.40
  - para 5 ....3.40
  - para 6 ....3.40
  - para 7 ....3.40
  - para 8 ....3.40
  - para 9 ....3.40
    - (4) 13.01
  - para 10 ....3.40

Taxes Management Act 1970
- s 6 ....3.43
- s 19A 3.35
- s 20
  - (1) 16.13
  - (3) 3.35, 10.04, 14.62, 16.13
  - (8) 10.20
  - (8A) 10.20
  - (8C) 10.04
- s 20A(1) 16.13
- s 20B
  - (3) 3.35, 16.12
  - (8) 16.12, 16.13
- s 20BA 14.62
  - (1) 14.62
- s 20C 14.62, 14.63, 14.66, 16.13
  - (1) 14.30
- (3) 14.66, 16.13
  - (c) 14.65
- (3A) 14.66
- (4) 14.67, 16.12
- (4A)–(4B) 14.67
- s 73(a) 13.19
- Sch 1 ....3.43
- Sch 1AA 14.62
  - para 3 ....14.63

Telecommunications Act 1984
- s 43 ....16.35
- s 45 ....3.43

Terrorism Act 2000 ....10.11, 10.24, 10.25, 10.32, 14.46
- s 1 ....10.11, 10.24, 14.46
- s 15 ....10.02
- ss 15–18 ....12.14
- s 16 ....10.02
- s 18 ....10.02, 16.03
- s 19 ....3.36, 10.02, 10.11, 12.14
  - (2) 10.01, 10.25
  - (3) 10.11, 10.29
  - (4) 10.27
  - (5) 10.13, 10.30
  - (6) 10.13, 10.30
- s 20 ....12.14
  - (3) 10.02, 10.26, 12.14
- s 21(1) 10.13
- s 21(8) 10.13
- s 21(5)(6) 10.13
- s 21A 3.36, 10.01, 10.11, 10.28, 12.14
  - (5) 10.11, 10.13
- s 21B 10.26
  - (1) 10.02
- s 32 ....14.46
- s 38B 3.36, 3.40, 10.02, 10.11, 10.13
  - (4) 10.11, 10.13
- s 39 ....10.17
  - (5) 10.17
  - (6) 10.17
- Sch 3, para 7(4) 10.01
- Sch 5
  - para 1
    - (2)–(3) 14.47
    - (4) 14.47
    - (5)(b) 14.47
  - para 2 ....14.47
  - para 3 ....14.47
  - para 4 ....14.47
  - para 5 ....14.48
    - (8)(1)(b) 14.48
    - (9) 14.48
    - (11) 14.48

Terrorism Act 2000 (*cont.*):
- (13) 14.49
- (2) 14.49
- (3) 14.49
- (14) 14.49
- para 6
  - (1)(b) 14.48
  - (2) 14.48
  - (3) 14.48
- para 7(1) 14.48
- para 8(1)(b) 14.48
- para 13(3) 16.23
- para 15 ....14.48
- Sch 6 ....14.18, 14.50
  - para 7 ....14.50
- Sch 6A, para 2(5) 14.18

Theatres Act 1968,
- s 4 ....6.87
- s 7 ....6.87

Theft Act 1968 ....6.70, 21.17
- s 1 ....6.68
- (2) 6.68
- s 3(1) 6.68
- (2) 6.85
- s 4(1) 6.68, 6.70, 6.82
- s 9(1) 6.82
- s 13 ....6.72

s 15 ....6.73
- (4) 6.74
s 21 ....6.82
s 22(1) 6.85
s 31 ....16.03
s 34(2) 6.82

Torts (Interference with Goods) Act 1977
- s 3(3)(b) 7.19

Tribunals of Inquiry (Evidence) Act 1921 ....15.48, 15.54
- s 1 ....15.50
- s 2 ....15.50

Value Added Tax Act 1994
- Sch 11
  - para 10 ....14.37
    - (3) 14.68
      - (b) 14.68
      - (c) 14.68
  - para 11 ....14.68
    - (4) 14.68

Venereal Diseases Prevention Act 1980 (Can) 4.51

Wireless Telegraphy Act 1649 ....6.67
- s 5 ....6.86, 7.43
  - (b) 6.67
- s 19(1) 6.67

TABLE OF STATUTORY INSTRUMENTS

Abortion Regulations 1968,
 reg 5 .... 16.60
Abortion Regulations 1991 (SI 1991/499)
 reg 4 .... 3.36, 10.03
 reg 5 .... 3.42
  (g) 13.08
Access to Health Records (Control of Access) Regulations 1993 (SI 1993/746)
 reg 2 .... 1.05
Adoption Agencies Regulations 1983 (SI 1983/1964)
 reg 15(2)(a) 5.47

Child Support (Information, Evidence and Disclosure) Regulations 1992 (SI 1992/1812) 3.40
 reg 2(2)
  (d) 3.40
  (f) 10.03
Children's Homes Regulations 1991 (SI 1991/1506)
 reg 19 .... 3.36
Civil Procedure (Modification of Enactments) Order 1998 (SI 1998/2940) 14.05
Civil Procedure Rules 1998 (SI 1998/3132) 3.04, 6.99, 6.100, 6.108, 6.110,
                                                 8.02, 8.28, 8.66, 8.69, 14.05, 16.02, 16.21, 17.16
 r 1.1 .... 6.100, 15.17
 r 3.1(2)(m) 14.08
 r 5.4(2)(c) 17.22
 r 10.20(3) 17.22
 r 24 .... 4.15
 Pt 25 .... 8.08
  PD 8.08
 r 25.1(1)(a) 8.08
 r 25.3(1) PD 14.17
 r 25.7(2) PD 14.16
  (3)(2) PD 14.17
 r 25.8(1) PD 14.16
 r 27.2 .... 14.14
 r 31 .... 12.32
 r 31.1(1) PD 14.14
 r 31.11 .... 14.14
 r 31.12 .... 14.08, 14.14
 r 31.13(3)(d) 14.13
 r 31.14 .... 14.14, 16.34
 r 31.15 .... 14.14
  (4) 14.06
 r 31.16(3) 14.13
  (4)(a) 14.13
 r 31.17 .... 14.05, 14.08, 14.12, 17.16
 r 31.19 .... 14.05

Civil Procedure Rules 1998 (SI 1998/3132) (*cont.*):
   r 31.19(1) 14.14
        (3) 14.14
   r 31.20 .... 6.99, 6.108
   r 31.22(1) 17.16
        (a) 17.16, 17.26
        (b) 17.16
        (c) 17.16
   r 31.22(2) 17.16, 17.23
   r 31.3(1)(b) 14.05
        (2) 14.05, 14.14
   r 31.4 .... 15.02
   r 31.5 .... 14.14
   r 31.6 .... 14.08, 14.14
   r 31.7(3) 14.06
   r 31.8 .... 14.14
   r 32 .... 6.95
   r 32.1 .... 6.99, 15.12, 15.17
   r 32.12 .... 17.25
        (2)(c) 17.26
   r 32.13(1) 17.25, 17.27
        (2) 17.25
        (3) 17.25
        (4) 17.25
   Pt 34 .... 15.02
   r 34.2(4) 15.10
   r 34.3 .... 15.03
        (4) 15.05
   r 34.4 .... 15.41
   Pt 35 PD 16.34
   r 35.10 .... 16.34
   r 38.14 .... 15.02
   r 39.1(2) PD 17.26
        (4A) PD 17.33
        (5) PD 17.32
        (9) PD 17.33
        (10) PD 17.33
        (11) PD 17.32
        (12) PD 17.33
   r 39.2 .... 17.42
        (1) 17.26, 17.32
        (2)(c) 17.34
        (3) 17.32, 17.45
           (a) 17.42
           (b) 17.42
           (c) 17.32, 17.34
           (d) 17.35
        (4) 17.38, 17.40, 17.42
   r 48.7(3) 12.28
Commission for Health Improvement (Functions) Regulations 2000 (SI 2000/662)
   reg 17 .... 3.37
   reg 18 .... 3.35
County Court Rules 1981 (SI 1981/1687)
   Ord.20 r 12 .... 15.02

Criminal and Care Proceedings (General) Regulations 1992 (SI 1989/344)
  reg 56 ....10.03
Crown Court (Amendment) Rules 1991
  r 31(2) 14.137
  r 32 ....14.137
Crown Court (Criminal Procedure and Investigations Act 1996) (Disclosure)
  Rules 1997 (SI 1997/698) 14.127
Crown Court Rules 1982 (SI 1982/1109)
  r 23 ....14.131
    (3)(d) 15.07
  r 24A 17.31

Data Protection (Conditions under Paragraph 3 of Part II of Sch 1) Order 2000
  (SI 2000/185) 18.17
Data Protection (Designated Codes of Practice) Order 2000 (SI 2000/418) 3.08
Data Protection (Designated Codes of Practice) (No 2) Order 2000 (SI 2000/1864) 18.40
Data Protection (Miscellaneous Subject Access Exemptions) Order 2000
  (SI 2000/419) 19.26, 19.40, 19.41, 19.45
Data Protection (Miscellaneous Subject Access Exemptions) (Amendment) Order 2000
  (SI 2000/1865) 19.41
Data Protection (Notification and Notification Fees) Regulations 2000 (SI 2000/188) 18.03
Data Protection (Processing of Sensitive Personal Data) Order 2000
  (SI 2000/417) 13.44, 13.49, 18.27
  r 9 ....18.43
  Sch
    para 1 ....18.27
    para 2 ....18.27
    para 3 ....18.27
    para 4 ....18.27
    para 5 ....18.27
    para 7 ....18.27
    para 8 ....18.27, 18.43
    para 9 ....18.27
    para 10 ....18.27
Data Protection (Subject Access) (Fees and Miscellaneous Provisions) Regulations 2000
  (SI 2000/191) 19.21
  reg 2 ....19.24
Data Protection (Subject Access Modification) (Education) Order 2000 (SI 2000/414)
  r 4 ....19.42
  r 5 ....19.44, 19.89
    (2) 19.87, 19.89, 19.115
  r 7 ....19.32, 19.76, 19.81
Data Protection (Subject Access Modification) (Health) Order 1987 (SI 1987/1903)
  para 9 ....19.39
Data Protection (Subject Access Modification) (Health) Order 2000 (SI 2000/413)
  r 4 ....19.42
  r 5 ....19.76
    (1) 19.39, 19.68, 19.87, 19.108
    (2) 19.89
    (3) 19.115
      (c) 19.72
  r 8(a) 19.32
Data Protection (Subject Access Modification) (Social Work) Order 2000 (SI 2000/415),
  r 5 ....19.41, 19.42, 19.63, 19.76

Data Protection (Subject Access Modification) (Social Work) Order 2000 (SI 2000/415) (*cont.*):
   (3) 19.115
   (4) 19.114
  r 7(2) 19.41
Data Protection Tribunal (Enforcement Appeals) Rules 2000 (SI 2000/189)
  r 15 .... 15.41
  r 19 .... 15.47
  r 22 .... 18.49

Education (Pupil Information) (England) (Amendment) Regulations 2001 (SI 2001/1212)
  reg 4 .... 19.83
  reg 6
    (1) 19.83
    (2) (b) 19.83
Education (Pupil Information) (England) Regulations 2000 (SI 2000/297) 19.76, 19.79, 19.80
  reg 3(1) 19.80, 19.81
  reg 5 .... 19.80
  reg 6
    (2)(a) 19.82, 19.83
    (3) 19.83
    (7) 19.83
  reg 9 .... 19.45, 19.83
  Sch 1 .... 19.83
Education (Special Educational Needs) (England) (Consolidation) Regulations 2001
  (SI 2001/3455) 13.18
  reg 24 .... 3.42
    (1) 13.14
      (c) 13.56
    (2) 13.14
    (3) 13.17
    (4) 6.32
Employment Tribunals (Constitution and Rules of Procedure) Regulations 1993 (SI 1993/2687)
  reg 4(2) 15.41
Employment Tribunals (Constitution and Rules of Procedure) Regulations 2001
  (SI 2001/1171)
  Sch 1
    r 10(3) 15.47
    r 16 .... 15.47

Family Procedure Rules 1991 (SI 1991/1247) 13.14, 14.05, 15.02, 16.39, 17.17
  r 2.62 .... 14.04
  r 4.11 .... 13.14
  r 4.12 .... 13.14
  r 4.16(7) 17.31, 17.32
  r 4.23 .... 11.34, 17.16, 17.22
  r 9.2A 13.14
  r 10.20(1) 17.27
    (3) 17.22, 17.27
Family Proceedings Courts (Children Act 1989) Rules 1991 (SI 1991/1395) 17.17
  r 23 .... 17.17
General Osteopathic Council (Health Committee) (Procedure) Rules Order of Council 2000
  (SI 2000/242)
  r 16(1) 15.45
  r 39 .... 15.44

Table of Statutory Instruments

Health Service (Control of Patient Information) Regulations 2002 (SI 2002/1438)
    reg 2 ....13.54
    reg 3 ....13.54
    reg 7(2) 13.54
Human Organ Transplants (Supply of Information) Regulations 1989 (SI 1989/2108)..........3.36

Insolvency Rules 1986 ....15.39
    r 9.5..15.39
Investigatory Powers Tribunals Rules 2000 (SI 2000/2665)
    r 9(6) 14.87

Legal Services Commission (Disclosure of Information) Regulations 2000 (SI 2000/442) 10.03

Magistrates' Courts (Advance Information) Rules 1985 (SI 1985/601)...............................14.123
Magistrates' Courts (Children and Young Persons) Rules 1992 (SI 1992/2071)
    r 10...3.40
Magistrates' Courts (Criminal Justice (International Co-operation) Rules) 1991 (SI 1991/ 1074)
    r 6...14.137
Mental Health Review Tribunals Rules 1983 (SI 1983/942)
    r 12(2) 19.68
        (3) 17.02
    r 21...15.45
Misuse of Drugs (Notification of and Supply of Addicts) Regulations 1973 (SI 1973/799)
    reg 3 ....10.03
Money Laundering Regulations 1993 (SI 1993/1933) 10.24, 10.25, 10.27
Money Laundering Regulations 2001 (SI 2001/3641)
    reg 10 ....3.37
    reg 11 ....14.69
    reg 14 ....14.69

National Care Standards Commission (Inspection of Schools and Colleges) Regulations 2002
    (SI 2002/552)...3.37
National Health Service (General Medical Services) Amendment (No 4) Regulations 2000
    (SI 2000/2383)...21.16
National Health Service (General Medical Services) Regulations 1992 (SI 1992/635)...........21.16
    Sch 2 ....21.16
        para 25 ....21.16
        para 36 ....21.16
        (6) 21.16
National Health Service (Notification of Births and Deaths) Regulations 1982
    (SI 1982/286)...10.03
National Health Service Trusts and Primary Care Trusts (Sexually Transmitted Diseases)
    Directions 2000..3.41
National Health Service Trusts (Venereal Disease) Regulations 1991......................................4.51
National Health Service (Venereal Diseases) Regulations 1974 (SI 1974/29) 3.42, 4.51
    reg 2 ....12.14
National Health Service (Venereal Diseases) Regulations 1974 (SI 1974/29) 3.42, 10.03

Offshore Installations (Safety Representative and Safety Committees) Regulations 1989
    (SI 1989/971)
    reg 18 ....1.05
Open-Ended Investment Companies (Investment Companies with Variable Capital)
    Regulations 1996 (SI 1996/2827)
    reg 23(2)...10.04

Police and Criminal Evidence Act 1984 (Application to Customs and Excise) Order 1985
  (SI 1985/1800) 14.19
Probation Rules 1984 (SI 1984/647) 3.42
  reg 22 ....3.42
Protection of Children Act Tribunal Regulations 2000 (SI 2000/2619)
  reg 21(2) 15.48
Protection of Children and Vulnerable Adults and Care Standards Tribunal Regulations 2002
  (SI 2002/816)
  reg 15 ....15.48
  reg 16 ....15.41
  reg 19 ....15.47
  reg 21 ....15.47
Public Health (Infectious Diseases) Regulations 1988 (SI 1988/1546) 3.36, 10.03
Public Interest Disclosure (Prescribed Persons) Order 1999 (SI 1999/1549) 21.25, 21.26

Reporting of Injuries, Diseases and Dangerous Occurrences Regulations 1985
  (SI 1985/2023) 3.36
Reporting of Injuries, Diseases and Dangerous Occurrences Regulations 1995
  (SI 1995/3163) 10.03
Representation of the People (England and Wales) Regulations 2001 (SI 2001/341) 3.40
  reg 23 ....3.40
  reg 43 ....12.14
Rules of the Supreme Court 1965 (SI 1965/1776) 14.05
  Ord.32, r 7 ....15.02
  Ord.85, r 2 ....12.38

Social Security (Disclosure of State Pension Information) Regulations 2000 (SI 2000/3188)
  reg 3(1) (a) 13.01

Telecommunications (Data Protection and Privacy) Regulations 1999 (SI 1999/2093) 14.104

Wireless Telegraphy (Short Range Devices) (Exempt) Regulations 1993 (SI 1993/1591) 6.67

EUROPEAN CONVENTION ON HUMAN RIGHTS

European Convention on Human Rights..................3.51, 3.54, 8.24, 8.31, 10.13, 10.15, 11.55,
13.17, 14.18, 14.77, 14.121, 16.09, 16.48, 17.34
- Art 1 ....20.05
- Art 2 ....3.16, 3.26, 3.30, 11.23, 15.53, 16.40, 17.35, 20.05
- Art 3 ....3.16, 3.26, 3.30, 11.23, 16.40, 20.05
- Art 6 ....2.16, 3.10, 3.11, 3.16, 3.23, 6.29, 6.102, 8.44, 10.15, 11.69, 12.24,
  12.25, 12.29, 13.63, 14.97, 14.101, 14.122, 14.130, 15.09, 15.47, 15.55, 16.02,
  16.09, 16.15, 16.25, 16.27, 16.40, 16.50, 16.63, 16.64, 17.13, 17.34, 20.13
  - (1) 3.10, 3.23, 3.24, 3.26, 6.95, 6.100, 12.25, 12.28,
    15.17, 15.18, 15.45, 15.46, 17.08, 17.34, 17.35, 17.36, 17.37, 17.38
  - (2) 3.10
  - (3) 3.10
    - (c) 3.10, 3.11
- Art 8 ....1.12, 3.04, 3.08, 3.09, 3.10, 3.15, 3.19, 3.22, 3.26, 3.28, 3.29, 3.30,
  3.32, 4.15, 4.46, 4.59, 5.04, 5.20, 5.51, 6.12, 6.16, 6.17, 6.19, 6.26, 6.28,
  6.34, 6.100, 8.18, 8.19, 8.31, 8.55, 8.56, 8.57, 8.62, 8.65, 10.08, 10.09, 10.12,
  10.13, 10.15, 11.13, 11.23, 11.50, 12.07, 12.17, 12.25, 13.63, 14.07, 14.09, 14.10,
  14.27, 14.40, 14.55, 14.59, 14.65, 14.77, 14.82, 14.88, 14.97, 14.98, 14.117,
  14.130, 15.09, 15.18, 15.19, 15.54, 16.02, 16.09, 16.26, 16.40, 16.401, 17.11,
  17.38, 17.51, 18.20, 18.37, 18.40, 18.58, 18.60, 19.01, 19.20, 19.75, 19.82, 21.30
  - (1) 1.07, 1.55, 3.03, 3.06, 3.19, 3.26, 3.28, 3.44, 5.20, 5.40, 6.28,
    9.21, 10.08, 10.13, 11.06, 11.37, 11.46, 12.22, 12.28, 13.18, 14.82, 14.104, 14.122,
    16.50, 16.51, 17.35, 17.36, 17.39, 17.51, 19.18, 19.87, 19.91, 19.92, 20.05
  - (2) 3.19, 3.28, 5.20, 10.08, 10.13, 10.14, 10.40, 11.13, 11.28, 11.42,
    11.55, 12.07, 12.17, 12.22, 12.28, 14.104, 16.26, 16.50, 18.28, 18.37, 19.87
- Art 9...3.16, 16.49, 16.50, 16.51
- Art 10 ....2.26, 3.17, 3.18, 3.19, 3.22, 3.26, 3.28, 3.29, 3.31, 3.32, 4.15, 5.61,
  6.16, 6.46, 6.47, 6.87, 7.09, 7.16, 7.28, 7.38, 8.11, 8.14, 8.18, 8.19, 8.25, 8.70, 11.42,
  11.65, 11.73, 15.55, 17.35, 17.50, 17.51, 18.20, 18.40, 18.60, 21.29, 21.30
  - (1) 3.17, 3.19, 3.27, 3.28, 17.35, 21.29, 21.30
  - (2) 3.19, 3.27, 3.28, 3.31, 8.22, 11.46, 17.50
- Art 13 ....14.101
- Art 14 ....3.19, 13.18
- Art 15 ....3.19
- Art 16 ....3.19
- Art 17 ....3.19
- Art 41 ....8.31, 8.69

ABBREVIATIONS

AID	artificial insemination by donor
BMA	British Medical Association
BSC	Broadcasting Standards Commission
CPR	Civil Procedure Rules 1998
CRB	Criminal Records Bureau
DfEE	Department for Education and Employment
DfES	Department for Education and Skills
DoH	Department of Health
DPA	Data Protection Act 1998
DPWP	Article 29, Data Protection Working Party
ECHR	European Convention on Human Rights
ECtHR	European Court of Human Rights
ERA	Employment Rights Act 1996
FOIA	Freedom of Information Act 2000
FOM	Faculty of Occupational Medicine of the Royal College of Physicians
GMC	General Medical Council
HFEA	Human Fertilization and Embryology Authority
HGC	Human Genetics Commission
HRA	Human Rights Act 1998
IC	Information Commissioner
ICCPR	International Covenant on Civil and Political Rights
ITC	Independent Television Commission
LPP	legal professional privilege
NCIS	National Criminal Intelligence Service
NHS	National Health Service
NMC	Nursing and Midwifery Council
PACE	Police and Criminal Evidence Act 1984
PCC	Press Complaints Commission
PII	public interest immunity
PIU	Performance and Innovation Unit
RIPA	Regulation of Investigatory Powers Act 2000
SAR	subject access right
UKCC	UK Central Council for Nursing Midwifery and Health Visiting
UNHRC	United Nations Human Rights Commission

Part I

INTRODUCTION

1

DEFINITIONS AND RATIONALES

A. Use of Terms in the Book	1.02	B. Justifying and Limiting Professional	
Personal Information	1.02	Confidentiality	1.35
Privacy, Confidentiality and Privilege	1.06	Justifying Confidentiality	1.35
Professionals and their Clients	1.23	Justifying Breaches of Confidentiality	1.54
Third Parties, Interceptors and Strangers	1.33		

The purpose of this book is to examine the legal obligations that professionals owe their clients in respect of confidential personal[1] information concerning the clients. It is written from the premise that in matters of confidentiality and disclosure of personal information the same fundamental legal principles apply to all professionals and that any variations in the obligations of different professional groups need to be rationally justified by differences in the nature of the service provided to the client or the information that the professional handles. **1.01**

A. Use of Terms in the Book

Personal Information

Information about an individual

Sensitive and non-sensitive personal information

Information is 'that which informs, instructs, tells or makes aware'.[2] Personal information is information about an individual, that is a natural person.[3] In common parlance it refers to such things as a person's political and religious beliefs, medical history, mental stability, emotions, sexuality, intimate relationships, **1.02**

---

[1] Occasionally the discussion branches out to include disclosure by the professional of information that is not strictly personal. The main examples are found in ch 19 where disclosure of information *to* the client is considered and in ch 5 when disclosure of information in breach of fiduciary duty is discussed. It is unclear in England and Wales whether the disclosure or misuse of personal information can constitute a breach of fiduciary duty.

[2] *Commissioner of Police v Ombudsman* [1988] 1 NZLR 385, 402.

[3] Cp Information Act 1982 (Aus); *Australian Privacy Charter* 1994 at http://www.apcc.org.au/Charter.html.

genetic makeup, IQ, criminal history and financial affairs.[4] This is information that the individual can reasonably expect to keep to himself[5] or which, as Wacks puts it, the individual is likely to view as 'intimate or sensitive'.[6] The sensitivity of information depends very much upon the purposes for which it is used.[7] Seen as raw data an individual's name and address are not normally sensitive information,[8] but a list of persons engaged in controversial research involving experimental work on animals[9] or who are thought to be unfit to work with children is. What impact use for a particular purpose has for the sensitivity of information depends upon societal expectations, the personal circumstances of the individual and that individual's personal sensitivities and culture.[10]

1.03 Legal definitions of personal information vary. In the Police Act 1997[11] 'personal information' is defined as '[i]nformation concerning an individual (living or dead) who can be identified from it and relating to his physical or mental health or to spiritual counselling or assistance given or to be given to him'. In other words, it is restricted to certain types of sensitive information. The Data Protection Act 1998 (DPA) is narrower in its coverage in that it is confined to recorded data[12] about a living individual but wider in that it includes any fact, opinion or expression of intention about an individual, whether true or false and whether sensitive or not.[13] The Local Government Finance Act 1992 defines 'personal information' as 'information which relates to an individual (living or dead) who can be identified from that information or from that and any other information supplied to any person by the authority' and includes 'any expression of opinion about the individual and any indication of the intentions of any person in respect of the individual'.[14] Except when dealing with data protection, in this book personal information means knowledge about a person (whether alive, dead

---

[4] cp A Hedges, *Confidentiality: the Public View* DSS Research Report No 56 (London: 1996) 19.
[5] NZLRC, *Protecting Personal Information from Disclosure* PP 49 (2002) ch 3, para 56.
[6] R Wacks, *Personal Information: Privacy and the Law* (Oxford: 1993) 26. One could say that 'personal information' has a wide and a narrow meaning: (1) information about a person, and (2) private or sensitive information about a person.
[7] cp *R (on the application of Robertson) v City of Wakefield Metropolitan Council* [2001] EWHC Admin 915; [2002] 2 WLR 889, para 34.
[8] Personal circumstances may mean that it is. Cp Press Complaints Commission, *Renate John v Sunday Mirror*, 4 June 2000.
[9] cp *Imtran v Uncaged Campaigns Ltd* [2001] 2 All ER 385, para 8.
[10] cp P Roth, 'What is "Personal Information"?' (2002) New Zealand Universities L Rev 40, 42. For a striking example of the importance of the individual's personal circumstances for the sensitivity of information about name and address see *Venables v NGN Ltd* [2001] 1 All ER 908.
[11] s 99(2).
[12] On the distinction between data and information see para 18.02 below.
[13] DPA, s 1. The DPA has a special category of sensitive personal data which is more intensely protected: see para 18.23 below.
[14] Local Government Finance Act 1992 s 68 and Sch 2, para 17(3). cp Audit Commission Act 1998, s 15(4).

or still unborn).[15] The information need not be 'personal' in the popular sense of being private or sensitive and it need not be created, or even known of, by the individual to whom it relates. It can exist in someone's head, be recorded in any manner known to mankind or exist as physical matter, for instance, blood or genetic material.

Information not merely associated with, but about, an individual

Personal information is information *about* an individual. Whether information satisfies this condition depends upon context.[16] Information that concerns a small group (a band, a partnership, a club, a family business) will not be information about anyone belonging to the group unless the group and its individual members are closely connected.[17] When a professional makes a work communication, that communication may be personal information about the professional, but only in so far as the communication tells us something about the professional or the opinions that she holds.[18] The Canadian Privacy Commissioner has ruled that a doctor's prescription is not personal information about the prescribing doctor: 'While it can be revealing with regard to the patient—the nature of an illness or condition, for instance, and perhaps its severity—it discloses little or nothing about the physician *as an individual*.'[19] More controversially, the Canadian Privacy Commissioner, says that information gleaned by examining the doctor's prescribing patterns is not personal information either. It is information 'about the tangible result of his or her work activity, namely the work product'.

1.04

Who is identifiable

To constitute personal information in law, information must not just be about an individual, it must be about someone who can be identified. That some individual must be identifiable for information to be considered personal information is

1.05

---

[15] For the case for treating an embryo as having a private life and a personal integrity deserving of legal protection see P Blume, *Protection of Informational Privacy* (Copenhagen: 2002) 5.

[16] P Roth, 'What is "Personal Information"?' (2002) 20 New Zealand Universities L Rev 40, 56 argues that a telephone number with nothing to associate it with an individual is not 'about' anyone and therefore is not 'personal' information. It becomes personal information if 'included in an individual's file as a means of contacting the individual'. Similarly, an e-mail address is personal information if it can be used to identify someone on its own (eg R.Pattenden@uea.ac.uk) or together with other available information (eg if the e-mail address is included in a file as the contact address of a named individual).

[17] *Montana Band of Indians v Canada (Minister of Indian and Northern Affairs)* [1989] 1 FC 143, 153. Cp Information Commissioner, *Data Protection Act 1998—Legal Guidance* (2001) para 2.2.1. Contrast *C v ASB Bank Ltd* (1997) 4 HRNZ 306, 307–311, discussed by P Roth, 'What is "Personal Information"?' (2000) 20 New Zealand Universities L Rev 40, 56.

[18] When a professional expresses an opinion about a client that opinion may tell you more about the professional (her likes and dislikes) than about the client.

[19] 'Finding on the Prescribing Patterns of Doctors', 2 October 2001 at http://www.privcom.gc.ca. See also *E.H. v the Information Commissioner* (H.C. Eire, 21 December 2001), available at www.oic.gov.ie/23ae_3C2.htm.

Chapter 1: Definitions and Rationales

attested to by numerous statutes.[20] Identification does not have to proceed from the information alone. The condition is met if it is possible to trace the information to a single person. The EU Data Protection Directive[21] states that an identifiable person is someone who can be identified, directly or indirectly, by reference to an identification number or to one or more factors specific to his physical, physiological, mental, economic, cultural or social identity.[22] Information about individuals that has been aggregated and presented in a statistical format that does not allow information about any one person to be extracted or traced is not personal information.

Privacy, Confidentiality and Privilege

Privacy

1.06 This book is about *confidential* personal information handled by professionals. The term 'confidentiality' is often used interchangeably with 'privacy'. Some people think the two terms are synonymous. This is a misconception.[23] Though the two are related, privacy is in all but one respect[24] a wider concept. Both privacy and confidentiality are about interaction between an individual and others. They share the supposition that the individual lives in a community.[25] Privacy depends upon there being a community of at least two individuals. Confidentiality requires a community of at least three. Where A, B and C make up the community, confidentiality is achieved if A and B keep something from C, privacy if A is able to keep something from B *and* C.[26] Confidentiality presupposes trust between individuals—between A and B in the example given. Privacy can exist in a world where there is no trust. Confidentiality requires some privacy, privacy requires no confidentiality. Privacy rights precede obligations of confidentiality in respect of personal information and are more fundamental.[27] The following discussion will expand on this resumé.

---

[20] Local Government Finance Act 1992 s 68(2); Police Act 1997 s 99(2); Learning and Skills Act 2000 s119(4)(3); Financial Services and Markets Act 2000, s 348 (4)(b). cp Offshore Installations (Safety Representative and Safety Committees) Regulations 1989, SI 1989/971 reg 18; Human Fertilization and Embryology Act 1990 s 31(2); Access to Health Records (Control of Access) Regulations 1993, SI 1993/746, reg 2; DPA ss 1(1), 59(1)(b); Immigration and Asylum Act 1999 s 93(2)(b).
[21] (EC) 95/46 Art 2.
[22] Art 2. Account must be taken of possible identification through data mining.
[23] *R v BSC, ex p BBC* [2000] 3 All ER 989, 1002: 'But privacy and confidentiality are not the same' per Lord Mustill.
[24] See para 1.18 below.
[25] P Blume, *Protection of Informational Privacy* (Copenhagen: 2002) 9–10.
[26] Consequently A's privacy is breached when information is obtained about A by B or C, A's confidentiality is breached when information about A is disclosed by B to C.
[27] W Lawrance, 'Privacy and Health Research' (US: 1997) 3, at http://aspe.hhs.gov/admnsimp/PHR1.htm; M Collingridge, S Miller and W Bowles, 'Privacy and confidentiality in Social Work' (2001) 54 (2) Australian Social Work 3, 12.

Defining privacy

1.07 The distinction between the public (in the sense of political) and private spheres was well understood in antiquity but people laid no claim to a right to privacy.[28] As a concept privacy had negative connotations:[29] it suggested dereliction of duty and rejection of the social order.[30] The idea that we are all entitled to hide personal information about ourselves from others is a by-product of urban anonymity and prosperity and a recent development in the history of Western ideas.[31] 'Privacy' as a right made its debut in legal discourse in *Boyd v US*[32] roughly 100 years ago. It remains an amorphous idea in legal and non-legal usage incapable of precise definition by lawyer or philosopher.[33] There has been no greater success in defining the related right to respect for 'private life' guaranteed by Article 8(1) of the European Convention on Human Rights.[34]

1.08 Shils, looking at the term 'privacy' from a sociologist's perspective, observed the following:

> Numerous meanings crowd in the mind . . . the privacy of private property; privacy as a proprietary interest in name and image; privacy as the keeping of one's affairs to oneself; the privacy of the internal affairs of a voluntary association or of a business; privacy as the physical absence of others who are unqualified by kinship, affection or other attributes to be present; respect for privacy as the desire of another person not to disclose or have disclosed information about what he is doing or has done; the privacy of sexual and familial affairs; the desire for privacy as the desire not to be observed by another person or persons; the privacy of the private citizen as opposed to the public official; and these are only a few.[35]

---

[28] There is no word in Latin or Greek that corresponds to the modern idea of 'privacy'. 'Idios' meaning private or personal is found in Homer (*Odyssey* 3.82, 4.314).

[29] L Velecky, 'The Concept of Privacy' in J Young (ed), *Privacy* (Chichester: 1978) 17.

[30] B Moore, *Privacy* (New York: 1984) 82.

[31] NZLRC, *Protecting Personal Information from Disclosure* PP 49 (2002) ch 3, paras 39–41. See also P Blume, *Protection of Informational Privacy* (Copenhagen: 2002) 9–10.

[32] 116 US 616, 630 (1885).

[33] There is a vast literature about privacy. Useful materials include, J Young (ed), *Privacy* (Chichester: 1978); R Wacks, 'The Poverty of "Privacy" ' (1980) 96 LQR 73; F Schoeman (ed), *Philosophical Dimensions of Privacy: An Anthology* (Cambridge: 1984); J Inness, *Privacy, Intimacy and Isolation* (New York: 1992) ch 5; E Barendt, 'Privacy and the Press' [1995] 1 Media & Entertainment L 27; J Wagner DeCew, *In Pursuit of Privacy* (Ithaca: 1997) chs 3, 4; F Cate, *Privacy in the Information Age* (Washington: 1997) ch 3; E Byrne, 'Privacy' in R Chadwick (ed), *Encyclopedia of Applied Ethics* (California: 1998) 649.

[34] *PG v UK* Application 44787/98 [2002] Crim LR 308, para 56; *Rose v Secretary of State for Health* [2002] EWHC 1593, para 45. No attempt has been made to define precisely the German right of personality which covers much the same ground as privacy in the common law world: B Broomekamp, 'The Human Rights Act 1998 in Comparison with the Protection of Privacy and Personality in Germany' [2000] Yearbook of Media and Copyright L 66, 70.

[35] E Shils, 'Privacy: Its Constitutional Vicissitudes' (1966) 31 L and Contemporary Problems 281.

Chapter 1: Definitions and Rationales

All these usages have several things in common: they are culturally,[36] socially and contextually[37] determined and in some way or other they involve exclusion of others.

1.09 Expanding on the last quality of privacy, some writers describe privacy in terms of the ability to restrict, or the individual's interest in restricting, access to or interference with the self.[38] By 'self' these writers mean not just the physical self but also the 'internal man', the individual's mental world. By 'access' they mean not only perception through the senses but access to knowledge about the exterior and interior self.

1.10 A criticism of control definitions is that they focus upon rights.[39] Privacy can also be viewed as a condition; as a state of accessibility to the self or some aspect of the self.[40] This state of affairs should be voluntary: the shipwrecked sailor on a deserted island and the prisoner in solitary confinement have solitude but not privacy because privacy presupposes community and autonomy.[41]

1.11 The most famous legal definition of privacy—the 'right to be left alone'—was used by Warren and Brandeis, who as long ago as 1890 were disturbed by intrusive press reporting,[42] to describe the idea that each one of us is entitled to a private realm that is not just spatial.[43] In this realm we can let down our guard and be at odds with the appearance we present to the world.[44] As a definition of privacy, however, the Warren–Brandeis formulation is flawed.[45] It overlooks that privacy is

---

[36] A Westin, *Privacy and Freedom* (London: 1967) 26–30; C Fried, 'Privacy' (1968) 77 Yale LJ 475, 487.
[37] *R v BSC, ex p BBC* [2000] 3 All ER 989, 994.
[38] M Powers, 'A Cognitive Access Definition of Privacy' (1996) 15 L and Philosophy 369, 373.
[39] G Laurie, *Genetic Privacy* (Cambridge: 2002) 51–55, 67–69.
[40] T Beauchamp and J Childress, *Principles of Biomedical Ethics* (5th edn, Oxford: 2001) 294; M Powers, 'A Cognitive Access Definition of Privacy' (1996) 15 L and Philosophy 369, 375; *R v Department of Health, ex p Source Informatics* [1999] 4 All ER 185, 195.
[41] cp G Laurie, 'Challenging Medico Legal Norms' (2001) 22 J of Legal Medicine 1, 31.
[42] This definition was first formulated by Judge Cooley (*Cooley on Torts* (2nd edn, 1888) 29) and taken up by Brandeis (later a justice of the US Supreme Court) and Warren in a now famous article in the Harvard Law Review of 1890 (S Warren and L Brandeis, 'The Right to Privacy' (1890) 4 *Harvard L Rev* 193). cp Council of Europe, Resolution 1165 (1998) *Right to privacy* para 4: 'The right to privacy, guaranteed by article 8 of the European Convention on Human Rights, has . . . been defined by the Assembly . . . within Resolution 428 (1970), as "the right to live one's own life with a minimum of interference".' Warren and Brandeis's primary concern seems not to have been with keeping others at bay, as their definition implies, but with how to keep one's domestic affairs private.
[43] Judge Bonello said in *Rotaru v Romania* Application 28341/95 8 BHRC 449, para 2 in a partly dissenting opinion that '[t]here are reserved zones in our person and in our spirit which [the Art 8 right to respect for privacy] requires should remain locked. It is illegitimate to probe for, store, classify or divulge data which refer to those innermost spheres of activity, orientation or conviction . . .'.
[44] This permits emotional release which is one of the benefits of privacy: A Westin, *Privacy and Freedom* (London: 1967) 33 et seq.
[45] And not only as stated in the main text. The definition conflates privacy and liberty: *Report of the Committee on Privacy* (Cmnd 5012, 1972) 18–19; G Laurie, *Genetic Privacy* (Cambridge: 2002) 71.

A. Use of Terms in the Book

not just about the right to be, or condition of being, left undisturbed, it is also about the right to be, or condition of being, unknown and unnoticed. 'A journalist infringes the privacy of a person . . . if he or she intrudes uninvitedly into the person's home and takes a picture of this person. . . . Furthermore, the journalist infringes this person's privacy indirectly by publishing the photograph in a newspaper to inform the readers about the person's personal sphere. The readers who are thus informed infringe this person's privacy directly, albeit non-voluntarily.'[46] To sum up: privacy is a state of voluntary physical, psychological and informational[47] inaccessibility to others to which the individual may have a right and privacy is lost and the right infringed when without his consent 'others obtain information about [the] individual, pay attention to him or gain access to him'.[48]

Privacy and secrecy

Privacy should not be equated with secrecy. First, secrecy is relied upon to conceal the truth. It is at least arguable that privacy can be invaded by the circulation of information that is false:[49] '[t]he publication of defamatory comments constitutes an invasion of the individual's personal privacy and is an affront to that person's dignity.'[50] Secondly, it is not only people who have secrets; companies and governments[51] have secrets too. In fact, in law, secrecy is generally associated with the public sphere.[52] Privacy, however, is about the protection of the individual's dignity[53] and personality.[54] In *Douglas v Hello! Ltd* Sedley LJ described privacy as a legal principle drawn from the fundamental value of personal autonomy.[55] In *R v BSC, ex p BBC* Lord Mustill said that he found 'the concept of a company's privacy hard to grasp. To my mind the privacy of a human being denotes at the same time the personal "space" in which the individual is free to be itself, and also the carapace, or shell, or umbrella, or whatever other metaphor is preferred, which protects that space from intrusion. An infringement of privacy is an affront to the personality, which is damaged both by the violation and by the demonstration

1.12

---

[46] A Vedder, 'Medical Data, New Information Technologies, and the Need for Normative Principles Other than Privacy Rules' in M Freeman and A Lewis (eds), *Law and Medicine* (Oxford: 2000) 448.
[47] Cp Council of Europe, Resolution 1165 (1998) *Right to privacy*, para 5: 'In view of the new communication technologies which make it possible to store and use personal data, the right to control one's own data should be added to this definition.'
[48] per Latham J, *R v Department of Health, ex p Source Informatics* [1999] 4 All ER 185, 195.
[49] M Tugendhat, 'Privacy and Celebrity' in E Barendt and A Firth (eds), *Yearbook of Copyright and Media Law 2001/2* (Oxford: 2002) 18.
[50] per Cory J, *Hill v Church of Scientology of Toronto* [1995] 2 SCR 1130, 1179. The DPA, which sets out to protect the individual's informational privacy (see para 18.01 below), applies to information that is true or false (see para 18.05 below).
[51] *Att-Gen v Jonathan Cape* [1975] 3 All ER 484.
[52] eg the Official Secrets Act 1989.
[53] *ABC v Lenah Game Meats Pty Ltd* [2001] HCA 63, para 43 and paras 1.37–1.38 below.
[54] See para 1.36 below.
[55] *Douglas v Hello! Ltd* [2001] 2 All ER 289, para 126.

Chapter 1: Definitions and Rationales

that the personal space is not inviolate. . . . I do not see how it can apply to an impersonal corporate body, which has no sensitivities to wound, and no selfhood to protect.'[56] A company cannot feel mental pain and cannot be stripped of dignity. Privacy for a company is an intermediate good, not an end in itself.[57] When, as has occasionally happened, a court has interceded to protect a company's privacy[58] what it has actually done is protect its goodwill.[59]

1.13 A third difference is that a secret is always something that is intentionally concealed because disclosure may discredit or otherwise damage the owner of the secret.[60] Privacy may, and often does, protect secrets but '[i]t should not be assumed that a desire for privacy means that a person has "something to hide"'.[61] Privacy is a state in which A has made some part of himself inaccessible to B because that part of the self is something that A thinks is no concern of B's[62]—excretion and copulation, for example, which even from the most puritanical moral standpoint may involve no impropriety. Barendt calls this 'social privacy'.[63] Feldman explains: 'We all have things we would rather not make accessible to others, from a sense of decency, dignity, or respect for intimacy.'[64] Put bluntly: 'All of us want to be able to go about the business of our lives without having someone looking over our shoulder, demanding to know what we're doing, and why . . . In that context, you might say privacy means having the right to say "*none of your damn business*".'[65]

Forms of privacy

1.14 Rather than attempt to find an all-embracing definition of privacy, some legal theorists describe the forms that it takes. All of the following in one setting or another

---

[56] [2000] 3 All ER 989, para 48.
[57] D'Amato, 'Comment: Professor Posner's Lecture on privacy' (1978) 12 Georgia L Rev 497, 499–500.
[58] eg *R v BSC, ex p BBC* [2000] 3 All ER 989 where the Court of Appeal held that 'privacy' in s107(1) of the Broadcasting Act 1996, s107(1) extended to unwarranted inference with the privacy of a company. This decision was a result of the express language of the Act (s111(1)) which allowed complaints by a 'body of persons whether incorporated or not' and the legislative purpose of upholding standards. In South Africa privacy has also been applied to corporations: *Financial Mail (Pty) Ltd v Sage Holdings* 1993 (2) SA 451, 460–466. See also *Investigating Directorate v Hyundai Motor Distributors* [2000] ZACC 13, paras 17–18. The European Court of Human Rights has decided that companies have some Art 8 rights: *Stes Colas Est v France* Application 37971/97 (16 April 2002).
[59] *ABC v Lenah Game Meats Pty Ltd* [200] HCA 63, paras 120–128.
[60] J Wagner De Cew, *In Pursuit of Privacy* (Ithaca: 1997) 48; S Bok, *Secrets: The Ethics of Concealment and Revelation* (Oxford: 1984) 10. Secrecy does not have to involve negative facts—trade secrets, for example, may be very good and valuable.
[61] *Australian Privacy Charter* 1994, available at http://www.apcc.org.au/Charter.html.
[62] J Wagner DeCew, *In Pursuit of Privacy* (Ithaca: 1997) 56.
[63] E Barendt, 'Privacy as a Constitutional Right and Value' in P. Birks (ed), *Privacy and Loyalty* (Oxford: 1997) 6.
[64] D Feldman, *Civil Liberties and Human Rights in England and Wales* (2nd edn, Oxford: 2002) 512.
[65] Privacy Commissioner of Canada, Address to the Canadian Medical Association, 24 November 2000, available at http://www.privcom.gc.ca/speech/02_05_a_001124_e.asp.

A. Use of Terms in the Book

have—whether rightly or wrongly is disputed is some cases—been described as aspects of privacy:

- not to be identified (*anonymity*);[66]
- not to be subjected to physical interference through, for example, involuntary body searches and drugs testing (*physical or bodily privacy*);[67]
- freedom from unwanted surveillance by, amongst others, stalkers, paparazzi, busybodies, voyeurs and agents of the state (*access privacy*);
- not to have communications monitored or intercepted (*privacy of communications*);
- not to make known with whom one associates (*relational or associational privacy*);
- physical space in which to conduct one's personal affairs free from unwanted observation or intrusion (*spatial or territorial privacy*);
- independence in making decisions about 'quintessentially private' matters such as contraception, abortion, marriage, child rearing and where to live[67a] (*decisional privacy*);
- control over the collection, storage, retrieval and sharing and use of personal information (*informational privacy*, also known as data protection);[68]
- control of one's identity including image,[69] bodily products and genetic profile (*proprietary privacy*);[70]
- not to have one's time wasted by unsolicited communications (junk mail and spam) (*attentional privacy*);[71] and
- the right to develop close relationships with human beings of one's choice (*intimacy*).[72]

There is obvious overlap between the forms.[73] Directly or indirectly the goal in almost every case is to stop unwanted intrusion, unwanted circulation of personal information or both. Spatial and physical privacy fall into the third group: they prevent intrusion *and* disclosure. Looked at another way, the aim is to establish

1.15

---

[66] *Valiquette v Gazette* (1991) 8 CCLT (2d) 302.
[67] eg *R v Dyment* (1988) 26 DLR (4th) 399, 514–515; *Henderson v Chief Constable of Fife* 1988 SLT 361, 367.
[67a] *Godbout v Longueiul (City)* [1997] 3 SCR 844, para 66 per La Forest J.
[68] A Westin, *Privacy and Freedom* (London: 1967) 7. Genetic privacy is a subcategory of informational privacy which has come to the fore with rapid advances in genetic testing.
[69] *Les Editions ViceVersa Inc v Aubry* (1998) 50 CRR (2d) 225.
[70] See further, W Prosser, 'Privacy' (1960) 48 California L Rev 383; W Robinson, 'Privacy and the Appropriation of Identity' in G Collste (ed), *Ethics and Information Technology* (Delhi: 1998) 43; T Beauchamp and J Childress, *Principles of Biomedical Ethics* (5th edn, Oxford: 2001) 294–295.
[71] D Friedman, 'Privacy and Technology' (2000) 17 Social Philosophy and Policy 186, 187.
[72] *X v Iceland* (1976) 5 DR 86, 87; *Niemetz v Germany* (1992) 16 EHRR 97, para 29. I myself see this as something that privacy facilitates rather than another form of privacy.
[73] C Bennett, 'The Political Economy of Privacy' at http://web.uvic.ca/~polisci/bennett/research/gnom.htm; D Friedman, 'Privacy and Technology' (2000) 17 Social Philosophy and Policy 186, 187. For example, between communications privacy and informational privacy and between proprietary privacy and informational privacy.

control over something which is closely associated with the individual—be it (as Feldman puts it) space (including property), time, action or information.[74]

Confidentiality

Confidentiality in ethics

1.16 Confidentiality is about keeping information secure and controlling its disclosure. As an ethical concept, it may be defined as an obligation to protect information that is not generally known[75] and to use or disclose it only to approved persons, for agreed purposes.[76] In Hohfeld's terms,[77] it involves a right and a correlative duty. The obligation is confined to information that is true.[78] No purpose is served in protecting false material.

1.17 In professional–client relationships the issue of confidentiality arises when some personal information has been disclosed and some privacy has, in consequence, been surrendered.[79] Its function is to surround the privacy that remains with a protective barrier. By disclosing to his doctor that he has the symptoms of a sexually transmitted disease, the patient foregoes a little of his privacy but because the doctor has promised confidentiality the infringement of privacy is contained; beyond the doctor and other health professionals engaged in his treatment no one should become aware of the condition. Westin's definition of confidentiality is a good one:

> Confidentiality is the question of how personal data collected for approved social purposes shall be held and used by the organization that originally collected it, what other secondary or further uses may be made of it, and when consent by the individual will be required for such uses.[80]

1.18 The information that an ethical obligation of confidentiality protects does not have to be intimate (my health) or personal (my bank balance). In a business set-

---

[74] D Feldman, 'Privacy-related Rights: Their Social Value' in P Birks (ed), *Privacy and Loyalty* (Oxford: 1997) 24.

[75] G Laurie, *Genetic Privacy* (Cambridge: 2002) 212, says that information in the public domain cannot be confidential and therefore be protected by an obligation of confidentiality. This is only true up to a point. A can agree not to publicize information about B that is in the public domain. If A reneges on this obligation, A acts unethically and, in terms of contract law, unlawfully: see para 4.10 below. The public domain is, moreover, a flexible concept. Information can be imparted by B to A which at the time of impartation is in the public domain, but thereafter it ceases to be in the public domain: see para 5.16 below.

[76] cp A Allen, *Uneasy Access: Privacy for Women in a Free Society* (Totowa, NJ: 1988) 24.

[77] W Hohfeld, 'Some Fundamental Legal Conceptions as Applied in Legal Reasoning' (1913) 23 Yale LJ 16.

[78] See also, E Cameron, 'Confidentiality in HIV/AIDS: Some Reflections on India and South Africa' (2001) 1 Oxford U Commonwealth LJ 35, 36. See also para 1.21 below.

[79] A Cavoukian, 'The Promise of Privacy-Enhancing Technologies: Applications in Health Information Networks' in C Bennett and R Grant (eds), *Visions of Privacy: Policy Choices for the Digital Age* (Toronto: 1999) 116, 121.

[80] A Westin, *Computers, Health Records and Citizen Rights* (Washington: 1976) 6.

A. Use of Terms in the Book

ting the information may be a trade secret. While companies ought not to be entitled to privacy, they are entitled to confidentiality to protect their commercial interests. In this respect confidentiality is wider than privacy.

Confidentiality in law

When the protected information is personal information, the individual who authorized its collection and who is entitled to specify the audience to whom the information is revealed is typically, but not invariably,[81] also the subject of the information. When confider and subject are identical and certain conditions laid down in the law are met,[82] writes Gurry, confidentiality becomes a legal device for securing the privacy of personal information received in confidence by another.[83]

1.19

> [I]f the confidential information is personal to the confider, the [legal] action for breach of confidence allows him the right to ensure that a confidant does not disseminate the information to others thereby granting greater access over the confider to others and causing a loss to the confider's state of privacy.[84]

Recent developments in the law have removed the need for impartation of the information within a relationship of trust as assumed by Gurry. A professional (like anyone else) who somehow acquires confidential personal information may be saddled with an obligation of confidentiality toward X, the subject of the information, whether there was direct, indirect or no contact with X. All that is necessary is that the professional was aware, or a reasonable person in her position would have been aware, that the information is private to X.[85]

1.20

In law there is an obligation not to disseminate false personal information that is injurious to another, but this is the province of the torts of defamation[86] and injurious falsehoods[87] and not of an equitable or contractual obligation of confidentiality. In law it is the function of the obligation of confidentiality to safeguard information that is true,[88] or at least substantially true.[89] In *Church of Scientology of*

1.21

---

[81] There are two exceptions. The first is when A, the subject of the information, is incompetent to give consent to the collection of the information and B has legal authority to give the necessary consent; the second is where A provides C with information about B that is relevant to A on the understanding that the information about B is confidential. For example, a wife who has failed to become pregnant might inform her doctor that impotence on the husband's part cannot be the cause because his previous girlfriend/current mistress has had two abortions.

[82] See paras 4.04 et seq and 5.06 et seq.

[83] It is not a device that is always available or that can protect against all forms of privacy invasion.

[84] F Gurry, *Breach of Confidence* (Oxford: 1984) 14.

[85] See para 6.13 et seq below.

[86] *Malik v BCCI* [1997] 3 All ER 1,10; see para 4.34 below.

[87] See para 4.41 below.

[88] *Interbrew SA v Financial Times Ltd* [2002] EWCA Civ 274; [2002] 2 Lloyd's Rep 229, para 45. Contrast *Initial Services Ltd v Putterill* [1967] 3 All ER 145, 150. However, an opinion may be confidential even though incapable of being true or false.

[89] *Campbell v MGN* [2002] EWHC 499, QB; [2002] EMLR 30, para 52. But see [2002] EWCA Civ 1373, para 57, and para 6.13 below.

Chapter 1: Definitions and Rationales

California v Kaufman[90] relief was refused to preserve the confidentiality of cult teachings which were described by the judge as 'pernicious nonsense' and 'absolutely nonsensical mumbo jumbo'. The overlap between defamation and confidentiality that occurs in law when personal information is wrongfully disseminated is in respect of the harm that is suffered. Defamation always, and confidentiality sometimes, affects the victim's reputation. It is a moot point whether a claimant can recover compensation for injury to reputation in an action for breach of confidence because he has lost a reputation that he did not deserve.[91] But in both actions recovery of compensation for mental distress is now possible.[91a]

Privilege

1.22 Privilege is the name given to a rule of law that permits a lawful demand for information to be refused. Unlike an obligation of confidentiality, it operates exclusively as a shield. Traditionally the rule has been applied to the right to keep back confidential communications that are relevant to litigation. Once the claim is made out, the right to withhold the information is absolute.[92] In 1958 in *Parry-Jones v Law Society* Diplock LJ said that legal professional privilege was:

> irrelevant when one is not concerned with judicial or quasi-judicial proceedings because, strictly speaking, privilege refers to a right to withhold from a court, or a tribunal exercising judicial functions, material which would otherwise be admissible in evidence.[93]

Whether it is still true that legal professional privilege is nothing but a rule of evidence or whether it has become a fundamental legal right that operates beyond the litigation arena and can be removed by Parliament only in compelling circumstances is an issue pursued in chapter 16.[94]

Professionals and their Clients

Professionals

1.23 Who are these professionals? In the first chapter of his book *Professional Ethics* Bennion points out that 'profession' is one of the least precise terms in the English language. In its wider meaning it is used to describe 'virtually any occupation where some degree of intellectual discipline is required'.[95] Having surveyed the field of possible professions he concludes that a profession has the following characteristics: an intellectual basis, a foundation in private practice, an advisory

---

[90] [1973] 1 RPC 627, 658.
[91] See para 8.62 below.
[91a] See para 8.56 below.
[92] See para 16.25 below.
[93] Per Diplock LJ, *Parry-Jones v Law Society* [1968] 1 All ER 177, 180.
[94] See para 16.12 below.
[95] F Bennion, *Professional Ethics* (London: 1969) 14.

function, a tradition of service, a representative institute and a code of conduct. Bennion's criteria, however, exclude many people who regard themselves, and are widely accepted within the community, as professionals. Teachers and social workers are two cases in point. Importantly for this book, teachers and social workers handle as much sensitive personal information as anyone in the classical professions of medicine, divinity and law.

This book rejects the Bennion formulation in favour of a much broader one. Professionals are people in occupations with the following attributes: **1.24**

- a specialist training conferring esoteric knowledge and skills;
- a professional culture sustained by professional associations;
- access to the client's property or person;
- an ideal of working in the service of others; and
- substantial autonomy in the way they work.[96]

Some examples of occupational groupings that match these criteria and handle confidential *personal* information are physicians, surgeons, dentists, pharmacists, barristers, solicitors, accountants, ministers of religion, psychologists, psychiatrists, nurses, social workers, stockbrokers, university lecturers and teachers. Bankers are included in this book even though those who work for large banking corporations may have no sense of 'calling' or service ideal. Inclusion is unavoidable because in law there exists between the bank and its customer a personal relationship that imposes on the bank an obligation of confidentiality that is very similar to that imposed on the members of the non-banking professions. Decisions on the confidentiality obligations of banks are a potent indicator of the confidentiality responsibilities of all professionals. **1.25**

In separating the professional from the non-professional, no importance is attached to such matters as licensing, certification, self-employment, the existence of a governing body and self-regulation or the existence of a written code of ethics. Further comment will be made in chapter 3 about codes of ethics. It is virtually certain that a written code of professional ethics, if it exists, will have something to say about confidentiality and what it says may have an impact on the legal obligations which are the main concern of this book. A professional's status as an employee may also have ramifications for the confidentiality of client information. This subject is pursued in chapter 21. **1.26**

---

[96] See further, W Moore and G Rosenblum, *The Professions: Roles and Rules* (New York: 1970) 51 et seq; M Bayles, 'The Professions' in J Callahan (ed), *Ethical Issues in Professional Life* (Oxford: 1988) 27 et seq; T Airaksinen, 'Professional Ethics' in R Chadwick (ed), *Encyclopedia of Applied Ethics* (California: 1998) 671.

Clients and Examinees

Professional engaged by the client

1.27 A client for the purposes of this book is the individual whom the professional most immediately serves.[97] Payment by the client is not necessary. Sometimes the state makes the services of a professional available free of charge to the end-user[97a] (as in the case of the National Health Service, local authority social services and state education), at other times a third party such as an employer foots the bill.[98] Professionals have been known to waive their fees.

Professional engaged by a third party

1.28 Situations in which a third party (A) is responsible for the intervention of a professional (P) fall into two categories:[99]

(1) *A engages P to serve B's interests.* Examples include:

- the doctor retained to treat a child by a parent;
- the nurse employed by the occupier of premises to attend to persons injured on those premises.

In the first example the parent has a say about what the professional does and a right to information from the professional,[100] but it is the child who is the 'true' client. If the interests of parent and child clash, the professional must promote the child's best interests. In the second example, the injured person is at liberty to decline the professional's assistance but if that assistance is accepted the client is entitled to the same duty of confidentiality that he would have been owed had he hired the nurse himself. The position is more complicated in an indemnity insurance situation if the insurer has a contractual right under the insurance policy to choose the solicitor who acts for the insured and an absolute right to control the conduct of proceedings under the retainer. In these circumstances the insurer's interests will prevail over those of the insured and in the event of a serious conflict of interest between the insurer and the insured about the disclosure of information, the only course the solicitor can properly pursue is to stop acting for the insured.[101]

---

[97] As to who is the 'client' in relation to the provision of legal services see *Apple v Wily* [2002] NSWSC 855.
[97a] To the recipient of the services, if not to the taxpayer.
[98] When this happens the third party may have a contractual right to a say about the way the service is provided and some information about what is being done.
[99] In social work the situation may be more complex. For a discussion about the complexities of determining who the social work client is see M Davies, *The Essential Social Worker* (3rd edn, Aldershot: 1994) ch 10.
[100] As to parental rights to information about a child see para 19.72 below.
[101] cp *Groom v Crocker* [1938] 2 All ER 394.

A. Use of Terms in the Book

(2) *A engages P to examine B, for A's benefit.* Particularly in the case of doctors, the 'true' client may be the third party who engaged the professional and not the person examined (the examinee). Examples include:

- the consultant forensic psychiatrist engaged by a court or the Parole Board to form an objective opinion about a defendant's mental state;
- the psychiatrist asked by local authority social services to assess whether a child has been subjected to sexual abuse;[102]
- an occupational health professional who carries out a pre-employment health check for a prospective employer;[103]
- the doctor who medically examines a personal injury claimant for an insurance company.

Duties owed by professional to examinee

The professional–examinee relationship is outside the scope of the book but for the sake of completeness a few comments will be made here about the professional's duties toward the examinee in respect of the examinee's confidential personal information. First, as there is no intention to provide a service to the examinee (in the case of a doctor, there is no intention to provide clinical care), the professional has no professional (therapeutic) relationship with the examinee, who should have no reasonable expectations of confidentiality vis-à-vis the third party.[104] At the outset of the examination, the professional should (as a matter of ethics,[105] and of law[106]) tell the examinee (if capable of understanding the information) that:

1.29

- the usual seal of confidentiality in a professional relationship does not apply[107] and (if the examinee has any choice in the matter) that he must consent to being seen on this basis: this is vital in clinical settings because it is common for examinees to assume that what they say will be treated by the doctor as confidential;[108]

---

[102] *X v Bedfordshire CC* [1995] 3 All ER 353.
[103] *Baker v Kaye* (1996) 39 BMLR 12. Cp *Hoesl v US,* 451 F Supp 1170, 1176 (1978).
[104] cp *R v Smith* (1979) 69 Cr App R 378, 384; *Farnsworth v Hammersmith and Fulham LBC* [2000] IRLR 691, para 20.
[105] Set out most clearly in GMC, *Confidentiality: Protecting and Providing Information* (London: 2000) para 34 and Faculty of Occupational Medicine, *Guidance on Ethics for Occupational Physicians* (5th edn, London: 1999) para 1.11.
[106] cp *R v Gayle* [1994] Crim LR 679.
[107] T Gutheil, 'Ethics and forensic psychiatry' in S Bloch, P Chodoff and S Green, *Psychiatric Ethics* (3rd edn, Oxford: 1999) 347. The correct procedure was followed in *R v Gayle* [1994] Crim LR 679. See also, *Farnsworth v Hammersmith and Fulham LBC* [2000] IRLR 691, para 20; *R v Davies* [2002] EWCA Crim 85, para 33. If it is not made plain to the individual that the seal of confidentiality does not apply, anything that the individual says to the professional is vulnerable to be disallowed under Police and Criminal Evidence Act 1984, s 78 as evidence in criminal proceedings against the individual: cp *R v Souter* [1995] Crim LR 729.
[108] The danger is particularly acute in prisons when a prison doctor with clinical responsibility for a prisoner is asked to prepare an independent, objective report. This can present difficulties and some commentators are of the view that clinical and forensic roles should not be mixed: K Rix, 'Privilege and the prison inmate medical record' (2000) 11 J of Forensic Psychiatry 654. Cp *Re B* [2000] 1 FLR 871.

- the information will not be used or disclosed for any purpose inconsistent with the purpose of the examination without the examinee's consent unless this is either compelled or permitted by law, for example, where disclosure is in the public interest.[109]

1.30 Secondly, the examinee has no entitlement to see the professional's report unless this is a legal requirement[110] or disclosure has been agreed with the third-party client. There has been debate as to whether a health professional has an ethical and legal obligation to disclose to the examinee a serious health problem of which the examinee is unaware if this creates no conflict of interest with the third party. Commentators favour a legal obligation.[111] There is no English legal authority directly in point. In *Kapfunde v Abbey National plc*[112] the claimant brought an action in negligence against Abbey National and a doctor who had prepared a pre-employment assessment for Abbey National about the claimant. The Court of Appeal said that the duty of a doctor who conducts a medical examination is simply to avoid making the condition of the person examined worse.[113] However, in this case there was no physical examination and the claim was for economic loss.

1.31 There is a danger that if there is no duty to warn, the examinee might be lulled into a false sense of security about his health if the doctor says nothing. An examinee who is not forewarned against drawing inferences from silence is likely to assume that no news is good news.[114] In *Re N*[115] Clarke LJ suggested that it was 'at least arguable that where an FME [forensic medical examiner] carries out an examination and discovers that the person being examined has, say, a serious condition which needs immediate treatment, he or she owes a duty to that person to inform him or her of the position. None of the authorities considers such a case and it is not necessary to do so here.'[116]

---

[109] cp *Hellwell v Chief Constable of Derbyshire* [1995] 4 All ER 473; *Woolgar v Chief Constable of Sussex Police* [1999] 3 All ER 604. Disclosure in the public interest is examined in ch 11.
[110] eg Access to Medical Reports Act 1988. This applies only to doctors who have an established doctor–patient relationship with the applicant: see para 19.49 below.
[111] See 'Commentary' [1998] Medical L Rev 367; D Kloss, 'Pre-Employment Health Screening' in M Freeman and A Lewis (eds), *Law and Medicine* (Oxford: 2000) 463–464.
[112] [1998] IRLR 583.
[113] Following *X v Bedfordshire CC* [1995] 2 AC 633, 752.
[114] cp *Betesh v US* 400 F Supp 238, 246 (1974).
[115] [1999] Lloyd's Rep Med 257, 263.
[116] In *R v Croydon Health Authority* (1997) 40 BMLR 40, which reached the Court of Appeal on the issue of damages, the health authority accepted that it was liable in negligence for the failure of a radiologist who had examined a chest X-ray of a female of child-bearing age as part of a pre-employment assessment to diagnose a significant untreatable abnormality which diminished her life-expectation and would be seriously exacerbated if she became pregnant, as in fact happened. Had the Health Authority's occupational therapy section been informed of the condition, as it should have been, it would have advised against employing her but would have informed the claimant's doctor. This case does not settle that the radiologist, who was not sued, owed the claimant a duty to examine the X-ray with care and pass on any adverse discoveries.

B. *Justifying and Limiting Professional Confidentiality*

Journalist–informer relationships

This is not a professional-client relationship. Journalists themselves say that journalism is not a profession 'but the exercise by occupation of the citizen's right to freedom of expression'.[117] Even if one is not prepared to take this at face value, it would not be right to deal with journalists in this book, except peripherally in connection with tracing personal information that has been disclosed without permission.[118] Journalists serve a readership with whom they have a very public relationship. Their confidential relationships are with their sources and this is limited to protection of identity. If journalists could not promise anonymity to sources, the amount of information reaching the media, and ultimately the public, would be greatly reduced.[119]

1.32

Third Parties, Interceptors and Strangers

A third party is anyone who is neither the professional nor the client. When information generated in a professional relationship is disclosed by the professional to someone other than the client, the recipient of the information is referred to as a third party whether or not the disclosure is lawful. When disclosure of information is the result of illicit interception of personal information, the person responsible is designated an 'interceptor' and anyone to whom the interceptor conveys the information (often a newspaper) is referred to as a 'stranger'. An innocent stranger does not know, and has no reason to suppose, the murky origins of the information.

1.33

The disagreement between feminists and those who hold to traditional rules of grammar is solved by treating all professionals, third parties and strangers as feminine and all clients and interceptors as masculine unless this is factually inaccurate for a specific case.

1.34

B. Justifying and Limiting Professional Confidentiality

Justifying Confidentiality

The best way to understand why confidentiality matters is to ask what function it serves for the client, the professional and society. It will emerge that confidentiality is something that benefits society just as much as the individuals who are in a professional relationship. The House of Lords has acknowledged this by treating the protection of confidences as a matter of public interest.[120]

1.35

---

[117] G Robertson and A Nicol, *Media Law* (4th edn, London: 2002) 274.
[118] See para 7.12 et seq below.
[119] *Goodwin v UK* (1996) 22 EHRR 123, para 39.
[120] *Att-Gen v Guardian Newspapers (No 2)* [1988] 3 All ER 545, 640, 659.

Chapter 1: Definitions and Rationales

Value to clients

Privacy and confidentiality as aids to autonomy[121]

1.36 Confidentiality, privacy and personal autonomy[122] are closely intertwined. Privacy creates the ideal condition for autonomous choice and allows individuals to develop the maturity and psychological resilience[123] to choose wisely. It facilitates choice by removing scrutiny, criticism, hostility, domination, manipulation and anything else that puts pressure on the individual to conform to social norms. In a dark age of the future in which the word 'I' has dropped out of the English language, it is only the discovery of a secret tunnel to which he can escape to write, ruminate and experiment and the willingness of his companion road sweeper not to report him to the authorities that enables Equality 7–2521, the hero of Ayn Rand's novella *Anthem*,[124] to develop the ability to think and act independently, a capacity he had not previously had because of the total absence of privacy in the society into which he was born. By allowing the client to decide when, how, and to what extent 'his' information is communicated to others, the professional encourages and upholds the client's autonomy.[125] The mere threat of unauthorized disclosure of confidential personal information may undermine the client's personal autonomy.

Protection of human dignity

1.37 Respect for human dignity is a non-instrumental justification for confidentiality. 'The man ... whose every need, thought, desire, fancy or gratification is subject to public scrutiny, has been deprived of his individuality and human dignity' writes Bloustein.[126] It is no accident that the International Covenant on Civil and Political Rights[127] and the Universal Declaration of Human Rights[128] juxtapose

---

[121] See generally, A Westin, *Privacy and Freedom* (London: 1967); C Fried, 'Privacy' (1968) 77 Yale LJ 477; J Rachels, 'Why Privacy is Important' [1975] 4 Philosophy and Public Affairs 323; J Schonsheck, 'Privacy and Discrete "Social Spheres" ' (1997) 7 Ethics & Behavior 221; A Gewirth, 'Confidentiality in Child-Welfare Practice' (2001) 75 Social Service Rev 479.

[122] The meaning of personal autonomy is as fuzzy as that of privacy. On this subject see O O'Neill, *Autonomy and Trust in Bioethics* (Cambridge: 2002).

[123] This is where functions of privacy mentioned by commentators such as emotional release, opportunity for self-reflection, experimentation, protected communication and intimacy with chosen partners come into their own.

[124] Since the expiry of the US copyright of this book, which was written in 1937, it has become available on-line at http://www.gutenberg.org.

[125] V Alexander, 'The Corporate Attorney-Client Privilege: A Study of the Participants' (1989) St John's L Rev 191, 217–218.

[126] E Bloustein, 'Privacy as an Aspect of Human Dignity: An Answer to Dean Prosser' (1964) 39 New York U L Rev 962, 1003.

[127] ICCPR Art 17(1) 'No one shall be subjected to arbitrary or unlawful interference with his privacy, family, home or correspondence, nor to unlawful attacks on his honour and reputation . . .'.

[128] Art 12.

B. Justifying and Limiting Professional Confidentiality

interference with privacy with attacks on honour and reputation. The following passage shows how confidentiality, privacy and dignity interact in the context of medical treatment.

> The principle of medical confidentiality can be based squarely on this general right of privacy. The patient, in distress, shares with the physician detailed information concerning problems of body or mind. To employ the imagery of concentric circles, the patient admits the physician to an inner circle. If the physician in turn, were to make public the information imparted by the patient—that is, if he were to invite scores or thousands of other persons into the same inner circle—we would be justified in charging that he had violated the patient's right of privacy and that he had shown disrespect to the patient as a human being.[129]

To have his dignity respected is something to which a client is entitled even if he is incapable of acting autonomously because of youth, mental disability,[130] or unconsciousness. Lord Hoffman said of Anthony Bland, a comatose patient without hope of recovery, that the Official Solicitor had offered a seriously incomplete picture of the patient's interests when 'he confine[d] them to animal feelings of pain or pleasure. It is demeaning to the human spirit to say that, being unconscious, he can have no interest in his personal privacy and dignity . . .'.[131] 'The degradation of an incapacitated person shames us all, even if that person is unable to appreciate it . . .'[132] An ethicist makes the same point:

1.38

> We do not normally think that attending a patient who lacks autonomy absolves health professionals of their duty to maintain confidentiality . . . Perhaps what is wrong with breaching confidentiality in cases of nonautonomous patients is that it involves, in some sense, a violation of the *self* (as might be the case, for example, if health professionals were to compromise the *bodily* privacy of such patients).[133]

Treating personal information with respect is a means of demonstrating respect for the individual who is its subject.[134]

Harmful consequences

Quite apart from any affront to their dignity and the threat to their autonomy, clients do not want personal information that professionals hold about them released without their permission because of the potentially harmful consequences.

1.39

---

[129] L Walters, 'Ethical Aspects of Medical Confidentiality' in T Beauchamp and L Wallas (eds), *Contemporary Issues in Bioethics* (California: 1978) 171 as quoted by N Moore, 'Limits to Attorney–Client Confidentiality: A "Philosophically Informed" and Comparative Approach to Legal and Medical Ethics' (1985–6) 36 Case Western Reserve L Rev 177, 191.
[130] cp *R (on the application of Stevens) v Plymouth City Council* [2002] EWCA Civ 388; [2002] 1 FLR 1177, para 47.
[131] *Airedale NHS Trust v Bland* [1993] 1 All ER 821, 854.
[132] *R (on the application of Willkinson) v Responsible Medical Officer, Broadmoor* [2001] EWCA Civ 1545; [2002] 1 WLR 419, para 79.
[133] J Oakley, 'The Morality of Breaching Confidentiality to Protect Others' in L Shotton (ed), *Health Care, Law and Ethics* (Katoomba, NSW: 1997) 116.
[134] G Laurie, *Genetic Privacy* (Cambridge: 2002) 64.

'The definite connection between harm and the invasion of privacy explains why we place a value on not having undocumented personal information about ourselves widely known.'[135] To lose control over confidential information is to run the risk of rejection.

> The average patient doesn't realize the importance of the confidentiality of medical records. Passing out information on venereal disease can wreck a marriage. Revealing a pattern of alcoholism or drug abuse can result in a man's losing his job or make it impossible for him to obtain insurance protection.[136]

1.40 In *Venables v NGN Ltd*[137] Butler-Sloss P was in no doubt that if the media made known the new appearances, identities and whereabouts of Thompson and Venables, two child murderers who had grown to adulthood and were soon to be released from detention, their lives would be at risk from revenge attacks. This is an extreme case. Very grave consequences may, however, follow breaches of confidentiality by professionals. A commonly cited example is the disclosure that a client is HIV seropositive. 'HIV/AIDS and those affected by it have attracted unique levels of opprobrium and ostracism.'[138] Access to foreign countries, employment, education, insurance, credit, housing and other necessities may be severely damaged. Social isolation may ensue leading to depression and psychological conditions that hasten the onset of full-blown AIDS.[139] Even physical ill-treatment is a possible outcome.[140] Disclosure of mental health problems can wreck the client's life just as badly.

1.41 One of the most important uses of personal information is to enable governments, organizations and individuals to discriminate between individuals. These two examples draw attention to the role confidentiality plays in preventing *unfair* discrimination.[141] For example, the refusal of insurance to someone because he has undergone genetic testing when further inquiry would have established that he is a carrier of a genetic disorder and is not personally affected, or denial of employment to a young person because in later life he might develop Huntington's

---

[135] W Parent, 'Privacy, Morality and the Law' in J Callahan (ed), *Ethical Issues in Professional Life* (New York: 1988) 218.
[136] M Todd, President of the American Medical Association quoted by J Rachels, 'Why Privacy is Important' (1974) 4 Philosophy and Public Affairs 323, 324.
[137] [2001] 1 All ER 908, 933.
[138] E Cameron, 'Confidentiality in HIV/AIDS: Some Reflections on India and South Africa' (2001) 1 Oxford U Commonwealth LJ 35, 36. The extreme reactions that this complaint elicits is demonstrated by the case of *A & B v Tameside & Glossop Health Authority* [1997] 8 Med LR 91 in which an action was brought on behalf of patients who had allegedly suffered psychiatric illness because they had been informed by letter instead of face to face from an experienced health worker of the fact that a health professional by whom they had been treated was HIV seropositive.
[139] E Cameron, 'Confidentiality in HIV/AIDS: Some Reflections on India and South Africa' (2001) 1 Oxford U Commonwealth LJ 35, 45.
[140] M Gunderson, D Mayo and F Rhame, *Aids: Testing and Privacy* (Salt Lake City: 1989) 66.
[141] Confidentiality prevents both fair and unfair discrimination. The issue of what is fair and unfair is often complex.

B. Justifying and Limiting Professional Confidentiality

Disease.[142] Part of the reason that people want to control information about themselves is the knowledge that intolerance is rife and that people are quick to draw false conclusions,[143] particularly when based on fragments of personal information communicated out of context.[144] According to Tugendhat, 'privacy is necessary to protect the reputation a person has in the minds of *wrong* thinking members of society.... It protects society from making decisions on a factual basis which is true but irrelevant.'[145] It is this kind of thinking that best explains the list of 'sensitive personal data' in the DPA.[146] Some categories of sensitive personal data—racial origin for example—are not obviously private information but like all the selected categories historically there is a high risk that the information will be put to objectionable uses.[147]

1.42 It should not be assumed that it is only information that reflects badly on a person that may be damaging. Virtually any leaked information has the capacity to cause harm. 'There are no harmless data. Or to put it another way, it is not the data that are harmless, it is what people do with them that is the problem.'[148] Information that shows the client in a favourable light may present a threat to a third party or excite jealousy. Either way it may lead to unfavourable treatment. In *Prince Albert v Strange* Knight Bruce VC said that '[a] man may employ himself in private in a manner very harmless, but which, disclosed to society, may destroy the comfort of his life, or even his success in it'.[149]

1.43 Even if a disclosure does not actually lead to harm, the client may fear that it will do so and this fear is of itself injurious. The Supreme Court of India has wryly noted that disclosure 'has the tendency to disturb a person's tranquility. It may generate many complexes in him and he may, thereafter, have a disturbed life all through.'[150] Added to this, the indignity of a breach of confidentiality is likely to produce mental distress in a healthy adult of average sensitivity; no one enjoys the feeling of being betrayed. So the short answer to Barendt's question—should we be concerned about an invasion of privacy only if it is damaging to the individual

---

[142] Examples taken from Human Genetics Commission, *Inside Information,* May 2002, paras 6.18, 6.41, box 10.
[143] See eg *Adenjii v Newham LBC* (QBD, 16 October 2001).
[144] W Bogaert reviewing ' "The Unwanted Gaze: The Destruction of Privacy in America" by J Rosen' (2000) 10 Boston U Public Interest LJ 196, 197.
[145] M Tugendhat, 'Privacy and Celebrity' in E Barendt and A Firth (eds), *Yearbook of Copyright and Media Law 2001/2* (Oxford: 2002) 13. A contrast is drawn with libel which is 'necessary to protect the reputation that a person has in the minds of *right* thinking members of society'.
[146] See para 18.23 below.
[147] Private communication from M Tugendhat. See also Rehabilitation of Offenders Act 1974.
[148] P Sieghart, 'Information Privacy and the Data Protection Bill' cited in C. Bennett, *Regulating Privacy* (Ithaca: 1992) 34.
[149] (1849) 64 ER 293, 312. cp *Campbell v MGN* [2002] EWCA Civ 1373, para 52.
[150] *Mr X v Hospital Z* (1998) 8 SCC 296, 307.

Chapter 1: Definitions and Rationales

concerned?—is that if it involves a breach of confidentiality it is *always* at some level damaging.[151]

Value to society

Privacy and democracy

1.44 The independent-minded citizens that a democracy requires to flourish are most likely to be found in a society that protects privacy.[152] Privacy allows one to question mainstream ideas and to try out new ones. Moreover, it is possible that without the opportunity for social retreat no one would be willing to become a public figure.[153] Thus Cameron contends,[154] and the Australian Privacy Charter assumes,[155] privacy (and, through its supporting role, confidentiality) are essential to the survival of a pluralistic democratic society. But this is not a universally held view. It has also been argued that privacy, at any rate excessive emphasis on privacy, threatens democracy by supporting self-indulgence and the disengagement of individuals from society.[156] For this reason privacy is not popular with communitarians but even they are likely to endorse an instrumental rationale for confidential professional-client relationships.

Protection of the vulnerable

1.45 The professional–client relationship tends to be one of inequality with the professional having the upper hand. This is particularly so if the relationship is involuntary. An obligation of confidentiality is one way of preventing the professional from exploiting the asymmetry of the relationship.

> Differences in vulnerability, medical knowledge, and in physical and psychological functioning frequently exist between the two parties to a clinical relationship. Where there is such inequality the powerful party has moral obligations towards the weaker

---

[151] E Barendt, 'Privacy as a Constitutional Right and Value' in P Birks (ed), *Privacy and Loyalty* (Oxford: 1997) 4. A Capron, 'Genetics and Insurance: Accessing and Using Private Information' in E Paul, F Miller and J Paul (eds), *The Right to Privacy* (New York: 2000) 235.

[152] It is no coincidence that the society to which Equality 7–2521 (see para 1.36 above) belongs in Ayn Rand's novella is a totalitarian one.

[153] R Gavison, 'Privacy and the Limits of Law' (1980) 89 Yale LJ 421, 456. In this respect the impeachment of Bill Clinton for private consensual sexual acts was most undesirable; Presidents and Prime Ministers must be allowed privacy or no reasonable person will be willing to take on such an onerous civic job.

[154] E Cameron, 'Confidentiality in HIV/AIDS: Some Reflections on India and South Africa' (2001) 1 Oxford U Commonwealth LJ 35, 38. See also P Blume, *Protection of Informational Privacy* (Copenhagen, 2002) 23; H Oliver, 'Email and Internet Monitoring in the Workplace: Information Privacy and Contracting Out' (2002) 31 Industrial LJ 321, 323.

[155] 'A free and democratic society requires respect for the autonomy of individuals, and limits on the power of both state and private organizations to intrude on that autonomy', *Australian Privacy Charter* 1994 at http://www.apcc.org.au/Charter.html.

[156] cp D Feldman, 'Privacy-related Rights: Their Social Value' in P Birks (ed), *Privacy and Loyalty* (Oxford: 1997) 19–20; A Etzioni, *The Limits of Privacy* (New York: 1999).

B. Justifying and Limiting Professional Confidentiality

one—at the very least the negative duty not to take advantage of the weaker party (non-malfeasance): not taking advantage includes protecting patient's secrets.[157]

The very young and those with mental disabilities who are unable to protect their own privacy are in particular need of protection.[158]

Unreserved candour

The ethical argument Proponents of professional confidentiality most frequently rely on the consequentialist argument that unless the public has confidence in the confidentiality of their communications with professionals, there is a risk that professionals will not be consulted by some potential clients and others will delay contact and/or withhold information.[159] The legal officer of the Community Health Councils for England and Wales, for example, has warned that '[c]ertain groups of patients now routinely withhold information from medical practitioners in the NHS because they do not trust the health service to protect their confidences. Many gay men, for example, will not tell their GPs they have been tested for HIV for fear that if this information is recorded in their medical records they will be unable to secure the insurance that they may need to obtain a mortgage. Many doctors do not tell their own GPs about conditions such as anxiety or depression, believing that this information may become known to their employers and damage their careers.'[160] **1.46**

Every missed client and every client who conceals relevant information reduces the capacity of the professional to discourage anti-social behaviour or, in the case of health professionals, the prolongation or spread of disease. There is empirical evidence that lawyers play an important role in preventing illegal conduct by their clients.[161] Anything that discourages the public from consulting lawyers is therefore bad for society as well as the individuals concerned. **1.47**

The judicial response The importance to society of candid exchanges between professionals and clients and of the need for confidentiality to secure candour has been endorsed in respect of doctors and lawyers by the judiciary at the highest levels.[162] **1.48**

---

[157] B Hurwitz, 'Informed consent for access to medical records for health services research' in L Doyal and J Tobias (eds), *Informed Consent in Medical Research* (London: 2001) 231.
[158] *R (on the application of Stevens) v Plymouth City Council* [2002] EWCA Civ 388; [2002] 1 FLR 1177, para 47.
[159] L Doyal, 'Human Need and the Right of Patients to Privacy' (1997) 14 J of Contemporary Health Law and Policy 1, 12; R Tur, 'Medical Confidentiality and Disclosure: Moral Conscience and Legal Constraints' (1998) 15 J of Applied Philosophy 15, 17.
[160] M Chester, 'The patient's perspective on medical privacy' (2001) 18/5 British J of Healthcare Computing & Information Management 20, 21. The position is the same in the US: W Lowrance, *Privacy and Health Research: A Report to the US Secretary of Health and Human Services* (May 1997) endnote 14 at http://aspe.hhs.gov/datacncl/PHR.htm.
[161] L Levine, 'Testing the Radical Experiment: A Study of Lawyer Response to Clients who Intend to Harm Others' (1994) 41 Rutgers L Rev 81, 97.
[162] For pharmacists see *R v Department of Health, ex p Source Informatics* [1999] 4 All ER 185, 198.

Chapter 1: Definitions and Rationales

Respecting the confidentiality of health data is a vital principle in the legal systems of all the Contracting Parties in the Convention. It is crucial not only to respect the sense of privacy of a patient but also to preserve his or her confidence in the medical profession and health services in general.

Without such protection, those in need of medical assistance may be deterred from revealing such information of a personal and intimate nature as may be necessary in order to receive appropriate treatment and, even from seeking such assistance, thereby endangering their own health and, in the case of transmissible diseases, that of the community. The domestic law must therefore afford appropriate safeguards to prevent any such communication or disclosure . . .[163]

The foundation of [legal professional privilege] is not difficult to discover . . . [I]t is out of regard to the interests of justice, which cannot be upholden, and to the administration of justice, which cannot go on, without the aid of men skilled in jurisprudence, in the practice of the Courts, and in those matters affecting rights and obligations which form the subject of all juridical proceedings. If the privilege did not exist at all, everyone would be thrown upon his own legal resources; deprived of all professional assistance, a man would not venture to consult any skilled person, or would only dare to tell his counsellor half his case.[164]

1.49 **Weaknesses in the candour argument** The argument that candour is necessary for effective practice, and that confidentiality is necessary for candour, rests upon a number of assumptions on which empirical research could usefully be done.[165] First, how much does client candour really matter for effective professional work? In psychotherapy, which depends almost entirely on self-revelation of intimate thoughts, unreserved communication by the patient is recognized to be of crucial importance[166] but some professionals rely less upon what the client has to say than on direct observation and their own researches. Secondly, what role does confidentiality actually play in persuading clients to seek timely advice and to speak frankly? Inability to cope, fear, or a desire for emotional release may be as, or even more, important.

---

[163] *Z v Finland* (1997) 25 EHRR 371, para 95. See also *X v Y* [1988] 2 All ER 648, 653; *MS v Sweden* (1999) 28 EHRR 313, para 41; *A Health Authority v X* [2001] EWCA Civ 2014, [2002] 2 All ER 780, para 15.

[164] per Lord Brougham, *Greenough v Gaskell* (1833) 39 ER 618, 620–621. See also *R v Derby Magistrates' Court, ex p B* [1995] 4 All ER 526, 540; *Bolkiah v KPMG* [1999] 1 All ER 517, 529; *R v McClure* [2001] SCC 14, paras 2, 39.

[165] R Loder, 'When Silence Screams' (1996) 29 Loyola of Los Angeles L Rev 1785, 1787. This comment was made in respect of legal professional confidentiality.

[166] S Saltzburg, 'Privileges and Professionals: Lawyers and Psychiatrists' (1980) 66 Virginia L Rev 597, 620–621; Manitoba Law Reform Commission, *Report on Medical Privilege* R56 (Winnipeg: 1983) 24; *Ashworth Security Hospital v MGN Ltd* [2002] UKHL 29; [2002] 1 WLR 2033, para 63. Likewise, the importance of confidentiality to sacramental confession is not in doubt: W Cole, 'Religious Confidentiality and the Reporting of Child Abuse' (1987) 21 Columbia J of L and Social Problems 1, 15.

B. Justifying and Limiting Professional Confidentiality

1.50 While there is convincing empirical evidence that without confidentiality patients would be deterred from undergoing psychotherapy,[167] there is scant evidence that confidentiality is the primary reason for candour in many other professional relationships. It has been suggested with respect to lawyers that:

> [p]eople would have ample incentives to disclose adverse information to counsel even without confidentiality safeguards because they are honest and law abiding, because they cannot make reliable judgments about when it is in their interests to withhold, or because in many business contexts they risk liability by failing to seek good legal advice.[168]

It has also to be borne in mind that not all who consult professionals do so voluntarily. What the involuntary client conceals from the professional is likely to be determined more by the consequences of non-disclosure than apprehension that the information will be passed on.

1.51 If one assumes that confidentiality has some impact—intuitively this seems right—how robust does the promise of confidentiality have to be to achieve full disclosure by the client? Solicitors are forbidden by English law from disclosing the confidential communications of a client to a court without client consent[169] and Law Society rules forbid nonconsensual disclosure of confidential information elsewhere except to prevent *future* serious bodily harm,[170] child-abuse[171] and in the interests of the lawyer's self-defence.[172] No other professional group is subject to such a strict confidentiality regime. Would other professional relationships work better if their rules of confidentiality were tightened? Probably not. First, there is no evidence that the existing rules that apply to non-lawyer professionals are causing clients to hold back information.[173] Secondly, there is evidence from the United States[174] and

---

[167] H Roback, 'Effects of Confidentiality Limitations on the Psychotherapeutic Process' (1995) 4 J of Psychotherapy Practice and Research 185. See also, D Joseph and J Onek, 'Confidentiality in psychiatry' in S Bloch, P Chodoff and S Green (eds), *Psychiatric Ethics* (3rd edn, Oxford: 1999) 108 and Australian Law Reform Commission, *Evidence,* Report No 26, vol 1 (1985) 516 where empirical evidence is reviewed.

[168] W Simon, 'Ethical Discretion in Lawyering' (1988) 101 Harvard L Rev 1083, 1142.

[169] Legal professional privilege is discussed in ch 16. The courts have recently extended legal professional privilege beyond the legal arena.

[170] The Law Society, *The Guide to the Professional Conduct of Solicitors* (8th edn, London: 1999) 325, 16.02 para 3.

[171] ibid, 16.02 para 4.

[172] ibid, 16.02 para 12.

[173] No difference in the willingness of clients to make disclosures to psychiatrists and psychologists in US states in which the law does not confer privilege on such communications and those states in which it does has been detected: Note, 'Functional Overlap between the Lawyer and other Professionals: Its Implications for the Privileged Communications Doctrine' (1962) 71 Yale LJ 1226, 1225.

[174] Note, 'Functional Overlap between the Lawyer and other Professionals: Its Implications for the privileged Communications Doctrine' (1962) 71 Yale LJ 1226, 1236; F Zacharias, 'Rethinking Confidentiality' (1989) 74 Iowa L Rev 351, 376 et seq. cp R Jagim et al, 'Mental Health Professionals' Attitudes Toward Confidentiality, Privilege and Third-Party Disclosure' (1978) Professional Psychology 458, 463.

Chapter 1: Definitions and Rationales

Canada[175] that lay knowledge of the scope of professional confidentiality is extremely confused; clients often assume that their communications with professionals are entitled to greater protection than is the case.

1.52 If there is no need to tighten up the rules for non-legal professionals, would lawyer–client relationships suffer if the rules of confidentiality for lawyers were brought into line with those that apply to doctors? Or if the courts were to distinguish between communications in aid of litigation and more routine legal communications related, for example, to conveyancing and will-making?[176] Cranston doubts that empirical research would back up the judicial belief that the present absolute rule for all lawyer–client communications[177] encourages client disclosures.[178] It is noteworthy that the absence of legal professional privilege for communications between clients and accountants has not hampered accountants from capturing a large chunk of tax-planning work from solicitors, although the Office of Fair Trading has suggested that the share of tax advising work done by non-lawyers might be greater still were legal professional privilege not restricted to lawyers.[179] A Yale study found that 30 per cent of the lay respondents believed that lawyer–client communications were protected in circumstances where they were not.[180] These findings were confirmed 25 years later in another small study.[181] Any reduction in the current level of protection for confidences given to lawyers might therefore have a negligible impact—at any rate, if not accompanied by an obligation to explain clearly to each client the specific limits of confidentiality.

Value to professionals

1.53 For professionals, confidentiality serves numerous ends. It:

- encourages clients to speak freely and to trust them;
- reinforces the professional's claim to professional status;[182]

---

[175] D Schuman et al, 'The Privilege Study (Part III): Psychotherapist–Patient Communications in Canada' (1986) 9 Intl J of J Law and Psychiatry 393, 407. On the subject of public awareness of medical privilege see Manitoba Law Reform Commission, *Report on Medical Privilege* Report 56 (Winnipeg: 1983) 14 where a number of empirical studies are discussed.

[176] See para 16.46 below.

[177] See para 16.25 below.

[178] R Cranston (ed), *Legal Ethics and Professional Responsibility* (Oxford: 1995) 9. US empirical research into corporate attorney–client privilege suggests that it is only litigation privilege that deserves to be near absolute: V Alexander, 'The Corporate Attorney–Client Privilege: A study of the Participants' (1989) St John's L Rev 191.

[179] *Restrictions on Competition in the Provision of Professional Services*, Report of OFT by LECG Ltd, December 2000, paras 188–189.

[180] Note, 'Functional Overlap Between the Lawyer and Other Professionals: Its Implications for the Privileged Communications Doctrine' (1962) 71 Yale LJ 1126, 1262.

[181] C Zacharias, 'Rethinking Confidentiality' (1989) 74 Iowa L Rev 351, 379.

[182] S Bok, *Secrets: The Ethics of Concealment and Revelation* (Oxford: 1983) 116.

B. Justifying and Limiting Professional Confidentiality

- may relieve the professional from some difficult ethical decisions[183] and offer a shield against criticism;[184]
- may protect the professional from being brought to account for incompetent or unethical conduct by hindering its discovery. This may be good for the professional, and in those situations when the client benefits from unethical professional conduct, also the client, but it is a very bad thing for clients collectively.

There is a further *ex post facto* argument for confidentiality. In a society in which professional confidentiality is the norm, the professional who breaches confidentiality runs the risk of destroying her livelihood, or confidence in the organization employing her.

Justifying Breaches of Confidentiality
Confidentiality cannot be allowed to be absolute

A client cannot be permitted to insist on absolute confidentiality because this would prevent disclosures necessary to maintain the social order. **1.54**

> As long as we view confidentiality as an isolated phenomenon, most of us will see it as an unquestionable good. But if we take into account the consequences it has for other crucial values in society, we have to choose between these values and the advantages of keeping the principles of confidentiality in their present form.[185]

Confidentiality may, as already indicated, shield malpractice by the professional[186] and conceal dangers (for which the client is not necessarily responsible)[187] to third parties. Confidentiality may impede detection and punishment of those (not necessarily the client) who have committed or are intending to commit crimes. Confidentiality may be an obstacle to social science and medical research[188] if researchers have to obtain the client's consent to the disclosure of information either because this is an impractical exercise or because too many would refuse their consent. Use of anonymous data is not always an option. Cancer data must be linked to individuals to allow subsequent data flows into the registry from, for example, a death certificate.[189] Unless comprehensive medical information can be

---

[183] S Watson, 'Keeping Secrets that Harm Others: Medical Standards Illuminate Lawyer's Dilemma' (1992) 71 Nebraska L Rev 1123.
[184] F Zacharias, 'Rethinking Confidentiality' (1989) 74 Iowa L Rev 351, 359–360. The lawyer who knew that her client was flouting the law in retaining an undeserved payment or engaging in risky conduct can offer the excuse that she was not entitled to speak out.
[185] E Oyen, 'Trend Report: The Social Functions of Confidentiality' (1982) 30 Current Sociology 1, 36.
[186] See para 1.53 above.
[187] See discussion of whether information about genetic defects (i) can be disclosed without client consent (para 11.53 below) and (ii) whether it should be disclosed (para 20.37 below).
[188] J Sstrobl, 'Data Protection Legislation: Interpretation and Barriers to Research' (2000) 321 British Medical J 890; C Verity and A Nicoll, 'Consent, confidentiality, and the threat to public health surveillance' (2002) 324 British Medical J 1210.
[189] P Brown, 'Cancer Registries Fear Imminent Collapse' (2000) 321 British Medical J 849; Cambridge Health Informatics Ltd, *Gaining Patient Consent to Disclosure* (Cambridge: 2001) 19.

collected for cancer research results will be flawed and suffering from disease may be unnecessarily prolonged.

> [Confidentiality] is a means by which the law protects the patient's right to privacy, but privacy itself is simply one interest which is to be balanced against many others ... [T]he patient is entitled to demand confidentiality only so long as this does not conflict with some greater interest of another person, or of society itself.[190]

From the perspective of the common good, there are worse harms than a very limited loss of confidentiality.[191]

1.55 For this reason, the client cannot always be allowed to dictate when, and under what conditions, his private facts are disseminated; a balance must be struck between the competing public (and private) interests that pull away from and towards privacy and confidentiality. This is not only the conclusion that most[192] ethicists have reached, but also the framers of the European Convention on Human Rights and the English judiciary. Interference with the right to respect for private life guaranteed in Article 8(1) of the Convention, which amongst other things, protects confidentially communicated personal information,[193] can be justified so long as the interference is not arbitrary and has a lawful foundation.[194] In *W v Egdell* Bingham LJ said: 'the law treats [confidentiality] not as absolute but as liable to be overridden when there is held to be a stronger public interest in disclosure.'[195] The challenge is to know when the point has been reached where confidentiality undermines the common good.

Obligatory versus discretionary disclosure

1.56 Is there any reason why professionals should have a choice about breaching professional confidentiality where a breach is justified? If the harm or risk of harm that non-disclosure perpetrates is sufficient to warrant disclosure in breach of a pledge of professional confidentiality, should disclosure not be mandatory? Might compulsion not reduce the risk of arbitrary and inconsistent disclosure decisions and strengthen the hand of a professional trying to dissuade a client from wrongdoing?[196]

---

[190] K Norrie, 'Medical Confidentiality' (1988) 36 Forensic Science Int 143, 145.
[191] A Gewirth, 'Confidentiality in Child-Welfare Practice' (2001) 75 Social Service Rev 479, 482.
[192] Contra M Kottow, 'Medical Confidentiality: An Intransigent and Absolute Obligation' (1986) 12 J of Medical Ethics 117. His objections to exceptions to medical confidentiality are that it leads to inconsistent and arbitrary decisions to disclose information.
[193] See para 3.03 below.
[194] See para 3.19 below.
[195] [1990] 1 All ER 835, 848. See also *Campbell v Frisbee* [2002] EWCA Civ 1374, para 23: 'The right to confidentiality, whether or not founded on contract, is not absolute. That right must give way where it is in the public interest that confidential information should be made public.' Per Lord Phillips MR.
[196] L Levin, 'Testing the Radical Experiment: A Study of Lawyer Response to Clients Who Intend to Harm Others' (1994) 47 Rutgers L Rev 81, 141.

B. Justifying and Limiting Professional Confidentiality

Opponents of mandatory disclosure would argue that professionals can be trusted to do the right thing, or conversely, that the confidentiality ethic in some professions is so strong that a mandatory reporting rule that is not backed by criminal sanctions will be disobeyed. A US study of lawyers supports this conclusion.[197] Far from strengthening the professional's hand, a cut-and-dried duty to disclose information could hamper the professional's efforts to win the client's trust and dissuade client misconduct.[197] The most compelling argument against compulsory disclosure is, however, the unpredictability of human conduct and circumstances; no single response is *always* the right one. **1.57**

> The human beings who make up a clientele, while they may be similar, do not operate in standard or predictable ways. What is good for one cannot be assumed to be good for another. This is a danger of any standardization involving people, and care should be taken that codes of ethics do not make the position worse than better.[198]

As the ensuing chapters will show, the English legal system has opted for a mixture of permissive and compulsory disclosure.

---

[197] ibid, 126–127, found that the threat of exposure was not an important tactic in discouraging wrongdoing.

[198] J Pritchard, 'Codes of Ethics' in R Chadwick (ed), *Encyclopedia of Applied Ethics* (California: 1998) 527, 530.

2

THE SOCIAL CONTEXT

A. Technological, Political and Social Change	2.01	Public Attitudes to Professional Confidentiality	2.26
Increased Recording and Storage of Information	2.02	Children's Rights	2.29
New Technology	2.04	Public Trust in the Protection of Personal Information	2.30
Pressures for Disclosure to Third Parties	2.11	Attitudes of Professionals to Confidentiality	2.32
Employed Professionals	2.21	B. The Issues Confronting the Law	2.34
Workplace Pressures	2.25		

A. Technological, Political and Social Change

Law exists to fulfil societal needs. The law relevant to confidentiality in professional-client relationships is no exception. Law does not serve society properly unless it is responsive to (amongst other things) changing technology, social outlook and changing behavioural patterns. The following pages detail the developments that have taken place over the past 50, and more particularly 20 years, that have implications for professional confidentiality and which, to varying degrees, have stimulated developments and exposed gaps in the law that regulates professional confidentiality. **2.01**

Increased Recording and Storage of Information

Fifty years ago many professionals kept minimal records and those that were kept were mainly notes of consultations with the client. Now detailed records are the norm and the records often contain information garnered from a host of sources. For example, medical records may contain correspondence with laboratories, health professionals to whom the patient has been referred, schools, health officials, medical researchers and, possibly, insurers. Causes of this recording boom include: **2.02**

- a need for more reliable data as procedures become more sophisticated;
- in some disciplines, the availability of more information;[1]

---

[1] DNA screening and other new scientific techniques are the prime cause.

- pressure to provide a better service in a competitive environment;
- more detailed auditing;
- increased inspection and regulation; and
- a more litigious environment.

For professionals who operate as part of a team, as increasing numbers do, records provide an essential medium of communication between team members who do not meet face to face.

2.03 It is not only professionals that have expanded their record-keeping activities. Vast quantities of personal information are collected, handled and stored by a wide spread of public agencies. Some of this information may have had its genesis in a professional-client relationship and have been obtained, either from the professional or the client, through the use of coercive powers.[2]

New Technology

2.04 The growth in record-keeping might have been more limited had it not been for the emergence of the personal computer. Computers (and, to a lesser extent microfilm technology) have enormously increased the amount of information that can be conveniently and inexpensively recorded, stored, retrieved, combined, collated and disseminated. Most professionals, or the organizations for which they work, keep information about current clients in word processor and database program files. In some large organizations, such as the NHS, that deliver professional services information has been aggregated into very large databases. The NHS has ambitious plans to link up all GPs and hospitals electronically to allow electronic patient records to be transmitted instantaneously to all treatment locations. The goal is fast, convenient and 'seamless' patient care.[3]

2.05 There have been security gains from the new technology,[4] but also losses. Computerization has destroyed one of the chief barriers that ensured the privacy of personal information, namely 'the sheer costs of retrieving personal information; the impermanency of the forms in which that information was stored; and the inconvenience experienced in procuring access (assuming that its existence was known)'.[5] Networked computers in association with telecommunications

---

[2] See para 3.33 and ch 10.
[3] DoH, *Information for Health* (London: 1998) available at http://www.nhsia.nhs.uk; *The NHS Plan, A Plan for Investment, A Plan for Reform* (Cm 4818-I, 2000) available at http://www.nhs.uk/nationalplan/.
[4] PIU, *Privacy and Data-sharing* (April 2002) 3.14, 8.10, 8.25. Transmitting encrypted e-mail messages is safer than sending the same information by post and suspicious patterns of computer access can be picked up by intrusion detection systems: R. Anderson, 'Security in Clinical Information Systems' (Cambridge, 1996) available at http://www.cl.cam.ac.uk/~rja14/policy11/policy11.html.
[5] M Kirby, 'Privacy in Cyberspace' (1998) 21 U of New South Wales LJ 323, 325.

A. Technological, Political and Social Change

allow unauthorized access to data without the interloper setting foot on the premises of the victim. Computers connected to the internet are particularly vulnerable.

> With world-wide Internet connections, someone could get into your system from the other side of the world and steal your password in the middle of the night when your building is locked up. Viruses and worms can be passed from machine to machine. The Internet allows the electronic equivalent of the thief who looks for open windows and doors; now a person can check hundreds of machines for vulnerabilities in a few hours.[6]

Once access is gained to a computer, data can be copied and transmitted almost instantaneously often without leaving tell-tale signs of interception.

2.06 It is estimated that in the United States hackers have illicitly gained access to sensitive information held on computers in hundreds of thousands of cases.[7] Professionals are as susceptible as anyone to hacking. A US textbook on counselling gives the example of a professor who left test results and personal data about clients on an unsecured hard drive to which a student hacker gained access.[8] It has been discovered that the head of admissions at Princeton repeatedly hacked into Yale's applications website and read the files of students who had applied to both institutions.[9] There is anecdotal evidence of hackers targeting UK hospital computers to alter or acquire patient data.[10] When hacking occurs the interception of personal information may be on a scale that was inconceivable in previous eras.[11] The encryption of information may frustrate the objectives of hackers. However, much confidential personal information stored by professionals, especially those who do not work for large organizations, is not encrypted.

2.07 Computer hacking is, of course, not the only threat to the privacy of computer data. Software bugs and viruses can re-route data,[12] and, with the right equipment, it is possible to intercept confidential information as it is being legitimately transmitted to, or received by, a computer. Alternatively, electromagnetic

---

[6] IETF, *Site Security Policy Handbook* at http://www.net.ohio-state.edu/hypertext/rfc1244/Toc.html.

[7] L Mizell, *Invasion of Privacy* (New York: 1998) xx. In 1995 hackers broke into the US Defence Department's computer more than 160,000 times: *Computer Misuse* NZLC R54 (Wellington: 1999) para 2.

[8] L Swenson, *Psychology and Law for the Helping Professions* (2nd edn, Pacific Grove: 1997) 93.

[9] 'Ivy League university investigated for hacking', The Times, 27 July 2002.

[10] D Tribe, 'NHS Medical Records—How Safe Can They Be' (2001), available at http://www.herts.ac.uk/extrel/news/oct01/1a_info.htm.

[11] N Ellis, 'Security, privacy and confidentiality in health care: a human and organization perspective', paper presented to the Primary Health Care Specialist Group of the British Computer Society, Cambridge 1999 (see http://www.phcsg.org.uk/conferences/Cambridge1999/camb99–12.htm).

[12] See T Branigan, 'Measure for measure', The Guardian, 14 September 2002 where this is referred to as key stroke logging.

radiation 'leaks' from the monitor can be captured and reconstituted as visual images.[13]

2.08 If these forms of interception strike the reader as fanciful, consider the possibility of misuse of computerized personal information by employees. '[T]he most common threat to confidentiality', according to electronic patient records experts, 'is the inappropriate accessing of information by authorized providers'.[14] Encryption may offer no protection. The threat of unauthorized access by employees is greatest where data is aggregated in huge centralized databases within a dispersed networked computer system as in high street banking[15] and the NHS.[16]

> The sheer number of authorized users, the potential for lawful access without explicit authority, and the threat of fraudulent access render it virtually impossible to ensure significant levels of privacy for patients. . . .[17]

2.09 Information that is not on a computer has, because of technological advances, also become much more vulnerable. Telephone-tapping equipment allows the interception of landline telephone calls. Non-digital wireless communication can be easily intercepted with a scanner or even a baby monitor.[18] There is a frightening array of other surveillance devices. Conversations can be picked up from the vibration of window glass by laser beams[19] and by microphones coupled to transmitters that can hear through walls.[20] A camera fitted with a telescopic lens or a video concealed inside a clock, smoke detector or ceiling sprinkler allows those outside a room to see what is going on inside. Photographs can be taken in the dark using

---

[13] Law Com Working Paper 110, *Computer Misuse* (1988) para 2.13; A Newbold, 'Safeguarding client information' (1988) 85 LS Gaz 10; *Computer Misuse* NZLC R54 (Wellington: 1999).

[14] D Rind et al, 'Maintaining the Confidentiality of Medical Records Shared over the Internet and the World Wide Web' (1997) 127 Annals of Internal Medicine 138, available at http://www.acponline.org/journals/annals/15jul97/mronnet.htm.

[15] Instances of unauthorized access to customer banking details by tellers have been reported: N Luck and J Burns, 'Your Secrets for Sale', Daily Express, 16 February 1994; D Bainbridge and G Pearce, 'Tilting at Windmills—Has the New Data Protection Law Failed to make a Significant Contribution to Rights of Privacy' (2000) 2 J of Information, L and Technology, available at http://elj.warwick.ac.uk/jilt/00-2/bainbridge.html.

[16] R Anderson, 'Security in Clinical Information Systems' (Cambridge: 1996) available at http://www.cl.cam.ac.uk/~rja14/policy11/policy11.html; R Anderson, 'Information Technology in Medical Practice: Safety and Privacy lessons from the UK' (1998) extract from article in Australian Medical Journal, available at http://www.cl.cam.ac.uk/users/rja14/austmedjour/node7.html.

[17] L Gostin, 'Health Information Privacy' (1995) 80 Cornell L Rev 451, 489.

[18] T Loscalzo, 'Cell phones and client confidentiality' (2001) 37 Trial 19. In the UK internet service providers can be required to fit devices to allow the police and other agents of the state to intercept digital communications: see para 14.95 below.

[19] T Branigan, 'Measure for Measure', Guardian, 14 September 2002. This contains a full description of some of the more unusual surveillance devices on the market.

[20] D Sim, 'The Right to Solitude in the US and Singapore: A Call for a Fundamental Reordering' (2002) 22 Loyola of Los Angeles Entertainment L Rev 443, 452.

A. Technological, Political and Social Change

infra-red cameras. Wearable computers that can secretly record and transmit visual images to third parties at lightening speed are just around the corner.[21]

2.10 It is not only the police and security services that have access to this new technology. Highly sophisticated bugging and communications interception devices can be purchased over the internet.[22] It may be that interception of client data by persons not acting for the state is a relatively uncommon phenomenon because such interception can be expensive. But it can and it does happen. In 2001 an electronic bug was found in a room used for private discussions about college business in an Oxbridge college.[23] When Geoffrey Robertson QC was acting for the gym-owner who surreptitiously photographed the Princess of Wales during her workouts at his gym, the mobile telephone of the solicitor who briefed Robertson was intercepted and conversations with a potential witness recorded.[24] Cases of eavesdropping that one hears about are probably only the tip of the iceberg. Either the eavesdropping was bungled or the information extracted was passed to the media, as in the case of Geoffrey Robertson's instructing solicitor.

Pressures for Disclosure to Third Parties

2.11 The number of people and organizations claiming a 'need to know' personal information about individuals is constantly growing.[25] Twenty years ago in *Secrets: On the Ethics of Concealment and Revelation* Bok painted a grim picture:

> Employees, schools, government agencies and mental health and social service organizations are among the many groups now delving into personal affairs as never before. Those with fewest defenses find their affairs most closely picked over. Schools, for instance, are looking into home conditions of students with problems, sometimes even requesting psychiatric evaluations of entire families . . . And access to public welfare assistance, work training programs, and many forms of employment may depend on the degree to which someone is willing to answer highly personal questions.[26]

2.12 Unfortunately, this description is, for present-day circumstances, an understatement. Personal information has become a valuable, saleable commodity that is

---

[21] R Turkington and A Allen, *Privacy Law: Cases and Materials* (St Paul: 1999) 335.
[22] See the list of products advertised at http://www.globalspyshop.com.
[23] Information from the author's husband who had the bug examined by experts. In 1993 hidden electronic listening devices were discovered in the administration offices of an American university: L Mizell, *Invasion of Privacy* (New York: 1998) 89.
[24] *The Justice Game* (London: 1999) 348. cp *Edwards v State Farm Insurance Co and 'John Doe'* 833 F 2d 535 (1987) (radio scanner recorded mobile telephone call between claimant and his lawyer).
[25] On the pressures on doctors to disclose personal information see A Kaul, 'Confidentiality in Dual Responsibility Settings' in C Cordess (ed), *Confidentiality and Mental Health* (London: 2001) ch 6 and the BMA, 'Confidentiality and disclosure of health information' (London: 1999) available at http://www.bma.org.uk. All those interested in an individual's genetic information are documented by G Laurie, *Genetic Privacy* (Cambridge: 2002) 113–181.
[26] S Bok (Oxford: 1984) 117.

Chapter 2: The Social Context

sought after by a very wide range of organizations and individuals. The kind of personal information that a professional might possess about a client may be of interest to any of the following: regulators (including those regulating the professions), the police, the institutions of the criminal justice system, licensing authorities, benefit fraud investigators, immigration authorities, social services, the intelligence services, public service planners, the Inland Revenue, businesses looking for customers to target, employers, personal injury and family law litigants, insurers, debt collection agencies, researchers (scientists, social scientists, journalists, historians). This list, which is not intended to be exhaustive, contains representatives of both the public and private sectors. Enforced subject access, a now partially illegal[27] practice which involves putting pressure on an individual to exercise his personal data access rights for the benefit of a third party, is a symptom of the hunger of third parties for personal information about others.

2.13 Amongst the people and organizations that want access to personal information are some who are prepared to go to almost any lengths to get it. Sometimes there is a public interest justification for resorting to underhand methods,[28] but often there is not. The result is a strong black market for personal information[29] that encourages the abuse of legitimate access to personal information, hacking, identity theft,[30] stealing,[31] deception and covert surveillance.[32] The existence of this undercover trade in personal data prompted the creation of three new criminal offences in the Criminal Justice and Public Order Act of 1994.[33]

Public sector data-sharing[34]

2.14 The Information Commissioner commented in her annual report to Parliament in 2000 that one of 'the key issues we face in the public sector is the increasing pressure for public bodies to share personal information with other public bodies

---

[27] DPA s 56.
[28] A report appeared in the Sunday Times on 28 April 2002 by undercover journalists who had spent a week working for the Crown Prosecution Service in its Thames branch to expose the muddle and confusion prevailing in that service. The Press Complaints Commission's Code, para 11(iii), says that 'subterfuge can be justified only in the public interest and only when material cannot be obtained by any other means'. Use of listening devices is prohibited (para 8). The state also undertakes clandestine investigations. Its powers to do so are described in ch 14.
[29] 'Big Brother', The Guardian, 21 September 2002, 4–7.
[30] Theft, followed by use, of passwords of those who have access to data.
[31] Computer disks holding the names of thousands of children whose parents had refused the MMR vaccine and opted instead for single jabs were stolen from a clinic in Liverpool covering patients from all over the north of England. The motive may have been to 'out' politicians and health professionals who have rejected the government's MMR policy: Guardian, 24 March 2002.
[32] According to N Peacock, 'Human Rights and Clinical Guidelines' in J Tingle and C Foster (eds), *Clinical Guidelines: Law, Policy and Practice* (London: 2002) 135, covert surveillance is common in big medical and personal injury cases, eg *Jones v University of Warwick* [2003] EWCA Civ 151.
[33] Data Protection Registrar (now Information Commissioner), 'Confidentiality: Problems Prior to February 1995'.
[34] See 'Big Brother' The Guardian, 21 September 2002, 16–17.

or to use such information for purposes beyond those for which it was originally obtained'.[35] The benefits of data-sharing include better informed decisions, better targeted services, having to request the same information less often or only once[36] and more effective detection of benefit fraud, child abuse, illegal working, illegal immigration, smuggling and tax evasion.[37]

2.15 Data-sharing is driven by two powerful catalysts. The first is the desire to improve public services. Data-sharing, where possible with the aid of advances in information technology, enables the government to personalize public services and improve their quality.[38] Initiatives include the NHS goal of 'seamless' patient care and the joint delivery of health and social care by the NHS and local authority social service departments.[39] The second is public safety.[40] Since the attacks on the United States of 11 September 2001, facilitating information exchanges in the search for terrorists has become a top priority at EU and national level, but this is not the only public safety reason for sharing information. Concern for public safety lies at the heart of such initiatives as List 99 (renamed the Department for Education and Employment List by the Protection of Children Act 1999),[41] a national database of persons considered to be unsuitable for working with children,[42] the new Criminal Records Bureau[43] and the controversial proposal for a database of potential youth offenders.[44]

---

[35] Information Commissioner, 2000 annual report, ch 5, available at http://www.dataprotection.gov.uk.
[36] Privacy Advisory Group Minutes, 18 April 2001, para 9, at http://www.cabinet-office.gov.uk/innovation/2000/privacy/privag4.shtml.
[37] PIU, *Privacy and Data-sharing* (April 2002) 10.12.
[38] ibid, 3.19.
[39] Further examples are mentioned in PIU, *Privacy and Data-sharing* (April 2002) 10.08.
[40] This philosophy is explicit in a letter dated 1 February 2002 that the author received from the National Probation Service, National Directorate (Home Office): 'There is no central policy on information sharing, rather each area has its own local protocols with other criminal justice agencies and other agencies such as housing. Such information sharing will of course be in line with the requirements of the Data Protection Act, but the primary concern of the probation service will always be protection of the public.'
[41] Protection of Children Act 1999 ss 5–6.
[42] The DoH maintains two further lists by authority of the Protection of Children Act 1999 s 3 and the Care Standards Act 2000 ss 80–89.
[43] This CRB service when fully operational will allow checks of criminal records and other information held by the police and certain government departments to provide employers with information to make safer recruitment decisions. The facilitating legislation is the Police Act 1997 Pt V. A basic disclosure certificate is issued to persons applying on their own behalf. This shows convictions, if any, recorded nationally that are not 'spent' under the Rehabilitation of Offenders Act 1974. The more comprehensive standard disclosure certificate, application for which must be supported by a registered body, contains spent and unspent criminal convictions and details of cautions, reprimands and warnings held on the Police National Computer and, for those who will have regular contact with children or vulnerable adults in education or health care or who are entering certain professions, information from DoH (Protection of Children Act List) and Department for Education and Skills (List99). Enhanced disclosure is available for people in positions of special

note 44 on p. 40

Chapter 2: The Social Context

2.16 The events of 11 September may have accelerated,[45] but certainly did not initiate the policy of sharing personal information more freely between public sector organizations. The Performance and Innovation Unit (PIU) was asked to examine the issue of public-sector information sharing well before 11 September 2001. Its report, which contains no reference to the events of 11 September, strongly supports the exchange of information by public bodies.[46] The report identifies a number of obstacles:

(1) data protection legislation restrictions on the processing of data for purposes not announced when the data was originally collected;[47]

(2) specific statutory bars to the disclosure by public servants of personal information for purposes that differ from those for which the information was collected;[48]

(3) frequently, a lack of statutory authority for data-sharing by statutory authorities[49] with the result that data-sharing, even with the data subject's consent,[50] is unlawful[51] because the disclosing body has no administrative power (vires) to disclose the information;[52]

(4) the possibility that when personal information is disclosed without the consent of the data subject, this is an actionable breach of confidence unless disclosure is a legal requirement or done for overriding public interest reasons.[53]

---

sensitivity including sole charge of children. This will include information held locally by the police, including relevant non-conviction information. The background to this initiative is described in the Home Affairs Committee, *Second Report, Criminal Records Bureau*, 20 March 2001. The CRB website is http://www.crb.gov.uk/. See also T Thomas, 'Employment Screening and the Criminal Records Bureau' (2002) 31 Industrial LJ 55.

[44] 'Alarm at Met database on likely young criminals', The Guardian, 22 January 2002. The database is to be based on information from schools and social services about children involved in truancy, minor vandalism or causing a nuisance.

[45] The immediate outcome was an emergency Anti-terrorism, Crime and Security Act 2001.

[46] *Privacy and data-sharing: The way forward for public services* (April, 2002) available at http://www.piu.gov.uk/2002/privacy/report.

[47] PIU, *Privacy and Data-sharing* (April 2002) A.45. The obstacles are the fair processing code that is part of the first data protection principle (see para 18.10 below) and the second data protection principle that forbids use of personal data for collateral purposes (see para 18.29 below).

[48] See paras 3.43 and 10.35 below.

[49] A public body that is the creature of statute can only do things that are expressly or impliedly authorized by statute: *R v Brentwood BC, ex p Peck* [1998] EMLR 697.

[50] PIU, *Privacy and Data-sharing* (April 2002) 10.07–10.08.

[51] *A Health Authority v X* [2001] 2 FLR 673 confirmed that a court does not have the power to grant a public body a mandatory order for the disclosure of documents needed to carry out its functions.

[52] PIU, *Privacy and Data-sharing* (April 2002) A.47 et seq. Disclosure of personal information is ultra vires in administrative law terms. This will have the knock-on effect of making the disclosure unlawful under HRA, s 6 (see para 3.05 below) because the interference with the right to respect for private life (Art 8) which disclosure involves will not be in accordance with law (see para 3.19 below).

[53] See ch 11.

A. Technological, Political and Social Change

One recommendation is to increase statutory gateways allowing data-sharing.[54] Steps in this direction have already been taken in the Health and Social Care Act 2001[55] and the Social Security Fraud Act 2001. The former permits sharing of medical data without patient consent,[56] the latter allows authorized officials to require information about an individual from public and private sector organizations including banks and educational establishments when there are reasonable grounds for believing that the individual, or a member of his family,[57] has become involved in benefit fraud.[58]

For the most part, what the PIU regards as 'obstacles' to dissemination of personal data across the public sector are not there by chance; they exist for the protection of the freedom and rights of the individual. Legislation that facilitates data-sharing is at variance with the purpose of laws,[59] including the Data Protection Act 1998 (DPA), designed to protect privacy. Shifting the balance between privacy and compulsory disclosure more in favour of the latter by non-transparent data-sharing, whilst possibly still consistent with Article 8(2) of the European Convention on Human Rights if proportionate to a legitimate aim and subject to safeguards,[60] could have undesirable consequences. If a large proportion of the public does not trust the authorities to keep its personal information secure, as an opinion poll commissioned by the Guardian suggests,[61] and suspects that the

2.17

---

[54] Other key recommendations include having a named senior manager responsible for the handling of personal information, a 'Public Services Trust Charter' setting out key commitments to protecting privacy and personal information and improved mechanisms to ensure data is accurate: PIU, *Privacy and Data-sharing* (April 2002) ch 12. Data-sharing compounds problems of inaccuracy.

[55] See para 13.53 below. See also Crime and Disorder Act 1998 s 115 (as to which see 12.15) and Social Security Administration (Fraud) Act 1997 ss 1, 2 amending ss 122 and 122A of the Social Security Administration Act 1992 (supply of information held by tax authorities and other government information for fraud prevention and checking the accuracy of social security information).

[56] s 60.

[57] A family is defined in s 137 of the Social Security Contributions and Benefit Act 1992 and associated regulations. See also the Code of Practice on Obtaining Information (Version 2)(April 2002) para 2.13. Children and dependants are included.

[58] A new s 109B has been inserted into the Social Security Administration Act 1992 by the Social Security Fraud Act 2001. Hitherto banks, building societies, credit providers, utilities and apparently some public bodies were unwilling to disclose information relevant to the detection of benefit fraud because of confidentiality considerations in spite of DPA s 29 and the public interest exception to contractual and equitable obligations of confidentiality. The new legislation makes disclosure compulsory and in a new s179A allows for the mutual exchange of relevant information with overseas authorities. For an analysis and critique of the Bill see House of Commons Library Research Paper 01/32 21 March 2001 at http://www.parliament.uk/commons/lib/research/rp2001/rp01–032.pdf. There is a detailed explanation of the legislation in the Draft Code of Practice on Obtaining Information (Version 2)(April 2002) at http://www.dwp.gov.uk/publications/dwp/2002/fraud-cop-i/chapter1.htm.

[59] See para 3.42 below.

[60] To avoid abuse and ensure accuracy.

[61] An ICM poll between 12 and 14 July 2002 for the Guardian's 'Big Brother' special report, 7 September 2002 found that 58% of those questioned do not trust the government to keep personal information secure.

government will, without notice, put that information to unexpected uses that are contrary to its interests, the candour of compulsory disclosures will decline and there will be fewer voluntary disclosures.

The widening circle of confidentiality

2.18 When a client consults a professional the circle of confidentiality usually extends beyond the two. Almost all professionals rely on the back-up of administrators or clerical workers and some rely on computing experts who have access to client records. From time to time professionals consult colleagues about the best way to handle a client's affairs or seek advice about the ethics of disclosing information from a professional organization.[62] This is generally considered desirable professional behaviour[63] even though it may impinge on client confidentiality if disguising the identity of the client is not possible.

2.19 Professional services are, as already adumbrated, often delivered by a team. This is the norm within medicine[64] and education and, on a lesser scale, is found also in accountancy and law.

> Few patients are aware how widely drawn the confidentiality circle in practice can become. In the United States, the medical record of the average hospital inpatient is accessed by some 75 health professionals and hospital personnel. In the United Kingdom, NHS financial flows linked to (and triggered by) healthcare provision delivered to identifiable individuals, the development of electronic records, and legal requirements . . . have all resulted in a significant shift: from a small circle of people 'in the know', to a larger circle whose access to, and routine use of, personal medical information requires to be carefully controlled.[65]

The more people who have access to confidential information the greater the risk of unauthorized disclosures. When confidential records are freely available to many people, as in a hospital or a social services department, the dangers of unauthorized disclosure increase disproportionately because responsibility for maintaining confidentiality is dispersed and those who handle the information may have no tie of personal loyalty to the client.

Multi-disciplinary partnerships

2.20 A multi-disciplinary approach is strongly encouraged in social work. In child protection, mental health and youth justice multi-disciplinary teams may involve

---

[62] The British Medical Association is constantly consulted by doctors about whether or not to disclose information.
[63] R Swain, 'Ethical codes, confidentiality and the law' (1996) 17 Irish J of Psychology 95, 101.
[64] J Montgomery, 'Confidentiality in the modernized NHS: the challenge of data protection' [1999] Bulletin of Medical Ethics 18.
[65] B Hurwitz, 'Informed consent for access to medical records for health services research' in L Doyal and J Tobias (eds), *Informed consent in Medical Research* (London: 2001) 232. See also Human Genetics Commission, *Inside Information* (May 2002) para 3.34.

A. Technological, Political and Social Change

representatives from the police, social services, probation service, housing departments, education and health sectors necessitating information-sharing across professions and between agencies.[66] A Department of Health document on child protection stresses that '[p]rofessionals can only work together to safeguard children if there is an exchange of relevant information between them'.[67] There is judicial recognition and support for this:

> The consequence of the inter-disciplinary investigation is that there has to be free exchange of information between social workers and police officers together engaged in an investigation. . . . The information obtained by social workers in the course of their duties is . . . confidential . . . It can, however, be disclosed to fellow members of the child protection team engaged in the investigation of the possible abuse of the child concerned.[68]

The members of an inter-disciplinary team who are professionals will all have an ethical commitment to confidentiality, but their ideas about how confidentiality should be handled in a given situation may be very different.[69] Social services have a tradition of readily exchanging information with other agencies.[70] This may inhibit professionals with a stricter confidentiality culture, especially doctors, from passing information to social workers.[71] The Home Office recommends that confidentiality be discussed at the commencement and conclusion of all inter-agency meetings at which information is exchanged in complex child abuse investigations.[72]

Employed Professionals

Codes and conflicts

Large numbers of professionals are salaried and many of them work in the public sector. Employed professionals may be obligated by the terms and conditions of their employment to maintain the confidentiality of client records.[73] So long as

2.21

---

[66] See eg guidance issued by the Home Office on *Complex Child Abuse Investigations: Inter-Agency Issues* (2002), available at http://www.homeoffice.gov.uk/pcrg/child_abuse_guidance.pdf.
[67] DoH, *Working Together to Safeguard Children* (London: 1999) para 7.29, available at http://www.doh.gov.uk/quality5.htm. Cp Report of the Committee of Enquiry into the Education of Handicapped Children and Young People (1978) para 16.2.
[68] per Butler-Sloss LJ, *Re G* [1996] 2 All ER 65, 68.
[69] K and J Williams, 'Vulnerable Adults—Confidentiality and Inter-Disciplinary Working' in A Garwood-Gowers, J Tingle and T Lewis (eds), *Healthcare: The Impact of the Human Rights Act 1998* (London: 2001) 154. See also S Daniel, *Confidentiality and Young People* (Leicester: 1997) 21, 45, 55.
[70] This includes releasing information about suspected abusers to the DoH for inclusion in the Protection of Children Act List or the Department for Education and Skills for inclusion on List 99.
[71] This problem is hinted at in DoH, 'Child Protection: Medical Responsibilities—Guidance for Doctors Working with Child Protection Agencies' para 4.4.
[72] *Complex Child Abuse Investigations: Inter-Agency Issues: Guidance* (2002) para 5.03.
[73] The DoH recommends that NHS bodies incorporate an express obligation of confidentiality into employment contracts: DoH, *Protection and Use of Patient Information* HSG (96) 18 (1996) para 4.7.

the terms and conditions of employment reinforce the professional's duty of confidentiality to the client this is a good thing. But the existence of a managerial hierarchy may be inimical to professional confidentiality if the employer expects the professional to put loyalty to the employer ahead of loyalty to the client when other parts of the employing organization want access to client information in circumstances not allowed by the relevant code of professional ethics, the general law, or both.[74]

2.22 A steady stream of public sector codes, circulars and protocols about protection and disclosure of confidential information has turned into a torrent.[75] The PIU sees them as valuable tools for achieving consistency, transparency and accountability[76] and wants more of them. Sometimes, however, the guidance pays insufficient attention to traditions of confidentiality within the professions,[77] particularly the strict rules that clinicians are required to observe. 'While cloaked in a rhetoric of maintaining confidentiality, in effect, they mostly tend towards the disclosure of patients' healthcare information.'[78] A doctor who follows an employer's code in preference to the General Medical Council's (GMC's) guidelines faces potential disciplinary action by the GMC.[79]

Child abuse reporting by college counsellors

2.23 Two examples from the field of education illustrate the dilemma that employer guidelines can pose for the professional. In 1996 the Association of Colleges issued a circular for counsellors working in further education requiring them to report all instances of child abuse within two hours.[80]

> This mandatory duty to report all child abuse would place therapists working in colleges in a quandary regarding confidentiality. For example, in counselling a mature student for depression, the client may reveal having lost her temper and hit her teenage son for being 'out of order'. If the counsellor is under a blanket requirement to report all abuse, then doing so might jeopardize the therapeutic work being done with the mother . . . Failure to report abuse might also be seen as a breach of the employment contract or conditions of service by the college authorities.[81]

---

[74] This is often a problem for occupational health professionals: see para 21.05 below.
[75] In the pages of this book there are many references to government guidelines. See also J Montgomery, 'Confidentiality in the modernized NHS: the challenge of data protection' [1999] Bulletin of Medical Ethics 18, 19.
[76] PIU, *Privacy and Data-sharing* (April 2002) para 6.12.
[77] Lord Bingham commented in *R v Secretary of State for the Home Department, ex p Daly* [2001] UKHL 26; [2001] 2 AC 532, para 4 that the inquiry that resulted in the prison rules about cell searches 'gave no consideration at any stage to legal professional privilege or confidentiality'.
[78] C Cordess, 'Confidentiality and Contemporary Practice' in *Confidentiality and Mental Health* (London: 2000) 43.
[79] V Hapwood, 'Guidelines in medical practice: the legal issues' (1998) *Cephalalgia* Suppl 21, 57, 62.
[80] Circ 13/96.
[81] D Daniels and P Jenkins, *Therapy with Children* (London: 2000) 87.

A. Technological, Political and Social Change

On behalf of the Association for University and College Counselling, the British Association for Counselling sought legal advice from John Friel, a barrister. His opinion concluded that '[a] contract which obliges disclosure in all cases where abuse is suspected or reported has . . . the effect of abrogating the duty of confidence. It effectively places the duty on the counsellor to disclose in all circumstances where some sort of abuse is reported, outside the law of confidentiality, without any consideration of their own professional judgment and duty . . .'.[82]

Teachers and contraceptive advice

The second example concerns teachers and the controversial issue of contraceptive advice to pupils. In December 1993 what is now the Department of Education and Skills issued draft guidelines that stated that if a teacher is led to believe that a pupil has embarked upon or is contemplating engaging in under-age sex the teacher should normally inform the head teacher who should 'ensure that the parents are made aware'.[83] Michael Beloff QC[84] was consulted by a number of teaching associations. He advised that it was up to the professional judgment of the individual teacher to decide in the pupil's best interests whether to respect a confidence but that a term in the teacher's employment contract obliged the teacher to inform the head teacher if the head teacher expressly asked to be informed.[85] The guidance finally issued was more inimical to confidentiality than the draft version. It stated that where the pupil was under age the teacher 'should arrange . . . for the parents to be made aware, preferably by the pupil himself or herself (and in that case checking that it has been done)'.[86] In 2000 this guidance was withdrawn and replaced by guidance that recognized that when sexual abuse is not suspected teachers are 'not legally bound to inform parents or the head teacher of any disclosure unless the head teacher has specifically requested them to do so'.[87] This still means that teachers may have to disclose the information to the head teacher who may decide to give information to the pupil's parents against the better judgment of the teacher in whom the pupil confided.

2.24

---

[82] ibid.
[83] DFE Draft Circ, *Sex Education in Schools,* para 39.
[84] H Mountfield and M Beloff, Joint Opinion for Association of Teachers and Lecturers, *Sex Education in Schools,* 2 August 1994, unpublished.
[85] Teachers were bound by the Teachers' Statutory Terms and Conditions to work under the 'reasonable direction' of the head teacher. See now School Teachers' Pay and Conditions Document 2002, para 64.1.1, available from http://www.askatl.org.uk.
[86] DFE, *Education Act 1993: Sex Education in Schools,* Circ 5/94.
[87] DfEE, *Sex and Relationship Education Guidance,* July 2000 DfEE 0116/2000, 33 and paras 7.11 and 7.13, available at http://www.dfee.gov.uk/circulars/dfeepub/jul00/030700/confi.htm. For the extent to which a professional can offer confidentiality to a person under the age of 16 under the general law see paras 19.93 et seq.

Workplace Pressures

2.25 Inevitably, overworked professionals and their support staff make mistakes and cut corners. More unauthorized disclosure of confidential personal information is probably caused by carelessness than intentional misconduct. There are numerous reported cases of lawyers accidentally posting or faxing privileged documents to litigation opponents.[88] Everyday causes of inadvertent disclosure include:

- leaving confidential records, either on paper or on screen, where they can be read by unauthorized persons;
- disposal of records in a manner that allows their retrieval by unauthorized persons;[89]
- misdialing of fax numbers[90] and dispatch of e-mails to unintended recipients (easily done if a response is mistakenly sent to a mailing list address);
- discussing a client with a colleague where the conversation can be overheard;
- leaving a message on an answerphone or transmitting a letter to a fax machine to which unauthorized persons have access;
- using client information to illustrate a talk without removing all identifying information;
- failing to verify the identity of a person seeking information by telephone[91] or the authenticity of an e-mail;[92]
- working on client files in a public place (including an aircraft) without taking appropriate safeguards to ensure privacy;[93]
- taking files home and losing them[94] or leaving them unguarded in a place, such as a car,[95] to which a thief has easy access;
- recycling erased disks and tapes from which the supposedly erased data can be recovered by those with technical expertise.

---

[88] For examples see ch 8.

[89] A London trainee solicitor bolstered his income by rummaging through bags of rubbish put out for collection by law firms and chambers and selling some of the contents: V Tunkel, 'Lawyers and their Waste Products' (2000) 150 NLJ 384.

[90] G Negus (2000) 97 (18) LS Gaz 4.

[91] On the subject of deception see N Ellis, 'Security, privacy and confidentiality in health care: a human and organisational perspective', paper presented to the Primary Health Care Specialist Group of the British Computer Society, Cambridge 1999, available at http://www.phcsg.org.uk/conferences/Cambridge1999/camb99-12.htm. For evidence of extreme laxness in GP surgeries see L Mansfield (2001) 322 British Medical J 421.

[92] Forging e-mail identities is easy if electronic signatures are not used.

[93] During a conference, the author sat behind a civil servant who, instead of listening to the speaker, was editing on a laptop computer a document containing recommendations for the promotion and appointment of persons to public office. The text could be easily read.

[94] Patient files detailing mental health problems were discovered by a roadside: M Chester, 'Practice Points' (2001) 98 LS Gaz 50.

[95] In 2000 a laptop containing the Queen Mother's medical history was stolen from the car of her consultant. cp *Swinney v Chief Constable* [1996] 3 All ER 449.

A. *Technological, Political and Social Change*

Public Attitudes to Professional Confidentiality

Communication of confidential information to the client

Clients are today much better informed about their rights, partly because of wider media coverage of ethical and legal misconduct by professionals. As a result the balance of power between professionals and clients is more level.[96] Also, society has become more open. 'Secrecy nowadays has to be justified where previously it did not.'[97] Twenty years ago professionals, especially doctors, felt justified in withholding opinions and information from clients on the grounds that the client lacked the expertise to understand it. This type of paternalism is no longer acceptable to clients. A Harris poll in the United States in 1993 found that 96 per cent of Americans thought that individuals should have the legal right to a copy of their medical records.[98] Clients want to know—or at least be able to find out should they wish to[99]—what professionals know and think about them and whether errors are being made or covered up. Article 10 of the European Convention on Human Rights and Biomedicine reflects this change. It states that '[e]veryone is entitled to know any information collected about his or her health. However, the wishes of individuals not to be so informed shall be observed'.[100] Only in 'exceptional cases' and 'in the interests of the patient' does the Convention allow restrictions to be placed by law on the exercise of these rights.

2.26

Public attitudes to disclosure of personal information

In the industrialized Western world members of the public place a high value on their informational privacy. In *R (on the application of Robertson) v City of Wakefield*[101] Maurice Kay J drew attention to the 'convergence of views throughout Europe about the need to protect personal data from disclosure to third parties without consent'. High up on the list of things that people want to protect are medical and financial information. A 1993 Harris Poll[102] in the United States found that:

2.27

- 85 per cent believe that protecting the confidentiality of medical records is 'absolutely essential' or 'very important';

---

[96] J Pritchard, 'Codes of Ethics' in R Chadwick (ed), *Encyclopedia of Applied Ethics* (California: 1998) 527, 528.
[97] *Rose v Secretary of State for Health* [2002] EWHC 1593, para 47. The Freedom of Information Act 2000 is indicative of the fashion for greater transparency.
[98] Harris Equifax, *Health Information Privacy Survey* (1993), available at http://www.epic.org/privacy/medical/polls.html.
[99] Actual up-take of rights of access may not be great: see eg S Gelman, 'Client access to agency records: a comparative analysis' (1991) 34 Intl Social Work 191, 200.
[100] http://conventions.coe.int.
[101] [2001] EWHC Admin 915; [2002] 2 WLR 889, para 30.
[102] Harris Equifax, *Health Information Privacy Survey* (1993), at http://www.epic.org/privacy/medical/polls.html.

- 60 per cent believe that it is unacceptable for pharmacists to pass medical information about themselves, without their individual approval, to direct marketing firms;
- 64 per cent did not want medical researchers to have access to their records, even if they were not personally identified, unless the researchers first got their consent;
- 75 per cent were concerned that medical information from a computerized national database would be used for non-health purposes and 38 per cent were very concerned.[103]

A Gallup survey in 2000 of a national cross-section of US households found that public concern about maintaining financial confidentiality exceeded concern about protecting medical confidentiality (84 per cent as opposed to 78 per cent).[104]

2.28 Accurate data about public attitudes to the confidentiality of the kind of personal information professionals handle is harder to come by for the United Kingdom but undoubtedly there is concern about informational privacy. The Information Commissioner commissions market research on an annual basis into public attitudes to data protection. In 2001, for the first time, interviewees were asked for their spontaneous reaction to the types of information that caused them concern. Financial and medical information, along with home address, headed the list.[105] An unpublished report from Sheffield University suggests that over 20 per cent of patients would refuse to allow their medical data to be used for medical research if given a choice.[106] A poll conducted for the Patients Association in May 2002 found that 70 per cent of patients did not want medical researchers to have access to their medical records without their consent.[107] Disclosure of health care information to persons not directly involved in clinical care such as social workers, receptionists, managers and researchers is disapproved of.[108] A Caldicott Guardian working with researchers at Teeside University using focus groups,

---

[103] Gallup Organization, *Public Attitudes Toward Medical Privacy* (2000), at http://forhealthfreedom.org/Gallupsurvey/IHF-Gallup.html. This survey found strong opposition to non-medical groups gaining access to medical records.
[104] ibid.
[105] *Annual Report 2001* 'Data subject and individual research' available from http://www.dataprotection.gov.uk/ar2001/annrep/research.htm.
[106] M Oswald, 'A Question of Balance', letter to the British Medical J, 7 March 2001, athttp://www.bmj.com/cgi/eletters/322/7284/442.
[107] J Meikle, 'Bodies of Evidence', The Guardian, 7 September 2002, 'Big Brother' survey.
[108] Bolton Research Group, 'Patients' knowledge and expectations of confidentiality in primary health care' (2000) *British J of General Practice* 901; D Schickle, 'What do the public think about the use of their health information?' Confidentiality and Security Conference, 27 February to 1 March 2001, available at http://www.n-i.nhs.uk/dataprotection/trainingmanchester_event/manchester_home.htm.

A. Technological, Political and Social Change

commissioned surveys and literature searches, concluded the following about public attitudes to medical confidentiality:[109]

1) The data gathered from a person belongs to that person, and we use it and share it only with their consent.
2) People have the right to identify how each item of data may be used or shared.
3) People have the right to change their mind about use and sharing of data.
4) Some of the uses of data which are inferred by organizations run contrary to the Data Protection Act 1998 (DPA).
5) People have a right to explicit description of how their data will be used.
6) Most people do not wish to control their record, but many wish to view it.
7) People trust their GP with their medical record, but not other surgery staff.
8) People have a right to know who has seen their data.

Children's Rights

2.29 Children are no longer viewed as the property of their parent but as independent beings with rights. Increasingly these rights are seen as including the right to participate actively in decisions that affect their lives.[110] The Children Act 1989 recognizes this by requiring that decision-making bodies including courts and social services take into account the views of children to an extent commensurate with age and understanding. Under normal circumstances, legal parents remain the decision-makers for their children on questions of upbringing, medical treatment and welfare, but there is a consensus that the privacy of family life and obligations of professional confidentiality should not be used to hide sexual and other child abuse.

Public Trust in the Protection of Personal Information

Attitudes to privacy

2.30 The strong desire for privacy already mentioned[111] is matched by growing public concern about privacy.[112] The three principal causes of this are:

- an unduly intrusive media catering for a mass voyeuristic, prurient audience;[113]
- the ease with which databases can be combined to create new information; and

---

[109] M Thick et al, *Initial Findings of the Consent and Confidentiality Project: Setting the Scene* (March 2001) para 6.11 at http://www.tees-ha.org.uk/erdipo/documents/pro3_initial_findings.pdf. See also http://www.nhsia.nhs.uk/erdip/archive/erd_030401/mt2_030401.pdf.

[110] UN Convention on the Rights of the Child 1989, especially Art 12. See also A Garwood-Gowers, 'Time for Competent Minors to have the same right of self-determination as competent adults with respect to medical intervention?' in A Garwood-Gowers, J Tingle and T Lewis (eds), *Healthcare Law: The Impact of the Human Rights Act 1998* (London: 2001) 241.

[111] See para 2.27 above.

[112] There is evidence of rising concerns about privacy in the UK including a three-fold increase in the number of referrals for assessment to the Information Commissioner between 1993–94 and 2000–01: PIU, *Privacy and Data-sharing* (April 2002) 3.57–3.58, 6.04.

[113] Cp R Singh, 'Rights Time', Guardian, 21 September 2002.

- a not wholly accurate perception that information stored electronically is not as safe as information contained in paper-based files.[114]

These fears are widespread in western societies and have led more than thirty countries to enact laws for the protection of personal data. At the supra-national level European states have sought to placate these concerns in the recommendations and conventions of the Council of Europe,[115] the EU Data Protection Directive[116] and the Charter of Fundamental Rights which in Article 8 declares that '[e]veryone has the right to the protection of personal data concerning him. Such data must be processed fairly for specified purposes on the basis of the consent of the person concerned or some other legitimate basis laid down by law . . .'.

Trust in professionals

2.31 Little empirical research has been done about how far the public trusts professionals to safeguard the privacy of their personal information. Annual surveys in the early 1990s by the Information Commissioner showed widely differing perceptions of the integrity of the different professions. The best outcome was for doctors and the NHS (92 per cent) and banks and building societies (78 per cent). For schools and colleges the level of trust fell to 70 per cent.[117] A small exploratory investigation of public beliefs by Ormrod and Ambrose in 1999 found a substantial discrepancy between the degree of confidentiality members of the public thought that they deserved from doctors, lawyers, psychiatrists, general practitioners, clinical psychologists, nurses and social workers and what they thought they got.[118] US and Australian studies of public opinion show disapproval of breaches of confidentiality by professionals except when the client reveals murder, suicide plans, child abuse, treason and, in the United States, major theft.[119] The overall impression these disparate studies give is of a public that believes that it is entitled to a high level of confidentiality from professionals but is somewhat sceptical about whether these expectations are met in real life. Older children complain of a lack of confidentiality in their dealings with social workers. Butler and Williamson found 'a pervasive feeling amongst children and young people that even a commitment to confidentiality is, too often, a "false promise" and that information divulged will them be "spread around" without the consent of the

---

[114] VLRC, *Technology and the Law* (1999) para 8.38, at http://www.parliament.vic.gov.au/lawreform/tech/8.html.
[115] See para 3.52 below.
[116] (EC) 95/46.
[117] A Hedges, *Confidentiality: the Public View*, DSS Research Report No 56 (London: 1996) 32.
[118] J Ormrod and L Ambrose, 'Confidential communications—public opinion' (1999) 8 J of Mental Health 413.
[119] ibid.

A. Technological, Political and Social Change

individual concerned'.[120] This is one reason why independent helplines which allow the child to remain anonymous are so popular.

Attitudes of Professionals to Confidentiality

There has been very little empirical research into the attitude of professionals to their obligations of confidentiality. A study by Watson[121] found a disturbing disposition on the part of social workers and community nurses to give relatives and other professionals information contrary to strict instructions against disclosure from the client and without justification in law or under the applicable ethical code. The main reasons for breaching confidentiality found by Watson were the best interests of the client, loyalty to colleagues and responsibilities to third parties. A much stronger confidentiality ethic exists amongst doctors, lawyers, non-medical psychotherapists and counsellors. Which is not to say that these groups insist on absolute confidentiality. Such research as has been undertaken shows support amongst most medical practitioners, psychologists and psychiatrists for limited disclosures in the public interest.[122] The legal profession (as evidenced by its codes) tolerates public interest disclosures least.[123] The strong support amongst doctors for medical confidentiality does not mean that there is no unauthorized disclosure of medical information. A South Australian survey of doctors and hospitals as data custodians using a sample of 3,013 randomly selected residents over 15 years of age found that 3.6 per cent had experienced the release of medical information without their consent.[124] Hospitals and GPs were the main culprits. Of the unauthorized disclosures at least 1 per cent were not legally defensible.[125]

2.32

---

[120] I Butler and H Williamson, *Children Speak: Children, Trauma and Social Work* (London: 1994) 78. Later research found similar dissatisfaction by children with standards of confidentiality: E Munro, 'Empowering looked-after children' (2001) 6 Child and Family Social Work 129.

[121] F Watson, 'Overstepping boundaries' (1999) *Professional Social Work*, September 14–15. A similar lack of respect for confidentiality emerged in a 1981 study: see K Prince, *Boring Records?* (London: 1996) 16. The author remarks that '[t]he description of unguarded baskets of files left overnight on desks, free exchange of information between agencies, and the informality of neighbourhood grapevines must resonate within the consciences of many practitioners and with the worst suspicions of their clients'.

[122] B McSherry, 'Confidentiality of Psychiatric and Psychological Communications: The Public Interest Exception' (2001) 8 Psychiatry, Psychology and L 12, 14.

[123] See paras 1.51 above and 11.15 below.

[124] Figures for unauthorized disclosure of medical information in the US are much higher and approach 20% of adults: Princeton Survey Research Associates, *Medical Privacy and confidentiality survey* (Sacramento: 1999). Health care practices and expectations vary considerably from country to country and therefore the results of Australian and US surveys do not necessarily give any insight into the position in England and Wales.

[125] E Mulligan (2001) 174 Medical J of Australia 637. The unlawful disclosures included disclosures by practitioners of pregnancy, contraceptive use or diagnosis to family members. Two patients had received personally addressed advertisements for respiratory medications which they attributed to their addresses and diagnosis having been released to a pharmaceutical company.

2.33 Studies have not been done in the United Kingdom of the attitude of professionals to disclosing information *to* their clients. A 1995 Australian study showed widespread ignorance amongst doctors about the full extent of their legal and ethical obligation to inform patients of the risks involved in treatment. Doctors who were aware of the rules were often critical of them and ignored them.[126] Many doctors were willing to disclose information to relatives which they had withheld from the patient on therapeutic grounds.[127] The legality of giving medical information to relatives without the patient's consent under both English and Australian law is dubious.[128]

B. The Issues Confronting the Law

2.34 The changes in society detailed in this chapter, the need to set limits to obligations of confidentiality and the ignorance of many professionals about the scope of their obligations of confidentiality raise a host of practical issues that the law should address, including the following:

Existence and scope of the legal obligation of confidentiality

- Must confidentiality be explicitly or implicitly promised for a legal obligation of confidentiality to arise?
- How long does the legal obligation of confidentiality last? Does it survive the death of the client? Does the professional owe the deceased client's relatives a duty not to cause them distress by disclosing confidential information about the deceased?
- Does the obligation of confidentiality cover personal information provided by a third party about the client or, conversely, personal information about a third party provided by the client? If the answer to the second question is yes, is the professional answerable to the third party or to the client or both?
- Does a professional's obligation of confidentiality extend to personal information that has been or is in the public domain?
- Does the obligation of confidentiality include personal information about the client acquired outside the professional relationship?

Breaches of confidentiality

- At what point does disclosure of personal information to a colleague within a firm or organization such as the NHS become a breach of confidence?

---

[126] L Skene and S Millwood, 'Informed Consent to Medical Procedures: the Current Law in Australia, Doctors' Knowledge of the Law and their Practices in Informing Patients' in L Shotton (ed), *Health Care, Law and Ethics* (Katoomba: 1997) 92.
[127] ibid, 89.
[128] See para 13.57 below.

B. The Issues Confronting the Law

- When professionals from several public sector agencies are working together to assist a client, does a professional working for one agency (say the NHS) who shares information about the client with a professional working for another agency (say social services) breach a legal obligation of confidentiality?
- Is it proper for a public agency that obtained confidential information (possibly under compulsion) for one purpose to use it or share it with another public agency for some other purpose?
- Does disclosure of anonymized personal information breach the obligation? Does the answer depend upon the effectiveness of the anonymization process?
- Is the obligation breached if personal information reaches a third party who does not access the information, for example, if a doctor leaves files in a restaurant which are returned unread?
- If the client provides confidential information about a family member, is the consent of the family member also required before that information is disclosed?

Obligations of third parties

- What obligations, if any, should a third party who obtains confidential personal information about a client from a professional have to the client? What, if any, difference does it make that the third party acquired the information without the consent of the professional?

Exceptions to confidentiality

- When can a client be said to have consented to the disclosure of confidential personal information?
- What happens if the client lacks the capacity to consent?
- What sort of potential harm (physical, mental, economic) and what degree of harm (trivial, moderate, substantial) to a third party warrants disclosure without client consent?
- How likely must the potential harm be to trigger disclosure?
- What, if any, difference should it make that the potential victim is a child or elderly or otherwise particularly vulnerable?
- Does it make any difference that the harm to others threatened by the client is unintentional?[129]
- Is the professional ever under a positive duty to disclose confidential information about a client to avert harm to a third party? If so, is the duty owed to the third party or to society generally?

---

[129] This is particularly relevant to the discussion of whether a health professional treating a patient with a genetic disability has a duty to disclose the condition to relatives who are also at risk: see para 20.37 below.

- Is a professional entitled to disclose personal information without consent if disclosure is perceived to be in the client's best interests? If this is not as a general rule permitted, is the professional nevertheless entitled to make a disclosure in a medical emergency or to avoid serious self-harm?
- Are there any circumstances in which personal information can be disclosed without client consent when harm to the client or a third person is not threatened? For example, can the professional breach the obligation to assist crime detection or in self-defence?

Giving information to clients

- Should professionals volunteer to clients the legal limits of confidentiality at the outset of the professional relationship and at periodic intervals thereafter? In other words, should clients be cautioned in the same way that the police have to caution suspects before questioning?
- Should the client be given notice immediately before the professional makes a disclosure without the client's consent? If so, are there exceptions? If the client is not warned in advance, should the client be informed immediately after the disclosure?
- Is a professional entitled to withhold information from a client? If so, when and why?

Other

- Are all professions to be treated alike or are the obligations of confidentiality that members of some professions owe their clients deserving of greater protection than others? If so, which ones?
- How may a professional dispose of her client records if she sells or terminates her business or, if employed, changes employers?
- Can a professional accept a client whose interests conflict with those of an existing or former client?
- How is an employed professional to avoid situations in which she simultaneously owes an obligation of confidentiality to the client and a contractual obligation of disclosure to the employer?
- Can a client, who has suffered no pecuniary or tangible injury from the unauthorized disclosure of confidential personal information about himself by a professional, recover damages for mental distress, damage to reputation or loss of privacy caused by the disclosure?

2.35 The rest of the book will combine a detailed analysis of the law surrounding professional confidentiality with a search for answers to these questions. To some the law provides a satisfactory answer, to others there is no answer or the answer is inadequate. Where appropriate, ways in which the law may be improved will be suggested.

3

THE LEGAL FRAMEWORK

A. **Human Rights**	3.02	C. **Professional Codes of Ethics**	3.46
Article 8(1)	3.03	Purpose of a Code	3.46
Relevance of Other Convention Articles	3.10	Legal Significance of an Ethics Code	3.47
Justified and Unjustified Interference with Convention Rights	3.19	D. **Domestic 'Soft Law'**	3.48
When Convention Rights Collide	3.26	Public Sector Guidance	3.48
B. **Legislating About Confidentiality**	3.33	Information Commissioner's Guidance	3.50
Compulsory Disclosure	3.33	E. **The International Dimension**	3.52
Non-disclosure	3.41	Supranational and International Instruments	3.52
Disclosure to the Subject of the Information	3.45		

The object in this chapter is to draw attention to some of the main features of the legal, quasi-legal and ethical landscape in which decisions about professional confidentiality are taken. Legislation, such as the Data Protection Act 1998 (DPA), that is looked at in detail later in the book is mentioned in passing only, but the Human Rights Act 1998 (HRA), which impacts on many chapters of this book, is analysed—from the point of view of its significance for the law of professional confidentiality—in some depth here. The later parts of the chapter are devoted to a discussion of the nature and standing of the many ethical codes and extensive 'soft law' that offer guidance to those making disclosure decisions about confidential personal information. **3.01**

A. Human Rights

In 1998 Parliament passed a Human Rights Act to give effect in domestic law to the majority of rights set out in the European Convention on Human Rights (ECHR), an international instrument which the United Kingdom had ratified some 47 years earlier. The HRA enables these rights to be enforced directly before courts and tribunals[1] in the United Kingdom. Previously, complaints about **3.02**

---

[1] Defined in HRA, s 21 as 'any tribunal in which legal proceedings can be brought'. This wide definition would include disciplinary tribunals.

violations of these rights had to be taken to the Commission and Court at Strasbourg. A number of the incorporated rights have a bearing on the law of confidentiality as it applies to professional–client relationships.

Article 8(1)

Relevance to professional confidentiality

3.03 The Convention rights absorbed into English law include a broad right on the part of individuals to 'respect for'[2] 'private and family life . . . home and . . . correspondence'. While the full reach of the right to respect for private life may be obscure,[3] it is uncontroversial that Article 8(1) is engaged when personal 'information protected by the duty of professional secrecy'[4] is collected, held or disclosed. The European Court of Human Rights (ECtHR) has said that:

> the protection of personal data, not least medical data, is of fundamental importance to a person's enjoyment of his or her right to respect for private and family life as guaranteed by Article 8 of the Convention.[5]

Specifically, unjustified encroachment on 'professional secrecy' between lawyer and client was held to infringe Article 8(1) in *Foxley v UK*[6] and to require particularly compelling justification.

---

[2] Notice that the protection is not 'freedom from interference' with private life but 'respect for' private life which D Feldman, *Civil Liberties and Human Rights in England and Wales* (2nd edn, Oxford: 2002) 524, suggests may be a weaker right.

[3] The concept of respect for private life extends far beyond the protection of personal information; it includes notions of physical and moral integrity (*X v Netherlands* (1985) 8 EHRR 235); freedom to establish and develop relationships with other human beings (*Amann v Switzerland* (2000) 30 EHRR 843); freedom to develop one's own personality (*Gaskin v UK* (1989) 12 EHRR 36). For a discussion of the scope of the article see F Tulkens, 'Freedom of expression and information in a democratic society and the right to privacy under the ECHR . . .', paper presented to the Strasbourg Conference on *Freedom of expression and the right to privacy*, 23 September 1999, 29, available from http://www.humanrights.coe.int/media. D Feldman, 'Information and Privacy' in *Freedom of Expression and Freedom of Information: Essays in Honour of Sir David Williams* (Oxford: 2000) 307 points out that Art 8 'has been the subject of particularly vigorous and dynamic interpretation'.

[4] per Bingham LJ, *W v Egdell* [1990] 1 All ER 835, 853. Cp *Police v Georghiades* (1983) 2 Cyprus LR 33, 55. 'Correspondence' in Art 8(1) is not qualified by the word 'private' and was held not to be restricted to letters in *Klass v Germany* (1978) 2 EHRR 214, para 41 where it was applied to telephone conversations. See also *Malone v UK* (1984) 7 EHRR 14; *Halford v UK* (1997) 24 EHRR 523; *Bugallo v Spain* Application 58496/00, 18 February 2003; *MM v Netherlands* Application 39339/98, 8 April 2003. E-mail and other newer forms of communication are likely to be classified as 'correspondence'.

[5] *Z v Finland* (1997) 25 EHRR 371, para 94. See also *MS v Sweden* (1999) 28 EHRR 313, para 41. As regards application of Art 8 to personal data generally, see *X v UK* (1982) 30 DR 239; *Leander v Sweden* (1987) 9 EHRR 433; *Hilton v UK* (1988) 57 DR 108; *Murray v UK* (1995) 19 EHRR 193, paras 78–79; *Peck v UK* Application 44647/98, 28 January 2003, para 78.

[6] (2001) 31 EHRR 25, para 44. See also *Niemietz v Germany* (1992) 16 EHRR 97, para 37; *Campbell v UK* (1993) 15 EHRR 137, paras 50–54; *Domenichini v Italy* (2001) 32 EHRR 4, paras 26–33 (inspection of prisoner's correspondence with his lawyer).

A. Human Rights

Impact of the Human Rights Act 1998 on professional confidentiality

The interpretive obligation

3.04 Article 8 has far-reaching implications for all professionals—those who are employed by, and carry out acts on behalf of, public authorities and those who work in the private sector performing wholly private functions. The impact of the HRA on professional confidentiality is threefold. First, '[s]o far as it is possible to do so' s3(1) requires *all* primary legislation and subordinate legislation to be read and given effect to 'in a way that is compatible with the Convention rights'[7] in *all* litigation.[8] The practical result is that legislation affecting confidentiality such as the Crime and Disorder Act 1998,[9] the Social Security Fraud Act 2001[10] and the Regulation of Investigatory Powers Act 2000[11] must be interpreted if at all possible to comply with Article 8.[12] Subordinate legislation, such as the Civil Procedure Rules 1998, that is not compatible with adopted Convention rights may be held ultra vires.[13]

Indirect horizontal effect

3.05 **Implication of public authority status of courts** Secondly, HRA s6(1) makes it 'unlawful for a public authority to *act* in a way which is incompatible with a Convention right'.[14] 'Act' includes a failure to act.[15] Courts and tribunals as public authorities[16] must avoid infringing Convention rights.[17] This demands more of them than Convention-compliant procedures. A court must strive as best it can to achieve effective compliance with Convention rights in procedural, remedial[18] and substantive law terms,[19] regardless of whether the litigants are private parties or

---

[7] See para 3.55 below.
[8] If it is not possible, the law must be applied but the court may make a 'declaration of incompatibility' (s 4).
[9] See para 12.15 below.
[10] See para 2.15 above.
[11] See para 14.83 below.
[12] Quite apart from the HRA, legislation such as the DPA that implements EU law must be interpreted to comply with the ECHR: *Rutili v Minister of the Interior* [1975] ECHR 1219.
[13] eg *General Mediterranean Holdings v Patel* [1999] 3 All ER 673; *R v Secretary of State for the Home Department, ex p Daly* [2001] UKHL 26; [2001] 2 AC 532. Subordinate legislation cannot be held ultra vires if primary legislation prevents removal of the incompatibility: s 3(1)(c).
[14] Italics added.
[15] HRA, s 6(6).
[16] HRA, s 6(3).
[17] *R v Lambert* [2001] UKHL 37; [2001] 3 All ER 577, para 28.
[18] Provided a right exists under the common law, the Convention will influence the remedy that is awarded for a breach of that right, eg if the claimant is the victim of a breach of confidence, Arts 8 and 10 will be taken into account in determining whether to grant an injunction. This is specifically required by HRA, s 12.
[19] But see *R (on the application of Wooder) v Feggetter* [2002] EWCA Civ 554; [2002] 3 WLR 591, para 48, where Sedley LJ, said : '[i]t is probable, though as yet undecided, that "acting" governs remedies and procedures rather than doctrines of substantive law.'

emanations of the state. In *R v Lambert* Lord Hope said that the interpretation of legislation and the formulation of the common law are 'act[s]'.[20]

> [T]he prohibition in s. 6(1) . . . affects matters of substance. It will be unlawful within the meaning of s. 6(1) for a court to determine a criminal charge on an interpretation of a statute which ignores the interpretative obligation in s.3(1), or on a proposition of law which is incompatible with a convention right. It will be unlawful in the convention sense for an appellate court to do likewise.[21]

This is the HRA's so-called indirect horizontal effect.[22]

3.06 A court that fails to prevent or rectify an interference with a client's right to respect for private life whatever the nature of the litigation, when it lies within its power to do so by developing domestic remedial law (and arguably substantive common law doctrines) incrementally, acts unlawfully in those proceedings.[23] This unlawfulness provides grounds for an appeal.[24] A comparison may be made with the positive obligation of a member state[25] to take active steps to ensure that private life is respected even where no public authority is responsible for the interference complained of.[26] The difference between the court and a member state is that the

---

[20] *R v Lambert* [2001] UKHL 37; [2001] 3 All ER 577, para 114. Contrast P Mirfield, 'Regulation of Investigatory Powers Act 2000 (2) Evidential Aspects' [2001] Crim LR 91, 92–93. In Lord Hope's opinion, the word 'act' should be given 'a broad and purposive meaning'.

[21] *R v Lambert* [2001] UKHL 37; [2001] 3 All ER 577, para 114. See also *Douglas v Hello! Ltd* [2001] 2 All ER 289, para 166.

[22] Sedley LJ, *London Regional Transport v Mayor of London* [2001] EWCA Civ 1491, para 59 prefers the phrase 'cascade effect'. For a discussion of competing theories of horizontal effect see I Hare, 'Verticality Challenged: Private Parties, Privacy and the Human Rights Act' [2001] EHRLR 526; A Young, 'Remedial and substantive horizontality: the common law and *Douglas v Hello! Ltd* [2002] PL 232.

[23] *R v Sutherland* (Nottingham Crown Court, 29 January 2002) transcript, 41: '[i]f the Court relieves a party to proceedings from the consequences of a flagrant breach of a fundamental right against the opposing party in the proceedings, which right is recognized by the Convention and the breach takes place in the context of the very proceedings before the Court, it is not difficult for it to be seen that the Court could be regarded as acting in those proceedings in a way which is incompatible with the Convention.' See also *Heather v Leonard Cheshire Foundation* [2001] EWHC Admin 429, para 106; *McKenna v British Aluminium*, The Times, 16 January 2002 where, in refusing to strike out a cause of action, Neuberger J said: 'the potential unsatisfactory possibilities canvassed . . . during argument satisfy me that there is a real possibility of the court concluding that in light of the different landscape, namely article 8.1 now being effectively part of our law, it is necessary to extend or change the law, even though, in circumstances where the Convention was no part of English law, the majority of the House of Lords thought otherwise.'

[24] HRA, s 9.

[25] It is arguable that as an emanation of the state the court shares the positive obligation described by the ECtHR in *X & Y v Netherlands* (1986) 8 EHRR 235, paras 23 to adopt measures 'designed to secure respect for private life even in the sphere of the relations of individuals to themselves'.

[26] *Airey v Ireland* (1980) 2 EHRR 305, para 32; *Stjerna v Finland* (1997) 24 EHRR, para 38; *Sheffield and Horsham v UK* (1999) 27 EHRR 163, para 52. Where positive obligations are concerned, the state has a wide margin of appreciation in determining what steps are appropriate.

obligation of a court under HRA, s 6 does not (on current thinking)[27] include invention of an entirely new cause of action. This was firmly disavowed by Dame Butler-Sloss in *Venables v NGN Ltd*.[28] The President of the Family Division explained that

> [t]he obligation on the court does not . . . encompass the creation of a free-standing cause of action based directly upon the articles of the convention . . . The duty on the court . . . is to act compatibly with convention rights in adjudicating upon existing common law causes of action, and that includes a positive as well as negative obligation.[29]

So long as the courts observe the constraint that breaches of the ECHR are not actionable per se, how they set about achieving alignment with the Convention is left to their discretion (just as it is in the discretion of the state to decide how best to implement a positive Convention obligation). The favoured method at the moment is to expand the action for breach of confidence so that it protects informational privacy.[30]   **3.07**

Duty to consider privacy codes   Where Article 8 is concerned, the HRA achieves horizontal effect indirectly also by a second route.[31] In any case in which the court is considering whether to grant relief which might affect the exercise of the right of freedom of expression in a journalistic, literary or artistic context, the court is required by s12(4)(b) to have regard to 'any relevant privacy code'. The HRA does not name them[32] but they include the Press Complaints Commission's Code,[33] the Broadcasting Standards Commission's Code[34] and the Independent Television Code.[35] These codes assume a right to privacy and some explicitly embody Article 8. Because of s 12, a substantial portion of the judgment in *Douglas v Hello! Ltd*,[36] an action between private parties, was devoted to a discussion of Article 8. Brooke LJ remarked that: **3.08**

---

[27] The orthodox view is that new causes of action cannot be invented because of the restrictions on proceedings contained in HRA s 7(1) and on remedies in s 8(1). But there are some who predict that over time the courts will move toward full horizontality and allow Convention rights to give rise to fresh causes of action: see J Cooper, 'Horizontality: The Application of Human Rights Standards in Private Disputes' in R English and P Havers (eds), *Human Rights and the Common Law* (Oxford: 2000) 69. Furthermore, even now it is possible to get an injunction without a cause of action if there is interference with a 'legitimate interest': see para 8.02 below. A Convention right ought to count as a legitimate interest.
[28] [2001] 1 All ER 908. See also *Douglas v Hello! Ltd* [2001] 2 All ER 289, para 81.
[29] per Butler-Sloss P [2001] 1 All ER 908, para 27. See also para 111 (emphasis added).
[30] See ch 6. See also R Scott, 'Confidentiality' in J Beatson and Y Cripps (eds), *Freedom of Expression and Freedom of Information: Essays in Honour of Sir David Williams* (Oxford: 2000) 271.
[31] *Douglas v Hello! Ltd* [2001] 2 All ER 289, para 133. That this was the intention is clear from remarks by the Home Secretary in Parliament: *Hansard*, HC vol 315, cols 536, 553 (2 July 1998). But see N Moreham, '*Douglas and others v Hello! Ltd*—the Protection of Privacy in English Private Law' (2001) 64 MLR 767, 772.
[32] Contrast Data Protection (Designated Codes of Practice) Order 2000, SI 2000/418.
[33] See para 9.10 below.
[34] See para 9.17 below.
[35] See para 9.20 below.
[36] [2001] 2 All ER 289.

[u]nlike the court in *Kaye v Robertson*, Parliament recognized that it had to acknowledge the importance of the article 8(1) respect for private life, and it was able to do so untrammelled by any concerns that the law of confidence might not stretch to protect every aspect of private life. It follows that on the present occasion it is not necessary to go beyond s.12 of the Human Rights Act and clause 3 of the [Press Complaints Commission's Code of Practice] to find the ground rules by which we should weigh the competing considerations of freedom of expression on the one hand and privacy on the other.[37]

3.09 **Liability of public authorities**   Thirdly, under the HRA someone who suffers a breach of a Convention right at the hands of a 'public authority':[38]

- is given a cause of action against the offending authority[39] (if not a court)[40] and
- may rely on the breach in legal proceedings brought on other grounds,

unless an Act of Parliament or valid subordinate legislation prevented the public authority from acting differently.[41] In consequence, if a professional working for a public authority breaches an obligation of confidentiality owed to a client, the potential exists to bring proceedings under the HRA against the public authority.[42] A breach of Article 8 does not require a breach of confidence and therefore there may be circumstances in which a client can sue the authority though unable to maintain an action for breach of confidence against the professional because, for example, the professional refused to give an unqualified promise of confidentiality.

Relevance of Other Convention Articles

Article 6

Communications with lawyers

3.10   Besides Article 8, up to five other Convention rights may affect professional confidentiality. First, there is Article 6[43] which may, if the professional is a lawyer, do so in a positive or in a negative way. The positive impact stems from Article 6(1)'s guarantee of a fair hearing in the determination of 'civil rights and obligations or of any criminal charge'. Article 6(2) and (3) spell out some of the manifestations of a fair hearing in criminal proceedings. One is the right to legal assistance.[44]

---

[37] *Douglas v Hello! Ltd* [2001] 2 All ER 289, paras 94–95.
[38] See para 4.47 below.
[39] See para 4.45 below.
[40] The only remedy if a court breaches the Convention is an appeal or, in the case of an inferior court, judicial review HRA s 9.
[41] HRA ss 6, 7.
[42] As regards principles of vicarious liability see para 21.31 below.
[43] An attempt by a litigant to use Art 6(1) as a shield to avoid disclosure of confidential personal information to litigation opponents was rejected as manifestly ill-founded in *Vernon v UK* Application 38753/97 (2001) 29 EHRR CD 264 and *L v UK* [2000] 2 FLR 322.
[44] Art 6(3)(c).

A. Human Rights

Legal professional privilege,[45] the rule of English law that communications between lawyer and client do not have to be disclosed, buttresses unimpeded access to the courts and to legal advice.[46] This protection is considered by the English courts to be essential for uninhibited discussions between lawyer and client.[47] Hence Article 6(1) requires the secrecy of communications with lawyers in the preparation and conduct of a criminal case. The right is implied, though less obviously, for civil proceedings as well.[48]

The jurisprudence of the ECtHR backs up these claims. In *Niemietz v Germany* **3.11** the court commented that 'where a lawyer is involved, an encroachment on professional secrecy may have repercussions on the proper administration of justice and hence on the rights guaranteed by Article 6'.[49] Surveillance of conversations between a lawyer and a detained client[50] and interception of correspondence between the two[51] have been found by the ECtHR to violate the right to a fair trial, most recently in *Brennan v UK*.[52] The complaint there was as to the presence of a police officer during some of the applicant's discussions with his solicitor. It was argued that '[t]his destroyed the confidentiality of lawyer/client communication and was extremely prohibitive of the necessary frankness with which a client must be permitted to express himself if he is to be properly, usefully and meaningfully advised and assisted by his lawyer'.[53] The ECtHR concluded that:

> an accused's right to communicate with his advocate out of hearing of a third person is part of the basic requirements of a fair trial and follows from article 6(3)(c). If a lawyer were unable to confer with his client and receive confidential instructions from him without surveillance, his assistance would lose much of its usefulness, whereas the Convention is intended to guarantee rights that are practical and effective . . . The importance to be attached to the confidentiality of such consultations, in particular that they should be conducted out of the hearing of third persons, is illustrated by the international provisions cited above [American Convention on Human Rights, Article 8; Council of Europe Standard Minimum Rules for the Treatment of Prisoners, Article 93; European Agreement Relating to Persons

---

[45] See para 16.08 below.
[46] *R v Secretary of State, ex p Leech* [1993] 4 All ER 539, 550.
[47] See para 1.48 above. See also *R v McClure* (2001) 151 CCC (3d) 321, 331–332.
[48] No significance attaches to the fact that Art 6 does not spell out expressly a right to effective legal assistance in civil proceedings. Plainly legal assistance is needed in civil proceedings just as much as criminal proceedings if the hearing is to be fair.
[49] (1993) 16 EHRR 97, para 37. See also *Tamosius v UK* [2002] STC 1307.
[50] *S v Switzerland* (1992) 14 EHRR 670, para 48; *Campbell v UK* (1993) 14 EHRR 137, paras 46–47. See also *R (on the application of M) v Commissioner of Police for the Metropolis* [2001] EWHC Admin 553, [2002] Crim LR 215; *R v Sutherland* (Nottingham Crown Court, 29 January 2002, Newman J).
[51] *Campbell v UK* (1993) 14 EHRR 137, paras 46–47.
[52] (2002) 34 EHRR 507, para 63.
[53] ibid, para 56.

Participating in Proceedings of the European Court of Human Rights, Article 3(2)(c)].[54]

3.12 It is problematic as to whether Article 6[55] can be invoked to protect communications with lawyers when litigation is not contemplated. Does it, for example, cover instructions to a solicitor to draw up a will? The opening words of Article 6(1) refer to the '*determination* of . . . civil rights and obligations'[56] which could be taken to imply that protection of lawyer-client communications is limited to those made in aid of a trial or its preparation.[57]

Article 6 induced loss of confidentiality

3.13 Article 6 can demolish professional confidentiality in several ways:

(1) The entitlement in Article 6 to a fair trial may mean that confidential personal information that is relevant to litigation has to be disclosed to the parties and to the court. The paradigm case is confidential information known to, or held by, a professional that establishes a criminal defendant's innocence. In so far as the common law rule of legal professional privilege may deny an accused access to such vital evidence,[58] it may breach the ECHR and require reconsideration.[59]

(2) Article 6 guarantees to litigants a public hearing.[60] Disclosure of confidential client information in open court is likely to destroy the confidentiality of the information. Ways of minimizing the damage to professional confidentiality without impinging on the absolute[61] right of the parties to a fair hearing are explored in chapter 17.

Effect of breach of Article 8 on Article 6

3.14 Use in trial proceedings of evidence obtained by means that violated Article 8 need not infringe Article 6. In criminal proceedings the accused has reason to complain of an Article 6 violation only if the trial as a whole is unfair[62] and even

---

[54] ibid, para 58. Contrast *R (on the application of M) v Commissioner of Police for the Metropolis* [2001] EWHC Admin 553; [2002] Crim LR 215 which was decided before *Brennan v UK* (2001) 34 EHRR 507.
[55] Even if Art 6 does not apply, Art 8 would apply.
[56] Italics added.
[57] J Auburn, *Legal Professional Privilege* (Oxford: 2000) 40–43. This writer points out, however, that the ECtHR has an expansionist approach to Art 6.
[58] *R v Derby Magistrates' Court, ex p B* [1995] 4 All ER 526.
[59] See paras 16.25 to 16.27 below. Note that under the Freedom of Information Act 2000, s 42 privileged information has only a qualified exemption.
[60] *Axen v Germany* (1984) 6 EHRR 195, para 25.
[61] See para 3.23 below.
[62] *Schenk v Switzerland* (1988) 13 EHRR 242; *Khan v UK* (2000) 31 EHRR 45; *R v Mason* [2002] EWCA Crim 385, para 66. For an example of a case in which a breach of Art 8 meant that the trial would be unfair see *R v Sutherland* (Nottingham Crown Court, 29 January 2002).

A. Human Rights

then unfairness may be cured by an appeal.[63] In *R v Khan*[64] the House of Lords condoned the used of evidence obtained by fixing a listening device to the wall of the house of the accused who was suspected of being involved in the importation of prohibited drugs. This bugging, which was done without the knowledge or consent of the accused, was both an unlawful trespass and an unjustified invasion of the accused's right to respect for private life in that it was not done 'in accordance with the law'.[65] The House of Lords rejected an appeal by the accused against conviction, Lord Nolan saying that it would be 'a strange reflection on our law if a man who has admitted his participation in the illegal importation of a large quantity of heroin should have his conviction set aside on the grounds that his privacy has been invaded'.[66]

3.15 The ECtHR accepted that despite the interference with the accused's privacy rights, there was no interference with Article 6 because the applicant had had the opportunity to challenge the authenticity and use of the evidence. 'Had the domestic courts been of the view that the admission of the evidence would have given rise to substantive unfairness, they would have had a discretion to exclude it under s 78 of the 1984 Act.'[67] In *Schenk v Switzerland*[68] the ECtHR seems to have thought that it was important that the evidence obtained in breach of Article 8 was not the sole or main basis of conviction but in *Khan*,[69] where it was, this was disregarded because of the compelling character of the impugned evidence and the absence of challenge to its reliability.[70] No wonder that in *R v P* Lord Hobhouse said that 'any remedy for a breach of art 8 lies outside the scope of the criminal trial'.[71] Ashworth finds the pronouncements on the interface between Articles 6 and 8 'confusing and unconvincing'. His opinion is that the ECtHR has never squarely addressed 'the argument that to base a trial on evidence obtained through a breach of another Convention right must undermine the fairness of the trial'.[72]

Articles 2, 3, 9

3.16 The Article 9 right to freedom to manifest one's religion or beliefs may be engaged when confidential personal information is obtained, held, or disclosed by a spiritual

---

[63] *Edward v UK* (1992) 15 EHRR 417.
[64] [1996] 3 All ER 289.
[65] The relevant law lacked clarity and therefore qualitatively failed to meet the standard of certainty required by *Malone v UK* (1984) 7 EHRR 14. See para 3.19 below.
[66] [1996] 2 All ER 289, 302.
[67] *Khan v R* (2000) 31 EHRR 45, para 39.
[68] *Schenk v Switzerland* (1988) 13 EHRR 242, para 47.
[69] (2000) 31 EHRR 45.
[70] Reliability and proportionality are seen as the key concerns in *R v McLeod* [2002] EWCA Crim 989, para 30.
[71] [2001] 2 All ER 58, 70. Contrast *Police v Georghiades* (1983) 2 Cyprus LR33.
[72] Commentary *PG v UK* [2002] Crim LR 308. See also D Ormrod, 'ECHR and the Exclusion of Evidence: Trial Remedies for Article 8 Breaches' [2003] Crim LR 61, 65.

counsellor.[73] Article 2 (the right to life) and Article 3 (the right to protection from torture or inhuman or degrading treatment) may be brought into play if a client poses a serious physical threat to a third party. In these circumstances there is an issue as to whether the third party, or someone capable of protecting the third party, should be warned about the danger the client presents. This topic is pursued in chapter 20. Suffice it to say here that Article 3 is unqualified which means that there can be no interference with this right to accommodate some other person's interest. The Article 2 right to life is also unqualified 'save in the execution of a sentence of a court following . . . conviction of a crime'. The absence of qualification is, however, tempered by the considerable flexibility that the courts have to determine the scope of these rights.[74]

Article 10[75]

3.17 Article 10(1) is about freedom of expression. One aspect of freedom of expression is the right to impart information and ideas (including those that shock, disturb and offend)[76] without interference from a public authority. Since legal, as well as natural, persons are entitled to freedom of expression,[77] Article 10 is implicated when a media organization is sued because it has published, or intends to publish, confidential personal information of which a professional (willingly or unwillingly) is the source.[78] Courts are reminded of this by HRA, s 12.[79] When a litigant invites the court to enjoin publication of 'material which the respondent claims, or which appears to the court, to be journalistic',[80] s 12(4) requires the court to 'have particular regard to . . . the extent to which—(i) the material has, or is about to, become available to the public; or (ii) is, or would be, in the public interest for the material to be published'. The media is the recipient of special treatment because it: keeps the public informed of matters of public interest; offers a forum of political debate outside Parliament; acts as a safety valve for public discontent; exposes corruption and abuse of power in government.[81] These roles are summed up in the description of the media as the watchdog of democracy. To perform its checking and informative functions, there must be a free flow of information and ideas to and from the media.

---

[73] See para 16.49 below.
[74] A Young, 'Judicial Sovereignty and the Human Rights Act 1998' [2002] CLJ 53, 61.
[75] See G Robertson and A Nicol, *Media Law* (4th edn, London: 2002) ch 2.
[76] *Handyside v UK* (1976) EHRR 737, para 49.
[77] *Autronic AG v Switzerland* (1990) 12 EHRR 485, para 47. eg *Re X* [2001] 1 FCR 541.
[78] *de Haes v Belgium* (1997) 25 EHRR 1, para 39.
[79] See para 8.14 below.
[80] HRA, s12(4).
[81] *R v Secretary of State for the Home Department, ex p Simms* [1999] 3 All ER 400, 408.

A. Human Rights

Freedom of information is also about the right to receive information unhindered by state intervention.[82] Both the media[83] and members of the public[84] have this right, but the information must be information that someone is *willing* to impart.[85] The freedom to seek out and take receipt of information does not entitle the media, or anyone else, to information from a source who has no wish to share it.[86] Article 10 imposes no positive obligation on the state to institute effective access to information.[87] Indeed, freedom of expression benefits from laws protecting privacy because without these no communication might take place: 'assurance of privacy helps to overcome our natural reluctance to discuss private matters when we fear that our private conversations may become public.'[88]

3.18

Justified and Unjustified Interference with Convention Rights
Interference with Articles 8 and 10

Neither the right to respect for private life (Article 8(1)) nor the right to freedom of expression (Article 10(1)) are absolute. 'In a democratic society there are many circumstances in which freedom of expression must, of necessity, be restricted. In particular, untrammelled exercise of freedom of expression will often infringe the "rights of others", both under the Convention and outside it.'[89] Similarly, qualification of the privacy rights protected by Article 8 is necessary. Interference (which includes collection and storage)[90a] with Article 8 and 10 Convention rights by a public authority (including a court) is permitted so long as the interference, *in the particular case*,[90] meets the following criteria.

3.19

(1) *It is 'in accordance with law' (Article 8(2)) or 'prescribed by law' (Article 10(2))*

The rule of law requires that any interference with the rights of a citizen must have a legal foundation. The ECtHR examined what 'prescribed by law'

---

[82] *London Regional Transport v Mayor of London* [2001] EWCA Civ 1491, para 55; *Howard v Secretary of State for Health* [2002] EWHC 396, para 103.
[83] *De Haes v Belgium* (1997) 25 EHRR 1, para 39.
[84] *Herczegfalvy v. Austria* Series A No 244, (1993) 15 EHRR 437; *Open Door Counselling Ltd and Dublin Well Woman v Ireland* Series A No 246, (1993) 15 EHRR 244.
[85] *R (on the application of Pelling) v Bow County Court* [2001] UKHRR 165, paras 35–36.
[86] *Leander v Sweden* (1987) 9 EHRR 433, para 74.
[87] *Guerra v Italy* (1998) 26 EHRR 357. Cp *Z v Austria* Application 10392/83 (1998) 56 DR 13. See also *Howard v Secretary of State* [2002] EWHC 396, paras 103, 112 and *Persey v Secretary of State for the Environment* [2002] EWHC 371, paras 52–53 disapproving the approach of Kennedy LJ in *R v Secretary of State for Health, ex p Wagstaff* [2001] 1 WLR 292.
[88] per Breyer J, *Bartnicki v Vopper* 532 US 514, 538 (2001). See also Rehnquist CJ, ibid at 543. The case concerned the constitutional validity of a statutory provision making disclosure of a previously intercepted electronic communication illegal.
[89] per Lord Phillips MR, *Ashdown v Telegraph Group* [2001] 4 All ER 666, para 25.
[90a] *Amann v Switzerland* (2000) EHRR 843, para 65.
[90] 'The Convention cannot be used to complain of laws in the abstract, however Draconian their effect. There must be a "victim" who has suffered a real "violation"': G Robertson and A Nicol, *Robertson & Nicol on Media Law* (4th edn, London: 2002) 40. Conversely, though a law may, generally, be Convention-compliant, in a particular application it may not be.

entails in *Sunday Times v UK*.[91] The first principle that emerges from that judgment is that the interference must have a basis in domestic law, that is legislation or common law.[92] Administrative guidelines which lack the force of law will not do.[93] A second principle is publication: 'the law must be adequately accessible: the citizen must be able to have an indication that is adequate, in the circumstances, of the legal rules applicable to a given case.'[94] In surveillance cases, this applies not only to the susceptibility to surveillance but also to the subsequent use of the intercept.[95] A third principle is certainty: 'a norm cannot be regarded as a "law" unless it is formulated with sufficient precision to enable the citizen to regulate his conduct: he must be able—if need be with appropriate advice—to foresee, to a degree that is reasonable in the circumstances the consequences which a given action may entail.'[96] The degree of precision that the Convention requires depends on the subject matter.[97] When the law touches on areas of subjective judgment such as obscenity where public opinion may shift, the law is not expected to be over-precise.[98] But when the law allows intrusive surveillance precision is called for.[99]

[T]he domestic law . . . must give an adequate indication of the circumstances in which, and the conditions under which, such surveillance can occur: see *Malone v UK*. The rules must also define with clarity the categories of citizens liable to be the subject of such surveillance, the offences which might give rise to an order for surveillance, the permitted duration of the interception, and the circumstances in which recordings are to be destroyed: *Huvig v France*.[100]

A law that confers wide discretionary powers may provide the necessary legal certainty provided the discretion is limited[101] and an indication is given to those likely to be affected as to how it will normally be exercised so that they can regulate their conduct accordingly.[102] Guidance can be given in non-statutory guidelines.[103] Exactly how the doctrine of legal certainty will be

---

[91] (1979) 2 EHRR 245.
[92] *PG v UK* Application 44787/98 [2002] Crim LR 308, para 62.
[93] *Malone v UK* (1984) 7 EHRR 14; *Khan v UK* (2000) 31 EHRR 45.
[94] *Sunday Times v UK* (1979) 2 EHRR 245, para 49.
[95] *R v P, C & S* (CA, 16 May 2000) para 15.
[96] *Sunday Times v UK* (1979) 2 EHRR 245, para 49.
[97] *Malone v UK* (1984) 7 EHRR 14, para 68.
[98] *Muller v Switzerland* (1988) 13 EHRR 212, para 29.
[99] *Malone v UK* (1984) 7 EHRR 14; *Valenzuela Contreras v Spain* (1998) 28 EHRR 483; *Rotaru v Romania* Application 28341/95, 8 BHRC 449, para 57.
[100] per Potter LJ, *R v P, C & S* (CA, 16 May 2000). See also *Valenzuela v Spain* (1998) 28 EHRR 483, para 46.
[101] *Leander v Sweden* (1987) 9 EHRR 433, para 55; *Rotaru v Romania* Application 28341/95, 8 BHRC 449, para 57.
[102] *Hentrich v France* (1994) 18 EHRR 440, para 42.
[103] *Silver v UK* (1983) 5 EHRR 347, para 88; *Leander v Sweden* (1987) 9 EHRR 433, para 55. cp *R (on the application of ProLife Alliance) v BBC* [2002] EWCA Civ 297; [2002] 2 All ER 756, para 56.

A. Human Rights

applied in situations of professional secrecy is necessarily speculative and may vary according to the professional relationship. In *Domenichini v Italy*[104] the ECtHR held that an Italian law which allowed a judge to authorize monitoring of correspondence between a prisoner and his lawyer without saying 'anything about the lengths of the measure or the reasons that may warrant it' infringed Article 8. When professional confidentiality is invaded the ECtHR may insist on a framework of rules regulating when, by whom, why and by what procedures interference is lawful, what may be recorded, for how long it may be retained and who has access to the information. An effective remedy against abuse of power is a likely further requirement.[105]

(2) *It serves a specific legitimate aim*
Section 8(2)[106] of the Convention allows Article 8(1) to be infringed by a public authority for the following purposes: in the interests of national security, public safety, the economic well-being of the country; the protection of health or morals, the prevention of disorder or crime or the protection of the rights of others. Prevention of disorder or crime has been held to include disclosure for the purpose of investigating and prosecuting crime[107] and the country's economic well-being includes the tax and revenue system.[108] According to Article 10(2),[109] the Article 10(1) freedom of expression may be subject to restrictions for the following purposes: in the interests of national security, territorial integrity, public safety; for the prevention of disorder or crime, protection of health or morals, protection of the reputation or rights of others, to maintain the authority and impartiality of the judiciary, for the protection of the reputation or rights of others and to prevent the disclosure of information received in confidence.[110] The ECtHR has shown greater concern about curbs on the dissemination of true information than false information[111] and about interference with the Convention rights of others

---

[104] (2001) 32 EHRR 4, para 32. The court acknowledged that it was 'impossible to attain absolute certainty in the framing of the law, and the likely outcome of any search for certainty would be excessive rigidity' but that the law left the authorities with 'too much latitude'.

[105] This is implicit in the judgment in *Tamosius v UK* [2002] STC 1307 where it was pointed out that if the Inland Revenue exceeded its powers and removed legally privileged material, the Revenue could be sued.

[106] For an analysis of Strasbourg cases in which infringement of Art 8(1) has been held to be justified see R Clayton and H Tomlinson, *The Law of Human Rights* (Oxford: 2000) 830 et seq.

[107] *Murray v UK* (1994) 19 EHRR 193; *Z v Finland* (1997) 25 EHRR 371; *R v Secretary of State for the Home Department, ex p The Kingdom of Belgium* (QBD, 15 February 2000); *R v P* [2001] 2 All ER 58, 74. The rationale may be that, unless caught, the offender may re-offend.

[108] *Lundvall v Sweden* (1985) 45 DR 121; *R v Inland Revenue Commissioners, ex p Banque Internationale a Luxembourg SA* [2000] STC 708.

[109] For an analysis of the cases in which infringement of Art 10(1) has been found justified see R Clayton and H Tomlinson, *The Law of Human Rights* (Oxford: 2000) 1079 et seq.

[110] In addition to the aims mentioned in Art 10(2), freedom of speech may be restricted under Arts 15, 16 and 17. The last contains a safeguard against subversion of Convention rights.

[111] *Markt Itern and Beermann v Germany* (1987) 11 EHRR 212, para 234.

than their non-Convention rights.[112] The high importance attached to freedom of expression, and media freedom in particular,[113] is reflected in the ECtHR's practice of construing the exceptions to Article 10(1) narrowly.[114]

(3) *It is not discriminatory*

Discriminatory interference with Convention rights is forbidden by Article 14. This article is not autonomous but has effect in relation to other Convention rights.[115] A 'distinction is discriminatory if it "has no objective and reasonable justification", that is, if it does not pursue a "legitimate aim" or if there is not a "reasonable relationship of proportionality between the means employed and the aims sought to be realized" '.[116]

(4) *It is 'necessary in a democratic society'*[117]

In *Sunday Times v UK* the ECtHR said that for an infringement of Article 10 to be justified

[i]t is not sufficient that the interference involved belongs to that class of exceptions listed in Art 10(2) which has been invoked; neither is it sufficient that the interference was imposed because its subject matter fell within a particular category . . . ; the court has to be satisfied that the interference was necessary having regard to the facts and circumstances prevailing in the specific case before it.[118]

An interference will be 'necessary' in a democratic society if

- it meets 'a pressing social need';[119] that a measure that interferes with a Convention right is useful, desirable, logical or reasonable or has been done in good faith is not enough,[120]
- the reasons adduced for encroaching on the Convention right are 'relevant and sufficient',[121]
- the restriction is proportionate to the legitimate aim pursued.[122]

---

[112] *R (on the application of ProLife Alliance) v BBC* [2002] EWCA Civ 297; [2002] 2 All ER 756, para 52.
[113] See para 3.17 above.
[114] *Vogt v Germany* (1996) 21 EHRR 205, para 52.
[115] *Van Raalte v Netherlands* (1997) 24 EHRR 503, para 33.
[116] *Marckx v Belgium* (1979–80) 2 EHRR 330, para 33.
[117] Arts 8(2) and 10(2) ECHR.
[118] (1979) 2 EHRR 245, para 65.
[119] *Handyside v UK* (1976) 1 EHRR 737, para 48; *Att-Gen v Guardian Newspapers (No 2)* [1988] 3 All ER 545, 660; *Vogt v Germany* (1996) 21 EHRR 205.
[120] *Sunday Times v UK* (1979) 2 EHRR 245, para 59. See also *R v Secretary of State for the Home Department, ex p Daly* [2001] UKHL 26; [2001] 2 AC 532, para 27.
[121] *Goodwin v UK* (1996) 22 EHRR 123, para 45; *Z v Finland* (1997) 25 EHRR 371, para 94. cp *Anne-Marie Andersson v Sweden* (1998) 25 EHRR 722.
[122] *Ashworth v MGN* [2001] 1 All ER 99, 1009. See also *R v Secretary of State for the Home Department, ex p Daly* [2001] UKHL 26; [2001] 2 AC 532, para 27.

A. Human Rights

Proportionality

The nature of the proportionality test

To decide whether a response is proportionate is not to engage in a review of the merits of the act, rule or decision but it 'may require the reviewing court to assess the balance which the decision maker has struck, not merely whether it is within the range of rational or reasonable decisions'.[123] The balance referred to is that between 'the demands of the general interest of the community and the requirements of the protection of the individual's fundamental rights'.[124] Lord Steyn[125] has endorsed the three-stage test formulated by Lord Clyde in the Privy Council whereby the court asks: **3.20**

> whether (i) the . . . objective is sufficiently important to justify limiting a fundamental right; (ii) the measures designed to meet the . . . objective are rationally connected to it; and (iii) the means used to impair the right or freedom are no more than is necessary to accomplish the objective.[126]

Such an assessment involves the court in determining the relative weight of competing interests[127] and to that extent judicial human rights decisions are political.

Factors affecting proportionality in relation to an interference with Article 8(1)

A court conducting a proportionality review of an infringement of professional confidentiality will be interested in some or all of the following: **3.21**

- whether the interference goes beyond the minimum necessary to achieve the stated objective;[128]
- availability of the information from another source;[129]
- whether the decision-making process is procedurally unfair;[130]

---

[123] per Lord Steyn, *R v Secretary of State for the Home Department, ex p Daly* [2001] UKHL 26, [2001] 2 AC 532, para 27.
[124] *Sporrong v Sweden* (1982) 5 EHRR 35, para 69. See also *Brown v Stott* [2001] 2 All ER 97, 130.
[125] *R v Secretary of State for the Home Department, ex p Daly* [2001] UKHL 26; [2001] 2 AC 532, para 27.
[126] *De Freitas v Permanent Secretary of Ministry of Agriculture, Fisheries, Lands and Housing* [1999] 1 AC 69, 80.
[127] *R v Secretary of State for the Home Department, ex p Daly* [2001] UKHL 26; [2001] 2 AC 532, para 27.
[128] *Campbell v UK* (1993) 15 EHRR 137, para 48; *Z v Finland* (1997) 25 EHRR 371, para 103; *MS v Sweden* (1999) 28 EHRR 313, para 43. cp *Anne-Marie Andersson v Sweden* (1998) 25 EHRR 722.
[129] *Vereniging Weekblad 'Bluf' v Netherlands* (1995) 20 EHRR 189, para 44; *Fressoz v France* (2000) 31 EHRR 2, para 53.
[130] *TP v UK* Application 28945/95 (20 May 2001) para 72. cp *Z v Finland* (1997) 25 EHRR 371, para 101.

- safeguards against abuse of the power to compel disclosure[131] and misuse of information that has been compelled;[132]
- availability of a remedy if professional confidentiality is unjustifiably infringed;[133]
- reason for the interference—courts are more deferential to claims of interference on grounds of national security than the pursuit of some other public interests, for instance, tax collection;[134]
- effect, if any, on freedom of expression, particularly media freedom;[135]
- extent to which the information is disseminated;[136]
- measures that interfere with confidential communications with lawyers require particularly compelling justification;[137]
- the financial burden of disclosure on the professional;
- sensitivity of the information and the impact of its disclosure on the client.[138]

3.22 The last factor is an important one. In *Dudgeon v UK*,[139] a case concerning sexual orientation, the ECtHR said that the more intimate the aspect of private life that is interfered with, the more serious must be the reasons for legitimate interference.[140] In *Z v Finland*[141] the ECtHR held that protecting the confidentiality of the applicant's HIV seropositive status should have had priority over the transparency of the criminal proceedings against her husband.[142] *MGN Ltd v Attard*[143] is a case at the other extreme. The case arose from an application by MGN Ltd to publish photographs of the surviving Siamese twin without the consent of the

---

[131] *Malone v UK* (1984) 7 EHRR 14, 45; *Khan v UK* (2001) 31 EHRR 45. Independent assessment of whether an intercepted communication was protected by legal professional privilege was required in *Kopp v Switzerland* (1999) 27 EHRR 527, paras 73–75.

[132] cp *X v UK* (1982) 30 DR 239; *Anne-Marie Andersson v Sweden* (1998) 25 EHRR 722; *Z v Finland* (1997) 25 EHRR 371, para 102; *MS v Sweden* (1999) 28 EHRR 313, para 43; *Huvig v France* (1990) 12 EHRR 528.

[133] *Tamosius v UK* [2002] STC 1307, where the ECtHR pointed out that the Inland Revenue could be sued if it seized items subject to legal professional privilege.

[134] See para 10.14 below. D Feldman, 'Information and Privacy' in J Beatson and Y Cripps (eds), *Freedom of Expression and Freedom of Information: Essays in Honour of Sir David Williams* (Oxford: 2000) 312.

[135] See para 3.17 above.

[136] See *K & T v Finland* (1994) 76A DR 140, 150–151 where there was a complaint about disclosure of intimate details of the applicant's sex life to people outside the social welfare administration. This was not pursued before the ECtHR. See also *Peck v UK* Application 44647/98, 28 January 2003, para 62.

[137] *Niemietz v Germany* (1992) 16 EHRR 97, para 37; *Foxley v UK* (2001) 31 EHRR 25, para 44.

[138] cp *Leander v Sweden* (1987) 9 EHRR 433 where disclosure impacted on the applicant's employment prospects. See also *Peck v UK* Application 44647/98, 28 January 2003.

[139] (1982) 4 EHRR 149, para 52.

[140] See also *Douglas v Hello! Ltd* [2001] 2 All ER 289, para 168.

[141] (1997) 25 EHRR 371, paras 78, 113.

[142] The Finnish courts had been wrong to refuse to suppress the applicant's medical records for longer than 10 years and the Court of Appeal was wrong to disclose in the text of its judgment that she was HIV seropositive and name her. The judgment was made available to the press and given widespread publicity.

[143] 19 October 2001. Judgment was given in open court.

parents. The newspaper had obtained photographs of Jodie taken in a pram being pushed along a highway in Malta by her mother. Connell J described the interference with Jodie's right to privacy as 'minimal' and said that if he had jurisdiction in the case, he would allow publication: 'although anyone who sees them in the press might be able to identify Jodie if they were particularly observant over the next two or three months, those photographs are unlikely so clearly to reveal her appearance that she will be immediately recognizable thereafter'. A court can also be expected to adopt a less protective attitude to private financial information, especially in the case of a public figure.[144] In *Fressoz v France*[145] the ECtHR found a violation of Article 10 in the conviction of journalists for handling stolen photocopies of a tax assessment that had been leaked in breach of professional confidentiality by an unknown public servant working for the French tax authorities. The ECtHR noted that under the Court of Cassation's case law, publication of a person's income or assets, especially if that person exercised public or quasi-public functions, was not an interference with Article 8 at all.[146]

Interference with Article 6

Right to a fair trial

3.23 There is no provision in the Convention for interference with the Article 6(1) right to a fair hearing: 'the right to a fair trial is absolute in its terms and the public interest can never be invoked to deny that right to anybody under any circumstances.'[147] Though the right may be absolute, its contents is not fixed. 'What a fair trial requires cannot . . . be the subject of a single unvarying rule or collection of rules. It is proper to take account of the facts and circumstances of particular cases.'[148] Human rights jurisprudence allows pre-trial disclosure of documents and the way the trial is conducted to be adjusted to accommodate the legitimate privacy concerns of individuals (be they parties or non-parties), so long as the accommodation does not cause disproportionate interference with the fair trial interests of any of the litigants,[149] particularly, in a criminal trial, those of the defence.[150] Article 6 is 'result-focused. In criminal proceedings, the

---

[144] This is borne out by Lord Levy's failure to obtain an injunction to prevent disclosure of his tax bill in the Sunday Times: *Lord Levy v Times Newspapers Ltd* (HC, 23 June 2000).
[145] (2000) 31 EHRR 2.
[146] (2000) 31 EHRR 2, para 56.
[147] per Lord Hope, *Brown v Stott* [2001] 2 All ER 97, 129.
[148] per Lord Bingham, *Brown v Stott* [2001] 2 All ER 97, 106. See also *R v Forbes* [2001] 1 All ER 686, 697; *R v A* [2001] 3 All ER 1, 15.
[149] *Re B* [2001] 2 FLR 1017: '[t]here may accordingly be circumstances in which, balancing a party's prima facie art 6 right to see all the relevant documents and the art 8 rights of others, the balance can compatibly with the Convention be struck in such a way as to permit the withholding from a party of some at least of the documents.' per Munby J, para 67.
[150] *MK v Austria* (1997) 24 EHRR CD 59, 60–61; *Doorson v Netherlands* (1996) 22 EHRR 330 para 3; *Van Mechelen v Netherlands* (1998) 25 EHRR 647, para 56. cp *R v A* [2001] UKHL 25; [2002] 1 AC 45, para 38.

Chapter 3: The Legal Framework

ultimate question must be whether the right [of the defence to a fair trial] is still effective.'[151]

Right to a public hearing

3.24 The fact that the fairness standard is not something to be evaluated without regard to affected privacy interests is underscored by the second part of Article 6(1) which deals with the conduct of hearings in public. The right to a 'public hearing' may be violated on grounds that include 'the interest of morals', the 'interests of juveniles' and 'the protection of the private life of the parties'.[152] Interestingly, there is no express mention of interference for the purpose of safeguarding the reputations and private lives of adult third parties. This has not stopped the ECtHR from approving a private hearing to protect the right to private life of a third party about whom a professional is compelled to give evidence in breach of professional confidentiality.[153]

Communications with lawyers

3.25 Limited qualification of the constituent rights of a fair trial is acceptable 'if reasonably directed by national authorities towards a clear and proper public objective and if representing no greater qualification than the situation calls for'.[154]

When Convention Rights Collide

Conflicting Convention rights and proportionality

3.26 The right to respect for private life (Article 8(1)) may collide with the right to life (Article 2) or prohibition on torture (Article 3) or, more frequently, the right to freedom of expression (Article 10(1)) or to a fair trial (Article 6(1)). Of these rights, the prohibition on torture, the right to a fair trial and, for current purposes, the right to life are absolute. How is such conflict to be handled? The Convention does not rank the rights that it gives: all are of equal value.[155] '[W]here one right clashes with another right it is necessary to find a "reasonable balance".'[156] In *N v Sweden* the Commission commented that 'where a question arises of interference with private life through publication in mass media, the state must find a proper

---

[151] Law Commission Report 273, *Evidence of Bad Character in Criminal Proceedings* (Cm 5257, 2001) para 3.28.
[152] Art 6(1).
[153] See para 17.37 below.
[154] per Lord Bingham, *Brown v Stott* [2001] 2 All ER 97, 115. cp *R (on the application of Canaan) v Governor of HMP Full Sutton* [2003] EWHC 97 Admin.
[155] Council of Europe Resolution 1165 (1998), *Right to privacy*, para 11; *Campbell v Frisbee* [2002] EWHC 328; [2002] EMLR 31, para 24; *Cream Holdings Ltd v Banerjee* [2003] CA Civ 103, para 51.
[156] F Tulkens, 'Freedom of expression and information in a democratic society and the right to privacy under the ECHR . . .', p 33 of a paper presented to Strasbourg Conference on *Freedom of expression and the right to privacy*, 23 September 1999, available from http://www.humanrights.coe.int/media. See also J Craig and N Nolte, 'Privacy and Free Speech in Germany and Canada: Lessons for an English Privacy Tort' [1998] European Human Rights L Rev 162, 165.

balance between the two Convention rights, namely the right to respect for private life guaranteed by Article 8 and the right to freedom of expression guaranteed by Article 10 of the Convention'.[157] This balance must be achieved in the light of the facts of the particular case.

In *Douglas v Hello! Ltd* the Court of Appeal acknowledged that the right to respect for private life is not subordinate to freedom of expression[158] and, by implication, any other right. **3.27**

> By virtue of s.12(1) and (4) [of the HRA] the qualifications set out in art. 10(2) are as relevant as the right set out in art. 10(1). This means, for example, the reputations and rights of others—not only but not least their convention rights—are as material as the defendant's right of free expression . . . [S].12 of the 1998 requires the court to have regard to art. 10 . . . this cannot . . . give the art 10(1) right to freedom of expression a presumptive priority over other rights. What it does require the court to consider is art 10(2) along with 10(1), and by doing so bring into the frame the conflicting right to privacy. This right, contained in art 8 and reflected in English law, is in turn qualified in both contexts by the right of others to free expression. The outcome, which self evidently has to be the same under both articles, is determined principally by considerations of proportionality.[159]

Strictly speaking, this analysis describes how an interference permitted by Article 10(2) is to be justified and not how a conflict between Articles 8(1) and 10(1) is to be resolved.[160] 'In the presence of the "logical contradiction of two conflicting provisions of the same international instrument", it is not the principle of proportionality that should be applied.'[161] It is true that the language of Articles 8(2) and 10(2) each bring in the competing rights contained within the other Article by mentioning protection of the rights of others, but it does not follow that the courts should apply a proportionality test to resolve conflict between the two articles. Proportionality is relevant in determining whether what is complained of interferes with each of these rights[162] but once it has been decided that it does a solution to the conflict must be found—as in the case of conflict between two absolute rights—elsewhere. There is no mention of proportionality in Lord Woolf's description of the balancing process in *A v B plc & C*. **3.28**

---

[157] (1986) 50 DR 173, 175. Cp Council of Europe, Resolution 1165 (1998) para 10.
[158] This view was expressed in Parliament by the Home Secretary too: *Hansard* HC vol 315, col 542 (2 July 1998).
[159] per Sedley LJ, *Douglas v Hello! Ltd* [2001] 2 All ER 289, para 136. For criticism of this analysis of the effect of HRA, s12 see P Plowden, 'Right to Privacy' [2001] J of Civil Liberties 57, 68–69.
[160] But see *Tammer v Estonia* Application 41205/98, 10 BHRC 543, paras 69–70.
[161] F Tulkens, 'Freedom of expression and information in a democratic society and the right to privacy under the ECHR . . .', p 32 of a paper presented to Strasbourg Conference on *Freedom of expression and the right to privacy*, 23 September 1999, available from http://www.humanrights.coe.int/media.
[162] If the court can be persuaded that, say, disclosure of certain personal information about the applicant in a media soundbite has not in fact interfered with Art 8 then the collision between Arts 8 and 10 is avoided. cp paras 16.50–16.51 below.

There is a tension between the two articles which requires the court to hold the balance between the conflicting interests they are designed to protect. This is not an easy task but it can be achieved by the courts if, when holding the balance, they attach proper weight to the important rights both articles are designed to protect. Each article is qualified expressly in a way which allows the interests under the other article to be taken into account.[163]

Sedley LJ himself commented in *Douglas v Hello! Ltd*[164] that the outcome 'self-evidently has to be the same under both articles'. This is not possible if a conflict between Convention rights 'is determined principally by considerations of proportionality'.[165] Outcome will be determined whichever right is selected as the starting point for the proportionality analysis.[166] If it is Article 8, the incursion into respect for private life must be minimized. If it is Article 10, interference with freedom of expression must be kept to a minimum. It is not possible to minimize both since minimizing one occurs at the expense of minimizing the other.

Achieving an appropriate balance between Articles 8 and 10

3.29 When a court is asked to strike a balance between two Convention rights it must, in effect, decide where the greater public interest lies. This is essentially a political question. Because of the importance attached to freedom of expression, and press freedom in particular,[167] the ECtHR and the English courts insist on convincing reasons and probative evidence that it is necessary to circumscribe freedom of expression to achieve some greater public good.

> [A]n interference with the exercise of press freedom cannot be compatible with art. 10 . . . unless it is justified by an overriding requirement in the public interest.[168]

> If freedom of expression is to be impeded . . . it must be on cogent grounds recognized by law.[169]

> There are a large number of recent cases where the importance, and sometimes the 'primacy' of the right of freedom of expression is underlined . . .[170]

3.30 The ECtHR generally favours press freedom where the publication is of public (usually political) interest and a conflict with another Convention right has

---

[163] [2002] EWCA Civ 337; [2002] 3 WLR 542.
[164] [2001] 2 All ER 289, para 137.
[165] ibid. Munby J fell into the same trap in *Clibbery v Allan* [2001] 2 FLR 819, para 140. See also *Jockey Club v BBC* [2002] EWHC 1866, QB, para 57.
[166] M Tugendhat and I Christie (eds), *The Law of Privacy and the Media* (Oxford: 2002) para 10.64.
[167] See para 3.17 above.
[168] *Fressoz v France* (2000) 31 EHRR 2, para 51. This condition was satisfied in *Z v Switzerland* Application 10343/83 (1983) 35 DR 224.
[169] per Sedley LJ, *Douglas v Hello! Ltd* [2001] 2 All ER 289, para 136.
[170] per Gray J, *Jockey Club v BBC* [2002] EWHC 1866, QB.

A. Human Rights

arisen, but very few of the cases have involved Article 8.[171] In Resolution 1165 (1998), which the Court of Appeal has described as 'useful guidance',[172] the Council of Europe said that press freedom must sometimes give way to respect for private life. The two relevant resolutions are:

- '[T]the right to privacy afforded by Article 8 . . . should not only protect an individual against interference by public authorities, but also against interference by private persons or institutions, including the mass media.'[173]
- 'Editors and journalists should be rendered liable for invasions of privacy by their publications, as they are for libel.'[174]

Domestically, press freedom has been trumped by the right to respect for private life in conjunction with the right to life (Article 2) and the prohibition on torture (Article 3). This was in *Venables v NGN Ltd*,[175] where publication of the new identities and whereabouts of the applicants was thought to carry a 'real and serious risk'[176] to their lives.[177]

A real risk of physical harm is not essential for the right to respect for private life to take priority over that of freedom of expression. As long ago as 1981, Lord Denning said that the right to keep highly confidential information confidential may 'be so important that it takes priority over the freedom of the press. An injunction may be granted restraining the newspaper from breaking the confidence. The principle is well expressed in art 10(2) of the European Convention. It recognizes that the freedom of expression may be restricted whenever a restriction is "necessary in a democratic society . . . for preventing the disclosure of information received in confidence".'[178] An English court has held that freedom of expression

3.31

---

[171] Two cases with a privacy angle in which press freedom won the day are *Fressoz v France* (2001) 31 EHRR 28 and *Krone Verlag GmBH v Austria* Application 34315/96 (21 March 2002). But there are other cases in which it has not: *A Neves v Portugal* Applicaton 20683/92 (20 February 1995); *Tammer v Estonia* Application 41205/98, 10 BHRC 543, para 68.

[172] *A v B plc & C ('Flitcroft')* [2002] EWCA Civ 337; [2002] 3 WLR 542, para 11, guideline xii.

[173] para 12.

[174] para 14(ii).

[175] [2001] 1 All ER 908.

[176] [2001] 1 All ER 908, para 86.

[177] Credible threats had been made to harm the applicants who were about to be released from detention which was the result of their having committed a particularly horrible murder of a toddler when they were 10 years old. In *Mills v NGN Ltd* [2001] EMLR 957 relief was refused because the judge considered the evidence of a real risk to the applicant to be 'very slight' (para 34). In *Beckham v MGN Ltd* (QBD, 28 June 2001) security concerns influenced the court. On how to handle a risk of physical injury through loss of privacy see also *Douglas v Hello! Ltd* [2001] 2 All ER 289, paras 134–135.

[178] *Schering Chemicals v Falkman Ltd* [1981] 2 All ER 321, 333. Note that in *Jockey Club v BBC* [2002] EWHC 1866, para 57 one of the factors that led Grey J to sanction disclosure of confidential documents about corruption in the horse racing industry was that the claimant was 'a public authority . . . rather than an individual seeking to protect personal or private information . . .'.

must give way to respect for private life if disclosure of the identity of litigants would nullify an injunction for breach of confidence or pre-empt the decision of the court.[179] Beyond breach of confidence situations, the Family Court in the exercise of its paternal jurisdiction regularly restrains publication of information concerning the upbringing of a child to protect the child's privacy and this is unlikely to change.[180] Further guidance on how to reconcile conflict between the two rights is available in the Strasbourg jurisprudence. In *Markt Intern and Beermann v Germany* the ECtHR noted that 'even the publication of items which are true and describe real events may under certain circumstances be prohibited: the obligation to respect the privacy of others or the duty to respect the confidentiality of certain commercial information are examples'.[181] In *A Neves v Portugal*[182] a photographer alleged a breach of Article 10 because he had been convicted of defamation and invasion of privacy for publishing photographs of well-known businessmen engaging in sexual activity. An application was rejected as manifestly ill-founded. In *Tammer v Estonia*[183] the ECtHR unanimously held that the conviction of a journalist for publishing an interview with a fellow journalist that contained insulting remarks[184] about aspects of the private life of the wife of a politician was compatible with Article 10; the journalist could have 'formulated his criticism . . . without resorting to such insulting expressions'.[185]

3.32 Lord Woolf has said that in the event that the Article 8 and 10 rights are in balance,[186] relief against the media should be refused.[187] Press freedom is treasured more, all things being equal, than respect for private life.[188]

---

[179] *H (A Healthcare Worker) v Associated Newspapers Ltd* [2002] EWCA Civ 195; [2002] EMLR 23, para 43.

[180] *X CC v A* [1985] 1 All ER 53 (the Mary Bell case); *Re C* [1989] 2 All ER 791; *Re M* [1990] 1 All ER 205; *Re W* [1992] 1 All ER 794. See also *R v Central Independent Television plc* [1994] 3 All ER 641. In *MGN Ltd v Attard* (Fam Div, 19 October 2001) the likelihood of financial loss to Jodie did not deter Connell J from deciding that MGN should be allowed to publish photographs of the child where interference with her privacy was minimal because the photographs were not very clear and the baby's growth was likely to make her unrecognizable within two or three months. The judge was influenced by the fact 'that Jodie's situation has been placed in the public domain (a) because of her unfortunate circumstances, but (b) also because of the cooperation of her family' with certain newspapers who for reward were allowed to print photographs and interviews with the parents.

[181] (1989) 12 EHRR 161, para 35. Also (1989) 11 EHRR 313, para 235.

[182] Application 20683/92 (20 February 1995) as to which see S Naismith, 'Photographs, Privacy and Freedom of Expression' [1996] European Human Rights L Rev 150, 156–157.

[183] Application 41205/98, 10 BHRC 543; see para 8.23 below.

[184] 'A person breaking up another's marriage . . . an unfit and careless mother deserting her child . . . It does not seem to be the best example for young girls.'

[185] Application 41205/98, 10 BHRC 543, para 67.

[186] Since there are no rules for determining how much weight each right attracts, it is within the discretion of the judge to either produce or avoid a situation of balance.

[187] *A v B plc & C ('Flitcroft')* [2002] EWCA Civ 337; [2002] 3 WLR 542, para 12.

[188] Press freedom is described by Lord Phillips MR in *H (A Healthcare Worker) v Associated Newspapers Ltd* [2002] EWCA Civ 195; [2002] EMLR 23, para 32 as 'of paramount importance'.

B. Legislating About Confidentiality

Compulsory Disclosure

Legislation compelling disclosure of confidential personal information

3.33 There is now a considerable miscellany of legislation that allows obligations of professional confidentiality to be ignored by officials who need access to information either about a client or about a professional. Major pieces of legislation include the Police and Criminal Evidence Act 1984 which governs police powers of search and seizure and the Regulation of Investigatory Powers Act 2000 which makes provision for intrusive and directed surveillance and interception of communications by public officials. The impact of these two statutes on professional confidentiality is examined in chapter 14.

Forms of compulsion

3.34 There are many other measures that allow officials to extract confidential information from professionals about their clients in particular circumstances.[189] Mostly the empowering legislation allows this without application to a court.[190] Statutory disclosure powers come in various guises.

Orders to produce documents or information This kind of provision is common.[191] In August 2000 the General Medical Council acquired the power to force a medical practitioner who is not herself under investigation or 'any other person' to supply information or produce documents to assist the Council, or any of its committees, to carry out its functions in respect of professional conduct, professional performance or fitness to practise.[192] There are exemptions for information that would not have to be disclosed to a court in civil proceedings[193] and information the disclosure of which 'is prohibited . . . under any other enactment'.[194] The Taxes Management Act 1970, s 20(3)[195] enables the Inland Revenue to issue

---

[189] eg Charities Act 1993, s 9(1); Companies Act 1985, s 434(2); Companies Act 1989, ss 83(2), 84, Sch 14, pt 1, s 4(2); National Audit Act 1983, s 8; Health and Safety Act 1974, s 20; Housing Act 1996, s 30; Nationality Immigration and Asylum Act 2002, s 135.

[190] For cases in which a court order is required see Insolvency Act 1986, ss 236, 366, Proceeds of Crime Act 2002, ss 345, 357, 370.

[191] Even the Information Commissioner has such powers: DPA, s 44. By a recent addition to the public sector's armoury of compulsory disclosure powers, when the Treasury makes a freezing order under the Anti-Terrorism, Crime and Security Act 2001 it may include provisions requiring disclosure of information and production of documents (see Sch 6, paras 5 and 6).

[192] Medical Act 1983, s 35A(1). Medical information may also have to be produced under Commission for Health Improvement Functions (Regulations) 2000, SI 2000/662, reg 18.

[193] Medical Act 1983, s 35A(6).

[194] Medical Act 1983, s 35A(4).

[195] See also Income and Corporation Taxes Act 1988, s 767C by which documents may be required from third parties for the purpose of determining whether, in connection with a change in ownership of a company, the previous owner was liable for outstanding corporation tax liability. This information required is unlikely to be personal.

production notices to third parties—typically bankers, brokers, lawyers and other professional advisers—requiring production of documents relevant to a taxpayer's tax liability. In one case the Inland Revenue[196] demanded that a taxpayer's solicitor[196a] provide 'all correspondence, tax messages, telexes, notes of meetings and telephone conversations' with the taxpayer within the previous six years.[197] Moses J was unmoved by the firm's complaint that its client was not legally bound to reimburse the firm's expenses. Section 19A of the same Act permits inspectors looking into the tax affairs of a professional to require production of documents. In one case it was used by the Revenue to compel access to client ledgers, client cash books and various supporting documents for the purpose of determining a solicitor's personal tax liability.[198]

3.36 Reporting requirements A statutory reporting requirement obliges the professional to pass on information without a specific request.[199] Reporting obligations are a feature of the medical profession. Under legislation that can be traced back to the nineteenth century, doctors have an obligation to report food poisoning and thirty diseases or disease groups including cholera, plague, TB, measles, mumps, acute meningitis and small pox (but not AIDS) to the Public Health Laboratory Service.[200] A doctor must give notice of the termination of a pregnancy, including the name and address of the woman concerned, to the relevant Chief Medical Officer.[201] Occupational health practitioners have to report serious work accidents[202] and doctors doing organ transplant work must report details of donors and recipients.[203] The other professions are not immune from reporting obligations. Many professionals are potentially affected by the terrorism reporting requirements[204] and the obligation to pass on suspicions

---

[196] An inspector cannot give notice to a barrister, advocate or solicitor but s 20B(3) allows the Board to do so. This power can be delegated (in theory) to a junior officer: *R v Inland Revenue Commissioners, ex p Ulster Bank Ltd* [2000] STC 537.

[196a] Bankers and stockbrokers (eg *TC Coombs & Co v Inland Revenue Commissioners* [1991] 3 All ER 623) are also popular targets amongst professionals.

[197] *R v Inland Revenue Commissioners, ex p Davis Frankel & Mead (a firm)*, The Times, 11 July 2000.

[198] *Guyer v Walton* [2001] STC (SCD) 75. See also 'Confidentiality Fear', LS Gaz, 9 June 1999.

[199] Reporting provisions are relatively uncommon and where found may not require disclosure of personal information. For example, the auditors of regulated financial institutions are required to pass on information about irregularities to the industry regulator. See Y Cripps, 'New Statutory Duties of Disclosure for Auditors in the Regulated Financial Sector' (1996) 112 LQR 667.

[200] Public Health (Control of Disease) Act 1984; Public Health, England and Wales (Infectious Disease) Regulations 1988. A health professional who is responsible for running a community home, voluntary house or registered children's home is required by the Children's Homes Regulations 1991, SI 1991/1506, reg 19 to report child abuse to the local authority.

[201] Abortion Regulations 1991, SI 1991/499, reg 4.

[202] Health and Safety at Work Act 1974; Reporting of Injuries, Diseases and Dangerous Occurrences Regulations 1985, SI 1985/2023.

[203] Human Organ Transplants Act 1989, s 3; Human Organ Transplants (Supply of Information) Regulations 1989, SI 1989/2108.

[204] Terrorism Act 2000, ss 19, 21A, 38B.

B. Legislating About Confidentiality

of money-laundering.[205] The money-laundering provisions are considered in chapter 10.

Powers of entry Entry powers allow an official to go into premises uninvited without a warrant[206] for the purpose of obtaining information[207] and, in some instances, to carry out an inspection.[208] Officials of the Health and Safety Executive and local authorities have extensive powers of entry and inspection under the Health and Safety at Work Act 1974[209] and carry out 'pro-active' visits without prior notice.[210] For the purpose of enforcing safety legislation, once on premises officials can demand the production, inspection, and copying of documents, and question persons found there whom it is reasonable to suppose can provide answers to relevant questions.[211] It is an offence to contravene any requirement imposed by an inspector.[212] There is no exemption for health professionals and medical records. Thus an occupational health professional may have to supply information about the medical condition of employees in her care. 3.37

Powers of oral examination The Disability, Sex Discrimination and Race Relations Commissions, when conducting a formal investigation, may serve a notice on 'any person' requiring that person 'to attend and give oral information about any matter specified in the notice' as well as to produce documents.[213] Information that would not have to be disclosed in civil proceedings is exempt.[214] Other Acts conferring power to require a person to attend under compulsion to provide information (in some cases on oath) include the Explosive Substances Act 3.38

---

[205] See para 10.24 below.
[206] Powers of entry pursuant to warrant by the police and others are examined in ch 14.
[207] eg Child Support Act 1991, s 15(4) gives an inspector power to enter premises used for the purpose of carrying on a profession to make such examination and inquiry there as he considers appropriate. By s 15(6) he may require any person carrying on a profession from the premises to 'furnish . . . all such information and documents as the inspector may reasonably require'. See also Commission for Health Improvement (Functions) Regulations 2000, SI 2000/662, reg 17 and Children Act 1989, s 80(5), (7).
[208] eg Misuse of Drugs Act 1971, s 23(1); Mental Health Act 1983, s 115; Children Act 1989, s 80; Education Act 1997, s 40; Money Laundering Regulations 2001, SI 2001/3641, reg 10; National Care Standards Commission (Inspection of Schools and Colleges) Regulations 2002, SI 2002/552. The Secretary of State is empowered by Health Act 1999, s 23 to make regulations conferring on persons authorized by the Commissioner for Health Improvement the power to enter NHS premises to inspect those premises and require prescribed persons at such places to produce documents or information.
[209] Health and Safety at Work Act 1974, s 20.
[210] JUSTICE briefing to the Data Protection Bill, 20 April 1998, 11.
[211] Health and Safety at Work Act 1974, s 20(2)(j), (k).
[212] Health and Safety at Work Act 1974, s 33.
[213] Race Relations Act 1976, s 50(1)(b); Sex Discrimination Act 1975, s 59(1)(b); Disability Rights Commission Act 1999, s 4 (1)(b).
[214] Race Relations Act 1976, s 50(3)(a); Sex Discrimination Act 1975, s 58(3)(a); Disability Rights Commission Act 1999, s 4(3)(a).

1883,[215] Official Secrets Act 1920,[216] Companies Act 1985,[217] Financial Services Act 1986,[218] the Financial Services and Markets Act 2000,[219] and the Local Government Act 2000.[220]

Effect on professional confidentiality

3.39 Every provision allowing coercive disclosure, not matter how compelling the reasons for it, diminishes professional confidentiality.

> In any given instance, the public interest will seem overriding; yet in the long run protection of the interest of every individual in privacy will have gone by default; the piecemeal erosion of the privilege may never have been halted, to take an overall view of the total consequences. In this respect privacy resembles environmental values; the particular damage rarely seems sufficient to outweigh the promised benefits, but the cumulative consequences may be disastrous.[221]

Data-sharing

3.40 Confidential client information that has been supplied, whether voluntarily or under compulsion, by a professional to a public servant may be passed from one official to another without reference back to the professional or her client under a host of statutory provisions.[222] Statutory data-sharing provisions are supplemented by common law powers to exchange personal information.[223] Toulson

---

[215] s 6.

[216] s 6.

[217] This allows for officials appointed to investigate the affairs of a company (s 432) or share dealings by director's families (s 446) to examine the company's agents, including its bankers, solicitors and auditors, on oath (ss 434(3), 446). The DTI proposes to widen the power of oral examination by allowing investigators appointed to conduct a confidential fact-finding investigation under s 447 to require any person with relevant information to attend before them and provide information, material or an explanation: DTI, *Company Investigations: Powers for the Twenty-first Century* (October 2001) para 74.

[218] s 177(3).

[219] s 173.

[220] An ethical standards officer investigating an alleged breach of a code of conduct within a local authority may require 'any person' to appear before him to provide information (s 62(1)).

[221] S Benn, 'The Protection and Limitation of Privacy' (1978) 52 *Australian LJ* 686, 691.

[222] Statutes that permit onward transmission of confidential information without consent include Finance Act 1972, s 127; Local Government Act 1974, s 29; Children Act 1989, ss 27, 42(1), 47; Security Service Act 1989, s 4(4); Social Security Administration Act 1992, s 122; Intelligence Services Act 1994, s 8(4); Finance Act 1997, s 110; Access to Justice Act 1999, s 94; Financial Services and Markets Act 2000, s 350; Tax Credit Act 2002, Sch 5, paras 4, 6; Crime and Disorder Act 1998, s 115; Representation of the People (England and Wales) Regulations 2001, SI 2001/341, reg 23; Proceeds of Crime Act 2002, ss 436, 438. The *Draft Data Protection and Personal Information Code of Practice* (1999) para 11.3 contains a long list of persons and bodies to whom social services departments will disclose confidential personal information either on a discretionary basis or because of a legal obligation.

[223] Prison governors have a non-statutory duty to share information about sex offenders (including information about spend convictions): *R (on the application of N) v Governor of HM Prison Dartmoor* [2001] EWHC Admin 93. An education authority has a lawful interest in receiving information about an applicant for a teaching post from the police: *R (on the application of A) v Chief Constable of C* [2001] 1 WLR 461. Councillors have a common law right to inspect information in

B. Legislating About Confidentiality

and Phipps liken the possibilities of public sector data-sharing (which are constantly being increased) to the permutations on a football pool coupon.[224] From the standpoint of the client or professional, it makes no difference whether onward transmission is required by law or is by voluntary act; it is done without their consent. The disclosure may be for purposes entirely unrelated to the purpose for which the information was collected.[225] For example,[226] the Criminal Cases Review Commission, when conducting an investigation into an alleged miscarriage of justice, may require under Criminal Appeal Act 1995, s 17 *any* public body to produce '*any* document or other material which may assist the Commission in the exercise of any of [its] functions'.[227] The Commission has used this power to obtain sensitive information about intra-family sexual assaults from local authorities.[228] As a further unexpected consequence of secondary disclosure some of the protection provided under the legislation that compelled or allowed its original disclosure may be lost.

Non-disclosure

The legislation

Data Protection Act 1998

By far the most important statutory provisions restricting the disclosure of personal information are the HRA, which has already been described,[229] and the

3.41

---

the possession of an authority if it is reasonably necessary for the proper performance of the councillor's duties: *R v Birmingham City Council, ex p O* [1983] 1 All ER 497. See also Ogden, 'Councillors win right to see ritual files', *Social Work Today*, 27 August 1992, 18–19.

[224] R Toulson and C Phipps, *Confidentiality* (London: 1996) 99.

[225] The original disclosure by the professional may have been either permissive or under statutory compulsion.

[226] Further examples are found in Child Support (Information, Evidence and Disclosure) Regulations 1992, SI 1992/1812, reg 2(2)(d); *Re R* [2000] 2 FLR 751; Terrorism Act 2000, s 38B, Tax Credits Act 2002, Sch 5, paras 5, 7, 8, 9, 10. Regulation of Investigatory Powers Act 2000, s 22(2) envisages disclosure of communications data for much wider purposes than its retention is permitted under Anti-Terrorism Crime and Security Act 2002, s 102(3) (see para 14.105 below). Youth Courts have statutory authority under the Children and Young Persons Act 1969, s 9 and Magistrates' Courts (Children and Young Persons) Rules 1992, SI 1992/2071, r 10 to require an educational authority to produce a school report for sentencing purposes based on school records which were compiled for quite another purpose from information supplied *inter alia* by teachers and others. Guidance on the content of the report is set out in the Judicial Studies Board's *Youth Court Bench Book* para 7.20 (http://www.jsboard.co.uk/magistrates/index.htm). Apart from educational data, it may disclose family or health information on a need-to-know basis and incorporate information from other agencies. Note that school information should also appear in the pre-sentence report prepared pursuant to the Criminal Justice Act 1991: S Ball and J Connolly, 'Requiring School Attendance: A Little Used Sentencing Power' [1999] Crim LR 183.

[227] Italics added.

[228] L Elks, 'Disclosure by local authorities: An examination of the Criminal Appeal Act 1995' [2000] J of Local Government 32, 34.

[229] See para 3.02 above.

notoriously complex DPA, which governs all processing of data relating to living individuals that is contained in structured manual records and in computer records.[230] Details of this legislation can be found in chapters 18 and 19. The DPA does not prohibit the disclosure of personal data without consent (known in German constitutional law as informational self-determination)[231] but it regulates the circumstances in which disclosure can lawfully take place, requires notification of the data subject, lays down requirements of data quality and limits third-country transmission of personal data. Data protection principles can be ignored only in so far as exemptions in the DPA (and its subordinate legislation)[232] or a more recent statute allow.[233] Failure to do so, however, is not a criminal offence. The DPA gives the client important rights:

- to compensation if the professional (or whoever is the data controller)[234] is unable to prove that reasonable care was taken to comply with the requirements of the DPA;[235]
- to prevent disclosures by the data controller likely to cause the client unwarranted damage or distress unless disclosure is a legal or contractual obligation or necessary to protect the client's vital interests;[236]
- to disallow processing for purposes of direct marketing and automated decision-making;[237]
- to invoke the Commissioner's assessment powers.[238]

Other legislation barring disclosure

3.42 There is much legislation that protects the confidentiality of personal information.[239] There is no particular pattern. Sometimes the legislation forbids disclosure of certain kinds of information as in the case of the Probation Rules 1984,[240] the NHS Venereal Disease Regulations 1974, the NHS Trusts and Primary Care

---

[230] From 2005 all records held by public authorities will be subject to the data protection regime.
[231] J Maxeiner, 'Freedom of Information and the EU Protection Directive' (1995) 48 Federal Communications LJ 93, 97.
[232] See para 18.37 (exemptions from the data protection principles), and para 19.28 (exemptions from subject access rights).
[233] *R (on the application of Robertson) v City of Wakefield Metropolitan Council* [2001] EWHC Admin 915; [2002] 2 WLR 889, para 24.
[234] See para 18.11 below.
[235] DPA, s 13. See para 4.49 below.
[236] DPA, s 10, Sch 2, paras 1–4.
[237] DPA, ss 11, 12.
[238] DPA, s 42. See para 18.47 below.
[239] A good example, though not one that impinges directly on professional-client relationships, is a confidentiality order under the Companies Act 1985 (ss 723B–F) and supporting regulations. This disapplies the normal requirement that company directors and secretaries disclose their residential address if disclosure is likely to attract a serious risk of violence or intimidation, eg from animal rights protestors.
[240] SI 1984/647, reg 22.

B. Legislating About Confidentiality

Trusts (Sexually Transmitted Diseases) Directions 2000,[241] the Human Fertilization and Embryology Act 1990,[242] the Abortion Regulations 1991[243] and the Education (Special Educational Needs) (England) (Consolidation) Regulations 2001.[244] Certain personal information that may be sourced from a professional including information relating to an individual's financial or business affairs[245] or relating to his adoption, care fostering or education[246] is exempt from local authority public access provisions.

3.43 In addition there are measures that forbid disclosure of *any* information obtained under specified statutory powers for unspecified purposes. Anti-Terrorism, Crime and Security Act 2001, Sch 4 lists fifty-three statutory non-disclosure provisions that bind public authorities and therefore professionals in their employment.[247] The actual number of non-disclosure provisions is much higher[248] and although much of the information involved is commercial, some provisions safeguard the privacy of personal information.[249] Usually disclosure of information for an unauthorized purpose is a criminal offence.[250] Under a few statutes the disclosure offence can be committed by anyone including the person who receives the information.[251]

Multi-layered legal protection of professional confidences

3.44 Protection of confidential personal information has become multi-layered. A professional who is contemplating disclosing confidential personal information about a client will break the law if she proceeds with the disclosure unless she can give affirmative answers to *all* of the following questions:

---

[241] This and the 1974 venereal diseases regulations (SI 1974/29 r 2) prevent disclosure of identifying information about a patient examined for a sexually transmitted disease, including HIV and AIDS, other than to the treating medical practitioner.
[242] This restricts the circumstances in which information may be disclosed by centres licensed under the Act. An unauthorized disclosure is a criminal offence (s 41). See also Human Fertilization and Embryology Authority Code of Practice (2001) para 5, available from http://www.hfea.gov.uk.
[243] SI 1991/499, reg 5.
[244] SI 2001/3455, reg 24. This restricts disclosure of special educational needs statements.
[245] Local Government Act 1972, Sch 12A, para 6.
[246] ibid, Sch 12A, para 5.
[247] Much of it is, of course, not going to be confidential personal information, let alone information extracted from a professional.
[248] See *Second Report to Parliament on the Review of Legislation Governing the Disclosure of Information* (November 2002), available at www.lcd.gov.uk/foi/foid.irpt2.htm.
[249] eg Census Act 1920, s 8(2)(3); Parliamentary Commissioner Act 1967, s 11; Taxes Management Act 1970, s 6 and Sch 1; Sex Discrimination Act 1975, s 61; Race Relations Act 1976, s 52; Telecommunications Act 1984, s 45; Official Secrets Act 1989, s 1; Health Act 1999, s 24; Data Protection Act 1998, s 59; Disability Rights Commission Act 1999, Sch 3, para 22(2)(f); Proceeds of Crime Act 2002, s 437.
[250] eg Finance Act 1989, s 182. See also para 10.35 below.
[251] eg Electronic Communications Act 2000, s 4.

(1) Does the DPA allow disclosure?
(2) Is disclosure compatible with the client's Article 8(1) right to respect for private life and, if not, is disclosure necessary and proportionate to an Article 8 (2) aim?
(3) Does the disclosure contravene legislation other than the DPA?
(4) If the professional is acting on behalf of a public body, is there legislation enabling the public body to make the disclosure?[252]
(5) Is the disclosure lawful at common law?[253]

To avoid accusations of professional misconduct, the professional may also have to comply with her profession's ethical code. For reasons to be explained in chapter 18,[254] a negative answer to questions 3, or 4 and often 5 will produce a negative answer to 1.

Disclosure to the Subject of the Information

3.45 The DPA gives individuals the right of access to personal data about themselves held by others[255] (including information in the possession of professionals) and rights in relation to rectification, blocking erasure and destruction of inaccurate data.[256] These subject access rights are examined in chapter 19. As a result of amendments to the DPA by the Freedom of Information Act[257] which will come into force in January 2005[258] existing subject access rights will be enlarged so as to make all personal information held by public authorities accessible.[259] In other countries access rights to personal information have been amongst the most widely exercised rights conferred by Freedom of Information legislation.[260]

C. Professional Codes of Ethics

Purpose of a Code

3.46 Most professions have a formal written code[261] setting out minimal ethical standards to which members are expected to adhere in the conduct of their professional

---

[252] Crime and Disorder Act 1998, s 115 (see para 12.15 below) was enacted because of doubts about the ability of public bodies to disclose information for crime prevention purposes. A public body created by statute can only do things expressly or impliedly authorized by statute: *R v Brentwood BC, ex p Peck* [1998] EMLR 697.
[253] The principal issue here will be whether disclosure is possible without contravening contractual or equitable duties of confidentiality.
[254] See para 18.09 below.
[255] DPA, ss 7–9.
[256] DPA, s 14. See para 19.48 below.
[257] See s 40(1) and Pt VII.
[258] Lord Chancellor, *Hansard*, HL vol 628, cols 457–458 (13 November 2001).
[259] The enlargement involves giving a right of access to personal data in unstructured manual files.
[260] *Your Right to Know: The Government's Proposals for a Freedom of Information Act* (Cm 3818, 1997) para 4.1.
[261] See N Harris, *Professional Codes of Conduct in the United Kingdom: A Directory* (2nd edn, London: 1996). A code may be supplemented by non-mandatory guidelines.

C. Professional Codes of Ethics

lives. A code with the title 'code of ethics' tends to be more general than one designated as a 'code of conduct' but both serve similar ends. These include some or all of the following:

- to protect and promote the profession's status;
- to establish professional standards for those professions that are self-regulating;
- to sensitize and educate members of the profession about the ethical dimensions of their work;
- to inform non-members (clients, other professional groups, the general public) about the standards of the profession with a view to instilling trust.

Whether a code is intended to be inspirational or regulatory, if the members of the profession to which it relates handle sensitive personal information it will have something to say about confidentiality. The more detailed codes will not only state that the client is owed a duty of confidentiality but also when that duty may be breached without the client's consent. But however detailed the code, the exercise of judgment will be required except in the most blatant case. Some professional codes of ethics have international or EU versions.[262]

Legal Significance of an Ethics Code

In describing the law relating to professional confidentiality the ethical codes of the professions cannot be disregarded. The codes are part of the background to law and may influence its formulation, particularly where the body responsible for the code has, like the General Medical Council (doctors),[263] the Nursing and Midwifery Council, the Social Care Council (social careworkers) and the Law Society (solicitors), a statutory role in setting and enforcing ethical standards for the profession.[264] **3.47**

Observations about professional codes

(1) The typical code will instruct members of the profession to comply with legal requirements. Should the code omit to do so, the professional must still put

---

[262] eg World Medical Association, *International Code of Medical Ethics* (Geneva: 1949, 1968, 1983) reproduced in BMA, *Medical Ethics Today* (London: 1993) Appendix 2 or see http://www.bma.org.uk; World Medical Association, *Declaration of the Rights of the Patient* (Lisbon: 1981, 1995) http://www.wma.net; ICOH, *International Code of Ethics for Occupational Health Professionals* (Singapore: 1992); International Council of Nurses, *Code of Ethics for Nursing* (2000) http://www.icn.ch/ethics.htm; *Code of Conduct for Lawyers in the European Union*, http://www.barcouncil.org.uk, issued by the Council of the Bars and Law Societies of the European Union (1988).

[263] GMC rules were relied upon in *W v Egdell* [1990] 1 All ER 835, 843, 849. C Foster and N Peacock, *Clinical Confidentiality* (London: 2000) 15 suggest that in a case involving a health professional other than a doctor in a situation analogous to one dealt with in the GMC guidelines on confidentiality, the GMC guidelines might still be found helpful by the court. The GMC guidelines are to be found at http://www.gmc-uk.org.

[264] On the very variable quality and authority of codes of professional ethics and practice see further J Kultgen, *Ethics and Professionalism* (Philadephia: 1988) ch 10.

the law first to the extent that there is any conflict between law and code because a professional code, even one with a foundation in statute, does not set legal standards.[265] The decision of the Court of Appeal in *W v Egdell*[266] has as its premise that the courts and not responsible professional opinion determine when a breach of confidence (in that case by a psychiatrist) is lawful.[267]

(2) What a code says about privacy or confidentiality, if relevant to litigation, may be considered by the court.[268] This is not just because a code written by a professional association or institution is a source of informed opinion but because it is confusing for professionals and threatening to justice for the common law and a code to pull in opposite directions. 'If judges pay insufficient respect to the ethos and ethics of health care professionals, there will be increased tension and health care professionals will be tempted to alter or conceal the truth out of a legitimate commitment to the ethics of their calling.'[269] To debate any professional confidentiality point in the courts without reference to the relevant professional code of conduct is ill-advised.[270] The same applies to a relevant non-statutory government guideline.

(3) Where the legal issue is whether the professional was negligent in failing to disclose information, breach of professional rules is evidence of conduct falling below the required standard of care.[271] Foster, Wynn and Ainley go so far as to say that '[d]eparture from a professional code raises a clear (but rebuttable) presumption of fault'.[272] Whether they are right may depend upon the legal status of the code and its standing within the profession. Conversely, adhering to a professional code is an indication, though not a conclusive one, that the required standard of care has been met.[273] In *Johnson v Bingley* Hytner QC (sitting as a High Court judge) said (with reference to the Law Society's

---

[265] *David Lee & Co (Lincoln) Ltd v Coward Chance* [1991] 1 All ER 668, 672.
[266] [1990] 1 All ER 835.
[267] C Foster, T Wynn and N Ainley, *Disclosure and Confidentiality: A Practitioner's Guide* (London: 1996) 323.
[268] The courts are directed by HRA, s 12(4) to take into account certain media privacy codes when making decisions that might affect the media's Art 10 right of freedom of expression.
[269] R Tur, 'Medical Confidentiality and Disclosure: Moral Conscience and Legal Constraints' (1998) 15 J of Applied Philosophy 15, 20.
[270] C Foster, T Wynn and N Ainley, *Disclosure and Confidentiality: A Practitioner's Guide* (London: 1996) 322.
[271] *Furniss v Fitchett* [1958] NZLR 396, 405.
[272] C Foster, T Wynn and N Ainley, *Disclosure and Confidentiality: A Practitioner's Guide* (London: 1996) 321.
[273] There will be no finding of negligence if a medically qualified professional adheres to accepted professional standards unless the professional standard is incapable of withstanding logical analysis: *Calver v Westwood Veterinary Group* [2001] Lloyd's Rep Med 20. As regards other professionals see para 19.64 n 241. Contrast *Gold v Haringey Health Authority* [1987] 2 All ER 888, 893–894.

C. Professional Codes of Ethics

Guide to Professional Conduct of Solicitors): 'whilst I have found the Guide... relevant, both to foreseeability and the reasonableness of the steps to be taken to avoid risk, I do not find that either, taken on its own without more, to be conclusive of liability, or indeed the absence of it.' In *Harvest Trucking v Davis*[274] Dimond J found the Code of Practice of the British Insurance Association 'not unhelpful' in determining whether the defendant insurance intermediary had been negligent. This was first 'because it was part of the context in which [the insurance intermediary] ... had to operate. Second, because in deciding whether a professional man has been negligent, a Court has to be careful not to adopt too high or perfectionist a standard, and to some extent it may be helpful to refer to the code to ensure that the standard of care which the Court is otherwise minded to apply is not considered unrealistic in the industry'.

(4) '[I]t is a common feature of professional rules that they impose a higher duty on the members of the profession than does the law itself.'[275] Some examples of this are:

- The Law Society's rules and guidance on conflict of interests which set standards that are higher than those required by law.[276]
- The obligation to continue confidentiality after the death of the client[277] mentioned in the *Code of Ethics and Practice for Counsellors*,[278] the *Guide to the Professional Conduct of Solicitors*,[279] the *Professional Practice Guidelines 1995*[280] of the British Psychological Society, Division of Clinical Psychology and the GMC's booklet, *Confidentiality: Protecting and Providing Information*.[281] It is doubtful whether an equitable obligation of confidentiality survives the death of the client when there is no property interest at stake.[282]

---

[274] [1991] 2 Lloyd's Rep 638, 644.
[275] *David Lee & Co (Lincoln) Ltd v Coward Chance* [1991] 1 All ER 668, 672 per Browne-Wilkinson VC.
[276] See para 6.92 below.
[277] cp DoH, *AIDS/HIV Infected Health Care Workers: Guidance on the Management of Infected Health Care Workers and Patient Notification* (1999) para 10.5; WHO, *Declaration on the Promotion of Patients' Rights in Europe* (Amsterdam: 1994) para 4.1.
[278] British Association for Counselling (Rugby, 1997) (http://www.bac.co.uk) para B.3.2: '[a]greements about confidentiality continue after the client's death unless there are overriding legal or ethical considerations.'
[279] Law Society, *The Guide to the Professional Conduct of Solicitors* (8th edn, London: 1999) 324, 16.01, para 3. At the trial of a man called Waddell for a murder for which Patrick Meehan was wrongly convicted, a Scottish judge said that the solicitor of Waddell's alleged accomplice, a man by the name of McGuinness, was bound by his obligation of confidence to his client even though his client was dead: L Kennedy, *A Presumption of Innocence: The Amazing Case of Patrick Meehan* (London: 1976).
[280] para 6.3.5 (http://www.bps.org.uk).
[281] (London: 1995) para 13. Cp *Re C* [1996] 1 FCR 605, 608 (publicity after life-support machine is switched off).
[282] See para 5.48 below.

- The GMC's guidance to doctors mandates disclosure of the threat of physical violence to a third party; the law does not.[283]

(5) It is possible for the law to be stricter than the professional code. The Law Society recognizes a self-defence exception to confidentiality[284] where it is arguable that the law does not. This issue is discussed in chapter 12.

(6) Only a small fraction of the type of situations in which disclosure issues arise are likely to come before a court. What should a psychiatrist do if, as happened to one US psychiatrist,[285] she becomes aware that a patient is considering politically defecting with sensitive material? The more detailed codes of professional practice are an important supplement to the law.[286] They may not provide complete answers, but they will indicate the ethical principles to be applied. 'The management of confidentiality on a day-to-day basis is much more a matter of professional ethics than of legal requirements.'[287]

(7) When it comes to confidentiality, there are marked variations in the obligations imposed by the professional codes. Points on which codes differ include whether all information about a client is confidential,[288] whether information provided by the client about another person falls within the ambit of confidentiality,[289] how obligations of confidentiality arise,[290] whether new clients must be informed about confidentiality standards at the point of first contact,[291] and the scope of the public interest exceptions to the obligation of confidentiality.[292]

(8) In a fully regulated profession, the professional code is authoritative for disciplinary purposes. A member discovered to have disobeyed the code can be

---

[283] GMC, *Confidentiality: Protecting and Providing Information* (London: 2000) para 36: '[w]here third parties are exposed to a risk so serious that it outweighs the patient's privacy interest . . . you should disclose information promptly to an appropriate person or authority.' As to the legal situation see para 20.23 below.

[284] Law Society, *The Guide to the Professional Conduct of Solicitors* (8th edn, London: 1999) 327, para 16. 02, para 12.

[285] D Joseph and J Onek, 'Confidentiality in Psychiatry' in S Block, P Chodoff and S Green (eds), *Psychiatric Ethics* (3rd edn, New York: 1999) 121.

[286] F Zacharias, 'Specificity in Professional Responsibility Codes' (1993) 69 Notre Dame L Rev 223, 232.

[287] D Joseph and J Onek, 'Confidentiality in Psychiatry' in S Block, P Chodoff and S Green (eds), *Psychiatric Ethics* (3rd edn, New York: 1999) 108.

[288] P Cain, 'The Limits of Confidentiality in Healthcare' in C Cordess (ed), *Confidentiality and Mental Health* (London: 2001) 128.

[289] P Moodie and M Wright, 'Confidentiality, Codes and Courts: An Examination of the Significance of Professional Guidelines on Medical Ethics in Determining the Legal Limits of Confidentiality' (2000) 29 Anglo-American L Rev 39, 46–47.

[290] P Cain, 'The Limits of Confidentiality in Healthcare' in C Cordess (ed), *Confidentiality and Mental Health* (London: 2001) 129.

[291] eg BPS Division of Clinical Psychology, *Professional Practice Guidelines* (1995) para 6.1.1, available at http://www.bps.org.uk.

[292] See paras 11.14 et seq below.

disciplined.[293] Sanctions may range from a formal warning to restrictions on practice, suspension and loss of the right to practice. When the code adopts higher standards than the law, the professional may face disciplinary proceedings yet be immune from legal action. In his judgment in *Tournier v National Provincial and Union Bank of England*,[294] Scrutton LJ attributed the dearth of litigation against professionals for breach of confidence to the integrity of professionals: '[t]he absence of authority appears to be greatly to the credit of English professional men, who have given so little excuse for its discussion.'[295] The existence of professional codes and sanctions for their violation may be an even more significant cause.

D. Domestic 'Soft Law'

Public Sector Guidance

3.48 Attention was drawn in the previous chapter to the large body of official guidance sometimes referred to as 'soft law' or quasi-law that exists about confidentiality.[296] This guidance comes in many forms: departmental circulars, executive letters, privacy statements, codes of practice, charters, memoranda of understanding and recommendations in departmental and inter-departmental reports. There have been many initiatives especially in the health and social services field. In March 2000 the Department of Health set up a national body, the National Confidentiality and Security Advisory body, to set standards for the confidentiality and security of patient information.[297] Prior to this the *Report on the Review of Patient-Identifiable Information*[298] by the Caldicott Committee (led by Dame Fiona Caldicott) and other reports[299] had stressed the importance of developing local procedures and access protocols to allow proper exchange of patient identifiable information for non-clinical purposes within the NHS and between NHS and non-NHS organizations.[300] The Home Office is also keen on protocols to

---

[293] See para 9.07 below.
[294] [1924] 1 KB 461.
[295] [1924] 1 KB 461, 479.
[296] See para 2.22 above. This guidance is referred to as 'organisational rules and procedures' by the Department of Health, Social Services and Public Safety in its consultation paper *Health and Personal Social Services: Protecting Personal Information* (Northern Ireland, June 2002) para 2.15.
[297] Press release, 15 March 2000, http://www.doh.gov.uk/ipu/whatnew/newadvis.htm.
[298] *Report on the Review of Patient-Identifiable Information* (1997) available at http://www.doh.gov.uk/confiden/crep.htm. Six principles for testing whether to disclose patient-identifiable informaton were recommended and later adopted in NHS guidance available at http://www.doh.gov.uk/confiden/cgmintro.htm.
[299] eg *Reform of the Mental Health Act 1983—Proposals for Consultation* (Cm 4480, 1999), available from http://www.official-documents.co.uk; DoH, *No Secrets: The Protection of Vulnerable Adults* (2000) para 1.5, available from http://www.doh.gov.uk.
[300] For an example see General Protocol for Sharing Information between Suffolk Social Services and Felixstowe RD Medical Practice, at http://www.nhsia.nhs.uk.

facilitate the exchange at local level of information that will contribute to the reduction of crime and disorder.[301] Many areas have protocols between social services, the police and the Crown Prosecution Service for child abuse investigations.[302] A national protocol regulating disclosure by social services in child abuse investigations is being developed.

3.49 For the most part, official guidance has no legal status.[303] In practice it is closely followed by public sector professionals because failure to do so will breach their terms and conditions of employment and may be relied upon as evidence of non-compliance with an administrative law duty.[304] Local authorities and their employees are in fact bound by the Local Authority Social Services Act 1970[305] 'in the exercise of their social services functions, including the exercise of any discretion', to apply general guidance issued by the Secretary of State unless there are exceptional circumstances that justify a variation. The latest (and very extensive) guidance dealing with the confidentiality of social work records was issued in March 2000.[306] There is an earlier document on exchanging confidential information to protect children.[307] Beyond the public sector, government guidance may set standards of reasonable conduct.[308] Social workers in the voluntary sector disregard the Department of Health's advice to social services about issues of confidentiality at their peril. Official guidance and protocols do not necessarily solve confidentiality dilemmas for professionals. If the guidance is at variance with that issued by their own professional organizations the problem of deciding what to do is compounded.[309]

Information Commissioner's Guidance

3.50 The Information Commissioner combines a number of roles: consultant, educator, policy adviser, negotiator, ombudsman, auditor, enforcer and international ambas-

---

[301] Joint Statement by the Information Commissioner and Home Office, 'Disclosure of Information in Connection with Crime and Disorder' (1998), available from http://www.homeoffice.gov.uk.

[302] Home Office, *Complex Child Abuse Investigations: Inter-Agency Rules: Guidance* (2002) para 5.6, available from http://www.homeoffice.gov.uk. A national protocol is being devised.

[303] *Re G (A Minor)* [1996] 2 All ER 65, 69. The court nevertheless encouraged adherence to the guidelines in Home Office, DoH, Dfee *Working Together under the Children Act 1989* (1991). See also *R (on the application of A) v Chief Constable of C* [2001] 1 WLR 461, paras 34, 43.

[304] *R (on the application of A) v Chief Constable of C* [2001] 1 WLR 461, para 34.

[305] s 7.

[306] DoH, *Social Care Policy* LASSL (2000) 2 ch 6, available at http://www.doh.gov.uk/scg/datap.htm.

[307] DoH, *Working Together to Safeguard Children* (London: 1999) ch 7, available at http://www.doh.gov.uk.

[308] P Moodie and M Wright, 'Confidentiality, Codes and Courts: An Examination of the Significance of Professional Guidelines on Medical Ethics in Determining the Legal Limits of Confidentiality' (2000) 29 Anglo-American L Rev 39, 40.

[309] BMA, *Confidentiality and disclosure of health information* (London: 1999) 15.

D. Domestic 'Soft Law'

sador.[310] Several of these roles require the Commissioner 'to promote good practice by data controllers'.[311] This is done by disseminating information to the public about the operation of the Act, good practice and other matters within the scope of his functions.[312] At the direction of the Secretary of State, or on his own initiative, the Commissioner is also required to prepare and disseminate codes of practice after consultation with appropriate trade associations and the representatives of data subjects.[313] These codes must be laid before Parliament.[314] Thus far there have been two codes. The draft code on the use of personal data in employer/employee relationships has some relevance to the concerns of this book.[315] There is no legal requirement to comply with the Commissioner's codes but anyone who does so can be assured of meeting the legal requirements of the DPA. A code may be cited by the Information Commissioner in enforcement proceedings.

The Information Commissioner and his support staff have issued a great deal of general guidance (much of which is available on the internet)[316] that explains how the data protection legislation works and how to achieve compliance. Later chapters of this book draw heavily on the Information Commissioner's *Data Protection Act 1998—Legal Guidance* and *The Use and Disclosure of Health Data*.[317] As the Commissioner himself recognizes his advice is not legally binding: **3.51**

> The Commissioner can only give general guidance; the final decision in cases of dispute is a question for the Courts.[318]

One would, however, expect the courts to pay attention to how the Commissioner interprets the DPA and to any relevant code of practice issued or approved by the Commissioner. In the absence of case law the Commissioner's compliance advice is the most authoritative guidance available. This guidance must be consistent with the ECHR both because the Information Commissioner as a public authority must act compatibly with the ECHR[319] and because of the interpretative obligation imposed by HRA s 3.[320]

---

[310] C Bennett, 'Data Protection Authority—Regulator, Ombudsman, Educator or Campaigner?', Data Protection and Privacy Commissioners Conference Report, 11 September 2002, available on Mason's website at http://www.masons.com.
[311] DPA, s 51(1). There is a similar duty under Freedom of Information Act 2000, s 47 to promote good practice by public authorities.
[312] DPA, s 1(2).
[313] DPA, s 51(3).
[314] DPA, s 52(3).
[315] Found at http://www.dataprotection.gov.uk.
[316] ibid.
[317] May 2002. Available on the Information Commissioner's website.
[318] Data Protection Act 1998 Legal Guidance, para 2.1.
[319] HRA, s 6.
[320] See para 3.04 above.

E. The International Dimension

Supranational and International Instruments

3.52 Such is the interest in privacy internationally that professional confidentiality is either specifically addressed in, or affected by, a large number of international and regional instruments.[321] Worthy of notice are:

- Organisation for Economic Co-operation and Development (OECD)

    —Guidelines on the Protection of Privacy and Transborder Flows of Personal Data (1980)[322]

- United Nations

    —*Convention of the Rights of the Child* (General Assembly: 1989)
    —WHO, Declaration on the Promotion of Patients' Rights in Europe (Amsterdam: 1994)[323]
    —WHO, Proposed International Guidelines on Ethical Issues in Medical Genetics and Genetic Services (Geneva: 1997)[324]
    —Guidelines for the Regulation of Computerised Personal Data Files (1990)[325]
    —International Guidelines on HIV/AIDS and Human Rights (1997)[326]
    —UNESCO, Universal Declaration on the Human Genome and Human Rights (1999)[327]

- Council of Europe[328]

    —Recommendation R (83) 10 on the protection of personal data used for scientific research and statistics (1983)
    —Recommendation R (86) 1 on the protection of personal data for social security purposes (1986)
    —Recommendation R (89)14 on the ethical issues of HIV infection in the healthcare and social settings (1989)

---

[321] There is some discussion of the international plane in D Feldman, 'Information and Privacy' in Y Cripps and J Beatson (eds), *Freedom of Expression and Freedom of Information: Essays in Honour of Sir David Williams* (Oxford: 2000) ch 19. Some of the international instruments are reproduced in M Rotenberg, *The Privacy Law Sourcebook 2000* (Washington DC: 2000); almost all are available on the internet.

[322] These guidelines attempt to harmonize privacy laws to prevent privacy becoming a barrier to international trade.

[323] This endorsed 'Principles of the Rights of Patients in Europe: A Common Framework'.

[324] Available from http://www.who.int. See particularly para 9.

[325] Final version E/CN.4/1990/72, adopted by the General Assembly pursuant to Art 10 of the UN Charter A/Res/95 (1991).

[326] UNCHR Res 1997/33, UN Doc E/CN.4/1997/150, guideline 5 which advises states to enact laws to ensure privacy and confidentiality for HIV/AIDS sufferers.

[327] Particularly Art 9 (http://www.unesco.org).

[328] http://www.coe.int.

E. The International Dimension

—Recommendation R (91) 10 on the communication to third parties of personal data held by public bodies (1991)

—Recommendation R (92) 3 on genetic testing and screening for health care purposes (1992)[329]

—Recommendation of the Committee of Ministers R (97) 5 on the protection of medical data (1997)

—Recommendation of the Committee of Ministers R(98) 7 concerning the ethical and organizational aspects of health care in prisons (1998)[330]

—Recommendation of the Committee of Ministers Rec (00)10 on codes of conduct for public officials (2000)[331]

—Recommendation of the Committee of Ministers Rec (00) 21 on freedom of exercise of the profession of lawyer (2000)[332]

—Committee of Ministers, *Guidelines on human rights and the fight against terrorism*, 15 July 2002[333]

—*Right to Privacy*, Parliamentary Assembly Resolution 1165 (1998)[334]

—Convention for the Protection of Human Rights and Fundamental Freedoms (1950)[335]

—Convention for the Protection of Individuals with regard to the Automatic Processing of Personal Data (1981)[336]

—Convention on Human Rights and Biomedicine (1997)[337]

—Convention on Cybercrime (2001)[338]

- European Union

—European Union Data Protection Directive (1995)[339]

—Charter of Fundamental Rights of the European Union (2000)[340]

—European Union regulation on the protection of individuals with regard to the processing of personal data by Community institutions (2001)[341]

—European Union regulation on access to confidential data for scientific statistical purposes (2002)[342]

---

[329] See particularly principles 8, 9.
[330] See particularly para 13.
[331] See particularly Art 22, para 2.
[332] See particularly paras 28–32, 42–43.
[333] Arts V, VI.
[334] Described as 'useful guidance' in *A v B plc & C ('Flitcroft')* [2002] EWCA Civ 337; [2002] 3 WLR 542, para 11, guideline xii.
[335] Referred to in this book as the European Convention on Human Rights or ECHR.
[336] Similar in content to the OECD guidelines. Many of the Convention principles are to be found in EU Data Protection Directive (EC) 95/46 and the DPA which implements this directive.
[337] Particularly Art 10.
[338] http://conventions.coe.int/Treaty/EN/WhatYouWant.asp?NT=185. See particularly Title 1, 'Offences against the confidentiality, integrity and availability of computer data and systems'.
[339] (EC) 95/46. This is implemented by the DPA.
[340] The legal status of this instrument, which is to be reviewed in 2004, is uncertain.
[341] Commission Regulation (EC) 45/2001.
[342] Commission Regulation (EC) 831/2002.

—Directive on the processing of personal data and the protection of privacy in the e-communications sector (2002)[343]

—Opinions of the Working Party established by Article 29 Directive 95/46/EC

Domestic impact of supranational and international instruments

3.53 The recommendations of the Council of Ministers and the UN and OECD Guidelines and Declarations are 'soft law' that is intended to set standards for the development of law and practice at national level. International and multinational instruments may influence the drafting and construction of statutes and the development by the courts of the common law. Reference will therefore be made in this book to 'soft law' when it provides a helpful pointer on how to resolve an issue of professional confidentiality for which there is no clear answer in English law. Because the United Kingdom is a dualist system,[344] conventions to which the United Kingdom is a signatory, even after ratification, do not impose obligations or confer rights within the domestic legal system.[345] Effect must be given to the Convention through legislation passed, or authorized, at Westminster. Of course there is a strong presumption in favour of interpreting English law (whether common law or statute) in a way which does not place the United Kingdom in breach of an international obligation.[346]

3.54 Most of the European Convention on Human Rights has been 'brought home' by the HRA. The EU regulations are automatically part of domestic law because of the European Communities Act 1972. The EU Data Protection Directive[347] has been implemented at national level by the DPA.[348] The effect of the European Communities Act 1972 and EU law is to require domestic law (including the DPA) to be interpreted as far as possible to achieve the results that this Directive envisages and also any decisions of the Court of Justice about the Directive.[349]

---

[343] (EC) 2002/58 (available on the Oftel website at http://www.oftel.gov.uk). Art 15 allows member states to lift the protection of privacy for electronic communications for the purpose of safeguarding 'national security . . . defence, public security and the prevention, investigation, detection and prosecution of criminal offences or of unauthorized use of the electronic communication system' where this is a 'necessary, appropriate and proportionate measure within a democratic society'. Data may be retained for a limited period under legislation that conforms with the general principles of EU law. Lawful interceptions of electronic communications must be in accordance with the ECHR.

[344] *Maclaine Watson & Co Ltd v International Tin Council* [1990] 2 AC 418.

[345] *Wainwright v Home Office* [2001] EWCA Civ 2081; [2002] 3 WLR 405, para 91.

[346] per Lord Hoffmann, *R v Lyons* [2002] UKHL 44, para 27.

[347] (EC) 95/46 (1995).

[348] The DPA applies EU principles to the processing of personal data across the board—to systems operating within and without the remit of EU law.

[349] *R (on the application of Robertson) v Wakefield Metropolitan Council* [2001] EWHC Admin 915; [2002] 2 WLR 889, paras 17–18; *Campbell v MGN* [2002] EWCA Civ 1373, para 97. See further, A. Arnull, A Dashwood, M. Ross and D Wyatt (eds), *Wyatt & Dashwood's European Union Law* (4th edn, London: 2000) 92 et seq.

E. The International Dimension

This may mean implying words into or reading down legislation that pre-dates the EU directive.[350] EU law additionally requires that the DPA be interpreted to comply with the ECHR.[351]

Impact of the European Convention on Human Rights on domestic law

When a convention that is not EU-related has been implemented domestically, a court may normally consider the convention only when construing the implementing statute if ambiguity is found, but not as a reason for finding ambiguity.[352] The HRA sets aside the conventional rule in favour of an idiosyncratic arrangement:

3.55

(1) Courts and tribunals must 'take into account' judgments, decisions and opinions of the ECtHR, the Commission and the Committee of Ministers whenever a question arises in connection with a Convention right.[353] This could happen either when interpreting and applying legislation or when developing the common law. That courts and tribunals are not *bound* by the Strasbourg jurisprudence reflects the continually evolving nature of the Convention[354] and the 'margin of appreciation' doctrine. These make it desirable to leave domestic tribunals with some leeway of choice. In the absence of special circumstances,[355] however, the domestic courts of the United Kingdom are expected to follow 'any clear and constant jurisprudence of the European Court of Human Rights'—not least because the losing party can take the matter before the ECtHR which 'is likely in the ordinary case to follow its own constant jurisprudence'.[356]

(2) Courts and tribunals are required by HRA s 3(1) to construe domestic legislation of any vintage, including the HRA itself, 'so far as it is possible to do so',[357] and, if needs be, by reading in words or adopting a linguistically strained interpretation,[358] 'in a way which is compatible with the Convention rights'.[359] Young, having analysed the possible interpretations of 'so far as it is possible',

---

[350] cp *R v Department of Health, ex p Source Informatics* [2000] 1 All ER 786, 797, 798.
[351] *Rutili v Minister of the Interior* [1975] ECR 1219.
[352] *R v Home Secretary, ex p Brind* [1991] 1 All ER 720, 722–723.
[353] HRA, s 2.
[354] *Tyrer v UK* (1976) 2 EHRR 1. In *Cossey v UK* [1991] 2 FLR 492, 501 the ECtHR said that the interpretation of the Convention must reflect 'societal changes and remain in line with present-day conditions'.
[355] Possible reasons for departure include that the ECtHR has misunderstood domestic law and that the Strasbourg decisions compel a conclusion fundamentally at odds with the British constitution: see R Clayton, 'Developing Principles for Human Rights' [2002] European Human Rights L Rev 175, 177–178.
[356] per Lord Slynn, *R (on the application of Holding & Barnes plc) v Secrtary of State for the Environment* [2001] UKHL 23; [2001] 2 WLR 1389, para 26.
[357] HRA, s 3(1).
[358] *R v A* [2001] UKHL 25; [2002] 1 AC 45, para 44; *R v Lambert* [2001] UKHL 37; [2001] 3 WLR 206, paras 78–81.
[359] HRA, s 3(1).

concludes that in practice s 3(1) imposes no fetters on the capacity of the judges to interpret statutes to achieve compatibility with Convention rights.[360] Even if the courts take a more restrictive view of their interpretative powers, legislation intended to implement human rights obligations, such as the DPA and the Regulation of Investigatory Powers Act 2000, is bound to be interpreted, however much contortion and manipulation it takes, in a manner compatible with the Convention for this was plainly Parliament's intention.

These two HRA innovations make extensive reliance on Convention jurisprudence necessary in this book to establish the content of the English domestic law of professional confidentiality.

---

[360] A Young, 'Judicial Sovereignty and the Human Rights Act 1998' [2002] CLJ 53, 65.

Part II

RESPONDING TO DISCLOSURE

4

CONTRACT AND TORT SOLUTIONS TO INTENTIONAL DISCLOSURE

A. **Contract**	4.02	Defamation	4.34
Contract Basics	4.02	Injurious Falsehood	4.41
Confidentiality as a Contractual Term	4.04	Conspiracy	4.43
B. **Tort**	4.19	Breach of Statutory Duty	4.45
Negligence	4.20	Infringement of Privacy	4.53
Intentional Infliction of Distress	4.29	Breach of Confidence	4.60

This chapter and the next examine the circumstances in which the intentional unjustified disclosure or planned disclosure, of confidential personal information by a professional gives rise to legal liability on the professional's part in contract, tort, copyright or equity. Intentional here does not mean any intentional act that has the effect of violating an obligation of confidentiality. Rather, it more narrowly refers to an intention to do something which the professional knows, or should know, will cause that obligation to be breached. This chapter sets out the possibilities for suing in contract or tort. The following deals with actions in equity and copyright. **4.01**

A. Contract

Contract Basics

The existence of a contract

An action in contract requires an express or implied[1] contract for services between the professional and the client. In *Quarles v Sutherland*[2] a Tennessee court held that a shopper who, after suffering an accident in a shop, was sent to the shop's regular physician for free medical treatment could not sue the physician in contract for sending a copy of his diagnosis and the treatment he had prescribed to the shop **4.02**

---

[1] *X v Y (No 1)* [1954] VLR 709, 711.
[2] 289 SW2d 249, 252 (1965).

owner's lawyer. There was no contract here because no charge had been made for the physician's services: if there is no deed (and it would be most unusual if there were) a contract requires an intention to create a legal relationship for consideration (reward).[3] Many professionals, including the clergy, social workers, teachers in state schools and health professionals working for the NHS[4] are not paid by the people they help and therefore have no contractual relationship with them. Barristers in private practice are forbidden at common law from entering a contract with the lay client. Although this rule has been abolished by the Courts and Legal Services Act 1990,[5] the Bar Council has exercised its statutory power in the Bar's *Code of Conduct*[6] to continue the prohibition. A barrister cannot sue for unpaid fees or, consequently, be sued for breach of contract.[7] Of course, barristers do not work for nothing. By tradition barristers receive an honorarium from their instructing solicitor.[8]

Privity of contract

4.03 At common law, rights and obligations created by a contract affect only the parties to the contract.[9] A client, therefore, was unable to sue a professional for services given under a contract that was made not with the client or the client's agent but with someone such as an employer. Payment of the professional's fee by A, who is not the client, however, does not have to mean that B, the client, has no contract with the professional. In *Furniss v Fitchett*,[10] an action brought by a patient against a doctor whose account had been settled by the patient's husband, the court agreed with *Charlesworth on Negligence*[11] that 'there is in most cases a contract between patient and medical practitioner, even if the patient himself is not liable for payment of the services rendered, such payment being made by someone else'. The Contracts (Rights of Third Parties) Act 1999 has reversed the common law in that it now allows a person upon whom a contract confers a benefit, but who is not a party to it, to sue on the contract except where this is contrary to the intention of the contracting parties.

---

[3] For the requirements of a valid contract, including consideration, see J Beatson (ed), *Anson's Law of Contract* (27th edn, Oxford: 1998).

[4] On the absence of a contractual relationship between doctors and patients in the NHS see *Pfizer Corp v Minister of Health* [1965] AC 512; A Grubb and D Pearl, 'Medicine, Health, the Family and the Law' [1986] Family L 227, 240.

[5] s 61.

[6] *Code of Conduct of the Bar of England and Wales* (8th edn, London: 1999) Annexe B, paras 25 and 26.

[7] *Kenney v Brown* (1863) 13 CBNS 677.

[8] M Seneviratne, *The Legal Profession: Regulation and the Consumer* (London: 1999) 37. Modification of the rule that there must be a solicitor intermediary between a lay person and a barrister is proposed: *Direct Access to the Bar* (London: April 2002)

[9] *Tweddle v Atkinson* (1861) 1 B & S 393, 121 ER 762.

[10] *Furniss v Fitchett* [1958] NZLR 396, 399.

[11] (London: 1956) 471. Now *Charlesworth & Percy on Negligence* (9th edn, London: 1997) 574.

A. Contract

Confidentiality as a Contractual Term
Establishing an obligation of confidentiality

For a client to be in a position to bring an action in contract over the disclosure, or planned disclosure, of confidential information, the contract must contain an express or implied term forbidding the disclosure. Contracts with public figures often contain an express non-disclosure clause.[12] The clause may be as wide or narrow as the parties desire, but not so obscure that it is void for vagueness.[13]

4.04

Many contracts for professional services are not in writing and, even where they are, the promise of non-disclosure has to be implied.[14] An obligation will be implied if at the time the bargain was struck the parties would have testily replied 'Oh, of course' to an officious bystander who asked whether the contract included a non-disclosure clause.[15] The burden of proving the implied term (and its breach) lies with the claimant.[16] It will not be difficult to persuade a court that the parties to a contract creating a professional relationship for personal services intended an obligation of confidentiality.[17] Codes of professional ethics invariably accept the existence of an ethical duty of confidentiality and maintaining professional duties of confidence is in the public interest.[18] The Court of Appeal has acknowledged that contracts between doctor and patient, accountant or solicitor and client, and bank and customer contain an implied term to keep the patient's affairs confidential.[19]

4.05

The extent of the duty of confidentiality

Trivial information

If confidentiality is an implied term of a contract between professional and client, what does it forbid the professional from disclosing? Clearly, it covers information imparted by the client either to the professional, the professional's employee or the professional's agent but, as in equity,[20] a court might exclude trivial information

4.06

---

[12] eg *Att-Gen v Barker* [1990] 3 All ER 257, 259 (this confidentiality covenant, entered into in return for employment in the royal household, was worldwide and unlimited in time); *Campbell v Frisbee* [2002] EWHC 328; [2002] EMLR 31.
[13] *Adams v Attridge* (QBD, 8 October 1998). Clause upheld that defined confidential as including any information which the defendant 'might reasonably expect [the claimants] . . . or any of their professional advisors to regard as confidential'.
[14] It has become common for solicitors to provide a written contract setting out the obligations of the parties in full at the commencement of the relationship.
[15] *Shirlaw v Southern Foundries (1926) Ltd* [1939] 2 All ER 113, 124 applied *W v Egdell* [1989] 1 All ER 1089, 1105. cp *Hilton v Barker, Booth & Eastwood* [2002] EWCA Civ 723, para 29.
[16] *Tournier v National Provincial and Union Bank of England* [1924] 1 KB 461, 483.
[17] cp *Parry-Jones v Law Society* [1968] 1 All ER 177, 178.
[18] *W v Egdell* [1990] 1 All ER 835, 848. Cp *Att-Gen v Guardian Newspapers Ltd (No 2)* [1988] 3 All ER 545, 640.
[19] *Parry-Jones v Law Society* [1968] 1 All ER 177, 178, 180.
[20] See para 5.08 below.

that the parties could not have intended to be private. As with the equitable obligation of confidence, triviality depends upon context. To reveal the town to which the client has moved to a known stalker is altogether different from revealing it to a former student of the client who is trying to trace the client to obtain a reference.

Information from third parties

4.07 In *Tournier v National Provincial and Union Bank of England*[21] the issue was whether the implied obligation covers information from sources other than the client. The bank was sued by Tournier, a customer, because the acting manager of a branch had told the claimant's employer that the claimant had paid money to a bookmaker. The consequence of this was that the claimant lost his job. The bank had obtained the information from another bank. A majority in the Court of Appeal held that the bank's duty of non-disclosure included information concerning the client acquired from third parties by the bank in its character of banker during the currency of its contractual relationship with the customer. While admitting that the duty of non-disclosure which a professional owes a client may vary from profession to profession, Bankes LJ thought that the underlying principles for other options were similar.[22]

4.08 Kennedy and Grubb have speculated as to whether medical confidentiality extends to information acquired by a doctor about a patient from a third party who is unaware of the doctor–patient relationship.[23] This question could just as easily arise if the recipient were some other professional. Two situations need to be distinguished. The first is where the professional finds it expedient to conceal the professional relationship when seeking information. In these circumstances the professional should be bound to keep the information confidential unless it fails at the triviality hurdle. The second is where the information is acquired accidentally when not acting in a professional capacity. The old American Bar Association Model Code obliges a lawyer to protect her client's secrets 'without regard to the nature or source of the information'[24] but coverage is limited to information 'gained in the professional relationship'. This would exclude gossip picked up at a cocktail party or learnt unexpectedly from another client in a discussion about an unrelated matter. This is likely to be the understanding of the English courts for most, if not all, professionals.[25] Kennedy and Grubb, however, argue for a wider obligation for doctors:

---

[21] [1924] 1 KB 461.
[22] ibid at 474. Also Scrutton LJ at 481.
[23] I Kenedy and A Grubb, *Medical Law* (3rd edn, London: 2000) 1062. See also C Foster and N Peacock, *Clinical Confidentiality* (London: 2000) 5.
[24] ABA, *Model Code of Professional Responsibility* (1969) DR4–101 and E4–4. This has been dropped from the ABA's Model Rules of Professional Conduct.
[25] cp *Tournier v National Provincial and Union Bank of England* [1924] 1 KB 461, 481 (bank); *Ott v Fleishman* (1983) 5 WWR 720 paras 6–7 (lawyer). In neither case was the point fully discussed. *Ott v Fleishman* cites *Re Holloway; Young v Holloway* (1887) 12 PD 167 inappropriately.

A. Contract

On one view, since the doctor does not receive the information *qua* professional vis-à-vis the third party, he has no professional obligation of confidence. The better view, perhaps, is that a court would recognize a duty to respect confidentiality since what lies at the root of the doctor patient relationship is the patient's trust that the doctor will not reveal any clinical information to another without permission.[26]

As a matter of ethics this must be right, but is there any reason for the doctor's legal obligation to be more extensive than that of a lawyer or an accountant? Is it the law's function to police the professional's personal integrity?

Information by direct observation

It is a logical inference from *Tournier's* case that a professional's obligation of confidentiality extends to information and opinions arising from direct observation of, or examination of, the client. Should this be done clandestinely, for example by secretly spying on, photographing[27] or filming the client, the very acquisition of the information may itself be contrary to an implied term of the contract.[28] **4.09**

Information in the public domain or known already

An express contractual promise of non-disclosure may extend to all information that the professional has about the client. This may include information of which the recipient is aware[29] and information that is in the public domain.[30] In this respect a contractual promise of non-disclosure may be wider than an equitable obligation of confidentiality which may be confined to information that has not been widely circulated.[31] **4.10**

The scope of an implied promise of confidentiality depends upon all the circumstances but members of the public generally expect very high standards of integrity from the professionals who handle their personal information. They would not expect a doctor, lawyer or accountant to mention personal information that has become widely known without the consent of the client. General Medical Council (GMC) guidelines on *Media Inquiries about Patients*[32] state quite explicitly that 'information which a doctor has learnt in a professional capacity should be regarded as confidential, whether or not the information is also in the public **4.11**

---

[26] I Kennedy and A Grubb, *Medical Law* (3rd edn, London: 2000) 1062.
[27] *Clayman v Bernstein* 38 Pa D & C 543 (1940).
[28] cp *HRH Princess of Wales v MGN Ltd* (QB, 8 November 1993).
[29] *Christofi v Barclays Bank plc* [1999] 4 All ER 437, 446.
[30] Law Commission, *Breach of Confidence* Report No 110 (1981) para 6.132. See also *Att-Gen v Blake* [2000] 3 WLR 625, 645; *Att-Gen for England and Wales v Television New Zealand Ltd and X* (1998) 44 IPR 123 (available from http://www.brookers.co.nz/legal/judgments); *Ashworth Security Hospital v MGN Ltd* [2002] UKHL 29; [2002] 1 WLR 2033, para 32.
[31] cp *Att-Gen v Blake* [2000] 3 WLR 625, 645. However, there is a possibility that a professional's equitable obligation of confidentiality extends to information in the public domain: see para 5.14 below.
[32] (London: 1996). Available at http://www.gmc.uk.org.

domain'.[33] It would be unprofessional, and might be a breach of contract, for a professional to draw to the attention of a third party that a client has a criminal history, information of which the third party is ignorant and of which the client would wish the third party to remain ignorant. In *Christofi v Barclays Bank plc*[34] the judge at first instance held that a bank's implied obligation of confidentiality extended to information that was not a secret and which could be got from another source, but that it did not include information which the bank would have expected the recipient to know already. This decision was confirmed on appeal.[35]

Limits of confidentiality

4.12 An implied promise of professional confidentiality is not absolute.[36] An express contractual term purporting to require confidentiality under *all* circumstances would not be in the public interest for reasons explained in chapter 1[37] and would therefore be against public policy.[38] The leading authority on the limits of an implied contractual promise of confidentiality is *W v Egdell*.[39] W, who had admitted to killing five people, had been ordered to be detained without limit of time for the public safety at a secure hospital. His solicitors instructed Dr Egdell to provide an independent report on W's mental state which they hoped to use to support an application to a Mental Health Appeal Tribunal for W's transfer from the hospital to a regionally secure unit. The report was unfavourable to W and the application for the transfer was withdrawn. Dr Egdell, who, unlike the doctor treating W, considered W to pose a danger to the public, took it upon himself to provide the superintendent of the hospital with a copy of the report and recommended that a copy be sent to the Home Office, which was done. In doing this it was held that he had not acted in breach of his contractual obligation of confidentiality to W.

4.13 To determine the limits of the doctor's obligation of confidentiality Scott J, at first instance, applied the 'officious bystander' test:[40] would the doctor have readily agreed that he should under no circumstances whatsoever disclose his report without W's consent? Scott J did not think the answer would have been a testy 'Of course'.

> [A]fter consideration he would, I think, have said that he would regard himself as entitled to disclose his report to the relevant authorities if, in his judgment, the

---

[33] November 1996.
[34] [1998] 2 All ER 484, 488.
[35] See also *Schering Chemicals v Falkman Ltd* [1981] 2 All ER 321, 344–346.
[36] *Tournier v National Provincial and Union Bank of England* [1924] 1 KB 461, 472, 479, 484; *W v Egdell* [1990] 1 All ER 835, 848.
[37] See paras 1.54–1.55 above.
[38] cp *Att-Gen v Guardian (No 2)* [1988] 3 All ER 545, 572.
[39] [1989] 1 All ER 1089.
[40] *W v Egdell* [1989] 1 All ER 1089, 1105.

public interest so required. If he had given that answer he would, in my judgment, have been right.[41]

In the Court of Appeal Bingham LJ said that the breadth of a duty of confidentiality 'is . . . dependent on circumstances'.[42] Had the doctor sold his report to the media,[43] or discussed the case in a learned article without concealing W's identity,[44] he would have breached the contract. The limits of a duty of confidentiality are to be determined by 'weighing the public interest in maintaining confidence against a countervailing public interest favouring disclosure'.[45] Guidance may be sought in the relevant professional ethical code.[46]

Duration of the obligation of confidentiality[47]

Termination of the professional-client relationship

There are few precedents on the duration of professional obligations of confidentiality. If nothing is expressly stated, the promise of confidentiality will last at least for the duration of the professional-client relationship. One would expect the courts to imply an intention to keep information confidential for considerably longer in the majority of cases. Obviously important factors in deciding how long the obligation was intended to survive will be the nature of (1) the information and (2) the service provided by the professional. The courts may take the view that the parties intended sensitive personal information such as medical information to be protected indefinitely.[48] There was a division of opinion in *Tournier v National Provincial and Union Bank of England* about just how long the banker's contractual duty of confidentiality lasts. Bankes LJ and Atkin LJ said that the duty extends beyond the period of the relationship.[49] No opinion was ventured as to what determines it. Scrutton LJ thought that the duty expired when the professional relationship did.[50] The British Banking Association's Banking Code promises to maintain confidentiality when the client has ceased to be a customer.[51]

4.14

---

[41] ibid at 1105.
[42] [1990] 1 All ER 835, 848.
[43] ibid.
[44] [1990] 1 All ER 835, 848.
[45] *Att-Gen v Guardian Newspapers Ltd (No 2)* [1988] 3 All ER 545, 659 as quoted in *W v Egdell* [1990] 1 All ER 835, 849. Bingham LJ relies here on the public interest defence: see ch 11.
[46] *W v Egdell* [1990] 1 All ER 835, 843, 849.
[47] For retention and storage of records see para 5.56 below.
[48] cp the duty of confidentiality of a secret agent which is lifelong: *Att-Gen v Guardian Newspapers (No 2)* [1988] 3 All ER 545, 647, 650; *Att-Gen v Blake* [1996] 3 All ER 903, 908–909.
[49] [1923] 1 KB 461, 473, 485. Atkin LJ stated that the obligation of confidentiality did not extend to information obtained after the customer ceased to be a customer of the bank.
[50] [1923] 1 KB 461, 481.
[51] para 4.1 (London: 1998).

Effect of repudiation of the contract

4.15 The professional's obligation of confidentiality in equity,[52] and possibly in contract,[53] is unaffected by repudiatory breach of the contract by the client. In *Campbell v Frisbee*, an action against a defendant formerly employed by the claimant under a contract for services, Lightman J said:

> It is plain beyond question that the obligation of confidence of e.g. a lawyer, doctor or security consultant survives acceptance by the service provider of the repudiation of his contract by the client. Indeed that is surely the premise upon which the relationship between client and service provider is created . . .[54]

The Court of Appeal, which reversed the decision to enter summary judgment under CPR r 24 for Campbell, reached no conclusion on this point but suggested that the assumption of a contractual obligation of confidentiality enhanced the case for restricting freedom of expression.[55] Freedom of expression is necessarily infringed by the post-contract survival of the obligation of confidentiality either at law or in equity. This interference with Article 10 must be weighed against the interference that will be occasioned to Article 8 if the confidential information loses its protection.

Death of the client

4.16 The decision of the US Supreme Court in *Swidler and Berlin v US*[56] that attorney–client privilege survives the death of the client implies that in the United States the attorney's contractual obligation of confidentiality continues posthumously. Law Society guidance agrees with this[57] and many other codes of professional ethics adopt this position.[58] Disclosure of personal information that in the lifetime of the client was confidential is felt to be disrespectful of the memory of the deceased and possibly an invasion of the privacy of the deceased's family. However, the client's death may allow for further exceptions to the obligation.[59]

4.17 The one relevant case in English law is *Fogg v Gaulter and Blane*[60] where the executors of two estates, that of a father and son, were in dispute about the beneficial

---

[52] The equitable obligation of confidentiality is described in ch 5 below.
[53] In *Hurst v Bryk* [2002] 1 AC 185, para 53 Lord Millett said that '[r]ights and obligations which arise by the partial execution of the contract continue unaffected'. It is arguable that the obligation not to disclose confidential information without authorization falls into this category.
[54] [2002] EWHC 328; [2002] EMLR 31, para 22.
[55] [2002] EWCA Civ 1394, para 22. Contrast *London Regional Transport Ltd v Mayor of London* [2001] EWCA 1491, para 46. In a professional–client relationship, the client's Art 8 right should outweigh the professional's Art 10 right.
[56] (1998) 118 S Ct 2081.
[57] Law Society, *The Guide to the Professional Conduct of Solicitors* (8th edn, London: 1999) 324, 16.01, para 3.
[58] See para 3.47 above.
[59] GMC, *Confidentiality: Protecting and Providing Information* (London: 2000) paras 40–41.
[60] (1960) 110 L J 718. See also K Edwards, 'Accountants' Duty of Secrecy and Care' (1960) 110 LJ 714.

ownership of some property. The court awarded £100 to the executor of the son's estate against the son's accountants who, without the consent of the son's personal representative, disclosed to the executors of the father's estate the records they held about the son's affairs. The disclosed information was very damaging to the son's estate: an income tax return acknowledged that the father was beneficial owner of the disputed property. Arguably, this case is authority that a contractual obligation of confidentiality by any professional can survive the client's death if disclosure of information prejudices the property interests of the estate.[61]

Breach of the obligation

A contractual obligation of confidentiality may be breached either by disclosure or exploitation of the protected information. Information may be used without being disclosed.[62] In an unusual Canadian case a lawyer took advantage of his knowledge that his client was having marital problems to embark on a sexual relationship with the client's wife. He was held to have compromised his obligation of confidentiality to the client.[63]

4.18

B. Tort

To breach an ethical obligation of confidentiality to a client is a moral wrong but not necessarily a tort. To be actionable in tort the professional's conduct must satisfy the criteria of an established tortious cause of action. None is tailor-made to provide relief against the intentional or reckless disclosure of confidential personal information by a professional. Depending on the circumstances, a number of torts may provide an adequate fit.

4.19

Negligence

Relevance of negligence

The law of negligence is about those relationships in which the law imposes liability on defendants who have acted carelessly. It may seem strange to consider the tort of negligence, which involves liability for unintended consequences in a chapter on intentional disclosure[64] but the fact is that quite unintended consequences may flow from an intentional disclosure.

4.20

Not all careless acts attract liability in negligence. Liability arises[65] where (1) the law imposes on the defendant a duty to take care, which is to say an obligation to

4.21

---

[61] For the position in equity see para 5.46 below.
[62] eg if the professional blackmails the client.
[63] *Szarfer v Chodos* (1986) 54 OR (2d) 663. See para 5.72 below.
[64] For accidental disclosure see ch 6.
[65] For a summary of the law see *E v UK* Application 33218/96 (26 November 2002), para 70.

avoid behaviour that creates an unreasonable risk of injury, *and* (2) a failure in that duty has caused actual damage that is not too remote. To establish a duty of care, the claimant must show that the facts of which he complains fall within an established duty of care situation.[66] Alternatively, where the relationship is one that has not previously been before a court, the claimant must satisfy the judge:[67]

(1) of a special relationship of sufficient proximity between claimant and defendant;
(2) that harm to persons like the claimant was reasonably foreseeable;
(3) that it is fair, just and reasonable to impose a duty of care on the defendant.

4.22 Two points need emphasizing:

(1) the discussion that follows is highly speculative as there is no precedent in English law for imposing a duty on a professional not to disclose confidential personal information about a client;
(2) in the final analysis the existence of a duty of care is a question of public policy. Requirements of 'reasonable foreseeability', 'proximity' and 'fairness, justness and reasonableness' overlap and are just convenient labels.[68] The prevailing judicial approach is one of caution: new duty situations are created pragmatically, incrementally and with an eye to preserving certainty and predictability in the law. A duty of care is thus unlikely to be found to exist unless a similar one exists already.[69]

Duty of care and improper disclosure of personal information

Proximity

4.23 It is acknowledged that a professional relationship is sufficiently proximate to give rise to a duty of care to the client. Where the relationship is contractual, the very existence of a contract gives rise to a duty of care.[70] But a contract is not vital:

> The normal duty of a doctor to exercise reasonable skill and care is well established as a common law duty of care. In my judgment, the same duty applies to any other person possessed of special skills, such as a social worker. It is said, rightly, that in general such professional duty of care is owed irrespective of contract and can arise even where the professional assumes to act for the plaintiff pursuant to a contract with a third party.[71]

---

[66] *TP v UK* Application 28945/95 (2002) 34 EHRR 2, para 46.
[67] *Caparo Industries plc v Dickman* [1990] 1 All ER 568, 573–574.
[68] ibid at 574.
[69] P Kaye, *English Law of Torts* (Chichester: 1996) 48.
[70] *Mouat v Clarke Boyce* [1992] 2 NZLR 559, 566.
[71] per Lord Browne-Wilkinson, *X (minors) v Bedfordshire CC* [1995] 3 All ER 353, 383, HL. cp *Phelps v Hillingdon LBC* (1997) 147 NLJ 1421.

B. Tort

The fact that the relationship is one in which the claimant has passed confidential personal information to the defendant is indicative of proximity.[72]

Reasonable foreseeability of harm

Satisfaction of the reasonable foreseeability element of the duty test is a question of fact. The court must ask itself, in the circumstances, was injury of the kind sustained reasonably foreseeable? In *Furniss v Fitchett*[73] a New Zealand court concluded that harm to a patient resulting from the intentional non-consensual disclosure of confidential personal information by her doctor fell into this category. The claimant had accused her husband of cruelty, insanity and trying to poison her. The doctor gave the distraught husband a certificate for his lawyer expressing the opinion that the claimant required treatment for paranoia. In providing the husband with the certificate the doctor breached his obligation of confidentiality to the wife who was his patient. A year later the marital discord had reached the point of separation and maintenance proceedings. During cross-examination of the wife, the husband's solicitor showed her the doctor's certificate. Seeing the certificate caused her psychiatric injury. Barrowclough CJ concluded that the doctor ought reasonably to have foreseen that the information was likely to become known to the wife if he disclosed it to the husband without placing restrictions on its use, and further, that if it did become known to her, her health would suffer.[74] 4.24

Furniss v Fitchett is unusual as breach of confidence situations go in that the disclosure complained of was not of information confided by the claimant to the defendant but of observations by the professional which he had not communicated to the patient. Also, the doctor's liability in negligence arose not so much from the fact that he had intentionally disclosed confidential information to a third party as in his failure to guard against the patient learning the information for the first time via the third party in highly charged circumstances. 4.25

Policy arguments for a duty

The decision in *Furniss v Fitchett* was handed down long before the threefold test for determining the existence of a duty of care became accepted and does not isolate for separate discussion the third element of the test, namely the fairness of imposing a duty of care. The judge did, however, point out that the doctor's tortious duty is far less onerous than that imposed by the medical profession in its ethical codes.[75] This, and the fact that the disclosure was voluntary, are reasons 4.26

---

[72] cp *Swinney v Chief Constable* [1996] 3 All ER 449, 467: '[p]roximity is shown by the police assuming responsibility, and the plaintiffs relying upon that assumption of responsibility, for preserving the confidentiality of the information . . .' per Peter Gibson LJ.
[73] [1958] NZLR 396.
[74] ibid at 403.
[75] ibid at 404.

why on the facts recognition of a duty of care was justified. In *Swinney v Chief Constable*,[76] a case of inadvertent disclosure by police, Hirst LJ said that it was 'unthinkable' that if the police promised to preserve a confidence by an informer and deliberately broke that promise the law would countenance such conduct. There is every reason to think that the same attitude would prevail if:

- a professional ignored an obligation of confidentiality, and
- in consequence her client suffered tangible injury, the risk of which was reasonably foreseeable.

Breach of duty and damage that is not too remote

Additional requirements for liability

4.27 Establishing that the professional owed the claimant a duty of care not to put confidential personal information into circulation if it was reasonably foreseeable that disclosure could cause the client harm is only the first step in a successful negligence action. The claimant must also show that:

(1) *The duty of care was breached.* English judges show considerable deference to professional standards when determining what could reasonably have been expected of a professional.[77] Disclosure of information in violation of the requirements of a professional code of conduct or, semble, government guidelines is powerful evidence, albeit not conclusive evidence, of negligence.[78] Breach of a statutory confidentiality obligation would similarly be evidence that conduct fell below the required standard of care.[79]

(2) *The breach caused the claimant injury.* Causation in a historical and physical sense is often so obvious that it is not discussed. In *Furniss v Fitchett* the usual 'but for' causation test was applied *sub silento*.

(3) *The injury is not too remote.*[80]

Remoteness

4.28 The law does not make a defendant pay for every tangible injury the defendant may have caused; only for those that a reasonable individual would have foreseen.[81] In *Furniss v Fitchett* the defendant argued that the claimant's injury was too remote to be compensated because it depended upon the intervening act of a third party (a *novus actus interveniens*),[82] namely the solicitor showing the certificate to

---

[76] [1996] 3 All ER 449, 464. See also Peter Gibson LJ at 466.
[77] See para 3.47 above.
[78] *Furniss v Fitchett* [1958] NZLR 396, 405
[79] *R in Right of Canada v Saaskatchewan Wheat Pool* [1983] 1 SCR 205, 227–228.
[80] For details about the law of causation and remoteness see W Rogers, *Winfield & Jolowicz on Tort* (16th edn, London: 2002) ch 6.
[81] per Viscount Simonds, *The Wagon Mound (No 1)* [1961] 1 All ER 404, 415.
[82] cp *Rademaker v Number Ten Holdings Ltd* (1983) 47 BCLR 376. There is disagreement in the cases as to whether a novus actus should be treated as an issue of factual causation or of remoteness.

Mrs Furniss. This was not accepted: the intervening event 'was foreseeable by the doctor and was the very thing which the law required him to take care to avoid'.[83] Had Mrs Furniss' employer been in court to lend her moral support and, on hearing the certificate read out, sacked her, it is possible that the court's opinion might have been different. Predicting how a court will decide an issue of remoteness is difficult because the decision is ultimately one of policy. The vexed issue of whether injury in the shape of mental distress is too remote to be compensated is discussed in chapter 8.

Intentional Infliction of Distress[84]

Elements of the tort

In *Furniss v Fitchett* the defendant intentionally disclosed confidential information without being aware that his action might cause the claimant harm. The injury (as opposed to the precipitating act) was therefore not intended. His culpability lay in 'the manner in which he released the report, and in not foreseeing that at some stage, Mrs Furniss might be confronted with it in circumstances which might injure her'.[85] Suppose instead that: 4.29

(1) the doctor's disclosure of the confidential information has been deliberate; *and*
(2) was intended to cause the wife physical harm or was done with a state of mind that could be described as reckless in circumstances where there was a high risk that the wife would come to grief.

These changed facts make the well-known but rarely litigated tort of intentional infliction of distress relevant. This originated in the case of *Wilkinson v Downton*[86] where the defendant told the claimant that her husband had met with an accident in which his legs were broken. This was untrue and was intended as a sick joke. The gullible claimant suffered a severe shock that resulted in a physical illness with lasting consequences. Although the tort is one of intention, it is not necessary to prove that the defendant wanted to cause the claimant severe emotional distress. The tort can be committed recklessly.[87] 4.30

---

[83] [1958] NZLR 396, 408.
[84] N Mullany and P Handford, *Tort Liability for Psychiatric Damage* (London: 1993) ch 14.
[85] per Barrowclough CJ [1958] NZLR 396, 401.
[86] [1897] 2 QB 57.
[87] *Janvier v Sweeney* [1919] 2 KB 316, 318; *Home Office v Wainwright* [2001] EWCA Civ 2081; [2002] 3 WLR 405, paras 44–50. See also *Abramzik v Brenner* (1967) 65 DLR (2d) 651, 654; *Bradley v Wignut Films* [1993] 1 NZLR 415, 422.

Application to intentional disclosure of personal information

Unresolved issues

4.31 *Tucker v News Media Ownership Ltd*[88] is a good vehicle for exploring the potential application of *Wilkinson v Downton* to the intentional disclosure of personal information. Tucker, the claimant, was propelled into the public eye by an appeal to raise money to send him to Australia for a heart transplant operation that could not be performed in New Zealand. Relying on *Wilkinson v Downton*, and armed with a medical opinion that the stress induced by public exposure might kill him, his lawyers obtained interim injunctions to prevent media organizations from disclosing Tucker's criminal convictions for indecency. In later proceedings a judge decided that there was a serious issue to be tried and refused to discharge the injunctions.[89]

4.32 Two issues had to be resolved in the claimant's favour before there could be any question of liability under the rule in *Wilkinson v Downton*. These were whether

- offensive disclosure has to be in the claimant's presence; and
- the information has be untrue[90] (as it was in *Wilkinson v Downton*).

These same issues will often (though not always) arise in cases of intentional disclosure of confidential personal information by a professional. At least by implication, the judge in *Tucker v News Media Ownership Ltd* was satisfied that *Wilkinson v Downton* does apply to true statements[91] that were not made to, or in the presence of, the claimant.[92] Bollas and Sundelson[93] mention the case of a licensed clinical psychologist who examined a girl at her father's request and provided the father with a written opinion of his belief that the girl had been sexually abused while in her mother's custody. The father contacted officials and the psychologist repeated his statement to them. Further investigation showed the

---

[88] [1986] 2 NZLR 716. cp *Pierre v Pacific Press Ltd* (1994) 113 DLR (4th) 511.
[89] Whether his action was ultimately successful is not known.
[90] The claimant in *G v Day* [1982] 1 NSWLR 24, 31 alleged intentional infliction of harm by a newspaper that planned to disclose his identity. Yeldham J found the tort inapplicable because disclosure of G's identity was not 'conduct devoid of any social utility'.
[91] But in *D v NSPCC* [1976] 2 All ER 993, 998 Lord Denning doubted that *Wilkinson v Downton* extended to 'a statement which is made honestly and in good faith'.
[92] On the last point see also: *Stevenson v Basham* [1922] NZLR 225; *Bielitski v Obadiak* (1922) 65 DLR 627. Contrast *Bunyan v Jordan* (1937) 57 CLR 1 where the claimant saw another handling a revolver, overheard him say that he was going to 'shoot someone' and, after he had left, heard a shot. No liability was found. This case is distinguishable from *Tucker* in that the comments had nothing to do with the claimant; they were remarks she had chanced to overhear. In the US presence is required. Claimants were unable to rely on the tort of negligent infliction of mental distress to claim damages against persons who had appropriated and misused autopsy photographs of dead relatives in *Reid v Pierce County* 961 P2d 333 (1998) because they were not present when the photographs had been displayed.
[93] C Bollas and D Sundelson, *The New Informants* (London: 1995) 33–35.

allegations to be groundless whereupon the mother sued the psychologist for intentional infliction of distress. The outcome is not recorded but on these facts the success of the action depended amongst other things upon the court not insisting on direct contact between claimant and defendant.[94]

Mental distress

In *Tucker* the anticipated injury was of a physical nature; in many breach of confidence situations it is purely emotional. In the United States this does not matter so long as the defendant's conduct was outrageous[95] and the emotional distress severe,[96] whereas in England it does.[97] Damages cannot be recovered for mental distress falling short of psychiatric illness[98] although an injunction has been granted to prevent further harassment of a claimant who had, at the time of trial, suffered no recognizable illness but whose health was at serious risk if the harassment continued.[99] It is only in extreme circumstances that illness will result from the intentional disclosure of personal information.

4.33

Defamation

Elements of the action

Defamation compensates the claimant for injury to reputation and hurt feelings.[100] In this—and only this—respect it is an ideal cause of action for a client who is the victim of the unauthorized publication of confidential personal information to a third party but who has suffered no tangible loss as a result. In defamation it does not matter whether the information is confidential so long as it is personal (that is to say, it refers to the claimant)[101] and (whether intentional or not) defamatory. Information is defamatory if it exposes the claimant to 'contempt or ridicule'[102] or causes the claimant to be 'shunned and avoided'[103] or

4.34

---

[94] There might also be an issue about whether the defendant had the right mental state for liability.
[95] *Urbaniak v Newton* 226 Cal App 3d 1128, 1143 (1991).
[96] The *Restatement (Second) of Torts* (1977) para 46(1) states that '[o]ne who by extreme and outrageous conduct intentionally or recklessly causes severe emotional distress to another is subject to liability for such emotional distress'. Resulting bodily harm is an indication of severe emotional distress, but is not necessary.
[97] R Townsend-Smith, 'Harassment as a Tort in English and American Law: The Boundaries of Wilkinson v Downton' (1995) 24 Anglo-American L Rev 299, 322–325.
[98] *Wong v Parkside Health NHS Trust* [2001] EWCA Civ 1721, paras 11–12,; *Home Office v Wainwright* [2001] EWCA Civ 2081; [2002] 3 WLR 405, para 49. Examples of psychiatric illness include post-traumatic stress disorder and morbid depression.
[99] *Khorasandjian v Bush* [1993] 3 All ER 669, 677, 685. Clients confronted by an on-going threat of disclosure of confidential information by a professional have no need to turn to *Wilkinson v Downton* to obtain an injunction. The action for breach of confidence described in ch 5 is tailor-made.
[100] *Fielding v Variety Inc* [1967] 2 All ER 497, 500, 503. See also para 8.49 below.
[101] The reference need not be intentional; liability is strict. See *Hulton v Jones* [1910] AC 20. But see now *O'Shea v MGN Ltd* [2001] EMLR 943.
[102] *Parmiter v Coupland* (1840) 9 LJ Ex 202, 203.
[103] *Youssoupoff v Metro-Goldwyn Mayer Pictures Ltd* (1934) 50 TLR 581, 584.

lowered in the estimation of right-thinking members of society.[104] Information may have this effect by way of innuendo as in *Peters-Brown v Regina General Hospital*[105] where the claimant's name was included in a list of those whose body fluids required special precautions. As social attitudes shift, so too do the things that lower a person in the estimation of reasonable persons.

Application to improper disclosure of personal information

General unsuitability of defamation

4.35 When a professional reneges on a promise of confidentiality defamation is not usually a suitable vehicle for making her account for her actions. One reason is that defamation protects but a small part of that which is personal to the individual: his reputation. A great deal of the confidential personal information that a professional holds about a client may be completely neutral in terms of discrediting the client in the eyes of the right-thinking person,[106] though some may do so.[107] A second reason is that unless the defamatory statement is in permanent form (libel),[108] it is not usually actionable without proof of special (that is, specific financial) damage such as loss of income or employment. Imputations of the commission of an offence punishable by imprisonment, contagious disease, unchaste conduct or adultery by a woman, and unfitness for a profession or calling are the exceptions.[109] Mental distress on its own does not constitute special damage.

> Mental pain or anxiety the law cannot value, and does not tend to redress, when the unlawful act complained of causes that alone; though where a material damage occurs, and is connected with it, it is impossible a jury, in estimating it, should altogether overlook the feelings of the party interested.[110]

Defences

4.36 The third drawback of defamation is that it is subject to a number of broad defences. It is normally a complete defence for the defendant to prove the defamatory statement is substantially true.[111] 'If a publication can be proved true, then it does not matter how private the information may be, or how humiliating its

---

[104] *Sim v Stretch* [1936] 2 All ER 1237, 1240.
[105] (1995) 58 ACWS (3d) 1044. In *Kaye v Robertson* [1991] FSR 62 the Court of Appeal thought that it was possible that the claimant might establish libel by innuendo.
[106] *Kaye v Robertson* [1991] FSR 62.
[107] As it did in *Cornelius v De Taranto* [2001] EMLR 12. See also *AB v CD* (1904) 7 Sess Cas (5th ser) 72, a defamation action brought against a doctor who had disclosed that his patient had intended to procure an illegal abortion.
[108] *Malik v BCCI* [1997] 3 All ER 1, 10. General damages for libel may include damages for mental distress: *McCarey v Associated Newspapers Ltd* [1964] 3 All ER 947, 959. And see para 8.49 below.
[109] *Clerk & Lindsell on Torts* (17th edn, London: 1995) paras 21–28.
[110] per Lord Wensleydale, *Lynch v Knight* (1861) 9 HL Cas 577, 598.
[111] *Furniss v Fitchett* [1958] NZLR 396, 398; *Cornelius v De Taranto* [2001] EMLR 12. See also *Hollinsworth v BCTV* (1998) 83 ACWS (3) 525.

publication may be. It does not matter how lacking in public interest it may be.'[112] There is one statutory exception to this; a defence of justification involving a spent conviction can be defeated by proof of malice.[113] The other defences are called privileges. Fair comment protects anything said or written that is within the bounds of fairness and on a matter of public interest.[114] Qualified privilege applies when an untrue factual statement is made by someone with a legitimate interest or duty (legal, social or moral) to make it and the recipient has a special interest in receiving it.[115] Both defences can be destroyed by showing that the defendant acted maliciously.[116]

In *Kenney v Gurley* the dean of a women's college informed the mother of a student that her daughter would not be re-admitted to the college because she suffered from a venereal disease, a circumstance that indicated that she 'had not been living right'. The student sued the dean and the doctor responsible for the diagnosis. The action failed because she was unable to prove malice. The court said that '[e]ven if the diagnosis then made, after the professional care and skill shown to have been then availed of, was erroneous, or subsequently proved to be a mistake, that error of judgment, unimpeached in respect of its bona fides could not serve to afford evidence of actual or express malice'.[117] **4.37**

What would the outcome have been if the disclosure to the mother had been a breach of confidence to the daughter? Or suppose that a doctor wrongly diagnosed a husband as suffering from AIDS and in good faith, but without his consent, told his wife.[118] It was said in a Canadian case that **4.38**

> the fact that defamatory matter has originated in breach of confidence, to the knowledge of the defamer, or, indeed, the fact that it was produced under a system which contemplated the violation of confidence as a source of information, may constitute a conclusive reason for rejecting the claim of privilege.[119]

In *Halls v Mitchell*[120] a doctor revealed to a Compensation Board information that he mistakenly believed had been confided to him by a patient who was seeking compensation from the Board. When the outraged patient discovered this and sued him in defamation the court disallowed a defence of qualified privilege. The

---

[112] M Tugendhat, 'Privacy and Celebrity' in E Barendt and A Firth (eds), *Yearbook of Copyright and Media Law 2001/2002* (Oxford: 2002) 6.
[113] Rehabilitation of Offenders Act 1974, s 4(5).
[114] *Reynolds v Times Newspapers* [1999] 4 All ER 609, 614–615.
[115] ibid at 615.
[116] On the meaning of malice see ibid at 616. For relevant examples see para 4.40 below and *Chaudhary v Cowan* (1973) British Medical J 181.
[117] McClellan J, *Kenney v Gurley* (1923) 208 Ala 623, 627.
[118] The facts are taken from *Molien v Kaiser Foundation Hospitals* 616 P 2d 813. The claimant, however, did not sue for defamation. cp A O'Neill, 'Matters of Discretion—the Parameters of Doctor/Patient Confidentiality' (1995) 1 Medico-Legal J Ireland 94,100.
[119] per Duff J, *Halls v Mitchell* [1928] 2 DLR 97, 114.
[120] [1928] 2 DLR 97, 109.

answer in the hypothetical AIDS case would appear therefore to turn on whether the doctor's breach of confidence was lawful as a public interest disclosure.[121]

4.39 Sometimes the public interest in uninhibited expression is so great that an untrue defamatory statement attracts absolute privilege and even a malicious statement is protected. Absolute privilege attaches to statements made in the course of judicial proceedings and proceedings before a tribunal that acts judicially such as the Disciplinary Committee of the Law Society or the GMC.[122]

> [A] medical practitioner, unlike a solicitor, can be compelled to disclose, as a witness, relevant confidential information received in connection with professional services rendered, so that the statements complained of, when made in the witness box, were [sic] absolutely privileged : . .[123]

4.40 There are two reported English actions involving the disclosure of professional secrets in which malice has been established. In *Kitson v Playfair*[124] a physician of great eminence told his wife and brother-in-law, Sir James Kitson, that their brother's wife, whom he had treated professionally, had miscarried a child which was not that of her husband. This resulted in her discredit and loss of an allowance from Sir James.[125] Kitson was unable to prove the truth of his allegations and was therefore thrown back on the defence of qualified privilege.[126] The jury found that the communication was outside the scope of his duty as a doctor and further held that the communication had not been made in good faith and without malice. Mrs Kitson received £12,000 in damages, a very large sum in 1896 and £7,000 more than she had asked for. In *Groom v Crocker*[127] a solicitor engaged by an insurance society to conduct the defence of the insured admitted liability for a motor collision without the insured's consent. The three members of the Court of Appeal found that if the letter admitting liability was written on a privileged occasion, which was doubted, there was evidence of malice in that the admission of liability had no basis in fact and was intended to obtain an improper advantage for the society. 'In these circumstances' said Sir Wilfred Greene 'it appears . . . to be idle to say that malice or indirect motive did not exist.'[128]

---

[121] See para 11.58 below *et seq*.
[122] Law Commission, Consultation Paper 163, *Publication of Local Authority Reports* (2002) paras 6.11, 6.13.
[123] per Smith J, *Halls v Mitchell* [1928] 2 DLR 97, 116.
[124] (1896) 1 British Medical J 815.
[125] As the allegation was one of unchastity the claimant, in fact, did not have to show the existence of any special damage.
[126] The British Medical Journal's legal correspondent suggested that justification was not run as a defence because of the risk that if the defence failed it would involve the defendant in greatly enhanced damages: (1896) 1 British Medical J 869.
[127] [1938] 2 All ER 394.
[128] ibid at 403.

B. Tort

Injurious Falsehood

4.41 The essence of this tort is that the defendant published a false statement about the claimant maliciously, that is, with the intention of injuring the claimant.[129] There is no need for the statement to be defamatory but it must be false. Malice will be inferred if the words were calculated to produce damage and the defendant either knew the statement to be untrue or was reckless about its truth.[130] At common law the claimant had to prove special damage (that is specific pecuniary loss)[131] but this requirement has been softened by s 3 of the Defamation Act 1952.[132]

4.42 The specifications of the injurious falsehood tort make it an unsuitable vehicle for recovering damages from a professional in most circumstances. For the action to prosper the professional must disclose false information that interfered with the client's economic interests. Putting it about that the client is terminally ill might, if the client is in business or self-employed, have this effect.[133] In *Kaye v Robertson*[134] the claimant's right to make money by selling his story to the press was undermined by the publication of a photograph and article by the defendant newspaper. In the United States a claimant failed in an action for injurious falsehood against a pharmacist who put about a false report that the claimant had submitted a prescription for venereal disease.[135] Once special damage (that is specific pecuniary loss) is established, or s 3 satisfied, the client is entitled to recover aggravated damages for distress and injury to feelings.[136]

Conspiracy

Elements of the action

4.43 There are two reported English cases in which the tort of conspiracy has been used to restrain the dissemination of information.[137] Neither, as it happens, involved personal information. The tort has two forms: simple conspiracy and unlawful means conspiracy. They differ in that although both require two or more persons

---

[129] *Douglas v Hello! Ltd* [2001] 2 All ER 289, para 155.
[130] *Kaye v Robertson* [1991] FSR 62, 67; *Bradley v Wignut Films* [1993] 1 NZLR 415, 427.
[131] Whether mental distress satisfies this requirement is uncertain: *Joyce v Sengupta* [1993] 1 All ER 897, 907.
[132] Provided the claimant can show that the statement is 'calculated' to cause pecuniary damage to him and that the words were published in writing, or other permanent form, no actual pecuniary loss need be shown.
[133] cp *Younger Committee Report* (Cmnd 5012, 1972) para 8.
[134] [1991] FSR 62.
[135] *Evans v Rite Aid Corp* 478 SE 2d 846 (1996). The holding in this case, however, was not lack of special damage but that a pharmacist does not owe an obligation of confidentiality to the customer. This holding would not be followed in England.
[136] *Joyce v Sengupta* [1993] 1 All ER 897, 906–907; *Khodaparast v Shad* [20001] 1 All ER 545, 556. See also paras 8.50 and 8.66 below.
[137] *Gulf Oil (Great Britain) Ltd v Page* [1987] 3 All ER 14; *Femis-Bank (Anguilla) Ltd v Lazar* [1991] Ch 391, 394.

to agree to injure the client (and succeed in doing so), in 'simple conspiracy' the act is lawful in itself and in 'means' conspiracy it is not.[138] What constitutes 'unlawful means' is the subject of controversy. It could be that a breach of confidence will do.[139] Why bring an action for conspiracy if the act itself is a civil wrong? One reason is that suing for conspiracy may enlarge the available range of remedies.[140] Another is that it enables the client to sue someone who did not participate in the unlawful act.

Drawbacks of conspiracy

4.44 A client contemplating suing a professional for either version of conspiracy faces formidable difficulties, though not the principal problem which confronts the claimant in a defamation action, namely the availability of the defence of truth.[141] First, conspiracy is useful only where there is an agreement between the professional and a third party to disclose the information. Secondly, conspiracy has so far only been applied in this country in situations involving interference with commercial interests[142] and to pecuniary losses.[143] In *Lonrho plc v Fayed (No 5)* the Court of Appeal said that actual pecuniary damage, such as loss of salary or medical expenses, was an essential ingredient of the tort[144] and that non-pecuniary (non-financial) damages were not obtainable, even tacked on parasitically to a pecuniary loss.[145] Thirdly, if the allegation is one of simple conspiracy the client must prove that the predominant motive of the disclosure was to injure him;[146] with unlawful means conspiracy there must be an intention to injure but not a predominant purpose or intention to do so.[146a] This would prevent recovery if the predominant purpose of the professional and his co-conspirators was to line their own pockets.[147]

---

[138] *Lonrho plc v Fayed* [1991] 3 All ER 303.
[139] H Carty, 'Intentional Violation of Economic Interests: The Limits of Common Law Liability' (1988) 104 LQR 250, 266.
[140] Y Cripps, *The Legal Implications of Disclosure in the Public Interest* (London: 1994) 222. *Spermolin v John Winter* [1962] CLR 2441 is given as an example.
[141] *Lonrho plc v Fayed (No 5)* [1994] 1 All ER 188, 192.
[142] The possibility of applying it in personal injury litigation has been recognized in Canada in *Damien v O'Mulvenny* (1981) 34 OR (2d) 448, 451 and in Singapore in *X Pte Ltd v CDE* [1992] SLR 996. Unlawful means conspiracy was alleged in *Douglas v Hello! Ltd* [2002] EWHC 2560, [2003] EWCA Civ 139 where disclosure of personal information caused a financial loss.
[143] per Evans LJ, *Lonrho plc v Fayed (No 5)* [1994] 1 All ER 188, 210.
[144] [1994] 1 All ER 188, 193, 200, 210. See also *Quinn v Leathem* [1901] AC 495, 498. Arguably, the court's comments in *Lonrho plc* about recovery for non-pecuniary losses were obiter.
[145] [1994] 1 All ER 188, 203, 210. But see *Quinn v Leathem* [1901] AC 495, 498 and *Pratt v BMA* [1919] 1 KB 244, 231–232. The implication in *Lonrho plc* that general damages are not recoverable for personal injury is obiter since the claim was for damage to reputation.
[146] *Marrinan v Vibart* [1963] 1 QB 528, 537.
[146a] *Kuwait Oil Tanker Co v Al-Bader* [2002] 2 All ER (Comm) 271, para 107.
[147] *Lonrho plc v Fayed (No 5)* [1994] 1 All ER 188, 200, 209; *Douglas v Hello! Ltd* [2002] EWHC 2560, para 33.

B. Tort

Breach of Statutory Duty

Human Rights Act 1998[148]

Cause of action

Under the terms of the HRA it is unlawful for a 'public authority' to act in a manner which is incompatible with those Convention rights that the Act incorporates, unless the action was required by primary legislation.[149] If it does, or proposes to do, so the 'victim'[150] can bring an action under HRA s 7 in the domestic courts. The victim's right to damages for a loss caused by breach of a Convention right is not automatic and therefore there is some debate about whether this cause of action should be called tortious.[151] Normally the victim has one year from the date of the violation to commence the proceedings[152] which are additional to any other cause of action that the victim may have.[153] **4.45**

Effect of disclosure of confidential personal information

A client will be a victim within the meaning of s 7 if he can show a 'reasonable likelihood'[154] that his Article 8 privacy related rights have been violated by disclosure of personal information by a public authority or someone for whose actions a public authority is vicariously responsible.[155] In surveillance cases where evidence of the infringement of Article 8 may be impossible to obtain, the client can impugn an intelligence gathering regime without offering evidence of the surveillance.[156] Someone who is not the client, but who is indirectly affected by the breach of confidence, such as a member of the client's family, may also be a 'victim' and have standing to sue the public authority.[157] The public authority will escape liability if it can demonstrate that the interference was justified.[158] **4.46**

---

[148] Whether it is correct to categorize an action under the HRA for damages as a statutory tort is a controversial point. This was the classification favoured by the Law Commission in *Damages under the Human Rights Act 1998* (Law Com No 266, 2000) para 4.20, available from http://www.lawcom.gov.uk/library/library.htm, and arguably by A Lester and D Pannick (2000) 116 LQR 380, 382 but it has been rejected by Lord Woolf in 'The Human Rights Act 1998 and Remedies' in M Andenas and M Fairgrieve (eds), *Judicial Review in International Perspective* II (The Hague: 2000) 432.

[149] HRA, s 6. If it is authorized by subordinate legislation, that legislation must be valid.

[150] For a discussion of who may be a victim see Law Commission, *Damages under the Human Rights Act 1998* (Law Com No 266, 2000) para 2.15.

[151] D Fairgrieve, 'The Human Rights Act 1998, Damages and Tort Law' [2001] PL 695, 696. Damages at common law are not discretionary.

[152] HRA, s 7(5). This one-year limitation period can be extended if this is equitable in all the circumstances.

[153] HRA, s 11.

[154] *Hilton v UK* (1988) 57 DR 108, 119; *Halford v UK* (1997) 24 EHRR 523, paras 48, 57.

[155] See para 21.31 below.

[156] *Klass v Germany* (1980) 2 EHRR 214, para 34.

[157] *McCann v UK* (1995) 21 EHRR 97; *Osman v UK* (1998) 29 EHRR 245.

[158] For the circumstances in which interference is justified see para 3.19 above.

What is a public authority?[159]

4.47 'Public authority' is not precisely defined in the HRA. The Lord Chancellor told the House of Lords that the definition had been left deliberately vague 'because we want to provide as much protection as possible for the rights of individuals against the misuse of power by state'.[160] The HRA has been drafted with two types of public authority in mind:[161]

(1) Obvious public authorities such as central and local government, the courts and tribunals, government agencies and non-departmental public bodies. This category includes the prison service, the police, NHS bodies, health authorities, social services, the Crown Prosecution Service, public defenders, the community legal service, statutory regulators, local education authorities, maintained schools and colleges. Every act or omission by these bodies that is not Convention-compliant is actionable.

(2) Hybrid public authorities, that is bodies that have both public and private *functions*.[162] Acts of a private nature by a hybrid body are not actionable under the HRA.[163] Regulatory bodies of the professions such as the GMC, the Royal Pharmaceutical Society[164] and the Law Society would seem to be hybrid public authorities. The Lord Chancellor told the House of Lords that GPs were public authorities in relation to their NHS patients but not their private patients.[165] The same may be presumed of dentists, opticians and pharmacists. It is likely that universities will be public authorities when providing education[166] but not when engaged in commercial ventures. It is not clear how far, if at all, independent schools[167] and churches performing charitable functions are public authorities. The English courts have adopted a very narrow approach to the concept of a hybrid public authority. A private body does not become a hybrid body by discharging a function such as education that would otherwise be performed as a public function by a public body.[168] For

---

[159] M Carss-Frisk, 'Public Authorities: The Developing Definition' [2002] European Human Rights L Rev 319.
[160] Lord Chancellor, *Hansard*, HL vol 583, col 808, 24 November 1997.
[161] ibid col 811.
[162] HRA, s 6(3)(b). For a detailed discussion of who may be a hybrid authority see L Mulcahy (ed), *Human Rights and Civil Practice* (London: 2001) paras 8.17 et seq.
[163] HRA, s 6(5).
[164] *R (on the application of Panjawani) v Royal Pharmaceutical Society of GB* [2002] EWHC 1127, para 11.
[165] Lord Chancellor, *Hansard*, HL vol 583, col 811, 24 November 1997. cp *Eldridge v Att-Gen of British Columbia* (1997) 3 BHRC 137.
[166] They are designated as public authorities in Freedom of Information Act 2000, Sch 1, Pt IV.
[167] In *Heather v Leonard Cheshire Foundation* [2001] EWHC Admin 429; [2001] ACD 75, para 79 Stanley Burnton J was not inclined to treat an independent school as a 'public authority'. They are not listed amongst the educational institutions listed as public authorities in Freedom of Information Act 2000, Sch 1, Pt IV.
[168] *Donoghue v Poplar Housing Association* [2001] 4 All ER 604, paras 58–60.

B. Tort

the act to involve the performance of a public function the private body must stand in the shoes of the state.

> Statutory authority for what is done can . . . help to mark the act as being public; so can the extent of control over the function exercised by another body which is a public authority. The more closely the acts that could be of a private nature are enmeshed in the activities of a public body, the more likely they are to be public.[169]

Similarly a contract with a public authority and public funding do not necessarily mean that a private body is performing a public function.[170]

4.48 To sum up, a client who has a grievance about the disclosure (or proposed disclosure) of confidential personal information by a professional employed by a 'public authority' in circumstances in which the disclosure constitutes an unjustified interference with the right to respect for private life is likely to have a freestanding statutory right of action against the public authority under the HRA.

Data Protection Act 1998

4.49 Legislation may create a statutory duty not to disclose information without consent and expressly impose civil liability if that duty is breached.[171] The DPA does just that. The 1998 Act requires a professional who controls the 'processing'[172] of personal information about a client held in a computer or structured manual filing system[173] to comply with a set of data protection principles unless an exemption in Pt V of the Act applies. The effect of the DPA is to create a statutory tort of unfair disclosure of personal information which does not depend upon the personal information disclosed being either untrue or confidential.[174] Its reach is therefore much greater than the torts of defamation or injurious falsehood or the equitable action for breach of confidence. Unlike breach of confidence, there is no defence of public interest or public domain defence (unless the data subject was responsible for the publicity).[175] Details of the requirements that must be observed to avoid committing the data protection tort are given in chapter 18. There is an exemption for data processed for journalistic, literary or artistic

---

[169] per Lord Woolf, *Donoghue v Poplar Housing Association* [2001] 4 All ER 604, para 65.
[170] *Heather v Leonard Cheshire Foundation* [2001] EWHC Admin 429; [2001] ACD 75.
[171] It is possible that Regulation of Investigatory Powers Act 2000 s 1(3) may be of use to the client. This gives a civil right of action if interception of telecommunications occurs without consent to or through a private network.
[172] A broad term defined to include 'obtaining, recording or holding', 'carrying out any operation or set of operations on the information' and 'disclosure . . . dissemination or otherwise making available' the information.
[173] See para 18.06 below.
[174] M Tugendhat, 'Privacy and Celebrity' in E Barendt and A Firth (eds), *Yearbook of Copyright and Media Law 2001/2002* (Oxford: 2002) 7.
[175] See paras 18.25 and 18.26 below. Public interest and previous publication might affect the award of damages.

purposes (the 'special purposes')[176] where the data controller reasonably believed that compliance with the DPA was incompatible with the special purposes.[177] By s 13(1), if the client suffers 'damage' because of a contravention of any of the requirements of the DPA, the client is entitled to compensation, unless the professional can show that reasonable care was taken to avoid the contravention.[178] A client cannot be compensated under s 13 *and* for breach of confidence.[179]

Statutory non-disclosure provisions that confer no express cause of action

4.50 Statutes that create a duty often fail to specify whether a breach gives rise to a civil cause of action. The existence of other statutory remedies, such as a criminal penalty or loss of a licence, makes it difficult[180] but not impossible to infer an intention to allow a private law remedy.[181]

> [A] private cause of action will arise if it can be shown, as a matter of construction of the statute, that the statutory duty was imposed for the protection of a limited class of the public and that Parliament intended to confer on members of that class a private right of action for breach of the duty.[182]

4.51 There are statutory provisions that prohibit the disclosure of confidential personal information except for specified purposes.[183] A case in point is the statutory duty to ensure that information capable of identifying a person with a sexually transmitted disease (including, it has been suggested, HIV/AIDS)[184] shall not be disclosed other than to a medical practitioner in connection with, and for the purpose of the treatment, or to prevent the spread of the disease.[185] It would be a small step for an English court[186] to hold a doctor liable for failing to comply with this statutory duty (in the absence of some public interest in the disclosure).[187] In the United

---

[176] DPA, s 3.
[177] See para 18.39 below.
[178] DPA, s 13(3).
[179] *Campbell v MGN Ltd* [2002] EWHC 499; [2002] EMLR 30, para 124.
[180] Prima facie the fact that there exists a statutory remedy tells against a private law right of action: *X (Minors) v Bedfordshire CC* [1995] 3 WLR 152, 166. See also *Att-Gen v Blake* [1996] 3 All ER 903, 910.
[181] *Argyll v Argyll* [1967] 1 Ch 392, 339 et seq; *Lonrho Ltd v Shell Petroleum Ltd* [1981] 2 All ER 456, 461; *Francome v MGN Ltd* [1984] 2 All ER 408, 412.
[182] *Pickering v Liverpool Daily Post and Echo Newspapers plc* [1991] 1 All ER 622, 632.
[183] See paras 3.42–3.43 above.
[184] *X v Y* [1988] 2 All ER 648, 656.
[185] NHS (Venereal Diseases) Regulations 1974, NHS Trusts (Venereal Diseases) Regulations 1991.
[186] Such an argument was advanced in *Damien v O'Mulvenny* (1981) 34 OR (2d) 448, 450, a case in which a doctor had disclosed to the claimant's employer that the claimant had a venereal disease. The statute that was said to confer a civil cause of action on the claimant was the Venereal Diseases Prevention Act 1980 (Can). The reported decision concerns a preliminary procedural point.
[187] See ch 11.

B. Tort

States patients have pursued actions for breach of statutory duty against doctors for disclosing confidential medical information.[188] An Australian case has held that a witness who was named in a newspaper after the medical tribunal before whom she had given evidence in disciplinary proceedings had ordered her identity to be withheld had an arguable action for breach of statutory duty.[189]

Mental distress

If the client has suffered only mental distress[190] as a result of the breach of statutory duty the court must be persuaded that Parliament contemplated recovery for injury of this kind. In a New Zealand case a government department disclosed to an adopted child the identity of his natural mother despite the mother having notified the appropriate official in accordance with the relevant statute that she did not want the child to be told. The court refused to strike out her action pointing out that the emotional injury suffered by the claimant was just the kind of harm that the statute was designed to prevent and that if a private law action were ruled out no means existed of enforcing the statutory duty.[191] The claimant in *Pickering v Liverpool Daily Post* fared less well. This was an action for an injunction to enforce observance of the prohibition in the Mental Health Tribunal Rules 1983 on publication of applications to Mental Health Tribunals. While conceding that unauthorized publication 'may in one sense be adverse to the patient's interest' Lord Bridge said that it is incapable of causing the claimant loss or injury of a kind for which the law awards damages.[192]

4.52

> I know of no authority where a statute has been held . . . to give a cause of action for breach of statutory duty when the nature of the statutory obligation or prohibition was not such that a breach of it would be likely to cause to a member of the class for whose benefit or protection it was imposed either personal injury, injury for property or economic loss.[193]

---

[188] eg *Schaffer v Spicer*, 215 NW 2d 134 (1974). See further B Watson, 'Disclosure of Computerized Health Care Information: Provider Privacy Rights Under Supply Side Competition' (1981–82) 7 American J of L and Medicine 281, 283.

[189] *CS v News Ltd* (NSW SC, 10 February 1999, NSW LEXIS 441). Under the Medical Practice Act 1992 (NSW) Sch 2, cl 16 it is a criminal offence to disclose the name of any witness that the tribunal directs is not to be published.

[190] Such cases must be distinguished from those where there is both reasonably foreseeable mental anguish *and* tangible loss: *Reed v Madon* [1989] 2 All ER 431, 442.

[191] *G v Att-Gen* [1994] 1 NZLR 714.

[192] per Lord Bridge, [1991] 1 All ER 622, 632.

[193] ibid.

Infringement of Privacy[194]

Characteristics of the action

4.53 Many common law jurisdictions have a common law or statutory tort of infringement of privacy.[195] The tort, which has many possible formulations, tends to have the following characteristics:

- it protects true information so long as it is private information;[196]
- after a suitable lapse of time, information originally available from a public source may become private information;
- a special relationship between claimant and defendant is not required;
- damages are recoverable for mental distress.[197]

The US privacy tort[198]

4.54 The first common law country to recognize a tort of invasion of privacy was the United States. This development was stimulated by an academic article by Brandeis and his law partner Warren who felt that newspapers were going too far in their truthful reporting of matters of a personal nature. They analysed various English property, contract, confidence and defamation cases and concluded that all were based on a broad common law principle that protected the individual against the infliction of mental suffering through the infringement of privacy.[199] A common law tort of invasion of privacy flowing from natural law and the constitutional guarantees of personal liberty and security was recognized by the Georgia Supreme Court in 1905.[200] By 1949 the new tort had gained sufficient recognition to be included in the Restatement of Torts.[201] A celebrated article by Prosser published in 1960 demonstrated that the US tort of privacy is in fact four separate torts:[202]

---

[194] R Bagshaw, 'Obstacles on the Path to Privacy Torts' in P Birks (ed), *Privacy and Loyalty* (Oxford: 1997) ch 6.

[195] New Zealand and most US jurisdictions have a common law tort of privacy. A common law tort exists in some Canadian jurisdictions, but many have a statutory tort: E Paton-Simpson, 'Privacy and the Reasonable Paranoid: The Protection of Privacy in Public Places' (2000) 50 U of Toronto LJ 305, 309.

[196] L Warren and S Brandeis in 'The Right of Privacy' (1890) 4 Harvard L Rev 193, 216 included in this category any information about the private life, habits, acts and relations of an individual. Much of this is not confidential. It may even concern something that happened in a public place: *Daily Times Democrat v Graham* 162 So 2d 474 (1964) (photograph of claimant with her dress blown up as she left a fair). See also *Bradley v Wingnut Ltd Films* [1993] 1 NZLR 415, 424.

[197] The Canadian statutory privacy torts are actionable without proof of damage: eg Privacy Act 1970 (Man), s 2(2); Privacy Act 1990 (Nfld), s 3(1).

[198] R Sack, *Sack on Defamation* (3rd edn, New York: 2002) vol 1, ch 12; E Bohlman, 'Privacy in the Age of Information' (2002) J Information, L and Technology 2.

[199] L Brandeis and S Warren, 'The Right to Privacy' (1890) 4 Harvard L Rev 193.

[200] *Pavesich v New England Life Insurance Co.* 50 SE 68 (1905).

[201] s 867 (1939).

[202] W Prosser, 'Privacy' (1960) 48 California L Rev 383.

B. Tort

(1) intrusion upon seclusion;
(2) public disclosure of private facts;
(3) publicity placing a person in a false light;
(4) appropriation of name or likeness.

4.55 The public disclosure of private facts tort branch of the privacy tort is the one most likely to be relevant where a breach of confidentiality by a professional has occurred, although in the right circumstances another form might apply.[203] Liability for the private facts tort is confined to situations where the fact made public is highly offensive to a reasonable person with ordinary sensibilities[204] and the disclosure was made to a large number of people.[205] A university was held not liable for disclosing a transcript of a student's grades to a third party because the communication was not made to enough people.[206] These requirements seem to be based more on floodgates concerns than anything else. The difference in the injury a person suffers from the disclosure of information to fifty people rather than five is one of degree[207] and it is arguable that the disclosure of *any* fact in breach of a professional obligation of confidentiality is highly offensive to a reasonable person.

4.56 There are two potential defences to the private facts tort. On the principle that it cannot be wrong to publish a fact that is true when it would not be wrong to publish the same fact were it false, American courts apply to the private facts tort the defences of absolute and qualified privilege found in defamation.[208] To accommodate the potential conflict between the desire for privacy and other social values, such as freedom of speech, free circulation of information and disclosure of iniquity, it is another defence that the information is 'of legitimate concern to the public',[209] a phrase that, for constitutional reasons, has been generously interpreted in favour of the press to include anything which is 'newsworthy' according to the mores of the community and does not offend against common decency.[210] So few claimants have won suits against the media that one commentator has described the privacy action as a 'phantom tort'.[211]

---

[203] eg, photographing a client without consent would be an intrusion upon seclusion and using the photograph to illustrate a book without the client's consent could constitute appropriation of his likeness.

[204] *Restatement (Second) of Torts* (1977) para 652D, comment (c).   [205] ibid, comment (a).

[206] *Porten v University of San Francisco* 64 Ca App 3d 825, 828 (1976). But not all jurisdictions insist on disclosure to a large number of people: R Sack, *Sack on Defamation* (3rd edn, New York: 2002) vol 1, para 12.4.2.

[207] J Mintz, 'The Remains of Privacy's Disclosure Tort: an Exploration of the Private Domain' (1996) 55 Maryland L Rev 425, 438.

[208] *Carr v Watkins* 177 A 2d 841, 843 (1962); *Munsell v Ideal Food Stores* 494 P 2d 1063, 1075 (1992).

[209] *Restatement (Second) of Torts* (1977) para 652D, and comment d.

[210] ibid, comments g and h. Merciless exposure of details about a former mathematical prodigy was held to be 'of legitimate public interest' in *Sidis v F-R Publishing Corp* 113 F 2d 806, 809 (1940).

[211] D Zimmerman, 'Requiem for a Heavyweight: A Farewell to Warren and Brandeis's Privacy Tort' (1983) 68 Cornell L Rev 291, 362.

No right of privacy in pre-HRA English law

4.57 In 1931 Winfield reviewed the American scene in an article in the *Law Quarterly Review* and recommended that England too recognize a discrete tort of privacy actionable without proof of special damage.[212] The suggestion was not taken up by the courts[213] even when presented with a golden opportunity in *Kaye v Robertson*.[214] Here a trespassing journalist and a photographer from a tabloid newspaper 'interviewed' and photographed a well-known actor while he was recovering from brain surgery. The claimant, who was unable to recall the visit 15 minutes after it had happened, sought an interlocutory injunction to stop publication of the material. The judges felt only able to give relief on the grounds of injurious falsehood. Bingham LJ admitted that the claimant had suffered a gross invasion of privacy:

> If ever a person has a right to be let alone by strangers with no public interest to pursue, it must surely be when he lies in hospital recovering from brain surgery and in no more than partial command of his faculties. It is this invasion of his privacy which underlies the plaintiff's complaint. Yet it alone, however gross, does not entitle him to relief in English law.[215]

Glidewell LJ saw the facts as 'a graphic illustration of the desirability of Parliament considering whether and in what circumstances statutory provision can be made to protect the privacy of individuals'.[216] The third judge, Leggatt LJ, said that the right of privacy had so long been disregarded that it could only be recognized by the legislature.[217]

Failed bills and proposals

4.58 In Britain six private members' Bills creating a tort of privacy have come before Parliament.[218] None has reached the statute book. The Younger Committee[219] pronounced itself against a general tort of invasion of privacy,[220] preferring to recommend a reference of the law relating to breach of confidence, which it was felt was

---

[212] P Winfield, 'Privacy' (1931) 47 LQR 23.
[213] *Re X (A Minor)* [1975] Fam 47, 58.
[214] [1991] FSR 62.
[215] [1991] FSR 62 at 70.
[216] ibid at 66.
[217] ibid at 71.
[218] Details are given in *Infringement of Privacy*, Consultation Paper, Lord Chancellor's Department (1993) Appendix D and C Hartmann, 'The emergence of a statutory right to privacy tort in England' [1995] 6 J of Media L and Practice 10.
[219] *Report of the Committee on Privacy* (Cmnd 5012, 1970).
[220] The Calcutt Committee which reported in 1990 agreed: *Report of the Committee on Privacy and Related Matters* (Cm 1102, 1992) para 12.5. But see *Review of Press Self-Regulation* (Cm 2135, 1993) para 7.34.

potentially capable of affording considerable protection of privacy,[221] to the Law Commission and a new tort of disclosure or use of information unlawfully acquired.[222] Three things led the Committee to reach this conclusion: the difficulty of defining privacy;[223] the fact that there is a competing public interest in the free circulation of information and a desire not to involve the judiciary in the determination of controversial issues of social policy (an argument which it is difficult to take seriously in the post-HRA era). Further objections to a general tort of infringement of privacy is its breadth and the uncertainty this creates.[224] That is why in 1992 the National Heritage Committee preferred to recommend a number of civil offences which, cumulatively, created a tort of infringement of privacy, and criminalization of certain forms of physical intrusion.[225] The torts put forward in the 1992 report most directly relevant to this book are (1) obtaining and/or publishing harmful or embarrassing personal material or photographs and (2) obtaining and/or publishing private information or photographs without the permission of the person concerned. After consultation the Government decided that there was insufficient public consensus on which to base legislation.[226]

Effect of Human Rights Act 1998

The prospects for a dedicated privacy tort improved with the incorporation into English law by the HRA of much of the European Convention on Human Rights. The effect is to recognize a right to respect for private life in English law for the first time which must be protected in domestic law.[227] Because *Kaye v Robertson*[228] was not a decision of the House of Lords, it cannot be regarded as the last word as to whether a privacy tort exists still hidden in the depths of the common law. As far back as 1993, when Drake J granted the Princess of Wales an interlocutory injunction against a newspaper to prevent publication of photographs secretly taken of her at her fitness club, he suggested that it did.[229] But it is unlikely that his expectations will be fulfilled. Expansion of the parameters of the existing action

4.59

---

[221] *Report of the Committee on Privacy* (Cmnd 5012, 1972) para 630.
[222] ibid para 632.
[223] See also *Report of the Committee on Privacy and Related Matters* (Cm 1102, 1992) para 12.9.
[224] In New Zealand where a tort of invasion of personal privacy has been tentatively recognized, mainly in decisions at interlocutory level, its ingredients after more than ten years were still very unclear: see J Katz, 'Sex, Lies, Videotapes and Telephone Conversations: The Common Law of Privacy from a New Zealand Perspective' [1995] 1 EIPR 6. For subsequent developments see *P v D* [2000] 2 NZLR 591.
[225] Fourth Report, *Privacy and Media Intrusion* (HC 294-I, March 1993).
[226] *Privacy and Media Intrusion: the Government's Response* (Cm 2918, July 1995) para 4.13.
[227] Art 8 and HRA, s 6.
[228] [1991] FSR 62.
[229] (QB, 8 November 1993): 'I think that that the law would act in common law as well and, if there cannot be found yet an example where the common law has so intervened, then the causes of action are never closed in tort and this is a case for a door to open.'

for breach of confidence is the method preferred by most of the judiciary for giving effect to the Article 8 privacy right in domestic English law.[230] Lord Woolf said in *A v B plc & C*:

> It is most unlikely that any purpose will be served by a judge seeking to decide whether there exists a new cause of action in tort which protects privacy. In the great majority of situations, if not all situations, where the protection of privacy is justified, relating to events after the Human Rights Act came into force, an action for breach of confidence now will, where this is appropriate, provide the necessary protection.[231]

Moreover, a general tort of invasion of privacy which either left privacy undefined or defined it in the most general of terms might not be sufficiently foreseeable to qualify as 'law' by the European Court of Human Rights in a situation of conflict with Article 10.[232]

Breach of Confidence

4.60 In *Kaye v Robertson*[233] the claimant did not allege breach of confidence. Today an action for breach of confidence might succeed on the facts of that case.[234] There are some who believe that breach of confidence, notwithstanding its equitable origins, is a tort.[235] This is not the generally held view[236] although it received judicial endorsement from Butler-Sloss P in *Venables v NGN Ltd*.[237] In 1981 the Law Commission recommended turning breach of confidence from an equitable cause of action into a statutory tort exercisable against anyone who improperly obtained possession of information subject to an obligation of confidence.[238] Such a reclassification would involve more than a change in terminology: it would affect the range of available remedies[239] and remove the discretionary element in the award of compensation.[240] The Law Commission did not recommend that the new tort should, like libel, be actionable per se but did recommend that damages be

---

[230] *Douglas v Hello! Ltd* [2001] 2 All ER 289; *Venables v NGN Ltd* [2001] 1 All ER 908. Cp *Wainwright v Home Office* [2001] EWCA Civ 2081; [2002] 3 WLR 405, para 98.
[231] *A v B plc & C* [2002] EWCA Civ 337; [2002] 3 WLR 542, para 11, principle vi.
[232] *Sunday Times v UK* (1979) 2 EHRR 245, para 49.
[233] [1991] FSR 62.
[234] cp *Douglas v Hello! Ltd* [2001] 2 All ER 289; *Barber v Time* 159 SW 2d 291 (1942).
[235] R Scott, 'Developments in the Law of Confidentiality' [1990] Denning LJ 77, 83; S Todd, 'Protection of Privacy' in N Mullany (ed), *Torts in the Nineties* (North Ryde: 1997) 187. The issue of whether there is a tort of breach of confidence was raised but not decided in *O'Neill v DHSS* [1986] 5 NI 290, 294, 299–300.
[236] US courts have awarded damages in tort for the unauthorized disclosure of confidential information obtained in a confidential relationship between doctor and patient: *MacDonald v Clinger* 84 D 2d 482 (1982); *Humpers v First Interstate Bank of Oregon* 696 P 2d 527 (1985).
[237] [2001] 1 All ER 908, 922, 932. See also *Douglas v Hello! Ltd* [2001] 2 All ER 289, para 117.
[238] Report No 110, *Breach of Confidence* (Cmnd 8388, 1981) paras 5.5, 6.28 et seq.
[239] eg loss of account of profits as a remedy.
[240] All equitable remedies are discretionary.

B. Tort

allowed for mental distress[241] and that punitive damages be available against a defendant who behaved outrageously.[242] A suggested widening of liability to allow the subject of the confidential information to sue, if the confider did not, was rejected.[243] No legislative activity has followed this report.[244]

---

[241] Report 110. *Breach of Confidence* (Cmnd 8388, 1981) paras 6.105–6.106.
[242] S Giles, 'Promises Betrayed; Breaches of Confidence as a Remedy for Invasions of Privacy' (1995) 43 Buffalo L Rev 1, 58.
[243] Report 110, *Breach of Confidence* (Cmnd 8388, 1981) para 5.9.
[244] The Government gave implementation of the Law Commission's report a low priority, *Hansard*, HC, col 257w, 2 March 1989. The National Heritage Select Committee supported the Law Commission (Fourth Report, *Privacy and Media Intrusion* (HC 294-I, March 1993) para 50) but still nothing happened.

5

EQUITY AND COPYRIGHT SOLUTIONS TO INTENTIONAL DISCLOSURE

A. Equity	5.02	B. Copyright	5.84
Breach of Confidence	5.02		
Breach of Fiduciary Duty	5.64		

Equity has been at the forefront in inventing remedies against the intentional disclosure of confidential personal information. Equitable causes of action, together with the action for breach of copyright are examined in this chapter. **5.01**

A. Equity

Breach of Confidence

Origins of the cause of action

Although equity has had a long-standing interest in protecting confidences, it was not until the nineteenth century that breach of confidence became a distinct equitable cause of action. The seminal case was *Prince Albert v Strange*,[1] an action brought in 1848 in the Court of Chancery by the Prince Consort with the dual object of preventing the exhibition of impressions taken from etchings made by the Royal Family and of preventing publication of an unauthorized catalogue describing them. As far as anyone could tell, the copies had been surreptitiously made by a dishonest employee of the Royal Printers to whom the original copperplates had been sent but it could not be proven that the defendant, Mr Strange, knew this. Prince Albert could claim the impressions on a property theory basis, but the existence of a property interest in the catalogue was dubious.[2] Lord **5.02**

---

[1] (1849) 41 ER 1171, Ch.
[2] Prince Albert's counsel argued that publication of the catalogue interfered with his property right in the etchings which entitled him to determine when they were to be made public: ibid at 1176.

Cottenham's decision to enjoin publication of the catalogue was put on alternative grounds: the Prince had a property interest in the information used to write the catalogue,[3] alternatively, because of the improper means by which the etchings came into the defendant's possession, the Prince had a right of action founded on 'breach of trust, confidence or contract'.[4] On either theory, the decision went beyond precedent, though Lord Cottenham claimed otherwise.

5.03 The courts were at first confused about the exact juristic basis of the breach of confidence action[5] and this remains a hotly debated subject amongst academics[6] and, to a lesser extent, judges.[7] The courts usually treat the action for breach of confidence as equitable.[8] Within equity the action has been variously attributed to a requirement of good faith, trust principles, a fiduciary obligation and principles of unjust enrichment.[9] Since the action was revived by the Court of Appeal in 1948 in *Saltman Engineering Co Ltd v Campbell Engineering Co Ltd*[10] most courts have opted for a 'good faith' basis.[11] In *Stephens v Avery*,[12] which, unusually for a case decided before 2000, involved personal information, Sir Nicolas Browne-Wilkinson said that equity intervened because 'it is unconscionable for a person who has received information on the basis that it is confidential subsequently to reveal that information'.

Breach of confidence and personal information

5.04 An action for breach of confidence arises independently of any pre-existing relationship between the parties[13] or any right of property.[14] Since 1948 the action for breach of confidence has been used chiefly to protect trade secrets, particularly exploitation of information by ex-employees. Before the Human Rights Act 1998 (HRA) few cases were about personal information, notable exceptions being *Argyll v Argyll*[15] (marital confidences); *Stephens v Avery*[16] (sexual orientation and

---

[3] This is contrary to most modern case law in which confidential information is not viewed as property: see paras 7.31 and 19.04 below.
[4] ibid at 1179.
[5] *Morison v Moat* (1851) 68 ER 492, 498.
[6] Lord Goff alluded to the debate in *Att-Gen v Guardian Newspapers Ltd (No 2)* [1988] 3 All ER 545, 659. For summaries of the conflicting views see M Neave and M Weinberg, 'The Nature and Function of Equities' (1978) 6 U of Tasmania L Rev 115, 118 et seq.; G Jones, 'Restitution of Benefits Obtained in Breach of Another's Confidence' (1970) 86 LQR 463.
[7] *General Mediterranean Holdings v Patel* [1999] 3 All ER 673, 681.
[8] *Kitechnology BV v UNCOR GmbH Plastmaschinen* [1995] FSR 765, 777–778; *Att-Gen v Guardian Newspapers (No 2)* [1988] 3 All ER 545, 625.
[9] R Wacks, 'Breach of Confidence and the Protection of Privacy' [1977] NLJ 328.
[10] (1948) 65 RPC 203.
[11] per Lord Denning MR, *Fraser v Evans* [1969] 1 All ER 8, 11.
[12] [1988] 2 WLR 1280, 1286.
[13] See para 6.07 below.
[14] *Stephens v Avery* [1988] 2 WLR 1280.
[15] [1967] 1 Ch 302.
[16] [1988] 2 WLR 1280.

A. Equity

conduct); *X v Y*[17] (identity of AIDS victims); and *Barrymore v NGN Ltd* (details of sexual conduct).[18] In 1993 Princess Diana instigated an action alleging breach of confidence against Mirror Group Newspapers[19] and the manager of Fitness LA, a private gym, to stop publication of photographs taken by a concealed camera which showed her exercising in a leotard and cycling shorts.[20] The case was settled out of court. With the incorporation into domestic law of Article 8 by the HRA, breach of confidence has become popular in the absence of a free-standing tort of privacy as a means of securing personal privacy.[21]

5.05 According to Finn breach of confidence is 'is pre-eminently one of the fields of law which we know in part and prophesy in part'.[22] This observation is particularly apposite for breaches of confidence by professionals. There are only two reported English breach of confidence cases (both involving contracts) against professionals alleging unlawful disclosure of personal information that have gone to full trial.[23] One succeeded.[24]

Elements of the action for breach of confidence

The Megarry test

5.06 In the test formulated by Megarry J in *Coco v AN Clark (Engineers) Ltd*[25] (and confirmed in many later cases) there are three elements[26] to an action for breach of confidence for misuse or disclosure of a trade secret:

---

[17] [1988] 2 All ER 648.
[18] [1997] FSR 600.
[19] (QB, 8 November 1993).
[20] The following year the Prince of Wales is said by the Data Protection Registrar to have commenced a breach of confidence action against an ex-employee: *The Eleventh Report of the Data Protection Registrar* (HC 629, June 1995) 68. Years earlier he had obtained an injunction to prevent publication of a tape recording allegedly containing conversations with Lady Diana, before their marriage.
[21] eg *R v Department of Health, ex p Source Ltd* [2000] 1 All ER 786 (pharmaceutical prescriptions); *Douglas v Hello! Ltd* [2001] 2 All ER 289 (wedding photographs); *A v B plc & C* [2002] EWCA Civ 337, [2002] 2 All ER 545 (adultery); *Mills v NGN Ltd* [2001] EMLR 957 (address); *Beckham v MGN Ltd* (QB, 4 June 2001) (home interior); *Theakston v MGN Ltd* [2002] EWHC 13, [2002] EMLR 22, QB (sexual activity); *Campbell v MGN Ltd* [2002] EWCA 499, [2002] EMLR 30, QB (drug addiction therapy); *Campbell v Frisbee* [2002] EWHC 328, [2002] EMLR 31, Ch (sexual activity). A number of other actions are neither reported nor available on a commercial database.
[22] P Finn, *Fiduciary Obligations* (Sydney: 1977) 130.
[23] The claim against the solicitor in *Re Kavanagh* [1949] 2 All ER 264, 265 was settled out of court.
[24] *Fogg v Gaulter and Blane* (1960) 110 LJ 718. See para 4.17 above. The one that failed was *W v Egdell* [1989] 1 All ER 1089 (see paras 4.17 and 11.21).
[25] [1969] RPC 41, 49. These elements were endorsed by Lord Griffiths in *Att-Gen v Guardian Newspapers Ltd (No 2)* [1988] 3 All ER 545, 649.
[26] In personal injury cases there is possibly a fourth requirement for information that is capable of being either true or false and that is that the information is substantially true: see para 1.21 above.

(1) the information has a 'quality of confidence about it';
(2) the information was communicated in circumstances importing an obligation of confidence;
(3) unauthorized disclosure or use of the information 'to the detriment of the party communicating it'.

The manner in which the confidential information has been preserved by the defendant is irrelevant; it can be on paper, as a photograph,[27] a drawing,[28] a model,[29] as computer data or inside the defendant's head.[30]

5.07 In *Hollinsworth v BC*[31] the British Columbia Court of Appeal said that the three elements listed by Megarry 'should not be treated with statutory rigidity in other cases. The tests determine the general scope of the obligation but do not define it precisely for all cases.' For actions for breach of confidence involving personal information there is good reason to think that all three elements of the Megarry test, if they still apply, do not apply in the manner he envisaged. Certainly, the second no longer does.[32]

Quality of confidentiality

5.08 **Information of a trivial character**   The court must be satisfied that the information that is the subject of the action is confidential. This means first and foremost that the information is not already public knowledge,[33] an issue that will be addressed in some detail. But it also means that there is something worth protecting.[34] The court will not help a claimant if in its view the information is of a trivial character.[35] Clients (and people generally) must not be encouraged to go to court every time a piece of information about them is disclosed that they had rather had not been disclosed. Whether the requirement that the information be of some significance judged by the standards of the reasonable person in the claimant's position is a substantive requirement of the action[36] or a discretionary bar to the intervention of equity is debatable.[37]

---

[27] *Pollard v Photographic Co* (1889) 40 Ch D 345; *Hellewell v Chief Constable of Derbyshire* [1995] 1 WLR 804, 807.
[28] *Nichotherm Electrical Co Ltd v Percy* [1957] RPC 207.
[29] In *Franklin v Giddins* [1978] 1 Qd R 72 the information was preserved as a budwood from a tree.
[30] *Printers & Finishers v Holloway* [1965] RPC 239, 255. Cp H Fenwick and G Phillipson, 'Confidence and Privacy: A Re-Examination' (1996) 55 CLJ 447, 450.
[31] (1998) 83 ACWS (3d) 525.
[32] See para 6.13 below.
[33] *Saltman Engineering Co Ltd v Campbell Engineering Co Ltd* (1948) 65 RPC 203, 215.
[34] *Att-Gen v Guardian Newspapers Ltd (No 2)* [1998] 3 All ER 545, 624 per Bingham LJ.
[35] [1988] 3 All ER 545, 659. See also *Att-Gen v Blake* [1996] 3 All ER 903, 908, 909. Art 8 will not be engaged if an interference with respect for private life is trivial: *Costello-Roberts v UK* (1993) 19 EHRR 112.
[36] *Att-Gen v Guardian Newspapers Ltd (No 2)* [1998] 3 All ER 545, 659.
[37] *Stephens v Avery* [1988] 2 WLR 1280, 1285.

A. Equity

Information in the public domain Equity does not act in vain and therefore does not protect information that has been widely disseminated. This aspect of the confidentiality requirement is sometimes referred to as the public domain defence.[38] In truth it is not a defence but something that prevents an obligation of confidentiality from existing in the first place. **5.09**

> [C]onfidentiality only applies to information to the extent that it is confidential . . . [O]nce it has entered what is usually called the public domain (which means no more than that the information in question is so generally accessible that, in all the circumstances, it cannot be regarded as confidential) then, as a general rule, the principle of confidentiality can have no application to it.[39]

Confidential information may be mixed with information in the public domain.[40] The solution is to sever that which is in the public domain from the rest if this is possible. If it is not, equity may protect the lot.[41]

Deciding whether personal information is in the public domain is problematic.[42] Trade secrets precedents are not useful guides. A trade secret loses its commercial value immediately it becomes accessible to competitors.[43] Establishing that personal information has lost its confidential character is more difficult.[44] Referring to *Argyll v Argyll*,[45] Lord Keith suggested in *Spycatcher (No 2)* that had the duke published information about the marriage in American newspapers the duchess might still have been able to restrain publication of the same information in England.[46] **5.10**

The courts approach the public domain issue in two different ways. The first involves asking whether the information was known to a substantial number of **5.11**

---

[38] M Tugendhat, 'Privacy and celebrity' (2001) 37 Amicus Curiae 3, 5.
[39] per Lord Goff, *Att-Gen v Guardian Newspapers Ltd (No 2)* [1988] 3 All ER 545, 659. Note, that it may still be a breach of the DPA to disclose sensitive personal data about a client that is in the public domain without consent: see paras 18.25–18.26 below.
[40] eg *Campbell v MGN Ltd* [2002] EWHC 499, [2002] EMLR 30, QB; *CMI-Centers for Medical Innovation BmbH v Phytopharm plc* [1999] FSR 235, para 53.
[41] *Falconer v ABC* [1992] 1 VR 662, 669. A mix of confidential and non-confidential information may hinder an application for an injunction: *Times Newspapers v NGN Ltd* [1993] EMLR 443 and see para 8.10 below.
[42] In *Att-Gen v Times Newspapers Ltd* [2001] 1 WLR 885, 896 the Court of Appeal held that a newspaper could not be required to seek confirmation from the Attorney-General or a court that facts intended for republication had been sufficiently brought into the public domain by prior publication.
[43] R Dean, *The Law of Trade Secrets* (Sydney: 1990) 133, 134.
[44] *B v H Bauer Publishing Ltd* [2002] EMLR 8, para 26.
[45] [1967] 1 Ch 302.
[46] [1988] 3 All ER 545, 643. An injunction was granted to the parents of Gracie Attard, the surviving cojoined twin, to prevent republication of a photograph taken without the consent of the parents and published once in the Manchester Evening News: M Tugendhat and I Christie (eds), *The Law of Privacy and the Media* (Oxford: 2002) para 4.09.

people.[47] If Lord Keith's views are accepted, these people must be in the jurisdiction in which the court is sitting. This test allows for friends,[48] family and even some strangers[49] to be privy to the personal information without it ceasing to be confidential. What constitutes a substantial number of people is a question of circumstance and degree[50] and can only be decided on a case-by-case basis.[51] There have been occasions when information has been circulated widely to people upon whom no obligation of confidentiality has been impressed without destroying its confidentiality.[52]

5.12 The other approach is to ask whether the information is 'generally accessible'[53] which is to say, easily found by members of the public who have no special expertise. On this approach most information on the internet is in the public domain.[54] However, coded messages left on internet sites by terrorist groups for their members, for example, are not. In *Att-Gen v Greater Manchester Newspapers Ltd*[55] information was located in a specialist government publication held by many public libraries and on a government website. The information was provided in a statistical format that the average person could not readily decipher. Dame Elizabeth Butler-Sloss asked: '[d]oes the existence of information which can be accessed but is unlikely to be known to be available to the general public, not engaged in statistics or research of some sort, amount to being as a matter of reality in the public domain?'[56] She decided that it did not. The Law Reform Commission of Hong Kong has suggested that information is not in the public domain if a significant amount of labour, skill or money is required to access it.[57] Thus an action for breach of confidence will not be defeated by evidence that the information could be found by a prolonged manual search of newspaper backfiles.

5.13 Feldman's assessment is that the range of information that can be protected by an action for breach of confidence will expand as the breadth of what the Article 8 right to respect for private life protects comes to be appreciated.[58] The fact that private information has had a public airing will not preclude its disclosure being

---

[47] *Stephens v Avery* [1988] 2 WLR 1280, 1285; *Barrymore v NGN Ltd* [1997] FSR 600, 603.
[48] In *Prince Albert v Strange* (1849) 41 ER 1171, Ch the Prince Consort had given copies of the Royal Family's etchings to friends. See also *Douglas v Hello! Ltd* [2001] 2 All ER 289, para 165, where 250 wedding guests had seen the bride and groom.
[49] *R v Galvin* [1987] 2 All ER 851, 856.
[50] *Franchi v Franchi* [1967] RPC 149, 153.
[51] *Att-Gen v Guardian Newspapers Ltd (No 2)* [1988] 3 All ER 545, 575.
[52] cp *Caird v Sime* (1887) 12 App Cas 236; *Exchange Telegraph Co Ltd v Central News Ltd* [1897] 2 Ch 48; *Foster v Mountford & Rigby Ltd* (1976) 29 FLR 233; *R v Galvin* [1987] 2 All ER 851, 856.
[53] *Att-Gen v Guardian Newspapers Ltd (No 2)* [1988] 3 All ER 545, 659. See also *Coulthard v Disco Mix Club* [1992] 2 All ER 457, 474.
[54] cp *Att-Gen v Times* [2001] 1 WLR 885, para 24.
[55] [2001] TLR 688.
[56] [2001] TLR 688, para 27.
[57] *Civil Liability for Invasion of Privacy* (1999) 139.
[58] D Feldman, *Civil Liberties and Human Rights in England and Wales* (Oxford: 2002) 622.

an interference with Article 8(1). Most obviously this is so when the information concerns a stale criminal conviction.[59] Previous public disclosure will have a bearing on the question whether any interference with the right to respect for private life is proportionate. The effect of the HRA may therefore be to convert prior publicity from an automatic bar to liability to a factor to be considered in deciding whether there has been a breach of confidence or the relief sought should be granted.

Professionals and information in the public domain In the case of a professional it was probably already the case before 2000 that information in the public domain could be the subject of an obligation of confidentiality to the client because of the Court of Appeal's decision in *Schering Chemicals v Falkman Ltd*.[60] In this case the defendant, an experienced broadcaster, was hired as a sub-contractor on a freelance basis to provide public relations training to Schering's executives to counter the bad publicity the company had received over a drug that might have been the cause of deformities in children born to women who had taken the drug during pregnancy. A large amount of information about the drug passed from Scherings to the sub-contractor which the defendant accepted was received in confidence. When the training course was over, the sub-contractor made a television documentary programme about the drug based entirely on information in the public domain. The company obtained an injunction to prevent the film being shown on the ground of breach of duty of confidence arising out of the trust that Schering had placed in him when acting as their confidential professional adviser. Shaw LJ described the defence that the information was in the public domain as 'cynical; some might regard it as specious. Even in the commercial field, ethics and good faith are not to be regarded as merely opportunist or expedient.'[61] 5.14

If this is the position for commercial information, how much more must this be so for personal information disclosed to a professional. No professional code exempts information in the public domain from the professional's obligation of confidentiality[62] and with good reason. Disclosure of personal information 5.15

---

[59] See para 5.20 below.
[60] [1981] 2 All ER 321.
[61] [1981] 2 All ER 321, 338. The matter was put more mildly by Templeman LJ (ibid at 346) who said '[a]s between Scherings and Mr Elstein, if Mr Elstein had obtained information from sources other than Scherings, then it would of course not have been confidential in his hands, but in agreeing to advise Scherings and by accepting information from them to enable him to advise Scherings, Mr Elstein placed himself under a duty . . . not to make use of that information without the consent of Scherings in a manner which Scherings reasonably considered to be harmful to their cause'.
[62] The GMC's guidelines on handling *Media Inquiries about Patients* (November 1996) forbid disclosure of information that is in the public domain if it was learnt in a professional capacity; see http://www.gmc-uk.org/standards/MEDIA.HTM. When a hospital released details about the treatment that Mrs Rose Addis had received in the Accident and Emergency Department of an NHS hospital after her daughter and grandson complained to the media about her treatment, a

beyond the trivial is a breach of trust which undermines the client-professional relationship and the dignity of the client.[63]

5.16 **Does information remain in the public domain forever?** If the *Schering* approach is followed, it becomes immaterial whether the information disclosed by a professional is or was in the public domain. But given that Lord Denning delivered a powerful dissenting judgment in *Schering Chemicals v Falkman Ltd*[64] based on Article 10 of the European Convention on Human Rights (ECHR), it is best to assume for now the contrary and consider what effect it might have that the information disclosed was once, but is no longer, widely known. In these circumstances does the professional have a defence? The issue is whether information can pass out of, as well as into, the public domain. In dismissing the public domain argument in *Schering Chemicals v Falkman Ltd* Shaw LJ said that, 'though facts may be widely known, they are not ever-present in the minds of the public. To extend the knowledge or to revive the recollection of matters which may be detrimental or prejudicial to the interests of some person or organisation is not to be condoned because the facts are already known to some and linger in the memories of others.'[65] This is some acknowledgement that information may regain the necessary quality of confidentiality to be the subject of an action for breach of confidence when no longer widely known by, or readily accessible to, members of the public.[66] Whether this point has been reached will depend upon the notoriety of the information and the ease with which records can be accessed.[66a] Short of the destruction of our civilization, information about the death of Princess Diana may never escape the public domain but more mundane news may be quickly forgotten.[67] In *G v Day*,[68] an Australian court granted an injunction to restrain publication of the identity of a police informant who had been promised anonymity by the police notwithstand-

---

GMC spokesman (as reported in 'Doctors concerned patients may lose confidence in confidentiality', the Telegraph, 25 January 2001) commented: '[i]f information is in the public domain a common law interpretation might be that there is no problem with disclosure, but we believe that doctors have a duty above and beyond that.'

[63] P Blume, *Protection of Informational Privacy* (Copenhagen: 2002) 7. But see Health Information Privacy Code 1994 (NZ), r 11(i)(d) available at http://www.privacy.org.nz.

[64] [1981] 2 All ER 321, 333–334. See also *Att-Gen v Blake* [1996] 3 All ER 903, 907, 909. Blake, a former intelligence officer, was assumed not to have breached the obligation of confidentiality to which, on leaving the intelligence services, he had been subject because all the information that he had disclosed in his book was at the date of publication in the public domain.

[65] per Shaw LJ, [1981] 2 All ER 321, 338. See also *Mills v NGN Ltd* [2001] EMLR 957, para 25. Lord Oliver expressed a preference for Lord Denning's judgment in *Att-Gen v Guardian Newspapers* [1987] 3 ALL ER 316, 374.

[66] Contrast PCC, *Submission to the Culture, Media and Sport Select Commitee* (February 2003) § C (3) para 15 available www.pccpapers.org.uk/docs.php.

[66a] Putting the back issues of newspapers on-line is going to prolong the time they remain in the public domain.

[67] cp *Briscoe v Reader's Digest Ass Inc* 93 Cal Rptr 866 (1971).

[68] [1982] 1 NSWLR 24, 40.

ing that his name had been twice mentioned in television news broadcasts. The court treated the television broadcasts as transitory phenomena.[69]

5.17 The strongest judicial support for treating the public domain as something that does not claim personal information forever is found in *R v BCC, ex p Granada Television Ltd* where the Court of Appeal upheld the dismissal of an application for a judicial review of the Broadcasting Complaints Commission's[70] ruling that Granada Television had infringed the privacy of two sets of parents by giving publicity to the deaths of their respective daughters several years after the event without forewarning them. Balcombe LJ said:

> Even in those States of the USA which recognize the tort of invasion of privacy it is by no means clear that the fact that the matter is already in the public domain precludes there being an invasion of privacy . . . In my judgment it is clear that the fact that a matter has once been in the public domain cannot prevent its resurrection, possibly many years later from being an infringement of privacy.[71]

5.18 The Australian court in *G v Day* might have taken a different view had the original disclosure been to, or by, a court.[72] In its report on *Breach of Confidence* the Law Commission[73] drew a sharp distinction between personal information that had lost its notoriety through passage of time and personal information disclosed in litigation[74] or recorded in a public register. In *Elliott v Chief Constable of Wiltshire*[75] Sir Richard Scott refused to treat a criminal conviction pronounced in open court as confidential.[76] Any contrary argument was treated as unarguable by the Divisional Court in *R v Chief Constable of North Wales, ex p AB*,[77] a case in which the police had disclosed the applicants' previous convictions for paedophile offences. When the case was before the Court of Appeal[78] Lord Woolf MR did not contradict this. He

---

[69] cp *Kwok v Thang* [1999] NSWSC 1034: '[b]ut a prior transitory publication of information, which may not be remembered or discovered by all those who would be interested in it, does not necessarily defeat an obligation of confidentiality, where what is sought to be restrained is a more permanent and enduring form of disclosure.' per Austin J (LEXIS *15).

[70] Predecessor of the Broadcasting Standards Commission.

[71] [1995] EMLR 163, 168.

[72] See E Paton-Simpson, 'Private Circles and Public Squares: Invasion of Privacy by the Publication of "Private Facts" ' (1998) 61 MLR 318, 326 et seq.

[73] Law Commission Report 110, *Breach of Confidence* (Cmnd 8388, 1981) para 6.69.

[74] In the US an action in tort for breach of privacy cannot be maintained if the information was a matter of public record because such facts are not private ones and matter disclosed in court proceedings is inherently of legitimate public concern: K Rhodes, 'Open Court Proceedings and Privacy Law' (1996) 74 Texas L Rev 881, 909.

[75] The Times, 5 December 1996. This could subvert the policy of the Rehabilitation of Offences Act 1974 of conferring a measure of confidentiality on convictions for lesser offences after a prescribed time: Michael, 'Open Justice: Publicity and the Judicial Process' [1993] CLP 190, 202.

[76] See also *Bunn v BBC* [1998] 3 All ER 552, 557 where Lightman J took this view of a statement read out in court.

[77] [1997] 4 All ER 691, 701.

[78] [1998] 3 All ER 310, 321.

Chapter 5: Equity and Copyright Solutions to Intentional Disclosure

did, however, hold that absent any public interest in disclosure, the police had a *public law duty* not to disclose the applicants' criminal record. This is consistent with the Data Protection Act 1998 (DPA) which treats criminal convictions as sensitive personal data.[79]

5.19 If the police were prima facie not entitled to disclose the applicants' criminal past, would the applicants' doctor, dentist or lawyer—people the applicants could reasonably expect not to disclose adverse personal information without their consent—have disclosed the information with impunity in the absence of a public interest in the disclosure? It seems obvious that if the courts attach importance to candid exchanges between professionals and their clients[80] and the successful reintegration of criminals into society,[81] disclosure of a client's criminal past by a professional should be treated as a breach of confidence unless there is a public interest defence.[82]

5.20 Whatever the legal position before 2000, in the HRA era the disclosure of information that was, but is no longer, well known may interfere with the right to respect for private life guaranteed by Article 8(1). '[T]he fact that a matter has once been in the public domain cannot prevent its resurrection, possibly many years later, from being an infringement of privacy.'[83] In *Botta v Italy* the European Court of Human Rights (ECtHR) said that the purpose of Article 8 was 'to ensure the development, without interference, of the personality of each individual in his relations with other human beings'.[84] Disclosure of past convictions impedes a fresh start.[85] Therefore, although a past conviction is a public fact, its unauthorized disclosure after an individual has paid his debt to society 'could conceivably constitute an interference with his private life'.[86] This human rights angle was flagged by Buxton J in *R v Chief Constable of North Wales, ex p AB*:

---

[79] See para 18.23 below.
[80] See para 1.46 above.
[81] cp *Melvin v Reid* 112 Cal App 285, 292 (1931). It was accepted that the facts of the crime could be republished. What the court thought was wrong was the identification of the claimant, a former prostitute, who had been acquitted of the murder, had married and become respectable.
[82] See ch 11.
[83] per Balcombe LJ, *R v BCC, ex p Granada* [1995] EMLR 163, 168.
[84] (1998) 26 EHRR 241, para 32.
[85] This is the thinking behind the Rehabilitation of Offenders Act 1974 which requires a person who has not been sentenced to more than two and a half years' imprisonment to be treated for all purposes of law as if he had no prior convictions after a specified period. M Tugendhat, 'The Data Protection Act 1998 and the Media' in *Yearbook of Copyright and Media Law 2000* 115, 134 draws attention to the French right to be forgotten ('droit a l'oubli') which prevents the individual from being crushed by his past. See also *Briscoe v Reader's Digest Assoc Inc* 93 Cal Rptr 866, 872 where the court said that 'identification of the actor in reports of long past crimes usually serves little independent public purpose'. But see *Cox Broadcasting Corp v Cohn* 420 US 469 (1975).
[86] *X v Norway* (1977) 14 DR 228, 229. It was assumed that disclosure of a spent conviction was a breach of Art 8 in *R v Governor of HM Prison Dartmoor, ex p N* (QBD Admin, 13 February 2001). But see *R (on the application of Pearson) v DVLA* [2002] EWHC 2482 para 15. Note that in

A. Equity

I . . . consider that a wish that certain facts in one's past, however notorious at the time, should remain in the past is an aspect of the subject's private life sufficient at least potentially to raise questions under art. 8 of the Convention for the Protection of Human Rights . . .[87]

Thus it would appear that if a professional were to disclose that her client has a conviction, the professional would have to show that the disclosure was for an aim mentioned in Article 8(2), proportionate and necessary in a democratic society.[88] If the professional cannot do this, HRA, s 6 requires the court to provide the client with a remedy.[89] Although a rule that prevents a professional from arbitrarily disclosing a client's convictions interferes with the professional's own right of freedom of expression, this interference is easily justified.

5.21

A quite different view might be taken, given the importance attached to media freedom,[90] if the press were to receive information about the conviction from a professional and want to publish the fact, whether or not there was a current public interest in the information amongst the newspaper's readers.[91] The Strasbourg jurisprudence shows that the ECtHR will rarely find an interference with media freedom justified.[92]

5.22

Rotaru v Romania Application 2834/95, 8 BHRC 449, para 43 the ECtHR said that public information can fall within the scope of private life where it is systematically collected and stored by the state and that this 'is all the truer where such information concerns a person's distant past'. In other words, passage of time increases the privacy of information.

[87] [1997] 4 All ER 691, 704. See also Lord Bingham at 702. The Divisional Court (ibid at 702, 704) held that the disclosure was a justified interference with the applicant's Art 8 rights. The issue is bound to be explored when Mary Bell's application for a permanent injunction to protect her new identity comes before the High Court. At the time of writing, an interim injunction has been granted to preserve the status quo until that hearing: The Telegraph, 14 April 2002, Independent, 18 April 2002. Mary Bell, now aged 45, was convicted at the age of 11 of killing two small children. She served 12 years and was then released.

[88] See para 3.19 above. The disclosure in *R v Chief Constable of North Wales, ex p AB* [1997] 4 All ER 691 would very probably have been found to be a justified interference with Art 8. On this point see also *R v Secretary of State for Health, ex p SW* (2000) HRLR 702. Literature includes R Mullender, 'Privacy, Paedophilia and the European Convention on Human Rights: A Deontological Approach' [1998] PL 384.

[89] See para 3.05 above.

[90] See paras 3.17 and 8.14.

[91] cp *Kelly v BBC* [2001] 1 All ER 323, 357–358.

[92] *Jersild v Denmark* (1995) 19 EHRR 1, para 25; *Bladet Tromso v Stensas Norway* (1999) 29 EHRR 125. When the information concerns a past criminal conviction, a court that embarks on the task of striking a balance between press freedom and the individual's right to respect for private life might consider the factors suggested by the Law Reform Commission of Hong Kong in its *Consultation Paper on the Regulation of Media Intrusion* (Hong Kong: 1999) 46:

'• whether he is a public figure and, if so, whether there is a connection between the offence for which he was convicted and his public office or mandate;
• whether the offence in question is consistent with his public image;
• the seriousness of the offence;
• how many years have elapsed since he was convicted of the offence;
• whether the individual had become fully rehabilitated; and whether the publication of the identity of the individual could be justified on other grounds.'

5.23 Obviously private information The broadening of the action for breach of confidence[93] to include information that was not imparted to the defendant under circumstances of trust and confidence (the second element of the Megarry test, shortly to be discussed) has opened up the need for a more rigorous test of confidential quality. That the information is not trivial and prior to disclosure was not public knowledge will (subject to remarks earlier about the unique obligations of a professional to her client[94]) remain requirements, but where there is no pre-existing relationship there will have to be something more to mark out information as 'obviously confidential',[95] that is, as information which according to contemporary standards of social behaviour a reasonable person would understand to be intended to be kept secret or to be available to a limited group to which the defendant does not belong.[96] Several tests for divining private facts are mentioned in the cases and these together with examples of information that in the past has been said to be confidential are considered in chapter 6. When information is imparted in the course of, or generated within a relationship of trust,[97] looking for indicia of confidentiality beyond those already discussed in this chapter should be unnecessary.

Confidential impartation of information

5.24 General test One way in which private information becomes the subject of an obligation of a confidence in equity is if it is acquired for a limited purpose within a relationship of trust.[98] The relationship need not be one that the law recognizes for any other purpose.[99]

> If information is accepted on the basis that it will be kept secret, the recipient's conscience is bound by that confidence, and it will be unconscionable for him to break his duty of confidence by publishing the information to others.[100]

5.25 The existence of a relationship of trust can be established by asking whether:

(1) a reasonable person standing in the defendant's shoes would have realized (even if the actual confidant did not) that the information was provided on a confidential basis;[101] or

---

[93] See paras 6.07–6.08 below. In *Mills v NGN Ltd* [2001] EMLR 957, para 26 Collins J summed up the change by saying that it is 'no longer a necessary element of the cause of action that information arises from a confidential relationship'.

[94] See paras 5.14 et seq.

[95] per Lord Goff, *Att-Gen v Guardian Newspapers (No 2)* [1988] 3 All ER 545, 659.

[96] *ABC v Lenah Game Meats Pty Ltd* [2001] HCA 63, para 42. cp *Dagg v Canada (Minister of Finance)* [1997] 2 SCR 403, para 71.

[97] See para 5.24 below.

[98] *Barrymore v NGN Ltd* [1997] FSR 600, 602.

[99] eg *Stephens v Avery* [1988] 2 WLR 1280, *A v B & C* (HC, 10 August 2001). The confider and confidant (before the disclosure) were in the first case two friends and in the second lovers.

[100] *Douglas v Hello! Ltd* [2001] 2 All ER 289, para 65.

[101] *Coco v AN Clark (Engineers) Ltd* [1969] RPC 41, 48. The duty may be imposed unilaterally 'by the confider telling the confidant that the information is given "in confidence" ' per Browne-Wilkinson V-C, *Marcel v Commissioner of Police of the Metropolis* [1991] 1 All ER 845, 853.

(2) the confidant gave an express undertaking of confidentiality.[102]

A variant to these tests was suggested by Lord Woolf in *A v B plc and C ('Flitcroft')*:

> A duty of confidence will arise whenever the party subject to the duty is in a situation where he either knows or ought to know that the other person can reasonably expect his privacy to be protected.[103]

5.26 Whatever test is adopted the communication of personal information to a professional in her professional capacity is bound to satisfy it.[104] In *R v Department of Health, ex p Source Informatics*, Simon Brown LJ referred to the pharmacist's 'undoubted duty of confidentiality to a patient' who presented a prescription[105] and in a New Zealand case Anderson J said:

> It should be so obvious as to go without saying that when a person seeking psychological support consults, even gratuitously as here, a professional psychologist acting in such capacity for psychological advice then the usual confidentiality of a psychologist/patient relationship must apply.[106]

5.27 **Established professional relationships of confidentiality** An obligation of confidentiality has long been associated with the following professional relationships: lawyer;[107] accountant;[108] stockbroker;[109] social worker[110] and client; health professional and patient;[111] priest and penitent;[112] and bank and customer.[113] Whenever a person provides personal information within one of these categories of relationship, the law presumes the communication and any information generated by the relationship to be confidential: '[t]he nature of the subject matter or the

---

[102] *Stephen v Avery* [1988] 2 WLR 1280, 1286.
[103] [2002] EWCA Civ 337; [2002] 3 WLR 542, para 11 guideline ix.
[104] cp *H (A Healthcare Worker) v Associated Newspapers Ltd* [2002] EWCA Civ 195; (2002) 65 BMLR 132, para 28.
[105] [2000] 1 All ER 786, 790.
[106] *JD v Ross* [1998] NZFLR 951, LEXIS transcript 15. That all those involved in the care of a patient in a hospital owe a duty of confidence in respect of information acquired about the patient was recognized in *Re C (A Minor) (No 2)* [1989] 2 All ER 791, 795, 800.
[107] *Re Van Laun, ex p Chatterton* [1907] 2 KB 23, 29; *Parry-Jones v Law Society* [1969] 1 Ch 1, 7; *Sidaway v Bethlem Royal Hospital* [1984] 1 All ER 1018, 1032; *Att-Gen v Guardian Newspapers Ltd (No 2)* [1988] 3 All ER 545, 595, 639; *Nelson v Nelson* [1997] 1 All ER 970, 974.
[108] *Weld-Blundell v Stephens* [1919] 1 KB 520; *Fogg v Gaulter and Blane* (1960) 110 LJ 718; *W v Egdell* [1990] 1 All ER 835, 848; *Agip (Africa) Ltd v Jackson* [1992] 4 All ER 451, 466.
[109] *Brown v Inland Revenue Commissioners* [1964] 3 All ER 119, 127.
[110] *Venables v NGN Ltd* [2001] 1 All ER 908, 940.
[111] *Parry-Jones v Law Society* [1969] 1 Ch 1, 7; *Goddard v Nationwide Building Society* [1986] 3 All ER 264, 271; *W v Egdell* [1990] 1 All ER 835, 848; *Venables v NGN Ltd* [2001] 1 All ER 908, 941.
[112] *Goddard v Nationwide Building Society* [1986] 3 All ER 264, 271; *Att-Gen v Guardian (No 2)* [1988] 3 All ER 545, 639; *W v Egdell* [1990] 1 All ER 835, 848; *Marcel v Commissioner of Police of the Metropolis* [1991] 1 All ER 845, 853.
[113] *Tournier v National Provincial and Union Bank of England* [1924] 1 KB 461; *Parry-Jones v Law Society* [1969] 1 Ch 1, 7; *Att-Gen v Guardian Newspapers Ltd (No 2)* [1988] 3 All ER 545, 639; *W v Egdell* [1990] 1 All ER 835, 848.

circumstances of the defendant's activities ... suffice ... to give rise to liability for breach of confidence'.[114] There is no need for the client to be able to communicate or to have sufficient understanding to have an expectation of confidentiality: in law,[115] as in ethics,[116] a doctor (and by analogy any other professional) owes clients who are incompetent a duty of confidentiality. Ungoed-Thomas J explained in *Argyll v Argyll* that the choice of relationships deserving of protection by an obligation of confidentiality is ultimately a matter of policy: '[i]t is sufficient that the court recognizes that the communications are confidential, and their publication within the mischief which the law as its policy seeks to avoid.'[117]

Unauthorized disclosure or use of confidential information

5.28 **Co-existence of contractual and equitable obligations of confidentiality** In the reported cases there is a tendency to assume that contractual and equitable obligations of confidentiality co-exist and are co-extensive.[118] This assumption has made it unnecessary to consider whether the claimant who is owed a contractual obligation of confidentiality can sue on an equitable obligation of confidentiality. Meagher, Gummow and Lehane suggest that 'where there is a contract then it is to the contract that the court should look to see from express words or necessary implication what the obligations of the parties are and the introduction of equitable concepts should be resisted.'[119] This is what happens when an employee is accused of leaking confidential information. The courts concentrate on the employee's contractual duty of confidentiality which is rooted in an obligation of mutual trust and confidence.[120] A contractual obligation of confidentiality can modify or expand the equitable obligation; the parties can agree to keep confidential that which equity would refuse to protect because it is trivial or is in the public domain.

5.29 **Scope of the equitable obligation of confidentiality** There is little case law of any substance on the breadth of a professional's obligation of confidentiality. The

---

[114] per Keene LJ, *Douglas v Hello! Ltd* [2001] 2 All ER 289, para 166.
[115] *Re C (No 2)* [1989] 2 All ER 791 (a minor); *Re Z* [1995] 4 All ER 961, 979 (a minor); *R (on the application of Stevens) Plymouth City Council* [2002] EWCA Civ 388; [2002] 1 FLR 1177, para 33 (doctors and social workers have obligations of confidentiality to an incompetent adult). See also para 19.94 below.
[116] BMA, *Consent, Rights and Choices in Health Care for Children and Young Persons* (London: 2000) 79: '[a]ll patients, regardless of their age, status or mental capacity, are entitled to expect that information about themselves provided or discovered in the course of their health care will not be revealed to others without their consent.' See also para 1.38 above.
[117] [1967] 1 Ch 302, 330.
[118] *Att-Gen v Guardian Newspapers Ltd (No 2)* [1988] 3 All ER 545, 573; *London Regional Transport v Mayor of London* [2001] EWCA Civ 1491, para 46. In *Collins (Engineers) Ltd v Roberts & Co Ltd* [1965] RPC 429, 431 the test used to find an equitable obligation of confidentiality was used to decide whether a term of confidentiality should be implied into a contract. See also *Bolkiah v KPMG* [1999] 1 All ER 517, 527.
[119] *Equity, Doctrine and Remedies* (4th edn, Sydney: 2002) paras 41–020.
[120] See para 21.17 below.

A. Equity

extent of liability for breach of confidence in equity ultimately turns on all the factual circumstances and 'the law's policies and purposes'.[121] In the context of professional practice these policies are protection of the client's privacy[122] and ensuring candour.[123] With these aims in mind, prima facie the equitable obligations of confidentiality of a professional might include:

(1) *Disclosure or use of personal information supplied by the client (including information from the client about others) for purposes for which it was not intended by the client to be used.*[124] In *China Light & Power Co Ltd v Ford*[125] a barrister who retained confidential papers belonging to a client after his retainer was terminated and used these to institute proceedings on his own behalf in the United States was found liable for breach of confidence. Information provided by the client during an abortive attempt to establish a professional relationship is subject to an obligation of confidentiality.[126] Release of more information than necessary in an authorized disclosure might convert it into an authorized disclosure attracting liability for breach of confidence.[127] Use does not have to involve disclosure. It is a breach of confidence to exploit the trade secrets of another without disclosing them.[128] Just so, it is a breach of confidence to use confidential personal information for an unauthorized purpose such as blackmail or as a lead to other sources of the same or related information.[129]

(2) *Disclosure or use of information about the client obtained from third parties*[130] *or by examining the client or from personal observation of private events involving the client*[131] *or by the professional's own researches*[132] *for a purpose not intended by the*

---

[121] P Finn, 'Professionals and Confidentiality' (1992) 14 Sydney L Rev 317, 324.
[122] *R v Department of Health, ex p Source Informatics Ltd* [2000] 1 All ER 786, 797.
[123] See para 1.46 above.
[124] cp *Norwich Pharamacal v Customs & Excise Commissioners* [1972] 3 All ER 813, 818; *Moorgate Tobacco Co Ltd v Philip Morris Ltd (No 2)* (1984) 156 CLR 414, 437.
[125] [1996] HKC LEXIS 250.
[126] The position is the same where legal professional privilege is claimed: see para 16.16 below.
[127] cp *Urbaniak v Newton* 226 Cal App 3d 1128, 1142.
[128] *Franklin v Giddins* [1978] Qd R 72; *CMI-Centers for Medical Innovation GmbH v Phytopharm plc* [1999] FSR 235.
[129] cp *Terrapin Ltd v Builders' Supply Co Ltd* [1960] RPC 128.
[130] *Tournier v National Provincial and Union Bank of England* [1924] 1 KB 461; *Att-Gen v Guardian (No 2)* [1988] 3 All ER 545, 571.
[131] In *A v B plc & C*, the confidants, C and D, had not received information in a literal sense. The information was the result of personal observation. This was deemed irrelevant by the judge at first instance and Lord Woolf in the Court of Appeal did not disagree with him about this: *A v B plc & C* [2002] EWCA Civ 337; [2002] 3 WLR 542, para 29. cp *Argyll v Argyll* [1965] 1 All ER 611. The injunction covered all private information about the Duchess that the Duke had acquired during their marriage, not just information she had given him. The court noted at 625 that the Duchess had acted in breach of confidence by revealing in an earlier newspaper article that the Duke had taken purple heart tablets. Case 01 HDCO 4859, NZ Health and Disability Commissioner available at http://www.hdc.org.nz is instructive on this point.
[132] *Att-Gen v Guardian Newspapers Ltd (No 2)* [1988] 3 All ER 545, 571.

client. The understanding of clients will be that all non-trivial information that the professional acquires about the client in a professional capacity is confidential.[133] Sometimes personal information about a client is provided to a professional by a third party, say a relative, on the understanding that it is to be used for the client's benefit but that the information, and/or its source, is not to be disclosed to the client. In these circumstances the professional owes the third party an obligation to keep the information and/or its source from the client,[133a] and the client an obligation not to disclose the information to anyone else.

(3) *Passing body samples or other items that the client provided to a third party for a purpose that has not been agreed*. In *R v Dyment* La Forest J said that a '[blood] specimen taken for medical reasons becomes part of the patient's personal medical record which should be kept confidential'.[134] If a doctor were to hand over a blood specimen taken for treatment purposes to police without the patient's consent this would prima facie constitute a breach of confidence.

(4) *Naming the client or admitting a professional relationship, except with the express or implied consent of the client, where the client's identity or the existence of the relationship is sensitive information*. The identity of a client is not automatically confidential.[135] It is to be noted that English law does not treat the identity of the lawyer's client as privileged information.[136] Whether the client's identity is sensitive enough to be confidential information will depend upon the extent of previous disclosure, the circumstances in which the professional relationship arose, the age of the information, efforts made to conceal the existence of the relationship and the purpose of the disclosure.[137] In *Lavallee, Rackel and Heintz v Canada (Att-Gen)* Veit J pointed out that:

> in some situations, it may be critically important for a client to be confident that no one will know that she has consulted a divorce lawyer, or a lawyer who specializes in sterilization claims, or in claims for individuals who contracted AIDS through the blood supply, or in defending drunk driving charges.[138]

5.30 The actual scope of the obligation of confidentiality will depend very much upon the circumstances of the individual case. For example, an employed professional may be in a position to give only a qualified promise of confidentiality.[139] She may

---

[133] cp Health and Social Care Act 2001, s 60 (a)(b).
[133a] Unless the professional refused to receive the information on the basis that it would be kept from the client.
[134] (1988) 26 DLR (4th) 399, 510.
[135] cp *Geisberger v Willuhn* 390 NE 2d 945 (1979).
[136] See para 16.23 below.
[137] cp *Dalgleish v Lothian & Borders Police Board* [1991] IRLR 422.
[138] (1998) 160 DLR (5th) 508, para 9. It is implicit in Law Society guidance to solicitors that the client's identity except where a matter of public record is confidential: see Law Society, *The Guide to the Professional Conduct of Solicitors* (8th edn, London: 1999) 324, para 16.01. The client's identity is asserted to be confidential in *Cordery on Solicitors* (9th edn, London: 1995) F [163].
[139] See para 21.09 below.

reserve the right to discuss confidential information or certain such information with people more senior than herself in the organization in which she is employed and to disclose suspicions of iniquity to the appropriate external authorities. To be enforceable, the obligation must exempt any legal obligation to disclose the information[140] and the discretion to disclose information in the public interest.[141]

Unauthorized disclosures that do not breach the obligation of confidentiality 5.31
Not every use or disclosure of confidential personal information for a purpose that has not been agreed is a breach of confidence. To be a breach of confidence, it must be unconscionable.

> To avoid taking unfair advantage of information does not necessarily mean that the confidee must not use it except for the confider's limited purpose... [T]here can be no breach of the equitable obligation unless the court concludes that a confidence reposed has been abused, that unconscientious use has been made of the information ... [C]ourts exercising equitable jurisdiction should not be too ready to import an equitable obligation of confidence in a marginal case. There is the distinction between use of confidential information in a way of which many people might disapprove, on the one hand, and illegal use on the other.[142]

In *R v Department of Health, ex p Source Informatics Ltd*[143] the issue before the 5.32 Court of Appeal was whether pharmacists could sell information contained on GPs' prescription forms to a commercial firm doing market research on the prescribing habits of GPs if no client could be identified from the information disclosed. The Department of Health had issued a policy document stating that the process breached patients' legal rights of confidence and right to privacy and this was challenged by the defendants. Simon Brown LJ asked

> [W]ould a reasonable pharmacist's conscience be troubled by the proposed use to be made of the patients' prescriptions? Would he think that by entering Source's scheme he was breaking his customers' confidence, making unconscientious use of the information they provided.[144]

He found that he would not.

The vagueness of the troubled conscience test makes it a poor predictor of when 5.33 disclosure is a breach of confidence. Indeed, it could be said that whether the

---

[140] See para 10.01 below.
[141] See para 11.04 below.
[142] *Smithkline & French Laboratories (Australia) Ltd v Department of Community Services and Health* (1999) 99 ALR 679, 691 as quoted in *R v Department of Health, ex p Source Informatics Ltd* [2000] 1 All ER 786, 793 by Simon Brown LJ.
[143] [2000] 1 All ER 786. For a strongly critical commentary see D Beyleveld and E Histed, 'Betrayal of Confidence in the Court of Appeal' (2000) 4 Medical L Intl 277.
[144] [2000] 1 All ER 786, 796. It has been suggested that Simon Brown LJ should have used the standard of the reasonable patient and not that of the reasonable pharmacist to decide whether the disclosure was conscionable: Y Dunkel, 'Medical Privacy Rights in Anonymous Data: Discussion of Rights in the United Kingdom and the United States in the Light of the Source Informatics Cases' (2001) Loyola of Los Angeles Intl & Comparative L Rev 41.

professional's conscience should be troubled is determined by the nature of the customer's rights.[145] Sedley LJ criticized the test in *London Regional Transport v Mayor of London*[146] saying that he would have preferred the Court of Appeal in *Source Informatics* to have applied a test of proportionality. This is no more helpful because the question addressed in *Source Informatics* was whether disclosure of anonymous information interfered with a customer's rights; only if this receives an affirmative answer does the question of proportionality (along with legitimate aim and necessity) arise.

5.34 In *Source Informatics* it was held that the obligation of confidentiality existed to protect the customer's privacy, and that a data collection system that relied on anonymous information[147] did not disturb the customer's privacy,[148] a view that is shared by the British Medical Association (BMA) which has consistently argued that disclosure of 'truly anonymous information does not breach confidentiality'[149] or Article 8 of the ECHR. In the words of Simon Brown LJ,

> The patient has no proprietorial claim to the prescription form or to the information it contains. Of course he can bestow or withhold his custom as he pleases—the pharmacist, note, has no such right: he is by law bound to dispense to whoever presents a prescription. But that gives the patient no property in the information and no right to control its use provided only and always that his privacy is not put at risk . . . his only legitimate interest is in the protection of his privacy.[150]

Arguably[151] *Source Informatics* stands for the proposition that if a professional discloses personal information about a client in a form in which the client cannot be identified[152] for a purpose that has not been agreed there is no breach of confidence.

5.35 Thus, for example, a professional does not need to obtain the consent of a client before releasing personal data for the purposes of recognized medical or social science research provided that the data has been properly anonymized.[153] In *Source*

---

[145] P Fennell, *The All England Reports Annual Review 2000* (London: 2001) 254.
[146] [2001] EWCA Civ 1491, para 58.
[147] Query: whether anonymized information has the quality of confidentiality required to give rise to a duty of confidence when the information is not a trade secret.
[148] A number of statutes make disclosure of confidential personal information unlawful only where the person to whom the information relates is identifiable: see para 1.05 above. See also Health and Social Care Act 2002, s 60 (9)(a); Disability Discrimination Act 1995, s 31 B (4), (6) (a).
[149] BMA, 'Confidentiality and disclosure of health information' (London: 1999), http://www.bma.org.uk.
[150] *R v Department of Health, ex p Source Informatics Ltd* [2000] 1 All ER 786, 797.
[151] There is a potential alternative ratio: because of acceptable anonymization the data passed to the applicants did not have the necessary quality of confidence to be protected by an action for breach of confidence. The Court of Appeal chose not to distinguish the two arguments: [2000] 1 All ER 786, 797.
[152] The burden of proving this lies on the professional.
[153] See para 13.50 below.

A. Equity

Informatics the litigation was brought by a public authority, but the reasoning in no way suggests that this was germane to the decision and that the position is any different in private law disputes.[154] But there is also an argument that when a professional makes an unauthorized disclosure about a client, the dissemination of information about the client to a third party is just a part of the wrong done to the client. The latter may feel a justifiable sense of betrayal which does not depend upon his being identified to a wider audience. The decision in *Source Informatics* itself has been criticized for adopting an unduly narrow view of privacy.[155] If privacy is about dignity, autonomy and control over the dissemination of information,[156] privacy may be damaged whether or not there is identification. The House of Lords might not therefore treat identification as a prerequisite for liability for breach of confidence. In *L v G*, a New Zealand tort action for infringement of privacy, disclosure of information anonymously was said to reduce the level of damages but not to prevent recovery.[157]

On the assumption that for now a court would follow *Source Informatics* in any case of anonymous disclosure, several important caveats are necessary. First, in *Source Informatics* an acceptable level of anonymity had been achieved. The risk of a client being identified from the data disclosed was 'remote'.[158] Deleting or changing the name of the client is often not enough to guarantee that the client cannot be identified, particularly if the client is described in fine detail and has unusual characteristics.[159] Secondly, equity does not allow *use* of information for private gain by a fiduciary who owes a client a duty of undivided loyalty.[160] The fact that the client's privacy is not endangered is irrelevant. 5.36

> Whether founded on contract or equity, the [solicitor's] duty to preserve confidentiality is unqualified . . . Moreover, it is not merely a duty not to communicate the information to a third party. It is a duty not to misuse it, that is to say, without the

---

[154] Contrast M Thomson, 'Privacy before and after the Human Rights Act' [2001] 6 Communications L 180.
[155] D Beyleveld and E Histed, 'Betrayal of Confidence in the Court of Appeal', (2000) 4 Medical L Intl 277, 294. Cp G Laurie, *Genetic Privacy* (Cambridge: 2002) 225; Y Dunkel, 'Medical Privacy Rights in Anonymous Data: Discussion of Rights in the United Kingdom and the United States in Light of the Source Informatics Cases' (2001) 23 Loyola of Los Angeles Intl & Comparative L Rev 41, 45 et seq.
[156] See para 1.15 above.
[157] *L v G* [2002] DCR 234, 2002 NZDCR LEXIS 2 [*32 et seq]. For a critique of *L v G* see K Evans, 'Of Privacy and Prostitutes' (2002) 20 NZLR 71.
[158] The Court of Appeal treated the personal data as anonymous despite the defendant's admission that there was 'a remote risk that certain information of a rare kind might conceivably enable a patient to be identified' [2000] 1 All ER 786, 789. This would suggest that personal data that includes identifiers such as part of a postcode, the client's sex or year of birth is acceptable if, in a particular context, it is extremely difficult to trace the identifier to any one individual.
[159] Query, must steps always be taken so that no one, not even the client, is able to recognize the client? To avoid recognition by all, clinical (especially psychiatric) data used in medical textbooks and for teaching purposes might have to be disguised so heavily that its scientific value might be lost.
[160] See para 5.65 below. cp para 5.83 below.

consent of the ... client to make any use of it or to cause any use to be made of it by others otherwise than for his benefit.[161]

Thirdly, there may be uses of client information (not involving disclosure and therefore loss of privacy) in non-fiduciary relationships that equity may regard as unconscionable.[162]

5.37 Fourthly, it is possible that a client might wish to impose an obligation on the professional not to disclose information even in anonymous format. A patient, for example, might be concerned about the use of his health data for research to which he had ethical or religious objections. If the professional-client relationship is contractual and non-disclosure of anonymous data is agreed, this obligation will be enforced. If the relationship was not contractual and the client made it clear that information was provided on the basis that it would not be disclosed anonymously without the patient's consent, it is still possible that a court would decide that disclosure of the data in an anonymous form for the forbidden purpose is unlawful.

5.38 The third caveat[163] may be one reason why the Court of Appeal referred to the conscience of the pharmacist. The Court of Appeal saw nothing objectionable about a pharmacist using patient prescriptions for stock-taking purposes[163a] but the Court of Appeal might react very differently if a psychiatrist exploited commercially valuable information about a pending takeover learnt from a patient to make a killing on the stock exchange. It is not unlikely that equity would force the psychiatrist to disgorge the profit.[164] Likewise it might be considered unconscionable to allow the professional to use client information as a 'springboard' to the obtaining of other accessible information that is then disclosed for personal advantage.[165] This was part of the UK Government's submission to the European Commission in *Spencer v UK*.[166]

5.39 **Proving breach of confidence** Disclosure or use of information in breach of confidence may be proved directly or inferentially.[167] Disclosure to just one person may suffice,[168] as for defamation.[169] Positive action by the professional is not

---

[161] per Lord Millett, *Bolkiah v KPMG* [1999] 1 All ER 517, 527. cp *Universal Thermosensors Ltd v Hibben* [1992] 3 All ER 257 where employees stole a confidential customer list from their employer and used it to locate customers for a rival business.
[162] See para 5.38 below.
[163] See para 5.36 above.
[163a] [2000] 1 All ER 786, 800.
[164] cp *SEC v Willis* 787 F Supp 58 (1992).
[165] cp *Schering Chemicals Ltd v Falkman Ltd* [1981] 2 All ER 321, 345.
[166] *Spencer v UK* (1998) 25 EHRR CD 105, CD 113. The argument is derived from *Seager v Copydex* [1967] 2 All ER 415, a trade secrets case.
[167] *CMI-Centers for Medical Innovation GmbH v Phytopharm plc* [1999] FSR 235, 257–258. See also F Gurry, *Breach of Confidence* (Oxford: 1984) 256.
[168] Contrast the US private facts tort which requires disclosure to the public at large: see para 4.55 above.
[169] P Milmo and W Rogers (eds), *Gatley on Libel and Slander* (9th edn, London: 1998) para 6.1.

A. Equity

required. Tacit consent to another consulting or removing confidential personal records is a breach of confidence.

Harmful and harmless disclosures In a trade secret case such as *Coco v AN Clark (Engineers) Ltd* the claimant is expected to show that the breach of confidence caused financial loss. This is a reasonable requirement when the information is commercially valuable and the court's goal is to prevent the defendant from using confidential information 'without paying for it'.[170] When personal information is disclosed the result may be economic[171] or physical loss, but more often the harm is damage to reputation and emotional injury that is not of lasting consequence and does not trigger psychiatric illness. No ethical code distinguishes between harmful and harmless disclosures and it makes no sense for the courts to do so if their goal is to protect the client's personal autonomy and dignity and to encourage the client to be candid with the professional.[172] Moreover, interference with the right to respect for private life is not dependent upon tangible harm.[173] The courts will be acting in violation of the ECHR if they ignore breaches of Article 8(1) simply because the only damage or apprehended damage is emotional distress[174] or injury to reputation.

5.40

Fortunately, there is ample material in the case law to justify a judge in awarding damages to a claimant who has suffered no tangible loss but who has a legitimate interest in preserving the privacy of the information. Indeed this was the position in *Prince Albert v Strange*,[175] the well-spring of the cause of action. In *Coco v AN Clark (Engineers) Ltd* Megarry J said that he could 'conceive of cases where a plaintiff might have substantial motives for seeking the aid of equity and yet suffer nothing which could fairly be called detriment to him'[176] and in *X v Y*[177] Rose J doubted that detriment was necessary for injunctive relief.[178] Differing views were expressed on this point in *Spycatcher No 2*[179] (a case in which government, not

5.41

---

[170] per Lord Denning, *Seager v Copydex Ltd* [1967] 2 All ER 415, 417.

[171] In *Albert v Devine* 479 NE ed 113 (1984) the patient, a clergyman, failed to be renewed in his post of minister to a Boston church because of disclosures by his psychiatrist to his clerical superiors about his mental health. The unauthorized disclosures reduced his earning capacity and caused other financial losses as well as damage to his reputation and mental distress.

[172] See ch 1.

[173] See para 8.55 below.

[174] G Phillipson and H Fenwick, 'Breach of Confidence as a Privacy Remedy in the Human Rights Act Era' (2000) 63 MLR 660, 691.

[175] (1849) 41 ER 1171, Ch.

[176] [1969] RPC 41, 48.

[177] [1988] 2 All ER 648, 675. In *Cornelius v De Taranto* [2001] EMLR 12 Morland J followed Rose J holding that the claimant did not have to prove that any detrimental use was made of a confidential medico-legal report that a psychiatrist had disclosed in breach of confidence to other health professionals.

[178] The issue was put on one side by the Court of Appeal in *R v Department of Health, ex p Source Informatics Ltd* [2000] 1 All ER 786, 797.

[179] [1988] 3 All ER 545, 650. cp Lord Goff (at 659): detriment 'may not be necessary'.

Chapter 5: Equity and Copyright Solutions to Intentional Disclosure

personal, information was disclosed), but even Lord Griffiths, who insisted that detriment must be found, gave an example that involved intangible loss.[180] Lord Keith expressed the opinion that:

> Information about a person's private and personal affairs may be of a nature which shows him up in a favourable light and would by no means expose him to criticism. The anonymous donor of a very large sum to a very worthy cause has his own reasons for wishing to remain anonymous, which are unlikely to be discreditable. He should surely be in a position to restrain disclosure in breach of confidence of his identity in connection with the donation. So I would think it a sufficient detriment to the confider that information given in confidence is to be disclosed to persons whom he would prefer not to know of it, even though the disclosure would not be harmful to him in any positive way.[181]

5.42 It may be that the absence of financial detriment affects the choice of relief rather than whether the plaintiff has a cause of action.[182]

Who can bring an action for breach of confidence?

5.43 According to long-standing precedent, the professional's obligation of confidentiality to the client is personal to the client.[183] This has the consequence that when the client's confidentiality rights are interfered with by X it is the client who must sue X. The professional cannot bring legal proceedings against X on the client's behalf[184] though in some cases the professional may have an independent cause of action for breach of confidence.[185] The rule that the obligation is personal to the client meant also that if A, the client, told B, a professional, information in confidence about C, his spouse, A could sue B for disclosing the information but C could not. The result was that if A was dead or estranged from C, C had no remedy. Finn saw this as a serious gap in the law, especially in the doctor–patient context, given the frequency with which patients provide their doctors with personal information about other family members.[186] But this second consequence is based on the supposition that an action for breach of confidence requires a pre-existing relationship between defendant and claimant and this was rejected by the Court of Appeal in *Douglas v Hello! Ltd*[187] and *Venables v NGN Ltd*.[188] This rejection allows

---

[180] Loss of friendship.
[181] *Att-Gen v Guardian Newspapers Ltd (No 2)* [1988] 3 All ER 545, 640. cp *R v Department of Health, ex p Source Informatics Ltd* [1999] 4 All ER 185, 194: 'the breach of confidence in itself might carry with it sufficient detriment to justify the grant of a remedy' per Latham J.
[182] R Wacks, *Personal Information, Privacy and the Law* (Oxford: 1989) 56.
[183] *Fraser v Evans* [1969] 1 All ER 8, 11, 12. See also *Moorgate Tobacco v Philip Morris* (1982) 64 FLR 387, 404–405.
[184] *Broadmoor Special Hospital Authority v Robinson* [2000] 2 All ER 727, para 30.
[185] cp *Ashworth Special Hospital v MGN Ltd* [2001] 1 All ER 991, 1003–1004 where the hospital but probably not the patient could bring an action for breach of confidence.
[186] P Finn, 'Professionals and Confidentiality' (1992) 14 Sydney L Rev 317, 322.
[187] [2001] 2 All ER 289, para 126. See para 6.07 below.
[188] [2001] 1 All ER 908.

A. Equity

for an independent obligation of confidentiality by the doctor to the family member.[189]

Cessation of the obligation of confidentiality

Effect of the termination of the professional relationship

An obligation of confidentiality can outlive a professional relationship whatever the reason for its termination—it may survive even a repudiation of a contract for professional services.[190] In *Hollinsworth v BCTV*[191] the surgeon's obligation of confidentiality was undiminished seven years after hair graft surgery when all contact with his patient had long ceased. Even if the relationship and the obligation are coterminous, it is unlikely that equity would tolerate the professional ending the relationship in order to be able to disclose or use confidential client information.[192] **5.44**

Many professional codes assume that the duty of confidentiality owed to a client lasts indefinitely.[193] Treating personal information in the hands of a professional, whether or not the professional still has a professional relationship with the client, as the subject of an obligation of confidentiality presents equity with no difficulties so long as the client is living, the information is not in the public domain, and the client has not released the professional from the obligation. The clients of many kinds of professionals (dentists, doctors, lawyers, accountants to name a few) can reasonably expect confidentiality for the duration of their lives and anything less might deter some members of the public from speaking frankly to them. In 1820 Lord Eldon observed in *Wyatt v Wilson* shortly after King George III's death: '[i]f one of the late king's physicians had kept a diary of what he heard and saw, this Court would not, *in the king's lifetime*, have permitted him to print and publish it.'[194] **5.45**

Dead clients

Why confidentiality might be necessary after the client has died The situation once the client has died is uncertain. There are reasonable grounds for continuing **5.46**

---

[189] Even before the decisions in *Douglas v Hello! Ltd* and *Venables v NGN Ltd*, R Toulson and C Phipps, *Confidentiality* (London: 1996) 156 argued that if a patient disclosed to his doctor information about X, a family member, 'it would be open to a court to hold that publication by the doctor on the patient's death would be unconscionable conduct towards X'.
[190] See para 4.15 above.
[191] (1998) 83 ACWS (3d) 525.
[192] A fiduciary cannot avoid liability for breach of fiduciary duty by terminating the relationship and thereafter exploiting information obtained within it: *CMS Dolphin Ltd v Simonet* [2001] 2 BCLC 704, para 96 where a number of authorities are discussed.
[193] See para 3.47 above.
[194] Cited in *Prince v Strange* (1849) 41 ER 1171, 1179 (italics added).

Chapter 5: Equity and Copyright Solutions to Intentional Disclosure

to withhold information,[195] at least for a time and for allowing an action to be brought if information is disclosed without the consent of the deceased's personal representative.

> Clients may be concerned about reputation, civil liability, or possible harm to friends or family. Posthumous disclosure of such communications may be as feared as disclosure during the client's lifetime.[196]

If post-mortem disclosure of medical information were to become routine, patient trust of doctors, the utilitarian raison d'être for medical confidentiality,[197] might be eroded.

5.47 Disclosure of personal information about a dead person may be particularly offensive to relatives when the disclosure is about the circumstances of the death. In one US case families successfully sued the county medical examiner's office when they discovered that his employees had obtained and displayed graphic autopsy pictures of their dead relatives (including one of the county governor) at cocktail parties, school road safety classes and in personal scrapbooks.[198] But the court decided in their favour on the basis that the defendant's conduct had violated an independent protectable privacy interest in the autopsy records.[199] English courts that declare that life-sustaining treatment can lawfully be discontinued, frequently also order that the identity of the patient continue to be suppressed after the patient's death to protect the privacy of the medical staff and the patient's family.[200] Once again, however, the privacy interest that is being protected is that of the survivors and not that of the deceased.

5.48 **Post-mortem legal protection of the equitable obligation of confidentiality** In Toulson and Phipps' view it 'is open to the courts to regard divulgence by a doctor of information supplied in confidence by a patient who has since died as being unconscionable as well as unprofessional . . . there is no reason in principle why equity should not regard the doctor as owing a duty of confidence to the

---

[195] For a detailed analysis of the ethical arguments for postmortem confidentiality see J Berg, 'Grave Secrets: Legal and Ethical Analysis of Postmortem Confidentiality' (2001) 34 Connecticut L Rev 81.
[196] per Rehnquist CJ, speaking of attorney–client privilege in *Swidler and Berlin v US* (1998) 118 St Ct 2081, 2086.
[197] See para 1.46 above.
[198] *Reid v Pierce County* 961 P 2d 333 (1998). In *Katz v National Archives & Records Admin* 68 F 3d 1438 (1995), the court held that the Kennedy family had a privacy interest in preventing the disclosure of the x-rays and optical photographs taken during President Kennedy's autopsy. See also *Douglas v Stokes* 149 SW 849 (1912) (illicitly taken photograph of dead Siamese twins who died shortly after birth).
[199] *Reid v Pierce County* 961 P.2d 333, 342 (1998). In *Fitch v Voit* 624 So 2d 542 (1993) the court held that relatives could not sue a newspaper for depicting a relative lying in a hospital bed and describing her as dying of cancer two years after her death because there is no relational right of privacy.
[200] *Dobson v North Tyneside Health Authority* [1996] 4 All ER 474; *B v NHS Hospital* [2002] EWHC 429; [2002] 2 All ER 449.

A. Equity

deceased's estate, consonant with the maxim that equity will not suffer a wrong to be without a remedy'.[201] To an extent their conclusion is supported by *Russo v Nugent Care Society*.[202]

5.49 In the *Russo* case a High Court judge was confronted with the question whether a voluntary adoption agency could refuse the claimant access to the complete records of her adoption over 50 years after the event by which time her natural and adoptive parents were all dead. The Adoption Agencies Regulations 1983[203] gave the agency a discretion to provide access to all the records, but the agency had decided to limit the claimant's access. Judgment was given against the agency on the grounds that it had adopted an inflexible policy of treating information as confidential regardless of how much time had elapsed or the death of the people concerned. Scott Baker J said that 'the duration of . . . such duty [of confidentiality] will vary according to the nature of the information and the nature of the relationship. Nor does the death of the confider necessarily bring the confidentiality to an end, for example where a patient has confided confidential information to a doctor and then dies.'[204] After citing Toulson and Phipps, he said that 'in principle a duty of confidentiality should cease if the information loses the quality of confidence, whether through the passage of time, loss of secrecy or other change of circumstances'.[205] In the instant case 'the fact that none of the relevant people other than the claimant, is still alive suggests that there is little if any purpose in maintaining confidentiality from the viewpoint of those who imparted the information. Balanced against this is the genuine interest to the Claimant in receiving the information. Viewed on this basis it seems to me that the scales would be likely to come down firmly in favour of disclosure.' In the circumstances of the case, this conclusion was not offset by a public interest in maintaining the confidentiality of the adoption process generally.

5.50 *Russo* is an unusual case in that the complaint was that the defendant had *refused* to break a confidence. What if the Adoption Agencies Regulations 1983 had not existed? Could anyone have stopped the adoption agency from showing the records to the claimant? The first question to address is whether there is anyone with standing to sue. The deceased's relatives have no relationship of confidence with the professional unless the information implicates them also[206] (in which case they may independently be owed an obligation of confidentiality)[207] and therefore

---

[201] R Toulson and C Phipps, *Confidentiality* (London: 1996) 155. See also p 72 where an analogy is drawn with legal professional which can survive the death of the privilege-holder.
[202] [2001] EWHC Admin 566; [2002] 1 FLR 1.
[203] SI 1983/1964, reg 15(2)(a).
[204] para 51.
[205] para 52.
[206] eg, disclosure that a dead person suffered from a genetic disorder might implicate relatives and intrude on their privacy.
[207] See para 5.43 above.

cannot bring proceedings for breach of confidence. If anyone has standing to sue it will be the client's personal representative. But the estate suffers a legal wrong only if records that form part of the estate are disclosed[208] or the obligation of confidentiality passed to the estate as a thing in action. This requires the information to have a commercial value.[209] If the injury is to the reputation of the deceased, the action must fail because such damages are personal to the client and cannot be assigned.[210] If the complaint is of the distress disclosure caused to the relatives one comes once again up against the problem that they have no standing to sue. Toulson and Phipps avoid this issue by treating disclosure as unconscionable conduct toward the relatives much as the American court did in *Reid v Pierce County*.[211] This would be a new departure for equity since the information is not confidential information about the relatives.[212]

5.51 **Legislative and other analogies** The Law Commission[213] thinks it would be illogical to allow a posthumous action for non-pecuniary loss resulting from a breach of confidence given that personal representatives cannot sue for defamation. In so far as it provides guidance by analogy, legislation points largely away from an obligation of confidentiality:

- personal data of a dead person is not protected by the DPA[214] and therefore from disclosure under the Freedom of Information Act 2000;
- once the patient has died, it ceases to be a criminal offence to reveal information disclosed to the Commission for Health Improvement under the Health Act 1999 about an identifiable patient;[215]
- it is not an offence to disclose information relating to an individual who has died under the Electronic Communications Act 2000;[216]
- death certificates which must state the cause of death are public documents and a copy can be obtained upon payment of a fee;[217]

---

[208] As regards ownership of records see paras 19.03 et seq.
[209] This condition is satisfied if the information disclosed is a trade secret, as to which see *Morison v Moat* 68 ER 492. Some personal information has a commercial value but most does not.
[210] *Ord v Upton* [2000] 1 All ER 193, 205–206.
[211] 961 P 2d 3 33 (1998); see para 5.47 above.
[212] There is the further issue of whether recovery will be allowed for mental distress as to which see para 8.51 below.
[213] Law Commission Report 110, *Breach of Confidence* (Cm 8388, 1981) 83. Cp I Kennedy and A Grubb, *Medical Law* (3rd edn, London: 2000) 1082. But a breach of confidence will not necessarily be damaging to the client's reputation—it might improve it: J McHale, 'Paper on Confidentiality and Mental Health' (2000) 8, available at http://www.doh.gov.uk/mhar/paper.htm.
[214] DPA, s 1(1) defines 'personal data' as 'data which relate to a *living* individual' (italics added).
[215] Health Act 1999, s 24.
[216] s 4.
[217] Births and Deaths Registration Act 1953, s 32.

A. Equity

- personal representatives may bring an action for false attribution of authorship for up to 20 years after the deceased's death under the Copyright Designs and Patents Act 1988.[218]

Soft law offers more support for post-mortem liability:

- The closure period for public records can be extended beyond the 30-year period laid down in the Public Records Act 1958 to avoid 'substantial distress' to descendants.[219] The Freedom of Information Act 2000, however, will abolish this regime.[220]
- The BSC's Code of Guidance forbids crime reconstructions without the consent of a deceased victim's close relatives except where the programme has an overriding public interest justification 'such as the illumination of public policy or the disclosure of significant new facts'. Also a complaint about the invasion of an individual's privacy may be made by relatives if the victim has died.[211]
- Department of Health guidance about HIV infected health care workers states that 'duties of confidentiality still apply even if the infected health care worker has died . . .'.[222]

The ECtHR accepts that heirs who are family members have sufficient interest to justify the continuation of an application alleging violation of a Convention right after the applicant's death,[223] but does not permit executors to institute an application in the deceased's name.[224] Disclosure of information distressing to relatives might be considered to interfere with their right to respect for *family life* but this would have to be balanced against the professional's right of freedom of expression and that of the intended recipient of the information.[225] If the recipient is a media organization, the ECtHR is unlikely to find the interference with freedom of expression justified.

Doctors The professional most likely to be asked to release confidential personal information about a client posthumously is a doctor. The moral case for suppressing information about the dead is obviously affected by the length of time that has elapsed since the death and the purpose of the disclosure. Society has an

5.52

5.53

---

[218] Copyright, Designs and Patents Act 1988, ss 84, 95(5).
[219] http://www.pro.gov.uk/recordsmanagement/dispositionpolicy/dispositionquestions.htm.
[220] If no exemption applies, subject to the Art 8 right to respect for private and family life, members of the public have a legal right to the information.
[221] See para 9.04 below.
[222] DoH, *HIV Infected Health Care Workers* (September 2002) available at http://www.doh.gov.uk/aids.htm, para 10.5. This guidance is still the subject of consultation.
[223] *X v France* Series A, No 234-C, (1992) 14 EHRR 483, para 26; *Scherer v Switzerland* (1994) 18 EHRR 276, para 31; *Anne-Marie Andersson v Sweden* (1998) 25 EHRR 722, para 29.
[224] Only the 'victim' can make an application (Art 25).
[225] Other Convention rights might be engaged if the information discloses a serious risk to a third party.

interest in access to the medical records of the dead to determine the causes of disease, for research and for epidemiological purposes; individuals may want the information for religious or financial reasons or to promote their own health by discovering whether they have been exposed to, or have a predisposition toward, certain diseases. The police may want information to clear up a crime.[226] The doctor himself may need the information for a personal audit or research.[227] Once someone is dead consent to an unanticipated disclosure is obviously no longer an option. Confidentiality protection therefore, if it persists, needs to be much more flexible for the dead than for the living.[228]

5.54 The American Medical Association, looking at the issue from an ethical perspective, has made the following recommendations:

(1) 'All information contained within a deceased patient's medical record, including information entered postmortem, should be kept confidential to the greatest possible degree.'
(2) If information about a patient could be disclosed during the patient's lifetime it may be disclosed after the patient's death.
(3) 'Disclosure of medical information postmortem for research and educational purposes is appropriate as long as confidentiality is maintained to the greatest possible degree by removing any individual identifiers.'
(4) In other cases, the decision to disclose identified information about a dead patient should take into account: '(1) the imminence of harm to identifiable individuals or the public health, (2) the potential benefit to at-risk individuals or the public health . . . (3) any statement or directive made by the patient regarding postmortem disclosure, (4) the impact disclosure may have on the reputation of the deceased patient, and (5) personal gain for the physician that may unduly influence professional obligations of confidentiality.'[229]

'Dead' professionals: retirement, death or change of employment

5.55 Professionals discontinue their professional activities for many reasons: death, retirement, a career change, transfer to another employer or a different location, the sale of the business, bankruptcy, imprisonment, disqualification for professional misconduct. Whatever the reason, means must be found of preserving the confidentiality of information in client files. These files, when compiled by a self-

---

[226] See para 13.09 below.
[227] J Savulescu and L Skene, 'Who has the Right to Access Medical Information from a Deceased Person? Ethical and Legal Perspectives' (2000) 8 J of L and Medicine 81, 84.
[228] A Maixner, 'Confidentiality of Health Information Postmortem' (2001) 125 *Archives of Pathology & Laboratory Medicine* 1189, 1190–1191.
[229] ibid at 1192.

A. Equity

employed professional in the private sector, are the property of the professional and when compiled by an employed professional, belong either to the professional or her employer.[230] In the public sector, preservation of record confidentiality when personnel change is not likely to be an issue because the public sector has corporate records and detailed institutional rules about their retention and storage.[231]

Storage and retention of papers and documents can be provided for in a contract between the professional and client. For instance, the terms of engagement of a solicitor may state that the client's file will be kept for 15 years after payment of the final bill and then destroyed except for any documents that the client asks to be placed in safe custody.[232] When there is no contract, or no relevant contractual term, it might be appropriate for the professional to turn over the client's file to the client, securely destroying the file[233] or, with the consent of the client, transferring the file to another professional.[234] In *Anonymous v CVS Corp* a New York judge dismissed an argument that the out-going owner of a pharmacy could lawfully transfer customer records to the new owner, a national pharmaceutical chain, without reference to the customers.[235]

5.56

If the departing professional is an employee the record is most probably the physical property of the employer even if the professional has exclusive access to the files.[236] On change of employment the professional cannot take the client's files away.[236a] Suitable arrangements will have to be made to transfer control to another professional within the employer's organization. The client's consent might not be needed for this.

5.57

Transfer of confidential personal records between professionals when, for example, a practice is sold or a professional retires, is rarely dealt with in professional codes of ethics. The Faculty of Occupational Medicine's guidelines are unusual in this respect. They provide:

5.58

---

[230] As to ownership of records see paras 19.03 et seq.
[231] For the NHS see Health Service Circular HSC 1999/053.
[232] For issues relating to the use of legal documents for historical research see A Thick and D Chun, 'Depositing old documents' (1992) 89(30) LS Gaz 21.
[233] If the professional owns the file, the client cannot prevent this: '[h]e or she may be restrained from using the information in them to make an unauthorized profit or from disclosing that information to unauthorized persons. But otherwise the records are his or hers to save or destroy.' per *Breen v Williams* (1996) 138 ALR 259, 288.
[234] See also para 19.09 below.
[235] 3/9/01 NYLJ 19 (col 6) (NY Sup Ct, March 5 2001). It was a feature of this case that after transfer the records became part of a database that was accessible to tens of thousands of employees of the pharmaceutical chain and by health plan organizations who had contracts with that chain.
[236] See para 21.03 below.
[236a] *Healys v Mischon de Reya* [2002] EWHC 2480.

Arrangements should be made in advance by occupational health record holders to ensure that when they leave, retire or die, the records can be transferred to a new holder and that the subjects of these records are informed of the transfer and retain their rights to information under the Data Protection Acts. It is the responsibility of the current holder to ensure that health records are transferred only to an appropriate health professional . . .

Within an in-house occupational health service, the records are the property of the employer . . . If an organization is transferred to a new owner (and a new occupational health provider), the occupational health records should normally be transferred. There is no requirement for individual consent in such circumstances, but employees should be advised of the transfer and given the opportunity to ask for their clinical record to be archived rather than transferred. The same considerations apply when an in-house occupational health service is contracted out.[237]

Once a client has left professional A for professional B, whether through choice or because A has withdrawn her services, there would seem to be no justification for A to continue to have access to client records that have been transferred to B. The Health Service Commissioner has taken the view that it is improper for a patient's previous doctor to see records once the patient has changed to another doctor.[238]

Effect of information entering the public domain

5.59 **The general rule** The general rule is that the equitable obligation of confidentiality dissolves when the information enters the public domain.[239] '[O]nce confidence escapes, like air from a punctured tyre, the confidence is no more.'[240] When the schoolboy son of the then Home Secretary was arrested on a drugs offence an injunction was initially granted to prevent publication of his name. This injunction was lifted shortly afterwards when it was realized that his name was freely available on the internet.[241] The rule that the obligation of confidentiality goes when the information escapes into the public domain is, however, only a prima

---

[237] Faculty of Occupational Medicine, *Guidance on Ethics for Occupational Physicians* (5th edn, London: 1999) paras 2.23–2.24.
[238] J Montgomery, *Health Care Law* (2nd edn, Oxford: 2002) 266.
[239] *Bunn v BBC* [1998] 3 All ER 552, 557; *Att-Gen v Times Newspapers Ltd* [2001] EMLR 19, para 6. As to whether information remains permanently in the public domain see para 5.16 above.
[240] per Leggatt J, *X A G v A Bank* [1983] 2 All ER 464, 475.
[241] A Nicol, G Millar and A Sharland, *Media Law and Human Rights* (London: 2001) 84. Contrast *Venables v NGN Ltd* [2001] 1 All ER 908, 941, para 105 where Butler-Sloss P directed that the injunction should continue in force even if the claimants were identified on the internet or in foreign newspapers. Morland J also confirmed an ex parte injunction granted by Jackson J restraining use of extracts of the memoirs of the Blair family's former nanny who had entered into a confidentiality agreement with the Blairs notwithstanding that one and a half million copies of the Mail on Sunday had reached the public and the information was available on the internet by the time the injunction was issued. These facts are taken from R English, 'Confidentiality and Defamation' in R English and P Havers (eds), *Human Rights and the Common Law* (Oxford: 2000) 187. See also *Blair v Lister* (2000) WL 3116509, QB.

facie rule.[242] There may be reasons why the confidant should not be released from an existing obligation of confidentiality.[243]

Defendant responsible for putting information into the public domain In 5.60 *Speed Seal Products Ltd v Paddington*[244] Fox LJ distinguished three situations. The first is where publication was by or with the consent of the claimant. This destroys the obligation of confidentiality. The second is where neither claimant nor defendant had anything to do with the publication. Normally this will free the defendant to disclose the information. The third is where the defendant was responsible for the information entering the public domain. In this third situation the law is in a state of flux. When the issue was considered in *Att-Gen v Guardian Newspapers Ltd (No 2)*[245] their Lordships were divided. Lord Griffiths thought that when information entered the public domain through the wrongful actions of the confidant the obligation of confidentiality continued.[246] Lord Goff disagreed:

> [I]t is difficult to see how a confidant who publishes the relevant confidential information to the whole world can be under any *further* obligation not to disclose the information, simply because it was he who wrongfully destroyed its confidentiality . . . For his wrongful act, he may be liable in damages, or may be required to make restitution; but . . . the confidential information, as confidential information, has ceased to exist, and with it should go, as a matter of principle the obligation of confidence.[247]

Lord Goff's position is supported by two decisions of the ECtHR in which prior 5.61 public dissemination of confidential information by the applicant, in breach of domestic law, defeated the respondent state's defence that interference with the applicant's right to freedom of expression was justified.[248] Underlying the English judicial division of opinion are different conceptions of what the duty of

---

[242] *Att-Gen v Guardian Newspapers Ltd (No 2)* [1988] 3 All ER 545, 575 per Scott J: 'The question . . . whether the public accessibility of the information sought to be protected is fatal to an attempt to restrain the use or disclosure of the information by enforcing a duty of confidence cannot be answered in any absolute terms. The answer will depend on the circumstances of the particular case. It will depend on the nature of the information, the nature of the interest sought to be protected, the relationship between the plaintiff and the defendant, the manner in which the defendant has come into possession of the information and the circumstances in which and the extent to which the information has been made public.'
[243] *Cranleigh Precision Engineering Ltd v Bryant* [1965] 1 WLR 1293, 1319. See also A Stewart and M Chesterman, 'Confidential Material: The Position of the Media' (1992) 14 Adelaide L Rev 1, 12–13.
[244] [1986] 1 All ER 91, 94–95.
[245] [1988] 3 All ER 545, 651, 661–663.
[246] cp *Euro Banking Corp v Fourth Estate* [1993] 1 NZLR 559, 565.
[247] Lord Goff, [1988] 3 All ER 545, 662–663 (italics added).
[248] *Weber v Switzerland* (1990) 12 EHRR 508, paras 49–51; *Vereinigung Weekblad Bluf! v Netherlands* (1995) 20 EHRR 189, paras 43–45. Had the authorities acted against the applicant in the first case at the time of the original disclosure the ECtHR would not have found a violation of Art 10. In other words, the initial disclosure was plainly wrong, but this did not deflect the ECtHR from finding in favour of the applicant.

confidence protects: a relationship of trust (Lord Griffiths)[249] or the privacy of information (Lord Goff).[250] When the subject of the confidence is personal information and the confidant is a professional, Lord Griffiths' approach is to be preferred.

> If the law seeks to encourage full and frank disclosures in certain relationships, then a confidant should be burdened by a special disability not 'to mention in public what is now common knowledge.'[251]

5.62 Lord Goff, and the majority of Law Lords who sided with him on this point, left open the possibility of an injunction against further disclosure based not on a fresh breach of a subsisting obligation of confidentiality but on the undesirability of allowing the confidant to profit from his own past breach of confidence.[252] Suppose that a dentist were responsible for a tabloid story that a famous male cinema idol had false teeth. It is conceivable that the dentist would be enjoined by a court from exploiting the fact that she was chosen by the cinema idol to fit his dentures in literature advertising her dental practice. The conceptual difficulties of allowing an injunction to prevent unjust enrichment are discussed by R Toulson and C Phipps.[253] They point out that an injunction that is not based on a continuing duty of confidence, but on the broader principle that wrongdoers should not be allowed to take advantage of their wrongdoing, could not be limited to cases of breach of confidence.[254]

5.63 Authentication of information in the public domain It was suggested earlier that information may be in the public domain and yet might remain subject to an ethical obligation of confidentiality by a professional.[255] If this is right, then the fact that information has escaped into the public domain through no fault of the professional may make no difference to the professional's obligation of confidentiality. Speaking of a confidential professional adviser who had used commercial information in the public domain without the consent of his company client, Shaw LJ said in *Schering Chemicals v Falkman Ltd*:[256] '[i]t is not the law that where confidentiality exists it is terminated or eroded by adventitious publicity.' If Shaw

---

[249] 'It would make a mockery of the duty of confidence owed by members of the Security and Intelligence Services if they could discharge it by breaching it', per Lord Griffiths, [1988] 3 All ER 545, 651.

[250] 'The information has, after all, already been so fully disclosed that it is in the public domain: how, therefore, can he thereafter be sensibly restrained from disclosing it? Is he not even to be permitted to mention in public what is now common knowledge?' per Lord Goff, [1988] 3 All ER 545, 662–663.

[251] D Laster, 'Commonalities Between Breach of Confidence and Privacy' (1990) 14 New Zealand Universities L Rev 144, 155.

[252] [1988] 3 All ER 545, 664. See also 642, 647.

[253] *Confidentiality* (London: 1996) 61.

[254] In *Kaye v Robertson* [1991] FSR 62, 69 an injunction was refused to prevent defendants profiting from their own trespass.

[255] See para 5.14 above.

[256] [1981] 2 All ER 321, 339. Under DPA, Sch 3, para 5 sensitive personal data in the public domain cannot be processed by the data controller unless it was the client who put it there.

A. Equity

LJ is wrong in his approach, there will nevertheless be situations where a professional may do great harm to a client by discussing information that has become public knowledge because it confirms the accuracy of personal information about the client that cannot be tested experientially.[257] Thus a doctor who publishes an autobiography stating that she is treating a famous actor for AIDS may authenticate stories from unattributed sources in tabloid newspapers of his illness. Her disclosure violates the actor's Article 8 right to respect for private life and suppression of the offensive passage in the autobiography is likely to be found to be a justifiable interference with her freedom of expression.

Breach of Fiduciary Duty[258]

Who is a Fiduciary?

The boundaries of the law of fiduciaries are frustratingly vague.[259] The term 'fiduciary' has been applied by some judges to those who owe an equitable obligation of confidentiality and nothing more.[260] To the purist this is an abuse of the term 'fiduciary'.[261] Fiduciaries in the true sense are those who for reasons of legal policy have their interests completely subordinated to those of others with whom they are in a relationship.

5.64

> The fiduciary duty arises where one party to the relationship (A) is reasonably entitled to expect of the other (B) that B will act in the interests of A, not in the interests of B or a third party and not merely having regard to A's interests. Under the fiduciary standard the fiduciary must act solely and selflessly in the interests of the beneficiary.[262]

---

[257] cp *Schering Chemicals v Falkman Ltd* [1981] 2 All ER 321, 338 where Shaw LJ said that '[t]o extend the knowledge or to revive the recollection of matters which may be detrimental or prejudicial to the interests of some person or organisation is not to be condoned because the facts are already known to some and linger in the memories of others'.

[258] See generally, S Baughan, *Professionals and Fiduciaries: Perils and Pitfalls* (Saffron Walden: 2002). R Dean, The Law of Trade Secrets and Personal Secrets (2nd edn, Sydney, 2002) [4.385]–[4.450].

[259] See P Finn, *Fiduciary Obligations* (Sydney: 1977).

[260] Fiduciary is used with reference to the equitable obligation of confidentiality in *Schering Chemicals Ltd v Falkman Ltd* [1981] 2 All ER 321, 337, 338; *Att-Gen v Blake* [1998] 1 All ER 833, 842.

[261] Counsel cited Shaw LJ's comment in *Schering Chemicals Ltd v Falkman Ltd* [1981] 2 All ER 321, 338 to Harman J in *Andersen Consulting v CHP Consulting Ltd* (Ch, 26 July 1991). His response was that Shaw LJ had erred in calling the equitable obligation of confidentiality a fiduciary one. 'In my judgment a fiduciary obligation . . . arises from a relationship properly described as a fiduciary relationship. The most obvious and well known is trustee and beneficiary . . . [E]quity will impose an obligation of confidence and enforce it by injunction if, for example, one friend confides to another friend in circumstances where the communication is plainly intended to be (and therefore to be kept) confidential . . . But the relationship of friend is not a relationship having a fiduciary nature and the obligation is not a fiduciary obligation: it is simply an obligation of equity imposed in conscience.'

[262] per Richardson J, *DHL International (NZ) Ltd v Richmond Ltd* [1993] 3 NZLR 10, 23.

The rationale for imposing fiduciary obligations tends to be the vulnerability and reliance of the principal and the discretionary authority and power of the fiduciary, though all four elements are not necessarily present.[263] Fiduciary duties do not depend upon the existence of a contract[264] and there is therefore no need for the relationship between fiduciary and beneficiary to be for reward.[265]

5.65 In equity the relationship between a client and a solicitor, accountant, stockbroker or other financial adviser is presumed to be a fiduciary relationship of trust and confidence.[266] In the case of the solicitor, the purpose for which the solicitor was consulted does not matter.[267] The duty owed by professionals in a relationship of trust and confidence is that of undivided loyalty.

> This core liability [of loyalty] has several facets. A fiduciary must act in good faith; he must not make a profit out of his trust; he must not place himself in a position where his duty and his interest may conflict; he may not act for his own benefit or the benefit of a third party without the informed consent of his principal.[268]

5.66 Any other professional who enters into an agency relationship with the client will assume these obligations.[269] The category of fiduciaries is not fixed. The facts of a particular professional-client relationship, although not one of agency, may lead a court to hold that a relationship of trust and confidence arose. Unfortunately, there are no agreed criteria for recognizing non-agency relationships that attract the duty of loyalty.[270]

---

[263] P Michalik, 'Doctors' Fiduciary Duties' (1998) 6 J of L and Medicine 168, 170–173.

[264] *Bristol & West Building Society v Merrimans* [1996] 2 All ER 801, 815. But they may be superimposed on contractual obligations.

[265] See eg *JD v Ross* [1998] NZFLR 951.

[266] Solicitors: *Re Van Luan, ex p Chatterton* [1907] 2 KB 23; *Nelson v Nelson* [1997] 1 All ER 970, 974; *McKaskell v Benseman* [1989] 3 NZLR 75; *Beach Petroleum NL v Kennedy* (1999) 48 NSWLR 1, 45. Accountants: *Evitt v Price* (1827) 57 ER 659. Stockbrokers: *Brown v Inland Revenue Commissioners* [1964] 3 All ER 119, 127; *Brandeis (Brokers) Ltd v Black* [2001] 2 All ER (Comm) 980. Financial adviser: *Cook v Evatt (No 2)* [1992] 1 NZLR 676. cp *Daly v Sydney Stock Exchange Ltd* (1986) 160 CLR 371, 377; *Estate Realities v Wignall* [1991] 3 NZLR 482.

[267] Solicitors representing persons facing criminal charges are bound by the solicitor's normal fiduciary obligations. See para 5.80 n316 below. Particularly high standards of conduct are imposed on solicitors by virtue of the fact that they are officers of the court: *Rakusen v Ellis* [1912] 1 Ch 831, 834–835, 840.

[268] per Millett LJ, *Bristol & West Building Society v Mothew* [1996] 4 All ER 698, 712. The fiduciary's obligations may be modified by contract: *Kelly v Cooper* [1993] AC 205. Regarding the solicitor's obligation of loyalty to the client see *R v Neil* [2002] SCC 70, paras 16–17. For the respective obligations of the solicitor and her firm see paras 15, 29.

[269] The relationship between agent and principal is a fiduciary one: *Breen v Williams* (1996) 138 ALR 259, 265.

[270] Some indicia of a fiduciary relationship are suggested in *Breen v Williams* (1996) 138 ALR 259, 284. See also *Duke Group v Pilmer* (1999) 73 SASR 64, 219.

Disclosure of confidential information and breach of fiduciary duty

Confidentiality as an aspect of the fiduciary duty

Duty of loyalty   Maintaining confidentiality is treated as integral to the fiduciary's duty of loyalty in recent cases.[271] An Australian judge has said: '[t]he fiduciary duties of a solicitor to his client include the duty to preserve confidentiality of information.'[272] Confidentiality is a natural partner to loyalty. As part of the duty of loyalty, the fiduciary has a duty to report material facts to the client.[273] The fiduciary has a corresponding duty not to report material facts about the client to others without the client's consent.[274] Breach of the duty to report facts to the client does not have to involve dishonesty; the test is whether the fiduciary acted intentionally and consciously.[275] Is the same true of a legitimate complaint of intentional unauthorized use or disclosure of confidential information? 5.67

Breach of fiduciary duty or breach of confidence?   A solicitor who discloses or uses confidential information relating to an existing client for a purpose other than to benefit the client[276] may simultaneously breach: 5.68

(1) a contractual duty of confidentiality;
(2) an equitable obligation of confidentiality;
(3) a fiduciary obligation of loyalty.

This immediately raises the question: when a fiduciary duty of loyalty and an equitable obligation of confidence co-exist, can the claimant elect to bring an action for breach of fiduciary duty in preference to an action for breach of confidence? To answer this one must first consider how the actions for breach of fiduciary duty and breach of confidence relate to each other. 5.69

Are breach of confidence and breach of fiduciary duty two separate causes of action?[277]   This preliminary point was addressed by La Forest J in *Lac Minerals* 5.70

---

[271] *McLean v Arklow Investments Ltd* [1998] 3 NZLR 680, 733; *Arklow Investments Ltd v Maclean* [2000] 1 WLR 594, 598; *Brandeis (Brokers) Ltd v Black* [2001] 2 All ER (Comm) 980, para 38. See also *R v Neil* [2002] SCC 70, para 17. According to this judgment a conflict of interest (a form of disloyalty) can arise with or without misuse of confidential information. Some commentators view the conflation of the obligation of loyalty and confidentiality as a mistake: see J Glover, 'Is breach of confidence a fiduciary wrong? Preserving the reach of judge made law' [2001 LS 594 and L Clarke, 'Breach of Confidence and the Employment Relationship' (2002) 31 Industrial LJ 353, 356–347.
[272] per Mullane J, *Griffis v Griffis* (1991) FLC 92–233, 78–595.
[273] See para 19.58 below.
[274] *Hilton v Barker Booth & Eastwood* [2002] EWCA Civ 723; see para 5.76 below.
[275] *Bristol & West Building Society v Mothew* [1996] 4 All ER 698, 713.
[276] cp the submission of Crown counsel in *Att-Gen v Blake* [1996] 3 All ER 903, 907.
[277] For the case that they are not see D Klinck, ' "Things of Confidence": Loyalty, Secrecy and Fiduciary Obligation' (1990) 54 Saskatchewan L Rev 73.

Ltd v International Corona Ltd, a case involving the wrongful disclosure of confidential commercially valuable information. His conclusion was that 'while distinct, [they] are intertwined'.[278] As evidence of their separate identities La Forrest J pointed to the following:

(1) A claim for breach of confidence (at least in commercial cases)[279] needs detriment to the confidor; '[f]iduciary law, being concerned with the exaction of a duty of loyalty, does not require the harm in the particular case to be shown to have resulted'.[280]
(2) '[D]uties of confidence can arise outside a direct relationship, where for example a third party has received confidential information from a confidee in breach of the confidee's obligation to the confidor . . . It would be a misuse of the term to suggest that the third party stood in a fiduciary position to the original confidor.'[281]
(3) '[B]reach of confidence also has a jurisdictional base at law, whereas fiduciary obligations are solely equitable creation.'[282]

He might also have mentioned that an obligation of confidence that allows an action for breach of confidence can exist where there is no fiduciary obligation of loyalty between confider and confidant.[283]

5.71 It does not follow from the fact that the two causes of action are separate that equity will place both at the disposal of the claimant. In *Lac Minerals Ltd v International Corona Ltd* Sopinka J said:

> No doubt one of the possible incidents of a fiduciary relationship is the exchange of confidential information and restrictions on its use. *Where however the essence of the complaint is misuse of confidential information, the appropriate cause of action in favour of the party aggrieved is breach of confidence and not breach of fiduciary duty.*[284]

In *Indata Equipment Supplies Ltd v ACL Ltd*[285] Otton LJ agreed but since the Court of Appeal held that the claimant and defendant were not in a fiduciary relationship his view is obiter.

---

[278] (1989) 611 DLR (4th) 14, 35.
[279] This may not be a requirement in cases involving personal information: see paras 5.40–5.42 above.
[280] (1989) 61 DLR (4th) 14, 36.
[281] ibid. But see *Schering Chemicals Ltd v Falkman Ltd* [1981] 2 All ER 321, 337.
[282] (1989) 61 DLR (4th) 14, 36. He is referring to an action for breach of contract.
[283] See para 5.04 above. See also *International Corona Resources Ltd v Lac Minerals Ltd* (1987) 44 DLR (4th) 592, 639.
[284] (1989) 61 DLR (4th) 14, 64 (emphasis added). Cp *Att-Gen (UK) v Heinemann Publishers* (1987) 10 NSWLR 86, 150.
[285] [1998] 1 BCLC 412.

A. Equity

Gurry in his influential book on *Breach of Confidence*[286] gives only qualified support to this approach. He argues that the principal in a fiduciary relationship can pursue an action for breach of fiduciary duty over the exploitation of confidential information when the fiduciary's misconduct is bound up with a breach of a fiduciary duty *other* than a simple breach of confidentiality. *Szarfer v Chodos*[287] may be an example. The defendant lawyer was engaged by the claimant to represent him in an employment matter. During the retainer the lawyer discovered that for various reasons, including impotence, the client's marriage was failing. The lawyer exploited this information to commence a sexual relationship with the claimant's wife. The claimant successfully sued the lawyer for breach of his fiduciary duty to avoid a conflict of interests. In Gurry's language, the abuse of confidential information was the medium for a breach of the duty to avoid a conflict of interests.[288] The trial judge in *Szafer v Chodos* indicated that the client would also have succeeded in an action for breach of confidence because the lawyer's wrong involved misuse of confidential information.[289] One has to be cautious about this decision. In English law so far breach of fiduciary duty has involved the defendant taking advantage of some property interest of the claimant.[290] There has been no recovery for breach of confidence in circumstances remotely similar to the facts of this Canadian case. Something more about this will be said later in this chapter.

5.72

Some further judicial support for allowing an action for breach of fiduciary duty and of confidence on the same facts is to be found in the judgments of La Forest and Wilson JJ in *Lac Minerals Ltd v International Corona Ltd*,[291] a more traditional decision in that it involved commercial exploitation of the claimant by the fiduciary. The judgment of the High Court of Australia in *Moorgate Tobacco Co Ltd v Philip Morris Ltd (No 2)*[292] and of the New Zealand Court of Appeal in *Maclean v Arklow Investments Ltd*[293] both proceed on the assumption that the actions for breach of confidence and breach of fiduciary duty can be concurrently available. Thomas J said:

5.73

---

[286] F Gurry, *Breach of Confidence* (Oxford: 1984) 161.
[287] (1986) 54 OR (2d) 663. Confirmed on appeal (1988) 66 OR (2d) 250. For further examples involving professionals see *Evitt v Price* (1827) 57 ER 659; *Carter v Palmer* (1842) 8 ER 256; *Guertin v Royal Bank of Canada* (1983) 1 DLR (4th) 68 (bank).
[288] *Breach of Confidence* (Oxford: 1984) 161–162.
[289] (1986) 54 OR (2d) 663, 679.
[290] See para 5.80 below.
[291] These two judges, unlike Sopinka J, found that a fiduciary relationship existed between the parties: (1989) 61 DLR (4th) 14, 17–18, 42. McIntyre J concurred with Sopinka J. Latimer J agreed with Sopinka J that the evidence did not establish the existence of a fiduciary relationship. He expressed no view as to whether, in the event that a fiduciary relationship arose, the claimant would be confined to an action for breach of confidence where the core complaint was the misuse of confidential information.
[292] (1984) 156 CLR 414, 436–438. As in *Indata Equipment Supplies Ltd v ACL Ltd* [1998] 1 BCLC 412 no fiduciary relationship was found to exist.
[293] [1998] 3 NZLR 680.

I . . . consider that [counsel] presses the distinction too far in claiming that, where the facts disclose an obligation of confidence the appropriate cause of action is breach of confidence, not breach of fiduciary duty. This may be so in some circumstances, but it is not necessarily or invariably the case. The two causes of action are not mutually exclusive. Lord Woolf MR made the point succinctly in . . . *Attorney-General v Blake* . . . [B]oth a duty not to act contrary to the interests of the other party and an obligation to retain and not misuse confidential information may arise and overlap in the same case.[294]

5.74 Comparison of breach of confidence and breach of fiduciary duty There is no point to the client bringing an action for breach of fiduciary duty instead of breach of confidence unless this secures the client an advantage. The remedies available to a successful claimant in the two actions are largely the same.[295] The word 'largely' is used to flag the uncertainty about whether a court can impose a constructive trust (a standard remedy for breach of fiduciary duty) in an action for breach of confidence.[296] However, the circumstances in which an action for breach of fiduciary duty and an action for breach of confidence can succeed are not.

> They [the obligation of loyalty and the obligation of confidentiality] may co-exist between the same parties at the same time. But they generate different obligations, and their duration may be different.[297]

To confine the client to an action for breach of confidence, as Sopinka J suggested in the *Lac Minerals* case,[298] may in some circumstances therefore deprive the client of relief.

5.75 The first difference between the two obligations concerns the range of information protected. Under fiduciary law the information must be acquired by the fiduciary in his capacity of fiduciary; there is no need for the information to have the quality of confidentiality necessary to support an action for breach of confidence.[299]

> This prohibition on pursuing . . . self-interest must apply irrespective [of] whether the information making up the business opportunity is confidential information in the strict sense or not.[300]

---

[294] [1998] 3 NZLR 680 at 733. His was a dissenting judgment, but not on this point.
[295] But if there is a contract an action for breach of confidence can lead to damages and not merely equitable compensation.
[296] See para 8.78 below. The answer is likely to be yes: *Att-Gen v Blake* [1996] 3 All ER 903, 912. Reservations expressed in *Satnam Investments Ltd v Dunlop Heywood* [1999] 3 All ER 652, 671 are unlikely to apply where (1) the information exploited for profit is confidential personal information and (2) the person making the profit is not a third party but the person with the primary obligation of confidentiality.
[297] per Lord Woolf, *Att-Gen v Blake* [1998] 1 All ER 833, 842.
[298] (1989) 61 DLR (4th) 14, 64.
[299] *Canadian Aero Service Ltd v O'Malley* (1973) 40 DLR (3d) 371, 388; *Investors Syndicate Ltd v Versatile Investments* (1983) 42 OR (2d) 397, 403; *Moorgate Tobacco Co Ltd v Philip Morris Ltd (No 2)* (1983–84) 156 CLR 414, 438; *Att-Gen v Guardian Newspapers Ltd* [1987] 1 WLR 1248, 1319.
[300] per Thomas J, *Maclean v Arklow Investments Ltd* [1998] 3 NZLR 680, 724.

A. Equity

A professional who has a fiduciary relationship with a client may not disclose the client's criminal record unless, semble, there are public interest reasons for this.[301] In *Hilton v Barker Booth & Eastwood*[302] a solicitor was held to have acted correctly in not telling client A the very material piece of information that client B had in the recent past been convicted of criminal offences relating to his bankruptcy and sentenced to nine months' imprisonment, 'matters of public record and so not confidential in any strict legal sense'.[303] It is possible, though not probable, that an action for breach of confidence against a professional will be defeated by the fact that information is in the public domain.[304]

5.76

A second difference lies in the duration of the duty of confidence and the duty of loyalty. The obligation of confidentiality can survive the demise of the professional relationship that gave rise to the obligation,[305] the fiduciary duty of loyalty arising from the retainer disappears when the professional relationship is at an end.[306]

5.77

> Where the court's intervention is sought by a former client . . . [t]he court's jurisdiction cannot be based on any conflict of interest, real or perceived, for there is none. The fiduciary relationship which subsists between solicitor and client comes to an end with the termination of the retainer. Thereafter the solicitor has no obligation to defend and advance the interests of his former client. The only duty to the former client which survives the termination of the client relationship is a continuing duty to preserve the confidentiality of information imparted during its subsistence.[307]

An action for breach of fiduciary duty after termination of the fiduciary relationship must normally[308] relate to something that happened before termination.[309]

---

[301] See para 11.02 below.
[302] [2002] EWCA Civ 723. cp *Stewart v Canadian Broadcasting Commission* (1997) 150 DLR (4th) 24.
[303] per Sir Robert Morritt, [2002] EWCA Civ 723, para 11.
[304] See paras 5.14 et seq.
[305] See para 5.44 above.
[306] But the fiduciary will be in breach of the fiduciary duty if she terminates the fiduciary relationship with the express purpose of exploiting confidential information acquired within it: *CMS Dolphin Ltd v Simonet* [2001] 2 BCLC 704.
[307] per Lord Millett, *Bolkiah v KPMG* [1999] 1 All ER 517, 527. Cp *Faccenda Chicken Ltd v Fowler* [1986] 1 All ER 617, 625; *Att-Gen v Blake* [1998] 1 All ER 833, 842; *R v Neil* [2002] SCC 70, para 27. cp *Dranez Anstalt v Nayek* [2002] 1 BCLC 693, para 75. Contrast *McMaster v Byrne* [1952] 1 All ER 1362, 1368 and *Stewart v Canadian Broadcasting Association* (1997) 150 DLR (4th) 24, esp 138–141 where various cases, including *Allison v Clayhills* (1907) 97 LT 709, are discussed in which the formal relationship of lawyer and client had ended but the fiduciary relationship continued. In the *Stewart* case an Ontario court decided that an advocate who had acted for a client at the sentencing and appeal stages of a criminal case had a continuing fiduciary duty to his client which made it wrong for him to attract business to himself by publicity about the case that was adverse to the client even though this happened years after his retainer had ended.
[308] The fiduciary relationship arising from the retainer may, in some circumstances, be replaced by a similar fiduciary relationship which is independent of the retainer: *Longstaff v Birtles* [2001] EWCA Civ 1219; [2002] 1 WLR 470: '[a] solicitor proposing either to buy property from, or to sell property to, a client is under a duty to cause the client to obtain independent advice. That duty may

Footnote 309 on following page

5.78 A third possible difference may lie in liability for inadvertent disclosure. In *Seager v Copydex*[310] unconscious use of confidential information supported a finding of breach of confidence. If detriment is necessary to found an action for breach of confidence (which is doubtful in a case involving personal information)[311] this is yet another difference between the two actions. Liability for breach of fiduciary duty is strict.[312]

5.79 The differences between the action for breach of confidence and for breach of fiduciary duty may be attributable to the slightly different goals of the two actions. While both aim to promote good faith, breach of fiduciary duty is about maintaining the integrity of a relationship and breach of confidence in actions concerning personal information is primarily about protecting reasonable expectations of privacy.[313]

Breach of fiduciary duty of loyalty and personal information

5.80 The value of the action for breach of fiduciary duty as a solution to the disclosure of confidential information by a professional depends upon two overlapping issues:

(1) whether professionals in recognized fiduciary relationships with clients owe their clients a duty of loyalty in respect of personal information that is of no commercial value; and

(2) the extent to which courts will impose fiduciary duties on professionals who do not manage their client's assets.

Thus far, in England[314] and Australia[315] the fiduciary duty of undivided loyalty has been restricted to relationships in which, at least when the fiduciary label was first applied,[316] the beneficiary entrusted the fiduciary with control and management

---

endure beyond the relationship of solicitor and client. . . . The source of the duty is not the retainer itself, but all the circumstances (including the retainer) creating a relationship of trust and confidence, from which flow obligations of loyalty and transparency . . .' per Mummery LJ.

[309] J Glover, 'Is breach of confidence a fiduciary wrong? Preserving the reach of judge-made law' [2001] LS 594, 613–614.

[310] [1967] 2 All ER 415. See para 6.91 below.

[311] See para 5.40 above.

[312] *English v Dedham Vale Properties Ltd* [1978] 1 WLR 93, 112; *Canadian Aero Service Ltd v O'Malley* (1973) 40 DLR (3d) 371, 383–385; *Moorgate Tobacco Co Ltd v Philip Morris Ltd (No 2)* (1983–84) 156 CLR 414, 437.

[313] See para 6.14 below.

[314] 'Equity imposes on certain people fiduciary obligations in relation to *the property* of their clients or patients . . .' per Browne-Wilkinson LJ, *Sidaway v Bethlem Royal Hospital Governors* [1984] 1 All ER 1018, 1031 (italics added).

[315] See *Paramasivam v Flynn* 1998 Aus Fed Ct, Lexis 1161, paras 45 et seq.

[316] The solicitor–client relationship is an established fiduciary relationship. Although it may have gained this characterization because solicitors have responsibility for the economic well-being of their clients, the client's economic interests do not have to be at stake for the obligation of loyalty to be engaged. The duty to avoid a conflict of interest arises just as much when a solicitor represents a

A. Equity

of property or money.[317] Because doctors do not normally handle their patients' assets, English law says that they do not owe their patients a fiduciary duty of loyalty.[318] The only fiduciary duty of the doctor is to abstain from obtaining property from the patient through the exercise of undue influence.[319]

In Canada no judicial inhibition has been felt about imposing full fiduciary duties across the spectrum of doctor–patient transactions.[320] The Canadian doctor owes a fiduciary duty of loyalty to the patient which may be breached by sexual exploitation,[321] non-disclosure of information[322] and, semble, disclosure or misuse of confidential information.[323] It does not seem likely that English courts will follow the Canadian precedents since there is no obvious lacuna in English law. Adequate protection when information is improperly disclosed or used is available in the shape of an action for breach of confidence, and in other cases of disloyalty by the torts of deceit, conversion and negligence[324] or the law of contract. **5.81**

---

client in a criminal matter as in a civil case in which the client stands to gain or lose financially: see *R v Neil* [2002] SCC 70 where at para 12 the solicitor's duty of loyalty (like legal professional privilege) is seen as essential to the integrity of the administration of justice. In *Hilton v Barker Booth & Eastwood* [2002] EWCA Civ 723 it was held that a solicitor had acted correctly in not disclosing a client's criminal conviction.

[317] R Cooter and B Freedman, 'The Fiduciary Relationship: Its Economic Character and Legal Consequences' (1991) 66 New York UL Rev 1045, 1046. The case against treating property as the defining characteristic of a fiduciary relationship of trust and confidence is argued by R Magnusson, 'A Triumph for Medical Paternalism: *Breen v Williams*, Fiduciaries and Patient Access to Medical Records' (1995) Tort LJ 12, 31 et seq.

[318] *Sidaway v Bethlem Royal Hospital Governors* [1984] 1 All ER 1018, 1032; see para 19.15 below.

[319] If a patient gives an unusual gift to a doctor there is a presumption of undue influence: *Johnson v Buttress* (1936) 56 CLR 113. This presumption also applies to spiritual advisers (*Nottidge v Prince* (1860) 66 ER 103, 113; *Allcard v Skinner* (1887) 36 Ch D 145) and to solicitors: cp *Rhodes v Bate* (1865–66) LR 1 Ch App 252; *Naidoo v Naidu,* The Times, 1 November 2000.

[320] Fiduciary relationships have been recognized in a variety of relationships not involving management of money or property. See eg the Supreme Court decision in *M(K) v M(H)* (1992) 96 DLR (4th) 289 which involved a parent–child relationship.

[321] *Norberg v Wynrib* [1992] 2 SCR 226; *Taylor v McGillivray* (1993) 110 DLR (4th) 64. Cp *L v Robinson* [2000] 3 NZLR 499, paras 26 et seq. See further, A Grubb, 'The Doctor as Fiduciary' [1994] CLP 311; I Kennedy 'The Fiduciary Relationship and its Application to Doctors and Patients' in P Birks (ed), *Wrongs and Remedies in the Twenty-first Century* (Oxford: 1996) 120–140; P Michalik, 'Doctors' Fiduciary Duties' (1998) 6 J of L and Medicine 168. The term 'fiduciary' is bandied about in *Furniss v Fitchett* [1958] NZLR 396, 404 and *Duncan v Medical Disciplinary Committee* [1986] 1 NZLR 513, 521 but it is unclear whether this is intended to signify anything beyond the rebuttable presumption that a gift is the consequence of undue influence.

[322] *McInerney v MacDonald* (1992) 93 DLR (4th) 415.

[323] cp *Lac Minerals Ltd v International Corona Resources Ltd* (1989) 611 DLR (4th) 14.

[324] eg *L v Robinson* [2000] 3 NZLR 499 a case of sexual exploitation in which the defendant was held to owe his patient a duty not to engage in sexual activity with her while she was his patient and not to engage in actions which would cause further psychological or psychiatric harm. Exemplary damages were awarded.

Chapter 5: Equity and Copyright Solutions to Intentional Disclosure

5.82 Even if the action for breach of fiduciary duty is confined to commercially valuable information it is not wholly useless as a solution to the disclosure of confidential personal information. Sometimes confidential personal information does however have considerable commercial value[325] and it may happen that a professional who is in an established fiduciary relationship with a client, say a solicitor or an accountant, has the opportunity to profit financially by exploiting the client's *personal* information. Inside information about a client with a high public profile may be a highly saleable commodity.

5.83 In *Breen v Williams*[326] the High Court of Australia envisaged doctors as having wider fiduciary obligations than the English courts have recognized so far, but the duties are still entirely prescriptive (negative).[327] Australian doctors were held not to be under an obligation to give their patients access to or to permit them to copy their patient records (the actual holding of *Breen v Williams*)[328] but it was hinted that they could not make a secret profit from the relationship by, for example, advising the patient to undergo treatment at a particular private hospital in which the doctor has an undisclosed financial interest[329] or patenting the patient's genes.[330] This seems a sensible compromise.[331]

B. Copyright

Nature of copyright

5.84 Copyright is a property right.[332] It prevents all except the owner of the copyright and those licensed by the owner from expressing information in the form of the copyright work.[333] All original work is copyright[334] (regardless of its artistic merit)[335] for the duration of the creator's[336] lifetime plus 70 years.[337]

---

[325] eg *Douglas v Hello! Ltd* [2001] 2 All ER 289.
[326] (1996) 138 ALR 259, esp 306–307.
[327] (1996) 138 ALR 259, 289.
[328] See para 19.12 below. Contrast *McInerney v MacDonald* (1992) 93 DLR (4th) 415.
[329] *Breen v Williams* (1996) 138 ALR 259, 274, 285, 286, 307.
[330] cp *Moore v Regents of University of California* 271 Cal Rptr 146 (1990).
[331] cp *Guide to Professional Conduct of Solicitors* (1999) para 16.05: '[a] solicitor must not make any profit by the use of confidential information for his or her own purposes.'
[332] *Hyde Park Residences v Yellard* [2000] 3 WLR 215, para 38.
[333] *Ashdown v Telegraph Group* [2001] 1 All ER 666, para 30. Copyright can be owned jointly. One owner cannot exploit the copyright without the consent of the other owner(s): *USP Strategies plc v London General Holdings Ltd* [2002] EWHC 2557.
[334] Copyright, Designs and Patents Act 1988, s 1.
[335] ibid s4(1)(a). All that is necessary is some skill and labour: *Ladbroke (Football) Ltd v William Hill (Football) Ltd* [1964] 1 WLR 273, 278. The composition of medical notes was acknowledged to create copyright by Gummow J in *Breen v Williams* (1996) 138 ALR 259, 300.
[336] The owner of copyright is generally the creator or author: Copyright, Designs and Patents Act 1988, ss 9, 11.
[337] Copyright, Designs and Patents Act 1988, s 12.

B. Copyright

In a professional relationship, the client will own the copyright in letters written to the professional and any other documents created and submitted to the professional such as drawings, photographs or a diary.[338] The professional (or her employer)[339] will own the copyright in letters sent to the client or to third parties about the client and in the notes and documents prepared for, or about, the client.[340] The professional's terms of engagement may expressly state that copyright in documents that she prepares remains with her (or her firm) and is licensed to clients for use in the particular matter for which they were drawn up. Under current copyright legislation[341] the copyright in a photograph (whether commissioned or not) belongs to the photographer.[342] If this was the professional (or her employee) it belongs to the professional.[343] If the photograph was commissioned by the client, for the duration of copyright the client has the right to object to copies being issued to the public, displayed in public, broadcast or included in a cable programme.[344] 5.85

Copyright and disclosure of confidential information

Copyright cannot usually be relied upon to prevent or redress unauthorized disclosure or use of confidential personal information because copyright does not protect confidentiality as such.[345] There is no breach of copyright when an image or drawing is described or the contents of a literary work retold in different words. Infringement requires copying without permission. In *Nottinghamshire Healthcare National Health Service Trust v NGN Ltd*,[346] The Sun was found to have infringed the copyright of an NHS Trust by reproducing a photograph stolen from the medical records of an inmate of Rampton Hospital. 5.86

Copyright is not infringed if the copying is done for the purposes of judicial proceedings.[347] 5.87

---

[338] cp *A v B* [2000] EMLR 1007, para 11.
[339] An employer usually owns the copyright in work created by an employee in the course of employment: Copyright Designs and Patents Act 1988, s 11(2).
[340] Medical records upon which doctors, nurses and counsellors had made entries were treated as the subject of copyright in *Auckland Medical Aid Trust v Commissioner of Police* [1976] 1 NZLR 485, 488.
[341] This came into force on 1 August 1989.
[342] Copyright, Designs and Patents Act 1988, ss 9,11.
[343] ibid ss 3, 11.
[344] ibid ss 85, 86(1).
[345] *Fraser v Evans* [1969] 1 All ER 8,12; *Fraser v Thames Television* [1983] 2 All ER 101, 117. See also *Philip v Pennell* [1907] 2 Ch 577.
[346] [2002] EWHC 409; [2002] EMLR 33.
[347] Copyright, Designs and Patents Act 1988, s 45(1). It is at least arguable that s 45 is not limited to copies made after the issue of originating process: *A v B* [2000] EMLR 1007, para 13.

6

DEALING WITH UNINTENTIONAL DISCLOSURE

A. Interception and Disloyalty	6.02	B. Accidental Disclosure	6.89
Civil Actions: Client v Interceptor	6.02	The Professional's Liability	6.90
Civil Actions: Client v Professional	6.32	Admissibility of Accidentally Disclosed and Intercepted Materials in Court Proceedings	6.95
Civil Actions: Professional v Employee	6.38		
Civil Actions: Professional v Interceptor	6.48		
Prosecuting Interceptors and Disloyal Employees in the Criminal Courts	6.54	Restraining the Use of Materials by Means of the Action for Breach of Confidence	6.103
Prosecuting a Stranger in the Criminal Courts	6.84		
Committing a Criminal Offence in the Public Interest	6.88		

A professional may be confronted by a situation of unintentional disclosure of confidential client information in two distinct circumstances. **6.01**

(1) Information has been intercepted without authority by someone working for the professional or by an outsider. Chapter 2 contains comments about the many technical devices available that may be used for this purpose. The leaking to the press of the proof of evidence given by Paul Burrell, Princess Diana's butler, to his solicitors is an instance of this kind of unintentional disclosure.[1]
(2) The professional or an employee has disclosed the information not intending to do so; in other words, disclosure was accidental.

Part A of this chapter considers:

(1) what sort of civil action the client and the professional might bring against the disloyal employee or the interloper (not acting for the state)[2] who manages to get hold of confidential personal information and discloses or misuses it;[3]
(2) the criminal offences that the wrongdoer commits.

---

[1] 'Burrell proof probe' 15 November 2002, http://www.lawgazette.co.uk.
[2] The powers of the police, security services, customs and excise officials and other public officials to intercept confidential information are considered in ch 14.
[3] Actions against a stranger to whom an interceptor or corrupt employee may have passed the confidential information are dealt with in ch 7.

Part B of this chapter deals with the consequences of, and solutions to, accidental disclosure. Part C looks at the use of intercepted or accidentally disclosed confidential in the course of litigation.

A. Interception and Disloyalty

Civil Actions: Client v Interceptor

Breach of confidence

The rationale of the action

6.02 When a professional intentionally discloses confidential information about a client without the client's permission, usually the most suitable cause of action against the professional is an action in equity for breach of confidence.[4] This can be used to secure an injunction to prevent further dissemination of the information or compensation for any loss inflicted or both.[5] Can this action also be maintained against an interceptor? For many years the answer was no. The action for breach of confidence was understood to be a mechanism to prevent opportunistic conduct by someone to whom confidential information has been entrusted. The element of trust generated what some courts have called a fiduciary relationship, but this is not a fiduciary relationship in the strict sense of the term.[6] To support an action for breach of confidence there does not have to be anything economic about the relationship between claimant and defendant. What attracts the intervention of equity is quite simply the defendant's unconscionable betrayal of the claimant's trust.[7]

The elements of the action

6.03 In *Coco v AN Clark (Engineers) Ltd* Megarry J declared that the action for breach of confidence involved three elements.[8] The second of these is that the 'information was imparted in circumstances importing an obligation of confidence'.[9] Megarry J said that this element would be satisfied if 'the circumstances are such that any reasonable man standing in the shoes of the recipient of the information would have realised that upon reasonable grounds the information was being given to him in confidence'.[10] These words presuppose reliance by the claimant on

---

[4] See ch 5.
[5] See ch 8.
[6] See para 5.64 above.
[7] cp R Flannigan, 'Fiduciary Regulation of Sexual Exploitation' (2000) 79 Canadian Bar Rev 301, 302.
[8] See para 5.06 above.
[9] [1969] RPC 41, 47.
[10] [1969] RPC 41, 48.

A. Interception and Disloyalty

the defendant. In *Malone v Commissioner of Police* Sir Robert Megarry V-C assumed that the absence of a relationship of trust between claimant or defendant (or between the claimant and the source upon whom the defendant drew for the information)[11] was fatal to an action for breach of confidence.

> In the present case, the alleged misuse is not by the person to whom the information was intended to be communicated, but by someone to whom the plaintiff had no intention of communicating anything: and that, of course, introduces a somewhat different element, that of the unknown overhearer. It seems to me that a person who utters confidential information must accept the risk of any unknown overhearing that is inherent in the circumstances of communication . . . No doubt a person who uses a telephone to give confidential information to another may do so in such a way as to impose an obligation of confidence on that other; but I do not see how it can be said that any such obligation is imposed on those who overhear the conversation, whether by means of tapping or otherwise.[12]

Consequence of insisting on a relationship of trust

The Megarry approach leaves the confidant without protection in equity when confidential personal information is stolen and either the thief, or someone to whom the thief has passed the information, proposes to, or has in fact, published it. In 1988 a Crown Court recorder was unable to get an injunction to prevent The Sun from publishing correspondence that had been stolen from his homosexual lover.[13] 'What system of jurisprudence would regard as tortious the publication of the material by the confidant but would permit the publication of the material by the thief?' Sir Richard Scott asked in an article published in 1990.[14] As long ago as 1970 Jones argued that if equity can intervene against a third party who receives information which has been disclosed in breach of an obligation of confidence and only learns of the breach through the bringing of the action,[15] equity ought also to be able to intervene where information has been obtained by clandestine means.[16] Gurry said that the action for breach of confidence should lie because 'espionage offends the same ethical norm on which the policy of the breach of confidence action is founded'.[17] Although the spy has not abused a confidence, he has obtained involuntary disclosure of information that he must know is confidential, otherwise why use underhand means to get it?[18]

6.04

---

[11] See para 7.25 below.
[12] *Malone v Commissioner of Police* [1979] 2 All ER 620, 645, 646. Contrast *Franklin v Giddins* [1978] Qd R 72, 80; *Kennedy v Ireland* [1987] IR 587.
[13] G Robertson and A Nicol, *Robertson and Nicol on Medial Law* (4th edn, London: 2002) 227.
[14] Scott J, 'Developments in the Law of Confidentiality' [1990] Denning LJ 77, 85.
[15] See para 7.23 below.
[16] G Jones, 'Restitution of Benefits Obtained in Breach of Another's Confidence' (1970) 86 LQR 463, 482.
[17] F Gurry, *Breach of Confidence* (Oxford: 1984) 164.
[18] Articles that consider the issue include G Wei, 'Surreptitious taking of confidential information' (1992) 12 LS 302; M Richardson, 'Breach of confidence, surreptitiously or accidently obtained information and privacy: theory versus law' (1994) 19 Melbourne UL Rev 673.

Chapter 6: Dealing with Unintentional Disclosure

The law changes direction

6.05 **Decisions preceding *Douglas v Hello! Ltd*** In 1984 the Court of Appeal in *Francome v MGN Ltd*[19] allowed an action for breach of confidence involving the interception of telephone conversations to proceed to trial. The case was argued on the basis that the newspaper to whom the interceptor had passed the intercepted information stood in the shoes of the interceptor. *Malone* was distinguished on the grounds that the tapping of the claimant's telephone had been *unlawful*.

> The Vice-chancellor was only dealing with a case of authorised tapping by the police and he makes that clear. . . . Illegal tapping by private persons is quite another matter, since it must be questionable whether the user of a telephone can be regarded as accepting the risk of that in the same way as, for example, he accepts the risk that his conversation may be overheard in consequence of the accidents and imperfections of the telephone system itself.[20]

6.06 In the 1990s the English courts became bolder and, in interlocutory proceedings involving covert acquisition of confidential information (including photographs), assumed that when a third party was sued for breach of confidence a relationship of confidence between the claimant and the defendant or the defendant's source was unnecessary.[21] In *Hellewell v Chief Constable of Derbyshire* Laws J ventured the opinion that:

> If someone with a telephoto lens were to take from a distance and with no authority a picture of another engaged in some private act, his subsequent disclosure of the photograph would, in my judgment, as surely amount to a breach of confidence as if he had found or stolen a letter or diary in which the act was recounted and proceeded to publish it. In such a case, the law would protect what might reasonably be called a right of privacy, although the name accorded to the cause of action would be breach of confidence.[22]

6.07 ***Douglas v Hello! Ltd* and *Venables v NGN Ltd*** By 2001 it was widely believed in legal circles that a duty of confidence may arise in equity independently of any extant confidential relationship between the parties. This had been the spring-

---

[19] [1984] 1 WLR 892. According to G Robertson and A Nicol, *Robertson and Nicol on Media Law* (4th edn, London: 2002) 232 the Prince of Wales was awarded an ex parte injunction to prevent publication of a tape recording which allegedly contained conversations with Lady Diana, as she then was during their engagement.
[20] per Fox LJ, [1984] 1 WLR 892, 900.
[21] *X Ltd v Morgan-Grampian Ltd* [1990] 1 All ER 1, 5; *Shelley Films Ltd v Rex Features Ltd* [1994] EMLR 134; *Creation Records Ltd v NGN Ltd* [1997] EMLR 444. See also *HRH Princess of Wales v MGN* (QB, 8 November 1993) where Drake J said that equity would intervene if a passing doctor came to the assistance of a patient in extremis and then, without consent, photographed him. It is possible to argue that in this situation there is a relationship of confidence by reason of the doctor treating the patient.
[22] [1995] 1 WLR 804, 807. Several years earlier, in August 1992, Latham J had refused an injunction to prevent publication of photographs of the Duchess of York in the company of John Bryan by Mirror Group Newspapers Ltd.

A. Interception and Disloyalty

board for the United Kingdom's exegesis of the law to the European Commission of Human Rights in *Earl Spencer v UK*.[23] This was confirmed in *Douglas v Hello! Ltd*.[24] The first two claimants were a Hollywood couple who had contracted with OK! magazine, the third claimant, to publish exclusive photographs of their wedding. An unidentified photographer, who could have been a guest, a member of the catering staff or an intruder, had secretly taken photographs of this happy occasion and sold them to a rival of the third claimant, Hello! magazine. Although the Court of Appeal discharged an interlocutory injunction restraining the defendants from publishing the photographs,[25] the court confirmed that the claimants' success against the defendant in an action for breach of confidence did not depend upon whether the photographs were taken by an insider with whom the first two claimants had had a reciprocal relationship[26] or an outsider with whom they had not. Keene LJ said:

> Already before the coming into force of the Human Rights Act 1998 (HRA) there have been persuasive dicta . . . to the effect that a pre-existing confidential relationship between the parties is not required for a breach of confidence suit. The nature of the subject matter or the circumstances of the defendant's activities may suffice in some instances to give rise to liability for breach of confidence.[27]

Had the claimants not intended to publish the wedding photographs in a popular magazine, he said, 'I might have concluded that in the current state of English law the claimants were likely to succeed [in obtaining an injunction] at any eventual trial'.[28]

6.08 Very shortly after judgment was handed down in the *Douglas* case, Butler-Sloss P allowed an injunction on a breach of confidence theory to prevent the media exposing the whereabouts and new identities of two teenagers who were about to be released after serving sentences for a particularly horrendous murder of a small child while they themselves were children.[29] Identification, Butler-Sloss P decided, might put their lives at risk. The decision demonstrates that subject matter and consequences can determine whether disclosure of personal information is a breach of confidence irrespective of the circumstances of its obtaining.[30]

---

[23] (1998) 25 EHRR CD 105. See *Douglas v Hello! Ltd* [2001] 2 All ER 289, paras 123–124; *B v H Bauer Publishing Ltd* [2002] EMLR 145, para 30.

[24] [2001] 2 All ER 289.

[25] A money remedy was considered sufficient: see para 8.17 below.

[26] If the photographer was a wedding guest or a member of the staff engaged to assist at the wedding then there was a pre-existing relationship of confidence. Staff had given confidentiality undertakings and guests had been warned that photography was not permitted in their invitations and by a notice at the entrance to the Plaza Hotel where the reception took place. It has since emerged that the photographer was an intruder.

[27] *Douglas v Hello! Ltd* [2001] 2 All ER 289, para 166. See now also *A v B & C plc* [2002] EWCA Civ 337; [2002] 3 WLR 542, para 11, guideline viii.

[28] *Douglas v Hello! Ltd* [2001] 2 All ER 289, para 167.

[29] *Venables v NGN Ltd* [2001] 1 All ER 908.

[30] J Wright, *Tort Law and Human Rights* (Oxford: 2001) 181. cp *Att-Gen v Guardian Newspapers Ltd (No 2)* [1988] 3 All ER 545, 658–659.

Interception of privileged communications

6.09 It is surprising that the courts took so long to dispense with the impartation requirement in breach of confidence actions involving improperly obtained information because it has been accepted since the decision in *Lord Ashburton v Pape*[31] in 1913 that equity will restrain the use of legally privileged documents that have found their way into the hands of an opponent by surreptitious means. In *Lord Ashburton v Pape*, Swinfen Eady J did not rest his decision in favour of Lord Ashburton on the fact that the leaked documents were privileged. He said that that equity would 'restrain the publication of *confidential* information improperly or surreptitiously obtained . . .'.[32] In *ITC Film v Video Exchange* Warner J said:

> [W]here A has improperly obtained possession of a document belonging to B, the court will, at the suit of B, order A to return the document to B and to deliver up any copies of it that A has made, and will restrain A from making any use of any such copies or of the information contained in the document.[33]

Breach of confidence or breach of informational privacy?

6.10 **A *de facto* law of privacy** If equity intervenes to protect confidential personal information that has been surreptitiously intercepted, it is highly artificial to talk of a relationship of confidence and an obligation of confidentiality. Semantically, confidentiality means information given in trust from the Latin *fido* (I trust) and *con/cum* (with/together with).[34] Where the claimant and defendant or, at least, the first person in the chain of knowers leading to the defendant, have no connection, equity's object in granting relief is to protect the claimant's reasonable expectation of privacy. The interceptor's obligation (and that of a stranger)[35] is more appropriately described as an obligation to respect the claimant's informational privacy.

6.11 In *Douglas v Hello! Ltd* Keene LJ acknowledged that breach of confidence has become, in effect, a de facto law of privacy when, after stating that a pre-existing confidential relationship between the parties was not required to have a cause of action, he said:

> Whether the resulting liability is described as being for breach of confidence or for breach of a right to privacy may be little more than deciding what label is to be attached to the cause of action, but *there would seem to be merit in recognising that the original concept of breach of confidence has in this particular category of cases now devel-*

---

[31] [1913] 2 Ch 469.
[32] ibid at 475 (italics added). See also *Exchange Telegraph Co v Howard* (1906) 22 TLR 375, 378. Contrast *Corelli v Wall* (1906) 22 TLR 532.
[33] [1982] 2 All ER 241, 244.
[34] E Cameron, 'Confidentiality in HIV/AIDS: Some Reflections on India and South Africa' (2001) 1 Oxford University Commonwealth LJ 35, 37, n 7.
[35] See para 7.27 below.

A. Interception and Disloyalty

oped into something different from the commercial and employment relationships with which confidentiality is mainly concerned.[36]

Sedley LJ thought the same:

> I would conclude, at lowest, that [counsel for the claimants] has a powerfully arguable case to advance at trial that his two first-named clients have a right of privacy which English law will today recognise and, where appropriate, protect . . . To say this is in my belief to say little, save by way of a label that our courts have not said already over the years. . . . What a concept of privacy does . . . is accord recognition to the fact that the law has to protect not only those people whose trust has been abused but those who simply find themselves subjected to an unwanted intrusion into their personal lives. The law no longer needs to construct an artificial relationship of confidentiality between intruder and victim: it can recognise privacy itself as a legal principle drawn from the fundamental value of personal autonomy.[37]

Sedley LJ's words have been interpreted to support a free-standing tort action for breach of privacy.[38] This may not have been what he intended; all three judges were satisfied that recovery was available on a breach of confidence theory.[39] In *A v B plc and C* ('*Flitcroft*') Lord Woolf was opposed to an independent right of action based on infringement of privacy. The courts, he said, could give effect to Article 8 by a generous approach to the action for breach of confidence.[40]

6.12

> In the great majority of situations, if not all situations, where the protection of privacy is justified . . . an action for breach of confidence now will, where this is appropriate, provide the necessary protection. This means that at first instance it can be readily accepted that it is not necessary to tackle the vexed question of whether there is a separate cause of action based upon a new tort involving the infringement of privacy.[41]

Only the House of Lords can now create a privacy tort. The difficulty of defining privacy[42] and the remedial issues that would arise if the equitable action were reclassified as a tort[43] makes it unlikely that the House of Lords will move the law in this direction.

---

[36] [2001] 2 All ER 289, para 166 (emphasis added). See also *John v Joulebine* (QB, 26 January 2001).
[37] *Douglas v Hello! Ltd* [2001] 2 All ER 289, para 126.
[38] *Home Office v Wainwright* [2001] EWCA Civ 2081; [2002] 3 WLR 405, paras 96–97.
[39] It is quite clear from his exposition that Sedley LJ saw the action for breach of confidence as an available remedy for privacy intrusion: *Douglas v Hello! Ltd* [2001] 2 All ER 289, paras 117, 123–125, 138.
[40] [2002] EWCA Civ 337; [2002] 3 WLR 542, paras 4, 6.
[41] per Lord Woolf, ibid, para 11, guideline vi.
[42] See paras 1.07 and 4.58 above.
[43] Equity compensates pure mental distress. Would the common law do the same? Classifying the wrong as a tort also removes the discretion (exercised on settled grounds) to refuse compensation. The common law has to rely on concepts of mitigation, remoteness and contributory fault. These issues are discussed in ch 8.

Breach of informational privacy

Breach of confidentiality v breach of informational privacy

6.13 In time, the courts may admit that original breach of confidence action has branched into two forks: protection of trade secrets and breach of informational privacy.[44] There is nothing improper about this: 'breach of confidence is a developing area of the law, the boundaries of which are not immutable but may change to reflect changes in society, technology and business practice.'[45] The advantage of admitting the split is that the courts can then freely develop the rules laid down in *Coco v AN Clark (Engineers) Ltd*[46] with trade secrets in mind in a form that is appropriate to situations involving the disclosure of personal information by an interceptor. In practice, this has happened already. The three requirements that Megarry laid down, namely:

(1) confidential information;
(2) imparted in confidence;
(3) disclosed or used without authority to the detriment of the client;

are in the process of being transformed into two

(1) a reasonable expectation in the privacy of information;[47]
(2) detriment through unauthorized disclosure or use (though even this requirement is becoming academic).[48]

In personal information cases there is possibly a further requirement for information that is capable of being true or false that the court had no need to consider in *Coco v AN Clark (Engineers) Ltd* and other trade mark cases. This is whether the information (if factual) is true.[48a] The Court of Appeal in *Campbell v MGN Ltd*[49] suggested that the inaccuracy of some of the information published about Campbell strengthened the case against judicial intervention. If an action for breach of informational privacy will fail because what has been disclosed is inaccurate (either because truth is a substantive law requirement or because discretionary relief will be refused) upon whom does the burden of proving that the information is inaccurate fall? By analogy with defamation, this should be the

---

[44] In *Campbell v MGN* [2002] EWCA Civ 1373, paras 69–70 Lord Phillips MR admitted that an action arising from non-consensual disclosure of confidential personal information is more accurately described as a breach of privacy than a breach of confidence.
[45] per Keene LJ, *Douglas v Hello! Ltd* [2001] 2 All ER 289, para 165.
[46] [1969] RPC 41, 47; see para 5.06 above.
[47] cp *Halford v UK* (1997) 24 EHRR 523, para 44; *Dagg v Canada (Minister of Finance)* [1997] 2 SCR 403, para 7.
[48] See para 6.26 below.
[48a] A free-standing tort of infringement of privacy might, arguably, protect information that is either true or false: see para 1.12 above. By sticking with breach of confidence the courts avoid having to settle a boundary between privacy and defamation.
[49] [2002] EWCA Civ 1373, para 57.

A. Interception and Disloyalty

defendant; the claimant should not have to confirm the truth of the information.[50]

Reasonable expectation of privacy

The reasonable expectations test For personal information, the test of impartation in circumstances importing an obligation of confidentiality[51] has been replaced by a test of reasonable expectation of privacy: '[a] duty of confidence will arise whenever the party subject to the duty is in a situation where he either knows or ought to know that the other person can reasonably expect his privacy to be protected.'[52] One circumstance that may give rise to a reasonable expectation of privacy is disclosure of personal information within a relationship of trust.[53] But a reasonable expectation of privacy may also arise from: **6.14**

(1) the circumstances in which the information was disclosed, such as in the course of a telephone call that the claimant was entitled to assume was private,[54] or
(2) the nature of the information itself.

'[C]ertain kinds of information are categorised as private and for that reason alone ought not to be disclosed.'[55] These words are taken from the Law Commission's Report, *Breach of Confidence*, but the same opinion was expressed by Lord Goff in *Att-Gen v Guardian Newspapers (No 2)*: some information is 'obviously confidential'.[56]

In connection with the Fourth Amendment right to freedom from unreasonable searches and seizures, the US Supreme Court has promulgated a reasonable expectation of privacy standard which addresses the huge variation in the notions that individuals have about their privacy. Those who claim the protection of the Fourth Amendment must show that their expectation of privacy was (1) actually held *and* (2) reasonable based on societal standards.[57] The expectation test with its **6.15**

---

[50] H Tomlinson, *Privacy and the Media: The Developing Law* (London: 2002) 75.
[51] *Coco v AN Clark (Engineers) Ltd* [1969] RPC 41, 47.
[52] per Lord Woolf, *A v B plc and C ('Flitcroft')* [2002] EWCA Civ 337; [2002] 3 WLR 542, para 11, guideline ix.
[53] See para 5.24 above.
[54] *Halford v UK* (1997) 24 EHRR 523, para 45; *Bugallo v Spain* Application 58496/00, 18 February 2003. cp *Moreton v Police* [2002] 2 NZLR 236. Contrast *Malone v Commissioner of Police of the Metropolis* [1979] 2 All ER 620, 646; *Edwards v State Farm Insurance Co and 'John Doe'* 833 F 2d 535 (1987).
[55] (Cmnd 8388, 1981) para 2.3.
[56] [1988] 3 All ER 545, 658–659.
[57] *Katz v US* 389 US 357, 361 (1967). In practice the first prong of the test is said only to be used in situations where a reasonable expectation of privacy is found not to exist: R Julie, 'High-Tech Surveillance tools and the Fourth Amendment: Reasonable Expectations of Privacy in the Technological Age' (2000) 37 American Crminal L Rev 127, 133. Julie also mentions the common criticism that the reasonable expectation of privacy test is circular: the only expectations that are reasonable are those that the court will protect.

separation of the public from the private has been transferred by US courts to the US private facts tort.[58]

6.16 The problem of establishing whether an expectation of privacy is reasonably based was glossed over in *A v B plc and C ('Flitcroft')*. Lord Woolf said that there 'must be some interest of a private nature which the claimant wishes to protect, but usually the answer to the question whether there exists a private interest worthy of protection will be obvious. In those cases in which the answer is not obvious, an answer will often be unnecessary.'[59] Lord Woolf's last sentence has to be understood in the context in which it was made, namely an application for an injunction against a newspaper. An uncertain claim to privacy is likely to be outweighed by a newspaper's competing claim to disclosure based on freedom of expression.[60] A potentially more helpful test is Morland J's suggestion in *Campbell v MGN Ltd*, derived from *ABC v Lenah Game Meats Pty Ltd*,[61] and ultimately from the US private facts tort,[62] that the information must be 'easily identifiable as private and disclosure of the information would be highly offensive to a reasonable person of ordinary sensibilities'.[63] Whether this test is compatible with Article 8, especially in cases in which the media and Article 10 are not involved, has not been addressed. In some contexts a test of 'highly offensive' may set a threshold that is too high.[64]

6.17 Information capable of being confidential (private)[65] Warby and co-authors have trawled the case law for personal information that the courts have treated as confidential in past actions for breach of confidence or have indicated to be of an intrinsically confidential nature. This is information that might be capable of being the subject of an obligation of confidentiality even though there was no relationship of trust and confidence between the claimant and defendant (or the defendant's ultimate source). His findings have been supplemented to compile the following list:

---

[58] R Turkington, *The Privacy Primer*, 14, available at http://vls.law.villanova.edu/prof/turk/privacynotes/PRIVACYPRIMER.pdf. See also para 4.54 above.
[59] [2002] EWCA Civ 337; [2002] 2 3 WLR 542, para 11, guideline vii.
[60] See para 3.17 above.
[61] [2001] HCA 63, para 42. The relevant passage appears in Lord Woolf's judgment in *A v B plc & C ('Flitcroft')* [2002] EWCA Civ 337; [2002] 3 WLR 542 para 11, guideline vii.
[62] See para 4.54 above.
[63] [2002] EWHC 499; [2002] EMLR 30, para 40(1). Approved [2002] EWCA Civ 1373, paras 49–50. There is also implicit approval of this test in *A v B plc & C ('Flitcroft')* [2002] EWCA Civ 337; [2002] 3 WLR 542, para 11, guideline vii.
[64] M Tugendhat and I Christie (eds), *The Law of Privacy and the Media* (Oxford: 2002). Update, ch 4, available from http://www.media-ent-law.co.uk/privacy.
[65] cp *Report of the Committee on Privacy and Related Matters* (Cm 1102, 1990) para 3.5; Lord Chancellor, *Infringement of Privacy* (July 1993) para 5.22.

A. Interception and Disloyalty

- medical information,[66] especially psychiatric information;[67]
- circumstances surrounding birth and death;[68]
- information about sexual activity and orientation;[69]
- information about personal relationships;[70]
- a person's visual image at a particular moment in time;[71]
- information about identity;[72]
- financial information;[73]
- information about the care, upbringing and education of children including social work records;[74]

---

[66] *Campbell v MGN* [2002] EWCA Civ 1373, para 47.

[67] *Argyll v Argyll* [1967] 1 Ch 302, 331; *W v Egdell* [1990] 1 All ER 835; *R v Department of Health, ex p Source Informatics Ltd* [2000] 1 All ER 786; *P v D* [2000] NZLR 591; *Venables v NGN Ltd* [2001] 1 All ER 908, para 103; *Ashworth Hospital Authority v MGN Ltd* [2002] UKHL 29, [2002] 1 WLR 2033; *Campbell v MGN Ltd* [2002] EWHC 499, [2002] EMLR 30.

[68] The French law of privacy protected photographs of the corpse of President Mitterrand that had been taken surreptitiously: M Tugendhat and I Christie (eds), *The Law of Privacy and the Media* (Oxford: 2002) para 7.62. cp *Reid v Pierce County* 961 P 2d 3 33 (1998).

[69] *Stephens v Avery* [1988] 2 WLR 1280; *Barrymore v NGN Ltd* [1997] FSR 600. Cp *Theakston v MGN Ltd* [2002] EWHC 137, [2002] EMLR 22; *ADT v UK* (2001) 31 EHRR 33; *A v B plc & C ('Flitcroft')* [2002] EWCA Civ 337, [2002] 3 WLR 542. These two cases limit the relationships to which protection applies.

[70] *ABC v Lenah Game Meats Pty Ltd* [2001] HCA 63, para 42. See also *Argyll v Argyll* [1967] 1 Ch 302.

[71] *Prince Albert v Strange* (1849) 41 ER 1171, Ch; *Pollard v Photographic Co* (1889) 40 Ch D 345; *Hellewell v Chief Constable of Derbyshire* [1995] 1 WLR 804, 807; *Shelley Films Ltd v Rex Features Ltd* [1994] EMLR 134; *Creation Records Ltd v NGN Ltd* [1997] EMLR 444; *Khodaparast v Farrokh-Shad* (CA, 26 February and 28 April 1997); *Douglas v Hello! Ltd* [2001] 2 All ER 289; *W v W* (HC, 22 February 2001); *Re A* (HC, 16 June 2001) (photograph of the surviving co-joined twin); *Theakston v MGN Ltd* [2002] EWHC 137, [2002] EMLR 22, paras 78–80. cp *L v G* [2002] DCR 234, 2002 NZDCR LEXIS 2. Sir Richard Scott published an article in 1990 in which he wrote with reference to the case of *Kaye v Robertson* [1991] FSR 62: '[i]f the photographs of Mr. Kaye's head had, with Mr. Kaye's consent, been taken by a doctor for the purpose of use in a teaching hospital or for an illustration in a learned journal, the doctor would have been restrained from general publication . . .', 'Developments in the Law of Confidentiality' [1990] Denning LJ 77, 87–88.

[72] Informer: *G v Day* [1982] 1 NSWLR 24; *Nicholls v BBC* [1999] EMLR 791; cp *Swinney v Chief Constable of Northumbria* [1996] 3 All ER 449, 452. AIDs and HIV patients: *X v Y* [1988] 2 All ER 648; *H (A Healthcare Worker) v Associated Newspapers Ltd* [2002] EWCA Civ 195, [2002] EMLR 23; cp *Estate of Behringer v Medical Center at Princeton* 592 A 2d 1251 (1991). Natural parent: *G v Att-Gen* [1994] 1 NZLR 714. Youth offender: *Venables v NGN Ltd* [2001] 1 All ER 908.

[73] *Argyll v Argyll* [1967] 1 Ch 302, 329–330; *John Reid Enterprises Ltd v Pell* [1999] EMLR 675. Cp *Lord Levy v Times Newspapers Ltd* (HC, 23 June 2000), The Guardian, 26 June 2000; *ABC v Lenah Game Meats Pty Ltd* [2001] HCA 63, para 42. The ECtHR recognized that a person's tax affairs were confidential in *Fressoz v France* (1999) 31 EHRR 2, paras 43, 53.

[74] *Re Z* [1995] 4 All ER 961; *Venables v NGN Ltd* [2001] 1 All ER 908, para 103; see para 16.59 below.

- diaries,[75] private correspondence,[76] internal memoranda[77] and private conversations.[78]

This is, at best, a provisional list because there is 'no bright line which can be drawn between what is private and what is not'.[79]

6.18 It has been suggested that the sensitive personal data category in the Data Protection Act 1998 (DPA) is an indicator of confidential information.[80] Caution is required here. Some of the data that the DPA rightly treats as sensitive does not relate to information in respect of which anyone could have, in any abstract sense, a reasonable expectation of privacy:[81] for example, racial and ethnic origins.[82] A recent charge[83] or conviction,[84] although classified as sensitive personal information in the DPA, is public domain information.[85] It looks as if only some of the personal data classified as sensitive in the DPA ('sexual life', for instance and 'physical or mental health or condition')[86] has been selected for this classification because its disclosure threatens the individual's dignity and exposes his private life. The unifying characteristic of all the categories in the list is that historically the information has been widely used as the basis for unfair discrimination and the individual concerned therefore must be kept informed of why and when such information will be circulated from his records.

6.19 **Determining whether information is confidential (private)** Whether or not information that falls into any of these categories is deserving of protection by equity in a specific case will depend upon all the facts and circumstances including:

---

[75] *Att-Gen v Guardian Newspapers Ltd (No 2)* [1988] 3 All ER 545, 659; *Hellewell v Chief Constable of Derbyshire* [1995] 1 WLR 804, 807; *A v B* [2000] EMLR 1007; *Ashdown v Telegraph Group* [2001] 4 All ER 666.

[76] *Thompson v Stanhope* (1774) 27 ER 476; *Philip v Pennell* [1907] 2 Ch 577; *John Reid Enterprises Ltd v Pell* [1999] EMLR 675 (letter from accountant). cp *Re Aitken* (HC, 10 September 1999). Art 8 expressly protects correspondence without regard to subject matter.

[77] *Beloff v Pressdram Ltd* [1973] 1 All ER 241. cp *Lion Laboratories Ltd v Evans* [1984] 2 All ER 417.

[78] *Francome v MGN Ltd* [1984] 1 WLR 892. cp *Kennedy v Ireland* [1987] IR 587; *Halford v UK* (1997) 24 EHRR 523; *Ludi v Switzerland* (1992) 15 EHRR 173; *Armstrong v UK* Application 48521/99, The Times, 6 August 2002. Contrast *Malone v Commissioner of Police of the Metropolis* [1979] 2 All ER 620.

[79] per Gleeson CJ, *ABC v Lenah Game Meats Pty Ltd* [2001] HCA 63, para 42.

[80] M Tugendhat and I Christie (eds), *The Law of Privacy and the Media* (Oxford: 2002) para 6.69.

[81] Some, such as the data subject's 'sexual life' and 'physical or mental health or condition', obviously deserves a high privacy rating.

[82] DPA, s 2(a).

[83] DPA, s 2(g).

[84] DPA, s 2(h).

[85] See para 5.18 above.

[86] DPA, s 2(e)–(f).

A. Interception and Disloyalty

- whether the claimant can be identified from the information;[87]
- extent of previous publicity;[88]
- circumstances in which the information was created including public visibility[89] or access by members of the public at that time;[90]
- method of obtaining used by the defendant[91] (illegality may be a compelling factor);[92]

---

[87] *R v Department of Health, ex p Source Informatics Ltd* [2000] 1 All ER 786, 797. But see *L v G* [2002] DCR 234, 2002 NZDCR LEXIS 2, where identification was found unnecessary.

[88] See para 5.09 above. The courts tolerate more in the way of prior publicity where personal information is concerned than trade and government secrets because of the continuing capacity for personal information to injure even when widely disseminated. It is noteworthy that there is no public domain defence to defamation (false personal information) see para 7.38 below. Each republication is a fresh tort.

[89] *Woodward v Hitchins* [1977] 1 WLR 760; *MGN Ltd v Attard* (Fam Div, 19 October 2001); *R (on the application of Ford) v PCC* [2001] EWHC Admin 683, [2002] EMLR 5; *Theakston v MGN* [2002] EWHC 137, [2002] EMLR 22, para 5 (anyone passing by could have seen him going in and coming out—it was likely that other customers and staff could see who came and went); *Campbell v MGN* [2002] EWCA Civ 1373, para 33 (photograph of Campbell in the street did not convey confidential information). US and Canadian courts generally reject privacy claims in respect of information acquired in a public place: E Paton-Simpson, 'Privacy and the Reasonable Paranoid: The Protection of Privacy in Public Places' (2000) 50 U of Toronto LJ 305. The PCC similarly rejects complaints about photographs taken at a location that is visible to the public, eg Sean Connery and the Sunday Mail, 25 April 1999; *R (on the application of Ford) v PCC* [2001] EWHC Admin 683, [2002] EMLR 95; Michaelangelo and Rina Attard (parents of the conjoined twins) and Manchester Evening News, 16 June 2001. For clients the visibility factor is unlikely to be a problem except when receiving assistance from a professional in a public place. Has a patient a reasonable expectation of privacy when a doctor is carrying out emergency surgical procedures at the scene of a road accident? The BSC found an infringement of privacy in the filming and transmission of close-ups of a road accident victim trapped semi-conscious in the driver's seat of his car in a public place and later being treated by paramedics in an ambulance when the victim had expressed objection to the filming; 'the infringement was unwarranted as there was no overriding public interest': Complaint of Mr Graeme Oswald, 9 January 2002. cp *Bathurst City Council v Saban* [1985] 2 NSWLR 704, 708; *Peck v UK* Application 00044647/98, 28 January 2003, paras 56–62. In *Leverton v Curtis Pub Co* 192 F 2d. 974 (1951) a car nearly ran over a girl on a bicycle. A newspaper photographer who happened to be present took a dramatic photograph. The claimant admitted that the defendant was entitled to publish the photograph the next day in a newspaper but objected to it being used to illustrate an article about careless pedestrians 20 months later. The court held that the privilege to publish the photograph was not lost by the passage of time, but that the bounds of privilege had been exceeded by using it to support an article that had nothing whatsoever to do with the accident and was in fact misleading as the child's accident had been caused by the carelessness of the driver, not of the child.

[90] In *Camenzind v Switzerland* Application 21353/93, partial decision 27 February 1995, the Commission refused to entertain a complaint from a German lawyer that his Art 8 rights were infringed by the interception of a radio-telephone call made with an unauthorized apparatus using a frequency reserved for civil and military aircraft that others could access.

[91] *Hellewell v Chief Constable of Derbyshire* [1995] 1 WLR 804, 807 (telephoto lens). Contrast *R (on the application of Ford) v PCC* [2001] EWHC Admin 683; [2002] EMLR 5 (telephoto lens but location was accessible to the public). All the privacy codes prohibit use of clandestine devices for obtaining information unless disclosure is in the public interest and the information cannot be obtained by other means. On the undesirability of clandestine filming see *R v BSC, ex p BBC* [2000] 3 All ER 989, paras 37, 43; *R v Loveridge* [2001] 2 Cr App R 29, para 30.

[92] *A v B plc & C ('Flitcroft')* [2002] EWCA Civ 337; [2002] 3 WLR 542, para 11, guideline x.

- amount of disclosed detail;[93]
- medium of disclosure (because photographs and films convey information in a uniquely vivid way[94] their disclosure may be enjoined where a written account would not);[95]
- age of the information (if unfavourable information has been forgotten, antiquity may have restored the client's expectations of privacy);
- possible consequences of disclosure (physical injury,[96] unfair discrimination,[97] significant emotional distress);[98]
- measures by the claimant to avoid publicity or disclosure such as 'no entry' or 'no photograph' signs, restricted access, secure storage;[99]
- whether the client impressed on the professional the confidentiality of the information ('if something is expressly said to be confidential, then it is much more likely to be so held by the courts');[100]
- scale of the disclosure (e.g. to a few friends and acquaintants or to a tabloid newspaper);[101]
- whether the client is a 'public figure' (a point which will be explored further);
- any special vulnerability (for example, youth or serious illness).[102]

It seems improbable that, if there is no medical emergency and A talks loudly to his doctor in the street about his health, equity will lend its assistance to prevent B, who happened to be passing by at the time, from talking about A's health to others. In these circumstances A had no reasonable expectation of privacy, however intrinsically private the information. If, on the other hand, the conversation

---

[93] *Barrymore v NGN Ltd* [1997] FSR 600, 603; *Theakston v MGN Ltd* [2002] EWHC 137; [2002] EMLR 22, para 75; *Campbell v MGN Ltd* [2002] EWCA 499; [2002] EMLR 30.

[94] 'It has been said that a picture is worth a thousand words.... The same result is not obtainable through the medium of words alone, nor by recollected drawings with their inevitable inaccuracy'. per Keene LJ, *Douglas v Hello! Ltd* [2001] 2 All ER 289, para 165. cp *R (on the application of ProLife Alliance) v BBC* [2002] EWCA Civ 297; [2002] 2 All ER 756, paras 57, 61–62.

[95] *Theakston v MGN Ltd* [2002] EWHC 137; [2002] EMLR 22, paras 78–80. Contrast *Service Corp International plc v Channel Four* [1999] EMLR 83, 90.

[96] *Venables v NGN Ltd* [2001] 1 All ER 908.

[97] *X v Y* [1988] 2 All ER 648; *H (A Healthcare Worker) v Associated Newspapers Ltd* [2002] EWCA Civ 195, 65 BMLR 132 (AIDs and HIV infected persons).

[98] In *Campbell v MGN Ltd* [2002] EWHC 499; [2002] EMLR 30, para 40.1 Morland J asked whether disclosure would 'be highly offensive to a reasonable person of ordinary sensibilities'.

[99] *Faccenda Chicken v Fowler* [1986] 1 All ER 617, 627; *Creation Records Ltd v NGN Ltd* [1997] EMLR 444; *Shelley Films Ltd v Rex Features Ltd* [1994] EMLR 134; *R v Law* [2002] SCC 10 (theft of safe containing documents; police recovered the safe but before returning it to the owners photocopied the documents). The PCC also considers the measures taken to protect privacy: JK Rowling and *OK! Magazine*, 17 August 2001.

[100] per Jacob J, *Barrymore v NGN Ltd* [1997] FSR 600, 603. cp *Creation Records Ltd v NGN Ltd* [1997] EMLR 444.

[101] In *A v B plc and C ('Flitcroft')* [2001] 1 WLR 2341, 2354 the judge at first instance drew a distinction between disclosures by the prostitutes to acquaintances and by a tabloid to a mass readership. cp *Stephens v Avery* [1988] 2 WLR 1280; *Peck v UK* Application 44647/98 28 January 2003, para 62.

[102] See para 9.10 below.

A. Interception and Disloyalty

took place in the doctor's surgery and B trespassed on the doctor's property to listen through a slightly open window,[103] there is every likelihood that equity will aid A. The outcome in cases that are further from either of these extremes will depend on their particular facts.

Public policy has also to be considered. Policy dictates that information disclosed in open court loses its confidentiality even if it is never reported and no one but the lawyers and the parties hear it.[103a] Conversely, there are powerful policy reasons for continuing to treat information disclosed to public authorities as confidential. '[A] civilized society must . . . allow its citizens space. It must protect the information they have provided to the state from the eyes of others, except when there are clear grounds for overriding that right to privacy.'[104] Communications that are a step in the commission of a crime or fraud are not privileged for the purposes of the law of evidence[105] and are unlikely to be worthy of protection in an action for breach of confidence. The public policy argument for denying protection may be weaker when the information concerns completed criminal acts. In *Francome v MGN Ltd*[106] an interim injunction was obtained to restrain publication of conversations between the claimant, a jockey, and his wife that revealed possible criminal conduct by the jockey. Rehabilitation of offenders may make ancient crimes for which they have paid the penalty worthy of protection.[107] **6.20**

In any case involving journalistic literary or artistic material the courts are obliged by the HRA to consult the media privacy codes.[108] Under the code that applies to the press an intention to rectify misleading information previously fed to the public is relevant.[109] HRA s 12(4) requires the court, when deciding whether to grant relief, to take into account the extent to which material has, or is about to, become public knowledge. An intention to publish the information does not, however, preclude relief.[110] **6.21**

---

[103] cp *Police v Georghiades* (1983) 2 Cyprus LR 33 (bugging of conversation between doctor and patient without trespass).
[103a] See paras 17.26–17.27 below.
[104] E France, 'Privacy, data protection and freedom of information' (2000) 2 Interactive Marketing 11, 12. The Council of Europe has recommended that where an individual has been forced to provide a public body with personal information, 'processing . . . by third parties should either be subject to obtaining the express and informed consent of [the individual] or be in accordance with statutory requirements'. Council of Europe, Committee of Ministers, *Personal Data held by Public Bodies* Recommendation R (91) 10 (9 September 1991) para 6.1. See also *R v Chief Constable of North Wales Police, ex p AB* [1997] 4 All ER 691, 698.
[105] See para 16.35 below.
[106] [1984] 1 WLR 892.
[107] cp Rehabilitation of Offenders Act 1974. cp *Melvin v Reid* 112 Cal App 285, 292 (1931).
[108] See para 8.13 below.
[109] See paras 9.10 and 11.10 below.
[110] In *Khashoggi v Smith* (1980) 124 SJ 14 Roskill LJ said: 'I do not think that the fact that the plaintiff was in negotiation with the second defendants for the sale of her memoirs . . . deprives her of any right to confidentiality to which she would otherwise be entitled.' And Sir David Cairns said: '[i]t seems to me that a person may well be entitled . . . to say: "I am willing for the details of my

6.22 **Public figures** According to Lord Woolf in *A v B plc and C ('Flitcroft')*[111] a 'public figure' has a lessened expectation of privacy compared to someone whose life has not come to the public's attention. In that case a professional footballer was not entitled to suppress information about his extra-marital affairs. The meaning of 'public figure' is not explored in the judgment. It is a concept well established in other legal systems. In the Council of Europe's Resolution *Right to Privacy*[112] public figures are 'persons holding public office and/or using public resources and, more broadly speaking, all those who play a role in public life, whether in politics, the economy, the arts, the social sphere, sport or in any other domain'. This description is slightly narrower than the US definition of the public figure but wider than that used in Canada. The Canadian public figure is a person whose 'professional success depends on public opinion'.[113] The 'public figure' of US law is a 'person who, by his accomplishments, fame, or mode of living, or by adopting a profession[114] or calling which gives the public a legitimate interest in his doings, his affairs, and his character, has become a "public personage" '.[115] The reasons that US courts tend to give for the public figure's loss of privacy are: (1) that those who seek out and benefit from publicity cannot later complain about bad publicity (an argument adopted in *Theakston v MGN Ltd*);[116] (2) their fame means that their personality and affairs have ceased to be their own private business; and (3) the public has a right to be kept informed by the media about the doings of public figures.[117]

6.23 These reasons do not, however, explain the extensive loss of privacy of a further category of public figure recognized in US law. These are people involuntarily thrust into the limelight as a result of their involvement in, commission of, or association with, an accident, a health epidemic or a crime[118] or because they have a relationship (husband, parent, etc.) with a voluntary public figure.[119] English law has been

---

private life to be made known to the public by me in the form which I choose and for my financial-benefit; but not for them to be published through information disclosed by my confidential servant in a form chosen by her and others and to the profit of her and others".' cp *Douglas v Hello! Ltd* [2001] 2 All ER 289.

[111] [2002] EWCA Civ 337; [2002] 3 WLR 542, para 11, guideline xii.
[112] 1165 (1998) para 7.
[113] *Les Editions Vice Versa Inc v Aubry* [1998] 1 SCR 591, paras 57–58.
[114] It is questionable whether the ECtHR will take such a wide view of a 'public figure'. In *Rotaru v Romania* Application 2834/95, 8 BHRC 449, para 43 the ECtHR reiterated that 'there is no reason of principle to justify excluding activities of a professional or business nature from the notion of "private life" (see the *Niemietz v Germany* . . . and the *Halford v United Kingdom* . . .)'.
[115] W Prosser, 'Privacy' (1960) 48 California L Rev 383, 410. See further G Williams, ' "On the QT and very Hush Hush": A Proposal to extend California's Constitutional right to Privacy to Protect Public Figures from Publication of Confidential Personal Information' (1999) 19 Loyola of Los Angeles Entertainment L Rev 337, 347.
[116] [2002] EWHC 137; [2002] EMLR 22, paras 48, 68.
[117] *Cabaniss v Hipsley* 151 SE 2d 496 (1966).
[118] *Florida Star v BJF* 491 US 524 (1989).
[119] *Carlisle v Fawcett Pub Inc* 20 Cal Rptr 405 (1962); Williams, op cit n 107 above, 348.

A. Interception and Disloyalty

more inclined to protect the privacy of those whose notoriety is not of their own doing[120] and because of Article 8 this is likely to continue to be the case.[121]

What public figures can reasonably expect to remain confidential (private)   **6.24**
Amongst those who are public figures, Lord Woolf says that those who speak to the media about their private lives have the lowest expectation of privacy.[122] But even such persons do not relinquish all claim to privacy forever.[123] The media is not entitled to expose 'private facts which a fair-minded person would consider it offensive to disclose'.[124] A public figure can, for example, expect to keep out of the news that she is receiving treatment for drug addiction and the details of that treatment *provided she has not previously stated falsely to the media that she has no drug problem.*[125] Where this proviso applies, the media may rebut the lies along with sufficient background detail to give the media report credibility.[126] Medical information fits the classic mould of information protected by an obligation of confidentiality.[127] If the facts of *Kaye v Robertson*[128] were repeated today, an action for breach of confidence would probably succeed.[129] A public figure or celebrity, and a fortiori a person who is not a public figure, has in this writer's opinion a reasonable expectation that personal information (medical or non-medical) that has been disclosed to a professional for the purpose of obtaining a personal professional service will remain private (confidential) if not already in the public

---

[120] eg *Williams v Settle* [1960] 1 WLR 1072 (sale of wedding photograph to newspaper after the bride's father was murdered); *Stephens v Avery* [1988] 2 WLR 1280 ('friend' told a newspaper about the claimant's lesbian past after her husband's murder). See also *X NHS Trust v A* (HC, 31 July 2002) as to which see para 17.41 below. The PCC too protects families of public figures, eg Lilley and Daily Mirror Report 29. See PCC, *Submission to the Culture, Media and Sport Select Committee* (February 2003) §C(3) paras 17–18.

[121] The PCC's code forbids identification of friends or relatives of persons accused or convicted of crime. In Peter Lilley and the Daily Mirror, 19 January 1995, there was a finding against a newspaper that had publicized the fact that the nephew of a cabinet minister was dying of AIDS.

[122] *Theakston v MGN Ltd* [2002] EWHC 137; [2002] EMLR 22, para 68.

[123] [2002] EWCA Civ 337; [2002] 3 WLR 542, para 11, guideline xii. See on this point also *Lingens v Austria* (1986) 8 EHRR 407; *Krone Verlag GMBH v Austria* Application 34315/96 (26 February 2002). Cp *Diaz v Oakland Tribune* 188 Cal Rptr 762, 773 (1983). Has the individual who courts publicity a reduced expectation of privacy for all time? Can a public figure sink back into obscurity and recover the privacy expectations of the ordinary man or woman? If information can cease to be in the public domain (see para 5.16 above) then this too must be a possibility.

[124] per Lord Phillips, *Campbell v MGN* [2002] EWCA Civ 1373, para 40, and cp para 56.

[125] ibid, paras 36, 38, 43.

[126] ibid, paras 62, 64.

[127] S Thomas, 'Does Campbell make model law?' (2002) 152 NLJ 716, 717. Cp *Police v Georghiades* (1983) 2 Cyprus LR 33, 55. In *Campbell v MGN Ltd* [2002] EWCA Civ 1373, para 48 the Court of Appeal refused to equate therapy from Narcotics Anonymous with clinical treatment. Implicit in this rejection is the acceptance that clinical medical information is protected information.

[128] [1991] FSR 62, see para 4.57 above. cp *Barber v Time, Inc* 159 SW 2d 291, 296 (1942) (the facts of which are uncannily similar to *Kaye v Robertson*): 'whatever may be the right of the press, tabloids or news reel companies to take and use pictures of persons in public places, certainly any right of privacy ought to protect a person from publication of a picture taken without consent while ill or in bed for treatment and recuperation', per Hyde C.

[129] *Douglas v Hello! Ltd* [2001] 2 All ER 289, paras, 73, 167.

Chapter 6: Dealing with Unintentional Disclosure

domain and not trivial.[130] Triviality is not an absolute standard but depends on context.[131]

6.25 The California Constitution guarantees a right to privacy that is enforceable against governmental and non-governmental actors.[132] A reasonable expectation of privacy test based on widely accepted community norms is used to determine whether this right has been violated.[133] Decisions of the Court of Appeal of California about constitutionally founded claims of violations of professional confidentiality are of interest. The Californian court has held that:

- a client has a reasonable expectation of privacy in his medical records[134] and in disclosures made to a psychotherapist;[135]
- an examinee in discovery proceedings who discloses to a nurse that he tested positive for the HIV virus after the medical examination was over in order to alert her to the need to take precautions in handling electrodes contaminated with his blood has a reasonable expectation that his HIV status will not be unnecessarily disclosed;[136]
- a private university which discloses a student's grades to a government scholarship and student loans agency without the student's consent abridges the student's reasonable expectation of privacy;[137]
- a bank interferes with its customer's reasonable expectation of privacy if it reveals the customer's banking affairs except under compulsion of legal process.[138]

None of these cases involved interception of personal information, but if those who legitimately hold the information cannot disclose it for an unauthorized purpose without consent, a third party who intercepts the information should not be entitled to do so either without legal authority.

---

[130] cp *John v Joulebine* (QB, 26 January 2001).
[131] *Att-Gen v Guardian (No 2)* [1998] 3 All ER 545, 624; *Campbell v MGN* [2002] EWCA Civ 1373, para 57.
[132] California Constitution, s 1, Art 1 provides: '[a]ll people are by nature free and independent and have inalienable rights. Among these are enjoying and defending life and liberty, acquiring, possessing, and protecting property, and pursuing and obtaining safety, happiness, *and privacy*' (italics added). On the application to non-governmental actors see *Hill v National Collegiate Athletic Association* 865 P 2d 633. Nine other US states have constitutional guarantees of privacy but offer protection only against government encroachment.
[133] *Hill v National Collegiate Athletic Association* 865 P 2d 633, 655 (1994).
[134] *Board of Medical Quality Assurance v Gherardini* 93 Cal App 3d 669, 679 (1979).
[135] *Cutter v Brownbridge* 228 Cal. Rptr 545 (1986).
[136] *Urbaniak v Newton* 266 Cal App 3d 1138 (1991). In this case, the examinee had said that he did not want the information disclosed in the report.
[137] *Porten v University of San Francisco* 64 Cal App 3d 825, 833 (1976). To escape liability, the court said, the University must demonstrate a compelling public interest in the disclosure.
[138] *Valley Bank of Nevada v Superior Court* 15 Cal 3d 652 (1975). And even if disclosure is to a court, the bank must take reasonable steps to give the customer advance notice of the disclosure so that the customer can enter an objection.

A. Interception and Disloyalty

Detriment caused by unauthorized disclosure

The Megarry requirement of detriment has been relaxed to the point that in personal information cases it barely exists. Summing up the previous pronouncements of the court, Latham J said in *R v Department of Health, ex p Source Informatics* that 'there must be some effect on the confider, from which the court considers that he is entitled to protection'.[139] In *Campbell v MGN Ltd*[140] Morland J looked for detriment that went beyond the 'significant distress' that Campbell felt when the Mirror published details of her attendance at meetings of Narcotics Anonymous and found it in the deterrent effect on her continuing with the drug therapy.[141] In the Court of Appeal Lord Phillips said that '[g]ratuitous disclosure of confidential information may be objectionable even where it shows the complainant in a good light'.[142] Mental distress is all that is required for Article 8 of the European Convention on Human Rights (ECHR) to be infringed,[143] and it can only be a matter of time before the courts accept that in an action for breach of confidence involving disclosure or misuse of personal information that is the subject of an obligation of professional confidentiality, all the client has to show is some legitimate interest in preserving the privacy of the information.

6.26

Interception without disclosure

Mostly when A sets about obtaining confidential personal information about B by underhand means, it is with the object of using or disclosing the information. But there are exceptions. A computer enthusiast may be out to circumvent the target computer's security without any interest in reading or downloading what he finds. A stalker might intercept information about the person he is stalking for himself or as a means of harassing his victim[144] but have no wish to disclose the information to a third party. The courts have yet to tackle the question of whether an interceptor 'misuses'[145] information for the purposes of an action for breach of confidence simply by the act of reading or obtaining it.[146] In *R v Brown*[147] a majority of the House of Lords decided that a police officer who had run an unauthorized check

6.27

---

[139] [1999] 4 All ER 185, 194. At 197 the judge suggested that 'the breach of confidence in itself might carry with it sufficient detriment to justify the grant of a remedy'. See also paras 5.40–5.41 above.

[140] [2002] EWCA 499; [2002] EMLR 30.

[141] ibid, para 40.

[142] *Campbell v MGN Ltd* [2002] EWCA Civ 1373, para 52.

[143] See para 8.55 below. See also G Phillipson and H Fenwick, 'Breach of Confidence as a Privacy Remedy in the Human Rights Act Era' (2000) 63 MLR 660, 691. cp Law Commission Report 266, *Damages under the Human Rights Act 1998* (Cm 4853, 2000) para 3.26.

[144] cp *Nader v General Motors Corp* 255 NE 2d 765 (1970).

[145] Misuse as well as disclosure will ground an action for breach of confidence: see para 5.29 above.

[146] Either of these activities would involve 'processing' within the meaning of s 1 of the current DPA.

[147] [1996] 1 All ER 545.

of vehicle registration numbers for a friend on the Police National Computer did not 'use' the data within the meaning of s 5 of the Data Protection Act 1984. This provision made it an offence for a registered data user knowingly or recklessly to hold or use personal data for any other than a registered purpose. In his dissenting judgment, Lord Griffiths argued that 'use' should be broadly construed.

> To read the personal data about an individual displayed on a computer screen or in a print-out is an invasion of that person's privacy, if there is no legitimate purpose for doing so ... It is not straining the meaning of language to say that a person is using the information stored in a computer if he informs himself of its contents. Whether or not he then goes on to apply the information for a particular purpose, and to use it in that sense, will depend on the value of the information to him: but whether or not he applies the information does not alter the fact that he has wrongly invaded the privacy of the individual, and now has the information available to apply at any time in the future. Once information has entered the public domain it is impractical to attempt to place any restraints on its use or further dissemination.[148]

6.28 A court operating under the HRA and Article 8(1) of the ECHR may find Lord Griffith's analysis of what protection of privacy requires attractive. Unauthorized accessing of a computer is a criminal offence.[149] The absence of a corresponding wrong in civil law exposes the courts to the charge of not adequately protecting the client's Article 8 right to respect for private life. If the courts no longer insist on a relationship of trust, it hardly seems controversial to award compensation for intentional unauthorized access to confidential information when no disclosure followed or was intended to follow.[150]

Tort

Intentional infliction of distress, conspiracy, injurious falsehood and defamation

6.29 A number of the torts that might succeed against a professional who intentionally breaches a confidence[151] might succeed against an interceptor. The tort of intentional infliction of distress does not require a pre-existing relationship. Whether the tort is a serious option depends, amongst other things, upon whether the tort encompasses the disclosure of true information to someone other than the claimant, something that has not been decided in England.[152] When more than one person is involved in the interception of information, the tort of conspiracy might apply.[153] If untrue information has been intercepted and disclosed to others, the client may be able to sue for injurious falsehood, but this will require

---

[148] [1996] 1 All ER 545, 554–555.
[149] See para 6.60 below.
[150] cp RIPA, s 2(2). But see *Wainwright v Home Office* [2001] EWCA Civ 2081; [2002] 3 WLR 405, para 87.
[151] See ch 4.
[152] See para 4.32 above.
[153] See para 4.33 above.

A. Interception and Disloyalty

proof of malice.[154] If the information is both untrue and discreditable, an action for defamation may lie.[155]

Breach of statutory duty

To hold[156] intercepted personal data on a computer or in a relevant manual filing system[157] is to breach the fair processing code of the DPA.[158] If the client suffers damage as a result of this or any other contravention of the DPA by the interceptor,[159] the client can bring an action for compensation under DPA, s 13(1).[160] Recovery for distress is allowed provided 'damage' was also suffered.[161]

6.30

Copyright

An interceptor who surreptitiously copies a substantial portion of a confidential document written by the client breaches the client's copyright.[162]

6.31

Civil Actions: Client v Professional

Interception by someone who is not an employee

Negligence

Professionals, it is submitted, have a private law duty to protect the confidences of their clients.[163] They must take reasonable precautions to protect client information from loss, theft and unauthorized access, copying, disclosure and use. If this duty is neglected and tangible[164] harm results, the client should have an action in negligence against the professional.[165] The ethical duty to keep client information secure is acknowledged in General Medical Council guidelines:

6.32

---

[154] See para 4.41 above.
[155] See para 4.34 above.
[156] See paras 18.08 and 18.11 below.
[157] See para 18.06 below.
[158] See para 18.10 below. Under s 17(1) it is a further contravention to hold the data without being registered.
[159] If the interceptor uses or discloses data held in the relevant formats there will be further breaches of the DPA.
[160] See para 4.49 above. If the data is used or disclosed there are further contraventions. Under s 17(1) it is unlawful to hold data without being registered.
[161] DPA, s 13(2).
[162] See para 5.84 above.
[163] The seventh data protection principle (see para 6.35 below) makes it difficult to deny the existence of such a duty. Cp para 6.90 below. Note also the express statutory duty to secure special educational needs statements and supporting documentation from unauthorized access: Education (Special Educational Needs) (England) (Consolidation) Regulations 2001, SI 2001/3455, reg 24(4). This might support a private law action for breach of statutory duty: see para 4.50 above.
[164] Damages are not at present recoverable for mental distress not accompanied by physical injury to person or property: see para 8.49 below.
[165] Negligence by a fiduciary (eg a solicitor) is actionable as negligence, not as breach of fiduciary duty: *Henderson v Merrett Syndicates Ltd* [1994] 3 All ER 506, 543; *Bristol & West Building Society v Mothew* [1996] 4 All ER 698, 712.

When you are responsible for personal information about patients you must make sure that it is effectively protected against improper disclosure at all times.[166]

A professional may be liable for negligence even if the act complained of was by an employee[167] either on the theory that the employee was acting in the course of his employment (vicarious liability)[168] or because the professional should have had rules and procedures to guard against unauthorized access to, or insecure disposal of, confidential material (direct liability).[169]

6.33 Liability in negligence for the interception of information depends upon the extent to which the defendant can reasonably be expected to have guarded against the risk of interception. Following Hughes' analysis,[170] the pertinent issues are:

(1) magnitude of risk of third party interception;
(2) the gravity of the consequences of interception;
(3) the protective measures that could have been taken and their cost and inconvenience relative to the risk of interception;
(4) common practice in the profession, although this is not decisive;
(5) the amount of risk of third party interception that the client assumed.

6.34 The Bar Council has warned that the courts might impose liability 'for negligence for losses arising out of the sending of e-mails of confidential . . . litigation sensitive or privileged communications in an unencrypted or unprotected form which are misdirected or published to the disadvantage of the owner or intended recipient'.[171] This is particularly so if systems for encryption are not expensive.[172]

Breach of statutory duty

6.35 Where lax technical or organizational security practices make interception possible, the seventh data protection principle may have been breached. This principle requires a data controller to take:

[a]ppropriate technical and organisation measures . . . against unauthorised or unlawful processing of personal data and against accidental loss or destruction of, or damage to, personal data.[173]

---

[166] GMC, *Confidentiality: Protecting and Providing Information* (London: 2000) s 1, para 2.
[167] Examples: *Estate of Behringer v Medical Center at Princeton* 592 A 2d 1251 (1991); *Peters-Brown v Regina General Hospital* 58 ACWS (3d) 1044 (1995).
[168] See para 21.31 below.
[169] cp *Ott v Fleishman* [1993] 5 WWR 721, para 9; DPA, Sch 1, Pt II, para 10.
[170] G Hughes, *Data Protection in Australia* (Melbourne: 1991) 237.
[171] *Guidance on E-Mail Security, Web-Sites and Use of the Internet,* http://www.barcouncil.org.uk.
[172] A Mulcahy, 'Consumer Protection and Advertising' in L Mulcahy (ed), *Human Rights and Civil Practice* (London: 2001) para 19.64 argues that sending personal information that is not encrypted by e-mail without the client's consent infringes the client's Art 8 rights.
[173] DPA, Sch 1.

A. Interception and Disloyalty

Disclosure may be evidence of a breach of the obligation but does not in itself constitute a breach.[174]

An individual who suffers damage because of a contravention of the seventh data protection principle is entitled to be compensated by the data controller for any 'damage'.[175] If damage *and* distress are suffered, compensation is recoverable for the distress.[176] It is a defence that the data controller 'had taken such care as in all the circumstances was reasonably required to comply with the requirement concerned'.[177] Relevant factors include the state of technology, the cost of implementing safeguards, the risks presented, the nature of the data and the reliability of the employees with access to personal data.[178] Should the professional contract out any part of the processing of client data to another organization (known in the DPA as a 'data processor'),[179] there will be a breach of the seventh data protection principle unless there is a written contract containing suitable indemnification clauses and the processor is given formal written instructions.[180] **6.36**

Interception by a corrupt employee

An employer's vicarious liability in tort, contract or equity for the acts of an employee is discussed in chapter 21. The employer might be personally liable in negligence if the interception was facilitated by lack of adequate safeguards or a failure to vet employees with access to the personal data.[181] **6.37**

Civil Actions: Professional v Employee

Breach of contract[182]

Disclosure while employed by the professional[183]

Keeping client information confidential is an implied,[184] and often also an express, term of an employee's contract of employment.[185] Subject to any possible public **6.38**

---

[174] *Lord Ashcroft v Att-Gen* [2002] EWHC 1122, QB, para 35.
[175] DPA, s 13(1). The client could not recover damages for negligence and under s 13 since this would involve double compensation.
[176] DPA, s 13(2)
[177] s 13(3).
[178] Sch 1, Pt II, para 9.
[179] DPA, s 1, 'data process' means 'any person (other than an employee of the data controller) who processes the data on behalf of the data controller'.
[180] DPA, Sch 1, Pt II, paras 11–12.
[181] See also Sch 1, Pt II, para 10.
[182] A Stewart, 'Confidentiality and the Employment Relationship' (1988) 1 Australian J of Labour L 1; R Dean, The Law of Trade Secrets and Personal Secrets (2nd edn, Sydney: 2002) [4.35] et seq.
[183] See also para 21.17 below.
[184] cp *Initial Services Ltd v Putterill* [1967] 3 All ER 145, 148; *Khashoggi v Smith* (1980) 124 SJ 14.
[185] eg *Blair v Associated Newspapers Ltd* (QBD, 13 November 2000, 2000 WL 3116509).

interest defence,[186] the employee who intentionally discloses confidential information for an unauthorized purpose breaches the terms of the employment contract. For this the employee can be sued in contract or, subject to the observance of disciplinary procedures, be summarily dismissed for misconduct.[187] A justifiable fear that an employee is planning to reveal confidential personal information about a client may allow summary dismissal.[188] The professional may be able to sue the employee for disclosing confidential client records where the client cannot because the client has put the information into the public domain.[189]

Disclosure after termination of employment[190]

6.39 An employee whose employment has ended remains subject to an implied (and often also an express) contractual duty to preserve the confidentiality of the employer's trade secrets and their equivalents.[191] This is a less stringent duty than the duty of fidelity imposed on the employee during the currency of the employment. In order to allow the ex-employee to pursue his livelihood without restriction, the ex-employee is entitled to exploit general knowledge and skills and information inseparable from general knowledge and skills acquired during the employment. But this would not include confidential personal information about clients. Such information satisfies the indicia of a trade secret: obvious sensitivity and confidentiality, restricted access, isolation from other information, employer emphasis on security and confidentiality.[192] Disclosure in the public interest is a potential defence.[193]

Disclosure to the media

6.40 Even if confidential client information did fall into the category of exploitable information, the ex-employee would not be entitled to sell the information to the media. The court in *Faccenda* specifically left:

> open . . . for further examination . . . whether additional protection should be afforded to an employer where the former employee is not seeking to earn his living by making use of the body of skill, knowledge and experience which he has acquired in the course of his career, but is merely selling to a third party information which he acquired in confidence in the course of his former employment.[194]

---

[186] See ch 11 and paras 21.23 et seq.
[187] cp *Golden Cross Hire Co Ltd v Lovell* [1979] IRLR 267. See further, B Napier, 'Confidentiality and Labour Law' in L Clarke (ed), *Confidentiality and the Law* (London: 1990) 110–111, 120–121.
[188] *Skyrail Oceanic Ltd v Coleman* [1980] IRLR 226.
[189] *Ashworth Hospital Authority v MGN Ltd* [2002] UKHL 29; [2002] 1 WLR 2033, para 32.
[190] See also paras 21.19–21.21 below.
[191] *Faccenda Chicken Ltd v Fowler* [1986] 1 All ER 617, 626.
[192] ibid, 626–627.
[193] See ch 11.
[194] per Neill LJ [1986] 1 All ER 617, 627.

A. Interception and Disloyalty

Breach of confidence

Employees and former employees owe an employer an equitable obligation of confidentiality that is co-extensive with the contractual obligation of confidentiality.[195]

6.41

Tort

Conversion and conspiracy

If the disclosure involved the employee asserting rights over any property of the professional, for example a floppy disk, a letter or a computer print-out, in a way that was inconsistent with the professional's rights, the employee may be liable for conversion.[196] It is uncertain whether memorizing a document or accessing and reading data on a computer amounts to conversion.[197] A court would have to be persuaded that the document or the computer was converted by the extraction of the information. Damages may extend beyond the intrinsic value of the converted item to a consequential loss.[198]

6.42

Where the intentional act of an employee acting in collusion with a stranger has caused the professional financial loss, the professional has a possible cause of action in tort for conspiracy or interference with business interests.[199]

6.43

Trespass

Physical contact with the professional's documents or equipment by an employee not authorized to handle them may constitute the tort of trespass to goods.[200] An employee who enters the professional's premises outside working hours or enters a forbidden part of the premises in order to gain access to confidential client information commits trespass to land. Cripps speculates that lawful presence on premises can be converted into unlawful presence at the point at which a decision is taken to engage in unlawful conduct.[201] If this is right, an employee who is lawfully on the professional's premises for the purposes of employment becomes a trespasser when he forms the intention of converting property or disclosing confidential information in breach of confidence.

6.44

---

[195] *Att-Gen (UK) v Heinemann Publishers* (1987) 10 NSWLR 86, 153; *Independent Management Resources Pty Ltd v Brown* [1987] VR 605, 611–612.
[196] For details of the tort see A Grubb (ed), *The Law of Tort* (London: 2001) 434 et seq. and for its application to personal data, G Hughes, *Data Protection in Australia* (Sydney: 1991) 243–244.
[197] R Dean, *The Law of Trade Secrets* (Sydney: 1990) 347–348.
[198] Torts (Interference with Goods) Act 1977, s 3.
[199] See para 4.43 above.
[200] A Grubb (ed), *The Law of Tort* (London: 2001) 489.
[201] Y Cripps, *The Legal Implications of Disclosure in the Public Interest* (2nd edn, London: 1994) 212.

Chapter 6: Dealing with Unintentional Disclosure

Copyright

6.45 An employee who, without permission, photocopies, photographs or copies his employer's documents verbatim by hand infringes the professional's copyright in them. No breach of copyright, however, occurs if the employee reads and memorizes information belonging to the employer and then discloses it in his own words to a stranger; copyright protects format not content.[202]

Identifying the Employee

6.46 The fact of disclosure may be known but the identity of the disloyal employee responsible may not. Equity may compel an individual or organization with information that would enable the professional to identify the employee to disclose it to the employer.[203] If that person happens to be a journalist or a media organization, Article 10 of the ECHR and s10 of the Contempt of Court Act 1981 rear their heads.[204] Before 1998 the English courts were generally sympathetic towards employers who used discovery proceedings to unmask corrupt employees in spite of s10.[205] In *Camelot v Centaur Communications Ltd*[206] the defendants were ordered to hand over leaked confidential documents which compromised the claimant's ability to run the National Lottery:

> Clearly there is unease and suspicion amongst the employees of the company which inhibits good working relationships. Clearly there is a risk that an employee who has proved untrustworthy in one regard may be untrustworthy in a different respect and reveal the name of, say, a public figure who has won a huge lottery prize.[207]

6.47 There is reason to think that judicial willingness to help the employer has not waned in the HRA era if the employee poses a continuing threat to the confidentiality of personal records, especially those containing sensitive personal information. Article 10, to which HRA, s 12 requires the courts to have specific regard, allows the right of freedom of expression to be curtailed for the purpose of 'preventing the disclosure of information received in confidence'[208] if there is a pressing social need for this and the interference is proportionate to the legitimate aim pursued.[209] Protection of patient information was seen by Lord Phillips in *Ashworth Security Hospital v MGN Ltd*[210] as a matter of vital concern to the NHS.

---

[202] See para 5.86 above.
[203] See paras 7.04 et seq.
[204] See para 7.12 below.
[205] eg *British Steel Corp v Granada Television Ltd* [1981] 1 All ER 417; *X Ltd v Morgan-Grampian Ltd* [1990] 2 All ER 1; *Camelot v Centaur Communications Ltd* [1998] IRLR 80.
[206] [1998] IRLR 80.
[207] per Schiemann LJ, *Camelot v Centaur Communications Ltd* [1998] IRLR 80, 84.
[208] It also permits curtailment 'for the protection of health or morals' and 'for the protection of the reputation or rights of others'. Either or both of these may be applicable to some professions.
[209] See para 3.19 above.
[210] [2001] 1 All ER 991.

A. Interception and Disloyalty

He described the unauthorized disclosure of confidential medical records to the press by an unknown employee of the applicant, a hospital, as 'an attack on an area of confidentiality which should be safeguarded in any democratic society'.[211]

Civil Actions: Professional v Interceptor

Tort

Conspiracy and interference with trade, business or economic interest

Along with conspiracy,[212] an action for interference with the professional's business by unlawful means[213] is a possibility. This tort differs from conspiracy in not requiring the involvement of more than one person. As with conspiracy, the meaning of 'unlawful' is unsettled. At its widest, 'unlawful' may mean a breach of any statutory duty regardless of whether it is capable of generating a civil or a criminal action.[214] This would include breaches of DPA duties.

6.48

The sticking point with the interference tort is the requirement that the defendant intended to injure the claimant. In nine times out of ten the defendant's motive in making the disclosure will not have been to undermine the professional's business. As a rule, therefore, this tort will not assist the professional unless the courts decide that liability extends to economic loss that is an incidental but probable[215] (or, on a stricter view, an inevitable)[216] consequence of intentional unlawful conduct.[217]

6.49

Trespass and conversion

When physical items embodying confidential information are illicitly removed from the professional's premises (even dustbins)[218] both the torts of trespass and conversion are likely to have occurred.[219] Unauthorized manipulation of the professional's computer system may be a trespass to the professional's goods.[220] So too

6.50

---

[211] ibid at 1012.
[212] See para 4.43 above. The professional would have to establish inter alia that the conspiracy has caused pecuniary damage. This requirement is readily satisfied if, as a result of the conspiracy, the professional has lost a fee-paying client.
[213] *Acrow (Automation) Ltd v Rex Chainbelt Inc* [1971] 1 WLR 1676, 1682. See further, W Rogers (ed), *Winfield & Jolowicz on Tort* (15th edn, London: 1998) 588; A Grubb (ed), *The Law of Tort* (London: 2002) 27.88.
[214] A Grubb (ed), *The Law of Tort* (London: 2002) 27.92–27.98.
[215] G Fridman, 'Interference with Trade or Business' (1993) 1 Tort L Rev 19, 113.
[216] H Carty, 'Intentional Violation of Economic Interests; The Limits of Common Law Liability' (1988) 104 LQR 250, 280.
[217] In *Lonrho plc v Fayed* [1993] 1 All ER 303 the House of Lords held that the tort of conspiracy to injure by unlawful means could be established without showing that injury to the claimant was the defendant's immediate goal.
[218] *Dubai Aluminium Co Ltd v Al Alawi* [1999] 1 WLR 1964, 1968.
[219] The only point in suing the interceptor for trespass is to obtain compensation. The fact that the interceptor trespassed gives the client no right to restrain disclosure of the information acquired.
[220] G Hughes, *Data Protection in Australia* (Sydney: 1991) 241. The goods in question are the professional's computer hardware and software.

is the removal of a document from a filing cabinet for the purpose of copying, reading or photographing. Opinion differs as to whether illicit use without physical contact can be trespass: for example, photographing a document that has been left lying about.[221] According to Lord Camden in *Entick v Carrington*, 'the eye cannot by the laws of England be guilty of a trespass'.[222] This issue is important if information was extracted by computer hacking. The hacker has no physical contact with the professional's computer. Trindade and Cane maintain that 'any act which sets in motion an unbroken series of continuing consequences the last of which ultimately causes contact with the goods of the plaintiff will be regarded as sufficiently "direct" for the purposes of the tort of trespass to goods'.[223]

6.51 An interceptor who has no permission to be on the professional's premises when intercepting confidential information may be liable to the professional for trespass to land.[224] No damage to the property is required.[225] Most implied invitations are for limited purposes and in such cases an entry unrelated to those purposes, for example obtaining confidential information by stealth, will be a trespass from the outset.[226] In *Savoy Hotel plc v British Broadcasting Corp*[227] Comyn J thought that the BBC's conduct in entering the Savoy Hotel with concealed cameras and television equipment in order to surreptitiously film employees serving short measure to customers was a trespass. In *Malone v Commissioner of Police for the Metropolis*[228] Megarry V-C said that '[i]f some wire or other tapping device is attached to a telephone wire in the airspace over the plaintiff's land, no doubt there would be some remedy in trespass'. Damages for all injury reasonably connected to the trespass are recoverable from a trespasser.[229] Covert surveillance of the professional's premises from the air or from adjacent land does not give rise to an action in trespass.[230]

Deceit

6.52 The tort of deceit might apply if interception was made possible by deception; for example by the interceptor gaining entry to the professional's premises by pre-

---

[221] There is no common law definition of trespass to goods. M Lunney, in A Grubb (ed), *The Law of Tort* (London: 2001) 489 says the action 'lay for an intentional and *direct* interference with another's possession of goods' (italics added).
[222] (1765) 19 How St Tr 1029, 1066.
[223] F Trindade and P Cane, *The Law of Torts in Australia* (Melbourne: 1985) 106–107. See also W Rogers (ed), *Winfield & Jolowicz on Tort* (15th edn, London: 1998) 473.
[224] In *Francome v Mirror Group Newspapers Ltd* [1984] 1 WLR 892, 895 the defendants conceded that the eavesdroppers had committed a trespass to the claimant's land.
[225] *Entick v Carrington* (1765) 19 How St Tr 1029, 1066; *Thurston v Charles* (1905) 21 TLR 659. But some writers have reservations: see F Trindade and P Cane, *The Law of Torts in Australia* (Melbourne: 1985) 108; W Rogers (ed), *Winfield & Jolowicz on Tort* (15th edn, London: 1998) 588–590.
[226] *Lincoln Hunt Australia Pty Ltd v Willesee* (1986) 4 NSWLR 457, 460.
[227] [1983] NLJ 105.
[228] [1979] 2 All ER 620, 644.
[229] *Thurston v Charles* (1904) 21 TLR 659, 660.
[230] *Bernstein v Skyviews* [1977] 2 All ER 902.

A. Interception and Disloyalty

tending to be a prospective client. The technical requirements of deceit are a wilfully false representation or statement [231] made with intent that it should be acted upon by the claimant, reliance upon the representation or statement and resulting loss.[232] Is the tort committed by a defendant who deceived the professional's computer by keying in another person's password?[233] In the criminal law it has been assumed that only a person can be the victim of deception:[234] '[d]eception is something that operates on the mind—we have not yet arrived at the stage of attributing mental facilities to machines, however sophisticated the machine'.[235] But if the intention was to deceive, and damage resulted, why should it matter that the conduct operated directly on a machine?

Copyright

This is a possibility if the confidential records written by the professional are removed and a substantial unaltered part published.[236] **6.53**

Prosecuting Interceptors and Disloyal Employees in the Criminal Courts[237]
Confidential information and the criminal law

The criminal law is not geared to protecting the confidentiality of information. The two exceptions to this are the communications interception and computer accessing offences.[238] Otherwise, the criminal liability of an interceptor or disloyal employee, if it arises at all, depends upon the commission of an offence that has nothing to do with protecting information. **6.54**

Many of the potential crimes are property offences. The property in question is never the information; it is always the thing that contains the information. The criminal courts regard information as too ephemeral to be property.[239] When the Privy Council decided that export quotas are property it said: '[i]t would be strange indeed if something which is freely bought and sold and which may clearly be the subject of dishonest dealing which deprives the owner of the benefit it confers were not capable of being stolen.'[240] In this so-called 'information age' data is **6.55**

---

[231] Silence or concealment will not do: *Peek v Gurney* (1893) LR 6 HL 377, 391.
[232] *Derry v Peak* (1889) 14 App Cas 337. See further, A Grubb (ed), *The Law of Tort* (London: 2002) citing *Steed v Neal* (CA, 30 July 1986).
[233] G Hughes, *Data Protection in Australia* (Sydney: 1991) 247–248.
[234] *Davies v Flackett* [1973] RTR 8, 11; *R v Thompson* [1984] 3 All ER 565.
[235] Law Reform Committee, Report No 47, *Computer Misuse* (Hobart: 1986) 17.
[236] See para 5.86 above.
[237] Details of many of the offences discussed below are to be found in: E Griew, *The Theft Acts* (7th edn, London: 1995); A Smith, *Property Offences* (London: 1994); J Smith, *The Law of Theft* (8th edn, London: 1997).
[238] See paras 6.64 and 6.60 below.
[239] See para 6.70 below. See further J Cross, 'Trade Secrets, Confidential Information, and the Criminal Law' (1991) 36 McGill LJ 525.
[240] per Lord Bridge, *Att-Gen for Hong Kong v Nai-Keung* (1988) 86 Cr App R 174, 177.

traded as a commodity and the refusal to treat information as property is in need of reconsideration. But as things stand, generally, a person who gains access to premises without forcing entry and reads documents lying on a desk, fully aware that he has no right to do so, behaves dishonestly but commits no crime.[241]

Data protection offences

6.56 It is not a criminal offence to breach the principles for the lawful processing of personal data laid down in the DPA. Subject to certain exceptions,[242] however, s 55(1) and s 55(3) of the DPA make it an offence for a person knowingly or recklessly[243] and without the data controller's[244] consent to:

- obtain[245] or disclose 'personal data';[246] or
- obtain or disclose information extracted from personal data; or
- procure the disclosure to another person of the information contained in that data.[247]

Resort to deception (for example, by posing as the client or a relative of the client) to obtain the information would be cogent evidence of awareness of lack of entitlement to the information.[248] There are a number of defences: prevention or detection of crime, lawful authority, order of a court, the public interest and a reasonable belief that obtaining or disclosing or procuring was lawful or that the data controller would have consented had he known.[249] The burden of proof rests on the accused. It is more likely that a public interest defence will be made out if disclosure was to a public authority rather than to the media.

6.57 A person who tries unsuccessfully to obtain disclosure can be charged with an attempt to obtain the data.[250] Aiding, abetting, counselling or procuring a disclos-

---

[241] Law Commission Consultation Paper 150, *Legislating the Criminal Code: Misuse of Trade Secrets* (1997) para 1.24.

[242] s 28(1)(c) creates an exemption in respect of data acquired 'for the purpose of safeguarding national security'.

[243] On the meaning of 'recklessly' see *Data Protection Registrar v Amnesty International* [1995] Crim LR 633; *Information Commissioner v Islington LBC* [2002] EWHC 1036.

[244] It would depend on the organizational structure whether the professional was the data controller or not. See para 18.11 below.

[245] The question was left open in *R v Brown* [1996] 1 All ER 545, 549 whether the unauthorized transfer of data from the database of one computer to the database of another could amount to disclosure.

[246] That is data which relates to a living identifiable individual: see para 10.04 below.

[247] DPA, s 55. cp *R v Rees* (CA, 20 October 2000).

[248] A private investigator who obtained personal data about famous people from BT by deception and sold it to newspapers was prosecuted for procuring and selling the information under provisions of the DPA 1984 similar to s 55: Data Protection Registrar, *Fourteenth Annual Report* (London: 1998) 21, 54.

[249] s 55(2).

[250] *R v McShane* (1977) 66 Cr App R 97, 102.

ure is a crime. Offering to sell (or inviting to treat to sell)[251] personal data having committed the obtaining, disclosing or procuring offence or subsequently obtaining personal data in these circumstances is a crime.[252] Selling personal data that has been obtained in contravention of s 55 is another crime.[253] The majority of data protection prosecutions are for illegal trading in personal data.

6.58 Processing personal data held on a computer, unless an exemption applies, without being registered with the Information Commissioner is a strict liability offence.[254] Since holding information on a computer falls within the statutory definition of 'processing',[255] a hacker who stores personal data obtained from elsewhere on his own computer commits the processing as well as the obtaining offence.

6.59 Proceedings for any offence under the DPA must be brought by the Information Commissioner or with the consent of the Director of Public Prosecutions[256] and, although triable either way, all are punishable with a fine.[257] On summary conviction the maximum fine is £5,000; on conviction in the Crown Court the fine is unlimited. Additionally, the court can order that the data taken be erased or forfeited.[258]

Unauthorised computer access

Computer Misuse Act 1990, s 1

6.60 An interceptor who extracts confidential personal information from a professional's computer commits a summary offence, punishable by up to six months' imprisonment and/or a fine of up to £2,000, under the Computer Misuse Act 1990. Section 1 provides:

(1) A person is guilty of an offence if—
    (a) he causes a computer to perform any function with intent to secure access to any program or data held in any computer;
    (b) the access he intends to secure is unauthorised; and
    (c) he knows at the time when he causes the computer to perform the function that that is the case.

6.61 Access can take four forms: altering or erasing data; copying or moving data; using data or outputting data (for example, to a screen or a printer).[259] The phrase 'any computer' in s 1(1)(a) allows the offence to be committed by:

---

[251] In the case of advertisements, all indications of the availability for sale of personal data is treated as an offer for sale: s 55(6).
[252] DPA, s 55(5).
[253] DPA, s 55(4).
[254] DPA, s 21(1). It is a defence for the person charged to show that he exercised all due diligence to comply with the duty to register.
[255] DPA, s 1(1).
[256] DPA, s 60(1).
[257] DPA, s 60(2).
[258] DPA, s 60(4).
[259] Computer Misuse Act 1989, s 17(2).

(1) an employee of the professional with direct access to the targeted computer;[260] or

(2) an interceptor who accesses the professional's computer by using another computer on the same network or remotely, including from outside the United Kingdom.[261]

The offence of unauthorized access may be committed by an employee who has authority to access one kind of data and accesses another.[262] An employee who has authority to access data and who does so for an unauthorized purpose commits no offence. This is why a prosecution against a BT operator who had demonstrated to a journalist just how easy it was to obtain sensitive information from a BT computer (contrary to the claims of the company) failed.[263] The employee used entry protocols provided by his employer and did not stray into any forbidden databases. The decision was in line with the recommendations of the Law Commission.[264]

6.62 For a conviction, the defendant must cause the target computer to perform a 'function'. A hacker does so by copying data from the professional's computer to his own.[265] Monitoring radiation leaks from a VDU screen, looking over someone's shoulder to read the VDU screen or a print-out or bugging a telephone line transmitting information to or from the computer are outside s 1 because the eavesdropper does not cause the targeted computer to perform a function. Electronic eavesdropping as such is not an offence. The presence of the words 'with intent' in s 1(1)(a) and the content of s 1(1)(c) means that the interceptor's conduct must be intentional, though not necessarily vis-à-vis any particular data or any particular computer.[266] A teenage hacker who offered a defence of computer addiction was acquitted by a jury.[267] An employee who supplies a hacker with a confidential password enabling the hacker to contravene s 1 is an accessory.[268]

Computer Misuse Act 1990, ss 2–3

6.63 Section 2 of the Computer Misuse Act 1990 creates a more serious offence, triable summarily or on indictment punishable with imprisonment for up to five years or a fine or both. To be convicted the hacker must commit the s1 offence with intent

---

[260] *Att-Gen's Reference (No 1 of 1991)* [1992] 3 All ER 897, 901–902.
[261] Computer Misuse Act 1989 s 4.
[262] *R v Bow Street Magistrates' Court, ex p Government of the US* [1999] 4 All ER 1, 9–10.
[263] *R v Arlidge* discussed in P Davies, 'Computer Misuse' (1995) 145 NLJ 1776.
[264] Law Commission Report 186, *Criminal Law: Computer Misuse* (Cm 819, 1989) para 3.38.
[265] Computer Misuse Act 1990, s 17.
[266] ibid s 1(2). See further, P Murphy (ed), *Blackstone's Criminal Practice 2001* (11th edn, London: 2001) 730.
[267] *R v Bedworth* (17 March 1993), see http://www.eff.org/Net_culture/Hackers/uk_court_acquits_teenage_hacker.article.
[268] Magistrates' Courts Act 1980, s 44(1).

to commit or to facilitate the commission of some 'further' offence for which the sentence is fixed by law or for which a person aged 21 years without prior convictions may be sentenced to imprisonment for a term of five years. It is not necessary for the further offence to have been committed, or even to be possible, so long as it was envisaged by the defendant.[269] An offence would be committed under s 2 by someone who gained unauthorized access to confidential personal information held on a computer with the intention of using the information for blackmail.[270] It would not be committed by a hacker who conceived the idea of blackmail *after* gaining access to a doctor's database and discovering the identity of her HIV seropositive patients. Section 3 makes it an offence to modify the contents of a computer system without authorization. This offences could be committed by someone who de-encrypts personal data knowing that he had no authority to do so.

Interception of communications offences

Regulation of Investigatory Powers Act 2000

By the Regulation of Investigatory Powers Act 2000 (RIPA) it is an offence intentionally and without lawful authority to intercept anywhere within the United Kingdom a communication in the course of its transmission through a public postal service or a public telecommunications system.[271] The period of transmission includes the time during which the communication is stored in the system awaiting collection or access by the intended recipient.[272] A 'public telecommunications system'[273] is defined as a system made available to the public or a substantial part of the public (whether by a public or private organization) 'which exists (whether wholly or partly in the United Kingdom or elsewhere) for the purpose of facilitating the transmission of communications by any means involving the use of electrical or electro-magnetic energy'.[274] This definition captures all the newer forms of communication including the internet, e-mail, radio-pagers and mobile and satellite telephones.

6.64

There is a similar offence of intercepting a communication in the course of its transmission through a private telecommunications system, that is a private network such as a hospital or office switchboard that is connected directly or indirectly to a public system.[275] No offence is committed where the interceptor has the right to control the operation of the system or has the express or implied consent of the person who does.[276] Interception of a communication passing through a

6.65

---

[269] Computer Misuse Act 1990, s 2(4).
[270] P Murphy (ed), *Blackstone's Criminal Practice 2001* (11th edn, London: 2001) 732.
[271] RIPA, s 1(1). See also paras 14.86 and 14.91 below.
[272] RIPA, s 2(7); *R (on the application of NTL Group Ltd) v Ipswich CC* [2002] EWHC 1585.
[273] RIPA, s 2 (1). [274] ibid.
[275] ibid. [276] RIPA, s 1(6).

telecommunications system requires the contents of the communication to be disclosed either to the interceptor or to a stranger.[277]

6.66 On conviction of unlawful interception by a magistrates' court, the interceptor may be fined up to £5,000; conviction in the Crown Court carries a possible prison sentence of two years, an unlimited fine, or both.[278] A prosecution requires the consent of the Director of Public Prosecutions.[279] The consent requirement is important because the Act contains no public interest defence. The News of the World newspaper used a telephone sting operation to obtain evidence of Lord Archer's perjury. A telephone conversation between Francis (who was co-operating with News of the World) and Archer was tape recorded. In it Archer admitted having asked Francis to provide a false alibi. Had RIPA been in force the sting operation might have been illegal.[280]

Wireless Telegraphy Act 1949

6.67 The Wireless Telegraphy Act 1949 makes it an offence to use (or possess with the intention of using)[281] an apparatus for wireless telegraphy[282] unless the apparatus is licensed or in a licence-exempt category.[283] Radio scanning devices, listening devices that convert sound into radio signals and radio receivers that convert these sounds back into audio form are all apparatuses for wireless telegraphy.[284] The use of a wireless telegraphy receiving apparatus (licensed, unlicensed or exempt) for the purpose[285] of intercepting messages which the defendant was not authorized to receive and disclosure of the intercepted information (whoever did the intercepting) except in the course of legal proceedings or reporting legal proceedings are offences under s 5(b).[286] Interception of signals to a cordless telephone by means of an FM radio falls within s 5(b).

---

[277] RIPA, s 2(2).   [278] RIPA, s 1(7).
[279] RIPA, s 1(8).
[280] D Tench, 'Don't pull the dog's teeth', Guardian, 23 July 2001.
[281] But not to sell such equipment.
[282] This expression is defined in the Wireless Telegraphy Act 1949, s 19(1) to mean 'the emitting or receiving, over paths which are not provided by any material substance constructed or arranged for that purpose, of electro-magentic energy of a frequency not exceeding three million megacycles a second, being energy which . . . (a) serves for the conveying of messages, sound or visual . . .'.
[283] ss 1,1A. Exempt apparatus are set out in the Wireless Telegraphy (Short Range Devices) (Exemption) Regulations 1993 SI 1993/1591.
[284] Irish Law Reform Commission, *Privacy: Surveillance and Interception of Communications* (Dublin: 1996) 100.
[285] The interception must be done with intent. Lack of evidence of intent would have prevented a prosecution of the person responsible for intercepting the alleged conversations between the Prince of Wales and Camilla Parker-Bowles in the Camilla tapes episode.
[286] *Malone v Commissioner of Police of the Metropolis (No 2)* [1979] 2 All ER 620, 644. They are not repealed by the RIPA.

A. Interception and Disloyalty

Theft

6.68 Theft is defined in s1 of the Theft Act 1968 as the dishonest[287] appropriation[288] (whether or not for gain)[289] of 'property belonging to another with the intention of permanently depriving the other of it'. ' "Property" includes money and all other property, real or personal, including things in action and other intangible property.'[290] The interceptor who removes a physical object containing confidential personal information that is the property of, or in the 'possession or control of',[291] a professional such as a file or an X-ray or a computer print-out with no intention of returning it commits this offence. So does a person who comes by the property innocently (perhaps he finds a medical file left behind on a train) and later decides to keep it or deals with it as if he were the rightful owner.[292] And so also does a person who receives property by mistake (perhaps a solicitor to whom privileged documents are mistakenly disclosed in litigation) and ignores an obligation to make restoration.[293]

6.69 The interceptor who borrows a document, floppy-disk or CD-rom intending to return what was taken after making a copy on some other premises is not guilty of theft unless the borrowing is 'for a period and in circumstances making it equivalent to an outright taking or disposal'.[294] In *R v Lloyd* the Court of Appeal explained that:

> mere borrowing is never enough to constitute the necessary guilty mind unless the intention is to return the 'thing' in such a changed state that it can truly be said that all its goodness or virtue has gone.[295]

The fact that by his actions the borrower inflicts substantial financial loss on the person in rightful possession (in *Lloyd*, by making a master video from which to manufacture pirate videos) does not make the conduct of the borrower theft.

6.70 For a conviction under s1 of the Theft Act 1968, it is quite irrelevant that the property taken embodies confidential information. Confidential information itself is not property and therefore cannot be stolen.[296] This was settled in *Oxford v Moss*,[297] a case in which a student from Liverpool University was caught returning the proof

---

[287] *R v Ghosh* [1982] QB 1053.
[288] 'Any assumption by a person of the rights of an owner amounts to appropriation...': Theft Act 1968, s 3(1).
[289] ibid s 1(2).
[290] ibid s 4(1).
[291] ibid s 5(1). 'Control' covers a wide raqnge of situations and would include removing documents from a dustbin on the professional's property: cp *R v Woodman* [1974] 2 All ER 955.
[292] ibid s 3(1).
[293] ibid s 5.
[294] ibid s 6(1).
[295] per Lord Lane CJ, *R v Lloyd* [1985] 2 All ER 661, 667.
[296] R Hammond, 'Theft of Information' (1984) 100 LQR 252.
[297] (1979) 68 Cr App R 183. See also *R v Absolom*, The Times, 14 September 1983.

of an examination paper he was soon to sit which he had copied. It was an agreed fact that the defendant had no intention to steal the paper on which the questions were written. Indeed, the success of his plan depended upon his being able to return the paper without the interception being detected. The Divisional Court held that confidential information is neither tangible nor intangible property within the meaning of the Theft Act 1968, s 4(1).[298] Had the Divisional Court decided otherwise, the student would still have been acquitted because he had no intention of permanently depriving the university of the information. The current thinking is that 'goodness and virtue'[299] is not lost by destruction of value through loss of confidentiality.[300]

6.71 From time to time the idea has been floated of creating a specific offence of theft of information. The Younger Committee rejected this in 1972, preferring to recommend a new criminal offence for the unlawful use of technical devices and greater reliance on civil causes of action.[301] The Scottish High Court of Judiciary declined to declare the dishonest exploitation of confidential information by a former employee a crime in *Grant v Allan*[302] inter alia because of the serious implications for the mobility of labour.[303] The Supreme Court of Canada in *R v Stewart* gave three further reasons why unauthorized appropriation of confidential information should not be criminalized:

(1) When someone 'steals' information the person in rightful possession is forced to share it; she is not (except in exceptional circumstances) deprived of it.[304]
(2) There would be practical problems in defining confidential information precisely.[305]
(3) There might be an overriding public interest in the free flow of information. 'Would society be willing to prosecute the person who discloses to the public a cure for cancer, although its discoverer wanted to keep it confidential?'[306]

Abstracting electricity

6.72 Obtaining information may require the use of electricity. Theft Act 1968, s 13 makes it an offence (with a maximum penalty of five years' imprisonment) to dis-

---

[298] cp *R v Stewart* (1988) 50 DLR (4d) 1.
[299] *R v Lloyd* [1985] 2 All ER 661, 667.
[300] Commentary [1979] Crim LR 119, 121.
[301] Report of the Committee on Privacy (Cmnd 5012, 1972) paras 489 et seq.
[302] 1988 SLT 11.
[303] ibid at 11, 14.
[304] (1988) 50 DLR (4d) 1, 14. For deprivation to occur the information must become unavailable to the person with the legal right to the information, eg the original copy is destroyed in the copying process.
[305] (1988) 50 DLR (4d) 1, 12. Is confidentiality to be determined subjectively or objectively? When does information cease to be confidential?
[306] per Latimer J, *R v Stewart* (1988) 50 DLR (4d) 1, 12. See also J Cross, 'Trade Secrets, Confidential Information and the Criminal Law' (1991) 36 McGill LJ 524, 534–535.

A. Interception and Disloyalty

honestly use any electricity without due authority, or to dishonestly cause electricity to be wasted or diverted.[307] An employee who uses his employer's electricity to access or copy information when he ought not to do so, or an interceptor who installs a bugging device that uses electricity from the victim's telephone or power supply, may commit this offence. Applying this provision to punish hackers may prove problematic. Sometimes less of the victim's electricity is used during the hacking process than when the targeted computer is in an idle state. This is because the copy command is generated by the hacker's computer which is powered by electricity paid for by the hacker.[308]

Deception

Theft Act 1968, s 15 provides that '[a] person who by any deception dishonestly obtains property belonging to another, with the intention of permanently depriving the other of it' commits an offence. If tried on indictment this offence is punishable by up to ten years' imprisonment. The elements of deception are similar to those of theft: both crimes require dishonesty and permanently depriving a person of property. Deception is the usual charge where the victim was tricked into parting with property.[309]

6.73

All the remarks made in connection with theft about the need for tangible property to be taken and either an intention to deprive the victim of that property permanently or to return it in a useless state apply to deception. Importantly, the crime requires more than merely the practice of deception;[310] there must be deception that operated successfully[311] upon a human mind.[312] These requirements are satisfied when a professional is led by the interceptor to believe something, for example, that the interceptor is the client, and in consequence parted with confidential information about the client. A hacker who gains access to confidential information held on the professional's computer by using a password without authority deceives the machine, not the professional, and cannot be convicted under s 15.[313] A prosecution under s1 of the Forgery and Counterfeiting Act 1981 will similarly fail because the hacker intends the computer, not a person, to respond to the password.[314] Additionally, such a prosecution would fail because a password, momentarily held by the targeted computer, is not a false 'instrument' within the meaning of s 8(1)(d) of the 1981 Act.[315]

6.74

---

[307] *R v McCreadie* [1992] Crim LR 872.
[308] This problem is discussed by R Brown, 'Crime and Computers' (1983) 7 Criminal LJ 68, 76.
[309] *Archbold, Criminal Pleading, Evidence and Practice 1997* (London: 1997) 1831.
[310] As to what constitutes deception see Theft Act 1968, s 15(4) and A Smith, 'The Idea of Deception' [1982] Crim LR 721.
[311] If it did not operate successfully there is only attempted deception.
[312] *DPP v Ray* [1973] All ER 131, 137.
[313] See C Tapper, ' "Computer Crime": Scotch Mist?' [1987] Crim LR 4, 12.
[314] *R v Gold* [1988] 2 All ER 186, 190.
[315] ibid at 192.

Corruption

6.75 The Public Bodies Corrupt Practices Act 1889 is contravened by a public sector employee who corruptly supplies information in return for a 'gift, loan, fee, reward or advantage' for himself or someone else.[316] Public and private sector employees alike offend against the Prevention of Corruption Act 1906 if they corruptly provide information in return for 'a gift or consideration'.[317] An interceptor who obtains information by bribery may contravene the Prevention of Corruption Act 1906[318] and, if the information is obtained from an employee of a public body, also the Public Bodies Corrupt Practices Act 1889.[319] There is also a common law offence of bribery of a public official.[320]

6.76 A charge of conspiracy to commit corruption is a possibility.[321] The Observer and an employee of the Ministry of Defence were prosecuted in 1987 after it was discovered that the newspaper had paid the employee £10,000 for information about financial mismanagement in the Department. The employee was convicted of corruptly accepting a bribe but, in a separate trial, the Observer, whose editor and journalists had believed that the employee had resigned before making the disclosures, was acquitted of offering the money corruptly.[322]

Conspiracy to defraud[323]

6.77 It may be possible to prosecute two or more persons jointly involved in the interception of confidential personal information for conspiracy even though prosecution of a solo interceptor who did the same thing could not be. This is *not* because an agreement by two or more persons to intercept confidential personal information is of itself a crime. In *DPP v Wither*[324] several people had implemented a plan to obtain confidential information from bank and building society officials about the accounts of customers by posing over the telephone as managers of similar institutions. Their convictions for conspiracy to effect a public mischief were quashed by the House of Lords. No such crime, their Lordships

---

[316] s 1(1).
[317] s 1.
[318] s 1(1). On conviction on indictment, the maximum penalty is seven years' imprisonment and an unlimited fine.
[319] s 1(2).
[320] Home Office, *Raising Standards and Upholding Integrity: The Prevention of Corruption* (Cm 4759, 2000) para 1.7.
[321] cp *R v Wilson* (1982) 4 Cr App R (S) 337 where the chief buyer of a manufacturing concern was convicted of conspiracy to commit corruption as well as corruption for accepting gifts of £2,500 in return for favouring one supplier. The person offering the bribe can be charged with conspiracy to make corrupt payments: *R v Att-Gen, ex p Rockall* [1999] 4 All ER 312.
[322] G Robertson and A Nicol, *Robertson and Nicol on Media Law* (4th edn, London: 2002) 229.
[323] D Kirk and A Woodcock, *Serious Fraud: investigation and trial* (2nd edn, London: 1997) ch 6.
[324] [1974] 3 All ER 984.

decided, is known to English law. Rather, it is because dishonest behaviour that is lawful if done by one person may in certain limited circumstances, if agreed to by two, constitute the crime of conspiracy to defraud.

6.78 Disclosure of a trade secret is a breach of confidence and may be a breach of contract but it is not a crime. The Law Commission believes, however, that a prosecution for conspiracy to defraud is possible against two or more people who dishonestly use or disclose a trade secret.[325] Trade secrets are a type of confidential information. If the Law Commission is right, an action for conspiracy to defraud might be possible against those who conspire to remove confidential personal client information from a professional without authority. A defendant proved to have committed the conspiracy offence faces the prospect of up to ten years' imprisonment or a fine or both.[326]

6.79 The elements of conspiracy to defraud are unsettled, and this makes it difficult to be certain whether such a prosecution would succeed. There is no doubt about two of the elements: deceit or an intention to deceive is unnecessary but there must have been an agreement by at least two people to dishonestly deprive another of something to which he was entitled.[327] The presence of dishonesty is assessed according to the ordinary standards of reasonable and honest people.[328]

6.80 To take confidential personal information from a professional intentionally without authority and then to disclose without authority may be seen as dishonest behaviour. Since it can give rise to civil liability in an action for breach of confidence, it further involves an interference with the professional's rights. Therefore these two basic requirements are satisfied. Additionally, according to Lord Diplock in *Scott v Metropolitan Police Commissioner*, the conspirators must have had the intention to cause their victim economic loss.[329] In a later case it was considered enough that the conspirators realized that their actions gave rise to a risk of economic loss.[330] In a prosecution against an interceptor, this could be a stumbling block as economic loss or risk of economic loss are not an inevitable consequence of the dishonest removal of confidential client information. However, there is an alternative well-supported theory that an intention[331] to risk any kind of prejudice to another's rights will suffice.[332] It is also well settled that economic

---

[325] Law Commission Consultation Paper 150, *Legislating the Criminal Code: Misuse of Trade Secrets* (1997) para 1.21; Law Commission Consultation Paper 104, *Criminal Law: Conspiracy to Defraud* (1987) para 4.42.
[326] Criminal Justice Act 1987, s 12(3).
[327] *Scott v Metropolitan Police Commissioner* [1974] 3 All ER 1032, 1038.
[328] *R v Ghosh* [1982] 2 All ER 689, 692, 696.
[329] [1974] 3 All ER 1032, 1040.
[330] *R v Allsop* (1976) 64 Cr App R 29, 31.
[331] This need not be the primary object; it is enough it is an inevitable by-product: *R v McPherson* [1985] Crim LR 508.
[332] *Welham v DPP* [1960] 1 All ER 805, 808; *Wai Yu-tsang v R* [1991] 4 All ER 664, 670; *Adams v R* [1995] 2 Cr App R 295, 308.

loss or the risk of economic loss is not necessary when the intended victim is a public official,[333] which some professionals are. A charge of conspiracy to defraud may be brought even when the evidence supports a charge of statutory conspiracy.[334]

6.81 Where two or more people agree to acquire confidential information by a course of action that necessarily involves the commission of any criminal offence by one of them (for example, theft or corruption) a charge of statutory conspiracy[335] is possible.

Other offences

6.82 In the process of obtaining the confidential information the interceptor may commit any one or more of a number of other crimes:

- If in the course of accessing information, an employee or interceptor intentionally or recklessly damages property belonging to the professional or the client (for example, damages a filing cabinet or diary lock), he can be prosecuted for intentional or reckless damage to property.[336] Any intentional or reckless physical alteration to tangible property, other than modification of data in a computer,[337] that temporarily or permanently impairs its usefulness or value to its owner[338] constitutes criminal damage for this purpose.
- In gaining access to the professional's premises the interceptor may commit burglary.[339]
- An interceptor who threatens the professional or an employee with violence in order to obtain the information is guilty of assault.[340]
- Although breaching copyright is not a crime,[341] the knowing sale or distribution of an infringing copy may be an offence under s 107 of the Copyright, Designs and Patents Act 1988.

---

[333] *Scott v Metropolitan Police Commissioner* [1974] 3 All ER 1032, 1038.
[334] Criminal Justice Act 1987, s 12.
[335] Criminal Law Act 1977, s 1.
[336] Criminal Damage Act 1972, s1 provides: '[a] person who without lawful excuse . . . damages any property . . . intending to . . . damage any such property . . . shall be guilty of an offence.' S 10(1) states: '. . . "property" means property of a tangible nature . . .'.
[337] Computer Misuse Act 1990, s 3(6).
[338] *R v Whitely* (1991) 93 Cr App R 25, 28. Whitely gained unauthorized access to a university computer network and altered data causing computer failure. His defence that he had caused no perceptible physical alteration of the computer or the computer disk was rejected. The decision, in so far as it relates to computer data, has been reversed by the Computer Misuse Act 1990, s 3(6) but is still good law in respect of other forms of property.
[339] Theft Act 1968, s 9(1).
[340] Criminal Justice Act 1988, s 32.
[341] Copyright is not property for the purposes of Theft Act 1968, s 4(1): *Frank Film v Video Information* [1981] 2 All ER 76, 83. See further A Smith, *Property Offences* (London: 1994) 56.

A. Interception and Disloyalty

- Obtaining a physical object containing confidential information by means of a threat is blackmail.[342] Obtaining the information itself by such means is not because information is not property.[343]

6.83 The Human Genetics Commission advocates making non-consensual or deceitful obtaining and/or analysis of personal genetic information for non-medical purposes a crime.[344] The Commission notes that in some EU countries deliberate unauthorized disclosure of confidential medical information or other professional secrets is a criminal offence and that in 1981 the Law Commission recommended the creation of a statutory offence of breach of confidence.[345]

Prosecuting a Stranger[346] in the Criminal Courts
Conspiracy, accessory, handling, theft and data protection offences

6.84 Where no property is stolen and passed to the stranger, it is difficult to convict the stranger who receives confidential personal information from an interceptor or disloyal employee of an offence unless:

(1) the stranger encouraged or assisted the interceptor to commit a crime—this makes the stranger an accessory;[347]
(2) an agreement can be proved between the stranger and the interceptor to obtain the information by unlawful means or to risk prejudice to the professional's rights, in which case a charge of conspiracy is a possibility;[347a]
(3) contrary to DPA, s 55(1), the stranger knowingly or recklessly obtained, disclosed or procured personal data or information contained in personal data without the consent of the data controller.

In situation (3) there are a number of possible defences including that 'the obtaining, disclosing or procuring was justified as being in the public interest'.[348] This might protect a journalist who received and published confidential personal information about the client well aware that it had been unlawfully intercepted by her informant.

6.85 If the stranger was not a party to the theft but dishonestly received an object stolen from the professional, such as a document containing confidential information, knowing or believing it to be stolen, she is guilty of handling.[349]

---

[342] Theft Act 1968, s 21.
[343] The demand with menaces must be made with a view to gain or loss; gain or loss means 'money or other property': Theft Act 1968, s 34(2). Information is not property: see para 6.70 above.
[344] HGC, *Inside Information* (May 2002) para 3.60.
[345] ibid para 3.48.
[346] A person who receives information from an interceptor.
[347] Accessors and Abettors Act 1861, s 8; Magistrates' Courts Act 1980, s 44.
[347a] See paras 6.67–6.80 above.
[348] DPA, s 55(2)(d). See further para 6.56 above.
[349] Theft Act 1968, s 22(1).

Mens rea is determined subjectively; wilful blindness does not suffice for guilt.[350] A bona fide purchaser for value of a stolen document who subsequently discovers that the document is stolen commits no offence by deciding to keep or sell it.[351] However, where value is not given, an innocent stranger who retains or disposes of the document after discovering that it was stolen commits theft and may in some circumstances also be guilty of handling.[352]

Wireless telegraph interception

6.86 By s 5 of the Wireless Telegraphy Act 1949 it is an offence for 'any person' (other than in the course of legal proceedings) to disclose details of a message illegally intercepted under the terms of that Act.[352a]

Criminal libel

6.87 The stranger may have published the client information. Intentionally publishing a statement in permanent form[353] that exposes a person to public hatred, contempt and ridicule or which is likely to injure him in his profession or trade is a criminal libel,[354] an indictable offence. Privilege is a defence to a charge of criminal libel[355] but truth is not in the absence of proof that 'it was for the public benefit that the said matters charged should be published'.[356] Private as well as public prosecutions may be brought, but both are rare[357] and there is doubt about whether imposing a burden on the accused to prove both truth and public interest conforms to Article 10 of the ECHR.[358] If the defendant is a 'proprietor, publisher, editor or any person responsible for the publication of a newspaper' a judge

---

[350] *R v Griffiths* (1974) 60 Cr App R 14.
[351] *R v Wheeler* (1991) 92 Cr App R 279, 283 and see Theft Act 1968, s 3(2). It is possible for the innocent purchaser of stolen goods who sells them on after learning they were stolen to commit the offence of deception by representing that she has a good title, or of aiding and abetting the commission by the purchaser of the offence of handling by receiving if both know that the goods were stolen.
[352] J Smith, *The Law of Theft* (7th edn, London: 1993) 210.
[352a] See para 6.67 above.
[353] Publication of words in the course of a theatre performance (Theatres Act 1968, ss 4, 7) or a broadcast programme (Broadcasting Act 1990, s 166(1)) is deemed a publication in permanent form.
[354] Libel Act 1843, s 5. For the meaning of 'defamatory libel' in s 5 see *Blackstone's Commentaries* (13th edn, 1796) vol 4, p 150, para 13. Risk of provoking a breach of the peace has ceased to be an essential element: *Gleaves v Deakin* [1979] 2 All ER 497, 498, 502, 504–505.
[355] *R v Rule* [1937] 2 KB 375.
[356] Libel Act 1843, s 6.
[357] It is not worth prosecuting if the libel is not of a serious character because, as Viscount Dilhorne pointed out in *Gleaves v Deakin* [1979] 2 All ER 497, 501, it is open to the judge to advise the jury that the libel is so trivial that they should return a verdict of not guilty. If despite his advice, they convict, he can grant an absolute discharge.
[358] *Gleaves v Deakin* [1979] 2 All ER 497, 498–499.

A. Interception and Disloyalty

must first be persuaded that a prosecution is *required* in the public interest.[359] The punishment, a fine and/or imprisonment, depends upon whether the defendant knew the libel to be false.[360]

Committing a Criminal Offence in the Public Interest

It is no breach of confidence or contract to disclose confidential client information without consent in the public interest.[361] In the criminal law the position is different. Disclosure in the public interest is not a defence to conspiracy or theft[362] and a person charged with breach of a statutory prohibition on disclosure of confidential information cannot, in the absence of an express statutory defence,[363] justify his conduct on public interest grounds.[364] Were disclosure in a particular case to be genuinely in the public interest, for example if documents were stolen as the only practical way of averting reasonably anticipated serious physical injury to an innocent person, the Director of Public Prosecutions might decide not to prosecute.[365] In *Buckoke v Greater London Council* Lord Denning accepted as correct the proposition that a fire-engine driver would have no defence if he proceeded through a red light when the road was clear to save a man in extreme peril in a blazing house 200 yards away. Lord Denning went on to say 'nevertheless such a man should not be prosecuted. He should be congratulated.'[366]

6.88

---

[359] Law of Libel Amendment Act 1888, s8, as to which see *Goldsmith v Pressdram Ltd* [1977] 2 All ER 557. There is no appeal from the judge's decision.
[360] Libel Act 1843, ss 4, 5.
[361] See ch 11.
[362] Y Cripps, *The Legal Implications of Disclosure in the Public Interest* (2nd edn, London: 1994) 209, 221 thinks that the public interest should be a defence to charges of theft and conspiracy 'provided that at the time an offence was allegedly committed, it was reasonable to anticipate that the serious harm to persons which would result from compliance with the criminal law would exceed the damage which would be caused by the conduct prohibited by the offence in question and that there were no other more proportionate means of averting the danger to which resort would first have been had by persons of reasonable steadfastness'.
[363] eg Banking Act 1987, s 83; Financial Services Act 1986, s 180; DPA, s 55(2).
[364] Y Cripps, *The Legal Implications of Disclosure in the Public Interest* (2nd edn, London: 1994) 170. It is worth noting that the Public Interest Disclosure Act 1998 which protects a whistleblower against dismissal or victimization by the employer does not apply if disclosure is in breach of the criminal law.
[365] Prosecution of Offences Act 1985, s 10.
[366] [1971] 2 All ER 254, 258.

B. Accidental Disclosure

6.89 What can be done if confidential personal information about a client escapes from a professional to a third party? The verb 'escape' has been chosen deliberately to convey the idea that disclosure was unintended even if the act that caused it was not. Cases in which client records are wafted out of windows by fans and are picked up by strangers in the street or professionals talk about clients in their sleep in crowded railway carriages are very much the exception. It is much more likely that disclosure of confidential information was an unintentional consequence of a voluntary act.[367] Examples include, careless talk in a public place, accidentally posting[368] or faxing confidential documents to the wrong person, selling a computer without deleting data from the hard drive[369] and leaving client documents behind on a train[370] or in a place in which they are vulnerable to theft such as a car boot or dustbin bags awaiting collection in the street.[371]

The Professional's Liability

Post-disclosure causes of action

Accidental disclosure and unconscious use

6.90 The obligation of a professional not to disclose a client's secrets without consent includes an obligation not to do so inadvertently.

---

[367] Chs 4 and 5 differ from this chapter in that the professional intended to disclose the confidential information to the party who initially received it. In this chapter the professional did not.

[368] eg *Ablitt v Mills & Reeve*, The Times, 25 October 1995; *DPP v Kane* (1997) 140 FLR 468.

[369] In one recorded incident in the US a self-employed computer technician who bought a second-hand IBM computer cast off by a pharmacy found that it still contained the full records of 2,000 persons on its hard disk. Some of the drugs prescribed were for AIDS, depression and alcohol abuse: see L Mizell, *Invasion of Privacy* (New York: 1998) 193. Independent, 11 January 2002 reports the disposal to an individual by the Law Department at Bristol University of a PC which still contained material about paedophiles and their victims supplied to the university by the police for a study of evidence in child abuse cases.

[370] A judge issued an order preventing publication of the contents of the trial bundle of the defendant in *Archer v Williams* after counsel representing Ms Williams admitted that he had left, but fortunately recovered, correspondence with his instructing solicitor and his client's evidence on a London underground train: Guardian, 23 March 2002, 7. The Audit Commission in *Setting the Records Straight. A Study of Hospital Medical Records* (1995) mentions a doctor who 'sold his car with patients' case notes still in the boot'.

[371] A Canadian hospital administrator ordered that eight boxes of sensitive medical records be burned on a beach instead of being shredded or incinerated. Because fires were not permitted on public beaches, the fire brigade put out the flames. The remains of the documents were washed up on the coast. 'People who helped scavenge the records were astonished to find all manner of their neighbours' medical records and even adoption documents': 'Bungled Bonfire of Medical Records Fuels Call for Records Protection Law' FIPA Bulletin (Fall, 1994) reproduced by A Cavoukian and D Tapscott, *Who Knows: Safeguarding your privacy in a networked world* (New York: 1997) 124. At the time of writing, the NTL internet news service reported an administrative blunder in which personal details of staff at a prison were handed to inmates by mistake to burn as rubbish. The documents had not been recovered.

B. Accidental Disclosure

A solicitor is under a duty not to communicate to others any information in his possession which is confidential to the former client. But the duty extends well beyond that of refraining from deliberate disclosure. It is the solicitor's duty to ensure that the former client is not put at risk that confidential information which the solicitor has obtained from that relationship may be used against him in any circumstances.[372]

An action for breach of confidence lies against a professional who discloses confidential client information negligently.[373] Alternatively, damages may be recoverable for contravention of the data security requirements of the DPA[374] and, if there is a contractual promise of confidentiality, breach of contract.[375] A judge of the Supreme Court of British Columbia awarded a patient $1,000 damages against a physician who had inadvertently disclosed information concerning the patient's treatment. This unintentional disclosure was found to be a breach of 'an implied term of the contract' between them.[376]

6.91 Unconscious use of confidential information has been recognized as a ground for finding a breach of confidence in trade secrets cases.[377] Copyright can be infringed subconsciously.[378] The fact that the wrong was committed unintentionally may affect the relief that equity is prepared to give. In *Seager v Copydex Ltd*,[379] a case of unconscious plagiarism of a commercial design for a carpet strip, the court refused an injunction and substituted damages. Such an outcome is less likely if a professional unconsciously uses confidential personal information about a client, say, in the professional's autobiography, because money is not usually an adequate substitute for loss of privacy.[380]

---

[372] per Lord Hope, *Bolkiah v KPMG* [1999] 1 All ER 517, 519.

[373] *Jackson v Royal Bank of Scotland* [2000] CLC 1457 (bank negligently sent documents to client's customer to whom the client had sold a consignment of goods), and see para 6.32 above. cp *Swinney v Chief Constable of Northumbria* [1996] 3 All ER 449, 453 (negligent disclosure of the identity of a police informant).

[374] See paras 6.35–6.36 above.

[375] Negligence by a fiduciary professional is actionable as negligence, not as a breach of fiduciary duty: *Bristol and West Building Society v Mothew* [1996] 4 All ER 698, 712.

[376] *Mammone v Baken* (10 February 1989) cited by D Casswell, 'Disclosure by a Physician of AIDS-Related Patient Information: An Ethical and Legal Dilemma' (1989) 68 Canadian Bar Rev 224, 230 n 24.

[377] *Seager v Copydex Ltd* [1967] 2 All ER 415; *Talbot v General Television Corp Pty Ltd* [1980] VR 224. Does this imply a proprietary interest in the information? M Neave and M Weinberg, 'The nature and function of equities' (1978) 6 U of Tasmania L Rev 115, 120–121 think so. It is not obvious why the accidental or unconscious disclosure of confidential personal information qualifies as a breach of confidence if good faith (see para 5.03 above) is the rationale for an action for breach of confidence.

[378] W Cornish, *Intellectual Property* (4th edn, London: 1999) 415.

[379] [1967] 2 All ER 415, 419.

[380] See para 8.10 below.

Conflicts of interest between clients[381]

6.92 There is no general principle of law that a professional cannot act for parties with competing interests if the professional is able to fulfil his obligations to one client without breaching his obligations to another. 'The large accountancy firms commonly carry out the audit of clients who are in competition with one another.'[382] The clients are taken to consent to this.[383] In spite of the fiduciary duty of loyalty that the solicitor owes the client, the better view is that at law a solicitor can act for a client in one matter and against that client (whether or not still a client) in a fresh and wholly unrelated matter, including litigation.[384] The secrets of a client or former client (A) are safe because of the professional's legal (and ethical) obligation of confidentiality to A which overrides any fiduciary obligation of disclosure that the professional may owe to another client (B).[385] Nothing must be disclosed about A to client B, without A's informed consent.

6.93 If there is a real risk (not merely a theoretical or fanciful one)[386] of a professional, P, unwittingly disclosing information about A, a client or former client, to B, another of P's clients, or alternatively, of P unconsciously using A's confidential

---

[381] See further, C Hollander and S Salzedo, *Conflicts of Interest and Chinese Walls* (London: 2000); C Nakajima and E Sheffield, *Conflicts of Interest and Chinese Walls* (London: 2002); J Griffiths-Baker, *Serving two masters: conflicts of interest in the modern law firm* (Oxford: 2002). B Watson, *Litigation Liabilities* (Bembridge: 2002) 60–70. See also, Regulation Review Working Party, *Conflict of Interest* (Law Society, June 2001) and proposed new rules and guidance on 'Conflict and Confidentiality' available at www.lawsocietyorg.uk.

[382] *Bolkiah v KPMG* [1999] 1 All ER 517, 526.

[383] ibid.

[384] City of London Law Society Working Party, *Review of Conflict Rules (draft)* (July 2000) paras 4.2, 4.14, 7.18, available at http://www.citysolicitors.org.uk/Legal_activities/ConflictReport.doc; Association of Pension Lawyers, Discussion Paper, *Pensions Litigation, Conflicts and Chinese Walls* (2000) para 2, available from http://www.apl.org.uk; *Skjevesland v Geveran Trading Co Ltd* [2002] EWCA Civ 1567, para 7 ('a legal adviser can "change sides" provided he does not misuse confidential information'). However, the Law Society rules seem to bar a firm automatically from acting for A if the firm holds relevant confidential information about B acquired in an unrelated matter in which B was represented by the firm: ibid paras 7.2, 7.5. Whether or not there is a risk of confidential information being misused, the solicitor's obligation of loyalty (see para 5.65 above) ought generally to preclude a solicitor or someone else within the firm to which she belongs acting for the opponent of an existing client in the same or in a related matter. (But to the contrary see *Rakusen v Ellis, Munday and Clarke* [1912] 1 Ch 831 where it was said that there is no general rule that a solicitor who has acted in a particular matter for one party may not act in that matter for his opponent. See also *Flanagan v Pioneer Building Society Ltd* [2002] QSC 346, para 10.) No obligation of loyalty prevents a solicitor from acting for a former client's opponent in the same or any other matter provided the solicitor did not discharge the client for the purpose of representing the opponent (ibid).

[385] For the disclosure to client obligation of professionals who owe their clients a fiduciary obligation of loyalty see para 19.58 below.

[386] *Bolkiah v KPMG* [1999] 1 All ER 517, 528; *Re T and A* [2000] 1 FLR 859. cp *Skjevesland v Geveran Trading Co Ltd* [2002] EWCA Civ 1567 (barrister knew no confidential information, but had been a friend of the client's opponent); *Farrow Mortgage Services Pty Ltd v Mendall Properties Pty Ltd* [1995] 1 VR 1, 19.

B. Accidental Disclosure

information for B's benefit,[387] the disclosure or misuse can be prevented by equity. The case law concerns:

- firms of solicitors[387a] and forensic accountants[388] who have accepted instructions from a new client whose interests are in conflict with those of an existing or former client;[389]
- merger of firms of solicitors where one of the amalgamated firms previously acted for one side in contentious litigation and the other for the other;[390]
- representation of an opponent in litigation by a firm of solicitors that has taken on as an employee or partner a solicitor who previously acted for the claimant in another firm;[391]
- a firm of solicitors initially instructed by all the participants in a joint project and which is later asked to act for one participant against another in litigation about the project.[392]

When the claimant is the existing client of a solicitor, or firm of solicitors, the vehicle for equitable intervention is an action for breach of fiduciary duty.[393] When the claimant is an ex-client, it is an action for breach of confidence.[394] To persuade equity to intervene, a former client must establish two things:[395]

6.94

(1) that the professional or her firm is in possession of information which was and remains[396] confidential to the former client, and to the disclosure of which he has not consented; and

(2) that such information is or might be relevant to the matter on which the professional is, or is to be, instructed by the new client.

---

[387] *Davies v Davies* [1999] 3 FCR 745, 756.
[387a] eg *In the Matter of a Firm of Solicitors* [2000] 1 Lloyd's Rep 31; *Re T* [2000] 1 FLR 859.
[388] *Bolkiah v KPMG* [1999] 1 All ER 517; *Young v Robson Rhodes* [1999] 3 All ER 524. Secondary literature includes T Leng, 'Protecting confidential client information' (2000) 16 Professional Negligence 103; H McVea, '"Heard it Through the Grapevine": Chinese Walls and Former Client Confidentiality in Law Firms' (2000) 59 CLJ 370
[389] As regards barristers from the same chambers representing opposing clients see *Laker Airways Inc v FLS Aerospace Ltd* [2000] 1 WLR 113. For a detailed analysis of conflict of interest at the Bar see J Griffiths-Baker, *Serving Two Masters* (Oxford: 2002) 56 et seq.
[390] *David Lee & Co (Lincoln) Ltd v Coward Chance* [1991] 1 All ER 668.
[391] *Halewood International v Addleshaw Booth & Co* [2000] Lloyd's Rep PN 298; *Koch Shipping Inc v Richards Butler* [2002] EWCA Civ 1280. In this situation the defendant had no contractual or fiduciary responsibility to the claimant. cp *MacDonald Estate v Martin* [1990] 3 SCR 1235.
[392] *Ball v Druces* [2002] EWCA Civ 157.
[393] Clients of professionals who do not owe fiduciary duties would have to rely on the action for breach of confidence.
[394] *Bolkiah v KPMG* [1999] 1 All ER 517, 526–527.
[395] ibid at 527.
[396] It is not enough that the information was confidential when imparted if it has ceased to be confidential information by, for example, being read out in open court: *Halewood International v Addleshaw Booth & Co* [2000] Lloyd's Rep PN 298.

The burden of doing this is not normally a heavy one.[397] There is a presumption that information circulates freely within a firm of solicitors.[398] If the claimant discharges this burden, the defendant must demonstrate by clear and convincing evidence that the risk of accidental disclosure has been effectively eliminated.[399] The method usually employed to prevent a leak is a 'Chinese wall'.[400] This phrase refers to an information barrier that prevents communication of confidential information from one part of a firm to another. The effect is to split the firm into two. It will be easier to set up a ring-fence in a large firm than in a small one, and where only one individual poses a risk than where a whole team of professionals does.

Admissibility of Accidentally Disclosed and Intercepted Materials in Court Proceedings[401]

Confidential information

6.95 It is no objection to the admissibility of evidence in a trial, civil or criminal, that it is confidential.[402] In his dissenting judgment in *Rumping v DPP*, Viscount Radcliffe said:

> A husband may gasp or mutter to his wife some agonised self-incrimination intended for no ear in the world but her's: yet the law will receive and proceed on the evidence of the successful eavesdropper, professional amateur or accidental... An incriminating letter may be intercepted by any means: it may be snatched from the wife's hand after receipt, taken into custody if she has mislaid it accidentally, withdrawn from her possession by one means or another: in all these cases... a trophy may be carried into the court by the prosecution and, given proof that the prisoner is its author, the law has no rule that excludes it from weighing against him as a confession.[403]

---

[397] *Ball v Druces* [2002] EWCA Civ 157. The point was made (at para 23) that if the client had to specify very precisely the confidential information that might be misused, that might destroy the very subject matter of the application.

[398] City of London Law Society Working Party, *Review of Conflict Rules (draft)* (July 2000) para 4.7.

[399] *Bolkiah v KPMG* [1999] 1 All ER 517, 529.

[400] Lord Millett said in *Bolkiah v KPMG* [1999] 1 All ER 517, 531 that an effective Chinese wall 'needs to be an established part of the organisational structure of the firm, not created ad hoc' within the same department. But see *Halewood International v Addleshaw Booth & Co* [2000] Lloyd's Rep FN 298 and *Young v Robson Rhodes* [1999] 3 All ER 524, 539 where Laddie J said: '[i]t seems to me that all Lord Millett was saying was that Chinese walls which have become part of the fabric of the institution are more likely to work than those artificially put in place to meet a one-off problem.' If the client establishes only a relatively weak case that the solicitor has confidential information and/or that it is, or might be, relevant to the affairs of the new client this is something which can be taken into account in deciding whether there is a real, as opposed to a theoretical, risk of disclosure adverse to the former client's interests: *In the Matter of a Firm of Solicitors* [2000] 1 Lloyd's Rep 31, 32, 33.

[401] See P Matthews, 'Breach of confidence and legal privilege' [1981] 1 LS 77; N Andrews, 'The Influence of Equity Upon the Doctrine of Legal Professional Privilege' (1989) 105 LQR 608.

[402] See paras 15.08, 15.13 and 16.02 below. Contrast *Slavutych v Baker* (1975) 55 DLR (3d) 224; *Police v Georghiades* (1983) 2 Cyprus LR 33.

[403] [1962] 3 All ER 256, 266–267.

B. Accidental Disclosure

Discretionary exclusion of the evidence is possible in civil[404] and in criminal proceedings,[405] if the court can be persuaded that admitting intercepted or inadvertently disclosed confidential information would undermine the fairness of the trial. The fairness of both civil and criminal hearings is underpinned by Article 6(1) of the ECHR.[406]

Privileged information

The original document

Communications between a lawyer[407] and a client tend not only to be confidential but also privileged.[408] It is unclear whether legal professional privilege in the original of a document is extinguished if it finds its way through inadvertent disclosure into the hands of the privilege holder's litigation opponent. In *Calcraft v Guest* Lord Lindley said 'I take it that, as a general rule, one may say once privileged always privileged'.[409] In *Great Atlantic Insurance Co. v Home Insurance Co*[410] Templeman LJ offered the opinion that '[a] man who is entitled to assert privilege over a document does not waive that privilege by suffering the misfortune of the theft of those documents from his custody or from the custody of his solicitor'. Australian, Canadian and New Zealand courts have said that unintended disclosure does not necessarily destroy privilege in the original document.[411] But there is English authority to the contrary. In *Webster v James Chapman & Co*, Scott J said '[i]f the document has been disclosed, be it by trickery, accident or otherwise, the benefit and protection of legal privilege will have been lost'[412] and in *Guinness Peat Properties Ltd v Fitzroy Robinson Partnership* Slade LJ said 'privilege is essentially privilege from compulsory disclosure . . . once a privileged document has not only been disclosed but also inspected in the course of discovery, it is too late to put the clock back: the privilege is lost'.[413]

6.96

Auburn[414] argues that although confidentiality may be a substantive requirement for legal professional privilege to arise, involuntary loss of confidentiality from

6.97

---

[404] CPR, r 32. See also *Grobbelaar v Sun Newspapers*, The Times, 12 August 1999 and para 15.17 below.
[405] PACE, s 78 and *R v Sang* [1979] 2 All ER 1222. See also para 15.18 below.
[406] 'In the determination of his civil rights and obligations or of any criminal charge against him, everyone is entitled to a fair . . . hearing . . .'
[407] The privilege applies not only to solicitors and barristers but also to patent and trademark agents in respect of legal proceedings, to licensed conveyancers and to authorized advocates and litigators: see para 16.42 below.
[408] For the conditions for legal professional privilege to arise see ch 16.
[409] [1898] 1 QB 759, 761–762.
[410] [1981] 2 All ER 485, 494.
[411] *Goldberg v Ng* (1994) 33 NSWLR 639, 675; *National Insurance Co Ltd v Whirlybird Holdings Ltd* [1994] 2 NZLR 513; *Meltend Pty Ltd v Restoration Clinics of Australia Pty Ltd* (1997) 145 ALR 391; *Re Stevens and Prime Minister of Canada* (1997) 144 DLR (4th) 553, 566–567.
[412] [1989] 3 All ER 939, 946.
[413] [1987] 2 All ER 716, 729.
[414] J Auburn, *Legal Professional Privilege: Law and Theory* (Oxford: 2000) 207–210. Many other writers whom he cites take a different view. R Toulson and C Phipps, *Confidentiality* (London:

whatever cause does not determine privilege. Loss of privilege requires waiver or some relevant exception to legal professional privilege such as communication in furtherance of a crime.[415]

Admissibility of secondary evidence

6.98 The fact that privilege probably does not lapse when a privileged document is unintentionally disclosed is not the end of the privilege holder's worries. Once his opponent is aware of the contents of the privileged document, under English law[416] the latter can circumvent the privilege by adducing secondary evidence of the privileged document in the form of a copy or oral testimony about its contents. Secondary evidence of a privileged communication is admissible no matter how improper the manner of its obtaining. In *Calcraft v Guest*[417] the claimant by accident obtained possession of privileged documents belonging to the defendant. Copies were made before the originals were returned.[418] The question arose incidentally during the trial as to whether the copies were admissible. The court held that they were. It would have made no difference had the claimant used stealth to obtain them:[419]

> [I]t does not matter how the document came into the hands of the adversary or his witness: the party who would otherwise have been entitled to claim privilege for it can no longer do so.[420]

An eavesdropper who overhears a conversation between a client and his lawyer can give evidence of the fruits of his surveillance.[421] The one exception, recognized subsequently to *Calcraft v Guest* on grounds of public policy, is where the privileged material was taken from the privilege-holder, without consent, from within the precincts of a court.[422]

Exclusion in civil proceedings

6.99 The situation of a client engaged in civil litigation who has lost control of the content of a privileged communication is not as grave as may at first appear. For

---

1996) 184 state that 'confidentiality is a pre-requisite of . . . privilege'. See also N Andrews, 'The Influence of Equity upon the Doctrine of Legal Professional Privilege' (1989) 105 LQR 608, 612.

[415] See para 16.35 below.

[416] Contrast *R v Uljee* [1982] 1 NZLR 561 where an accidentally overheard communication between lawyer and client that was intended to be confidential was held inadmissible; Uniform Rules of Evidence 26; Federal Rules of Evidence, r 503(a)(4).

[417] [1898] 1 QB 759.

[418] On being returned these once again were privileged.

[419] *Lloyd v Mostyn* (1842) 152 ER 558, 560; *Waugh v British Railway Board* [1979] 2 All ER 1169, 1177; *English and American Insurance Ltd v Herbert Smith* [1988] FSR 232, 239.

[420] *Sixteenth Report of the Law Reform Committee* 1967 para 31.

[421] Wigmore, *Evidence in Trials at Common Law* (Boston: 1961) vol 8, para 2326. Contrast *R v Uljee* [1982] 1 NZLR 561.

[422] *ITC Film Distributors v Video Exchange Ltd* [1982] 2 All ER 241, 246.

B. Accidental Disclosure

reasons that will be explained shortly,[423] so long as the client is sufficiently alert to take timely pre-emptive action in equity the rule in *Calcraft v Guest* can be circumvented. Furthermore, under the Civil Procedure Rules 1998 (CPR), where 'a party inadvertently allows a privileged document to be inspected, the party who has inspected the document may use it or its contents only with the permission of the court'.[424] A privileged communication inadvertently disclosed in other circumstances may be amenable to exclusion under a more general discretion conferred by the CPR to 'exclude evidence that would otherwise be admissible'.[425]

6.100 The CPR exclusionary discretion must be exercised in accordance with the overriding objective of the CPR which is to try cases justly.[426] Dealing with cases justly includes inter alia 'ensuring that the parties are on an equal footing' and 'ensuring that [the case] is dealt with . . . fairly'. The privilege-holder is likely to argue that to admit the evidence is a disproportionate infringement of Article 8 and therefore unfair. His opponent might counter with the argument that exclusion is an infringement of the Article 6(1) right to a fair hearing which is absolute.[427] But is it unfair, and does it lead to an unjust trial, to deprive a litigant of probative evidence to which he ought not to have had access under a rule—that of legal professional privilege—that is designed to enable his opponent to have effective access to justice?[428]

Exclusion in criminal proceedings

6.101 A criminal defendant who is unfortunate enough to have a privileged communication fall into the hands of the prosecution can ask the judge to exclude the communication under Police and Criminal Evidence Act 1984, s 78.[429] The courts are not disposed toward exercising the discretion in the criminal client's favour if there is no suggestion of sharp practice by the prosecution.[430]

6.102 Where there has been police malpractice, a stay of proceedings is a possibility. In *R v Sutherland*[431] the police had deliberately set out to intercept the privileged communications of a number of co-defendants and their solicitors in the exercise yard of various police stations. Newman J halted the trial having concluded that the police misconduct was incompatible with Article 6 and unlawful under HRA, s 6(1). He cautioned against expecting a court to stay proceedings if interception

---

[423] See para 6.109 below.
[424] CPR, r 31.20. See para 6.108 below.
[425] CPR, r 32.1.
[426] CPR, r 1.1. Dealing with cases justly includes inter alia 'ensuring that the parties are on an equal footing', 'ensuring that it is dealt with . . . fairly'.
[427] See para 3.23 above.
[428] See para 18.08 below.
[429] cp *R v Tompkins* (1977) 67 Cr App R 181, 184. See also, *Willis v Governor of Her Majesty's Prison, Winchester* (Ch D, 21 December 1994).
[430] *R v Cottrill* [1997] Crim LR 56.
[431] Nottingham Crown Court, 29 January 2002.

of privileged material was not intentional. 'Circumstances can arise in which the police come into possession of privileged material by mistake. For example, it is not unusual for a solicitor to attend at his client's home to tender advice. If the home is subject to covert surveillance, accidental recording will occur . . . [I]t has not been submitted, in my judgment rightly so, that whenever the prosecution come into possession of privileged material, by accident or mistake, a prosecution must be stayed.'[432] Later in the same judgment he said that the mischief in a case of inadvertent and unintentional acquisition of privileged material in the course of a properly authorized covert surveillance might be curable.

> A senior officer should be immediately informed of the mistake which has occurred. The defence solicitor should be immediately informed of the fact that it has occurred, of the details and the circumstances, and all the contents of the material which has been obtained. As necessary, any officer who has become aware of the material, who is in the inquiry, could, if the circumstances so required, be moved from that inquiry forthwith. Prompt, transparent action will obviate the difficulties.[433]

Restraining the Use of Materials by Means of the Action for Breach of Confidence

Privileged materials

Enjoining use of the communication in civil proceedings

6.103 A litigant who is lucky or dishonest enough to discover the contents of a privileged communication by an opponent[434] is well advised to conceal this good fortune until the moment it is tendered in evidence. This is because a privilege-holder who has not intentionally waived the privilege[435] and who gets wind of the leak may bring a breach of confidence action to restrain use of the information and the return of the original document and any copies that have been made.[436] Separate proceedings do not have to be launched for this purpose.[437] There has been no breach of confidence proceedings of this nature since the HRA came into force. Will the HRA make it more difficult for the privilege-holder to obtain this

---

[432] Transcript p 11.
[433] Transcript p 44.
[434] The same applies if the privilege-holder is not the opponent: see eg *Rockefeller & Co Inc v Secretary for Justice* [2000] 3 HKC 48.
[435] For the rules on waiver see para 16.31 below.
[436] *Lord Ashburton v Pape* [1913] 2 Ch 469; *Goddard v Nationwide Building Society* [1986] 3 All ER 264, 270. P Matthews, 'Breach of confidence and legal privilege' [1981] LS 77, 91–93 contends that equity cannot enjoin the use of secondary evidence of a privilege communication in a trial. This is not the view of the courts: see eg *Frank Truman Export Ltd v Metropolitan Police Commissioner* [1977] QB 952, 958. The distinction between admissibility and enjoinability is criticized as schizophrenic by D Vaver in 'Keeping Secrets, Civilly Speaking' (1991–92) 13 Advocates' Quarterly 334, 344.
[437] When injunctive relief is urgently needed against an opponent it can be obtained without issuing process if there is an undertaking to issue a pro forma writ: *Goddard v Nationwide Building Society* [1986] 3 All ER 264, 271; *Rockefeller & Co Inc v Secretary for Justice* [2000] 3 HKC 48.

B. Accidental Disclosure

equitable relief? The privilege-holder's opponent will argue that being enjoined from using the information interferes with his right to a fair hearing. There is a good chance that this argument will fail. If the opponent has not relied upon the inadvertently disclosed information to change his position, what detriment will he suffer if a court restores the privilege? It is no more than the loss of evidence to which he had no entitlement—an information windfall.

Def American Inc v Phonogram Ltd[438] illustrates how equity may come to the aid of the privilege-holder. A private telephone conversation involving the claimant's US attorney was intercepted and a tape recording made of the interception by a radio hack who then sold it to the defendants for £1,000. The claimant applied to the Chancery Division for an injunction to stop the defendant using the intercepted material. The defendant's response was that privilege had been lost because the tape had been used in open court in previous interlocutory proceedings. The claimant demonstrated that no more than 1 per cent of the tape's transcript had in fact been referred to in open court and the injunction was granted. *Def American Inc* involved impropriety by the hacker and, arguably, also the defendant. But the result would have been the same had this not been so.

6.104

The principle of *Ashburton v Pape* applies where there is 'an accidental escape of information to the third party'[439] and where the defendant to the breach of confidence action acted innocently though the person responsible for the escape did not.[440] The law's paramount concern is to maintain the sanctity of privilege.

6.105

> The court does not, so far as privileged documents are concerned, weigh the privilege and consider whether the privilege should outweigh the importance that the document should be before the court at the trial, or the importance that possession of the document and the ability to use it might have for the advocate.[441]

Communication required for criminal proceedings Equity is loathe to deprive a prosecutor of relevant evidence, even privileged communications,[442] that was not obtained in bad faith.[443] Equity will, however, aid a defendant against a prosecutor if use of a privileged material will undermine the efficacy of his access to

6.106

---

[438] The Times, 16 August 1994.
[439] per Sir Nicolas Browne-Wilkinson, *English & American Insurance Ltd v Herbert Smith* [1988] FSR 232, 237.
[440] *Goddard v Nationwide Building Society* [1986] 3 All ER 264, 272. See also *ITC Film Distributors Ltd v Video Exchange Ltd* [1982] 2 All ER 241, 247; *Nationwide Building Society v Various Solicitors (No 2)* [1998] All ER (D) 119.
[441] per Dillon LJ, *Derby & Co v Weldon (No 8)* [1991] 1 WLR 73, 99. See also *Goddard v Nationwide Building Society* [1986] 3 All ER 264, 272; *Pizzey v Ford Motor Co Ltd* [1994] PIQR P15. A contrary ruling at first instance in *Webster v James Chapman & Co* [1989] 3 All ER 939 has been disapproved.
[442] *Butler v Board of Trade* [1970] 3 All ER 593, 599–600; *R v Tompkins* (1977) 67 Cr App R 181,184. Contrast *R v Uljee* [1982] 1 NZLR 561.
[443] *R v Cotrill* [1997] Crim LR 56. The position is otherwise if the police have cynically disregarded legal constraints on the interception of privileged material: see para 14.122 below.

legal representation. In *Willis v Governor of Her Majesty's Prison, Winchester*[444] a privileged letter between the claimant and his solicitor was inadvertently intercepted in breach of prison rules by a prison correspondence officer. The letter contained highly incriminating material concerning the death of two people. Robert Walker J, noting the 'very strong public interest, backed by the European Commission of Human Rights and the European Court of Human Rights, in ensuring that remand prisoners have unimpeded access to legal advice for the purposes of their defence',[445] decided to grant a declaration against the Prison Service 'that the letter should be handed to the plaintiff's solicitors, and that copies of it should be handed over or destroyed, and that the contents of the letter should not be disclosed to any other person'.

6.107 Yet to be considered by a court is whether an injunction should be granted to restrain use of a privileged document or secondary evidence of it that helps to prove someone's innocence. Had the solicitors for the stepson in *R v Derby Magistrates' Court, ex p B*[446] inadvertently disclosed their instructions to the stepfather, would equity have prevented the stepfather from using the information in his defence? Just because the privilege-holder is entitled by a common law rule to resist disclosure of exculpatory evidence[447] does not mean that equity, a court of conscience, will compel the suppression of information inadvertently disclosed by the privilege-holder, or his agent, that exonerates the breach-of-confidence defendant of a serious crime in circumstances in which the privilege-holder will suffer no appreciable detriment.[448]

6.108 **Accidental disclosure of privileged material during pre-trial disclosure** Special rules apply in civil proceedings when a privileged document is through oversight included amongst documents made available for inspection by an opponent during the pre-trial disclosure stage of litigation.[449] The CPR allow the opponent to rely on the inadvertently disclosed privileged document or its content only with leave of the court.[450] Before 1998 the opponent could be prevented by the privilege-holder from using an inadvertently disclosed privileged document by an injunction.

6.109 In *Guinness Peat Properties Ltd v Fitzroy Robinson Partnership* the defendants' solicitors accidentally omitted to claim privilege for a letter from the defendants to their insurers and included it in the file of correspondence sent to the claimants.

---

[444] Ch D, 21 December 1994.
[445] per Robert Walker J, *Willis v Governor of Her Majesty's Prison, Winchester* (Ch D, 21 December 1994).
[446] [1995] 4 All ER 526.
[447] *R v Derby Magistrates' Court, ex p B* [1995] 4 All ER 526.
[448] cp *Rockefeller & Co Inc v Secretary for Justice* [2000] 3 HKLRD 351.
[449] And also when privileged documents are inadvertently disclosed in support of an application to strike out a claim: *Breeze v John Stacey* [2000] CP Rep 77.
[450] CPR, r 31.20. This shifts the onus from the privilege-holder to the party wishing to use the document

B. Accidental Disclosure

On discovering the error, the defendants' solicitors applied for an order restraining the claimants from using at the trial the copy they had made. Slade L J said:

(1) Where solicitors for one party to litigation have, on discovery, mistakenly included a document for which they could properly have claimed privilege... the court will ordinarily permit them to amend the list... at any time before inspection of the document has taken place.
(2) ... once in such circumstances the other party has inspected the document ... the general rule is that it is too late for the party who seeks to claim privilege to attempt to correct the mistake by applying for injunctive relief...
(3) If, however, the other party or his solicitor either (a) has procured inspection of the relevant document by fraud or (b) on inspection, realises that he has been permitted to see the document only by reason of an obvious mistake, the court has power to intervene for the protection of the mistaken party by the grant of an injunction... Furthermore... it should ordinarily intervene in such cases. ...[451]

The second and third of Slade LJ's principles remain relevant to an application for leave under the CPR.[452] If the privilege-holder can prove that it must have been obvious to a reasonable solicitor that the privileged document was disclosed in error, there is nothing unfair about depriving the opponent of its use. Other factors that may be relevant include:

- the extent of the claim to privilege in the documents;
- the nature and purpose of the disclosed documents;
- the complexity of the discovery;
- the way in which discovery was made;
- the surrounding circumstances;
- equitable grounds for refusing relief such as inordinate delay or anything that makes it impossible to restore the status quo.[453]

6.110

Confidential information

Confidential material is not accorded the same protection as privileged material. An injunction will be refused to stop the use of confidential information in litigation unless legislation forbids its use or a claim to public interest immunity is made out:

[The equitable jurisdiction] can prevail over the rule of evidence only in cases where privilege can be claimed. The equitable jurisdiction is well able to extend, for example,

6.111

---

[451] [1987] 2 All ER 716, 730–731. See also *Nationwide Building Society v Various Solicitors (No 2)* [1998] All ER (D) 119.
[452] *Breeze v John Stacey & Sons Ltd* [2000] CP Rep 77; *Al Fayed v Commissioner of Police of the Metropolis* [2002] EWHC 562, QB.
[453] per Curtis J, *Al Fayed v Commissioner of Police of the Metropolis* [2002] EWHC 562, QB, para 27. In this case it was relevant that the two inadvertently disclosed documents had been amongst 3,900 documents copied in 16 volumes. Also, that the documents, which contained the opinion of counsel, were subject to class public interest immunity.

to the grant of an injunction to restrain an unauthorised disclosure of confidential communications between priest and penitent or doctor and patient. But those communications are not privileged in legal proceedings and I do not believe that equity would restrain a litigant who already had a record of such a communication in his possession from using it for the purposes of his litigation. It cannot be the function of equity to accord a de facto privilege to communications in respect of which no privilege can be claimed. Equity follows the law.[454]

The courts cannot consistently hold at trial that evidence given in confidence that is relevant and necessary is compellable (as to which see *Att-Gen v Mulholland*)[455] *and* prior to the trial issue an injunction restraining a party from using information that is relevant but has been inadvertently disclosed.

---

[454] per Nourse LJ, *Goddard v Nationwide Building Society* [1986] 3 All ER 264, 271.
[455] [1963] 1 All ER 767, 771 and see para 15.16 below.

7

SUING AND TRACING THIRD PARTIES AND STRANGERS

A. Tracing	7.02	Breach of Confidence	7.20
Introduction	7.02	Breach of Fiduciary Duty	7.35
Discovery Proceedings	7.03	Tort	7.36
B. Actions Against Third Parties and Strangers	7.20	Copyright	7.44

The subjects of this chapter are: **7.01**

(1) the problem of tracing those who are or were in possession of personal information when they should not have been as a prelude to taking action against the person(s) responsible for the unauthorized dissemination of confidential personal information; and
(2) the potential civil liability of third parties[1] and strangers[2] for the unauthorized use or disclosure of personal information and the amenability of such parties to injunctions.

A. Tracing

Introduction

In order for the client to seek an injunction to prevent disclosure of confidential **7.02** personal information by an interceptor, stranger or third party, or compensation from such persons for any disclosure that has already occurred, the client must know who to sue. There may be not just one but many third parties or strangers. The opportunities for the disclosure of information are infinite. If A intercepts information about B, A can pass that information to C, D and E, and each of these

---

[1] Someone who, directly or indirectly, receives information from a confidant who has disclosed the information in breach of confidence.
[2] Someone who receives information from an interceptor.

persons can pass it on to numerous others. Like an ink drop on blotting paper, the information can spread in many directions in no time. To prevent further dissemination, the client will have to identify and muzzle every person with knowledge of the information. If the identity of these people is not volunteered by those who know it, the only way the client can compel disclosure of their identity is by bringing discovery proceedings.[3]

Discovery Proceedings

Introduction

7.03 It is useful to distinguish between:

(1) an application for discovery against someone who has received and has passed on, or simply received, information unaware that it is the subject of an obligation of confidentiality (the innocent stranger or third party); and

(2) an application for discovery against a wrongdoer.

Discovery proceedings against persons in the second category are likely to be a procedural remedy that forms an interlocutory part of ordinary litigation. Discovery proceedings against those in the first category are likely to be a stand-alone affair. As the courts move toward treating anyone who acquires obviously confidential information as owing the client a duty of confidentiality,[4] the number of persons falling into the first category will shrink.

Discovery against innocent facilitators

Discovering the identity of a wrongdoer

7.04 It is a long-standing principle that discovery cannot be obtained against someone who had no involvement in the wrong of which a complaint is made.[5] However, in *Norwich Pharmacal Co v Customs and Excise Commissioners*[6] the House of Lords confirmed that equity can compel a person who unwittingly 'facilitated' wrongdoing by an unidentified party, but who incurs no personal liability for the wrongdoing, to identify the wrongdoer.[7] In the *Norwich Pharmacal* case discovery was obtained against the Customs and Excise Commissioners who, through the exercise of their statutory powers, had given clearance for the importation of chemicals infringing the claimant's patents.

---

[3] Supreme Court Act 1981, s 37(1).
[4] See para 6.07 above.
[5] *Norwich Pharmacal Co v Customs and Excise Commissioners* [1973] 2 All ER 943, 948; *Ricci v Chow* [1987] 3 All ER 534, 540–541. This is known as the 'mere witness' rule.
[6] [1973] 2 All ER 943.
[7] See now also *Ashworth Hospital Authority v MGN Ltd* [2002] UKHL 29; [2002] 1 WLR 2033, paras 1, 26.

A. Tracing

[I]f through no fault of his own a person gets mixed up in the tortious acts of others so as to facilitate their wrongdoing he may incur no personal liability but he comes under a duty to assist the person who has been wronged by giving him full information and disclosing the identity of the wrongdoers. I do not think that it matters whether he became so mixed up by voluntary action on his part or because it was his duty to do what he did. But justice requires that he should co-operate in righting the wrong if he unwittingly facilitated its perpetration.[8]

The Data Protection Act 1998 (DPA) is not an obstacle to disclosure[9] so long as the applicable conditions of its first and second Schedules are satisfied.[10] To achieve compliance the court must consider whether the disclosure is warranted having regard to the rights and freedoms or the legitimate interests of the client.[11]

Discovering the identity of an innocent stranger or third party

Suppose that an interceptor, X, unlawfully acquires confidential information about a client from a professional and passes it to A. Thereafter, A, who is not aware of the breach of confidence, passes the information to B. Suppose also that innocent receipt of the information is sufficient to make B 'mixed up' in X's wrongdoing. Can the client obtain an order from a court against B (whose identity is known) to disclose the identity of A (whose identity is unknown) in order to make a discovery application against A to identify X? 7.05

The extension of the *Norwich Pharmacal* jurisdiction to permit disclosure of the identity of innocent parties was considered in *CHC Software Care Ltd v Hopkins & Wood*[12] and in *Roberts v Jump Knitwear Ltd*,[13] respectively malicious slander and copyright actions. In *CHC Software Care Ltd v Hopkins & Wood*[14] Mummery J held that the *Norwich Pharmacal Co* jurisdiction was 'not confined to the case of identifying wrongdoers'. An order for discovery was made to enable the claimants to contact recipients of a letter that was said to amount to a trade libel to enable the claimant to mitigate his loss. 7.06

In *Roberts v Jump Knitwear Ltd* the claimant wanted the names and addresses of customers to whom the defendants, the wrongdoers, had supplied knitwear that infringed the claimant's copyright. The customers' lack of knowledge of the infringing character of the garments meant that they could not be sued for selling 7.07

---

[8] per Lord Reid, *Norwich Pharmacal Co v Customs and Excise Commissioners* [1973] 2 All ER 943, 948.
[9] DPA, s 35(2) permits disclosure for the purposes of legal proceedings or prospective legal proceedings or for the purpose of obtaining legal advice or exercising, establishing or defending legal rights.
[10] *Totalise plc v Motley Fool Ltd* [2001] EWCA Civ 1897; [2002] 1 WLR 1233, para 23.
[11] DPA Sch 2, para 6; *Totalise plc v Motley Fool Ltd* [2001] EWCA Civ 1897; [2002] 1 WLR 1233, para 24.
[12] [1993] FSR 241.
[13] [1981] FSR 527.
[14] [1993] FSR 241, 250.

or offering the knitwear for sale.[15] *Norwich Pharmacal*, said Falconer J, was 'quite clearly restricted to pursuing wrongdoers'.[16] If wrongdoers who are defendants to the substantive action will not be ordered to give discovery of the identity of innocent third parties then a fortiori an innocent third party will not be ordered to do so.

7.08 *CHC Software Care Ltd v Hopkins* rather than *Roberts v Jump Knitwear Ltd* was followed by Jacob J in *Jade Engineering (Coventry) Ltd v Antiference Window Systems Ltd*,[17] a copyright case in which the claimant wanted to discover the identity of an Italian manufacturer of a grooving machine (who was assumed not to have notice of the claimant's copyright) in order to prevent him from supplying further machines in the United Kingdom and abroad that infringed the claimant's design right. As a matter of principle it seems quite unobjectionable to allow discovery of the identity of an innocent intermediary.[18] The courts will order an innocent banker to disclose the identity of an innocent party to whom the claimant's money has been fraudulently transferred so that it can be traced.[19] Why then not assist the client who wants to protect his privacy to discover against whom to take out injunctions or the professional to discover the mole in his practice?

Discovery against wrongdoers

7.09 If there is no Article 10 issue,[20] neither client nor professional will have difficulty persuading a court to exercise the *Norwich Pharmacal* jurisdiction to compel a wrongdoer to disclose the identity of:

- the source of the leak;[21]
- intermediaries, innocent[22] or otherwise.[23]

In *Michael O'Mara Books Ltd v Express Newspapers plc*[24] the claimant was said to be entitled 'virtually as of right' to an order requiring a defendant to state the names and addresses of all those whom they had supplied with material the copy-

---

[15] Copyright Act 1956, s 5(3).
[16] [1981] FSR 527, 534. But see *Sega Enterprises Ltd v Alca Electronics Ltd* [1982] FSR 516.
[17] [1996] FSR 461. A third party without knowledge who is in possession of infringing copies of copyright material is a tortfeasor under the Copyright, Design and Patents Act 1988. Technically, therefore, *Roberts v Jump Knitwear Ltd* [1981] FSR 527 could have been distinguished.
[18] This is possibly implicit in *Ashworth Hospital Authority v MGN Ltd* [2002] UKHL 29; [2002] 1 WLR 2033, paras 26, 30, 34. cp *Carlton Film Distributors v VDC Ltd* [2003] EWHC 616 (ch).
[19] *Bankers Trust Company v Shapira* [1980] 1 WLR 1274, 1282. Strictly, this is not an exercise of the discovery jurisdiction: *Re Murphy's Settlement* [1998] 3 All ER 1, 9.
[20] See para 7.12 below.
[21] eg *Mersey Care NHS Trust v Ackroyd* [2002] EWHC 2115.
[22] *Jade Engineering (Coventry) Ltd v Antiference Window Systems Ltd* [1996] FSR 461. See also *Adams v Attridge* (QB, 8 October 1998).
[23] *Ashworth Hospital Authority v MGN Ltd* [2001] 1 All ER 991, 1005, CA.
[24] [1998] EMLR 383.

A. Tracing

right of which was vested in the claimant. Discovery will be ordered even if the claimant has no intention of bringing legal proceedings against anyone. The only requirement is that the claimant has the intention to vindicate his rights.[25] In *British Steel Corporation v Granada Television Ltd*[26] Granada was made to reveal the identity of a disloyal employee who had passed confidential documents to the television company during a strike at BSC so that BSC could sack the employee.

Parameters of the jurisdiction

The *Norwich Pharmacal* jurisdiction is still evolving and certain details have either only recently been clarified or remain to be worked out: 7.10

(1) A wrong for the purpose of the *Norwich Pharmacal* jurisdiction includes all of the following: a criminal offence,[27] breach of confidence,[28] breach of contract,[29] infringement of copyright,[30] defamation and injurious falsehood.[31]

(2) In *Axa Equity & Life Assurance Plc v National Westminster Bank Plc*[32] Morritt LJ said that it was not 'necessary that, as facilitators, [the discovery defendants] should have come under any liability themselves but they must have been so involved as to justify treating them differently from the bystander with whom such a person was contrasted by Lord Reid'. The fact that the claimant's property passed through the defendant's hands is enough.[33] By analogy innocent receipt of information (without further transmission) should suffice to attract the jurisdiction.

(3) Opinion is divided as to whether the claimant to discovery must show a strong prima facie case that his rights have been infringed.[34] In *P v T Ltd*[35] the claimant did not know whether a tort had been committed. Equity lent its assistance so that he could discover whether he had a viable cause of action for

---

[25] *BSC v Granada Television* [1981] 1 All ER 417, 479.
[26] [1981] 1 All ER 417. See also *Camelot Group Plc v Centaur* [1998] 1 All ER 251; *Ashworth Hospital Authority v MGN Ltd* [2002] UKHL 29; [2002] 1 WLR 2033.
[27] *Ashworth Hospital Authority v MGN Ltd* [2002] UKHL 29; [2002] 1 WLR 2033, paras 53 et seq.
[28] *BSC v Granada Television* [1981] 1 All ER 417, 442–443, 457, 479; *Interbrew SA v Financial Times Ltd* [2002] EWCA Civ 274; [2002] Lloyd's Rep 229. The tracing order in *Blair v Lister* (QB, 2000, WL 33116509) was presumably made on this basis. If there is a public interest defence to the disclosure there is no wrongdoing: cp *Mersey Care NHS Trust v Ackroyd* [2002] EWHC 2115, paras 22, 27.
[29] *Ashworth Hospital Authority v MGN Ltd* [2001] 1 All ER 991, CA; *Carlton Film Distributors v VDC Ltd* [2003] EWHC 616 (ch), para 14.
[30] *RCA Corp v Reddingtons Rare Records* [1974] 1 WLR 1445, 1446.
[31] *P v T Ltd* [1997] 4 All ER 200, 209.
[32] [1998] CLC 1177.
[33] *Norwich Pharmacal Co v Customs and Excise Commissioners* [1973] 2 All ER 943.
[34] Cases that favour this include: *D v NSPCC* [1976] 2 All ER 993, 998; *RCA Corp v Reddingtons Rare Records* [1974] 1 WLR 1445, 1447; *Doyle v Commissioner of An Garda Siochana* [1998] 1 ILRM 229.
[35] [1997] 4 All ER 200, 208.

defamation or injurious falsehood. Protection of the claimant's reputation was considered of paramount importance.[36]

(4) Does the *Norwich Pharmacal* jurisdiction allow a court to order disclosure of anything besides the identity of the wrongdoer?[37] It seems so, if the information is essential to enable an action to proceed to trial.[38]

Points of procedure

7.11 The costs of an application are likely to have to be borne by the client.[39] The order for discovery is discretionary[40] and may be refused if the advantage of the order to the client is outweighed by the detriment to the defendant or to the party whose identity is sought[41] or would involve a violation of the latter's Convention rights. For this reason a defendant who owes an obligation of confidentiality to the third party should not volunteer information in anticipation of a *Norwich Pharmacal* order.[42] Where appropriate,[43] the defendant can tell the third party what is going on and offer to pass on to the court the third party's objections to the order. Indeed, the court may require that this to be done.[44] The chances are that the third party's objections will be rejected. To date the courts have attached supreme importance to righting legal wrongs,[45] except in cases involving media defendants.

Discovery of media sources[46]

Contempt of Court Act 1981, s 10

7.12 Purpose of s 10 A journalist has an absolute professional obligation, laid down in the National Union of Journalists' code of conduct, to protect sources.[47] The

---

[36] ibid, 209.
[37] *Axa Equity & Life Assurance Plc v National Westminster Bank Plc* [1998] CLC 1177.
[38] *Société Romanaise de la Chaussure FA v British Shoe Corporation Ltd* [1991] FSR 1, 5; *P v T Ltd* [1997] 4 All ER 200, approved on this point in *Ashworth Hospital Authority v MGN Ltd* [2002] UKHL 29; [2002] 1 WLR 2033, para 57; *Kalmneft v Denton Wilde Sapte* QB Leeds Mercantile Court MERC No 1 MC 000410 (2002), para 17; *Carlton Film Distributors v VDC Ltd* [2003] EWHC 616 (ch).
[39] *Norwich Pharmacal Co v Customs and Excise Commissioners* [1973] 2 All ER 943, 970; *Totalise plc v Motley Fool Ltd* [2001] EWCA Civ 1897; [2002] 1 WLR 1233, paras 29–30; *Ashworth Hospital Authority v MGN Ltd* [2002] UKHL 29; [2002] 1 WLR 2033, para 26.
[40] *Ashworth Hospital Authority v MGN Ltd* [2002] UKHL 29; [2002] 1 WLR 2033, paras 2, 36.
[41] cp *Arab Monetary Fund v Hashim (No 5)* [1992] 2 All ER 911, 919; *Merchantile Group (Europe) AG v Aiyela* [1994] 1 All ER 110, 115.
[42] *Totalise plc v Motley Fool Ltd* [2001] EWCA Civ 1897; [2002] 1 WLR 1233.
[43] It would not be appropriate if communicating with the third party is likely to trigger evasive action by the third party.
[44] cp *Totalise plc v Motley Fool Ltd* [2001] EWCA Civ 1897; [2002] 1 WLR 1233, para 27.
[45] Y Cripps, 'Judicial Proceedings and Refusals to Disclose the Identity of Sources of Information' [1984] CLJ 266, 275.
[46] M Tugendhat and I Christie (eds), *The Law of Privacy and the Media* (Oxford: 2002) ch 14; M Moncrieff, 'No names . . . unless the court decides otherwise', Guardian, 8 April 2002, 6–7.
[47] G Robertson and A Nicol, *Robertson and Nicol on Media Law* (4th edn, London: 2002) 253 et seq. See also Council of Europe, Committee of Ministers, Recommendation R (2000) 7 on the right of journalists not to disclose the sources of their information, http://www.coe.int/cm.

A. Tracing

exercise of the *Norwich Pharmacal* jurisdiction runs counter to this professional obligation. If the defendant treats the professional obligation as paramount the defendant may put himself in contempt of court. This dilemma for the media industry is addressed in s 10 of the Contempt of Court Act 1981 which states:

> No court may require a person to disclose, nor is any person guilty of contempt of court for refusing to disclose, the source of information contained in a publication for which he is responsible, unless it be established to the satisfaction of the court that disclosure is necessary in the interests of justice or national security or for the prevention of disorder or crime.

Section 10, it will immediately be apparent, does not give unqualified support to the journalist's professional obligation of confidentiality to a source.

The pre-1981 position Before s 10 was enacted, it was the practice of courts to take into account the conscientious objections of journalists to breaching undertakings of confidentiality to their sources but the court would order disclosure if satisfied that the public interest in disclosure exceeded the public interest in non-disclosure which was generally held to be the case.[48] Section 10 'varied this discretion or practice to the extent that, unless the exceptional circumstances were established to its satisfaction, the court was bound to refuse to require any person to disclose the source of information contained in a publication'.[49]   7.13

Scope of s 10 Section 10 has been given a wide construction.[50] The section applies both to information that has been and is to be published.[51] 'Publication' includes any speech, writing, broadcast or other communication addressed to the public or any section of the public.[52] 'Information' includes photographs.[53] The media is the chief beneficiary of s 10, but does not have to be involved.[54] The section applies to all courts and any other tribunal or body exercising judicial power[55] irrespective of the nature of the proceedings or cause of action.[56] If the defendant shows that there is 'a reasonable chance' that the identity of a source will be exposed,[57] the prohibition bites and the client has the burden of showing a   7.14

---

[48] eg *BSC v Granada Television* [1981] 1 All ER 417, 455.
[49] per Sir John Donaldson MR, *Secretary of State for Defence v Guardian Newspapers Ltd* [1984] 1 All ER 453, 457.
[50] *X Ltd v Morgan-Grampian (Publishers) Ltd* [1990] 2 All ER 1, 7; *Mersey Care NHS Trust v Ackroyd* [2002] EWHC 2115, para 31.
[51] *X Ltd v Morgan-Grampian (Publishers) Ltd* [1990] 2 All ER 1, 7, 17.
[52] Contempt of Court Act 1981, ss 2(1), 19.
[53] *Handmade Films (Productions) Ltd v Express Newspapers plc* [1986] FSR 463.
[54] *Secretary of State for Defence v Guardian Newspapers Ltd* [1984] 3 All ER 601, 608. There must, however, be an intention to publish to the public at large or to a section of the public.
[55] This does not include the Professional Conduct Committee of the GMC: *GMC v BBC* [1998] 1 WLR 515.
[56] *Secretary of State for Defence v Guardian Newspapers Ltd* [1984] 3 All ER 601, 606–607.
[57] There is no need to show that the source would definitely be identified: *Secretary of State for Defence v Guardian Newspapers Ltd* [1984] 3 All ER 601, 607.

'compelling case'[58] (but nevertheless to the civil standard)[59] 'that disclosure is *necessary* in the interests of justice or national security or for the prevention of disorder or crime'.[60] There are no exceptions to this. If the source disclosed material subject to legal professional privilege, the client must still make out one of the four permitted grounds for ordering disclosure.[61] The application of s10 is not confined to the pre-trial stages of litigation: it may justify refusal to answer questions in the witness box.

7.15 **Presumption against disclosure** The 'interests of justice' exception is the most obvious reason for removing the shield when it is a client or professional who is trying to trace the route by which confidential personal information reached the media.[62] The phrase has been generously interpreted to include 'the exercise of legal rights and self-protection from legal wrongs, whether or not by court action'.[63] In deciding whether outing the source is 'in the interests of justice', the court starts from the presumption that it is contrary to the public interest to require the media to disclose information that may lead to the identification of a source.[64]

Impact of Article 10 of the ECHR

7.16 The interpretation and application of s 10 must conform to Article 10 of the European Convention on Human Rights (ECHR) as far as possible.[65] The key to this is the word 'necessary' in s 10. To be 'necessary', 'disclosure must meet a pressing social need, must be the only practical way of doing so, must be accompanied by safeguards against abuse and must not be such as to destroy the essence of the primary right'.[66] The net effect is to require that the client show a substantial private interest in identifying the wrongdoer which 'on the facts of the case is so important that it overrides the public interest in protecting jour-

---

[58] *John v Express Newspapers Ltd* [2000] 3 All ER 257, para 24.
[59] *Secretary of State for Defence v Guardian Newspapers Ltd* [1984] 3 All ER 601, 617–618.
[60] Italics added.
[61] *Saunders v Punch Ltd* [1998] 1 All ER 234, 241; *John v Express Newspapers* [2000] 3 All ER 257.
[62] In *X v Y* [1988] 2 All ER 648, 665 a health authority failed to persuade Rose J, on the balance of probabilities, that disclosure was necessary for the prevention of crime since prevention of crime was not one of the claimant's tasks and a criminal investigation was not the intended or likely consequence of disclosure.
[63] per Sedley LJ, *Interbrew SA v Financial Times Ltd* [2002] EWCA Civ 274; [2002] 2 Lloyd's Rep 229, para 17. This is confirmed in *Ashworth Hospital Authority v MGN Ltd* [2002] UKHL 29; [2002] 1 WLR 2033.
[64] *John v Express Newspapers* [2000] 3 All ER 257, 266. See also *Interbrew SA v Financial Times Ltd* [2002] EWCA Civ 274; [2002] 2 Lloyd's Rep 229, para 50.
[65] *Ashworth Hospital Authority v MGN Ltd* [2001] 1 All ER 991, para 78; *Interbrew SA v Financial Times Ltd* [2002] EWCA Civ 274; [2002] 2 Lloyd's Rep 229, paras 32, 38.
[66] *Interbrew SA v Financial Times Ltd* [2002] EWCA Civ 274; [2002] 2 Lloyd's Rep 229, para 50.

A. Tracing

nalistic sources in order to ensure free communication of information to and through the press'.[67]

From the cases the following factors can be culled as relevant to the decision whether an order is 'necessary': **7.17**

(1) The existence of a justifiable fear of future leaks.[68]
(2) All other reasonable means have been tried unsuccessfully to identify the source.[69]
(3) The *claimant* had no plans to make the leaked information public.[70] Past or future public disclosure of the information by someone other than the claimant (for example, if the claimant is the professional, by the client) does not rule out an order that is needed to track down a wrongdoer.[71]
(4) The type of information leaked. When the information that was leaked is personal the Article 8 right to respect for private life has to be considered. In *Ashworth Hospital Authority v MGN* Lord Phillips MR described the disclosure to a tabloid newspaper of the hospital records of a notorious child-murderer, Ian Brady, by an unknown hospital employee as:

> an attack on the area of confidentiality which should be safeguarded in any democratic society. The protection of patient information is of vital concern to the National Health Service and, I suspect, to health services throughout Europe. This is an exceptional case. If the order . . . discourages press sources from disclosing similar information in the future, this will be no bad thing.[72]

---

[67] per Lord Phillips, *Ashworth Hospital Authority v MGN Ltd* [2001] 1 All ER 991, CA, para 90. See also *Camelot Group v Centaur Ltd* [1998] 1 All ER 251, 259; *Interbrew SA v Financial Times Ltd* [2002] EWCA Civ 274; [2002] 2 Lloyd's Rep 229, paras 25–26. cp *X Ltd v Morgan-Grampian (Publishers) Ltd* [1990] 2 All ER 1, 9, 16.

[68] *Ashworth Hospital Authority v MGN Ltd* [2002] UKHL 29; [2002] 1 WLR 2033, para 17. cp *John Reid Enterprises Ltd v Pell* [1999] EMLR 675 (serious effect of failing to detect the leak on the claimant's business emphasized).

[69] *Special Hospital Service Authority v Hyde* (1994) 20 BMLR 75; *John v Express Newspapers* [2000] 3 All ER 257, 265; *Ashworth Hospital Authority v MGN Ltd* [2002] UKHL 29; [2002] 1 WLR 2033, para 19.

[70] HRA, s 12(4)(i) requires courts to have regard to the extent to which material is about to become publicly available.

[71] *Ashworth Hospital Authority v MGN Ltd* [2002] UKHL 29; [2002] 1 WLR 2033, paras 4, 31, 66. In this case a patient in a secure hospital had put his medical information into the public domain. This did not prevent the hospital obtaining a disclosure order against a newspaper to enable it to discover the identity of the employee responsible for supplying the patient's medical record to the newspaper, in breach of his contract of employment. Because of the action of the patient, the hospital would not have been able to maintain an action for breach of confidence in equity against the source, the intermediary or the newspaper.

[72] *Ashworth Hospital Authority v MGN Ltd* [2001] 1 All ER 991, CA, para 99. Approved *Ashworth Hospital Authority v MGN Ltd* [2002] UKHL 29; [2002] 1 WLR 2033, paras 65–66. See also *Mersey Care NHS Trust v Ackroyd* [2002] EWHC 2115, paras 29–30.

The court may be less concerned about the leaking of non-sensitive personal information even if the information affects a professional-client relationship.[73]

(5) how effective an order is likely to be in establishing the identity of the source.[74]

Judicial opinion is divided about the relevance of two further factors: (1) the motive or purpose of the source in making the disclosure,[75] and (2) the method by which the leaked information was obtained, for example, theft.[76]

7.18 Decisions about the application of s10 are decisions of law and not discretion.[77] However, once the court has decided that s10 permits a journalist to be ordered to disclose a source, the court still has a residual discretion whether or not to make the order.[78]

Delivery up of property that discloses the source of a leak

7.19 There are occasions when obtaining the return of some physical object might enable the identity of the person responsible for disseminating the confidential personal information to be discovered. This method of tracing can only be used where the client has a property right in the physical object, usually a document, and the physical object has not been destroyed.[79] The court has a discretion to refuse delivery up of property[80] and, apart from this, will refuse an order to return

---

[73] Consider *John v Express Newspapers* [2000] 3 All ER 257.

[74] *Att-Gen v Lundin* (1982) 75 Cr App R 90; *Interbrew SA v Financial Times Ltd* [2002] 1 Lloyd's Rep 542, Ch, para 32.

[75] Against considering: *Ashworth Hospital Authority v MGN Ltd* [2001] 1 All ER 991, CA, para 101. cp *A v B plc & C ('Flitcroft')* [2002] EWCA Civ 337; [2002] 3 WLR 542,. In favour of considering: *Interbrew SA v Financial Times Ltd* [2002] EWCA Civ 274; [2002] 2 Lloyd's Rep 229, para 60; *Mersey Care NHS Trust v Ackroyd* [2002] EWHC 2115, paras 16, 25. cp *X Ltd v Morgan-Grampian (Publishers) Ltd* [1990] 2 All ER 1, 9–10. In practice, little may be known of the source's motive or purpose.

[76] In favour of considering method of obtaining: *X Ltd v Morgan-Grampian (Publishers) Ltd* [1990] 2 All ER 1, 10; *John Reid Enterprises Ltd v Pell* [1999] EMLR 675. Against considering method of obtaining: *Ashworth Hospital Authority v MGN Ltd* [2001] 1 All ER 991, CA, para 101. Cp para 11.61 below.

[77] *Interbrew SA v Financial Times Ltd* [2002] EWCA Civ 274; [2002] 2 Lloyd's Rep 229, paras 63–65. The media defendant can appeal a disclosure order to a higher court, but a journalist who is not the media defendant cannot.

[78] *X Ltd v Morgan-Grampian* [1990] 2 All ER 1, 15–16. See further M Tugendhat and I Christie (eds), *The Law of Privacy and the Media* (Oxford: 2002) paras 14.43–14.46.

[79] It is not a contempt of court to destroy a document before legal proceedings have been formally initiated. G Robertson and A Nicol, *Robertson & Nicol on Media Law* (4th edn, London: 2002) 268 recommend that journalists and media organizations destroy documents received from an informer that belong to someone else as soon as they get wind that the owner might want them returned. The risk of a civil action for conversion (see para 6.42 above) is small and would net the claimant minimal damages. A criminal prosecution for theft (see para 6.68 above) is not likely. If the source supplied a copy, then there is not even this risk.

[80] The common law discretion to refuse delivery up of a document is confirmed, according to Sir John Donaldson MR in *Secretary of State for Defence v Guardian Newspapers Ltd* [1984] 1 All ER 453, 458, by Torts (Interference with Goods) Act 1977, s 3(3)(b).

property where the effect would be to circumvent Contempt of Court Act 1981, s 10.[81]

B. Actions Against Third Parties[82] and Strangers[83]

Breach of Confidence

Information disclosed by professional without authority

Client v third party

Accessory liability of dishonest third party It is possible for a third party who receives information directly or indirectly from a professional who disclosed the information in breach of confidence to be liable as an accessory to the professional's breach of confidence.[84] Until recently it was unclear what mental state was required for accessory liability.[85] In *Royal Brunei Airlines v Tan*,[86] in a decision since followed by the House of Lords,[87] the Privy Council held that in an action for assisting in a breach of trust the claimant must prove dishonesty (in the sense of conscious impropriety)[88] on the part of the assister. It was decided in *Thomas v Pearce*[89] that the same principle governs liability for breach of confidence. But, if information is obviously confidential (for example, medical records)[90] the third party may owe the client an independent obligation of confidentiality making it unnecessary to consider accessory liability.[91] It may be that this is what Lord Phillips had in mind when in *Campbell v MGN Ltd*[92] he said in the context of third party liability: 7.20

> The suggestion that complex tests of the mental state of the publisher have to be satisfied before breach of confidence can be made out in respect of publication of information which violates the enjoyment of private or family life is not acceptable.

---

[81] *Secretary of State for Defence v Guardian Newspapers Ltd* [1984] 3 All ER 601, 607; *Camelot Group v Centaur Ltd* [1998] 1 All ER 251, 256. The defendant is at a disadvantage since he may not know whether the document contains clues about the identity of the source.

[82] Someone who, directly or indirectly, receives information from a confidant who has disclosed the information in breach of confidence.

[83] Someone who receives information from an interceptor.

[84] *Campbell v MGN Ltd* [2002] EWCA 1373, para 66. cp *Schering Chemicals v Falman Ltd* [1981] 2 All ER 321, 338.

[85] J Stuckey, 'When, If at All, Does a Third Party Innocently Implicated in Another's Breach of Confidence Become Liable to the Discloser' (1981) 4 U of New South Wales LJ 80.

[86] [1995] 3 All ER 97, 109.

[87] *Twinsectra Ltd v Yardley* [2002] UKHL 12; [2002] 2 AC 164.

[88] [1995] 3 All ER 97, 105–106. Objectively, the conduct must be dishonest *and* the defendant must have realized that the conduct was dishonest.

[89] [2000] FSR 718.

[90] cp *Venables v NGN Ltd* [2001] 1 All ER 908, 939.

[91] See para 6.14 above and para 7.27 below.

[92] [2002] EWCA 1373, para 66.

7.21 *Thomas v Pearce* was neither concerned with the disclosure of personal nor obviously confidential information. It was an action against a former employee and her new employer arising from the disclosure by the employee to the new employer of a list of the claimant's clients. In the Court of Appeal the primary breach of confidence was not disputed but liability was denied by the second defendant. The judge found that the second defendant's agent had acted negligently in failing to check whether there was any legal restriction on the use of the information, but not dishonestly; she was not aware that the information was confidential and had not deliberately closed her mind to that possibility.[93] The Court of Appeal agreed with Phipps and Toulson that 'for a third party to be liable in equity for a breach of confidence, more is required than merely careless, naive or stupid behaviour. There must be awareness that the information was confidential or willingness to turn a proverbial blind eye.'[94]

7.22 **Accessory liability of innocent third party**   Accessory liability cannot be pinned on a third party recipient of confidential personal information who is unaware, and not deliberately so, of the breach of confidence.

> In the present case, the defendant was not a *bona fide* purchaser without notice. . . . However, they did not know of the plaintiffs' right to the information. In my view . . . it did not bind their conscience. Thus, although the court may step in to grant injunctive relief, I do not believe that it would be right to grant an inquiry as to damages. I believe that only in cases where the conscience of the defendant is bound would it be appropriate to grant relief by way of damages.[95]

7.23 **Obtaining an injunction against a third party**   Lack of knowledge of the breach of confidence (as the passage in the previous paragraph indicates) is no bar to an injunction to prevent *future or continuing* disclosure or misuse of the information.[96]

> The duty of confidence is, as a general rule, also imposed on a third party who is in possession of information which he knows is subject to an obligation of confidence. If this was not the law the right would be of little practical value: there would be no point in imposing a duty of confidence in respect of the secrets of the marital bed if newspapers were free to publish those secrets when betrayed to them by the unfaithful partner in

---

[93] [2000] FSR 718, 723. cp *British Industrial Plastics Ltd v Ferguson* [1938] 4 All ER 504, 510 (mental state required for liability for inducing a breach of contract in respect of disclosure of confidential information).

[94] R Toulson and C Phipps, *Confidentiality* (London: 1996) 93. The nature of the information or the circumstances under which it must have been obtained may be strongly suggestive of a breach of confidence, for example, a photograph of Princess Diana exercising in a gym or a tape-recording of a private conversation. If this is the case, this will make the claimant's task of proving conscious dishonesty easier.

[95] per Aldous J, *Valeo Vision SA v Flexible Lamps Ltd* [1995] RPC 205, 228. See also *PCR Ltd v Dow Jones Telerate Ltd* [1998] FSR 170, 180.

[96] *Butler v Board of Trade* [1970] 3 All ER 593, 599; *Goddard v Nationwide Building Society* [1986] 3 All ER 264, 271–272; *G v Day* [1982] 1 NSWLR 24, 35. See also *Malone v Commissioner of Police of Metropolis (No 2)* [1979] 2 All ER 620, 634; R Dean, *The Law of Trade Secrets and Personal Information* (2nd edn, Sydney: 2002) [6.45]–[6.64].

B. Actions Against Third Parties and Strangers

the marriage. When trade secrets are betrayed by a confidant to a third party it is usually the third party who is to exploit the information and it is the activity of the third party that must be stopped in order to protect the owner of the trade secret.[97]

The proceedings for injunctive relief against the third party fix the third party however innocently he obtained the information with notice of the breach of confidence. The third party may, however, have a defence: that disclosure was in the public interest,[98] that the information is in the public domain,[99] estoppel or bona fide purchaser without notice.[100] It is not in any case an 'absolute rule . . . that a third party who receives the confidential information will be restrained from using it'.[101] Each case will depend upon its own facts and whether in the circumstances the third party's conscience is affected.

Third party on notice of an injunction[102]   In *Att-Gen v Times Newspapers Ltd*[103] the House of Lords decided that the actus reus of a common law criminal contempt is committed if X, who is aware that A has been awarded an interim injunction against B to prevent the disclosure of confidential information (here official secrets) puts the protected information into the public domain and thereby frustrates the operation of B's injunction.[104] A number of questions left open[105] have subsequently been answered. First, the rule applies to personal information[106] but not to the flouting of a final injunction.   **7.24**

> The juridical basis on which a third party may be affected by an order made in proceedings to which he is not a party lies in contempt. The underlying principle is that if a person, with knowledge of an order of the court, does some act which has the effect of interfering with or wholly undermining the manifest purpose of such an order then he will be guilty of contempt even though the order was not against him. The essence of the contempt consists in the interference by the third party with the course of justice in the proceedings in which the order was made.[107]

---

[97] per Lord Griffiths, *Att-Gen v Guardian Newspaper (No 2)* [1988] 3 All ER 545, 649. See also *Att-Gen v Observer Ltd* [1989] 2 FSR 3, 26 *per* Millett J: 'equity gives relief against all the world, including the innocent, save only a *bona fide* purchaser for value without notice.'

[98] See ch 11.

[99] See para 5.10 above and para 7.33 below.

[100] See para 7.31 below.

[101] per Lord Griffiths, *Att-Gen v Guardian Newspapers Ltd (No 2)* [1988] 3 All ER 545, 652.

[102] J Berryman, 'Injunctions—The Ability to Bind Non-Parties' (2002) 81 Canadian Bar Rev 207.

[103] [1991] 2 All ER 398. *Att-Gen v Newspaper Publishing plc* [1987] 3 All ER 276, 304, 308, 313.

[104] There is no need for X to have aided and abetted a breach of the injunction by B. What matters is that X's act had a significant and adverse effect on the administration of justice: *Att-Gen v Punch* [2002] UKHL 50, para 4.

[105] A Stewart and M Chesterman, 'Confidential Material: The Position of the Media' (1992) 14 Adel LR 1.

[106] *H (A Healthcare Worker) v Associated Newspapers Ltd* [2002] EWCA Civ 195; (2002) 65 BMLR 132, para 43. cp *Re L* [1988] 1 All ER 418, 421–422; *Att-Gen v Greater Manchester Newspapers Ltd* [2001] TLR 688.

[107] per Grey J, *Jockey Club v BBC* [2002] EWHC 1866, QB, para 23. But see *Pharaon v BCCI* [1998] 4 All ER 455, 458.

A final injunction is not enforceable against a third party to the proceedings unless expressly made contra mundum as was the case in *Venables v NGN Ltd*.[108] Secondly, the offence is not committed unless the purpose of the injunction is wilfully interfered with by the third party.[109]

Intercepted information

Client v stranger

7.25 **The traditional position** Formerly the client could not sue an interceptor for breach of confidence to recover compensation or an account of profits and therefore could not sue a stranger to whom the interceptor passed the information. This legal lacuna was pointed out by the Younger Committee in 1972: 'the damaging disclosure . . . of information acquired by means of any unlawful act, with knowledge of how it was acquired is an objectionable practice' but not unlawful.[110] It recommended enacting legislation to make it a civil wrong 'to disclose or otherwise use information which the discloser knows, or in all the circumstances ought to have known, was obtained by means of an unlawful act'.[111] This has not happened.

7.26 **The new law on interceptor liability** The premise on which the Younger Committee's analysis rested—that the action for breach of confidence depends upon a pre-existing relationship of trust—was questioned by Lord Goff in *Att-Gen v Guardian Newspapers Ltd (No 2)*. He preferred to rest liability for breach of confidence on awareness that the information was confidential. This allows an interceptor to be sued after disclosure for breach of confidence.

> I start with the broad general principle . . . that a duty of confidence arises when confidential information comes to the knowledge of a person (the confidant) *in circumstances where he has notice*, or is held to have agreed, *that the information is confidential*, with the effect that it would be just in all the circumstances that he should be precluded from disclosing the information to others . . . The existence of this broad general principle reflects the fact that there is such a public interest in the maintenance of confidences, that the law will provide remedies for their protection . . . I have expressed the circumstances in which the duty arises in broad terms, *not merely to embrace those cases where a third party receives information from a person who is under a duty of confidence in respect of it*, knowing that it has been disclosed by that person to him in breach of his duty of confidence, but also to include situations, beloved of law teachers, where *an obviously confidential document* is wafted by an electric fan out of a window into a crowded street, or where an *obviously confidential document*, such as a private diary, is dropped in a public place, and is then picked up by a passer-by . . .[112]

---

[108] [2001] 1 All ER 908.
[109] *Att-Gen v Punch* [2002] UKHL 50.
[110] *Report of the Committee on Privacy* (Cmnd 5012, 1972) para 632.
[111] ibid.
[112] *Att-Gen v Guardian Newspapers Ltd (No 2)* [1988] 3 All ER 545, 658–659 (italics added).

B. Actions Against Third Parties and Strangers

As regards the liability of an interceptor, Lord Goff's approach has prevailed.[113] An interceptor may today be:

(1) restrained from disclosing or using the intercept;[114] and
(2) held liable for damage caused by the disclosure of intercepted information which the interceptor knew, or ought to have known, was confidential.[115]

The stranger's liability The position of a stranger[116] has not been explored in any depth by the courts. Undoubtedly, an injunction may issue to prevent the stranger using or disclosing confidential personal information.[117] And the stranger may be made to deliver up property such as a stolen document taken by the interceptor and passed to the stranger.[118] If recent commercial cases of accessory liability are followed, the liability of a stranger for damage caused through the use or disclosure of the information will, like that of a third party, depend upon the stranger having acted dishonestly.[119] But, in cases where informational privacy has been violated it would make more sense for the courts to consider whether the stranger (and similarly, where the professional has made an unauthorized disclosure, the third party)[120] owes the client independent an obligation not to disclose the information further or use it. An independent obligation will exist if the stranger (ditto the third party) is aware,[121] or should have realized, that the client had a reasonable expectation of informational privacy.[122] In *John v Joulebine*[123] Countess Joulebine, the defendant, operated a website devoted to celebrity gossip on which visitors posted messages on a bulletin board. An unknown person posted a message that included stolen legal advice from counsel to Sir Elton John and others. The defendant linked the message to her home page. She claimed: 7.27

(1) that she had no idea whether the message was genuine or a prank; and
(2) that the test as to whether she knew or must have known the information was confidential was subjective.

---

[113] *Douglas v Hello! Ltd* [2001] 2 All ER 289, paras 58, 118, 166; *Venables v NGN Ltd* [2001] 1 All ER 908, 933 ; *B v H Bauer Publishing Ltd* [2002] EMLR 145, para 30; *A v B plc & C ('Flitcroft')* [2002] EWCA Civ 337; [2002] 3 WLR 542, para 11, guideline ix.
[114] See para 8.02 below.
[115] See paras 5.23 and 6.14 above.
[116] That is, someone who receives information from an interceptor.
[117] See para 7.23 above.
[118] In *Att-Gen of Ontario v Gowling & Henderson* (1984) 12 DLR (4th) 623, 634 the court said that legal professional privilege did not entitle a lawyer to refuse to disclose possession of intercepted Cabinet documents which the lawyer had received from or on behalf of a client. Further, the lawyer had to deliver up the documents to their rightful owner. In short, a stranger is no better placed that the interceptor from whom he received the information.
[119] See para 7.20 above.
[120] ibid.
[121] cp *Ashworth Hospital Authority v MGN Ltd* [2001] 1 All ER 991, CA, para 63.
[122] See para 6.14 above.
[123] QB, 26 January 2001, WL 98221.

This defence was rejected. The question, Master Leske said, was not what she knew or must have known but what she ought to have known. He said:

> Any intelligent person . . . must know or ought to know, if they do not actually know, that an advice from counsel is confidential and privileged, and whether or not she thought it might be a prank she ought to have known that there was a risk that it was being imparted in breach of confidence and therefore ought not to have continued to have it on her website; far less should she have created the link.

7.28 Because of the requirement to prove conscious dishonesty by the stranger or third party,[124] accessory liability is less favourable to the victim of a breach of confidence or an interception than liability for breach of an independent equitable obligation of confidentiality. Dishonesty is not an element of the action for breach of confidence. On the contrary, an obligation of confidentiality can be breached unconsciously.[125] One cannot be absolutely certain, however, that the courts will by-pass accessory principles. In cases involving media defendants the very difficulty of proving conscious dishonesty may prove attractive to a court mindful of its statutory obligation under s 12 of the Human Rights Act 1998 (HRA) to have 'particular regard' to Article 10. A test of dishonesty will have less of a 'chilling effect' on freedom of expression because the number of defendants against whom this can be proven will be small.[126] If the courts do feel this attraction, it is to be hoped that they will resist it. To allow the character of the defendant to determine liability (as opposed to the remedy) will distort this newly emerging area of substantive law,[127] undermining the development of universally relevant principles.[128]

Professional v stranger

7.29 In interception and accidental disclosure cases, only the client or his agent can sue a third party or stranger for breach of confidence.[129] Solicitors who inadvertently disclosed confidential (and privileged) documents to untraceable former clients were held not to have locus to make applications restraining the use of those documents in pending litigation between themselves and the third party in *Nationwide Building Society v Various Solicitors (No 2)*.[130]

---

[124] It must be proved by clear evidence: *ABK Ltd v Foxwell* [2002] EWHC 9, Ch.
[125] *Seager v Copydex Ltd* [1967] 2 All ER 415, 417: 'I have no doubt that the defendant company honestly believed the alternative grip was their own idea; but I think that they must unconsciously have made use of the information which the plaintiff gave them', per Lord Denning.
[126] A White, 'Privacy—Two Problems for Practitioners: Accessory Liability, Public Interest Defence' Matrix Chambers Seminar Programme, 14 February 2001, 4, available at http://www.matrixlaw.co.uk/seminars/seminar.html.
[127] cp *R v Department of Health, ex p Source Informatics* [2000] 1 All ER 786, 801.
[128] The danger of this happening is apparent in *A v B plc & C ('Flitcroft')* [2002] EWCA Civ 337; [2002] 3 WLR 542, where Lord Woolf formulated principles wholly in terms of a media defendant.
[129] cp para 5.43 above.
[130] [1998] All ER (D) 119.

B. Actions Against Third Parties and Strangers

[T]he right of confidence (or, if you wish, the privilege) is that of the former clients and it is therefore for them, and them alone, to take action to protect the confidentiality of the information in question. The fact that a solicitor is subject to a duty to preserve the confidentiality of privileged communications does not mean that if, for whatever reason, the communications come into the possession of a third party, the solicitor acquires a locus to assert his client's (or former client's) right of confidence. The fact, if fact it is, that the client (or former client) cannot be contacted for instructions is irrelevant.[131]

7.30 If the breach of confidence is a result of the activities of a disloyal employee, the professional has a cause of action for breach of confidence against the employee[132] and, consequently, potentially against anyone to whom the information is passed by the employee.

Defences (other than public interest)[133]

7.31 **Bona fide purchaser for value** There is a great deal of conflicting authority as to whether the defence of bona fide purchaser without notice for value may be relied upon by a third party recipient of confidential information.[134] The defence of bona fide purchaser is a property law concept. 'The proposition that confidential information may be regarded as property is highly controversial. It has had distinguished supporters from time to time, but it presents formidable conceptual difficulties.'[135] If confidential information is not property, then 'purchaser for value' must be understood in a metaphorical sense.

7.32 But is the defence really relevant? Accessory liability is foreclosed by the decision in *Thomas v Pearce*[136] that the liability depends upon proof of conscious dishonesty. Liability as principal depends upon whether the confidentiality of information

---

[131] per Blackburne J, *Nationwide Building Society v Various Solicitors (No 2)* [1998] All ER (D) 119.
[132] See para 6.38 above.
[133] As regards this defence see ch 11.
[134] Against the defence are *Wheatley v Bell* [1984] FSR 16, 22; *G v Day* [1982] 1 NSWLR 24, 34, 35; *Stevenson, Jordan & Harrison Ltd v MacDonald & Evans* (1951) 190, 195, (1952) RPC 10, 16. For the defence are *Morison v Moat* (1851) 68 ER 494, 501–502; *Att-Gen v Observer Ltd* [1989] 2 FSR 3, 26; *Goddard v Nationwide Building Society* [1986] 3 All ER 264, 270; *Att-Gen v Guardian (No 2)* [1988] 3 All ER 545, 596. See also *Schering Chemicals v Falkman Ltd* [1981] 2 All ER 321, 346; *Valeo Vision SA v Flexible Lamps Ltd* [1995] RPC 205, 228. For a discussion of the issue see G Forrai, 'Confidential Information—A General Survey' (1968–71) 6 Sydney L Rev 382, 391–392; Jones, 'Restitution of Benefits Obtained in Breach of Another's Confidence' (1970) 86 LQR 463, 478–481. For the position of an innocent volunteer see *Printers and Finishers Ltd v Holloway* [1965] RPC 239, 253.
[135] per Toulson J, *Fyffes Group v Templeman* [2000] 2 Lloyd's Rep 643. Cp *Breen v Williams* (1996) 138 ALR 259, 264; *R v Department of Health, ex p Source Informatics* [2000] 1 All ER 786, 797. For a discussion of the issues see R Meagher, W Gummow and J Lehane, *Equity, Doctrines and Remedies* (Sydney: 1992) 877–881; N Palmer and P Kohler, 'Information as Property' in N Palmer and E McKendrick (eds), *Interests in Goods* (London: 1993), ch 7; G Jones (ed), *Goff and Jones, The Law of Restitution* (6th edn, Sweet & Maxwell, 2000) 754–755. Cases that indicate a property view of confidential information include *Prince Albert v Strange* (1849) 1 Mac & G 25; *Argyll v Argyll* [1965] 1 All ER 611, 617; *Att-Gen v Guardian Newspapers Ltd* [1987] 3 All ER 316, 327–328. See, also para 19.04 below.
[136] [2000] FSR 718.

was,[137] or should have been, obvious to the defendant.[138] If either condition is satisfied, the purchaser cannot have been a bona fide purchaser without notice. The idea of applying the bona fide purchaser without notice defence in breach of confidence actions originated in trade secrets cases. The retail of a trade secret to an unsuspecting customer is plausible, the sale of confidential personal information to an unsuspecting customer much less so. The confidentiality of the information tends to be self-evidently private, for example the medical notes of a public figure, and the purchasers are usually worldly-wise media organizations.[139] Even if this is not so, there is really no need for a defence of bona fide purchaser for value without notice. Since all equitable remedies (including equitable compensation) are discretionary, where someone has innocently laid out money to acquire the information, and the more so if she then relied upon the information to change her position, the court can make the claimant submit to terms as a condition of relief or refuse relief altogether.[140]

7.33 **Information in the public domain** An action to enjoin publication by an innocent third party will fail if, before the case gets to court, the information becomes so widely disseminated that it enters the public domain.[141]

> The courts have to evolve practical rules and once the confidential information has escaped into the public domain it is not practical to attempt to restrain everyone with access to the knowledge from making use of it.[142]

Lord Griffiths in *Spycatcher (No 2)* wanted to except situations in which the third party was associated with the wrongdoing that put the information into the public domain.

> Each case will depend upon its own facts and the decision of the judge as to whether or not it is practical to give injunctive protection and whether the third party should, as a matter of fair dealing, be restrained or, to use the language of the equity lawyer, whether the conscience of the third party is affected by the confidant's breach of duty. There is certainly no absolute rule even in the case of a breach of a private

---

[137] In *Att-Gen v Guardian Newspapers Ltd (No 2)* [1988] 3 All ER 547 the liability of The Sunday Times for breach of confidence in publishing the first serialized extract from *Spycatcher* depended simply on awareness 'that the material was confidential in character and had not as a whole been previously published anywhere', per Lord Keith at 655. See also Lord Griffiths at 649: '[t]he duty of confidence is ... imposed on a third party who is in possession of information which he knows is subject to an obligation of confidence.'

[138] See para 6.14 above.

[139] M Tugendhat and I Christie (eds), *The Law of Privacy and the Media* (Oxford: 2002) para 9.27. cp *Lady Anne Tennant v Associated Newspapers* [1979] FSR 298; *Att-Gen v Observer Ltd* [1989] 2 FSR 3, 26.

[140] F Gurry, *Breach of Confidence* (Oxford: 1984) 280.

[141] *Att-Gen for UK v Wellington Newspapers* [1988] 1 NZLR 129, 175. See also *Jockey Club v BBC* [2002] EWHC 1866, QB, para 43.

[142] per Lord Griffiths, *Att-Gen v Guardian Newspapers Ltd (No 2)* [1988] 3 All ER 545, 652.

B. Actions Against Third Parties and Strangers

confidence that a third party who receives the confidential information will be restrained from using it.[143]

Lord Goff who disagreed with Lord Griffiths' view that the obligation of confidentiality continues to bind a confidant who is responsible for putting information wrongfully into the public domain,[144] also disagreed with him about the position of a third party recipient of information that has been published to the world in breach of confidence.

> [T]he artificial perpetuation of the obligation, despite the destruction of the subject matter, leads to unacceptable consequences. Take the case of confidential information with which we are here concerned. If the confidant who has wrongfully published the information so that it has entered the public domain remains under a duty of confidence, so logically must also be anybody who, deriving the information from him, publishes the information with knowledge that it was made available to him in breach of a duty of confidence. If Peter Wright is not released from his obligation of confidence neither, in my opinion, are [his publishers] nor anybody who may hereafter publish or sell the book in this country in the knowledge that it derived from Peter Wright, even booksellers who have in the past, or may hereafter, put the book on sale in their shops, would likewise be in breach of duty. If it is suggested that this is carrying the point to absurd lengths, then some principle has to be enunciated which explains why the continuing duty of confidence applies to some, but not others, who have wrongfully put the book in circulation.[145]

Anonymous information It is not necessarily a breach of confidence to use or disclose personal information that has been anonymised.[146] Rose LJ was not, however, persuaded to refuse an injunction by the defendants' promise not to name the hospital and the doctors in *X v Y*.[147] Simon Brown LJ suggested in *R v Department of Health, ex p Source Informatics Ltd* that this was because the leak by a health authority employee had involved a flagrant breach of confidence (a fact of which the newspaper must have been aware): 'the judge was concerned to prohibit any further use of it as the fruit of the poisoned tree.'[148] For the same reason, it is unlikely that a stranger can avoid an injunction by cloaking illegally obtained information in anonymity unless there is an overriding public interest in publication.[149]

7.34

---

[143] ibid at 652.
[144] See para 5.60 above.
[145] [1988] 3 All ER 545, 663.
[146] See para 5.34 above.
[147] [1988] 2 All ER 648.
[148] [2000] 1 All ER 786, 793.
[149] cp *A v B plc & C ('Flitcroft')* [2002] EWCA Civ 337; [2002] 3 WLR 542, para 11, guideline x.

Breach of Fiduciary Duty

Client v third party

7.35 Similar principles govern accessory liability for breach of fiduciary duty and breach of confidence. A third party who receives the information as a result of a breach of fiduciary duty by a professional is prima facie liable to be restrained from making use of or further disclosing the information[150] but liability to the client for past use or disclosure will depend upon the stranger's mental state when he took advantage of the opportunity afforded by the professional's breach of fiduciary duty.[151] In *Satnam Ltd v Dunlop Heywood Ltd*[152] the Court of Appeal decided that mere knowledge of the breach of fiduciary duty does not (at least in a commercial setting) expose the third party to liability for having used the information that was disclosed in breach of a fiduciary duty. For liability, the third party must have acted with conscious dishonesty.[153]

Tort

Client v third party

7.36 Interference with contractual relations between professional and client A contract 'not only binds the parties to it by the obligation entered into, but also imposes on all the world the duty of respecting that contractual obligation'.[154] The possibility exists that a third party, say a newspaper, that encourages or otherwise induces a professional to breach a contractual promise of confidentiality to the client without lawful excuse could be sued by the client for the tort of procuring a breach of contract.[155] The claimant must prove that the defendant 'acted with knowledge of the contract, and with the intention to interfere with the claimant's contractual rights'.[156] In 1993 the Princess of Wales instigated proceedings against Mirror Group Newspapers in which she alleged that Mirror Group Newspapers had induced a gym owner to breach his contract with her by covertly photographing her exercising at the gym.[157] The action was settled out of court. The claimant has a right of action whether or not specific damage has accrued.[158] It is

---

[150] *Satnam Ltd v Dunlop Heywood Ltd* [1999] 3 All ER 652, 670.
[151] *Royal Brunei Airlines v Tan* [1995] 3 All ER 97.
[152] [1999] 3 All ER 652, 671.
[153] per Nourse LJ, [1999] 3 All ER 652, 671. On the meaning of dishonesty in a similar context see *Twinsectra Ltd v Yardley* [2002] 2 All ER 377.
[154] per Lopes LJ, *Temperton v Russell* [1893] 1 QB 715, 730.
[155] *Church of Scientology of California v Kaufman* [1973] RPC 635, 640; *X v Y* [1988] 2 All ER 648, 661. On the tort generally see *British Industrial Plastics Ltd v Ferguson* [1940] 1 All ER 479.
[156] per Henry J, *Cardinal Packaging Ltd v Atkinson* (CA, 24 March 2000) para 5. The liability of the third party can be based either on direct knowledge or imputed knowledge 'derived from wilful or fraudulent ignoring of the facts', per Slesser LJ, *British Industrial Plastics v Ferguson* [1938] 4 All ER 504, 510 (affirmed on appeal to the House of Lords [1940] 1 All ER 479).
[157] QB, 8 November 1993.
[158] *Exchange Telegraph Co Ltd v Gregory & Co* [1896] 1 QB 147, 153.

B. Actions Against Third Parties and Strangers

a defence that the third party acted with 'sufficient justification'.[159] Those who disclose information because of an overriding public interest[160] therefore have nothing to fear.

Inducing breach of an equitable obligation The existence of a tort of inducing a breach of equitable obligation mirroring the tort of inducing a breach of contract was mooted in *James v Commonwealth*.[161] Since then the Court of Appeal has held that there is no tort of procuring a breach of trust[162] but an action of procuring a breach of confidence[163] has been acknowledged. 7.37

Defamation Libel and slander do not require the claimant and defendant to have a pre-existing relationship. Every re-publication of a defamatory statement that is a natural probable consequence of the original publication is a fresh libel or slander.[164] The fact that the defamatory statement had been widely circulated at the time of re-publication does allow the defendant to avoid liability; there is no public domain defence.[165] It is possible to defame a person of whom one has never heard, to whom one does not intend to refer and without any awareness that one is making a defamatory imputation.[166] Someone who is not an editor or commercial publisher may, however, have a defence of innocent dissemination in these circumstances.[167] A newspaper that publishes an untrue, defamatory statement emanating from a professional may have a defence of qualified privilege if the statement is about a matter of genuine public concern such as the health of the Prime Minister.[168] 7.38

---

[159] *X v Y* [1988] 2 All ER 648, 661. The parameters of this defence have not been fully explored. Presumably it would apply where there was a public interest in disclosure. See generally A Grubb (ed), *The Law of Tort* (London: 2001) 1237 et seq.
[160] See ch 11.
[161] (1939) 62 CLR 339, 370.
[162] *Metall und Rohstoff AG v Donaldson Lufkin and Jenrette Inc* [1990] 1 QB 391, 408–409.
[163] *Printers and Finishers Ltd v Holloway* [1965] RPC 239; *X v Y* [1988] 2 All ER 648, 661; *O'Neill v Department of Health (No 2)* [1986] NILR 290. cp *Alberts v Devine* 479 NE 2d 113 (1984); *Morris v Consolidation Coal Co* 446 SE 2d 648 (1994). In these two US actions the courts held that a cause of action lay against a third party who induced, respectively, a psychiatrist and a physician to breach the obligation of confidentiality owed to a patient.
[164] *Slipper v BBC* [1991] 1 All ER 165.
[165] As there is in equity in an action for breach of confidence: see para 5.09 above.
[166] *Hulton v Jones* [1910] AC 20, 23. But see *O'Shea v MGN Ltd* [2001] EMLR 943 where, because of Art 10, the strict liability principle was not applied to a look-alike photograph used in commercial advertising for an 'adult only' internet website.
[167] Defamation Act 1996, s 1.
[168] *Reynolds v Times Newspapers Ltd* [1999] 4 All ER 509, 626 sets out the relevant considerations. See further M Tugendhat, 'Privacy and Celebrity' in E Barendt and A Firth (eds), *Yearbook of Copyright and Media Law 2001/2002* (Oxford: 2002) 5.

Chapter 7: Suing and Tracing Third Parties and Strangers

7.39 Conspiracy The client may have an action for conspiracy against a third party who induces one of the professional's employees to disclose confidential information about the client in breach of the employee's contractual obligations to the employer.[169] A conspiracy may also exist between an interceptor and a stranger.

7.40 Protection from Harassment Act 1997 In the Protection from Harassment Act 1997 Parliament made it both a crime and a tort to knowingly 'pursue a course of conduct' (including through speech)[170] 'which amounts to harassment of another'.[171] Harassment is not defined, but its effects include alarm and distress.[172] In *Thomas v NGN Ltd*,[173] a county court judge decided that the press can be sued for harassment. The Court of Appeal agreed. The claimant was a civilian working for the City of London police who had reported to her superiors racist remarks made by three police officers about an asylum seeker for which the police officers were disciplined. The defendants published a 'strident, aggressive and inflammatory' article criticizing the claimant, who was identified by name and place of work and described as 'black'. Readers' letters attacking the claimant for ruining the officers' careers were published along with a further article in which she was again referred to as 'black'. In consequence of this, the claimant received race hate mail at her place of work. The Court of Appeal held that harassment was any course of conduct targeted at an individual 'which is calculated to produce the consequences described in section 7 [ie alarm or distress] and which is oppressive and unreasonable'.[174] In this case the conduct 'was foreseeably likely to stimulate a racist reaction on the part of . . . readers and cause [the claimant] distress'.[175]

7.41 The Protection from Harassment Act 1997, although enacted principally to protect the victims of stalking and racial harassment, has the potential to curb media door-stepping and persistent pursuit of celebrities.[176] Its scope for redressing disclosure of confidential personal information by the media is limited by the need to show a 'course of conduct'[177] (in other words repeated disclosure) and uncertainty about what sort of disclosures by the media might be classed as harassment. The decision reached in *Thomas v NGN Ltd*[178] is surprising given the

---

[169] See para 4.43 above.
[170] s 7(4).
[171] ss 1, 2, 3, 7.
[172] s 7(2).
[173] [2001] EWCA Civ 1233; [2002] EMLR 4, noted in J Coad, 'Harassment by the Media' [2002] Entertainment L Rev 18.
[174] *Thomas v NGN Ltd* [2001] EWCA Civ 1233; [2002] EMLR 4, para 30.
[175] The claimant had received hate-mail at her place of work and had become afraid to go out in public.
[176] Clause 4 of the PCC's privacy code provides guidelines on the avoidance of harassment by the media.
[177] Protection from Harassment Act 1997, s 7(3).
[178] [2001] EWCA Civ 1233; [2002] EMLR 4.

B. Actions Against Third Parties and Strangers

importance attached by the domestic courts,[179] the European Court of Human Rights and Parliament,[180] to press freedom. If there is no race angle, the courts may decline to use the tort to curb the activities of the media unless a media organ pursues a vendetta intending to cause an individual distress. Damages may then be awarded for (among other things) any anxiety caused . . . and any financial loss resulting from the harassment'.[181]

Professional v third party

A stranger or third party who receives converted property can be sued for the tort of conversion.[182] It was agreed by Megarry V-C in *British Steel Corp v Granada Television Ltd*[183] that televising the contents of confidential documents that had been intercepted by stealth and passed to the defendants was conversion. The liability of the recipient of a converted object is not contingent on proof of guilty knowledge.[184] But, it does depend on the defendant taking receipt of the object embodying the information, and not just the information in it because information cannot be converted.

7.42

The professional will have an action for inducing a breach of contract against a stranger who persuaded a corrupt employee to hand over confidential information in breach of his contract of employment.[185] Other causes of action may be conspiracy,[186] and, in rare cases, breach of statutory duty.[187] Should a communication be intercepted in the course of its transmission through an external telecommunications system or a private telecommunications system linked to a public one without appropriate consent, the interceptor may be liable to the professional under Regulation of Investigatory Practices Act 2000, s 1(3).

7.43

Copyright

A third party or stranger who reproduces something composed or created by the client (or professional) without authorization may infringe the client's (or professional's) copyright.[188] If the infringement is unwitting, the third party or stranger is protected by s 97(1) of the Copyright, Designs and Patents Act 1988 from

7.44

---

[179] cp *A v B plc & C ('Flitcroft')* [2002] EWCA Civ 337; [2002] 3 WLR 542.
[180] HRA, s 12(4).
[181] s 3(2).
[182] *Fine Arts Society Ltd v Union Bank of London Ltd* (1886) 17 QBD 705; *Healys v Mishcon de Reya* [2002] EWHC 2480, para 22 (conversion by unlawful retention of client files).
[183] [1981] 1 All ER 417, 423.
[184] *AL Underwood Ltd v Bank of Liverpool & Martins* [1924] 1 KB 776, 791. See further A Grubb (ed), *The Law of Tort* (London: 2002) 435.
[185] cp *British Plastics Ltd v Ferguson* [1940] 1 All ER 479, 481.
[186] See para 4.43 above.
[187] *Francome v Mirror Group Newspapers Ltd* [1984] 1 WLR 892, 896–897 where breach of a duty created by s 5 of the Wireless Telegraphy Act 1949 was alleged.
[188] *Lady Anne Tennant v ANG* [1979] FSR 298. cp *A v B plc & C ('Flitcroft')* [2002] EWCA Civ 337; [2002] 3 WLR 542, para 49.

having to pay damages (including additional damages pursuant to s 97(2))[189] so long as he had no reason to believe that copyright subsisted in the work.[190] It is specifically stated that this defence is without prejudice to any other remedy. Thus the innocent third party can be made to give an account of profits, to deliver up the client's (or professional's) property[191] and to be restrained by an injunction.

> The policy lying behind the preserving of all other rights of relief against the innocent infringer is entirely comprehensible; even the innocent must be stopped from continuing to infringe, and have no prima facie right, moral or legal, to be allowed to keep the benefits derived from their infringements. Nor should the innocent infringer be allowed to retain possession of property which is plainly that of the copyright owner.[192]

Damages will be awarded against a third party who knew, or should as a result of reasonable inquiries have known, of the client's (or professional's) copyright.

---

[189] *Redrow Homes Ltd v Betts Brothers Plc* [1997] 24 FSR 828, 839.
[190] Copyright Design and Patents Act 1988, s 97(1).
[191] In *Laidlaw v Lear* (1898) 30 OR 26 a firm of solicitors obtained an injunction for the return of draft letters by a member of the firm that had been surreptitiously removed by a former employee and handed over to the defendant.
[192] per Lord McCluskey, *Redrow Homes Ltd v Betts Brothers Plc* [1997] FSR 828, 839.

8

REMEDIES

A. Prior Restraint	8.02	B. After-the-Event Remedies	8.28
Permanent Injunction	8.02	Monetary Awards	8.28
Interim Injunctions	8.08	Account of Profits	8.71
Data Protection Compliance Order	8.26	Delivery Up and Destruction of Items	8.74
		Constructive Trusts	8.76

8.01 What substantive relief is available to a professional or a client who has a civil cause of action arising from the wrongful past or prospective disclosure of confidential information? How is prior restraint to be reconciled with freedom of expression and media freedom? Which, if any, of the after-the-event sanctions will enable the client to obtain financial compensation for mental distress if this is the sole injury suffered and how much will the client recover? These and related issues are addressed in this chapter.

A. Prior Restraint

Permanent Injunction[1]

General principles

Availability

8.02 The Civil Procedure Rules (CPR) glossary defines an injunction as '[a] court order prohibiting a person from doing something or requiring a person to do something'. Invented by the Court of Chancery, this equitable remedy is an effective way of preventing repetition or continuance of conduct[2] by a professional,[3] interceptor, third

---

[1] P Baker and P St J Langan (eds), *Snell's Equity* (29th edn, London: 1990) 645; F Gurry, *Breach of Confidence* (Oxford: 1984) chs xix, xx; A Burrows *Remedies for Torts and Breach of Contract* (2nd edn, London: 1994) ch 9; P Parkinson (ed), *The Principles of Equity* (Sydney: 1996) ch 18.

[2] The client must adduce evidence in support of a claim that the misuse or disclosure is set to continue or to be resumed. The professional, stranger or third party may be able to avoid an injunction by giving an undertaking not to act in this way.

[3] In *Doe v Roe* 400 NYS 2d 668 (1977) a psychiatrist was enjoined from circulating a book which reported verbatim and extensively a patient's most intimate thoughts. An accountant was restrained by an injunction in *Evett v Price* (1827) 1 Sim 483, 57 ER 659.

party or stranger that infringes the claimant's legal or equitable rights or, possibly, interferes with his legitimate interests.[4] In cases of unintentional disclosure, the professional as well as the client may have standing to seek an injunction.[5] The injunction may be given extra-territorial effect[6] and in exceptional circumstances can be expanded to take in the whole world (contra mundum).[7] Those without a presence in the jurisdiction, however, can ignore a worldwide injunction.

8.03 *Quia timet* injunctions   Relief may be given before any information has been disclosed[8] where disclosure is probable[9] or, if not probable, its consequences particularly grave.[10] A lower standard of probability applies in situations in which a professional owes the client a fiduciary duty of undivided loyalty. The profession this is most likely to affect is the legal profession. If a solicitor has taken on a new client whose interests are opposed to those of an existing or former client and there is a real risk that confidential information about the old client will, consciously or unconsciously, be put at the disposal of the new client, equity may force the solicitor to withdraw from the more recent relationship.[11]

Unavailability

8.04 **Information in the public domain**   It is an equitable maxim that equity does not act in vain. An injunction will not be granted if it would be 'idle and ineffectual'.[12]

---

[4] Normally a claimant with no rights cannot obtain an injunction, but there are exceptions, eg *Burris v Azadani* [1995] 4 All ER 802, 807–808: '[i]t would not seem to me to be a valid objection to the making of an exclusion zone order that the conduct to be restrained is not of itself tortious or otherwise unlawful, if such an order is reasonably regarded as necessary for the protection of a plaintiff's legitimate interests', per Sir Thomas Bingham MR. At this stage the courts are not willing to treat infringement of Art 8 as a legitimate interest entitling the applicant to an injunction where no legal or equitable right has been interfered with: *Venables v NGN Ltd* [2001] 1 All ER 908, para 27.

[5] See para 7.29 above. cp *H (A Healthcare Worker) v Associated Newspapers Ltd* [2002] EWCA Civ 195, (2002) 65 BMLR 132, para 32; *Ashworth Hospital Authority v MGN Ltd* [2002] UKHL 29; [2002] 1 WLR 2033, paras 22, 32. A public authority employer may have standing to apply for an injunction by virtue of its need to perform its statutory responsibilities: *Broadmoor Special Hospital Authority v R* (1999) 52 BMLR 137, 145.

[6] In *Att-Gen v Barker* [1990] 3 All ER 257 an injunction to prevent publication of a book, *Courting Disaster*, by a former employee of the Royal household in breach of an express worldwide, perpetual confidentiality covenant was granted worldwide.

[7] *Re X* [1984] 1 WLR 1422; *Venables v NGN Ltd* [2001] 1 All ER 908, 938. An injunction contra mundum means that it applied directly to newspapers that had notice of it that were not a party to the proceedings and not merely as an indirect result of the law of contempt (as to which see para 7.24 above). Also, violation of the injunction is a civil contempt. cp *Kelly v BBC* [2001] 1 All ER 323, 359.

[8] *H (A Healthcare Worker) v Associated Newspapers Ltd* [2002] EWCA Civ 195, (2002) 65 BMLR 132, para 19.

[9] *Att-Gen v Manchester Corp* [1893] 2 Ch 87, 92; *Hooper v Rogers* [1975] 1 Ch 43, 50.

[10] eg *Venables v NGN Ltd* [2001] 1 All ER 908.

[11] *Bolkiah v KPMG* [1999] 1 All ER 517, 529. Relief will be refused if the solicitor can satisfy the court on the basis of clear and convincing evidence that all effective measures have been taken to ensure that no disclosure will occur. See further para 6.92 above.

[12] *Wookey v Wookey* [1991] Fam 121, 131.

A. Prior Restraint

This has led courts to refuse an injunction[13] when confidential information has been put into the public domain by a third party.[14] But not in all cases.[15] In *Venables v NGN Ltd*[16] Butler-Sloss P made a contra mundum order forbidding publication of information about the assumed identities, appearances and whereabouts of the applicants. The injunction was to continue even if information was published on the internet or abroad. If information is in the public domain as a result of rumour, gossip, and speculation, enjoining further disclosure by a professional may still serve a worthwhile purpose.[17]

Wrongdoer will benefit from his own wrong In *Att-Gen v Guardian Newspapers Ltd (No 2)*[18] the House of Lords laid the groundwork for restraining persons responsible for wrongfully putting information into the public domain from profiting from their own wrongdoing. Thus if it was an earlier indiscretion on the part of the professional that was the cause of the information losing its confidential quality, an injunction is still likely to be forthcoming. 8.05

What the court might do

Courts have a statutory power to substitute damages for a prohibitory injunction[19] but it is improbable that this will be done if the effect is to license the intentional use or disclosure of confidential personal information acquired in the course of a professional relationship. An injunction, if granted, will last as long as the court directs, which could be indefinitely.[20] However, since an injunction against disclosure[21] of information is, by definition, a restriction on freedom of expression,[22] it cannot be for longer than absolutely necessary in a democratic society.[23] If through no fault of the defendant the injuncted information enters the public domain, a court might lift the injunction.[24] 8.06

---

[13] *Universal Thermosensors Ltd v Hibben* [1992] 3 All ER 257, 270. This does not rule out the possibility of damages in contract for breach of a contractual promise of confidentiality (see para 4.10 above) or compensation for breach of the DPA (see para 4.49 above, *Att-Gen for England and Wales v R* (NZCA, 21 May 2001) or possibly even for breach of confidence in equity (see para 5.14 above). In any case, establishing that personal information is in the public domain may be difficult: *B. v H Bauer Publishing Ltd* [2002] EMLR 8, para 26; see paras 5.10 et seq.

[14] For the position when it is in the public domain as a result of the act of the defendant see para 5.62 above.

[15] H Tomlinson (ed), *Privacy and the Media* (London: 2002) 37 eg *Re S* [2003] EWHC 254 (Fam) para 20.

[16] [2001] 1 ALL ER 908, para 105.

[17] See para 5.63 above.

[18] [1988] 3 All ER 545, 664. See also 642, 647 and para 5.62 above.

[19] Supreme Court Act 1981, s 50 re-enacting Lord Cairns' Act. And see *Shelfer v City of London Electric Co* [1895] 1 Ch 287, 315.

[20] *Doe v Roe* 400 NYS 2d 668 (1977). cp *Att-Gen v Jonathan Cape* [1975] 3 All ER 484, 495.

[21] But not use without disclosure.

[22] To which the courts are obliged to have regard: HRA, s 12.

[23] *Imutran Ltd v Uncaged Campaigns Ltd* [2001] 2 All ER 385, para 21.

[24] *Att-Gen v Guardian Newspapers Ltd (No 2)* [1988] 3 All ER 545. See also *Att-Gen v Times Newspapers Ltd* [2001] EMLR 19; *Borax Europe Ltd v Cave* [2002] EWCA Civ 741, para 8.

Judicial discretion

8.07 As an equitable remedy, an injunction is a discretionary remedy.[25] The discretion, however, is 'a judicial and not an arbitrary discretion';[26] it is exercised according to settled legal principles.[27] Reasons for refusing an injunction include: delay[28] or acquiescence, lack of 'clean hands',[29] difficulty of enforcement,[30] the public interest, and, arguably, if these matters do not go to the existence of a substantive cause of action, the triviality of the disclosure or absence of detriment: 'the remedy has been fashioned to protect the confider not to punish the confidant, and there seems little point in extending it to the confider who has no need of the protection.'[31] If an injunction involves any interference with a Convention right such as freedom of expression, the Convention principles of necessity and proportionality must be observed. This, of itself, should prevent enjoinder of a trivial interference with confidentiality.[32]

Interim Injunctions[33]

General principles

Maintaining the status quo

8.08 To obtain a perpetual injunction after a full trial may take a considerable time. To maintain the status quo in the meantime the client can apply for an interim injunction.[34]

---

[25] For details of the discretionary bars to an injunction see P Baker and P St J Langan (eds), *Snell's Equity* (29th edn, London: 1990) 653–655.

[26] per Lord Selborne, *Goodson v Richardson* (1874) 9 Ch App 221, 223.

[27] *Beddow v Beddow* (1878) 9 Ch D 89, 93.

[28] cp *Bunn v BBC* [1998] 3 All ER 552, 557.

[29] *Hubbard v Vosper* [1972] 1 All ER 1023, 1033.

[30] *Khashoggi v Smith* (1980) 124 SJ 14: 'I am not satisfied that any injunction could be framed which would at the same time protect the plaintiff against some disclosure which ought not to be made and which would be damaging to her, while not being unreasonably restrictive of the right of publication, and which would be capable of enforcement', per Sir David Cairns.

[31] per Lord Griffiths, *Att-Gen v Guardian Newspapers Ltd (No 2)* [1988] 3 All ER 545, 650. In this respect, confidentiality is different from legal professional privilege which continues even when the client has no substantial reason for asserting privilege: see para 16.28 below.

[32] If triviality remains a substantive element of the breach of confidence action in cases involving personal information (see para 5.08 above), trivial cases should be eliminated before the court addresses the question of whether to grant an injunction.

[33] An interim injunction, known formerly as an interlocutory injunction, applies until further order of the court or the final hearing in the case: see CPR, Pt 25 and PD 25. Power to grant an interim injunction is conferred by r 25(1)(1)(a).

[34] eg *Kaye v Robertson* [1991] FSR 62. Paul Burrell, formerly butler to Princess Diana, obtained a temporary interim injunction halting publication in the press of further extracts from the witness statement that he had given to his solicitors in a criminal action in which he was accused of stealing the Princess' possessions after her death: the Guardian, 7 November 2002. The matter was settled out of court. Not long afterwards in the Court of Sessions, lawyers acting for the Prince of Wales won an interim interdict banning a Glasgow newspaper from describing the behaviour of the Prince and his family: http://icwales.icnetwork.co.uk 16 November 2002.

A. Prior Restraint

The American Cyanamid *principles*

The principles that determine whether an interim injunction should be granted were laid down in *American Cyanamid v Ethicon*.[35] The client must show: **8.09**

(1) that there is 'a serious question to be tried' or 'a real prospect of succeeding . . . to a permanent injunction at the trial'; and, if so,
(2) that damages would not be an adequate remedy for the client, if an injunction were refused but the client were to win at trial; and
(3) if the defendant is able to show that he too cannot be adequately compensated by damages for delayed disclosure, that the balance of convenience favours an injunction.

Application of American Cyanamid *in breach of confidence cases*

In actions by clients that involve no serious freedom of expression issue,[36] an interim injunction will probably be granted if the client has an arguable case[37] that a breach of confidentiality is threatened[38] or is continuing and: **8.10**

- the claimant is not planning to disclose the confidential information for financial gain—if he is, damages may be an adequate remedy,[39] though not in all cases;[40]
- the defendant has not raised a plausible defence of disclosure in the public interest;[41]
- there are no discretionary grounds for refusing relief;[42] and
- the client is able to particularize the confidential information precisely.[43]

---

[35] [1975] 1 All ER 504, 510. These rules apply to contract and equitable actions to prevent a breach of confidence: *Lion Laboratories Ltd v Evans* [1984] 2 All ER 417; *Att-Gen v Barker* [1990] 3 All ER 257; *Graham v Delderfield* [1992] FSR 313.

[36] By definition freedom of speech will arise in any case in which a professional is prevented from disclosing information, but a priest cannot seriously claim to have a right to broadcast the contents of a religious confession or a doctor what her patient told her.

[37] *Francome v Mirror Group Newspapers Ltd* [1984] 2 All ER 408, 415; *HRH Princess of Wales v MGN* (QB, 8 November 1993).

[38] per Lightman J, *Bunn v BBC* [1998] 3 All ER 552, 558.

[39] *Douglas v Hello! Ltd* [2001] 2 All ER 289, 315 discussed below in the main text. The fact that the client intends to make the information public may strengthen the case for an injunction if disclosure ruins the market for the information in a way that cannot be compensated in money.

[40] eg *Creation Records Ltd v NGN Ltd* [1997] EMLR 444, 445–446.

[41] See ch 11 and HRA, s 12(4).

[42] See para 8.07 above.

[43] The injunction must be framed with sufficient precision that the professional knows what it is she must not disclose: *Woodward v Hutchins* [1977] 1 WLR 760, 764; *A v B* [2000] EMLR 1007, para 8; *CMI for Medical Innovation GmbH v Phytopharm plc* [1999] FSR 235. A whole book is unlikely to be suppressed if the breach of confidence is contained in only a few pages. Cp *Amway Corp v Eurway International Ltd* [1974] RPC 82, 86–87; *Times Newspapers Ltd v MGN Ltd* [1993] EMLR 442.

The reason the courts are easily persuaded of the need for an interim injunction is that loss of confidentiality is irreversible.

> Confidential information is like an ice cube... Give it to the party who has no refrigerator or will not agree to keep it in one, and by the time of the trial you just have a pool of water.[44]

To refuse an interim injunction is to deprive the client of his only worthwhile remedy.[45] Interim relief will not be refused even if the client's cross-undertaking in damages[46] is worthless.

> [T]o insist strictly on the ability to meet the cross-undertaking would be oppressive and give to those with ample means eager to exploit confidential information for their own profit the passport to ride roughshod over the obligations of confidentiality owed to those without means.[47]

Injunctions that undermine freedom of expression

Human Rights Act 1998, s 12

8.11 **Protection of freedom of expression** Getting an injunction before trial is much more difficult if the injunction will interfere with freedom of expression—particularly that of the press.[48] The European Court of Human Rights (ECtHR) requires the 'the most careful scrutiny' if the media is to be gagged.[49] Lord Woolf explained in *A v B plc & C ('Flitcroft')* that:

> [a]ny interference with the press has to be justified because it inevitably has some effect on the ability of the press to perform its role in society. This is the position irrespective of whether a publication is desirable in the public interest. The existence of a free press is in itself desirable and so any interference with it has to be justified.[50]

An interim injunction against the media may be tantamount to a permanent injunction if by the date of trial the information has lost its topicality.[51] Even before Article 10 was incorporated into domestic law by the Human Rights Act 1998 (HRA), in the interests of free speech the courts would refuse an interim injunction to restrain publication of an allegedly defamatory statement if the

---

[44] per Sir John Donaldson MR, *Att-Gen v Newspaper Publishing plc* [1987] 3 All ER 276, 291.
[45] *A v B plc and C ('Flitcroft')* [2002] EWCA Civ 337; [2002] 3 WLR 542, para 11, guideline i. See also *Adams v Attridge* (QB, 8 October 1998).
[46] A party who is awarded an interim injunction has usually to promise to compensate the enjoined party against any loss incurred through the injunction if at the trial the enjoined party is successful.
[47] per Lightman J, *Bunn v BBC* [1998] 3 All ER 552, 558.
[48] Even in the pre-HRA era a claimant who sought to muzzle the press had to satisfy the court that he would succeed at trial in order to obtain an interim injunction: *William Coulson & Sons v James Coulson & Co* [1887] 3 TLR 46; *Herbage v Times Newspapers Ltd*, The Times, 1 May 1981.
[49] *Observer and Guardian v UK* (1991) 14 EHRR 153, para 60.
[50] per Lord Woolf, [2002] EWCA Civ 337; [2002] 3 WLR 512, para 11, guideline iv.
[51] G Robertson and A Nicol, *Robertson and Nicol on Media Law* (4th edn, London: 2002) 224. cp *Kelly v BBC* [2001] 1 All ER 323, 355.

A. Prior Restraint

defendant intended to plead justification,[52] privilege or fair comment except in the rarest of cases where that plea was bound to fail.[53] Where the cause of action was not defamation interim injunctions were sometimes refused if it was felt that the true motive behind the application was to protect the applicant's reputation and the very strict criteria for interim injunctions in defamation cases had not been met.[54] In the main, however, interim injunctions were granted to prevent breaches of confidence.[55] No anomaly was perceived in allowing prior restraint of true information when enjoining publication of false information was forbidden.[56] This discrepancy will continue so long as interim injunctions are denied in defamation actions in which the defendant indicates an intention to plead justification, but are allowed in breach of confidence actions on the claimant showing that the action is likely to succeed at trial.[57]

Prior notice The purpose of HRA, s 12 is to provide an additional layer of protection for freedom of expression in general, and the media in particular.[58] HRA, s 12(2) requires a court to whom application is made for an interim injunction to be satisfied that all practical steps have been taken to notify the defendant of the application so that the defendant may be represented at the hearing of the application, if he so wishes.[59] There must be 'compelling reasons' if the defendant has not been notified.[60] In Parliament the Home Secretary gave the example of a case raising national security issues where there was a risk that the respondents would rush into print if they got wind of an application for an interim injunction.[61] **8.12**

---

[52] *Hubbard v Vosper* [1972] 1 All ER 1023, 1030.
[53] *Bonnard v Perryman* [1891] 2 Ch 269, 284.
[54] eg *Hubbard v Vosper* [1972] 1 All ER 1023, 1029–1030; *Woodward v Hutchins* [1977] 1 WLR 760, 764; *Service Corporation International plc v Channel Four Television Corporation* [1999] EMLR 83.
[55] eg *Francome v MGN Ltd* [1984] 1 WLR 892; *A v B plc and C ('Flitcroft')* [2001] 1 WLR 2341 (reversed on appeal, but not because the motive was to protect reputation).
[56] cp *Fraser v Evans* [1969] 1 All ER 8, 11. See M Tugendhat and I Christie (eds), *The Law of Privacy and the Media* (Oxford: 2002) para 7.44.
[57] The gap between the treatment of defamation actions and breach of confidence actions has narrowed in so far as HRA, s 12(3) requires the claimant in application for an interim injunction in a breach of confidence action to show that 'the application is likely to establish that publication should not be allowed'. Tugendhat and Marzec in M Tugendhat and I Christie (eds), *The Law of Privacy and the Media* (Oxford: 2002) para 7.50, advocate that courts apply the Woolf guidelines laid down in *A v B plc & C ('Flitcroft')* [2002] EWCA Civ 337; [2002] 3 WLR 542 in defamation actions of a private nature. The premise of their argument is that there is no clear distinction between privacy and defamation. This is not the view taken in this book: see para 6.13 above.
[58] *Hansard*, HC vol 306, col 775 (16 February 1998). There is no need for a public authority to be involved.
[59] HRA, s 12(2)(a).
[60] HRA, s 12(2)(b). Before the HRA temporary interim injunctions were regularly obtained without notice outside normal office hours against the media.
[61] *Hansard*, HC vol 314, col 535 (2 July 1998).

8.13 **Media cases** By s 12(4), if the action relates to journalistic, literary or artistic material,[62] which will be the case whenever the application is to restrain publication by a newspaper or in a broadcast, the court must consider:

(1) The extent to which the material 'has, or is, about to become available to the public'.[63] In Parliament the Home Secretary gave as an example that the information was shortly to be published abroad or had already been published in Scotland.[64] Section 12(4) does not make previous or prospective publication a barrier to an injunction.[65]

(2) Whether 'it is, or would be, in the public interest for the material to be published'.[66] There is a complimentary provision in the Data Protection Act 1998 (DPA)[67] which exempts processing of data for the special purposes of journalism, literature and art from most of the requirements of the DPA prior to publication if 'the data controller reasonably believes that, having regard in particular to the special importance of the public interest in freedom of expression, publication would be in the public interest'[68] if compliance is incompatible with the special purpose.

(3) Any relevant privacy code.[69] This allows the court to take into account compliance (or non-compliance) with media industry privacy codes and is therefore supportive of media self-regulation. The DPA likewise requires the courts to consider the privacy codes when deciding whether the data controller's belief that publication for one of the special purposes would be in the public interest was or is a reasonable one.[70]

8.14 **'Particular regard' to freedom of expression** The combined effect of s 12(1) and s 12(4) is that the court must have 'particular regard' to freedom of expression whenever deciding (not just at the interlocutory stage) whether to allow relief of any kind (damages included) which might undermine free speech. This does not mean that the court should place *extra weight* on freedom of expression.[71] Section 12(4) and Article 10 do not give freedom of expression a presumptive priority over

---

[62] These terms are not defined. In *Campbell v Frisbee* [2002] EWHC 328; [2002] EMLR 31, para 26 Lightman J adopts a definition of 'journalistic material' based on Police and Criminal Evidence Act 1984, s 13, namely 'material acquired or created for the purpose of journalism and conduct connected with such material'.
[63] s 12(a)(i).
[64] *Hansard*, HC vol 315, col 538 (2 July 1998).
[65] See *Venables v NGN Ltd* [2001] 1 All ER 908, para 105 and see para 8.04 above.
[66] s 12(a)(ii).
[67] DPA, s 32.
[68] DPA, s 32(1)(b). See *Campbell v MGN Ltd* [2002] EWCA Civ 1373.
[69] s 12(4)(b). Whether a source can rely on a privacy code was left open in *Campbell v Frisbee* [2002] EWCA Civ 1374, paras 24–25.
[70] DPA, s 31(3). Under the DPA only codes designated in a statutory instrument may be consulted (see para 18.40 below) whereas under the HRA there are no restrictions.
[71] *Ashdown v Telegraph Group* [2001] 4 All ER 666, para 27.

other rights.[72] Indeed, where proceedings relate to material which the defendant claims, or which appears to the court, to be journalistic, literary or artistic material, s 12(4) directs the court to have regard to 'any relevant privacy code'.[73] For the print media this will be the Press Complaints Commission's Code of Practice.[74] One of the functions of the PCC's Code, and that of other similar codes, is to protect privacy rights.

Human Rights Act 1998, s 12(3) and American Cyanamid

Effect of s 12(3) on the burden of proof In a freedom of expression case s 12(3) forbids a court from granting an interim injunction 'unless the court is satisfied that the applicant is likely to establish that publication should not be allowed'. The intention is to make the courts consider the relative strengths of the cases the two sides have put forward,[75] as the Scots courts have long done,[76] at the interlocutory stage. Hitherto this only happened in English law where the decision to grant or refuse interim relief effectively disposed of the action. This tends to be the case where the applicant seeks to enjoin publication of confidential personal information by the media. An interim injunction not to publish a story, if granted, will kill it. Conversely, if interim relief is refused there will be nothing left to protect at the trial and it may be impossible to offer realistic compensation for the privacy that has been destroyed.[77] **8.15**

By virtue of s 12(3) a court must be satisfied that upon a final determination of the case the applicant is *likely* to succeed (in the sense of having a real prospect of success, convincingly established)[78] taking into account the full range of relevant Convention rights.[79] If it is not known what the information is that the defendant proposes to disclose it will be almost impossible to obtain an interim injunction.[80] Where the information is known, the matters to be considered include 'not **8.16**

---

[72] *Campbell v Frisbee* [2002] EWHC 328; [2002] EMLR 31, para 29. cp Council of Europe, Resolution 1165 (1998) *Right to Privacy*, para 11: 'The Assembly reaffirms the importance of every person's right to privacy, and of the right to freedom of expression, as fundamental to a democratic society. These rights are neither absolute nor in any hierarchical order, since they are of equal value.'
[73] HRA, s 12(4)(b). See also *A v B plc & C ('Flitcroft')* [2002] EWCA Civ 337; [2002] 3 WLR 542, para 11, guideline xiv. On the extent to which the privacy codes may set standards of conduct for others who have obligations of confidentiality see: *Campbell v Frisbee* [2002] EWHC 328; [2002] EMLR 31, para 29 and [2002] EWCA Civ 1374, paras 24–25.
[74] http://www.pcc.org.uk and see para 9.10 below. Apart from the PCC's Code, other possible codes are those of the Broadcasting Standards Commission (see para 19.17 below), the Independent Television Commission (see para 19.20 below), the Radio Authority's Programme Code and the Producers Guidelines of the BBC.
[75] *Hansard*, HC vol 315, col 536 (2 July 1998).
[76] *NWL Ltd v Woods* [1979] 3 All ER 614, 628.
[77] cp *Cambridge Nutrition Ltd v BBC* [1990] 3 All ER 523.
[78] *Cream Holdings Ltd v Banerjee* [2003] EWCA Civ 103 overruling previous announcements that the standard was 'more probable than not'.
[79] *Douglas v Hello! Ltd* [2001] 2 All ER 289, para 134.
[80] cp *Dickson Minto WS v Bonnier Media Ltd* [2002] SLT 776, para 5.

merely the evidence about how great is the risk of that right being breached, but also a consideration of the gravity of the consequences for an applicant if the risk materializes'.[81] In *Mills v NGN Ltd*,[82] Collins J refused an interim injunction to restrain publication of the location of the residence of Ms Mills, the girlfriend of ex-beatle Sir Paul McCartney, because the information was 'relatively trivial' and the evidence of a 'real risk' to her personal safety if the information was disclosed 'very slight'.[83] Several judges have said that s 13(3) will not appreciably affect the ability to get an interim injunction compared with the situation before the HRA came into force[84] and this could be true for those seeking to gag the media; in personal information actions the perishable nature of the information meant that the relative merits of both sides had to be considered even before the HRA.

8.17 **The balance of convenience** Should the applicant for an injunction manage to satisfy the requirements of s 12(3), an interim injunction may still not be forthcoming[85] if, for example, the consequences of an injunction for the defendant would be graver than the consequences of refusing an injunction for the claimant. To this extent the *American Cyanamid* principles[85a] remain relevant. In *Douglas v Hello! Ltd*[86] the Court of Appeal discharged the interim injunction granted by the lower court to prevent the defendants spoiling a contract for the exclusive right to publish photographs of a celebrity wedding because the claimants had intended to publicize the occasion in a magazine anyway and injury to the claimants, unlike the defendants, could be adequately compensated by damages.[87]

The Woolf guidelines

The guidelines

8.18 Lord Woolf offered practical guidance on how to approach s 12 when an interim injunction is sought against the media in *A v B & C plc ('Flitcroft')*.[88] He said that the existence of an obvious public interest in publication strengthens[89] the case for refusing the injunction.[90] The fact that the claimant is a role model for some mem-

---

[81] per Keene LJ, *Douglas v Hello! Ltd* [2001] 2 All ER 289, para 150.
[82] [2001] EMLR 957.
[83] ibid paras 33, 34. These are factors, that could be considered as part of the balance of convenience when applying the *Cyanamid* test, though possibly only as a last resort.
[84] *Imutran Ltd v Uncaged Campaigns Ltd* [2001] 2 All ER 385 para 17; *A v B plc and C ('Flitcroft')* [2002] EWCA Civ 337; [2002] 3 WLR 542, para 11, guideline iii.
[85] *Cream Holdings Ltd v Banerjee* [2003] EWCA Civ 103, para 61.
[85a] See para 8.09 above.
[86] [2001] 2 All ER 289, paras 99–102.
[87] ibid at paras 97–99, 142, 171.
[88] [2002] EWCA Civ 337; [2002] 3 WLR 542.
[89] A substantial public interest may be offset by other considerations such as deterring suspects from making statements to the police (*Bunn v BBC* [1998] 3 All ER 552, 557) or persons suffering from a sexually transmitted disease seeking treatment (*X v Y* [1988] 2 All ER 648).
[90] *A v B plc and C ('Flitcroft')* [2002] EWCA Civ 337; [2002] 3 WLR 542, para 11, guideline viii. If it is not obvious whether there is a public interest in disclosure judges should not hear detailed

A. Prior Restraint

bers of the public may be a reason why correction of a false image is in the public interest.[91] However, the fact that there is no identifiable public interest in the press publishing material:

> does not mean that the court is justified in interfering with the freedom of the press ... [s]uch an approach would turn section 12(4) upside down. Regardless of the quality of the material which it is intended to publish *prima facie* the court should not interfere with its publication.[92]

There is, he said, a public interest in newspapers publishing anything which is of interest to the public. Sales keep newspapers afloat, and stories about well-known figures sell newspapers. 'Once it is accepted that freedom of the press should prevail, then the form of reporting in the press is not a matter for the courts but for the Press Complaints Commission and the customers of the newspapers concerned.'[93] A person may be a legitimate subject of public attention whether or not he has courted publicity and even trivial facts about a public figure can be of great interest to a newspaper's readers.[94] Obtaining confidential information that is not of public interest by unlawful means, however, may be a compelling argument in favour of restraint.[95]

8.19 Taking everything relevant into account, when the court faces an application for an injunction, the court must balance press freedom against the rights of others, particularly rights conferred under Article 8. The weight to be attached to each relevant factor depends upon the precise circumstances.[96] If the balance between the claimant's Article 8 privacy rights and a newspaper's Article 10 right to

---

argument on the point, as it is unlikely to determine whether interim relief should be granted. For the public interest as a defence to an action for breach of confidence see ch 11.

[91] [2002] EWCA Civ 337; [2002] 3 WLR 542, para 11, guideline xii. But see *Campbell v MGN Ltd* [2002] EWCA Civ 1373, para 41. Ironically, if the role model continues to be admired by impressionable members of the public, the exposé may do more harm than good.

[92] per Lord Woolf, *A v B plc and C ('Flitcroft')* [2002] EWCA Civ 337; [2002] 3 WLR 542, para 11, guideline v.

[93] *A v B plc & C ('Flitcroft')* [2002] EWCA Civ 337; [2002] 3 WLR 542, para 48. See also para 11, guideline xiii.

[94] ibid, para 11, guideline xii. In saying this, Lord Woolf would appear to be saying that publication of some information that, objectively viewed, is not actually in the public interest, is justifiable despite the infringement of privacy involved to an individual, because it contains information that is of interest to the public. In these circumstances the distinction between what is of interest to the public and what is in the public interest ceases to be important. Contrast Council of Europe, Resolution 1165 (1998) *Right to privacy*, para 8: '[i]t is often in the name of a one-sided interpretation of the right to freedom of expression ... that the media invade people's privacy, claiming that their readers are entitled to know everything about public figures.' In *Campbell v MGN Ltd* [2002] EWCA Civ 1373, para 40, the Court of Appeal tried to distance itself from Lord Woolf's approach by suggesting that he had not quite meant what he had said: 'Lord Woolf was not speaking of private facts which a fair-minded person would consider it offensive to disclose. That is clear from his subsequent commendation of the guidance or striking a balance between Article 8 and 10 rights provided by the Council of Europe Resolution 1165 of 1998.'

[95] *A v B plc & C ('Flitcroft')* [2002] EWCA Civ 337; [2002] 3 WLR 542, para 11, guideline x.

[96] ibid, para 12.

freedom of expression is in equilibrium, the court should not intervene.[97] Whatever decision the trial judge comes to, it will be accorded considerable deference by an appellate court.[98]

Criticism of the guidelines

8.20 Inconveniently for Lord Woolf, his advice contradicts the Press Complaints Commission's (PCC) own Code of Practice which requires a media intrusion to be justified by the public interest in a much narrower sense.[99] The BBC's Producer's Guidelines, another media privacy code to which the courts might have to refer, takes a very strict line:

> Public figures are in a special position, but they retain their rights to a private life. The public should be given the facts that bear upon the ability or the suitability of public figures to attain or hold office or to perform their duties, *but there is no general entitlement to know about their private behaviour provided that it is legal and does not raise important wider issues.* As a general principle, BBC programmes should not report the private legal behaviour of public figures unless broader public issues are raised either by the behaviour itself or by the consequences of its becoming widely known. The mere fact that other parts of the media have reported private behaviour . . . is not of itself sufficient to justify the BBC reporting it too. . . . Even when the personal affairs of public figures become the proper subject of enquiry they do not forfeit all rights to privacy. BBC programmes should confine themselves to relevant facts and avoid gossip. The information we broadcast should be important as well as true. It is not enough to say that it is interesting.[100]

8.21 Not long before Lord Woolf delivered his judgment, the Prime Minister's wife had obtained an injunction to prevent her former nanny and relatives from contravening an express confidentiality agreement by publishing reminiscences of their life as part of the Blair household. In giving a repeat judgment Wright J stated that there was no public interest in the publication of the material. 'I agree . . . with the view taken by Morland J that publication of this material is quite plainly not justified by any conceivable public interest, bearing in mind as I do the expression "public interest" means information that the public has an interest in receiving and not that which the public might be interested in hearing about, which is of course the justification that

---

[97] ibid, para 12. Contrast *Douglas v Hello! Ltd* [2001] 2 All ER 289, paras 135.
[98] *A v B plc & C* [2002] 2 All ER 545 [2002] EWCA Civ 337, para 46.
[99] The Code of Practice says that there may be exceptions from the privacy clauses (see para 9.10 below) of the code 'where they can be demonstrated to be in the public interest'. Grounds justifying intrusion into privacy include 'detecting or exposing' serious crime, and 'preventing the public from being misled by some statement or action of an individual or an organization'. There is no suggestion that this category includes items that titillate or satisfy the idle curiosity of readers and hence sell newspapers. The Code further states that where the public interest is invoked the editor must give a full explanation demonstrating how the public interest was served. In cases involving children the editor must demonstrate an exceptional public interest to override the normally paramount interest of the child. See also PCC, *Submission to the Culture, Media and Sport Select Committee* (February 2003) §C (4). Seven principles are identified, including whether 'there is a genuine public interest in intrusion'.
[100] Producer's Guidelines, ch 4.2, http://www.bbc.co.uk (italics added).

A. Prior Restraint

is so often put forward, because it sells newspapers.' The view of these judges is shared by the Broadcasting Standards Commission which has criticized programmes that infringe privacy without any public interest justification.[101]

The ECtHR is a strong supporter of press freedom when the item published contributes to public debate.[102] No support has been expressed by the Court or the Commission for the publication of gossip that interferes with someone's right to respect for private life and is not in the public interest.[103] The Committee of Ministers has said that the purpose of the Convention is not to protect the commercial interests of particular newspapers.[104] This accords with French and German law which treat publication of private information for purely commercial reasons as an invasion of privacy.[105] Moreover, the Court of Appeal itself has said that issues of taste, decency and offence (which Lord Woolf treats as exclusively the concern of the PCC) are capable of providing a justification for a prior restraint under Article 10(2) by reference to 'the rights of others'.[106]

8.22

Tammer v Estonia,[107] in which the ECtHR unanimously rejected the claim of a journalist that his conviction was incompatible with Article 10, is a telling case. The reason for the conviction were derogatory remarks contained in an interview with a fellow journalist about aspects of the private life[108] of a politician's wife who was in a dispute with the interviewed journalist about the authorship of her memoirs. The ECtHR said that the words the journalist had published:

8.23

> [had to be] seen against the background which prompted their utterance *as well as their value to the general public*[109] [and that despite her involvement in a political party] the Court does not find it established that the use of the impugned terms in relation to [her] private life *was justified by considerations of public concern or that they bore on a matter of general importance. In particular, it has not been substantiated that her private life was among the issues that affected the public in April 1996. The applicant's remarks could therefore scarcely be regarded as serving the public interest*... [T]he Court observes that the Estonian courts fully recognized that the present case

---

[101] M Tugendhat and I Christie (eds), *The Law of Privacy and the Media* (Oxford: 2002) para 13.49.
[102] See paras 3.17, 3.19 and 3.29 above.
[103] See for example, *A Neves v Portugal* Application 20683/92 (20 February 1995) which involved conviction of the owner of a magazine for defamation and violation of privacy following the publication of photographs of a well-known businessman engaging in sexual acts with several young women.
[104] *de Geillustreerde Pers v Netherlands* (1976) DR 8, p 5; Resolution of the Committee of Ministers DH (77) 1 of 17 February 1977.
[105] J Craig, 'Invasion of Privacy and Charter Values' (1997) 42 McGill LJ 355, 393 citing *Princess Caroline* BGH NJW 1996, 1128, 1130; *Philipe v France Editions* Gaz Pal 1966 1er sem Jur 38.
[106] *R (on the application of ProLife Alliance) v BBC* [2002] EWCA Civ 297; [2002] 2 All ER 756, paras 26, 52, 56.
[107] Application 41205/98, 10 BHRC 543.
[108] Breaking up his previous family and letting her parents look after their child.
[109] ibid, para 66.

involved a conflict between the right to impart ideas and the reputation and rights of others. It cannot find that they failed properly to balance the various interests involved in the case.[110]

8.24 Jack J's assessment in *A v B plc and C ('Flitcroft')* of what the European Convention on Human Rights (ECHR) requires, if not his actual decision on the facts, is more in keeping with the privacy codes, the structure of the Convention and the relevant Strasbourg jurisprudence than Lord Woolf's judgment on appeal.

> [I]t follows as a matter of logic, and is consistent with the structure of Article 10 in two paragraphs, that where the public interest, the public benefit, in the publication of a matter is great, any justification for suppressing that publication must be very strong in order to prevail. Conversely, where the public interest in publication is very slight, or non-existent, a lesser justification may exist.[111]

Summary of relevant factors

8.25 At this point it is useful to sum up the factors that domestic and European case law, the HRA and the privacy codes indicate are relevant to the decision whether to grant an interim injunction that interferes with Article 10. They include

(1) how[112] and where[113] the information was acquired;
(2) whether disclosure was in flagrant breach of an express confidentiality covenant;[114]
(3) the public or private status of the victim;[115]
(4) intimate or non-intimate nature of the information;[116]
(5) the extent to which the information has already been disseminated;[117]

---

[110] ibid, para 68 (italics added). cp *Report of the Committee on Privacy* (Younger Committee) (Cmnd 5012, 1972) para 157.

[111] [2001] 1 WLR 2341, para 31.

[112] *R (on the application of Ford) v PCC* [2001] EWHC Admin 683; [2002] EMLR 95, para 30 (clandestine photography). A newspaper that flouts clause 3 of the PCC code (see para 9.10 below) 'is likely . . . to have its claim to an entitlement to freedom of expression trumped by Article 10(2) considerations of privacy', per Brooke J, *Douglas v Hello! Ltd* [2001] 2 All ER 289, para 94. Any breach of a media privacy code is evidence of abuse of press freedom.

[113] *R (on the application of Ford) v PCC* [2001] EWHC Admin 683; [2002] EMLR 95, paras 31, 33; *MGN Ltd v Attard* (Fam Div, 19 October 2001) (photograph of Jodie Attard being pushed along a public highway in a pram by her mother). See also para 6.19 above.

[114] cp *Att-Gen v Barker* [1990] 3 All ER 257, 261c; *Adams v Attridge* (QB, 8 October 1998); *Campbell v Frisbee* [2002] EWHC 328; [2002] EMLR 31, para 40; *Hitchcock v TCN Channel Nine Pty Ltd* [2000] NSWSC 198.

[115] *Dalban v Romania* (2001) 31 EHRR 39, paras 48, 50; *A v B plc & C ('Flitcroft')* [2002] 2 All ER 545 [2002] EWCA Civ 337; [2002] 3 WLR 542, para 11, guideline xii; *Peck v UK* Application 44647/98 28 January 2003, para 62. For an analysis of 'the public figure' see para 6.22 above.

[116] Compare *Ashworth Hospital Authority v MGN Ltd* [2001] 1 All ER 991, CA, para 99; approved *Ashworth Hospital Authority v MGN Ltd* [2002] UKHL 29; [2002] 1 WLR 2033, paras 65–66 (medical data) and *Fressoz v France* (2000) 31 EHRR 3 (financial). Triviality is a reason for refusing an injunction, but will simultaneously negate the public interest in disclosure.

[117] *Att-Gen v Guardian Newspapers Ltd (No 2)* [1988] 3 All ER 545, 645, 665; *Tucker v News Media Ownership Ltd* [1986] 2 NZLR 716, 736.

A. Prior Restraint

(6) extent of planned dissemination;[118]

(7) adverse consequences of disclosure beyond loss of privacy;[119]

(8) the public interest in disclosure,[120] especially the contribution the information can make to public debate;[121]

(9) whether the personal information that is the subject of complaint was gratuitous to that debate;[122]

(10) disclosure in visual or non-visual format.[123]

Data Protection Compliance Order

8.26 Should the professional or third party be a data controller,[124] the client is entitled to require the cessation (or non-commencement) of processing[125] of his personal information provided:

(1) the information is held as 'personal data' on a computer or in structured manual files;[126] *and*

(2) the processing is causing or likely to cause unwarranted and substantial damage or distress to the client or to someone else.[127]

8.27 If the request goes unheeded, the client can apply to a court for a compliance order which the court, in its discretion, may grant.[128] Should such an application be met by a claim that the personal data is being processed solely for journalistic, literary or artistic purposes with a view to first publication, the court must stay the

---

[118] See paras 11.62–11.65 below. cp *Peck v UK* Application 44647/98 28 January 2003, para 62.

[119] *Venables v NGN Ltd* [2001] 1 All ER 908 (risk to life); *H (A Health Worker) v Associated Newspapers Ltd* [2002] EWCA Civ 195, (2002) 65 BMLR 132, para 27 (health workers will be discouraged from reporting they are HIV seropositive).

[120] HRA, s12(4).

[121] cp *Fressoz v France* (2001) 31 EHRR 2, paras 50–51; *A v B & C* (21 March 2001); *A v B plc and C ('Flitcroft')* [2001] 1 WLR 2341, QB, para 31; *Tammer v Estonia* Application 41205/98, 10 BHRC 543, para 68; *H (A Health Worker) v Associated Newspapers Ltd* [2002] EWCA Civ 195, (2002) 65 BMLR 132, para 24. But see *A v B plc and C ('Flitcroft')* [2002] EWCA Civ 337; [2002] 3 WLR 542, para 11, guideline v; *Mills v NGN Ltd* [2001] EMLR 95, para 32.

[122] *Tammer v Estonia* Application 41205/98, 10 BHRC 543, para 67. Cp *Barber v Time, Inc* 159 SW 2d 291, 295–296 (1942); *X v Y* [1988] 2 All ER 648, 656; *Peck v UK* Application 44647/98 28 January 2003, para 74. It is a requirement of German law that the court consider whether public debate was possible 'without any interference—or a less far-reaching interference—with the protection of personality': *Lebach* BVerfGE 35,202 (1973) in B Markesinis, *A Comparative Introduction to the German Law of Torts* (3rd edn, Oxford: 1994) 390. The PCC takes a similar view. It has found against newspapers that have identified CJD sufferers: Mrs Janet Rutherford and The Scottish Daily Mail, 10 June 1996, Annual Report 2001, 'Protecting ordinary people'. cp *R (on the application of ProLife Alliance) v BBC* [2002] EWCA Civ 297; [2002] 2 All ER 756, paras 19, 62.

[123] See para 6.19 above.

[124] A data controller is defined in DPA, s 1(1) as a person who (alone or jointly) determines the purposes for which and manner in which personal data is processed.

[125] This includes holding, using and disclosing: DPA, s 1(1).

[126] See DPA s 1(1) and para 18.06 below.

[127] DPA, s 10(1).

[128] DPA, s 10(4). It is assumed here that no exemption applies.

proceedings[129] until such time as the claim is withdrawn or the Information Commissioner has made a determination[130] about the validity of the claim.[131] The stay procedure applies also to an action for statutory damages pursuant to DPA, s 13.[132]

B. After-the-Event Remedies

Monetary Awards[133]

Causes of Action

Contract and tort

8.28 The glossary to the CPR describes 'damages' as '[a] sum of money awarded by the court as compensation to the claimant'. Damages may be awarded in contract for breach of a contractual promise of confidentiality. All tortious causes of action support claims for damages.

Breach of copyright

8.29 The successful claimant in an action for breach of copyright has the option of damages or securing an account of profits[134] made by the defendant by using the claimant's work or damages. The measure of damages is the depreciation the infringement has caused to the value of the copyright.[135]

Recovering damages from a public authority under the Human Rights Act 1998[136]

8.30 When a client brings a successful action under HRA, s 7 against a public authority for violation of an adopted Convention right, HRA, s 8 enables the court to grant such remedy as it thinks 'just and appropriate'. This includes damages, but

---

[129] DPA, s 32(4).
[130] The Commissioner can require the defendant to provide information about the processing (s 44), but, except in urgent cases (s44(6)), the defendant can delay providing the information until a right of appeal to the Data Protection Tribunal has been exhausted (ss 44(5), 48(1)).
[131] DPA, s 45.
[132] See para 4.49 above. The procedure has no relevance for any other cause of action arising out of the threatened disclosure of information.
[133] A Burrows, *Remedies for Torts and Breach of Contract* (2nd edn, London: 1994); F Gurry, *Breach of Confidence* (Oxford: 1984) ch xxiii; P Parkinson (ed), *The Principles of Equity* (Sydney: 1996) ch 22; D Harris, D Campbell, R Halson, *Remedies in Contract and Tort* (2nd edn, London: 2002).
[134] See para 8.71 below.
[135] *Beloff v Pressdram Ltd* [1973] 1 All ER 241, 264; *Surrey CC v Bredero Homes Ltd* [1993] 3 All ER 705, 710–711.
[136] D Fairgrieve, 'The Human Rights Act 1998, Damages and Tort Law' [2001] PL 695; T Eicke and D Scorey, *Human Rights Damages: Principles and Practice* (London: 2001); L Mulcahy (ed), *Human Rights and Civil Practice* (London: 2001) paras 9.18 et seq.

damages are not obtainable as of right. The court must be satisfied, after taking into account the effect of other relief granted and the consequences of the decision, that 'the award is necessary to afford just satisfaction' to the successful claimant.[137] This points to damages as a residual remedy: a stop-gap if other relief is inadequate.

8.31 In applying s 8 the courts are required to have regard to the principles that the ECtHR applies to determine compensation under Article 41.[138] The ECtHR's general approach is to try to put the applicant in the position that he would have been in had there been no breach of the Convention (restitutio in integrum).[139] It has no settled principles for measuring damages. In *Secretary of State for the Home Department v Wainwright*[140] Buxton LJ commented that it 'it is wholly unclear what are the rules of remoteness attaching to a claim under s 7; whether breaches of the ECHR by public authorities are actionable per se; and if they are, what heads of damage and amounts of damages are recoverable'. The ECtHR sometimes refuses non-pecuniary damages, taking the view that a finding of a violation is sufficient compensation.[141] Factors that appear to influence the amount of damages awarded are the seriousness of the interference and the conduct of the parties.[142]

8.32 Extra-judicially[143] Lord Woolf has deduced a number of principles from the Strasbourg jurisprudence which he has suggested should inform decisions of the domestic courts about whether, and to what extent, to allow damages under the HRA:

(1) if there is any other viable remedy, damages should only be granted in addition if necessary to afford satisfaction;
(2) the award should be of a sum that is no greater than necessary to achieve just satisfaction;
(3) the quantum of damages should be moderate and 'normally on the low side by comparison to tortuous awards';

---

[137] HRA, s 8(3).
[138] HRA, s 8(4). For a discussion of the applicable principles see Law Commission Report 266, *Damages under the Human Rights Act 1998* (Cm 4853, 2000) available from http://www.lawcom.gov.uk.
[139] Law Commission Report 266, *Damages under the Human Rights Act 1998* (Cm 4853, 2000) para 3.19.
[140] [2001] EWCA Civ 2081; [2002] 3 WLR 405, para 94.
[141] *Domenichini v Italy* 21 October 1996, para 45; *Kopp v Switzerland* (1998) 27 EHRR 91, para 83; *Amann v Switzerland* (2000) 30 EHRR 843. All three cases involved interferences with Art 8 rights.
[142] Law Commission Report 266, *Damages under the Human Rights Act 1998* (Cm 4853, 2000) paras 3.45–3.57.
[143] M Andenas and M Fairgrieve (eds), *Judicial Review in International Perspective* II (The Hague: 2000) 429.

(4) the claimant should receive compensation only for what happened in so far as the unlawful conduct exceeded what could happen lawfully;

(5) the sum awarded can be reduced to take account of the failure of the claimant to mitigate his injuries.

'Damages' in equity

8.33 In common law tort and contract actions There are two distinct circumstances in which a client might receive monetary relief in equity in proceedings relating to the disclosure or threatened disclosure or misuse of confidential personal information. The first is where the client brings an action at common law. Since the enactment of Lord Cairns' Act in 1858 a court exercising equitable jurisdiction has been able to grant statutory damages *in addition* to an injunction in aid of a legal right.[144] Normally when Lord Cairns' Act (now s 50 of the Supreme Court Act 1981) is applied to an already committed legal wrong the claimant will recover in equity what he would have recovered at common law.[145] Because statutory damages in equity (unlike common law damages) are discretionary,[146] the client may sometimes recover less in equity than he would have done at common law, or nothing at all, because of factors such as delay, acquiescence or a lack of 'clean hands' on his part.

8.34 Lord Cairns' Act also entitles a court to *substitute* statutory damages for an injunction, provided the injunction is refused on non-jurisdictional grounds.[147] Damages in lieu of an injunction relate to the future and therefore go beyond what could be recovered at common law where damages are only given for past injury.[148] It is difficult to envisage circumstances in which a court would prefer to give damages to injunctive relief where there is a continuing threat of disclosure of confidential personal information by a professional.

Recovering 'damages' for interference with an exclusively equitable interest

8.35 The second circumstance in which the question of monetary relief may arise in equity is if the client pursues an equitable cause of action. The two possibilities are breach of confidence and breach of fiduciary duty.

8.36 Breach of fiduciary duty An account of profits is the standard remedy for breach of fiduciary duty but in *Nocton v Lord Ashburton*[149] Viscount Haldane

---

[144] Chancery Amendment Act 1858, s 2. See now Supreme Court Act 1981, s 50.
[145] *Johnson v Agnew* [1980] AC 367, 400; *Jaggard v Sawyer* [1995] 2 All ER 189.
[146] *Price v Strange* [1978] Ch 337, 359, 368–369.
[147] Non-jurisdictional examples include acquiescence, delay, lack of 'clean hands' or, possibly, the trivial nature of the information disclosed. Another possible reason for refusing an injunction might be that the information disclosed in breach of a contractual obligation of confidentiality has become universally known. However, there is uncertainty as to whether this is a jurisdictional or a discretionary factor.
[148] *Jaggard v Sawyer* [1995] 2 All ER 189, 204, 211.
[149] [1914] AC 932, 956, 958. See also *Swindle v Harrison* [1997] 4 All ER 705, 733.

B. After-the-Event Remedies

confirmed that equitable compensation is an alternative.[150] The power to compensate derives from the court's inherent equitable jurisdiction and not from Lord Cairns' Act.[151] Where the claimant has suffered actual loss, equitable compensation for breach of fiduciary duty is assessed on the principle that the claimant should be put in as good a position as that in which he was before the breach of fiduciary duty occurred.[152] Equitable compensation can be awarded though the claimant benefited from the breach of fiduciary duty.[153]

Breach of confidence[154]   It has become routine for a complainant alleging the disclosure of personal information in a breach of confidence action to ask for 'damages',[155] usually, but not necessarily, coupled with an application for an injunction to prevent future or continued disclosures. That a court is entitled to award money to the claimant in a breach of confidence action, with or without an injunction, is now certain.[156] The source of the power to award compensation is not. The juristic basis of the 'damages' is tied up, in part, with the issue of the origins of the breach of confidence action.[157] If, as some think, it is tortious, then the damages are common law damages[158] which are obtainable as of right. If, as seems more likely, it is equitable then the 'damages' are, like all equitable remedies, discretionary. 8.37

There are three theories about equity's ability to award monetary compensation for a breach of confidence: 8.38

(1) The 'damages' are awarded pursuant to Lord Cairn's Act (now s 50 of the Supreme Court Act 1981) either as a substitute for, or in addition to, an injunction.[159]

---

[150] See also *Longstaff v Birtles* [2001] EWCA Civ 1219; [2002] 1 WLR 470. It is not possible to have an account of profits and equitable compensation: *Tang Man Sit (dec'd) v Capacious Investments Ltd* [1996] 1 All ER 193, 197.

[151] *US Surgical Corp v Hospital Products International Pty Ltd* [1982] 2 NSWLR 766, 816.

[152] *Swindle v Harrison* [1997] 4 All ER 705.

[153] *Boardman v Phipps* [1967] 2 AC 47.

[154] D Capper, 'Damages for breach of the equitable duty of confidence' [1994] 14 LS 313; M Gronow, 'Damages for Breach of Confidence' (1994) 2 Australian Intellectual Property J 95.

[155] *Woodward v Hutchins* [1977] 1 WLR 760, 764, 765; *W v Egdell* [1990] 1 All ER 835; *Khodaparast v Farrokh-Shad* (CA, 28 February 1997); *Adjenii v Newham LBC* (QB, 16 October 2001). See also, *Douglas v Hello! Ltd* [2001] 2 All ER 289, para 142.

[156] *Adjenii v Newham LBC* (QB, 16 October 2001). Cp *Seager v Copydex Ltd (No 1)* [1967] 2 All ER 415, 419; *Seager v Copydex Ltd (No 2)* [1969] 2 All ER 718.

[157] See para 5.03 above.

[158] *O'Neill v DHSS (No 2)* [1986] NI 290, 294, 299.

[159] *Nichrotherm Electrical Co Ltd v Percy* [1957] RPC 207, 214. See also *Saltman Engineering Co Ltd v Campbell Engineering Co Ltd* [1963] 3 All ER 413 n, 415; *Att-Gen v Guardian Newspapers Ltd (No 2)* [1988] 3 All ER 545, 662; *O'Neill v DHSS (No2)* [1986] NI 290, 298; *Douglas v Hello! Ltd* [2001] 2 All ER 289, para 122.

(2) Independently of s 50, on the assumption that law and equity have fused, courts can come to the aid of an equitable right with an award of common law damages.[160]

(3) The court awards equitable compensation.[161] In *Campbell v MGN Ltd*[162] Morland J treated this as self-evident.[163]

8.39 In *Malone v Metropolitan Police Commissioner* Megarry VC said in relation to an action for breach of confidence arising from the disclosure of confidential information:

> if there is no case for the grant of an injunction, *as when the disclosure has already been made*, the unsatisfactory result seems to be that no damages can be awarded under this head . . .[164]

This obiter passage implies that:

(1) the 'damages' that are recoverable depend upon Lord Cairns' Act;
(2) statutory damages cannot be awarded unless the court had *jurisdiction* to grant an injunction;
(3) an injunction will be refused if there is no risk of the wrong recurring; and
(4) refusal on ground (3) goes to *jurisdiction.*

The third assumption is well settled,[165] and the second also.[166] The other two are controversial.

8.40 If Megarry VC is right then the action for breach of confidence is seriously deficient as a remedy for the improper disclosure of confidential personal information. A professional can breach a duty of confidentiality to her client with

---

[160] *Aquaculture Corp v New Zealand Green Mussel Co* [1990] 3 NZLR 299, 301. See also *Mouat v Clark Boyce* [1992] 2 NZLR 559, 566. For a critique of *Aquaculture Corp* see P Michalik, 'The availability of compensatory and exemplary damages in equity: A Note on the Aquaculture decision' (1991) 21 Victoria U of Wellington L Rev 391, 399 et seq. cp *Metall und Rohstoff AG v Donaldson Lufkin & Jenrette Inc* [1990] 1 QB 391, 473 where the Court of Appeal refused to award damages for a breach of trust.

[161] R Toulson and C Phipps, *Confidentiality* (London: 1996) 31 et seq.

[162] [2002] EWHC 499; [2002] EMLR 30, para 42.

[163] In *O'Neill v DHSS* [1986] 5 NI 290, where the court did not think that Lord Cairns' Act could be relied upon because an injunction could not be obtained, the court did not consider the alternative of equitable compensation.

[164] [1979] 2 All ER 620, 633 (italics added). See also *O'Neill v DHSS* [1986] 5 NI 290, 297.

[165] 'Now an injunction is granted for prevention, and where there is no ground for apprehending the repetition of a wrongful act there is no ground for an injunction', per Fry LJ, *Proctor v Bayley* (1889) 42 Ch D 390, 401.

[166] The wording of Supreme Court Act 1981, s 50 makes this clear. See also *O'Neill v DHSS (No 2)* [1986] NI 290, 296; *Jaggard v Sawyer* [1995] 2 All ER 189, 205. In *HRH Princess of Wales v MGN* (QB, 8 November 1993) the contention that no injunction was warranted because 'there is nothing left to hide; the ice has been melted because the photographs have already been published' was rejected on the grounds that there were known to be more photographs in existence. Presumably if there had not been, an injunction might have been refused.

impunity so long as (1) she makes sure that she disseminates the information so widely that it enters the public domain, and (2) her financial position is not improved by the disclosure. The first condition makes an injunction pointless, and therefore statutory damages unobtainable, and the second rules out an account of profits. Yet it is hard to conceive that equity would send the victim of a wrongful disclosure of confidential personal information by a professional away empty handed, if the victim made a timely application for compensation.[167]

The better view must be that: **8.41**

(1) 'damages' may be awarded independently of s 50 of the Supreme Court Act 1981 in the form of as equitable compensation, or
(2) impossibility (or unlikelihood) of repetition is only a discretionary reason for refusing an injunction;[168] or
(3) both (1) and (2) are correct.

Heads of Damage

Tangible injury

There is no problem about the client recovering common law damages for a pecuniary[169] or physical injury[170] suffered in consequence of a breach of confidence or associated wrong, provided the injury was caused by the wrong and is not too remote. It is beyond the scope of this book to discuss theories of causation and remoteness of damage in tort and contract[171] except for one point. For torts of intention such as the rule in *Wilkinson v Downton*, injurious falsehood and interference with contractual relations, the client can recover for injuries that were *not* of a foreseeable nature but were intended or were a direct consequence of the disclosure.[172] **8.42**

The client who suffers 'damage'[173] by reason of a contravention of the DPA may recover his 'special or financial'[174] losses under s 13 of that Act. **8.43**

---

[167] Morland J did not in *Cornelius v de Taranto* [2002] EMLR 12.
[168] D Capper, 'Damages for breach of the equitable duty of confidence' [1994] *LS* 313, 320.
[169] eg *G v Att-Gen* [1994] 1 NZLR 714, 719 (cost of restoring secrecy after a breach of statutory duty).
[170] eg *Furniss v Fitchett* [1958] NZLR 396 (psychiatric injury).
[171] See also J Cartwright, 'Remoteness of Damage in Contract and Tort' [1996] CLJ 488, 510–511.
[172] In *Home Office v Wainwright* [2001] EWCA Civ 2081; [2002] 3 WLR 405, para 50 Lord Woolf said: '[w]e are here concerned with an intentional tort and intended harm. In such a situation, unlike negligence, problems as to forseeability do not arise. If the conduct is actionable then compensation should be payable for the intended harm.' See also *Smith New Court Securities Ltd v Scrimgeour Vickers (Asset Management) Ltd* [1996] 4 All ER 769, 792 (deceit). But a defendant may escape liability for the unintended republication of a libel: *Weld-Blundell v Stephens* [1920] AC 956.
[173] DPA, s 13(2)(a).
[174] *Campbell v MGN Ltd* [2002] EWHC 499; [2002] EMLR 30, para 123.

8.44 HRA, s 7 supports the award of damages to cover for pecuniary loss.[175] Strasbourg jurisprudence requires a direct link between the damages claimed and the Convention violation.[176] This principle has caused many claims for pecuniary loss to founder in the ECtHR.[177]

8.45 Equitable compensation is available to make good a financial loss[178] inflicted by the defendant by the breach of an equitable duty. There are statements in English[179] and Commonwealth[180] cases that when assessing equitable compensation common law concepts of causation and remoteness are irrelevant. But even in equity, there must be some causal connection between breach and loss. In *Target Holdings Ltd v Redferns*[181] Lord Browne-Wilkinson approved an observation by a judge of the Canadian Supreme Court that 'it is essential that the losses made good are only those which, on a common sense view of causation, were caused by the breach'.[182] A New Zealand judge confined the claimant's damages against a psychologist 'to the actual, not the perceived nature' of the breach of his confidence. The psychologist had, the judge decided, legitimately disclosed to a government department information about the claimant's daughter who was accusing her father of sexual abuse. What was wrong was the additional disclosure of information about the father that was not necessary in the daughter's best interests. Modest damages were allowed for this excessive zeal because, in the judge's opinion, this information was of no significance or consequence: '[t]he plaintiff

---

[175] The principles of the ECtHR must be applied (HRA, s8(4)); the ECtHR allows recovery of pecuniary losses: *Jabardo v Spain* (1994) 11 EHRR 360 (Art 6 case), Law Commission Report 266, Damages under the Human Rights Act 1998 (Cm 4853, 2000) paras 3.19–3.21, 3.23–3.25, 4.61–4.62.

[176] *Sekanina v Austria* (1993) 17 EHRR 221.

[177] Law Commission Report 266, *Damages under the Human Rights Act 1998* (Cm 4853, 2000) para 3.58.

[178] In *X v Att-Gen* [1997] 2 NZLR 623 a New Zealand judge allowed X to recover pecuniary losses arising from the breach of confidence by the police (the expense of obtaining an injunction and moving his wife and child to a place of safety). In *Cornelius v de Taranto* [2001] EMLR 12, para 86 the claimant recovered the expense of retrieving copies of the report that should not have been disclosed.

[179] *Bartlett v Barclays Bank Trust Co Ltd (No 2)* [1980] Ch 515, 543; *Swindle v Harrison* [1997] 4 All ER 705, 733. See also *Brickenden v London Loan & Savings Co* [1934] 3 DLR 465, 469.

[180] *Re Dawson* [1966] 2 NSWLR 211, 216; *Commonwealth Bank of Australia v Smith* (1991) 102 ALR 453, 479; *Bennett v Minister of Community Welfare* (1992) 66 ALJR 550, 557; *Pilmer v Duke Group Ltd* [2001] HCA 31, paras 85, 150–156. But see *Day v Mead* [1987] 2 NZLR 443; *Stewart v Canadian Broadcasting Corp* (1997) 150 DLR (4th) 193, 169.

[181] [1995] 3 All ER 785, 798. See also *Swindle v Harrison* [1997] 4 All ER 705, 733.

[182] *Canson Enterprises Ltd v Boughton* (1991) 85 DLR (4th) 129, 163 per McLachlin J The members of the court were divided as to how this result was to be achieved. 'A wrongdoer is only liable for the consequences of his being wrong and not for all the consequences of a course of action', per Mummery LJ, *Swindle v Harrison* [1997] 4 All ER 705, 718, 735. Consider also *Hilton v Barker Booth & Eastwood* [2002] EWCA Civ 723 where solicitors who had acted in breach of contract and of their fiduciary duty of loyalty by not telling the client that they were unable properly to act for him were not held liable for a loss that the client had sustained that he could not prove he would have avoided had he been represented by other solicitors.

B. After-the-Event Remedies

. . . is not entitled to compensation for all the anxiety and unhappiness caused by the dealings of the Department of Social Welfare with M, only for the actual consequences of the breach of the confidence.'[183]

Mental distress

Contract When personal information is disclosed by a professional without authority, the client is bound to be distressed. In some cases this may be the only injury flowing from a broken promise of confidentiality. Distress can take many forms of varying degrees of seriousness: annoyance, anger, grief, bitterness, anxiety, frustration, tension, disappointment, aggression, low self-esteem, shame, embarrassment, worry, indignation. English courts have traditionally been reluctant to compensate loss of mental tranquillity. In contract, damages for mental disturbances falling short of psychiatric illness are not generally allowed:[184]

8.46

> A contract-breaker is not in general liable for any distress, frustration, anxiety, displeasure, vexation, tension or aggravation which his breach of contract may cause to the innocent party. This rule is not, I think, founded on the assumption that such reactions are not foreseeable, which they surely are or may be, but on considerations of policy . . .[185]

There are some limited exceptions to the general rule:[186] distress resulting directly from physical inconvenience caused by the breach of contract[187] and contracts whose very object is to provide peace of mind or enjoyment.[188] It cannot be said that peace of mind is of the very essence of most contracts between professionals and their clients.[189] In *Groom v Crocker* a solicitor made an admission that a motor accident was caused solely by his client without consulting the client for his approval. The admission was not made in the client's best interests but to gain an advantage for the insurance company that was funding the retainer. The solicitor was held to have been in breach of contract to his client but the client recovered only nominal damages. Sir Wilfrid Greene MR said:

8.47

---

[183] *JD v Ross* [1998] NZFLR 951, 24–25.
[184] *Addis v Gramophone Co* [1909] AC 488.
[185] per Bingham LJ, *Watts v Morrow* [1991] 4 All ER 937, 959. See also *Johnson v Gore Wood & Co* [2001] 1 All ER 481, 505; *Farley v Skinner* [2001] UKHL 49, [2001] 4 All ER 801, paras 16, 47.
[186] N Enonchong, 'Breach of Contract and Damages for Mental Distress' [1996] OJLS 617; K Wheat (ed), *Recovering Damages for Psychiatric Injury* (2nd edn, Oxford: 2002) 30.
[187] *Perry v Sidney Phillips & Son* [1982] 3 All ER 705.
[188] *Hayes v Dodd* [1990] 2 All ER 815, 824, 826; *Farley v Skinner* [2001] UKHL 49, [2001] 4 All ER 801, paras 19–24. See also P Clarke, 'Damages in Contract for Mental Distress' (1978) 52 Australian LJ 626, 631.
[189] *Channon v Johnstone* [2002] EWCA Civ 353; [2002] Lloyd's Rep PN 342, para 54. In *McLeish v Amoo-Gottfried & Co*, The Times, 13 October 1993 Scott Baker J held that the very essence of a contract to act for the claimant in preparation for and at his trial for a criminal trial 'was to ensure his peace of mind by taking all appropriate steps to secure his acquittal, if possible, and if not, to make the best possible case for him'. Accordingly, damages for mental distress were recovered in this action for professional negligence in which liability was admitted.

I should have been glad if I could have found the law to be different from what I have conceived it to be. Professional men such as solicitors and doctors are in a position where a breach of duty may often lead to mental suffering and social discredit without any real pecuniary damage. In some cases, the client may, on the facts, have some other cause of action—for example, defamation. If, however, his sole cause of action depends on breach of contract, it is unfortunate if the damages recoverable in such circumstances are only nominal. Nevertheless, in the absence of authority, I am not prepared to hold otherwise than that the £1,000 awarded under this head must be reduced to 40s.[190]

8.48 If the professional has profited from the unauthorized disclosure of confidential information about the client, the client might try for restitutionary damages. In *Att-Gen v Blake*[191] the House of Lords held that a defendant could be made to disgorge the profit he had made through breaching a contract 'in exceptional circumstances' where other 'remedies are inadequate'. 'A useful guide' said Lord Nicholls was 'whether the plaintiff had a legitimate interest in preventing the defendant's profit-making activity.' This is true when a client who has suffered no tangible loss sues a professional for breach of confidence in contract. Even if the professional is not in a fiduciary relationship with the client (and some professionals are), the relationship has a fiduciary-like quality: the client expects loyalty.[192]

8.49a **Tort**[193]   The position is only a little brighter for the client in tort. Mental distress not amounting to psychiatric illness[194] cannot be compensated in negligence[195] unless it can be tacked[196] on to a physical effect.[197] 'The law expects the ordinary person to bear the mishaps of life with fortitude and . . . customary phlegm.'[198] Similarly, damages for mental distress under DPA, s 13 must be linked[199] to 'special or financial damages in contra-distinction to distress in the shape of injury to

---

[190] *Groom v Crocker* [1930] 2 All ER 395, 402.
[191] [2000] 4 All ER 385, 398.
[192] cp ibid at 404. See also *CMS Dolphin Ltd v Simonet* [2001] 2 BCLC 704.
[193] N Mullany and P Handford, *Tort Liability for Psychiatric Damage* (London: 1993); P Giliker 'A "new" head of damages: damages for mental distress in the English law of torts' [2001] LS 19.
[194] There was no difficulty in recovering damages in *Furniss v Fitchett* [1958] NZLR 396, 408 because the claimant suffered psychiatric injury. cp *Gogay v Hertfordshire CC* [2000] IRLR 703. Post-traumatic stress disorder, known to lawyers as 'nervous shock', is the most likely kind of mental illness to be caused by the disclosure of information, eg *Peters-Brown v Regina General Hospital* (1995) 58 ACWS (3d) 1044, affirmed (1996) 67 ACWS (3d) 924 where medical evidence of the nervous shock was not insisted upon.
[195] *Hunter v London Docklands Development Corp* [1997] 2 All ER 426, 453.
[196] 'The ordinary measure of compensatory damages will cover all they have suffered as a result of that breach, physically, psychologically and mentally. Full account will be taken of the distress and anxiety which such an event necessarily causes', per Sir Thomas Bingham MR, *AB v South West Water Services Ltd* [1993] 1 All ER 609, 628.
[197] *Joyce v Sengupta* [1993] 1 All ER 897, 907; *Shelley v Paddock* [1978] 3 All ER 129,136. See also *Kralj v McGrath* [1986] 1 All ER 54, 62; *Salih v Enfield Health Authority* [1991] 2 Med LR 235. cp *Archer v Brown* [1984] 2 All ER 267, 281–283.
[198] per Dillon LJ, *Khorasandjian v Bush* [1993] 3 All ER 669, 677.
[199] DPA, s 13(2)(a).

B. After-the-Event Remedies

feelings'[200] unless disclosure or use of the personal data was for literary, artistic or journalistic purposes.[201] It seems that damages for mental distress cannot be awarded at all for unlawful means conspiracy.[202]

Mental distress without other tangible harm will be compensated in an action for libel.[203] **8.49**

> In an action for defamation, the wrongful act is damage to the plaintiff's reputation. The injuries that he sustains may be classified under two heads: (i) the consequences of the attitude adopted to him by other persons as a result of the diminution of the esteem in which they hold him because of the defamatory statement; and (ii) the grief or annoyance caused by the defamatory statement to the plaintiff himself.[204]

Damages for both injury to reputation and grief or annoyance are 'at large'.[205]

Damages for pure mental distress can be awarded for many intentional torts,[206] though not at present intentional infliction of distress.[207] There is some hope that if a case reaches the House of Lords this bar will be lifted. Lord Hoffmann said in *Hunter v Canary Wharf Ltd* that he could see 'no reason why a tort of intention should be subject to the rule which excludes compensation for mere distress, inconvenience or discomfort in actions based on negligence'.[208] If a tort of infringement of privacy is recognized in this jurisdiction, it will doubtless allow recovery for pure mental distress.[209] There is no point in having a privacy tort if recovery is restricted to those rare situations in which the claimant suffered pecuniary or physical injury as well. The Law Commission proposed a statutory tort of breach of confidence that was to be actionable when the only injury was emotional.[210] **8.50**

---

[200] per Morland J, *Campbell v MGN Ltd* [2002] EWHC 499; [2002] EMLR 30, para 123. cp *Pascal v Barclays Bank plc Mayor's and City of London Court* May 1999 LTL 18 May 2001.
[201] DPA., s13(2)(b).
[202] *Lonrho plc v Fayed (No 5)* [1994] 1 All ER 188, 195.
[203] *Cleese v Clark* (QBD 2 February 2003). Mental distress on its own does not supply the special damage necessary for an action for slander: see para 4.35 above.
[204] per Diplock LJ, *McCarey v Associated Newspapers Ltd* [1964] 3 All ER 947, 959. See also, *John v MGN Ltd* [1996] 2 All ER 35, 47. In *Carson v John Fairfax & Sons Ltd* (1993) 178 CLR 44, 60–61 the High Court of Australia split defamation damages further into reparation for harm to reputation, vindication of the claimant's good reputation and consolation for personal distress.
[205] *Broome v Cassell & Co Ltd* [1972] AC 1027, 1125.
[206] Defamation, as already discussed, trespass to the person (*Appleton v Garrett* [1996] PIQR P1), malicious prosecution (*Clark v Chief Constable of Cleveland Police*, The Times, 13 May 1999), trespass to property (*Ashgar v Ahmed* (1995) 17 HLR 25), nuisance through abusive telephone calls intended to cause distress (*Perharic v Hennessey* (CA, 9 June 1997)), injurious falsehood (*Khodaparast v Shad* [2000] 1 All ER 545) and harassment (see para 7.40 above). There is no authority on compensation for distress caused by intentional interference with a contract. If it were allowed, liability of the third party would be more extensive than that of the contract-breaker who, in most cases, could not be compelled to compensate mental distress (see paras 8.46–8.47 above).
[207] See para 4.33 above.
[208] [1997] 2 All ER 426, 452. See also *D v NSPCC* [1976] 2 All ER 993, 998. See also F Trindade, 'The Intentional Infliction of Purely Mental Distress' (1986) 8 OJLS 219, 222.
[209] cp *L v G* [2002] DCR 234, 2002 NZDCR Lexis 2 [* 19].
[210] Law Commission Report 110, *Breach of Confidence* (Cmnd 8388, 1981) 176.

8.51 Equity Can compensation be recovered in equity for mental distress? Scott J said no in *W v Egdell*[211] and in *O'Neill v DHSS*,[212] another breach of confidence action, recovery of statutory damages under Lord Cairns' Act for shock and distress was seen as doubtful.[213] But there is authority the other way. In *Stephens v Avery*[214] the defendant, the claimant's 'friend', disclosed to a newspaper that the claimant had had a lesbian relationship with a woman who had been murdered by her husband. There is no mention in the arguments of counsel or the judgment of tangible harm yet the judge and both parties assumed that if the claimant was owed a duty of confidentiality she could ask for 'damages'[215] as her sole relief.[216]

8.52 *Egdell*, *O'Neill* and *Stephens v Avery* all predate the HRA and have limited value as precedent. If Lord Woolf has his way they will be treated as 'largely of historic interest'.[217] There is no reason in principle why damages for mental distress should not be recoverable in equity. In a New Zealand breach of confidence action by an informer against the police the judge said that the claimant was 'entitled to an award of equitable compensation or damages . . . to an amount which will reflect the effect on both parties in a just and equitable way and which will endeavour to compensate him for the value to him of the information disclosed'.[218] Apart from his pecuniary losses, the informer was allowed a sum by way of general damages to cover his concerns for the safety of his family and the effect of the publication on his state of mind.[219] In a second New Zealand breach of confidence case where there was no financial loss a patient recovered compensation for injury to feelings from his psychologist for wrongful disclosure of information. Anderson J said:

> That no economic loss has been suffered is no more a barrier to suit than, for example, the absence of economic loss in a case of defamation. The damage to the plaintiff is the loss of the confidence and the emotional sequelae are matters in augmentation of the damages which must be paid for the breach of confidence. If a breach having no economic loss were not compensatable, then there would be no sanction against the unjustifiable, inequitable, disregard of privacy which modern society regards as a social value. The law acknowledges a right to compensation for the inequitable breach of private, albeit non-commercial, confidences where the duty to observe such confidences is founded in contract . . . or solely in equity. Where equity could restrain a prospective breach it must be able to remedy a part breach, and such remedy will usually be

---

[211] [1989] 1 All ER 1089, 1108–1109.
[212] [1986] NI 290, 300.
[213] The question did not have to be decided because the impugned acts of the DHSS clerk were held to be outside the scope of her employment. The question of whether there can be recovery for mental distress is tied up with the question of whether the claimant must show detriment in an action for breach of confidence: see paras 5.40–5.41 above. It is only if no detriment need be shown by the claimant, or if disclosure is of itself considered sufficient detriment, that recovery for pure mental distress becomes possible.
[214] [1988] 2 WLR 1280. [215] [1998] 2 WLR 1280 at 1281.
[216] See also *Re Kavanagh* [1949] 2 All ER 264.
[217] *A & B plc & C ('Flitcroft')* [2002] EWCA 337; [2002] 3 WLR 542, para 9.
[218] [1997] 2 NZLR 623, 637.
[219] ibid at 638.

possible only by way of damages. That a person is likely to be distressed on learning of a disclosure in breach of confidence is a principal reason why a breach which does not cause economic loss should be visited with damages, in order to acknowledge the breach, deter their occurrence, and recognise the usual effects of them.[220]

Policy considerations It is easy to understand why the courts should be hesitant about awarding damages for mental distress where this is the claimant's sole injury: people should not be encouraged to go to court every time they feel upset. Not only might claims spiral out of control, there is the risk of fabrication and the difficulty of proving and assessing a subjective form of injury.[221] Against this, however, it can be argued that more than bad manners and the rough and tumble of day-to-day existence[222] is at stake when a professional *intentionally* betrays her client or someone deliberately intercepts information that forms part of the professional's records about the client in circumstances that would attract compensation were tangible injury to result. It is in the public interest that members of the public consult professionals; this may be discouraged if professionals can ignore their obligations of confidentiality toward their clients without good cause.[223] In some EU countries breaches of professional secrecy by doctors and certain other professionals is a criminal offence.[224] Discouraging members of the public from interfering with professional-client communications and professional records is an equally worthy goal. 8.53

The risk of a client feigning distress is small: the Court of Appeal has indicated that there can be no recovery unless disclosure is seriously offensive and objectionable to a reasonable person.[225] When severe distress is claimed, information is likely to be discreditable.[226] Had the information been untrue, the claimant might have recovered damages in an action for defamation or injurious falsehood. The 8.54

---

[220] *JD v Ross* [1998] NZFLR 951, 23–24. Other Commonwealth cases which recognize that equity can award compensation for mental distress include *Szarfer v Chodos* (1986) 54 OR (2d) 663; *Stewart v Canadian Broadcasting Corp* (1997) 150 DLR (4th) 193, 169; *X v Att-Gen* [1997] 2 NZLR 623.

[221] Though this has not prevented the recovery of damages in contract for such intangible losses as pain and suffering.

[222] cp W Keeton (ed), *Prosser and Keeton on the Law of Torts* (5th edn, St Paul: 1984) 56.

[223] The extent to which the lack of a remedy will discourage consultations is admittedly uncertain and controversial: see para 1.49 above. Also in many professions, abuse of confidence is a disciplinary matter.

[224] The first provision of this kind was Art 458 of the Napoleonic Criminal Code of 1810: '[s]hould physicians, surgeons, health officers, pharmacists, midwives and all others who through their status or profession be in possession of information confided to them reveal such secrets, they shall be punished with imprisonment for 8 days to six months and a fine of 100 to 150 francs—unless called to testify as a witness in a court of law or compelled by a court or the law to divulge the secret.'

[225] See para 6.16 above. In any case it is not beyond the courts to distinguish genuine and feigned distress: cp *Ogle v Chief Constable of Thames Valley* [2001] EWCA Civ 598, paras 14–15.

[226] But not always: see *Pierre v Pacific Press Ltd* (1994) DLR (4th) 511 where the claimant's distress was induced by the media's intentional disclosure (against her wishes) of her name and address and appearance, information that might have enabled those who had committed a murder that she had witnessed to seek her out and silence her. Note the suggestion in *Campbell v MGN Ltd* [2002] EWCA Civ 1373, para 55 that an over-sensitive claimant cannot recover more than a person of average sensitivity.

fact that the information is true should not improve the position of the intentional wrongdoer[227] and the difficulty of quantifying the damage should not disqualify the claimant. In *Perharic v Hennessey*[228] Sir Richard Scott commented: '[i]t is very difficult to express in money terms an interference with a facility which is essentially non-monetary. But that is something that the courts have to deal with time and time again in a variety of different types of case.' Those whose distress is slight and who bring the action to vindicate the confidentiality of information can be awarded a nominal sum. More dfficult is the question whether damages should be allowed if the information is already in the public domain. It is argued elsewhere that this fact should not rule out an action in contract or equity for breach of confidence against a professional.[229] It may, however, restrict recovery to the mental distress occasioned by the client's sense of betrayal.

8.55 **Impact of the Human Rights Act 1998** Compliance with Article 8, obligatory for a court as a public authority,[230] may force the judiciary to compensate pure mental distress if the claimant's right to respect for private life has been invaded. The ECtHR does not share the compunction of English judges about allowing damages for pure mental distress.[231] Compensation is recoverable for a wide range of non-pecuniary losses,[232] which the court is sometimes prepared to assume were suffered without proof.[233] Mulcahy says that the ECtHR has awarded non-pecuniary damages (not necessarily for a breach of Article 8) for all of the following: injury to feelings and distress, loss of reputation, harassment, humiliation, stress, anxiety and deterioration in way of life, psychological harm, feelings of helplessness and frustration, moral damage, inconvenience and feelings of injustice.[234] In *Z v Finland*[235] an award of £12,500 was made to an applicant whose HIV status was disclosed in breach of Article 8. No pecuniary loss is mentioned. Lord Woolf's extra-judicial guidelines[236]

---

[227] But, unfortunately, it did in *Robertson v Canadian Imperial Bank* [1995] 1 All ER 824, 831 where wounded feelings and injured pride were disregarded in determining whether the claimant had suffered damage as a result of the disclosure by his banker that his account was overdrawn.

[228] (CA, 9 June 1997.) This gives the lie to Lord Wensleydale's famous claim in *Lynch v Knight* (1861) 9 HLC 577, 598 that the law cannot value mental pain or anxiety.

[229] See paras 4.10 and 5.14 above.

[230] See para 3.05 above.

[231] eg *Gaskin v UK* (1990) 12 EHRR 36; *Halford v UK* (1997) 24 EHRR 523. See also I Leigh and L Lustgarten, 'Making Rights Real: The Courts, Remedies and the Human Rights Act' [1999] CLJ 509, 529. But sometimes a finding that Art 8 has been breached is considered a sufficient remedy for non-pecuniary injury, eg *Schönenberger & Durmaz v Switzerland* (2000) 11 EHRR 202.

[232] Law Commission Report 266, *Damages under the Human Rights Act 1998* (Cm 4853, 2000) paras 3.26, 4.63, 4.69. Sometimes a finding that Art 8 has been breached is considered to be an adequate remedy: para 8.31 above.

[233] T Eicke and D Scorey, *Human Rights Damages: Principles and Practice* (London: 2001) A2–206. See in particular *Abdulaziz v UK* [1985] ECHR 9214/80, para 96; *Peck v UK* Application 44647/98, 28 January 2003, para 118.

[234] L Mulcahy (ed), *Human Rights and Civil Practice* (London: 2001) para 9.33.

[235] (1998) 25 EHRR 371.

[236] M Andenas and M Fairgrieve (eds), *Judicial Review in International Perspective* II (The Hague: 2000) 429.

on the award of compensation in an action brought under HRA, s 7 state that the loss must be clearly attributable to breach of a Convention right but it is immaterial whether the loss is pecuniary or non-pecuniary.

In *Cornelius v de Taranto* a patient sued a psychiatrist in contract and in equity for breach of confidence for disclosing to other health professionals without her consent a medico-legal report which contained defamatory material, inaccuracies and embarrassing details about her life and medical history. Morland J referred to Article 8 and said 8.56

> In my judgment it would be a hollow protection of that right if in a particular case in breach of confidence without consent details of the confider's private and family life were disclosed by the confidant to others and the only remedy that the law of England allowed was nominal damages. In this case an injunction or order for delivery up of all copies of the medico-legal report against the defendant will be of little use to the claimant. The damage has been done. The details of the claimant's private and family life are within the archives of the National Health Service and she has been unable to retrieve them . . .[237]

> [I]n my judgment recovery of damages for mental distress caused by breach of confidence, when no other substantial remedy is available, would not be inimical to 'considerations of policy' but indeed to refuse such recovery would illustrate that something was wrong with the law. Although the 'object of the contract' was the provision of a medico-legal report, that object could not be achieved without the defendant's examination and assessment of confidential material relating to the claimant's private and family life. The duty of confidence was an essential, indeed fundamental, ingredient of [the] contractual relationship between the claimant and the defendant which she breached.[238]

The same judge awarded Naomi Campbell, the international model, damages against the Mirror for disclosing the details of her therapy for drug addiction. The award was set aside on appeal, but not on the grounds that in an action for breach of confidence no compensation is payable for mental distress.[239]

Assessing damages for mental distress for breach of confidence The sum awarded for mental distress is in the discretion of the court.[240] Awards made for mental distress in breach of confidence actions have so far not in any way been comparable to the sums awarded (mostly by juries) in defamation cases.[241] The reported awards are in line with those of the ECtHR which tends to make modest 8.57

---

[237] *Cornelius v de Taranto* [2001] EMLR 12, para 66.
[238] ibid, para 68. Contrast *W v Egdell* [1989] 1 All ER 1089, 1108.
[239] *Campbell v MGN Ltd* [2002] EWCA Civ 13730. 'Damages' were awarded in equity in *John v Joulebine* QB, 26 January 2001, WL 98221.
[240] *Reed v Madon* [1989] 2 All ER 431, 442.
[241] This impression is reinforced by an award of £2,000 for passing off in a false endorsement case in which the image of a Formula One racing driver was manipulated and used without his consent to advertise a radio station: *Irvine v Talksport Ltd* [2002] EWHC 367; [2002] 1 WLR 2355, Ch D. Appropriation of a person's likeness is a species of invasion of privacy.

awards for breaches of Article 8.[242] In *Cornelius v de Taranto* the judge, taking into account what the defendant knew of her client's psychological make-up, 'the nature and detail of the confidential material disclosed, the character of the recipients of the disclosure and the extent of disclosure', gave the claimant £3,000 for the 'significant' injury to her feelings engendered by the unauthorized disclosure of the medico-legal report.[243] The fact that the disclosure was well-intended (for the client's future health care) was treated as irrelevant: '[i]t was for the claimant to decide what details of her private life and family life and medical history were revealed to others.'[244] The client recovered a further £750 compensation for her efforts to retrieve copies of the report from NHS records.

8.58 Naomi Campbell's award against the Mirror which the Court of Appeal set aside[245] was for a mere £2,500 even though the judge found that the disclosure of the details of her drug addiction had caused her to suffer 'a significant amount of distress'[246] and had deterred her from continuing wholeheartedly with therapy when in England.[247] When the defendant is a newspaper, it is inevitable that a relatively small sum will be awarded because the judge must take account of the 'chilling effect' of a large award on freedom of expression.[248]

8.59 If the award is made in equity, the court may reduce the amount to reflect the claimant's bad conduct. The flexibility of equitable 'damages' is a good reason for continuing to treat breach of confidence as an equitable cause of action and not a tort. However, in *Cornelius v De Taranto* Morland J noted the anomaly that a claimant who proves that she has suffered injury through a breach of confidence 'would be entitled as of right in contract to full compensation for that injury without regard to her post-breach conduct to the confidant, however wounding that

---

[242] eg *Funke v France* (1993) 16 EHRR 297 (£6,325); *Gaskin v UK* (1990) 12 EHRR 36 (£5,000); *Halford v UK* (1997) 24 EHRR 523 (£10,000); *Lambert v France* [1999] EHRLR 123 (£1,000); *Z v Finland* (1998) 25 EHRR 371 (£12,500 for disclosure of HIV status). But see *Lustig-Prean v UK* (2000) 31 EHRR 734, also an Art 8 case, where the applicants received £19,000 non-pecuniary damages for discharge from the army on discovery of their homosexual sexual orientation.

[243] In 1983 in *Ott v Fleishman* [1985] 5 WWR 721 a Canadian court awarded $500 (by way of nominal damages) to a client whose barrister in divorce proceedings had disclosed to her husband, the professional body of private investigators and the Law Society of British Columbia, that his client had begun an affair with the private investigator engaged to find evidence of her husband's adultery. As a result the wife had twice had to appear before a disciplinary body as a witness for the private investigator. This had 'caused the plaintiff some concern because she did not wish her two grown-up daughters to know the details of her relationship with Mr. Britton [the investigator]' per McEachern CJSC at 726.

[244] per Morland J, *Cornelius v de Taranto* [2001] EMLR 12 para 80.

[245] The Court of Appeal [2002] EWCA Civ 1373 found for the newspaper on the issue of liability and said nothing about the size of the award by the trial judge.

[246] *Campbell v MGN Ltd* [2002] EWHC 499; [2002] EMLR 30, para 136.

[247] ibid, paras 40, 128, 129. There was evidence that the upset had been transitory (ibid, para 133) and much of Campbell's distress had been caused by the disclosure of her drugs problem which the newspaper had been entitled to make (ibid, paras 113, 136).

[248] HRA, s 12. See para 8.14 above.

B. After-the-Event Remedies

conduct may have been to the confidant but if the claimant's only remedy was "equitable" damages the position might be otherwise'.[249]

Injury to reputation

Injury to reputation (what others think of X) is distinguishable from mental distress (X's hurt feelings) though injury to reputation may be an integral part of the mental distress suffered (anxiety about what others might think of X).[250]

8.60

> If the vicar's wife is, through her solicitor's negligence, wrongfully convicted of shoplifting and her mental anguish is increased by what she believes the parishioners think of her, I cannot see why that does not enhance her damages. Mental distress that sounds in damages comes in different forms in different categories of case.[251]

Prior to the HRA, the only torts other than defamation for which recovery of damages was allowed for injury to reputation (as opposed to mental distress inseparable from loss of reputation) were malicious prosecution and false imprisonment.[252] The courts were concerned to avoid claimants circumventing the defamation defences of privilege and fair comment which constitute 'a worthy balancing of competing interest in free speech [and] reputation'.[253] In addition courts were reluctant to compensate for loss of an unfounded reputation: 'one can only suffer an injury to reputation if what is said is false.'[254] The position in contract was that loss of reputation was not a head of damage[255] except where the very object of the contract was to protect the reputation (deserved or not) that was lost in consequence of breach of the contract.[256] Exceptionally, a claimant could be compensated for financial loss occasioned by reduction in employment prospects flowing from a loss of reputation.[257]

8.61

The possibility of recovering damages for injury to reputation when the right to respect for private life is interfered with is problematic. The injury, and correspondingly the compensation, could be substantial if extensive publicity were to

8.62

---

[249] [2001] EMLR 12, para 74.

[250] *McLeish v Amoo-Gottfried & Co*, The Times, 13 October 1993 where Scott Baker J said that the claimant could recover damages for his distress at what his family and workmates thought of him following his (wrongful) conviction. See also *CS v News Ltd* (NSWSC, 20 February 1998, NSW LEXIS 441).

[251] per Scott Baker J, *McLeish v Amoo-Gottfried & Co*, The Times, 13 October 1993.

[252] *Lonrho plc v Fayed (No 5)* [1994] 1 All ER 188, 203–204.

[253] R Magnusson, 'Recovery for Mental Distress in Tort, with Special Reference to Harmful Words and Statements' (1994) 2 Tort LJ at 145 cited in *CS v News Ltd* (NSWSC, 20 February 1998, NSW LEXIS 441).

[254] *Lonrho v Fayed (No 5)* [1994] 1 All ER 188, 202. See also ibid at 195. Hence the fact that truth is a complete defence to defamation. Query whether damages for breach of confidence will be reduced if a public figure who has neither courted publicity nor misled the public is 'demonstrated to have feet of clay'. per Lord Phillips in *Campbell v MGN Ltd* [2002] EWCA Civ 1373, para 41.

[255] *Addis v Gramophone Co Ltd* [1909] AC 488; *Groom v Crocker* [1938] 2 All ER 401, 402, 415. Where damages for mental distress are recoverable either as parasitic damages or (as in *McLeish v Amoo-Gottfried & Co*, The Times, 13 October 1993) because the object of the contract was peace of mind, account will be taken of the effect on the claimant of his perceived loss of reputation.

[256] *Cambridge Nutrition Ltd v BBC* [1990] 3 All ER 523, 540.

[257] *Malik v BCCI SA* [1997] 3 All ER 1, 10–11, 21

be given to a criminal history that is unknown in the local community.[258] In *Niemietz v Germany*[259] the ECtHR refused the applicant, a lawyer, non-pecuniary damages for the violation of his Article 8 right, the court being of the opinion that the finding was sufficient to counter the damage done to his reputation by the search of his business premises for evidence of the identity of a client. Account, however, must also be taken of the ECtHR's more recent decision in *Rotaru v Romania*.[260] The applicant who had complained about the existence, contrary to Article 8, of secret official files on him containing false and defamatory information and the lack of any effective remedy did receive non-pecuniary damages. But it is of obvious significance that the information that had been stored and was later disclosed was *false*.

8.63 Closer to home, it is arguable that compensation for injury to reputation was recovered in *Adenjii v Newham LBC*,[261] a breach of confidence action. Damages of £5,000 were approved[262] against a local authority that had kept, stored and years later used without parental authority the photographs of a child attendee at one of its nurseries. The photographs had been used to illustrate local authority brochures that went by the titles of 'The Strategy for Children and Young People who are Affected or Infected by HIV or AIDs' and 'Strategy for Preventing Youth Crime'. Circulation of these brochures had caused the claimant, who was 10 years old at the time, distress. One of the causes may have been injury to her reputation. Friends had stopped playing with her and it was thought that this might have been because people drew the *false* conclusion that the titles applied to her, an inference the more easily made because she suffered from certain disabilities. In the judgment the following factors are treated as relevant to the assessment of compensation: absence of commercial exploitation and malice, repetition of the disclosure after promise of cessation, and the 'unhappy connotations'. English law is without precedent for the recovery of damages for injury to reputation consequent on the disclosure of *true* information. Whatever position the English courts adopt on this point, it is submitted that the client cannot be compensated for injury to reputation consequent on the disclosure of information that is both true and already in the public domain.[263]

---

[258] As happened in *Melvin v Reid* 112 Cal App 285, 292 (1931) and *Briscoe v Reader's Digest Ass Inc* 483 P 2d 34, 40 (1971). But in some contexts disclosure vindicates reputation, eg *Kennedy v Ireland* [1987] IR 587.
[259] (1992) 16 EHRR 97.
[260] Application 2834/95, 8 BHRC 449, paras 81–83.
[261] (QB, 16 October 2001.)
[262] This was necessary because the claimant was a child: CPR, r 21.10.
[263] It is argued in para 5.14 above that a professional's liability for breach of confidence in equity should extend to information in the public domain. If this happens, damages should be restricted to mental distress attributable to a feeling of betrayal and to tangible loss.

B. After-the-Event Remedies

Loss of privacy[264]

In an action for defamation the claimant can recover damages for injury to reputation *and* injury to feelings.[265] Might the victim of a breach of confidence claim compensation for both mental distress[266] and loss of privacy? Recovery for loss of privacy takes on added significance if injury to reputation resulting from disclosure of *true* information is not compensatable[267] or the mental distress that can be proven is slight. In *Halford v UK*, a case of covert interception of an employee's private telephone calls, the ECtHR rejected the applicant's claim for alleged distress caused by the interception of her telephone calls[268] but awarded £10,000 damages for 'a serious infringement of her rights by those concerned'.[269]

8.64

In other Article 8 cases no clear distinction is made between the non-pecuniary heads of damage for which damages are recoverable and in some it is possible that the applicant received aggravated damages rather than damages for loss of privacy *and* distress. There is a policy objection to courts awarding damages (however modest) against the media for loss of privacy and that is that it could subvert self-regulation which HRA, s12 with its reference to media privacy codes seems designed to promote. However, this should not be used to deprive claimants of the opportunity to vindicate privacy rights in cases raising no issue of media freedom. This argument should not be understood as an endorsement of loss of privacy damages where information in the public domain is disclosed: only damages for mental distress attributable to the professional's betrayal of the client should be allowed here.

8.65

Aggravated damages

The CPR glossary defines aggravated damages as '[a]dditional damages which the court may award as compensation for the defendant's objectionable behaviour'. Lord Woolf has stated in extrajudicial guidelines that aggravated damages are not

8.66

---

[264] M Tugendhat and I Christie (eds), *The Law of Privacy and the Media* (Oxford: 2002) paras 10.94–10.95.

[265] See para 8.49 above.

[266] The mental distress of the client at the unauthorized disclosure of confidential information by a professional may have up to three separate causes: a sense of betrayal, anxiety about what others may think of him, loss of control over further dissemination of the information. This mental distress is distinct from injury to reputation. Whether the claimant's interest in vindicating his right to privacy and being compensated for mental distress are as distinct is more doubtful.

[267] The extent of the individual's distress may in part reflect the effect on his reputation. This will not apply in all cases, because reputation is not adversely affected by the disclosure of all confidential information eg *Kennedy v Ireland* [1987] IR 587.

[268] *Halford v UK* (1997) 24 EHRR 523, para 75: 'there is no evidence to suggest that the stress Ms Halford suffered was directly attributable to the interception of her calls, rather than to her other conflicts with the Merseyside police.'

[269] ibid, para 76. cp *Kennedy v Ireland* [1987] IR 587.

available in actions brought against public authorities under the HRA.[270] Their availability in actions for breach of confidence, however, is not in doubt. At first instance a sum of £1,000 was awarded by way of aggravated damages to Naomi Campbell[271] to compensate for the increased distress caused by her vilification[272] in a second newspaper article. Had the trial judge's findings on liability been valid, the Court of Appeal said that it would have been open to him to award the aggravated damages.[273] It will often be difficult to decide in a disclosure case whether a sum allowed for mental distress was intended to compensate for the primary wrong or for the defendant's manner of committing it or response to a complaint.[274]

8.67 Damages for mental distress are recoverable in copyright by way of aggravated damages. The common law authority is *Williams v Settle*.[275] A photographer sold a wedding photograph to a national newspaper when the bride's father was murdered. The groom, who owned the copyright, obtained substantial damages for the injury to his feelings—including the distress of seeing his wife upset.[276] Sellers LJ said that the defendant had acted in total disregard of the legal rights of the claimant regarding copyright and 'of his feelings and his sense of family dignity and pride. It was an intrusion into [the claimant's] life, deeper and graver than an intrusion into a man's property.'[277]

8.68 Damages for mental distress were also recoverable in *Williams v Settle* under s 17(3) of the Copyright Act 1956. This provision has been superseded by s 97(2) of the Copyright, Designs and Patents Act 1988 which states that a court may, 'having regard to all the circumstances, and in particular to (a) the flagrancy of the infringement, and (b) any benefit accruing to the defendant by reason of the infringement, award . . . additional damages'. Section 97(2) is open-ended as to the type of circumstances that qualify for an award of additional damages: it is not necessary for both (a) and (b) to be satisfied.[278] The section would enable a

---

[270] M Andenas and M Fairgrieve (eds), *Judicial Review in International Perspective* II (The Hague: 2000) 429. There is no ECtHR precedent for the award of aggravated damages. A claim for aggravated damages in *Lustig-Prean v UK* (2000) 31 EHRR 734 was dismissed. Contrast *Kennedy v Ireland* [1987] IR 587.
[271] [2002] EWHC 499; [2002] EMLR 30, para 161.
[272] The article called her a 'chocolate soldier' (which she took to be a racist remark) and 'trashed her as a person in a highly offensive and hurtful manner': [2002] EWHC 499; [2002] EMLR 30, para 164.
[273] *Campbell v MGN Ltd* [2002] EWCA Civ 1373, para 139.
[274] The view is held in some quarters that (defamation apart) damages for mental distress are recoverable *only* as an ingredient of aggravated damages: *Lonrho plc v Fayed (No 5)* [1994] 1 All ER 188, 194. This produces the startling result that although the immediate distress flowing from the wrongful act cannot be compensated, additional distress arising from the way the wrongful act was done can be compensated.
[275] *Williams v Settle* [1960] 1 WLR 1072, 1082. The damages were seen as non-compensatory but at 1083 Sellers LJ stressed the foreseeability of the mental distress.
[276] [1960] 1 WLR 1072, 1087.
[277] ibid at 1082.
[278] *Redrow Homes Ltd v Betts Brothers Plc* [1997] FSR 828, 836.

court to compensate a client for injury to his feelings and permit an element of restitution.[279]

Exemplary damages[280]

Exemplary damages are defined in the CPR glossary as '[d]amages which go beyond compensating for actual loss and are awarded to show the court's disapproval of the defendant's behaviour'. They are designed to deter and punish: to teach the defendant that wrongdoing does not pay. The availability of exemplary damages in tort in certain defined circumstances[281] is well established. Exemplary damages are not available in contract[282] and the ECtHR[283] does not award them. The Woolf extra-judicial guidelines[284] for awarding compensation under the HRA state that the court should not award exemplary damages.

8.69

In parts of the Commonwealth[285] exemplary damages have been awarded in equity. It is uncertain whether an English court would do the same in a breach of confidence action.[286] The Law Commission's view is that outrageous disregard of equitable rights should be capable of attracting exemplary damages.[287] In *Francome v Mirror Group Newspapers*[288] the claimant, a well-known jockey, asked for exemplary damages in an action for breach of confidence against a newspaper. The case reached the Court of Appeal, but not on this point. If exemplary damages are available at all, they are most likely to be considered in a situation in which the defendant made a cynical

8.70

---

[279] cp *Nottinghamshire Healthcare NHS Trust v NGN Ltd* [2002] EWHC 409; [2002] EMLR 33, paras 33, 40, 51.

[280] L Aitken, 'Developments in Equitable Compensation: Opportunity or Danger?' (1993) 67 Australian LJ 596, 599; D Jensen, 'Punitive Damages for Breach of Fiduciary Obligation' (1996) 19 U of Queensland LJ 125.

[281] Oppressive, arbitrary or unconstitutional action by government servants; where the defendant's conduct was calculated to make a profit that exceeds the compensation payable to the claimant; where statute permits: *Rookes v Barnard* [1964] AC 1129; *AB v South West Water Services Ltd* [1993] 1 All ER 609, 620, 627; *Kuddus v Chief Constable of Leicestershire Constabulary* [2001] UKHL 29, [2001] 3 All ER 193.

[282] *Johnson v Unisys Ltd* [2001] 2 All ER 801, 807.

[283] Although Art 41 does not preclude exemplary damages the court does not openly make such an award. Awards of non-pecuniary and pecuniary damages have possibly sometimes contained a punitive element, eg *Gaygusuz v Austria* (1996) 23 EHRR 364, 385. See further D Fairgrieve, 'The Human Rights Act 1998, Damages and Tort Law' [2001] PL 695, 704.

[284] M Andenas and M Fairgrieve (eds), *Judicial Review in International Perspective* II (The Hague: 2000) 429.

[285] Canada: *Schauenberg Industries Ltd v Borowski* (1979) 101 DLR (3d) 701,712; *Norberg v Wynrib* (1992) 92 DLR (4th) 449. Both cases involved breach of fiduciary duty. New Zealand: *Aquaculture Corp v New Zealand Green Mussel Co Ltd* [1990] 3 NZLR 299, 301 (breach of confidence).

[286] Exemplary damages are seen as anomalous: *Rookes v Barnard* [1964] AC 1129, 1221. The main objections to exemplary damages are: that only the criminal law should be used to punish; that punishment should not be imposed without the procedural and evidential safeguards of a criminal trial; that the 'fine' should go to the state not to the claimant.

[287] Law Commission Consultation Paper 132, *Aggravated, Exemplary and Restitutionary Damages* (1993) para 1.20.

[288] [1984] 2 All ER 408, 409.

calculation that his profit would exceed compensation payable to the client.[289] There is a clear danger of newspapers thinking this way, especially now that it looks like awards of damages for disclosure of personal information will be modest. Although there is not necessarily any correlation between the exemplary damages and the defendant's gain, an award of damages combined with exemplary damages is likely to strip away his profit.[290] However, an award of exemplary damages against the press is virtually ruled out by Article 10 and HRA, s12[291] because of the 'chilling effect' on freedom of expression.

Account of Profits[292]

8.71 An account of profits is an equitable remedy that allows the client to recover the profit which a professional, stranger or third party made by wrongfully using or disclosing confidential information about the client. It is available for breaches of confidence, fiduciary duty, copyright, torts involving infringement of intellectual property rights, and in exceptional circumstances in contract actions.[293] Where the defendant has made a significant gain from the disclosure of the claimant's information but the claimant is likely to recover only modest damages because of the nature of his injury (mental distress) this is the most appropriate remedy.

8.72 By law, the defendant is required to draw up an account, and then pay over the net gain. This may include a profit that the claimant could never have made for himself.[294] Where the defendant's profit is only partially derived from the wrongful use of information, as where a book published by a professional contains confidential information about a client but much else besides, the account of profits runs into problems of apportionment.[295] Working out what should count as profit and what should be allowed by way of deductions[296] can be immensely difficult.[297] These

---

[289] Possibly unauthorized disclosures by professionals employed by the state (NHS doctors, Community Legal Service lawyers, etc) fall within the oppressive, arbitrary or unconstitutional conduct by government servants category: M Tugendhat and I Christie (eds), *The Law of Privacy and the Media* (Oxford: 2002) paras 10.110–10.111.

[290] A more certain way of achieving this result is to award a restitutionary remedy: *Kuddus v Chief Constable of Leicestershire Constabulary* [2001] UKHL 29; [2001] 3 All ER 193 para 109.

[291] HRA, s 12(4) (see para 8.13 above) may not apply after publication, but this statutory provision adds very little to the effect of Art 10 itself.

[292] F Gurry, *Breach of Confidence* (Oxford: 1984) ch xxii; P Baker and P St J Langan (eds), *Snell's Equity* (29th edn, London: 1990) 637; P Parkinson (ed), *The Principles of Equity* (Sydney: 1996) ch 26; M Gronow, 'Restitution for Breach of Confidence' (1996) 10 Intellectual Property J 219.

[293] See para 8.47 above.

[294] *Regal (Hastings) Ltd v Gulliver* (Note) [1967] 2 AC 134.

[295] In *Spencer v UK* (1998) 25 EHRR CD 105, 115 the Spencers complained about 'the major evidential difficulties associated with proving to a court that the inclusion of . . . confidential information in a newspaper containing many other articles directly led to an identifiable and calculable profit which could be awarded to the plaintiff'.

[296] In actions against third parties and strangers, the cost of acquiring the personal information from the professional or interceptor is *not* deductible: *Att-Gen v Guardian Newspaper Ltd (No 2)* [1988] 3 All ER 545, 645, 647–648, 655, 667.

[297] G Jones, 'Restitution of Benefits Obtained in Breach of Another's Confidence' (1970) 86 LQR 463, 487.

B. After-the-Event Remedies

practical problems do not arise where the defendant has been rewarded for selling information about a client to the media. As the remedy is personal, it is unnecessary to trace the profit to a particular fund.

Like all equitable remedies an account of profits is discretionary.[298] The remedy may be combined with an injunction and an order for the delivery up of items,[299] but not with other monetary relief. This is to avoid the claimant receiving a double benefit from the same wrong.[300] **8.73**

Delivery Up and Destruction of Items[301]

The professional, third party or stranger who breaches or threatens to breach an equitable obligation of confidentiality or the client's copyright[302] may be ordered to deliver up to the client any item (usually a document) belonging to the client.[303] The remedy is available on its own[304] or as a supplement to other remedies. If the client has no proprietary interest in items containing his personal information, for example, the professional's records, the court can order the defendant to destroy the items or, if the defendant is not to be trusted, to deliver them up to the claimant or to the court for destruction. In *Prince Albert v Strange*[305] the defendant was ordered to deliver up for destruction copies of impressions made of the Royal Family's etchings and copies of a catalogue describing them. In a breach of confidence action, the defendant may be ordered to deliver up a document containing a mixture of confidential and non-confidential material.[306] The defendant assumes the risk that 'he may subsequently lose all his own effort if the document itself, when looked at as a whole, is covered by confidentiality'.[307] **8.74**

The delivery up remedy is discretionary. If litigation is in prospect to which the document is relevant an order may be refused. Instead the court may require the **8.75**

---

[298] See eg *Seager v Copydex Ltd* [1967] 2 All ER 415, 419 where both an injunction and an account of profits was refused because the defendant's breach of confidence was unconscious.

[299] *Peter Pan Manufacturing Corp v Corsets Silhouette Ltd* [1964] 1 WLR 96.

[300] Law Commission Report 110, *Breach of Confidence* (Cmnd 8388, 1981) para 4.86. It has been suggested that if damages for mental distress are recoverable in an action for breach of confidence (which is now virtually certain, see paras 8.55–8.56 above) it should be possible to combine these non-pecuniary damages with an account of profits: H Tomlinson (ed), *Privacy and the Media: The Developing Law* (London: 2002) 86.

[301] F Gurry, *Breach of Confidence* (Oxford: 1984) ch xxii, A Burrows, *Remedies for Torts and Breach of Contract* (2nd edn, London: 1994) 457–461.

[302] Copyright, Designs and Patents Act 1988, s 230 seems inapplicable.

[303] *Prince Albert v Strange* (1849) 64 ER 293, 321. cp *A v B* [2000] EMLR 1007. Such an order was made against Paul Attridge, chauffeur to the Spice Girls, who broke a confidentiality agreement not to reveal their business, sex or shopping habits: The Times, 25 July 1998. cp *Blair v Lister* (QB, 13 November 2000, WL 33116509).

[304] *Franklin v Giddins* [1978] Qd R 72. But see *Mergenthaler Linotype Co v Intertype Co Ltd* [1926] 43 RPC 381, 382.

[305] (1849) 64 ER 293, 321.

[306] *A v B* [2000] EMLR 1007, para 8.

[307] per Wright J, *Blair v Lister* (QB, 13 November 2000, WL 33116509).

Constructive Trusts[310]

Breach of fiduciary duty

8.76 Constructive trust is a device used by equity to allow recovery of property misappropriated by a fiduciary. Unconscionable use of property or funds is not necessary.[311] Where a fiduciary obtains confidential information by virtue of her position and in breach of a fiduciary duty of loyalty uses it to produce a private gain, a constructive trust may be imposed over assets derived from or acquired from the breach of duty.[312] No detriment to the claimant is required: the object is to keep fiduciaries 'up to the mark'. But what is necessary is a complete discrete item of property to which the constructive trust can attach.[313]

8.77 Were a solicitor, in breach of fiduciary duty, to sell confidential personal information about a client to a newspaper for reward and then invest money received in shares, the solicitor would hold the shares in trust for the client.[314] The actions of the solicitor can be likened to the acceptance of a bribe. The Privy Council held in *Att-Gen for Hong Kong v Reid*[315] that a fiduciary who takes a bribe in breach of his duty holds the bribe (or any property purchased from it) in trust for the person to whom the duty is owed. If the same principles apply to personal as to commercial information,[316] a third party to whom information is disclosed in breach of fiduciary duty will not hold any gain made by exploiting the information as a constructive trustee for the client unless the third party acted as a dishonest accessory to the fiduciary's breach of duty.

---

[308] *A v B* [2000] EMLR 1007, para 21.
[309] cp *Saltman Engineering Co Ltd v Campbell Engineering Co Ltd* [1963] 3 All ER 413, 415.
[310] P Parkinson (ed), *The Principles of Equity* (Sydney: 1996) ch 21 and pp 469–470; A Oakley, *Constructive Trusts* (3rd edn, London: 1997); T. Wu, 'Confidence and the constructive trust' (2003) LS 135.
[311] '[I]t is not in all cases that a pre-existing right of property will exist when a constructive trust is ordered. The imposition of a constructive trust can both recognize and create a right of property.' per La Forest J, *Lac Minerals v International Corona Resources* (1989) 61 DLR (4th) 14, 50.
[312] *Boardman v Phipps* [1967] 2 AC 46. Their Lordships were divided as to whether information is property.
[313] *Ocular Sciences Ltd v Aspect Vision Care Ltd* [1997] RPC 289, 416.
[314] cp *Carter v Palmer* (1841) 8 Cl & Fin 657. If the money is absorbed into his cash-flow a constructive trust is not possible.
[315] [1994] 1 All ER 1. The Privy Council declined to follow *Lister v Stubbs* (1890) 45 Ch D 1. In *Att-Gen v Blake* [1996] 3 All ER 903, 912 Sir Richard Scott, while recognizing that the Court of Appeal was bound by *Lister v Stubbs*, expressed support for the Privy Council's approach.
[316] *Satnam Ltd v Dunlop Heywood Ltd* [1999] 3 All ER 652, 671.

B. After-the-Event Remedies

Breach of confidence

The imposition of a constructive trust in an action for breach of confidence is con- **8.78**
troversial.[317] In *Ocular Sciences Ltd v Aspect Vision Care Ltd* Laddie J thought that
it could be attached to the gain made through a breach of confidence because 'in
most, if not all, cases where obligations of confidence arise, it will be in circumstances where the court will find that a fiduciary relationship exists also'.[318] There
is some support in *Att-Gen v Guardian Newspapers Ltd (No 2)* for treating a constructive trust as flowing directly from a breach of confidence. Lord Goff suggested that a confider who published a book containing information that was
disclosed in breach of confidence holds the copyright in the book in trust for the
confidant.[319] Nowhere in the judgment is it stated that a fiduciary relationship
(other than one that gives rise to an action for breach of confidence)[320] is necessary.
Both Lord Griffiths and Lord Keith agreed that the copyright was probably vested
in the confider—which in this case was the Government.[321] These views are obiter
since the Crown declined to advance its claim in copyright. Moreover, the
Government was refused an injunction to restrain publication of the book. The
House of Lords did not address the anomaly of allowing a proprietary remedy for
the misuse of something (information) that in most cases is not regarded as property.[322]

Should the copyright analysis come to be accepted it would mean that whenever **8.79**
a professional deliberately publishes a book or article of which confidential personal information about a client forms a substantial component, the copyright—
or a share of the copyright, if the courts are prepared to make an allowance for the
innocuous parts—belongs to the client and not to the professional.

---

[317] The Canadian Supreme Court was divided on this point in *International Corona Resources v LAC Minerals Ltd* (1989) 61 DLR (4th) 14. In *Satnam Ltd v Dunlop Heywood Ltd* [1999] 3 All ER 652, 671 a constructive trust is treated as the remedy for breach of fiduciary duty and an account of profits as the remedy for breach of confidence.
[318] [1997] RPC 289, 413. This is not true unless 'fiduciary' is used in a restricted sense to designate a relationship in which the only obligation owed is confidentiality.
[319] [1988] 3 All ER 545, 664.
[320] See para 5.64 above. A full fiduciary relationship—that is, one that gives rise to a duty of undivided loyalty and not simply of confidentiality—is not necessary for the recognition of a constructive trust in Canada: G Fridman, *Restitution* (2nd edn, Toronto: 1992) 441.
[321] [1988] 3 All ER 545, 645, 654. See also, *Att-Gen v Blake* [1996] 3 All ER 903, 912.
[322] See para 7.31 above. If the courts allow claimants in cases such as *Douglas v Hello! Ltd* [2001] 2 All ER 289 to recover all the commercial loss occasioned by the premature publication of personal information then there is little to distinguish privacy/confidentiality rights from property rights such as copyright.

9

ALTERNATIVES TO LITIGATION

A. Litigation	9.01	B. Litigation Alternatives	9.04
Selecting Civil Causes of Action	9.01	The Alternatives	9.04
Pros and Cons of Civil Litigation	9.02	Media Regulatory Bodies	9.08

A. Litigation

Selecting Civil Causes of Action

The previous chapters have shown that there is a whole range of causes of action potentially open to the victim of a breach of confidence by a professional. The choice of cause of action may depend not only on its substantive law requirements but also upon a number of other considerations: **9.01**

- the limitation period:[1] tort,[2] contract[3] and copyright[4] have statutory limitation periods within which the action must be commenced, breach of confidence and breach of fiduciary duty have no set time limits,[5] nevertheless excessive delay may give rise to the defence of laches;[6]
- whether the client has suffered detriment beyond pure mental distress;[7]

---

[1] Defined in the CPR glossary as '[t]he period within which a person who has a right to claim against another person must start court proceedings to establish that right. The expiry of the period may be a defence to the claim'.

[2] Limitation Act 1980, s 2 (general), s 4A (libel and malicious falsehood).

[3] ibid, s 5. Although the statutory time limit for contract and most tort actions is the same, different methods are used to calculate the limitation period which may mean that the limitation period has expired for one form of action but not the other: see A McGee, *Limitation Periods* (2nd edn, London: 1994) chs 5, 10.

[4] Limitation Act 1980, s 2, Copyright, Designs and Patents Act 1988, s 113.

[5] See *Nocton v Lord Ashburton* [1914] AC 932, 957. However, Limitation Act 1980, s 36(1) may require a time limit to be applied by analogy. In *Swinney v Chief Constable of Northumbria* [1996] 3 All ER 449, 452 it was assumed that the six-year tort limitation period applied. For a fuller discussion of the issues see M Tugendhat and I Christie (eds), *The Law of Privacy and the Media* (Oxford: 2002) paras 9.116–9.117.

[6] See A McGee, *Limitation Periods* (2nd edn, London: 1994) 20.

[7] On the question of when recovery is permitted for pure mental distress see paras 4.33 and 8.46 et seq.

- what sort of remedy the client wants if he wins the action;[8]
- availability of aggravated and exemplary damages.[9]

Where there is concurrent liability in more than one legal category the client may sue in whatever manner suits him best, provided that where a contract exists any non-contractual remedy which the client elects to pursue has not been limited or excluded by the contract.[10]

Pros and Cons of Civil Litigation

Advantages

9.02 The advantage of bringing an action in the civil courts lies principally in the remedies that a court has at its disposal.[11] If the client is lucky enough to know that a professional is intending to disclose confidential personal information he can seek an injunction. Montgomery, writing about health care, comments that 'this is not usually the case and where it is patients can usually confront the health professionals and persuade them to respect their privacy without recourse to the courts'.[12] After the disclosure, the client can ask for damages or other financial relief. But where no tangible injury has been suffered, or the injury is minor, compensation may not be what the client wants. Rather, the client may want an explanation of what happened, to receive an apology and to be reassured that nothing similar will happen in future, to himself or to others—all without having to spend money.[13] Litigation cannot deliver any of this.

Disadvantages

9.03 The drawbacks of a civil action are considerable:

(1) Important though the principle of open justice is,[14] it is an unattractive feature of litigation as far as the claimant in an action for breach of confidence is concerned.[15] To obtain compensation for loss of confidentiality, the client may have to endure further loss of privacy. Naomi Campbell had to disclose more details about her private life in court than were disclosed by the news-

---

[8] An account of profits, for example, requires an equitable cause of action.
[9] As to which actions allow recovery of exemplary and aggravated damages see paras 8.66–8.70 above.
[10] *Henderson v Merrett Syndicates Ltd* [1994] 3 All ER 506, 532–533, 544.
[11] Litigation does have the advantage that allegations are protected by absolute privilege. Complaints to other bodies probably are not. An unfounded complaint could result in the complainant facing a defamation action.
[12] *Health Care Law* (Oxford: 1997) 267–268.
[13] J Stone and J Matthews, *Complementary Medicine and the Law* (Oxford: 1996) 186; Editorial, 'Angered patients and the medical profession' (1999) 170 Medical J of Australia 576.
[14] See para 17.28 below.
[15] Victorian Legal and Constitutional Committee, *Report Upon Privacy and Breach of Confidence* (Melbourne: 1990) 44.

A. Litigation

paper she was suing.[16] When Victoria and David Beckham settled their action against Andrew Morton, their unauthorized biographer, and his publisher, after proceedings had begun for an injunction, the defendants thanked the claimants for the free publicity: '[t]he Beckhams have probably tripled the sales and for that I thank them roundly.'[17] It is unlikely that the Beckhams had wanted to promote the book.

(2) Litigation is costly (even for an outright winner). The litigant-in-person is rarely successful so most people who go to law engage legal representation. As soon as lawyers get involved, costs escalate.[18] Naomi Campbell's legal costs at first instance are estimated at £400,000.[19] The Woolf reforms of the civil justice system may have reduced the delay, uncertainty and complexity of civil litigation but the process remains costly and is therefore still inaccessible to victims of unlawful disclosure who are not wealthy. Civil legal aid has never been available for actions in defamation and for other tort, contract and equity actions it has largely been replaced by the speculative conditional fee. This is an arrangement whereby the client pays his lawyers nothing if he loses; if he wins he pays the normal charge plus an additional uplift. A conditional fee agreement removes the financial risk of going to court, but only as regards the client's own fees; the client still has to pay the defendant's fees should he lose, unless he insures against this outcome.[20] The modest size of awards of damages for breach of confidence[21] more or less rules out contingency fee arrangements except where the claimant seeks an account of profits.[22] The Press Complaints Commission (PCC) in its 2001 Annual Report draws attention to the fact that fewer than 12 privacy cases were brought in the courts in the first 18 months that the HRA was in force, 'a very small number that underlines the fact that actions under the legislation have proved cumbersome, inaccessible and practically useless for ordinary people'.[23] A claimant poor enough to qualify for public funding may be forced to accept any reasonable settlement offered because of the refusal of the Legal Services Commission to provide funding for a trial.

---

[16] *Campbell v MGN Ltd* [2002] EWHC 499; [2002] EMLR 30.
[17] 'Beckhams drop Morton book battle', Guardian, 31 August 2000.
[18] J Stone and J Matthews, *Complementary Medicine and the Law* (Oxford: 1996) 186.
[19] 'Privacy on parade', Guardian, 18 February 2002. This figure probably included the cost of interlocutory proceedings and possibly also satellite litigation by Naomi Campbell against an employee. The costs in *A v B pc & C ('Flitcroft')* [2002] EWCA Civ 337; [2002] 3 WLR 542, which went to the Court of Appeal, were said to be £200,000 by the Independent, 31 March 2002.
[20] Under Access to Justice Act 1999, s 29 the defendant, if he loses, can be ordered to reimburse the insurance premium.
[21] See para 8.57 above.
[22] ibid.
[23] http://www.pcc.org.uk.

B. Litigation Alternatives

The Alternatives

Advantages of the litigation alternatives

9.04 A client who is concerned about a breach of confidentiality has a number of options that do not involve litigation. Most are cost-free, easily accessible, informal and many produce results much more quickly than going to court. If there is no threat of costly litigation, those at fault may be more willing to apologize, compromise and set up procedures that will prevent unauthorized disclosures in the future. Unlike at law, the death of the person affected by the disclosure may be no impediment to relief.[24]

Complaints procedures

9.05 If the professional is an employed professional, one possibility is to complain to the employer who may take disciplinary action. The NHS,[25] local authorities[26] and the banks all have established internal complaints procedures. The Law Society requires every firm of solicitors to have one.[27] A second possibility is to ask the Information Commissioner for an assessment of whether the Data Protection Act 1998 (DPA) has been contravened.[28]

Ombudsmen

9.06 Some breaches of confidentiality can be investigated by an ombudsman.[29] In particular, breaches of confidentiality by professionals working for banks,[30] for local

---

[24] The PCC (see para 9.08 below) may accept complaints from third parties. The BSC (see para 9.18 below) can accept complaints made up to five years after the death of the person affected.

[25] The current NHS complaints procedure dates from 1996. All GPs and all NHS trusts must have a complaints procedure. If the complaint cannot be resolved at local level, the patient can ask for an independent review: see further, Royal College of General Practitioners, *Information Sheet No 15* (1996), available from http://www.rcgp.org.uk, and DoH, *NHS Complaints Procedure National Evaluation* (March 2001) ch 2, available from http://www.doh.gov.uk/.

[26] Under Child Care Act 1980, s 76 an inquiry can be conducted into a local authority's exercise of its child care functions.

[27] Solicitors' Costs Information and Client Care Code, available from http://www.lawsociety.org.uk.

[28] See para 18.47 below.

[29] For more information about the ombudsmen schemes see National Consumer Council, *A–Z of Ombudsmen* (London: 1997); M Seneviratne, *Ombudsmen: Public Services and Administrative Justice* (London: 2002). The Legal Services Ombudsman can only investigate the way that the professional's own body investigated a complaint.

[30] The Office of the Banking Ombudsman handled 127 complaints concerning confidentiality in 1997 and can order compensation. For information about this ombudsman see S Sugar, 'Banking on dispute resolution' (2001) 145 SJ 338 and http://www.bba.org.uk. Prior to approaching the ombudsman the complainant must have tried the bank's own complaints procedure unsuccessfully.

B. Litigation Alternatives

authorities,[31] for the NHS[32] and in prisons or the probation service[33] or in the personal investment services sector. The powers of ombudsmen vary. Some can make binding decisions,[34] others recommendations.[35] As a rule decisions and recommendations are not based purely on legal principles, but also on good practice and what is just and reasonable. Ombudsmen regularly order or recommend financial compensation for 'distress',[36] including stress, anxiety, frustration and inconvenience. Recourse to the Parliamentary Commissioner for Administration is a cheap solution in situations in which information obtained under compulsion has been unlawfully shared by a public authority causing distress but no tangible loss to the client.[37] A client who is dissatisfied with the outcome of an ombudsman's investigations is still able to go to court.

Disciplinary proceedings

Intentional unauthorized disclosure of personal information may constitute professional misconduct. A complaint to the appropriate professional body may lead to disciplinary proceedings against the offending professional by the relevant professional body.[38] The Law Society's Rules of Professional Conduct state: **9.07**

---

[31] The ombudsmen are officially known as the Local Commission for Administration. Each local government ombudsman has power to compel the attendance of witnesses and production of documents: Local Government Act 1974, s 29.

[32] The Health Service Commissioner has handled complaints relating to privacy/breach of confidence and non-disclosure of information. Complaints cannot be taken direct to the Commissioner; the NHS complaints procedure must be exhausted first. The website is http://www.parliament.ombudsman.org.uk. The Health Service Commissioner's role is examined in S Kerrison and A Pollock, 'Complaints as Accountability? The Case of Health Care in the United Kingdom' [2001] PL 115, 120.

[33] The Prison and Probation Ombudsman for England and Wales came into existence on 1 September 2001. His remit includes breaches of confidentiality in prisons and by probation officers. In a private communication the ombudsman informed the author that he investigated at least two allegations of breaches of medical confidentiality in a prison in 2001. The ombudsman's website is http://www.homeoffice.gov.uk/ppoweb/.

[34] Banking Ombudsman, Office of the Investment Ombudsman, Personal Investment Authority Ombudsman Bureau.

[35] The Local Government Ombudsmen for England and the Health Service Commissioner may recommend compensation. Local authorities usually pay the recommended compensation: *E v UK* App 33218/96, 26 November 2002, para 76.

[36] Commission for Local Administration in England, *Guidance on Good Practice 6: Remedies* (London: 1997) para 30.

[37] cp Parliamentary Commission for Administration, Case C. 172/99 where an Inland Revenue inspector told the applicant's former accountants that the applicant was planning to sue the accountants. The ombudsman concluded that there had been a breach of confidence and that the test of 'harm done' was irrelevant. The Revenue paid a consolatory payment of £100 and £500 to meet the applicant's additional costs (see http://www.parliament.ombudsman.org.uk).

[38] For details of disciplinary proceedings consult B Harris, *The Law and Practice of Disciplinary and Regulatory Proceedings* (2nd edn, Chichester: 2000) and the internet supplement at http://www.regulatorylaw.co.uk/.

Disclosure of a client's confidences which is unauthorized by the client or by the law would lead to disciplinary proceedings against a solicitor . . .[39]

Geoffrey Bindman, a well-known solicitor and human rights campaigner, was fined £12,000 by the Solicitors' Disciplinary Tribunal following a prosecution by the Office for the Supervision of Solicitors over two charges of conflict of interest and one charge of improperly passing on confidential information.[40] The General Medical Council's (GMC's) guidelines warn doctors that though the courts are the ultimate arbiters of whether a disclosure is in the public interest, 'the GMC may also require you to justify your actions if we receive a complaint about the disclosure of personal information without a patient's consent'.[41] A doctor has been struck from the medical register for casually discussing a patient with another health professional.[42] Proceedings have also been brought against three doctors who published an article in the British Journal of Psychiatry about a patient from which she could be identified. The tribunal found that adequate consent had not been obtained but made no serious finding of professional misconduct.[43]

Media Regulatory Bodies[44]

Press Complaints Commission[45]

Constitution and powers

9.08 If the UK print media[46] has abused the client's privacy, it is open to the client to submit a written complaint to the press's non-statutory self-regulatory body, the PCC.[47] This is a free service but must be pursued promptly and before any court action is taken because the PCC will not consider a case that is the subject of current legal proceedings. The Commission normally has 16 members of whom the majority have no connection with the work of newspapers and magazines. There are also seven serv-

---

[39] Law Society, *The Guide to the Professional Conduct of Solicitors* (8th edn, London: 1999) 324, 16.01, para 2. The Bar too treats failure to keep the lay client's affairs confidential as professional misconduct: see Bar Council, 'Complaints: About the System' at http://www.barcouncil.org.uk.

[40] Anyone can bring proceedings before the tribunal but the Office for the Supervision of Solicitors, an arm of the Law Society, is responsible for the majority of cases and in cases of professional misconduct acts as prosecutor.

[41] GMC, *Confidentiality: Protecting and Providing Information* (London: 2000) para 20.

[42] Medical Defence Union, *Confidentiality* (London: 1997) 28.

[43] *Eagles v GMC* (1995) 311 British Medical J 1240, 1245.

[44] M Tugendhat and I Christie (eds), *The Law of Privacy and the Media* (Oxford: 2002) ch 13; T Cassels, 'Professional Regulatory Bodies' in *Tom Crome: Law and the Media*, ed P Alberstat et al (4th edn, Oxford: 2002) ch 17. Oral evidence to House of Commons Select Committee on Culture, Media & Sport March–April 2003.

[45] Law Reform Commission of Hong Kong, *Consultation Paper on The Regulation of Media Intrusion* (Hong Kong: 1999) 78–81; R Pinker, 'Press freedom and press regulation—current trends in their European context' (2002) 7 Communications L 102; PCC, *Submission to the Culture, Media and Sport Select Committee* (February 2003) available at http: www.pccpapers.org.uk

[46] Magazines as well as newspapers are covered.

[47] http://www.pcc.org.uk The PCC received 3,033 complaints in 2001, of which almost a quarter concerned privacy issues. There is a Privacy Commissioner to supervise privacy complaints.

B. Litigation Alternatives

ing editors on the Commission drawn from across the national, regional and periodical press. The PCC has a good record of after-publication conciliation and, should conciliation fail either because the editor does not accept that there is anything to complain about or because the complainant is not satisfied with what the newspaper offers to say or do, the Commission will make a formal adjudication based on the complaint, the editor's written response and the article complained about.[48] There is no hearing. The commitment of the industry to self-regulation he is supposed to ensure that the offending party prints the adjudication giving it full prominence.[49]

Adjudications by the PCC are based on a Code of Practice written by a committee of editors and ratified by the PCC. Adherence to the Code of Practice is a condition in the contracts of employment of most newspaper editors and a significant number of journalists.[50] The PCC's privacy code, and other media industry privacy codes, have taken on an added significance because the courts are directed by s12(4) of the Human Rights Act 1998 (HRA) to take the relevant code into account when 'considering whether to grant any relief which, if granted, might affect the exercise of the Convention right to freedom of expression' if the proceedings relate to journalistic, literary or artistic material. The DPA allows compliance with the codes to be considered for the purpose of determining whether a data controller had or has a reasonable belief that publication of personal data for journalism, literature or art is in the public interest.[51] Lord Woolf has advised against taking into account the actual decisions of the PCC[52] which he said, at best, are illustrative of how the PCC performs its responsibilities. A differently constituted Court of Appeal took just the opposite approach in *R (on the application of ProLife Alliance) v BBC* with Simon Brown LJ citing adjudications of the Broadcasting Standards Commission (BSC) and the Independent Television Commission (ITC) to refute the BBC's case.[53]

9.09

The PCC and privacy

Privacy Code The Privacy Code (which applies to the on-line as well as paper editions of newspapers) mirrors the language of Article 8(1) of the European Convention on Human Rights (ECHR). It provides:

9.10

Privacy[54]
(i) Everyone is entitled to respect for his or her private and family life, home, health and correspondence. A publication will be expected to justify intrusions into

---

[48] R Pinker, 'Human Rights and self-regulation of the press' (1999) 4 Communications L 51. Pinker, ibid at 52, gives the average time for resolving complaints as 12 weeks but in the Annual Report for 2001 this had been reduced to 32 working days.
[49] There is no legal compulsion. The ultimate threat is expulsion from membership of the PCC.
[50] *Venables v NGN Ltd* [2001] 1 All ER 908, 929.
[51] DPA, s 32(3). Only codes designated in a statutory instrument may be considered (see para 18.40 below). This does not apply to the HRA, but in practice this is an irrelevant distinction.
[52] *A v B plc and C ('Flitcroft')* [2002] EWCA Civ 337; [2002] 3 WLR 542, para 11, guideline xv.
[53] [2002] EWCA Civ 297; [2002] 2 All ER 756, para 61.
[54] Clause 3.

any individual's private life without consent. (ii) The use of long-lens photography to take pictures of people in private places without their consent is unacceptable. Note—Private places are public or private property where there is a reasonable expectation of privacy.

Harassment[55]

They must not photograph individuals in private places . . . without their consent; must not persist in telephoning, questioning pursuing or photographing individuals after having been asked to desist; must not remain on their property after having been asked to leave and must not follow them . . .

Children[56]

Young people should be free to complete their time at school without unnecessary intrusion. Journalists should not interview or photograph a child under the age of 16 . . . in the absence of or without the consent of a parent . . . Pupils must not be approached or photographed while at school without the permission of the school authorities. . . . Where material about the private life of a child is published, there must be justification for publication other than the fame, notoriety or position of his or her parents or guardian.

Hospitals[57]

i) Journalists or photographers making enquiries at hospitals or similar institutions should identify themselves to a responsible executive and obtain permission before entering non-public areas. ii) The restrictions on intruding into privacy are particularly relevant to enquiries about individuals in hospitals or similar institutions.[58]

Privacy intrusions may be justified on a number of public interest grounds.[59] They include

(i) Detecting or exposing crime or a serious misdemeanour.
(ii) Protecting public health and safety.
(iii) Preventing the public from being misled by some statement or action of an individual or an organization.

An editor claiming publication served the public interest must demonstrate this with a full explanation. The Code recognizes that there is a public interest in freedom of expression and the Commission will therefore have regard to the extent to which material has, or is about to, become available to the public. In cases involving children editors must demonstrate 'an exceptional public interest to override the normally paramount interest of the child'.

9.11 **Privacy complaints** The privacy provisions of an earlier[59a] version of the Code were considered in 1995 when a number of tabloids published a photograph of Countess Spencer, taken without her consent, walking in the grounds of the clinic

---

[55] Clause 4. [56] Clause 6. [57] Clause 9.
[58] http://www.pcc.org.uk/cop/cop.asp. This version dates from December 1999. Also of interest are clauses 8 (listening devices) and 11 (misrepresentation).
[59] For more details see PCC, *Submission to the Culture, Media and Sport Select Committee* (February, 2003) §C (4).
[59a] The Code was re-worded after the death of Princess Diana to strengthen the protection for her children against media intrusion: M Tugendhat, 'Privacy and Celebrity' in E Barendt and A Firth (eds), *Yearbook of Copyright and Media Law 2001/2002* (Oxford: 2002) 8.

B. Litigation Alternatives

where she was being treated for an eating disorder.[60] The photograph was accompanied in each instance by an article about her health. The reaction of the News of the World, one of the newspapers complained of, was reminiscent of the reaction of the Mirror in the Naomi Campbell case.[61] It printed an article entitled 'Hypocrisy of the Arrogant Earl Spencer' which attempted to justify its decision to publish the photograph on the grounds that this was necessary to prevent the Earl disputing the story of his wife's eating disorder. The PCC decided that publication of a photograph 'taken with a telephoto lens of an indisputably unwell person walking in the private secluded grounds of an addiction clinic' breached the Code and that while the Earl's past relationship with the press may have reduced the amount of privacy to which he was entitled, it could not justify intrusion into the private life of the Countess. The PCC considered that matters of health fell within the ambit of an individual's private life and that as the Countess had not opened her illness to public scrutiny, reports about the Countess's health and psychological state were not justified.

9.12 There have been a number of other adjudications that may interest professionals.[62] In 1996 the PCC upheld a complaint by the actor Hugh Grant about the publication by the Sunday Mirror of confidential medical information about him.[62a] On another occasion the PCC held that a newspaper should not have published the name and medical details of a teenager whose mother was prosecuted for possession of cannabis which she had been giving to him as a drug.[63] A complaint about the publication of a photograph of the surviving conjoined twin taken with a long-lens camera when the baby was in a hospital car park was rejected.[64] In the same adjudication the PCC said that it is not its function to protect the financial interests of complainants through the privacy sections of the Code. It would not, therefore, have adjudicated in favour of Mr and Mrs Douglas had they complained about the undermining of their exclusive deal with OK! magazine by the publication of photographs of their wedding in Hello! magazine. '[W]here a complainant releases or sells information or photographs then they may become disentitled to the protection of the Code in certain circumstances. Privacy is . . . not a commodity which can be sold on one person's terms.'[65]

9.13 The *PPA Privacy Handbook* offers the following summary, derived from past decisions of the PCC, of the factors that this body regards as significant when deciding whether there has been a breach of the PCC's privacy code:

---

[60] Details of the adjudication are to be found in *Spencer v UK* (1998) 25 EHRR CD 105.
[61] See para 8.66 above.
[62] Also McCartney and Hello! 30 May 1998; Tonner and News of the World (Scotland), 21 July 2002; Blair and Mail on Sunday, 24 January 1999; Blair and Daily Telegraph, 18 December 2001; Munro and Bancroft and Evening Standard, 21 March 2001; Brown and Kentish Express, 25 April 1996.
[62a] Hugh Grant and Sunday Mirror, 23 June 1996.
[63] A Woman and Hastings and St Leonard's Observer 9 January 1998.
[64] Michaelangelo and Rina Attard (parents of the conjoined twins) and Manchester Evening News, 16 June 2001.
[65] ibid.

1. the extent to which the material has, or is about to, become available to the public;
2. whether the complainant has openly discussed similar matters in the past;
3. whether the complainant has sold private material about themselves;
4. whether there is a public interest in publishing private details or pictures; and
5. whether photographs complained of were taken in a place where the complainant could expect to have a reasonable expectation of privacy.[66]

Shortcomings of the PCC

9.14 A complainant who is dissatisfied with a PCC privacy adjudication might find that the PCC's decision influences the outcome of subsequent civil litigation because the courts are required by the HRA to take the PCC's Privacy Code (though not its adjudications) into account when considering whether to grant '*any* relief which, if granted, might affect the exercise of the Convention right to freedom of expression'.[67] There is, of course, no obligation to resort to the PCC before seeking a legal remedy.

9.15 The deference paid by the courts to the decisions of the PCC makes it difficult to challenge the PCC's adjudication.[68] In *R v PCC, ex p Stewart-Brady*[69] the applicant, a convicted murderer, applied for leave to obtain a judicial review of the Commission's finding that a photograph taken of him in hospital with a long-lens camera did not breach the Code. Leave was refused. In *R (on the application of Ford) v PCC*[70] leave was once again refused to review an adjudication, Silber J holding that 'the courts will . . . not be keen to interfere with decisions of the Commission on [privacy] issues unless . . . it is clearly desirable to do so'.[71] In the judge's opinion, the Commission was much better equipped because of the expertise of its members than a court to strike a balance between the privacy rights of the complainant and the freedom of expression of the publisher.[72] But is this true? Calcutt did not regard the PCC as an effective regulator or that it held the balance fairly between the press and individuals.[73] This view is shared by the Chairman of

---

[66] C Hutchings and S Thomas, *PPA Privacy Handbook* (Charles Russell, London: 2001) 20. See also PCC, *Submission to the Culture, Media and Sport Select Committee* (February, 2003) §C (2), (3).

[67] s 12(1). The word 'any' has been put in italics to draw attention to the fact that the Code is not only relevant in cases of prior restraint. An award of damages against the press may have a chilling effect on press freedom.

[68] The BSC and ITC are public bodies (see Freedom of Information Act 2000, Sch 1, Pt VI) which, if they fail to give effect to Convention rights can be said to have acted unlawfully: see para 3.05 above. It is uncertain whether the PCC is a public authority.

[69] [1997] EMLR 185.

[70] [2001] EWHC Admin 683; [2002] EMLR 95. The PCC had refused to recognize a qualitative disitnction between being seen by a few people and millions of readers.

[71] ibid, para 17.

[72] ibid, paras 23–25.

[73] D Calcutt, 'Freedom of the Press, Freedom from the Press' [1994] Denning LJ 1. See also *Review of Press Self-Regulation* (Cm 2135, 1993) of which Calcutt was the chairman. For an examination of the early privacy adjudications of the PCC see L Blom-Cooper and L Pruitt, 'Privacy, Jurisprudence of the Press Complaints Commission' (1994) Anglo-American L Rev 133.

B. Litigation Alternatives

the BSC.[74] Barendt accuses the PCC of failing to distinguish reporting which is in the public interest and reporting which the public finds interesting: 'how otherwise can one explain its rejections of complaints regarding the publication of the photo in hospital of the victim of a brutal attack and publication of a sequence of photographs of someone jumping to death from a bridge.'[75] The PCC's privacy adjudications have been criticized by others as inconsistent.[76]

9.16 One particular failing to which Calcutt drew attention was the absence of a 'hot-line' for anticipated breaches of the code.[77] Like all the media regulators, the PCC has no legal power to stop publication of material,[78] but this does not mean that it should not try to intercede before publication. Preventing an infringement of privacy is much more useful than commenting adversely on it after it has happened. Other drawbacks include inability to order payment of compensation,[79] the absence of any mechanism for investigating disputed facts, lack of jurisdiction over newspapers from abroad and the anomaly that the PCC can adjudicate only on the contents of books serialized in newspapers.[80] When the PCC finds against a newspaper, the newspaper is required to print the adjudication in full with due prominence. Should a newspaper fail to do so, there are no legal sanctions.

Broadcasting Standards Commission[81]

9.17 If the client's informational privacy is violated by the commercial or public broadcasting media,[82] the client can turn to the BSC,[83] a 15-member body independent of both government and the media which has a statutory duty to produce and keep under review a code of conduct for all British broadcasters regarding 'unwarranted infringement of privacy in . . . and . . . in connection with the obtaining of material included in' programmes.[84] Like the PCC, it has a code that deals with

---

[74] See interview with the new chairman of the BSC in the 2000/01 Annual Review on the BSC website.

[75] E Barendt, 'Media intrusion: the case for legislation' in D Tambini and C Heyward (eds), *Ruled by Recluses?* (London: IPPR, 2002) 17. See also *Peck v UK* Application 44647/98 28 January 2003.

[76] H Tomlinson (ed), *Privacy and the Media: The Developing Law* (London: 2002) 99. eg compare Anna Ford and Daily Mail 15 September 2000 with HRH Prince William amd OK! magazine 27 October 2000.

[77] The PCC now has a general helpline.

[78] This weighed with the court in *Venables v NGN Ltd* [2001] 1 All ER 908, para 96.

[79] In the 2001 Annual Report it is reported that a national newspaper had published a photograph of a man in the company of a well-known entertainer, along with details of the man's private life. The man received an apology and a payment. The photograph was destroyed.

[80] M Tugendhat and I Christie (eds), *The Law of Privacy and the Media* (Oxford: 2002) para 4.08.

[81] Law Reform Commission of Hong Kong, *Consultation Paper on The Regulation of Media Intrusion* (Hong Kong: 1999) 82–83; Lord Dubs, 'The Broadcasting Standards Commission and privacy complaints' in D Tambini and C Heyward (eds), *Ruled by Recluses?* (London: IPPR, 2002) ch 5.

[82] The remit covers radio and television, BBC and commercial broadcasters, terrestrial, satellite and cable operators.

[83] See eg *R v Brentwood BC, ex p Peck* [1998] EMLR 697, 702, 707.

[84] Broadcasting Act 1996, s 107(1).

privacy but in much greater detail.[85] The BSC considers and adjudicates written complaints about breaches of the Code that are not the subject of litigation or best dealt with by litigation.[86] The Commission has power to require recordings of broadcast material, to call for written statements and to hold a hearing[87] in private.[88] The hearing takes place before a panel of three lay Commissioners and is attended by the complainant, broadcaster and, if the broadcaster is licensed, the relevant licensing regulator.[89] Legal representation is allowed.

9.18 Far fewer privacy complaints are received by the BSC than the PCC.[90] Only the victim of an unwarranted infringement of privacy may make a complaint, but posthumous complaints are allowed by a personal representative, relative or person closely connected with the victim.[91] The Broadcasting Act 1996 requires the BSC to publish a summary of the complaint and its findings.[92] The BSC 'may, if they think fit, omit from any summary which is included in a report . . . any information which would lead to the disclosure of the identity of any person connected with the complaint' other than the broadcaster.[93] For clients who do not want additional exposure to publicity, this is a boon. If a complaint is upheld, the BSC may require the broadcaster to publish a summary of the complaint and the BSC's findings 'in such manner . . . as may be specified in the directions'. This is normally on air and in print. The broadcaster must comply with the BSC's directions and report back.[94] If the broadcaster is licensed, the BSC can ask the relevant regulator to direct the licensee to publicize the complaint and finding.[95] There are no other sanctions open to the Commission; it has no power to prevent a broadcast.

9.19 In 1998 the BSC upheld a complaint that the secret filming of a shop by the BBC was an infringement of the shop's privacy. This finding was unsuccessfully challenged in the courts in judicial review proceedings.[96] If secret filming of a place to which the public has access is, without adequate justification,[97] improper, then

---

[85] The Code on Fairness and Privacy is available from http://www.bsc.org.uk.
[86] Broadcasting Act 1996, s 114(2).
[87] This is a matter of discretion: ibid, s 115(1).
[88] ibid, s 115(2).   [89] ibid, s 115(2).
[90] According to the 2000/01 Annual Review the BSC received a total of 360 complaints about privacy and fairness out of a grand total of 5,280 complaints. Of these 80 were entertained, 9 were about privacy alone and 2 were upheld.
[91] Broadcasting Act 1996, s 111. In any case, a person's own privacy may be invaded by disclosure of information about a close relative: *R v Broadcasting Complaints Commission, ex p Granada Television Ltd* [1995] EMLR 163.
[92] Broadcasting Act 1996, s 119(8).
[93] ibid, s 119(10).
[94] ibid, ss 119, 120.
[95] ibid, s 119.
[96] *R v BSC, ex p BBC* [2000] 3 All ER 989. There is no right of appeal against decisions of the BSC.
[97] Code on Fairness and Privacy, para 14: '[a]n infringement of privacy has to be justified by an overriding public interest in disclosure of the information. This would include revealing or detecting crime or disreputable behaviour, protecting public health or safety, exposing misleading claims made by individuals or organizations, or disclosing significant incompetence in public office. Moreover, the means of obtaining the information must be proportionate to the matter under investigation.'

intrusion into the workplace of a professional, whether open to the public or not, to obtain information confidential to a client should be. In fact the BSC has found an invasion of privacy in the filming and transmission without consent of close ups of a seriously injured driver trapped in his car after a road accident and later while receiving medical assistance in an ambulance.[98] So long as there is some connection with material that was broadcast, a complaint may be made about the obtaining of material that was not in the end broadcast.[99]

The BSC (as well as the ITC) is to be abolished during 2003 and replaced by a new regulator, the Office of Communications (OFCOM).[100] OFCOM is expected to adopt the BSC's procedures and will have the ITC's wider powers of sanction. Already in anticipation of OFCOM, the BSC considers privacy complaints made to the ITC and the Radio Authority.[101]   **9.20**

Independent Television Commission[102]

This body is a programme regulator for independent television broadcasting by UK based operators. Its jurisdiction over privacy complaints overlaps with that of the BSC.[103] Standards for programme content are set in a Programme Code[104] which the BSC enforces on its own initiative and in reaction to viewers' complaints. Unlike the PCC and BSC, it will consider a complaint that is the subject of litigation.[105] Section 2 of the Code deals with privacy. Broadcasters are expected to respect rights to private and family life guaranteed by Article 8(1).[106]   **9.21**

Included in the Code is the rule that 'the individual's right to privacy at times of bereavement or extreme distress must in particular be respected'.[107] It was this requirement that the ITC found to have been breached when Channel 5 broadcast a programme about road traffic accidents in November 2000 in which it disclosed the medical prognosis for the victim of a motor-cycle crash 16 weeks earlier.[108] The victim was not named but was a viewer and was able to identify   **9.22**

---

[98] Complaint of Graeme Oswald, 9 January 2002 about 'Back to the Floor' broadcast on BBC2 27 November 2001.
[99] Code of Fairness and Privacy, para 15; *R v Broadcasting Complaints Commission, ex p BBC* [1993] EMLR 419. See also *R v Broadcasting Complaints Commission, ex p Barclay* [1997] EMLR 62.
[100] Office of Communications Act 2002.
[101] Lord Dubs, 'The Broadcasting Standards Commission and privacy complaints' in D Tambini and C Heyward (eds), *Ruled by Recluses?* (London: IPPR, 2002), 63.
[102] http://www.itc.org.uk.
[103] The BSC alone has jurisdiction over BBC television and S4C.
[104] April 2001. The Code is authorized by the Broadcasting Act 1990 and reflects the general effect of the BSC's Code.
[105] If there is no on-going litigation the ITC tends to refer privacy complaints to the BSC.
[106] Programme Code 2.1.
[107] Programme Code 2.2(iv).
[108] 'Crash—Picking Up the Pieces: Channel 5, Monday 20 November 2000: 8 p.m'., http://www.itc.org.uk.

himself from the description given of the accident. The breach was serious because the commentary stated that he 'would never walk or ride again', something that the victim's doctor had not told him and which the victim eventually disproved. The programme-maker's source was a police officer to whom the information had been inappropriately disclosed by a hospital employee.

9.23 When privacy is infringed the ITC, unlike the BSC, is not limited to commenting on the complaint. It has a wide range of sanctions at its disposal. Minor infringements are dealt with by contacting the offending broadcaster and offering guidance. For more serious breaches and persistent breaches of the Programme Code the ITC can issue a formal warning, order the offending company to broadcast an apology or correction, impose a fine, forbid repeats, shorten the term of a licence or, in an extreme case, withdraw the licence. But it cannot compensate the complainant.

Part III

DEFENCES

10

COMPELLED DISCLOSURE

A. Coercive Statutory Disclosure	10.02	B. Money Laundering	10.24
The Targets of Coercive Disclosure	10.02	Reporting Obligation	10.25
Confidentiality and Coercive Disclosure	10.04	Related Offences	10.32
Legal Professional Privilege and Coercive Disclosure	10.13	C. Use of Information Disclosed Under Compulsion	10.34
Making the Disclosure and Notifying the Client	10.16	In a Criminal Prosecution	10.34
		For a Collateral Purpose	10.35
Consequences of Non-Disclosure	10.22		
Compulsory Disclosure Under Foreign Law	10.23		

Situations abound in which a professional is entitled to disclose confidential personal information concerning a client without the client's consent although the professional owes the client a legal obligation of confidentiality. This chapter looks at those in which disclosure is mandatory and occurs for reasons not immediately related to litigation. Most codes of professional ethics expressly recognize that where the law compels disclosure, the professional must oblige. It may be a criminal offence not to do so.[1] By complying the professional will not violate the first data protection principle[2] or become exposed to an action for breach of confidence in equity or contract or violate any subsisting injunction restraining disclosure:[3] 10.01

> [A] duty of confidence is subject to, and overridden by, the duty to the party to that contract to comply with the law of the land. If it is the duty of such a party to a contract . . . to disclose in defined circumstances confidential information, then he must do so, and any express contract to the contrary would be illegal and void.[4]

---

[1] eg Terrorism Act 2000, ss 19(2), 21A, Sch 3, para 7(4).
[2] See para 18.19 below.
[3] *A v B Bank (Bank of England intervening)* [1992] 1 All ER 778.
[4] per Diplock LJ, *Parry Jones v Law Society* [1969] 1 Ch 1, 9.

However, a disclosure obligation imposed by law would not seem to preclude liability for defamation[5] or negligence in contract or tort if the professional failed to exercise reasonable care in making the compelled disclosure.[6]

A. Coercive Statutory Disclosure

The Targets of Coercive Disclosure

10.02 Compulsory disclosure, except in connection with litigation, is almost[7] always a statutory affair. Many legislative provisions exist that allow officials to demand of professionals personal information about their clients either with the object of investigating the client or with the object of investigating the professional.[8] Some of this legislation is general; it imposes a disclosure obligation on everyone.[9] For example, Family Law Act 1986, s 33 provides that 'where in proceedings . . . in respect of a child there is not available to the court adequate information as to where the child is, the court may order *any person* who it has reason to believe may have relevant information to disclose it to the court'.[10] Courts routinely make orders under this power against solicitors,[11] social services and the NHS.[12] Other legislative provisions target professionals as a group. Section 15 of the Child Support Act 1991 empowers an inspector to enter any premises used for the pur-

---

[5] cp *Shah v Standard Chartered Bank* [1998] 4 All ER 155. There may be a defence of qualified privilege: cp *Mahon v Rahn* [1997] 3 All ER 687, 709.

[6] cp *Swinney v Chief Constable of Northumbria Police* [1996] 3 All ER 449.

[7] In the exercise of its wardship jurisdiction a court has an inherent power to order a solicitor to disclose information in his possession material to the recovery of an abducted child: *Re B* [1995] 1 FLR 774, 776; *Re H* [2000] 1 FCR 499. The legal representatives of the parties also have a duty to disclose to the court and other parties information material to the welfare of a child in family proceedings notwithstanding that the information is contrary to the interests of the client and within the scope of legal professional privilege: *Re R* [1993] 4 All ER 702, 705, *Re DH* [1994] 1 FLR 679; *Oxfordshire CC v M* [1994] 2 All ER 269. The correctness of these decisions was left open in *Re L* [1996] 2 All ER 78, 86–87. Lord Nicholls who was in the minority had reservations about the existence of the duty, at 93. See also para 10.11 below.

[8] As in *Parry-Jones v Law Society* [1968] 1 All ER 177; *R v Inland Revenue Commissioners ex p Taylor (No 2)* [1990] 2 All ER 409 and *Cowell v Law Society* (Ch D, 12 October 2001). The client will not always be willing to consent to the disclosure of confidential personal information in aid of an official investigation.

[9] See also Health and Safety at Work Act 1974, s 27; Local Government Act 1974, s 29(1); Insolvency Act 1986, s 366; Income and Corporation Taxes Act 1988, S745, Children's Act 1989, s 50(3)(c); Competition Act 1998, s 25, as to which see A Riley, 'Saunders and the Power to Obtain Information in Community and United Kingdom Competition Law' (2000) 25 ELR 264; Disability Rights Commission Act 1999, s 4; Financial Services and Markets Act 2000, ss 161, 172, 173, 175; Terrorism Act 2000, s 38B (see para 10.11 below).

[10] Italics added. See also Child Abduction and Custody Act 1985, s 24A and *Re H* [2000] 1 FLR 766 where a firm of solicitors was ordered to disclose any information they had about the whereabouts of their client and the client's child, who was missing.

[11] *Re H* [2000] 1 FLR 766.

[12] See also *Chief Constable of West Yorkshire Police v S* [1998] 2 FLR 973 where the police successfully resisted an order.

A. Coercive Statutory Disclosure

poses of carrying on a profession 'to make such examination and enquiry there as he considers appropriate' and to insist that a person carrying on a profession at those premises 'furnish to the inspector all such information and documents as the inspector may reasonably require'.[13] Not to do so without reasonable excuse is a criminal offence.[14] Under Terrorism Act 2000, s 19 it is a criminal offence for a professional in the unregulated sector who 'believes or suspects' that another person has committed an offence under ss 15 to 18 of that Act based on information derived from her work not to report her suspicions as soon as 'is reasonably practicable'.[15] The disclosure obligation for professionals in the regulated sector[16] is even stricter. The professional commits an offence if she 'knows or suspects' or 'has reasonable grounds for knowing or suspecting' that another person has committed any of these offences and fails to report 'as soon as is reasonably practicable'.[17] The offences range from money laundering (which is discussed in greater depth later in this chapter)[18] to arranging or raising funds for terrorism or using or possessing money or property collected for purposes of terrorism.

Most common of all are the measures directed at the members of specific named professions. The Jack Report[19] on banking drew attention to two disclosure provisions restricted to the banking fraternity: Taxes Management Act 1970, s 17(1)[20] and Criminal Justice Act 1987, s 2(10). Probation officers have reporting duties under the Children Act 1989.[21] Accountants must co-operate with the Child Support Agency.[22] A solicitor is obliged to pass client information to the legal aid authorities,[23] to a client's trustee in bankruptcy,[24] to the Law Society when the Society is investigating her affairs[25] and, where the Secretary of State has appointed investigators to examine the management of an insurance company, to the insurance company's solicitor, though this information is not very likely to be of a

10.03

---

[13] s 15(4), (6).
[14] s 15(9)(b).
[15] The professional cannot be sued for making the disclosure: s 20(3).
[16] This is broadly anyone who is obliged to comply with the Money Laundering Regulations. Once the second EU Money Laundering Directive is implemented (before June 2003) this will include accountants, lawyers, auditors and tax advisers.
[17] s 21A. The professional cannot be sued for making the disclosure: s 21B(1).
[18] See para 10.24 below.
[19] *Banking Services: Law and Practice Report* (Cm 622, 1989).
[20] See also Income and Corporation Taxes Act 1988, s 745(5).
[21] Children Act 1989, s 7.
[22] Child Support (Information, Evidence and Disclosure) Regulations 1992 SI 1992/1812, reg 2(2)(f).
[23] Legal Aid in Criminal and Care Proceedings (General) Regulations 1989 SI 1989/344, reg 56; Legal Services Commission (Disclosure of Information) Regulations 2000 SI 2000/442.
[24] Insolvency Act 1986, ss 311(1), 312(2).
[25] Solicitors Act 1974, ss 35, 44B. Without the power to override confidentiality the Office for the Supervision of Solicitors would be unable to investigate complaints unless the complainant was the client. cp Administration of Justice Act 1985, s 31 (licensed conveyancers).

personal nature.[26] Doctors have many statutory reporting duties. The British Medical Association sums these up as being concerned with 'potential dangers to society from serious diseases, control of illegal substances sought by addicts and the interests of order and justice, which oblige the reporting of abortions, births, deaths and accidents'.[27] Along with everyone else who works for the NHS, doctors must provide the Health Service Commissioner with documents and information.[28]

Confidentiality and Coercive Disclosure

Statutory protection for confidential information

10.04 Legislation that mandates disclosure of information rarely exempts from this obligation information that is the subject of an obligation of confidentiality.[29] Where it does, the protection may be limited. By Criminal Justice Act 1987, s 2(10) it is provided that:

> [a] person shall not . . . be required to disclose information or produce a document in respect of which he owes an obligation of confidence by virtue of carrying on any banking business unless—
> (a) the person to whom the obligation of confidence is owed consents to the disclosure or production; or
> (b) the Director has authorized the making of the requirement or, if it is impracticable for him to act personally, a member of the Serious Fraud Office designated by him . . .

The Director of the Serious Fraud Office regularly authorizes breaches of banking confidentiality.[30] There are other provisions similar to s 2(10).[31]

---

[26] Insurance Companies Act 1982. s 43A (repealed).

[27] BMA, *Medical Ethics Today* (London: 1998) 57. The provisions are: notification of infectious diseases: Public Health (Control of Disease) Act 1984, NHS (Venereal Diseases) Regulations 1974, Public Health (Infectious Diseases) Regulations 1988; notification of drug addicts: Misuse of Drugs (Notification of and Supply of Addicts) Regulations 1973 SI 1973/799, reg 3; notification of accidents and dangerous occurrences at work and work-related disease: Reporting of Injuries, Diseases and Dangerous Occurrences Regulations 1995 SI 1995/3163; notification of abortions: Abortion Regulations 1991 SI 1991/499, reg 4; notification of births and deaths: NHS Act 1977, s 124; NHS (Notification of Births and Deaths) Regulations 1982 SI 1982/286.

[28] Health Service Commissioner Act 1993, s 12.

[29] But see Taxes Management Act 1970, s 20(8C) which excludes from a production notice made pursuant to s 20(3) 'personal records' as defined in Police and Criminal Evidence Act 1984, s 12 and 'journalistic material' within the meaning of s 13 of that Act. For an explanation of 'personal records' and 'journalistic material' see para 14.22 below. See also s 20B(9) which exempts auditors' working papers and relevant communications between a tax adviser from production and s 20B(2) which exempts documents relating to the conduct of a pending appeal by the taxpayer.

[30] M Levi, 'Covert Policing and the Investigation of Organized Fraud: The English Experience in International Context' in C Fijnaut and G Marx (eds), *Police Surveillance in Comparative Perspective* (The Hague: 1995) says that in 1993–94 this was done on 657 occasions. See also para 14.59 below.

[31] Companies Act 1985, s 452(1A) and (1B); Companies Act 1989, s 84(4); Open-Ended Investment Companies (Investment Companies with Variable Capital) Regulations 1996 SI 1996/2827, reg 23(2). cp Financial Services and Markets Act 2000, s 175(5). For an exhaustive

A. Coercive Statutory Disclosure

Rather than exempt confidential documents and information, some legislation expressly requires its disclosure.[32] Criminal Appeal Act 1995, s 17(4) provides that: 10.05

> the duty to comply with a requirement under this section is not affected by any obligation of secrecy or other limitation on disclosure (including any such obligation or limitation imposed by or by virtue of an enactment) which would otherwise prevent the production of the document . . .

Judicial interpretation

Before the Human Rights Act 1998 came into force

When, as is often the case, disclosure legislation is silent about whether information subject to an obligation of confidentiality has to be disclosed or not, the question becomes one of statutory construction for the courts. Before 2000 courts were not receptive to arguments that confidential information was exempt from compulsory disclosure.[33] By the Road Traffic Act 1988, s 172(b), where the driver of a vehicle or rider of a bicycle is alleged to be guilty of a road traffic offence: 10.06

> *any other person* shall if required . . . give such information which it is in his power to give and may lead to identification of the driver.[34]

In *Hunter v Mann*[35] the Divisional Court held that the statutory predecessor of s 172(2)(b) overrides medical confidentiality.[36] A doctor who refused to answer questions from the police about the identities of a man and a girl whom he had treated after a motor accident caused by dangerous driving was convicted and fined. Courts tended to take the view that an exemption for confidential information would undermine the purpose for which the power to compel disclosure had been given.[37] In *Price Waterhouse (a Firm) v BCCI Holdings (Luxembourg) SA*[38] Millett J held that not even the public interest in banking confidentiality[39] warranted the court implying into Banking Act 1987, s 39 an exception for confidential documents held by accountants that in litigation in the High Court would

---

survey of legislation under which a bank may be obliged to disclose confidential information see P Cresswell et al (eds), *Encyclopaedia of Banking Law* (London: 1998) vol 1, C351. cp Financial Services and Markets Act 2000, s 175(5)(d).

[32] Health Service Commissioner Act 1993, s 12(3).
[33] eg *A v B (Bank of England Intervening)* [1992] 1 All ER 778, 786–790; *Guyer v Walton* [2001] STC (SCD) 75, paras 24–28.
[34] Italics added.
[35] [1974] 2 All ER 414.
[36] The case concerned the same provision in an earlier act: Road Traffic Act 1972, s 168(2)(b).
[37] eg *Parry-Jones v Law Society* [1968] 1 All ER 177.
[38] [1992] BCLC 583.
[39] Banking Act 1987, s 82(1) makes (subject to exceptions) the disclosure of the banking affairs of any person a criminal offence. See *BCCI (Overseas) Ltd (In Liquidation) v Price Waterhouse* [1997] 4 All ER 781.

have been shielded from production by legal professional privilege.[40] This decision has since been disapproved by the House of Lords.[41]

Recent judicial interpretation

10.07 Compulsory disclosure of confidential personal information, and in particular personal information about clients, to anyone in the public sector without the subject's consent may be an interference with the right to respect for private life. One would therefore expect the courts to be more protective of confidential personal information in the Human Rights Act (HRA) era but there is no sign of this yet. In *H (A Healthcare Worker v Associated Newspapers Ltd*[42] a health authority which had employed an HIV dentist sought the dentist's private patient records in order to carry out a 'look-back' exercise to advise exposure prone patients.[43] Claiming that disclosure of his patients' records breached their clinical confidentiality and that the 'look-back' exercise was unnecessary, the dentist resisted the application. During the hearing in the Court of Appeal the dentist agreed to disclose his private patient records over the last ten years 'if the court declares it necessary'.[44] The Court of Appeal did, holding that 'he should make available such records as are reasonably required for the purpose of evaluation'[45] but on terms that they were not to be disclosed, or any action taken on the basis of them, without the permission of the dentist or the permission of the court. The Court of Appeal did not explain by what authority the health authority was entitled to examine the records. The best explanation is that the power to obtain them was a necessary implied statutory power derived from the health authority's other statutory functions and duties.[46]

Impact of the Human Rights Act 1998

10.08 A possible reason that Article 8 went unmentioned[47] in *H (A Healthcare Worker v Associated Newspapers Ltd* was the ease with which a 'look-back' exercise could be

---

[40] Lawyers are in a better position. Banking Act 1987, s 39(13) expressly allows lawyers to refuse to produce legally privileged documents. It was, indeed, the fact that Parliament had expressly stated that lawyers did not have to disclose information that led the court to infer that accountants did. Millett J reasoned that if Parliament had intended accountants to be in the same position, Parliament would have said so.

[41] *R v Special Commissioner, ex p Morgan Grenfell & Co Ltd* [2002] UKHL 21; [2002] 2 WLR 1299, para 37.

[42] [2002] EWCA Civ 195, (2002) 65 BMLR 132.

[43] The most recent guidelines on 'look back' exercises and patient notification are to be found in DoH, *HIV Infected Health Care Workers* (September 2002) para 10.5, available from http://www.doh.gov.uk/aids.htm. This guidance is still the subject of consultation.

[44] ibid para 6.

[45] [2002] EWCA Civ 195, (2002) 65 BMLR 132, para 62.

[46] H Hyam. 'Disclosure of confidential information' (2002) 152 NLJ 1129, 1130. cp *Broadmoor Special Hospital v Robinson* (1999) 52 BMLR 137, 145.

[47] Only the justification for interfering with freedom of expression is referred to: [2002] EWCA Civ 195, (2002) 65 BMLR 132, para 43.

justified under Article 8(2). Interference with Article 8 in the circumstances of this case was in line with the Strasbourg jurisprudence on the interface between Article 8, medical confidentiality and compulsory disclosure of personal information to officials.[48] In *Andersson (Anne-Marie) v Sweden*[49] a psychiatrist had submitted a report containing information about the applicant's mental and physical health to the social authorities out of concern about the detrimental effect on the applicant's under-age son of the applicant's condition. Submission of a report was compulsory under Swedish law though its contents were left to the discretion of the author of the report. The Commission held the application inadmissible as being manifestly ill-founded. Contrary to the submission of the applicant, the Commission thought that the psychiatrist's concern did not lack substance and that it was necessary for the authorities to have information about her health and not just that of her son. Legitimate aims were being pursued, namely 'protection of health or morals' and 'protection of the rights and freedoms of others', and the disclosure 'was of a limited nature, as the information did not become public but remained protected by the same level of confidentiality as that applicable to psychiatric records'.[50] Moreover, the applicant was notified of the disclosure.

10.09 Another case in point is *MS v Sweden*[51] where medical records were disclosed to a Social Securities Insurance office that was investigating a claim to worker's compensation. Interference with the applicant's right to private life was found to be justified: the interference was proportionate to the legitimate aim of ensuring that public funds were allocated to deserving claimants. The court pointed out that the disclosure of the medical records was subject to important limitations[52] and was accompanied by effective and adequate safeguards against abuse.

10.10 The Strasbourg cases were reviewed by Munby J in *X v A Health Authority*.[53] Having held that NHS regulations empowered the health authority to demand patient records for the purpose of investigating the extent to which a GP and his partners had complied with their terms of service, he considered the compatibility of the demand with Article 8. His conclusion was that disclosure of confidential medical records without patient consent for a purpose other than the patient's best interests was an interference with Article 8 that had to be for a compelling public interest satisfying the criteria of necessity and proportionality. His order for

---

[48] cp *Z v Finland* (1997) 25 EHRR 371 where requiring doctors to give evidence in a court of law about the HIV status of a patient was held to be a justified interference with Art 8(1).
[49] (1997) 25 EHRR 722.
[50] ibid, para 41.
[51] (1997) 45 BMLR 133. See also *R v Secretary of State for the Home Department, ex p Kingdom of Belgium* (DC, 15 February 2000) where the Divisional Court said that disclosure of the medical report on General Pinochet's fitness to stand trial was justified under Art 8.
[52] The office had to request the information which had to be important to the application of the Insurance Act and the office was obliged to protect the confidentiality of the medical records.
[53] [2001] Lloyd's Rep Med 349.

disclosure was made conditional on efficient and adequate safeguards against abuse of the disclosed records: measures to maintain the confidentiality of the records,[54] minimum public disclosure of information in them and protection of patient anonymity. These safeguards were to apply not only to the initial disclosure but to any subsequent transmission by one public body to another. On appeal these conditions were endorsed by the Court of Appeal which accepted the submission of the doctor's counsel that it was for a judge and not for the public authority to resolve the conflict of interests between the private/public interest in medical confidentiality and any competing public interest.[55]

'Reasonable excuse' for non-disclosure

10.11 A number of statutes permit information to be withheld if the person from whom the information is demanded has a 'reasonable excuse'.[56] Statutes which do this include:

(1) The Child Support Act 1991[57] which empowers an inspector to enter certain premises and, having entered, to question a person found there who is over 18 or require documents to be furnished. It is a defence to a prosecution for failing to provide information or a document that the defendant had a 'reasonable excuse'.

(2) The Terrorism Act 2000 which makes it a criminal offence for 'a person' not to disclose information which he 'knows or believes' might be of 'material assistance' in preventing the commission of an act of terrorism or securing the capture and conviction of a terrorist in the United Kingdom as soon as reasonably practicable.[58] Terrorism is defined[59] as including the use or threat of action 'designed to influence the government' for the purpose of advancing 'a political, religious or ideological cause' and action as including 'serious damage to property'. It is a defence for a person charged with this offence 'to prove that he had a reasonable excuse for not making the disclosure'.[60]

(3) The Children Act 1989[61] which imposes a duty on those employed by local authorities, local education authorities, local housing authorities, health

---

[54] cp *Re V* [1999] IFLR 267, 274; *Re L* [2000] 1 FLR 913.
[55] per Thorpe LJ, [2001] EWCA Civ 2014; [2002] 2 All ER 780, paras 14, 25.
[56] eg Financial Services and Markets Act 2000, ss.161(6), 177(2); Proceeds of Crime Act 2002, s 330(1).
[57] s 15.
[58] Terrorism Act 2000, s 38B as amended by the Anti-Terrorism, Crime and Security Act 2001. Cp *Att-Gen's Ref (No 3) of 1993* [1993] NI 50. Summary conviction carries a sentence of up to six months' imprisonment and/or a fine and conviction on indictment a five years' maximum prison sentence and/or a fine.
[59] s 1.
[60] Terrorism Act 2000, s 38B(4). The offences created by s 19 and 21A (see para 12.02 below) have the same defence (ss 19(3), 21A(5)). See also Sch 3 (freezing orders), para 7(4).
[61] s 47(9).

A. Coercive Statutory Disclosure

authorities and others authorized by the Secretary of State to assist social service investigations into alleged child abuse by providing information if called upon to do so unless 'doing so would be unreasonable in all the circumstances'.[62]

Does an obligation of professional confidentiality excuse non-disclosure under any of these three statutes?

The prevailing lay opinion is that professional confidentiality is a reasonable excuse for not disclosing information under the Children Act provision.[63] These expectations may be disappointed. It is possible that a court will decide that, subject to compliance with Article 8, the public interest in discovering the whereabouts of a missing child is greater than the public interest in maintaining a professional confidence.[64] It is improbable that professional confidentiality is a reasonable excuse for non-compliance with the disclosure provision in the Terrorism Act, a provision introduced in the wake of 11 September 2001, though fear of reprisals might be. A Home Office circular states that 'having a legal or familial relationship with someone does not constitute immunity from the obligation to disclose information'.[65] In *Sykes v DPP*[66] it was Lord Denning's view that a solicitor's, doctor's or lawyer's obligation of confidentiality offered a reasonable excuse defence to the offence of misprision of felony. The master of a college too might be excused for having failed to report a student. But Lord Denning might have taken a different view had the offence been failure to supply information that might have averted an act of terrorism.

10.12

Legal Professional Privilege and Coercive Disclosure

Article 8

The Terrorism Act 2000 exempts 'a professional legal adviser' from the duty to disclose information about terrorist funding obtained 'in privileged circumstances' or a belief or suspicion based on such information.[67] There is no express exemption from the obligation to report information that the professional legal adviser 'knows or believes' might be of material assistance in preventing an act of terrorism or detecting and convicting a terrorist.[68] Thus it will be left to the courts

10.13

---

[62] Children Act 1989, s 47(10).
[63] T Bond, *Confidentiality: Counselling and the Law* (3rd edn, Rugby: 1999) 9.
[64] cp *Re H* [2000] 1 FLR 766 (the need to find an abducted child outweighed the public interest in legal professional privilege to the extent that a firm of solicitors had to disclose all the information they had about the whereabouts of the child, but the court refused to make an order preventing the solicitors from disclosing the existence of the order to the client). See also *Re DH* [1994] 1 FLR 679.
[65] Circular 7/2002, 5, available at http://www.homeoffice.gov.uk/circulars/2002/hoc7.htm.
[66] [1961] 3 All ER 33, 42.
[67] ss 19(5), 21A(5)(b). Privilege is defined in ss 19(6) and 21A(8). See para 10.30 below.
[68] Terrorism Act 2000, s 38B.

to decide whether legal professional privilege is a 'reasonable excuse'.[69] A number of other coercive disclosure provisions expressly require disclosure of information that in litigation in the High Court could be the subject of a successful claim to legal professional privilege.[70] In *R v Derby Magistrates' Court, ex p B*[71] Lord Taylor CJ flagged the possibility that the European Convention on Human Rights (ECHR) may restrict statutory qualification of legal professional privilege. Strasbourg jurisprudence bears this out. Five years on in *Foxley v UK*[72] the European Court of Human Rights (ECtHR) held that the interception of correspondence between the applicant and his legal advisers by the applicant's trustee in bankruptcy, although apparently lawful under the Insolvency Act 1986, s 371[73] interfered with Article 8(1) of the Convention and therefore had to be justified under Article 8(2). The court saw no pressing social need for the interference and found a violation of the Convention.

10.14 Abrogation of legal professional privilege in furtherance of one of the purposes mentioned in Article 8(2) can, if done for a sufficiently compelling reason, be lawful.[74] Lord Hoffman has doubted that collection of the revenue is such a reason.[75] The courts take the view that the welfare principle enshrined in Children Act 1989, s 1 overrides professional privilege in relation to family proceedings.[76] A breach of legal professional privilege to avert an act of terrorism may be seen as legitimate and necessary. But no matter how pressing the reason for the abrogation of legal professional privilege, the courts are likely to hold interference with this important legal right a disproportionate interference with Article 8 where there are no safeguards against the abuse of power.[77] In *Foxley* the ECtHR said that steps to intercept letters to a bankrupt:

> must be accompanied by adequate and effective safeguards which ensure minimum impairment of the right to respect for his correspondence. This is particularly so where, as in this case, correspondence with the bankrupt's legal advisers may be intercepted. The Court notes in this connection that the lawyer-client relationship is, in principle, privileged and correspondence in that context, whatever its purpose, concerns matters of a private and confidential nature.[78]

---

[69] ibid, s 38(B)(4).
[70] See para 16.08 below.
[71] [1995] 4 All ER 526, 541.
[72] Application 33274/96 (2000) 8 BHRC 571. For a case comment see (2000) 150 NLJ 1296.
[73] In accordance with that section a court had ordered that for a period of three months all postal packets directed or addressed to the bankrupt be re-directed by the Post Office to the trustee.
[74] See para 3.19 above.
[75] *R v Special Commissioners, ex p Morgan Grenfell & Co Ltd* [2002] UKHL 21; [2002] 2 WLR 1299, para 39. Passing reference had been made to the economic well-being of the country in the Court of Appeal ([2002] 1 All ER 776, para 18).
[76] *Re R* [1993] 4 All ER 702, 705, *Re DH* [1994] 1 FLR 679. See para 20.03 n9 below. cp *Re H* [2000] 1 FLR 766.
[77] cp *Kopps v Switzerland* (1999) 27 EHRR 91; *R v Special Commissioner, ex p Morgan Grenfell & Co Ltd* [2002] UKHL 21; [2002] 2 WLR 1299, para 32.
[78] Application 33274/96 (2000) 8 BHRC 571, para 43.

A. Coercive Statutory Disclosure

In *R v Secretary of State for the Home Department, ex p Daly*[79] Lord Bingham decided that prison rules that interfered with a prisoner's right to respect for his correspondence with a lawyer violated Article 8 because they interfered with legal professional privilege 'to an extent much greater than necessity requires'.[80]

Article 6

The applicant in *Foxley* had alleged that the interception of the applicant's correspondence with his lawyer had violated not only his Article 8 rights but also his Article 6 right to a fair procedure in respect of the receivership proceedings. The court did not decide this point as the applicant had not provided the court with any information on the conduct and outcome of the receivership proceedings. But, the court did vouchsafe to comment that

10.15

> where a lawyer is involved, an encroachment on professional secrecy may have repercussions on the proper administration of justice and hence on the rights guaranteed by Article 6 of the Convention (see the *Niemietz v Germany* judgment . . .).[81]

The argument that Article 6 is infringed might need to be explored further if legally privileged documents extracted by public officials under compulsion are thereafter offered as evidence against the client in civil or criminal proceedings.[82] In *Saunders v UK*[83] the ECtHR held that self-incriminating evidence (other than pre-existing items) obtained from the applicant by DTI inspectors relying on coercive statutory powers could not subsequently be used against the applicant in a criminal prosecution.

Making the Disclosure and Notifying the Client

The disclosure

Personal data may be disclosed under compulsion of law without breaching the provisions of the Data Protection Act 1998 (DPA).[84] The professional should be careful to disclose no more information than is strictly necessary,[85] and to do so only in the manner prescribed by law.[86] If the information disclosed is inaccurate or misleading, the professional could expose himself to an action in negligence by the client, if the client suffered economic loss in consequence. There might also be

10.16

---

[79] [2001] UKHL 26; [2001] 2 AC 532, para 23.
[80] See para 16.14 below. cp *R (on the application of Cannan) v Governor of HMP Full Sutton* [2003] EWHC 97 Admin.
[81] Application 33274/96 (2000) 8 BHRC 571, para 50.
[82] The fair trial concept applies to criminal proceedings and to proceedings in which civil rights and obligations are determined.
[83] (1996) 23 EHRR 313. As regards pre-existing documents, see *Att-Gen's Ref* (No 7 of 2000) [2001] EWCA Crim 888; *R v Allen* [2001] UKHL 45.
[84] See DPA, Sch 2, para 3 and Sch 3, paras 2, 7, 8, 9.
[85] cp *Robertson v Canadian Imperial Bank of Commerce* [1995] 1 All ER 824, 830–831.
[86] cp *Simonsen v Swenson* 177 NW 831, 832 (1920).

an actionable contravention of the DPA entitling the client to compensation without proof of negligence.[87]

Notifying the client of disclosures relating to money laundering

10.17 Under money-laundering legislation tipping off a client, by word or by deed,[88] about a money laundering investigation, if likely to prejudice the investigation, is a criminal offence.[89] Tipping off a client about information that has been revealed in the course of a criminal trial or that is in a file that has long been closed is unlikely to cause prejudice and therefore to be an offence.[90] Under the Terrorism Act 2000 it is a defence to a tipping off charge that the defendant 'had lawful authority or reasonable excuse for the disclosure'.[91] In *R v Central Criminal Court, ex p Francis & Francis*[92] Lord Griffiths agreed with the judge at first instance that the need to take instructions from the client about whether to contest the order provided a reasonable excuse for notifying the client. All current money laundering legislation makes special arrangements for the client to receive legal advice from a lawyer.[93] Feldman doubts that the courts would view as a reasonable excuse a claim by any other category of professional that she needed to take instructions from the client. 'It has been held that bankers have no contractual obligation to inform their customers about production orders . . . *A fortiori* social workers . . . with no contractual obligations to their "clients", would find it hard to base a reasonable excuse or lawful justification on the . . . relationship which links them to the "client".'[94]

10.18 The money laundering tipping-off offences create something of a catch–22 situation for the banks (and indeed some other professionals).[95] If, as part of the investigation, the suspect customer's accounts are frozen, how is the bank to explain to the customer

---

[87] DPA, s 13.
[88] *The Bank v A Ltd* (HC, 23 June 2000, WL 774924).
[89] Criminal Justice Act 1988, s 93D (as to which see *C v S* [1999] 2 All ER 343 and *Governor and Company of the Bank of Scotland v A Ltd* [2001] All ER (D) 81); Drug Trafficking Act 1994, s 53; Terrorism Act 2000, s 39; Proceeds of Crime Act 2002, s 333 (which supersedes s 93D and s 53). It is a defence under the Criminal Justice Act 1988, s 93D(6) and Drug Trafficking Act 1994, s 53(6) that the professional 'did not know or suspect that the disclosure was likely to be prejudicial' and under Terrorism Act 2000, s 39(5), that he 'had no reasonable cause to suspect that the disclosure . . . was likely to affect a terrorist investigation'.
[90] HM Treasury, *The UK's Anti-Money Laundering Legislation and the Data Protection Act 1998: Guidance Notes for the Financial Sector* (April 2002) para 11. Available from http://www.hm-treasury.gov.uk.
[91] Terrorism Act 2000, s 39(5).
[92] [1988] 3 All ER 775, 791–792.
[93] A solicitor who discloses information to a client about a money laundering investigation commits no offence provided the disclosure is in connection with the giving of legal advice or in contemplation of legal proceedings and not in furtherance of a criminal purpose: Criminal Justice Act 1988, s 93D(4), (5); Drug Trafficking Act 1994, s 53(4), (5); Terrorism Act 2000, s 39(6); Proceeds of Crime Act 2002, s 333(2)(c), (3).
[94] D Feldman, *Civil Liberties and Human Rights in England and Wales* (Oxford: 2002) 658.
[95] A solicitor who refused to accept further instructions from the client might alert the client to the fact that she was suspicious.

why he cannot use his funds without making the client suspicious? If the bank ignores the freezing order so as to avoid committing the tipping-off offence, the bank risks being held liable as constructive trustee to third parties for the funds paid out.[96] In *Bank of Scotland v A Ltd*[97] the Court of Appeal recommended that the bank seek an accommodation with the Serious Fraud Office and if that failed, that the bank seek the directions of a court naming the Serious Fraud Office as the defendant. The Proceeds of Crime Act 2002, s 335 allows police to consent to an unlawful transaction.

Notifying the client of disclosures relating to a missing child

10.19 A court that directs a professional to disclose information to enable a missing child who is the subject of court proceedings to be found may, if it is felt necessary, include in the order a direction not to inform the client of the order or that it has been complied with. The order will prevent the professional from feeling a moral duty to alert the client of the efforts being made to trace the child.[98] This does not apply to solicitors because this would disable them from giving clients the advice that they need. At the very most, a solicitor should be barred for a brief period from disclosing the fact of the order to the client to enable the information to be followed up.[99]

Notifying the client of other disclosures

10.20 In cases not involving child abduction or money laundering, should a professional tell the client that he is about to disclose, or has disclosed, confidential personal information that she holds about the client for a purpose that the client has not authorized?[100] This is not a requirement of human rights law if the client has no right to prevent the communication from taking place[101] and statutes that compel disclosure of confidential personal information do not usually[102] require that the client be notified. Nevertheless, if not prevented by law from notifying the client then, normally,[103] the client should be told of the disclosure. The DPA requires personal data to be processed fairly[104] and it is a condition of the fair processing of data obtained from the data subject[105] that, so far as practicable, the data subject is

---

[96] The bank also risks committing an offence under s 93A (assisting another to retain the benefits of criminal conduct).
[97] [2001] 3 All ER 58, noted (2001) 151 NLJ 634. It is unlikely that a freezing order will be given in such circumstances in future.
[98] *Re H* [2000] 1 FLR 766.
[99] ibid.
[100] Under Taxes Management Act 1970, ss 20(8), (8A) the Inland Revenue can require a third party to hand over documents relevant to a tax inquiry without naming the taxpayer. It is obviously not possible to warn the client of the demand for information if it is not possible to identify the taxpayer from what is demanded: see eg *R v Inland Revenue Commissioners, ex p Ulster Bank Ltd* [2000] STC 537.
[101] *MS v Sweden* (1997) 45 BMLR 133, paras 49–50.
[102] But see Health Service Commissioner Act 1993, s 15(e)(1C).
[103] But see para 12.40 below.
[104] DPA, Sch 1, Pt I, first principle. See para 18.10 below.
[105] If the data to be disclosed was obtained from a third party, notification of the data subject is not necessary: DPA, Sch 1, Pt II, para 3 (2)(b).

informed of an intended disclosure,[106] except where an exemption applies, for example, where:

- disclosure is for the purpose of national security[107] or
- crime prevention or detection[108] or certain regulatory activity for the protection of the public would be prejudiced.[109]

Subject access rights to personal data can be withheld on the same grounds.[110] The crime exemption allows a professional who suspects and reports money laundering to avoid committing the tipping-off offence without infringing the DPA.[111] It also explains why a bank need not inform its customer of a police application for access to the customer's account. The courts have said that the professional ought not to inform the client if the police request this.[112] This is a moral and not a legal obligation.

10.21 Some professionals warn new clients of the legal limits of confidentiality and caution a client who seems to be about to say something that might have to be disclosed. There is nothing in existing case law that this is a legal requirement except in family proceedings involving a child. In *Re DH* Wall J said that 'the client needs to be told authoritatively at an early stage in the relationship that whilst the advocate has a duty to represent the client's case to the best of his or her ability, the advocate has a higher duty to the court and to the child whose interests are paramount to disclose relevant material to the court even if that disclosure is not in the interests of the client'.[113]

Consequences of Non-Disclosure

10.22 The methods used to enforce disclosure vary. Failure to disclose information that a court has ordered to be disclosed is a contempt of court. Non-observance by a lawyer of a duty to disclose information to a court could attract disciplinary

---

[106] DPA, Sch 1, Pt II, para 2(1)(a) to which para 1(2) is subject (disclosure 'authorized by or under an enactment to supply it' or 'required to supply it by or under an enactment' is 'to be treated as obtained fairly'), See also paras 18.11, 18.13 below. cp Information Commissioner, Draft Code of Practice on the use of personal data in employer/employee relationships, para 3.8: '[a]lways inform the employee at the time a non-routine disclosure is to be made unless prevented by law from doing so or the information would be a "tip off" prejudicing the crime or taxation purposes.'
[107] DPA, s 28. See para 18.44 below.
[108] DPA, s 29. See paras 14.44 and 18.44 below.
[109] DPA, s 31. But see *Woolgar v Chief Constable of Sussex Police* [2000] 1 WLR 25, 26.
[110] See para 19.30 below. The Law Gazette in 'Act may hand clients money laundering reports', 26 January 2002, reports the view of the Information Commissioner that while reports to the police would be exempt from subject access rights, reports of money laundering suspicions raised within an organization might have to be disclosed.
[111] HM Treasury, *The UK's Anti-Money Laundering Legislation and the Data Protection Act 1998: Guidance Notes for the Financial Sector* (April 2002).
[112] *Barclays Bank plc v Taylor* [1989] 3 All ER 563, 569. See also para 14.43 below.
[113] [1994] 2 FCR 2, 43.

B. Money Laundering

measures. Under some statutes non-compliance may be reported to the High Court where the defaulter can be punished as if in contempt of court.[114] Failure to comply with a notice from the Race Relations, Sex Discrimination or Disability Commissions may be followed up by an application for an order from the county court.[115] The most common sanction for non-compliance, destruction of documents or provision of false and misleading information, is the commission of a summary offence punishable on conviction by a fine.[116] The power to demand documents may be backed up by the power to obtain a warrant to enter premises and seize documents that should have been, but have not been, produced.[117]

Compulsory Disclosure under Foreign Law

Situations arise in which a professional whose relationship with a client is governed by English law faces compulsion to disclose confidential information about the client in a foreign jurisdiction. This danger is greatest in professions that have multi-national firms: banks, solicitors, accountants. US regulatory authorities and courts feel no compunction about ordering overseas branches of banks incorporated in the United States to disclose confidential information in the possession of their English branches even though, as far as the English courts are concerned, the client–bank relationship is governed by English law.[118] Whether a professional who complied with a coercive foreign disclosure order would have a defence against an action for breach of contract or breach of confidence in the English courts is not the subject of binding authority.[119]

10.23

B. Money Laundering[120]

In England and Wales there are at the time of writing three major statutory regimes the object of which is to counter money laundering (ie schemes designed

10.24

---

[114] Companies Act 1985, ss 436, 451; Financial Services and Markets Act 2000, s 177.
[115] Race Relations Act 1976, s 50 (4); Sex Discrimination Act 1975, s 58(4); Disability Rights Commission Act 1999, s 4(5).
[116] eg Companies Act 1985, s 447(6); Child Support Act 1991, s 15(9)(b); Competition Act 1998, s 42(1). Contrast Children Act 1989, s 47.
[117] eg Consumer Credit Act 1974, s 162(3); Companies Act 1985, s 448; Banking Act 1987, s 43; Pensions Act 1995, s 100; Financial Services and Markets Act 2000, s 176(1).
[118] F Neate, *Banking Secrecy: Financial Privacy and Related Restrictions* (London: 1980) 35; *X AG v A Bank* [1983] 2 All ER 464. The Canadian courts are not averse to ordering disclosure of confidential banking information held by branches outside Canada: *Spencer v R* (1985) 21 DLR (4th) 756.
[119] In *X AG v A Bank* [1983] 2 All ER 464, 479, an application by the customer for an interlocutory injunction to prevent disclosure abroad, Leggatt J was not convinced that the American bank would suffer detriment if it obeyed an English injunction not to disclose the confidential information (ibid at 480).
[120] See R Bosworth-Davies and G Saltmarsh, *Money Laundering* (London: 1994); R Fortson, *Misuse of Drugs and Drug Trafficking Offences* (4th edn, London: 2002); D McLean, *International Co-operation in Civil and Criminal Matters* (Oxford: 2002) 279 et seq; P Alldridge, *Money Laundering Law* (Oxford: 2003).

to disguise the criminal origins of money).[121] They are to be found in the Drug Trafficking Act 1994, the Criminal Justice Act 1988 and the Terrorism Act 2000 as amended by the Anti-Terrorism, Crime and Security Act 2001. The first two Acts concern themselves with money laundering associated with drug-dealing and the proceeds of other non-terrorist crimes,[122] the Terrorism Act criminalizes involvement in money laundering of terrorist funds.[123] The Criminal Justice Act 1988 is supplemented by the Financial Services Authority rules on money laundering,[124] and the Money Laundering Regulations 1993.[125] The latter requires those who conduct 'relevant financial business'[126] to set up identification, record-keeping, and internal reporting procedures. Parliament has passed the Proceeds of Crime Act 2002. From 24 February 2003 the provisions in this Act replace the money laundering provisions of the 1994 and 1998 Acts. The Terrorism Act will remain in force.

Reporting Obligation

The obligation

10.25 By Drug Trafficking Act 1994, s 52[127] 'a person' must report to a constable (in practice the National Criminal Intelligence Service (NCIS)) as soon as is reasonably practicable knowledge or suspicion of 'drug money laundering'[128] acquired 'in the course of [a] trade, profession, business or employment'. The suspicion may be of on-going or past money laundering.[129] Failure to do so is a criminal offence.[130] By the Terrorism Act 2000 a crime is committed by a professional who believes or suspects (or has reasonable grounds for believing or suspecting) that another person is laundering terrorist funds and who does not disclose 'to a con-

---

[121] For background information see M Levi, 'Taking financial sources to the cleaners' (1995) 145 NLJ 26.
[122] s 93A(1).
[123] Terrorism is widely defined in Terrorism Act 2000, s 1 as the use or threat, for the purpose of advancing a political, religious or ideological cause, of action which involves serious violence against any person or property, endangers the life of any person, or creates a serious risk to the health or safety of the public or a section of the public. Action includes action outside the UK.
[124] Draft Money-Laundering Sourcebook (2000), available at http://www.fsa.gov.uk.
[125] Implementing EU Council Directive (EEC) 91/308 of 10 June 1991.
[126] Solicitors and accountants are currently affected when conducting investment business. As regards solicitors see D Corker, [1999] LS Gaz 28.
[127] Implementing EU Council Directive (EEC) 91/308 of 10 June 1991.
[128] This means doing any act which constitutes an offence under the Drug Trafficking Act 1994, ss 49, 50 or 51.
[129] D Corker 'Money-laundering: a cautionary tale' about *R v Duff* [2002] EWCA Crim 2117 warns that any past transaction which becomes suspicious in the light of later developments such as the prosecution of the client for drug trafficking has to be reported. See also, D Barton, 'Washing your hands of dirty money', The Times, 10 September 2002, 8.
[130] The solicitor convicted in *R v Duff* was given a prison sentence even though the trial judge accepted that he had made a genuine mistake of law in failing to report his client, namely that the statute only required him to report money laundering that was on-going.

B. Money Laundering

stable' the information upon which the belief or suspicion is based 'as soon as is reasonably practicable'.[131] The Proceeds of Crime Act 2002 simultaneously extends and restricts the obligation to report suspicions of money laundering that were imposed in the Acts it supersedes. Under the 2002 Act[132] professionals conducting business in the 'regulated sector'[133] have to report knowledge or suspicion (objectively determined)[134] which they acquire in the course of exercising their profession that another person is engaged in laundering the proceeds of *any* criminal conduct to the NCIS or a nominated money laundering reporting officer. Failure to do so is punishable on conviction by a maximum of five years' imprisonment, a fine or both.[135] 'Criminal conduct' includes any conduct (serious or not) wherever it takes place that would constitute a criminal offence if committed in the United Kingdom.[136] There is no need to know the exact nature of the criminal offence. Included in the reporting obligation are suspicions arising from business that was turned away. The professions most likely to be affected by the 2002 Act, once the Second EU Directive on Money Laundering[137] is implemented, will be accountants, bankers, auditors, tax advisers, art dealers, real estate agents, and solicitors, all of whom will be part of the regulated sector for all, or almost all, of their activities. The Proceeds of Crime Act 2002 makes arrangements so that those outside the regulated sector may report suspicions of the laundering of the proceeds of any crime[138] but failure to do so is not a criminal offence.

Immunity from being sued

All the money laundering Acts state that reporting suspicions of money laundering (whether voluntarily or under legal compulsion) does not offend against any statutory or other restriction on the disclosure of information.[139] This immunizes the professional against an action for breach of contract, confidence or fiduciary duty for reporting her suspicions, but possibly not against an action for defamation if information is misreported.[140]

10.26

---

[131] s 19(2).
[132] s 330.
[133] See Proceeds of Crime Act 2002, Sch 9 and Money Laundering Regulations 1993 SI 1993/1933 which will be amended to take account of the Second EU Money-Laundering Directive (EC/2001/97) no later than 15 June 2003.
[134] See para 10.28 below.
[135] By failing to make the report the professional may also commit a money laundering offence.
[136] Proceeds of Crime Act 2002, s 340(2). It need not have been a criminal offence where it took place, if that place was outside the UK
[137] EC/2001/97.
[138] Proceeds of Crime Act 2002, s 337.
[139] Drug Trafficking Act 1994, s 52(4), (6); Criminal Justice Act 1988, s 93B(5)(a); Terrorism Act 2000, ss 20(3), 21B; Proceeds of Crime Act 2002, ss 337(1), 338(4). Disclosure of a mere suspicion might not fall within the common law public interest defence, as to which see ch 11.
[140] C Williams, 'The Effect of Domestic Money-Laundering Countermeasures on the Banker's Duty of Confidentiality' (1998) 13 Banking & Finance L Rev 25, 57.

Employees

10.27 The non-disclosure offence may be committed by an employee. In organizations that have an internal regime for reporting suspicions of money laundering,[141] the employee has a defence if she has reported her suspicions to the internal person with responsibility for making a disclosure to the authorities.[142] The Financial Services Authority's rules[143] require firms over which it has oversight to have a money laundering reporting officer (MLRO) to whom employees must report suspicion of money laundering. If, having considered the report, the MLRO suspects that a person has engaged in money laundering he must report this promptly to the NCIS.[144] Under the Criminal Proceeds Act 2002 it is a defence for someone employed within the regulated financial sector who is charged with failing to report suspicions of money laundering that the training required by regulations about the detection of money laundering has not been given.[145]

Reasonable suspicion

10.28 'Suspicion' rather than 'belief' is the reporting criterion in the more recent money laundering legislation. The intention is to maximize the flow of intelligence information to the authorities[146] and to facilitate convictions. In other contexts 'belief' has been held to mean a state of mind inclining a person to assent to a proposition but leaving something to surmise or conjecture.[147] 'Suspicion' is a mental state falling short of belief but with some factual foundation.[148] In *Commissioner for Corporate Affairs v Guardian Investments* it was treated as 'a degree of satisfaction and not necessarily amounting to belief but at least extending beyond speculation as to whether an event has occurred or not'.[149] Doubt as to whether suspicion is to be assessed subjectively (actual suspicion) or objectively (reasonable grounds for suspicion) is laid to rest in the Proceedings of Crime Act 2002[150] by requiring a transaction to be reported if the professional knows, suspects or has reasonable grounds for knowing or suspecting that another person is

---

[141] The setting up of an internal reporting regime is governed by the Money Laundering Regulations 1993 SI 1993/1933. See J Wadsley, 'Money Laundering: Professionals as Policemen' [1994] *Conveyancer and Property Lawyer* 275, 285.

[142] Drug Trafficking Act 1994, s 52(5), Terrorism Act 2000, s 19(4).

[143] Money Laundering Sourcebook, r 5.

[144] Proceeds of Crime Act 2002, s 331.

[145] s 330(7).

[146] R Fortson, *Misuse of Drugs and Drug Trafficking Offences* (4th edn, London: 2002) 648.

[147] *George v Rockett* (1990) 179 CLR 104, 116.

[148] *Hussein v Chong Fook Kam* [1969] 3 All ER 1626, 1630–1631. cp *Robert v Commissioner of Police* [2002] 1412 HKCU 1, para 131: 'to "suspect" ... does not carry with it a connotation of mere surmise.'

[149] [1984] VR 1019, 1023–1025. On the subject of what constitutes 'suspicion' see A Brown, 'Money Laundering: A European and U.K. Perspective' [1997] 8 *J of Intl Banking L* 307, 309.

[150] s 330(2).

B. Money Laundering

laundering the proceeds of any criminal activity.[151] It includes wilful blindness and situations where the defendant did not have suspicions but a reasonable and honest person would have had on the information known to the defendant.[152]

In determining whether failing to report a particular transaction is an offence, the court is to have regard to guidance notes issued by a supervising authority or other appropriate body approved by the Treasury.[153] The guidance notes are expected to include a definition of 'reasonable grounds for suspicion' and examples of situations in which it would be appropriate to report. The Minister said in Committee that if employees have followed the guidance, and did not know or suspect that money laundering was taking place, they would not be convicted of a failure to report such an offence.[154] A professional facing a non-reporting charge will avoid conviction if able to make out a 'reasonable excuse' for the omission.[155] Whether this defence is open to someone who was coerced into silence or remained silent out of fear of reprisals has not been judicially determined. An obligation of professional confidentiality is most certainly not an acceptable excuse.[156]

10.29

Legal professional privilege

No offence is committed by a lawyer who fails to disclose information 'which has come to him in privileged circumstances'.[157] Information comes to a lawyer in privileged circumstances if it is communicated by a client, or a representative of the client, in connection with the provision of legal advice to the client or it is given to the lawyer by a person (who need not be an existing client) seeking legal advice or in connection with legal proceedings or contemplated legal proceedings.[158] The saving does not include acts by the client observed by the professional[159] or instructions given by the client for a criminal purpose such as money laundering.[159a] If the construction of Police and Criminal Evidence Act 1984, s 10[160] that was adopted

10.30

---

[151] See also Terrorism Act 2000, s 21A.
[152] cp *Seng Yuet-fong v HKSAR* [1999] 2 HKC 833, 836. cp PIU, 'Recovering the Proceeds of Crime' (June 2000) paras 9.59–9.60, available at http://www.cabinet-office.gov.uk/innovation/2000/crime/recovering/contents.htm.
[153] s 330(8).
[154] House of Commons Standing Committee B, 29 January 2002, col 1169 (Mr Ainsworth).
[155] Drug Trafficking Act 1994, s 52(3); Terrorism Act 2000, s 19(3); Proceeds of Crime Act 2002, s 330(6)(a).
[156] See para 10.26 above.
[157] Drug Trafficking Act 1994, s 52(2), (8); Terrorism Act 2000, s 19(5); Proceeds of Crime Act 2002, s 330(6)(b).
[158] Proceeds of Crime Act 2002, s 330(10). This derives from s 52 of the Drug Trafficking Act 1994 almost without alteration.
[159] *Robert v Commissioner of Police* [2002] 1412 HKCU 1, para 34.
[159a] Drug Trafficking Act 1994, s 52(9); Terrorism Act 2000, s 19(6); Proceeds of Crime Act 2002, s 330(11).
[160] s 10(2): '[i]tems held with the intention of furthering a criminal purpose are not items subject to legal privilege.'

in *Francis & Francis (A Firm) v Central Criminal Court*[161] is applied to the money laundering legislation, the criminal purpose need not be that of the client but may be that of an unknown third party with the client an innocent facilitator. The adoption of a negligence standard for reporting suspicions of money laundering in the Proceeds of Crime Act 2002 means that if a court were to conclude that information of money laundering was not obtained in privileged circumstances, the solicitor could potentially be prosecuted for failing to report the information despite having genuinely believed that she had received the information in privileged circumstances.[162] This creates a dilemma for solicitors because their professional ethics do not allow a policy of defensive reporting. Consultation with the Law Society before making disclosure is recommended in a Hong Kong case.[162a]

10.31 The Second EU Money Laundering Directive contains a discretionary provision that allows Member States to extend legal privilege to accountants and tax advisers giving advice to clients about their legal position under tax law. The Government has said that it will not extend legal privilege beyond the members of the legal profession.[162b] This restriction may contravene EU law.

Related Offences

Assisting the money laundering of the proceeds of crime

10.32 The Criminal Justice Act 1988 makes it an offence to:

(1) assist another to retain the benefit or proceeds of criminal conduct and acquisition,[163] or
(2) possess or use proceeds of criminal conduct.[164]

Theoretically, a solicitor who notifies suspicions of money laundering to the NCIS and goes on acting for the client (as she may have to avoid tipping off the client)[165] could commit the assisting or possessing offence. Prosecution is improbable and might be held to be an abuse of process. The 'proceeds of criminal conduct' are defined to exclude terrorist funds and drug money,[166] but otherwise include money obtained from any crime wherever committed which would constitute an indictable offence in the Crown Court or a Schedule 4 offence in a

---

[161] [1988] 3 All ER 775.
[162] But see Lord Rooker, *Hansard*, HL, vol 635 col 1078, 27 May 2002: 'the courts would read in a requirement that he could not be convicted if he did not know.'
[162a] *Robert v Commissioner of Police* [2002] 1412 HKSU 1. Is this consistent with Proceeds of Crime Act 2002, s 330(4)?
[162b] House of Commons Standing Committee B, 29 January 2002, col 1166 (Mr Ainsworth).
[163] Criminal Justice Act 1988, s 93A. The maximum sentence is 14 years' imprisonment.
[164] ibid s 93B.
[165] ibid s 93D.
[166] ibid s 71(9)(c).

magistrates' court if the crime had taken place in the United Kingdom.[167] Lawyers and accountants need to be on the lookout for the proceeds of financial crimes. The Drug Trafficking Act 1994[168] and the Terrorism Act 2000[169] contain similar offences. The Proceeds of Crime Act 2002[170] makes it an offence to acquire, possess, conceal, disguise, transfer, convert, use or remove from the UK criminal property[171] and anyone who enters into or becomes concerned in an arrangement which he knows or suspects facilitates acquisition, retention, use or control of criminal property also commits an offence.[172]

Defences

It is a defence under all the legislation that the accused: 10.33

(1) disclosed to a constable the money laundering *before* committing the act *and* continued with the consent of the constable,[173] or
(2) disclosed the money laundering *after* committing the act on his own initiative and as soon as it was reasonable for him to do so.[174]

The second defence protects the innocent professional who inadvertently undertook a laundering transaction and subsequently became aware before being confronted by investigators of the true nature of her actions. It is a defence that the accused intended to report her suspicions and has a reasonable excuse for failing to do so.[175] There is no defence of legal professional privilege.

---

[167] ibid s 93A(7). Examples include theft, fraud, robbery, forgery, counterfeiting, illegal deposit taking, blackmail and extortion.

[168] s 50 (assisting another person to retain the benefit of drug trafficking), s 51 (acquisition, possession or use of proceeds of drug trafficking).

[169] s 16 (use and possession of money or other property for terrorism), s 17 (involvement in funding arrangements).

[170] ss 327–329.

[171] 'Criminal property' is defined in s 340(3) as 'a person's benefit from criminal conduct'. The accused need not receive any benefit from the criminal conduct and that conduct can have occurred at any time and, provoded it would be an offence in the UK, anywhere.

[172] s 328(1).

[173] Criminal Justice Act 1988, s 93B(5)(b)(i); Drug Trafficking Act 1994, ss 50(3)(b)(i), 51(5)(b)(1); Terrorism Act 2000, s 21(1) (which omits the requirement that there must be disclosure before any offence is committed); Proceeds of Crime Act 2002, s 329(2)(a). Under the 2002 Act the NCIS is allowed seven working days to decide whether to consent. If the NCIS fails to respond within this period or refuses consent but a further 31 days passes before the NCIS is treated as having consented.

[174] Criminal Justice Act 1988, s 93B(5)(b)(ii); Drug Trafficking Act 1994, ss 50(3)(b)(ii), 51(5)(b)(ii); Terrorism Act 2000, s 21(2)–(3). cp Proceeds of Crime Act 2002, s 329(2)(b).

[175] Criminal Justice Act 1988, s 93B(7); Drug Trafficking Act 1994, ss 50(4), 51(7); Terrorism Act 2000, s 21(5). See also Proceeds of Crime Act 2002, s 329(2)(b).

C. Use of Information Disclosed under Compulsion

In a Criminal Prosecution

10.34 Many regulatory bodies have the power to compel the disclosure of confidential information as part of an investigation to discover whether a criminal offence has been, or is being, committed with a view to bringing a prosecution if the outcome is positive. As a result of the judgment of the ECtHR in *Saunders v UK*,[176] information obtained under compulsion cannot generally be adduced as evidence in subsequent criminal proceedings against the person from whom it was obtained.[177] The judgment does not restrict use of information compulsorily acquired from A about B against B—for example, information secured from a professional about a client, if in making disclosure the professional did not act as the client's agent. If the statute under which the professional was compelled to provide the information says nothing about its use as evidence in a prosecution of the client of the kind envisaged by the legislation, the expectation must be that the information can be used for this purpose, if relevant. This is particularly so if the statute expressly forbids use of compelled information against the person who supplied the information.[178]

For a Collateral Purpose

Express and implied statutory restrictions

10.35 Statutes that enable confidential information to be collected under compulsion by public authorities from professionals usually forbid, on pain of criminal sanction, onward disclosure of the information for a purpose not authorized by legislation without the consent of the provider.[179] The absence of such a provision is not, however, a green light to disclose information obtained under compulsion (or threat of compulsion)[180] for a purpose collateral to the purpose for which it was obtained.

---

[176] (1997) 23 EHRR 313.

[177] The general rule does not apply where the person who provided the information introduces compelled statements as evidence or where he is prosecuted for lying to investigators. The *Saunders* judgment does not prevent use of the information by a public authority in civil proceedings or by the police for the purpose of investigating any crime and it does not prohibit use of pre-existing documents disclosed under compulsion.

[178] eg Financial Services and Markets Act 2000, s 174.

[179] There are many statutory provisions restricting use of information collected by public authorities but the majority have no relevance to personal information. For a selection that do, see Banking Act 1987, s 82; Finance Act 1989, s 182; Courts and Legal Services Act 1990, s 49(4); Child Support Act 1991, s 50 (as to which see *Re C* [1995] 1 FLR 201); Social Security Administration Act 1992, s 123; Health Commissioner Act 1993, s 15. cp Local Government Act 1974, s 32; Security Service Act 1989, s 2(a); Criminal Appeal Act 1995, s 25. See also Y Cripps, 'Disclosure in the Public Interest: The Predicament of the Public Sector Employee' [1983] PL 600, 628; P Birkinshaw, 'Freedom of Information' (1990) 140 NLJ 1637.

[180] 'In my judgment, it makes no difference that the information is obtained informally, not by the use of the court's compulsory powers but under the threat of them' per Millett J, *Re Barlow Clowes Gilt Managers Ltd* [1991] 4 All ER 385, 392.

C. Use of Information Disclosed under Compulsion

Action for breach of confidence

In *Marcel v Commissioner of Police of the Metropolis*[181] the police seized documents from the claimants under the powers of search and seizure conferred by the Police and Criminal Evidence Act 1984. The Court of Appeal agreed[182] with the judge at first instance that the police were entitled to seize, retain and use the documents for purposes related to the investigation and prosecution of crime and the return of stolen property to the true owners but for no other purpose.[183] Voluntary communication of the contents of the documents or their transfer to third parties was authorized to the extent that this was reasonably incidental to the performance of the approved purposes,[184] but not otherwise.[185] Unauthorized disclosure to a third party, the court held, gives rise to a cause of action for breach of confidence against a public agency that obtains documents or information under compulsion.[186]

10.36

> [W]here the police or any other public authority use compulsory powers to obtain information or documents from the citizen, the relationship between them is such that the information or documents are received solely for those purposes for which the power was conferred and equity imposes on the public authority a [private law] duty [of confidentiality] not to disclose them to third parties . . .[187]

Volunteered information

It is not necessary for information to be compelled for an obligation of confidentiality to arise.

10.37

> Relationships with employees, with trade secrets, with doctor and patient, with banker and customer may in law restrict the use that may be made of information, or its disclosure. There are we consider undoubtedly similar restrictions on confidential information that is in the possession of public bodies, including that received from others, held for the purpose of exercising public powers and duties. Examples include information relating to crime, tax, benefits, health and welfare.[188]

This passage is taken from a judgment of the Data Protection Tribunal (now the Information Tribunal) but the courts have expressed support for imposing on public agencies both a public[189] and a private law duty to use information only for the purposes for which it was collected.

---

[181] [1991] 1 All ER 845.
[182] *Marcel v Commissioner of Police of the Metropolis* [1992] 1 All ER 72, 81, 85.
[183] [1991] 1 All ER 845, 852.
[184] Once the information is in the hands of a third party, the information may be used in any proper way: *BOC Ltd v Instrument Technology Ltd* [2001] EWCA Civ 854, [2002] QB 537, CA.
[185] [1992] 1 All ER 72, 87.
[186] ibid, 89.
[187] per Browne-Wilkinson VC, *Marcel v Commissioner of Police of the Metropolis* [1991] 1 All ER 845, 854 (italics added). See also [1992] 1 All ER 72, 86.
[188] *British Gas Trading Ltd v Data Protection Registrar* [1997–98] Info TLR 393. Passages are cited from *Att-Gen v Guardian Newspapers Ltd (No 2)* [1988] 3 All ER 545 which make it clear that the tribunal means to include information that was volunteered.
[189] See para 10.39 below.

In *Hellewell v Chief Constable of Derbyshire*[190] the claimant applied to the High Court for a declaration that the police had acted unlawfully in showing shopkeepers a photograph taken of him when he was in police custody for the purpose of warning them about his criminal propensities. Lord Woolf said in *R v Chief Constable of the North Wales Police, ex p AB*[191] that 'the plaintiff may have had an action in private law for breach of confidence in relation to the disclosure of [the] photograph' though he agreed with the judge who had tried the case that on the facts the police had a public interest defence. The police's private law duty was unaffected by the absence of a statutory regime regulating the use to which the photograph could be put or by the fact that the claimant had no proprietary interest in the photograph and had not been photographed under compulsion.[192]

Information lawfully obtained by covert means

10.38 It is argued in another chapter, that covert state interception of information is a form of compulsory disclosure.[193] Shah contends that no action for breach of confidence for the improper disclosure of covertly acquired information is possible against the government.[194] He must be right if no action for breach of confidence lies against a private individual who obtains confidential personal information by illicit means. But the courts now accept that an action may lie in equity against the individual who steals information.[195] It is not a big step to say that, as a rule, the government (or police) may be sued for the unauthorized disclosure of intercepted information,[196] always assuming that the government (or police) can be held responsible for the leak according to principles of vicarious responsibility.[197] Overriding public policy considerations probably rule out a civil action against the government for abuses of power by MI5 or MI6.[198] However, disclosure of covertly acquired 'intelligence' by any civil servant is a criminal offence.[199] It also contravenes the Civil Service Code.[200]

Public law duty

10.39 In addition to the private law obligation of confidentiality, a public law authority that compels disclosure of confidential personal information has, independently

---

[190] [1995] 4 All ER 473. See also *Bunn v BBC* [1998] 3 All ER 552, 556.
[191] [1998] 3 All ER 310, 321.
[192] *Hellewell v Chief Constable of Derbyshire* [1995] 4 All ER 473, 478.
[193] See para 14.70 below.
[194] R Shah, 'Private lives—the government's ability to make information about individuals the property of the public' (1994) 91 LS Gaz 28.
[195] See para 6.07 above.
[196] This would apply whether interception was lawful or unlawful.
[197] See paras 21.31 et seq.
[198] This does not mean that the government cannot sue the offending civil servant; the Spycatcher saga testifies to that: see *Att-Gen v Guardian Newspapers Ltd (No 2)* [1988] 3 All ER 545.
[199] Official Secrets Act 1989, ss 1, 4; Regulation of Investigatory Powers Act 2000, s 19.
[200] http://www.cabinet-office.gov.uk/central/1999/cscode.htm, paras 8, 10.

C. Use of Information Disclosed under Compulsion

of any statutory provision forbidding onward disclosure, a public law duty not to disclose the information for an unauthorized purpose. In *R v Chief Constable of North Wales Police, ex p AB*,[201] a case in which convicted paedophiles unsuccessfully challenged the right of the police to disclose their identity after their release from prison, Lord Bingham said in the Divisional Court:

> When, in the course of performing its public duties, a public body . . . comes into possession of information relating to a member of the public, being information not generally available and potentially damaging to that member of the public if disclosed, the body ought not to disclose such information save for the purpose of and to the extent necessary for performance of its public duty or enabling some other public body to perform its public duty. . . . The principle does not . . . rest on the existence of a duty of confidence owed by the public body to the member of the public, although it might well be that such a duty of confidence might in certain circumstances arise. The principle . . . rests on a fundamental rule of good public administration which the law must recognise and if necessary enforce.[202]

Unlike the private law obligation of confidentiality, it is not a prerequisite of the public law duty of non-disclosure that the information is confidential.[203] When *ex p AB* reached the Court of Appeal Lord Woolf said:

> The fact that the convictions of the applicants had been in the public domain, did not mean that the police as a public authority were free to publish information about their previous offending.[204]

A public servant who without lawful authority discloses information knowing that the disclosure will probably cause the client harm can be sued for misfeasance in public office by the client if the disclosure causes him loss.[205]

Disclosure in the public interest

Disclosure may be justified in spite of a private law obligation of confidentiality on public interest grounds.[206] Likewise, the public interest may override a public law duty of non-disclosure. The public interest exception to the public law duty, which was held to apply in *ex p AB*, comes into play when there is a pressing public interest in disclosure.[207] It was held in *R v A Local Authority in the Midlands, ex*

10.40

---

[201] [1997] 4 All ER 691.
[202] [1997] 4 All ER 691, 698.
[203] For a private law obligation of confidentiality to arise information must have a quality of confidentiality: see para 5.08 above.
[204] *R v Chief Constable of the North Wales Police, ex p AB* [1998] 3 All ER 310, 320.
[205] *Three Rivers District Council v Bank of England* [2000] 3 All ER 1, 8. Such an allegation was made in *Lord Ashcroft v Att-Gen* [2002] EWHC 1133, though the complaint was not of disclosure but authentication by the third defendant, the Deputy Head of the News Department in the Foreign and Commonwealth Office, of already disclosed information.
[206] *Preston BC v McGrath*, The Times, 19 May 2000. See also Solicitors' J 24 January 2003, 83.
[207] Note the absence of an imminent risk to an identifiable third party. Public interest reasons for disclosure may go beyond those described in ch 11. In *R v Secretary of State for the Home Department, ex p Kingdom of Belgium* (QBD 15 February 2000) in which an issue was whether states requesting

p LM [208] that the decision to disclose allegations of child sex abuse to a third party required the public authority to balance the public interest in the need to protect children against the need to safeguard the right of an individual to a private life. Factors that would usually have to be considered include the strength of the public bodies' belief in the truth of the allegation,[209] the intensity of the interest of the third party in obtaining the information and the degree of risk posed by the subject of the information if disclosure is not made. Dyson J concluded that a decision to disclose to a local authority with whom LM had contracted to provide a bus service that LM had 10 years earlier been accused of sexually abusing his daughter and another child when these allegations had not resulted in proceedings or in a caution would be irrational. The judge was not persuaded that there was real and cogent evidence of a pressing need for the disclosure which would have very damaging social and employment consequences for LM. Where disclosure does meet a pressing public interest it will still need to be for a purpose listed in Article 8(2)[210] and proportionate[211] in order to comply with the requirements of the Human Rights Act 1998.

---

his extradition should be given sight of a confidential medicalreport about General Pinochet's health which was critical to the Home Secretary's provisional decision not to extradite him, the public interest lay in operating a procedure that would be perceived to apply fairly to all concerned.

[208] [2000] 1FCR 736.

[209] 'At one end of the spectrum will be the case . . . where the person about whom the information is held has actually been convicted in a criminal court. At the other end will be the case where the authority has investigated the allegation, and has concluded that there is no substance in it' per Dyson J, [2000] 1 FCR 736, 746–747.

[210] See para 3.19 above. In *R v Secretary of State for the Home Department, ex p Kingdom of Belgium* (QBD 15 February 2000) disclosure of the Pinochet medical report was found to be 'necessary in a democratic society . . . for the prevention of disorder or crime'.

[211] As to what this might involve see para 10.10 above.

11

DISCLOSURE IN THE PUBLIC INTEREST

A. The Public Interest	11.02	H. Interceptors, Strangers and Third Parties	11.72
B. Disclosure of Iniquity	11.09	I. The Public Interest and Privileged Communications	11.77
C. Incriminating Physical Evidence	11.39		
D. Disclosure Without Iniquity	11.41	J. Tort Defences and the Public Interest	11.81
E. Genetic Information	11.53		
F. HIV Infection	11.58	K. Copyright and the Public Interest	11.82
G. Procedural and Miscellaneous Matters	11.60		

In *Tournier v National Provincial and Union Bank of England*, a leading banking case, Bankes LJ listed the qualifications to a bank's contractual duty of confidentiality to a customer: **11.01**

> On principle I think that the qualifications can be classified under four heads:
> (a) where the disclosure is under compulsion by law
> (b) where there is a duty to the public to disclose
> (c) where the interests of the bank require disclosure
> (d) where the disclosure is made by the express or implied consent of the customer.[1]

This chapter is devoted to the second of these exceptions, namely disclosure in the public interest. Unlike 'disclosure under compulsion of law' this is a discretionary disclosure: it is permitted but not mandated.[2] In *Parry-Jones v Law Society*[3] Lord Denning cited *Tournier* as an authority for implying an obligation of confidence into the contract between a solicitor and his clients.[4] It is reasonable to suppose that where an obligation of confidentiality exists between any other kind of professional and the client, the Bankes list of qualifications applies also.

---

[1] [1924] 1 KB 461, 473.
[2] But see para 20.06 below.
[3] [1968] 1 All ER 177, 178.
[4] Both Bankes and Scrutton LJJ make reference ([1924] 1 KB 461, 474, 480–481) to obligations of confidentiality owed by other professionals indicating that general principles are involved, albeit they might apply with particular strictness to bankers.

Chapter 11: Disclosure in the Public Interest

A. The Public Interest[5]

Causes of action to which it applies

11.02 A professional who discloses confidential information about a client without the client's consent but in the public interest cannot be held accountable at law for the disclosure in an action for breach of confidence in equity[6] or in contract.[7] Disclosure in the public interest is a defence to a prosecution under the Data Protection Act 1998 (DPA) for unlawful disclosure[8] but is not an answer to an action for compensation for failing to comply with the requirements of the DPA.[9] Disclosure in the public interest may be a valid reason for infringing copyright[10] and for overriding a public law duty of non-disclosure.[10a] Whether the public interest can justify breach of a fiduciary duty is not something that the courts have yet been asked. The solicitor–client relationship is a fiduciary one and according to the Law Society's guidance disclosure of confidential information by solicitors is permitted on the public interest grounds of preventing serious bodily harm or child abuse.[11]

Nature of the public interest

The public good

11.03 The courts have repeated many times that public interest means for the public's good and not public curiosity.[12] Though Lord Woolf appeared willing to allow the media to ignore this distinction in the *Flitcroft* case,[13] the Court of Appeal has since drawn back from this position,[14] and, importantly for this book, there has never been the slightest hint that anyone apart from the media would be allowed such licence.[15]

11.04 Gurry describes 'the public interest' in these terms:

---

[5] See generally, Y Cripps, *The Legal Implications of Disclosure in the Public Interest* (2nd edn, London: 1994).
[6] Examples are given in the text of this chapter.
[7] *Tournier v National Provincial and Union Bank of England* [1924] 1 KB 461. cp *London Regional Transport v Mayor of London* [2001] EWCA Civ 1491. The public interest defence may be applied more strictly where there is an express contractual promise of confidentiality than where the obligation arises by implication in contract or only in equity because of the substantial public interest in seeing that freely made contractual promises of confidentiality are honoured: *Campbell v Frisby* [2002] EWHC 328, [2002] EMLR 31, para 30. The Court of Appeal [2002] EWCA Civ 1374 did not offer an opion about this.
[8] DPA, s 55(2)(d). It is not a general criminal law defence: para 6.88 above.
[9] DPA, s 13; see para 4.49 above.
[10] See para 11.80 below.
[10a] See para 10.40 above.
[11] See para 11.15 below.
[12] eg *Lion Laboratories Ltd v Evans* [1984] 2 All ER 417, 423; *Francome v MGN Ltd* [1984] 1 WLR 892, 897–898.
[13] *A v B plc & C ('Flitcroft')* [2002] EWCA Civ 337; [2002] 3 WLR 542 and see para 8.18 above.
[14] *Campbell v MGN Ltd* [2002] EWCA Civ 1373, para 40.
[15] cp *W v Egdell* [1990] 1 All ER 835, 848; *R v C* (1991) 7 BMLR 138, 144.

A. The Public Interest

The public interest is a reincarnation of the older common law principle of public policy, which was described by Winfield as 'a principle of judicial legislation or interpretation founded on the current needs of the community'. Its function in the enforcement of confidences is the same as the role played by public policy in the formulation of contract law. It provides a starting point for the courts' intervention and circumscribes the scope of that intervention.[16]

The effect of this rationale is to prevent the validation of any contractual provision prohibiting disclosure absolutely. If the community, or some public authority, ought to be told certain facts, a covenant forbidding disclosure will be against public policy.[17] An absolute contractual ban on disclosure by a public authority will also fall foul of s 6(1) of the Human Rights Act 1998 (HRA) by impinging on Article 10.[18]

> Whether or not undertakings of confidentiality had been signed, both domestic law and art. 10(2) would recognize the propriety of suppressing wanton or self-interested disclosure of confidential information; but both correspondingly recognize the legitimacy of disclosure, undertakings notwithstanding, if the public interest in the free flow of information and ideas will be served by it.[19]

Vagueness

11.05 The fact that the courts have not attempted to define the 'public interest'[20] or to subject the concept to close analysis makes disclosure of confidential personal information by a professional a risky business.[21] In *A v B plc & C ('Flitcroft')* Lord Woolf said that in the majority of situations whether the public interest was involved would be 'obvious'.[22] But is this true?[23] The British Medical Association (BMA) spearheaded a campaign to put disclosure of medical information on a statutory footing because application of the public interest test in the healthcare field was not easily predictable.[24] Legislation would not improve the position of

---

[16] *Breach of Confidence* (Oxford: 1984) 5.
[17] *Weld-Blundell v Stephens* [1919] 1 KB 520, 527; *Initial Services Ltd v Putterill* [1967] 3 All ER 145, 151. cp *Price Waterhouse (A Firm) v BCCI Holdings (Luxembourg) SA* [1992] BCLC 583, 601.
[18] *London Regional Transport v Mayor of London* [2001] EWCA Civ 1491, para 60.
[19] per Sedley LJ, *London Regional Transport v Mayor of London* [2001] EWCA Civ 1491, para 55.
[20] For the varying approaches to the concept of the 'public interest' adopted by the courts, Parliament and regulators of the press and broadcasting see D Parsons, 'The meaning of "public interest" ' (2001) 6 Communications L 191.
[21] For an example where a professional (a lawyer) wrongly predicted that disclosure was in the public interest see *Ott v Fleishman* [1983] WWR 721.
[22] *A v B plc & C ('Flitcroft')* [2002] EWCA Civ 337; [2002] 3 WLR 542, para 11, guideline viii.
[23] Contrast *NZ Post Ltd v Prebble* [2001] NZAR 360, para 30. Even in *A v B plc & C ('Flitcroft')* [2002] EWCA Civ 337; [2002] 3 WLR 542 the trial judge and the Court of Appeal disagreed about whether there was a public interest in disclosing the identity of a well-known footballer who had had extra marital affairs.
[24] Disclosure and Use of Personal Health Information Bill, HL Bill 37 (1996) tabled by Lord Walton. See also J Montgomery, *Health Care Law* (2nd edn, Oxford: 2002) 288. An empirical study by the Institute of Public Policy Research using focus groups concluded that regulators and the media industry lacked an authoritative definition of the public interest: D Morrison and M Sevennevig, *The Public Interest, The Media and Privacy* (March 2002) available from http://www.radioauthority.org.uk/. Ironically, the BBC interviewee said that 'the last person [he]

health professionals, however, unless it is tightly drawn and specific.[25] A solution to the professional's dilemma, albeit one that is only possible in cases that are not urgent and when funds permit, is to seek a declaration of legality from a court before making the disclosure.[26] A firm of accountants was granted a declaration that an obligation of confidentiality owed to BCCI did not prevent it from supplying information and documents to a public inquiry.[27]

11.06 The fact that the nature and extent of the public interest is not spelt out must raise doubts about whether disclosure on common law public interest grounds by or to those working for a public authority is always compatible with the Article 8(1) right to respect for private life.[28] An interference with that right must be 'in accordance with law'.[29] Can the client (even with legal advice) predict with reasonable accuracy when it is in the public interest for a professional to ignore the obligation of confidence owed to the client? For some types of public interest disclosure guidance may be available in non-statutory guidelines. If these are reasonably specific, the Convention requirement of reasonable foreseeability may be satisfied.[30] But there are bound to be countless situations where legal precedent and specific guidance, statutory or otherwise, are entirely lacking.

A defence or a limiting principle?

11.07 In *Gartside v Outram*, an early breach of confidence action in which the claimant's clerk had removed documents allegedly showing fraudulent transactions in the conduct of the claimant's wool broking business, Wood VC said:

> there is no confidence as to the disclosure of iniquity. You cannot make me the confidant of a crime or a fraud and be entitled to close my lips upon any secret which you have the audacity to disclose to me relating to any fraudulent intention on your part; such a confidence cannot exist.[31]

---

would expect to know what was in the public interest was a high court judge' (para 3.2). Some Australian judges have shunned the broad English 'public interest' test precisely because of its fluidity: *Castrol Australia Pty Ltd v Emtech Associates Pty Ltd* (1980) 33 ALR 31; *Corrs Pavey Whiting and Byrne v Collector of Customs* (1987) 74 ALR 428, 445–450.

[25] eg the Public Interest Disclosure Act 1998. To enact something along the lines of Immigration and Asylum Act 1999, s 93(3)(d) would not be an improvement. This section confers legality on a disclosure that would otherwise be unlawful under the confidentiality provisions of the Act if 'having regard to the rights and freedoms or legitimate interest of any person, the disclosure is necessary in the public interest'.

[26] As in *Jones v Smith* [1999] 1 SCR 455. And see *Pharaon v BCCI* [1998] 4 All ER 455.

[27] *Price Waterhouse (A Firm) v BCCI Holdings (Luxembourg) SA* [1992] BCLC 583.

[28] Contrast D Feldman, 'Information and Privacy' in *Freedom of Expression and Freedom of Information: Essays in Honour of Sir David Williams* (Oxford: 2000) 317.

[29] See para 3.19 above.

[30] Even where guidance exists, its application in the many and varied factual circumstances that arise may be uncertain. There will always be borderline public interest cases. cp *A v B plc & C ('Flitcroft')* [2002] EWCA Civ 337; [2002] 3 WLR 542, para 40, guideline viii.

[31] (1856) 26 LJ Ch (NS) 113, 114.

A. The Public Interest

This passage assumes that iniquity prevents an obligation of confidence from arising ab initio just as it prevents material from being privileged in the law of evidence.[32] There are also passages in more recent judgments that treat the public interest as something that determines whether an obligation of confidentiality exists at all.[33] In *R v Harrison*, for example, a remand prisoner facing a murder charge blurted out to a prison chaplain that he had got such a buzz out of killing that he wanted to kill someone else. Delivering the judgment in which his appeal against conviction was dismissed, Rougier LJ said: '[w]e doubt whether there exists any confidentiality or any right to privacy for someone who announces that he intends to continue a career of murder.'[34] In *R v Department of Health, ex p Source Informatics Ltd* the Court of Appeal said that where a duty of confidentiality undeniably arises,[35] the scope of the duty of confidentiality 'is circumscribed to accommodate [the public interest]'.[36]

There are many cases, however, that say that it is unlawful to disclose confidential information unless disclosure can be shown to be in the public interest.[37] On this approach the public interest is a defence that overrides the obligation of confidentiality.   11.08

> No person is permitted to divulge to the world information which he has received in confidence, *unless he has just cause or excuse for doing so.*[38]

Perhaps the divergent approaches arose originally because equitable relief is discretionary and will be refused if the claimant comes with unclean hands. Where the only obligation of confidentiality owed to the client is equitable or the remedy sought is an injunction the court will not enforce the professional's obligation of confidentiality if to do so is against the public interest. If the confidentiality obligation is contractual and the claim is for damages, the way that the public interest excuse is expressed has implications for the burden of proof. If the public interest is relevant to the content or existence of the obligation then the claimant has to negate a public interest in disclosure. This is what happens when the information disclosed is a government secret.[39] In no case involving personal information, however, has it

---

[32] See para 16.36 below.
[33] *Initial Services Ltd v Putterill* [1967] 3 All ER 145, 149, 151; *Malone v Commissioner of Police of the Metropolis (No 2)* [1979] 2 All ER 620, 646; *Re a Company's Application* [1989] 2 All ER 248, 251. cp *Re C* [1991] 2 FLR 478.
[34] (CA, 10 July 2000.) Cp R Toulson and C Phipps, *Confidentiality* (London: 1996) 87.
[35] The court was dealing with a case that did not involve iniquity.
[36] [2000] 1 All ER 786, 800–801. This approach was said to be preferable to a 'public interest defence'. See also *Tournier v National Provincial and Union Bank of England* [1924] 1 KB 461, 473.
[37] eg *Hubbard v Vosper* [1972] 1 All ER 1023, 1030; *Lion Laboratories Ltd v Evans* [1984] 2 All ER 417, 432; *Re Barlow Clowes Gilt Managers Ltd* [1991] 4 All ER 385, 392; *Hellewell v Chief Constable of Derbyshire* [1995] 4 All ER 473, 479. cp *London Regional Transport Ltd v Mayor of London* [2001] EWCA Civ 1491, para 36.
[38] per Lord Denning, *Fraser v Evans* [1969] 1 QB 349, 361, italics added.
[39] *Att-Gen v Guardian Newspapers (No 2)* [1998] 3 All ER 545, 660. The law may be moving in this direction too where the defendant is a media organization because of the importance attached to freedom of the press. On this point see *Jockey Club v BBC* [2002] EWHC 1866, QB.

been suggested that the claimant must demonstrate that disclosure was *not* in the public interest. It seems inherently unlikely that the client would have to do so in an action against a professional for breach of a contractual obligation of confidentiality and in *W v Egdell*[40] the Court of Appeal's judgment proceeded on the basis that it was for the doctor to prove that he had acted in the public interest.[41]

B. Disclosure of Iniquity

The meaning of 'iniquity'

11.09 Iniquity was at first understood to mean crime[42] and fraud,[43] then certain civil wrongs[44] and finally anything anti-social. In *Initial Services Ltd v Putterill*[45] Lord Denning refused to strike out the public interest defence to a contract action against an ex-employee who had revealed that his former employers had falsely attributed a price increase to the imposition of a selective employment tax and had, in breach of statutory duty, failed to register a restrictive trade agreement.

Correcting a false image

11.10 More controversially, in *Woodward v Hutchins*[46] Lord Denning condoned disclosure of confidential information about the lives of pop-stars by their ex-press agent and public relations manager on the grounds that '[t]he public should not be misled'[47] by the false picture of themselves that the claimants had put about. 'Outing' hypocrisy has achieved legal respectability with the passage of the HRA. In litigation raising an issue of freedom of expression and the media, s 12(4) requires the court to have regard to the relevant media privacy code.[48] The print media's privacy code endorses publication to prevent 'the public being misled by

---

[40] [1990] 1 All ER 835, 845. See also *Price Waterhouse (A Firm) v BCCI Holdings (Luxembourg) SA* [1992] BCLC 583, 597.

[41] The defendant must do so on information known to the defendant when the information was disclosed: *Campbell v MGN Ltd* (QB, 21 December 2001) transcript p 14. But the court will take into account the information disclosed: *Nationwide Building Society v Various Solicitors (No 2)* [1998] All ER (D) 119.

[42] *Malone v Commissioner of Police of the Metropolis (No 2)* [1979] 2 All ER 620, 646; *Tournier v National Provincial and Union Bank of England* [1924] 1 KB 461, 473, 481, 486.

[43] *Gartside v Outram* (1857) 16 LJ Ch (NS) 113.

[44] *Weld-Blundell v Stephens* [1919] 1 KB 520. The view expressed in that case that the public interest exception is limited to *proposed* civil wrongs has been widely rejected: see *Initial Services Ltd v Putterill* [1967] 3 All ER 145, 148 and F Gurry, *Breach of Confidence* (Oxford: 1984) 332–334. It has been suggested that negligence does not justify a breach of confidence: *Distillers Co v Times Newspapers* [1975] 1 All ER 41, 50.

[45] [1967] 3 All ER 145.

[46] [1977] 1 WLR 760. This approach was said not to be relevant when the claimant sued on an express contractual promise of confidentiality in *Adams v Attridge* (QB, 8 October 1998).

[47] [1977] 1 WLR 760, 764.

[48] See para 8.13 above.

B. Disclosure of Iniquity

some statement or action of an individual . . .'.[49] In *A v B plc & C ('Flitcroft')*[50] Lord Woolf took the matter one step further saying that there is a legitimate public interest in exposing the fact that a role model who has not courted publicity has behaved badly.[51] In *Campbell v MGN Ltd*,[52] however, reservations were expressed by the Court of Appeal about this:

> We do not see why it should necessarily be in the public interest that an individual who has been adopted as a role model, without seeking this distinction, should be demonstrated to have feet of clay.[53]

Disclosures of iniquity by professionals

Balancing interests

Dicta abound that professionals may disclose iniquity,[54] and the courts have approved public interest disclosures by doctors.[55] The iniquity need not be that of the client,[56] but may be that of a spouse or an associate of the client.[57] But disclosure of iniquity by a professional is not permissible in all circumstances.[58] In *Bunn v BBC* Lightman J said:

11.11

---

[49] See para 9.10 above. cp ITC Programme Code, para 2.1(i). See also *Theakston v MGN Ltd* [2002] EWHC 137; [2002] EMLR 22, para 69. Exposure of false publicity is not a qualifying disclosure for the purposes of the Public Interest Disclosure Act 1998; see para 21.25, below.

[50] [2002] EWCA Civ 337; [2002] 3 WLR 542, para 11, guideline xii.

[51] See also *Campbell v MGN Ltd* [2002] EWHC 499; [2002] EMLR 30 where Morland J said that the press was entitled to expose the fact that Campbell had lied when she had denied taking drugs.

[52] [2002] EWCA Civ 1373.

[53] ibid, para 41. Reservations about *Woodward v Hutchins* were also expressed by the Court of Appeal in *Campbell v Frisbee* [2002] EWCA Civ 1374. D Howarth, 'Privacy, Confidentiality and the Cult of Celebrity' [2002] CLJ 264, 267 comments that newspapers sometimes create celebrities for their own commercial purposes: 'To allow the cult [of celebrity] to count as a reason for the invasion of privacy amounts to allowing newspapers to manufacture their own defence in advance.' The Court of Appeal's reservations put in doubt the broadcasting media's Code of Guidance (1998), para 14, which treats exposure of 'disreputable behaviour' as justification for encroaching on an individual's privacy. See M Tugendhat, 'Privacy and Celebrity' in E Barendt and A Firth (eds), *Yearbook of Copyright and Media Law 2001/2002* (Oxford: 2002) 9.

[54] *Weld-Blundell v Stephens* [1919] 1 KB 520, 527, 533 (chartered accountant); *Hunter v Mann* [1974] 2 All ER 414, 417–418 (doctor); *Re M* [1990] 1 All ER 205, 213 (social worker). Cases beyond this jurisdiction include: *Halls v Mitchell* [1928] 2 DLR 97, 105 (medical practitioner); *Duncan v Medical Practitioners' Disciplinary Committee* [1986] NZLR 513, 521 (medical practitioner).

[55] *W v Egdell* [1989] 1 All ER 1089; *R v Crozier* (1991) 8 BMLR 128. Cp *Re DH* [1994] 1 FLR 679.

[56] cp Law Society, *The Guide to the Professional Conduct of Solicitors* (8th edn, London: 1999) 16.02, para 3.

[57] In *Re DH* [1994] 1 FLR 679 doctors disclosed to the police video evidence of abuse of the patient (a toddler) by his mother without the consent of either the mother or the father, who was not implicated.

[58] *A v Hayden* (1984) 156 CLR 532, 545. cp *Weld-Blundell v Stephens* [1919] 1 KB 520.

> The public interest may on occasion require disclosure of confidential information disclosing iniquity, but this is not invariably so. The public interest does not require a solicitor to disclose confessions made to him by his client . . .[59]

11.12 The public interest in a professional disclosing iniquity must be weighed against the public interest in maintaining obligations of professional confidence.[60] These obligations are not to be lightly set aside.[61] *Woodward v Hutchins*[62] sets a precedent for breaching a confidence to correct a false public image,[63] but it would take quite exceptional circumstances for a professional to be justified in doing this to her client. In *Campbell v Frisbee* Lightman J said:

> [W]hen a public figure has painted a false picture of himself or herself, there may be a public interest in correcting that picture. Whether the public interest is such as it overrides an obligation of confidence depends upon the facts of the particular case. Two factors or sets of factors appear to me to be of particular significance. The first set of factors is the status of the public figure, the respect in which the picture was false, the nature of the correction and the means taken to effect the correction. The second factor is the nature of the confidentiality obligation owed. Plainly the relationship between the parties owing and owed the duty of confidentiality is significant: it can scarcely be suggested that e.g. a lawyer, accountant or doctor is free to use the confidential information which he possesses to make public revelations about his client or patient to correct any false impression which the client or patient has created. The trust to be placed by clients in their advisers or other confidants and their legitimate expectation that the Courts will protect confidences reposed should not lightly be undermined.[64]

Disclosure may be more harmful to society than concealment of wrongdoing or false publicity. Breaches of confidence by doctors, for example, may endanger public health if patients are deterred from presenting themselves for treatment.[65] Factors to be considered in assessing a defence of iniquity by a professional include the kind of service the professional provides, the expectations of members of the public with respect to the particular profession in question, the nature of the client's wrongdoing and the immediacy of the threat.[66]

11.13 **Impact of the Human Rights Act 1998** The HRA requires a revision of the way that professionals and courts approach the public interest defence. Disclosure of confidential personal client records by or to a public authority[67] without the client's

---

[59] [1998] 3 All ER 552, 557.
[60] *W v Egdell* [1990] 1 All ER 835, 848. cp *Att-Gen v Guardian Newspapers Ltd (No 2)* [1988] 3 All ER 545, 640.
[61] cp *Campbell v Frisbee* [2002] EWHC 328; [2002] EMLR 31, para 42.
[62] [1977] 1 WLR 760.
[63] See para 11.10 above.
[64] [2002] EWHC 328; [2002] EMLR 31, para 32. See also para 35.
[65] *X v Y* [1988] 2 All ER 648, 653 (AIDS). Contrast *W v Egdell* [1989] 1 All ER 1089, 1105.
[66] The public interest in disclosure may be outweighed by that in non-disclosure if the danger has passed: *Schering Chemicals Ltd v Falkman Ltd* [1981] 2 All ER 321.
[67] The indirect horizontal effect of HRA, s 6 (see para 3.05 above) probably means that non-consensual disclosure of personal client records by a professional in private practice to a private third

B. Disclosure of Iniquity

consent interferes with the client's Article 8 right to respect for private life[68] and must therefore be justified. Justification requires that the disclosure be for one of the aims listed in Article 8(2).[69] The most likely candidates are 'public safety',[70] 'the protection of health or morals',[71] 'prevention of disorder or crime'[72] or 'protection of the rights and freedoms of others'.[73] But this is not enough. The disclosure must also be shown to be for a pressing social need in a democratic society and satisfy a test of proportionality.[74] The proportionality test replaces the more impressionistic pre-HRA era balancing of competing interests test. Feldman explains: '[a]lthough the tests under Article 8(2) involve the exercise of judgment, the ECtHR typically sets out all the interests (public and private) favouring the enforcement of the right to privacy and favouring interfering with it, and gives an indication of the weight which it attaches to each of the facts of the case and the reasons for those weights.'[75]

What the professional codes of ethics say

Professional codes of ethics may offer guidance (not, of course, binding on the courts)[76] as to when disclosure is in the public interest. Different views are advanced in the codes by different—even related—professions. There is room for only a sample here. It is interesting that despite their many differences, the English codes only very rarely compel,[77] as opposed to allow, the disclosure of iniquity. This is unlike some Canadian and US professional codes of ethics that unambiguously mandate lawyers to disclose prospective crimes of violence.[78]

11.14

---

party also potentially interferes with Art 8, eg if a psychiatrist discloses to a husband suing for divorce that his wife, who is the psychiatrist's private patient, is receiving treatment for drug addiction.

[68] *MS v Sweden* (1997) 28 EHRR 83; *Martin v UK* 21 EHRR CD 112 at CD 114; *Z v Finland* (1997) 25 EHRR 371; *Foxley v UK* (2000) 8 BHRC 571. It may involve interference with respect for his correspondence as well.

[69] Art 8(2).

[70] eg, *W v Egdell* [1990] 1 All ER 835, 853.

[71] eg, *L v UK* [2000] 2 FLR 322.

[72] eg, *W v Egdell* [1990] 1 All ER 835, 853.

[73] eg, *L v UK* [2000] 2 FLR 322.

[74] See para 3.19 above. Defensive disclosures will therefore be unlawful.

[75] D Feldman, 'Information and Privacy' in *Freedom of Expression and Freedom of Information: Essays in Honour of Sir David Williams* (Oxford: 2000) 317.

[76] See para 3.47 above.

[77] But see GMC, *Confidentiality: Protecting and Providing Information* (London: 2000) para 36 which may impose a duty to disclose information to an appropriate person where third parties are exposed to a serious risk by the patient.

[78] Nova Scotia Law Society, *Legal Ethics and Professional Conduct Handbook,* para 5.12, available at http://www.nsbs.ns.ca; Law Society of Alberta, *Code of Professional Conduct*, ch 7, para 8(c); Law Society of Manitoba, *Code of Professional Conduct,* commentary 11. On the US position see L Levin, 'Testing the Radical Experiment: A Study of Lawyer Response to Clients who Intend to Harm Others' (1994) 47 Rutgers L Rev 81, 84. At one time even in England it was thought that a solicitor who came by information about a serious prospective crime had to inform the appropriate authorities: T Lund, *A Guide to the Professional Conduct and Etiquette of Solicitors* (London: 1960) 105, 107 cited by R Cranston, 'Legal Ethics and Professional Responsibility' in R Cranston (ed), *Legal Ethics and Professional Responsibility* (Oxford: 1995) 26.

Lawyers

11.15 Lawyers have the most limited capacity to make disclosures on public interest grounds. The Law Society says that a solicitor may reveal confidential information to the extent necessary to prevent the client or a third party committing a criminal act that is reasonably believed to be likely to result in serious bodily harm,[79] and in cases of continuing or anticipated child abuse provided disclosure is in the public interest.[80] The Law Society, however, treats any communication by a client to a solicitor made with the intention of obtaining legal assistance to further a crime or fraud as outside the bounds of confidentiality.[81] This extends the crime-fraud exception to legal professional privilege (LPP)[82] to the solicitor's obligation of confidentiality.[83] The Law Society's rules do not allow disclosure of information by a solicitor about completed[84] crimes (even if they are a continuing source of harm),[85] on-going torts that physically endanger members of the public[86] and 'asides'[87] about future crimes or frauds that are likely to occasion serious damage to property, the environment or the financial interests of third parties.

---

[79] Law Society, *The Guide to the Professional Conduct of Solicitors* (8th edn, London: 1999), 16.02, para 3. This might include a crime not designed to cause bodily harm that carried a high risk of violence such as armed robbery.

[80] The Law Society's guidance is reproduced in D Herschman and A MacFarlane, *Children Law and Practice* (London: 2001). Solicitors are advised not to disclose child abuse if the client refuses consent and is a *Gillick* competent minor unless the solicitor 'knows or strongly suspects that younger siblings are being abused or where the child is in fear of his or her life or of serious injury'. When the client is an immature child, the abuser or a third party the solicitor has a discretion to disclose the abuse to a third party if the solicitor believes 'that the public interest in protecting children at risk outweighs the public interest in maintaining the duty of confidentiality' . For a comment on this advice see G Brasse, 'The Confidentiality of a Child's Instructions' [1996] Family L 733.

[81] Law Society, *The Guide to the Professional Conduct of Solicitors* (8th edn, London: 1999) 16.02, para 1.

[82] See para 16.35 below.

[83] K Wheat, 'Lawyers, Confidentiality and Public and Private Interests' (2000)1 Legal Ethics 184, 193. Cp *Smith v Jones* [1999]1 SCR 455. See also N Moore, 'Limits to Attorney-Client Confidentiality: a "Philosophically Informed" and Comparative Approach to Legal and Medical Ethics' (1985–86) 36 Case Western Reserve L Rev 177, 201 and D Layton, 'Ethics, Confidentiality and Privilege: Comment on *Smith v Jones*' (1999), available at http://www.crimlaw.org/def brief48.html.

[84] Distinguishing between past and future crimes may be difficult: D Friend, 'Too High a Price for Truth: The Exception to the Attorney-Client Privilege for Contemplated Crimes and Frauds' (1986) 64 North Carolina L Rev 443, 444.

[85] A Scottish solicitor felt constrained by the Scottish rules not to disclose that a client had confessed responsibility for a murder for which another man was serving a life sentence until after the client had died and his widow had given her consent: R Tur, 'Confidentiality and Accountability' (1992) 1 Griffith L Rev 73, 76–77 citing J Beltrami, *A Deadly Innocence* (Edinburgh: 1989) 19.

[86] M Brindle and G Dehn, 'Confidence, Public Interest, the Lawyer' in R Cranston (ed), *Legal Ethics and Professional Responsibility* (Oxford: 1995) 122.

[87] Asides are communications not made with the object of facilitating the crime or to obtain legal advice and therefore potentially confidential.

B. Disclosure of Iniquity

The Code of Conduct of the Bar of England and Wales unhelpfully[88] states that a barrister 'must not without the prior consent of the lay client *or as permitted by law* . . . communicate to any third person . . . information which has been entrusted to him in confidence'.[89] This has been interpreted by the head of the Professional Standards and Legal Services Department of the General Council of the Bar to mean, 'if the lay client has told a barrister that he is likely to commit a crime, the barrister is prevented from informing the authorities'.[90]

11.16

Healthcare professionals

The codes of some[91] healthcare professionals[92] are broadly worded and would permit disclosure to assist the detection and prosecution of a serious crime and disclosure of tortious conduct that threatens to be the cause of serious injury.[93] Disclosure by pharmacists is approved 'where necessary to prevent serious injury or damage to the health of the patient or a third party'.[94] Pharmacists may also disclose confidential information 'to a police officer who provides in writing confirmation that disclosure is necessary to assist in the prevention, detection of or prosecution of serious crime'.[95] The Nursing and Midwifery Council's code[96] states that disclosure is 'justified in the public interest (usually where disclosure is essential to protect the patient or client or someone else from the risk of significant harm)'. Further guidance explains that 'public interest means the interests of an individual or groups of individuals or of society as a whole, and would, for

11.17

---

[88] D Nicolson and J Webb, *Professional Legal Ethics* (Oxford: 1999) 253 criticize the Bar Code for creating uncertainty: 'depending on how the phrase "permitted by law" is interpreted, the exceptions to the barrister's professional duty could be either narrower or wider than those provided by the LSG [Law Society Guidance].'

[89] *Code of Conduct of the Bar of England and Wales* (7th edn, London:1999) para 702 (italics added).

[90] M Stobbs, 'Ethical Issues Facing the Bar' (1998)1 Legal Ethics 27, 28. The authority cited is *R v Derby Magistrates' Court, ex p B* [1995] 4 All ER 4, 4–6.

[91] *The General Dental Council's code, Maintaining Standards* (2000), para 3.5, recognizes that '[t]here may be . . . circumstances in which the public interest outweighs a dentist's duty of confidentiality and in which disclosure would be justified' but does not spell out in any way what these might be.

[92] As regards most healthcare professionals see P Moore and M Wright, 'Confidentiality, Codes and Courts' (2000) 29 Anglo-American L Rev 39.

[93] To this writer it seems absurd to allow a professional to disclose a risk of serious injury to a third party through crime but not an equally serious risk of physical injury through tortious conduct falling short of the criminal.

[94] Royal Pharmaceutical Society, *Standards of Professional Performance* Part 2, C(iv), (v), available at http://www.rpsgb.org.uk.

[95] According to Department of Health Advice, a serious crime is a 'serious arrestable offence' within the meaning of Police and Criminal Evidence Act 1984, s116. See DoH, *The Protection and Use of Patient Information* HSG (96) 18 (1996) para 5.7–9 and Annex D. The Police and Criminal Evidence Act 1984 definition of a 'serious arrestable offence' includes 'serious financial loss' and allows seriousness to be determined by reference to the person who suffers the loss.

[96] Nursing and Midwifery Council (NMC) *Code of Professional Conduct* (2002) para 5.3.

example, cover matters such as serious crime, child abuse, drug trafficking or other activities which place others at serious risk'.[97]

11.18 The General Medical Council's (GMC's) guidelines,[98] the benchmark for health professionals, condone disclosure of personal information without consent 'where failure to do so may expose the patient or others to risk of death or serious harm'[99] and 'where a disclosure may assist in the prevention or detection of a serious crime'.[100] Serious crimes are ones that 'will put someone at risk of death or serious harm, and will usually be crimes against the person, such as abuse of children'.[101] The medical profession regards harm as encompassing omissions, such as neglect and psychological injury.[102] The BMA's advice is that the seriousness of the harm should be assessed subjectively, that is, from the viewpoint of the person likely to suffer it.[103] The BMA has also recommended that doctors satisfy themselves that material released will be destroyed when no longer needed.[104] Under the GMC rules disclosure of suspected child abuse is virtually mandatory:

> If you believe a patient to be a victim of neglect or physical, sexual or emotional abuse and that the patient cannot give or withhold consent to disclosure, you should give information promptly to an appropriate responsible person or statutory agency, where you believe that the disclosure is in the patient's best interests. . . . Such circumstances may arise in relation to children, where concerns about possible abuse need to be shared with other agencies such as social services. If, for any reason, you believe that disclosure of information is not in the best interests of an abused or neglected patient, you must still be prepared to justify your decision.[105]

A similar position is adopted by the British Psychological Society in respect of child abuse but not crime detection. Its guidance states that disclosure without client consent may be necessary 'in situations in which failure to disclose appropriate information would expose the client, or someone else, to a risk of serious harm (including physical or sexual abuse) or death. Such disclosure may particularly be required where there is a risk of, or actual, sexual or physical abuse of children.'[106]

---

[97] *News*, 'Practitioners face dilemma about reporting illegal acts' 1 March 2001, available at http://www.nmc-uk.org/cms/content/News/.
[98] Royal College of Psychiatrists, *Good Practice Guidance on Confidentiality* (London: 2000) basing itself on this guidance sets out factors to be considered when deciding whether or not disclosure is justified in the public interest.
[99] GMC, *Confidentiality: Protecting and Providing Information* (June 2000) para 36. This may permit non-consensual disclosure in domestic violence situations.
[100] ibid, para 37, p 17. cp Royal College of Psychiatrists, *Good Psychiatric Practice: Confidentiality* (London: 2000) 6, available from http://www.rcpsych.ac.uk.
[101] GMC, *Confidentiality: Protecting and Providing Information* (June 2000) para 37c, p 17.
[102] BMA, *Confidentiality and disclosure of health information* (London: 1999) 8.
[103] ibid.
[104] BMA, *Philosophy and Practice of Medical Ethics* (London: 1988) 23–24.
[105] GMC, *Confidentiality: Protecting and Providing Information* (London: 2000) para 39.
[106] *Professional Practice Guidelines 1995* (2001) 6.3.2, available from http://www.bps.org.uk.

B. Disclosure of Iniquity

Social workers and counsellors

11.19 The British Association of Social Workers' *Code of Ethics for Social Work* recognizes that breaches of confidentiality may occur 'where there is clear evidence of serious danger to the client, worker, other persons or the community or in other circumstances judged exceptional on the basis of professional consideration and consultation'.[107] Superseded guidance from the Department of Health encouraged social workers to assist the police with information especially where helpful 'to prevent, detect or prosecute a serious crime'.[108] This is not repeated in the current guidance which, however, approves disclosure to enable statutory functions to be performed by public bodies including the police.[109]

11.20 Counselling organizations, the Samaritans in particular, make referral of terrorist bomb warnings a specific exception to their promise of virtually absolute confidentiality to clients.[110]

The Law

Prevention of harm to the person

11.21 **Doctors** There is a paucity of case law on just when iniquity might warrant disclosure of confidential personal information by a professional. Most of what exists relates to health care professionals.[111] In *W v Egdell*[112] a psychiatrist was held to have lawfully disclosed to the responsible public authorities that his client, a patient detained in a secure hospital after killing five people and seriously injuring two others, posed a 'real risk of . . . danger to the public'[113] if released because of an unhealthy fascination with firearms and home-made bombs.[114] The court said that the doctor's opinion as to the risk posed by the patient, while not conclusive, was something to which it attached weight.[115] There is a strong implication that

---

[107] *The Code of Ethics for Social Work* (1996) principle xi, available from http://www.basw.co.uk.
[108] 'DoH, 'Personal Social Services: Confidentiality of Personal Information', Circular LAC (88) 17 discussed in B Hebenton and T Thomas, 'The Police and Social Services Departments in England and Wales: the exchange of personal information' [1992] J of Social Welfare & Family L 114, 115.
[109] DoH, *Social Care Policy* LASSL (2000) 2, para 6.18, available from http://www.doh.gov.uk.
[110] P Jenkins, 'Terrorism and the law' (2001) 12 Counselling & Psychotherapy J 42.
[111] See M Jones, 'Medical confidentiality and the public interest' (1990) 6 Professional Negligence 16.
[112] [1990] 1 All ER 835. For a case involving the clergy see *R v Harrison* (CA, 10 July 2000) and for a case involving a probation officer see *R v Kennedy* [1999] Cr App R 54.
[113] per Bingham LJ, [1990] 1 All ER 835, 853.
[114] It is unclear whether Dr Egdell discovered new facts about W's criminal propensities or whether he simply disagreed with the diagnosis of those treating the patient. W. L Kennedy and A Grubb, *Medical Law* (3rd edn, London: 2000) 1101 suggest that there is a greater justification for disclosing factual information than an opinion unless all relevant information takes the form of an opinion which, when dealing with psychiatric issues, might well be the case.
[115] ibid at 851.

the risk of a minor crime being committed would not have swayed the court in the same way.

11.22 Breach of medical confidentiality was also the issue in *Jones v Smith*[116] in which the Supreme Court of Canada ruled that a doctor was entitled to disclose confidential information if—and by implication *only* if—reasonable grounds exist to believe that disclosure is necessary to prevent a crime involving death or serious bodily harm and that there is a clear risk to an identifiable[117] group or person or group of persons that is imminent. There are three elements to this test:

(1) the consequence of non-disclosure;
(2) the probability of that consequence happening; and
(3) urgency.[118]

On the evidence of *W v Egdell*[119] urgency is not essential under English law for a lawful disclosure by a doctor: there is nothing in the facts to suggest that a third party was in immediate danger. Indeed, there is nothing to suggest that an identifiable person or group of persons would have been put at risk if W had been released. From the facts and outcome one might deduce that English law requires no more than a real risk of serious physical harm to someone.[120]

11.23 In both *Jones v Smith* and *W v Egdell* the doctors who made the disclosures were engaged by defence lawyers exclusively for the purpose of providing the defence with a medical opinion. In circumstances where the disclosing doctor is the patient's regular treating physician, a disclosure might not only cause mental distress to the patient and weaken public confidence in doctors generally (certainly if such disclosures occur with any frequency), but might have serious therapeutic consequences for the patient.[121] Where such a risk exists, this too must be consid-

---

[116] [1999] 1 SCR 455. This case has the additional complication that disclosure was a breach of solicitor–client privilege.

[117] Cory J referred to this as the 'clarity' factor. A general threat directed at everyone might be too vague unless the threat is extremely serious and imminent.

[118] See P Moore and M Wright, 'Confidentiality, Codes and Courts' (2000) 29 Anglo-American L Rev 39, 54–55.

[119] [1990] 1 All ER 835. The Court of Appeal disregarded W's argument (see 845) that the danger must be 'immediate'. See also *R v Crozier* (1990) 8 BMLR 128 where disclosure was made in circumstances where there was no imminent risk of the patient injuring anyone. It is questionable whether there was a risk to the public at all from a defendant who had murdered his sister during a family argument. But see *Duncan v Medical Practitioners Disciplinary Committee* [1986] 1 NZLR 513, 521 where there is a reference to a 'clear and present danger to life or limb' exception for doctors. See also Case Note: 30372 (June 2001), NZ Privacy Commissioner available at http://www.privacy.org.nz.

[120] Even on this more liberal test, the disclosure that occurred in *R v Wilson* [1996] 3 WLR 125 was probably actionable by the accused's wife as a breach of confidence by her doctor. In this criminal case the accused had burnt his initials into his wife's buttocks at her instigation with a hot blade. When she consulted her doctor about the after-effects, he reported the 'branding' to the police.

[121] One could attribute the death of Ms Tarasoff in *Tarasoff v Regents of the University of California* 529 P 2d 553, 554 (1974) to the refusal of Poddar (the patient who killed her) to

B. Disclosure of Iniquity

ered.[122] A factor likely to tilt the balance the other way is the vulnerability of the individual at risk. It is unimaginable that a court would disapprove of a decision to disclose information of potential, or actual, sexual abuse or cruel or degrading treatment of a child.[123] In the case of a normal adult, Articles 2 and 3 of the European Convention on Human Rights (ECHR) may, if there is a real and immediate risk of serious avoidable injury,[124] provide reasons for disclosure that outweigh the client's Article 8 right to privacy.[125]

Other professionals An entirely uniform judicial approach to disclosure across the professions is not to be expected because of the very different circumstances in which, and frequency with which,[126] disclosure issues will arise and the differing impact of disclosure on different kinds of professional relationship. Disclosure by a lawyer or a psychotherapist is, for example, much more likely to frustrate the objective of the consultation than disclosure by a physician or a banker.[127] A psychotherapist who was subpoenaed to testify at a trial attempted to justify his refusal by telling the judge: 11.24

> For me the need to retain secrecy was not just a moral imperative such as might exist, for example, for a general practitioner who was treating a patient for pneumonia. If such a doctor were to talk indiscreetly about his patient, he might not be behaving ethically, but he might still have treated the pneumonia adequately. But if I were to speak indiscreetly about a patient, I should not only be behaving unethically, but I should also be destroying the very fabric of my therapy.[128]

Still, it would be surprising if English law forbade a member of any profession from breaking a professional confidence to reveal a real risk of serious *physical* harm to an identifiable third party. The Court of Appeal has thought it proper for a prison chaplain to disclose that a remand prisoner planned to pursue a career of murder.[129] Would they have taken the same view if the disclosure had been made by his lawyer? Judicial concern to protect the confidentiality of communications 11.25

---

continue treatment after his psychologist had informed the campus police that he was threatening to murder her when she returned from Brazil: see paras 20.07 and 20.10 below.

[122] cp DoH, *The Protection and Use of Patient Information* HSG (96) 18 (1996) para 5.7.
[123] cp UN, The Convention of the Rights of the Child (1989) Arts 34, 37. cp *Re D* [1993] 2 All ER 693, 699 (child abuse an exception to conciliation privilege; as to which see paras 16.07 and 16.38 below).
[124] cp *Osman v UK* (1998) 5 BHRC 293, para 116.
[125] cp *Venables v NGN Ltd* [2001] 1 All ER 908. Does this apply in cases of possible self-harm? Cp para 12.07 below.
[126] It has been suggested that for lawyers such conflicts are likely to be more frequent than for doctors: N Moore, 'Limits to Attorney-Client Confidentiality: "A Philosophically Informed" and Comparative Approach to Legal and Medical Ethics' (1985–86) 36 Case Western Reserve L Rev 177, 209.
[127] cp M Brindle and G Dehn, 'Confidence, Public Interest, the Lawyer' in R Cranston (ed), *Legal Ethics and Professional Responsibility* (Oxford: 1995) 122.
[128] The Lancet, 16 October 1965, 785–787.
[129] *R v Harrison* (CA, 10 July 2000).

between professionals and lawyers is well known.[130] The answer may well depend on whether there is an imminent risk of serious injury to an identifiable person or persons. If there is, the societal interest in disclosure, it is submitted, outweighs the societal interest in non-disclosure even in the case of a lawyer, or in HRA terms the client's Article 8 right is outweighed by the Article 2 or 3 rights of the person at risk. Consistent with this conclusion, a US court has held that an attorney was entitled to warn the lawyer for a client's ex-wife that the client had 'cased' the ex-wife's home and threatened to kill her.[131] At the other end of the scale of threatened wrongs are minor violations of the criminal law that are unlikely to attract imprisonment. It would be surprising if the courts were to sanction a breach of confidence by any professional to avert shoplifting.[132] Disclosure of such a minor offence would very likely fail the proportionality test for a valid infringement of the right to respect for private life guaranteed by Article 8(1).[133] The Information Commissioner has suggested that a hospital may consider disclosure of medical information to police justified if a member of staff was assaulted but unjustified in the context of a minor theft.[134]

Prevention and exposure of on-going financial wrongdoing

11.26 **Lawyers** In *Re a Company's Application*[135] Scott J refused to grant an injunction to prevent an employee of a financial services company from disclosing confidential information about the company to a regulatory authority. Would the outcome have been different had the whistle-blower been a professional and the information concerned a client?

11.27 Law Society guidelines do not permit a solicitor to disclose financial wrongdoing by a client[136] except where a solicitor's advice is sought to further a financial crime or civil fraud.[137] In *R v Derby Magistrates' Court, ex p B*[138] Lord Nicholls assumed that LPP could not be breached to bring a defendant alleged to have defrauded

---

[130] See para 16.08 below.
[131] *Mulka v Fain* (Conn Sup Ct, 14 April 1994, WL 146793). The arguments for and against disclosure by lawyers are discussed in K Wheat, 'Lawyers, Confidentiality and Public and Private Interests' (2000)1 Legal Ethics 184.
[132] Notice also that in *Kitson v Playfair*, The Times, 28 March 1896, 5 Hawkins J thought that it would be 'a monstrous cruelty' for a doctor to inform the police that a patient had been trying to procure an abortion—in spite of the existence at that time of the common law offence of misprision of felony.
[133] See para 3.19 above.
[134] *Guidance on Use and Disclosure of Health Data* (May 2002) 14.
[135] [1989] 2 All ER 248.
[136] The situation might be different if an employed solicitor disclosed misconduct by the partners of the firm to the Law Society.
[137] Is there any difference between a situation in which a client actively seeks legal assistance to carry out of a fraud or crime (where there certainly is no privilege or confidentiality) and one in which the client simply reveals his involvement in an on-going fraud or his intention to commit some crime to a lawyer?
[138] [1995] 4 All ER 526, 545

B. Disclosure of Iniquity

hundreds of people of their pensions or life savings to book. He might have taken a different view of disclosure to avert financial loss arising from on-going or planned fraud if the victim was not legally represented and the transaction was not a commercial one.[139]

Other professionals In principle there is no reason why a professional who is not a lawyer should not disclose financial wrongs and financial risks in the public interest.[140] Although Article 8 might be infringed by the disclosure, in some circumstances this could be justified in terms of protecting the economic well-being of the country[141] or the rights of others.[142] In any given case the question is whether there is a pressing social need and proportionality.[143]   11.28

There is no English judicial guidance on the rights or wrongs of disclosing confidential financial information about a client. A Canadian court has permitted breach of the banker's duty of confidentiality to thwart deception of a third party by the customer.[144] But a Scottish court has condemned accountants auditing the accounts of a dissolved firm of solicitors for disclosing to the income tax authorities underpayment of taxes by one of the firm's clients.   11.29

> . . . I have never read or heard that the duty of assisting the Treasury in the collection of the public revenue was of such a paramount nature that it must be carried out by private individuals at the cost and betrayal of confidence and the invasion of the proprietary rights of other people.[145]

Would a court take the same view of a disclosure to prevent a patient defrauding the NHS or an insurance company? This is not an issue to which the ethical codes of health professionals provide a clear lead. The BMA's advice about illicit benefit claims is that 'wherever possible, doctors should raise the issue with the patient concerned and make it clear that health professionals will not collude with fraudulent claims, thereby encouraging the patient to desist from such action'.[146]   11.30

---

[139] cp *Seaway Trust Co v Markle* (1991) 47 CPC (2d) 258.
[140] In *Price Waterhouse v BCCI Holdings (Luxembourg) SA* [1992] BCLC 583 the public interest in effective Bank of England supervision of banking institutions was held to justify a breach of confidence. While not directly in point, this decision does show that disclosure may be justified by reasons other than public or individual safety. Lord Levy was refused an injunction when he applied by telephone to prevent The Sunday Times from publishing findings about his tax bill (*Lord Levy v Times Newspapers Ltd* (HC, 23 June 2000)). According to the Guardian ('Lord Levy denies Tory sleaze allegation', 26 June 2000) Toulson J 'declared that there was an overriding public interest in the information being made public'. Other cases in which the danger was of economic loss include *Gartside v Outram* (1856) 26 LJ Ch (NS) 113; *Re a Company's Application* [1989] 2 All ER 248.
[141] But in *British Steel Corp v Granada* [1981] 1 All ER 417 the House of Lords held that there was no public interest in disclosure of mismanagement and government intervention in a nationalized industry during a national strike.
[142] Art 8(2).
[143] See para 3.19 above.
[144] *CIBC v Sayani* (1993) 83 BCLR (2d) 167.
[145] per Lord M'Laren, *Brown's Trustees v Hay* (1898) 35 SLR 877, 880.
[146] *Confidentiality and disclosure of health information* (London: 1999) 7.

And if the patient does not desist? On the one hand the BMA says that '[i]n general, threats to people are significant in a way that threats to property or financial interests are not'.[147] On the other, it states that '[s]erious fraud or theft involving NHS resources ... would be quite likely to harm individuals awaiting treatment'.[148] The European Court of Human Rights (ECtHR) attaches particular importance to the protection of medical data[149] and requires the state to demonstrate very serious reasons for invading intimate parts of an individual's life.[150] It has, nevertheless, found the disclosure of medical information to protect public funds justified.[151]

11.31 The Institute of Chartered Accountants in its Handbook[152] envisages members disclosing fraud or non-compliance with law or regulations. Members are advised to weigh the public interest in maintaining confidential client relationships against the public interest in disclosure to the proper authority, taking into account: (a) the extent to which members of the public are likely to be affected; (b) whether the directors have rectified the matter or are likely to take effective corrective action; (c) the extent to which non-disclosure is likely to enable the misconduct to recur with impunity; (d) the gravity of the matter; and (e) the weight of evidence and the degree of the member's suspicion that there has been misconduct. A court might find these guidelines helpful.

Detection of completed crimes

11.32 **Professionals who are not lawyers** From time to time professionals are approached for information by the police or other public officials conducting a criminal investigation. The professional should establish whether the person making the request has a statutory right to the information.[153] If he has not then, barring circumstances where there is an overriding public interest in the information being provided or where legislation expressly authorizes voluntary disclosure (which will be based on Parliament's assessment of where the public interest lies),[154] confidential personal information about a client should not be released.[155]

---

[147] BMA, *Consent, Rights and Choices in Health Care for Children and Young Persons* (London: 2000) 82.
[148] *Confidentiality and disclosure of health information* (London: 1999) 7.
[149] *MS v Sweden* (1997) 45 BMLR 133, para 41.
[150] *Dudgeon v UK* (1981) 4 EHRR 149, para 52.
[151] *MS v Sweden* (1997) 45 BMLR 133.
[152] Institute of Chartered Accountants in England and Wales, *Members Handbook 2001* (London: 2001) 371–372, section 1.306, paras 14–17.
[153] Under the Anti-Terrorism, Crime and Security Act 2001, s 117 it is an offence to withhold information about acts of terrorism from the police.
[154] eg Anti-Terrorism, Crime and Security Act 2001, ss 17, 19.
[155] Refusal of information for reasons of confidentiality will not constitute wilful obstruction of a police officer in the execution of his duty under Police Act 1964, s 51(3) or the doing of an act contrary to Criminal Law Act 1967, s 4.

B. Disclosure of Iniquity

A police officer goes to a bank to make an enquiry about a customer of the bank. He goes to the bank, because he knows that the person about whom he wants information is a customer of the bank's. The police officer is asked why he wants the information. He replies, because the customer is charged with a series of frauds. Is the bank entitled to publish that information? Surely not.[156]

There are formal channels regulated by legislation containing safeguards for the individual by which the police can get information.[157]

11.33 When might a professional be justified on public interest grounds in voluntarily disclosing information to assist crime detection? The BMA and the Department of Health envisage disclosure of confidential medical information to the police in the context of serious offences.[158] The seriousness of the offence alone, however, would not justify[159] the police or other investigator in by-passing normal channels for obtaining information (where applicable) unless there is a serious risk of further mishap and insufficient time to obtain it through those channels.[160]

11.34 Case law on voluntary disclosure of confidential personal information by professionals to the police and other investigators is sparse and contradictory. In *Re G*[161] it was held that a social worker should disclose to the police any admissions that the parents had made about unexplained injuries to the child. The child was the subject of pending care proceedings and the argument was about whether the court's leave was necessary for further disclosure to the police.[162] The parents had not been given an unqualified promise of confidentiality.

11.35 Elsewhere in the common law world courts have both upheld and objected to disclosure of confidential medical information to police for crime detection purposes. In *R v Dersch*[163] a hospital doctor, in response to a police request, and

---

[156] per Bankes LJ, *Tournier v National Provincial and Union Bank of England* [1924] 1 KB 461, 474. cp GMC, *Confidentiality* (1995) para 21: '[i]n the absence of a court order, a request for disclosure by a third party, for example, a ... police officer ... is not sufficient justification for disclosure without a patient's consent.' But see *A v Hayden (No 2)* (1984) 56 ALR 82; *Grofam Pty Ltd v KPMG Peat Marwick* [1993] 27 IPR 215, 222.

[157] See paras 14.19 et seq.

[158] BMA on-line guidance on 'Confidentiality and disclosure of health information' (London: 1999) 'Disclosure in the public interest', available from http://www.bma.org.uk. DoH, *Protection and Use of Patient Information* HSG (96) 18 (1996) para 5.8. Cp Health Act 1999, s 24(6) which states that disclosure of information obtained during an investigation by the Commission for Health Improvement is to be regarded as made with lawful authority if made 'in connection with the investigation of a serious arrestable offence'. cp (1914) 78 JP 604.

[159] Any disclosure of confidential medical information would have to be justified under Art 8(2) and this imposes requirements of proportionality and necessity.

[160] Normal channels cannot apply if the crime is unknown to police. The GMC's position on gun-shot wounds is that in the overwhelming majority of cases disclosure is appropriate (private communication 5 January 2003).

[161] [1996] 2 All ER 65, 73.

[162] Family Proceedings Rules 1991 SI 1991/1247, r 4.23.

[163] (1993) 18 CRR (2d) 87. See also *Morris v Consolidation Coal Co* 446 SE 2d 648 (1994) where detection of a possibly fraudulent claim to disability benefit by the patient's employer was not held to justify disclosure by the doctor.

without the patient's consent, prepared a report that included the results of a blood alcohol test (taken against the patient's express wishes) and a diagnosis that the patient (who had been involved in a fatal road accident) had been intoxicated when admitted to the hospital. The Canadian Supreme Court held that provision of the information to the police by the doctor violated the doctor's common law duty of confidentiality to the patient, and the obtaining of the information by the police without a search warrant violated the patient's Charter right to be free from unreasonable seizures. In *R v Dyment*,[164] a similar case in which a doctor provided police with a blood specimen taken from the patient for treatment purposes, La Forest J said that 'to use an individual's blood or other bodily substances confided to others for medical purposes for purposes other than these seriously violates the personal autonomy of the individual'. Absent a pressing necessity, he concluded, it was a breach of the Charter for the police to obtain evidence in this way.[165]

11.36 A quite different approach was taken in *Brown v Brooks*,[166] a New South Wales case, where a clinical nurse specializing in mental health informed police of admissions by her client during counselling sessions that were directly relevant to charges that had been laid against him of assault and indecency involving his stepdaughter. The client applied for an injunction to restrain the nurse from making further disclosures and the police from using the confidential information already obtained. This was refused by McClelland J who was of the view that it would be contrary to public policy for the courts to enforce an obligation of confidentiality if this would impede the proper investigation and prosecution of a felony.[167] McClelland J emphasized the serious nature of the charge laid against the client: 'the position may well be different in the case of a trivial offence.'

11.37 The different outcomes in *R v Dersch* and *R v Dyment* on the one hand, and *Brown v Brooks* on the other are explicable on a number of grounds. First, in the Australian case there may have been an on-going risk to the victim.[168] In the two Canadian cases, both of which arose out of motor vehicle accidents, there was not.[169] Secondly, the Canadian cases involve an infringement of a Charter right to be secure from 'unreasonable search or seizure' which protects privacy interests. This factor makes the Canadian cases more relevant than the Australian one

---

[164] (1988) 55 DLR (4th) 503, 520.
[165] Under the English Road Traffic Act 1988, s 7A under certain circumstances a blood sample may be taken from a patient incapable of giving consent but the sample must be taken by a doctor who is not responsible for the clinical care of the patient.
[166] (1998) NSW LEXIS 9221. See also *R v Singleton* [1995] 1 Cr App R 431, 439.
[167] cp *Butler v Board of Trade* [1970] 3 All ER 593.
[168] See also *Re DH* [1994] 1 FLR 679.
[169] The cases are also distinguishable by the fact that the Australian case involved confessional evidence and the Canadian real evidence but traditionally courts have been more scrupulous about admitting confessional evidence than real evidence. Confessions must be voluntary (or pass Police and Criminal Evidence Act 1984, s 76), real evidence is admissible no matter how obtained: *Kuruma v R* [1955] 1 All ER 236.

C. Incriminating Physical Evidence

because Article 8(1) of the ECHR requires respect for the accused's private life and any interference with that right has to be justified.[170] Disclosure of information to the police to assist crime detection and prosecution falls within the legitimate aim of preventing crime or disorder,[171] but this is not, of itself, enough to make the interference Convention-compliant. The authorities must also demonstrate a pressing social need and proportionality.[172] Something that needs to be borne in mind when deciding whether there is proportionality and a pressing social need is La Forest J's warning in *R v Dyment*[173] that if '[a] free exchange of information between physicians . . . and the police' were permitted it might deter persons in need of health care, in some circumstances, from seeking it.[174]

Lawyers   The position of lawyers is different from that of other professionals. It is well settled that a lawyer who is consulted for the purpose of defending a criminal charge cannot be a turncoat and pass information to the prosecution[175] or, semble, the police. If the client confesses and still pleads 'not guilty', the lawyer will have to withdraw from the case if the client insists on giving or presenting evidence of his innocence or challenging prosecution evidence that the lawyer knows to be true but the prosecution or court should not be told why.[176] If a lawyer could incriminate a client, the client could not trust the lawyer and legal representation would become illusory. If a lawyer is not consulted for the purpose of conducting a criminal defence but, say, to draw up a will and reveals acts of past criminal wrongdoing, there is still a danger that if the lawyer could disclose the information to the authorities recourse to lawyers might be discouraged to the detriment of wider societal interests.[177] Disclosure is prevented under the Law Society rules[178] and by legal advice privilege.[179]   11.38

C. Incriminating Physical Evidence[180]

Handing the evidence to the authorities

There is no English authority, and no English guidance, on how a professional should react when a client hands over physical evidence of a crime. Solicitors and clergy are   11.39

---

[170] See para 3.19 above.
[171] ibid.   [172] ibid.
[173] (1988) 26 DLR (4th) 399, 518.
[174] In *Weld-Blundell v Stephens* [1919] 1 KB 520, 527 at a time when suicide was a criminal offence it was taken for granted that a doctor must not disclose that a patient had attempted suicide.
[175] *Weld-Blundell v Stephens* [1919] 1 KB 520, 544.
[176] *Tuckiar v R* (1934) 52 CLR 335.
[177] There is scope for argument about the extent of this danger and whether lawyers should be treated differently from other professionals: see para 1.52 above and para 16.46 below.
[178] See para 11.15 above.
[179] See para 16.16 below. Query, would legal advice privilege prevent disclosure if the client in the course of seeking legal advice quite gratuitously boasted to the lawyer about some past criminal act?
[180] For an analysis of the law from the perspective of Canadian law and ethics with specific reference to lawyers see M Proulx and D Layton, *Ethics and Canadian Criminal Law* (Toronto: 2001)

Chapter 11: Disclosure in the Public Interest

the ones most likely to be confronted with this dilemma. What is the lawyer to do if the client lays the gun used in an armed robbery on her desk? Canadian and US authority requires a lawyer to whom a client presents the instrument or product of a crime to hand what she receives to the authorities within a reasonable period regardless of whether the authorities know of, and ask for, the item.[181] Failure to do so, if it hinders a criminal investigation, amounts in the United States or Canada to the English crime of obstructing a police officer in the execution of his duty.[182]

Disclosing how, and from whom, the physical evidence was obtained

11.40 A professional who is not a lawyer who hands over physical evidence received from a client can be compelled, unless this would involve self-incrimination, to give evidence about how the evidence came into her possession and what was said at the time. In 1860 a priest was found guilty of contempt for refusing to divulge the identity of the person who had given him a stolen watch.[183] Under US law an attorney can refuse to divulge the identity of the source of physical evidence and any communications that accompanied the handing-over by claiming attorney–client privilege.[184] So long as the iniquity exception to LPP does not apply,[185] the position in English law will be the same. The physical item itself will not be privileged.[186] Should the client tell the lawyer where to find the physical evidence instead of handing it over, this communication too would be privileged. In *People v Belge*,[187] a US case, a client gave his lawyers directions where to find two people whom he had murdered. The lawyers found the site and photographed the bodies, but the information was not divulged until the client went into the witness box and, as part of a defence of insanity, told the court himself. One of the lawyers was charged with interfering with burial rights and failing to give notice of death without medical assistance. The charges were successfully defended on the grounds that the lawyer's knowledge and observations at the burial site were

---

ch 9. See also Law Society of Upper Canada, Special Committtee on Lawyers' Duties with Respect to Property Relevant to a Crime or Offence, *Report to Convocation*, 21 March 2002, available at http://www.lsuc.on.ca.

[181] *R v Murray* (2000) 144 CCC (3d) 289, paras 118 et seq. LPP does not apply to an object that was not brought into existence for the purposes of the professional-client relationship: see para 16.23 below.

[182] Police Act 1964, s 51(3). cp *R v Murray* (2000) 144 CCC (3d) 289.

[183] *R v Hay* (1860) 175 ER 933.

[184] *Washington Olwell* 394 P 2d 681 (1964). cp *People v Meredith* 631 P 2d 46 (1981).

[185] See para 16.35 below. If the client's purpose in handing over evidence of a crime is to conceal the crime, the item ought not to be privileged because the intention is to obstruct a police investigation which is itself a crime under Police Act 1964, s 51(3).

[186] *R v Peterborough Justices, ex p Hicks* [1977] 1 WLR 1371; *R v King* [1983] 1 All ER 929.

[187] 372 BYS 2d 798 (1975) aff'd 376 NYS 2d 771, aff'd 359 NE 2d 377 (1976). cp *Sanford v State* 21 SW 3d 337 (2000).

D. Disclosure Without Iniquity

A balancing of interests

In *Initial Services Ltd* and *Woodward* we see the beginning of a shift of emphasis in the law from the claimant's conduct to the effects of non-disclosure on third parties.[189] This shift was completed in *Lion Laboratories Ltd v Evans*[190] where the defence was applied to a claimant who had not done anything that could be classified as anti-social.[191] The claimant was the sole manufacturer licensed by the Home Office to supply the police with a device used to measure the blood alcohol level of motorists. The defendants were a national newspaper and two of the claimant's ex-employees who had passed to the newspaper internal memoranda of the claimant that cast doubt on the accuracy of the claimant's instruments. The claimant initially succeeded in obtaining an interlocutory injunction to restrain the former employees and the newspaper from disclosing or making use of the confidential information but this was discharged by the Court of Appeal which accepted that the defendants had an arguable defence of public interest to an action for breach of confidence. Iniquity, the court held, was merely an instance of a just cause and excuse for breaking a confidence in the public interest.[192] Griffiths LJ said:

11.41

> I believe that the so-called iniquity rule evolved because in most cases where the facts justified a publication in breach of confidence, the plaintiff had behaved so disgracefully or criminally that it was judged in the public interest that his behaviour should be exposed. No doubt it is in such circumstances that the defence will usually arise, but it is not difficult to think of instances where, although there has been no wrongdoing on the part of the plaintiff, it may be vital in the public interest to publish a part of his confidential information.[193]

The Court of Appeal explicitly applied the balancing approach forged in later iniquity cases[194] which involves weighing the public interest in disclosure against the public interest in maintaining confidentiality.[195] This approach was endorsed in *Att-Gen*

11.42

---

[188] See para 16.23 below. The fact that the lawyer knew the location because of something the client said would have been privileged.
[189] See also *Malone v Commissioner of Police of the Metropolis (No 2)* [1979] 2 All ER 620, 635.
[190] [1984] 2 All ER 417.
[191] Cp *Malone v Commissioner of Police of the Metropolis (No 2)* [1979] 2 All ER 620, 635.
[192] [1984] 2 All ER 417, 423, 431, 432, 433. See also *Malone v Commissioner of Police of the Metropolis (No 2)* [1979] 2 All ER 620, 635.
[193] [1984] 2 All ER 417, 432–433.
[194] See paras 11.12, 11.13 above.
[195] [1984] 2 All ER 417, 424.

v Guardian Newspapers Ltd (No 2).[196] In the HRA era the balancing test must be replaced by the language of human rights law. Since a breach of professional confidentiality always involves interference with the right to respect for private life,[197] it will have to be shown to be necessary in a democracy and proportionate to a legitimate aim mentioned in Article 8(2).[198] Conversely, if disclosure is suppressed, interference with Article 10 (freedom of expression) must be justified.[199]

Indirect benefit to client

11.43 Reported cases show that there are two very different kinds of circumstance in which the balance may come down in favour of disclosure of confidential personal information in the public interest without there being any iniquity. The first involves disclosure of information for some purpose collateral to the purpose for which the professional was engaged, but which nevertheless may indirectly benefit the client or persons like the client. Usually the disclosure will be for purposes of training other professionals, research, investigation of professional misconduct, peer assessment or to monitor professional standards or financial probity.[200] Obtaining express consent may be impossible because the client is dead or not contactable or, alternatively, contacting the client may be impracticable because of lack of time or the cost or undesirable on therapeutic grounds.[201]

Interference with medical confidentiality

11.44 The issue of disclosure without consent is one that has only been explored in any depth in relation to medical confidentiality. In *R v Department of Health, ex p Source Informatics Ltd*,[201a] advice from the Department of Health to pharmacists that they should not collect and sell anonymized data of the drug prescribing habits of GPs was challenged. Having held that the disclosure of the information did not involve a breach of confidence because no patient could be identified and therefore patient privacy was not imperilled,[202] the Court of Appeal went on to say

---

[196] [1988] 3 All ER 545, 649, 659.
[197] *W v Egdell* [1990] 1 All ER 835, 853.
[198] See para 3.19 above.
[199] cp *London Regional Transport v Mayor of London* [2001] EWCA Civ 1491. See also para 3.29 above.
[200] See generally K Cohen, 'Some Legal Issues in Counselling and Psychotherapy' (1992) 20 British J of Guidance and Counselling 10, 22. Self-interest (see para 12.23 below) does not seem an adequate explanation for disclosures of this nature unless self-interest is viewed from the perspective of the profession as a whole and then self-interest means essentially public interest. On the latter point see *Turner v Royal Bank of Scotland plc* [2001] EWCA Civ 64; [2001] 1 All ER (Comm) 1057, para 31.
[201] Case Note: 21451 (July 2001), NZ Privacy Commissioner, available at http://www.privacy-org.nz.
[201a] [2000] 1 All ER 786.
[202] The Court of Appeal adopted as its standard for assessing whether there was a breach of confidence the conscience of the reasonable pharmacist: [2000] 1 All ER 786, 796. It is, however, debatable whether the information disclosed, given its anonymous form, had the requisite quality of

D. Disclosure Without Iniquity

that the public interest might, in any event, justify the disclosure of confidential personal information about identifiable individuals:

> [F]or certain limited purposes patient information is used in identifiable rather than anonymised form. As the Department states:
>
> 'thorough research and management depend in part upon the possibility of others checking that anonymised and aggregated information does correspond to the real world, by audit procedures which must inevitably involve checking identifiable cases.'
>
> [P]rovided . . . the use of such identifiable data is very strictly controlled, there appears to be no reason to doubt that this is acceptable—whether because it falls within the public interest defence or as is perhaps the preferable view, because the scope of the duty of confidentiality is circumscribed to accommodate it.[203]

11.45 The GMC's position on use of patient information for research purposes[204] is that the express and informed consent of the patient should normally be obtained but confidential personal information can be used without consent[205] if obtaining consent is not practicable provided the lack of consent has been drawn to the attention of a research ethics committee and the latter has concluded that the likely benefit of the research outweighs the need for confidentiality.[206]

Implications of the Human Rights Act 1998

11.46 Disclosure of confidential personal information without consent for purposes of training, research and similar reasons will prima facie violate Article 8(1) of the ECHR but provided the interference is proportionate it may be justifiable as being necessary 'in a democratic society in the interests of . . . public safety or the economic well-being of the country . . . for the protection of health or morals, or for the protection of the rights and freedoms of others'.[207] Proportionality will depend upon there being efficient and adequate safeguards against improper dissemination and use of the information[208] and, semble, no feasible means of obtaining consent.

Interference with legal confidentiality

11.47 There is one case from another jurisdiction involving disclosure of personal information by a lawyer for a purpose that cannot have been foreseen, and therefore

---

confidentiality (see para 5.08 above) required for information to be subject to an obligation of confidentiality in the first place.

[203] per Simon Brown LJ, [2000] 1 All ER 786, 800. Cp *AB v CD* (1851) 14 D 177, 179–180.
[204] The GMC guidance does not envisage use of confidential patient information for teaching or audit purposes without consent.
[205] So long as consent has not been refused.
[206] *Confidentiality: Protecting and Providing Information* (June 2000) para 31. Criteria for deciding when it is ethical to dispense with patient consent in epidemiological research are suggested by L Doyle, 'Informed consent in medical research' (1997) 314 British Medical J 1107.
[207] Art 8(2).
[208] *A Health Authority v X* [2001] Lloyd's Rep Med 349 and see para 10.10 above.

consented to, by the client but which was arguably in the public interest. Notwithstanding the very strict approach of the courts to LPP, it is likely that were the facts of *R v Jack* to be repeated in England the decision of the Manitoba Supreme Court would be followed. Jack was accused of murdering his wife who, shortly before her death, had sought advice from a lawyer about a divorce. The husband objected to the deceased's lawyer giving evidence of what was said. Scott CJM ruled that 'if the evidence of the lawyer strayed into communications of a confidential nature, it was in the interests of both the client, Christine Jack, and the administration of justice that the communications in question be admitted in evidence'.[209]

11.48 It seems improbable that the Law Society or the English courts would accept that confidential legal records that have not been completely anonymized can be used (as medical information probably can) without client consent for the purposes of research.[210] On the one hand, there is not the same pressing social need for the fruits of legal research as medical research and on the other, the courts attach greater sanctity to legal confidences than to any other.

Protecting third parties

Disclosing information to protect third parties

11.49 A client's condition or activities though not in any way criminal or misleading may expose third parties to an unacceptable risk of harm. Examples include:

- the person who, although unfit to drive because of poorly controlled diabetes or epilepsy or a serious cardiac condition, refuses to give up driving;[211]
- the medical professional who suffers from a complaint that may be transmitted to patients;[212]
- the employee whose state of health threatens the safety of his fellow workers.

---

[209] (1992) 70 CCC (3d) 67, 91. The judge also held (at 90) that legal privilege 'cannot be invoked by a party whose interest in the proceedings is manifestly contrary to that of the client'.

[210] Given the judicial pronouncements that LPP lasts forever (see para 16.28 below), historical researchers may have a problem.

[211] The GMC says that a doctor may inform the medical adviser at the DVLA that a patient has ignored health-related warnings to stop driving: GMC, *Confidentiality: Protecting and Providing Information 2000* supplement faq. By analogy a doctor would be entitled to warn the police that it is unsafe for a mentally unstable patient to possess firearms.

[212] See DoH, *AIDS/HIV Infected Health Care Workers: Guidance on the Management of Infected Health Care Workers and Patient Notification* (1999) paras 6.8, 10.3. For new draft guidelines see DoH, *HIV Infected Health Care Workers* (September 2002), available at http://www.doh.gov.uk/aids.htm. This states at para 10.3 that 'the identity of infected individuals may be disclosed with their consent or without consent in exceptional circumstances where it is considered necessary for the purpose of treatment, or prevention of spread of infection'. As to whether a doctor is entitled to notify the sexual partner of a patient who has been diagnosed as being HIV without the patient's consent see paras 11.58 et seq.

D. Disclosure Without Iniquity

In *Re C*[213] a doctor volunteered to solicitors acting for a couple who were seeking to adopt a baby against the wishes of the mother that the baby's mother, her patient, was unfit to care for the baby. The court expressed the opinion, albeit obiter, that the doctor had not breached her duty of confidence to her patient.

Impact of the Human Rights Act 1998

Had Article 8 of the ECHR been part of domestic law at the time that *Re C* was decided, the disclosure could have been easily defensible despite the interference with the mother's right to respect for private life as necessary for the 'protection of health' and 'protection of the rights or freedoms of [the baby]'.[214] Disclosure of confidential information by a professional without client consent is unlikely to be justified unless the danger to a third party is both serious and immediate.[215] In *X v Y*[216] a health authority obtained an injunction against a journalist and newspaper to restrain use of leaked information about two practising doctors who had contracted AIDS. Since the doctors presented no hazard to patients,[217] Rose J concluded that the public interest in protecting the confidentiality of the medical records of AIDS victims who might otherwise be deterred from seeking treatment exceeded the public interest in the press's freedom to publish. The judge pointed out that discussion about AIDS and about the wisdom of doctors with the disease continuing to practise was not stifled by suppressing the leaked information; a general debate on this very subject had already taken place in the columns of the defendant's newspaper.[218]

11.50

Parameters of the public interest

The kind of risk to which the third party is exposed does not have to be physical. One can see why such a restriction would be unjust from the facts of *R v Ross*.[219] Ross was convicted by a jury of sexual assault after a trial at which he and the complainant gave radically different accounts of events in his apartment. When the complainant's former psychiatrist heard of Ross's conviction he became alarmed that there might have been a miscarriage of justice because of the possibility that

11.51

---

[213] [1991] 2 FLR 478, 484, 486. cp *Simonsen v Swenson* (1920) 177 NW 831. See also *Re R* [1998] 1 FLR 433 where the court condoned disclosure to the chief probation officer of advice received by the Official Solicitor from a consultant psychiatrist about the father of two young children, the subject of contact proceedings. That advice suggested that the continued employment of the father as a probation officer—a job that brought him into contact with families, the young and the vulnerable—might not be in the public interest.

[214] Art 8(2). cp *TV v Finland Application* 21780/93, 76A DR 140.

[215] cp *Jansen van Vuuren NNO v Kruger* 1993(4) SA 842 (A).

[216] [1988] 2 All ER 648, 661. cp *H (A Healthcare Worker) v Associated Newspapers Ltd* [2002] EWCA Civ 195; [2002] EMLR 23.

[217] [1988] 2 All ER 648, 653, 654–655.

[218] It is questionable whether Art 10 would allow a court today to agree with Rose J ([1988] 2 All ER 648, 657–658, 661) that publication that HIV doctors were working in the NHS should be suppressed if all means of identifying them were removed.

[219] 1993 NSR (2d) LEXIS 1982; 121 NSR (2d) 242 (CA); 1993 NSR (2d) LEXIS 1981; 119 NSR (2d) 177 (SC). J Dawson, 'Compelled Production of Medical Records' [1998] McGill LJ 25, 54.

the complainant had hallucinated.[220] The psychiatrist—arguably in breach of the Canadian Medical Association Code of Ethics[221]—voluntarily notified the Crown of his fears (without disclosing specific information) and the Crown alerted the defence. The defence applied to the Nova Scotia Court of Appeal for permission to conduct a discovery of the psychiatrist, which was granted. Subsequently a retrial based on the new evidence from the psychiatrist was ordered.

11.52 In England at first instance a judge has upheld on public interest grounds the banking practice of supplying certain credit reference agencies with information about customer debt without customer knowledge or consent. Unfortunately, when the case went on appeal the Court of Appeal did not consider whether this decision was correct.[222] In *B (A Minor) v RP*, an adoption application by the natural father of a child born to an unmarried mother, Butler-Sloss LJ criticized the unwillingness of social services to trace the fathers of children born to unmarried women who wanted the child put up for adoption without the father learning of the birth. 'Confidentiality', she said, 'is not in itself a reason for not giving the father an opportunity to be heard as to the future of his child.'[223] This presumably means that if a social worker does promise confidentiality to the mother, that promise can be broken in the wider public interest.

E. Genetic Information[224]

Does the public interest excuse apply?

11.53 There has been speculation as to whether the public interest excuse would justify disclosure of genetic information without patient consent when genetic testing discloses that a patient has a serious genetic disorder that has familial implications and the patient declines to pass this information on to affected relatives. This type of case has features that distinguish it from other situations in which a third party is at risk of physical harm:

(1) the source of the risk of harm to the third party is not the client's conduct;
(2) the third party may not want to be given the information;

---

[220] cp Employment Rights Act 1996, s 43B(1)(c) and para 21.25 below.
[221] This provides that a psychiatrist 'will keep in confidence information derived from his patient ... and divulge it only with the permission of the patient except when the law requires him to do so'. An annotation further provides that 'it is ethical to reveal confidential information when, in the opinion of the psychiatrist, the patient's behaviour is likely to endanger himself *and* others, and no alternative course will procure their safety' (italics added).
[222] *Turner v Royal Bank of Scotland plc* [2001] EWCA Civ 64; [2001] 1 All ER (Comm) 1057, para 31.
[223] [2001] 1 FLR 589, para 45.
[224] cp J Montgomery, *Health Care Law* (2nd edn, Oxford: 2002) 276–277; D Madden, *Medicine, Ethics and Law* (Dublin: 2002) 102–106.

E. Genetic Information

(3) genetic information is unique in that it goes to the very essence of who and what an individual is.

The BMA[225] is at one with the Nuffield Council on Bioethics,[226] the Human Genetics Commission,[227] the World Medical Association,[228] the World Health Organization[229] and the Council of Europe[230] in the belief that a health care professional may be justified in overriding the patient's desire for absolute confidentiality. The House of Commons Science and Technology Committee, on the other hand, wants no disclosure without the patient's approval.

11.54

> [I]f counselling cannot persuade someone to consent to sharing information with their relatives the individual's decision to withhold information should be paramount.[231]

If a warning would enable a relative to avoid a serious illness in the future, the moral case for disclosure by the professional without patient consent is a powerful one.

The difficulty is in knowing whether—and if so, when—an English court would allow a health care professional to ignore the wishes of the patient on public interest grounds. Society pays a price, sometimes a very high one, for genetic illnesses in terms of the cost of medical treatment, lost productivity and human suffering. It can therefore be argued that a disclosure that reduces the number of persons born with, or predisposed to, serious genetic conditions and improves the prospects of those already born who have the genetic predisposition is not only in the interests of those who receive the warning but in the public interest.[232] The ECHR permits the right to respect for private life, which protects medical confidentiality,[233] to be breached to protect the rights of others[234] and the DPA allows sensitive personal information to be disclosed when this is necessary to protect the vital interests of another person.[235]

11.55

---

[225] *Human Genetics—Choice and Responsibility* (Oxford: 1998) 71.
[226] Nuffield Council on Bioethics, *Genetic Screening: Ethical Issues* (London: 1993) para 5.3.
[227] *Inside Information* (May 2002) para 3.68.
[228] Declaration on the Human Genome Project, 44th World Medical Assembly (Spain, 1992), available at http://www.wma.net/e/policy/17-s-1_e.html.
[229] WHO, *Proposed International Guidelines on Ethical Issues in Medical Genetics and Genetic Services* (Geneva: 1997) para 9.
[230] Council of Europe, *On Genetic Testing and Screening for Health Care Purposes*, Recommendation R (92) 3, principle 9.
[231] *Human Genetics: The Science and Its Consequences*, Report of the House of Commons Science and Technology Committee (London: 1995), para 228.
[232] C Ngwena and R Chadwick, 'Genetic Diagnostic Information and the Duty of Confidentiality: Ethics and Law' (1993) 1 Medical L Intl 73, 81. See also W Flanagan, 'Genetic Data and Medical Confidentiality' (1995) 3 Health LJ 269; D Bell and B. Bennett, 'Genetic Secrets and the Family' [2001] Medical L Rev 130, 148.
[233] See para 3.03 above.
[234] Art 8(2).
[235] See paras 18.19–18.20.

When is disclosure in the public interest?

11.56 The GMC has offered no guidance on when disclosure is appropriate but there is guidance elsewhere.[236] The Social Issues Subcommittee on Familial Disclosure of the American Society of Human Genetics has recommended that disclosure without consent be confined to exceptional circumstances, these being where: attempts to encourage disclosure on the part of the patient have failed; the harm is highly likely to occur and is serious, imminent, and foreseeable; the at-risk relative is identifiable; and the disease is preventable, treatable or medically accepted standards indicate that early monitoring will reduce the genetic risk.[237] The BMA's advice is similar. The doctor should consider:

1. The severity of the disorder;
2. the level of predictability of the information provided by testing;
3. what, if any, action the relatives could take to protect themselves or to make informed reproductive decisions, if they were told of the risk;
4. the level of harm or benefit of giving and withholding the information; and
5. the reason given for refusing to share the information.[238]

11.57 The BMA factors mirror those mentioned in *W v Egdell*,[239] *R v Crozier*[240] and *Re C*[241] as being relevant to a decision to disclose patient information in the public interest: magnitude of harm, the degree of risk and the extent to which disclosure would avert or reduce that risk.[242] It is implicit in the BMA guidelines that the benefit of disclosure to those at risk should be considerable and outweigh any distress non-consenting disclosure might cause to the patient.[243] Another factor that would weigh with a court is whether disclosure is possible without identifying the patient.[244] The courts attach great importance to maintaining medical confidentiality[245] and if disclosure is likely to discourage patients from undergoing testing

---

[236] eg Ontario IRC, *Report on Genetic Testing* (Ontario: 1996) 226; Nuffield Council on Bioethics, *Genetic Screening: Ethical Issues* (London: 1993) para 5.31.

[237] B Knoppers et al, 'Professional Disclosure of Familial Genetic Information' (1998) 62 American J of Human Genetics 474.

[238] BMA, *Human Genetics—Choice and Responsibility* (Oxford: 1998) 72. These factors could be expanded to include also the reliability and accuracy of the genetic testing and the protections afforded to the tested individual against discrimination: D Bell and B Bennett, 'Genetic Secrets and the Family' [2001] Medical L Rev 130, 156.

[239] [1990] 1 All ER 835.

[240] (1990) 8 BMLR 128.

[241] [1991] 2 FLR 478, 484, 486.

[242] C Ngwena and R Chadwick, 'Genetic Diagnostic Information and the Duty of Confidentiality: Ethics and Law' (1993) 1 Medical L Intl 73, 81–84.

[243] This guideline is recommended by the Human Genetics Commission, *Inside Information* (May 2002) 3.68.

[244] cp *R v Department of Health, ex p Source Informatics Ltd* [2000] 1 All ER 786. The Human Genetics Commission, *Inside Information* (May 2002) para 3.68 recommends that the information be, as far as possible, anonymized but in a family context this is often impossible.

[245] *Ashworth v MGN* [2001] 1 All ER 991, 1012.

F. HIV Infection

and treatment this must be kept in mind.[246] As regards the extent of the disclosure, the WMA restricts this to 'the relevant genetic information'.[247] The Human Genetics Commission says that the information disclosed should be 'restricted to that which is strictly necessary for the communication of risk'.[248] One would expect an English court to agree with this.

F. HIV Infection[249]

11.58 There is a broad ethical consensus that a doctor is entitled to breach confidentiality to a patient as a last resort to protect a third party from HIV infection. The Council of Europe has recommended that '*as a general rule* there is no partner notification without the consent of the patient' but envisages non-consensual disclosure in an 'extreme case where a patient refuses to cooperate in the notification of an unsuspecting third party known to the health care worker'.[250] The GMC's position is that a doctor:

> *may* disclose information about a patient, whether living or dead, in order to protect a person from risk of death or serious harm. For example, you *may* disclose information to a known sexual contact of a patient with HIV where you have reason to think that the patient has not informed that person, and cannot be persuaded to do so. In such circumstances you should tell the patient before you make the disclosure, and you must be prepared to justify a decision to disclose information.[251]

11.59 In view of these guidelines, it is probable that if an infected patient evinces signs of deliberately or recklessly infecting someone who is not infected, for example, by refusing to use condoms or to stop sharing needles, disclosure of the danger to the person at risk can be justified[252] as being in the public interest[253] notwithstanding the possibility that anything less than absolute confidentiality might keep some

---

[246] *X v Y* [1988] 2 All ER 648.
[247] Declaration on the Human Genome Project, 44th World Medical Assembly (Spain, 1992).
[248] *Inside Information* (May 2002) para 3.68.
[249] J Montgomery, *Health Care Law* (2nd edn, Oxford: 2002) 268–9.
[250] Recommendation R (89) 14 (24 October 1989).
[251] GMC, *Serious Communicable Diseases: Guidance to Doctors* (October 1997) italics added, available from http://www.gmc-uk.org.
[252] In *Chizmar v Mackie* 896 P 2d 196, 208 (1995) a US court held that when a physician diagnoses a patient with a fatal sexually transmitted disease such as HIV, the physician's disclosure of this diagnosis to the patient's spouse is privileged as a matter of law.
[253] Knowingly engaging in high-risk behaviour with an unsuspecting partner is a criminal offence in Canada: *R v Cuerrier* [1998] 2 SCR 371. See also *HMA v Kelly* (HC Glasgow, 23 March 2001) where an HIV positive man who transmitted the infection to an unsuspecting partner was convicted of 'reckless and culpable conduct'. Therefore in disclosing the information the doctor may be preventing iniquity. See further R Wacks, *Personal Information, Privacy and the Law* (Oxford: 1989) 189 and M Jones, *Medical Negligence* (London: 1996) 2–117. Although HIV infection is sensitive personal data, the DPA allows this to be disclosed without the client's consent to protect the vital interests of a third party: DPA, Sch 3, para 3.

people from undergoing HIV testing.[254] In *TV v Finland*[255] the Commission upheld the disclosure of a prisoner's HIV status to prison staff saying that this was necessary for the protection of their health and other rights. The pros and cons of disclosure are more evenly balanced when the issue is whether to alert a partner who is probably already infected. Whose autonomy matters more: that of the patient or that of the individual who, if not told, cannot decide to seek treatment?

G. Procedural and Miscellaneous Matters

Mental state and motive of the professional

11.60 There is no public interest in the disclosure of iniquity or potential harm that is a figment of the professional's imagination. Therefore the professional's suspicions or concerns must be reasonably held (albeit they may turn out to have been mistaken).[256]

> [A] mere allegation of iniquity is not of itself sufficient to justify disclosure in the public interest. Such an allegation will only do so if, following such investigations as are reasonably open to the recipient, and having regard to all the circumstances of the case, the allegation in question can reasonably be regarded as being a credible allegation from an apparently reliable source.[257]

When disclosure is to the public at large it seems that there must be prima facie evidence of the iniquity or other danger.[258]

11.61 Some cases say that the motive of the person making a public interest disclosure is irrelevant.

> There is confidential information which the public may have a right to receive and others, in particular the press, now extended to the media, may have a right and even a duty to publish, even if the information has been unlawfully obtained in flagrant breach of confidence *and irrespective of the motive of the informer*.[259]

---

[254] This is an empirical question to which there is not at present a clear answer: I Kerridge, M Lowe and J McPhee, *Ethics and Law for the Health Professional* (North Sydney: 1998) 281.

[255] Application 21780/93, 76A DR 140.

[256] *Malone v Commissioner of Police of the Metropolis (No 2)* [1979] 2 All ER 620, 646. The care taken in reaching the disclosure decision may be evidence of an honest and reasonable belief (or lack thereof). Belief matters if false information is disclosed and the professional is sued in defamation: para 4.36 above.

[257] per Lord Goff, *Att-Gen v Guardian Newspapers Ltd (No 2)* [1988] 3 All ER 545, 660. cp *Hellewell v Chief Constable of Derbyshire* [1995] 1 WLR 804, 810.

[258] *Re A Company's Application* [1989] 2 All ER 248, 252. See also *Att-Gen v Guardian Newspapers Ltd (No 2)* [1988] 3 All ER 545, 644.

[259] *Lion Laboratories Ltd v Evans* [1984] 2 All ER 417, 422 per Stephenson LJ (italics added). See also *Re A Company's Application* [1989] 2 All ER 248, 251.

G. Procedural and Miscellaneous Matters

Others assume the opposite.[260] As a matter of principle, if the disclosure is in the public interest, it does not become less so because the disclosing party was motivated by the financial rewards of disclosure (something that was almost certainly true of the defendant in *Woodward v Hutchins*).[261] Greed may, nonetheless, be relevant in so far as it may cause the professional to disclose the information to an inappropriate person[262] or more information than necessary or put into question the honesty and reasonableness of the belief that disclosure was in the public interest. If the professional is in employment an improper motive might affect the fairness of a dismissal.

Manner of disclosure

Recipients

The public interest that prevents formation of an obligation of confidence, or alternatively, provides a defence to an action based on breach of such an obligation, does not give a professional carte blanche to disclose confidential personal information to whomsoever she pleases. It is only in the public interest to disclose confidential information to an appropriate recipient.[263] **11.62**

> Even if the balance comes down in favour of publication, it does not follow that publication should be to the world through the media. In certain circumstances the public interest may be better served by a limited form of publication perhaps to the police or some other authority who can follow up a suspicion that wrongdoing may lurk beneath the cloak of confidence.[264]

In *W v Egdell* Bingham LJ said:

> A consultant psychiatrist who becomes aware, even in the course of a confidential relationship, of information which leads him, in the exercise of what the court considers a sound professional judgment, to fear that . . . decisions may be made on the basis of inadequate information and with a real risk of consequent danger to the public is entitled to take such steps as are reasonable in all the circumstances to communicate the grounds of his concern *to the responsible authorities*.[265]

---

[260] *Initial Services Ltd v Putterill* [1967] 3 All ER 145, 149. It was considered significant in *London Regional Transport v Mayor of London* [2001] EWCA Civ 149, para 40 that a disclosure in breach of an express contractual promise of confidentiality was not made for private gain.

[261] [1977] 1 WLR 760.

[262] *W v Egdell* [1989] 1 All ER 1089, 1102. On the subject of to whom disclosure should be made see para 11.60 above.

[263] *Initial Services Ltd v Putterill* [1967] 3 All ER 145, 148; *Francome v Mirror Group Newspapers* [1984] 1 WLR 892, 898. The professional code may expressly restrict disclosure to appropriate people, eg British Association for Counselling, *Code of Ethics and Practice for Counsellors* (Rugby: 1997) para B.3.4.2, available from http://www.bac.co.uk.

[264] per Lord Griffiths, *Att-Gen v Guardian Newspapers Ltd (No 2)* [1988] 3 All ER 545, 649–650. See also *Imutran Ltd v Uncaged Campaigns Ltd* [2001] 2 All ER 385, para 20.

[265] [1990] 1 All ER 835, 853 (italics added).

11.63 The responsible authorities may be a Minister of the Crown,[266] or the police,[267] or some other relevant public agency[268] such as the Crown Prosecution Service[269] or, particularly where the professional is an accountant, the Serious Fraud Office, or the disciplinary body of the relevant profession.[270] When a particular individual is at risk it may be right to disclose the information to that person or those responsible for his welfare.[271] In *R v Devon County Council, ex p L*[272] parents of young children who were in contact with a man suspected of (but never prosecuted for) indecently assaulting a 4-year-old child were given a warning by social workers. A court refused to intervene.

11.64 There are sound reasons for limiting the audience to whom disclosure is made to public authorities if this is possible. These 'will be under a duty not to abuse the confidential information and to use it only for the purpose of their inquiry. If it turns out that the suspicions are without foundation, the confidence can then still be protected'.[273] To ensure this a court can extract an undertaking from the professional to limit disclosure to the responsible authorities and not to publicize the fact of disclosure.[274] A second advantage is that public authorities may be able to protect the identity of the informant. In *Solicitor-General of Canada v Royal Commission of Inquiry into Confidentiality of Health Records in Ontario*[275] the Supreme Court held that the police informer privilege allows the police to withhold from criminal and civil proceedings the identity of a physician who voluntarily passes on confidential information about a patient without the latter's consent, except where disclosure of the identity of the informer could help to show that an accused is innocent of an offence for which he is on trial.[276]

---

[266] cp *W v Egdell* [1990] 1 All ER 835.
[267] *Malone v Commissioner of Police for the Metropolis (No 2)* [1979] 2 All ER 620, 635, 646; *R v Singleton* [1995] 1 Cr App R 431. The police would not be an appropriate choice if they have an interest in suppressing the information. In *Cork v McVicar*, The Times, 31 October 1984 Scott J decided that disclosure of police corruption by the press was justifiable.
[268] *Initial Services Ltd v Putterill* [1967] 3 All ER 145, 148; *Re A Company's Application* [1989] 2 All ER 248; *Imutran v Uncaged Campaigns Ltd* [2001] 2 All ER 385, paras 25–26.
[269] In *R v Crozier* (1991) 8 BMLR 128 the psychiatrist made his disclosure to prosecuting counsel.
[270] *Woolgar v Chief Constable and UKCC* [1999] 3 All ER 604. cp *Re L* [2000] 1 FLR 913.
[271] Whether there is any kind of duty to make disclosure is pursued in ch 20.
[272] [1991] 2 FLR 541.
[273] *Att-Gen v Guardian Newspapers Ltd (No 2)* [1988] 3 All ER 545, 649. See also para 10.39 above.
[274] *Re a Company's Application* [1989] 2 All ER 248, 252.
[275] [1981] 2 SCR 494, 537. For English authority on the police-informer privilege (a form of public interest immunity) see: *Marks v Beyfus* (1890) 25 QBD 494, 498; *R v Turner* [1995] 1 WLR 264. Police-informer privilege has been applied in England by analogy to the National Society for the Prevention of Cruelty to Children: see *D v NSPCC* [1977] 1 All ER 589.
[276] The Supreme Court held, further, that it did not matter whether the disclosure was lawful or unlawful: '[t]he privilege . . . is not given to the informer and, therefore, misconduct on his part does not destroy the privilege. The privilege is that of the Crown . . .' per Martland J [1981] 2 SCR 494, 538.

G. Procedural and Miscellaneous Matters

Before the HRA a professional who disclosed confidential personal information directly to the media had to convince a court that some lesser form of disclosure would not have sufficed. Defendants succeeded where the responsible authorities had publicly committed themselves to a position at variance with the information,[277] or had failed to act.[278] The prominence given to Article 10 in HRA, s 12 has encouraged a more lenient approach. In *Theakston v MGN Ltd* Ouseley J rejected the argument that the defendant newspaper should have told the BBC, who employed the claimant as a TV presenter, that the claimant had visited a Mayfair brothel instead of publishing the information in the Sunday People.

11.65

> The free press is not confined to the role of confidential police force; it is entitled to communicate directly with the public for the public to reach its own conclusions.[279]

How much may be disclosed

When information is disclosed in the public interest it should be kept to the minimum necessary to achieve that purpose.[280] Like the question whether disclosure should occur at all, the degree of legitimate disclosure may involve fine judgments. The Canadian Supreme Court was divided as to how much could lawfully be disclosed by the doctor in *Jones v Smith*.[281] The authors of a casebook on medical law suggest that 'the revelation that a woman is HIV positive . . . may occasionally be justified. A doctor who, at the same time, points out that this was discovered in the course of an abortion procedure will be in breach of confidence.'[282]

11.66

In *JD v Ross*[283] a psychologist was found to have exceeded the limits of what the public interest might have entitled him to disclose about the claimant, a man accused of (but in the end not prosecuted for) sexually abusing his adopted daughter. The defendant had informed the New Zealand equivalent of social services, who were caring for the girl, that the father had telephoned requesting information

11.67

---

[277] This was the position in *Lion Laboratories Ltd v Evans* [1984] 2 All ER 417, 435. cp *Cork v McVicar*, The Times, 31 October 1984.
[278] *Att-Gen v Guardian Newspapers (No 2)* [1988] 3 All ER 545, 650. In *Jockey Club v BBC* [2002] EWHC 1866, QB the BBC argued that the responsible public authority, the Jockey Club, was not doing enough about corruption in the horse racing industry. But apart from that, Grey J felt that the issues at stake—the integrity and fairness of bookmaking to the betting public—was one of proper and serious concern to the public as a whole (para 47).
[279] [2002] EWHC 137; [2002] EMLR 22, para 69. cp *Grobbelaar v NGN Ltd* [2001] 2 All ER 437, paras 47, 201.
[280] cp *Pharaon v BCCI* [1998] 4 All ER 455, 466.
[281] [1999] 1 SCR 455. Major J said that the authorities should have been told only that the doctor had formed the opinion as a result of a consultation that Jones posed a threat to prostitutes in the Vancouver area without disclosing substantive details of communications from Jones. The majority, on the other hand, sanctioned the disclosure of Jones' confession to the doctor of a plan to assault and kill a number of prostitutes in Vancouver and that the assault for which he had been arrested was a 'trial run' to see if he could 'live with' what he had done.
[282] M Stauch et al, *Sourcebook on Medical Law* (London: 1998) 259.
[283] [1998] NZFLR 38.

about counselling for himself, that he had referred the father to a Mr Jacobs, and that the father had previously consulted the defendant about an application to have his daughter sent to a school outside the district in which the family lived. The judge held that it was unnecessary in the girl's interests to pass on this information about the claimant. Sometimes non-essential information may have to be disclosed to set essential information in its proper context.[284]

11.68 When information is disclosed by a professional in the public interest, agreement between the professional and the recipient about the retention, further disclosure and use of the information is desirable[285] but may not always be possible. A professional who decides to disclose information in the public interest is best advised to keep detailed records about the circumstances of the disclosure and any colleagues who were consulted. These records will be crucial if the client sues the professional over the disclosure or complains about the professional to her professional body.

Taking advice before making the disclosure

11.69 A professional minded to breach a professional confidence in the public interest may wish to obtain legal advice or consult with a colleague before taking action. The better view is that disclosure of the information to a lawyer (who will be bound to keep the information secret) or to a colleague, in strictest confidence, is not actionable as a breach of confidence or of contract. This may be either because such an act does not count as a breach of confidence or, alternatively, although it does, disclosure for the purpose of obtaining advice about releasing client information is defensible as being in the public interest (even if subsequent disclosure to others might not be).[286]

Alerting the client to the disclosure

Ethics

11.70 Some professional codes advise a professional who thinks that confidential information should be divulged for reasons of public interest to first consult with the client and attempt to obtain his consent.[287] Guidance issued by the Law Society on confidentiality and privilege in child abuse and abduction situations states:

---

[284] *W v Egdell* [1990] 1 All ER 835, 853. See also *Campbell v MGN Ltd* [2002] EWCA Civ 1373.

[285] cp *Re R* [1998] 1 FLR 433.

[286] M Brindle and G Dehn, 'Confidence, Public Interest and the Lawyer' in R Cranston (ed), *Legal Ethics and Professional Responsibility* (Oxford: 1995) 119. cp Employment Rights Act 1996, s 43. D Brindle and Dehn suggest that a rule penalizing disclosure to a lawyer would fall foul of Art 6 of the ECHR.

[287] British Association for Counselling, *Code of Ethics and Practice for Counsellors* (Rugby: 1997) para B.S.4.1; Royal College of Psychiatrists, *Good Psychiatric Practice: Confidentiality* (London: 2000) 7.

G. Procedural and Miscellaneous Matters

> [I]f a solicitor is about to breach his or her duty of confidentiality there is a high expectation that the solicitor will tell the client of his or her decision and explore with the client how this should be done. However, in the end it is for the solicitor to exercise his or her professional judgment about when and how to explain the duty of confidentiality to any client; it is impossible to formulate a rule that can be applied in all circumstances. Any solicitor who tells the client that the solicitor will breach the duty of confidentiality should inform the client that the client is entitled to terminate the solicitor's retainer if such disclosure is contrary to the client's wishes.[288]

The GMC says that where disclosure of personal information without consent is justified, doctors 'should generally inform the patient before disclosing the information'.[289] It is obviously better for the professional-client relationship that information be disclosed with the consent of the client than without, and, in the absence of consent, with notice rather than without. In some circumstances, forewarning a client about an intention to disclose information without consent may persuade the client to take steps that eliminate the need for the disclosure. If there are reasons for avoiding advance notice, notification after the event may be a requirement of the relevant code of ethics.[290]

Law

Whether notice to the client before or after disclosure is ever a legal requirement is another matter. Dr Egdell did not warn W of what he was planning to do.[291] He was not criticized for this by any of the courts that considered W's action against him. There may, however, be circumstances in which a client must be informed of a proposed disclosure. In *R v Chief Constable of North Wales, ex p AB* Lord Woolf MR said this about the failure of the police to seek the views of the applicants, convicted paedophiles who had been released from prison, before warning the public of their presence in a locality:

11.71

> [T]he police require as much information as can reasonably practicably be obtained in the circumstances. In the majority of the situations which can be anticipated, it will be obvious that the subject of the possible disclosure will often be in the best position to provide information which will be valuable when assessing the risk. In this case the gist of what Det Sgt Lewis had learnt about the applicants should have been disclosed to them. At least consideration should have been given as to whether to disclose the report from the Northumbria Police. This did not happen and we were not made aware of any reason why there could not have been disclosure. The applicants might have had information which would have caused the sergeant to

---

[288] The Law Society, *The Guide to the Professional Conduct of Solicitors* (7th edn, London: 1996) Annex 16A, 297–298.
[289] GMC, *Confidentiality: Protecting and Providing Information* (June 2000) paras 36. See also para 39. cp Dfee, *Sex and Relationship Education Guidance* (July 2000) Dfee 0116/2000 para 7.6, available from http://www.dfee.gov.uk.
[290] eg BPS Division of Clinical Psychology, *Professional Practice Guidelines* (1995) para 6.1.3, available from http://www.bps.org.uk.
[291] *W v Egdell* [1989] 1 All ER 1089. Nor did Dr McDonald in *R v Crozier* (1991) 8 BMLR 128.

re-assess the degree of risk. . . . Having said that, we do not accept that any information which the applicants could have given, if they had been given the opportunity to comment, would have altered the outcome.[292]

In *Halls v Mitchell* in finding the defendant, a medical practitioner, liable for defamation, the Supreme Court of Canada was influenced inter alia by the fact that the disclosures by the defendant to the Compensation Board (made with the intention of thwarting a claim for compensation) were 'made secretly without communicating with the appellant giving him an opportunity of explanation . . .'.[293] In *ex p AB* Lord Woolf recognized that there may be good reason for not consulting with the affected person prior to the disclosure such as triggering the very thing that the professional is seeking to prevent by speaking out.[294]

H. Interceptors, Strangers and Third Parties

Third parties

11.72 It was assumed by Lord Donaldson MR in *Att-Gen v Guardian Newspapers (No 2)*[295] that the public interest defence is open to third parties and strangers and this has been confirmed.[296] It could indeed be argued that vis-à-vis an interceptor or stranger the client has no reasonable expectation of privacy[297] in information disclosing criminality or risk of injury to another and therefore no obligation of confidentiality arises. The public interest is a specific defence to the offence of obtaining, disclosing or procuring personal data or information in personal data under the DPA.[298] Lord Donaldson cautioned against the presumption that whenever the confidant can invoke the public interest a third party can do likewise, and vice versa.

> The third party recipient may be subject to some additional and conflicting duty which does not affect the primary confidant or may not be subject to some special duty which does affect that confidant. In such situations the equation is not the same . . . and accordingly the result may be different.[299]

---

[292] [1998] 3 All ER 310, 320. Query, whether only a public law duty and public disclosure trigger a duty to consult.

[293] per Duff J, [1918] 2 DLR 97, 116. See also *Woolgar v Chief Constable of Sussex Police* [1999] 3 All ER 504, 615 where Kennedy LJ said that if the police were minded to disclose the record of an interview with a suspect against whom no charges were brought to a professional body they should 'inform the person affected of what they proposed to do in such time as to enable that person, if so advised, to seek assistance from the court'.

[294] cp Institute of Family Therapy, *Code of Ethics*, para 7.2.

[295] See also *Pharaon v BCCI* [1998] 4 All ER 455, an action between a bank's customer and the bank's accountants, in which the accountants were able to rely on the public interest to disclose to a foreign court any documents relating to the customer that were relevant to an alleged fraud committed by the bank.

[296] *A v B plc & C ('Flitcroft')* [2002] EWCA Civ 337; [2002] 3 WLR 542.

[297] See para 6.14 above.

[298] DPA, s 55(2)(d).

[299] per Donaldson MR, *Att-Gen v Guardian Newspapers Ltd (No 2)* [1988] 3 All ER 545, 600. See also Scott J at first instance, ibid 480.

H. Interceptors, Strangers and Third Parties

The media compared to other third parties

11.73 This is easy to understand when one compares the situation of a professional to that of a media organization. A professional may be entitled to disclose confidential information in breach of an obligation of confidentiality to a client only to a limited category of persons.[300] Because the media has a duty to provide information to the public,[301] a media organization that obtains possession of the information may be entitled to publish the information to a much wider audience[302] or when the professional would not be entitled to publish the information at all.[303] The position must be that described by Scott J in *Att-Gen v Guardian Newspapers (No 2)* with 'professional' transposed for 'ex-officer of MI5' and client for 'government':

> [T]he balance to be struck as between the [client] and [the professional] is not . . . an identical balance to that which has to be struck between the [client] and the press. Here a duty of confidence is sought to be enforced against a newspaper which has come into possession of confidential information knowing it to be confidential, the existence and scope of the alleged duty will depend . . . on the relative weight of the public or private interests for the protection of which the duty is claimed, on the one hand, and of the public or private interests to be served by disclosure of the information on the other.[304]

The strength of the media's claim has been increased by the incorporation of Article 10 and by HRA, s 12.[305]

11.74 The media privacy codes,[306] which the courts must consider when contemplating relief that could have a chilling effect on media freedom,[307] give some indication of when it may be in the public interest to publish information to the world

---

[300] See para 11.62 above.
[301] 'There is confidential information which the public may have a right to receive and others, in particular the press, now extended to the media, may have a right and even a duty to publish . . .', per Stephenson LJ, *Lion Laboratories Ltd v Evans* [1984] 2 All ER 417, 422 (italics added). See also, *Re M* [1990] 1 All ER 205, 210.
[302] But see *Att-Gen v Guardian Newspapers Ltd (No 2)* [1988] 3 All ER 545, 600 : '[i]f the public interest forbids indiscriminate publication, but permits or requires that disclosure be to a limited category of person, e.g. the police, the government, the opposition or members of Parliament, the media will have a correspondingly limited right and duty', per Lord Donaldson MR. This comment was made in the pre-HRA era. See para 11.65 above. For a more liberal approach to press freedom see the judgment of Hoffmann LJ in *R v Central Independent Television plc* [1994] 3 All ER 641, 651 et seq. The media must not make allegations without carrying out such investigations as are open to it: para 11.60 above.
[303] eg, a professional might be required to keep the criminal history of a client secret, where the press might have a free hand to discuss the offender's criminal record, a matter of public record: see paras 5.21–5.22 above.
[304] [1988] 3 All ER 545, 580.
[305] See paras 8.13–8.14 above. And see *Theakston v MGN Ltd* [2002] EWHC 137; [2002] EMLR 22, para 69.
[306] Discussed at length in M Tugendhat and I Christie (eds), *The Law of Privacy and the Media* (Oxford: 2002) ch.13.
[307] See para 8.13 above. In *Campbell v Frisbee* [2002] EWCA Civ 1374, paras 24–25 the Court of Appeal left open the question whether the media's source coudl treat a media privacy code as setting standards by which to judge whether the source's disclosure of confidential personal information to the media was justified.

at large that invades an individual's privacy. The Independent Television Commission Code, for example, states that the public interest includes: '(i) detecting or exposing crime or a serious misdemeanour; (ii) protecting public health or safety; (iii) preventing the public from being misled by some statement or action of an individual or organization; (iv) exposing significant incompetence in public office' and 'ensuring the fair conduct of judicial proceedings or protecting public morals'.[308] The Code requires a public interest defence to be proportional to the interest served. 'Where, for example, there is a significant intrusion into an individual's private affairs, particularly where the individual is innocent of any offence and/or where there is a significant risk of distress, an important public interest is likely to be required.'[309] Public figures must expect greater scrutiny of their private lives than ordinary folk.[309a]

Interceptors and strangers

11.75 In *Malone v Commissioner of Police of the Metropolis (No 2)* Megarry VC was willing to apply the public interest defence to police who had tapped the claimant's telephone, thereby indicating that the defence is open to an interceptor. In *Malone* the interception was legal. What if it had not been?

> There is confidential information which the public may have a right to receive and others, in particular the press, now extended to the media, may have a right and even a duty to publish, *even if the information has been unlawfully obtained* in flagrant breach of confidence and irrespective of the motive of the informer.[310]

In *Francome v Mirror Group* tapes had been obtained by illegally bugging the telephone line of a well-known jockey. Sir John Donaldson MR did not think it in the public interest that the information should be disclosed to the public at large but accepted that if the tapes:

> reveal evidence of the commission of a criminal offence or a breach of the rules of racing . . . it may well be in the public interest that the tapes and all the information to be gleaned therefrom be made available to the police and to the Jockey Club. Accepting the defendants' expressed desire to promote the public interest, it will be open to them to apply to the appropriate minister of the Crown for authority to disclose all the information to one or other or both of these authorities.[311]

11.76 To say that illegality in the acquisition of information can be ignored (and when it is the press that is doing the disclosing, might be ignored because of the importance attached to press freedom)[312] does not mean this should invariably happen.[313]

---

[308] For the PCC's guidance see para 9.10 above.   [309] Programme Code 2.1(i).
[309a] *A v B plc & C ('Flitcroft')* [2002] EWCA Civ 337 para 11 (xii).
[310] per Stephenson LJ, *Lion Laboratories Ltd v Evans* [1984] 2 All ER 417, 422 (italics added).
[311] [1984] 1 WLR 892, 899.
[312] See *A v B plc & C ('Flitcroft')* [2002] EWCA Civ 337; [2002] 3 WLR 542, para 11, guideline x: '[b]ut the fact that the information is the result of unlawful activities does not mean that its publication should necessarily be restrained by injunction on the grounds of breach of confidence . . .', per Lord Woolf.
[313] A Coleman, *The Legal Protection of Trade Secrets* (London: 1992) 74.

Illegality covers a wide range of conduct from the mere tortious to serious crime; the means selected may be disproportionate to the end achieved. It is worth noting that whistleblowers who have been granted statutory protection for public interest disclosures cannot avail themselves of that protection if, by making the disclosure, they commit a criminal offence.[314]

I. The Public Interest and Privileged Communications

Privilege and the public interest excuse compared

11.77 The rebranding of LPP as a substantive rule of law that operates outside the litigation arena[315] raises issues about the interaction of LPP and the public interest defence. Formerly the fact that a document was protected by LPP did not inhibit a professional from disclosing it outside the judicial arena without the privilege-holder's consent when to do so was in the public interest. Now, prima facie, it is unlawful for the professional to disclose the document in any circumstance in which disclosure would involve a breach of LPP. There is no public interest exception to LPP. The nearest thing is the rule that there is no privilege in a communication 'sought or given for the purpose of effecting iniquity . . .'.[316] Iniquity in the context of LPP has, however, a fairly narrow meaning: it refers to a communication tainted by crime or fraud.[317] In *Crescent Farm (Sidcup) Sports Ltd v Sterling Offices Ltd*[318] the court refused to extend the doctrine to the tort of inducing breach of contract. The public interest as a defence to an action for breach of confidence extends far beyond crime and fraud.[319] And it includes crimes by associates of the client to which the client is not an accessory.

11.78 Consider *W v Egdell*.[320] Ten years after W had been committed to a mental institution as a result of pleading guilty to the manslaughter of a number of people, W's solicitors commissioned a report on W's mental state from a psychiatrist with the intention of using the report to back an application by W to a mental health review tribunal to be conditionally discharged or transferred to a regional secure unit. The report was unfavourable and W's solicitors decided to suppress it. On discovering this, Dr Egdell took it upon himself to disclose the report to the hospital at which W was being held. At first instance Scott J seems to have accepted that LPP prevented the report from being put before a mental health review

---

[314] See para 21.25 below.
[315] See paras 16.12 et seq.
[316] per Schiemann LJ, *Barclays Bank v Eustice* [1995] 4 All ER 511, 521. See also *Ventouris v Mountain* [1991] 1 WLR 607, 611.
[317] See paras 16.35 et seq.
[318] [1971] 3 All ER 1192.
[319] See paras 11.41 et seq.
[320] [1990] 1 All ER 835.

tribunal.[321] This had no repercussions for the disclosure of the report by Dr Egdell to the hospital because at that time LPP was viewed as purely a rule of evidence. Scott J said:

> The function of privilege is to protect material from being produced on discovery or being placed in evidence in legal proceedings. What is complained of in the present case is that Dr Egdell supplied a copy of his report to the hospital and, indirectly, to the Home Secretary. Legal professional privilege is not a basis on which this complaint can be constructed.[322]

In breach of confidence actions like *W v Egdell* it may no longer be possible to treat LPP as an irrelevance.[323]

How would W v Egdell fare today?

11.79 In *Russell McVeigh McKenzie Bartleet & Co v Auckland District Law Society*[324] at first instance Paterson J was confronted by a situation in which LPP was claimed for confidential documents which, but for the privilege claim, could be disclosed on the grounds of public interest. The facts briefly were that the claimants, a firm of solicitors, had provided the Law Society with documents relevant to a serious complaint of fraud involving one of the firm's former partners. They were provided under an agreement whereby LPP was not waived and the documents were not to be further copied by the investigating counsel. The Law Society breached this agreement and the claimants issued proceedings for delivery up of the documents. The Law Society entered a defence of public interest. Paterson J concluded that it was in the public interest to maintain public confidence in the Law Society and its ability 'to investigate complaints against the members of the profession in a proper manner'. Furthermore, the allegations against the former partner were very serious. Additional complaints against the former partner required a full investigation both in the public interest and in the interests of the legal profession. However, the public interest defence to an action for breach of confidence could not override LPP. His solution was to rely on the discretionary nature of the equit-able remedy to refuse to order delivery up of the documents.[324a] He ruled that the Law Society could retain the documents but was not to use them for the purpose of any investigation other than the initial complaint.[325]

11.80 The Canadian courts have reduced the area of potential conflict between LPP and the public interest defence by abandoning the idea that LPP is absolute.[326] The circumstances in which LPP may be lost have been enlarged to include:

---

[321] Though not oral evidence from Dr Egdell.
[322] [1989] 1 All ER 1089, 1108.
[323] cp paras 16.12–16.14 below.
[324] (HC, M 1539SD/99, 6 July 2000.)
[324a] See also *Istil Group Inc v Zahour* [2003] EWHC 165 (ch) paras 93–94.
[325] On appeal [2002] 1 NZLR 721 a majority of the Court of Appeal decided that LPP had been abrogated by statute and that, even if it had not been, LPP had been waived. Therefore it was unnecessary for the Court of Appeal to reconcile the public interest defence to breach of confidence with LPP.
[326] See para 16.25 below.

(1) disclosure in the interests of public security, where there is an imminent risk of serious bodily harm or death to an identifiable person or group;[327] and
(2) disclosure that establishes the innocence of an accused.[328]

The upshot is that in Canadian law the existence of a clear, serious and imminent threat to public safety empowers a professional (who need not be a lawyer)[329] to volunteer information to which LPP attaches to a court or to the police or to potential victims (as appropriate) without violating LPP.[330]

J. Tort Defences and the Public Interest[331]

There is no public interest defence as such to any tort action that might be brought by a client. However, the public interest is relevant to a number of defences to tort actions. A defendant sued for the tort of inducing a breach of contract can plead 'justification'.[332] The public interest is one way that this tort may be justified.[333] Justification is also a defence to the torts of unlawful interference with economic interests[334] and conspiracy.[335] An action for defamation will fail if the defendant can show that the statement was true or a fair comment on a matter of public interest.[336] Qualified privilege is available as a defence if the information was communicated to someone with an interest or duty to receive it by a defendant under a legal, social or moral duty to make the communication.[337] In an earlier chapter reference was made to the Law Commission's proposal that breach of confidence should become a statutory tort.[338] This tort, so far not enacted, was to be subject to a statutory defence of disclosure in the public interest.[339]

11.81

---

[327] *Smith v Jones* [1999] 1 SCR 455, 471, 485–490 and para 11.22 above. Major J (at 466) dissented on the grounds that although it was appropriate to allow privileged information to be disclosed on the grounds of a 'clear, serious and imminent' danger, to allow the privilege to be overridden (as in the instant case) 'to the extent of allowing disclosure of self-incriminating evidence ... might endanger the public more than the public safety exception would protect them'. Defence counsel might not refer dangerous clients to medical experts until after the trial, if at all.
[328] *Smith v Jones* [1999] 1 SCR 455, 477–478 . Contrast *R v Derby Magistrates' Court, ex p B* [1995] 4 All ER 526. See also para 16.27 below.
[329] See para 16.19 below.
[330] *Smith v Jones* [1999] 1 SCR 455.
[331] See Y Cripps, *The Legal Implications of Disclosure in the Public Interest* (2nd edn, London: 1994).
[332] *Brimelow v Casson* [1924]1 Ch 302, 311.
[333] *Church of Scientology v Kaufman* [1973] RPC 635, 648–649; *X v Y* [1988] 2 All ER 648, 661.
[334] Y Cripps, *The Legal Implications of Disclosure in the Public Interest* (2nd edn, London: 1994) 219.
[335] *Crofter Hand Woven Harris Tweed Co Ltd v Veitch* [1942] AC 435, 495; *Femis-Bank (Anguilla) Ltd v Lazer* [1991].
[336] See para 4.36 above.
[337] See para 4.46 above.
[338] See para 4.60 above.
[339] Law Commission Report 110, *Breach of Confidence* (Cmnd 8388, 1981) para 6.77.

K. Copyright and the Public Interest[340]

11.82 The ambit of the public interest defence is restricted in copyright cases because copyright is a property interest and application of the defence to copyright material is akin to expropriation of property without compensation.[340a] After the Court of Appeal's decision in *Hyde Park Residence Ltd v Yelland*[341] it was thought for a brief period that a copyright infringer could almost never rely on the public interest defence. Aldous LJ in *Yelland* stated the availability of the defence in copyright actions very narrowly:[342] the court has an inherent power to refuse to enforce copyright where use of the court's procedure to enforce copyright would offend against the policy of the law.[343] This might be because the material was 'immoral, scandalous or contrary to family life' or 'injurious to public life, public health or safety or the administration of justice'.[344] The Court of Appeal recanted in *Ashdown v Telegraph Group*,[345] an action for copyright infringement by Paddy Ashdown against the Sunday Telegraph, which had published on its front page an article about a meeting with Tony Blair in October 1997 about the possible formation of a coalition cabinet. The article had contained several verbatim quotations from his minutes of that meeting. Lord Phillips said that the public interest defence was less tightly circumscribed in copyright cases than Aldous LJ had thought; 'the circumstances in which public interest may override copyright are not capable of precise categorization or definition.'[346]

11.83 Copyright restricts freedom of expression, but generally this is justified. Its inhibiting effect on the dissemination of information is limited because it protects form and not content.[347] On rare occasions the inability to reproduce the exact text of copyright material may conflict with freedom of expression.[348] In such a case one of the statutory exceptions to copyright will usually apply; these include 'fair dealing' for the purpose of criticism or review, research, private study or reporting of current events.[349] If they do not, it may be necessary to invoke the public interest defence.[350] A professional might need to rely on the public interest

---

[340] G Davies, *Copyright and the Public Interest* (2nd edn, London: 2002) ch 4.
[340a] M Tugendhat and I Christie (eds), *The Law of Privacy and the Media* (Oxford: 2002) para 9.83.
[341] [2000] 3 WLR 215, para 43.
[342] Copyright, Designs and Patent Act 1988, s 171(3) specifically preserves 'any rule of law preventing or restricting the enforcement of copyright, on grounds of public interest or otherwise'.
[343] [2000] 3 WLR 215, para 64.
[344] ibid, para 66.
[345] [2001] 4 All ER 666.
[346] ibid, para 58.
[347] See para 5.86 above.
[348] cp *Fressoz v France* (2000) 31 EHRR 2.
[349] Copyright, Designs and Patents Act 1988, s 30. Photographs do not fall within the current events exception.
[350] [2001] 4 All ER 666, para 58.

K. Copyright and the Public Interest

defence when disclosing the unpublished work of the client for although unpublished work is not excluded from the fair dealing defence,[351] it is unlikely to apply to anything that has not been widely distributed.[352] Had the claimant in *W v Egdell*[353] made drawings of exploding bombs and corpses, Dr Egdell might have wished to submit copies with the report that he sent to the hospital authorities to add weight to his opinion that W was still a danger to the public and should be detained.[354] As the law now stands, to have done so would have been lawful.

---

[351] *Beloff v Pressdram Ltd* [1973] 1 All ER 241, 263.
[352] *Hyde Park Residences v Yellard* [2000] 3 WLR 215 paras 32–36.
[353] [1989] 1 All ER 1089. For the facts see para 4.12 above. In any case the 'fair dealing' defence might not allow such extensive reproduction: *A v B* [2000] EMLR 1007, para 16.
[354] cp *Nottinghamshire Healthcare NHS Trust v NGN Ltd* [2002] EWHC 409; [2002] EMLR 33, para 57.

12

OTHER LAWFUL VOLUNTARY DISCLOSURE

A. Disclosure in Client's Best Interests	12.02	C. Disclosure Motivated by Self-Interest	12.23
The Competent Adult	12.02	Breaching Confidentiality Defensively	12.23
The Incompetent Adult	12.09	Breaching Confidentiality Affirmatively	12.34
Children	12.11		
B. Disclosure With Statutory Authority	12.14		
Statutory Provisions Allowing the Disclosure of Confidential Information	12.14		

This chapter looks at circumstances in which the professional has a discretion to disclose confidential personal information about the client without the client's consent for reasons other than an overriding public interest. There may be some who are puzzled that 'need to know' appears nowhere in the chapter as a reason for non-consensual disclosure. This is because in the author's opinion the 'need to know' principle was developed to set limits to disclosure with consent[1] or disclosure in the public interest[2] and is not a free-standing justification for disclosing confidential personal information.[3]   **12.01**

A. Disclosure in Client's Best Interests

The Competent Adult

Competent clients must be consulted

Professionals are expected to act in the best interests of their clients[4] and therefore professionals sometimes try to excuse disclosure of information without the   **12.02**

---

[1] See ch 13.
[2] See ch 11 and *Birmingham DC v O* [1983] 1 All ER 497, 505.
[3] cp J Montgomery, *Health Care Law* (2nd edn, Oxford: 2002) 266: '[i]t may be more realistic to suggest that the justification for disclosure in "need to know" cases is the public interest.'
[4] eg Solicitors' Practice Rules 1990, r 1(c).

client's consent on the grounds that disclosure was in the client's best interests. In *Tournier v National Provincial and Union Bank of England* Scrutton LJ doubted that it was 'sufficient excuse for disclosure, in the absence of the customer's consent, that it was in the interests of the customer, *where the customer can be consulted and his consent or dissent obtained*'.[5] But for one aberrant case, the facts of which are set out below, there is no reason to think that what Scutton LJ said is not equally true for all professional-client relationships when it is possible to consult the client and obtain the client's consent.

12.03 The aberrant decision is *Howell-Smith v Price*,[6] an unreported judgment of the Court of Appeal. Consent to the disclosure made in this case, had it been sought from the client, would have been refused.[7] The jurisprudential basis on which the solicitor made the non-consensual disclosures is difficult to fathom. The claimant was a disturbed but not an incompetent woman[8] (certainly not at the time of the

---

[5] *Tournier v National Provincial and Union Bank of England* [1924] 1 KB 461, 481 (italics added). See also, ALRC 22, *Privacy* (1983) vol 1, 419. In *Guidance on Ethics for Occupational Physicians* (5th edn, London: 1999) 10, the Faculty of Occupational Medicine lists authorized disclosures without consent as including a disclosure that 'is clearly in the patient's interest *but it is not possible to seek consent*' (italics added).

[6] (CA, 26 April 1996.) Cp *R v Mid Glamorgan Family Health Services* [1995] 1 All ER 356 where the Court of Appeal decided that a doctor or health authority was entitled to *deny* a patient with a history of psychiatric problems access to his medical records if to allow him access would be detrimental to the patient's health. Nourse LJ at 363 said in passing that a 'doctor's general duty . . . is to act at all times in the best interests of the patient. Those interests would *usually* require that a patient's medical records should not be disclosed to third parties; conversely, that they should usually . . . be handed on by one doctor to the next or made available to the patient's legal advisers if they are reasonably required for the purposes of legal proceedings . . .' (italics added.) It is to be doubted that he meant to suggest (emergency medical treatment apart) that there might be unusual circumstances in which a doctor was entitled to disclose information about a patient with no mental health problem to a third party without the patient's express or implied consent.

[7] See also *R v P* [2001] NSWCA 473 where consent had been refused by the client but nonetheless the solicitor went ahead with the disclosures acting, in his view, in the client's best interests (paras 31–32). The case is distinguishable from *Howell-Smith* in that the client was alleged to be incapable of giving rational instructions to a solicitor (the respondent was her sixth solicitor) by reason of a mental illness. The disclosures were, moreover, made to a court in protective proceedings initiated by the solicitor.

[8] The Official Solicitor had defended an action against the claimant brought by her solicitor for unpaid professional fees (which supports an incompetence theory) but when these proceedings were over refused to act further for the claimant having concluded that she was able to handle her business affairs. A solicitor employed by the Official Solicitor wrote to the claimant: '[t]he Official Solicitor's role as guardian *ad litem* is limited to present proceedings which are, as I say, effectively at an end. I must therefore drop out of the picture as Dr Harding Price indicates that you are able to handle your business affairs and from our meeting and correspondence I believe this to be so'. It may be that the claimant was incompetent for the purposes of defending a legal action but not for the purposes of managing her day-to-day affairs. In *Masterman-Lister v Brutton & Co* [2002] EWCA Civ 1889, paras 12, 29, 58, 62, 72 the Court of Appeal said that capacity was issue and time specific and that different conclusions were possible in different contexts—particularly if a finding of incapacity must be backed by medical evidence in one context but not in another. It nevertheless seems improbable that the views of a client who is competent to manage her property and affairs can be ignored when deciding whether to report her doctor for unethical conduct.

proceedings) who suffered from episodes of mental illness. For many years she had been a patient of Dr Price, a consultant psychiatrist who had been managing her business affairs and exercised considerable influence over her. The claimant and Dr Price had reached an informal agreement whereby she was to assist him financially with the purchase of a private nursing home when the health authority contemplated closing the nursing home where she lived. On the advice of Dr Price's solicitor she saw the defendant, a solicitor (also called Price), to provide independent advice. The defendant, who had doubts about the ability of the claimant to manage her own affairs, considered the business arrangement between his client and Dr Price to be improper and, because of the absence of a written agreement, not in her best interests. Without being instructed to do so, he investigated Dr Price's behaviour towards the claimant. These investigations included discussions with third parties and culminated in a report to Mr Whitlock, the administrator of the nursing home where the claimant was a resident and Dr Price worked. A copy of the report was passed to the General Medical Council (GMC) and to the Regional Health Authority, which suspended Dr Price. The claimant regarded these actions as a breach of confidence. In the High Court Waller J decided that the solicitor had acted pursuant to a public law duty and said that

> where what the solicitor is concerned about is improper influence being brought to bear on his client which actually affects the instructions which the client is giving, there must be an entitlement in a solicitor to break any duty of confidence that there may be and report that matter to the authorities to enable some independent advice to be given to the client, and/or to make some check in relation to the activities of the person whom the solicitor is complaining [sic]

12.04 Piller LJ in the Court of Appeal disagreed about the public law duty—'[t]his case turns upon a solicitor's duty to his client'—and suggested that Waller J had stated the solicitor's entitlement to make the disclosure 'too broadly'. He, however, agreed with Waller J that the solicitor had acted lawfully.

> In our judgment Mr. Price had every reason to be concerned about the situation which existed... No criticism can be made of Mr. Price's actions. He had a duty to protect her position... [I]t was appropriate for him to report to Mr. Whitlock in the manner he did. Such a report to an employer should not of course be made lightly but in the circumstances of this case such action was required.

12.05 One asks oneself: why was it required? A solicitor's implied authority does not normally extend to disclosures of which he is aware that the client would disapprove if she knew[9] unless disclosure is compelled by statute or for an overriding public interest.[10] The likelihood that the client would have refused consent

---

[9] See para 13.40 below.
[10] A narrow view is taken by the Law Society of when disclosure by a solicitor is in the public interest: see para 11.15 above. This is consistent with the emphasis by the courts on the absolute character of LPP: see para 16.25 below.

unwisely had she been consulted is not a reason to by-pass the client.[11] If the explanation for the judgment is that the claimant was incompetent at the time the disclosure was made, the decision is out of step with authority that holds that the approval of the Court of Protection is needed for the disclosure of the affairs of an incompetent adult.[12]

'Best interests' and client autonomy

12.06 The conclusion that the client's 'best interests' is not an independent reason for disclosing personal information about a competent adult is, *Howell-Smith* apart, consistent with the law about consent to medical treatment. A mentally competent adult has an absolute right to refuse treatment for good reason, bad reason or no reason at all.[13] Further, no professional code of ethics seen by this writer treats the client's best interests *per se* as a valid ground for disclosure. This is not surprising. Leaving aside situations where the professional acts under agency powers,[14] voluntary disclosure of information about a client who has not been consulted when there is no medical emergency because disclosure is in that client's 'best interests' (as determined by the professional) severely compromises the client's autonomy.

12.07 For this reason, a non-consensual disclosure of personal information made in the client's 'best interests' by a public authority[15] would interfere with the client's Article 8 privacy rights. To be lawful the disclosure would have to satisfy the proportionality test and be for a purpose mentioned in Article 8(2).[16] Interference for the purpose of protecting the rights of *others* is a legitimate aim, but not interference for the purpose of protecting *other* rights of the individual who suffers the interference. There is one exception to this: the ECtHR accepts that Article 8 may be interfered with for the purpose of protecting the applicant's own health.[17] But even here, a test as broad and undefined as the client's 'best interests' might not

---

[11] *Re MB* (1997) 2 FLR 436.

[12] *Re W (EEM)* [1971] Ch 123 where Ungoed-Thomas J disapproved of a patient's doctor giving information about a patient's condition and prognosis without the approval of the Court of Protection to the patient's husband who was making enquiries for the purposes of divorcing her. Why should the fact that the disclosure in *Re W (EEM)* ibid was (possibly) against the client's best interests whereas in *Howell-Smith v Price* (see para 12.03 above) it was in the client's best interests make a difference to the need to involve the Court of Protection?

[13] *Re MB* (1997) 2 FLR 436.

[14] See para 13.39 below. Agency was not mentioned in *Howell-Smith v Price* (CA 26 April 1996).

[15] And possibly because of the horizontal effect of HRA, s 6 between any two parties: see para 3.05 above.

[16] See para 3.19 above.

[17] *Martin v UK* (1996) 21 EHHR CD 113. Query, does the exception include suicide prevention and stopping domestic violence suffered by the client and no one else? There is a need of an exception for a client who lacks the capacity to consent to disclosure but judicial approval might be necessary to avoid incompatibility with Art 8; cp *Masterman-Lister v Brutton & Co* [2002] EWCA Civ 1889, paras 16, 19.

A. Disclosure in Client's Best Interests

meet the need for legal certainty inherent in the requirement that any interference be in accordance with law.[18]

Emergencies

12.08 It is well established at common law that treatment, and therefore by implication, disclosure of medical information is permitted in a medical emergency[19] when it is impossible to consult the patient. Toulson and Phipps speculate that 'a court would be unlikely to hold that the doctor's duty of confidentiality extended to prevent him from taking what he believed to be necessary action for the purpose of saving [a clinically depressed] patient's life'.[20] This could be regarded as a medical emergency of sorts.[21] In *H (A Healthcare Worker) v Associated Newspapers Ltd*[22] the Court of Appeal approved the disclosure of the medical records of the patients of an HIV seropositive dentist to a health authority without the knowledge of the patients in order that the authority might decide whether it was necessary to hold a 'look-back' exercise to advise exposure prone patients. The disclosure was described as being in 'their best interests'.[23] There has been no occasion for the courts to consider whether there might be non-medical emergencies in which professionals might find it necessary to disclose information in a client's best interests without first seeking client consent. Global IT communications have greatly reduced the chances of a client being out of contact. It is possible that illness may prevent consultation but in these circumstances there may be an issue of competence.

The Incompetent Adult

12.09 The only person with authority to consent to anything (including disclosure of information) on behalf of an incompetent adult is a person who holds an activated enduring power of attorney.[24] An enduring power of attorney authorizes acts

---

[18] See para 3.19 above.
[19] See para 13.11 below. This does not necessarily apply if the patient gave specific instructions to the contrary before the emergency arose: cp. *Malette v Shulman* (1990) 67 DLR (4th) 321.
[20] R Toulson and C Phipps, *Confidentiality* (London: 1995) 155. See also *Weld-Blundell v Stephens* [1919] 1 KB 520, 527. In preventing suicide or serious self-harm it is possible to argue the professional acts in the public interest (a recognized head of disclosure) and not just in the client's best interests. Suicide is no longer a crime, but it is not encouraged; a person who assists someone to commit suicide can be prosecuted (*R (on the application of Pretty) v DPP* [2001] UKHL 61; [2002] 1 AC 800). The Law Society's professional ethics guidance team suggested in the Law Gazette (15 March 2002) that a solicitor would not be criticized for notifying the prison authorities that her client was contemplating suicide even though suicide does not involve a breach of the criminal law. cp Case Note: 5733 (July 2001) and Case Note: 30372 (June 2001) NZ Privacy Commissioner, available at http://www.privacy.org.nz.
[21] Lord Scarman has commented extrajudicially in L Scarman, 'Law and Medical Practice' in P Byrne (ed), *Medicine in Contemporary Society* (London: 1987) 137 that '[e]mergency is a big word . . .'. Interference with the Art 8 privacy right would be justified: see para 12.07 above.
[22] [2002] EWCA Civ 195; (2002) 65 BMLR 132.
[23] ibid, para 28. Surely this was an emergency? See para 10.07 above.
[24] On enduring powers of attorney see S Cretney and D Lush, *Enduring Powers of Attorney* (4th edn, Bristol: 1996).

Chapter 12: Other Lawful Voluntary Disclosure

relating to the donor's 'property and affairs'.[25] It does not permit proxy authorization of acts of a personal nature requiring skill or discretion or decisions concerning the donor's personal welfare.[26] Management and administration of the property and affairs of a person (the patient) who has not signed an enduring power of attorney and is 'incapable by reason of mental disorder' from managing and administering his property and affairs[27] falls to the Court of Protection. As part of its statutory remit to take all steps 'necessary and expedient' to secure 'the maintenance or other benefit of the patient' and administer the patient's 'affairs',[28] a term that has been broadly interpreted,[29] the Court of Protection can approve the disclosure of personal information.[30]

12.10 The Mental Health Act 1983, Pt IV permits treatment of an incompetent adult *for a mental disorder* without consent.[31] Department of Health guidelines state that other treatment is allowed without consent (provided consent was not refused in advance when the patient had the capacity to consent) when in the patient's 'best interests'. 'This doesn't just mean what might be best for the patient's physical health. It takes into account their general well-being and what they're known to believe in.'[32] In *Re A* Dame Elizabeth Butler-Sloss stated that 'best interests encompasses medical, emotional and all other welfare issues'.[33] Disclosure of personal information in aid of lawful treatment must be lawful.

Children

The best interests of the child as a ground for disclosure

12.11 In exceptional circumstances a professional may disclose confidential personal information about a child-client in the 'best interests' of the child without first obtaining either the consent of the parent or that of the child, should the child have the maturity to consent to the disclosure.[34] The obvious example (and pos-

---

[25] Enduring Powers of Attorney Act 1985, s 3(1).
[26] *Clauss v Pir* [1988] 1 Ch 267.
[27] Mental Health Act 1983, s 94.
[28] ibid, s 95.
[29] *Re W (EEM)* [1971] Ch. 123, 143.
[30] The parens patriae jurisdiction of the courts in relation to persons of unsound mind which might have allowed approval to be given was lost on the coming into force of the Mental Health Act 1959.
[31] Mental Health Act 1983, s 63. For certain specified kinds of treatment such as a surgical operation for destroying brain tissue in a non-emergency situation consent is required.
[32] DoH, 'Consent—A Guide for Relatives and Carers' (2001), available from http://www.doh.gov.uk>. cp Mental Health Act 1983, s 6(1).
[33] [2000] 1 FLR 549, 555. See also Thorpe LJ at 560.
[34] *Re DH* [1994] 1 FLR 679 where doctors undertook covert video surveillance of mother and child without informing either parent and, when the mother was seen injuring the child, brought in the police. This is in line with a long line of authority that the child's welfare is of paramount importance, eg *Gillick v West Norfolk and Wisbech Area Health Authority* [1985] 3 All ER 402, 412; *Re C* [1999] 2 FLR 1004 (HIV testing).

A. Disclosure in Client's Best Interests

sibly the only example) is a situation in which the child is at risk of sexual or other abuse.[35] To protect the child, even the fact that abuse was reported may have to be withheld from a parent.[36] In general, however, professionals may not override the refusal of the parent and, if the child is mature, both the child and parent, to consent merely because the professional takes a different view of where the child's 'best interests' lie without first obtaining the approval of a court. In essence, the professional can make a disclosure without consent only when there is an overriding public interest justification[37] in that disclosure.

Legal professional privilege and the child's best interests

12.12 It is generally assumed that a child of sufficient understanding to instruct a solicitor is owed the same obligation of confidentiality as any other client.[38] No English court has addressed the scope of legal professional privilege (LPP) in family proceedings where the privilege-holder is a child. Precedent holds that the litigation privilege, but not the legal advice privilege, of parties who are not children can be overidden in the child's 'best interests'.[39] What of the child himself?

12.13 A report produced jointly by the Australian Law Reform Commission and Human Rights Equal Opportunity Commission concluded that while LPP applies to communications between children and their legal representatives in family law and care and protection cases both forms of the privilege should be subject to the obligation of the legal representative to notify the court of matters:

(1) that may place at risk the safety or best interest of the child,[40]
(2) that the court would otherwise not have access to; and
(3) that would be likely materially to affect the court's deliberations.[41]

The report further recommended that the legal representative explain to the child at the first meeting the limits of the confidentiality that applies to their

---

[35] See paras 11.15, 11.17 and 11.18 above. cp UN, The Convention of the Rights of the Child (1989) Arts 34, 37. Four kinds of abuse are recognized for the purposes of the child protection register: neglect, physical injury, sexual abuse and emotional abuse (DfEE Circular 10/95, *Protecting Children from Abuse: The Role of the Education Service*).

[36] A professional may refuse to divulge information to a person with parental responsibility when disclosure is contrary to the child's best interests: see paras 19.87–19.89 below.

[37] See ch 11.

[38] I Hamilton and J Wilson, 'Representation of Children in Private Law Proceedings Under the Children Act 1989' (1998) 8 Representing Children 32, 35. cp *R v H* [2000] 2 NZLR 257, para 22.

[39] See para 16.39 below. See also para 20.03 n9 below.

[40] cp *Re R* [1993] 4 All ER 702, 704–705 where Thorpe J said that legal representatives of the parties have a positive duty to bring to the attention of the court and to the other parties material relevant to the welfare of the child (in that particular case the child's safety) notwithstanding that it is adverse to the interests of the client and covered by LPP.

[41] ALRC 84, *Seen and heard: priority for children in the legal process* (1997) ch 13, recommendation 73, available at http://www.austlii.edu.au/au/other/alrc/publications/reports/84/ALRC84.html.

communications and, where it becomes clear that disclosure of information is necessary in the child's best interests, the representative should meet with the child and formulate a disclosure strategy.[42]

B. Disclosure with Statutory Authority

Statutory Provisions Allowing the Disclosure of Confidential Information

General comments

12.14 With two exceptions (the Crime and Disorder Act 1998 and the Anti-terrorism, Crime and Security Act 2001) no useful purpose is served by examining individually the statutory provisions that permit but do not compel disclosure of information by professionals to public authorities.[43] But there are certain general points that need to be made.

(1) Statutory provisions legitimizing disclosures are not of uniform design. Those that allow discretionary disclosure tend to be directed at the public at large[44] but they could be aimed at a particular profession or professionals in general.[45] They may create a defence to legal action instigated in consequence of a legitimate disclosure[46] or they may expressly authorize disclosure as in the case of Crime and Disorder Act 1998, s 115[47] and Terrorism Act 2000, s 20. Section 20 legitimizes reporting by anyone of suspicion or belief that money or property is terrorist property or derived from terrorist property and also suspicion or belief that another person has committed an offence under ss 15 to 18 of the Act.[48] Since a professional has a legal obligation under either s 19[49] or s 21A[50] to report suspicions based on information acquired in the course of her profession that someone (client or not) has committed any of these

---

[42] ALRC 84, *Seen and heard: priority for children in the legal process* (1997), recommendation 74.

[43] Two recently added examples are Representation of the People (England and Wales) Regulations 2001, SI 2001/341, reg 23 and Road Traffic Act 1988, s 7A. The latter authorizes a medical practitioner to take blood from a patient who is unable to consent at the request of a constable. The blood cannot, however, be analysed without the patient's consent.

[44] eg Terrorism Act 2000, s 20(3).

[45] Proceeds of Crime Act 2002, s 337(1) (see para 10.25 above).

[46] eg Financial Services Act 1986, s 109(1); Banking Act 1987, s 47(1) as to which see Y Cripps, 'New Statutory Duties of Disclosure for Auditors in the Regulated Financial Sector' (1996) 112 LQR 667, 669; Friendly Societies Act 1992, s 79(8)(c); Building Societies Act 1986 s 82(8)(c); Immigration and Asylum Act 1999 s 93(1). cp DPA, s 58. See also para 10.26 above.

[47] See also NHS (Venereal Diseases) Regulations 1974, reg 2. I Kennedy and A Grubb (eds), *Medical Law* (2nd edn, London: 1994) suggest that the patient's consent is necessary but this is far from clear.

[48] The offences involve money-laundering, arranging funds for, raising funds for, or using or possessing funds connected with terrorism.

[49] A professional operating in the non-regulated sector. See para 10.02 above.

[50] A professional operating in the regulated sector. See para 10.02 above.

B. Disclosure with Statutory Authority

offences, this part of s 20 is unlikely to affect the professional unless the information came to her outside her professional work.

(2) When legislation authorizes disclosure of information it generally neither exempts nor expressly includes confidential information. This makes the question whether confidential information may be disclosed one of statutory interpretation. The more specific a statute is about the information that may be disclosed the easier it will be for a court to infer that confidential information is (or more rarely, is not) included. Some disclosure powers would be otiose if confidential information could not be revealed. An interpretation that interferes with an Article 8(1) right must be a proportionate response to a pressing social need.

(3) A professional who by law is entrusted with a choice as to whether or not to disclose confidential information may be under a *professional* obligation to make the disclosure. For example, the auditing guidelines of the Consultative Committee of Accountancy Bodies *obliges* auditors to provide the Bank of England with the information that Banking Act 1987, s 47(1) *allows* auditors to provide to the Bank.[51] A similar cleavage between what the law permits and what the profession insists on may exist in situations not regulated by statute. The GMC imposes a positive duty on doctors to report physical or sexual child abuse[52] but whether the law does is uncertain.[53]

(4) It would appear that some professionals (though not bankers) may respond voluntarily to an informal request for financial information if refusal would result in the requesting party exercising its statutory powers to compel disclosure.[54]

The Crime and Disorder Act 1998

The object of the Crime and Disorder Act 1998 is crime control. This is to be achieved by means of local crime partnerships to 'formulate and implement . . . a strategy for the reduction of crime and disorder in [their] area',[55] youth offending teams, anti-social behaviour orders, sex offender orders and local child curfew schemes. The success of these measures depends upon close co-operation between public and private agencies and the local community, including timely exchanges of information. Section 115 empowers 'any person' to make a disclosure to a 'relevant authority' that is, a chief constable, a police authority, a local or health

12.15

---

[51] Y Cripps, 'New Statutory Duties of Disclosure for Auditors in the Regulated Financial Sector' (1996) 112 LQR 667, 669.
[52] GMC, *Confidentiality: Protecting and Providing Information* (London: 2000) para 39.
[53] See paras 20.24 et seq on the question of a duty in negligence. As regards the possibility of a public law duty see para 20.05 below.
[54] *Re Barlow Clowes Gilt Managers Ltd* [1991] 4 All ER 385, 395–396 where the practice of giving voluntary disclosure of information to liquidators is discussed and, apparently, approved.
[55] Crime and Disorder Act 1998, ss 6–7.

authority or the probation service (or a person acting on behalf of such a body) where 'necessary or expedient' for the purposes of any provision of the Act.[56]

12.16 Section 115 does not say whether *confidential* information may be disclosed but if it cannot be, s 115 as an aid to crime control is castrated. Home Office guidance states that those who rely on s 115 to make disclosures must abide by the requirements of the Data Protection Act 1998 (DPA),[57] the Human Rights Act 1998 (HRA) and the common law. The last means no defamatory statements and no breaches of confidence that cannot be defended: 'anyone proposing to disclose information not publicly available and obtained in circumstances giving rise to a duty of confidence will need to establish whether there is an overriding [public interest][58] justification for doing so. If not, it is still necessary to obtain the informed consent of the person who supplied the information.'[59]

12.17 Under the HRA disclosure of confidential personal information on the grounds of expediency is unlawful. Interference with the Article 8 right to respect for private life must be *necessary* for the prevention of disorder or crime (or some other aim mentioned in Article 8(2)) to meet a pressing social need and be proportionate.[60] The HRA bites whoever makes the disclosure because the recipient will be a public authority. There may sometimes be doubt as to whether a s 115 disclosure meets the European Convention on Human Rights (ECHR) requirement of being in accordance with law.[61] It will be in accordance with a statute, but that statute (the Crime and Disorder Act 1998) contains only the vaguest indications of when disclosure is proper. Guidance may exist in local protocols, but even with legal advice these may not be sufficiently accessible or detailed to make the exercise of the s 115 discretion adequately predictable.

Anti-terrorism, Crime and Security Act 2001

12.18 Until recently, if the police wanted access to confidential documents held by a public authority they had no choice but to get a warrant or production or access order which meant that they had to have, and satisfy a magistrate or judge that they had, a reasonable suspicion of the commission of a serious arrestable offence.[62] This has been changed by the Anti-Terrorism, Crime and Security Act 2001 which by s 17 enables persons working for public authorities[63] to disregard

---

[56] s 115(1).
[57] If disclosure is for crime prevention there may be partial exemption from the first data protection principle: DPA, s 29. The fair processing code (see para 18.10 below) does not apply.
[58] See ch 11.
[59] Home Office, *Guidance on Statutory Crime and Disorder Partnerships* (1998) para 5.14.
[60] See para 3.19 above.
[61] ibid.
[62] See paras 14.19–14.25 below.
[63] Public authority has the same definition as in the HRA (see para 4.47 above) and therefore will include GPs.

B. Disclosure with Statutory Authority

confidentiality requirements imposed by a variety of statutory provisions[64] (and any further provisions in subordinate legislation added to the list by order),[65] if disclosure is for the purposes of

- facilitating or ending any criminal investigation anywhere;
- facilitating or ending any criminal proceedings anywhere;
- investigating whether any crime has taken place anywhere.[66]

It requires quite a feat of imagination to see a connection between the threat of terrorism which precipitated the 2001 Act and the disabled non-disclosure provisions of, for example, the Diseases of Fish Act 1983 and the Merchant Shipping (Liner Conferences) Act 1982. The explanation offered to Parliament for not confining the power to terrorist investigations was that the government wanted 'to make it simple for public officials to understand what they are supposed to disclose' by allowing disclosure in virtually all circumstances.[67]

Legal barriers preventing the Inland Revenue and Commissioners of Customs and Excise from disclosing confidential information about taxpayers for these purposes or to the security services are removed for the purposes of:[68] **12.19**

(1) any existing or future criminal investigation or proceedings anywhere in the world; or
(2) to assist any of the intelligence services in the performance of its functions.

The Inland Revenue expects to make the majority of its disclosures to the police, National Criminal Intelligence Service and the National Crime Squad and is reported to be planning to place memoranda of understanding with these organizations to ensure that confidential information is treated appropriately.[69] Disclosure of information that was collected before the anti-terrorism legislation came into force is permitted[70] and the investigation or proceedings for which the information is disclosed need not be within the United Kingdom. Ensuring effective protection of confidential information once it leaves the jurisdiction may be impossible and it has been suggested that this might be a worry for wealthy foreign investors who are at risk from robbery and kidnapping.[71] The Home Secretary has power to exclude disclosures by public authorities to overseas investigators in certain circumstances[72] but is not obliged to do so and cannot, in any

---

[64] Listed in Sch 4 to the Act.
[65] s 17(3).
[66] s 17(2).
[67] Ruth Kelly, *Hansard*, HC vol 375, cols 791, 794 (26 November 2001).
[68] s 19(2). There is a supporting code of practice without statutory force which gives guidance on how the Inland Revenue will exercise the discretionary disclosure power: see http://www.inlandrevenue.gov.uk.
[69] P Vaines, 'Taxing Matters' (2002) 152 NLJ 787. Further disclosure is restricted by s 19(5).
[70] ss 17(7), 19 (1).
[71] P Vaines, 'Taxing Matters' (2002) 152 NLJ 787, 788.
[72] s 18.

event, prevent disclosures by the revenue departments or a Minister of the Crown.[73]

12.20 Relatively little of the information that the anti-terrorism legislation frees public authorities to disclose will be sensitive personal information, still less personal information supplied by a professional about a client. But some public authorities do have in their possession personal information that has been sourced from professionals. The Inland Revenue is the obvious, but not the only, example. Another is the Commission for Health Improvement. In the course of investigating an NHS service failure the Commission may gather information from the medical records of thousands of identifiable patients.[74]

12.21 The Home Office has emphasized that there is no compulsion on a public body to respond to a request for information: the public body can insist upon a search warrant or a production or access order. This is not much of a safeguard since it is unlikely that most public authorities will adopt stringent disclosure policies and whatever policies they have may receive little or no publicity. More important is the fact that disclosure is forbidden unless the body from whom the information is requested is satisfied that 'disclosure is proportionate to what is sought to be achieved by it'.[75] This requirement is intended to avoid incompatibility with the HRA. Additionally, there is an express prohibition on the revenue departments making any disclosure which is prohibited by the DPA.[76] The Act does not state whether the s 17 disclosure power which liberates other public authorities from some of the effects of some of the non-disclosure provisions that bind them is subject to the DPA but during debate in the House of Lords the Government indicated that the DPA did not apply.[77]

12.22 The Joint Committee on Human Rights was critical of the absence in the anti-terrorism legislation of a requirement that 'there should be reasonable grounds for suspecting that the information in question would be relevant to a criminal inquiry or that the data subject has committed an offence'.[78] The omission is all the more serious because of the absence of any mechanism for reviewing a dis-

---

[73] s 18(4).
[74] Health Act 1999, s 24. In April 2001 the Commission for Health Improvement commissioned a review of over 100,000 patient files in order to identify women who should have been, but were not recalled for breast screening tests, see http://www.chi.nhs.uk.
[75] ss 17(3), 19(3).
[76] s 19(7).
[77] *Hansard*, HL vol 629, col 418 (28 November 2001) (Lord McIntosh). If the DPA applied then there might be obstacles to the transfer of data outside the EEA. The DPA contains exemptions covering national security (s 28) and the detection and prevention of crime (s 29) but in the latter case the data controller must be satisfied that non-disclosure 'would be likely to prejudice' the purpose of the disclosure. When disclosure is sought under s 28, it is arguable that the data controller must be satisfied that disclosure is required for the purpose of national security.
[78] Second Report, *Anti-Terrorism, Crime and Security Bill*, HL Paper 37, HC 372 (November 2001) Pt 3, para 53.

closure decision. There is a 'significant risk'[79] because of 'the lack of statutory criteria to guide decisions and the lack of procedural safeguards to be followed when deciding whether it is necessary and proportionate to make a disclosure of personal information'[80] that a disclosure of personal information will be found to be an unjustifiable interference with Article 8(1). As JUSTICE explains in a briefing paper, the ECtHR 'has stressed that the protection of personal data is fundamental to the right to respect for private life. Powers of disclosure such as those extended [in ss 17 and 19] therefore need to be closely confined, and subject to safeguards, in order to ensure that such interference can be justified under Article 8(2)'.[81]

C. Disclosure Motivated by Self-Interest

Breaching Confidentiality Defensively

Criminal and disciplinary actions against lawyers

Law Society guidance

12.23 The Law Society's guidance to solicitors allows a solicitor to break an obligation of confidentiality to a client in order to defend a formal accusation of wrongdoing.

> A solicitor may reveal confidential information concerning a client to the extent that it is reasonably necessary to establish a defence to a criminal charge . . . or where the solicitor's conduct is under investigation by the Office for the Supervision of Solicitors, or under consideration by the Solicitors' Disciplinary Tribunal.[82]

The rationale offered by Proulx and Layton for the Canadian counterparts of this rule 'is that lawyers would otherwise be defenceless against groundless charges of impropriety'.[83]

Common law

12.24 The Law Society's position is out of kilter with the common law. The confidences lawyers attract are very likely to be the subject not only of an obligation of confidentiality but also of LPP.[84] The Law Society guidance treats self-defence as an exception to both. In *R v Derby Magistrates' Court, ex p B*,[85] however, the House of Lords said that at common law LPP is, barring situations where the communication was

---

[79] Joint Committee on Human Rights, Fifth Report, *Anti-Terrorism, Crime and Security Bill*, HL Paper 51, HC 420 (December 2001) Pt 3, para 24.
[80] ibid.
[81] JUSTICE, 'Briefing on the Anti-Terrorism Crime and Security Bill: House of Lords Second Reading' (November 2001) para 3.3, available from http://www.justice.org.
[82] Law Society, *The Guide to the Professional Conduct of Solicitors* (8th edn, London: 1999) 327, 16.02, para 12. K Wheat, 'Lawyers, Confidentiality and Public and Private Interests' (2000)1 Legal Ethics 184, 190 argues that the exception is too widely drawn.
[83] M Proulx and D Layton, *Ethics and Canadian Criminal Law* (Toronto: 2001) 225.
[84] See ch 16 on the subject of LPP.
[85] [1995] 4 All ER 526.

made in furtherance of a crime or fraud,[86] absolute. If LPP prevails over the right of a third party to defend himself against a charge of murder (the scenario in *R v Derby Magistrates' Court, ex p B*),[87] is it likely (in the absence of parliamentary intervention[88] or waiver by the client) to give way to the self-interest of a solicitor defending himself against a disciplinary or criminal charge? Were it not for Article 6 of the ECHR the answer would be bound to be no.

12.25 Article 6(1), which confers a right to a fair trial, may require a re-assessment of *R v Derby Magistrates' Court, ex p B* because that judgment does not take into account the interests of anyone besides the privilege-holder. Can a criminal trial be fair if the accused (be she a lawyer or anyone else) is deprived—regardless of the circumstances- of evidence that could establish the accused's innocence? The possible need to allow exceptions to the absolute and paramount character of legal professional privilege in the context of Articles 6 and 8 of the ECHR was acknowledged by Lord Hobhouse in *Medcalf v Weatherill*.[89]

12.26 The Canadian Supreme Court has held that a criminal defendant's charter right to make full answer may override solicitor–client privilege.[90] In Canada a lawyer who was prosecuted for obstructing the course of justice by failing to surrender to the authorities videotapes of the sexual slaying of several young women by his client was allowed by the trial judge, against the strenuous objections of the client, to adduce evidence of conversations that he had had with the client. The court insisted that such a breach of privilege was permissible in very limited circumstances and emphasized that the client had already been convicted and had exhausted all avenues of appeal.[91]

Civil claims against lawyers

By the client

12.27 The Law Society guidance to solicitors permits a solicitor to break an obligation of confidentiality owed to a client in order to defend civil proceedings brought by

---

[86] See para 16.35 below. The crime-fraud exception would be relevant if lawyer and client are accused of joint involvement in money laundering.

[87] [1995] 4 All ER 526. cp *Carter v Managing Partner, Northmore, Hale, Davy and Leake* (1995) 185 CLR 83.

[88] There is no statutory provision which removes LPP in a courtroom context other than the Children Act 1989 which impliedly denies litigation privilege to reports obtained for the purposes of care proceedings that could not have been prepared had the court not given leave for papers to be shown to experts or the child to be examined: *Re L (A Minor) (Police Investigation: Privilege)* [1996] 2 All ER 78, 85 (see para 16.39 below).

[89] [2002] UKHL 27; [2002] 3 WLR 172, para 60.

[90] See para 16.27 below.

[91] *R v Murray* discussed in A Hutchinson, 'Sex, lawyers and videotapes—A Canadian blockbuster' (2000) 150 NLJ 1008. See also R Fogl, 'Sex, Laws and Videotape: The ambit of Solicitor–Client Privilege in Canadian Criminal Law as Illuminated in *R v Murray*' (2001) 50 University of New Brunswick LJ 187.

C. Disclosure Motivated by Self-Interest

the client.[92] There is no conflict here between the guidance and the law. A client who sues a lawyer will, in most circumstances, be treated as having impliedly waived confidentiality and privilege in any information in the professional's possession relevant to the action.[93] Canadian courts have permitted lawyers to respond to imputations by former clients during litigation between the clients and third parties on this theory.[94] There is the possibility, too, that a court might imply a term into the contract between the lawyer and client releasing the lawyer from the obligation of confidentiality and privilege in the event that the information is needed to defend a civil suit by the client.

By someone who is not the client

12.28 The Law Society's guidance to solicitors does not permit the solicitor to breach a confidence owed to the client to enable the solicitor to defend a civil action brought by a third party. As far as wasted costs applications against the lawyers for the opposing party are concerned, this is a fair reflection of the law. In *General Mediterranean Holdings SA v Patel*[95] a rule of court ousting LPP in the wasted costs jurisdiction was held to be ultra vires.[96] The invalid rule, in any event, conferred a discretion on the judge to order disclosure. Had it been valid, Toulson J said that he would have refused to compel disclosure of privileged communications because the client had a right under Article 8(1) ECHR to confidentiality save where interference with the right was justified under Article 8(2).[97] The judge doubted that disclosure of privileged material 'is necessary and proportionate for the purpose of doing justice to the legal profession' on an application for disputed costs 'particularly bearing in mind the point that the courts have been used on hearing wasted costs applications to making allowance for the lawyer's inability to disclose privileged information without the client's consent'.[98] Article 6(1), the fair trial provision, did not, in his opinion, affect the absolute nature of LPP.[99]

12.29 In *Medcalf v Weatherill*[100] the House of Lords subsequently decided that when the wasted costs jurisdiction[101] is invoked against an opponent's lawyers and the

---

[92] Law Society, *The Guide to the Professional Conduct of Solicitors* (8th edn, London: 1999) 327, 16.02, para 12.
[93] See para 16.34 below. *Medcalf v Weatherill* [2002] UKHL 27; [2002] 3 WLR 172, para 31.
[94] *R v Dunbar* (1982) 68 CCC (2d) 13, 39. See also *R v Thawer* [1996] OJ No. 989.
[95] [1999] 3 All ER 673.
[96] The subordinate legislation was CPR r 48.7(3). This was made pursuant to the Civil Procedure Act 1997, s 1 and Sch 1, para 4.
[97] See para 3.19 above.
[98] [1999] 3 All ER 683, 696.
[99] per Toulson J, [1999] 3 All ER 673, 695.
[100] [2002] UKHL 27; [2002] 3 WLR 172.
[101] Supreme Court Act 1981, s 51(7) empowers a court in a civil case to order a legal representative to pay costs incurred by a party 'as a result of any improper, unreasonable or negligent act or omission on the part of any legal or other representative . . .'.

privilege-holder refuses to waive privilege the court 'must be satisfied before it makes the wasted costs order that there is nothing that the lawyer could say, if unconstrained, to resist the order and that it is in all the circumstances fair to make the order'.[102] By adopting such exacting conditions which give the lawyer-defendant the benefit of the doubt and leave little scope for making wasted costs orders,[103] the House of Lords avoided the need to consider whether LPP must yield its absolute and paramount character (which the parties had not challenged) in the face of the Article 6 right to a fair trial.[104] The Article 6 issue might yet have to be confronted in a case in which a solicitor is sued by a third party for negligence.[105] To refer to confidential and privileged material concerning the transaction which the client refuses to disclose might be vital to the solicitor's defence.[106] Lord Hobhouse hinted that 'a balancing exercise may sometimes be necessary'.[107]

Criminal, civil and disciplinary proceedings against non-lawyers

12.30 Legal professional privilege is not usually going to be an obstacle to a self-defence disclosure of client information by a professional who is not a lawyer. Confidentiality is not a recognized ground of objection to the disclosure of evidence in litigation[108] and therefore one would expect that if confidential client information is relevant to litigation against a professional it can be disclosed by the professional with or without the consent of the client.[109] The Institute of Chartered Accountants instructs its members that they may disclose confidential client information:

---

[102] per Lord Hobhouse, *Medcalf v Weatherill* [2002] UKHL 27; [2002] 3 WLR 172, para 63.
[103] ibid, para 24.
[104] The principle of equality of arms, a component of the concept of a fair trial, requires that each party have a reasonable opportunity to represent his case under conditions that do not place him at a substantial disadvantage vis-à-vis his opponent: *de Haes v Belgium* (1997) 25 EHRR 1, para 53.
[105] cp *Al-Kandari v Brown* [1988] 1 All ER 833.
[106] cp R Toulson and C Phipps, *Confidentiality* (London: 1996) 50.
[107] *Medcalf v Weatherill* [2002] UKHL 27; [2002] 3 WLR 172, para 60. The possibility of adopting measures such as partially inquisitorial procedures and restrictions on the use to which disclosed material may be put are suggested as means of reducing the infringement of the client's privilege. Criticism of the absoluteness of LPP was noted by Lord Steyn at para 30.
[108] See paras 14.07, 14.126, 15.08 and 16.02 below. Query, does the fact of relevance to litigation always satisfy the proportionality requirement (see para 3.19 above) for an interference with Art 8? Suppose in a civil action in negligence a doctor accused of undertaking a complicated operation without relevant prior experience wishes to introduce evidence of previous operations involving other patients in which he used similar procedures. The records of the other patients would be relevant, but would their non-consensual disclosure be necessary in a democratic society and proportionate? Shaw LJ's warning in *Schering Chemicals v Falkman Ltd* [1981] 2 All ER 321, 339 may be apposite: '[t]he public interest may demand that the duty [of confidentiality] be gainsaid; but it cannot be arbitrarily cast aside . . . it is not to be sloughed off at will for self-interest.'
[109] DPA, Sch 2, para 6 permits disclosure of non-sensitive personal data 'for the purposes of legitimate interests pursued by the data controller' and Sch 3, para 6(c) allows sensitive personal data to be disclosed without consent when 'necessary for the purposes of . . . defending legal rights'.

C. Disclosure Motivated by Self-Interest

(a) to enable the member to defend . . . a criminal charge or to clear himself of suspicion; or (b) to resist proceedings for a penalty in respect of a taxation offence . . .; or (c) to resist a legal action brought . . . by his client or some third person; or (d) to enable the member to defend . . . disciplinary proceedings.[110]

Surprisingly, the GMC guidelines on confidentiality do not address the position of a doctor who wants to disclose information in self-defence.

12.31 Case law on the self-defence exception to confidentiality is slim. In *Duncan v Medical Practitioner's Disciplinary Committee*,[111] a judgment of the New Zealand High Court, it was accepted that 'a doctor may reveal confidences and secrets if he is required to defend himself, or others, against accusations of wrongful conduct'. Writing in the pre-HRA era, Toulson and Phipps comment that when professional disciplinary or criminal proceedings are brought against a doctor '[g]rave injustice might be done . . . if he were not free to disclose matters concerning the patient which he would otherwise be required to treat as confidential'.[112] The Article 6 right to a fair hearing strengthens the case for allowing the doctor to defend herself. Disclosures prior to the trial can very likely be made by relying on the public interest exception to confidentiality.[113] If the professional is sued by the client, or is the subject of a formal complaint by the client to a disciplinary body, disclosure may be justified on an implied consent theory.[114] In contractual relationships, it may be possible to argue for an implied term that permits the professional to disclose confidential information in self-defence.[115]

12.32 In *Sunderland v Barclays Bank Ltd*[116] a bank dishonoured a woman's cheque to her dressmaker. She telephoned the bank and handed the telephone over to her husband so that he could support her complaint. To explain why overdraft facilities had not been made available, the bank told the husband that the wife had drawn cheques in favour of bookmakers. The disclosure to the husband was held to be in the bank's interests and made with the wife's implied consent. The decision lends slight support to the pronouncement of the president of the Royal College of Physicians that doctors have the right 'to reveal details of individual patient care when they are subjected to totally unreasonable criticism by the media and

---

[110] Institute of Chartered Accountants in England and Wales, *Members Handbook 2001* (London: 2001) s 1.306, para 19, 372.
[111] per Jeffries J, [1986] 1 NZLR 513, 521. See also, *Re MP* [1997] NZFLR LEXIS 141, 60–61; cp *Meyerhofer v Empire Fire & Marine Insurance Co* 497 F 2d 1190, 1194–1195 (1974).
[112] R Toulson and C Phipps, *Confidentiality* (London: 1996) 50.
[113] '[I]t might be necessary to seek to invoke the general principle that the public interest in disclosure outweighed confidentiality (*W v Egdell* . . .)', per Hirst LJ, *R v Institute of Chartered Accountants in England and Wales, ex p Brindle* [1994] BCC 297, 312.
[114] cp *Hay v University of Alberta Hospital* (1990) 69 DLR (4th) 755. If not, the professional can always apply for a disclosure order under CPR, r 31.
[115] *R v Institute of Chartered Accountants in England and Wales, ex p Brindle* [1993] BCC 736, 745; [1994] BCC 297, 306.
[116] (1938) 5 LDAB 163.

families'.[117] The BMA is more cautious. It has said that if 'a patient has made information public a doctor or a hospital can comment on the information but not add to it'.[118]

12.33 Caution must be exercised in applying the implied waiver theory to medical and other sensitive personal records. In *MS v Sweden*[119] the ECtHR held that the applicant had not by initiating compensation proceedings, consented to the infringement of her private life involved in the disclosure of her medical records to the Social Security Insurance Office because this disclosure, although foreseeable, was not automatic. This, and the DPA requirement that consent to the disclosure of health data must be 'explicit',[120] may explain why the Court of Appeal did not rely upon the implied waiver theory in *Nicholson v Halton General Hospital NHS Trust*[121] and instead stayed the claimant's proceedings until such time as the claimant expressly consented to waiver of her right of confidentiality in the medical information sought by the defendants from the claimant's consultant.

Breaching Confidentiality Affirmatively

Fee recovery

Fee recovery by non-lawyers

12.34 A professional may commence proceedings to which confidential personal information about a client is relevant. The paradigm case is a fee dispute. The defendant may be either the client or a third party who assumed responsibility for paying the professional. It is well settled that a bank may disclose confidential information about a customer in order to enforce a guarantee or to sue on an overdraft.[122] Whether other professionals may do so for the purposes of fee collection is not something on which there is English legal authority. A rule excluding relevant client information might work to the disadvantage of future clients. Fees might have to rise to cover for defaulting clients who could not be successfully sued or clients might be made to pay upfront which might exclude some individuals from professional services.[123] To allow a client to take advantage of an equit-

---

[117] 'RCP Comment on issues surrounding the case of Mrs Rose Addis', 24 January 2002, available from http://www.rcplondon.ac.uk/news/news.asp?PR_id=117.

[118] This comment was made after an NHS hospital released details of the treatment that an elderly patient had received at an NHS hospital and her relatives had complained to the media about the way she had been treated in the hospital's Accident and Emergency Department: 'Doctors concerned patients may lose confidence in confidentiality', Telegraph, 25 January 2002.

[119] (1997) 45 BMLR 133.

[120] DPA, s 2, Sch 3, para 1.

[121] [1999] P IQR P 310. See also para 14.09 below.

[122] *Tournier v National Provincial and Union Bank of England* [1924] 1 KB 461, 486. See also *X AG v A Bank* [1983] 2 All ER 464, 477.

[123] This last factor has weighed with US courts. See F Folk, 'Two Exceptions to a Lawyer's Duty of Confidentiality: Defence of Reputation and Pursuit of Fees' (2000) 58 Advocate (Vancouver) 33, 44.

C. *Disclosure Motivated by Self-Interest*

able obligation of confidentiality to thwart payment of money properly due to a professional is also unconscionable. Therefore, it may be suggested that disclosure of the minimum amount of personal information required to enable the professional to sue for fees is necessary in a democratic society for the protection of the rights of the professional and is proportionate.[124]

Fee recovery by lawyers

The solicitor's[125] ability to use confidential information in aid of fee recovery is a particularly thorny topic. The American Bar Association's Model Code of Professional Responsibility states that '[a] lawyer may reveal . . . [c]onfidences or secrets necessary to establish or collect his fee . . .'[126] on the basis that the client, by breaching his legal duty to pay his lawyer, forfeits the right to confidentiality.[127] The Law Society has no comparable rule, and even if it did, there is still the problem that LPP, which belongs to the client,[128] may attach to documents needed to validate the claim.[129] It is Samuels' view that if a lawyer sues a client for failure to pay fees properly charged and it becomes necessary 'to investigate in court the nature of the work alleged to be done or not done, the court would not permit any confidence to be breached by reference to the substantive matters in the document'.[130] This must be the result if *R v Derby Magistrates' Court, ex p B*[131] applies. But does it? 12.35

There is something most unsavoury about allowing the client to use LPP to escape paying the lawyer—something that the lawyer and client did not contemplate when they entered into their contractual relationship. Disclosure could be justified either on an implied waiver[132] or an implied term[133] theory. Precedent for 12.36

---

[124] DPA, Sch 2, para 6 permits disclosure of non-sensitive personal data 'for the purposes of legitimate interests pursued by the data controller' and Sch 3, para 6(c) allows sensitive personal data to be disclosed without consent when 'necessary for the purposes of establishing, exercising or defending legal rights'.

[125] Barristers cannot sue for fees: *Kennedy v Broun* (1863) 13 CBNS 677.

[126] American Bar Association, *Model Code of Professional Responsibility* DR4-101(C)(4). cp American Law Institute, *Restatement of the Law, The Law Governing Lawyers*, Proposed Final Draft No 1 (1996) ss 117, 133; Model Rules of Professional Conduct, r 1.6.

[127] R Patterson, 'Legal Ethics and the Lawyer's Duty of Loyalty' (1980) 29 Emory LJ 909, 964.

[128] *Ventouris v Moutain* [1991] 1 WLR 607, 611.

[129] The fact that the professional relationship is at an end because the client has not paid the bill does not affect the continuation of the privilege: see para 16.28 below. Solicitors' bills are privileged but the client care letter and the payment calculations are not: *Dickinson v Rushmer* (2002) 152 NLJ 58.

[130] A Samuels, 'Confidence and Privilege and the Lawyer' in J Young (ed), *Privacy* (Chichester: 1978) 222. If the client were to counterclaim for whatever reason, the lawyer could introduce communications relevant to the counterclaim into evidence on a theory of waiver.

[131] [1995] 4 All ER 526. And see para 16.25 below.

[132] See para 16.34 below.

[133] See para 12.31 above.

an exception to LPP in fee recovery situations exists in US[134] and Canadian law.[135] In *Wilson, King & Co v Torabian* Thackray J of the British Columbia Supreme Court said:

> There is no common law bar to the commencement and pursuit of a lawyer's action for fees. Any privilege that attaches to the identity of the client and to the reasons for the retainer and the extent of the retainer are waived by the client to the very limited extent necessary to resolve the dispute.[136]

Other disputes

12.37 A professional may commence proceedings against a client or a third party for a purpose other than recovery of unpaid fees to which information confidential to a client is relevant. One possibility is an action for defamation arising from allegations of professional incompetence.[137] Though not directly in point, the decision of the Supreme Court of Canada in *Slavutych v Baker*[138] is of interest. Professor Slavutych wrote a report about an academic colleague at the request of the University of Alberta where he was employed after repeated assurances of confidentiality. Later because of the contents of the report the University commenced arbitration proceedings against Professor Slavutych to secure his dismissal. The court held that the report was not admissible in evidence in these proceedings.[139] Spence J agreed with Sinclair JA in the lower court that

> ... a person who has obtained information in confidence is not allowed to use it as a springboard for activities detrimental to the person who made the confidential communication ...[140]

Even if this 'springboard' doctrine were to be applied in England to personal information,[141] it would not preclude the professional from breaching a confidence from reasons of self-interest in *all* litigation. The confidential personal information about the client would have to be central to the professional's claim.

---

[134] *Sokol v Mortimer* 225 NE 2d 496, 501 (1967); *McCormick on Evidence* (5th edn, St Paul: 1999) 142.

[135] F Folk, 'Two Exceptions to a Lawyer's Duty of Confidentiality: Defence of Reputation and Pursuit of Fees' (2000) 58 Advocate (Vancouver) 33, 42.

[136] (1991) ACWSJ LEXIS [*11].

[137] eg *Bergens Tidende v Norway* (2000) 31 EHRR 16.

[138] (1975) 55 DLR (3d) 224, 231.

[139] No previous case has held that evidence obtained by a breach of confidence is inadmissible. It is difficult to reconcile the exclusionary rule applied in *Slavutych v Baker* (1975) 55 DLR (3d) 224, 231 with *Calcraft v Guest* [1898] 1 QB 759 and *Lloyd v Mostyn* (1842) 152 ER 558, 560 which allow a copy of a privileged document to be admitted in evidence no matter how obtained (see para 6.98 above). For an analysis of *Slavutych v Baker* see J Avary, 'Privilege, Confidence and Illegally Obtained Evidence' (1977) 15 Osgoode Hall LJ 456.

[140] (1975) 55 DLR (3d) 224, 230. The words are taken from *Terrapin Ltd v Builders' Supply Co* [1960] RPC 128, 130 as cited in *Seagar v Copydex* [1967] 2 All ER 415, 417.

[141] The application of the 'springboard' doctrine in intellectual property actions for breach of confidence is well established: see F Gurry, *Breach of Confidence* (Oxford: 1984) 245.

C. Disclosure Motivated by Self-Interest

The 'springboard' principle would, moreover, not disbar disclosure in an action arising from the client's fraud or criminality. In *Finers v Miro*[142] the clamaint solicitors became concerned that assets which the firm held on behalf of the defendant might have been acquired from an insurance company by fraud and were therefore subject to a constructive trust in favour of the liquidator of the insurance company.[143] Anxious to avoid being held liable to the liquidator as a constructive trustee, the solicitors applied to the High Court[144] for a direction as to whether they should notify the US liquidator of the assets. The information at issue was both confidential and privileged. On appeal Dillon LJ asked

12.38

> Does it matter that it is the solicitor himself who is seeking in the present case to tear aside the client's privilege, and not a third party with a hostile claim? In my judgment it does not; the privilege does not require the court to compel the solicitor to continue, at his own personal risk, to aid and abet the apparently fraudulent ends of the defendant in covering up the original fraud of which there is such a prima facie case. The court is entitled, in my judgment, to give directions which would enable the liquidator to decide, with sufficient knowledge of the facts, whether or not to make any claim to the 'property investments monies and companies' which are now in the possession or under the control of the plaintiffs . . .[145]

Balcombe LJ agreed saying that

> fraud unravels all obligations of confidence. . . . If, therefore, the allegations are such that there is strong evidence of suspected fraud then it seems to me that is a matter which the court may, indeed must, take into account in deciding whether to give directions which would necessarily involve a breach of confidence.[146]

It would appear that fraud not only prevents LPP from arising,[147] it can also abrogate LPP that was valid at inception.

Extent of disclosure

Whatever the circumstances that allow the professional to disclose confidential information about a client to protect her own interests, only the minimum amount of information necessary to protect those interests may be disclosed.[148] The *Sunderland*[149] decision has been criticized on this front.[150] Why was it

12.39

---

[142] [1991] 1 All ER 182.
[143] *Agip (Africa) Ltd v Jackson* [1990] Ch 265. At the time of the proceedings no actual third party claim to the money had been made but the defendants had conceded that Finers had grounds for believing that the funds had been acquired from the misappropriation of assets in a US company.
[144] Under special rules for trustees: RSC Ord 85, r 2.
[145] [1991] 1 All ER 182, 187.
[146] [1991] 1 All ER 182, 191. There is no conflict between this decision and *R v Derby Magistrates' Court, ex p B* [1995] 4 All ER 526 because of the element of fraud.
[147] See para 16.36 below.
[148] *Tournier v National Provincial and Union Bank of England* [1924] 1 KB 461, 486.
[149] (1938) 5 LDAB 163. For the facts see para 12.32 above.
[150] M Ogilvie, *Canadian Banking Law* (Toronto: 1991) 627.

necessary for the bank to disclose to the husband the reason that his wife's account was overdrawn? If more than the necessary minimum is disclosed, the professional runs the risk of being sued by the client for breach of confidence, breach of contract or in negligence.[151]

12.40 A bank has no duty to tell the customer that it has passed the customer's confidential details to a third party[152] but all appropriate steps must be taken by the bank to ensure that the recipients of the information will themselves keep it confidential.[153] The reader should refer to the discussion in chapter 10 about the obligations of other professionals to notify clients about non-consensual disclosures.[154]

Withdrawal of services

12.41 The withdrawal of counsel or solicitors or both from a case, particularly mid-trial, may give rise to adverse inferences against the client. The decision of an accountant or an insurance broker to give up a client may have a similar effect. Any disclosure implicit in withdrawal has to be tolerated because it is cannot be avoided: the professional cannot be expected to continue to act for a client in breach of her code of professional ethics and, perhaps, the law. Counsel should not state the reasons for withdrawing if this might breach an obligation of confidentiality owed to the client. The American Bar Association allows an attorney to alert opponents to the possibility that the client has used the attorney's services fraudulently by a 'noisy' withdrawal.[155] This is unlikely to be condoned by the Law Society.

---

[151] cp *Robertson v Canadian Imperial Bank* [1995] 1 All ER 824.
[152] *El Jawhary v Bank of BCCI* [1993] BCLC 396, 400.
[153] ibid at 399. If, however, the information has to be tendered as evidence in open court the information will inevitably lose its confidentiality.
[154] See para 10.20 above.
[155] M Proulx and D Layton, *Ethics and Canadian Criminal Law* (Toronto: 2001) 623.

13

CONSENT

A. Express Consent	13.02	B. Implied Consent	13.34
Forms of Consent	13.02	Disclosure for Primary Purposes	13.34
Duration of Consent	13.05	Disclosure for Secondary Purposes	13.46
Capacity to Consent	13.08	Parameters of Express and Implied	
Reality of Consent	13.22	Consent	13.59
Informed Consent	13.28	C. Waiver	13.63
		English Waiver Cases	13.63
		Prerequisites of the Defence	13.67

It is perfectly proper for a professional to disclose confidential client information to a third party if the client consents[1] or, in cases of joint clients,[2] if all the joint clients consent.[3] Client consent qualifies the original contractual[4] or equitable[5] obligation of confidentiality; it negates breach of copyright[6] and libel;[7] and it ensures compliance with the first data protection principle.[8] This chapter explores   **13.01**

---

[1] A number of statutes allow disclosure of personal information with the consent of the subject of the information, eg Sexual Offences (Amendment) Act 1976, s 4(5A) (written consent required); Criminal Justice Act 1987, s 2(1)(a); Human Fertilization and Embryology Act 1990, s 33(6B); Immigration and Asylum Act 1999 s 93(3)(a); Social Security (Disclosure of State Pension Information) Regulations 2000 SI 2000/3188, reg 3(1)(a); Learning Skills Act 2000, s 119(4)(d); Tax Credits Act 2002, Sch 5, para 9(4).

[2] When a professional sees clients jointly the professional breaches no confidence by telling one client what the other has said: cp *Tatone v Tatone* (1980) 16 CPC 285, 286–287. A lawyer has a positive duty to keep each of the clients fully informed of material facts: see para 19.58 below.

[3] cp *Re Konigsberg* [1989] 3 All ER 289, 296; *Hellenic Mutual War Risks Association v Harrison* [1997] 1 Lloyd's Rep 160. A case in which a psychiatrist saw a couple together and obtained consent to disclosure from only one of them is reported in (1981) 283 British Medical J 1062.

[4] *Fomento (Sterling Area) Ltd v Selsdon Fountain Pen Co Ltd* [1958] 1 All ER 11, 23–24; *NRG v Bacon & Woodrow* [1995] 1 All ER 976, 984.

[5] A breach of confidence is an *unauthorized* disclosure or use of information: *Coco v AN Clark (Engineers) Ltd* [1969] RPC 41, 47; see para 5.06 above. See also *Fraser v Thames Television Ltd* [1983] 2 All ER 101, 122; *McKaskell v Bensemen* [1989] 3 NZLR 75, 88; *R v Department of Health, ex p Source Informatics* [2000] 1 All ER 786, 800.

[6] A copyright infringement is reproduction without licence: Copyright, Designs and Patents Act 1988, s 7.

[7] *Moore v News of the World Ltd* [1972] 1 All ER 915, 918.

[8] DPA, Sch 2, para 1. There are many situations in which disclosure without consent complies with data protection requirements: see para 18.19 below.

the parameters of consent. In actions for breach of confidence a fledgling defence of waiver shows signs of emerging.[9] There is an obvious parallel here with waiver in the law of evidence. Information that is not only confidential but privileged may be disclosed if the privilege-holder waives the privilege.[10] In US law waiver is a well-established defence to an allegation of invasion of privacy.[11] The last part of the chapter looks at the circumstances in which a court might hold that an obligation of confidentiality with respect to personal information has been waived. Waiver of legal professional privilege is summarized in Chapter 16.[12]

A. Express Consent

Forms of Consent

13.02 The professional or third party who relies upon consent as an answer to an action relating to the disclosure of information by a client must prove the client's consent on the balance of probabilities (the normal civil standard of proof). In English law consent comes in several versions: implied, express, explicit.[13] For most purposes all are equally effective.[14] Express consent involves active affirmation,[15] usually orally or in writing. Implied consent is discussed later in the chapter.[16] The Data Protection Act 1998 (DPA) requires 'explicit' consent to the processing of sensitive personal data.[17] The Information Commissioner understands it to be consent

---

[9] See para 13.63 below. Waiver means foregoing a legal or an equitable right. The informational privacy waiver is unusual. Normally 'waiver is an informed choice manifested in unequivocal conduct': S Wilkin, *The Law of Waiver, Variation and Estoppel* (2nd edn, Oxford: OUP, 2002) 43. Informational privacy waiver is not and this puts a question mark over the legitimacy of the defence.

[10] Waiver is primarily associated with legal professional privilege. Public interest immunity (see para 16.53 below) cannot normally be waived but conciliation privilege (see paras 16.07 and 16.38 below) may be if both spouses consent.

[11] J Ghent, 'Waiver or loss of Right of Privacy' 57 ALR 3d 16 (1974); R Sack, *Sack on Defamation* (3rd edn, New York: 2002) vol 1, para 12.4.8.

[12] See paras 16.31 et seq.

[13] EU Directive (EC) 95/46 which has been implemented in the UK by the Data Protection Act 1998 has a fourth variant: 'unambiguous consent'. This is required before personal data is processed (Art 7(a)) and allows personal data to be transmitted to a third country without adequate data protection laws (Art 26(a)). In the DPA 'unambiguous' has been dropped. There may be scope for arguing that the DPA does not properly implement the EU Directive: see H Oliver, 'Email and Internet Monitoring in the Workplace: Information Privacy and Contracting-Out' (2002) 31 Industrial LJ 321, 345.

[14] The Information Commissioner thinks that only express consent will do if (a) the purpose for which it is proposed to process personal data changes after collection (see para 18.13 below), or (b) personal data was collected before the DPA came into force without relevant fair processing information having been provided: *Guidance on the Use and Disclosure of Health Data* (May 2002) 17.

[15] *Bell v Alfred Franks & Bartlett Co Ltd* [1980] 1 All ER 356, 360.

[16] See para 13.34 below.

[17] See para 18.25 below. In Danish law consents in all contexts must be explicit: P Blume, *Informational Privacy* (Copenhagen: 2002) 44.

A. Express Consent

that is 'absolutely clear'[18] in the sense that it is specific about what it covers.[19] If the various formats of consent are viewed as a continuum then implied consent is potentially the most ambiguous and explicit consent the clearest.

Some government guidance assumes that 'explicit' consent means written consent[20] but this is probably incorrect.[21] Written consent merely facilitates proof of express consent. The Independent Television Commission's Programme Code[22] recommends that consent be obtained in writing in 'particularly sensitive situations' as when filming intensive care patients and some professional codes of ethics also advise that consent be given in writing.[23] However, putting consent in writing does not necessarily avoid disagreements. 'It may be claimed that the document was signed under duress, that the consent was given for a different purpose, or that the act complained of falls without the scope of the written consent.'[24] **13.03**

It is all too easy to falsify consent, therefore it is advisable that a professional who is told by a third party that a client has consented to the disclosure of confidential personal information ask for proof or check with the client before acting on the consent.[25] Depending upon the circumstances, it may be advisable to consult the client even before confirming the existence of the professional-client relationship.[26] Guidance provided to those working in clinics treating those suffering from sexually transmitted diseases states that '[i]f a health care professional from outside GUM[27] or another person requests information about a patient, evidence of permission from the patient is required before any information is disclosed, *even confirmation of attendance*'.[28] **13.04**

---

[18] *Data Protection Act 1998—Legal Guidance*, 3.1.5. The guidance is available on the Information Commissioner's website at http://www.dataprotection.gov.uk.

[19] 'In appropriate cases it should cover the specific detail of the processing, the particular type of data to be processed (or even the specific information), the purposes of the processing and any special aspects of the processing which may affect the individual, for example, disclosures which may be made of the data.' *Data Protection Act 1998—Legal Guidance*, 3.1.5.

[20] *Information Sharing between the NHS and Local Authorities: Guidance*, para 38 states that 'explicit' consent means 'in practice, signed consent, with no ambiguity and a full statement of the purposes for which consent is given'. Available at http://ww.ssimg.freeserve.co.uk/Guidance/managing_personal_data.htm.

[21] Consent would have to be in writing whenever sensitive data is disclosed if 'explicit' consent in the DPA, Sch 3, para 1 were to be interpreted as a reference to the record and not to the nature of the consent.

[22] See para 9.21 above.

[23] eg GMC, *Seeking patients' consent: the ethical considerations* (London: 2000) 15.

[24] M Tugendhat and I Christie (eds), *The Law of Privacy and the Media* (Oxford: 2002) para 9.06, n 7.

[25] S Ellis, a consultant neurologist, found that 20% of patients whom the Benefits Agency claimed had consented to the disclosure of personal information refused consent when he contacted them: (1997) 314 British Medical J 376.

[26] See para 5.29 above.

[27] Genito-Urinary Medicine.

[28] NCCG Training Manual, available at http://www.mssvd.org.uk/PDF/NCCG/nccgtraining.PDF. (Italics added.)

Duration of Consent

Retraction of consent

13.05 If consent to disclosure of confidential personal information follows the pattern in other areas of law where consent is a defence,[29] consent may be retracted with reasonable notice provided there is nothing contractual[30] or statutory to prevent this. Once consent is withdrawn, a disclosure is actionable subject to possible defences of estoppel or bona fide purchaser for value without notice.[31] The latter defence may assist an innocent third party who has relied on the information to change her position.[32] Conversely, since the former requires prior communication between claimant and defendant,[33] it cannot apply to interceptors or strangers.

Lapsing of consent

13.06 There is no English law on how long unretracted consent remains operative.[34] Section 14 of the Quebec Protection of Personal Information in the Private Sector Act 1993 provides that consent is valid 'only for the length of time needed to achieve the purposes for which it was requested'. It would be a mistake to assume that if a client consented at the outset of a professional relationship to the professional making all disclosures reasonably necessary for the professional to provide an effective service, that this consent authorizes a particular disclosure at some much later date. All the circumstances must be reviewed in order to decide whether it does. If consent is given to a specific disclosure and there is a long delay before disclosure takes place or if circumstances change between the date of the consent and the date of the planned disclosure, it may be necessary to seek fresh consent.

---

[29] M Tugendhat and I Christie (eds), *The Law of Privacy and the Media* (Oxford: 2002) para 9.13. One example given is *Bowden Brothers v Amalgamated Pictorial Ltd* [1911] 1 Ch 386, a copyright case in which revocation of an arrangement for the publication of photographs prevented the defendants from publishing them.

[30] Consent for valuable consideration may become irrevocable. Even so, there may be reasons for equity to refuse specific performance or to grant the client an injunction to prevent the information from being disseminated in which case the client will only be liable to pay damages for withdrawing his consent: *Nicholls v BBC* [1999] EMLR 791.

[31] See para 7.31 above. cp [1981] 2 All ER 321, 346.

[32] Price et al in M Tugendhat and I Christie (eds), *The Law of Privacy and the Media* (Oxford: 2002) para 9.22 writing in the context of media publication suggest that the availability of the defence will depend inter alia on whether the claimant was fully informed about the intended disclosure at the outset, the nature and gravity of the harm to him which disclosure might cause, the extent of damage that non-disclosure might cause the defendant and the claimant's means.

[33] M Tugendhat and I Christie (eds), *The Law of Privacy and the Media* (Oxford: 2002) para 9.21.

[34] The Information Commissioner says that for the purposes of the DPA, a data subject may be able to withdraw consent and that consent may not endure forever: *Data Protection Act 1998– Legal Guidance*, 3.1.5.

A. Express Consent

13.07 It is possible in some circumstances for a client's consent to survive the client's death. In the Canadian case of *Frenette v Metropolitan Life Insurance Co*[35] the defendant insurance company refused to pay out a supplementary indemnity on the death of the insured by drowning on the grounds that the insured had taken his own life or died as a result of taking drugs, both grounds of death excluded by the policy. The beneficiary and the hospital that held the relevant medical records refused to disclose them to the insurance company.[36] The Supreme Court of Canada ruled that the insurance company could not be refused access to the deceased's medical records because at the time that he had applied for life insurance the insured had signed a form expressly authorizing the insurer to have access to his medical records 'for the purposes of risk assessment and loss analysis'.

Capacity to Consent

Adults

Disclosure unlawful with or without consent

13.08 The client's consent to disclosure is irrelevant where disclosure of the information is prohibited by statute or the information is held by a public body that lacks statutory power to disclose it.[37] Before the enactment of the Human Fertilization and Embryology (Disclosure of Information) Act 1992 patients were unable to consent to the disclosure to their general practitioners that they were having infertility treatment. This was because Human Fertilization and Embryology Act 1990, s 33, as originally enacted, allowed disclosure of information about fertility treatment in just a few specified situations (of which this was not one).[38] If construed literally, the Abortion Regulations 1991[39] do not permit a health professional who performed an abortion to be reported to the General Medical Council (GMC) or the Nursing and Midwifery Council (NMC) for incompetence even with the consent of the woman whose pregnancy was terminated.

Authority to consent

13.09 A second condition is that the person who has given consent is the client or someone with authority to consent on the client's behalf.[40] In *R v Secretary of State for*

---

[35] (1992) 89 DLR (4th) 653.
[36] The Supreme Court of Canada said at 674 that the 'duties pertaining to and the principles governing the confidentiality of hospitals with respect to their records are analogous to professional secrecy between physician and patient', per L'Heureux-Dube J.
[37] See eg Local Government Finance Act 1992, Sch 2, para 17(2)(b).
[38] D Brahams, 'IVF Legislation: Error Causes Confidentiality Trap' (1991) 338 Lancet 1449–1450. The situation was rectified by the Human Fertilisation and Embryology (Disclosure of Information) Act 1992.
[39] SI 1991/499. Reg 5(g) allows information to be given 'to a practitioner, with the consent in writing of the woman whose pregnancy was terminated'. It is not stated that anyone else can be informed with her consent.
[40] If a professional receives information in confidence from a client, A, about B, B cannot by his own unauthorized act consent to the disclosure of the information by the professional: *Khashoggi v Smith* (1980) 124 SJ 14.

the Home Department, ex p Taj,[41] an illegal entry case, the court was faced with a conundrum: if, as the Home Secretary alleged, the applicant was not Mohammed Taj, the applicant's consent to the disclosure of Mohammed Taj's medical records to the Home Secretary was worthless. Yet disclosure of those records was expected to resolve who the applicant was. Scott Baker J pragmatically decided that the public interest in disclosure should prevail over medical confidentiality.[42] The issue of authority to consent may arise if the client is dead. Kingston has questioned the propriety of the police taking a blood sample from a man killed in an accident in Britain with the consent of relatives to establish whether he was the perpetrator of a crime in Ireland.[43] It is not known by whom or how the blood sample was taken. If the suspect had not died but had become incompetent his relatives could not have consented to the doctor treating him releasing the results of a blood test to the police.[44]

Capacity to consent

13.10 A more likely issue is whether the client has the legal capacity to consent. An adult's competence to consent is presumed[45] but this presumption can be rebutted.[46] The standard of proof for rebuttal is the balance of probabilities. There is no single test in English law of mental capacity: competence depends upon the context and is issue-specific.[47] For the disclosure of personal information there is no approved legal test.[48] One can confidently predict, however, that competence

---

[41] (QBD, 20 October 1999.)

[42] 'In conducting the balancing exercise, I have come to the conclusion that these records are potentially material and helpful as regards resolving the main issue in the case. In my judgment that overrides the principle of confidentiality.' Per Scott Baker J.

[43] M Kingston, 'Case closed by "dead man walking?"' (2000) 150 NLJ 705. The man had refused to consent to the taking of a sample in Ireland. The taking of intimate body samples (eg blood, semen, urine, pubic hair, dental impression, a swab from an orifice other than the mouth) from the living for the purpose of a criminal investigation is governed by Police and Criminal Evidence Act 1984, s 62. It requires inter alia the written consent of the person from whom the sample is taken (s 62(4)). The Act says nothing about whether consent can be given by that person's personal representatives or next of kin. A recent amendment to the Road Traffic Act 1988 (s 7A) permits a doctor to take a blood sample from a person who is not her patient and is incompetent to consent but the circumstances are strictly defined and nothing can be done with the sample without the consent of the person from whom the blood was taken.

[44] See para 13.11 below. Possibly the doctor would have a public interest defence if he had chosen to disclose the information. On this point see ch 11.

[45] *Masterman-Lister v Brutton & Co* [2002] EWCA Civ 1889, para 17.

[46] cp *Re C* [1994] 1 All ER 819, 824; *Re MB* (1997) 38 BMLR 175.

[47] English law has a range of approaches to mental incapacity with a stricter approach for consent to medical treatment (there must be a sufficient understanding of the nature, purpose and effect of the treatment) than for capacity to contract (the contracting party must be capable of understanding the general nature of what she was doing): *Re C* [1994] 1 All ER 819, 824. For a more detailed discussion see Law Commission Consultation Paper 119, *Mentally Incapacitated Adults and Decision-Making: An Overview* (1991) 19 et seq, and BMA, *Assessment of Mental Capacity* (London: 1995).

[48] No information is given about the test applied by the doctors in *R (on the application of Stevens) v Plymouth City Council* [2002] EWCA Civ 388; [2002] 1 FLR 1177.

A. Express Consent

will not be determined by intelligence quotient or prudence[49] but by the complexity of the disclosure decision, the capacity of the client to take in, understand and weigh up information[50] and the client's ability to communicate his wishes.[51] A client may be capable of consenting to the disclosure of some kinds of information and not others.

If competence to agree to a specific disclosure is lacking, whether temporarily (for example, due to unconsciousness) or permanently (for example, untreatable mental handicap, senile dementia or post-birth brain injury), and there is no relevant enduring power of attorney,[52] no individual (not a spouse, not a blood relative,[53] not a carer, not a Mental Health Act guardian[54]) can consent on the client's behalf.[55] The Family Division has been unable to consent since it lost its parens patriae jurisdiction for the mentally incapacitated.[56] Only the Court of Protection, the body responsible for the management of the property and financial affairs of patients suffering from a mental disorder, has the power to approve disclosure.[57] The Law Commission recognizes that there is a serious gap in the law.[58] In Scotland[59] legislation addressing this lacuna has already been passed and it can only be a matter of time before something is done about the gap in English

13.11

---

[49] '[T]he quality of the decision is irrelevant as long as the person understands what he is deciding', per Wright J, *Masterman-Lister v Jewell* [2002] EWHC 417; [2002] Lloyd's Rep Med 239, para 19.
[50] cp *Re C* [1994] 1 All ER 819, 824; *Re MB* (1997) 38 BMLR 175.
[51] cp *Masterman-Lister v Brutton & Co* [2002] EWCA Civ 1889, paras 26–27.
[52] See para 12.09 above.
[53] Relatives cannot consent to medical treatment for an adult and ipso facto they cannot consent to the disclosure of information. This point seems to have escaped the NHS Executive which proposes to allow disclosure of patient information to other public agencies on the say-so of relatives if the patient is too ill to consent: P Singleton, J Hunnable, R Mason, *Gaining patient consent to disclosure—a consultancy project for the NHS Executive* (DoH, 2001) available from http://www.doh.gov.uk.
[54] This is the authority or person appointed under the Mental Health Act 1983 to decide for an incompetent person received into guardianship (s 7) such matters as where he is to reside, what treatment he is to receive and how he is to be trained and occupied: *R (on the application of Stevens) v Plymouth City Council* [2002] EWCA Civ 388; [2002] 1 FLR 1177, para 18.
[55] The doctrine of implied consent (see para 13.34 below) may save the day for those clients who have not always been incompetent provided the information does not fall into the category of sensitive personal data for which 'explicit' consent is required by the DPA (see para 18.25 below).
[56] *T v T* [1988] Fam 52. Note, however, that the Family Division has assumed an inherent jurisdiction, which is not restricted to questions concerning medical treatment, to declare what is in an incapacitated adult's 'best interests' (*T v T* [1988] Fam 52; *A v A Health Authority* [2002] EWHC 18; [2002] Fam 213, paras 38–39). This jurisdiction can be invoked 'by anyone whose past or present relationship with the incompetent adult . . . gives him a genuine and legitimate interest in obtaining a decision', per Munby J, para 42. See also *Re S* [1995] 1 FLR 1075.
[57] The Court of Protection has jurisdiction over all the affairs of a patient bar the management or care of the patient's person: *Re W (EEM)* [1971] Ch 123, 143.
[58] See Law Commission, *Mental Incapacity* Law Com 231 (1995) and various government papers.
[59] Adults with Incapacity Act 2000.

Children

Young people between the ages of 16 and 18

13.12 When the client is a minor, competence to consent is not assumed. Scant attention has been paid, however, to the competence of someone under the age of 18 to consent to anything beyond medical treatment.[61] The Family Law Reform Act 1969 creates an irrebuttable presumption that a young person of 16 or 17 is legally competent to consent to medical, dental and surgical treatment without reference to a parent.[62] This would seem to imply competence to consent to the disclosure of medical information (otherwise treatment might not be possible). The Family Law Reform Act, by analogy,[63] points to the competence of a minor of 16 or above to consent to the disclosure of information that is not health-related.[64]

> [A] young person of this age is free to leave school, is not subject to employment restrictions, is free to consent to medical treatment and operations, free to marry with parental consent and, in the case of girls ... free to engage in sexual intercourse.[65]

It would be strange therefore if a 16 year old who did not suffer from any mental disability lacked the power to consent to the disclosure of personal information.

Mature children under 16

13.13 Ability of child to consent It was decided in *Gillick v West Norfolk and Wisbech Area Health Authority*[66] that a child under 16 who has the maturity and intelligence

---

[60] *F v West Berkshire Health Authority* [1989] 2 All ER 545, 551, 564–565; *Re F* [1990] 2 AC 1, 75; *Re A* [2000] 4 All ER 961, 991. See also, GMC, *Confidentiality: Protecting and Providing Information* (London: 2000) para 10; BMA on-line guidance on 'Confidentiality and disclosure of health information' (London: 1999), available at http://www.bma.org.uk. cp DoH, *Reference Guide for Examination or Treatment* (2001) para 8.5. See also, Council of Europe, Committee of Ministers, Recommendation R (99) 4 on principles concerning the legal protection of incapable adults, principle 26, available at http://cm.coe.int/ta/rec/1999/99r4.htm. Mental Health Act 1983, s 63 authorizes treatment for a mental order without consent and this must carry with it the power to disclose information necessary for the treatment to take place. See also para 19.70 below.

[61] As regards children and medical treatment see J Montgomery, *Health Care Law* (2nd edn, Oxford: 2000) ch 12, esp 308–311.

[62] s 8(1). cp s 21(2). The minor's consent 'cannot be overridden by those with parental responsibility for the minor' but can 'be overridden by the court' per Lord Donaldson, *Re W* [1992] 4 All ER 627, 639. Family Law Reform Act 1969, s 8(3) preserves the common law powers of consent.

[63] Statutory developments may influence the common law: *Erven Warnink Besloten Vennootschap v J Townsend & Sons* [1979] 2 All ER 927, 933. cp Age of Legal Capacity (Scotland) Act 1991.

[64] cp Age of Legal Capacity (Scotland) Act 1991.

[65] A Bainham, 'Sex education: a family lawyer's perspective' in N Harris (ed), *Children, Sex Education and the Law* (London: 1996) 37.

[66] [1985] 3 All ER 402, 413, 423, 425. See further J Fortin, *Children's Rights and the Developing Law* (London: 1998) 98 et seq; M Brazier and C Bridge, 'Coercion or Caring: Analysing Adolescent Autonomy' (1996) 16 LS 84. cp *Bellotti v Baird* 443 US 622 (1979).

A. Express Consent

to understand what is proposed and to reach a sensible decision is able to consent to medical treatment (in that case contraception) of which the parent is unaware.[67] Logically this competence must be accompanied by the capacity to consent to the receipt and disclosure of personal information relevant to that treatment. Department of Health guidelines assume that capacity to consent to treatment and to the disclosure of information go hand in hand.[68] Factors affecting the assessment of maturity should include the child's intellectual development, chronological, mental and emotional age and capacity to make up his own mind.

What of information that is not health-related? Can this be disclosed on the say-so of a mature child under 16?[69] There is legislation that for certain purposes expressly allows this. It is provided in the Education (Special Educational Needs) (England) (Consolidation) Regulations 2001 that except in circumstances laid down, a statement of special educational needs and supporting documentation may not be disclosed without the child's consent[69a] and, further, that '[a] child may consent to the disclosure of a statement . . . if his age and understanding are sufficient to allow him to understand the nature of that consent'.[70] That children younger than 16 may consent to the disclosure of personal information about themselves is supported by implication by the Children Act 1989 and Family Proceedings Rules 1991. These permit a child of 'sufficient understanding'[71] to instruct a solicitor directly for various family law related purposes.[72] **13.14**

As with consent to medical treatment, there can be no hard-and-fast rules about the disclosures that can be made on the basis of the child's consent. Everything will turn on the complexity of the issues and the seriousness of the decision: '[t]he graver the consequences of the decision, the commensurately greater the level of **13.15**

---

[67] If the parent becomes aware that the child has consented, the parent cannot overrule the 'Gillick' competent child's consent to treatment, though a court may do so: *Re R* [1991] 4 All ER 177, 187.

[68] DoH, *The Protection and Use of Patient Information* HSG (96) 18 (1996) para 4.10. While it may be true that a child that is competent to consent to treatment is competent to consent to disclosure of information the converse may not be true. A child who has the maturity to understand issues of disclosure may not yet have the maturity to appreciate the full implications of accepting treatment.

[69] The PCC assumes not. See Granton and Daily Post, 3 August 2002 (complaint by mother of 15 year old girl about a consensual interview with daughter upheld).

[69a] SI 2001/3455, reg 24(1).

[70] reg 24(2).

[71] The competence of a child to instruct a solicitor has been litigated on various occasions and the *Gillick* test applied: *Re S* [1993] 3 All ER 36; *Re SC* [1994] 1 FLR 96; *Re C* [1995] 1 FLR 927. See also, I Hamilton and J Wilson, 'Representation of Children in Private Law Proceedings under the Children Act 1989' (1998) 8 Representing Children 32, 34.

[72] Children Act 1989, s 10(8) and Family Proceedings Rules 1991 SI 1991/1247, r 9.2A recognize the ability of a child of sufficient understanding to instruct a solicitor to seek a s 8 order. See further I Hamilton and J Wilson, 'Representation of Children in Private Law Proceedings under the Children Act 1989' (1998) 8 Representing Children 32. Likewise, children can instruct their own solicitors in public law proceedings if of sufficient understanding: Family Proceedings Rules 1991, rr 4.11, 4.12.

Chapter 13: Consent

competence is required . . .'.[73] The Human Genetics Commission thinks that 'in general parental consent is advisable where any genetic test might have a major psychological effect or where it might have serious implications for other people or for family relationships'.[74]

13.16 **Ability of parent to consent** The fact that a minor (whether over or under 16 years of age) is able to consent to the disclosure of information does not have to mean that no one else can consent. Consent to life-saving medical treatment may be given by a court in its wardship jurisdiction[75] or by someone with parental authority for a patient of 16 who has refused the treatment.[76] Of necessity, this implies that those with authority to consent to treatment have authority also to disclose information required for that treatment to take place.[77] Is consent to (life-saving) medical treatment a particular application of a general rule that a person with parental authority can override a refusal of consent by a competent minor or a special case? Insight can be obtained by considering (1) legislative precedents (2) ECHR and (3) policy arguments.

13.17 The Access to Health Records Act 1990 (now superseded by the DPA) allowed a competent child to deny parental access to his medical records.[78] An independent parental right to access the medical records for the purpose of relaying information to a third party (say an insurer) is not consistent with this. The Education (Special Educational Needs) (England) Consolidation Regulations 2001 very specifically state: '[i]f a child *does not have sufficient age or understanding to allow him to consent to disclosure of his statement his parent may consent on his behalf.*'[78a] The clear

---

[73] per Butler-Sloss LJ, *Re MB* (1997) 38 BMLR 175, 186. cp *Secretary, Department of Health and Community Services v JWB* (1992) 175 CLR 215, 293.

[74] *Inside Information* (May 2002) para 4.40. Another area of uncertainty is disclosure for the purposes of research. There is on-going debate about the ethics of involving children in genetic research. If the research is not against the child's best interests, it does not seem objectionable to disclose information with the mature child's consent for this purpose if the information will be protected by an obligation of confidentiality.

[75] *Re A* [2000] 4 All ER 961, 992.

[76] *Re W* [1992] 4 All ER 627, 638.

[77] The DoH guidance, *Reference Guide to Consent for Examination or Treatment* (2001) para 8.3 allows parents to be given information about a competent child's medical condition where the child's refusal of treatment puts the child at serious risk stating: '[w]hile this will constitute a breach of confidence on the part of the clinician treating the child, this may be justifiable where it is in the child's best interests.'

[78] See para 19.72 below

[78a] SI 2001/3455, reg 24(3) (emphasis added). See also the DFEE's Code of Practice on the Identification and Assessment of Special Educational Needs (1994) para 2.52 which bars a doctor or health service worker from disclosing 'medical information without first obtaining the consent of the parents *and, where he or she has sufficient understanding, the child*. Exceptionally, children under age 16, who are judged to be competent by their doctors may give consent independently of their parents. When they first form an opinion that a child has special educational needs, doctors may find it convenient to alert parents *and children* to the possibility that they will be asked to give information to schools and the LEA. Doctors may then seek the consent of parents *and children* to the disclosure of necessary medical information to the school or LEA if they judge this would be

A. Express Consent

implication is that a child with the maturity to consent must be the one who consents. Nowhere has Parliament given parent and child concurrent rights to authorize disclosure of confidential personal information about the child to a third party.[79] Were Parliament to do so an issue of incompatibility with the European Convention on Human Rights (ECHR) might arise.

13.18 The right to privacy guaranteed by Article 8(1) is not restricted to adults.[80] Possibly a child has an even greater need for privacy than an adult. Unlike the UN Convention on the Rights of the Child,[81] there is no explicit requirement in the ECHR for a child to be consulted,[82] but it is arguable that the disclosure of confidential personal information about a competent child without consulting the child first, and even more so, against the child's known wishes, is disrespectful of the child's private life.[83] Referring to consent to invasive medical treatment, Balcombe LJ said: '[i]t will normally be in the best interests of a child of sufficient age and understanding to make an informed decision that the court should respect its integrity as a human being and not lightly override its decision . . .'[84] Hockton[85] (also writing in the context of consent to medical treatment) suggests that a different consent rule for the competent adult and the competent child discriminates unlawfully between the two, contrary to Article 14 of the ECHR.[86] Should the argument for seeking the child's consent, or, failing this, at least consultation, be accepted, a disclosure that has not involved the mature child will be unlawful unless the professional can show it is for a legitimate aim, a pressing social need and proportionate.[87]

---

helpful to the child' (emphasis added). Available at http://www.dfes.gov.uk/sen/documents/Code_of_Practice.htm.

[79] Disclosure of information about the child to a parent is discussed in ch 19.

[80] *Re A* [2001] 1 FLR 1, 98; *R (on the application of Addinell) v Sheffield City Council* [2001] ACD 61. cp *Nielsen v Denmark* (1989) 11 EHRB 175, 191; UN Convention on the Rights of the Child (1989) Art 16: '1. No child shall be subjected to arbitrary or unlawful interference with his or her privacy . . . 2. The child has the right to the protection of the law against such interference or attacks.'

[81] Resolution 44/25 (1989), Art 12(1): 'States Parties shall assure to the child who is capable of forming his or her own views the right to express those views freely in all matters affecting the child, the views of the child being given due weight in accordance with the age and maturity of the child.'

[82] U Kilkelly, *The Child and the European Convention on Human Rights* (Aldershot: 1999) 117. But see European Convention on the Exercise of Children's Rights, Art 3, reproduced at para 19.110 below.

[83] Kilkelly, ibid 118–119 writes that failure to consult a child has never been found to breach the Convention, but also that specific claims of this nature have never been brought on behalf of children. However, the Commission has used Art 8 to justify refusal of parental contact that is contrary to the wishes of the child.

[84] *Re W* [1993] Fam 64, 88.

[85] A Hockton, *The Law of Consent to Medical Treatment* (London: 2002) 82.

[86] See para 3.19 above. Article 14 does not mention age, but the list of objectionable grounds of discrimination is not exhaustive.

[87] See para 3.19 above. The Education (Special Educational Needs) (England) Consolidation Regulations 2001 allow disclosure of the education needs statement without the consent of either child or parent 'to persons to whom, in the opinion of the authority concerned, it is necessary to disclose the statement in the interests of the child'. Query: in the case of a mature child, is this

13.19 It was Lord Scarman's opinion in *Gillick v West Norfolk and Wisbech Area Health Authority* that parental rights derive from parental duties and lapse once the child becomes competent to make his own decisions.[88] Life-threatening situations apart, there is, it is submitted, no justification for allowing a competent child's decision to disallow disclosure to be overridden if no third party is adversely affected by non-disclosure. A different approach may be necessary if non-disclosure has adverse repercussions for a third party. For example, the parents of a child with a taxable personal income are liable for the tax in default of payment by the child.[89] The parents would be put in an unenviable position if the child were able to refuse consent to the disclosure of financial information to the Inland Revenue. Such a refusal would be evidence of immaturity and therefore incompetence but care must be taken to ensure that disclosure does not take place in the best interests of the parent rather than of the child. Leaving aside such problematic cases, a general rule that treats a mature child as competent to consent to, but not to stop, disclosure of confidential personal information undermines the principle of autonomy. If parent and child are at loggerheads about disclosure of information and there are potentially serious repercussions for the child from non-disclosure, there is always the option of seeking the intervention of a court in the exercise of its parens patriae jurisdiction. The High Court's powers under this jurisdiction are theoretically limitless. It can step into the shoes of anyone under 18 years of age and approve or disapprove the disputed disclosure.

Children of tender years

13.20 **Who can consent** When a child lacks the maturity to consent to the disclosure of confidential information, whether that information concerns the child's health or anything else, the consent must be sought from someone with parental responsibility[90] or a court: '[a] "*Gillick* incompetent" child cannot exercise the right of surrender, but the parent may exercise it on his behalf.'[91] In an emergency, if no one with parental responsibility is available to consent to the disclosure of

---

compatible with article 8? No safeguards are provided in the legislation for the information once disclosed.

[88] [1985] 3 All ER 402, 423–424 and L Scarman, 'Law and Medical Practice' in P Byrne (ed), *Medicine in Contemporary Society* (Oxford: 1987) 136–137.

[89] Taxes Management Act 1970, s 73(a).

[90] The following people may have parental responsibility: the child's mother; the child's father, if married to the mother at the time of or after the birth; the child's father if, though never married to the mother, he has acquired parental authority by order of a court or by agreement with the mother (Children Act 1989, s 4); the local authority, if child is the subject of a care order; anyone who has a residence order in relation to the child. Where more than one person has parental responsibility for the child, the consent of one of those persons suffices in law (Children Act 1989, s 2(7)). One person with parental responsibility cannot veto the consent of another person with parental authority without obtaining an order from a court, although there is obiter dicta by Glidewell LJ in *Re G* [1994] 2 FLR 964, 967 to the effect that some major decisions involving children ought to require consultation between all those with parental responsibility.

[91] per Ward LJ, *Re Z* [1995] 4 All ER 961, 983. See also 979, 980.

A. Express Consent

information, the person who has the care of the child at the time may do so provided consent 'is reasonable in all the circumstances of the case for the purpose of safeguarding or promoting the child's welfare'.[92]

Preventing parental consent A court exercising ordinary equitable principles may restrain a person with parental responsibilities from consenting to the disclosure of confidential personal information about a child.[93] In addition a court has a non-equitable jurisdiction 'to restrain any act by a parent that if unrestrained would or might adversely affect the welfare of the child'.[94] This could include disclosure of information.[95] This jurisdiction can be exercised either through a prohibited steps order under s 8 of the Children Act 1989[96] or by means of an injunction.[97] 13.21

Reality of Consent

Freely given consent

The client's consent or that of a proxy, where permitted, must be freely given. This means that the consent was not obtained under duress,[98] by coercion or as a result of significant deception or undue influence. 'Undue influence generally involves such moral pressure . . . [to consent] that there is domination by a wrongdoer of the mind and will [of the consenting party such] . . . that the mind of the latter becomes a mere channel through which the wishes of the former flowed.'[99] Children and young persons are highly vulnerable to pressure from those with whom they have emotional ties.[100] When a minor has consented to something that is to his disadvantage, the possibility of undue influence should be considered. 13.22

Consent that is compelled by law

When the ability to withhold consent to the disclosure of personal information is abrogated by domestic law, Article 8 is likely to be engaged.[101] If it is, the disclosure 13.23

---

[92] Children Act 1989, s 3(5).
[93] *Kelly v BBC* [2001] 1 All ER 323, 340.
[94] *Re G* [1999] 3 FCR 181, 187–188.
[95] In its wardship jurisdiction '[t]he court can . . . forbid the publication of information about the ward or the ward's family circumstances', per Lord Donaldson, *Re R* [1991] 4 All ER 177, 186.
[96] *Re Z* [1995] 4 All ER 961, 979, 980–981.
[97] *A v M* [2000] 1 FCR 1.
[98] In contractual situations duress exists where the victim would not have agreed to disclosure but for pressure exerted on him that the law regards as illegitimate or which left the victim without a practical choice: *Att-Gen for England and Wales v R* [2002] 2 NZLR 91 paras 59–69.
[99] per Tipping J, *Att-Gen for England and Wales v R* [2002] 2 NZLR 91 para 77. What constitutes undue influence is likely to be affected by the relationship of the parties and the reason that consent is needed.
[100] *Re T* [1992] 4 All ER 649, 662, 666–668, 669 (a case in which consent to medical treatment was refused under the undue influence of the mother).
[101] *R (on the application of Robertson) v City of Wakefield Metropolitan Council* [2001] EWHC Admin 915; [2002] 2 WLR 889, paras 29 et seq.

must be in accordance with law, in pursuit of a legitimate objective and proportionate. There are circumstances in which consent is compelled by the laws of another jurisdiction. US courts regularly issue consent directives that require defendants, on pain of being in contempt of court, to agree to the disclosure of confidential banking information held outside the United States.[102] In *Re Matter of ABC Ltd*[103] a Cayman Islands case, Summerfield CJ said:

> [W]here consent is a material element giving rise to a legal consequence, it must be voluntarily and freely given in the exercise of an independent and uncoerced judgment. This is a well-established principle in every sphere of our law, civil and criminal... To take any other view would result in allowing a foreign court to undermine and circumvent the provisions of the Confidential Relationships (Preservation) Law. This is not only important to this country where the law exists but would be equally important in many other common law countries which respect the principle in *Tournier v National Provincial & Union Bank of England* governing the duty of a bank to maintain secrecy.[104]

Absence of penalty-free choice

13.24 Deciding whether consent was 'real'[105] may be problematic where the client does not have a penalty-free choice. If a rape victim is told that the Crown Prosecution Service cannot prosecute unless allowed access to her rape counselling records in order to assess her credibility is the consent valid? Should a doctor disclose a patient's medical record to a prospective employer if he knows that the patient had no option but to provide the information to get the job?[106] The reality of consent may similarly be compromised if the patient knows that life insurance or a mortgage will be refused if consent to disclosure is not forthcoming. The Australian Privacy Charter states:

> ... 'consent' is meaningless if people ... have no option but to consent in order to obtain a benefit or service ...'[107]

13.25 In *R v A Local Authority in the Midlands, ex p LM*,[108] LM faced the choice of consenting to a police check or the contract upon which he depended for his livelihood would be terminated. Dyson J said that 'on a realistic view of the facts, if LM were to sign the form, he would not be consenting to the interference with his pri-

---

[102] *In the Matter of ABC Ltd* [1984] CILR 130, 132–133.
[103] [1984] CILR 130.
[104] ibid at 135.
[105] *Chatterton v Gerson* [1981] QB 432, 442.
[106] Contractual terms requiring a person to exercise his data subject access rights to obtain a health record and make it available are made void by DPA, s 57. The Act does not state that a professional must refuse subject access where she has good reason to believe that it is enforced. Legislation in some US states prohibits compelling consent to disclosure of information or records which identify an individual as HIV positive: H Edgar and H Sandomire, 'Medical Privacy Issues in the Age of AIDS: Legislative Options' (1990) 16 American J of L and Medicine 157, 173.
[107] (1994) 1 Privacy L and Policy Reporter 136. cp Art 29 DPWP Opinion 8/2001 5062/01/EN/Final p 3.
[108] *R v A Local Authority in the Midlands, ex p LM* [2000] UKHRR 143, 151.

A. Express Consent

vate life that the disclosure of the allegations would entail'. No specific test for determining genuine consent was suggested. In *Home Office v Wainwright*[109] Buxton LJ commented on the difficulty in crimes against the person of distinguishing between 'consent and submission' and of handling 'social' or 'forced' consent.

Psychological pressure

In addition to external pressure of the kind LM faced, the client may be subject to psychological pressures. Bollas and Sundelson, writing from the standpoint of the psychologist or psychiatrist, question whether there is such a thing as free consent.[110]   **13.26**

> The patient's or client's freedom of choice and freedom to negotiate are real and meaningful only if we forget about the unconscious . . . [T]he client or patient is not—and cannot—be aware of unconscious motives that may affect his contract 'negotiation'. At best, such motives make any true 'meeting of the minds', the essential condition of contract formation, difficult to achieve, at worst, they make it illusory.[111]

As pragmatic institutions, it is improbable that the courts will be swayed by arguments about the 'unconscious'.

Divining genuine consent

Consent, it is submitted, should be regarded as 'real' provided that: **13.27**

(1) there is a practical choice to agree or refuse consent to disclosure (even if the choice is an unpalatable one);
(2) the client intended to consent to disclosure; and
(3) consent to disclosure was not a consequence of pressure (or deception) that the courts regard as unacceptable.[112]

The Information Commissioner suggests, for example, that it would not be unfair that a patient should have to consent to his GP disclosing medical data to a Health Authority for administrative purposes as a condition of receiving treatment from the GP.[113] Factors affecting the legitimacy of external pressure include its nature and source, the nature of the information disclosed and the purpose of its disclosure.[114]

---

[109] [2001] EWCA Civ 2081; [2002] 3 WLR 405, para 117.
[110] This borders on the question: is there such a thing as free will?
[111] *The New Informants* (London: 1996) 164.
[112] cp *Re T* [1992] 4 All ER 649, 669 and see now *R v Att-Gen for England and Wales* [2003] UKPC 22. Sexual offences (Amendment) Act 1976, s 4(5B) offers a statutory analogy of unacceptable pressure to consent to disclosure of personal information.
[113] *Guidance on the Use and Disclosure of Health Data* (May 2002) 15.
[114] cp *Att-Gen for England and Wales v R* (NZCA, 21 May 2001). One medical law textbook comments: '[w]hat patient at a teaching hospital out-patient department is likely to refuse when the consultant asks: "You don't mind these young doctors being present, do you?"—the pressures are

Informed Consent[115]

The position at common law

13.28 There is no general principle in English law that consent has to be informed to be effective.

> [E]quity has developed a concept that a fiduciary cannot get rid of his fiduciary duties without the informed consent of the client[116] or patient. But I am not aware of any other type of case where English law provides that an apparently valid consent is invalid solely on the grounds of lack of knowledge of the surrounding circumstances or the consequences of giving consent. In my judgment there is no ground in English law for extending this limited doctrine of informed consent outside the field of property rights in which it is established.[117]

Nevertheless in *R v Department of Health, ex p Source Informatics* Lord Lester argued[118] (and Simon Brown LJ accepted)[119] that in the pharmacist–customer relationship, the customer must be told the purpose and extent of a proposed disclosure of confidential personal information[120] in order for the pharmacist to have the customer's valid consent. The same rule is followed in medical treatment cases:[121] the patient must be told 'in broad terms'[122] the nature and effect and risks of the proposed treatment.[123] If the doctor omits this information, the doctor is in breach of the duty of care to inform and can be sued in negligence (if all the other elements of the tort are satisfied).[124] If there is misfeasance (misrepresentation of

---

virtually irresistible . . .': J Mason, R McCall Smith and G Laurie, *Law and Medical Ethics* (London: 1999) 194. In this example the pressure is a social one. The training of doctors is important for society and the patient does not want to look like someone lacking in public spirit. It is improbable that a court would be concerned about this kind of pressure.

[115] This phrase was coined in the US in *Salgo v Leland Stanford Jr University Board Trustees* 317 P 2d 180 (1957) where it is associated with a specific standard, the 'reasonable person standard of disclosure' which requires a doctor to disclose to a patient what the reasonable person would want to know before consenting to medical treatment. The phrase is used in this book in a more general sense.

[116] See eg *Clark Boyce v Mouat* [1993] 4 All ER 268, 237: a solicitor may act for both parties in a transaction only if he has their informed consent. A solicitor may disclose to client A confidential information obtained from client B in another transaction only with client B's informed consent: *Hilton v Barker Booth & Eastwood* [2002] EWCA Civ 723, para 47.

[117] *Sidaway v Bethlem Royal Hospital Governors* [1984] 1 All ER 1018, 1032 per Browne-Wilkinson LJ. See also Lord Donaldson at 1026.

[118] The argument is reported in [2001] QB 425.

[119] [2000] 1 All ER 786, 800 [51].

[120] ie prescription details.

[121] Consent to medical treatment, by implication, also involves consent to the disclosure of information about that treatment to third parties. See para 13.41 below.

[122] per Lord Donaldson MR, *Re T* [1992] 4 All ER 649, 663.

[123] DoH, *Reference Guide to Consent for Examination or Treatment* (2001) para 4. Cp Convention on Human Rights and Biomedicine (1997) Art 5.

[124] A successful action in negligence for breach of duty to inform requires proof that the claimant would have withheld consent had the missing information been supplied: *Chatterton v Gerson* [1981] 1 All ER 257, 265; *Chester v Afshar* [2002] EWCA Civ 724; [2002] 3 All ER 552.

A. Express Consent

the risks or denial of information expressly or impliedly sought) and not merely non-feasance, consent to treatment may be vitiated.[125] There is no reason why the rule about informed consent that applies to doctors and pharmacists in England and Wales should not apply to other professionals who, like doctors and pharmacists, are not fiduciaries.[126]

Statutory requirements

Specific statutory requirements

13.29 The Human Fertilisation and Embryology Act 1990 states that 'consent to disclosure given at the request of another shall be disregarded unless, before it is given, the person requesting it takes reasonable steps to explain to the individual from whom it is requested the implications of compliance with the request'.[127]

Data Protection Act 1998

13.30 Whatever the position at common law, the DPA almost certainly requires the client to be given a substantial explanation of the effect of consenting to the disclosure of personal data even for consent that need not be 'explicit'.[128] Vague representations that information will be used to provide a service such as health care, education, or legal assistance might not be enough.[129] The client needs to receive sufficient information to make an informed decision about whether to consent to the processing of personal data. Article 2(h) of the EU Directive on Data Protection[130] upon which the DPA is based, and which may be considered in its interpretation,[131] defines the data subject's consent as

> any freely given *specific* and *informed* indication of his wishes by which the data subject signifies his agreement to personal data relating to him being processed.[132]

---

[125] *Re T* [1992] 4 All ER 649, 663. In medical treatment cases this means that treatment amounts to battery.

[126] For an indication of the professionals who are fiduciaries see para 19.58 below. They, certainly, must give the client full information before seeking consent for any purpose.

[127] Human Fertilisation and Embryology Act 1990, s 33(6D).

[128] Explicit consent is required for the disclosure of sensitive personal information unless the client has put the information into the public domain or disclosure is *necessary* for certain reasons laid down in the DPA: see para 18.25 below.

[129] In a consultation paper the Department of Health, Social Services and Public Safety, *Health and Personal Social Services Protecting: Personal Information* (NI: June, 2002), para 2.2 suggests that 'simply telling service users that their personal information will be used for health and social care purposes would be too general. On the other hand, an explanation that detailed all the administrative systems in which data might be recorded, the use of data for diagnosis for treatment, service provision etc. would be deemed excessive.' See also R Smith, 'Publishing information about patients' (1995) 311 British Medical J 1240.

[130] (EC) 95/46.

[131] If the DPA does not properly implement the EU Directive by dropping the requirement of unambiguous consent in Art 7(a) (see para 13.02 n13 above), under the doctrine of indirect effect the court must adopt an interpretation consistent with the EU Directive.

[132] Italics added. Art 2(h). The same definition of consent has been adopted in Directive (EC) 2002/58 on privacy and electronic communications: see preamble (17), Art 2(f).

This wording precludes blanket authorization to disclosures that are unlimited as to their duration, subject matter, purpose or recipient: '[a] patient cannot be deemed to have consented to something of which he or she is ignorant.'[133]

13.31 It is arguable that, because of the EU Directive, valid consent for the purposes of the DPA[134] requires that the client be made aware of all of the following:[135]

(1) the right to refuse consent to the disclosure or to limit the amount of information disclosed (if disclosure is optional);[136]
(2) the purpose(s) of the planned disclosure;
(3) the duration of the consent[137] (which can be for an unlimited period of time if a full explanation is given at the time consent is solicited);[138]
(4) the person(s) to whom disclosure may be made;
(5) whether those to whom information is disclosed are under an obligation of confidentiality;
(6) the type of information to be disclosed;
(7) that the client can be identified from the information that is disclosed;[139]
(8) any appreciable risk of adverse consequences from the disclosure;
(9) the right to freely withdraw consent at any time without giving reasons[139a] (unless withdrawal is a practical impossibility or by law not allowed).

There is an obvious overlap between the fair processing requirements of the DPA[140] and informed consent.[141] If insufficient information is given, the processing may not be fair.

13.32 Codes of professional ethics may offer guidance about what the professional should tell the client.[142] The Faculty of Occupational Medicine says:

---

[133] Information Commissioner, *Guidance on the Use and Disclosure of Health Data* (May 2002) 15.

[134] The word consent is not defined in the Act.

[135] cp Department of Health, Social Services and Public Safety, *Health and Personal Social Services Protecting: Personal Information; A Consultation Paper* (NI: June 2002) para 3.12.

[136] This is subject to para 13.27 above (service conditional on consent to reasonably necessary disclosures).

[137] The Information Commissioner says that the consent 'must be appropriate to the particular circumstances. For example, if the processing to which it relates is intended to continue indefinitely ... then the consent should cover those circumstances.' *Data Protection Act 1998—An Introduction*, ch 3.

[138] eg, consent by a banking customer when the customer opens an account to reference or status inquiries after the system has been clearly explained. To seek the client's express or implied consent every time the bank's opinion is sought would be administratively inconvenient.

[139] If identification is impossible the DPA does not apply: para 18.05 below.

[139a] cp Council of Europe, Committee of Ministers, Recommendation 5 (83) 10, *Protection of Personal Data used for Scientific Research and Statistics*, para 3.2.

[140] See paras 18.10 et seq.

[141] Information Commissioner, *Guidance on the Use and Disclosure of Health Data,* May 2002 16.

[142] cp *Human Fertilisation and Embryology Code of Practice* (1998) paras 3.6, 3.7, available at http://www.hfea.gov.uk/code/chapter3.htm.

Consent is only informed if the subject understands what information is being released, the purposes for which it will be used, and the possible consequences of that use.[143]

Contractual obligations

If there is a contractual relationship between client and professional, provision of erroneous or insufficient information to the client may be a breach of contract.

13.33

B. Implied Consent

Disclosure for Primary Purposes

Implied consent: an introduction

What is implied consent?

So long as consent does not have to be explicit,[144] consent may be implied from conduct. An inference of consent is warranted if the client was aware, or ought reasonably to have been aware,[145] that in the prevailing circumstances an action or inaction will be understood as incidentally indicating consent.[146] Examples are the failure of the client to tick a box for disallowing disclosure of personal information or posing for a photograph known to be intended for a website for an educational institution. In *Kampadia v Lambeth LBC*[147] the Court of Appeal held that a person bringing a disability discrimination complaint against his employer who had agreed to submit to a medical examination by the employer's medical expert had impliedly consented to the disclosure of the resulting report to the employer.[148]

13.34

Caution needs to be exercised when implying consent from conduct. In *Interbrew SA v Financial Times Ltd* sensitive (and probably false) commercial information concerning the claimant company had been passed to newspapers. Sedley LJ refused to treat a decision to comment on the record to the press about the information as dissolving its confidentiality. 'By going on the record . . . he was

13.35

---

[143] Faculty of Occupational Medicine, *Guidance on Ethics for Occupational Physicians* (5th edn. London: 1999) 1, 3.
[144] See para 18.25 below.
[145] The test is objective; unexpressed feelings do not matter.
[146] *O'Brien v Cunard Steamship Co* 28 NE 266, 273–275 (1891). cp *Abbasi v Minister for Immigration and Multicultural Affairs* [2001] FCA 1274, para 63.
[147] The Times, 4 July 2000.
[148] Can consent to disclosure of information by a professional be implied from the commencement of an action against the professional? The courts regard instigation of proceedings as amounting to waiver of legal professional privilege, eg *Lillicrap v Halder & Son* [1993] 1 All ER 724. See J Auburn, *Legal Professional Privilege* (Oxford: 2000) 217 and para 16.34 below. The same reasoning has been applied to actions against doctors in some other common law jurisdictions, eg *Hague v Williams* 181 A 2d 345 (1962); *Hay v University of Alberta Hospital* (1990) 105 AR 276, but not in England: see para 14.09 below. See also para 12.33 above.

trying [intelligently] to limit the harm . . . I see no possible case of waiver or acquiescence . . . unless it is to be the law that the victim of a leak is damned if he speaks to the media and damned if he does not.'[149] One can see that this might apply also to personal information. Furthermore implied consent cannot be based upon a professional practice or usage such as the banking practice of giving an opinion to another bank about a customer's credit-worthiness without reference to the customer unless it is notorious amongst the members of the public who make up the clientele.[150]

Inferring consent from silence

13.36 In *Theakston v MGN Ltd*[151] Ouseley J accepted the argument of counsel for the defendant newspaper that if an individual makes no complaint when information about him, in this instance aspects of his sex life, is put into the public domain he is to be taken as having consented to the publication of further personal information of a similar kind.[152] The objection from the claimant's counsel that consent must be specific to the particular material in question[153] was brushed aside.[154] The approach taken by the defence runs counter to the case law on consent.[155] It either confuses implied consent with the public domain argument[156] or a defence of waiver.[157] Consent must be 'real'[158] and to some extent degree informed.[159] In *Theakston* the 'consent' was neither.[160] Treating knowledge of a risk of disclosure as tantamount to consent is equally wrong.[161]

---

[149] [2002] EWCA Civ 274; [2002] 2 Lloyd's Rep 229, para 45.

[150] *Turner v Royal Bank of Scotland* [1999] 2 All ER Comm 664, 669–670. cp *R v Neil* [2002] SCC 70, para 28.

[151] [2002] EWHC 137; [2002] EMLR 22.

[152] ibid, paras 48, 75. For a similar argument see W. Keeton (ed), *Prosser and Keeton on The Law of Torts* (5th edn, St Paul: 1984) 860. Cp. *Granada Television complaint on behalf of Ms Jacqueline Pirie*, 23 January 2000, available from http://www.pcc.org.uk.

[153] [2002] EWHC 137; [2002] EMLR 22, para 53.

[154] ibid, para 66.

[155] Including consent as a defence in tort: see E Paton-Simpson, 'Privacy and the Reasonable Paranoid: The Protection of Privacy in Public Places' (2000) 50 U of Toronto LJ 305, 333–338. The sole exception is an obiter passage in *Malone v Commissioner of Police* [1979] 2 All ER 620, 645, 646.

[156] See para 5.10 above. The kind of argument made by the newspaper in *Theakston* was treated as relevant to whether the information was in the public domain by the Press Complaints Commission in *Granada Television complaint on behalf of MS Jacqueline Pirie*, 23 January 2000.

[157] See para 13.63 below. But see reservations about this defence, para 13.01 n above

[158] See para 13.22 below.

[159] See para 13.28 below.

[160] For the same reason the suggestion by Tugendhat ('The Data Protection Act 1998 and the Media' in [2000] Yearbook of Copyright and Media L 115, 124 and M Tugendhat and I Christie (eds), *The Law of Privacy and the Media* (Oxford: 2002) para 5.42) that a public figure consents to the disclosure of personal information is unacceptable. This is not to say that disclosure of personal information about public figures and the man on the Clapham omnibus does not need to be handled differently. Just that a fictitious notion of 'consent' should not be used as the basis of differentiation.

[161] *Edwards v State Farm Insurance Co and 'John Doe'* 833 F 2d 535 (1987) severely criticized by J Craig, 'Invasion of Privacy and Charter Values' (1997) 42 McGill LJ 355, 396. cp *Malone v Commissioner of Police* [1979] 2 All ER 620, 646.

B. Implied Consent

13.37 The Information Commissioner does not accept that for the purposes of data protection consent can be inferred from knowledge coupled with silence. Because the EU Directive[162] requires the data subject to 'signify' agreement, he says that there must be active communication between the parties.[163] The *Guidance on the Use and Disclosure of Health Data* states that it 'would not be sufficient . . . to write to patients to advise them of a new use of their data and to assume that all who had not objected had consented to that new use'.[164]

Primary and secondary purposes distinguished

13.38 When considering implied consent a distinction is necessary between:

(1) disclosures in the course of performing the very tasks for which the professional has been retained, and any necessary ancillary tasks such as billing;
(2) disclosures for some purpose that is unlikely to have personal consequences for the client.

In the first situation a court is very likely to hold (in the absence of an express contrary instruction or special circumstances) that the client did impliedly consent to the disclosure. This is because it is reasonable to infer foresight and agreement on the client's part. If a pupil fills in a UCAS (university application) form, a teacher can legitimately infer that he agrees to the disclosure of relevant confidential personal information in the teacher's UCAS reference. The position in the second situation is more complex and is discussed at length later in this chapter.[165]

Professionals in an agency relationship with the client

General principle

13.39 The obligation of confidentiality of a professional who has an agency relationship with the client will be qualified by the implied authority arising from the agency status.[166]

> Every agent has implied authority to do everything necessary for, and ordinarily incidental to carrying out his express authority according to the usual way in which such authority is executed.[167]

Information that if disclosed by a professional not in an agency relationship with the client would be a breach of confidence may be disclosed by the agent-professional provided the disclosure is within the scope of the agent's actual or implied authority.

---

[162] Directive (EC) 95/46, para 2(h).
[163] *Data Protection Act 1998—An Introduction*, ch 3.
[164] May 2002, 15. See also *British Gas Trading Ltd v Data Protection Registrar* [1997–98] Info TLR 393.
[165] See paras 13.46 et seq.
[166] On the subject of usual and implied authority see further F Reynolds, 'Apparent Authority' [1994] JBL 144; R Stone, 'Usual and Ostensible Authority—One Concept or Two' [1993] JBL 325.
[167] G Fridman, *The Law of Agency* (7th edn, London: 1996) 69.

Solicitors

13.40 Unless the client has given express instructions to the contrary,[168] a solicitor has extensive implied authority to make disclosures that are necessary to advance the client's interests.[169] For example, a solicitor may disclose information to the Crown Prosecution Service when negotiating a plea bargain or when addressing the court on the client's behalf.[170] Proulx and Layton suggest that when 'disclosing confidential information to third parties who are adverse in interest . . . authority should not be implied to permit disclosure that presents a real risk of harm to the client. Where the lawyer has any doubt on this score, the issue of disclosure should be fully canvassed with the client and express instructions obtained.'[171]

Implied consent and medical information

13.41 Many of the disclosures that occur within the NHS and in private medical practice depend for their legality upon implied consent. The Human Genetics Commission's *Inside Information* report says that in agreeing to treatment 'it is reasonable to assume that the patient implicitly consents to such disclosures as are necessary for the provision of care'.[172] The WHO's *Declaration on the Promotion of Patients' Rights in Europe* states: '[c]onsent may be presumed where disclosure is to other health care providers involved in that patient's treatment.'[173] Exceptionally, because of the very serious potential consequences and the GMC guidance on the subject,[174] Phipps and Touslon caution against implying consent to a blood sample being sent for HIV testing.[175] The ethical consensus is to take a

---

[168] Express instructions override usual or implied authority: *Fray v Voules* (1859) 1 El & El 839, 847. A third party to whom disclosure is made will be unaffected by the express instructions revoking authority to make the disclosure if unaware of them.

[169] eg *Kennedy v Diversified Mining Interests (Can) Ltd* [1949] 1 DLR 59, 61; *Causton v Mann Egerton (Johnsons) Ltd* [1974] 1 All ER 453, 457; *Great Atlantic Insurance v Home Insurance* [1981] 2 All ER 485, 492–493 (disclosures for the purpose of litigation); *Wright v Pepin* [1954] 2 All ER 52, 58 (acknowledging debt); *Bristol and West Building Society v Mothew* [1996] 4 All ER 698, 714; *Nationwide Building Society v Balmer Radmore* [1999] Lloyd's Rep PN 241 (confirming the absence of further borrowing in mortgage transactions); *Roy Dean v Allin & Watts (A Firm)* [2000] Lloyd's Rep PN 469 (answering buyer's inquiries during a conveyancing transaction). cp *Re Newen* [1903] 1 Ch 812; *Barazancha v Pannone Napier* (CA, 5 February 1998) (correspondence to avoid unnecessary work under a legal aid certificate).

[170] *Great Atlantic Insurance Co. v Home Insurance Co* [1981] 2 All ER 485, 493–494.

[171] M Proulx and D Layton, *Ethics and Canadian Criminal Law* (Toronto: 2001) 217. They cite *R v L (CK)* (1987) 39 CCC (3d) 476.

[172] May 2002, para 3.35. Cp GMC, *Confidentiality: Protecting and Providing Information* (London: 2000) para 7. There is no data protection problem about this because explicit consent is not required for the sharing of medical data amongst health professionals treating the patient: DPA, Sch 3, para 8(1).

[173] (Amsterdam: 1994) para 4.2.

[174] GMC, *Serious Communicable Diseases* (October 1997) para 4.

[175] R Toulson and C Phipps, *Confidentiality* (London: 1996) 148. But see J Koewn, 'The Ashes of AIDS and the Phoenix of Informed Consent' (1989) 52 MLR 790.

B. Implied Consent

similarly cautionary approach to consent to genetic testing.[176] The Committee of Ministers of the Council of Europe has said that genetic testing 'should be subject to ... express, free and informed consent'.[177] UNESCO's *Universal Declaration on the Human Genome and Human Rights*[178] similarly emphasizes the importance of prior informed consent before any testing of an individual's genome goes ahead.

When the patient does not consult the doctor to obtain treatment, implied consent to disclosure of medical information is more problematic. In *Cornelius v de Taranto* the claimant's solicitor arranged for the claimant to see a forensic psychiatrist to obtain a medico-legal report. Morland J held that if the claimant had not expressly consented, she had impliedly agreed to the psychiatrist publishing the medico-legal report to the solicitor.[179] What was the point of the claimant seeing the psychiatrist if the psychiatrist could not report back to her solicitor? But the judge also held, and the Court of Appeal agreed, that she had not impliedly consented to copies of the report being sent to a consultant psychiatrist (whom the Court of Appeal, but not the trial judge, held that she had (reluctantly) agreed to see) or to the disclosure of the report to her general practitioner. **13.42**

> Here was a document prepared primarily with a view to assisting in the prosecution of a civil claim. Although it certainly included matter which would have been of assistance to any doctor charged with the treatment of Mrs. Cornelius, at the same time it contained information which could have no conceivable bearing upon such treatment ... In my judgment what was required before the transmission of this report to any third person was the express consent of the client. Indeed, in the most unusual circumstances of this case, it would have been wise to obtain a specific written consent.[180]

Consultation with colleagues

In Chapter 2 attention was drawn to the large numbers of employed professionals. Consultation between employees is a feature of work in most organizations. 'In-house' discussions beneficial to the client are unlikely to be regarded as a breach of confidence even if there is no contract that expressly allows this.[181] **13.43**

---

[176] Human Genetics Commission, *Whose hands on your genes?* (2001) para 5.6, available from http://www.hgc.gov.uk.
[177] Recommendation R (92) 3, *Genetic Testing and Screening for Health Care Purposes*, principle 5.
[178] (1997) Art 5b.
[179] The judge, however, concluded that the defendant had been wrong in sending copies of the report to the claimant's GP or a consultant psychiatrist, whom the claimant was reluctant to see, without the claimant's express consent because these disclosures were not necessary: '[e]ven if the claimant had consented to therapeutic referral which in my judgment was not the case, it was not necessary to transmit the medico-legal report to the GP or consultant psychiatrist. Before doing so the defendant should have obtained the claimant's express consent preferably in writing.'
[180] per Mantell LJ, [2001] EWCA Civ 1511; [2002] EMLR 6, para 27.
[181] The terms of engagement of a firm of solicitors may provide that other lawyers in the firm may be brought in to deal with the client's affairs from time to time to cover absences and to deal with specialist points.

13.44 Consent to consultation with some persons not working for the same organization may also be implied. In *NRG v Bacon & Woodrow*[182] the claimant company's legal advisers had disclosed confidential information to the claimant's non-legal advisers. Colman J said,

> [A]s between NRG and its legal advisers the duty of confidence owed by those advisers to NRG was qualified to the extent that if, for the purpose of giving advice . . . the legal advisers exercising their professional judgment considered it necessary in the performance of their duties to disclose to any of the non-legal advisers written or oral communications or advice passing between them and NRG, it was open to those advisers to do so. They had a professional discretion in the matter. They were working in a developing transaction where negotiations in respect of the terms of the deal were progressing and where many of those terms related to matters on which the other non-legal advisers were retained to advise. It was obviously essential that in order to give further advice and in order that NRG should get the professional advice which it needed from the team, the legal advisers should from time to time be able to disclose to those other advisers their communications with NRG or the advice they were giving to NRG. This was clearly an implied qualification to the duty of confidence which [the legal advisers] owed to NRG.[183]

In *McKaskell v Bensemen*[184] an inexperienced solicitor sought guidance from a senior practitioner in another firm about what to do about a letter from a third solicitor that had gratuitously insulted his clients. The young solicitor did this without first seeking his clients' consent. The disclosure was held not to be a breach of the solicitor's obligation of confidentiality to his clients.[185] The Australian Bar Association Advocacy Rules expressly state that it is not a breach of confidentiality for a barrister to seek advice or professional assistance from another barrister.[186] The attention of the person consulted should be drawn to the fact that she is subject to an obligation to maintain the confidentiality of any client information that is disclosed.

Disclosure to support staff

13.45 It is a matter of common knowledge that in the normal operation of a professional's office (whether the professional is self-employed or employed by another), confidential client information will be seen by support staff. Client consent to necessary disclosures to assistants, secretaries and employees responsible for main-

---

[182] [1995] 1 All ER 976.
[183] *NRG v Bacon & Woodrow* [1995] 1 All ER 976, 984.
[184] [1989] 3 NZLR 75, 88
[185] This does not mean that in a parallel case in this country there would be no data protection issues about such a course of action, particularly if the information is sensitive personal data. Disclosure of sensitive personal data requires explicit consent unless the disclosure is 'necessary' for a purpose listed in DPA, Sch 3 or Data Protection (Processing of Sensitive Personal Data) Order 2000 SI 2000/417 see paras 18.25–18.27 below.
[186] ABA Advocacy Rules (1995) r 105.

B. Implied Consent

taining client records and client billing can reasonably be implied.[187] To be on the safe side, the GMC tells doctors to make sure that patients are aware that personal information about them will be shared within 'the health care team',[188] a category of persons defined to include administrative support staff.[189] To comply with the seventh data protection principle[190] professionals or their employers must impress upon support staff the importance of keeping client information confidential and take appropriate measures to prevent unauthorized access for example by locking files and offices when no one is about.

Disclosure for Secondary Purposes

The general position

When a professional discloses personal information for a purpose unrelated to the purpose for which the professional was engaged, it cannot be assumed that the client has either foreseen the type of disclosure or, if he has, would have agreed to it—even if the disclosure is in his 'best interests'. Thus a GP would not be justified in assuming a patient's consent to the disclosure to his social worker that he had been admitted to hospital. In *R v Department of Health, ex p Source Informatics* Simon Brown LJ commented on 'the well recognised reluctance of certain people to accept the views of those in authority as to just what is or is not good for them'.[191] A positive case must be made for implying consent.

13.46

According to Kennedy and Grubb, implied consent operates as 'a kind of estoppel whereby a [client] by virtue of his conduct and the circumstances is denied the ability to say "I did not consent to this". This means that it requires a consideration of all the circumstances such that it can be said that a reasonable person would, looking on, believe the [client] was consenting.'[192] Consent cannot be implied unless the client had effective advance notice of the disclosure.[193] Factors that need to be considered include the sort of notice that was given,[194] the specificity of that notice, the purpose of the disclosure, the nature of the information and the opportunity to object.

13.47

---

[187] *Slater v Bissett* (1986) 85 FLR 118, 121. cp *Duncan v Medical Disciplinary Committee* [1986] 1 NZLR 513, 521. Implied consent is assumed in *Code of Conduct of the Bar of England and Wales* (7th edn, London: 1999) para 702. See also Human Genetics Commission, *Inside Information* (May 2002) para 3.35.
[188] *Confidentiality: Protecting and Providing Information* (London: 2000) para 8.
[189] ibid p 2. This instruction may have been drawn up with the DPA fair processing code (as to which see paras 18.10 et seq below) in mind.
[190] DPA, Sch 1, Pt II.
[191] [2000] 1All ER 786, 800.
[192] I Kennedy and A Grubb, *Medical Law* (3rd edn, London: 2000) 1085. See also 1113.
[193] *Turner v Royal Bank of Scotland* [1999] 2 All ER (Comm) 664.
[194] Was the client told orally or in a personal letter? Or was the information only to be found in a leaflet in the waiting room or on a waiting-room wall? Whatever method is adopted, it will be important that the communication was in a language understood by the client.

Disclosure for training, research and management purposes

13.48 A professional may be asked to disclose confidential personal information for the purposes of teaching and training, quality assurance and monitoring of professional standards, financial audit, complaint-handling, managing services, future planning, research, and, in health care, clinical audit and public health functions. How should the professional respond? These are all secondary purposes: they are not for the immediate benefit of the client. The ethics of disclosing information about identifiable persons for such reasons has not been explored outside health care.[195]

The position in health care

13.49 The concerns about consent that arise in health care derive from the law of confidence. Consent to the processing of sensitive personal information for 'medical purposes', including research and management of health care services and reporting adverse drug reactions, is not required by the DPA.[196] Obtaining express consent to the disclosure of health information for secondary purposes may be impossible (the patient is dead, incompetent or his whereabouts unknown) or impracticable (insufficient time or cost). Department of Health Guidelines presume implied consent by patients to a wide range of disclosures for NHS purposes.[197] Although the guidance mentions that patients must be 'fully informed of the uses to which information about them may be put',[198] it is not suggested that a particular disclosure for NHS purposes depends upon this, or that the information about potential secondary uses must be anything other than very general. The guidance does not insist that patients be told before each disclosure that they have a right to object or that mechanism for objecting must be provided. If a strict approach were taken to implied consent, then consent is often lacking.[199]

---

[195] The health care literature includes 'Privacy and medical research' (1984) Medical J of Australia 620; I Kennedy and A Grubb, *Medical Law* (3rd edn, London: 2000) 1112–1118; M Ferriter and M Butwell, 'Confidentiality and Research in Mental Health' in C Cordess (ed), *Confidentiality and Mental Health* (London: 2001) ch 12.

[196] DPA, Sch 2, para 6 and, importantly, Sch 3, para 8 (see para 18.25 below). The Sch 3 condition may also be found in the exception for research that is in the 'substantial public interest' added by the Data Protection (Processing of Sensitive Personal Data) Order 2000 SI 2000/417 which is not restricted to medical research: see para 18.27 below.

[197] DoH, *The Protection and Use of Patient Information*, HSG (96) 18 (1996) para 2.5. The Royal College of General Practitioners, Committee on Medical Ethics, issued a paper in November 2000 that noted that implied consent was invoked to allow the use of patient identifiable information 'in teaching . . . examinations and assessments . . . for health service accounting . . . for audit, both clinical and financial . . . in disease registers . . . in research . . . to facilitate joint working and shared care by different members of the primary care team or similar multidisciplinary teams in other health care settings'. All but the last-mentioned uses are secondary uses. The paper also notes that implied consent is 'used to identify suitable patients who can then be approached for consent, or to retrieve the data that is to be anonymised'. Available from http://www.rcgp.org.uk.

[198] The DPA contains no exemption from the fair processing requirement for medical research.

[199] Cambridge Health Informatics Ltd, *Gaining Patient Consent to Disclosure* (Cambridge: 2001) 11–12.

B. Implied Consent

NHS guidance provides for draft posters for display to indicate the way in which information may be used, so that some force can be given to the idea that patient information is not being put to work without warning. However the reality is almost certainly that most patients have little idea how many people will have access to the information in their records.[200]

NHS practice also falls short of what is required by the fair processing requirements of the DPA.[201]

13.50 GMC guidelines on the disclosure of confidential patient-identifiable information for education, administration, research, audit and other non-treatment purposes are much stricter than the NHS rules. The guidance requires that express consent should be obtained for disclosures that are not for treatment, billing or to protect the patient or a third party from risk of death or serious harm. If it is not practical to get express consent, the data should be anonymized by a member of the health care team before disclosure.[202] The Court of Appeal held in *R v Department of Health, ex p Source Informatics Ltd*[203] that there was no breach of confidentiality when anonymized (unlinked) health information was disclosed.[204] This is because anonymous information lacks the quality of confidentiality necessary for disclosure to be a breach of confidence.[205] If it is not possible to anonymize patients, or if the disclosure is to enable someone who is not part of the health care team treating the patient to produce the anonymized data,[206] the GMC says that the patient must have been told, or had access to literature informing him, that his records might be disclosed for non-treatment purposes and given an opportunity to object.[207] Patients should also be informed that the person who is allowed access to their records will be subject to a duty of confidentiality.

---

[200] J Montgomery, 'Confidentiality in the modernized NHS: the challenge of data protection' [1999] Bulletin of Medical Ethics 18.

[201] Cambridge Health Informatics Ltd, *Gaining Patient Consent to Disclosure* (Cambridge: 2001) 10. On the fair processing code see paras 18.10 et seq.

[202] GMC, *Confidentiality: Protecting and Providing Information* (London: 2000) paras 13, 15, 16. cp WHO, *Declaration on the Promotion of Patients' Rights in Europe* (Amsterdam: 1994) paras 4.2, 4.7.

[203] [2000] 1 All ER 786.

[204] See paras 5.34 et seq.

[205] [2000] 1 All ER 786, 790, 797.

[206] Whether the process of anonymization is caught by the DPA is controversial: see para 18.08 below.

[207] GMC, *Confidentiality: Protecting and Providing Information* (London: 2000) para 16. See also Medical Research Council, *Personal Information in Medical Research*, available at http://www.mrc.ac.uk/pdf-pimr_summary.pdf. Cp Council of Europe, Recommendation R (89) 4 on collection of epidemiological data (6 March 1989) Appendix ii: '[d]ata subjects should be guaranteed the right to information about the nature and objectives of the data collection, and the methods to be used, as well as their rights in regard to the data stored and processed subsequent to collection. In particular, and subject to the existence of other effective safeguards laid down by domestic law, the express and informed consent of the data subjects should be sought before data can be collected and used . . .'

Disclosure in the public interest

13.51 The current GMC rules were a response to doubts[208] expressed about the legitimacy of relying on implied consent for disclosures for secondary purposes in *R v Department of Health, ex p Source Informatics Ltd*.[209] In his judgment Simon Brown LJ said:

> Lord Lester's arguments on implied consent, opposed though they were not merely by the department but also by the NPA and the MRC, to my mind appeared compelling. So far from patients being taken to have impliedly consented to such uses of the information they provide as are commonly accepted to be in the public interest, this is, submits Lord Lester, to conflate the issue of effective consent (which modifies the duty of confidence) with that of the public interest (which overrides the duty). The reference . . . in art 8(2) of the directive to the 'data subject [giving] his explicit consent' strongly supports this thesis. . . . Given, however, the department's submission that in any event, whenever patient consent could arguably be implied, so too could the public interest be invoked to the same end, it seemed pointless to carry the debate very far.[210]

There is a tendency to overlook that this passage, while questioning consent as a basis for disclosure, accepts that patient consent is superfluous if use or disclosure of information is in the public interest,[211] something *Source Informatics* had not suggested applied to the disclosures made to them.[212]

13.52 Disclosures of suspected adverse drug reactions to the Medicines Control Agency and the Committee on Safety of Medicines by doctors, dentists and pharmacists are quite obviously in the public interest.[213] If it were not allowed by legislation,[214] notification of infectious diseases would be justified by the public interest because of the serious public health risk. These disclosures, it is submitted, do not require the patient's consent, express or implied, to be lawful. Public health surveillance[215]

---

[208] Whether or not a breach of medical confidentiality can be justified on the grounds of either implied consent or the public interest is not a matter of great practical importance from the point of view of defending an action in equity for breach of confidence if detriment is an essential element of the cause of action and the claimant has suffered none. The indications are, however, that the claimant will not have to prove much in the way of detriment: see para 5.41 above.

[209] As suggested by G Aitken and M Spencer, 'Confidentiality—Medical Records' in M Powers and N Harris, *Clinical Negligence* (3rd edn, London: 2000) 261–262.

[210] *R v Department of Health, ex p Source Informatics* [2000] 1 All ER 786, 800.

[211] See also *AB v CD* (1851) 14 D 177, 179–180; *R v Department of Health, ex p Source Informatics Ltd* (1999) 49 BMLR 41, 52.

[212] [2001] 1 All ER 786, 789. *Source Informatics* (ibid at 797) relied (successfully) upon the fact that the patients who were the source of the information could not be identified to prevent liability for breach of confidence: see para 5.34 above.

[213] The Medicines Control Agency and Committee on Safety of Medicines have in fact dispensed with personal patient identifiers so as to comply with GMC guidelines on confidentiality: 'The Yellow Card Scheme: Protecting patient confidentiality' available at http://www.mca.gov.uk.

[214] See para 3.36 above.

[215] C Verity and A Nicoll, 'Consent, confidentiality and the threat to public health surveillance' (2002) 324 British Medical J 1210.

B. Implied Consent

may fall into the same category. Disclosure for a research purpose that has the approval of a Research Ethics Committee and for which the consent of the patient cannot practically be obtained is very likely to be held by a court to be in the public interest and therefore permits patient consent to be bypassed.[216] Kennedy and Grubb believe that the public interest justifies disclosure for financial audit and clinical audit. 'There is, in our view, an arguable public interest in maintaining and monitoring the efficient use of public funds within the NHS. Indeed, there is statutory backing for financial auditors to access patient information (National Health Service Act 1977 s 98).'[217] A New York court has doubted that public policy justifies the disclosure of psychiatric information about a patient whose identity has not been fully concealed for teaching purposes without the patient's consent.[218]

Health and Social Care Act 2001

13.53 The concept of disclosure in the public interest is ill-defined, its scope uncertain.[219] A much cited example is the notification of the United Kingdom's 11 cancer registries, which has been a requirement within the NHS since 1993. The usefulness of the statistics compiled in these registries for research into the causes, diagnosis, treatment and outcome of cancer would be undermined if even a small minority of patients[220] could prevent information from being passed to the registries by withholding consent.[221] Quite probably disclosure to the cancer registries without the client's consent is lawful at common law as being in the public interest. The GMC, however, had doubts and formulated guidance requiring explicit consent from every person newly diagnosed with cancer before information could be passed to the registries.[222]

---

[216] As regards data protection see para 13.49 above.

[217] I Kennedy and A Grubb, *Medical Law* (3rd edn, London: 2000) 1118.

[218] *Doe v Roe* 400 NYS 2d 668 (1977): '[i]n no case . . . has the curiosity of education of the medical profession superseded the duty of confidentiality. I do not reach the question of a psychiatrist's right to publish case histories where the identities are fully concealed for that is not our problem here, nor do I find it necessary to reach the issue of whether or not an important scientific discovery would take precedence over a patient's privilege of nondisclosure. I do not consider myself qualified to determine the contribution which this book may have made to the science or art of psychiatry. I do conclude, however, that if such contribution was the defendants' defense they have utterly failed in their proof that this volume represented a major contribution to scientific knowledge.' Per Stecher J.

[219] See para 11.05 above.

[220] This group includes adults who are incompetent to consent as well as the psychotic and simply bloody-minded.

[221] Department of Health, Social Services and Public Safety, *Health and Personal Social Services Protecting: Personal Information; A Consultation Paper* (NI: June 2002) paras 3.24–3.25.

[222] 'Medical Research Threatened by Patient Consent' Guardian, 12 April 2001. See also BioMed Central, 'Confusion reigns as data law continues to threaten research', 16 May 2001, http://www.biomedcentral.com/news/20010516/03; London School of Hygiene and Tropical Medicine, 'Confidentiality Rules Threaten Vital Medical Research', 10 May 2001, available at http://www.lshtm.ac.uk/events/rel-datarules.htm.

13.54 The Government responded by giving the Secretary of State for Health power in the Health and Social Care Act 2001[223] to make orders for medical purposes, after consultation with a Patient Information Advisory Group,[224] that override the common law duty of medical confidentiality where this is in the public interest or in the interests of improving patient care. For any disclosure that falls within the parameters of an order, patient consent is not required. Orders may be made only for circumstances in which it is not reasonably practicable to obtain patient consent and anonymized information will not do.[225] Regulations[226] came into force in June 2002 allowing processing of confidential patient information with a view to disclosure to cancer registries[227] and for the recognition, control and prevention of communicable diseases and other risks to public health.[228] By order the Secretary of State may approve the processing of patient information for medical purposes in circumstances set out in a Schedule.[229] Orders must comply with the requirements of the DPA[230] and the Human Rights Act (HRA). Various restrictions and exclusions apply when patient data is processed under the regulations including that no one should have access to the information who is not a health professional or a person subject to an equivalent duty of confidentiality.[231]

Disclosure in publications

13.55 It is implicit in the DPA[232] and several recommendations of the Committee of Ministers of the Council of Europe[233] that the client's express consent is required before information about the client is published in a form that permits the client

---

[223] The Government abandoned before enactment that part of the clause that permitted the Secretary of State to stop disclosure of anonymized or statistical data about NHS patients to data collection companies.
[224] ss 60(7), 61.
[225] Health and Social Care Act 2001, s 60(3)–(4). Satisfaction of these conditions is reviewed annually.
[226] Made pursuant to Health and Social Care Act 2001, s 64(3).
[227] Health Service (Control of Patient Information) Regulations 2002, SI 2002/1438, reg 2.
[228] ibid, reg 3. Doctors may be fined up to £5,000 if they refuse to co-operate.
[229] These include processing that makes patients less identifiable; that allows medical research into the geographical locations at which diseases and medical conditions occur; that permits identification of persons in order that they may be asked for consent; linking or validating confidential patient information; auditing, monitoring and analysing of health service care and treatment.
[230] Health and Social Care Act 2001, s 60(6).
[231] Health Service (Control of Patient Information) Regulations 2002, SI 2002/1438, reg 7(2).
[232] DPA, s 33(1)(b), (4).
[233] Council of Europe, Committee of Ministers, *Protection of Medical Data*, Recommendation No R (97) 5 (13 February 1997) para 12.5: '[p]ersonal data used for scientific research may not be published in a form which enables the data subjects to be identified, unless they have given their consent for the publication and publication is permitted by domestic law.' Council of Europe, Committee of Ministers, *Protection of Personal Data used for Scientific Research and Statistics*, Recommendation R (83) 10 (23 September 1983) para 8.1: '[p]ersonal data used for research should not be published in identifiable form unless the persons concerned have given their consent and in conformity with other safeguards laid down by domestic law.'

B. Implied Consent

to be identified.[234] If the client cannot be identified, consent is unnecessary. Sir Richard Scott published an article in 1990 in which he wrote with reference to the case of *Kaye v Robertson*:[235] '[i]f the doctor had taken the photographs without Mr. Kaye's consent he might have been able to justify publication in a medical journal or for teaching purposes provided he avoided identifying Mr. Kaye as the subject, but would not have a hope of justifying publication in a national newspaper which revealed the identity of Mr. Kaye as the subject of the photograph . . .'[236] If anything unusual about the client is disclosed, concealing the client's name and place of residence, and even age and sex, may not be sufficient to dispense with the necessity for consent.[237] The GMC reminds doctors that 'patients can be identified from information other than names or addresses. Details which in combination may reveal patients' identities include: their condition or disease, their age, their occupation, the area where they live, their medical history, the size of their family.'[238] Doctors who have published data about identifiable patients in journals without first obtaining adequate consent have faced disciplinary proceedings.[239] It is a wise precaution to allow the client to see a final draft of an article before it appears in print.

13.56 The Education (Special Needs) (England) (Consolidation) Regulations 2001 provide that information about a child's special education needs may be disclosed without the consent of the child or his parent 'for research which . . . may advance the education of children with special educational needs', 'if the person engaged in that research undertakes not to publish anything contained in, or derived from, a statement otherwise than in a form which does not identify any individual concerned including, in particular, the child concerned and his parent'.[240]

Disclosures to relatives

Sensitive data[241]

13.57 For many years health professionals assumed that they could inform a spouse or other close relative of a patient that their loved one was dying when the patient himself had not been told. In the 1995 edition of its guidance on confidentiality the GMC said:

---

[234] DoH, *Local Research Ethics Committees,* HSG 91(5) para 3.11; *W v Egdell* [1990] 1 All ER 835, 848.
[235] [1991] FSR 62.
[236] 'Developments in the Law of Confidentiality' [1990] Denning LJ 77, 87–88.
[237] cp C Cordess, 'Confidentiality and Contemporary Practice' in C Cordess (ed), *Confidentiality and Mental Health* (London: 2001) 38.
[238] *Media Inquiries about Patients* (London: 1996), available from http://www.Gmc-uk.org/standards/MEDIA.HTM.
[239] 'Publishing information about patients' (1995) 311 British Medical J 1240; 'GMC finds doctors not guilty in consent case' (1995) 311 British Medical J 1245; *Data Protection News,* Issue 25, Spring 1996, 12.
[240] reg 24(1)(c).
[241] See para 18.23 below.

[Y]ou may judge that it would be in a patient's interests that a close relative should know about the patient's terminal condition, but that the patient would be seriously harmed by the information. In such circumstances information may be disclosed without consent.[242]

The legal basis of this kind of disclosure was never properly explained. The status of a relative normally confers no right to information about an adult patient.[243] In its most recent advice on confidentiality the GMC has dropped all reference to disclosure of information to relatives without patient consent. This is probably because the DPA requires 'explicit' consent to the disclosure of sensitive data (which includes medical data), except for certain specified purposes none of which applies here.[244] It would appear that if the patient cannot be told the truth about his condition, the relatives cannot be told it either, even if they are the patient's main carers and need to know the prognosis. This is a matter that needs the attention of law reformers who might compare the position when a statutory after-care supervision order for a psychiatric patient is being considered. In the latter situation, the patient's nearest relative who will play a 'substantial part' in the care of the patient, may be consulted without the patient's consent if the patient has a 'propensity to violent or dangerous behaviour'.[245] This analogy is not intended to suggest that the dying are dangerous!

Non-sensitive data

13.58 There are no data protection reasons why professionals cannot base disclosure of non-sensitive data to a relative on implied consent, but there must be something in the circumstances and conduct of the client that justifies an inference of consent.

Parameters of Express and Implied Consent

Amount of detail

13.59 Paradoxically express consent may give rise to issues of implied consent. In expressly approving the disclosure of information, the client may have omitted to say anything about the amount of detail. 'It is a moot point', writes Clarke, 'whether medical practitioners should disclose on medical certificates the precise condition for which the certificate has been provided, a general indication of the condition, or nothing more than a statement of the period he or she considers the

---

[242] GMC, *Confidentiality* (1995) para 12.
[243] Blood ties confer no legal right to determine medical treatment for an adult (*Re T (Adult: Refusal of Medical Treatment)* [1992] 4 All ER 649, 653) and by analogy no right to confidential information.
[244] See paras 18.25–18.27 below. Empirical studies about the extent to which the non-disclosure rule is observed and if not, why not, would be interesting.
[245] Mental Health Act 1983, s 25B(3).

B. Implied Consent

person should be away from work.'[246] If there is any doubt about the extent of disclosure the client has sanctioned,[247] disclosure should be kept to a minimum.[248] The Faculty of Occupational Health advises that if an employee authorizes an occupational health professional to disclose information about his health 'it will normally be appropriate only to refer to the results of the health assessment and not the clinical details. Where details are necessary, this can only be with informed written consent.'[249] It is disturbing that evidence given to the Human Genetics Commission stated that some busy GPs send insurers who ask for a medical report about a patient who has applied for insurance a copy of the patient's full medical record.[250] These doctors not only ignore the Access to Medical Reports Act 1988,[251] they breach their obligation of confidentiality to their patients by making unnecessary disclosures.

Audience

A client who consents to the disclosure of confidential personal information (other than to the media) does not usually intend to authorize disclosure to all and sundry: there will be implied qualifications about the audience. 'A person seeking life insurance, who gives information about his health to his insurance broker, impliedly consents to the broker passing on the information to the underwriter, but not to the press.'[252] In a case that came before the NZ Privacy Commissioner, a woman had a blood test at a hospital to establish her suitability as an organ donor for a relative. She complained that the letter containing the blood test results was given to that relative to pass on to her and that the relative was told that she was a suitable donor. In its defence the hospital said that the physician had inferred from her agreement to undergo the blood test that she had consented to the disclosure of the results to the relative. The Privacy Commissioner found this not to be the case.[253]

13.60

Collateral use

Consent may be expressly or impliedly confined to disclosure for a particular purpose. In *Hollinsworth v BCTV*[254] a patient consented to his hair graft surgery

13.61

---

[246] 'Current Health Care Information Privacy Issues', paper presented to the Australian Medical Informatics Association Perth, April 1990, available at http://www.anu.edu.au/people/Roger.Clarke/DV/PaperMedical.html.
[247] eg *Frenette v Metropolitan Life Insurance Co; Hospital Jean-Talon, mis en cause* (1992) 89 DLR (4th) 653, 669.
[248] cp GMC, *Confidentiality: Protecting and Providing Information* (London: 2000) para 1.
[249] Faculty of Occupational Medicine, *Guidance on Ethics for Occupational Physicians* (5th edn, London: 1999) para 2.2.
[250] *Inside Information* (May 2002) para 7.33.
[251] See para 19.49 below.
[252] R Toulson and C Phipps, *Confidentiality* (London: 1996) 48.
[253] NZ Privacy Commissioner Case Note 6656, October 1995 (1995) 2 PLPR 171.
[254] (1998) 83 ACWS (3d) 525.

being videotaped for medical instructional purposes. The British Columbia Court of Appeal held that use of the videotape in a television programme about baldness was a breach of confidence.

Conditional consent

13.62 The client may impose other limitations on the consent. For example, the client may make consent to the professional using his personal information in an article conditional on his approving the final draft. In the United States a patient successfully sued a television station for mistakenly broadcasting his image for several seconds during a programme on AIDS. He had agreed to participate in the programme, but on condition that his identity would not be revealed.[255] Limited consent should be recorded for future reference. If this is not done and information is released at a later date in breach of the limitation, the disclosure may be actionable not only as a breach of confidence but as a breach of the seventh data protection principle[256] and negligence.[257]

C. Waiver[258]

English Waiver Cases

13.63 Some English courts have held it against a claimant that he previously put information about himself into the public domain.[259] One such case is *Theakston v NGN Ltd*.[260] Theakston, a TV presenter, gave interviews to the press about his personal and sexual life (though without giving details of sexual activity) and made no objection when more explicit detail was disclosed by women with whom he had slept. When the News of the World ran a story about his visit to a Mayfair brothel based on information from a prostitute he was refused an injunction except to prevent publication of a photograph. Ouseley J agreed with counsel for

---

[255] *Multimedia WMAZ v Kubach* 443 SE 2d 491 (1994). See also *Doe v Univision Television Group* 717 So 2d 63 (1998).
[256] Compensation can be sought for 'damage' caused by a breach of a data protection principle and for any associated distress: see para 4.49 above. As regards the seventh data protection principle see para 6.35 above.
[257] Tangible injury will have to be proved.
[258] M Tugendhat and I Christie (eds), *The Law of Privacy and the Media* (Oxford: 2002) ch 9.
[259] *Khashoggi v Smith* (1980) 124 SJ 14: 'if someone allows themselves to get into the public eye to the extent that this lady had done, she runs the risk of the whole story (if there be a whole story) and the whole truth (if it be the whole truth) being made public', per Roskill LJ; *Campbell v MGN Ltd* [2002] EWHC 499; [2002] EMLR 30, para 48; *A v B plc & C ('Flitcroft')* [2002] EWCA Civ 337; [2002] 3 WLR 542, para 11, guideline xii. cp *Tucker v News Media Ownership Ltd* [1986] 2 NZLR 716, 735.
[260] [2002] EWHC 137; [2002] EMLR 22.

C. Waiver

the defendant that the claimant should be treated as having consented to the publication of further information about his sexual life.[261]

> I consider that the Claimant has pleaded [sic] aspects of his private life, whom he has intimate relations with and his general attitude towards sexual relations and personal relationships into the public domain, discussing them willingly so as to create and project an image calculated to enhance his appeal to those who do or would employ him, through enhancing his fame, popularity and reputation as a man physically and sexually attractive to many women. He has not objected either to those with whom he has had sexual relations discussing those relations both in general and in more explicit and in more intimate detail... He has courted publicity of that sort and not complained of it when, hitherto, it has been very largely favourable to him ... The Claimant cannot complain if the publicity given to his sexual activities is less favourable in this instance.[262]

This writer is of the opinion that it is wrong to treat previous disclosures and tolerance of disclosures by others as constituting *consent* to the disclosure of information that is not already in the public domain.[263] But it may be possible to treat such voluntary conduct as a waiver of objection to further disclosures that do not exceed the intimacy of the earlier disclosures.[264] In US law waiver is a well-established defence to an allegation of invasion of common law privacy rights.[265] Unlike consent, it cannot be easily retracted and in US law it has very rarely been found to lapse.[266]

13.64 The waiver doctrine offers an explanation for two pre-Human Rights Act cases: *Lennon v NGN Ltd*[267] and *Woodward v Hutchins*.[268] The former was an action by

---

[261] ibid, para 68. For a similar argument see W. Keeton (ed), *Prosser and Keeton on The Law of Torts* (5th edn, St Paul: 1984) 860. cp *Granada Television complaint on behalf of Ms Jacqueline Pirie*, 23 January 2000, available from http://www.pcc.org.uk.
[262] [2002] EWHC 137; [2002] EMLR 22, para 68.
[263] See para 13.36 above. See also reservations about waiver para 13.01 n9.
[264] This is the approach of the PCC which 'has made it clear on a number of occasions that it will take into account the extent to which similar matters have been discussed by the complainant or have been published before without complaint. Privacy is a right which can be compromised and those who talk about their private lives on their own terms must expect that there must be others who will do so, without their consent, in a less than agreeable way.' Complaint of Venessa Feltz against the Sunday Times and the Mirror, 15 July 2001.
[265] J Ghent, 'Waiver or Loss of Right of Privacy' (1974) 57 ALR 3d 16; R Sack, *Sack on Defamation* (3rd edn, New York: 2002) vol 1. The readiness of US courts to treat public figures as having forfeited their privacy rights in media cases is not without its critics: see eg J Elwood, 'Outing, Privacy and the First Amendment' (1992) 102 Yale LJ 747, 760–762. The case for finding waiver where there is no informed consent is, however, surely weaker when what is foregone is a Convention right. ECtHR requires waiver of Art 6 rights to be made in an unequivocal fashion: *Sturesson v Sweden* (1990) 13 ECHR 1. One would expect this also for an Art 8 right.
[266] J Ghent, 'Waiver or loss of Right of Privacy' 57 ALR 3d 16 (1974) §33. A famous example is the mathematical child prodigy in *Sidis v F-R Pub Corp* 113 F2d 806 (1940) who could not escape his fame in adulthood.
[267] [1978] FSR 573. An alternative analysis suggested in H Tomlinson (ed), *Privacy and the Media* (London: 2002) 32, is that the notoriety of the marriage (the result of earlier disclosures) meant that a reasonable person of ordinary sensitivity would not find the disclosure to be offensive.
[268] [1977] 1 WLR 760.

John Lennon, the former Beatle, against a tabloid newspaper to avert publication of a feature article by his ex-wife about their six years of marriage. He was refused an injunction on the grounds that both he and his ex-wife had thrust their relationship into the limelight by previously giving interviews about their life together.[269] Finding for the newspaper, Lord Denning said:

> It seems to me as plain as can be that the relationship of these parties has ceased to be their own private affair. They themselves had put it into the public domain . . . One only has to read these articles all the way through to show that each of them is making money by publishing the most intimate details about one another, and accusing one another of this, that and the other, and so forth. It is all in the public domain.[270]

Lord Denning's assertion that it was '*all* in the public domain' is not correct. Not *everything* had been aired before in public.[271]

13.65 Waiver is also one possible explanation for the controversial decision in *Woodward v Hutchins*,[272] which involved an unsuccessful breach of confidence action by Tom Jones against his one-time public relations and press officer. This former employee, on leaving Jones' employment, had written a series of articles for the Daily Mirror containing much hitherto undisclosed information about the pop singer.[273] The press officer successfully defended an action against him for breach of confidence by Tom Jones. Price et al point out that the 'proposition that a person who puts an aspect of his or her personal life into the public domain waives to some extent the rights of privacy which they might otherwise enjoy has obvious attraction'.[274] It is a line of argument that has impressed the Press Complaints Commission.[275] So long as disclosures are proportionate to information already in the public domain the Commission will dismiss a complaint of infringement of privacy.[276]

13.66 English case law is not uniformly supportive of waiver as a defence. Michael Barrymore, the actor, was able to restrain publication by the Sun of articles that contained information about his sexual life and personal relationships that he had

---

[269] *Lennon v NGN Ltd* [1978] FSR 573.
[270] [1978] FSR 573 at 574–575.
[271] ibid at 575.
[272] [1977] 1 WLR 760.
[273] The alternative explanation, and the one for which there is most explicit support in the judgment, is disclosure in the public interest: see para 11.10 above.
[274] M Tugendhat and I Christie (eds), *The Law of Privacy and the Media* (Oxford: 2002) para 9.31A.
[275] ibid paras 9.33–9.34.
[276] Julia Carling and the Sun, 13 October 1995; Jacqueline Pirie and the News of the World, 23 January 2000 where the PCC said that 'even when individuals do put matters concerning their private lives into the public domain . . . the press cannot reasonably justify thereafter publishing articles on any subject concerning them'; Naomi Russell and the Sunday Sport, 11 November 2001, where the PCC was concerned about 'whether the details published in the story [were] proportional to those already in the public domain and whether the complainant [had] ever discussed similar matters'; Vanessa Feltz and the Sunday Mirror, 15 July 2001.

C. Waiver

not made public. Jacob J said that had the article merely indicated that there was a relationship there might have been no breach of confidence 'because Mr Barrymore had already disclosed that he was homosexual, and merely to disclose that he had had a particular partner would be to add nothing new. However, when one goes into details (as in *The Sun* article), about what Mr Barrymore said about his relationship with his wife and so on, one has crossed the line into breach of confidence.'[277] The *Barrymore v NGN Ltd* case was pre-HRA. The incorporation of Article 10 into English law has strengthened the argument for treating waiver as a defence to alleged intrusions into privacy by the press.

Prerequisites of the Defence

It is a feature of all the English cases that might support a defence of waiver that (1) information similar to that which is the subject of complaint was already in the public domain,[278] (2) the claimant was a public figure, and (3) the claimant had courted publicity.[279] There is nothing to suggest that information outside the public domain may be disclosed without consent about a private person.[280]

13.67

---

[277] [1997] FSR 600, 603.
[278] Not necessarily because of revelations by the claimant. In John Lennon's case some disclosures had been made by his wife. In *Theakston*'s case some of the disclosures had been made by the women with whom Theakston had had a sexual relationship.
[279] The latest comment by the Court of Appeal on the position of a public figure seems to rule out disclosure on a waiver theory if the public figure has not courted publicity. See para 11.10 above.
[280] See eg *Stephens v Avery* [1988] 2 All ER 477. Note also *Peck v UK* Applicatiion 44647/98, 28 January 2003, para 53.

Part IV

CONFIDENTIALITY AND PRIVILEGE IN THE LITIGATION PROCESS

14

INVESTIGATIONS AND PRE-TRIAL DISCLOSURES

A. Civil Cases	14.02	Covert Surveillance	14.70
Compulsory Pre-Trial Disclosure	14.02	Acquisition of Confidential	
Search Orders	14.15	Information by the Defence	14.123
Criminal Assets Recovery Authority	14.18	C. Proceedings Abroad	14.133
B. Criminal Cases	14.19	Civil Litigation	14.133
Acquisition of Confidential Information		Criminal Proceedings	14.137
by the Prosecution	14.19		

Chapters 14 and 15 cover disclosure of confidential personal information by a professional: **14.01**

(1) at all stages of the civil litigation process;
(2) during a criminal investigation by the police or by other agents of the state;
(3) during the preparatory stages before, and during, a criminal trial;
(4) in proceedings before a tribunal or public inquiry; and
(5) when evidence is sought by a foreign tribunal.

This chapter is concerned with disclosures that take place in the run up to a criminal or civil trial, including a hearing in a foreign jurisdiction. The analysis of criminal investigations includes both overt investigations and covert surveillance and interception of communications by law enforcement agencies.

A. Civil Cases

Compulsory Pre-Trial Disclosure

When neither professional nor client is a litigant

Introduction

An adversarial system of justice that aims for high standards of procedural fairness and accuracy must make provision for the parties to litigation to have unimpeded **14.02** access to all evidence material to their dispute.[1] Disclosure (known formerly as discovery) is the name given to this process. Originally all disclosure took place after the commencement of proceedings and was restricted to the parties. Someone who was not a party (a 'mere witness') could be compelled to give evidence or produce documents at the trial but not before.[2]

Norwich Pharmacal jurisdiction

14.03 To wait until the trial to get information from a non-party is at best inconvenient, at worst it may prevent the case from reaching trial. In *Norwich Pharmacal Co. v Commissioners of Customs and Excise* equity confirmed the existence of a jurisdiction to compel a non-party who innocently got 'mixed up in the tortious acts of others so as to facilitate their wrongdoing'[3] to disclose the identity of a wrongdoer to a prospective claimant to enable proceedings to be instigated.[4] This exception also allows discovery against a bank to enable funds to be traced.[5]

Legislation requiring disclosure

14.04 Pre-trial disclosure of material by a non-party professional or the employer of such a person is required under various legislative provisions: Access to Health Records Act 1990,[6] Data Protection Act 1998 (DPA),[7] Human Fertilisation and Embryology Act 1990[8] and, within narrow limits and with the agreement of a court,[9] the Bankers' Books Evidence Act 1879.[10] In family proceedings a court may require advance production by third parties of documents that could be compelled at the trial.[11]

---

[1] A Zuckerman, 'Privilege and public interest' in C Tapper (ed), *Crime Proof and Punishment: essays in memory of Sir Rupert Cross* (London: 1981) 248.
[2] *Re Barlow Clowes Gilt Managers Ltd* [1991] 4 All ER 385, 393.
[3] *Norwich Pharmacal Co v Customs and Excise Commissioners* [1973] 2 All ER 943, 948.
[4] See paras 7.04 et seq.
[5] *Bankers Trust Co v Shapira* [1980] 3 All ER 353. The existence of a relationship of confidence between the bank and the customer does not prevent access to the customer's account provided that there is prima facie evidence of fraud or other wrongdoing.
[6] See para 19.54 below. This allows access to the medical records of a deceased person in certain circumstances.
[7] See para 19.21 below. This only permits access to the claimant's own records.
[8] s 35(1): '[w]here for the purpose of instituting proceedings under section 1 of the Congenital Disabilities (Civil Liability) Act 1976 (civil liability to child born disabled) it is necessary to identify a person who would or might be the parent of a child . . . the court may, on the application of the child, make an order requiring the Authority to disclose any information contained in the register kept in pursuance of section 31 of this Act.'
[9] *MacKinnon v Donaldson, Lufkin and Jenrette Securities Corp* [1986] 1 All ER 653. See also *DB Deniz Nakliyatu TAS v Yugopetrol* [1992] 1 All ER 205, 208.
[10] See para 14.10 below.
[11] It was said in *A Health Authority v X (No 1)* [2001] Lloyd's Rep Med 349, Fam Div, paras 59–66 that a court has no power to order pre-trial disclosure of documents by a public body, but in *Re A and B (No 2)* [1995] 1 FLR 351, 369 Wall J suggested that in family proceedings the court may order the disclosure of relevant local authority material (which might include reports by professionals) subject to a suitable undertaking as to use and confidentiality. On this point see Family Proceedings Rules 1991, SI 1991/1247, r 2.62.

A. Civil Cases

Disclosure under the Civil Procedure Rules

Family proceedings apart,[12] most civil litigation disclosure is regulated by the Civil Procedure Rules 1998 (CPR). The Supreme Court Act 1981, s 34 and CPR 31.17 allow a court to order disclosure and production of documents in the possession of a non-party in all types of action[13] as soon as proceedings are underway. Production is enforced by application to the court. Disclosure cannot be compelled if: **14.05**

(1) production is disproportionate to the issues in the case,[14] or
(2) the documents are privileged,[15] protected by public interest immunity (PII)[16] or a statute overrides the normal obligation to produce the documents.[17]

Since the professional may not know whether a disclosure exception applies, the professional is best advised to wait for an order from a court before disclosing records. Furthermore, 'the process of discovery is not an uncontrolled juggernaut';[18] an order for production and inspection is not automatic once relevance and absence of entitlement to privilege are established.[19]

The CPR direct the court not to make an order unless 'the documents of which disclosure is sought are likely to support the case of the applicant or adversely affect the case of one of the other parties' *and* are 'necessary in order to dispose fairly of the claim or to save costs'.[20] It is no bar to an order for disclosure that the court is of the view that the document disclosed is as or more likely to support the case of another party than that of the applicant so long as it is 'likely' to support that of the applicant.[21] 'Likely' in this context means 'may well'.[22] This 'connotes a rather higher threshold of probability than merely "more than fanciful". But a prospect may be more than fanciful without reaching the threshold of "more **14.06**

---

[12] For family proceedings see the Family Proceedings Rules 1991, SI 1991/1247 and the Rules of the Supreme Court 1965, SI 1965/1776. For a detailed discussion of family proceedings see D Burrows, *Evidence in Family Proceedings* (Bristol: 1999). Even in family proceedings a court is likely to have regard to the CPR on disclosure, not least because the CPR costs regime applies.

[13] See Supreme Court Act 1981, s 34(2); County Courts Act 1984, s 53. These provisions formerly applied only to proceedings in respect of personal injury and wrongful death. The Civil Procedure (Modification of Enactments) Order 1998, SI 1998/2940 applies these provisions universally.

[14] CPR, r 31.3(2).
[15] See CPR, r 31.3(1)(b) and paras 16.08 et seq.
[16] See CPR, r 31.19 and paras 16.52 et seq.
[17] See *C v S* [1999] 2 All ER 343, 350.
[18] *Ventouris v Mountain* [1991] 1 WLR 607, 622 per Bingham LJ.
[19] *Sumitomo Corp v Credit Lyonnais Rouse Ltd* [2001] EWCA Civ 1152; [2002] 1 WLR 479, para 79.
[20] CPR, r 31.17(3).
[21] *Three Rivers District Council v Governor and Company of the Bank of England* [2002] EWCA Civ 1182, para 33.
[22] ibid, para 32.

probable than not".'[23] In deciding whether disclosure is necessary the court will have regard to the overriding objective which is to deal justly with the case but also to save expense and keep disclosure proportionate to the issues at stake.[24] The documents or class of documents to be disclosed must be specified.[25] If the order relates to a class of documents it must contain only documents likely to support the case of the applicant or adversely affect the case of one of the other parties and the non-party must not be given the task of identifying those documents within a composite class which meet this criteria.[26]

Confidential documents

14.07 If a document is necessary to dispose fairly of litigation, the fact that the information in it is confidential as between the professional and a third party is not a reason to refuse disclosure if the document is not privileged[27] though it might be a reason for conditional or restricted inspection.[28] Ackner LJ explained in *Campbell v Tameside MBC*:

> The fact that information has been communicated by one person to another in confidence is not, of itself, a sufficient ground for protection from disclosure. . . . The private promise of confidentiality must yield to the general public interest, that in the administration of justice truth will out.[29]

These words formed part of a judgment in which an education authority was directed to disclose reports by educational psychologists about the disposition and propensity towards violence of an 11-year-old boy who had attacked his teacher in class so seriously that she was forced to retire.[30] The court inspected the reports before ordering disclosure. In *Science Research Council v Nasse*,[31] the House of Lords reviewed the decisions of two industrial tribunals, one considering an allegation of racial discrimination and the other sexual discrimination, ordering defendants to produce to claimants the records of persons who had been interviewed for positions for which the claimants had unsuccessfully applied. Lord Wilberforce said:

---

[23] per Chadwick LJ, ibid, para 33.
[24] CPR, Pt 1.1. See *Simba-Tola v Trustees of Elizabeth Fry Hostel* [2001] EWCA Civ 1371.
[25] CPR, 31.15(4). See *Re Howglen Ltd* [2001] 1 All ER 376, 383.
[26] *Three Rivers District Council v Governor and Company of the Bank of England* [2002] EWCA Civ 1182, para 36.
[27] *Alfred Crompton Amusement Machines Ltd v Customs and Excise Commissioners* [1973] 2 All ER 1169, 1180; *O'Sullivan v Herdmans Ltd* [1987] 3 All ER 129, 135–136; *Marcel v Commissioner of Police of the Metropolis* [1992] 1 All ER 72, 82.
[28] See para 17.02 below.
[29] [1982] 2 All ER 791, 796–797.
[30] cp *Thompson v Inner London Education Authority* (1977) 74 LS Gaz 66.
[31] [1979] 3 All ER 673. See also *Kelly v Kelly* 1946 SLT 208 (disclosure of hospital records relating to the treatment of venereal disease); *Higgins v Burton* 1968 SLT 52 (disclosure of the records of a child guidance clinic).

A. Civil Cases

There is no principle in English law by which documents are protected from discovery by reason of confidentiality alone. But there is no reason why, in the exercise of its discretion to order discovery, the tribunal should not have regard to the fact that documents are confidential, and that to order disclosure would involve a breach of confidence. . . . *The ultimate test in discrimination (as in other) proceedings is whether discovery is necessary for disposing fairly of the proceedings.* If it is, then discovery must be ordered notwithstanding confidentiality. But where the court is impressed with the need to preserve confidentiality in a particular case, it will consider carefully whether the necessary information has been or can be obtained by other means, not involving a breach of confidence [32] . . . In order to reach a conclusion whether discovery is necessary notwithstanding confidentiality the tribunal should inspect the documents. It will naturally consider whether justice can be done by special measures such as 'covering up', substituting anonymous references for specific names, or, in rare cases, hearing in camera.[33]

Since the Human Rights Act 1998 (HRA) came into force there may be some scope for a non-disclosure argument based on Article 8 in some circumstances.[34]

When client, but not professional, is a litigant

Disclosure to client's opponent under the Civil Procedure Rules

There are a number of means by which a party to litigation, B, can secure documents concerning an opponent, A, that are relevant to the litigation if they (1) are held by a professional with whom A has or had a professional–client relationship, and (2) A could be ordered to disclose them under CPR 31.6 or 31.12, if they were with A. The first is to seek non-party disclosure against the professional pursuant to Supreme Court Act 1981, s 34[35] and CPR 31.17. The professional can oppose the disclosure on the grounds of PII, private privilege, disproportionality or a statutory bar but not normally because the records are confidential.[36] The second way is to apply for an order compelling A to produce the documents. This will only work if A is entitled to claim the original records or a copy from the professional. Under the CPR a party must disclose material documents in his control to an opponent.[37] A party has control of a document inter alia if he 'has or has had a right to inspect or take copies of it'.[38] In *Vernon v UK*[39] the European Court of Human Rights (ECtHR) rejected a complaint by the claimant in a personal injury action that his right to a fair trial had been violated by compulsion to disclose a

14.08

---

[32] See also *Yates v Buckley* (CA, 3 November 1997).
[33] [1979] 3 All ER 673, 679 (italics added). See also, *Lonrho plc v Fayed (No 4)* [1994] 1 All ER 870, 895; *Charnos plc v Donnelly* (EAT, 2000, WL 1151437); *Simba-Tola v Trustees of Elizabeth Fry Hostel* [2001] EWCA Civ 1371.
[34] See para 16.02 below.
[35] Or County Courts Act 1984, s 53.
[36] *O'Sullivan v Herdmans Ltd* [1987] 3 All ER 129, 135–136.
[37] CPR, r 31.8.
[38] CPR, r 31.8(2).
[39] Application 38753/97 (2001) 29 EHRR CD 264.

draft psychiatric report prepared for earlier custody proceedings.[40] A third solution is to seek an order requiring A to give specific authority to B's solicitors to inspect documents in the custody of the professional. The court 'has jurisdiction to make such an order having regard to the wide terms of the provisions of CPR ... including rule 3.1(2)(m)'.[41]

Medical confidentiality

14.09 In principle a patient should retain control over his own medical records and therefore an order under the Supreme Court Act 1981, s 34 to the professional requiring disclosure of those records should be reserved for exceptional cases and then only in carefully defined circumstances to avoid interfering with the patient's Article 8 rights.[42] The preferred approach prior to the CPR was to order proceedings to be stayed unless A consented to the disclosure of the medical records. This avoided any interference with medical confidentiality which in England (unlike Canada)[43] is not thought to lapse automatically upon instigation of litigation.[44] In *Nicholson v Halton General Hospital NHS Trust*[45] the claimant sued her former employer in negligence alleging injury to her wrist as a result of performing repetitive movements in her work. The claimant refused permission for the defendants' medical advisers to speak with the consultant who had performed an operation on the wrist and the consultant himself said that he would not be involved without a court order. The Court of Appeal made an order that unless the claimant consented to waive her right to confidentiality the action would be stayed. Sumner J said:

> There is no property in a witness, but there is the right of confidentiality between a patient and his treating doctor which the law will uphold. It is a right which it is for the patient to waive and he can only waive it voluntarily. The court will not order him to waive such a right. But in an appropriate case, the court can order

---

[40] The report had undermined his expert evidence and he had felt compelled to call its author to give oral evidence to counter its effect.
[41] *Bennett v Compass Group UK* [2002] EWCA Civ 642, para 26, per Clarke LJ.
[42] ibid, para 40.
[43] *Hay v University of Alberta Hospital* (1990) 105 AR 276, 281: 'the right of the patient to confidentiality ceases when he puts his health in issue by claiming damages in a lawsuit; the *raison d'être* for confidentiality is gone. The right to confidentiality is then eclipsed by the right of those who face the action to know the basis and scope of the claim advanced. The patient cannot use confidentiality to preclude the normal operation of the legal process and the adversary system.' Per Picard J. The judge (at 282) said that the right to confidentiality would be restored bar any information released for the purposes of the litigation should the action be abandoned. For a comment on the case see (1991) 337 Lancet 1276. cp *X v Y* [1954] VLR 708, 711. *Hay* was cited with approval in *NUR v John Wyeth & Brother Ltd* [1996] 7 Med LR 300 and *Skaw v Skeet* [1996] 7 Med LR 371. American law follows the Canadian pattern: *Hague v Williams* 181 A 2d 345, 349 (1962); *Tylo v Superior Court* 64 Cal Rptr 2d 731, 736 (1997).
[44] cp *Dunn v British Coal Corp* [1993] ICR 591 (see para 21.04 below). When the litigation is against the doctor and not a third party it is arguable that the patient has waived confidentiality in relevant documents by instigating the proceedings: cp. para 13.35 n above.
[45] [1999] PIQR 310.

A. Civil Cases

that the claim be stayed until such time as he consents to waive his right of confidentiality.

This may still be the best approach for a court to take.[46] The court uses its inherent discretion to stay proceedings to compel the claimant to submit to a medical examination.[47] There is no other way that the defendant can be obliged to provide personal information by direct examination. A medical examination is an invasion of personal liberty and will only be granted when reasonable in the interests of justice.[48]

Bankers' Books Evidence Act 1879[49]

Section 7 of the Bankers' Books Evidence Act 1879[50] allows 'a court or judge' to order that 'any party to legal proceedings . . . be at liberty to inspect and take copies of any entries in a bankers' book for any of the purposes of such proceedings'.[51] A s 7 order requires that legal proceedings be in existence.[52] 'Bankers' books' are defined in s 9 as including 'ledgers, daybooks, cash books, account books and other records within the ordinary business of the bank' whether in written, microfilm, electronic or magnetic format. 'Banker's' books do not encompass notes, letters or diaries.[53] The Act applies to civil and criminal[54] litigation. Section 7 does not enlarge the court's power to order disclosure, or the principles governing disclosure, in civil proceedings.[55] Fishing expeditions to discover if there is anything useful are not allowed. In exceptional circumstances the disclosure order may be framed to have extraterritorial effect.[56]

14.10

Disclosure to the client under the Civil Procedure Rules

In *C v C*[57] a doctor refused a patient's request to disclose details of a sexually transmitted disease from which she was suffering before presentation of a divorce

14.11

---

[46] cp dissenting judgment of Pill LJ in *Bennett v Compass Group UK* [2002] EWCA Civ 642, paras 85–86.
[47] *MGN Ltd v Jackson*, The Times, 29 March 1994. [48] *Lane v Willis* [1972] 1 All ER 430, 435–436.
[49] D Warne and N Elliott (eds), *Banking Litigation* (London: 1999) 292–294.
[50] The original intention of this Act was to spare bankers the inconvenience of their books and staff having to go to court. Discovery of information is an incidental effect.
[51] An order will not be made against a foreign bank in respect of records outside the UK recording transactions abroad when the bank is not a party to the litigation: *MacKinnon v Donaldson Lufkin and Jenrette Securities Corp* [1986] 1 All ER 653.
[52] The entries for which inspection is sought must be admissible in evidence at the trial: *Howard v Beall* (1889) 23 QBD 1, 2.
[53] See *Re Howglen Ltd* [2001] 1 All ER 376. See also *R v Leeds Crown Court, ex p Hill* [1991] Crim LR 376.
[54] See para 14.57 below.
[55] *Halsbury's Laws of England*, Butterworth Direct, Banking, Business of Banking, para 241.
[56] D McLean, *International Co-operation in Civil and Criminal Matters* (Oxford: 2002) 268.
[57] [1946] 1 All ER 562.

petition. Lewis J said that the doctor's silence until questioned in the witness box had not been justified; he should have given the information to the patient or to any named persons when asked by the patient to do so.[58] In *Walker v Eli Lilly & Co*,[59] a product liability case, Hirst J advised a health authority to respond readily and promptly to requests by patients for disclosure of medical records for litigation to which the health authority was not a party and not to compel the claimants to seek a court order.

14.12 Should a professional decline to disclose to a client for the purposes of litigation the client's own records, the client may apply, after commencement of proceedings, for disclosure pursuant to Supreme Court Act 1981 s 34[60] and CPR 31.17.

Litigation involving the professional

Preliminary disclosure

14.13 In all types of civil action, a professional (or the employer of a professional) who is a likely defendant may be ordered by a court to provide documents to a prospective claimant to enable the prospective claimant to discover whether he has a viable case.[61] This rule is often invoked against hospitals and doctors when an action for medical negligence is contemplated. Disclosure must be 'desirable in order to dispose fairly of the anticipated proceedings; assist the dispute to be resolved without proceedings; or save costs'[62] and the documents or class of documents whose disclosure is sought must be clearly specified.[63] As a further safeguard against 'fishing expeditions', a party cannot be made to disclose anything at this early stage that he could not be ordered to disclose by way of standard disclosure after instigation of proceedings.[64]

Ordinary disclosure under the Civil Procedure Rules

14.14 Once proceedings are underway the CPR require the professional bringing or defending[65] an action to disclose to opponents the existence of, and allow inspection and copying of, docu- uments in the professional's control.[66] An order for

---

[58] In *The Protection and Use of Patient Information* (1996) para 5.5 the Department of Health states that it 'is well-established practice that, at the patient's request, information relevant to legal proceedings may be released, usually to the patient's legal or medical adviser. . . . If the patient agrees, information may also be released to a third party involved in proceedings.'
[59] [1986] ECC 550.
[60] Or County Courts Act 1984, s 53. Or DPA subject access procedures: see para 19.21 below.
[61] Supreme Court Act 1981, s 33(2); County Courts Act 1984, s 52.
[62] CPR, r 31.16(3)(d).
[63] CPR, r 31.16(4)(a).
[64] CPR, r 31.16(3).
[65] A professional may not be joined as a party for the sole purpose of getting disclosure: cp *Douihech v Findlay* [1990] 3 All ER 118.
[66] CPR, rr 31.8, 11, 14, 15.

A. Civil Cases

standard disclosure of documents is the norm.[67] This covers documents upon which the professional relies, documents that adversely affect his case or another party's case and documents that support another party's case.[68] The only grounds for withholding documents are privilege,[69] that inspection would be disproportionate[70] or that a statute bars disclosure. The professional may apply to the court for an order permitting him to withhold disclosure of a document on the ground that disclosure would be damaging to the public interest.[71] If a professional were to refuse to allow inspection of relevant confidential client documents which did not fall into one of these exempt categories, it is unlikely that a court would refuse an order for specific disclosure.[72] In *Chantrey Martin v Martin*[73] the Court of Appeal forced a firm of chartered accountants to show working accounts and other papers that embodied information that was the subject of professional confidence between the firm and a client who was not a party to the litigation.

Search Orders[74]

Search orders are a device to prevent destruction of evidence required for impending or proposed litigation.[74a] They are most frequently used in intellectual property cases but might be useful in litigation in which the prospective defendant is a dishonest professional[75] or an interceptor.[76]

14.15

The applicant for a search order must be the person who is bringing or proposes to bring the action[77] but the respondent to the order does not have to be a defendant or proposed defendant.[78] If the order is granted the respondent must allow the applicant, accompanied by a suitably experienced[79] and independent[80] solicitor to

14.16

---

[67] CPR, r 31.5, PD 31 1.1. There is a power in r 31.12 to order specific disclosure. On the fast track disclosure is required only when ordered by the court in special directions: r 27.2, r 31.12.
[68] CPR, r 31.6.
[69] CPR, r 31.19(3).
[70] CPR, r 31(3)(2).
[71] CPR, r 31.19(1). The public interest is examined in ch 11.
[72] Such applications are made pursuant to CPR, r 31.12.
[73] [1953] 2 QB 286.
[74] R Dean, *The Law of Trade Sectrets and Personal Secrets* (2nd edn, Sydney: 2002) [13.05]–[13.215].
[74a] The jurisdiction was confirmed in *Anton Piller KG v Manufacturing Processes Ltd* [1976] Ch 55, 61 and set on a statutory basis in Civil Procedure Act 1997, s 7. See also *Chappell v UK* (1989) 12 EHRR 1.
[75] cp *Law Society v Y (A Solicitor)* (Ch D, 14 February 2000, WL 191148).
[76] cp *Universal Thermosensors Ltd v Hibben* [1992] 3 All ER 257 (documents containing confidential information stolen by former employees); *John Reid Enterprises Ltd v Pell* [1999] EMLR 675 (documents containing confidential information taken by an employee and passed to an investigative journalist).
[77] Civil Procedure Act 1997, s 7(2).
[78] ibid, s 7(3).
[79] CPR, PD 25, para 7.2.
[80] CPR, PD 25, para 8.1.

enter her premises. The respondent may be required: to allow a search or inspection of the premises for specified items; to produce specified items; to allow specified items to be copied, photographed, recorded or removed.[81] The order may also direct the respondent to provide information[82] and may contain an injunction restraining the respondent from informing others (except the respondent's lawyer) of the existence of the order for a limited period.[83]

14.17 To retain the element of surprise, a search order is normally obtained without notice to the respondent and the application is often heard in secret. The applicant for a search order must present affidavit evidence[84] to the court showing 'the probability that relevant material would disappear if the order were not made'.[85] In addition, the applicant must have an extremely strong prima facie case, the potential or actual damage to the applicant must be very serious (a requirement that would rule out clients whose only injury is mental distress), and there must be clear evidence that the incriminating material sought is in the respondent's possession.[86] The search order cannot be executed without the respondent's consent[87] (unlike a police search warrant) but if she does not co-operate she will be in contempt of court. Documents seized under the search order are subject to an implied undertaking of confidentiality and cannot be disclosed to anyone other than respondent without the respondent's consent or a court order.[88] To avoid abuse of the procedure, the applicant must make full and frank disclosure of all material facts[89] and will be required to give undertakings to the court to pay damages if the respondent sustains damage by reason of the order. An interceptor can invoke the privilege against self-incrimination to resist a search order.[90]

---

[81] Civil Procedure Act 1997, s 7(3), (4), (5).
[82] ibid s 7(5)(a).
[83] *Universal Thermosensors Ltd v Hibben* [1992] 3 All ER 257, 276.
[84] CPR, PD 25, para 3.1.
[85] CPR, PD 25, para 7.3(2). A search order should not be granted if an order to preserve the documents or deliver them up to a solicitor will achieve the desired end because the making 'of an intrusive order *ex parte* even against a guilty defendant is contrary to normal principles of justice and can only be done when there is a paramount need to prevent a denial of justice' per Hoffmann J, *Lock International plc v Beswick* [1989] 3 All ER 373, 384. In *Randolph M Fields v Watts*, The Times, 22 November 1984 the Court of Appeal took exception to a search order against practising members of the Bar who were not suspected of criminal activity.
[86] *Anton Piller KG v Manufacturing Processes Ltd* [1976] 1 All ER 779, 784.
[87] ibid at 782–783.
[88] *Customs and Excise Commissioners v AE Hamlin & Co* [1983] 3 All ER 654, 661.
[89] *Columbia Picture Industries v Robinson* [1986] 3 All ER 338, 350–351; *CMI-Centers for Medical Innovation GmbH v Phytopharm plc* [1999] FSR 235, 262.
[90] Civil Procedure Act 1997, s 7(7). The privilege has been removed for intellectual property cases by Supreme Court Act 1981, s 72 but not in other cases.

A. Civil Cases

Criminal Assets Recovery Authority[91]

14.18 The Criminal Assets Recovery Authority is a new body set up under the Proceeds of Crime Act 2002 to recover the proceeds of crime through confiscation and, where conviction is not possible, civil recovery and tax assessments. Upon application to a judge,[92] the Director can obtain compulsory powers of investigation. The compulsory powers available are a production order, a search and seizure warrant, a disclosure order, a customer information order and an account monitoring order. The production order[93] and search and seizure warrant[94] enlarge upon earlier investigatory powers found in the Drug Trafficking Act 1994 and the Criminal Justice Act 1988. A disclosure order[95] enables the Director to require *any* person whom the Director considers to have information relevant to an investigation to answer questions at interview and to provide information and documents.[96] A customer information order[97] requires targeted banks and other financial institutions to provide details of accounts held by the person under investigation. An account monitoring order[98] requires a bank or other financial institution to provide transaction information on a suspect account for a specified period. The Director is not alone in being given power by the 2002 Act to apply for a production order, a search warrant, a customer information order and an account monitoring order. The police and customs officials can use these powers in confiscation and (with the exception of disclosure orders)[99] money laundering investigations too.[100] Disclosure of information to the Director of the Criminal Assets Recovery Authority, police or customs in response to an order is not a breach of contract or confidence.[101] Legally privileged information and 'excluded material'[102] are exempt from production, search and seizure and disclosure orders.[103] The exercise of all coercive powers is limited by the HRA to what is compatible with the European Convention on Human Rights (ECHR).

---

[91] J Cassidy, 'Proceeds of Crime—Finally Enacted' (2002) 6 Tax LJ 55. D McLean, *International Co-operation in Civil and Criminal Matters* (Oxford: 2002) ch 10; P Alldridge, *Money Laundering Law* (Oxford: 2003) esp ch 10.
[92] Whether this must be a Crown Court or High Court judge depends on the type of order sought: s 343.
[93] ss 345–351. cp *R v Southwark Crown Court, ex parte Bowles* [1998] 2 All ER 193. The person named in the order must give access or produce material in his possession or control.
[94] s 352.
[95] ss 357–359.
[96] The Director of the Serious Fraud Office has similar powers: see para 14.58 below.
[97] ss 363–366. Cp Terrorism Act 2000, Sch 6.
[98] ss 370–373. Cp Terrorism Act 2000, Sch 6A, para 2(5) and para 14.50 below.
[99] Proceeds of Crime Act 2002, s 357(2).
[100] ss 352(5) (search warrant), 378.
[101] ss 348(4), 361(6), 368, 374.
[102] Defined at para 14.22 below. The meaning is as in PACE (Proceeds of Crime Act 2002, s 379).
[103] ss 348, 383(1) (production orders), 354 (search warrant), 361 (disclosure order).

B. Criminal Cases

Acquisition of Confidential Information by the Prosecution

General police powers[104]

Entry and search pursuant to a warrant from a magistrates' court

14.19 All professionals are potentially affected by the entry, search and seizure regime set up for the police (and customs officers)[105] in the Police and Criminal Evidence Act 1984 (PACE).[106] Section 8 provides for the issue by a justice of the peace of a warrant to enter and search premises for evidence of a 'serious arrestable offence'[107] on the written application of a constable. Certain conditions must be satisfied. These are that there exist reasonable grounds for believing:

(1) a serious arrestable offence has been committed; and
(2) material likely[108] to be of substantial value to the investigation is on the premises for which the warrant is sought; and
(3) the material is likely to be evidence admissible at the trial for the offence; and
(4) the material does not fall within a category exempt from s 8 warrants.

14.20 In addition the court must be satisfied of one of the following:

(1) it is not practicable to communicate with anyone entitled to grant entry to the premises; or
(2) it is not practicable to communicate with anyone entitled to grant access to the evidence; or
(3) entry will not be granted unless a warrant is produced; or
(4) the purpose of the search would be frustrated or seriously prejudiced unless a constable could obtain immediate access to the material.

---

[104] D Feldman, 'Access to Clients' Documents after the Police and Criminal Evidence Act 1984' [1985] Professional Negligence 24, 67; D Feldman, *Civil Liberties and Human Rights in England and Wales* (2nd edn, Oxford: 2002) 640 et seq.

[105] Police and Criminal Evidence Act 1984 (Application to Customs and Excise) Order 1985, SI 1985/1800.

[106] There are reported cases involving accountants (eg *R v Central Criminal Court, ex p Propend Finance Pty Ltd* [1996] 2 Cr App R 26; *R v Southwark Crown Court, ex p Sorsky Defries* [1996] Crim LR 195) and many involving lawyers (eg *R v Inner London Crown Court, ex p Baines & Baines* [1987] 77 Cr App R 111; *R v Maidstone Crown Court, ex p Wait* [1988] Crim LR 384; *R v Leeds Crown Court, ex p Switalski* [1991] Crim LR 559; *R v Lewes Crown Court, ex p Weller & Co* (DC, 12 May 1999).

[107] A 'serious arrestable offence' is defined in PACE, s 116 and Sch 5. A serious arrestable offence includes also 'any conduct which is an offence under the law of a country or territory outside the United Kingdom [that] . . . would constitute a serious arrestable offence if it had occurred in any part of the United Kingdom': Criminal Justice (International Co-operation) Act 1990, s 7(1).

[108] 'A likelihood is less than a probability', per Jowitt J, *R v Chief Constable, ex p Fitzpatrick* [1998] 1 All ER 65, 75.

B. Criminal Cases

The only one of these conditions that is likely to apply to a reputable professional is number 3.[109]

Special, excluded and legally privileged materials

14.21 A magistrates' court may not issue a warrant to search for information for 'special procedure material' or 'excluded material' or items subject to legal privilege. The burden of satisfying the court that materials sought under a warrant do not fall within these categories rests with the applicant for the warrant. 'Special procedure material'[110] is material subject 'to an express or implied undertaking to hold it in confidence' that was acquired or created by a professional in the course of his profession and that is not 'excluded material' or an item subject to legal privilege. Special procedure material passed in confidence from an employer to an employee remains special procedure material and anything created by the employee is 'special procedure material' if this is how it would have been classified had it been created by the employer.[111]

14.22 Items subject to legal privilege are defined in s 10.[112] These encompass:

(1) communications between 'professional legal adviser'[113] and client (or client's representative) for the purpose of giving legal advice;[114]
(2) communications between (a) the legal adviser and client (or client's representative) or (b) legal adviser and client (or client's representative) and a third party, in connection with or in contemplation of legal proceedings;[115]
(3) items enclosed with or referred to in such communications are also privileged provided they were created in connection with the giving of legal advice or for the purposes of legal proceedings.

---

[109] Not all professionals are reputable. In *R v Customs and Excise Commissioners, ex p Popely* [1999] STC 1016, customs and excise officers believed that P and his solicitor, H, had together been involved in the evasion of value added tax liabilities. Warrants were obtained to search and seize material from H's premises.

[110] PACE, s 14.

[111] s 14(4), (5).

[112] On the interpretation of s 10 see R Stone, 'PACE: Special Procedures and Legal Privilege' [1988] Crim LR 498, 504 et seq. The language of s 10 differs from LPP at common law (as described in ch 18). It is both wider and narrower. If a solicitor selects a number of documents that are not of themselves privileged, the resulting selection in her hands will be privileged at common law (*Dubai Bank Ltd v Galadari (No 7)* [1992] 1 All ER 658) but not under PACE s 10 (if interpreted literally) until the selection is communicated to someone. Derivative materials (see para 16.22 below), such as notes made by the solicitor will, for the same reason, not be covered by s 10.

[113] This phrase is undefined. S 10(1) has been stated to 'reflect the common law position': *Francis & Francis v Central Criminal Court* [1988] 3 All ER 775, 797 per Lord Goff. This surely means that it is confined to lawyers and does not extend to someone without a formal legal qualification who performs the functions of a legal adviser, eg an accountant advising on tax law. On this point see *R v Umoh* (1986) 84 Cr App R 138.

[114] Legal advice has been given a wide interpretation at common law: see para 16.17 below.

[115] LPP at common law extends only to a communication with a third party made with the dominant purpose of preparing for contemplated litigation: see para 16.21 below. There is no mention in s 10 of the dominant purpose test.

Provided one of these three tests is satisfied there is no need for the item to be in the custody of a 'professional legal adviser'. For example, a letter from a solicitor to a doctor seeking the doctor's opinion about the medical condition of a client is protected. Where items are held for the purposes of crime, they fall outside the ambit of legal privilege.[116] The criminal purpose may be that of a third party who is not a party to the lawyer–client relationship and of whose intentions the lawyer knows nothing.[117] The meaning of 'excluded material' is given in s 11. 'Excluded material' includes:

(1) 'personal records' which a person has acquired or created in the course of inter alia a profession, or
(2) human tissue or tissue fluid taken 'for the purposes of diagnosis or medical treatment'[118] or
(3) 'journalistic material'.[119]

In all cases the material must be '[held] in confidence'.[120] For material not acquired for journalism, this means subject to an express or implied undertaking of confidentiality or subject to a statutory restriction on disclosure.[121] 'Personal records' are:

> documentary and other records[122] concerning an individual (whether living or dead) who can be identified from them, and relating—
> (a) to his physical or mental health;[123]

---

[116] s 10(2). For an example involving items held by a solicitor see *R v Leeds MC, ex parte Dumbleton* [1993] Crim LR 866.

[117] *Francis & Francis v Central Criminal Court* [1988] 3 All ER 775. It was assumed in this case that both the client and solicitor were being used as innocent tools. For criticisms of the decision see A Newbold, 'The Crime/Fraud Exception to Legal Professional Privilege' (1990) 53 MLR 472, 481–483 and D Feldman, *Civil Liberties and Human Rights in England and Wales* (2nd edn, Oxford: 2002) 636–637.

[118] If a tissue or fluid sample is taken after death this cannot be for treatment though it might be for diagnosis. S 11 does not cover samples taken for research. Thus in the circumstances of a controversial Scottish case, *HMA v Kelly* (HC Glasgow, 23 March 2001), the medical research results obtained under a warrant from scientists by the Scottish police would have been special procedure but not excluded material in England. Briefly, the facts were that while in prison the accused had taken part in a study to find out the extent of an HIV outbreak through needle-sharing among prisoners. He had been assured confidentiality. At that particular prison all inmates were found to have a strikingly similar form of the HIV virus. Police used the research results to prove that the accused had infected his girlfriend who tested positive for the same strain of HIV.

[119] This is defined in s 13: '(1) . . . "journalistic material" means material acquired or created for the purposes of journalism. (2) Material is only journalistic material for the purposes of this Act if it is in the possession of a person who acquired or created it for the purposes of journalism. (3) A person who receives material from someone who intends that the recipient shall use it for the purposes of journalism is to be taken to have acquired it for those purposes.'

[120] A tissue or fluid sample taken after death might not be subject to a legal obligation of confidentiality; the law on this point is unsettled: see paras 5.46 et seq.

[121] s 11(2).

[122] eg computerized records, x-rays.

[123] This is not confined to clinical, nursing or surgical notes or treatment; it includes administrative records that concern an identifiable patient in his capacity of patient: *R v Cardiff Crown Court, ex p Kellam* (1993) 16 BMLR 76.

(b) to spiritual counselling or assistance given or to be given to him;
(c) to counselling or assistance given or to be given to him, for the purposes of his personal welfare.[124]

14.23 Some professionals, such as clergy and doctors,[125] will find that most of the confidential personal information that they hold about clients is 'excluded material'. For some other professionals such as bankers and accountants[126] the situation is reversed: the confidential personal information held is more likely to be 'special procedure material' because it is not concerned with the client's personal welfare. Social workers, educators, and probation officers will find that their counselling records and so much of their records as deal with assistance to an individual for his personal welfare are 'excluded material'. Much confidential information about clients in the possession of lawyers is protected by legal professional privilege (LPP). Where it is not the material may be 'excluded material' (for example, medical reports that were not prepared with litigation in mind) or 'special procedure material'. Each item must be assessed separately.

14.24 Anything that is legally privileged, is just as much privileged when in the possession of the client as in the possession of the lawyer. The very opposite is true for 'excluded material' and 'special procedure material'. 'Excluded' or 'special procedure' material in the hands of the client can be seized under an ordinary search warrant. '[T]he effect of the legislation is to protect the professional or voluntary adviser against invasion of privacy by the police, and to prevent the police, when seeking evidence against a suspect, from ransacking the records or premises of third parties with a duty of confidence. It does not protect the privacy of the suspect as such.'[127]

Access to special procedure and excluded material by production or access order

14.25 PACE has no procedure for allowing access to legally privileged materials.[128] Section 9(1), however, allows the police[129] access to 'special procedure material'

---

[124] PACE, s 12.
[125] See *R v Cardiff Crown Court, ex p Kellam* (1994) 16 BMLR 76 (administrative and clinical records of a psychiatric hospital excluded materials).
[126] See *R v Central Criminal Court, ex p Adegbesan* [1986] 3 All ER 113.
[127] D Feldman, *Civil Liberties and Human Rights in England and Wales* (2nd edn, Oxford, 2002) 642.
[128] *R v Southampton Crown Court, ex p J & P* [1993] Crim LR 962. Material subject to legal privilege is beyond the reach of a production order or search warrant because of the definition of 'special procedure material' in PACE s 14 and the absence of any mention in s 9 of items subject to legal privilege. In *Francis & Francis v Central Criminal Court* [1988] 3 All ER 775, 778 Lord Bridge said that embodied in s 9 and Sch 1 is 'a consistent thread that "items subject to legal privilege" as defined in section 10 of the Act of 1984 are placed beyond the reach' of the police.
[129] The PACE provisions dealing with special procedure and excluded materials do not apply to customs officers seeking access to materials acquired or created in the course of a trade, business or profession: Police and Criminal Evidence Act 1984 (Application to Customs and Excise) Order 1985 SI 1985/1800.

and some 'excluded material' for the purpose of investigating a serious arrestable offence.[130] Schedule 1 to the 1984 Act provides two routes by which the police can lay their hands on material for which they could not obtain a search warrant from a magistrates' court. Both routes entail making an application to a circuit judge who must give reasons for his decision.[131]

14.26 **First set of access conditions** The first route involves applying for an access order (to see the material in situ) or a production order (to take the material away)[132] Either one of two sets of conditions must be satisfied to obtain the order. The usual set of access conditions relied upon (of which the judge must be personally satisfied[133] by the police[134] on the balance of probabilities)[135] is laid down in Sch 1, para 2:

(1) there are reasonable grounds for believing that a serious arrestable offence has been committed;
(2) there is 'special procedure material'(not including 'excluded material') on specified premises;[136] and
(3) the desired material is likely to be of substantial value (whether by itself or together with other material) to the investigation and relevant, admissible evidence in a future trial;[137] and
(4) other methods of getting the material have failed or appear bound to fail;[138] and
(5) access to the material is in the public interest, having regard:
    (a) to the benefit likely to accrue to the police investigation from access and
    (b) the circumstances under which the person in possession of the material holds it.

14.27 In *R v Northampton Crown Court, ex p DPP*[139] the Divisional Court said that if condition (1) was satisfied it was unlikely that the public interest requirement laid

---

[130] This is defined by s 116 to include any arrestable offence likely to lead to serious interference with the administration of justice or the investigation of an offence; the death of any person; serious injury to any person; and substantial financial loss or gain to any person. Financial loss is measured according to the circumstances of the victim (s 116(7)).

[131] *R v CCC, ex p Propend Property* (1996) 2 Cr App R 26, 28; *R v Lewes Crown Court, ex p Nigel Weller & Co* (DC 12 May 1999).

[132] PACE, Sch 1, para 4. For information contained in a computer see para 5.

[133] *R v Lewes Crown Court, ex p Hill* (1990) 93 Cr App R 60; *R v Central Criminal Court, ex p Bright* [2000] 2 All ER 244, paras 78, 142.

[134] *R v Central Criminal Court, ex p Bright* [2000] 2 All ER 244 para 78.

[135] *R v Norwich Crown Court, ex p Chethams* [1991] COD 271.

[136] A speculative possibility is not enough: *R v Central Criminal Court, ex p Bright* [2001] 2 All ER 244 para 142.

[137] *R v Central Criminal Court, ex p Bright* [2001] 2 All ER 244, para 79.

[138] This includes, in the case of bank accounts, an order under Bankers' Books Evidence Act 1879, s 7: *R v Leeds Crown Court, ex p Hill* [1991] Crim LR 376.

[139] (1991) 93 Cr App R 376. The decision is criticized by D Feldman, *Civil Liberties and Human Rights in England and Wales* (2nd edn, Oxford: 2002) 646–647 as possibly incompatible with Art 8 in that it could be read to remove the judge's discretion to refuse the application on public interest grounds once access condition (1) is satisfied.

B. Criminal Cases

down in (5) was not satisfied. Nevertheless, there is no compulsion on the judge to issue an order if the access conditions have been met; he has an overarching discretion to refuse the application. Factors that do not fall to be considered under (1) to (5), but which might make an access or production order oppressive, may lead him to refuse the application.[140] These include the antiquity of the investigation, the risk of self-incrimination by the recipient of the order, the effect of the order on third parties, proportionality between the benefit to the police and the offence[141] and whether the material is being held in circumstances of confidentiality.[142] These last two factors have to be most carefully considered if an access or production order infringes an individual's Article 8 right to respect for private life or correspondence.[143] Material whose production will unjustifiably infringe Article 8 must be excluded from the production or access order.

Second set of access conditions The alternative set of conditions for obtaining an access or production order permits access to 'special procedure' *and* 'excluded materials'. This set requires the judge to be satisfied that: **14.28**

(1) there are reasonable grounds for believing that the desired material is on the premises specified, and
(2) 'a search of the premises for that material could have been authorised by the issue of a warrant to a constable under an enactment' prior to the coming into force of PACE[144] and
(3) the issue of such a warrant would have been appropriate.[145]

At first blush these conditions look less onerous than the previous set. There is, for example, no mention of a reasonable belief that a serious arrestable offence has been committed or that other methods of obtaining the material have been tried and failed. Failure to consider such matters when deciding whether to issue process to search for documents containing confidential personal information is likely, however, to constitute an unjustifiable interference with Article 8; to be appropriate an order must be proportionate which requires inter alia the nature of the offence and alternative methods of obtaining the material to be considered. It is impossible to get a production or access order for 'excluded material' in a murder inquiry because no statutory power to carry out a search existed before 1984.[146]

---

[140] *R v Central Criminal Court, ex p Bright* [2001] 2 All ER 244, para 84.
[141] per Judge LJ, ibid, para 85.
[142] ibid, para 160.
[143] ibid, para 162.
[144] The Official Secrets Acts are qualifying statutes.
[145] PACE, Sch 1, para 3.
[146] *R v Central Criminal Court, ex p Brown*, The Times, 7 September 1992; *R v Cardiff Crown Court, ex p Kellam* (1994) 16 BMLR 76; *R v Singleton* [1995] 1 Cr App R 431 (dental records).

Access to special procedure and excluded material by search warrant

14.29 The second route by which the police can get hold of 'special procedure' or 'excluded' material is to apply to the circuit judge for a search warrant.[147] Before issuing a search warrant the judge must be satisfied not only that one or other of the set of access conditions for obtaining a production or access order is satisfied, but also that

- one of several further conditions is fulfilled,[148] for example, the impracticality of communicating with anyone entitled to grant access; or
- the second set of access conditions[149] has been fulfilled and an order for production or access to the material has not been complied with.[150]

Opposing an access or production order or a search warrant

14.30 Applications for special procedure material should normally be made with notice.[151] A without notice application for a warrant to search the premises of a professional would be inappropriate unless the professional were a suspect,[152] and even then it might not be justified.

> [T]he fact that a solicitor is himself under investigation is not of itself necessarily a sufficient reason for ordering such an intrusion into his affairs and those of his clients. All the circumstances of the individual application must be taken into account, including, for example, the seriousness of the matter being investigated, the evidence already available to the police to found a prosecution based on it, and the extent to which the solicitor has already been put on notice of the interest in his affairs such as might have caused him to hide or destroy or otherwise interfere with incriminating documents.[153]

If the application is without notice, the police have a duty to ensure that all relevant material is brought to the attention of the judge whether it assists the application or militates against it.[154]

---

[147] PACE, s 15(3).

[148] Sch 1, para 14 specifies that the police must show one of the following: that it is not practicable to communicate (a) with a person entitled to grant entry to the relevant premises, or (b) with a person entitled to grant access to the material, or (c) the person in possession of the material holds it subject to a restriction on disclosure imposed by legislation which will be breached by disclosure without a warrant or (d) notification of person in possession 'may seriously prejudice the investigation'.

[149] See para 14.27 above.

[150] Sch 1, para 12(b).

[151] *R v Maidstone Crown Court, ex p Waitt* [1988] Crim LR 384.

[152] cp *Francis & Francis v Central Criminal Court* [1988] 3 All ER 775, 792.

[153] per Auld J, *R v Southampton Crown Court, ex p J & P* [1993] Crim LR 962. For an exceptional case where an application without notice for a warrant to search the premises of a solicitor was approved see *R v Leeds Crown Court, ex p Switalski* [1991] Crim LR 559. A warrant to search a solicitor premises issued *ex p* under the Taxes Management Act 1970, s 20C(1) was found to be Convention compliant in *Tamosius v UK* [2002] STC 1307.

[154] *R v Acton Crown Court, ex p Layton* [1993] Crim LR 458.

B. Criminal Cases

Pending a decision to issue a warrant, a professional who has been notified of the application must retain the information sought.[155] The s 9 application is a lis between the police and the professional. The police must give notice to the professional[156] but there is no obligation to notify the client.[157] The professional may oppose an application[158] on the grounds that it is excessively general[159] infringes Article 8[160] or includes items subject to legal privilege.

14.31

> It is . . . an important responsibility of a judge to look out for the possibility of legal privilege on an application . . . for access to material held by a solicitor. If there is such a possibility, he should consider carefully whether any part of the material to which the police seek access is or may be of a nature to which the privilege attaches and, if so, whether it has, or is likely to have, lost that privilege under section 10(2) and/or through waiver. When formulating an order or warrant he must only include items which he concludes are unlikely to be privileged.[160a]

Where there is a prima facie case that a file contains privileged and non-privileged material, it may be necessary to give provisional access to the entire file.[161]

A professional is not bound to oppose a police access application,[162] and in practice professionals who are not lawyers rarely do so if their own interests are not affected. For one thing, the client cannot be made to pay the expenses incurred and for another, the professional may not have enough information to raise objections without first contacting the client which the police, with the backing of the

14.32

---

[155] PACE, Sch 1, para 11. Not to do so may be a contempt if a para 11 exception does not apply. In *R (on the application of NTL Group Ltd) v Ipswich Crown Court* [2002] EWHC 1585; The Times, 6 August 2002, the Divisional Court held that lawful authority for an internet service provider to divert and store e-mails that are the subject of an application for special procedure material without the consent of the customer is implicit in Sch 1, para 11, read together with PACE, s 9. Accordingly, no offence is committed under RIPA. '[N]o harm will be caused to any third party in consequence of this being done because unless a judge is prepared to make the order and therefore remove the protection which would otherwise exist for third parties, the police have no right to be informed of the contents of the material retained', per Lord Woolf, ibid, para 25.

[156] PACE, Sch 1, para 8. On the subject of what constitutes proper notice see *R v Central Criminal Court, ex p Adegbesan* (1987) 84 Cr App R 219; *R v Inner London Crown Court, ex p Baines & Baines (A Firm)* [1987] 3 All ER 1025, 1029; *R v Manchester Crown Court, ex p Taylor* (1988) 87 Cr App R 358.

[157] *Barclays Bank v Taylor* [1989] 3 All ER 563.

[158] If representations to the circuit judge not to issue a production order are unsuccessful the circuit judge's decision may be challenged in judicial review proceedings or by the case stated procedure in the Divisional Court of the Queen's Bench Division: *R v Central Criminal Court, ex p Carr*, Independent, 5 March 1987.

[159] *R v Central Criminal Court, ex p AJD Holdings* [1992] Crim LR 669; *R. v. Southampton Crown Court, ex p J and P* [1993] Crim LR 962.

[160] See para 14.45. Cp *Schmidt v Luxembourg* Application 51772/99, 25 February 2003, paras 70–71.

[160a] per Auld J, *R v Southampton Crown Court, ex p J & P* [1993] Crim LR 962.

[161] ibid. Cp para 14.38.

[162] *Barclays Bank plc v Taylor* [1989] 3 All ER 563, 569; *R v CC at Lewes Crown Court, ex p Hill* (1990) 93 Cr App R 60.

courts, discourage.[163] In *Barclays Bank plc v Taylor*,[164] which concerned an application for access to bank accounts, Lord Donaldson said:

> Since the responsibility for deciding whether the access conditions are fulfilled is firmly placed on the circuit judge, and such an order cannot be made by consent of the parties, I can see no reason for implying an obligation to contest the application unless the bank knew something relevant to it which was not likely to be apparent on the face of the application or of the notice relating to it or might not be known to the police. The primary purpose of notice being given to the bank is to enable it to safeguard its own interests by, for example, pointing out that it did not hold the accounts to which the application related.

If the professional decides not to oppose access, a client who has become aware of the application has no right to oppose it in the professional's stead.[165] But if the application is opposed, the judge may find it helpful to hear what the client has to say before deciding whether to make an order.[166]

What an order or search warrant requires of the professional

14.33 An access or production order imposes a personal obligation on the professional to produce or grant access to the material specified. Failure to do so is punishable as a contempt of court.[167] Once the professional has been served with notice of an access or production order, destruction, concealment, disposal, or alteration of the subject-matter of the order is also a contempt of court.[168] Compliance is not a breach of contract or breach of confidence. A refusal to produce or allow access may lead to the issue of a search warrant.[169] It is not possible to oppose an application for a warrant since this takes place without notice. The professional or client can apply for judicial review to quash the warrant after its execution.[170]

14.34 A professional confronted with a warrant to search her premises has to admit the police and allow the police to carry out the search. If she does not, the police can deploy reasonable force to effect entry.[171] But the professional is not required to do anything personally to assist the police. '[She] is entitled to remain entirely passive.'[172] If the police do not find what they are looking for, she commits no wrong by failing to tell them where to look for it.

---

[163] See para 14.43 below.
[164] *Barclays Bank plc v. Taylor* [1989] 3 All ER 563, 569.
[165] *R v Leicester Crown Court, ex p DPP* [1987] 3 All ER 654, 656. Query, how can this be if the complaint is of infringement of Art 8? For a criticism of this interpretation see A Zuckerman, 'The Weakness of the PACE Special Procedure for Protecting Confidential Material' [1990] Crim LR 473, 478.
[166] *R v Lewes Crown Court, ex p Hill* (1990) 93 Cr App R 60.
[167] PACE, Sch. 1, para 15.
[168] PACE, Sch. 1, para 11.
[169] PACE, Sch. 1, para 12(b). See para 14.29 above.
[170] As was attempted in *R v Leeds Crown Court, ex p Switalski* [1991] Crim LR 559.
[171] PACE, s 117.
[172] per Judge LJ, *R v Central Criminal Court, ex p Bright* [2001] 2 All ER 244, para 114.

B. Criminal Cases

Police powers of seizure

PACE, s 19 enables a police constable to remove (or photocopy or photograph)[173] any items (including computer data)[174] authorized in a search warrant[175] (in which seizable items should be identified, so far as practicable).[176] The section also allows a police constable who is lawfully on premises (for whatever reason)[177] to recover (but not to search for)[178] material (including 'excluded' and 'special procedure' material which is exempt from a search warrant)[179] which he has reasonable cause to believe: **14.35**

(1) (a) has been obtained in consequence of the commission of an offence; *or*
    (b) is evidence in relation to an offence which he is investigating, or any other offence; *and*
(2) it is necessary to make the seizure in order to prevent it being concealed, lost, altered, destroyed or, in the case of the product of crime, damaged.[180]

Evidence of crimes quite different in character from the one for which the warrant or access order was issued (or their fruits) may be seized.[181] So also may evidence or the fruits of crimes committed by another client or even the professional himself. But in all but the last case, it is unlikely that it would be reasonable for the police constable to believe that, unless removed, the material would not, on request, be preserved. The fact that the police cannot get an access or production order in respect of the material because it is excluded material is not a legitimate reason to seize it. **14.36**

Preventing the seizure of legally privileged material

Material that a constable has reasonable grounds for believing to be subject to LPP cannot lawfully be seized or retained.[182] At one time police would remove material which they thought might be privileged in sealed bags for later sifting and **14.37**

---

[173] PACE, s 21(5).
[174] The police can demand a print-out: PACE, s 20.
[175] s 8(2)
[176] s 15(6)(b). See also *R v Central Criminal Court, ex p AJ Holdings* [1992] Crim LR 669. Identification of articles is desirable because it restricts the scope of the search.
[177] It could be, for example, to make a summary arrest, entry having been made under PACE, s 17.
[178] He may only carry out a search to the extent required for the purpose for which the warrant was issued: PACE, s 16(8).
[179] He may not seize anything that he has reasonable grounds for believing to be subject to legal privilege: PACE, s 19(6).
[180] PACE, s 19(4). Retention of the seized material is authorized by Criminal Justice and Police Act 2001, s 56.
[181] The crimes need not be arrestable crimes.
[182] s 19(6). In *R v Customs and Excise Commissioners, ex p Popely* [1999] STC 1016 the application of s 19(6) to a warrant issued to customs officers pursuant to Value Added Tax Act 1994, Sch 11, para 10 was considered.

assessment by independent counsel. The Divisional Court put an end to this practice in *R v Chesterfield Justices and Chief Constable of Derbyshire, ex p Bramley*.[183] Anticipating the incorporation into domestic law of Article 8, the court ruled that during a search the police could undertake a preliminary review of material to ensure that nothing outside the scope of the warrant was seized but without legislative authority they were not entitled to remove material from the premises for later examination. This decision made life difficult for the police when searching premises that contained a lot of documentation, some of which might be legally privileged.[184]

14.38 The Government's solution is in the Criminal Justice and Police Act 2001.[185] This confers on police and other law enforcement agencies, the power to remove from premises property that may be, or may contain, legally privileged material for the purpose of determining whether it falls within their power of seizure when it is not reasonably practicable to examine it in situ[186] because of constraints of time, manpower, technology or risk of damaging property or prejudicing the use of material that can be seized.[187] Once identified, legally privileged material (and any 'special procedure' or 'excluded' material found to which the investigators are not entitled) must be returned as soon as reasonably practicable[188] unless it is not reasonably practicable to separate what cannot lawfully be retained[189] from what can without prejudicing the use of material that can be retained.

14.39 To minimize the risk of abuse of power, the occupier of the premises from which material is taken must be notified of the seizure[190] and provision made for the occupier 'or a person with an interest in that property' to be present or represented when it is initially examined.[191] Application may be made to a judge by any person with a relevant interest in the seized property for the return of legally privi-

---

[183] [2000] 1 All ER 411.

[184] Independent counsel could be taken along to assist with the review, but this did not remove constraints of time, technology and manpower.

[185] A draft amended PACE Code B supplements this legislation. Officers must use the new powers only 'where it is essential to do so' and must not remove more material than 'absolutely necessary' (para 7.7). The sifting must be done 'at the earliest practicable time' (para 7.8) and all reasonable steps are to be taken to accommodate a reasonable request of an interested party to be present (Note 7D). Legally privileged, excluded or special procedure material that the police are not allowed to retain must be returned as soon as it is found, not when the whole examination is complete (para 7.9). If an interested party indicates an intention to apply to a judge for the return of the material, sifting is to stop and the material to be secured pending a judicial decision (para7.10). Where material that normally cannot be seized is 'inextricably linked' to that which can, the former must not be examined or copied except to prove the source and integrity of that which can (Note 7H). The final version of COPB, which differs from the draft, is available at www.homeoffice.gov.uk/pcrg/pacecodes/code_b_explan1_03.pdf.

[186] Criminal Justice and Police Act 2001, ss 50.

[187] ibid, s 50(3). S 51 contains a power of seizure from the person in terms similar to s 50.

[188] ibid, s 53(2)(c). For special procedure and excluded material see s 55(1).

[189] ibid, s 54(2)(b) (legally privileged), s 55(2)(b), (3)(b) ('special procedure' or 'excluded').

[190] ibid, s 52.

[191] ibid, s 52(4)

B. Criminal Cases

leged (or unseizable confidential) material which investigators are not entitled to retain.[192] Pending the hearing of the application, the investigator has a duty to secure the seized material[193] against examination, copying or use without the consent of the applicant or the judge.[194] Legally privileged (or unseizable confidential) material that is 'inextricably linked' to seizable property is a special case: it may be examined, copied and used to the extent that this will facilitate the use in any proceedings or investigation of material that can lawfully be seized.[195]

The new legislation eliminates any argument that seizure of confidential materials and items subject to LPP breaches Article 8 because it is not 'in accordance with law'.[196] It may not be compliant with the ECHR in other respects. Possible flaws include: **14.40**

(1) Safeguards in the Act may not prevent those who have seized confidential privileged material from examining it before application can be made to a court for its return.[197]

(2) Under the Act the police can retain and inspect confidential and privileged records of innocent clients that are inextricably linked to those of suspect clients. Nothing in the Act reminds investigators of the need for proportionality.

(3) Unless application is made for the return of the property seized to a court, it is the investigators who determine whether material is subject to LPP.[198] To avoid this, it is likely that applications will immediately be made for the return of documents whenever investigators remove legally privileged material. No provision is made in the Act for funding such applications.

(4) Feldman suggests that during the time that privileged documents are in the possession of the police, Article 8 will require the privilege-holder to be allowed to inspect and copy the material for legitimate purposes unless there is a pressing public interest reason for refusing access.[199] The same applies to other unseizable items. The Act does not provide for this.

Voluntary disclosure in the public interest

The existence of procedures for the police to procure 'special procedure material' and, sometimes, 'excluded material' does not stop a professional from voluntarily **14.41**

---

[192] ibid, s 59(3)(b).
[193] ibid, s 60.
[194] ibid, s 61.
[195] ibid, s 62.
[196] See para 3.19 above.
[197] The ECtHR might require the seized material to be deposited immediately in the custody of a neutral third party.
[198] In *Kopp v Switzerland* (1998) 27 EHRR 91, a case in which telephone communications to a lawyer were intercepted by the authorities, the ECtHR found it 'astonishing' that the task of distinguishing between privileged and non-privileged matters was not required by Swiss law to be supervised by a judge.
[199] D Feldman, *Civil Liberties and Human Rights in England and Wales* (2nd edn, Oxford: 2002) 638.

disclosing special procedure and even excluded material in the exceptional case where there is an overriding public interest in the disclosure. In *R v Singleton* a dentist chose to hand over the dental records and a dental impression of a client for comparison with bite marks on the chin of someone who had been murdered. This was 'excluded material' within the meaning of PACE. Farquharson LJ said that:

> the object of the Act is to protect disclosure of . . . confidential personal records. It seems equally clear that the person to be protected from disclosure is not the suspect in any particular case, but the person who has acquired or created the personal record.[200] Accordingly, if that person voluntarily discloses the record he does not seek or require the protection given by the Act to that class of record. It is for the person identified in section 11(1) to decide whether he wishes to make this disclosure, bearing in mind the degree of confidence reposed in him.[201]

14.42 The parameters of public interest disclosure are notoriously uncertain and extreme caution needs to be exercised by any professional minded to rely upon the public interest to justify disclosure of confidential client information.[202] If the professional misjudges the situation he exposes himself to civil liability for breach of contract or confidence or, if in the public sector, HRA s 6. Quite apart from this, professionals should be aware that if they are to retain the public's trust, they must avoid becoming part of the law enforcement machinery of the state.[203]

Warning the client

14.43 A banker is not obliged to warn a customer suspected of a criminal offence of a pending application under PACE for access to 'special procedure material' or 'excluded material' that concerns the client.[204] In *Barclays Bank plc v Taylor*[205] Lord Donaldson said that the banks had been at liberty to inform the Taylors of a police application to inspect their accounts but that he would have been disappointed if the banks had done so.[206] The defendants' argument that there is an implied term in the contract between banker and customer to inform the latter of any application for inspection or disclosure of confidential information was rejected.[207]

---

[200] A Grubb and I Kennedy, *Medical Law* (3rd edn, London, 2000) 1129 point out that this statement is not correct.
[201] [1995] 1 Cr App R 431, 439.
[202] For a full discussion of public interest disclosure see ch 11.
[203] cp Report of the Commission of Inquiry into the Confidentiality of Health Information, (Ontario: 1980) vol 2, 91.
[204] *R v Manchester Crown Court, ex p Taylor* [1988] 2 All ER 769, 777. No warning is required by the fairness criterion of the first data protection principle: See para 10.20 above.
[205] [1989] 3 All ER 563.
[206] Glidewell LJ, [1988] 2 All ER 769, 777, said that the police had no 'power to require the bank not to communicate with their account holder, but there is no reason why the police should not express in strong terms their view that it is undesirable . . .'.
[207] [1989] 3 All ER 563, 570.

B. Criminal Cases

There is judicial authority that a health care professional has no duty to inform a patient of an application under PACE for access to special procedure or excluded material concerning the patient.[208] Putting the patient on notice of a police investigation where this could prejudice[209] the investigation might arguably constitute the offence of obstructing a police constable in the execution of his duty.[210] When a court entertains an application without notice for an order for the disclosure of documents and information in the possession of a solicitor it is current practice to direct the solicitor, if the application is granted, not to communicate the existence of the order to the client until after it has been complied with it.[211]

14.44

Additional police powers

Police applications for search warrants under PACE, s 8 are relatively uncommon. Other statutes confer powers of search, entry and seizure for investigations into specific offences and quite often these powers are wider (and therefore more attractive) than anything found in PACE.[212] The following pages give details of some of these extraordinary powers together with powers of compulsory questioning that might be directed against professionals to discover confidential personal information about their clients. Since the coming into force of the HRA any exercise of these powers that invades the client's Article 8 rights[213] must be necessary in a democratic society in the sense of meeting a pressing social need and proportionate to the legitimate aim being pursued.[214] Data protection will not be an issue because the DPA contains an exemption for data processing for the purposes of prevention or detection of crime, apprehension and prosecution of offenders and assessment and collection of taxes.[215]

14.45

Terrorism[216]

Search and seizure Police conducting a terrorist investigation are given particularly wide powers of search and seizure in the Terrorism Act 2000. Terrorism is widely defined to involve the use or threatened use of serious violence against person or property or involving a serious risk to public health or public safety or

14.46

---

[208] *R v Singleton* [1995] 1 Cr App R 431.
[209] Prejudice is clearly possible if the professional has in his possession documents belonging to the client which the client can demand back.
[210] Police Act 1964, s 51(3) or even contravene Criminal Law Act 1967, s 4. Whether the prosecution could succeed has yet to be established.
[211] *Republic of Haiti v Duvalier* [1989] 1 All ER 456, 460.
[212] For an analysis of all the relevant provisions see R Stone, *Entry, Search and Seizure* (3rd edn, London: 1997) 93 et seq. For an account of the drug trafficking and serious fraud provisions see D Feldman, 'Press Freedom and Police Access to Journalistic Material' [1995] 1 Yearbook of Media and Entertainment L 3, 70, 74–78.[213] ie respect for private life and correspondence.
[214] See para 3.19 above. This applies also to the exercise of the PACE Powers.
[215] DPA, s 29. See para 18.44 below.
[216] J Rowe, 'The Terrorism Act 2000' [2001] Crim LR 527; C Walker, *The Anti-Terrorism Legislation* (Oxford: 2002) ch 4.

to electronic systems in order to influence the government or intimidate the public, 'for the purpose of advancing a political, religious or ideological cause'.[217] A 'terrorist investigation' is also widely defined to include conduct that is not necessarily criminal.[218] Counsellors,[219] social workers, doctors or, indeed, any other category of professional may be affected by the Terrorism Act if they have clients suspected of being involved in terrorism or if they themselves are suspects.

14.47 There are a number of search powers.[220] Under the first power police may apply to a justice of the peace for a warrant to enter and search the professional's premises and any person found there and to seize and retain any 'relevant material' that is not 'excepted material', that is to say 'excluded' or 'special procedure' material[221] as defined in PACE or material subject to legal privilege, also as defined in PACE.[222] If the application is made by a senior police officer the justice need be satisfied of only two things: (1) the warrant is sought 'for the purposes of a terrorist investigation' and (2) there are reasonable grounds for believing that there is material on the professional's premises which is likely to be 'of substantial value, whether by itself or together with other material, to a terrorist investigation'.[223] Once on premises pursuant to the warrant, material likely to be of substantial value to 'a' terrorist investigation (not necessarily 'the' terrorist investigation for which the warrant was issued) may be seized to prevent its loss, alteration or destruction, including special procedure and excluded material.[224]

14.48 Under a second search power application may be made without notice to a circuit judge for a production or access order for 'excluded'[225] and 'special procedure' material[226] including material 'which is expected to come into existence' within 28 days and to be in the professional's possession, custody or power within that period.[227] The police do not have to satisfy the circuit judge that grounds exist for

---

[217] Terrorism Act 2000, s 1.
[218] ibid, s 32. For example, it includes an investigation of the resources of a proscribed organization and the possibility of an order proscribing an organization.
[219] P Jenkins, 'Terrorism and the Law' (2001) 12 Counselling & Psychotherapy J 8, 42 comments that the legislation may have particular relevance to counsellors working with political refugees who have at some time been members of organizations banned under the Terrorism Act 2000.
[220] A search power relating to cordoned areas is not described below but is to be found in Terrorism Act 2000, Sch 5 para 3.
[221] ibid, Sch 5, paras 1(5)(b), 4. See para 14.21 above.
[222] ibid, Sch 5, paras 1(4). See para 14.22 above.
[223] Terrorism Act 2000, Sch 5, para 2.
[224] ibid, Sch 5, para 1(2)–(3).
[225] In *DPP v Channel Four Television Co Ltd* [1993] 2 All ER 517, 524 a production order was secured under previous terrorism legislation to compel a journalist to disclose journalistic information held in confidence (ie excluded material). See also *R v Middlesex Guildhall Crown Court, ex p Salinger* [1993] 2 All ER 310 where guidance was provided on how much information was to be provided to the circuit judge and to the person holding the desired material.
[226] Terrorism Act 2000, Sch 5, para 5.
[227] ibid, Sch 5, para 7(1).

B. Criminal Cases

believing that a serious arrestable offence has been committed or that the material is potential evidence, only that there are reasonable grounds for believing that the material is likely to be of substantial value to a terrorist investigation and that production or access is in the public interest.[228] Items subject to legal privilege are exempt[229] but all statutory disclosure restrictions are abrogated[230] and an order may be made in respect of material in the custody, possession or control of a government department.[231] There is a third power to apply to a circuit judge for a warrant if an order is disobeyed or it is not for specified reasons likely to succeed.[232] Under a fourth power, the powers of the circuit judge or justice of the peace may be exercised in an emergency by a senior police officer.[233]

14.49 Once the police have obtained relevant material they may apply to a circuit judge for an order requiring 'any person' to explain any of it.[234] The only lawful ground for refusing to obey an explanation order is that the information would be subject to LPP in legal proceedings in the High Court.[235]

14.50 **Account monitoring** In the Anti-terrorism, Crime and Security Act 2001 the police acquired the power to apply without notice to a judge of the Crown Court in chambers[236] for an order allowing continuous monitoring of the transactions of a named account at a financial institution[237] for up to 90 days.[238] There is no legal privilege exception on the assumption that LPP is not relevant.[239] The monitoring power[240] supplements an existing power to obtain an order requiring a financial institution to provide 'customer information' for the purposes of a terrorist investigation.[241] A customer information order does not permit disclosure of transactions or balances on the account. Either type of order is conditional on a judge being satisfied that the order is for the purposes of a terrorist investigation, that

---

[228] ibid, Sch 5, para 6(2),(3).
[229] ibid, Sch 5, paras 6(1)(b), 8(1)(a), 11(3)(a).
[230] ibid, Sch 5, para 5(8)(1)(b).
[231] ibid, Sch 5, para 5(9).
[232] ibid, Sch 5, para 5(11).
[233] That is, an officer of at least the rank of superintendent: ibid, Sch 5, para 15.
[234] ibid, Sch 5, para 5(13).
[235] ibid, Sch 5, para 5(13)(2). However, a lawyer may be required to provide the name and address of his client: para 5(13)(3). It is a criminal offence to make a false or misleading statement: Sch 5, para 5(14).
[236] ibid, Sch 6A, para 3(1).
[237] ibid, Sch 6, para 6(1). The definition includes banks, building societies and investment businesses.
[238] ibid, Sch 6A, para 2(5).
[239] *Hansard* HL vol 629, col 345 (28 November 2001) (Lord Rooker).
[240] cp Proceeds of Crime Act 2002, s 370.
[241] Terrorism Act 2000, Sch 6. Customer information is defined in para 7 as confirmation of a relationship between the financial institution and a customer, the customer's full name, account number, date of birth, date of opening and, or, ending the relationship with the financial institution, evidence received of the customer's identity, the identity of a person sharing an account with the customer. cp Proceeds of Crime Act 2002, s 363.

tracing terrorist property is desirable and that the order will enhance the effectiveness of the investigation.[242] The Act does not say that the customer must be a suspected terrorist. The police can, apparently, apply for an order to monitor the account of a professional suspected of having dealings with a terrorist. An account monitoring or customer information order overrides any legal restriction on the disclosure of information no matter how imposed.[243] Disobedience to a customer information order is a criminal offence.[244] Breach of an account monitoring order is a contempt of court.[245]

Drugs

14.51 Under the Misuse of Drugs Act 1971 a constable may obtain a warrant from a justice of the peace to search premises for controlled drugs and documents reasonably suspected to relate to drug dealing.[246] PACE, s 19(6) rules out seizure of items that the constable has reasonable grounds for believing to be subject to legal privilege.[247] A constable investigating a drug trafficking offence may apply to a circuit judge for a production order for particular material or material of a particular description[248] if there are reasonable grounds for suspecting:

(1) that a specified person has carried on or has benefited from drug trafficking;
(2) that the material to which the application relates (which does not have to be in the possession of the suspect) is likely to be of substantial assistance to the investigation; and
(3) that the order is in the public interest.[249]

The constable may obtain access to 'special procedure' but not legally privileged or 'excluded' material. A production order may be made against a professional who is not suspected of a drug trafficking offence and in relation to material in the possession of a government department.[250] Any 'restriction on the disclosure of information imposed by statute or otherwise' is abrogated.[251] If a production order fails, or would be inappropriate in the circumstances, there is provision for a constable to apply to a circuit judge for a search warrant.[252]

---

[242] Terrorism Act 2000, Sch 6, para 5, Sch 6A, para 2(2).
[243] ibid, Sch 6, para 1(2)(b), Sch 6A, para 6(2).
[244] ibid, Sch 6, para 1(3).
[245] This is the effect of ibid, Sch 6A, para 6(1).
[246] s 23(3).
[247] But items may be removed in order to establish whether they are legally privileged: Criminal Justice and Police Act 2001, s 50, Sch 1, Pt 1. See para 14.38 above.
[248] Drug Trafficking Act 1994, s 55(1), (2).
[249] ibid, s 55(4).
[250] ibid, s 55(10)(c).
[251] ibid, s 55(10)(b).
[252] ibid, s 56.

B. Criminal Cases

Serious fraud

The Director of the Serious Fraud Office has responsibility for investigating serious or complex fraud. He may apply to a justice of the peace for a warrant authorizing a constable to enter and search premises and to take possession of documents.[253] Documents covered by LPP may not be seized[254] but there is no protection for 'special procedure' or 'excluded material' or anything else confidential other than information held in the course of a banking business.[255]

14.52

Proceeds of crime

The Criminal Justice Act 1988 enables a court to order the confiscation of the proceeds of indictable offences and certain summary offences and gives the police powers to trace those proceeds.[256] A constable armed with an order or warrant obtained from a circuit judge pursuant to s 93H of the 1988 Act has powers of entry, search and seizure of premises not unlike those conferred on the police under PACE, Sch 1. A warrant may be obtained without notice where there exist 'reasonable grounds for suspecting that someone has benefited from criminal conduct'. There is no requirement that the conduct constitute a serious arrestable offence. Items subject to legal privilege and excluded material, as defined in PACE, are exempt.[257] 'Special procedure material' may be included in an order or warrant, as may material that is subject to 'any obligation as to secrecy or other restriction upon the disclosure of information imposed by statute or otherwise'.[258] A judge may issue a warrant only where the predominant reason for the police application is to recover the proceeds of criminal conduct. Police investigating a substantive offence may not use it to by-pass the stricter procedure laid down in PACE, s 9[259] for access to special procedure material.[260]

14.53

Espionage and disclosure of confidential government information

A justice of the peace, if satisfied by information on oath that there are reasonable grounds for suspecting that an offence is about to be, or has been, committed under one of the Official Secrets Acts,[261] may issue a constable with a warrant authorizing entry and search at any time of any premises named in the warrant.[262] Anyone on the

14.54

---

[253] Criminal Justice Act 1987, s 2(4)–(5).
[254] s 2(9). Items may be removed to establish whether they are subject to legal privilege: Criminal Justice and Police Act 2001, s 50, Sch 1, Pt 1. And see para 14.38 above.
[255] s 2(1). The Director, or a designated member of the Serious Fraud Office, may authorize disclosure of confidential banking information.
[256] For details see R Stone, *Entry, Search & Seizure* (3rd edn, London: 1997) 91. See now also new powers granted in respect of confiscation investigations by the Proceeds of Crime Act 2002: para 14.18 above.
[257] ss 93H(10), 93I(5).
[258] s 93H(10)(b).
[259] See para 14.25 above.
[260] *R v Southwark Crown Court, ex p Bowles* [1998] 2 All ER 193, a case involving an accountant.
[261] 1911 (spying and espionage) and 1989 (disclosure of secret government information).
[262] Official Secrets Act 1911, s 9.

premises may be searched and anything which the constable has reasonable grounds to suspect is evidence of an offence may be seized. The constable may not seize any item which he has reasonable grounds to believe is subject to legal privilege.[263]

14.55 The Secretary of State, or in an emergency, a chief officer of police, may authorize compulsory examination by the police of any person who is believed on reasonable grounds to be able to furnish information relevant to an espionage investigation.[264] It is an offence to refuse to attend the interview or to refuse to give information or to knowingly give false information. There is no reason why these powers cannot be used to extract information from a suspected spy's accountant, banker, psychiatrist or GP so long as any interference with the Article 8 right to respect for private life is necessary in a democratic society and proportionate to the aim pursued.[265] There is no express exception for communications that in litigation would be protected by LPP.[266]

Financial services

14.56 If an information requirement would be futile, a justice of the peace may issue a warrant to enable premises to be entered (with such force as may be reasonably necessary) and searched for documents or information relevant to an offence mentioned in s 168 of the Financial Services and Markets Act 2000[267] that has been or is being committed by anyone and for which the maximum sentence is at least two years imprisonment.[268] Documents and information appearing to be of the kind mentioned in the warrant may be seized or copied, except those that the constable has reasonable grounds for believing are protected by LPP,[269] and any person found on the premises may be required to explain them.

Bankers' Books Evidence Act 1879[270]

14.57 When proceedings have been instigated, the police can rely upon s 7 of the Bankers' Evidence Act 1879[271] for compulsory access to bankers' books.[272] In fact the police must use this route rather than PACE, s 9(1) if they are unable able to

---

[263] PACE, s 19(6). But items may be removed to establish whether they are legally privileged: Criminal Justice and Police Act 2001, s 50, Sch 1, Pt 1. And see para 14.38 above.
[264] Official Secrets Act 1920, s 6.
[265] See para 3.19 above. As far as data protection is concerned, disclosures would fall within the national security exemption in DPA, s 28 as to which see para 18.44 below.
[266] On the question whether LPP applies see paras 10.13 and 16.12 et seq.
[267] These include insider dealing, market abuse, misleading statements and practices, money laundering.
[268] Financial Services and Markets Act 2000, s 176.
[269] PACE, s 19(6). It is submitted that legally privileged documents are protected against copying and not just against seizure because they are not the kind of document for which a warrant could have been issued.
[270] D Warne and N Elliott (eds), *Banking Litigation* (London: 1999) 292–294.
[271] See also para 14.10 above.
[272] eg *Williams v Summerfield* [1972] 2 All ER 1334 where Lord Widgery CJ said that the proceedings must not be started solely for the purpose of gaining access to a bank account. See also *R v Marlborough Street Magistrates Court, ex p Simpson* (1980) 70 Cr App R 291.

B. Criminal Cases

satisfy the second set of access conditions laid down for 'special procedure material' in PACE, Sch 1.[273] The justice of the peace or judge to whom application is made for a s 7 order must:

(1) consider 'whether there is other evidence . . . to support the charge; or whether the application under s 7 is a fishing expedition';[274] and
(2) take into account the public interest in respecting the confidentiality of banking records:

> It is important that the Court should respect the confidence of a bank account. Before the confidence is impugned, the judge ought to see how the balance comes down. He should consider whether the public interest in helping the prosecution outweighs the private interest in keeping a customer's bank account confidential. It is only when the public interest prevails that he should order inspection.[275]

The period of disclosure should be limited to the period strictly relevant to the charge.[276]

Section 7 orders are almost always made against a party to the proceedings which means that an innocent professional is unlikely to be the subject of an order. It is desirable that the accountholder be given notice of a s 7 application although this is not a statutory requirement.[277]

Serious Fraud Office investigations[278]

14.58 Criminal Justice Act 1987, s 1 established a Serious Fraud Office (SFO) headed by a Director, a lawyer, under the supervision of the Attorney-General. Section 1(3) gives the Director wide powers to investigate cases of 'serious or complex' fraud. By s 2 the Director may, by notice in writing, require any person whom he has reason to believe has relevant information about the affairs of a person to be investigated, to answer questions or furnish information or produce relevant documents for inspection and copying or state where documents are to be found. The Serious Fraud Office regularly uses its powers to demand information and documents from lawyers, accountants and bankers. Failure to comply, without reasonable excuse, is a criminal offence punishable by a fine, imprisonment or both.[279] So too is purported compliance that involves making a false or misleading statement when this is done knowingly or recklessly.[280]

---

[273] See para 14.28 above. This is because the first set of access conditions (see para 14.26 above) found in Schedule 1 has as a requirement that 'other methods of obtaining the material (i) have been tried without success; or (ii) have not been tried because it appeared that they were bound to fail'. cp *R v Lewes Crown Court, ex p Hill* (1990) 93 Cr App R 60.
[274] per Lord Widgery CJ, *Williams v Summerfield* [1972] 2 All ER 1334, 1338.
[275] per Lord Denning, *R v Grossman* (1981) 73 Cr App R 302, 307.
[276] *Williams v Summerfield* [1972] 2 All ER 1334, 1338.
[277] *R v Marlborough Street Magistrates' Court, ex p Simpson* (1980) 70 Cr App R 291.
[278] D Kirk and A Woodcock, *Serious fraud: investigation and trial* (London: 1997); P Johnstone and R Jones, *Investigations and Enforcement* (London: 2001) paras 4.19–4.20.
[279] Criminal Justice Act 1987, s 2(13), (15).
[280] ibid, s 2(14).

14.59 The 1987 Act contains two express restrictions on the Serious Fraud Office's powers to extract information from professionals: LPP and banking confidentiality. Section 2(9) provides that 'a person shall not . . . be required to disclose any information or produce any document which he would be entitled to refuse to disclose or produce on the grounds of legal professional privilege in proceedings in the High Court'. Section 2(10) states that 'a person shall not . . . be required to disclose information or produce a document in respect of which he owes an obligation of confidence by virtue of carrying on any banking business unless (a) the person to whom the obligation of confidence is owed consents . . .', or (b) the Director or his delegate has personally authorized the demand.[281] The express partial exception for confidential banking documents implies that other confidential documents are not exempt.[281a] Since the coming into force of the HRA, any disclosure that impinges on the client's Article 8 privacy rights will have to be necessary in a democratic society in the sense of meeting a pressing social need and proportionate to the legitimate aim being pursued.[282]

14.60 Should a professional fail to hand over requested documents, or if surprise is essential, a warrant to search the professional's premises may be obtained by the Serious Fraud Office[283] from a justice of the peace.[284] There are no safeguards, such as are to be found in PACE,[285] for personal records (other than banking records) but legally privileged items are exempt.[286]

Other search and seizure powers[287]

14.61 A number of statutes allow public officials conducting an investigation to use a search warrant or a judicial production order to obtain information.[288] The investigations tend to be of more serious nature and are often the first step on the path to a prosecution.

---

[281] See para 10.04 above.
[281a] The House of Lords has given a wide interpretation to the Director's powers when self-incrimination has been claimed as a reason for non-disclosure: *Smith v Director of Serious Fraud Office* [1992] 3 All ER 456.
[282] See para 3.19 above.
[283] Execution of the warrant is left to the police: D Kirk and A Woodock, *Serious fraud: investigation and trial* (London: 1997) 50.
[284] s 2(4)–(5).
[285] See para 14.21 above.
[286] They can be seized in order to establish, elsewhere, whether they are legally privileged: Criminal Justice and Police Act 2001, s 50, Sch 1, Pt 1. See above 14.38 above.
[287] R. Stone, *Entry, Search and Seizure* (3rd edn, London: 1997) chs 6, 8, 9.
[288] It is more usual for a search warrant to be used as a back up to some less drastic power of mandatory disclosure: see para 10.22 above.

B. Criminal Cases

Tax investigations [289]

Production procedure   The Finance Act 2000[290] set up a procedure to enable specialist investigators in the Special Compliance Office of the Inland Revenue to obtain documents by means of a production order from an innocent third party such as a solicitor, bank or accountant.[291] The procedure is similar to that used by the police to obtain a production order for special material from a circuit judge,[292] however, there is no express protection for personal records (including medical records).[293] The applicant must satisfy the judge by information on oath that the documents may be required as evidence of a tax fraud that is reasonably suspected of having been, is being, or is about to be, committed and that they are in the power or possession of the third party.[294] If production will impinge on anyone's right to respect for private life or correspondence, the judge will have to be satisfied that the application is necessary in a democratic society and proportionate to a legitimate aim.[295]

14.62

In most cases, advance notice of the application must be given to the third party. The latter has a right of audience at the hearing of the application[296] but may not notify the suspect of the application.[297] This does not prevent a professional legal adviser from disclosing information in the course of giving legal advice in connection with legal proceedings.[298]

14.63

An order for production of documents must be complied with within 10 working days or such period as is specified in the order[299] and documents may not be destroyed.[300] Non-compliance is a contempt of court.[301] Items that are subject to legal privilege are immune whether they are in the possession of a lawyer or

14.64

---

[289] B Brown, 'Powers to combat serious fraud: the Inland Revenue Consultative Paper' [2000] BTR 61; J Walters, 'Information: Compliance v Confidentiality' (2001) 3 Corporate Tax Rev 161, 168–169; P Johnstone and R Jones, *Investigations and Enforcement* (London: 2001) paras 4.32–4.36.
[290] Finance Act 2000, ss. 149, 150 amending Taxes Management Act 1970, s 20C and inserting a new s 20BA and Sch 1AA. The amendments in the Finance Act 2000 were preceded by a consultation document, 'Powers to Combat Serious Tax Fraud', available from http://www.inlandrevenue.gov.uk.
[291] Production notices issued pursuant to Taxes Management Act 1970, s 20(3) (see para 3.35 above) are designed for civil investigations. They do not guarantee access to original documents, the procedure may take up to 60 days and interference by the subject of the investigation may occur.
[292] PACE, s 9(1). See para 14.25 above.
[293] There is also no exemption for documents relating to a pending tax appeal, audit papers and relevant communications with a tax adviser who is not a lawyer.
[294] Taxes Management Act 1970, s 20BA(1).
[295] See para 3.19 above.
[296] Taxes Management Act 1970, Sch 1AA, para 3.
[297] ibid, Sch 1AA, para 4(1)(b).
[298] ibid, Sch 1AA, para 4(3).
[299] ibid, s 20BA(2).
[300] ibid, Sch 1AA, para 4.
[301] ibid, Sch 1AA, para 9(1).

someone else.[302] Disputes about whether documents are subject to legal privilege are resolved by a judge.[303]

14.65 **Search and seizure powers** If use of the production procedure may seriously prejudice the investigation,[304] the Revenue can fall back on the powers conferred by s 20C of the Taxes Management Act 1970 to enter a professional's premises (by force if necessary)[305] and search for, and seize, evidence of serious fraud by a client.[306] The power of search includes a power to search the person of those found on the premises.[307] In *Inland Revenue Commissioners v Rossminster Ltd* where children's school reports were seized during the raid Lord Scarman described the Revenue's powers as 'a breath-taking inroad on the individual's right of privacy and right of property'.[308] Since the HRA has come into force, an interference with privacy which is not for a legitimate aim[309] and which is in any way disproportionate or lacking in procedural safeguards[310] is unlawful.[311]

14.66 Entry onto premises is pursuant to a warrant from a circuit judge who must have been satisfied that there were reasonable grounds for suspecting that an offence involving serious tax fraud[312] was being, or had been, or was about to be, committed and that evidence of it was to be found on specified premises.[313] While the warrant must state the premises to be entered and searched,[314] the nature and dates of the offences under investigation do not have to be specified.[315] Once on the

---

[302] Taxes Management Act 1970, Sch 1AA, para 5.
[303] Orders for the Delivery of Documents (Procedure) Regulations 2000 r7, SI 2000/2875, reg 7.
[304] Taxes Management Act 1970, s 20C(1AA).
[305] ibid, s 20C(1)(b).
[306] The high point of the use of s 20C search powers against professionals was *R v Inland Revenue Commissioners, ex p Kingston Smith* [1996] STC 1210 where the Inland Revenue obtained a warrant without notice to search the premises of a firm of chartered accountants who were not suspected of involvement in the suspected fraud and sought to remove the hard disk from the firm's computer. The alarmed accountants obtained an injunction by telephone which the Revenue officials ignored. The background to this tale is retold in [1997] British Tax Review 478–479.
[307] Taxes Management Act 1970, s 20C(3)(c). This power was exercised during the raid in *R v Inland Revenue Commissioners, ex p Kingston Smith* [1996] STC 1210.
[308] *Inland Revenue Commissioners v Rossminster Ltd* [1980] 1 All ER 80, 101.
[309] See para 3.19 above.
[310] Surprisingly, no Art 8 issue was raised in *H v Commissioners of Inland Revenue* [2002] EWHC 214, possibly because there was no claim to legal professional privilege.
[311] HRA, s 6. *Tamosius v UK* [2002] STC 1307.
[312] eg false accounting, forgery, conspiracy to defraud, perjury, false income tax statements.
[313] Taxes Management Act 1970, s 20C.
[314] *Inland Revenue Commissioners v Rossminster Ltd* [1980] 1 All ER 80, 102. If the documents are discovered to be archived on different premises a fresh search warrant must be obtained.
[315] *R v Inland Revenue Commissioners, ex p Tamosius* [2000] 1 WLR 453, 459. When the warrant is to search the premises of an innocent third party such as a bank the practice is to name the target of the investigation in a schedule to the warrant to avoid seizure and removal of confidential documents concerning innocent clients, a matter about which Lord Wilberforce expressed concern in *Inland Revenue Commissioners v Rossminster* [1980] 1 All ER 80, 83: J Walters, 'Revenue Raids' [1998] British Tax Review 213, 217.

B. Criminal Cases

premises, the Revenue may seize and remove anything they have 'reasonable cause to believe may be required as evidence'.[316] The power of seizure includes a power to require that information on a computer be produced in a visible and legible form.[317] In executing search warrants the Revenue have undertaken to observe the relevant parts of Code B of PACE except in so far as s 20C contains more stringent safeguards.[318]

14.67 The Inland Revenue are not entitled to seize and remove items subject to legal privilege[319] but under a power conferred by Criminal Justice and Police Act 2001, s 50 may remove items believed on reasonable grounds to be privileged to determine elsewhere whether or not this is the case if it is not reasonably practicable to do so in situ.[320] The Inland Revenue may seize personal records, documents relating to a pending tax appeal and audit papers. Draconian though the powers of the Revenue may be, the case law from Strasbourg does not hold out real hope that a raid on the premises of an innocent professional pursuant to s 20C will be held to contravene Article 8 of the ECHR.[321]

14.68 **Customs and Excise**[322] A justice of the peace on application by a Customs and Excise officer, if satisfied that there is reasonable ground for suspecting that evidence of a serious fraud offence in connection with value added tax is to be found on premises, may issue a warrant to enter (if necessary by force) and search those premises and any person found there if it is reasonable to believe that he has evidence.[323] The power may be used for the purpose of obtaining access to personal records. Once in possession of a warrant and on the premises the officer may seize and remove any documents or items 'which he has reasonable cause to believe may be required as evidence' except those that he had reasonable grounds for believing to be subject to LPP.[324] He may also 'search or cause to be searched any person

---

[316] Taxes Management Act 1970, s 20C(3).
[317] ibid, s 20C(3A).
[318] Inland Revenue, *Powers to Combat Serious Fraud* (29 November 1999), para 14, available from http://www.inlandrevenue.gov.uk.
[319] s 20C(4). Legal privilege is defined in s 20C(4A)–(4B) in the same terms as in PACE s 10 as to which see para 14.22 above. See also *Tamosius v UK* [2002] STC 1307.
[320] For details see para 14.38 above.
[321] P Baker, 'Taxation and the European Convention on Human Rights' [2000] BTR 211 who concludes at 256, '[o]verall, challenges under article 8 to information-seeking powers of revenue authorities have been unsuccessful, except where those powers were subject to inadequate supervision'. See particularly, *R v Austria* Application 12592/86, which involved a bank. Most recently in *Tamosius v UK* [2002] STC 1307 the ECtHR held that a raid on a solicitor's premises for evidence of a serious fraud carried out pursuant to a warrant issued by a circuit judge and under the supervision of independent counsel whose responsibility it was to prevent the removal of legally privileged material was a justifiable interference with the solicitor's Art 8 rights.
[322] P Johnstone and R Jones, *Investigations and Enforcement* (London: 2001) paras 4.59, 4.62.
[323] Value Added Tax Act 1994, Sch 11, para 10(3). For a case under previous legislation involving a solicitor see *R v Epsom Justices, ex p Bell* [1989] STC 169.
[324] PACE, s 19(6) as to which see *R v Customs and Excise Commissioners, ex p Popely* [1999] STC 1016, a case involving a solicitor. The fact that independent counsel was present during execution

found on the premises whom he has reasonable cause to believe to be in possession of any such documents or other things'.[325] No woman or girl may be searched except by a woman.[326] A warrant is not normally sought to enter the premises of an innocent third party such as a bank. Instead Customs and Excise will apply for a production order that mirrors that available to the Inland Revenue when investigating serious tax fraud.[327] Application should be made with notice whenever it is practicable to proceed that way.[328]

Other investigations

14.69 **Investigative powers of the Information Commissioner**   There are many other statutes that allow officials to apply to a judicial authority (in some cases a justice of the peace, in others a circuit court judge) for a search warrant.[329] One that may be of concern to professionals is the DPA. The Information Commissioner may apply to a judge for a warrant to enter and search premises and seize evidence of a suspected breach of the data protection legislation.[330] The powers of inspection and seizure do not apply to personal data processed for special purposes[331] or data which is exempted from the provisions of the Act on the grounds of national security.[332] There is an exemption for legally privileged communications, but only if the communication concerns the professional's compliance with the DPA and is in the possession of the legal adviser or the professional or his representative.[333] It is an offence intentionally to obstruct a person in the execution of the warrant or to fail, without reasonable excuse, to give the person executing the warrant such assistance as he may reasonably require.[334]

---

of the warrant and advised the officer that the material seized was not privileged would be cogent evidence that the officer had no reasonable cause to believe that what was seized was legally privileged.

[325] Value Added Tax Act 1994, Sch 11, para 10(3)(b), (c).
[326] ibid, s 10(3)(c).
[327] ibid, Sch 11, para 11. For two cases involving banks see *R v City of London Magistrates' Court, ex p Asif* [1996] STC 611; *R v City of London Magistrates' Court, ex p Peters* [1997] STC 141. Information held on a computer must be produced in a form which is visible, legible and can be removed: Sch 11, para 11(4).
[328] *R v City of London Magistrates' Court, ex p Asif* [1996] STC 611.
[329] eg Immigration Act 1971, ss 28D, 28E, 28F; Insolvency Act 1986, s 365(3); Solicitors Act 1974, s 22A; Companies Act 1985, s 448; Human Fertilisation and Embryology Act 1990, s 40; Competition Act 1998, s 28; Money Laundering Regulations 2001, SI 2001/3641, reg 11 (production order), reg 14 (search warrant).
[330] DPA, Sch 9.
[331] Unless the Commissioner has made a determination under s 45: Sch 9, para 1(2).
[332] Sch 9, para 8.
[333] Sch 9, para 9. Is this restriction, a prima facie breach of Art 8, justifiable? Anything held with the intention of furthering a criminal purpose is not protected. Items may be taken away to establish whether they are protected by legal privilege: Criminal Justice and Police Act 2001, s 50.
[334] DPA, Sch 9, para 12.

B. Criminal Cases

Covert Surveillance[335]

Introduction

Importance of covert surveillance

14.70 Agents of the state, especially the police, customs officials and the security services regularly undertake covert operations.[336] It is said that covert operations are the single most valuable law enforcement weapon against organized crime and drug trafficking.[337] A covert investigation may involve interception of communications to a person or an address and/or visual, aural (traditionally known as bugging) or audio-visual surveillance of a person or premises. Professionals may be the target of official surveillance either because they are suspected of being involved in crime or terrorism or because their clients are.[338] Except in those cases in which officials have enlisted the assistance of the professional, the professional will not be aware of the covert operation (not, at least, if it is handled competently) and will therefore be unable to prevent the disclosure of confidential personal information. Lawyers are particularly at risk of covert surveillance because legal services are 'indispensable to make organized crime organizations effective and profitable'.[339] Often there will be a risk of collateral intrusion, that is, interception of entirely innocent communications between the professional and clients who are not the target of the investigation.

Covert surveillance and the Human Rights Act 1998

14.71 Covert surveillance that intrudes upon a professional's relationship with a client is a prima facie interference with the right to respect for correspondence and private life of the client[340] and of the professional.[341] The interference will be justifiable[342] if necessary for a legitimate aim judged according to the standards of a democratic

---

[335] This is surveillance of which the target is intended to be unaware.
[336] Statistics are scarce. The Home Office estimates that 2,550 chief officer authorizations by the police and customs occurred throughout the UK in 1996, news release, 23 November 1998. The Financial Times on 7 May 2002 reported that the Office of Fair Trading is seeking surveillance powers to assist its investigations into anti-competitive behaviour.
[337] Home Office Press Release 454/98, 'UK: Safeguards for Intrusive Surveillance—Draft', available at http://www.nds.coi.gov.uk.
[338] For a striking example see *R v Lowe* (Vic 1996 LEXIS 1330) where the police tapped the telephone of the accused's therapist and installed a listening device in her room to monitor his conversations with her. For the first six months the therapist was unaware of the surveillance, thereafter she co-operated with the police.
[339] 'The Impact: Organized Crime Today' in *Report of the President's Commission on Organized Crime* (1986) 221 cited in M Goldsmith and K Balmforth, 'The Electronic Surveillance of Privileged Communications: A Conflict of Doctrines' (1991) 64 Southern California L Rev 903, 911.
[340] *R v Mason* [2002] EWCA Crim 385, para 65. cp *Malone v UK* (1984) 7 EHRR 14 ; *Hewitt and Harman v UK* (1991) 67 DR 88.
[341] cp *Niemietz v Germany* (1992) 16 EHRR 97; Schmit v Luxembourg Application 51772/99, 25 February 2003. That the client is the target is immaterial: *Kruslin v France* (1990) 12 EHRR 547.
[342] See para 3.19 above.

state, proportionate to a pressing social need and carried out in accordance with accessible and precise laws that contain adequate guarantees against abuse of power, including independent supervisory control[343] and adequate remedies for those whose privacy is wrongly invaded.[344] English domestic law now contains a raft of legislative measures designed to make covert surveillance by agents of the state Convention-compliant. The particular piece of legislation that applies depends on the agency carrying out the surveillance, the method of surveillance and the location of the surveillance.

Police Act 1997

Covert entry and interference with property

14.72 This Act legitimizes entry onto, and interference with, property or wireless telegraphy by the police and other law enforcement officers and by customs and excise officials that but for this Act would be contrary to law.[345] Section 92 provides:

> No entry on or interference with property or with wireless telegraphy shall be unlawful if it is authorised by an authorisation having effect under this Part.

In plain language, the police can be given permission to commit trespass and burglary. It is a condition of authorization that the purpose of the covert interference is to prevent or detect serious crime[346] and that other action would fail.[347] The property interfered with need not be the property of the person under surveillance.

14.73 Except in urgent cases,[348] and where the owner of the premises consents, the police are forbidden from entering office premises or a property used mainly as a dwelling or as a bedroom in a hotel without first obtaining the approval of both an authorizing officer (a chief constable or someone of equivalent seniority)[349] *and* a Surveillance Commissioner[350] (a serving or retired judge).[351] The premises maintained by a professional for consulting purposes should fall into one or other of

---

[343] *Klass v Germany* (1979) 2 EHRR 214, paras 56–57.
[344] Amongst the relevant cases are *Huvig v France* (1990) 12 EHRR 528; *Kopp v Switzerland* (1998) 27 EHRR 91.
[345] It has no application where the police use long-distance sensitive microphones, laser beam technology and other devices that do not have to be placed on the premises under surveillance.
[346] s 93(2)(a). Serious crime is defined in s 93(4) as a crime that '(a) ... involves the use of violence, results in substantial financial gain or is conduct by a large number of persons in pursuit of a common purpose, or (b) ... is an offence for which a person who has attained the age of eighteen and has no previous convictions could reasonably be expected to be sentenced to imprisonment for a term of three years or more'.
[347] Police Act 1997, s 93(2)(b).
[348] ibid, s 97(3).
[349] ibid, s 93(5).
[350] ibid, s 97(2)(a).
[351] There are six surveillance commissioners and a Chief Surveillance Commissioner. For their terms of appointment see s 91. The Office of Surveillance Commissioners has a website at http://www.surveillancecommissioners.org/.

B. Criminal Cases

these categories. Dual prior authorization is in any case required if the surveillance is likely to result in acquisition of knowledge of:[352]

- matters subject to legal privilege;[353] or
- confidential journalistic material; or
- confidential personal information[354] (defined in terms similar to 'personal records' in PACE).[355]

Provided that the police obtain the necessary permissions, they can lawfully use surveillance to detect the content of legally privileged material for which they could not have obtained a search warrant under PACE. Nothing confidential generated by, or within, a professional–client relationship is out of bounds. However, the police have given an undertaking not to breach the seal of confession between priest and penitent.[356] A written authorization by a recognized authorizing officer normally lasts for three months and can be renewed. 14.74

When dual approval is required, the 1997 Act [357] directs the Commissioner not to give it unless satisfied[358] that there are reasonable grounds for believing that 14.75

(1) 'it is necessary for the action specified to be taken for the purpose of preventing or detecting serious crime, and
(2) that the taking of the action is proportionate to what the action seeks to achieve[359] taking into account
(3) 'whether what it is thought necessary to achieve . . . could reasonably be achieved by other means'.[360]

The authorizing police officer, on whose say-so alone the interference can take place in an emergency,[361] must share these beliefs but is not required to have reasonable grounds for them.[362]

Admissibility in evidence of the fruits of the surveillance

The Police Act 1997 contains no restrictions on use in subsequent criminal proceedings of information obtained as a result of an authorization given under the 14.76

---

[352] ibid, s 97(2)(b).
[353] Defined in ibid, s 98. The definition excludes lawyer–client communications in furtherance of crime.
[354] Defined in ibid, s 99.
[355] See para 14.22 above.
[356] D Feldman, *Civil Liberties and Human Rights in England and Wales* (2nd edn, Oxford: 2002) 593.
[357] See also *Code of Practice on Covert Surveillance*, para 6.30.
[358] Making an independent assessment about whether the conditions for authorizing entry and interference have been met may be difficult because the application for authorization is made without notice and there is no provision for hearing evidence on oath.
[359] Police Act 1997, s 97(5) applying the criteria set out in s 93(2).
[360] ibid, s 93(2B).
[361] ibid, s 97(3).
[362] ibid, s 93(2).

Act. Information that in the absence of the authorized surveillance would have been inadmissible because it was legally privileged is admissible. This is a consequence of the common law rule that secondary evidence of a privileged communication is admissible no matter how obtained.[363]

14.77 The same rule renders evidence obtained by means of an unauthorized or improperly authorized surveillance admissible but the trial judge has a discretion to exclude it under s 78 if the fairness of the trial is thereby endangered.[364] Experience suggests that courts are reluctant to exclude probative evidence unless gross police misconduct is demonstrated.[365] A court that admits improperly or unlawfully obtained evidence, including evidence that interferes with the accused's right to respect for private life, does not per se act in a manner incompatible with the ECHR[366] and therefore contravene HRA, s 6. It is Article 6 and not Article 8 that counts. The Convention is violated if the overall effect of admitting evidence obtained in breach of Article 8 encroaches on the right to a fair trial.[367] The defence must be given the opportunity to challenge the use and admission in evidence of the unlawfully obtained evidence and 'a judicial assessment of the effect of its admission upon the fairness of the trial as is provided for by s 78'.[368] A cogent factor in favour of admitting evidence of an intercepted conversation is that one of the parties to it is going to be a witness and give evidence of what was said.[369]

Intelligence Services Act 1994 and Security Service Act 1989

The secret intelligence services

14.78 The Security Service (commonly known as 'MI5') is the United Kingdom's domestic security intelligence service. Its mission is to protect the United Kingdom against foreign espionage, subversion and terrorism and injury to the country's economic well-being. It has been claimed that the definition of its functions in the Security Service Act 1989[370] is so wide that it would justify surveillance of almost anyone.[371] Since 1996 the service has had added to its duties assisting the police, the National Criminal Intelligence Service, the National Crime Squad and other law enforcement agencies in the prevention and detection

---

[363] *Calcraft v Guest* [1898] 1 QB 759. See also para 6.98 above. Exclusion under PACE, s 78 is a possibility.
[364] *R v Cadette* [1995] Crim LR 229.
[365] cp *R v Khan* [1996] 3 All ER 289 where civil trespass and criminal damage to property were ignored.
[366] *R v Harrison* (CA, 10 July 2000); *R v P* [2001] 2 All ER 58, 68; *R v Wright* [2001] EWCA Crim 1394.
[367] See para 3.14 above
[368] per Lord Hobhouse, *R v P* [2001] 2 All ER 58, 69. See D Ormwood, 'ECHR and the Exclusion of Evidence: Trial Remedies for Article 8 breaches', [2003] Crim LR 61.
[369] ibid at 68.
[370] Security Service Act 1989, s 1(2), (3), (4).
[371] E Shorts and C De Than, *Civil Liberties* (London: 1998) 237.

B. Criminal Cases

of 'serious crime'.[372] This change was meant to enable 'MI5' to become a party to the fight against organized crime but the Act does not say so.[373] The Secret Intelligence Service (commonly known as 'MI6'), its sister organization, is in the business of foreign espionage.[374] Under the terms of the Intelligence Services Act 1994, 'MI6' is required to act in the interests of national security, the economic well-being of the United Kingdom and in support of the prevention or detection of serious crime.[375] Most of its operations take place abroad.

Covert entry and interference with property

14.79 The Security Service Act 1989 contained provisions for the issue of warrants by the Secretary of State authorizing interference with property or wireless telegraphy that have since been incorporated into the Intelligence Services Act 1994.[376] With such a warrant, bugging that involves trespass to property, copying of documents without the permission of the owner and theft are rendered lawful and information obtained by such means admissible in criminal proceedings.[377] Warrants are effective for six months and are renewable.[378]

14.80 It is a condition for granting a warrant that the Secretary of State thinks it is necessary for the purpose of assisting the Security Service to perform one of its functions, that he is satisfied that satisfactory arrangements have been made in respect of disclosure of any material obtained,[379] that he is satisfied that the taking of the action is proportionate and that what it is sought to be achieved cannot reasonably be achieved by other means.[380] These conditions are repeated in the Code of Practice on Covert Surveillance.[381]

14.81 Unlike the Police Act 1997, no special safeguards are provided for 'office premises'[382] or for 'special procedure material', 'excluded material' and items subject to legal privilege[383] even though 'MI5' may be helping the police who must observe such safeguards. The temptation for the authorities to circumvent the PACE search and seizure restrictions by relying on 'MI5' to obtain a warrant from the Secretary of State is reduced by a stipulation that a warrant to search property

---

[372] Security Service Act 1989, s 1(4). Inserted by Security Service Act 1996, s 1(1). Defined as in RIPA, s 81.
[373] H Fenwick, *Civil Liberties* (2nd edn, London: 1998) 355.
[374] Its functions are defined in Intelligence Services Act 1994.
[375] ibid, ss 1(2), 3(2).
[376] ibid, s 5. MI6 may not be issued with a warrant for the purpose of investigating serious crime in relation to property in the British Islands: s 5(3).
[377] ibid, ss 2(2)(a), 5(4). See also, *R v Khan* [1996] 3 All ER 289, 296.
[378] ibid, s 6(2)–(3).
[379] Official Secrets Act 1989, s 4(3)(b) prohibits disclosure of information obtained pursuant to the Secretary of State's warrant.
[380] Intelligence Services Act 1994, s 5(2), (2A).
[381] *Draft Code of Practice on Covert Surveillance*, para 6.32.
[382] See Police Act 1997, s 97(2)(a).
[383] Contrast ibid, ss 98–100.

in the British Isles for the purpose of investigating serious crime must relate to conduct that could attract a sentence of imprisonment of at least three years for a first-time adult offender or involve the use of violence, result in substantial financial gain or involve conduct by a large number of persons in pursuit of a common purpose.[384]

14.82 The breadth of the Home Secretary's warrant-issuing discretion coupled with the absence of independent judicial scrutiny before the warrant is issued may contravene Article 8.[385]

Regulation of Investigatory Powers Act 2000[386]

Regulated forms of surveillance

14.83 The Regulation of Investigatory Powers Act 2000 (RIPA) deals with:

(1) interception of all forms of communication;
(2) gathering of 'communications data', that is information identifying sender, recipient or message path;[387]
(3) *intrusive surveillance,* that is, covert[388] surveillance, usually from within, by human agency or technological device of what is being said or done in residential premises and private vehicles;[389]
(4) *directed surveillance,* that is, case specific surveillance[390] that is neither overt nor intrusive (for example the bugging of non-residential premises or the observation of private grounds with a telephoto lens) if likely to result in the 'obtaining of private information about a person'.[391]

14.84 RIPA does not regulate overt observation[392] or covert surveillance that is an immediate response to events.[393] The Code of Practice on Covert Surveillance refers to surveillance that falls outside RIPA as 'general law observation'. The distinction

---

[384] Intelligence Services Act 1994, s 5(3A), (3B).
[385] Such an apparently unfettered discretion may not comply with the requirement that any contravention of Art 8(1) is 'in accordance with law', see para 3.19 above. See also H Fenwick, *Civil Liberties* (2nd edn, London: 1998) 356; P Leach, 'The Security Service Bill' (1996) 146 NLJ 224.
[386] A Reid and N Ryder, 'For Whose Eyes Only? A Critique of the United Kingdom's Regulation of Investigatory Powers Act 2000' (2001) 10 Information and Communications Technology L 179; D Feldman, *Civil Liberties and Human Rights in England and Wales* (2nd edn, Oxford: 2002) 667 et seq.
[387] Access to communications data can be compared to reading the writing on the envelope of a letter without reading the letter itself.
[388] Meaning that the subject of the surveillance is unaware that it is taking place: RIPA, s 26(9)(a).
[389] For the meaning of 'intrusive surveillance' see para 14.107 below.
[390] Surveillance includes listening to or observing persons or monitoring their movements, with or without the assistance of a surveillance device, and recording the results: RIPA, s 48(2).
[391] RIPA, s 26(2).
[392] *Code of Practice on Covert Surveillance,* para 1.3, available at http://www.homeoffice.gov.uk/ripa/covert-surveillance.htm.
[393] RIPA, s 26(2).

B. Criminal Cases

between general law observation and surveillance regulated under RIPA may be a fine one.[394]

14.85 If surveillance that is regulated by RIPA involves entry onto private property, for example surreptitious planting of a bugging device on private property by police, authorization must be obtained under RIPA *and* one of the two preceding Acts described.[395] This can be done as a combined authorization, although the criteria for authorization under each Act must be considered separately.[396]

Sanctions

14.86 It is an offence to intercept communications intentionally and without lawful authority.[397] It is not an offence to conduct unauthorized intrusive or directed surveillance or to collect communications data without authority.

14.87 Complaints from those who believe themselves to be the victim of unlawful interception or unauthorized or improperly conducted surveillance (including non-compliance with Convention rights)[398] by police bodies, the intelligence services, the armed forces and Customs and Excise must be addressed to the Investigatory Powers Tribunal, an extra-judicial body.[399] This tribunal exercises a form of judicial review.[400] Its proceedings, including any oral hearing, must be conducted in secret,[401] it decides without giving reasons,[402] and outcomes are immune from challenge in the ordinary courts.[403] Remedies available include compensation and destruction of any records of information obtained, but all are discretionary.[404]

Interception of communications

14.88 **Interception of Communications Act 1985** In so far as RIPA regulates interception of communications by the police and other state investigators, it replaces the Interception of Communications Act 1985 (IOCA) which controlled interception

---

[394] H Fenwick, 'Covert Surveillance under the Regulation of Investigatory Powers Act 2000, Part II' (2001) J of Criminal L 521, 528. She asks, if there is prolonged observation of a house, is this still an immediate response to an unexpected turn of events?

[395] Intelligence Services Act 1994: see para 14.78 above. Police Act 1997: see para 14.72 above.

[396] *Code of Practice on Covert Surveillance*, para 2.11.

[397] RIPA, s 1.

[398] RIPA, s 65(2)(a).

[399] RIPA, s 65. Surveillance other than by the intelligence services, armed forces, police, NCIS, National Crime Squad and Customs and Excise may be challenged in the ordinary courts.

[400] RIPA, s 67(2).

[401] Investigatory Powers Tribunal Rules 2000, SI 2000/2665, r 9(6).

[402] RIPA, s 68(4).

[403] RIPA, s 67(8). The new tribunal is modelled on the tribunal set up under the Security Services Act 1996 which between 1996 and 2002 considered over 400 complaints but did not uphold a single one (information from Dr Chris Pounder of Masons, solicitors). It is arguable that the provisions for review do not comply with the *Guidelines of the Committee of Ministers of the Council of Europe on human rights and the fight against terrorism* (15 July 2002) which require that measures used in the fight against terrorism that interfere with privacy must be capable of challenge before a court.

[404] RIPA, s 67(7).

of post and communications passing through public telecommunications networks. The 1985 Act was passed in the wake of a decision of the ECtHR[405] that the United Kingdom was in violation of Article 8 of the ECHR by reason of the absence of a clear statutory framework regulating telephone-tapping.

14.89 The 1985 Act contained serious omissions. It did not regulate interception of communications passing through private networks[406] such as office switchboards (or for that matter communications from a base unit to a cordless telephone)[407] and it left unregulated interception of wireless telegraphy, telephone metering[408] and interception to which either the sender or the recipient had consented. Besides plugging these gaps, RIPA allows interception of newer forms of communication such as e-mail, web-mail, faxes, mobile and satellite telephones and radio-pagers. The wide definition of a public telecommunications service in RIPA catches all those who provide the public with a means of communicating that involves the use of electrical or electro-magnetic energy.[409]

14.90 **Lawful interception of communications under RIPA** RIPA regulates 'interception' of a communication as it passes through, or awaits collection from (1) a public telecommunications or public postal system (that is, a service available to a substantial section of the public)[410] or (2) a private telecommunications system that is linked within the United Kingdom to a public one.[411] In the latter case, RIPA applies to a communication even though no use is made of the external connection. 'Interception' requires some or all of the contents of a communication to be made available 'to a person other than the sender or intended recipient of the communication'.[412] There is no interception if a conversation is recorded from outside the system, for example, when sounds are picked up by a microphone positioned near a telephone receiver or attached to one party to the telephone conversation and transmitted to a tape-recorder.[413]

14.91 Intentional interception without lawful authority is a criminal offence.[414] Interception is lawfully carried out by the authorities when the interceptor satisfies one of the following conditions:

---

[405] *Malone v UK* (1984) 7 EHRR 14.
[406] *Halford v UK* (1997) 24 EHRR 523.
[407] *R v Effick* (1994) 99 Cr App R 312.
[408] Information relating to communications such as subscriber details, itemized billing and routing information.
[409] RIPA, s 2.
[410] The provider can be in either the public or the private sector.
[411] A private system that has no direct or indirect connection to a public system is not covered by RIPA (see s 2).
[412] RIPA, s 2(2). There is no interception if a party to a communication records it without the other party being aware of the fact: *R v Hardy* [2002] EWCA Crim 3012.
[413] Thus RIPA was not violated by the recording of a conversation between Lord Archer and Ted Francis who had a mini-microphone in his listening ear: M Tugendhat and I Christie, *The Law of Privacy and the Media* (Oxford: 2002) para 11.72.
[414] See para 6.64 above.

B. Criminal Cases

(1) the sender and recipient *both* consented;[415]
(2) either the sender or recipient has consented and surveillance has been authorized under RIPA, Part II,[416]
(3) the interception is being done by or with the consent of a private telecommunications system controller for an approved purpose;[417]
(4) interception is being carried out under a data content interception warrant issued by the Secretary of State.[418]

Content data interception warrants A content data interception warrant must be obtained in advance from the Secretary of State, or, in an emergency, a senior official.[419] The Secretary of State is prohibited from issuing a warrant unless satisfied that the warrant is 'necessary': 14.92

(1) in the interests of 'national security'; or
(2) for the purpose of preventing or detecting 'serious crime';[420] or
(3) for the purpose of safeguarding the 'economic well-being of the United Kingdom'; or
(4) for the purpose of giving effect to an international mutual assistance agreement in circumstances appearing to the Secretary of State to be equivalent to those in which he would issue a warrant on the first ground.[421]

No definition is provided of the first or third grounds, both of which are vague and could apply in a wide range of circumstances. RIPA adopts the wide definition of 'serious crime' found in the Police Act 1997.[422] It is therefore fortunate that the warrant must also satisfy a test of proportionality.[423] The proportionality test 14.93

---

[415] RIPA, s 3(1). Query: must the consent relate to the specific communication intercepted?
[416] In cases of participant-monitoring self-authorization under Part II of RIPA only is required: RIPA, s 3(2).
[417] RIPA, ss 1(6), 3(3); Telecommunications (Lawful Business Practice) (Interception of Communications) Regulations 2000, SI 2000/2699 discussed in H Oliver, 'Email and Internet Monitoring in the Workplace: Information Privacy and Contracting Out' (2002) 31 Industrial LJ 321, 339–343. Oliver points out that under the Regulations the controller has to make 'all reasonable efforts' to warn users about the risks of communications being monitored but no proportionality test has to be satisfied before monitoring takes place and there are no safeguards against the use of intercepted personal information for a purpose other than the purpose of the monitoring.
[418] This list of opportunities for lawful interception is not exhaustive. Additional ones include interception in prisons and high security psychiatric hospitals (RIPA, s 4(4), (5)), interception under statutory power to obtain stored information, documents on property (RIPA, s 1(5)(c)) and interception to enable an international mutual assistance agreement to be performed (RIPA, s 4(1)).
[419] RIPA, s 7. This does not apply if some other statute dispenses with the need to obtain authorization or the interception is an unplanned side-effect of intrusive surveillance: *Code of Practice on Covert Surveillance*, para 4.32.
[420] Telephone monitoring in the context of an investigation into a suspected conspiracy to commit armed robberies was held to be justified as a necessary measure in a democratic society in *PG v UK* Application 44787/98, [2002] Crim LR 308.
[421] RIPA, s 5(3).
[422] RIPA, s 81.
[423] RIPA, s 5(2)(b).

requires the Secretary of State to consider, inter alia, whether the information could reasonably be obtained by other means.[424]

14.94 Only specified persons may apply for a warrant.[425] They include the Director General of the Security Service, the Chief of the Secret Intelligence Service, the Director General of the National Criminal Intelligence Service (an organization that produces intelligence for UK law enforcement authorities), the Commissioners of Customs and Excise and the Commissioner of Police of the Metropolis.

14.95 If the Secretary of State decides to issue an interception warrant, it must specify the target (ruling out massive trawling of communications) unless what is intercepted is an 'external communication', that is, one sent or received outside the British Isles.[426] A target may be a person, an organization or a set of premises.[427] The warrant must also include one or more schedules that describe the communications to be intercepted.[428] Means of interception do not have to be stated. The initial period of validity is three months;[429] the warrant can be renewed. A communications service provider who is notified of a warrant must take all 'reasonable practicable' steps to give effect to it.[430] Failure to do so is a criminal offence.[431] Civil proceedings may also be brought against a recalcitrant service provider.[432] A provider of public telecommunications may be obliged to maintain an approved interception capability to implement interception warrants[433] and officials with a warrant are empowered to demand encryption keys or decryption of communications from 'any person'.[434]

14.96 Interception of legally privileged and other confidential material RIPA, unlike PACE, does not prohibit or restrict interception of sensitive confidential personal information or legally privileged communications. In the Code of Practice on Interception of Communications[435] it is stated that

---

[424] RIPA, s 5(4).
[425] RIPA, s 6(1).
[426] RIPA, ss 8(5), 20. However, according to the Guardian's 'Big Brother' report of 14 September 2002 even domestic internet traffic travels around the world en route thus falling within the exemption.
[427] RIPA, ss 8(1), 78(1).
[428] s 8(2). These may, for example, include telephone numbers and e-mail addresses.
[429] *Code of Practice on Interception of Communications*, para 2.11. Warrants made in the interests of national security or for safeguarding the economic well-being of the country can be issued for six months.
[430] RIPA, s 11(4).
[431] RIPA, s 11(7).
[432] RIPA, s 12(7).
[433] RIPA, s 12. See also, RIP (Maintenance of Interception Capability) Order 2002, SI 2002/1931. Obligations include to ensure 'filtering to provide only the traffic data associated with the warranted telecommunications identifier, where reasonable'.
[434] RIPA, ss 49–52. The person from whom an encryption key is requested must prove that he does not have it.
[435] Issued under RIPA, s 71, see http://www.homeoffice.gov.uk.

Particular consideration should also be given in cases where the subject of the interception might reasonably assume a high degree of privacy, or where confidential information is involved . . . For example, extra consideration should be given where interception might involve communications between a minister of religion and an individual relating to the latter's spiritual welfare, or where matters of medical or journalistic confidentiality or legal privilege may be involved.[436]

Consideration should be given to any infringement of the privacy of individuals who are not the subject of the intended interception, especially where communications relating to religious, medical, journalistic or legally privileged material may be involved. An application for an interception warrant should draw attention to any circumstances which give rise to an unusual degree of collateral infringement of privacy, and this will be taken into account by the Secretary of State.[437]

14.97 To avoid incompatibility with Article 8 by reason of the absence of any express exemption in RIPA for communications covered by LPP, the Government has put into the Code of Practice certain safeguards for lawyer–client communications. Strasbourg jurisprudence requires these communications to be accorded a high level of protection.[438] It may turn out that these safeguards are too flimsy to prevent the interception of legally privileged communications from violating articles 6 and 8 of the Convention.[439] Paragraph 3.7 of the Code[440] states that

Where a lawyer is the subject of an interception, it is possible that a substantial proportion of the communications which will be intercepted will be between the lawyer and his client(s) and will be subject to legal privilege. Any case where a lawyer is the subject of an investigation should be notified to the Interception of Communications Commissioner during his inspections . . .

14.98 In JUSTICE's view

the Code should make clear that the person applying for the warrant is personally responsible for ensuring that a proper assessment of the likelihood of legally privileged material being intercepted has taken place and that the results are properly reflected in the application. This would mean the Director General of NCIS having personal responsibility for this in the case of police applications. Similarly, the Secretary of State should not merely take the likelihood of privileged material being intercepted 'into account'; he should be satisfied that the Article 8 principles of necessity and proportionality are complied with in relation to this particular matter. In order to comply with proportionality, applications where there is a significant likelihood of privileged legal material being intercepted should only be authorised in exceptional and compelling circumstances. . . . [T]he Code should explicitly prohibit the interception of a lawyer's communications in any situation other than where the lawyers themselves are the object of criminal suspicions. Even then, valid

---

[436] *Code of Practice on Interception of Communications*, para 3.2.
[437] *Code of Practice on Interception*, para 3.1.
[438] See para 3.03 above.
[439] See para 14.117 below.
[440] The draft version said interception should be considered 'only in exceptional and compelling circumstances'. The final version does not. Legal privilege is as defined in Police Act 1997, s 98.

legal privilege will endure in respect of clients who are not involved in a criminal conspiracy with the lawyer. The safeguards necessary to protect this material should therefore be spelt out, including a restriction that a warrant is only to be granted in 'exceptional and compelling circumstances, irrespective of whether this other material represents a 'substantial proportion' or not of the overall material intercepted.[441]

Following the advice of JUSTICE, the Interception Code of Practice, like PACE,[442] includes definitions and descriptions of what amounts to confidential medical, journalistic and religious material.[443]

14.99 **Keeping the interception a secret** RIPA contains extensive measures to safeguard the secrecy of the fact of interception and the fruits of interception. It is an offence punishable by up to five years' imprisonment to disclose the existence and content of a warrant and any decryption that has taken place.[444] Normally[445] no mention may be made in legal proceedings of the existence of the warrant or, if application for or issue of a warrant or the commission of an offence of unlawful interception might be inferred, of the intercepted material itself.[446] This ban is unaffected by the probative value of the information that is suppressed. The prosecution in a criminal trial is, however, at liberty to adduce material lawfully intercepted by means that did not involve a warrant[447] and circumstantial evidence gathered as a result of interception under a warrant.[448] To prevent the conviction of someone whose innocence might be established by inadmissible intercepted material, RIPA allows the exonerating material to be shown to the prosecutor so that she can assess whether a prosecution is fair.[449] In exceptional circumstances the material may be disclosed to the judge. It remains to be seen whether these arrangements comply with the equality of arms principle that the ECtHR has implied into Article 6.[450]

---

[441] *Submissions on the draft Codes of Practice under the Regulation of Investigatory Powers Act 2000* (2000) paras 5, 6, available at http://www.fipr.org/rip/JusticeCoPSubNov00.doc.
[442] See paras 14.21 et seq.
[443] *Interception of Communications Code of Practice*, paras 3.9 to 3.11.
[444] RIPA, ss 19, 54
[445] Exceptionally, under s 18 intercepted material that would be inadmissible in criminal proceedings may be used in evidence in proceedings before the Special Immigration Appeals Commission and in any legal proceedings relating to an interception offence or to the fairness or unfairness of a dismissal on the grounds of the commission of an offence under RIPA.
[446] RIPA, s 17. See further, P Mirfield, 'Regulation of Investigatory Powers Act 2000(2): Evidential Aspects' [2001] Crim LR 91.
[447] RIPA, s 18(4). This is backed up by s 18(5) which allows the defence to challenge the prosecution's account of the provenance of the material, if necessary by suggesting things that are forbidden by s 17(1).
[448] This might not be allowed if the provenance of the material could not be challenged by the defence because of s 17(1).
[449] RIPA, s 17(7). Previously this was not permitted: *R v P* [2001] 2 All ER 58, 71–73.
[450] See *Foucher v France* (1998) 25 EHRR 234, para 34.

B. Criminal Cases

RIPA requires the Secretary of State to set up procedures to minimize dissemination and copying of intercepted material and to ensure that intercepted material is destroyed as soon as it is no longer needed.[451]

14.100

All the measures designed to keep the fact and result of interception secret mean that a person whose communications are intercepted is likely to be oblivious of the fact. This makes the complaints procedure set up under the Act something of a farce. Feldman believes that so long as there is no provision for the subject of an interception to be informed of the interception after it has taken place (unless this would threaten national security), the ECtHR will find that RIPA contravenes Article 13 by failing to provide an effective remedy for violations of Article 8 and, in some cases, Article 6.[452]

14.101

Communications data

Surveillance arrangements Communications data describes any detail about a communication that is not part of its contents.[453] Such data is used extensively by police investigating paedophile rings and smuggling rackets as a source of intelligence and evidence.[454] RIPA[454a] provides for the compulsory acquisition of communications data from telephone companies, internet providers and postal companies by the police, Customs and Excise, MI5 and MI6 and the Inland Revenue.[455] A supporting Code imposes a test of necessity and proportionality[456] but there is little oversight of the process which is essentially self-authorizing.[457] RIPA exempts the service provider from civil liability for disclosing communications data in response to a disclosure notice.[458]

14.102

---

[451] RIPA s 15.

[452] *Civil Liberties and Human Rights in England and Wales* (Oxford: 2002) 682–683.

[453] RIPA, ss 21(4), (6). This includes records of telephone calls made and received, the source, title, and destination of e-mails, websites visited and mobile phone location data. For a postal company it will include details of post received such as can be established without opening the letter or parcel.

[454] Between November 2000 and November 2001 the Metropolitan Police made 10,500 applications for communications data to BT and 13,000 to private sector providers: *Hansard*, HC, col 455W (6 December 2001). Cp All Party Internet Group, *Communications Data* (January 2003) para 8.

[454a] The scheme is not yet in force. Currently communications data is accessed under DPA, s 29 and disclosure is optional.

[455] RIPA, ss 21–22. A controversial draft order which would have extended these powers to seven government departments, local authorities and councils, the NHS, the Information Commissioner and even the Post Office was withdrawn by the Government. Extension of the powers is proposed again in Home Office consultation document, *Access to Communication Data, Respecting Privacy and Protecting the Public from Crime* (2003) www.homeoffice.gov.uk/ripa/part1/consult.pdf.

[456] *Accessing Communications Draft Code of Practice*, para 2.3, available www.homeoffice.gov.uk/ripa/pcdcpc.htm#Purposes. This embellishes RIPA, s 22(5) which requires access to be 'proportionate to what is sought to be achieved by so obtaining the data'.

[457] Account and subscriber details can be obtained by the police on the say-so of an inspector, and other information with the approval of a superintendent: *Accessing Communications Draft Code of Practice*, para 3.2. The application form is subject to inspection by a commissioner responsible for overseeing the powers conferred under RIPA.

[458] RIPA, s 21(3).

14.103 The grounds on which disclosure notices can be served on telecommunications and postal service providers are very broad: national security, preventing and detecting crime and disorder, safeguarding the economic well-being of the United Kingdom, public safety, public health, assessing and collecting taxes, preventing personal injury, any other purpose specified by the Secretary of State.[459] This part of RIPA represents a threat to professional confidentiality in that for relatively unimportant reasons (minor crimes and tax evasion) it allows investigators to identify a professional's clients and contacts or, vice versa, the professionals used by the individual who is the subject of the interception.

14.104 Under the Telecommunications (Data Protection Privacy) Regulations 1999[460] communications data cannot be retained for longer than necessary for billing or marketing purposes except where retention is required by law or by the order of a court or destruction would be likely to prejudice fraud prevention, detection or prosecution. This limits the usefulness of interception of communications data to investigators. Therefore in the Anti-terrorism, Crime and Security Act 2001 the Government put in place arrangements allowing communications data to be kept for longer 'for the purpose of safeguarding national security or the purposes of prevention or detection of crime or the prosecution of offenders which may relate directly or indirectly to national security'.[461] Communications service providers are expected to enter agreements with the Home Office to retain 'communications data'[462] and to abide by a voluntary[463] Code of Practice issued by the Secretary of State[464] which will be admissible in legal proceedings.[465] The period of retention proposed is 12 months. Under a proposed new EU Telecommunications Directive telecommunications and internet service providers will be required to keep traffic details of all telecommunications sent and received in the European Union in central computer systems for possibly as long as 24 months and, with judicial approval, make them available to EU governments on national security and other grounds.[466] The European Data Protection Commissioners have expressed serious reservations about the legitimacy and legality of this proposal which involves blanket retention of personal data for a set period. Their view

---

[459] RIPA, s 22; *Accessing Communications Draft Code of Practice*, para 4.1.
[460] SI 1999/2093, ss 6–10.
[461] s 102(3)(a)–(b).
[462] As defined in RIPA: Anti-terrorism, Crime and Security Act 2001, s 107.
[463] If the voluntary code does not work satisfactorily, the Home Secretary is able under s 104 Anti-terrorism, Crime and Security Act 2001, s 104 by order to activate a power to give directions to communications providers about the retention of data.
[464] Anti-terrorism, Crime and Security Act 2001, s 102. Is retention of data under of a *voluntary* code compatible with the requirement that an interference with respect for private life (Art 8(1)) be in accordance with law (Art 8(2))?
[465] s 102(5).
[466] Supplemental Regulatory Impact Assessment: Retention of communications data, available from http://www.statewatch.org.

B. Criminal Cases

is that Article 8[467] and the EU Directive concerning the processing of personal data and the protection of privacy in the electronic sector[468] permit retention only in specific cases where a demonstrable need is shown to exist, the period of retention must be as short as possible and there must be sufficient safeguards against unlawful access and other abuse.[469] Anything else is disproportionate.

Possible multiple illegality of the data retention arrangements The Earl of Northesk[470] told the House of Lords that preserving communications data to satisfy the needs of a body other than the service provider potentially engaged the second[471] and the fifth data protection principles. The latter provides that personal data 'processed for any purpose or purposes shall not be kept for longer than is necessary for that purpose or those purposes'.[472] In a submission to the Joint Committee on Human Rights, the Information Commissioner agreed and suggested that retention of all 'traffic data' might additionally breach the first[473] and third[474] data protection principles.[475] Lord Rooker, the Government spokesman in the Lords, insisted that a voluntary code and agreements could be drafted in a manner that would enable service providers who complied not to breach the DPA.[476] A further problem is that the anti-terrorism legislation only allows access to data on the grounds of national security but RIPA permits agents of the state to obtain access to communications data on much wider grounds including collection of taxes or other levies due to any government department. In an opinion obtained by the Information Commissioner, Emmerson and Mountfield state: 14.105

> The consequence of these two overlapping regimes [RIPA[477] and the anti-terrorism legislation][478] is that data may be retained for longer than they otherwise would be, on the grounds that their retention is necessary for the purposes of safeguarding national security, but that the data may then be accessed for a variety of collateral public purposes which have no connection (direct or indirect) with national security.[479]

---

[467] As further elaborated by the ECHR in Opinion 4/2001 of the Article 29 Working Party established by Directive (EC) 95/46 and the Declaration of Stockholm (April 2000).
[468] (EC) 2002/58. See Arts 1 and 15.
[469] See 'European Data Protection Commissioners oppose data retention' on the Statewatch website, http://www.statewatch.org.
[470] *Hansard*, HL, col 791 (4 December 2001).
[471] See para 18.29 below.
[472] Sch 1, Pt 1.
[473] See para 18.08 below.
[474] Personal data shall not be excessive in relation to the purpose for which it is processed. There was, for example, no reason why service providers should retain e-mail headers.
[475] Appendix, *Anti-Terrorism, Crime and Security Bill*, HL Paper 51, HC 420 (December 2001) Pt 3, para 24.
[476] *Hansard*, HL, col. 790 (4 December 2001). See also Home Office consultaion paper on Code of Practice for Voluntary Detention of Communications Data (2003) paras 11.4–11.9 available at www.homeoffice.gov.uk/oicd/antiterrorism/consult/htm.
[477] s 22(2).
[478] Anti-terrorism, Crime and Security Act 2001, s 102(3).
[479] The full opinion is available on the Privacy International website at http://www.privacyinternational.org.

Intrusive surveillance

14.106 **Definition** The provisions dealing with intrusive surveillance apply to all the emanations of the state that have an enforcement or investigative role including the police, customs and excise, the intelligence and security services and the armed forces.

14.107 Intrusive surveillance is covert surveillance of an individual that:

(1) takes place on any 'residential premises' (including movable structures)[480] or in a private vehicle; and
(2) involves the presence of an individual on the premises or vehicle or is carried out by means of a surveillance device.[481]

If the device is placed somewhere else it is still intrusive surveillance if 'the device is such that it *consistently* provides *information of the same quality* and detail as might be expected to be obtained from a *device actually present on the premises* or in the vehicle'.[482] This is intended to prevent evasion of statutory controls by the use of high-quality, long-distance equipment.[483] What quality off-premises surveillance must achieve to constitute intrusive surveillance is bound to be the subject of heated debate.[484]

14.108 The location of the surveillance is important. Residential premises are defined as 'premises . . . for the time being occupied or used, however temporarily, for residential purposes or otherwise as living accommodation'.[485] Hotels and prisons are given as examples.[486] The status of police cells is uncertain.[487] What is certain is that surveillance of office and business premises is directed surveillance. Surveillance of a conversation between doctor and patient is therefore intrusive surveillance if the conversation happens to take place in the patient's home or in a hospital but not if it takes place in the doctor's surgery. Similarly, the directed surveillance rules apply to surveillance of a consultation between lawyer and client in the offices of the lawyer or a prison yard but the stricter intrusive surveillance rules apply if the same consultation takes place in a prison cell.

---

[480] RIPA, s 48(1).
[481] RIPA, s 26(3).
[482] RIPA, s 26(5) (emphasis added). This is similar to the idea in Council of Europe Resolution 1165 (1998), *Right to Privacy,* para 14 (vi) that no distinction should be made between a person who trespasses to take photographs and make recordings and one who uses visual or auditory enhancement devices to capture information that would otherwise not have been captured without trespass.
[483] D Feldman, *Civil Liberties and Human Rights in England and Wales* (2nd edn, Oxford: 2002) 595.
[484] H Fenwick, 'Covert Surveillance under the Regulation of Investigatory Powers Act 2000, Part II' [2001] J of Criminal L 521, 535. Such uncertainty might cause this part of RIPA to contravene the requirement that an interference with Art 8(1) must be in accordance with law: see para 3.19 above.
[485] RIPA, s 48(1).
[486] ibid.
[487] *R v Mason* [2002] EWCA Crim 385, para 61.

B. Criminal Cases

This is an unsatisfactory state of affairs. Whether surveillance is intrusive should depend upon the content of the communication as well as its location and quality. Indeed, some would say that the quality of the information is irrelevant; that a poor recording of a confidential conversation between lawyer and client is as intrusive as a good one because what the victim of the intrusion of privacy finds objectionable is the loss of control over private information. The fundamental flaw of the legislation is that it is drawn up entirely from the perspective of the person carrying out the surveillance.

Grounds and procedures Intrusive surveillance by the intelligence and security services must be authorized by warrant by the Secretary of State.[488] For the police, intrusive surveillance must be authorized by a chief constable or the Commissioner of Police of the Metropolis or one of his Assistant Commissioners.[489] The approval of officials of similar standing is required when other arms of the state engage in intrusive surveillance.[490] Save in an emergency, approval for intrusive surveillance by persons other than the Secretary of State does not take effect without the additional approval of a Surveillance Commissioner (a judicial officer).[491] The Surveillance Commissioner has power to quash the order but if he does there is an appeal procedure to the Chief Surveillance Commissioner.[492] Once approved, the authorization is normally for three months and can be renewed.

14.110

It is arguable that surveillances authorized by the Secretary of State do not comply with the ECHR because there is no prior scrutiny by an independent judicial officer.[493]

14.111

The permitted grounds for intrusive surveillance are:[494]

14.112

(1) in the interests of national security;
(2) for the purposes of preventing or detecting serious crime;[495] or
(3) in the interests of the economic well-being of the United Kingdom.

As with interception warrants, requirements of necessity and proportionality must be satisfied.[496] In assessing proportionality, the Code of Practice of Covert Surveillance directs that consideration be given to whether the information could

14.113

---

[488] RIPA, s 42. The warrant is effective for six months unless cancelled.
[489] RIPA, s 32(6).
[490] ibid.
[491] RIPA, s 36. See para 14.73 above.
[492] RIPA, ss 38, 39.
[493] D Feldman, *Civil Liberties and Human Rights in England and Wales* (2nd edn, Oxford: 2002) 597.
[494] RIPA, s 32(3).
[495] This does not apply to the intelligence services, RIPA, s 42(3).
[496] RIPA, s 32(2); *Code of Practice on Covert Surveillance*, para 2.4.

reasonably be obtained by other means[497] and to collateral intrusion or interference with the privacy of persons who are not the subject of the surveillance.[498]

14.114 **Legally privileged and other confidential communications** The Code of Practice on Covert Surveillance makes special provision for interception of 'confidential information'. 'Confidential information' means:

(1) matters subject to legal privilege;[499]
(2) confidential journalistic material; and
(3) 'confidential personal information',[500] that is, information held in confidence:[501]

> relating to the physical or mental health or spiritual counselling concerning an individual (whether living or dead) who can be identified from it.[502]

This definition is so narrow that the only client–professional communications that will fall within its scope are those between lawyer and client, religious adviser and devotee and health professional and patient.

14.115 The Code of Practice para 2.7 specifies that any application for authorization which is likely to result in the acquisition of confidential material should include an assessment of the likelihood of this happening. If the targeted person handles a lot of confidential material (for example, a lawyer) an application should be considered only in exceptional and compelling circumstances with full regard to the proportionality issues this raises.[503] In *R v Sutherland*,[504] Newman J said that the authorizing official must consider 'in relation to the specific areas to be made subject to interception . . . (1) whether the proposed interception was proportionate and (2) whether there was a risk that privileged material might be intercepted or collateral intrusion might take place'. Confidential material obtained through covert surveillance should be destroyed as soon as it is no longer necessary to retain it for a specified purpose and should not be disseminated unless an appropriate officer is satisfied that it is necessary for a specific purpose.[505] Fenwick comments

---

[497] RIPA, s 32(4); *Code of Practice on Covert Surveillance*, para 2.5.
[498] *Code of Practice on Covert Surveillance*, para 2.7.
[499] Defined as in PACE, s 10.
[500] *Code of Practice on Covert Surveillance*, para 3.10.
[501] Para 3.10 specifies that information is held in confidence if (1) it is held subject to an express or implied undertaking to hold it in confidence; or (2) it is subject to a restriction on disclosure or an obligation of secrecy contained in existing or future legislation.
[502] *Code of Practice on Covert Surveillance*, para 3.10.
[503] *R v Robinson* [2002] EWCA Crim 2489, para 3.6. In this case a solicitors clerk was a police informant. Pill LJ said that it was 'a necessary ingredient of the rule of law that members of the public are able to obtain legal advice without the police obtaining access to what passes between lawyer and client'.
[504] (Nottingham Crown Court, 29 January 2002) transcript p 15.
[505] *Code of Practice on Covert Surveillance,* para 2.11. cp final version of Code, paras 2.16–2.19.

B. Criminal Cases

that there is no 'independent check ... even where material is most clearly of a private nature'.[506]

There are special safeguards for spiritual counselling, defined as 'conversations between an individual and a Minister of Religion acting in his official capacity where the individual being counselled is seeking or the Minister is imparting forgiveness, absolution or the resolution of conscience with the authority of the Divine Beings of their faith'.[507]   14.116

> Any person granting an authorization is reminded that police forces ... National Crime Intelligence Service, the National Crime squad and HM Customs & Excise have given an undertaking not to mount operations in circumstances covered by the Seal of the Confession. In addition, where they are satisfied that a Minister of Religion is not him/herself involved in the matter under investigation, and they believe that surveillance will lead to them intruding on spiritual counselling between the Minister and a member of his/her faith, they should, in preparing the case for authorization, give serious consideration to discussing the matter first with a relevant senior representative of the religious authority. The views of the senior representative would be included in the request for authorization.[507a]

In Liberty's view, legally privileged material should be put on a par with material given under the seal of confession. Article 8 does not actually require this. Interference with legally privileged material is acceptable provided that it is proportionate to a legitimate aim and subject to adequate safeguards.[508] Since RIPA does not expressly authorize the interception of legally privileged material, however, there must be a risk that a court will hold that the Code of Practice, in so far as it permits the interception of legally privileged communications, is ultra vires.[509] The judgment of Newman J in *R v Sutherland*[510] proceeds from the premise that the 'only relevant circumstances giving rise to an exception where the police could obtain authority to intercept privileged conversations would be that they had grounds to believe that communications would be made to facilitate crime or fraud'.[511] It is unclear whether Newman J regarded this as the only exceptional circumstance justifying police interception of legally privileged material or the only one that could be relevant in the factual circumstances of that case.[512]   14.117

---

[506] H Fenwick, 'Covert Surveillance under the Regulation of Investigatory Powers Act 2000, Part II' [2001] J of Criminal L 521, 530.
[507] Code of Practice on Covert Surveillance, para 3.11.
[507a] *Code of Practice on Covert Surveillance*, para 2.8. The final version is much weaker: See para 3.1.
[508] *Kopp v Switzerland* (1998) 27 EHRR 91. See also para 10.14 above.
[509] See paras 16.13–16.15 below.
[510] For details of this case see para 14.122 below.
[511] (Nottingham Crown Court, 29 January 2002) transcript p 12.
[512] In *Sutherland* the police surveillance amounted to directed covert surveillance, but the Code guidance for interception of confidential information material by intrusive or directed surveillance is identical.

14.119

Strictly speaking, when a communication is made to facilitate a crime or fraud it is not privileged anyway.[513]

14.118 **Admissibility of the fruits of surveillance in evidence** There are no statutory restrictions on the use of material garnered during an intrusive surveillance operation (or for that matter during directed surveillance) as evidence in subsequent civil or criminal proceedings. In criminal trials non-compliance with the Code of Practice or RIPA could lead to the exclusion of evidence under PACE, s 78.[514] If the police intentionally intercept legally privileged communications without complying with the Code of Practice, and in so doing endanger a fair trial, the trial must be stayed.[515] In civil litigation CPR r 32.1 allows exclusion of surveillance evidence. Alternatively, the court can mark its disapproval of the surveillance in its award of costs.[515a]

Directed surveillance

14.119 **Definition, grounds, procedures** Covert surveillance of the offices of a professional or of a meeting between professional and client elsewhere—say in a police interview room or exercise yard[516]—is directed surveillance. Directed surveillance is lawful[517] when carried out for any of the reasons for which intrusive surveillance can be lawfully carried out. Additionally, it may be approved:

(1) in the interests of public safety;
(2) for the purposes of protecting public health;
(3) for the purposes of preventing disorder;
(4) for the purpose of assessing or collecting any tax or revenue;[518]
(5) for any other purpose the Secretary of State may prescribe.

14.120 Directed surveillance operations require only self-authorization.[519] For the police, authorization is on the say-so of a superintendent or, in a case of urgency, an inspector.[520] For other public agencies someone of equivalent seniority must give approval.[521] Where it is likely that confidential material will be acquired, the Code of Practice recommends authorization by a chief constable.[522]

---

[513] See para 16.35 below.
[514] H Fenwick, 'Covert Surveillance under the Regulation of Investigatory Powers Act 2000, Part II' [2001] J of Criminal L 521, 533.
[515] *R v Sutherland* (Nottingham Crown Court, 29 January 2002).
[515a] *Jones v University of Warwick* [2003] EWCA Civ 151. See para 15.17 below.
[516] ibid.
[517] RIPA, s 28.
[518] Protection of tax revenues falls within the aim of advancing the economic well-being of a country: *Funke v France* (1993) 16 EHRR 297, para 52.
[519] Authorization of directed surveillance does not have to be notified to a Surveillance Commissioner but must be available for review during an inspection by the Commissioners and their associates.
[520] RIP (Prescription of Offices, Ranks and Positions) Order 2000, SI 2000/2417.
[521] RIP (Prescription of Offices, Ranks and Positions) Order 2000.
[522] *Draft Code of Practice on Covert Surveillance*, para 3.2.

B. Criminal Cases

14.121 The guidance for authorizing surveillance that is likely to turn up confidential/religious material is as for intrusive surveillance.[523] Authorization may not be granted unless it is believed to be necessary in a democratic society and proportionate to the aim pursued.[524] These two requirements are intended to ensure compatibility with the ECHR. In deciding on proportionality regard should be had to any interference with the privacy of persons who are not the subject of surveillance, particularly in cases where there are special sensitivities, for example in cases of premises used by lawyers or for any form of medical or professional counselling or therapy.[525]

14.122 **Compatibility with the European Convention on Human Rights** There is no requirement for advance approval of a directed surveillance by a surveillance commissioner, just general oversight of the regime by the Chief Surveillance Commissioner.[526] It has been suggested that this omission may cause the ECtHR to hold that the directed surveillance provisions in RIPA are not Convention-compliant.[527] That the safeguards put in place to support a legitimate interference with Article 8(1) privacy rights are inadequate was starkly demonstrated in January 2002 by the collapse of a £3 million murder trial. In *R v Sutherland*[528] Newman J found that police officers had planted bugging devices in police exercise yards intending to capture any conversation which might take place between the detained men and their solicitors, either before or between police interviews. In so doing they flagrantly breached the law by failing to satisfy the conditions for intercepting legally privileged communications laid down in the Code of Practice. In the circumstances (violation of private conversations protected by PACE, s 58 between detainees and their solicitors), the police conduct also contravened Article 6 of the ECHR and therefore HRA, s 6(1).[529] Both as a matter of principle and because the misconduct rendered a fair trial impossible,[530] the trial judge

---

[523] ibid, para 3.1–3.12.
[524] RIPA, s 28(2); ibid, paras 2.4, 2.5.
[525] cp Draft Code of Practice on Covert Surveillance, para 2.3. This advice is omitted from the final version.
[526] RIPA, s 62. This may satisfy the *Guidelines of the Committee of Ministers of the Council of Europe on human rights and the fight against terrorism* (15 July 2002) which requires that 'in the context of the fight against terrorism, the collection and the processing of personal data . . . may interfere with the respect for private life only if such collection and processing, in particular (iii) may be subject to supervision by an external independent authority' (Art V).
[527] Y Akdeniz, N Taylor and C Walker, 'Regulation of Investigatory Powers Act 2000(1): BigBrother.gov.uk: State surveillance in the age of information and rights' [2001] Crim LR 73, 85; H Fenwick, 'Covert Surveillance under the Regulation of Investigatory Powers Act 2000, Part II' [2001] J of Criminal L 521, 534–535.
[528] *R v Sutherland* (Nottingham Crown Court, 29 January 2002) transcript p 24.
[529] ibid at 29–30, 32.
[530] ibid at 47. The judge recognizes that his finding that the proceedings can be stayed as a matter of principle because of the damage done to the integrity of the administration of justice (ibid at 41) is obiter because the misconduct, for a number of reasons, had undermined the possibility of a fair trial.

decided that the only 'just and appropriate'[531] response was to stay the criminal proceedings, heinous though the crime was for which the defendants were standing trial. The prosecution was criticized for making a PII[532] application which, had it been successful, would have concealed the illegality that had taken place from the defence.[533]

Acquisition of Confidential Information by the Defence

Disclosure of used police material

14.123 An accused who is charged with an either-way or indictable offence is entitled to information about the evidence in the prosecution case before the commencement of the trial. For indictable offences the defence receives the statements or depositions relied on in the committal papers; for either-way offences the defence is either provided with copies of the prosecution evidence or a summary of the prosecution case before a decision is taken about where the trial is to be held.[534] If confidential personal information obtained from a professional forms part of the prosecution case it must be disclosed. The only way to avoid this is a successful claim to PII.

Disclosure of unused police material[535]

Procedures

14.124 **Material held by the investigating authorities** The Criminal Procedure and Investigations Act 1996 imposes a duty of primary disclosure on the prosecutor to allow the accused access to unused material collected in the course of the police investigation which the *prosecutor* holds or has inspected[536] and which, in the prosecutor's opinion, 'might undermine the case for the prosecution against the accused'.[537] A further duty of disclosure arises if the defence provides a statement setting out in general terms the nature of the accused's defence and indicating the matters on which the defence takes issue with the prosecution and why.[538] This

---

[531] HRA, s 8(1).
[532] See para 16.52 below.
[533] '[T]he basis of the claim for privilege advanced to the Court was that the material was not going to be relied upon as part of the prosecution's case, that it had not been used in the course of the inquiry, and that to give disclosure would reveal the techniques in relation to the covert surveillance, which could compromise future inquiries in which the use of such covert surveillance might be required. In my judgment, none of the grounds for non-disclosure were well founded.' Per Newman J, *R v Sutherland* (Nottingham Crown Court, 29 January 2002) transcript p 8.
[534] Magistrates' Courts (Advance Information) Rules 1985, SI 1985/601; *R v Stratford Justices, ex p Imbert* [1999] 2 Cr App R 276.
[535] J Epp, *Building on the Decade of Disclosure in Criminal Procedure* (London: 2001).
[536] s 3(2).
[537] s 3(1).
[538] s 5(5). Defence disclosure is voluntary if the case is tried summarily and compulsory if tried on indictment.

B. Criminal Cases

time the prosecutor must disclose material which has not already been disclosed that might reasonably be expected to assist the accused's defence as disclosed in the defence statement.[539] The accused may apply to a magistrates' court at this point for an order to disclose material held by the *police* which could have been, but has not, been inspected by the prosecutor and which does not, therefore, have to be automatically disclosed.[540]

Material held by third parties In criminal proceedings there is no duty of disclosure on third parties,[541] however, the equality of arms principle which the ECtHR has implied into Article 6, imposes an obligation on the investigating authorities to disclose any material they have *or can obtain* which might assist the defence.[542] Consistently with this obligation, the Attorney-General's Disclosure Guidelines say that if it is suspected that a third party such as a GP, forensic medical examiner, hospital, school or social services has material which, in the hands of the prosecution, might have to be disclosed, consideration should be given as to whether to seek access to the material. 'It will be important to do so if the material . . . is likely to undermine the prosecution case, or assist a known defence.'[543] If the third party refuses to part with the material voluntarily,[544] the prosecution is advised to apply to a court for a witness summons requiring its production.[545]

14.125

Confidential information

The prosecution cannot withhold material from the defence that falls within the relevant disclosure test simply because it is confidential and obtained through the use of coercive powers such as an access or production order.[546] The most that the prosecutor can do is to edit out anything confidential that would be of no assistance to the defence. The materiality test that must be satisfied before a professional can be forced to disgorge confidential client information in response to a summons or subpoena[547] is not applied to confidential client information in the possession of the police.[548]

14.126

---

[539] s 7(2).
[540] s 8(3)(c). Obligatory prosecution disclosure is confined to material held by, or inspected by, the prosecutor: s 7(3).
[541] *Mahon v Rahn* [1997] 3 All ER 687, 705.
[542] *Jespers v Belgium* (1981) 27 DR 61.
[543] *Att-Gen's Guidelines: Disclosure of Information in Criminal Proceedings* (2000) para 30.
[544] Those who volunteer information will only have qualified immunity from proceedings in libel: *Mahon v Rahn* [1997] 3 All ER 687, 709.
[545] *Att-Gen's Guidelines: Disclosure of Information in Criminal Proceedings* (2000) para 31. See para 14.129 below.
[546] See para 14.25 above.
[547] See paras 14.129 and 15.07 below.
[548] *R v Brushett* [2001] Crim LR 471. See also, J Temkin, 'Digging the Dirt: Disclosure of Records of Sexual Assault Cases' [2002] 61 CLJ 126, 132–133.

Public interest immunity

14.127 For some confidential unused material the prosecution may be able to make a PII claim.

> [Sensitive] [m]aterial must not be disclosed . . . to the extent that the court, on an application by the prosecutor, concludes it is not in the public interest to disclose it.[549]

The disclosure code gives 'material given in confidence' as an example of 'sensitive' material.[550] The court determines whether disclosure is contrary to the public interest according to common law principles.[551] These principles are discussed elsewhere.[552] A professional who directly or indirectly brought confidential information about a client to the prosecutor's attention (say a doctor or social worker who reported suspicions of child abuse) is entitled to be heard by the court.[553] The defence need not be informed of the non-disclosure application if the material is too sensitive to allow this.[554]

Material held by a professional

Voluntary disclosure

14.128 It is not at all uncommon for the defence to want to see statements of special education needs and reports by teachers, social workers, doctors and psychologists. A professional, and any body such as a hospital or social services that has possession of the original or a copy of such a document, is under no obligation to admit that it exists,[555] to preserve it[556] or to make it available to the defence except to the extent that legislation has created such an obligation.[557] In fact, if the document is the subject of an equitable obligation of confidentiality, voluntary disclosure without either the owner's consent or statutory authority may expose the third party to an action for breach of confidence.[558]

---

[549] s 3(6). See also ss 7(5), 8(5). In *R v K* [2002] EWCA Crim 2878 the Court of Appeal said that PII had been properly relied on to withhold material from social services that demonstrated that the 5-year-old rape complainant belonged to a seriously dysfunctional family and marked by sexual abuse. The evidence might have affected her credibility but it was not material to the alleged offence.
[550] *Criminal Procedure and Investigations Act, 1996 Code of Practice*, para 6.12.
[551] s 21(2).
[552] See para 16.52 below.
[553] s 16.
[554] Crown Court (Criminal Procedure and Investigations Act 1996) (Disclosure) Rules 1997, SI 1997/698.
[555] *Re Barlow Clowes Gilt Managers Ltd* [1991] 4 All ER 385, 393.
[556] *R v Carosella* [1997] 1 SCR 80, 155.
[557] *Re Barlow Clowes Gilt Managers Ltd* [1991] 4 All ER 385, 393. Cp *Re D* [1994] 1 FLR 346, 352.
[558] cp para 10.36 above.

B. Criminal Cases

Court-enforced disclosure[559]

14.129 If a professional refuses to give voluntary disclosure of confidential information about a client both prosecution and the defence can apply to the Crown Court under s 2(1) of the Criminal Procedure (Attendance of Witnesses) Act 1965[560] for a witness summons to produce it. This should be done as soon as reasonably practicable after the committal or notice of transfer. The applicant must describe what it is that is sought in an affidavit and satisfy the court that it will not be voluntarily produced and that it is 'material evidence', an undefined term that at common law means admissible evidence.[561] This does not include documents that are useful for cross-examining purposes[562] or anything which may assist a relevant line of inquiry. Without having seen the material, it is difficult for the applicant to discharge this burden[563] and applications for the production of confidential records in the possession of third parties are correspondingly rare.[564] Social services will, in any event, claim PII for files relating to children that are wanted by the defence.[565]

14.130 In every case in which application is made to extract documents containing confidential personal client information from a professional, the courts must engage in a balancing exercise weighing the Article 6 right of the applicant (usually the accused) to a fair trial against the Article 8 privacy rights of the client. However, the court will not necessarily know what view the client takes of the proposed disclosure. Crown Court Rules require the applicant for a witness summons to serve notice of the application on the professional[566] who may make written or oral representations but not on the client.

14.131 If a summons is issued, it may require that the documents are to be produced for inspection by the person applying for the summons in advance of the hearing.[567] There are no means of forcing a third party to disclose documents in advance of proceedings in magistrates' courts.

---

[559] J Epp, 'Production of confidential records held by a third party via witness summons in sexual offence proceedings' (1997) 1 Intl J of Evidence & Proof 122.
[560] The prosecution will rarely find a need to use this procedure. For details of the complicated regime see D Corker, 'Third party disclosure' (1999) 149 NLJ 1006.
[561] *R v Reading Justices, ex p Berkshire CC* [1996] 1 Cr App R 239.
[562] *R v Clowes* (1992) 95 Cr App R 440, 444.
[563] See D Corker, 'The CPIA Disclosure Regime: PII and Third Party Disclosure' (2000) 40 Medicine, Science & the L 116, 124; Home Office, *Research Findings No. 134* (2000). In *R v Westcott* [1983] Crim LR 545 Beldam J said that the Crown Court should refuse a witness summons to compel a GP to produce the medical records of a rape complainant unless substantial grounds are put forward for believing that the records contain material evidence.
[564] A Mackie and J Borrows, *A Study of Requests for Disclosure of Evidence to Third Parties in Contested Trials,* Home Office Research Findings 134 (London: 2000) 2.
[565] See paras 16.59 et seq.
[566] See Crown Court Rules 1982, SI 1982/1109, r 23.
[567] Criminal Procedure (Attendance of Witnesses) Act 1965, s 2A.

Bank accounts

14.132 Section 7 of the Bankers' Evidence Act 1879, s 7 empowers a court[568] to order inspection of the defendant's bank accounts or, in exceptional circumstances, those of someone else[569] once proceedings have been instigated. A professional cannot resist inspection on the grounds that the information is confidential—after all, all bank account information is confidential.

C. Proceedings Abroad[570]

Civil Litigation

14.133 A court or tribunal conducting civil proceedings in a foreign jurisdiction may require evidence from a witness who is in England and who is unable or unwilling to attend a trial abroad or voluntarily to make a deposition. The solution is to issue a letter of request (or 'letter rogatory') to the High Court. Under the terms of the Evidence (Proceedings in Other Jurisdictions) Act 1975[571] the High Court may, by order, arrange for the evidence to be obtained for the foreign court.[572] In effect, part of the foreign trial takes place in the High Court before an examiner or commissioner. The attendance of an unco-operative witness is secured by means of a subpoena.[573]

14.134 By s 3(1) of the 1975 Act a professional subpoenaed to give evidence before an examiner or commissioner cannot be made to give any evidence that she could refuse to give in English civil proceedings.[574] This includes anything that according to English law is privileged[575] or protected by PII.[576] Information that is privileged in civil proceedings under the law of the relevant foreign state is also protected.[577] Thus if the request emanates from the United States, the witness may claim accountant–client privilege, which is unknown in England. The High Court's decision to secure evidence for a foreign court is in any event discretionary.[578]

---

[568] This will usually be a magistrates' court. A judge of the High Court has a jurisdiction concurrent with the magistrates' court.
[569] *R v Grossman* (1981) 73 Cr App R 302.
[570] C Murray and L Harris, *Mutual Assistance in Criminal Matters* (London: 2000) ch 6.
[571] s 2.
[572] An order will be refused if the High Court concludes that the application is 'a fishing expedition', ie 'what is sought is not evidence as such, but information which may lead to a line of enquiry which would disclose evidence': *First American Corp v Clark M Clifford* (DC, 16 December 1997).
[573] Supreme Court Act 1981, s 36(6).
[574] Evidence (Proceedings in Other Jurisdictions) Act 1975, s 3(1)(a).
[575] *R v Rathbone, ex p Dikko* [1985] 2 WLR 375, 390; see para 16.05 below.
[576] See para 16.52 below.
[577] Evidence (Proceedings in Other Jurisdictions) Act 1975, s 3(1)(b).
[578] *Rio Tinto Zinc Corp v Westinghouse Electric Corp* [1978] 1 All ER 434, 455.

C. Proceedings Abroad

If fulfilling the foreign request involves a professional breaching a confidence, the High Court will weigh the public interest in preserving professional confidences against the public interest in assisting the foreign tribunal.[579] There is nothing to stop the High Court adopting measures to limit the injury that may be caused by, for example, confining production of the documents in the first instance to the petitioner's lawyers[580] or receiving the evidence at a hearing from which members of the public are excluded. It was said of earlier legislation[581] that an expert should not, as a rule, be required to give expert evidence against her wishes when she has no connection with the facts or history of the matter in issue, especially where the required evidence could not be given without a breach of confidence.[582] 14.135

US courts have been known to by-pass the letters of rogatory process by issuing subpoenas to the overseas branches of banks with offices in the United States commanding production of banking records.[583] In *XAG v A bank*[584] the High Court issued an interlocutory injunction restraining the English branch of a US bank from complying with a subpoena from a US court to disclose confidential documents relating to an account held in London. 14.136

Criminal Proceedings

Criminal trials

Criminal Justice (International Co-operation) Act 1990, s 4 regulates applications by authorities in foreign states for evidence from witnesses located in England for criminal trials abroad. Requests for compelled witness evidence must be directed to the Secretary of State who must be satisfied that there are reasonable grounds for suspecting that an offence under the law of the requesting state has been committed and that proceedings have been instituted. Having satisfied himself of these matters, the Home Secretary may, if he thinks fit, nominate a court 'to receive such of the evidence to which the request relates as may appear to the court to be appropriate for the purpose of giving effect to the request'.[585] This is usually a magistrates' court but may in a case of complexity be the Crown Court or the High Court. The nominated court can compel the witness to attend the court and/or to produce documents by issuing a witness summons.[586] Proceedings may 14.137

---

[579] *Re State of Norway's Application (No 2)* [1989] 1 All ER 701, 762. In this case the banker's duty of secrecy was the issue. On how a court should handle a request for confidential information by a foreign court see also the judgment of the Jersey Court of Appeal in *Wadman v Dick* [1998] 3 FCR 9.
[580] cp *Zakay v Zakay* [1998] 3 FCR 35.
[581] Foreign Tribunals Evidence Act 1856.
[582] *Seyfang v GD Searle & Co* [1973] 1 QB 148, 152.
[583] G Moscarino and M Shumaker, 'Beating the Shell Game: Bank Secrecy Laws and Their Impact on Civil Recovery in International Fraud Actions' (1997) 18 Comp. L 177, 179.
[584] [1983] 2 All ER 464.
[585] s 4(2).
[586] Criminal Justice (International Co-operation) Act 1990, Sch 1.

be conducted without notice and the court may, in the interests of justice, exclude the public.[587] When the s 4 procedure is applied, the witness must not be compelled to give evidence that she could refuse to give in criminal proceedings in England or in the requesting state.[588] This includes not just evidence that in either jurisdiction is privileged but also evidence that was not likely to be material evidence according to principles of English law.[589]

Criminal investigations

14.138 Criminal Justice (International Co-operation) Act 1990, s 4 allows a foreign state to secure evidence in connection with 'a criminal investigation'. The Secretary of State must be satisfied that an investigation into a particular offence is being carried out in the requesting state and that there are reasonable grounds for suspecting that the offence has been committed.[590] The s 4 procedure is anomalous in that it contains no restrictions on disclosure of 'special procedure material' and 'excluded material' in the possession of the witness. Theoretically, a professional could be compelled to disclose confidential personal information for the benefit of the FBI that she could not be compelled to disclose to English police acting under a search warrant or production order.[591]

---

[587] Magistrates' Courts (Criminal Justice (International Co-Operation)) Rules 1991, SI 1991/1074, r 6; Crown Court (Amendment) Rules 1991, rr 31(2), 32. See also *Eronat v Tabbah* [2002] EWCA Civ 950, para 24; International Court Act 2001, s 30(2).
[588] Criminal Justice (International Co-operation) Act 1990, Sch 1, para 4.
[589] *R v Bow Street Magistrates' Court, ex p King* (DC, 8 October 1997) where the evidence sought was held not to be admissible under English law though it was admissible under American law.
[590] Criminal Justice (International Co-operation) Act 1990, s 4.
[591] See paras 14.21 et seq.

15

TRIALS, TRIBUNALS AND INQUIRIES

A. Civil and Criminal Trials	15.02	B. Tribunals and Public Inquiries	15.41
Documentary Evidence	15.02	Tribunals	15.41
Oral Evidence	15.13	Statutory and Non-Statutory Inquiries	
Lawyer's Duty Not to Mislead the Court	15.31	Ordered by Ministers	15.49
Public Authority Disclosure of Confidential Information to a Court	15.36		

Disclosure of confidential personal client information by a professional may be unavoidable in the legal process. This chapter, a continuation of the previous one, looks at how disclosure is enforced at the trial stage and any discretion that a court may have to disallow disclosure. This is followed by a brief look at disclosure issues in tribunal proceedings and statutory inquiries. **15.01**

A. Civil and Criminal Trials

Documentary Evidence

Securing confidential documents for the trial

Civil proceedings

The presence in court of a document[1] in the possession, custody[2] or control of a professional who refuses to hand it over voluntarily is secured in civil proceedings by means of a witness summons[3] or in family proceedings in the High Court, a **15.02**

---

[1] As to what is a document see *Senior v Holdsworth, ex p Independent Television News Ltd* [1975] 2 All ER 1009. CPR, r 31.4 defines a document as 'anything in which information of any description is recorded'. This would include disks, audio cassettes, video cassettes, computer programs, photographs and plans.

[2] The person on whose behalf the professional has custody is entitled to object to production: *Falmouth v Moss* (1822) 147 ER 530, 533–534.

[3] For non-family civil proceedings see CPR, P 34. For family proceedings in the county courts see County Court Rules 1981, Ord 20, r 12.

subpoena duces tecum.[4] A summons or subpoena is issued at the instigation of a litigant. Normally this is done automatically: the issue of process is regarded as an administrative or ministerial act[5] and is done without notice to the holder of the document.[6]

15.03 Exceptionally, a subpoena will not be issued to produce sensitive personal information in family proceedings as a matter of course.[7] In *Re SL*,[8] a wardship case, a subpoena had been issued to secure the medical records of an adult that turned out not to be needed. Booth J said that the subpoena should not have been allowed.

> Medical records are confidential documents and are prima facie privileged from disclosure. But that privilege is qualified and is subject to any direction by the court that the records are relevant to the issue which the court has to determine, and to that extent they must then be disclosed to the court and to such other persons as the court may direct. Where it is sought to examine the medical records of a party or of a witness on the ground that they are, or may be, relevant to the issue, then their production to the court may be compelled by the writ of *subpoena duces tecum.* Once the documents in question are produced in court directions may then be sought as to their disclosure. The issue of a writ of *subpoena duces tecum* is a serious matter and, in the case of a hearing taking place in chambers, requires the leave of a registrar ... It is ... not a step which should be taken lightly. In my judgment, before leave is sought ... enquiries should be made to ascertain whether the required evidence may be made available by any other means. Further, in respect of documents which are protected by privilege from disclosure, the consent of the person concerned should first be sought for their production and disclosure.[9]

Criminal proceedings

15.04 A professional who possesses documents that contain material evidence who refuses to produce them voluntarily can be confronted by a summons from a magistrates' court issued under Magistrates' Courts Act 1980, s 97. The process by which a professional can be compelled to produce documents for proceedings in the Crown Court[10] was described in the previous chapter.[11] Failure to comply with the summons is a contempt of court with potential penal consequences.[12]

---

[4] Rules of the Supreme Court 1965, Ord 32, r 7; CPR, r 38.14. See also Family Proceedings Rules 1991, SI 1991/1247 which enable a party to require any person to come to court to produce specific documents that are 'necessary' for the fair disposal of the issues or for saving costs. The 1991 Rules were considered in *Roker International Properties Inc v Couvaras* [2001] 2 FLR 976.
[5] *Senior v Holdsworth, ex p Independent Television News Ltd* [1975] 2 All ER 1009, 1013–1014.
[6] *O'Sullivan v Herdmans Ltd* [1987] 3 All ER 129, 132.
[7] There does not seem to be any scope for a similar exception under the CPR. The language of r 34.3 with regard to the issue of a summons to produce a document at trial is mandatory. For a summons to produce a document at any other hearing leave is required.
[8] [1987] 2 FLR 412.
[9] ibid at 413.
[10] Criminal Procedure (Attendance of Witnesses) Act 1965, s 2.
[11] See paras 14.129–14.131 above.
[12] Criminal Procedure (Attendance of Witnesses) Act 1965, s 3.

Setting aside a summons or subpoena[13]

15.05 Irrespective of the court from which the summons or subpoena emanates, production of a document may be averted by a timely application to have it set aside.[14] If the professional does not act, the client may do so.

> It might be of no interest to a person subpoenaed to raise considerations of confidentiality or privacy and in a proper case I would think that the person entitled to the confidentiality or privacy may therefore be permitted to intervene.[15]

15.06 Because the client is entitled to have the summons set aside, it is normally highly desirable that the client should be told, if he can be contacted, about the summons.[16] 'In the ordinary way a customer in good standing could reasonably expect, if only as a matter of courtesy and good business practice, to be told by his bank that a subpoena had been received.'[17] There is no common law or statutory duty on a bank (or, semble, any other professional) to notify the customer of the receipt of a subpoena or summons[18] and the advent of the Human Rights Act 1998 (HRA) is unlikely to have changed this.[19] But if there is, the obligation is not absolute. There may be circumstances where the bank is 'entitled, for its own protection or compelled by public duty, to refrain from informing the customer'.[20] The ECtHR requires the client to be forewarned about a subpoena or summons to the professional to produce sensitive personal information about the client such as his medical records so that the client's views about this can be made known.[21]

---

[13] Anon, 'Application to set aside a witness summons' (2000) 19 Civil Justice Quarterly 1; P Matthews and H Malek, *Disclosure* (London: 2000) paras 8.26–8.31.
[14] A summons issued by a magistrates court can be set aside in judicial review proceedings. For the Crown Court see Criminal Procedure (Attendance of Witnesses) Act 1965, s 2(2); for mainstream civil proceedings see CPR, r 34.3(4). Instead of seeking to have a summons or subpoena set aside, a professional might choose to deliver the documents in person to the court and ask to be excused from producing them except at the direction of the court.
[15] Per Mance J, *London & Leeds Estates Ltd v Paribas Ltd (No 2)* [1995] 1 EGLR 102, 105. See also *Sphere Drake Insurance plc v Denby*, The Times, 20 December 1991.
[16] Australian Law Reform Commission, *Privacy and Personal Information*, DP 14 (Sydney, 1980) 65. cp *Marcel v Commissioner of Police of the Metropolis* [1992] 1 All ER 72, 82.
[17] per Lord Nolan, *Robertson v Canadian Imperial Bank* [1995] 1 All ER 824, 830.
[18] cp *Barclays Bank plc v Taylor* [1989] 3 All ER 563, 569.
[19] Contrast *Valley Bank of Nevada v Superior Court*, 15 Cal 3d 652, 657 (1975) where the opinion was expressed that protection of the customer should not be left to the election of the bank which might have its own axe to grind. The Californian constitutional right of privacy (which, unlike the HRA, binds governmental and non-governmental organizations alike) was held to require the bank to take reasonable steps to notify its customer of the pendency and nature of the proceedings and afford the customer a fair opportunity to assert his interests by objecting to disclosure.
[20] per Lord Nolan, *Robertson v Canadian Imperial Bank* [1995] 1 All ER 824, 830.
[21] This is clear from *Z v Finland* (1998) 25 EHRR 371, para 101.

15.07 If made out, privilege,[22] public interest immunity[23] and a statutory non-disclosure bar will automatically result in the summons or subpoena being quashed. Other valid grounds of objection are insufficient specificity,[24] oppression,[25] lack of necessity[26] and lack of materiality.[27] To be material evidence must be both relevant and admissible.[28] Lord Denning once said that a doctor called as a witness 'cannot be compelled to produce his notes'.[29] This most probably was an allusion to the fact that the notes were at that time inadmissible hearsay.[30]

Significance of information being confidential

15.08 The fact that documents are confidential is not on its own a reason to set aside a summons or a subpoena.[31] It was held in *R v Daye*[32] that a bank served with a subpoena[33] had to hand over to the court a document containing a secret chemical formula which the bank had promised not to deliver up without the consent of the depositors. The confidentiality of the document, however, is not to be completely ignored in deciding whether to enforce production of documents by subpoena.[34] The court, for example, will be at pains to ensure that the document is truly material. In *R v Azmy*[35] the Crown Court set aside a witness summons

---

[22] eg *R v Derby Magistrates' Court, ex p B* [1995] 4 All ER 526. For details of legal professional privilege see ch 16.

[23] eg *Morrow v DPP* (1993) 14 BMLR 54; *R v K* (1993) 97 Cr App R 342. For details of PII see paras 16.52 *et seq*. PII can be abrogated by statute: see *Re A subpoena issued by the Commissioner for Local Administration* [1996] 2 FLR 629 about the effect of Local Government Act 1974, s 29(4).

[24] *Re Howglen Ltd* [2001] 1 All ER 376. cp *R v Naviede* (Central Criminal Court, 9 November 1993) cited by D Kirk and A Woodcock, *Serious fraud: investigation and trial* (2nd edn, London: 1997) 145. An objection can usually be raised if the summons is for an entire file: *Panayiotou v Sony Music Ltd* [1994] Ch 142, 151–155.

[25] *Senior v Holdsworth* [1975] 2 All ER 1009, 1020.

[26] *Steele v Savory* [1891] WN 195.

[27] Criminal Procedure (Attendance of Witnesses) Act 1965, s 2(2); Crown Court Rules 1982, SI 1982/1109, r 23(3)(d); Magistrates' Courts Act 1980, s 97(1). See also, *R v Reading Justices, ex p Berkshire Crown Court* [1996] 1 Cr App R 239. For subpoenas see *Senior v Holdsworth*, [1975] 2 All ER 1009, 1020; *London & Leeds Estates Ltd v Paribas Ltd (No 2)* [1995] 1 EGLR 102.

[28] *R v Clowes* [1992] 3 All ER 440, 446. It may be legitimate to issue a subpoena directed to a third party to obtain documents which are to be used solely to impeach the credit of a witness: *Hunt v Judge Russell* (1995) 63 SASR 402, 410.

[29] *Re D (Infants)* [1970] 1 All ER 1088,1089.

[30] cp *Campbell v Tameside MBC* [1982] 2 All ER 791, 796. Hearsay evidence is no longer inadmissible in civil litigation (Civil Evidence Act 1995) and in criminal proceedings there is a wide statutory exception to the hearsay rule that will render a professional's notes admissible, when relevant, in most circumstances (Criminal Justice Act 1988, s 25).

[31] *A v B* [2000] EMLR 1007, para 10. cp *Senior v Holdsworth* [1975] 2 All ER 1009, 1017.

[32] [1908] 2 KB 333, 339. Cp *Robertson v Canadian Imperial Bank of Commerce* [1995] 1 All ER 824, 830.

[33] Before the CPR came into force a subpoena duces tecum was issued to force a person to produce documents to the court and a subpoena ad testificandum to force the person to give oral evidence.

[34] *Hassneh Insurance Co of Israel v Mew* [1993] 2 Lloyd's Rep 243, 250–251.

[35] (1996) 34 BMLR 45. Had the document been found to be material, the judge indicated at 54 that he would have set the summons aside on grounds of PII.

A. Civil and Criminal Trials

obtained by the defence in a rape case that required the clinical director of an NHS counselling centre to produce the records of counselling sessions with the complainant. The judge inspected the records and found nothing that might positively have advanced the defence case.[36]

15.09 The domestication of Article 8 of the European Convention on Human Rights (ECHR) by the HRA has strengthened the argument for setting aside a subpoena or summons (or, in the case of the Crown Court resisting its issue in the first place)[37] if the documents sought contain confidential personal information. When Article 8 is engaged, the court must balance the deleterious effect to the client's right to privacy against the applicant's Article 6 right to a fair trial. In *Re B*[38] in the context of children's proceedings, Munby J acknowledged that there may be circumsatnces:

> in which balancing a party's prima facie Art 6 right to see all the relevant documents and the rights of others, the balance *can* compatibly with the convention be struck in such a way as to permit the witholding from a party of some a least of the documents. The balance is to be struck in a way which is fair and which achieves a reasonable relationship of proportionality between the means employed and the aim sought to be acieved, having regard to the nature and seriousness of the interests at stake and the gravity of the interference with the various rights involved. . . . Bearing in mind the importance of the rights guaranteed by Art 6, and the fact that . . . Art 8 guarantees only 'respect' for and not inviolability of private and family life, any restriction of a party's right to see the documents in the case must . . . be limited to what the situation imperatively demands.

He added that:

> any difficulties caused to a litigant by a limitation on his right to see all the documents must be sufficiently counterbalanced by procedures designed to ensure . . . that he recieves a fair trial. . . . At the end of the day the court must be satisfied that whatever procedures are adopted and whatever limitations on a litigant's access to documents may be imposed, everyone involved in the proceedings receives a fair trial.

The availability of damage limitation measures[39] such as a hearing in private, restrictions on who can inspect the documents and reporting restrictions must be highly relevant to the balancing exercise.

---

[36] J Tempkins, 'Digging the Dirt: Disclosure of Records in Sexual Assault Cases' [2002] 61 CLJ 126, 129–130 explains why rape counselling records will rarely constitute 'material evidence'.
[37] The courts may be attracted to the two-stage process favoured by the Supreme Court of Canada in *R v O'Connor* [1995] 4 SCR 411 a case in which the issue was whether the defence should have access to the counselling records of the complainant in a sexual offence trial. Under the approach adopted, when asked for a subpoena for the production of third party records, a judge must concentrate on the likely relevance of the documentation and defer rights issues until the records are produced to the court.
[38] [2002] 2 FCR 32, para 67. *Re B* was approved by the Court of Appeal in *Re B* [2002] All ER (D) 167.
[39] See ch. 17.

The handling of confidential documents

15.10 Documents should be produced to the court, not to the party who applied for the summons or subpoena.[40] In civil proceedings it is common for the court to set a date for the production of the documents ahead of trial to give the party seeking the documents time to study them.[41]

15.11 When documents are produced into the custody of a court in response to a summons or a subpoena the court has a discretion to control their use. The following advice was given by an Australian judge in a case in which highly sensitive medical records of a party to an employment dispute were produced by a hospital to the court in response to a subpoena:

> [S]trong reasons may exist for allowing the party to whom the medical reports relate to inspect them ahead of any other party to the proceedings to ascertain what private or confidential information is contained in them. If this course is objected to, it may be necessary for the judge to consider the documents, and to form a view as to what restrictions, if any, should be placed upon the inspection of the documents, at least in the first instance. If there is private information within them that is likely to be regarded as confidential by the person to whom the records relate, and yet, at the same time, the information appears to have relevance to the issues before the Court, it is within the power of the judge to order that the documents in the first instance be examined only by counsel. In the event that counsel forms the view that it is in the interests of his or her client to use the documents, or information disclosed in them, in the course of the litigation, further application can be made to the judge for an order permitting that use. If necessary, permission can be granted subject to an order restricting the publication of the material. Similarly, if counsel considers that it is necessary to disclose the subpoenaed material in whole or in part to the client to obtain instructions, application can be made to the judge for an order permitting that to occur, subject if necessary to undertakings or other conditions designed to protect private or confidential information from publication beyond that which is strictly necessary in the attainment of justice.[42]

Unlawfully or unfairly obtained documents

15.12 The fact that papers or kindred items[43] containing confidential client information have been obtained by unlawful or unfair means[44] does not render them inadmissible in civil or criminal proceedings[45] unless legislation provides otherwise.[46] In civil proceedings governed by the Civil Procedure Rules (CPR) the evidence can be excluded under r 32.1 or if the manner of obtaining affects the interests of the

---

[40] *R v Wescott* [1983] Crim LR 545. See also *Re SL* [1987] 2 FLR 412, 414.
[41] *Khanna v Lovell White Durrant* [1994] 4 All ER 267; CPR, r 34.2(4). [42] per Von Doussa J, *Welfare v Birdon Sands Pty Ltd* (Aust Fed Ct, 1997) 900.
[43] The rule is the same whether the information is contained in documents, tape-recordings or video-recordings.
[44] cp *R v Khan* [1996] 3 All ER 289; *BOC Ltd v Barlow* [2001] All ER (D) 53.
[45] *Kuruma v R* [1955] 1 All ER 236; *Re DH* [1994] FLR 679.
[46] eg Disability Discrimination Act 1995, s 31B (7). See also para 14.99 above.

proper administration of justice, for example if the evidence was obtained in consequence of a contempt of court.[47] If the confidential client information is tendered by the prosecution in criminal proceedings, the defence can ask the judge to exclude the evidence under the discretion conferred in Police and Criminal Evidence Act 1984 (PACE), s 78. When the judge exercises this discretion the object will be to ensure that the trial is fair to both sides.[48] There has been no English pronouncement as to whether the judge may have regard to the privacy interests of third parties. The ECtHR would allow this so long as exclusion did not compromise the defendant's Article 6 right to a fair trial.[49]

Oral Evidence

Obligation to disclose confidential personal information

The attendance of a professional to give oral evidence before a court[50] is secured either by means of a witness summons or a subpoena ad testificandum. To ignore either is a contempt of court and may lead to arrest.[51] Once called upon to testify, the professional can be made to disclose confidential information about a client without the client's consent.[52]

15.13

> For example, in the case of banker and customer, the duty of confidence is subject to the overriding duty of the banker at common law to disclose and answer questions as to his customer's affairs when he is asked to give evidence on them in the witness box in a court of law . . . similar provisions as to disclosure apply to doctors.[53]

In *Nuttall v Nuttall*[54] a psychiatrist subpoenaed in divorce proceedings by the husband of a patient was asked what she had said during treatment. The psychiatrist protested about having to answer on the grounds of professional confidentiality. His objection was overruled by the Divorce Commissioner.[55]

---

[47] *ITC Film Distributors v Video Exchange Ltd* [1982] 2 All ER 241, 246; *Re DH* [1994] FLR 679.
[48] *Vel v Owen* [1987] Crim LR 496; *R v P* [2001] 2 WLR 463; *Att-Gen's Reference (No 3 of 1999)* [2001] 2 WLR 56.
[49] See para 3.23 above.
[50] The Coroners Act 1988 contains a special provision (s 21) for the summoning of medical witnesses to an inquest into a death to give evidence about the cause of death. See also *R v Southwark Coroner, ex p Hicks* [1987] 1 WLR 1642.
[51] Criminal Procedure (Attendance of Witnesses) Act 1965, ss 3, 4. A witness who fails to attend a coroner's inquest when summoned is punishable by a fine under Coroners Act 1988, s 10(2) or in the case of a medical witness, under s 21(5).
[52] It was established in the historic *Kingston (Duchess) case* (1776) 20 State Tr 335, 537 that a doctor is bound by the law to disclose communications between himself and his patient to a court.
[53] per Diplock LJ, *Parry-Jones v Law Society* [1968] 1 All ER 177, 180. See also, *R (on the application of Stevens) v Plymouth City Council* [2002] EWCA Civ 388; [2002] 1 FLR 1177, para 17.
[54] (1964) 108 SJ 605. cp *Hession v Health Commissioner for Wales* [2001] EWHC Admin 619.
[55] The Law Reform Committee's assertion in its Sixteenth Report, *Privilege in Civil Proceedings* (Cmnd 8472, 1967) para 51 that had the psychiatrist persisted in refusing to give evidence, the commissioner's direction would have probably been reversed by the Court of Appeal by relying on the discretion the comissioner had not to compel an answer (see text below), was criticized by Lord Edmund Davies in *D v NSPCC* [1997] 1 All ER 589, 618–620.

15.14 Just as it is a contempt for the professional to ignore a summons, it is a contempt to refuse to give evidence.[56] A Californian psychiatrist was imprisoned in 1977 for refusing to testify about a patient.[57] The only lawful grounds on which a professional can remain silent are privilege,[58] public interest immunity[59] or a statutory provision disallowing her evidence in a court of law. Should the professional take original notes into the witness box and use those to refresh her memory, opposing counsel is entitled to see these. Under some circumstances the notes may become an exhibit.[60]

Judicial discretion

Attitude of the courts

15.15 The courts are sympathetic toward professionals faced with the choice of betraying the confidences of a client or being held in contempt of court.[61]

> Courts have an inherent wish to respect [the] confidence, whether it arises between doctor and patient, priest and penitent, banker and customer, between persons giving testimonials to employees, or in other relationships.[62]

If a professional insists that she cannot breach a confidence to answer a question by counsel the judge may suggest to counsel not to press the matter[63] and to avoid antagonizing the judge counsel may not do so.

15.16 In *Att-Gen v Mulholland* the Court of Appeal mooted that the judge could go further. Donovan LJ said that courts would respect the professional's pledge of secrecy to the extent that the professional will not be directed to answer a question that would serve 'no useful purpose'.[64] In the same vein Lord Denning said:

> Take the clergyman, the banker or the medical man. None of these is entitled to refuse to answer when directed to by a judge. Let me not be mistaken. The judge will respect the confidences which each member of these honourable professions receives in the course of it, and will not direct him to answer unless *not only it is rele-*

---

[56] *Nuttall v Nutall* (1964) 108 SJ 605. See also *Att-Gen v Lundin* (1982) 75 Cr App R 90.
[57] P Jenkins, *Counselling, Psychotherapy and the Law* (London: 1997) 169.
[58] See ch 16.
[59] See paras 16.52 et seq.
[60] *Senat v Senat* [1965] P 172; *R v Britton* [1987] 2 All ER 412.
[61] 'If the courts . . . *restrain* a breach of confidence', Lord Denning once commented, 'surely they should not themselves *compel* a breach save when the public interest requires': *D v NSPCC* [1976] 2 All ER 993, 999.
[62] per Lord Wilberforce, *BSC v Granada Television Ltd* [1981] 1 All ER 417, 455. See also *Francome v MGN Ltd* [1984] 2 All ER 408, 412–413.
[63] *Cronkwright v Cronkwright* (1970) 14 DLR (3d) 168.
[64] [1963] 1 All ER 767, 772–773. In *Broad v Pitt* (1828) 3 C & P 518, 519 Best CJ stated that he would *never* compel a clergyman to disclose a communication made to him by a prisoner and in *R v Griffen* (1853) 6 Cox CC 219 the court exercised its discretion not to force a chaplain to disclose the content of a conversation with a man accused of murder.

vant but also it is a proper and, indeed, *necessary* question in the course of justice to be put and answered.[65]

The incorporation of Article 8 into English law will have heightened the concern of the judges not to invade professional confidences unnecessarily.

Civil proceedings

15.17 In its Sixteenth Report the Law Reform Committee attributed the judicial discretion not to compel an answer to the judge's general discretion in the conduct of a trial.[66] But at common law judges do not have a general discretion to exclude relevant, admissible evidence from civil proceedings.[67] A more likely explanation is that the judge exercises a discretion to waive punishment.[68] The issue has been laid to rest by CPR, r 32.1 which confers a general discretion to exclude admissible evidence in civil proceedings. This discretion must be exercised in accordance with the 'overriding objective' of the 1998 Rules.[69] It must also be exercised in a manner that is compatible with the Article 6(1) right to a fair hearing which is absolute.[70]

Criminal proceedings

15.18 In criminal proceedings both PACE, s 78 and the common law[71] confer a discretion on the court to exclude or limit the evidence of a prosecution witness. The courts have not had occasion to consider whether s 78 can be used to disallow a relevant question that, if answered, would breach an obligation of confidentiality.[72] If Parliament had had privacy interests in mind, one would have expected judges to have a statutory discretion to exclude evidence tendered by the defence, which is not the case.[73] On the other hand, HRA, s 3(1) directs courts to interpret

---

[65] [1963] 1 All ER 767, 771. The italicized words emphasize that the discretion enables the court to disallow relevant questions. See also *Hunter v Mann* [1974] 2 All ER 414, 418, 420; *D v NSPCC* [1978] AC 171, 227, 245 but cp 239; *BSC v Granada Television* [1981] 1 All ER 417, 455, 457; *Wadman v Dick* [1998] 3 FCR 9, 30. Donovan LJ's 'usefulness' test has proved more popular with the English judiciary than Lord Denning's more stringent 'necessity' test: *Senior v Holdsworth, ex p Independent Television News Ltd* [1975] 2 All ER 1009, 1017, 1022 (a document production case); *Garvin v Domus Publishing Ltd* [1989] 2 All ER 344, 352. The two tests are conflated in *Att-Gen v Lundin* (1982) 75 Cr App R 90, 99. Usefulness is to be assessed in the light of all the evidence available.
[66] *Privilege in Civil Proceedings* (Cmnd 3472, 1967) para 46. This was with specific reference to a priest, but it is clear from other parts of the report that the discretion applies more generally, see paras 41, 51.
[67] *Arab Monetary Fund v Hashim (No 2)* [1990] 1 All ER 673, 681.
[68] This was how the matter was handled by the judge in a case reported in The Lancet in 1965: A. Hayman 'Psychoanalyst Subpoenaed', 16 October 1965, p 785.
[69] CPR, r 1(1). Relevant factors include fairness, equality between parties, saving costs, proportionality, fair division of the court's resources and expedition.
[70] See para 3.23 above. See also *Jones v University of Warwick* [2003] EWCA Civ 151.
[71] *Att-Gen v Lundin* (1982) 75 Cr App R 90.
[72] But see *D v NSPCC* [1976] 2 All ER 993, 1000.
[73] *R v Myers* [1997] 4 All ER 314, 332–333.

legislation in a pro-Convention fashion and ought to persuade the Court of Appeal to allow trial judges to take a breach of Article 8 into account when exercising s 78. Even if the judges do this, they are unlikely to exclude relevant evidence simply because admitting it interferes with someone's privacy. Exclusion of relevant evidence interferes with the Article 6(1) right of both prosecution and defence to a fair trial. In the event of a conflict between a client's Article 8 privacy right and the right of one or more parties to an action to a fair trial it is likely that the right to a fair trial will prevail if the evidence has real probative value and the court can exclude the public whilst the witness gives the sensitive evidence.[74]

15.19 It was held in *Z v Finland*[75] that Article 8 was not violated when doctors were ordered to give evidence in camera about the HIV status of a patient whose husband was tried on several counts of sexual assault and attempted manslaughter. The ECtHR also upheld the compelled disclosure of Z's medical records to the court. Both the oral evidence and the records were relevant to the issue of whether the husband had known that he was HIV positive when he committed serious sexual offences.

Procedure

15.20 A professional who receives a witness summons is entitled to apply to have the summons set aside on the grounds that she has no 'useful' or admissible evidence to contribute.[76] If unsuccessful she must respond to the summons but after taking the oath the professional should consider telling the court that she will disclose no confidential client information until formally directed to do so by the court.[77] There are two reasons why this is desirable. First, it is better for future professional/client relations that the professional makes the disclosure in response to a court direction and secondly, it gives the court an opportunity to exercise any discretion it may have.[78] Commenting on the reluctance of an Anglican clergyman to disclose in divorce proceedings what the husband had said when the clergyman had attempted to effect a reconciliation between the couple, Wright J said:

---

[74] cp *Rockefeller & Co Inc v Secretary for Justice* (2000) 384 HKCU 1, 14.
[75] (1988) 25 EHRR 371.
[76] As regards civil proceedings see: *Senior v Holdsworth* [1975] 2 All ER 1009, 1015, 1017, 1021. As regards third party summons for Crown Court criminal proceedings see Criminal Procedure (Attendance of Witnesses) Act 1965, s 2C. The court must be satisfied 'that he cannot give any evidence, or produce any document or thing, likely to be material evidence'.
[77] 'If asked by a court to disclose information in breach of confidentiality, the doctor should explain why such disclosure should not be made . . .', BMA, *Medical Ethics Today* (London: 1993) 58. This was formerly also the advice of the GMC: ' If you are required to produce patients' notes or records under a court order you should disclose only so much as is relevant to the proceedings. You should object to the judge . . . if attempts are made to compel you to disclose other matters which appear in the notes . . .' (*Confidentiality* (1995) para 20). This advice does not appear in the current GMC guidance. cp *A Health Authority v X* [2001] Lloyd's Rep Med 349.
[78] Against this it can be argued that a professional can volunteer information to the police on public interest grounds, see *R v Singleton* [1995] 1 Cr App R 431, so why not to a court?

A. Civil and Criminal Trials

[T]he position that Canon Grigg has taken is a very proper one. He raised the point and asked for a ruling. It is my personal opinion that it is the position that ought to be taken by all persons who, by their profession or in the work in which they are engaged find themselves in a position of confidence. I think that professional people and people enjoying confidence of this kind, by reason of their office or special work, have a duty to endeavour to preserve that confidence as much and as far as it is open to them.[79]

Might failure to raise the matter of confidentiality constitute professional negligence if there is resulting loss? Or can the professional rely on the absolute immunity which a witness giving evidence in court enjoys? These points were left open by the Privy Council in *Robertson v Canadian Imperial Bank of Commerce*.[80] The bank, in response to a subpoena, had disclosed the claimant's bank statements for a particular month. Only an entry showing the receipt of $15,000 was relevant but there was no evidence that the unnecessarily wide disclosure (which had revealed that the claimant was overdrawn) had caused the claimant any injury beyond mental distress.[81] 15.21

Consequences of disclosure

No action lies against a professional who discloses a document in response to a summons or subpoena[82] and there is absolute immunity from civil suit in respect of evidence given in a court.[83] A contract in which the professional binds himself not to give evidence before a court is contrary to public policy and is therefore unenforceable.[84] Retaliating against a professional for providing the information to a court is a contempt of court.[85] Preventing retaliation in a foreign jurisdiction is problematical. 15.22

Bankers, accountants and lawyers who service clients abroad may find themselves directed to answer questions about work carried out outside the United Kingdom in the course of which confidential information was entrusted to them. In *Brannigan v Davison*[86] the claimants were New Zealand accountants who had done work in the Cook Islands and who retained connections with the Cook Islands that required them to visit there. The defendant was the commissioner in 15.23

---

[79] (1970) 14 DLR (3d) 168, 170. cp *R v Statutory Visitors to St Lawrence's Hospital Caterham, ex p Pritchard* [1953] 2 All ER 766, 772.
[80] [1995] 1 All ER 825, 831.
[81] After the statement was produced to the court an unknown person had telephoned the claimant and spoken of various of the transactions and the claimant's overdraft.
[82] cp *Barclays Bank v Taylor* [1989] 3 All ER 563.
[83] *Watson v McEwan* [1905] AC 480, 486; *Mahon v Rahn* [1997] 3 All ER 687, 709. Apart from immunity to an action for breach of confidence there is immunity from an action in defamation even if the evidence was given maliciously.
[84] *Harmony Shipping Co v Davis* [1979] 3 All ER 171, 182.
[85] *Chapman v Honig* [1963] 2 All ER 513.
[86] [1996] 3 WLR 859. See further R Pattenden, 'Self-incrimination and the threat of prosecution under foreign law: *Brannigan v Davison*' (1998) 2 Intl J of Evidence & Proof, 44.

charge of an inquiry into evasion of New Zealand income tax by means of the Cook Islands tax haven. He had directed the claimants to give oral evidence to the inquiry in spite of the fact that it was a criminal offence under Cook Islands law to do so. The Privy Council decided that a witness who feared foreign prosecution is not entitled to the privilege against self-incrimination as of right, but that the court has a discretion arising from 'its inherent power to conduct its process in a fair and reasonable manner'[87] to excuse a witness at risk of criminal prosecution in another state from answering questions. No guidance was offered as to when this discretion to excuse an answer should be exercised[88] or whether the discretion can be invoked by either the prosecution or the defence in criminal proceedings.

Expert witnesses

Confidentiality of expert reports

15.24 Professionals, particularly members of the medical profession, are regularly consulted by lawyers for their expert opinions about matters relevant to anticipated litigation. If an expert's opinion is not relied upon in the ensuing litigation by the party who retained her, her instructions[89] and, with two exceptions, her report[90] are protected by litigation privilege:[91]

> an expert witness's report prepared for a party to the litigation for the purposes of that litigation as a proof of evidence for the trial of an action, is a privileged document, the privilege being that of the litigation [sic] and not of the expert.[92]

The two exceptions to the rule that unused expert reports are privileged are expert reports obtained in children's cases[93] and for the prosecution during a criminal investigation.[94]

Calling an opponent's expert to give oral evidence

15.25 **No property in a witness** Privilege attaches to reports and other communications between the expert and the lawyer or client rendering them inadmissible; privilege does not attach to the expert witness.

---

[87] [1996] 3 WLR 859, 868.
[88] Factors that a court might consider include: the nature of the English proceedings, whether the witness is also a party, the importance of the evidence that the witness does not wish to give, whether exercising the discretion will deprive the court of all evidence from the witness (as in *Brannigan*), the nature of the crime under foreign law and the punishment which the witness might receive on conviction, the likelihood of the foreign state obtaining custody of the witness (or that it will bring proceedings in absentia) and the risk of the witness being prosecuted, should the witness voluntarily visit the foreign jurisdiction.
[89] *R v King* [1983] 1 All ER 929, 931.
[90] *Clough v Tameside & Glossop Health Authority* [1998] 2 All ER 971, 974.
[91] See para 16.20 below.
[92] per Dillon LJ, *Derby & Co Ltd v Weldon (No 9)*, The Times, 9 November 1990.
[93] See para 16.39 below.
[94] *R v Ward* [1993] 2 All ER 577, 618–629, 642–643.

A. Civil and Criminal Trials

[A] third party, who provided a report to the client, can be subpoenaed to give evidence by the opposing side.[95]

In criminal proceedings, however, account must be taken of Article 6 which requires the court to protect the right of an accused to a fair trial. Further, Article 6(3)(b) and (c) of the Convention may guarantee the confidentiality of communications with the expert adviser instructed by the defence. In *Wilson v HM Advocate*[96] the Scottish High Court, on appeal, held that although the defence does not, by instructing an expert witness, acquire an absolute veto over the use of the witness by the Crown, where the Crown proposes to call an expert previously instructed by the defence a balance must be struck between the interests of justice in the particular case and protection of the proper interests of the accused. Lord Coulsfield said that the court should consider:

(1) whether the Crown had good reason to require the expert's evidence;
(2) whether this evidence could be made available without any risk of information confidential to the defence being disclosed; and
(3) whether use of the witness would prejudice the defence by imposing additional burdens on the accused's advisers.[97]

Supporting the expert's oral evidence If the prosecution intends to rely upon an expert previously engaged by the defence[98] for an opinion, the prosecution must lay a foundation for that opinion in admissible evidence.[99] The prosecution has a problem if the expert's opinion is founded substantially or wholly on privileged material if privilege has not been waived. 15.26

In *R v R*[100] a scientist had carried out DNA tests at the request of defence solicitors on a blood sample provided by the accused to his general practitioner for that purpose and made available to the expert by the defence solicitors. This analysis had not proved helpful to the accused. At the trial the expert was called by the prosecution. It was held on appeal that her opinion had not been properly admitted. For the prosecution to have called an expert previously consulted by the accused's solicitors was not, of itself, wrong since there is no property in a witness.[101] The evidence which an expert witness can give is, however, 'limited by the normal rules 15.27

---

[95] per Bracewell J, *Clough v Tameside & Glossop Health Authority* [1998] 2 All ER 971, 974. See also, *Harmony Shipping Co v Davis* [1979] 3 All ER 171, 181 *Sender v Commonwealth* [2002] NSWSC 1109 (doctor instructed by B to examine and report on A called by A). Disclosure of the opinion outside the courtroom is likely to constitute a breach of contract.
[96] 2001 SCCR 633.
[97] ibid, paras 8, 11.
[98] eg *R v King* [1983] 1 All ER 929.
[99] *R v Abadom* [1983] 1 All ER 364, 368; *BCCI v Ali* [1999] IRLR 508, 520, para 108. See also R Pattenden, 'Expert Opinion Evidence Based on Hearsay' [1982] Crim LR 85.
[100] [1994] 4 All ER 260.
[101] See para 15.25 above.

of legal professional privilege'.[102] In this case the expert's evidence was founded in its entirety on the analysis of a blood sample. The Court of Appeal held that this sample qualified as 'items subject to legal privilege' within the meaning of PACE, s 10 because it was brought into existence 'in connection with or in contemplation of legal proceedings and for the purposes of such proceedings'.[103] This statutory provision, although enacted in the context of police powers of search and seizure, was said to set out the law in any situation in which 'the issue is whether the defendant can object to [an "item"] . . . being produced in evidence, or to oral evidence of opinion based upon it'.[104]

15.28 Evans LJ indicated in *R v R* that the outcome would have been different had the expert's opinion been based 'on examination and testing of a sample obtained in non-privileged circumstances[105] *or of the defendant himself*'.[106] The italicized words are a reference to a comment by Scott J sitting as judge of first instance in *W v Egdell*.[107]

15.29 Australian and Canadian courts have long treated the oral history provided by the accused to an expert retained by the defence as covered by the umbrella of litigation privilege and therefore inadmissible at the instance of the prosecution. Any opinion based on that evidence is similarly inadmissible.[108] Proulx JA said in *R v Perron*:

> When counsel requires the services of an expert in order to help him better prepare his defence, he acts within the scope of his mandate. It is the interest of his client which compels counsel to confer on a specialist the charge of evaluating the case and it follows that the accused must be able to undergo the evaluation in the same climate of confidence and in complete confidentiality as if he were communicating with his counsel. . . . The absence of counsel at the time of the performance of the evaluation does not have the effect of placing that meeting outside the relationship of confidence between a solicitor and his client.[109]

Without considering any of this case law, the Court of Appeal in *R v Davies*[110] reached the same conclusion. Davies' conviction was quashed because a psychiatrist instructed by the defence solicitor to examine the accused in prison and report was subsequently called to give evidence on behalf of the prosecution; the prosecution had correctly surmised that she did endorse his defence of diminished responsibility. The Court of Appeal held that:

> [her] opinion was based, at least to a material extent, on privileged communications. She received documents from the solicitors, some of which were privileged. She may

---

[102] *R v R* [1994] 4 All ER 260, 262.
[103] s 10(1)(c)(ii).
[104] [1994] 4 All ER 260, 265 per Evans LJ.
[105] Evans LJ had in mind a sample provided to the police under PACE, s 62.
[106] *R v R* [1994] 4 All ER 260, 264 (italics added).
[107] [1989] 1 All ER 1089, 1107.
[108] *R v Ward* (1981) 3 A Crim R 171, 179, 191; *Smith v Jones* [1999] 1 SCR 455, 463. See also, *Ex p Ochse* 238 P 2d 561 (1951); *R v Stone* (1997) 13 CCC (3d) 158, 173.
[109] *R v Perron* (1990) 54 CCC (3d) 108, 113.
[110] [2002] EWCA Crim 85.

A. Civil and Criminal Trials

have observed facts about the appellant which did not depend on him consciously communicating with her. But the occasion of her visit was privileged and his communications to her on that occasion were privileged. In her evidence, she was obliged to report things which he had said to her. Thus her opinion then was based on privileged material. In so far as it may also have been in part based on mere observation, the opinion was nevertheless inextricably dependent on privileged material.[111]

To permit disclosure of what passes between an expert and a party undermines the whole rationale of litigation privilege—to allow a party to prepare his case in safety.[112] And it does so in both civil and criminal proceedings when the expert's opinion is founded on a privileged communication.[113] It follows that Scott J's dicta in *W v Egdell* should be ignored in civil proceedings. Two reasons may be suggested why Scott J went wrong. First, he started from the premise that an expert's opinion is always admissible if it satisfies the rules for the admissibility of opinion evidence. This is not true: it is inadmissible if founded on material that 'is based on material which is privileged and which is provided to the expert in privileged circumstances'[113a] unless privilege has been waived.[114] Secondly, he may have been led astray by the consideration that, on public interest grounds, the expert, on the facts of the case, was entitled to disclose his report to the Home Secretary.[115] 15.30

Lawyer's Duty not to Mislead the Court[116]
Knowingly leading false evidence

All solicitors and barristers are officers of the court and because of this are subject to its supervisory jurisdiction. One duty this imposes is not to deceive or positively mislead the court about fact or law.[117] A lawyer takes part in deception of a court if she gives the court[118] information that she knows to be false with the intention of misleading the court or she knowingly allows her client to do so.[119] 15.31

---

[111] *R v Davies* [2002] EWCA Crim 85, para 32.
[112] See para 16.21 below. See also R Pattenden, 'Litigation privilege and expert opinion evidence' (2000) 4 Intl J of Evidence & Proof 213.
[113] What party A says to X, B's expert, is not privileged and therefore A can generally call X to give an opinion founded on what A said: *Sender v Commonwealth* [2002] NSWSC 1109.
[113a] per May LJ, *R v Davies* [2002] EWCA Crim 85, para 28.
[114] A passing reference to the expert's opinion in the report of another expert that is relied upon does not necessarily amount to waiver: *R v Davies* [2002] EWCA Crim 85, paras 37–38.
[115] See para 11.21 above.
[116] M Proulx and D Layton, *Ethics and Canadian Criminal Law* (Toronto: 2001) 265–280.
[117] Law Society, *The Guide to the Professional Conduct of Solicitors* (8th edn, London: 1999) 325, 16.02, para 5 and 374, 21.01. See also *Saif Ali v Sydney Mitchell & Co* [1978] 3 All ER 1033,1042–1043; *Medcalf v Weatherill* [2002] UKHL 27; [2002] 3 WLR 172, para 54; *Skjevesland v Geveran Trading Co Ltd* [2002] EWCA Civ 1567, para 37.
[118] eg confirms an inaccurate list of a client's past convictions as correct knowing that the list is inaccurate.
[119] In a civil action and when defending a criminal accused a lawyer need not correct false information given to the court by another party that is favourable to her client: *Saif Ali v Sydney Mitchell & Co* [1978] 3 All ER 1033, 1042.

15.32 In 1998 a solicitor represented a client in a magistrates' court who, to the solicitor's knowledge, put forward a false identity. The solicitor was subsequently tried and convicted on a charge of acting in a manner tending and intending to pervert the course of public justice and fined £2,000 by the Solicitors Disciplinary Tribunal.[120] After this case the criminal law committee of the Law Society issued the following advice to practitioners representing defendants in criminal trials:[121] try to persuade a client who seeks to give a false name address or date of birth to change his mind; if this fails, cease to act for the client. The Bar's code posits withdrawal 'if the client refuses to authorise [her counsel] to make some disclosure to the court which [her] duty to the court requires [her] to make'.[122] The Law Society has not recommended that a practitioner take it upon herself to inform the court of a client's intention to lie,[123] or, in the case of a legally-aided client, that the court be told why the practitioner is unable to continue to represent the client.[124] Such a disclosure is seen as a breach of confidentiality.[125]

Unwittingly leading false evidence

15.33 The Law Society has not considered what a solicitor should do if, after information essential to her client's case has been communicated to a court, the solicitor discovers that the information was false when given. In *Vernon v Bosley (No 2)*[126] the Court of Appeal decided unanimously that where there was a danger of the court being misled it was the duty of counsel to advise the client to disclose the true position.[127] Thorpe LJ[128] said that if the client demurred, counsel was under a duty, in civil litigation at least, to disclose the relevant material to the judge,[129] unless her opposite number agreed that this was unnecessary. If the client knew all along that the information conveyed to the court was false it could be argued that the client has deceived the lawyer and thereby forfeited the right to confidentiality.[130]

---

[120] [1988] 85(41) LS Gaz 53.
[121] See 'John Francis Bridgwood and solicitors' duty to client and court' [1988] 86(26) LS Gaz 11.
[122] General Council of the Bar, *Code of Conduct of the Bar of England and Wales* (London: 1998) r 506(e). See also, 'Letter to Heads of Chambers—Duty to Disclose Previous Convictions', 7 November 2001, available from http://www.barcouncil.org.uk.
[123] As is required in the US: *Nix v Whiteside* 475 US 157 (1986).
[124] When a client is legally-aided a solicitor who ceases to act for the client must apply to the court to be released from the legal aid order.
[125] For this reason a solicitor should decline to comment on the accuracy of a list of previous convictions presented for confirmation by a magistrates' clerk unless the client consents.
[126] *Vernon v Bosley (No 2)* [1997] 1 All ER 614, 629, 643, 652.
[127] Evans LJ dissented on the application of the rule to the particular facts of the case.
[128] [1997] 1 All ER 614, 654. See also Evans LJ, ibid at 644.
[129] cp US *Model Rules Professional Conduct* (1998) r 3.3(b). Contrast Stuart-Smith LJ [1997] 1 All ER 614, 631 who thought that if a barrister advised disclosure and the client did not act on that advice the barrister should withdraw from the case.
[130] This gets round the objection in *A v A* [2000] 1 FLR 701, 734–735 that disclosure interferes with professional privilege which is absolute.

A. Civil and Criminal Trials

Disclosure in these circumstances will encourage rather than discourage initial client candour.[131]

The client's criminal record

What is a lawyer to do if she realizes that a client who is about to be sentenced has a more serious criminal record than the prosecution and the court are aware of when no deception has been practiced on the court by the client? The dilemma for the lawyer is particularly acute if there is a stipulated minimum sentence for someone with the client's previous convictions. The judges collectively considered this issue and resolved that it was the lawyer's duty to expose the facts to the court in the interests of justice.[132] The Bar disagreed. The matter was resolved in the Bar's favour. The Professional Standards Committee has ruled that counsel is under no duty to reveal the client's criminal record to the prosecution or to the court; and there is no duty to withdraw if the client refuses to allow counsel to do so.[133] If the client insists on silence, counsel will be restricted in what she can say in mitigation. She must not, for example, suggest of a client whose previous convictions have been overlooked by the prosecutor, that he is of good character.[134] There is a good chance that an experienced prosecution counsel or judge will become suspicious if counsel fails to mention the client's antecedents. If this happens it could lead to an adjournment, to the matter being relisted for alteration of sentence or an Attorney-General's reference of the sentence to the Court of Appeal.[135] 15.34

The security of the court and its members

A US court has held that attorneys have a duty, founded on the attorney's role as an officer of the court, to warn of threats by clients against judges[136] and the Model Rules of Professional Conduct confirm this.[137] There is no Commonwealth authority on this point.[138] 15.35

Public Authority Disclosure of Confidential Information to a Court
General position

In chapter 10 it was explained that no public authority or official may disclose confidential information received from a professional for a purpose other than the 15.36

---

[131] N. Moore, 'Limits to Attorney–Client Confidentiality: A "Philosophically Informed" and Comparative Approach to Legal and Medical Ethics' (1985–86) 36 Case Western Reserve LR 177, 233.
[132] M.Berlins, Guardian, 31 October 2001, 17.
[133] 'Letter to Heads of Chambers—Duty to Disclose Previous Convictions', 7 November 2001, available from http://www.barcouncil.org.uk.
[134] *Tombling v Universal Bulb Co Ltd* [1951] 2 TLR 289, 297.
[135] Criminal Justice Act 1998, s 36.
[136] *State v Hansen* 862 P 2d 117 (1993).
[137] *Model Rules Professional Conduct* (1998) r 3.3(b).
[138] The HRA might provide a springboard for arguing for a duty to warn of threats to a judge: see para 20.05 below.

one for which it was obtained, whether or not this is stipulated in the legislation under which the public authority or official acquired the information.[139] Sometimes use of the information in litigation is one of the purposes for which the information was collected in the first place but just as often it is not—or the information was not intended for the particular litigation in which there is a desire now to use it.

15.37 In *Marcel v Commissioner of Police of the Metropolis*[140] the Court of Appeal decided that a document seized by the police may be made available for use in civil proceedings by a private litigant without the consent of the document owner in response to a subpoena.[141] This is because the true owner of the documents, if in possession of the documents, would have had to comply with the subpoena. To allow the owner of the documents to challenge the subpoena that person should be given notice that a subpoena has been served.[142] Any other public body that comes by confidential information through the use of its compulsory powers is similarly amenable to produce the information on subpoena or summons. Documents obtained by compulsion should not be voluntarily made available to private individuals for their private purposes.

Insolvency

15.38 In *Morris v Serious Fraud Office* a liquidator applied under Insolvency Act 1986, s 236 for an order that the Serious Fraud Office make available documents, some of which had been obtained from a firm of chartered accountants by the Serious Fraud Office under its compulsory powers and the rest seized by the police under search warrants. Nicholls V-C said that a s 236 order was discretionary and that in exercising the discretion the court must weigh up the advantages and disadvantages of making the order, including prejudice to the true owners.[143] The owners, together with the person from whom they were obtained under compulsion (if different), should normally be notified of the application.

15.39 The Insolvency Rules 1986 specify that information given to the court by a person examined in connection with the winding up of a company[144] is not to be put on the court file and the record of the examination is not to be open for inspection by anyone besides the liquidator and the Official Receiver unless the court orders otherwise.[145] Lord Browne-Wilkinson said of this rule in *Re Arrows Ltd (No 4)*:[146]

> The extraction of private and confidential information under compulsion from a witness otherwise than in the course of *inter partes* litigation is an exorbitant power. It is

---

[139] See para 10.35 above.
[140] [1991] 1 All ER 845.
[141] [1992] 1 All ER 72, 82, 84.
[142] *Marcel v Commissioner of Police of the Metropolis* [1992] 1 All ER 72, 82.
[143] [1993] 1 All ER 788, 796.
[144] Insolvency Act 1986, s 236.
[145] r 9.5.
[146] [1994] 3 All ER 814, 829.

right that such information should not be generally available but should be used only for the purposes for which the power was conferred. Although ... in my view there are severe limitations on the way in which such discretion can be exercised where prosecuting authorities are involved, it is important that no doubt should be cast on the discretion of the court to decide who shall have access to such information.

A liquidator may not voluntarily disclose a transcript of the examination to someone not entitled to apply for the examination, not even a defendant in criminal proceedings.[147] If the transcript is material to criminal proceedings, it must be made the subject of a witness summons.[148] If production is opposed, it will be up to the Crown Court to have to decide whether the transcript should be produced, if necessary after inspecting the transcript.[149]

15.40

B. Tribunals and Public Inquiries

Tribunals

Pre-hearing disclosure by a professional of confidential matters

Many of the regular tribunals that exist outside the ordinary court system have powers similar to those of courts enabling them to order disclosure of documents by professionals and to compel the attendance of professionals as witnesses.[150] Those tribunals that do not can call on the Queen's Bench Division for assistance.[151]

15.41

Where a tribunal is empowered to order the disclosure of documents before a hearing, confidentiality is not of itself a reason for not doing so if sight of the materials is necessary in order to dispose fairly of the proceedings.[152] In *Jindal v University of Glasgow*[153] the Employment Appeal Tribunal upheld the decision of the chairman of an employment tribunal directing the University of Glasgow, the respondents in race discrimination proceedings, to disclose in full the academic references received from third parties upon which the University had based a decision to refuse the applicant a personal chair. Lord Johnston said that the University could not be criticized for declining *voluntary* disclosure of such highly sensitive materials, but that the applicant needed to know the identity, professional and

15.42

---

[147] *Re Barlow Clowes Gilt Managers Ltd* [1991] 4 All ER 385.
[148] See para 14.129 above.
[149] *Re Barlow Clowes Gilt Managers Ltd* [1991] 4 All ER 385, 397.
[150] See eg Employment Tribunals (Constitution and Rules of Procedure) Regulations 1993, SI 1993/2687, reg 4(2) (employment tribunals); Solicitors Act 1974, s 46(11) (Solicitor's Disciplinary Tribunal); Data Protection Tribunal (Enforcement Appeals) Rules 2000, SI 2000/189, r 15 (Information (formerly Data Protection) Tribunal); Protection of Children and Vulnerable Adults and Care Standards Tribunal Regulations 2002, SI 2002/816, reg 16 (Care Standards Tribunal).
[151] *Soul v Inland Revenue Commissioners* [1963] 1 All ER 68, 113; *Currie v Chief Constable of Surrey* [1982] 1 All ER 89, 91; CPR, r 34.4.
[152] *Science Research Council v Nasse* [1979] 3 All ER 673, 679.
[153] (EAT/74/01, 31 May 2001.)

racial background of the referees in order to challenge their opinions and any factual circumstances that were mentioned in the references.

15.43 A tribunal investigating an allegation of professional misconduct is entitled to refuse a prosecutor access to the confidential records of a third party if the third party registers an objection and the tribunal concludes that the public interest in confidentiality outweighs the public interest in the tribunal doing justice.

> It was . . . right to distinguish between a case where a plaintiff in civil litigation puts his or her health in issue and a case where a patient is assisting a disciplinary tribunal. In the latter case a tribunal is likely to be much slower to override a patient's objection to the production of confidential records. If some alternative technique cannot be found to elicit the relevant evidence without the production of confidential documents, then the prosecutor may feel itself compelled to abandon that part of its case which relies on that patient's evidence rather than compel production against her will. It all depends on the circumstances.[154]

Oral evidence by a professional of confidential matters

15.44 A professional who is summonsed as a witness before a tribunal that has power to compel evidence or before whom witnesses cannot refuse to answer questions 'without sufficient cause'[155] or 'without lawful excuse' must divulge confidential personal information[156] unless a statute provides otherwise.[157] 'Sufficient cause' and 'lawful excuse' mean a reason that would be accepted by a court of law as justification for a witness to withhold evidence, and confidentiality does not figure among those reasons.[158] Legal professional privilege[159] (unless abrogated by statute)[160] and public interest immunity are valid grounds for refusing disclosure of documents or evidence even if the tribunal is one in which the law of evidence is not followed or is applied in modified form.[161] An employment tribunal should try, if at all possible, to adopt a compromise which avoids the disclosure of confidential personal information about employees who are not parties to the proceedings.[162]

---

[154] *Korsner v Royal Pharmaceutical Society of Great Britain* (DC, 19 February 1999) per Brooke LJ. This passage can be regarded as obiter because the person applying for disclosure was a witness, a doctor, whose credibility had been called into question.

[155] eg *Brannigan v Davison* [1996] 3 WLR 859.

[156] cp *Att-Gen v Mulholland* [1963] 1 All ER 767; *Att-Gen v Clough* [1963] 1 All ER 420. See also *Hession v Health Service Commissioner for Wales* [2001] EWHC Admin 619.

[157] eg Employment Rights Act 1996, s 202.

[158] See para 16.02 below. cp *Home or Away Ltd v Commissioners of Customs and Excise* VAT and Duties Tribunal, 17 January 2002.

[159] eg *Bradford Hospitals NHS Trust v Burcher* (EAT/958/01, 28 September 2001).

[160] *R v Secretary of State for the Home Department, ex p Daly* [2001] UKHL 26; [2001] 2 AC 532, para 23.

[161] eg General Osteopathic Council (Health Committee) (Procedure) Rules Order of Council 2000, SI 2000/242, r 39.

[162] *Charnos plc v Donnelly* (EAT (Scot) 27 July 2000).

B. Tribunals and Public Inquiries

Protecting confidential personal information

Public and media access

Mental health tribunals[163] and most disciplinary and regulatory bodies traditionally held their proceedings in private.[164] As a result of the incorporation of Article 6(1) by the HRA, however, public authorities that determine 'civil rights and obligations' must conduct their proceedings in public[165] unless one of the exceptions mentioned in that article applies[166] or the parties waive the right to a public hearing.[167] One such exception is 'the protection of the private life of the parties'. The ECtHR has allowed exclusion of the public to protect the private life of non-parties whose right to privacy is not mentioned in Article 6(1) but is protected by Article 8.[168]

15.45

Disciplinary proceedings inquiring into allegations of misconduct or incompetence against a professional must comply with Article 6(1).[169] The tribunal may be justified in closing the hearing of the proceedings while confidential personal information is disclosed about either the professional or her client.[170] In *Idenburg v General Medical Council*[171] the Privy Council rejected a complaint by a doctor about the disclosure of detailed medical information about her health when she had only consented to the GMC's Professional Conduct Committee approaching her doctors to inquire whether consultations had taken place. Lord Clyde said that it was well established in criminal proceedings that unlawfully obtained evidence was admissible[172] and that this principle was not restricted to criminal cases. Referring to General Medical Council Preliminary Proceedings Committee and Professional Conduct Committee (Procedure) Rules 1988, r 50 he said that it certainly applied 'to disciplinary proceedings such as that with which the present appeal is concerned'. The Privy Council was mindful of the fact that the Committee had excluded the public from the hearing when the content of the letters was being considered.

15.46

---

[163] Mental Health Review Tribunal Rules 1983, SI 1983/942, r 21 (as to which see *Pickering v Liverpool Daily Post* [1991] 1 All ER 622). If the patient requests the hearing may be in public if the tribunal is satisfied that this would not be against the interests of the patient.

[164] B Harris, *The Law and Practice of Disciplinary and Regulatory Proceedings* (2nd edn, Chichester: 1999) 202; General Osteopathic Council (Health Committee) (Procedure) Rules Order of Council 2000, r 16(1). cp Health Service Commissioners Act 1993, s 11(2).

[165] *Diennet v France* (1995) 21 EHRR 554. As to what constitutes a public hearing see *Storer v British Gas plc* [2000] 2 All ER 440.

[166] *Gautin v France* (1999) 28 EHRR 195, para 42. For the exceptions see para 3.24 above.

[167] *Le Compte Van Leuven & De Meyere v Belgium* (1982) 4 EHRR 1, para 59.

[168] ibid, para 59. See also para 17.37 below.

[169] *Konig v Germany* (1979) 2 EHRR 170; *Ginikawa v UK* (1988) 55 DR 251.

[170] *Le Compte Van Leuven & De Meyere v Belgium* (1982) 4 EHRR 1, para 59.

[171] (2000) 55 BMLR 101.

[172] *Kuruma v R* [1955] 1 All ER 236; *Jeffrey v Black* [1978] 1 All ER 555.

15.47 Article 6 applies to employment tribunals. Under regulations made since the HRA came into force, employment tribunals must sit in public but may sit in closed session when they receive information from a person '(a) ... which he could not disclose without contravening a prohibition imposed by or under any enactment, or (b) ... which has been communicated to him in confidence, or which he has otherwise obtained in consequence of the confidence reposed in him by another person'.[173] Recent legislation regulating hearings before the Information Tribunal and the Care Standards tribunal also recognize a general obligation to sit in public.[174]

Other safeguards

15.48 As a condition of making voluntary disclosure of confidential personal information to a party, a tribunal can impose a condition that the information disclosed remain confidential and not be used for a collateral purpose.[175] In exceptional circumstances, the Care Standards Tribunal can direct that a medical report submitted for its consideration shall not be disclosed to the applicant because disclosure would be harmful to his health or welfare.[176] Such a direction does not prevent disclosure of the report to the applicant's legal representatives.

Statutory[177] and Non-Statutory Inquiries Ordered by Ministers

Purpose and procedure

15.49 Inquiries are regularly set up by government to investigate political scandals, transport disasters, mismanaged child protection, non-accidental deaths in hospitals and other incidents of public concern. Their purpose is to discover some or all of the following: what happened, why it happened and how something similar can be prevented from happening again. In consequence, inquiries are, with rare exceptions, inquisitorial:[178] there are no parties and no lis.[179] The person conducting the inquiry decides what the documents are that the inquiry needs and from

---

[173] Employment Tribunals (Constitution and Rules of Procedure) Regulations 2001, SI 2001/1171, Sch 1, r 10(3). On the obligation to sit in public see *Storer v British Gas plc* [2000] 2 All ER 440. Employment tribunals may restrict reporting of personal information in certain circumstances: Sch 1, r 16.

[174] eg Data Protection Tribunal (Enforcement Appeals) Rules 2000, SI 2000/189 r 19; Protection of Children and Vulnerable Adults and Care Standards Tribunal Regulations 2002, SI 2002/816, regs 19, 21.

[175] *R v General Medical Council, ex p Toth* [2000] 1 WLR 2209.

[176] Protection of Children Act Tribunal Regulations 2000, SI 2000/2619, reg 21(2); Protection of Children and Vulnerable Adults Care Standards Tribunal Regulations 2002, r 15.

[177] The term 'statutory inquiry' is used in two different ways in the literature: to mean an inquiry set up under any statute (which is the way that the term is used in this chapter) or to mean an inquiry set up under the Tribunals of Inquiry (Evidence) Act 1921 (with all other inquiries, whether supported by a statute or not, being referred to as ad hoc inquiries).

[178] R Scott, 'Procedures at Inquiries—The Duty to Be Fair' (1995) 111 LQR 596, 597.

[179] Salmon LJ, *Report of the Royal Commission on Tribunals of Inquiry* (Cmnd 3131, 1966) para 30.

B. Tribunals and Public Inquiries

whom the inquiry should hear evidence. No two inquiries are exactly alike.[180] They make their own rules with the objectives of effectiveness, fairness, speed and economy in mind.[181] In the typical inquiry, questioning of witnesses is left to counsel to the inquiry (if there is one) and the chairman. Interested parties[182] are represented by lawyers but the lawyers, compared to trials, play a limited role.[183] There is no right of cross-examination though most chairmen allow some cross-examination by the lawyers of the interested parties.

Inquiries under the Tribunal of Inquiries (Evidence) Act 1921[184]

15.50 When a matter arises of 'urgent public importance'[185] the Tribunals of Inquiry (Evidence) Act 1921 allows a Tribunal of Inquiry to be set up by resolution of both Houses of Parliament. The Shipman Inquiry[186] into how a GP was able to murder his patients is a recent example. A Tribunal of Inquiry has power to compel the attendance of a professional to give evidence and to compel production of confidential client records.[187] Evidence must be given in public (otherwise public disquiet is unlikely to be allayed) but the tribunal has a discretion to take sensitive evidence in closed session when 'it is in the public interest expedient so to do for reasons connected with the subject matter of the inquiry or the nature of the evidence'.[188]

Other inquiries

Power to compel evidence from a professional

15.51 **Statutory inquiries** Tribunals of Inquiry are seldom used.[189] Ministers have plenty of powers to establish statutory inquiries inter alia under the Children Act 1989,[190] the Mental Health Act 1959,[191] the Police Act 1996,[192] the Local Authority Social Services Act 1970,[193] the Care Standards Act 2000[194] and the National Health Service Act 1977.[195] Statutory inquiries normally have the power

---

[180] See generally, R Wraith and G Lamb, *Public Inquiries as an Instrument of Government* (London: 1971) 163.
[181] Council on Tribunals Advice, para 2.3 cited in Law Commission Consultation Paper 163, *Publication of Local Authority Reports* (2002) para 8.52.
[182] eg victims and their families.
[183] The Victoria Climbie Inquiry, 'The Nature and Conduct of the Inquiry', paras 26, 34–39, available from http://www.victoria-climbie-inquiry.org.uk.
[184] *Royal Commission on Tribunals of Inquiry* (Cmnd 3121, 1966).
[185] Tribunals of Inquiry (Evidence) Act 1921, s 1.
[186] http://www.the-shipman-inquiry.org.uk/.
[187] s 1.
[188] Tribunals of Inquiry (Evidence) Act 1921, s 2.
[189] R Wraith & G Lamb, *Public Inquiries as an Instrument of Government* (London: 1971) 212. None was set up between 1977 (Fay Committee of Inquiry on the Crown Agents) and 1996 (Public Inquiry into the Shooting at Dunblane Primary School). Since then there have been a number of Tribunals of Inquiry Act inquiries.
[190] s 1.   [191] s 143.   [192] s 49.   [193] s 7C.   [194] s 10.
[195] s 84(1). The Secretary of State can also set up a tribunal under s 2.

to compel the attendance[196] of witnesses to give evidence on oath[197] and to order production of documents.[198] If these powers are used to require a professional to produce confidential personal information about a client, the professional must comply or face sanctions. An order to produce documents subject to public interest immunity (PII) can be challenged in judicial review proceedings.

15.52 If the inquiry chairman uses his powers to compel production of documents containing confidential personal information, he may make their availability to interested parties conditional on their undertaking to keep the material confidential, not to use them for any purpose other than the inquiry and to return them when the inquiry is over.[199] If the chairman does not take these steps the better view is that documents disclosed under compulsion are not subject to an implied obligation of confidentiality.[200]

15.53 Non-statutory inquiries A minister may rely upon prerogative authority to set up a non-statutory inquiry. Prominent examples are the BSE Inquiry[201] and the Scott Inquiry into Arms to Iraq.[202] A non-statutory inquiry has no coercive powers;[203] it must rely upon voluntary submission of evidence. A professional may volunteer confidential client information without client consent when there is an overriding public interest in her doing so.[204] Otherwise, the decision to submit information to the inquiry rests with the client.[205] This is the position also when a local authority orders an inquiry; under current law, a local authority lacks the power to set up an inquiry that can compel witnesses or produce documents.[206] Where there has been a loss of life the Government may have no choice but to

---

[196] A senior social worker with Harringey council was the first person prosecuted for failing to attend a public inquiry as a witness. See Daily Telegraph, 13 June 2002.

[197] Witnesses whose evidence is uncontroversial may be allowed to submit written statements in lieu of oral evidence.

[198] Acts that allow statutory inquiries to be set up often apply to the tribunal the powers set out in Local Government Act 1972, s 250(2)–(5).

[199] See eg *The Report of the Committee of Inquiry into the PDU, Ashworth Special Hospital* (1999) para 1.14.1.

[200] P Matthews and H Malek, *Disclosure* (London: 2000) para 17.61. They point out that when documents are disclosed to a public inquiry they are being disseminated to the public for the purpose of bringing facts out into the open.

[201] http://www.bseinquiry.gov.

[202] Sir Richard Scott, *Return to an Address of the Honourable the House of Commons dated 15th February 1996 for the report of the Inquiry into the export of Defence Equipment and Dual-use Goods to Iraq and Related Prosecutions* (London: 1996).

[203] *McGuiness v Att-Gen of Victoria* (1940) 63 CLR 73, 83, 91, 98–99; *Att-Gen for Quebec and Keable v Att-Gen for Canada* [1979] SCR 218, 240, 244; *Thompson v Commission of Inquiry* [1983] NZLR 98, 105. It was made clear to Sir Richard Scott that the power to compel testimony and production of witnesses would be given to him if he found that he needed them: *Hansard,* HC vol 214, cols 650–651 (23 November 1992).

[204] See ch 11.

[205] *Price Waterhouse (A Frm) v BCCI Holdings (Luxembourg) SA* [1992] BCLC 583, 601.

[206] Law Commission, Consultation Paper 163, *Publication of Local Authority Reports* (2002) para 9.99. The various kinds of inquiries that a public authority may order are listed in ch 2 of this report.

B. Tribunals and Public Inquiries

establish a statutory inquiry with power to compel testimony to avoid violating Article 2 of the ECHR.[207]

Media and public access

Statutes that allow a statutory inquiry to be held tend not to address the question of public and media access.[208] This is a matter for the Minister who sets up the inquiry. There is no presumption in favour of public access[209] unless the inquiry was established under the Tribunals of Inquiry (Evidence) Act 1921, though some ad hoc tribunals have sat and taken evidence in public and recently some inquiries have posted transcripts of the evidence of witnesses on websites to ensure the widest possible access to the hearing. In deciding whether an inquiry should be held in public, the Secretary of State may consider how the glare of publicity might affect the willingness of witnesses (including professionals) to come forward and give evidence.[210] Should an inquiry sit in public, it may still be necessary to sit in private when evidence is presented of sensitive personal matters such as confidential health records.[211] If the tests of necessity and proportionality are not satisfied, failure to do so will violate Article 8.

15.54

Article 10 (freedom of expression) does not require an inquiry to be conducted in public. Article 10 prohibits restrictions on the means available to individuals to impart information. It imposes no positive obligation on the state to provide additional facilities for the dissemination of information; a private inquiry promotes freedom of expression by giving individuals an opportunity to ventilate their views.[212] Article 6 is not engaged because there is no determination of 'civil rights'.[213]

15.55

A private inquiry is not a panacea from the point of view of protecting confidential client information. There may still be a considerable risk that evidence will find its way into the press if interested parties are given permission[214] to attend throughout and to talk freely about the evidence.

15.56

---

[207] *Edward v UK* Application 46477/99 (2002) 35 EHRR 19, para 87.
[208] But see Care Standards Act 2000, s 10(3), (4).
[209] *Howard v Secretary of State for Health* [2002] EWHC 396, para 77. The Alder Hey inquiry was held in private.
[210] *Howard v Secretary of State for Health* [2002] EWHC 396, para 85.
[211] cp *Thompson v Commission of Inquiry* [1983] NZLR 98, 105, 106.
[212] *Howard v Secretary of State for Health* [2002] EWHC 396, paras 104–105.
[213] cp *Thompson v Commission of Inquiry* [1983] NZLR 98, 102.
[214] cp *Howard v Secretary of State for Health* [2002] EWHC 396, para 101.

16

GROUNDS FOR NON-DISCLOSURE

A. Statutory Inadmissibility	16.02	B. Privilege	16.05
Admissibility of Confidential Informtion	16.02	Categories of Privilege	16.05
		Legal Professional Privilege	16.08
		Public Interest Immunity	16.52

This chapter takes a detailed look at the grounds upon which a professional can resist disclosure of confidential client information,[1] principally in legal proceedings. They are: **16.01**

(1) statutory inadmissibility;
(2) conciliation privilege;
(3) legal professional privilege (LPP);
(4) public interest immunity (PII).

The main concentration is on LPP: its relationship to the lawyer's obligation of confidentiality, when the privilege arises, its forms, its scope and how it may be lost.

A. Statutory Inadmissibility

Admissibility of Confidential Information

At common law and under the Civil Procedure Rules (CPR)[2] confidentiality is not a reason to refuse to disclose information that is needed for the conduct of legal or quasi-legal proceedings. **16.02**

> The court will order discovery of confidential material because the private rights and interests of the parties cannot be allowed to frustrate the public interest perceived to exist in full exchange of documents relevant to court proceedings.[3]

---

[1] The law is the same whether the information is personal information or not.
[2] See paras 14.07, 15.08, 15.13.
[3] per Laddie J, *BCCI v Price Waterhouse* [1997] 4 All ER 781, 797.

The Human Rights Act 1998 (HRA) may have introduced some scope for arguing that a party does not have to disclose sensitive personal information about himself or another if that information has marginal relevance to the litigation or is not needed because the fact that it is intended to prove can be proved as satisfactorily by other means.[4] The argument would be that disclosure is an interference with the right to respect for private life[5] and, because the evidence is not directly relevant to the issues in the case or essential, disclosure of the information is disproportionate to the aim of protecting the litigant's rights or bringing a criminal to justice.[6] Steps that can be taken to limit dissemination of the information would be something the court would wish to consider.[7] Any discretion to exclude relevant evidence must be exercised with regard to the litigant's absolute right under Article 6 to a fair hearing. The fact that the Article 6 right is absolute and the Article 8 right is not is perhaps an indication that in any conflict between the two, the greater public interest lies with Article 6. The balance that is struck is therefore likely to favour the right to a fair hearing more than respect for private life.

Confidential information obtained under compulsion

16.03 Legislation that allows confidential information to be collected under compulsion may expressly,[8] or by necessary implication, forbid the use of the compelled information for some, or all, kinds of litigation. Where the statute is silent about the matter and there is no issue of self-incrimination,[9] the courts are predisposed in favour of allowing the confidential information to be used for any purpose related to the administration of justice.[10] It has been held that a provision in money laundering legislation that makes it a criminal offence to tip someone off about a money laundering investigation[11] does not prevent disclosure of relevant information to a court. If there is a danger of prejudicing the money laundering investigation, the recommended procedure is to hand the information to the judge in a sealed envelope.[12] In *Garner v Garner*[13] a doctor was made to disclose

---

[4] See paras 15.09, 15.16 above.
[5] cp *MS v Sweden* (1999) 28 EHRR 313.
[6] Non-disclosure of confidential information in children's cases on Art 8 grounds is envisaged in *Re R* [2002] 1 FLR 955. See also *Re C* (Fam Div, 29 November 2001).
[7] See para 15.19 above and paras 17.30 et seq below.
[8] Statutes that allow confidential material to be used for the purposes of litigation are common, those that forbid it much less so. Examples of the latter include Theft Act 1968 s 31; Interception of Communications Act 1985, s 9; Regulation of Investigatory Powers Act 2000, s 17; Children Act 1989, s 98; Health Service Commissioner Act 1993, s 15(2).
[9] Art 6 contains an implied privilege against self-incrimination: *Funke v France* (1993) 16 EHRR 297; *Saunders v UK* (1996) 23 EHRR 313.
[10] cp *A v A* [2000] 1 FLR 701. In this case there was no relevant statutory provision.
[11] See para 10.17 above.
[12] *The Bank v A Ltd* (HC, 23 June 2000, WL 774924).
[13] (1920) 36 TLR 196. It is not possible to discover from the brief report of this case whether

information in divorce proceedings that had been obtained for the treatment of venereal disease under a legislative scheme which regulations required to be conducted confidentially.

Unusually, in *BCCI v Price Waterhouse*, an action in negligence by liquidators of a bank against the bank's auditors, the court refused to order the defendants to disclose confidential information that had been received under, and for the purposes of, the Banking Act 1987. An important factor was that the Banking Act 1987 expressly allowed the information to be used in certain specified types of litigation[14] and made it a criminal offence otherwise to disclose information to third parties without the consent of the persons to whom it related. The statutory draftsman had obviously given thought to the extent to which the embargoed material could be used in legal proceedings. This made it difficult to imply legislative approval for its use in any other kind of litigation.[15] Laddie J said:

16.04

> Where the legislature has determined that it is in the public interest that certain types of information should not be disclosed on pain of punishment save in defined and limited circumstances, the court should be wary of adding to the list of exceptions.[16]

B. Privilege

Categories of Privilege

The CPR glossary defines 'privilege' as '[t]he right of a party to refuse to disclose a document or produce a document or to refuse to answer questions on the ground of some special interest recognized by law'. Anything that is privileged can be withheld from a court, a tribunal acting judicially or an opponent although relevant and admissible evidence. Since privilege is a fetter on the discovery of truth, the privileges that the common law has chosen to recognize are few in number.[17] The principal surviving[18] privileges are LPP, the privilege against self-incrimination, and communications without prejudice in the course of negotiations to obtain a

16.05

---

unauthorized disclosure was a criminal offence. Contrast *Carter v Carter* (1974) 6 OR(2d) 603 where the evidence was held admissible but excluded as a matter of discretion on the grounds of public interest.

[14] s 82(1).
[15] *BCCI v Price Waterhouse* [1997] 4 All ER 781, 797.
[16] ibid.
[17] US jurisdictions recognize a much wider range of privileges, some as a result of legislation others through judicial law-making: S Stone and R Taylor, *Testimonial Privileges* (2nd edn, Colorado Springs: 1993); 12 Fed. Proc. § 33 (1988).
[18] The common law rule forbidding spouses from testifying for or against each other was abolished by PACE, s 80(9).

settlement of litigation.[19] A matrimonial-related conciliation privilege[20] that has taken on a life of its own has evolved from the last of these three.

Privilege against self-incrimination[21]

16.06 It is unlikely that the professional anxious not to divulge confidential client information during litigation will find the privilege against self-incrimination, useful. '[T]he privilege is not a privilege against incrimination; it is a privilege against *self*-incrimination.'[22] For a professional to be entitled to conceal anything that concerns a client on the grounds of self-incrimination, the communication must have a tendency to expose the professional to the risk of a criminal conviction or a penalty.[23] Even then, the professional must disclose the information if the court is able to find a way to neutralize the risk.[24]

Conciliation privilege

16.07 Conciliation privilege might be relevant when a professional such as a social worker, probation officer, counsellor or member of the clergy mediates between warring spouses (either on her own initiative or at the request of one or both partners).[25] The privilege bars the mediator from disclosing anything said during the attempted negotiations[26] unless both spouses have unequivocally waived privilege.[27] This privilege, unlike LPP[28] and the privilege against self-incrimination, cannot be claimed in criminal proceedings.[29]

---

[19] *Rush & Tompkins Ltd v Greater London Council* [1988] 3 All ER 737.
[20] The new privilege can be traced to *McTaggart v McTaggart* [1948] 2 All ER 754 where it is treated as an application of 'without prejudice' privilege. The new privilege has never been applied outside the family law context. The original rationale was 'the public interest in the stability of marriage' (per Lord Hailsham, *D v NSPCC* [1977] 1 All ER 589, 602), but the privilege now covers parental negotiations over the future of their offspring: see *Re D* [1993] 2 All ER 693. See also *Unilever plc v Proctor & Gamble* [2001] 1 All ER 783, 793.
[21] M Howard (ed), *Phipson on Evidence* (15th edn, London: 2000) 21.18 et seq.
[22] per Gibbs CJ, Mason and Dawson JJ, *Controlled Consultants Pty Ltd v Commissioner for Corporate Affairs* (1985) 59 ALJR 254, 257 citing *Andresen v State of Maryland* 427 US 463 (1976) (italics added).
[23] eg *Grofam Pty Ltd v Maccauley* [1994] 121 ALR 22.
[24] *Re O* [1991] 2 QB 461, 530; *AT & T Istel Ltd v Tully* [1993] AC 45, 63.
[25] *Henley v Henley* [1955] 1 All ER 590n. See also Disbability Discrimination Act 1995, s 31B(7).
[26] *McTaggart v McTaggart* [1948] 2 All ER 754; *Mole v Mole* [1950] 2 All ER 328. The conciliator was a probation officer in both cases.
[27] *Pais v Pais* [1970] 3 All ER 491.
[28] *R v Derby Magistrates' Court, ex p B* [1995] 4 All ER 526, 537.
[29] *R v Pabani* (1994) 89 CCC (3d) 437. Contra Disability Discrimination Act 1995, s 31B(7).

B. Privilege

Legal Professional Privilege[30]

Origins and rationale of legal professional privilege

Common law rationale LPP is the oldest of the privileges. Initially it was confined to situations of contemplated litigation. Historians disagree about its original purpose which has variously been attributed to protection of the lawyer's honour, the client's privilege against self-incrimination and the rule against party-witnesses.[31] Initially the privilege was that of the lawyer. By the mid-nineteenth century both the ownership and rationale of the privilege had undergone a sea change. The right to waive the privilege had passed to the client[32] and the purpose of the privilege had become the smooth working of the legal system which is too complex for laypersons to negotiate without professional assistance.[33] In the absence of lawyers to provide sound legal advice the courts would be swamped with meritless cases and legal compliance neglected through ignorance. This 'efficiency' rationale has been fulsomely expounded by the Supreme Court of Canada in *R v McClure*:

16.08

> The important relationship between a client and his or her lawyer stretches beyond the parties and is integral to the workings of the legal system itself. The solicitor–client relationship is a part of that system, not ancillary to it. . . . The prima facie protection for solicitor–client communications is based on the fact that the relationship and the communications between solicitor and client are essential to the effective operation of the system. . . . The law is complex. Lawyers have a unique role. Free and candid communication between the lawyer and client protects the legal rights of the citizen. It is essential for the lawyer to know all the facts of the client's position. The existence of a fundamental right to privilege between the two encourages disclosure within the confines of the relationship.[34]

A slightly narrower version of LPP than the English rule exists in EU law, a sign of the importance of the privilege to the operation of any legal system.[35]

---

[30] For fuller accounts of LPP: C Passmore, *Privilege* (Birmingham: 1998); R Desiatnik, *Legal Professional Privilege in Australia* (St Leonards: 2000); J Auburn, *Legal Professional Privilege: Law and Theory* (Oxford: 2000); M Howard (ed), *Phipson on Evidence* (15th edn, London: 2000) chs 20, 22.

[31] G Hazard, 'An Historical Perspective on the Attorney–Client Privilege' (1978) 66 California Law Rev 1061, 1070; Note ,'Developments—Privileged Communications' (1985) 98 Harvard Law Review 1501, 1502.

[32] *Wilson v Rastall* (1792) 4 Tr 753.

[33] *Greenough v Gaskell* (1833) 39 ER 618, 620.

[34] [2001] SCC 14, paras 36–39. Lord Hoffman said much the same thing more briefly in *R v Special Commissioner, ex p Morgan Grenfell & Co* [2002] UKHL 21; [2002] 2 WLR 1299, para 7. See also *Waugh v British Railways Board* [1979] 2 All ER 1169, 1176; *R v Derby Magistrates' Court, ex p B* [1995] 4 All ER 526, 540–541; *Bolkiah v KPMG* [1998] 1 All ER 517, 528.

[35] *AM & S Europe Ltd v EC Commission* [1983] QB 878. Communications with in-house lawyers are not protected. Rules of Procedure and Evidence of the International Tribunal, r 97 recognizes lawyer–client privilege for communications between lawyer and client and r 70 protects from disclosure 'reports, memoranda, or other internal documents prepared by a party, its assistants or representatives in connection with the investigation or preparation of a case'. See also ICC, Rules of Evidence and Procedure, r 73.

16.09 **Legal professional privilege and the Human Rights Act 1998** LPP is underpinned by the European Convention on Human Rights (ECHR). Article 6 guarantees to litigants a privilege against self-incrimination[36] and a right to effective legal assistance.[37] If a lawyer could be compelled to testify against her client these rights could easily be subverted.[38] Quite apart from this, can a trial be said to be fair that involves the lawyer informing on her client? It may be that when the occasion presents itself the European Court of Human Rights (ECtHR) will decide that Article 6 which guarantees the right to a fair hearing contains an implied right to LPP.[39] Additionally, in *Campbell v UK* the ECtHR said that correspondence with lawyers, 'whatever their purpose, concern matters of a private and confidential character. In principle, such letters are privileged under Article 8'.[40]

The nature of legal professional privilege

16.10 **Judicial proceedings** Initially, LPP was, like PII which is discussed later in this chapter, regarded as a rule of evidence that enabled the privilege-holder to avoid compulsory disclosure of material to an opponent or to the court[41] and forbade the court from drawing an adverse inference from the fact that privilege had been claimed.[42] The two rules of evidence were, however, distinguished by two important differences. The first is that LPP is preordained and absolute; there is no ad hoc balancing of public interests in individual cases as there is for PII[43] or under the Article 8(2) proportionality test.[43a] In formulating the law of LPP, the law has already undertaken the balancing process. The other major difference is that PII cannot be circumvented,[44] whereas LPP can. LPP attaches to the original document or communication, not the underlying information, and if other means can be found to prove its contents these can be used.[45]

16.11 If LPP is merely an evidential privilege then it has no relevance outside adjudication. In *Parry-Jones v Law Society* the Court of Appeal held that a rule made under

---

[36] *Saunders v UK* (1996) 23 EHRR 313, para 68.
[37] See para 3.10 above.
[38] R O'Dair, *Legal Ethics: Text and Materials* (London: 2001) 264. cp Note, 'Functional Overlap between the Lawyer and other Professionals: Its Implications for the Privileged Communications Doctrine' (1962) 71 Yale LJ 1226, 1237.
[39] I Dennis, *The Law of Evidence* (London: 1999) 309. Just as it has implied a privilege against self-incrimination: *Funke v France* (1993) 16 EHRR 297.
[40] (1992) 15 EHRR 137, para 48. Oral communications are also protected: para 3.03 above.
[41] *Privilege in Civil Proceedings* (Cmnd 3472, 1967) para 1.
[42] *Wentworth v Lloyd* (1864) 10 HLC 589. 'If adverse inferences are drawn in cases where the privilege . . . applies then it will undermine the privilege itself', per Sir Robert Morritt, *China National Petroleum v Fenwick Elliott* [2002] EWHC 60, Ch D, para 52.
[43] See para 16.55 below.
[43a] Para 3.19 above.
[44] Secondary evidence is not admissible of a document that is subject to PII: *Chatterton v Secretary of State for India* [1895] 2 QB 189, 193, 195; Lord Simon, 'Evidence Excluded by Considerations of State Interest' [1955] CLJ 62, 68–72. cp *Gain v Gain* [1961] 1 WLR 1469.
[45] *Calcraft v Guest* [1899] 1 QB 759; see para 6.98 above.

B. Privilege

the Solicitors Act 1957 to enforce compliance with the Solicitors' Accounts Rules and Solicitors' Trust Account Rules which enabled the Law Society to demand production of documents relating to his practice was not affected by LPP.

> [P]rivilege is irrelevant when one is not concerned with judicial or quasi-judicial proceedings because, strictly speaking, privilege refers to a right to withhold from a court, or a tribunal exercising judicial functions, material which would otherwise be admissible in evidence.[46]

The Court of Appeal indicated that the reason that a lawyer could withhold access to privileged client material outside the litigation arena was not LPP but the much broader obligation of confidentiality that a lawyer,[47] like any other professional, owes to a client.[48] The Court of Appeal did not choose to reflect on the fact that this reasoning undermines the raison d'être of LPP, namely perfect security[49] for lawyer–client communications so that advice can be candidly sought and given. LPP as a mere rule of evidence can protect communications from disclosure to a court without the client's consent, but it cannot guarantee that the same communications will not have to be disclosed to the police or some other public agency with power to compel production of documents or information.[50] This result can be avoided only by Parliament enacting a statutory substitute for LPP. So it was that during the 1970s and 1980s the common law courts of Canada, Australia and New Zealand decided to reinvent LPP as a substantive and fundamental common law right that limits the power to compel information in all contexts.[51] It was not long before this idea took root in England and Wales too.

Legal professional privilege in non-judicial contexts In *R v Derby Magistrates, ex p B*, Lord Taylor CJ, sitting unusually for a Lord Chief Justice in the House of Lords, said that: **16.12**

---

[46] per Diplock LJ, *Parry-Jones v Law Society* [1968] 1 All ER 177, 180.
[47] The lawyer's obligation of confidentiality is one of law and ethics. It encompasses all non-trivial information that the lawyer acquires from any source in the course of the professional relationship. Solicitors: Law Society, *The Guide to the Professional Conduct of Solicitors* (8th edn, London: 1999) 16.01, '[a] solicitor is under a duty to keep confidential to his or her firm the affairs of clients and to ensure that the staff do the same'. Barristers: *Code of Conduct of the Bar of England and Wales* (7th edn, London: 1999) para 702, '[w]hether or not the relation of counsel and client continues a barrister must preserve the confidentiality of the lay client's affairs and must not without the prior consent of the lay client or as permitted by law lend or reveal the contents of the papers in any instructions to or communicate to any third person (other than another barrister, a pupil or any other person who needs to know it for the performance of their duties) information which has been entrusted to him in confidence or use such information to the lay client's detriment or to his own or another client's advantage'.
[48] *Parry-Jones v Law Society* [1968] 1 All ER 177, 178, 180.
[49] per Knight Bruce V-C, *Pearse v Pearse* (1846) 63 ER 950, 957.
[50] *R v Special Commissioner, ex p Morgan Grenfell & Co* [2002] UKHL 21; [2002] 2 WLR 1299, para 30.
[51] *Baker v Campbell* (1983) 153 CLR 52, 117; *Goldberg v Ng* (1995) 185 CLR 83, 93–94; *Carter v Northmore Hale Davy & Leake* (1995) 183 CLR 121; *Descoteaux v Mierzwinski* [1982] 1 SCR 860, 875; *Smith v Jones* [1999] 1 SCR 455, 476–477; *Rosenburg v Jaine* [1983] NZLR 1.

[l]egal professional privilege is ... *much more than an ordinary rule of evidence*, limited in its application to the facts of a particular case. It is a fundamental condition on which the administration of justice as a whole rests.[52]

No one was quite sure what this change in the status of LPP meant for English law. *R v Derby Magistrates* was about the right to suppress a communication to a lawyer in criminal proceedings. It gave no clue about the working of LPP outside the judicial arena. Moreover, the change seemed at odds with the statutory provisions (of which there are a considerable number)[53] that expressly disallow compulsory disclosure of anything that would qualify for LPP in proceedings in the High Court. If LPP were a fundamental common law right, these provisions would be otiose. But then, as Buxton LJ observed in *R (on the application of Morgan Grenfell & Co Ltd) v Special Commissioner*,[54] 'it is not unusual for Parliament to say expressly what the courts would have inferred anyway'.

16.13 The response to *Ex p B* was to treat LPP as a prima facie defence to a statutory power to compel disclosure of information. To displace this presumption required 'clear words... or a compelling context'.[55] But the courts could be quite easily persuaded to find that Parliament had intended to remove the benefit of LPP.[56] Then came *R (on the application of Morgan Grenfell & Co Ltd) v Special Commissioner*.[57] The Inland Revenue had decided to investigate a tax avoidance scheme marketed by Morgan Grenfell, a merchant bank. There was no suggestion of criminality. Relying on Taxes Management Act 1970, s 20(1) a tax inspector, with the approval of a Special Commissioner, demanded to see counsel's instructions from and advice to the bank. First the Divisional Court and then the Court of Appeal held that s 20(1) authorized an inspector of taxes to issue a notice requiring a taxpayer to disclose material that in litigation would be subject to LPP. Although the Act contained no language that expressly overrode LPP, the Court of Appeal decided that the structure of the Act carried the inescapable implication that LPP was excluded except where it was expressly incorporated.[58] Documents in the

---

[52] [1995] 4 All ER 526, 540–541 (italics added).
[53] eg Taxes Management Act 1970, ss 20B(3), 20B(8), 20C(4); Health and Safety Act 1974, s 20(8); Local Government Act 1974, s 29(7); Sex Discrimination Act 1975, s 58(3)(a); Race Relations Act 1976, s 50(3)(a); Companies Act 1985, s 452(1)(a); Criminal Justice Act 1987, s 2(4); Companies Act 1989, s 83(5), Sch 14, Pt 1, 4(4); Drug Trafficking Act 1994, s 55(4)(b)(ii); Housing Act 1996, s 30(4)(a); Disability Rights Commission Act 1999, s 4(3); Competition Act 1998, s 30; Financial Services and Markets Act 2000, s 413. cp Medical Act 1983, s 5A(6). PACE, s 10 creates its own version of LPP: see para 14.22 above. Some legislation states that an informant cannot be compelled to disclose or produce information that could not be compelled in civil proceedings before the High Court. At other times the draftsman refers to 'professional privilege', 'legal privilege' or 'legal professional privilege'.
[54] [2000] All ER (D) 1729, para 26.
[55] per Lord Nicholls, *Re L* [1996] 2 All ER 78, 88.
[56] *S CC v B* [2000] 3 WLR 53, 72; *R v Inland Revenue Commissioners, ex p Lorimer* [2000] STC 751; *Guyer v Walton* [2001] STC (SCD) 75; *Cowell v Law Society* (Ch D, 12 October 2001).
[57] [2002] 1 All ER 776. cp *Guyer v Walton* [2001] STC (SCD) 75.
[58] [2002] 1 All ER 776, para 17.

B. Privilege

possession or power of a lawyer cannot be disclosed to the Inland Revenue without the client's consent.[59] The Court of Appeal took this as an indication that documents in the hands of the clients were not privileged. The House of Lords disagreed. The leading judgment is by Lord Hoffman who said:

> Why should Parliament want to preserve LPP for documents in the hands of the lawyer but not for documents (which may well be copies or originals of the same documents) in the hands of the taxpayer? . . . [Counsel] for the Inland Revenue said that there was no real anomaly because the inspector could indirectly obtain documents in the possession of the lawyer by applying to the taxpayer. . . . The purpose of section 20B(8) was to prevent the lawyer from being placed in a situation in which he had a statutory duty which conflicted with his duty to his client. . . . If Parliament had simply wanted to spare lawyers the difficulty of deciding which master to serve, it could just as easily have removed by the problem by providing that documents in the hands of lawyers also had to be produced. . . . If the client's consent is required when the documents are in the hands of the lawyer, why should it not be required when they are in the hands of the client himself? It seems to me strange to say that the lawyer could not produce the documents without the client's consent, but leave it to be inferred that a client served with a notice under section 20(1) would be obliged to give his consent.[60]

Lord Hoffman's analysis proceeds on the basis that LPP is 'a fundamental human right'[61] but that it can be abrogated 'by necessary implication'.[62] At first sight this caveat looks to be at variance with what Lord Bingham said in *R v Secretary of State for the Home Department, Ex p Daly*.[63] Speaking for the whole House in a case in which prison rules were held ultra vires that forbade prisoners to be present when their legal correspondence was examined by prison officers during a cell search,[64] Lord Bingham announced that LPP may be 'curtailed only by clear and express words, and then only to the extent reasonably necessary to meet the ends which justify the curtailment'.[65] It is probable, however, that Lord Bingham was not intending to cover the field and rule out removal of LPP by necessary implication;

16.14

---

[59] Taxes Management Act 1970, s 20B(8) prevents a lawyer from producing privileged documents in response to a s 20(3) or s 20A(1) notice without client consent and s 20C(3) prevents the Revenue from seizing privileged documents held by a lawyer under a s 20C warrant.
[60] per Lord Hoffman, [2002] UKHL 21; [2002] 2 WLR 1299, paras 23–24. See also, *AM & S Europe Ltd v Commission of the European Communities* [1983] QB 878, 913–914.
[61] [2002] UKHL 21; [2002] 2 WLR 1299, paras 7, 31. cp para 16.09 above.
[62] ibid, para 8.
[63] [2001] UKHL 26; [2001] 2 AC 532. Other House of Lords' decisions acknowledge the possibility of overruling by necessary implication.
[64] Lord Bingham said that a blanket policy that paid no attention to the prisoner's past or present conduct or whether the search was routine or an emergency measure provided 'for a degree of intrusion into the privileged legal correspondence of prisoners which is greater than is justified by the objectives the policy is intended to serve' (para 21) and was therefore not authorized by the parent Act under which the rules were made.
[65] *R v Secretary of State for the Home Department, ex p Daly* [2001] UKHL 26; [2001] 2 AC 532, paras 5, 31. Is *R (on the application of Cannan) v Governor of HMP Full Sutton* [2003] EWHC 97 Admin consistant with this?

the possibility of LPP being abrogated by necessary implication is envisaged in other House of Lords decisions.[66] Lord Hobhouse explained what this means in *Morgan Grenfell*:[67]

> [N]ecessary implication is not the same as a reasonable implication. . . . A *necessary* implication is one which necessarily follows from the express provisions of the statute construed in their context. It distinguishes between what it would have been sensible or reasonable for Parliament to have included or what Parliament would, if it had thought about it, probably have included and what it is clear that the express language of the statute shows that the statute must have included. A necessary implication is a matter of express language and logic not interpretation.

Statutory limitation of LPP by necessary implication is rare.[68]

16.15 There is a widespread suspicion in the Inland Revenue and elsewhere in law enforcement that legal privilege is abused to conceal misconduct.[69] In consequence there are statutes that expressly compel the disclosure of material covered by LPP.[70] Some of these provisions may not be Convention compliant. The ECtHR recognizes LPP as an important right to be overridden only in compelling circumstances.[71] For legislation abrogating LPP to comply with the Convention, it must be for a legitimate aim, meet a pressing social need, be proportionate to the aim[72] and not violate a litigant's absolute right to a fair trial (Article 6).[72a] Lord Hoffman doubted that collection of taxes could justify interference with LPP.[73] However, he approved of the outcome in *Parry-Jones v Law Society*[74] which allowed the Law Society to demand to see a solicitor's books on the grounds that this limited disclosure either did not breach the clients' LPP or, if it did, the breach was technical.

---

[66] *R v Secretary of State for the Home Department, ex p Leech* [1994] 3 All ER 539, 551 (mentioned without disapproval by Lord Bingham at [2001] UKHL 26; [2001] 2 AC 532, para 10); *Re L* [1996] 2 All ER 78, 88. cp *Pierson v Secretary of State for the Home Department* [1997] 3 All ER 577, 591.

[67] [2001] UKHL 26; [2001] 2 AC 532, para 45.

[68] *R v Secretary of State for the Home Department, ex p Leech* [1993] 4 All ER 439, 550. For a case in which a mandatory statutory obligation to report sexual abuse was held not to override litigation privilege see *Klassen v College of Physicians and Surgeons of Ontario* [2002] ACWSJ Lexis 6966, para 25. cp *Robert v Commissioner of Police* [2002] 1412 HKCU 1.

[69] D Corker, 'Legal privilege hangs in balance' (2002) 99 LS Gaz 10.

[70] eg Criminal Justice Act 1988, ss 93A, 93B; Drug Trafficking Act 1994, ss 50–52; Insolvency Act 1986, ss 236, 291, 311(1) (discussed in A Mithani, 'Disclosure in bankruptcy—the extent to which a trustee in bankruptcy is entitled to obtain documents from a bankrupt's former solicitor' (1994) 92(2) LS Gaz 20; *Re Murjani* [1996] 1 BCLC 272).

[71] *Foxley v UK* (2001) 32 EHRR 25, see para 3.03 above.

[72] Without safeguards there will be no proportionality, but safeguards may not ensure compliance. The TMA, s 20(1) had safeguards.

[72a] See paras 3.19, 3.23 and 10.14 above.

[73] [2001] UKHL 26; [2001] 2 AC 532, para 44.

[74] [1968] 1 All ER 177.

B. Privilege

Legal advice privilege

What it is and when it arises There are two strands to LPP: legal advice privilege (also known as lawyer–client privilege) and litigation privilege. Legal advice privilege protects communications, in whatever form, and whether or not litigation is in the offing,[75] between, on the one hand, a qualified[76] legal practitioner (who may be a foreign lawyer)[77] or the lawyer's agent[78] and, on the other hand, a client or prospective client.[79] An in-house corporate or government lawyer is treated in exactly the same way as an independent legal adviser in English, though not in EU, law.[80] If two people retain a lawyer (whether solicitor or counsel) jointly, the privilege that attaches to communications passing between them or any one of them and the lawyer is a joint privilege: as between themselves, each party is expected to be privy to all communications but against the outside world the communications are privileged unless both consent to waiver.[81] Should a dispute arise between the joint privilege-holders, either may insist that communications to the lawyer be disclosed.

16.16

There is no legal advice privilege unless the lawyer is acting in a professional capacity (not, for example, as a friend) at the time the communication is made[82] and the communication is related to the giving of legal advice,[83] a requirement that is nowadays liberally construed to cover most communications containing anything of substance between solicitor and client.[84] This takes account of the variety of

16.17

---

[75] *Buttes Gas and Oil v Hammer (No.3)* [1980] 3 All ER 475, 484. In *S CC v B* [2000] 3 WLR 53, 59 Charles J explains that originally the privilege 'was confined to advice or communication between solicitor and client concerning litigation'.

[76] In *New Victoria Hospital v Ryan* [1993] ICR 201, 203–20 an EAT refused to treat correspondence between a hospital and personnel consultants who had no legally qualified staff as privileged.

[77] *Great Atlantic Insurance v Home Insurance* [1981] 2 All ER 485, 490; *R v Inland Revenue Commissioners, ex p Tamosious* [1999] STC 1077.

[78] eg trainees, paralegals, clerks and accountants employed within a firm of solicitors. cp *Descoteaux v Mierzwinski* [1982] SCR 860, 873, 878–879. Interpreters are subject to the same obligations of confidentiality as the solicitor who is giving advice: *R (on the application of Bozkurt) v Thames Magistrates' Court* [2001] EWHC Admin 400; [2002] RTR 246, paras 18, 27.

[79] *Minter v Priest* [1930] AC 558, 573, 584; *Descoteaux v Mierzwinski* (1982) 70 CCC (2d) 385, 401; *R v Lory* [1997] 1 NZLR 44, 48–49; *Re H* [2000] 1 FLR 766.

[80] *Crompton (Alfred) Amusement Machines Ltd v Customs and Excise Commissioners (No.2)* [1972] 2 All ER 353, 376; *Waterford v Commonwealth* (1987) 163 CLR 54. EU law: *AM & S Europe Ltd v EC Commission* [1983] QB 878.

[81] *Rouchefoucauld v Boustead* (1896) 65 LJ Ch 794; *R v Dunbar* (1982) 68 CCC (2d) 13, 37; *Re Konigsberg* [1989] 3 All ER 289, 296; *Farrow v Mortgate Services Pty Ltd v Webb* (1996) 39 NSWLR 601, 608. And see para 19.59 below.

[82] *R v Woodley* (1834) 1 M & Rob 390; *Nederlandse Reassurantie Groep Holding NV v Bacon & Woodrow* [1995] 1 All ER 976, 982–983.

[83] A court famously ordered the solicitor to an Earl to disclose his client's statement that 'I would give £10,000 to have him hanged'; 'him' was a rival for the Earl's estate: *Annesley v Anglesea* (1743) 17 State Trials 1140, 1241.

[84] *R v Manchester Crown Court* [1999] 4 All ER 35, 42. See also, *Balabel v Air India* [1988] Ch 317, 330–331; *NRG v Bacon & Woodrow* [1995] 1 All ER 976, 982–983. But see *C v C* [2001] 1 FCR 756 where a communication intended to reduce the price of a conveyance and to press solicitors to complete the job was held not to have been made for the purpose of obtaining legal advice.

advice that the modern solicitor gives[85] and the difficulty clients may have in separating legal from non-legal advice.[86] Further, although secrecy need not be expressly stipulated, the communication must be made confidentially.[87] In an *obiter dictum* in *Three Rivers District Council v Bank of England* Langmore L.J., however, suggested that receipt of the communication by the legal adviser was unnecessary for legal advice privilege to apply.[87a] The death of the client while the communication is in transit, or loss in the post, would therefore not thwart what would otherwise be a valid claim to legal advice privilege.

16.18 Confidentiality is essential because the object of the privilege is to promote candour which, it is assumed, would be discouraged by fear of disclosure to the detriment of the legal system as well as the client.[88] So long as the conversation is confidential, it does not matter where it takes place. It could be the exercise yard of a police station.[89]

16.19 **Legal advice privilege and non-lawyer professionals** A professional who is not a lawyer is entitled to refuse to disclose a communication with a lawyer if, when it was made, the professional was acting:

(1) As the client's representative in dealing with the lawyer:[90]

[W]here an accountant is used as a representative, or one of a group of representatives, for the purpose of placing a factual situation or a problem before a lawyer to obtain legal advice or legal assistance, the fact that he is an accountant, or that he uses his knowledge and skill as an accountant in carrying out such task, does not make the communications that he makes, or participates in making, as such a representative, any the less communications from the principal, who is the client, to the lawyer; and similarly, communications received by such a representative from a lawyer whose advice has been so sought are none the less communications from the lawyer to the client.[91]

---

[85] D Feldman, *Civil Liberties and Human Rights in England and Wales* (Oxford: 2002) 633.
[86] Note, 'Functional Overlap between the Lawyer and Other Professionals: Its Implications for the Privileged Communications Doctrine' (1962) 71 Yale LJ 1236, 1235: 'if the client cannot separate legal from non-legal communications, the only way he can fully protect himself is by refraining from complete disclosure.'
[87] *Griffith v Davies* (1833) 110 ER 876; *Balabel v Air-India* [1988] 2 All ER 246, 254. See also *R v R* [1994] 4 All ER 260, 265. The presence of a third person during the communication may, depending upon who that person is, prevent privilege from arising: *R v Braham* [1976] VR 574. On the question whether unencrypted e-mail communications are sufficiently confidential to qualify for privilege see K Burden and P Gregoire, 'Client Communication by E-Mail' (1999) 15 Computer L & Security R 311.
[87a] [2003] EWCA Civ 474 para 21.
[88] See paras 16.08 and 1.48 above.
[89] *R v Sutherland* (Nottingham Crown Court, unreported 29 January 2002).
[90] *Wheeler v Le Marchant* (1881) 17 Ch D 675, 682, 684; *C-C Bottlers Ltd v Lion Nathan Ltd* [1993] 2 NZLR 445. See also *Att-Gen (NT) v Maurice* (1986) 65 ALR 230, 235. The terms 'agent' and 'representative' are interchangeable.
[91] per Jackett P, *Susan Hosiery Ltd v Minister of National Revenue* [1969] 2 Ex CR 27, 35–36.

B. Privilege

In some cases it may be difficult to decide whether the professional was

(a) employed as the client's representative to obtain legal advice from the lawyer (in which case the communication is privileged); or

(b) employed on behalf of the client to supply information that the lawyer requires to advise the client (in which case the communication is not privileged).[92]

(2) As the lawyer's agent.[93] Solicitors sometimes assemble a multi-disciplinary team to advise a client about a complex transaction. This will normally be a business transaction such as a corporate takeover. Communications between a non-legal adviser and the client or the solicitors are privileged where the adviser was acting as the solicitors' agent.[94]

Litigation privilege

Pre-conditions and rationale The distinctive feature of litigation privilege is that it allows communications between lawyers or their clients[95] and third parties to be withheld. A classic example is the report of an expert witness prepared for use in court.[96] In *Goldstone v Williams*[97] a statement of account prepared by an accountant at the request of the claimant's solicitors after litigation had commenced was held (prior to its use in litigation) to be privileged. It is not uncommon for accountants to prepare financial statements for matrimonial and personal injury litigation. In *S CC v B*[98] the instructions that medical experts had received, and the report they had prepared in support of the defence of a man accused of causing his young daughter to suffer serious non-accidental injuries were protected by litigation privilege and therefore not accessible to the child's guardian ad litem in care proceedings. Litigation privilege has been applied to a communication with a legal aid authority[99] but this may have been because of the wording of the statutory version of legal privilege found in Police and Criminal Evidence Act 1984 (PACE), s 10(1)(b). **16.20**

It is a pre-condition to common law litigation privilege that the dominant purpose of the communication was for use in connection with the preparation **16.21**

---

[92] *Wheeler v Le Marchant* (1881) 17 Ch 675, 684. *Great Atlantic Insurance v Home Insurance* [1981] 2 All ER 485, 489; *Price Waterhouse v BCCI (Luxembourg) SA* [1992] BCLC 583, 589.

[93] As in *Kowall v McRae* (1980) 108 DLR (3d) 486, 489.

[94] This point was not addressed in *NRG v Bacon & Woodrow* [1995] 1 All ER 976.

[95] *Chartered Bank of India v Rich* (1863) 32 LJQB 300; *Southwark and Vauxhall Water Company v Quick* [1878] 3 QBD 315, 320. It can be claimed by a litigant in person: *S CC v B* [2000] 3 WLR 53, 60. See also para 16.45 below.

[96] *British Coal Corp v Dennis Rye Ltd (No 2)* [1988] 3 All ER 816, 821. Privilege is lost if the report is exchanged or disclosed to the opponent.

[97] [1899] 1 Ch 47, 51.

[98] [2000] 3 WLR 53.

[99] *R v Snaresbrook CC, ex p DPP* [1988] 1 All ER 315, 318. Contrast *Legal Services Agency v Att-Gen* [2002] 1 NZLR 842, 851.

of existing or contemplated litigation.[100] There is disagreement about whether the protected information has to be confidential.[101] Those who argue that confidentiality is unnecessary point to the fact that information given by, and the identity of, prospective witnesses is privileged although none of this may be confidential;[102] a witness's proof of evidence may be a description of an event witnessed by hundreds of people and even if it is not, the information may not be confidential in the hands of the witness.[102a] Under these circumstances the purpose of litigation privilege is not to encourage candour but to create a 'zone of privacy' within which litigants can gather evidence from third parties without running the risk of having to hand it over to an opponent.

> Whereas solicitor–client privilege aims to protect a relationship (i.e. the confidential relationship between lawyer and client), litigation privilege aims to facilitate a process (i.e. the adversary process).[103]

Under the CPR this zone of privacy has shrunk.[104] But it is still not the case that a party has to disclose everything to an opponent during the disclosure process. For example, if a party commissions and then decides not to rely upon an expert report its contents do not have to be disclosed to an opponent.[105]

Scope of litigation and legal advice privilege

16.22 **Derivative materials** The protection of LPP extends beyond 'communications' to include:

---

[100] *Waugh v British Railways Board* [1979] 2 All ER 1169, 1181; *R v Davies* [2002] EWCA Crim 85, para 32.

[101] Against confidentiality: N Williams, 'Four Questions of Privilege: The Litigation Aspect of Legal Professional Privilege' in I Scott (ed), *International Perspectives on Civil Justice* (London: 1990) 233; G Watson and F Au, 'Solicitor–Client Privilege and Litigation Privilege in Civil Litigation' (1998) 77 Canadian Bar Rev 315, 331. In favour of confidentiality: R Mahoney in 'Evidence' [2001] NZLR 85 and 'Reforming Litigation Privilege' [2002] Common L World Rev 66. In *Health & Life Care Ltd v Price Waterhouse* (1997) 69 SASR 362, 369 the Full Court said that litigation privilege did not depend upon the information being confidential but on the purpose for which the communication was made. See also *General Accident Assurance Co v Chrusz* (1999) 92 ACWSJ 15134, para 23 which is consistent with *Re L (A Minor)* [1996] 2 All ER 78. But see *Goldstone v Williams* (1899) 1 Ch 47; *S CC v B* [2000] 3 WLR 53, 60; *Crisford v Haszard* [2000] 2 NZLR 729. Law Commission Consultation Paper 163, *Publication of Local Authority Reports* (2002) Pt IV treats confidentiality as an essential ingredient of litigation as well as legal advice privilege.

[102] *China National Petroleum Corp v Fenwick Elliott* [2002] EWHC 60, Ch D, para 45.

[102a] *Istil Group Inc v Zahoor* [2003] EWHC 165 (ch) paras 60, 63.

[103] G Watson and F Au, 'Solicitor–Client Privilege and Litigation Privilege in Civil Litigation' (1998) 77 Canadian Bar Rev 315, 331. But see *Istil Group Inc v Zahoor* [2003] EWHC 165 paras 56–58.

[104] eg, under CPR, r 35.10 the 'substance of all material instructions' to experts are stripped of privilege. Disclosure, however, requires a court order.

[105] *Causton v Mann Egerton Ltd* [1974] 1 WLR 162, 174. See further, R. Pattenden, 'Litigation privilege and expert opinion evidence' (2000) 4 Intl J of Evidence & Proof 213, 232.

B. Privilege

- samples created by the client for submission to an expert in anticipation of litigation;[106]
- working papers and drafts made by the lawyer for the purpose of giving legal advice.[107]

> [A] note made by a solicitor of a conference with his client will be privileged in so far as it is a record of the communication from the client... but also in so far as it might contain notes of the solicitor's own thoughts in regard to the matters communicated to him. Protection is afforded in the latter case on the ground that disclosure of that material might tend to reveal what had been communicated to the solicitor. There is much in the cases to support the view that this is the true basis upon which draft agreements, draft letters, draft pleadings and the like have long been accepted as privileged; that it is not so much because they are themselves 'advice' or 'communication' but because they will, if disclosed, reveal or tend to reveal, the content of privileged communications.[108]

The lawyer's protected work-product includes copies of unprivileged documents where their selection and copying reveals something about the legal advice given to, or the instructions received from, the client—but not otherwise.[109] Counsel can be asked whether she was shown an 'open' document by her client if this could not prejudice the client's interests.[110]

What is not protected The scope of LPP is a matter of law. The boundaries cannot be extended by agreement.[111] LPP does not cover: **16.23**

(1) facts underlying a privileged communication—the client must testify to facts within his knowledge that he communicated to the lawyer (unless the privilege against self-incrimination applies) as must a third party who provided the lawyer with information; it is only the version the lawyer was told that is protected;[112]
(2) original documents and items that pre-date the professional relationship[113] or were not created for the purpose of that relationship;[114]

---

[106] *R v R* [1994] 4 All ER 260 (blood sample given by the accused).
[107] *Lyell v Kennedy (No 3)* (1884) 27 Ch D 1; *M v L* [1997] 3 NZLR 424, 437. In the US this is referred to as the lawyer's 'work-product'.
[108] per Anderson J, *Dalleagles Pty Ltd v Australian Securities Commission* (1991) 4 WAR 325, 333.
[109] *Dubai Bank Ltd v Galadari* [1989] 3 All ER 769; *Sumitomo Corp v Credit Lyonnais Rouse Ltd* [2001] EWCA Civ 1152; [2002] 1 WLR 479, para 72. In *Ventouris v Mountain* [1991] 1 WLR 607, 621 Bingham LJ noted that 'in an age of indiscriminate photocopying' such a situation 'cannot occur often'.
[110] *Brown v Bennett* (HC (Ch), 18 December 2001) a case in which it was the lawyer, not the client, who was at risk of being prejudiced.
[111] *Federal Commissioner of Taxation v Coombes* (1999) 164 ALR 131. They can, however, be retracted. A party may be given contractual rights of access to legally privileged material.
[112] V Alexander, 'The Corporate Attorney–Client Privilege: A Study of the Participants' (1989) 63 St John's L Rev 191, 215.
[113] *R v King* [1983] 1 All ER 929.
[114] *Guyer v Walton* [2001] STC (SCD) 75, para 32. The opinion was tentative.

(3) translations[115] of documents sent to the lawyer in the course of obtaining legal advice or for litigation, if the originals are not privileged.
(4) facts observed by the lawyer in the course of the professional relationship[116] such as the date and time of a meeting with the client,[117] payments by the client,[118] the appearance of the client's handwriting,[118a] and, semble, the postmark on a letter;[119]
(5) the client's identity[120] (but some other jurisdictions treat identity as privileged if identity forms the crux of the communication);[121]
(6) information needed to find a missing child who is the subject of court proceedings or a ward of court.[122]

16.24 Anything confidential that is not privileged will have to be disclosed to a court or tribunal or opponent if relevant, subject to any discretion the court has to exclude it.[123]

> Though a lawyer is bound not to disclose his clients' affairs voluntarily, the law has always permitted and required him or her to disclose some of them under compulsion of court process, such as a subpoena, search warrant, or demand for an affidavit of documents. He or she can withhold only privileged papers. The limits of privilege mark the balance which the courts have mapped out between the demands of confidentiality, and the interests of society in compelling evidence.... If a paper was

---

[115] *Sumitomo Corp v Credit Lyonnais Rouse Ltd* [2001] EWCA Civ 1152; [2002] 1 WLR 479, para 44.
[116] *R v Jack* (1992) 70 CCC (3d) 67.
[117] *R v Manchester Crown Court, ex p Rogers* [1999] 4 All ER 35.
[118] *Re Furney* [1964] ALR 814; *Robert v Commissioner of Police* [2002] 1412 HKCU 1, para 34.
[118a] *Hurd v Moring* (1824) 1 C & P 372; *Dwyer v Collins* (1852) 21 LJ Ex 225, 227. cp *C v C* [2001] 1 FCR 756, para 23.7.
[119] *Ramsbotham v Senior* (1869) 8 LR Eq 575, 576.
[120] The English common law authorities on privilege and identity are numerous and include: *Parkhurst v Lowten* (1819) 2 Swans 194; *Brown v Foster* (1857) 1 H & N 736; *Bursill v Tanner* (1885) 16 QBD 1; *Pascall v Galinski* [1969] 3 All ER 1090; *Conoco (UK) Ltd v Commercial Law Practice* [1997] SLR 372, 378. See further A Pugh-Thomas, 'Who is your client?' (1997) SJ 44. Some statutes require a lawyer to disclose the client's identity and address: Inheritance Tax Act 1984, s 219(4); Criminal Justice Act 1987, s 2(9); Companies Act 1985, s 452(1)(a); Income and Corporation Taxes Act 1988, s 745(3), 745(4)(c); Terrorism Act 2000, Sch 5, para 13(3); Financial Services and Markets Act 2000, s 175(4). Query: in the absence of statute, can a lawyer be compelled to disclose the client's address? On this point see *Re Arnott* (1888) 60 LT 109 and *ex p Campbell, Re Cathcart* (1870) LR 5 Ch App 703, 705 where Stephen J said that an address is ordinarily something which is not part of any professional confidence. There are clearly circumstances where the client's address is confidential, for example, where the client is being stalked or at risk of assassination, but that does not mean the information is privileged.
[121] *Thorson v Jones* (1973) 38 DLR (3d) 312. See also *Conoco (UK) Ltd v Commercial Law Practice* [1997] SLR 372, 378.
[122] The High Court has both inherent powers (*Ramsbotham v Senior* (1869) 8 LR Eq 575, 579; cp *Re Bell, ex p Lee* (1980) 146 CLR 141) and statutory powers (Family Law Act 1986, s 33 or Child Abduction and Custody Act 1985, s 24A) to order a solicitor to disclose information that would allow the child to be found. On the exercise of these powers see *Re H* [2001] 1 FLR 766 and see para 10.19 above.
[123] See paras 15.15 et seq. Publicity may be controlled: see ch 17.

B. Privilege

not generated to give or get legal advice, or to run or defend litigation or a prosecution, I do not see why it should be sheltered from court process, for example.[124]

LPP when innocence is at stake English case law treats LPP as paramount and absolute once its definitional elements have been met unless waived.[125] It can be asserted by a privilege-holder who has no recognizable interest in maintaining it[126] against a litigant who has a pressing interest in obtaining the privileged material. The latter includes a criminal defendant who requires privileged evidence to establish his innocence,[127] a position that looks impossible to reconcile with the accused's right under Article 6 to a fair trial.[128]

16.25

LPP can arise in two contexts: when litigation is anticipated and when it is not. In the latter situation, it is supported by Article 8,[129] but Article 8(2) envisages exceptions to the right to respect for private life for 'the protection of the rights and freedoms of others'. Legal advice privilege cannot confer a more extensive right to privacy than that to which the client is entitled under Article 8. When litigation is anticipated, both Articles 6 and 8 come into play. The right to a fair trial guaranteed by Article 6, of which the right to access to a lawyer and LPP form a part,[130] is an absolute right,[131] but what is necessary for the privilege-holder to receive a fair trial cannot be considered in a vacuum. Let A be the privilege holder and B the person who wants access to the privileged material. A fair trial for B (who may or may not be A's opponent) cannot be sacrificed to ensure a fair trial for A. In civil proceedings, B's trial may possibly be fair even though B has not been able to use privileged material in the power or possession of A. But an accused who is prevented from showing that he is innocent because A has claimed LPP (especially if this is for a trifling reason) is deprived of a fair trial.[132] It is simply untenable to

16.26

---

[124] per Cote J, *Lavallee, Rackel and Heintz v Canada (Att-Gen)* (2000) Alta D Crim J 244, para 75.

[125] *R v Derby Magistrates' Court, ex p B* [1995] 4 All ER 526 (legal advice/litigation privilege); *General Mediterranean Holdings v Patel* [1999] 3 All ER 673 (legal advice/litigation privilege); *Linstead v East Sussex, Brighton v Hove* [2001] PIQR P25 (litigation privilege involving a third party communication). Contrast *Linstead* with *S CC v B* [2000] 3 WLR 53, 64 where Charles J suggested that a balancing exercise was required where the only reason that the communication was privileged was because the dominant purpose of a communication was in aid of litigation.

[126] See para 16.28 below. The argument for this is that it would make for uncertainty and undermine the privilege if a court had to decide whether the privilege-holder had a recognizable interest in asserting the privilege. Also, why would a privilege-holder claim privilege if he had no continuing interest in concealing the contents of the material?

[127] *R v Derby Magistrates' Court, Ex p B*, [1995] 4 All ER 526. See also *Carter v Northmore, Hale, Davey & Leake* (1995) 183 CLR 121. Criticisms of the English position: C Tapper, 'Prosecution and Privilege' (1996) 1 Intl J of Evidence & Proof 5 ; A Zuckerman, 'Legal Professional Privilege—The Cost of Absolutism' (1996) 113 LQR 535. For a defence: *General Mediterranean Holdings v Patel* [1999] 3 All ER 673, 694.

[128] See para 3.23 above.   [129] See para 3.03 above.   [130] See para 3.10 above.

[131] See para 3.23 above.

[132] Access to evidence is a prerequisite for a fair trial: *Jespers v Belgium* (1981) 27 DR 61, paras 57–58; *Edwards v UK* (1992) 15 EHRR 417. cp *McGinley v UK* (1998) 27 EHRRI, para 86.

argue that the HRA has made no difference and that Article 6 *never*[132a] gives a right to interfere with another person's legal confidentiality.[133]

16.27 The Canadian courts have recognized this. Solicitor–client privilege (as it is known in Canada) will be set aside to ensure that an accused can make full answer and defence, a right protected by the Canadian Charter of Rights and Freedoms, s 7.[134] To avoid damaging public confidence in the confidentiality of communications to lawyers the exception is narrowly confined. The accused must convince a court that there is a genuine risk of wrongful conviction if the privileged evidence is withheld. This involves showing that it relates to a core issue and that the same information cannot be obtained elsewhere.[135] The Canadian exception does not involve the ad hoc balancing of interests found in the criminal proceedings exception to LPP formulated in *R v Ataou*[136] which the House of Lords rejected in *R v Derby Magistrates' Court, ex p B*.[137] Transplanting the Canadian rule into English law would not, however, be problem-free:

- Should it apply to all criminal offences, or only serious crimes?
- Is the right confined to the defence? A defendant stands in a special position because he, and not the prosecutor, is in jeopardy, but Article 6 contains an implied equality of arms principle;[138]
- What happens if the protected material to which the accused seeks access is simultaneously subject to the privilege against self-incrimination?[139]
- To what extent, if at all, should the exception to LPP apply in circumstances where two persons are jointly standing trial and a communication by one co-defendant to his lawyer would materially assist the other?[140]

[132a] *General Mediterranean Holdings v Patel* [1999] 3 All ER 673, 695; *Linstead v East Sussex, Brigton v Hove* [2001] PIQR P25. Neither of these cases was a criminal case and in both the judge's refusal to find an exception to LPP was undoubtedly correct.

[133] Contrast the attitude of the courts to claims to PII in criminal proceedings: see para 16.63 below.

[134] *R v McClure* (2001) 151 CCC (3d) 321.

[135] G Murphy, 'The Innocence at Stake Test and Legal Professional Privilege: A Logical Progression for the Law. . . . But Not in England' [2001] Crim LR 728.

[136] [1988] 2 All ER 321

[137] [1995] 4 All ER 526, esp. 545.

[138] *De Haes v Belgium* (1997) 24 EHRR 11, para 53. Normally this is relied upon by an accused who complains of inferior treatment to that accorded to the prosecuting side. The answer may be that because the prosecution is not in jeopardy, the trial is fair even though the defence alone has a right of access to material covered by LPP.

[139] A privilege against self-incrimination has been held by the ECtHR to be inherent in Art 6 (*Funke v France* (1993) 16 EHRR 297; *Saunders v UK* (1996) 23 EHRR 313), therefore incriminating information extracted from the privilege-holder could not be used against the privilege-holder in a later criminal trial.

[140] In *R v Dunbar* (1982) 68 CCC (2d) 13, 16 the Ontario Court of Appeal suggested that 'an accused ought not to be required to disclose privileged information, the disclosure of which might assist a co-accused to the detriment of the accused who is required to disclose the privileged communication'.

B. Privilege

- If, in the interests of avoiding a miscarriage of justice, a privileged communication has to be disclosed, what practical steps should the court take to protect the confidentiality of the disclosed material?[141]

The operation of LPP in criminal cases is an issue worthy of the consideration of the Law Commission.[142]

Duration of legal professional privilege

General principles The general understanding is that the 'mouth of the attorney with respect to privileged communications is closed forever'.[143] The privilege-holder need no longer be the lawyer's client[144] or have a substantial interest in maintaining privilege.[145] LPP is not confined to the context in which it arose. If it came into being because litigation was contemplated with A, it can be asserted in later unconnected litigation against B.[145a] This makes sense for legal advice privilege.

16.28

> The reason of the privilege is that there may be that free and confident communication between solicitor and client which lies at the foundation of the use and service of the solicitor to the client; but, if at any time or under any circumstance such communications are subject to discovery, it is obvious that this freedom of communication will be impaired. The liability of such communications to discovery in a subsequent action would have this effect as well as their liability to discovery in the original action.[146]

It makes less sense for litigation privilege to persist in totally altered circumstances if its rationale is to protect the litigation brief.[147] This has led some Canadian courts to limit litigation privilege to the dispute in which the communication was

---

[141] What are the implications of abolishing the double jeopardy rule for some offences in the Criminal Justice Bill.

[142] It is worth noting that under Freedom of Information Act 2000, s 42, information covered by LPP has only a qualified exemption.

[143] per Sir James Wigram, *Chant v Brown* (1849) 7 Hare 84, 86. See also *Bullock v Corry* (1878) 3 QBD 356, 358–359; *Calcraft v Guest* [1898] 1 QB 759, 761; *R v Derby Magistrates' Court, ex p B* [1995] 4 All ER 526, 538, 543.

[144] *Bell v Smith* (1968) 68 DLR (2d) 751, 757; *Kershaw v Whelan* [1996] 2 All ER 404, 410.

[145] *R v Derby Magistrates' Court, ex p B* [1995] 4 All ER 526, 537, 542. Lord Nicholls at 546 reserved his 'final view' on whether a client who no longer has any interest to protect can claim privilege, but it is clear that the other members of the House did not share his reservations. Their Lordships' views were examined and compared in *Nationwide Building Society v Various Solicitors* (1998) 148 NLJ 241 where Blackburne J, concluded, 'notwithstanding Lord Nicholls' comments, I take the view that whether or not the client has any recognisable interest in continuing to assert privilege in the confidential communications, the privilege is absolute in nature and the lawyer's mouth is "shut: forever"'.

[145a] M Howard (ed), *Phipson on Evidence* (15th edn, (London: 2000) 572 contends that litigation privilege can be claimed for witness statements that are not used in open court against a different party, but the authority for this is slight. *Quinlivan v Tuohy* (Irish HC, 29 July 1992) (medical reports relating to an earlier accident).

[146] per Lord Esher, *Pearce v Foster* (1885) 15 QBD 114, 119–120.

[147] R Pattenden, 'Litigation Privilege and Expert Opinion Evidence' (2000) Intl J of Evidence & Proof 213 and see para 16.21 above.

made or closely related litigation.[148] The English position is that litigation privilege can be claimed in any subsequent litigation to which the privilege-holder is a party.[149]

16.29 **Death of the client** Neither legal advice nor litigation privilege is normally affected by the death of the client.[150] LPP vests in the client's personal representative or, once administration is complete, the person entitled to his estate.[151] Testamentary disputes are an exception.[152] In *Swidler and Berlin v US*[153] the Supreme Court, by a majority, refused to sanction an exception to attorney–client privilege for criminal proceedings to which the communication was of substantial relevance. Before the HRA it was likely that this decision would have been followed in England. Now, because of Article 6, the right of a litigant to a fair trial ought to have precedence.[154] The impact on the public's willingness to consult lawyers of a posthumous criminal proceedings exception to LPP is likely to be small.[155] To refuse to admit the evidence, unless privilege is waived by the deceased's personal representatives, may thwart a fair trial.

---

[148] *Boulianne v Flynn* [1970] 3 OR 84, 88–89; *Wujda v Smith* (1974) 49 DLR (3d) 476 *Att-Gen of Ontario v Holly Big Canoe* [2002] Ont CA Lexis 543, para 11. Contrast *The Aegis Blaze* [1986] 1 Lloyd's Rep 203, 211. See further N Williams, 'Four Questions of Privilege: the Litigation Aspect of Legal Professional Privilege' (1990) 9 Civil Justice Quarterly 139, 160–166.

[149] *The Aegis Blaze* [1986] 1 Lloyd's Rep 203; *Bradford Hospitals NHS Trust v Burcher* (EAT/958/01, 28 September 2001). cp *Schneider v Leigh* [1955] 2 All ER 173, 179. Neither the lawyer nor the client need be a party to the action in which legal advice privilege is claimed: *Minter v Priest* [1930] AC 558, 579. Recently never-ending litigation privilege was rejected in costs proceedings in *McCreery v Massey Plastic Fabrications Ltd* [2003] EWHC claim MA091748 (QB) para 82 et seq.

[150] *Bullivant v Att-Gen for Victoria* [1901] AC 196, 206; *Curtis v Beaney* [1911] PD 181; *R v Derby Magistrates' Court, ex p B* [1995] 4 All ER 526, 537, 540.

[151] *R v Molloy* [1997] 2 Cr App R 283. In this case the client died before his criminal appeal could be heard. His legal representatives were allowed to waive the privilege to enable the Court of Appeal to be shown his original statements and instructions to the lawyers who had acted for him at his trial. Other cases recognizing the survival of the privilege after the client's death are *Calcraft v Guest* [1898] 1 QB 759; *The Aegis Blaze* [1986] 1 Lloyd's Rep 203, 210. Contrast *Hitt v Stephens* 675 NE 2d 275 (1997).

[152] *Russell v Jackson* (1851) 9 Hare 387. This exception does not allow disclosure in all circumstances in which there is a dispute concerning a will: *Gordon v Gilroy* (1994) 5 ETR (2d) 289. See further H Laidlaw, 'Solicitor–Client Privilege: To Disclose or Not to Disclose . . . Remains the Question, Even after Death' (1995) Estates Trust J 56.

[153] (1998) 118 SCt 2081 (noted by H. Ho (1999) 115 LQR 27). Contrast *R v Jack* (1992) 70 CCC (3d) 67. Disclosure in *Jack* was in the client's interests and therefore might be classified as implied waiver.

[154] See paras 3.23 and 16.25 et seq.

[155] The fact that the client is dead minimizes the countervailing cost of lifting the privilege. If, as in *Swidler*, disclosure threatens no economic interests, reputation alone is protected by the privilege, something that the law of defamation refuses to protect after a person's death. How often will the possibility of posthumous disclosure of a communication with a lawyer in criminal proceedings deter a client from making a clean breast of his affairs, if disclosure has no economic consequences?

B. Privilege

Mechanics of legal professional privilege

A professional must not volunteer material that is covered by LPP without the consent of the client.[156] If the professional is the privilege-holder's lawyer or former lawyer it is her professional duty to assert LPP unasked[157] in any situation in which it is arguable that LPP exists.[158] A court will do its best to prevent a third party[159] or a solicitor making disclosures in breach of LPP. **16.30**

> [I]t would be the duty of any Court to stop him if he was about to disclose confidential matters . . . the Court knows the privilege of the client, and it must be taken for granted that the attorney will act rightly, and claim that privilege; or that if he does not, the Court will make him claim it.[160]

If the client chooses to waive LPP the lawyer cannot object.[161]

Loss of Legal Professional Privilege

Waiver[162]

Express waiver LPP may be intentionally waived.[163] If intentional waiver is asserted, it must be affirmatively proved.[164] Intentional waiver of privileged documents will prima facie amount to general waiver[165] but it is possible to waive privilege for a specific purpose in a specific context reserving it in relation to other uses in other contexts.[166] This is known as partial waiver.[167] Express reservation is not always necessary to achieve partial waiver. Waiver of LPP for documents relied on **16.31**

---

[156] *S C C v B* [2000] 3 WLR 53, 75.
[157] *Nationwide Building Society v Various Solicitors (No 2)* [1998] All ER (D) 119.
[158] *R v Derby Magistrates' Court, ex p B* [1995] 4 All ER 526, 538. See also *R v Ataou* [1988] 2 All ER 321, 325. The burden of laying an evidentiary foundation for LPP lies on the party asserting privilege.
[159] *Harmony Shipping v Saudi Europe Line* [1979] 3 All ER 177, 181.
[160] per Lord Eldon LC, *Beer v Ward* (1821) Jacob 77, 80.
[161] *R v Special Commissioner, ex p Morgan Grenfell & Co Ltd* [2002] UKHL 21; [2002] 2 WLR 1299, para 37. It is immaterial whether the solicitor owns the document containing the communication or not.
[162] The law on waiver of privilege is unsatisfactory. It is beyond the scope of this book to delve into the doctrine in all its details. For a critical examination see J Auburn, *Legal Professional Privilege* (Oxford: 2000) ch 11.
[163] Express waiver may be implied provided the waiver was intentional eg where the privilege-holder uses a privileged document to refresh a witness's memory. Intentional waiver needs to be distinguished from inadvertent disclosure (see paras 6.108 et seq).
[164] *Hilton v Barker Booth & Eastwood* [2002] EWCA Civ 723, para 29.
[165] Query: has a lawyer a duty to warn the client of this? On this point see *R v Kotapski* (1981) 66 CCC (2d) 78.
[166] *Bourns Inc v Raychem Corp* [1999] 3 All ER 154, 162; *Auckland District Law Society v B* [2002] 1 NZLR 721, paras, 156–157, 167. cp *Rockefeller & Co Inc v Secretary for Justice* [2000] 3 HKLRD 351, 371.
[167] 'A person who is offered information subject to limitations as to use has an option; he can either refuse the offer or accept it subject to the limitations', per Aldous LJ, *Bourns Inc v Raychem Corp* [1999] 3 All ER 154, 169.

in taxation extends only so far as the taxation.[168] In *British Coal Corp v Dennis Rye Ltd (No2)*[169] it was decided that if X, a party to a civil dispute against Y, voluntarily disclosed privileged information to the police, the prosecution or both and the prosecution then prosecuted Y and in doing so discloses the privileged material to Y, X could still assert privilege in the material against Y in the civil suit.

16.32 A disclosure made 'in confidence'[170] to someone with a common interest in the subject matter of the communication does not stop the privilege-holder from asserting LPP (in either form) against an opponent.[171] It has yet to be decided whether privilege survives voluntary[172] disclosure on a 'confidential basis' to a regulatory body.[173] There is a strong interest in LPP surviving because it will encourage disclosure of information that cannot be compelled but is needed for an effective investigation. The analogy with disclosure to the police and Crown Prosecution Service to enable a prosecution to be brought is a strong one.

16.33 How voluntary must waiver be? The motive of the privilege-holder and consequences for him of not waiving privilege are irrelevant. This emerges in the case law on the right to silence. In a criminal trial the judge will normally invite the jury to draw an adverse inference from the fact that when interviewed by the police the accused failed to mention something that he relied upon in his defence at his trial.[174] The accused does not waive LPP by giving as his reason for silence that he acted upon the advice of his solicitor,[175] but in order to dissuade the jury from drawing an adverse inference from his pre-trial silence, the accused may have to disclose why the advice was given. If, Lord Bingham has said, the accused discloses those reasons he 'voluntarily withdraws the veil of privilege which would otherwise protect confidential communications between his legal adviser and himself,

---

[168] *Bourns Inc v Raychem Corp* [1999] 3 All ER 154, 160–162. The rationale may be that the waiver is not truly voluntary.
[169] [1988] 3 All ER 816, 822.
[170] *Gotha City v Sotheby's* [1998] 1 WLR 114, 121; *CC Bottlers Ltd v Lion Nathan Ltd* [1993] 2 NZLR 445, 448.
[171] *Svenska v Sun Alliance* [1995] 2 Lloyd's Rep 84, 88. This decision extends the 'common interest privilege' recognized in *Buttes Gas & Oil Co v Hammer (No 3)* [1980] 3 All ER 475. See further, M Howard (ed), *Phipson on Evidence* (15th edn (London: 2000) 543–549; R Desiatnik, *Legal Professional Privilege* (St Leonards: 2000) 116–119. For the position in criminal trials where co-accused mount a joint defence that requires the pooling of information see *R v Dunbar* (1982) 68 CCC (2d) 13, 36–37.
[172] Disclosure to a regulatory body may be either under statutory compulsion (see ch 10) or voluntary. If disclosure is under compulsion there is no waiver. The extent to which privilege survives the disclosure depends upon the statute compelling disclosure.
[173] Consider *Goldberg v Ng* (1995) 185 CLR 183 and *R v NatWest Investment Bank* (23 January 1991) discussed by C Passmore, *Privilege* (Bristol: 1998) 181, n 54. See also *Rockefeller & Co Inc v Secretary for Justice* [2000] 3 HKC 48.
[174] Criminal Justice and Public Order Act 1994, s 34.
[175] *R v Roble* [1997] Crim LR 449.

B. Privilege

and having done so he cannot resist questioning directed to the nature of that advice and the factual premises on which it had been based'.[176]

Imputed waiver There are a number of situations in which the law deems a privilege-holder to have waived LPP although he may have had no actual intention of doing so. They are all situations in which the courts have decided that the continued existence of LPP would be unfair to an opponent. **16.34**

(1) When an ex-client sues a solicitor LPP is waived by operation of law in respect of anything relevant to the transaction sued on.[177] This includes relevant files of the client's earlier solicitors:[178] '[a] party cannot deliberately subject a relationship to public scrutiny and at the same time seek to preserve its confidentiality. He cannot pick and choose, disclosing such incidents of the relationship as strengthen his claim for damages and concealing from forensic scrutiny such incidents as weaken it. He cannot attack his former solicitor and deny the solicitor the use of materials relevant to his defence.'[179] Whether privilege is lost in documents needed to enforce the payment of fees to the lawyer by the client is discussed in chapter 12.[180]

(2) When the privilege-holder's state of mind is in issue and cannot be fairly assessed without examination of relevant local advice, privilege in the advice is deemed to be waived.[181]

(3) A privilege-holder who intentionally discloses a portion of a document will be treated as having waived privilege in the undisclosed portion if the document cannot be split into two separate and distinct parts[181a] or if partial disclosure would be misleading.[182]

(4) If the privilege-holder makes public his version of privileged communications with a lawyer he cannot, at the same time, enforce silence by others who disagree with that version.[183]

(5) When an expert witness is called as a witness, or his report is relied upon, by the party by whom he was instructed, waiver will be implied in respect of all privileged communications forming the basis of the opinion.[184]

---

[176] per Lord Bingham CJ, *R v Bowden* [1999] 4 All ER 43, 50 (examined in J Auburn, 'Implied Waiver and Adverse Inferences' (1999) 115 LQR 590). See also *R v Ali* [2001] EWCA Crim 863.
[177] *Lillycrap v Halder & Son* [1993] 1 All ER 724, 729, 731, 732–733; *Ball v Druces* [2002] EWCA Civ 157, para 27.
[178] *Kershaw v Whelan* [1996] 2 All ER 404, 415.
[179] per Lord Bingham, *Paragon Finance Plc v Freshfields* [1999] 1 WLR 1183, 1188. See also *NRG v Bacon & Woodrow* [1995] 1 All ER 976, 986.
[180] See para 12. 35 above.
[181] *BP Australia Pty Ltd v Nyran Pty Ltd* [2002] FCA 1302. But see *British Tobacco Australia Services Ltd v Cowell* [2002] VSCA 197, para 130.
[181a] *Great Atlantic Insurance Co v Home Insurance Co* [1981] 2 All ER 485, 490–491.
[182] *Paragon Finance Plc v Freshfields* [1999] 1 WLR 1183, 1188.
[183] *Benecke v National Bank of Australia* (1993) 35 NSWLR 110.
[184] CPR, rr 31.14, 35.10, PD 35. Instructions are not privileged: s 35.10(4). Whether background information, privileged or unprivileged, supplied to the expert, but not relied upon, must

A doctor... in a personal injury action can be asked what the claimant said on being examined for the purposes of the doctor's report, in so far as that is material to the doctor's opinion, for the claimant necessarily waives any privilege in what was said at the examination when calling the doctor to give evidence as to the opinion which he formed as a result of it.[185]

(6) Waiver of privilege between the clients is implicit in a joint retainer.[186]

(7) Accidental disclosure will not produce imputed waiver.

Iniquity

16.35 **Legal professional privilege** LPP does not exist in a communication tainted by 'iniquity'.[187] This vague term refers either to a communication that of itself constitutes misconduct[188] or one made (whether or not to the knowledge of the lawyer does not matter)[189] for one of the following purposes:

(1) to enable the client to better commit a crime[190] or fraud, broadly defined;[191]

---

be disclosed is unclear. *Clough v Tameside & Glossop Health Authority* [1998] 2 All ER 971 says so, but this case pre-dates the CPR and was not, in any case, applied in *Bourns Inc v Raychem Corp* [1999] 3 All ER 154, 163–167. The Court of Appeal's view was that there must at least be reference to the contents of the privileged documents and reliance on them. In criminal proceedings, a passing reference in an expert report for the defence to the opinion of another expert whose opinion the accused does not rely upon is not necessarily lost: *R v Davies* [2002] EWCA Crim 85, paras 37–38.

[185] per Toulson J, *General Mediterranean Holdings v Patel* [1999] 3 All ER 673, 694.

[186] *TSB v Robert Irving* [2000] 2 All ER 826. It was held that the waiver does not extend to communications to the solicitor after a conflict of interest has arisen of which the communicating client is ignorant.

[187] *Ventouris v Mountain* [1991] 1 WLR 607, 611; *Nationwide Building Society v Various Solicitors* (1998) 148 NLJ 241; *Barclays Bank v Eustice* [1995] 4 All ER 511, 524.

[188] *C v C* [2001] 1 FCR 756 where a threat by telephone to the solicitor to 'rip someone's throat out' was a criminal offence under Telecommunications Act 1984, s 43 and capable of constituting a threat to kill, contrary to Offences Against the Person Act 1861, s 16.

[189] *Banque Keyser Ullmann SA v Skandia (UK) Insurance Co Ltd* [1986] 1 Lloyd's Rep 336; *Walsh Automation (Europe) Ltd v Bridgeman* [2002] EWHC 1344, QB, para 16.

[190] *R v Cox* (1884) 14 QBD 153; *R v Special Commissioner, ex p Morgan Grenfell & Co Ltd* [2002] UKHL 21; [2002] 2 WLR 1299, para 38. If the client gratuitously announces that he intends to commit or is committing some crime, or that someone else is or is intending to do so, the communication might not be privileged but this would be because it was not related to the giving of legal advice rather than because it was made in furtherance of crime. The Law Gazette reported on 13 February 2002 the conclusion of the Office for the Supervision of Solicitors that when a solicitor received a letter from a client saying that he would not be answering his bail and had decided to abscond, the solicitor was not being used to facilitate a crime or fraud. Query: is a communication protected if made in furtherance of a crime that was not in the end committed? There is US authority that in this situation attorney–client privilege applies: Note, 'Functional Overlap between the Lawyer and Other Professionals: Its Implications for the Privileged Communications Doctrine' (1962) 71 Yale LJ 1226, 1243.

[191] eg selling property at less than its true value for the purpose of prejudicing the interests of creditors (*Barclays Bank v Eustice* [1995] 4 All ER 511, 521–522) or breaching an employee's duty of fidelity or confidence to the employer (*Walsh Automation (Europe) Ltd v Bridgeman* [2002] EWHC 1344, para 15). The court refused to go beyond the fraud exception, liberally construed, in *Crescent Farm (Sidcup) Sports Ltd v Sterling Offices Ltd* [1971] 3 All ER 1192, 1200. See also *Nationwide Building Society v Various Solicitors* [1998] All ER (D) 119. Notice that PACE, s 10(2) has an exception only for 'criminal purpose'.

B. Privilege

(2) in aid of a third party's crime or fraud (whether or not the client is aware of this);[192]
(3) to enable the client to take advantage of a third party's fraud;[193]
(4) to protect the proceeds of crime or fraud;[194]
(5) to cheat in litigation by developing a bogus defence[195] or by obtaining evidence by fraud or unlawful means.[196]

The traditional explanation for the iniquity exception is that a client who uses a lawyer to further iniquity is not consulting the lawyer in his professional capacity and the communication is therefore outside the ambit of the privilege.[197] An alternative explanation is that a communication made in bad faith is not deserving of protection.[198] Disclosure would not discourage honest citizens from consulting lawyers even if the dishonest might be put off. Denying LPP might have the positive consequence of making it more difficult for the dishonest to perpetrate fraud or crime.[199] But it might also deprive lawyers of opportunities to dissuade people from wrongdoing. A warning volunteered by a lawyer that certain conduct, if pursued, would be unlawful is protected by legal privilege.[200] Likewise, communications about the past commission of a crime or fraud are protected.[201] If they were not, those accused of criminal offences could not speak frankly to their lawyers. 16.36

The iniquity exception to LPP suffers from certain problems. First, the neat division between consulting a lawyer about iniquity that has already happened and planned iniquity on closer examination breaks down. 16.37

---

[192] This has not been finally settled. *Banque Keyser Ullmann SA v Skandia (UK) Insurance* [1986] 1 Lloyd's Rep 336 might be cited as authority that the criminal intent of someone who is not the solicitor or client does not destroy privilege but it is likely that the courts will hold that PACE, s 10(2) sets out the common law position. In *Francis & Francis (A Firm) v Central Criminal Court* [1988] 3 All ER 775, s 10(2) was interpreted as excluding privilege when anyone connected with the transaction had instigated it with a criminal intent: see para 14.22 above. Contrast US law; US courts require that the client knowingly use the attorney to perpetrate the iniquity: Note, 'Developments—Privileged Communications' (1985) 98 Harvard L Rev 1501, 1511.
[193] *Conoco (UK) Ltd v Commercial Law Practice* [1997] SLT 373, 379.
[194] cp *Francis & Francis (A Firm) v Central Criminal Court* [1988] 3 All ER 775.
[195] *Chandler v Church* (1987) 137 NLJ 451; *Dubai Bank Ltd v Galadari (No 6)*, The Times, 22 April 1991.
[196] *Dubai Aluminium Co Ltd v Al Alwai* [1999] 1 WLR 1964, 1970. C. Tapper, *Cross & Tapper on Evidence* (9th edn, London: 1999) 458 suggests qualifications.
[197] *R v Cox* (1884) 14 QBD 153, 168.
[198] *Banque Keyser Ullman SA v Skandia (UK) Insurance Ltd (No 1)* [1986] 1 Lloyd's Rep 336, 338. Note, 'Functional Overlap between the Lawyer and Other Professionals: Its Implications for the Privileged Communications Doctrine' (1962) 71 Yale LJ 1226, 1243.
[199] *Barclays Bank v Eustice* [1995] 4 All ER 511, 525.
[200] *Butler v Board of Trade* [1970] 3 All ER 593. Query: should it be if the client decides to pursue the course of conduct about which he was warned?
[201] *R v Derby Magistrates' Court, ex p B* [1995] 4 All ER 526, 541. See also *Weld-Blundell v Stephens* [1919] 1 KB 520, 544–545; *Crescent Farm (Sidcup) Sports Ltd v Sterling Offices Ltd* [1971] 3 All ER 1192, 1200.

In reality... future criminal activity is not neatly severable from past criminal activity. Moreover, clients asking for advice about on-going or future conduct may have mixed motives: obtaining legal advice about what is permissible and figuring out not only whether, but also how to engage in offensive conduct. Clients engaged in potentially unlawful commercial enterprises typically inquire about the legality of past conduct that the clients would like to continue.[202]

Secondly, it is often difficult to establish that a communication was a step in some criminal or iniquitous design, especially where the communication was made orally.[203] In an interlocutory application, the party seeking disclosure must produce a strong prima facie case of wrongdoing.[204] When the allegedly privileged communication is contained in a document, the document can be examined by the court for the purpose of deciding whether it was made for such purposes.[205]

Loss of other privileges

16.38 Express waiver (disclosure intended and consented to by the privilege-holder) applies to all forms of privilege.[206] The iniquity exception is also not unique to LPP. In *Unilever Plc v Proctor & Gamble Co*[207] Robert Walker LJ provided a summary of the numerous occasions on which, despite the existence of without prejudice negotiations, the without prejudice rule does not prevent the admission into evidence of what one or both of the parties said or wrote. The fourth exception is where the privilege would enable the exclusion of evidence so as to act as a cloak for perjury, blackmail or other unambiguous impropriety. This exception is similar to, but apparently wider than, the iniquity exception to LPP.[208] Because of its close connection to the without prejudice privilege, one would expect something similar for conciliation privilege. This is confirmed by *Re D* where Sir Thomas Bingham said that conciliation privilege does not prevent a statement made during the conciliation process from being given that 'clearly [indicates] that the maker has in the past caused or is likely in the future to cause serious harm to the well-being of a child',[209] if the judge, in his discretion, concludes that the public

---

[202] F Zacharias, 'Harmonizing Privilege and Confidentiality' (1999) 43 South Texas L Rev 69, 79. A Boon and J Levin in *The Ethics and Conduct of Lawyers* (Oxford: 1999) 253 suggest that *Barclays Bank v Eustice* [1995] 4 All ER 511 is a borderline case in which it is debatable whether the defendant consulted his lawyers in furtherance of fraud or to explain the legal effect of what had already been done.

[203] *Derby & Co Ltd v Weldon (No 7)* [1990] 3 All ER 161, 176–177.

[204] *Walsh Automation (Europe) Ltd v Bridgeman* [2002] EWHC 1344, para 17. On the need for prima facie evidence of fraud see also *O'Rourke v Darbishire* [1920] AC 581, 604; *Butler v Board of Trade* [1970] 3 All ER 593, 598. It is not necessary that the litigation is founded on the crime or fraud.

[205] *R v Governor of Pentonville Prison, ex p Osman* [1989] 3 All ER 701, 730. However, the point was not fully argued.

[206] For an example involving conciliation privilege see *Wilkinson v Wilkinson* [1994] HKC 58.

[207] [2001] 1 All ER 783, 791.

[208] See eg *Dora v Simper* (CA, 15 March 1999). In the course of settlement negotiations, the defendants threatened that steps would be taken to ensure that there would be no assets left out of which to pay the claimant's judgment. Evidence of the threats was held admissible.

[209] [1993] 2 All ER 693, 699.

B. Privilege

interest in protecting the interests of the child outweighs the public interest in preserving the confidentiality of the conciliation process. The possibility of a professional being compelled to disclose a relevant admission of child abuse made during parental negotiations in discovery or trial proceedings therefore exists.

Non-adversarial proceedings

Litigation privilege

It was decided in *Re L*[210] by the House of Lords that there is no litigation privilege in expert reports prepared for care proceedings with leave of the court and based on papers already before all the parties.[211] Other cases apply this rule to all reports prepared specifically for proceedings concerning the welfare of children.[212] The basis of the litigation privilege exception is the non-adversarial and investigative nature of the proceedings which derives from the court's paramount concern for the welfare of the child.[213] If the report is not protected by litigation privilege then, by implication, the letter of instruction to the expert also ceases to be privileged and must be disclosed.[214] It has been suggested that the same exception applies to an application for an order under Mental Health Act 1983 s 29 to displace someone as the nearest relative.[215] Litigation privilege that arises in relation to criminal proceedings continues (in the absence of statutory abrogation) to apply in related non-adversarial proceedings. 'It is one thing to conclude that the Children Act 1989 and the nature of proceedings under it has the result that a privilege does not arise in such proceedings and quite another to say that they remove, or affect, rights based on the public interest and which come into existence in, or in respect of, other proceedings.'[216]

16.39

---

[210] [1996] 2 All ER 78, 85 (noted J. McEwan, 'The Uncertain Status of Privilege in Children Act Cases: Re L' (1997) 1 Intl J of Evidence & Proof 80). The decision that LPP can only be abrogated by express language or necessary implication in *R v Special Commissioner, ex p Morgan Grenfell & Co Ltd* [2002] UKHL 21; [2002] 2 WLR 1299 (see para 16.13 above) makes *Re L* [1996] 2 All ER 78 vulnerable. See counsel's argument in *Oxfordshire CC v M* [1994] 2 All ER 269, 277.

[211] The Family Proceedings Rules 1991, SI 1991/1247 require the court's leave to have the child examined or to obtain disclosure of documents filed with the court. P Murphy, *Evidence* (7th edn, London: 2000) 425 argues that because the mother had initiated the disclosure of the court papers and had complied with the court's order to file and disclose the report she had plainly waived privilege in the report and it was therefore unnecessary for the House of Lords to decide that there is an exception to litigation privilege for reports prepared for care proceedings.

[212] *S CC v B* [2000] 3 WLR 53, 66, 68. Charles J leaves open the question whether litigation privilege arises in respect of communications with third party witnesses to the facts. See also *Re L (A Minor)* [1996] 2 All ER 78, 93; *Vernon v Bosley (No 2)* [1997] 1 All ER 614, 628.

[213] *Oxfordshire CC v M* [1994] 2 All ER 269, 278; *Re L* [1996] 2 All ER 78, 84–85. In *R v Secretary of State for the Home Department, ex p Gashi* [1999] INLR 276, 308 Thorpe LJ said (obiter) that litigation privilege could not be claimed for an expert report obtained for asylum proceedings because they were non-adversarial and 'the court has an overriding obligation to promote a welfare consideration'.

[214] *Re DH* [1994] 1 FLR 679.

[215] *R (on the application of Stevens) v Plymouth City Council* [2002] EWCA Civ 388; [2002] 1 FLR 1177, para 39.

[216] per Charles J, *S v CC v B* [2000] 3 WLR 53, 71.

Chapter 16: Grounds for Non-Disclosure

16.40 The compatibility of *Re L*[217] with Article 6 of the ECHR has not been judicially determined. Lord Nicholls delivered a powerful dissenting judgment in *Re L* in which he pointed out that family proceedings contained adversarial features: '[a] father who is alleged to have sexually abused his stepdaughter is concerned to protect his own reputation as well as his family life. He can hardly be blamed if he regards the proceedings as no less confrontational and adversarial than other civil proceedings.'[218] In his view the crucial question was not whether, and to what extent, children proceedings were inquisitorial but what was required for the proceedings to be fair. The rejoinder to this argument is that the right to a fair trial has no higher standing than the child's Article 2, 3 and 8 rights.[219] When Convention rights clash the court must decide where the greater public interest lies. If disclosure of an expert's report is necessary to protect the child, then the child's protection should be put ahead of the interests of a litigant-parent.[220] Both English domestic law and ECHR jurisprudence accept the paramountcy of the welfare principle which is enshrined in Children Act 1989, s 1.[221] Since there is no property in a witness,[222] it may be that sight of the report will not always be necessary. It will be unnecessary if the expert who made the report can appear as the court's witness to state the opinion orally and thereafter be examined by all the parties.[223] There is unlikely to be a breach of Article 6 if the party who commissioned and disowned the expert report is allowed to participate in the cross-examination.

Legal advice privilege

16.41 The majority in *Re L* assumed that legal advice privilege operated in children proceedings just as absolutely as in any other proceedings.[224] The instructions that a solicitor receives from a parent of a child who suffered serious injuries therefore do not lose their privileged status because the guardian ad litem thinks the court in care proceedings ought to know what account the parent gave the solicitor of the relevant events.[225] The difference in the treatment of legal advice privilege and litigation privilege presumably lies in the greater need for candour in communications between lawyers and clients than between lawyers and third parties many of

---

[217] [1996] 2 All ER 78. See also *Oxfordshire CC v M* [1994] Fam 151, 163 where a party was ordered to disclose an unfavourable report by a psychiatrist.
[218] *Re L* [1996] 2 All ER 78, 89.
[219] See para 3.26 above.
[220] cp *Re DH* [1994] 1 FLR 679.
[221] *Oxfordshire CC v M* [1994] 2 All ER 269, 278; *P v P* [2001] EWCA Civ 166; [2001] Fam 473, paras 38–39. See also *Sahin v Germany* (2002) 1 FLR 119.
[222] See para 15.25 above.
[223] *Re DH* [1994] 2 FCR 2, 44.
[224] [1996] 2 All ER 78, 86. See also *S CC v B* [2000] 3 WLR 53, 69. But see *Re R (A Minor)* [1993] 4 All ER 702. For critical comment see: A Zuckerman, 'Legal Professional Privilege—The Cost of Absolutism' (1996) 113 LQR 535, 538; D Burrows, 'Privilege and Disclosure after *Re L*' (1996) 140 SJ 560; J McEwan, 'The Uncertain Status of Privilege in Children Act Cases: *Re L*' (1996) 1 Intl J of Evidence & Proof 80.
[225] *S CC v B* [2000] 3 WLR 53, 58.

B. Privilege

whom, in children's cases, are likely to be professionals from whom candour is to be expected whether or not their communications are protected by privilege. It would be surprising if legal advice privilege impeded a lawyer's ability to inform a court of a serious risk to the safety of a child discovered in the course of a professional consultation whether or not the iniquity exemption applied.[226] The extent to which a child-client enjoys legal advice privilege in family proceedings was considered in chapter 12.[227]

Privilege for non-lawyers

The English situation

There are many cases in which judges have summarily dismissed the idea that communications between non-lawyers and their clients might be privileged in litigation and not simply subject to a contractual and/or equitable obligation of confidentiality.

16.42

> [T]he law has ... accorded to [confidential communications passing between lawyer and client] a degree of protection denied to communications, however confidential, between clients and other professional advisers.[228]

Professions that have been expressly singled out for mention by English courts as not benefiting from privileged communications with their clients include medical practitioners,[229] the clergy,[230] bankers,[231] accountants,[232] auditors[233] and journalists.[234] Lawyers aside, the only professionals to whom privilege applies in England

---

[226] cp *Re R* [1993] 4 All ER 702.

[227] See para 12.12 above.

[228] per Lord Bingham, *Paragon Finance Plc v Freshfields* [1999] 1 WLR 1183, 1188 (this passage does not deny that a communication between a client and an expert relating to litigation may fall under the umbrella of litigation privilege). See also *Wheeler v Le Marchant* (1881) 17 Ch D 675, 681; *McGuinness v Att-Gen for Victoria* (1940) 63 CLR 73, 102–103.

[229] *Duchess of Kingston's Trial* (1776) 20 How St Tr 355, 572–573; *Greenlaw v King* (1838) 48 ER 891, 894; *Russell v Jackson* (1851) 68 ER 558, 559–560; *Garner v Garner* (1920) 36 TLR 196, 197; *Nuttall v Nuttall* (1964) 108 SJ 605; *D v NSPCC* [1977] 1 All ER 589, 617. See also G Nokes, 'Professional Privilege' (1950) 66 LQR 88, 89–94; JRL, 'Privileged Communications, Part 3, Doctor and Patient' (1958) 13 Northern Ireland LQ 284.

[230] *Du Barre v Livette* (1790) 1 Peake 108; *Wilson v Rastall* (1792) 100 ER 1283, 1286–1287; *Broad v Pitt* (1828) 3 C & P 518, 519; *Wheeler v Le Marchant* (1881) 17 Ch D 675, 681; *Normanshaw v Normanshaw* (1893) 69 LT 468. See also G Nokes, 'Professional Privilege' (1950) 66 LQR 88, 94–100; JRL, 'Privileged Communications, Part 1, Communications with Spiritual Advisers' (1958) 13 Northern Ireland LQ 160.

[231] *Tournier v National Provincial and Union Bank* [1924] 1 KB 461, 473, 479, 486; *Parry-Jones v Law Society* [1968] 1 All ER 177, 180; *Robertson v Canadian Imperial Bank of Commerce* [1995] 1 All ER 824, 830.

[232] *Chantrey Martin (A Firm) v Martin* [1953] 2 All ER 691; *Home or Away Ltd v Commissioners of Customs and Excise* VAT and Duties Tribunal, 17 January 2002 (argument that Art 14 had been breached because a solicitor offering tax advice would be protected by privilege rejected).

[233] *Price Waterhouse v BCCI Holdings (Luxembourg) SA* [1992] BCLC 583.

[234] *Att-Gen v Mulholland* [1963] 1 All ER 767, 771.

and Wales by virtue of occupation are patent agents,[235] trade mark agents,[236] licensed conveyancers[237] and authorized advocates, litigators and probate practitioners[238] and this is because of legislation. Journalists have been accorded a limited capacity to shield their sources in Contempt of Court Act 1981, s 10.[239] Parliament and law reform bodies have not been impressed by arguments that communications involving other professionals should be privileged.[240]

Privilege in litigation for non-lawyers in other common law jurisdictions

16.43 In restricting privilege to legal and quasi-legal professionals England is out of step with much of the common law world.[241] Legislation confers privileged status in litigation on communications between clergy and penitent in Australia, New Zealand and parts of Canada.[242] Much of Australasia recognizes a limited doctor–patient privilege.[243] Canada and New Zealand shelter communications to marriage guidance counsellors.[244] In the United States[245] 50 states have enacted a statutory privilege for clergy–penitent communications and most recognize some form of physician–patient privilege. Many states protect the relationships of

---

[235] Copyright, Designs and Patents Act 1988, s 280. The Court of Appeal had previously refused to extend privilege to patent agents: *Wilder Pump & Engineering Co v Melvin Fusfeld* [1985] FSR 159.

[236] Copyright, Designs and Patents Act 1988, s 284.

[237] Administration of Justice Act, 1985, s 33; Courts and Legal Services Act 1990, s 63.

[238] Courts and Legal Services Act 1990, s 63.

[239] See paras 7.12 et seq.

[240] Law Reform Committee, *Privilege in Civil Proceedings* (Cmnd 3472, 1967); Criminal Law Revision Committee Eleventh Report, *Evidence (General)* (Cmnd 4991, 1976); Medical Practitioners' Communications (Privilege) Bill 1937 debated *Hansard,* HC vol 319, col 1982 (5 February 1937). cp German Code of Criminal Procedure §53 (Berufsgeheimnis).

[241] A judicial discretion to protect communications and records made in circumstances where one of the parties was under a legal, moral or ethical duty not to disclose them is supported by the Australian Law Reform Commission: ALRC Report 38, *Evidence* (Canberra: 1987) 116. See also ALRC Interim Report 26, *Evidence* (Canberra: 1985) vol 2, 51. The Canadian Law Reform Commission has recommended a discretionary professional privilege: Study 12, *Professional Privileges before the Courts* (Ottawa: 1975); First Report, *Evidence* (Ottawa: 1975) 30, 80, discussed in E Koroway, 'Confidentiality in the Law of Evidence' (1978) 16 Osgoode Hall LJ 260, 361.

[242] Australia: A Ligertwood, *Australian Evidence* (3rd edn, Sydney: 1998) 349–350. New Zealand: Evidence Amendment Act (No 2) 1980 (NZ) s 31; *R v Howse* [1983] NZLR 246. Canada: Quebec Charter of Human Rights and Freedoms, s 14; Newfoundland's Evidence Act 1970, s 6. Irish law has a privilege: *Cook v Carroll* [1945] IR 515. Roman Catholic priests have been granted immunity from testifying to the International Criminal Court about atrocities they have been told about in the confessional, The Times, 17 August 1999.

[243] Australia: A. Ligertwood, *Australian Evidence* (3rd edn, Sydney: 1998) 349–350. The Victorian doctor–patient privilege was considered by the High Court in *National Mutual Life Association of Australia Ltd v Godrich* (1909) 10 CLR 1. New Zealand: Evidence Amendment Act (No 2) 1980 (NZ), s 32. In criminal proceedings this privilege only protects communications by the defendant that relate to drug dependency or some other condition or behaviour that manifests itself in criminal conduct.

[244] Divorce Act 1986 (Can), s 10(5); Family Proceedings Act 1980 (NZ), s 18(1)(a).

[245] S Stone and R Liebman, *Testimonial Privileges* (New York: 1983); J Strong (ed), *McCormick on Evidence* (5th edn (St Paul: 1999) 123 et seq. and ch 10.

B. Privilege

accountant and client, psychotherapist and patient,[246] and in some states communications to schoolteachers, school counsellors, nurses, marriage counsellors, social workers and researchers[247] have some exemption.

Some jurisdictions have enacted legislation that is not specific to any one profession. New South Wales has amended its Evidence Act to create a 'professional confidential relationship privilege'[248] and both Victoria and New South Wales have a sexual assault communications privilege for communications to counsellors and medical practitioners by victims of sexual offences.[249] A New Zealand statute permits the judge to excuse a witness from giving evidence or producing a document that breaches a confidence *obtained* in the course of a 'special relationship'.[250] The latter is determined by having regard to 'the public interest in the preservation of confidences between persons in the relative positions of the confidant and the witness and the encouragement of free communication between such persons'.[251] **16.44**

Criticisms of the English refusal to accord wider privilege in litigation situations

The English policy of restricting privilege in litigation contexts to lawyers and quasi-lawyers has attracted criticism.[252] The first reason is that it ignores that some non-lawyers routinely offer tax advice, negotiate settlements and counsel lawful conduct, work which if undertaken by a lawyer would attract privilege.[253] The Office of Fair Trading claims that this distorts competition in the market for professional services to the detriment of accountants and other tax advisers.[254] If the **16.45**

---

[246] B Dickens, 'Legal Protection of Psychiatric Confidentiality' (1978) 1 Intl J of L and Psychiatry 255. See also Evidence Amendment Act (No 2) 1980 (NZ), s 32.

[247] C Knerr and J Carroll, 'Confidentiality and Criminological Research: The Evolving Body of Law' (1978) 69 Jn of Criminal L and Criminology 311.

[248] Evidence Act 1995 (NSW), s 126A–F allows a judge to direct evidence not be adduced if it would result in revealing a protected identity or a 'protected confidence', that is, a communication by a person in confidence to a confidant acting in a professional role. There is an obligation to suppress the information if the harm (including emotional harm) to the confidant exceeds the benefit of adducing the evidence.

[249] Evidence Act 1958 (Vic) Pt II Div 2A; Evidence Act 1995 (NSW), s 126G–I.

[250] Evidence Amendment Act No 2 (1980), s 35. It has been exercised to exclude evidence from a probation officer (*R v Secord* [1992] 3 NZLR 570), a psychiatric nurse (*R v Rapana* [1995] 2 NZLR 381), a counsellor (*M v L* [1997] 3 NZLR 424, 440) and a journalist (*European Pacific Banking Corp v Television NZ Ltd* [1995] 3 NZLR 381). The discretion applies to confidences received but not to confidences given. The client can therefore be compelled to disclose what he said to the professional.

[251] Evidence Amendment Act No 2 (1980), s 35(2).

[252] The debate about extending privilege to non-lawyers has been conducted entirely in terms of whether confidential communications can be withheld in litigation.

[253] See Note, 'Functional Overlap between the Lawyer and Other Professionals: Its Implications for the Privileged Communications Doctrine' (1962) 71 Yale LJ 1226. The legal profession's response might be that it is easier to control abuse of privilege by lawyers because they are subject to the court's control.

[254] *Restrictions on Competition in the Provision of Professional Services*, OFT Report by LECG Ltd. (December 2000) paras 188–189.

rationale for LPP is the desirability of lay persons being guided effectively through the labyrinth of the law,[255] the professional identity of the guide should be irrelevant. '[I]n the modern age it is not easy to see why the logic, purpose and public interest underlying the privilege when litigation is not contemplated supports the privilege in respect of communications with a lawyer but not, for example, communications with an accountant on the same subject matter.'[256] In *Bolkiah v KPMG*[257] the House of Lords conceded that an accountant who provided litigation support services might claim litigation privilege for third party communications. Can any other professionals who provide litigation support do so?[258]

16.46 The second weakness in the English position lies in the assumption—made by the courts with virtually no discussion—that effective legal representation is the only public interest in confidential professional–client communications of sufficient stature to outweigh the public interest in full disclosure to a court of all information relevant to litigation.[258a] This is not self-evident. There is, for example, a very substantial public health interest in successful medical treatment and therefore in candid doctor–patient consultations. What empirical evidence there exists, tends to, suggest that the clients of professionals such as doctors do not usually anticipate litigation when they seek out their services.[259] A propos the parishioner–spiritual counsellor relationship, the New Zealand Law Reform Commission has written:

> In most cases, the fear of revelation of the confession in court proceedings is probably not significant in determining whether people will take the opportunity of seeking spiritual guidance, either in the confessional or through some other form of contact with clergy.[260]

But this raises the question: would those who need legal advice be any more deterred from consulting lawyers by the possibility that their discourse might have to be disclosed in a court of law if, at the time of the consultation, there was no realistic prospect of litigation?[261] If there was no privilege, only an obligation of

---

[255] See para 16.08 above.
[256] per Charles J, *S CC v B* [2000] 3 WLR 53, 59.
[257] [1999] 1 All ER 517, 526.
[258] The principle of effective access implied by Art 6 (see *Golder v UK* (1975) 1 EHRR 524, para 36) may require this. In *Fahey v Att-Gen* [1993] 1 ERNZ 161 communications with lay industrial advocates were held to be privileged by the NZ Employment Court.
[258a] Reports that examine the question include Law Reform Committee, *Privilege in Civil Proceedings* (Cmnd 3472, 1967); Criminal Law Revision Committee Eleventh Report, *Evidence (General)* (Cmnd 4991, 1976); Ontario LRC, *Law of Evidence* (Ontario: 1976); Manitoba LRC, *Report on Medical Privilege* R56 (Winnipeg: 1983); ALRC Interim Report 26, *Evidence* (Canberra: 1985) vol 1; Report 1, *Report of the Royal Commission into Civil Rights in Ontario* (Ontario: 1988) vol 2, 822; NZLRC, Preliminary Report 23, *Evidence Law: Privilege* (Wellington: 1994) ch 11. See also G Peiris, 'Medical Professional Privilege in Commonwealth Law' (1984) 33 Intl and Comparative LQ 301.
[259] See eg M Weiner and D Shuman, 'Privilege—a comparative study' (1985) J of Psychiatry and L 373.
[260] NZLRC Preliminary Report 23, *Evidence Law: Privilege* (Wellington: 1994) 109.
[261] See para 1.52 above. See now also *Three Rivers District Council v Bank of England* [2003] EWCA Civ 474 para 26.

B. Privilege

confidentiality, would the public (any more than they do already) switch to DIY conveyancing and DIY wills? Would companies draw up their own contracts and set up their own companies? It may be the case that 'all legal advice is concerned with a possible ultimate resort to litigation',[262] but a high percentage of clients consult a solicitor in the expectation that this will prevent litigation.[263]

The Wigmore solution

The fact that most of the time nothing may be gained by conferring the mantle of privilege on confidential communications between non-lawyer professionals and their clients in litigation, does not mean this is invariably so. Recognizing this, the Canadian Supreme Court in *Slavutych v Baker*[264] instituted a case-by-case privilege founded on the utilitarian criteria set out in *Wigmore on Evidence*.[265] These are that: **16.47**

(1) the communication originated in a confidence;
(2) confidentiality was essential to full and satisfactory maintenance of the relation between the parties;
(3) the relation[266] is one which in the opinion of the community ought to be sedulously fostered;
(4) the injury that would inure to the relation from disclosure of the confidential information exceeds the benefit gained from correct disposal of the case.

There are a number of reported cases[267] in which communications between professionals and their clients have been analysed in terms of the Wigmore criteria. In most cases the conditions of the test were found not to have been satisfied but the Canadian Supreme Court has held communications to a psychiatrist providing sexual assault counselling to be privileged.[268] Sexual assault victim counselling is one circumstance in which the possibility of disclosure of the communication to

---

[262] P Murphy, *Evidence* (7th edn, London: 2000) 420.
[263] It would be interesting to carry out empirical research to see the extent to which LPP promotes candour. R Cranston, 'Ethics and Professional Responsibility' in R Cranston (ed), *Ethics and Professional Responsibility* (Oxford, 1995) 9 is sceptical: '[w]hether legal advice is sought depends in most cases on factors other than legal professional privilege. . . . It is highly likely anyway that most people are ignorant of the privilege.' For a similar view see S Ross, *Ethics in Law* (Sydney: 1998) 278–279.
[264] *Slavutych v Baker* (1975) 55 DLR (3d) 224 .
[265] McNaughton revision (1961) vol 8, para 2285. The Wigmore criteria were not intended to be applied case-by-case.
[266] Quaere: does this refer to the particular or generic relationship?
[267] *R v Gruenke* (1991) 67 CCC (3d) 289 (clergy); *R v Peddle* [2000] NJ No 311 (clergy); *Re SAS* (1977) 1 Legal Medical Quarterly 139 (psychiatrist); *R v S (RJ)* (1985) 19 CCC (3d) 115 (psychiatrist); *Gauthier v Solomon* (1990) 90 ACWS (3d) 39 (banker); *Union of Canada Life Insurance v Levesque Securities Inc* (1999) 42 OR (3d) 633 (banker); *R v Fehr* (1983) 6 DLR (4th) 281, 293 (counsellor for the hearing impaired).
[268] *M v Ryan* (1997) 143 DLR (4th) 1. Contrast *M v L* [1997] 3 NZLR 424; *R v Young* (1999) 46 NSWLR 681.

Chapter 16: Grounds for Non-Disclosure

a court is very likely to deter resort to a professional and openness by the client[269] because the possibility of a criminal prosecution is likely to be very much on the victim's mind.

Impact of the Human Rights Act 1998

16.48 As a consequence of the enactment of the HRA 'all law must now be looked at through the prism of human rights standards'.[270] A disclosure of a confidential personal information communicated by a client to a professional without the consent of the client is an interference with the client's right to respect for private life and correspondence guaranteed by Article 8(1) of the ECHR[271] which must be justified. If disclosure cannot be justified the evidence will have to be excluded. This, of itself, will not compel recognition of new forms of privilege. The courts have ample powers already to exclude relevant evidence.[272]

16.49 Compelling a Roman Catholic priest to disclose to a court what passed in the confessional may violate Article 9 which protects 'freedom to manifest one's religion or beliefs subject only to such limitations as are prescribed by law and are necessary in a democratic society in the interests of public safety, for the protection of public order, health or morals, or for the protection of the rights and freedoms of others'. The sacrament of confession, a fundamental tenet of Catholicism, is, it is submitted, a 'manifestation' within the meaning of Article 9.[273] Since at least 1693,[274] English judges have consistently denied the existence of clergy–parishioner privilege,[275] while in practice no disclosure has been forced (at least in a reported case) that would have been protected by clergy–parishioner privilege.[276] Perhaps court and counsel simply recognized the hopelessness of using the threat of contempt proceedings to extract information from a priest who would have to break a sacred trust to give it.

16.50 It must also, however, be borne in mind that withholding a confidential communication from a court may violate the absolute Article 6(1) right of a litigant to a

---

[269] G Bartley, 'Sexual assault communications privilege under siege' (2000–01) summer NSW Bar News, available from http://www.nswbar.asn.au.
[270] J Jowell and J Cooper, 'Introduction: Defining Human Rights Principles' in J Jowell and J Cooper (eds), *Understanding Human Rights Principles* (Oxford: 2001) 3.
[271] See para 3.03 above.
[272] These are described in ch 15.
[273] Disclosures to clergy outside the confessional would not constitute a manifestation. More difficult to decide is whether a communication in the confessional by a member of a denomination, such as the Anglican Church, that does not require confession would constitute a manifestation.
[274] *Anon* (1693) 90 ER 179.
[275] See para 16.42 above. JRL, 'Privileged Communications, Part 1, Communications with Spiritual Advisers' (1958) 13 Northern Ireland LQ 160.
[276] Lord Best CJ said in *Broad v Pitt* (1828) 3 C & P 518, 519 that he would never compel a clergyman to disclose communications made by a prisoner if the clergyman chose not to disclose them.

B. Privilege

fair trial.[277] A conflict between Article 8(1) or 8(1) and 9, on the one hand, and Article 6, is avoided only if

(1) a breach of Article 8(1) can be justified, that is, be shown to be in accordance with law, proportionate and necessary in a democratic society for one of the aims listed in Article 8(2), which include 'prevention of disorder or crime'[278] and 'the protection of the rights and freedoms of others';
(2) a breach of Article 9 can be justified, that is, shown to be prescribed by law, proportionate and necessary in a democratic society for one of the aims listed in Article 9 which include 'the protection of the rights and freedoms of others' or
(3) disclosure is unnecessary for the trial to be 'fair'.[279]

16.51 Factors that might be relevant in deciding either whether an interference with Article 8(1) or 9 is justified or disclosure is unnecessary for a fair trial or how two conflicting Convention rights are to be reconciled include the importance of the evidence to the litigation; the extent to which admitting the evidence invades the client's privacy; whether, and to what extent, the contents of the communication have already been disclosed; the mechanisms available to limit publication of the evidence; the availability of other evidence concerning the matters to which the evidence relates, and the nature of the litigation.[280] It is unlikely that a court would decide that the interests of a litigant in disclosure of a communication made for the purpose of receiving priestly absolution outweighed the interests of the penitent in privacy. Such was the outrage when a US District Attorney tape-recorded a confession by a prison inmate suspected of murder to a Roman Catholic priest that the District Attorney felt compelled to ask that the tape and transcript of it be sealed by court order and that all persons who had heard it be admonished never to reveal its contents.[281]

Public Interest Immunity[282]

General principles

16.52 In its consultation paper *Publication of Local Authority Reports* the Law Commission writes that it 'is a general rule of law founded on public policy and

---

[277] See para 3.23 above.
[278] This aim covers prosecution of criminal offences: See para 3.19 above.
[279] See para 3.23 above.
[280] The case for disclosure may be stronger if the litigation is criminal or concerns the welfare of a child than run-of-the-mill civil litigation.
[281] L Brocker, 'Sacred Secrets: The Clergy–Penitent Privilege Finds its Way into the News' (1996) 57 Oregon State Bar 15.
[282] There are many articles, but most are only marginally relevant to the position of a professional. See however, A Zuckerman, 'Public Interest Immunity—A Matter of Prime Judicial Responsibility' (1994) 57 MLR 703, R. Scott, 'The Use of Public Interest Immunity Claims in Criminal Cases' [1995] 2 Web J of Current Legal Issues 1. On the subject to PII generally, see M Howard (ed), *Phipson on Evidence* (15th edn, London: 2000) ch. 24.

recognized by Parliament[283] that any document may be withheld or an answer to any question may be refused on the ground that the disclosure of the document or the answering of the question would be injurious to the public interest'.[284] Once PII in a document or information has been established, its disclosure or use at any stage of the litigation process is ruled out.[285] This applies to civil, criminal[286] and tribunal proceedings of a judicial character.[287]

16.53 Save in exceptional cases, a professional who possesses material that is wanted for litigation but which falls prima facie within an immune class[288] (such as records relating to the welfare of a child) should assert PII in the material, leaving the court to decide whether the claim is well-founded.[289]

> Where a litigant asserts that documents are immune from production or disclosure on public interest grounds he is not (if the claim is well founded) claiming a right but observing a duty. Public interest immunity is not a trump card vouchsafed to certain privileged players to play when and as they wish. It is an exclusionary rule, imposed on parties . . . even where it is to their disadvantage in litigation . . . public interest immunity cannot in any ordinary sense be waived, since, although one can waive rights, one cannot waive duties.[290]

16.54 PII does not prohibit a professional from voluntarily disclosing information outside the litigation process when it is in the public interest to do so. In *Re W*[291] Butler-Sloss LJ recognized the need for the free exchange of information, including information protected by PII, between social workers, the police and others seeking to protect children from abuse. Vis-à-vis the public the information was confidential.

---

[283] Crown Proceedings Act 1947, s 28(1).
[284] Consultation Paper 163 (2002) para 5.23.
[285] PII cannot be avoided by holding proceedings in private (*Powell v Chief Constable of North Wales Constabulary*, The Times, February 2000) or, where a document is subject to PII, by admitting secondary evidence.
[286] Including magistrates' courts: *R (on the application of the DPP) v Acton Youth Court* [2001] EWHC Admin 402; [2001] 1 WLR 1828.
[287] See *Science Research Council v Nasse* [1980] AC 1028, 1071.
[288] See para 16.59 below.
[289] *Re G (A Minor)* [1996] 2 All ER 65, 69. cp *Re C* [1995] 1 FLR 204.
[290] *Makanjuola v Commissioner of Police of the Metropolis* [1992] 3 All ER 617, 623 per Bingham LJ. Bingham LJ's words were interpreted by government legal advisers as requiring ministers to automatically claim immunity in respect of documents of a class normally accorded PII. Lord Woolf dissociated the House of Lords from this interpretation in *R v Chief Constable of the West Midlands, ex p Wiley* [1994] 3 All ER 420, 437 to enable ministers and the Attorney-General to weigh the public interests themselves and disclose documents where they thought this to be in the public interest. But Lord Woolf did not dissent from Bingham LJ that officials should claim PII in any case of doubt and leave it to the court to resolve that doubt. If a party or witness does not claim PII, it is within the power of the court or any interested person to do so (*Rogers v Secretary of State for the Home Department* [1972] 2 All ER 1057, 1060) but judicial intervention in the post-*Wiley* era is unlikely unless documents are held by someone who is poorly placed to assess whether PII should be claimed.
[291] [1998] 2 All ER 801, 807. See also *Re M* [2002] EWCA Civ 1199.

B. Privilege

It is implicit in what has been said that PII, unlike LPP, is decided on a case-by-case basis. Unless legislation provides otherwise,[292] the final arbiter of its existence is a court.[293] The fact that information was given in confidence and that equity will protect that confidence, or even that without confidentiality a socially desirable communication might not have been made,[294] do not of themselves attract PII.[295] **16.55**

> The private promise of confidentiality must yield to the general public interest that in the administration of justice truth will out, unless by reason of the character of the information or the relationship of the information to the informant, a more important public interest is served by protecting the information or the identity of the informant from disclosure in a court of law.[296]

There is no PII unless the public interest in preserving the confidentiality of the information outweighs the public interest in securing justice.[297] Confidentiality is, however, 'a very material consideration'.[298] If confidentiality has been lost through wide dissemination of the information, it is improbable that a court will decide that it is not in the public interest to disclose it.[299] Why close the stable door after the horse has bolted?

Class and contents claims

Class and contents claims distinguished

Traditionally claims to PII were categorized as either 'class' claims or 'contents' claims. **16.56**

> [W]ith a class claim it is immaterial whether the disclosure of the particular contents of particular documents would be injurious to the public interest, the point being that it is the maintenance of the immunity of the 'class' from disclosure in litigation that is important. In the 'contents' claim, the protection is claimed for particular 'contents' in a particular document.[300]

Survival of class claims   Most (though by no means all) contents claims have related to state secrets, national security, the functioning of central government and law enforcement. PII was formerly known as Crown privilege for this very **16.57**

---

[292] See Local Government Act 1974 s 29(4).
[293] *Conway v Rimmer* [1968] 1 All ER 874.
[294] *Wheeler v Le Marchant* (1881) 17 Ch D 675, 681.
[295] *Norwich Pharmacal Co v Customs and Excise Commissioners* [1973] 2 All ER 943, 969; *Barrett v Ministry of Defence*, The Times, 24 January 1990.
[296] *D v NSPCC* [1977] 1 All ER 589, 594 per Lord Diplock. See also 605, 612, 618.
[297] *R v Chief Constable of the West Midlands, ex p Wiley* [1994] 3 All ER 420, 423 per Lord Templeman.
[298] *Alfred Crompton Ltd v Customs and Excise Commissioners (No 2)* [1973] 2 All ER 1169, 1184 per Lord Cross.
[299] Law Commission Consultation Paper 163, *Publication of Local Authority Reports* (2002) para 5.32.
[300] per Ralph Gibson LJ, *Halford v Sharples* [1992] 3 All ER 624, 646. 'Class' claims are said to encourage candour, avert ignorant criticism, allay fears of adverse legal consequences arising from disclosure, and protect confidences simpliciter: N Andrews, *Principles of Civil Procedure* (London: 1994) 359–360.

reason. After the publication of the Scott Report, the Attorney-General announced in Parliament that the 'division into class and contents claims will no longer be applied. Ministers will claim PII only when it is believed that a disclosure of a document would cause real damage or harm to the public interest'.[301] The real damage to the public interest would be clearly identified and ministerial certificates would be more detailed. These guidelines do not signal the end of class claims. The Attorney-General said that claims could involve 'class reasoning'.[302] The guidelines have had little impact in run-of-the-mill non-government cases.[303] Social services, for example, continue to make class claims for children's records.

16.58 **Judicial attitude to class-based claims**   A PII claim by a professional in respect of confidential client information is most probably going to be class-based.[304] Courts have become wary of class-based claims. They are most receptive to class claims when they fall into an established PII category. These categories are not closed,[305] but they are not readily expanded: '[t]he recognition of a new class-based PII requires clear and compelling evidence that it is necessary.'[306] A broad submission in *D v NSPCC*[307] that whenever a public interest would be served by refusing access to confidential information the court must balance that public interest against the countervailing public interest in allowing access was rejected by a majority in the House of Lords.[308] New immune classes are created 'by extension or analogy of recognized principles and reported precedents'.[309]

16.59 *Prima facie* **immune classes**   To date the recognized categories that might be either directly relevant, or relevant by way of analogy, when a professional asserts PII are social work and similar records about children that are wanted for private law proceedings,[310] child abuse complaints to a body with prosecuting powers,[311]

---

[301] *Hansard*, HC col 949 (18 December 1996) (Sir Nicholas Lyell). Confirmed as a written answer in the House of Commons on 11 July 1997. When pressed (col 951) the Attorney-General said that 'real damage' means the same as Lord Templeman's 'substantial harm' test in *R v Chief Constable of the West Midlands, ex p Wiley* [1994] 3 All ER 420, 424.

[302] *Hansard*, HC col 951 (18 December 1996) (Sir Nicholas Lyell).

[303] The guidelines are not binding on non-departmental bodies.

[304] Contents claims are not inconceivable, eg in time of war the state of the Prime Minister's health might be regarded as a state secret.

[305] *D v NSPCC* [1977] 1 All ER 589, 601.

[306] *R v Chief Constable of the West Midlands, ex p Wiley* [1994] 3 All ER 420, 446 per Lord Woolf.

[307] [1977] 1 All ER 589, 600, 613.

[308] The exception was Lord Edmund-Davies: see [1977] 1 All ER 589, 618. See also Lord Denning in *Riddick v Thomas Board Mills Ltd* [1977] 3 All ER 677, 687.

[309] per Lord Hailsham, *D v NSPCC* [1977] 1 All ER 589, 601.

[310] *Re M* [1990] 2 FLR 36; *Re G* [1996] 2 All ER 65, 68; *Venables v NGN* [2001] 1 All ER 908, 940. See also *Re D* [1994] 1 FLR 346, 352. Earlier authorities are cited in *Campbell v Tameside MBC* [1982] 2 All ER 791, 794 where PII was refused for school records. cp *McLeon v British Railways Board* [1997] SLT 434. It is unlikely that PII claims to social work records will be automatically accepted any longer. On this point see *Re R* [2002] 1 FLR 755 where Charles J said that the alleged harm from disclosure would have to be set out with particularity.

[311] *D v NSPCC* [1977] 1 All ER 589.

blood transfusion service records,[312] legal aid interviews with probation officers[313] and the abortion records of a licensed clinic.[314] Tentative findings of PII have been made in respect of probation records[315] and the counselling records of an NHS sexual assaults reference centre.[316] Attempts to extend PII to the whole class of medical records[317] and to journalists' sources[318] have foundered.

What the professional must establish Consistent with the refusal of the judicial system to accord privilege to communications between professionals (other than lawyers) and their clients, professionals asserting PII in client information must establish a public interest in non-disclosure over and above the normal public interest in preserving professional confidentiality.[319] In the abortion clinic record case PII was not recognized because of medical confidentiality but because women might have recourse to illegal abortions if not guaranteed absolute confidentiality. The existence of regulations[320] restricting disclosure of abortion information demonstrated the 'strong public interest in maintaining a high degree of confidentiality in respect of documents relating to abortions'.[321] The argument for treating sexual assault counselling records as confidential is the risk that victims will not report sex offences to the police.[322]   16.60

Public interest immunity claims in civil proceedings

The first question for a civil court faced with a PII application is whether the information is sufficiently relevant and material to the case of the party desiring the information to require its disclosure in the interests of justice; if it is not, there is no need for the court to decide whether there is a stronger public interest in   16.61

---

[312] *AB v Glasgow and West of Scotland Blood Transfusion Service* (1989) 15 BMLR 91. PII was recognized in the latter not because the records were confidential per se, but because the sufficiency of the national supply of blood for the purposes of transfusion might be put at risk if the confidentiality of the identity of blood donors could not be assured. Contrast *Long v Att-Gen* [2001] 2 NZLR 529.

[313] *R v Umoh* (1986) 84 Cr App R 138.

[314] *Morrow v DPP* (1993) 14 BMLR 54.

[315] *Re M* [1987] 1 FLR 46, 48, 49.

[316] *R v Azmy* (1996) 34 BMLR 45. In *R v K* (1993) 97 Cr App R 342 the evidence was found to be irrelevant. Contrast *R v Young* (1999) 46 NSWLR 681.

[317] *W v Egdell* [1989] 1 All ER 1089; *R v Crozier* (1990) 8 BMLR 128. See also *R v Statutory Visitors to St Lawrence's Hospital, ex p Caterham* [1953] 2 All ER 766, 772; *Flett v North Tyneside Health Authority* [1989] CLY 2968; *Re C* [1991] 2 FLR 478.

[318] *BSC v Granada Television* [1981] 1 All ER 417, 456.

[319] *R v Young* (1999) 46 NSWLR 681, 716.

[320] Abortion Regulations 1968, r 5. cp, the public interest in encouraging those suffering from venereal diseases coming forward for treatment—a fact demonstrated by legislation designed to preserve secrecy for information obtained about persons suffering from these complaints from doctors—led a Canadian court in *Carter v Carter* (1974) 6 OR (2d) 603 to exclude medical evidence on public interest grounds. The Ontario court, unlike the English courts, saw exclusion as a matter of discretion.

[321] *per* Farquharson LJ, *R v Morrow* (1993) 14 BMLR 54, 59.

[322] *R v Young* (1999) 46 NSWLR 681, 717.

non-disclosure than in giving access to the information.[323] The applicant cannot rely upon a private inspection of the documents by the judge to establish this threshold requirement. In *Air Canada v Secretary of State for Trade (No 2)* the House of Lords said that a judge ought not to inspect documents for which PII is claimed until he has definite grounds for expecting to find material of real importance to the party seeking disclosure.[324]

16.62 Once the disclosure applicant has demonstrated that the documents strengthen his case, the court will undertake the balancing operation[325] to determine whether on the particular facts the public interest dictates disclosure.[326] Many factors could be relevant to the balancing exercise. Amongst these are whether the information is already in the public domain, whether the information is available to the applicant from another source, whether the information is only capable of being used in cross-examination, and whether the source or recipient of the information objects to disclosure.[327] There is no point in suppressing confidential personal information about a professional's client if the client favours disclosure unless there remains a significant public interest, extraneous to the client's interest, in keeping the information under wraps.[328] In some cases partial non-disclosure may be an option.

Public interest immunity claims in criminal proceedings

16.63 Applications for PII are handled differently in criminal proceedings. Prosecution applications are generally made before the trial,[329] sometimes without notice to the defence (ex parte)[330] and in secret (in camera).[331] The judge must personally

---

[323] *R v Chief Constable of the West Midlands, ex p Wiley* [1994] 3 All ER 420, 423–424.
[324] [1983] 1 All ER 910, 917.
[325] Possibly after first inspecting the documents.
[326] See eg *Campbell v Tameside MBC* [1982] 2 All ER 791 in which the Court of Appeal ordered the disclosure of the confidential educational records of an 11-year-old schoolboy with entries by teachers and an educational psychologist.
[327] In *Campbell v Tameside MBC* [1982] 2 All ER 791, 795 Lord Denning suggested that PII may be waived if the maker of a confidential document does not object to disclosure. It is submitted, that the better approach is to treat the absence of an objection as affecting the weight of the public interest against disclosure.
[328] cp *Savage v Chief Constable of Hampshire* [1997] 2 All ER 631, 636. Contrast *C v C* [1946] 1 All ER 562, 563.
[329] See para 14.127 above.
[330] This is permitted by Art 6: *R v Botmeh* [2001] EWCA Crim 226; [2002] 1 WLR 531.
[331] *Jasper v UK* (2000) 30 EHRR 441. In this case the defence were informed of the application but not of the contents of the material that the prosecution wanted to withhold. The ECtHR (by a slender majority) found no violation of Art 6 because of effective procedural safeguards: the defence had been permitted to make submissions about the nature of the defence and to request disclosure of any evidence material to that defence; the undisclosed material played no part in the prosecution case; non-disclosure was constantly monitored by an independent and impartial judge; and the Court of Appeal had reviewed the case. See also *Fitt v UK* (2000) 30 EHRR 441. It has been suggested provision should be made for the court to appoint special counsel who would have access to the sensitive material, to represent the defendant's interests in ex parte applications. The government has so far rejected the suggestion on cost grounds: Auld, *A Review of the Criminal Courts of*

B. Privilege

inspect the material for which the claim is made.[332] It is something of a misnomer, as the Scott report noted, to describe the next step as a balancing exercise.[333] 'No judge could lawfully deny to the defence material which ... undermines the prosecution case and/or positively assists the defence'.[334] Disclosure must be ordered if the 'disputed material may prove the defendant's innocence or avoid a miscarriage of justice'.[335] If the prosecution is intent on preserving the confidentiality of the information, the only course it can follow after a disclosure ruling is to abandon the prosecution.

In *R v Thompson*[336] May J refused to set aside a witness summons issued to the Director of Family and Social Services in Sheffield to produce social work documents relating to witnesses who had once been in care whom the defendant, a social worker, was accused of having indecently assaulted and buggered. The judge recognized that PII was normally accorded to local authority records of child care investigations but decided that disclosure was necessary for a fair trial. To protect the privacy of the witnesses, he ruled that the documents were to remain confidential in the hands of the prosecution and the defendant and his lawyers and that none of the material was to be used publicly in the trial without his leave. A class or contents claim to PII is open to the defence, but there is no reported instance of the defence making such a claim.[337]

16.64

England and Wales (September 2001) paras 10. 193–194, available at http://www.criminal-courts-review.org.uk/auldconts.htm.

[332] *R v Clowes* [1992] 3 All ER 440, 455; *R v K* (1993) 97 Cr App R 342, 346.

[333] Sir Richard Scott, *Report of the Inquiry into the Expert of Defence Equipment and Dual-Use Goods to Iraq and Related Prosecutions* (HC (1995–96) 115) para K6.14.

[334] T Owen, 'Disclosure: the requirements of the ECHR and the PII problem', paper for the Auld Review of the Review of the Criminal Justice System, para 31, available at http://www.justice.org.uk/images/pdfs/cjs.pdf. Judicial support, pre-dating the HRA, for this is to be found in *R v Keane* [1994] 2 All ER 478, 484. If the material in respect of which PII is claimed is found not to assist the defence disclosure will not be ordered: *R v K* (1993) 97 Cr App R 342, 346–347.

[335] per Lord Taylor CJ, *R v Keane* [1994] 2 All ER 478, 484. If the material in respect of which PII is claimed is found not to assist the defence, disclosure will not be ordered: *R v K* (1993) 97 Cr App R 342, 346–347.

[336] (DC, 4 June 1992.) In *R v K* (1993) 97 Cr App R 342 production of the videos was not considered necessary for a fair trial.

[337] There is no information to which the prosecution has an absolute right regardless of the damage that disclosure may cause to the public interest.

17

PROTECTION OF PRIVACY

A. Control of Documents	17.02	B. Restricting Publicity	17.26
Withholding Information From a Party	17.02	Open Justice	17.26
Collateral Use of Documents	17.09	Hearing Evidence in Private	17.30
Access to Documentary Evidence by Non-Parties	17.22	Anonymity Orders	17.38
		Reporting Restrictions	17.44

17.01 Chapters 14 and 15 explained that in an adversarial legal system the parties to civil and criminal proceedings are entitled to have access to confidential documents belonging to opponents and third parties including records containing confidential personal information. This chapter examines the measures that exist in law to preserve as far as possible the confidentiality of the information that has had to be disclosed prior to trial or to a court of law.[1] Part A concentrates on how the courts may limit disclosure and subsequent use of documents. Part B is concerned with the publicity given to the proceedings.

A. Control of Documents

Withholding Information From a Party

Civil litigation

Limiting inspection of documents

Reasons and procedure When a party, a prospective party or a third party is **17.02** required to allow inspection of confidential documents in civil litigation, the court may limit production of the confidential documents such as medical and counselling records to the applicant's legal and professional advisers[2] or, if the

---

[1] For measures that can be adopted to protect the confidentiality of information provided to a tribunal or an inquiry see paras 15.45–15.48, 15.52, 15.54 above.
[2] In *Steele v Moule* [1999] CLY 326 the judge ordered the release of the claimant's entire medical history on the claimant's solicitors undertaking that they would only be released to their medical advisers and not to the defendants or the insurers. See also *Re B* [2002] All ER(D) 167. cp *Premier*

applicant is not legally represented, to his medical advisers.[3] Reasons for imposing restrictions on disclosure of documents about someone other than the party receiving disclosure include risk of harassment,[4] protection of privacy,[5] and the presence of irrelevant information of a private character in the document.

> It is not in dispute that the defendants' medical adviser should see all records, however sensitive, so that he can give proper advice on all the information known to the plaintiff's medical adviser. Justice demands no less. But I see no reason why the disclosure of sensitive records should go further than is necessary to secure that end. Documents which the medical adviser considers relevant will of course be disclosed to the defendants' legal advisers. . . . But the indiscriminate disclosure of all the plaintiff's medical records to the defendants' solicitors would, in my view, threaten a legitimate interest of the plaintiff in maintaining the confidentiality of her medical records, without securing any compensatory advantage or benefit to the defendants.[6]

Limiting access to documents to a party's lawyers can be embarrassing for counsel.

> [D]ifficulties are likely to arise where counsel appearing in, and advising their clients in respect of, protracted and complex proceedings acquire information which they are not free to use or to pass on to their clients. During the heat of battle an unwitting disclosure may occur. Frank and full advice becomes impossible. I am aware of cases in which, for reasons such as these, experienced counsel have declined to receive information which they are not free to share with their clients.[7]

However, the Article 8 right to privacy of the subject of the document may make such a restriction unavoidable.[8]

17.03 **Enforcement** The courts rigorously enforce orders for limited disclosure. When by oversight the solicitor for a mother sent her copies of hospital counselling records involving her children which she was not supposed to see, her firm was ordered to pay £1,000 for contempt of court and costs on an indemnity basis.

Profiles Ltd v Tioxide Europe Ltd (Commercial Court, 29 September 2002) para 39 (trade secret). cp Mental Health Review Tribunal Rules 1983, SI 1983/942, r 12(3). If there are legal advisers, the legal advisers must be given access to the documents: *Hipwood v Gloucester Health Authority* (1995) 24 BMLR 27. But see *Elliott v MEM Ltd* (CA, 11 March 1993).

[3] Supreme Court Act 1981, ss 33(2)(b)(iii), 34(2)(b)(iii). See also County Court Act 1984, ss 52(2), 53(2).

[4] *Church of Scientology v DHSS* [1979] 3 All ER 97. cp *B v B* [1991] 2 FLR 487 where the court directed that a video recording of an interview with a child in which allegations of sexual abuse by the father were made should be disclosed only to the doctors and lawyers involved in the case, and not to the child's parents.

[5] *M v L* [1997] 3 NZLR 424 (counselling records of the victims of sexual abuse).

[6] per Lloyd LJ, *Elliott v MEM Ltd* (CA, 11 March 1993).

[7] per Ryan J, *Grofam Pty Ltd v Macauley* [1994] 121 ALR 22, 37 citing Wilcox J, *Jackson v Wells* (1985) 5 FCR 296, 307.

[8] See para 15.09 above. cp *Re B* [2002] 2 FCR 32, paras 66–67 where it was recognized that in children cases not only the child (see para 17.05 below) but also an adult might need the protection of a non-disclosure order.

A. Control of Documents

The disclosure had breached a court order that the records should be kept back from all the parties.[9]

Therapeutic privilege Solicitors are generally under a duty to allow clients unfettered access to all relevant documentary evidence in their possession.[10] Law Society rules state that solicitors may withhold information from a client that might adversely affect the client's mental or physical condition.[11] An order for limited disclosure may deny the applicant sight of his own records if it is judged to be detrimental for him to read them.[12]

17.04

Protection of children

Normally anything that a court or tribunal is asked to take into account in reaching a decision must be disclosed to all the parties to the dispute.[13] 'It is a fundamental principle of fairness that a party is entitled to the disclosure of all materials which may be taken into account by a court when reaching a decision adverse to that party'.[14] But there are exceptions to this principle.

17.05

Disclosure of all documents is not required in non-adversarial bankruptcy proceedings[15] and in contested family law cases it has long been accepted that the court may receive information relevant to the welfare of a child that is withheld from some or all of the parties if disclosure is necessary to avoid 'real harm'[16] to the child.[17] In *Re X*[18] the Court of Appeal upheld a decision to withhold from birth parents who opposed the adoption of their children the identity of the prospective adopters, information which was known to their solicitor. In the lower court the

17.06

---

[9] *R v Solicitor* [1997] 1 FLR 101.
[10] See paras 19.07 and 19.58 below
[11] See para 19.63 below.
[12] The House of Lords' decision in *McIvor v Southern Health and Social Services Board* [1978] 2 All ER 625 holding that this restriction was not permissible under the Administration of Justice Act 1970 was reversed by Parliament in the Supreme Court Act 1981, s 34(2).
[13] *WEA Records Ltd v Visions Channel 4 Ltd* [1983] 2 All ER 589, 591; *R (on the application of Stevens) v Plymouth City Council* [2002] EWCA Civ 388; [2002] 1 FLR 1177, para 36. cp *R v Governors of Dunraven School, ex p B* [2000] BLGR 494 in which the governing body and appeal committee of a school were held to have acted unfairly in denying the applicant, a pupil who had been permanently excluded from the school, access to the written and oral evidence of another pupil who had informed on the applicant to the Headmaster.
[14] per Lord Mustill, *Re D* [1995] 4 All ER 385, 399.
[15] *Re Murjani* [1996] 1 All ER 65, 74–76.
[16] *Official Solicitor to the Supreme Court v K* [1963] 1 All ER 191; *Re M* [1994] 1 FLR 760; *Re D* [1995] 4 All ER 385, 399; *McGrath v McGrath* [1999] SLT 90, 92. See also *Re B* [2002] 2 FCR 32, *Re B* [2002] All ER (D) 167. Literature includes D Burrows, *Evidence in Family Proceedings* (Bristol, 1999) 107 et seq and D Ormerod, 'Confidentiality in children cases' (1995) 7 Child and Family LQ 1, 8.
[17] When a child is separately represented by a solicitor in family litigation, the solicitor can apply to the court for permission to withhold information from the child-client: see para 19.63 below. Cp *Re B* [1993] 1 FLR 191, 203.
[18] [2002] EWCA Civ 525.

judge had refused the solicitor permission to disclose the prospective adopters' identity to her clients because of a real possibility of significant harm to the children from two sources: (1) the intervention of the birth parents in their lives and (2) the increased anxiety of the adopters.

Criminal proceedings

Counsel to counsel disclosure in criminal litigation

17.07 The Professional Standards Committee has warned members of the Bar not to agree to counsel to counsel disclosures because it is not compatible with a transparent prosecution process.[19]

> [F]ailure to disclose material to a client could cause serious difficulties including an inability to take the lay client's instructions on the material, almost impossible difficulties in deciding how to conduct the defence in the client's best interests and generally a risk that disparity could develop in the practice of disclosure between counsel.[20]

Michael Mansfield QC, counsel for a woman accused of being involved in a conspiracy of a terrorist nature, offered the following explanation as to why he could not accept an offer to be told information for which PII was being claimed on condition that he kept the information to himself:

> [A] substantial risk of undermining public confidence and the clients' confidence in the profession; the inability of counsel to perform his duty advising his clients as to their best interests; proper instructions from a client not in a position to appreciate the significance of the material would be precluded; counsel might receive material adverse to his clients about which he could not obtain proper instructions; counsel would have serious practical difficulties in conducting the case without accidentally disclosing confidential material; and, if the material could not be disclosed to counsel's instruction solicitors, the matter could be compounded because of the solicitor's unrivalled knowledge of the case and professional duty of disclosure to the lay clients.[21]

Effect of Article 6

17.08 Under Article 6(1) of the European Convention on Human Rights (ECHR) all parties to civil and criminal trials and tribunal proceedings have an absolute right to a fair hearing[22] but the concept of a fair hearing is a flexible one.[23] Lack of access to all the documents may be counterbalanced by other measures.[24] In *Re X* the Court of Appeal said that departures from the usual requirements of an adversarial trial must be 'for a

---

[19] Bar Council, *PII Hearings and Disclosure*, available from http:www.barcouncil.org.uk.
[20] ibid. In *Orr v McFadyen* [2003] SLT 29 the High Court of Justiciary held that a defence solicitor was entitled to cross-examine a prosecution witness using information disclosed by the Crown to the defence solictor on condition of confidentiality.
[21] *R v Botmeh* [2001] EWCA Crim 226; [2002] 1 WLR 531, para 26.
[22] See para 3.23 above.
[23] *Re X* [2002] EWCA Civ 525, para 13.
[24] *Re B* [2001] 2 FLR 1017, para 67.

A. Control of Documents

legitimate aim and proportionate to that aim'. Protecting the welfare of children is one such aim.[25] So also is protection of an individual's right to respect for private life.

> There may accordingly be circumstances in which, balancing a party's prima facie art 6 right to see all the relevant documents and the art 8 rights of others, the balance can compatibly with the Convention be struck in such a way as to permit the withholding from a party of some at least of the documents. The balance is to be struck in a way which is fair and which achieves a reasonable relationship of proportionality between the means employed and the aim sought to be achieved, having regard to the nature and seriousness of the interests at stake and the gravity of the interference with the various rights involved.[26]

Collateral Use of Documents
Information gathered for a criminal investigation

Restrictions on subsequent use by the Crown

17.09 Disclosure by the police, the Serious Fraud Office or the Crown Prosecution Service to third parties of confidential[27] information procured in the course of a criminal investigation is governed by the principles laid down in *Marcel v Commissioner of Police of the Metropolis*.[28] According to these principles, anyone who makes unexpected use of confidential personal information is liable to be sued for breach of confidence.[29]

17.10 The following disclosures by the police do not run the risk of an action for breach of confidence either because of implied consent or because disclosure is in the public interest:

(i) the supplying of information and witness statements to interested parties where there is a possibility of civil litigation after a road accident, and in particular the supplying of the names and addresses of parties involved in the accident whom an injured party could well otherwise having difficulty tracing,

(ii) conferences with and the supplying of information to the social services and welfare agencies and doctors in relation to the welfare of a minor (even if there has been a decision not to prosecute) where there has been an allegation of child abuse, whether sexual or not, and

---

[25] *R (on the application of Stevens) v Plymouth City Council* [2002] EWCA Civ 388; [2002] 1 FLR 1177, para 37.
[26] per Munby J, *Re B* [2001] 2 FLR 1017, para 67.
[27] Once the contents of the documents has been read in open court, the documents lose their quality of confidentiality and can be disclosed: *Bunn v BBC* [1998] 3 All ER 552, 557. See also para 17.27 below.
[28] [1992] 1 All ER 72, see para 10.36 above.
[29] [1992] 1 All ER 72, 85. This applies also to disclosure of volunteered information if there was an expectation that the information would be used only for the purposes of a criminal prosecution.

(iii) the supplying of information to the Criminal Injuries Compensation Board where a victim has claimed compensation and there has been no prosecution because the alleged criminal has died or fled the country.[30]

In addition, the police may disclose confidential information which, in their reasonable estimation, should be disclosed in the interests of public health or safety[31] or in the interests of the administration of justice[32] without consent and without first notifying the person affected. In 1999 the then Data Protection Registrar approved guidance by the Association of Chief Police Officers that it is proper for the police to identify the victims of a major accident without consent in order to avoid unnecessary anxiety on the part of friends or relatives of those who are unharmed[33] and when the identity of a victim is in the public domain to provide further information to stop rumours and speculation.[34]

17.11 There is one area of uncertainty. The *Covert Surveillance Code of Practice*,[35] para 2.18 states:

> There is nothing in the 2000 Act which prevents material obtained from properly authorized surveillance from being used in other investigations. . . . Authorizing officers must ensure compliance with the appropritae data protection requirements and any relevant codes of practice produced by individual authorities relating to the handling and storage of material.

However, the absence of an express prohibition does not necessarily signify that collateral use is lawful. It is all a question of statutory construction and against the background of the existing common law it is doubtful that a court would imply power to use surveillance information for a purpose for which it was not obtained. Further, use of the information by any public agency whose activities are not regulated by the Regulation of Investigatory Powers Act 2000 is likely to fail the requirement that interference with the Article 8 right to respect for private life must be 'in accordance with the law' and proportionate.

Restrictions on subsequent use by the defence

17.12 At common law the defence gives an implied undertaking that unused documents disclosed by the prosecution will not be used in civil proceedings, for example in a

---

[30] per Dillon LJ, *Marcel v Commissioner of Police of the Metropolis* [1992] 1 All ER 72, 81.
[31] *Woolgar v Chief Constable and UKCC* [1999] 3 All ER 604.
[32] *Pamplin v Law Society* [2001] EWHC Admin 300.
[33] Association of Chief Police Officers, Media Advisory Group, *Guidance Notes* (2000) para 2.7. Except in such circumstances, 'a victim, witness or next of kind is entitled not to have their personal details released without their permission. They are not however entitled to request that police release no information of the incident whatsoever, provided that the information the police do release does not lead to their identification.' Dead victims may be named once relatives have been informed because the Data Protection Act 1998 does not apply to them (para 2.6); see http://www.acpo.police.uk/ policies/GN7.doc.
[34] ibid, para 2.8.
[35] Available on the Home Office website: http://www.homeoffice.gov.uk.

defamation action, or for any other purpose for which they were not disclosed.[36] The common law has been put on a statutory footing by Criminal Procedure and Investigations Act 1996, s 17.[37] Unused material disclosed by the prosecution to the defence is subject to an obligation of confidentiality and its use for any purpose other than preparing the accused's defence or an appeal[38] requires leave of the court.[39] This restriction lapses once the material has entered the public domain by being read or referred to in open court.[40] Improper use or disclosure is a contempt of court.[41] Only 'unused material', that is material that does not form part of the prosecution case, is protected by s 17; there is 'no statutory restriction on the use of *used* material',[42] that is, material disclosed to the defence because it forms part of the prosecution case and there is no statutory mechanism for a prosecutor or person with an interest in 'used' evidence to obtain an order restricting its use outside the criminal proceedings for which it is disclosed.[43] The alternative of a common law undertaking not to use the evidence outside the criminal proceedings was rejected by Otton LJ in *Mahon v Rahn*: 'I can find no justification for this court to proceed on the basis that prior to the Act there was any restriction in relation to used material other than public interest immunity.'[44] Since there were no common law restrictions on the use of 'unused' material displayed or disclosed in open court, there could be no overriding policy reasons for restrictions on the subsequent use of 'used' material.

Suppose the prosecution discloses material as part of its case but that material is not needed for the trial. This could happen if the accused decided to plead 'guilty' at the outset or during the course of the trial. In *Mahon v Rahn* Otton LJ and Staughton LJ did not consider that the absence of restriction on the subsequent use of 'used' material hinged on whether it was read out or referred to in open court.[45] Otton LJ's touchstone was Article 6 which gives a litigant an absolute right to a fair trial.[46] But he conceded that if he were wrong, 'I would be inclined to the view that the undertaking does continue to apply for so long as it remains **17.13**

---

[36] *Taylor v SFO* [1998] 4 All ER 801.
[37] s 17 does not apply to documents produced in response to a witness summons.
[38] Criminal Procedure and Investigation Act 1996, s 17(1), (2).
[39] ibid, s 17(4). Section 17(6) provides a mechanism whereby the prosecutor or a person claiming an interest in the information may apply to be heard by the court considering an application under s 17(4).
[40] *Mahon v Rahn* [1997] 3 All ER 687, 706–707; Criminal Procedure and Investigations Act 1996, s 17(3). Query, do documents enter the public domain if the court imposes reporting restrictions: see eg Contempt of Court Act 1981, s 4(2)? Surely not.
[41] s 18. This is punishable in the magistrates' court by imprisonment for six months or a fine of £5,000 or both and in the Crown Court by two years' imprisonment or a fine, or both.
[42] *Mahon v Rahn* [1997] 3 All ER 687, 706.
[43] ibid at 706–707.
[44] ibid at 708.
[45] ibid at 710, 711, 716. On this point the judgments are obiter because the 'used' material was relied upon in evidence-in-chief and cross-examination and 'certainly entered the public domain': [1997] 3 All ER 687, 715.
[46] ibid at 710.

unused and the court has made no order'.[47] No distinction was to be drawn between material obtained voluntarily or by compulsion.

> A prosecuting authority who discloses documents pursuant to its common law (and now statutory obligations) is not in the same position as a party to civil proceedings who voluntarily discloses documents at an interlocutory stage. . . . If one recognizes the underlying rationale of reassuring and not deterring informants, there is no logical reason for distinguishing between the means by which the documents were obtained. If such a distinction were recognized it might well be detrimental to the administration of justice, as it would discourage informers from volunteering information.[48]

A counter argument might be that when the prosecution does not have to rely on evidence disclosed as part of its case there is really nothing to distinguish 'used' material from 'unused' material. Logic would suggest that the 'used' material should, like the 'unused' material, be prevented from being used in other proceedings such as a libel action. Otherwise use in collateral proceedings of material disclosed only to the defence will depend entirely upon whether the prosecution selected the material to form part of a case which it did not in the end have to make. The flaw in this argument is to assume that 'unused' material that has not been read or referred to in open court will be unavailable for collateral proceedings other than in the exceptional case. Application may be made by the defence to use the 'unused' material[49] and Article 6 may require that that discretion be exercised in the applicant's favour whenever the evidence is relevant to the collateral proceedings. Furthermore, as Staughton LJ pointed out, there is no provision in s 17 for the court to give leave for 'used' material that was destined to be relied upon, but not in fact used, in the criminal proceedings to be made available in later civil proceedings.[50]

Information disclosed during civil proceedings[51]

Common law position

17.14 At common law a party[52] to whom documents are disclosed under compulsion by the process of civil disclosure (discovery) is forbidden from making collateral use

---

[47] *Mahon v Rahn* [1997] 3 All ER 687, at 711.
[48] ibid, 710.
[49] Criminal Procedure and Investigations Act 1996, s 17(4)–(6).
[50] *Mahon v Rahn* [1997] 3 All ER 687, 717. But since the implied undertaking would be common law in origin, there might be a corresponding common law discretion to allow the material to be used.
[51] S Gibbons, 'Subsequent Use of Documents Obtained Through Disclosure in Civil Proceedings—The "Purpose of the Proceedings" Test' (2001) 20 Civil Justice Q 303. For family proceedings see para 17.17 below.
[52] No obligation is implied on a stranger who happens to be in court (*Mahon v Rahn* [1997] 3 All ER 687, 712), but a stranger is only likely to discover the contents of the information if it is read out in open court. The obligation must extend to the party's agents, both solicitor and counsel.

A. Control of Documents

of the documents, confidential or otherwise, without the court's consent[53] unless the same documents or information become available to the party from another source.[54]

> Those who disclose documents on discovery are entitled to the protection of the court against any use of the documents otherwise than in the action in which they are disclosed.[55]

This is said to be the result of an implied undertaking to the court,[56] but this is a fiction: the obligation is imposed by law.[57] The non-disclosure obligation applies to both the documents and the information in the documents.[58] Its purpose is:

> to limit the invasion of privacy and confidentiality caused by compulsory disclosure of documents in litigation. It is generated by the circumstances in which the documents have been disclosed, irrespective of their contents. It excludes all collateral use, whether in other litigation or by way of publication to others. On the other hand, the undertaking may be varied or released by the courts if the interests of justice so require.[59]

Improper use of a document or its contents, whether by a party or a third party (including a court official),[60] may be restrained by an injunction[61] (unless needed as evidence in criminal proceedings)[62] or dealt with as a contempt of court.[63] It is unclear whether the party whose documents are misused can recover damages.

17.15 The undertaking of confidentiality dissolves once the document enters the public domain.[64] This normally happens when the document is used in open court or, semble, in contested proceedings in chambers that are neither secret nor family

---

[53] On application, the court may vary the obligation or release the applicant from it: *Miller v Scorey* [1996] 3 All ER 18, 25–26.

[54] *Mahon v Rahn* [1997] 3 All ER 687, 712–713: '[i]t cannot be the law that a litigant, having from the start information and evidence which would enable him to bring an action against another, becomes disqualified from using it if the information and that evidence are later disclosed to him on discovery in another action to which he is a party', per Straughton LJ.

[55] per Talbot J, *Distillers Co (Biochemicals) Ltd v Times Newspapers Ltd* [1975] 1 All ER 41, 48.

[56] Where there is a real risk of abuse an express undertaking of confidentiality may be required or a confidentiality order may be made by the court in relation to particular documents: *Riddick v Thames Board Mills Ltd* [1977] 3 All ER 677, 701; *Church of Scientology of California v DHSS* [1979] 3 All ER 97, 106; *Warner-Lambert Co v Glaxo Laboratories Ltd* [1975] RPC 354.

[57] *Mahon v Rahn* [1997] 3 All ER 687, 713.

[58] *Crest Homes plc v Marks* [1987] 2 All ER 1074, 1978.

[59] per Lord Hoffman, *Taylor v SFO* [1998] 4 All ER 801, 808. See also *Riddick v Thames Board Mills* [1977] 3 All ER 677, 687–688.

[60] *Bourns Inc v Raychem Corp* [1999] 1 All ER 908, 916, Ch D. See also *Distillers Co (Biochemicals) Ltd v Times Newspapers Ltd* [1975] 1 All ER 41, 48.

[61] *Prudential Assurance Co v Fountain Page Ltd* [1991] 3 All ER 878, 886.

[62] *Rank Film Distributors Ltd v Video Information Centre* [1981] 2 All ER 76, 81, 85.

[63] This is because the recipient's implied undertaking not to use documents disclosed during discovery is owed to the court: *Bourns Inc v Raychem Corp* [1999] 3 All ER 154, 169, CA.

[64] *Bourns Inc v Raychem Corp* [1999] 1 All ER 908, 915, Ch D. See also *Mahon v Rahn* [1997] 3 All ER 687, 693.

proceedings.[65] Voluntary disclosure does not attract the undertaking[66] unless disclosure is made under rules of court that by inference reserve rights of confidentiality or privilege.[67]

Civil Procedure Rules 1998

17.16 The common law has been superseded for most civil litigation by CPR, r 31.22(1) which states that litigants to whom documents have been produced[68] on disclosure may use them 'only for the purpose of the proceedings' for which they are provided. This rule disappears in the following circumstances:

(1) Where the document 'has been read to or by the court, or referred to, or at a hearing which has been held in public'.[69] A document to which this happens passes into the public domain. A document used in a private hearing[70] is not read out or referred to 'in public' and therefore by implication remains subject to the implied undertaking. It is to be noted that the CPR do not give a non-party an independent right of access to the document. Lord Bingham recognized the threat this poses for open justice and suggested that '[i]n some cases (especially cases of obvious and genuine public interest) the judge may in the interests of open justice permit or even require a fuller oral opening, and fuller reading of crucial documents, than would be necessary if economy and efficiency were the only considerations. . . . As the court's practice develops it will be necessary to give appropriate weight to both efficiency and openness of justice. . . . Public access to documents referred to in open court (but not in fact read aloud and comprehensibly in open court) may be necessary, with suitable safeguards, to avoid too wide a gap between what has in theory, and what has in practice, passed into the public domain.'[71]

(2) Where the court gives permission.[72] Leave is not readily granted to use a document that has not entered the public domain in collateral civil proceedings to pursue a remedy against a third party.[73] Leave is reserved for special circum-

---

[65] See para 17.30 below.
[66] *Derby v Weldon (No 2)*, The Times, 20 October 1988; *Esterhuysen v Lonrho plc*, The Times, 29 May 1989; *Mahon v Rahn* [1997] 3 All ER 687, 693, 697, 712. But see *Bourns Inc v Raychem Corp* [1999] 3 All ER 154, 170, CA, where the implied undertaking was applied to documents disclosed in proceedings for the taxation of costs in circumstances where a court would have ordered disclosure if voluntary disclosure had been refused.
[67] *Prudential Assurance Co Ltd v Fountain Page Ltd* [1991] 3 All ER 878, 890.
[68] There is no mention of the documents having had to be produced under compulsion.
[69] CPR, r 31.22(1)(a). See also *SmithKline Beecham Biologicals SA v Connaught Laboratories Inc* [1999] 4 All ER 498, 508–509.
[70] See paras 17.30 et seq.
[71] *Smithkline Beecham Biologicals SA v Connaught Laboratories Inc* [1999] 4 All ER 498, 512.
[72] CPR, r 31.22(1)(b).
[73] *A v A* [2000] 1 FLR 701, 718–720. If litigation is pursued against a third party, unless privileged the document will have to be produced in response to a summons or subpoena even if the court has previously refused leave under r 31.22(1)(b). There is also the possibility of an order for production before the trial under Supreme Court Act 1981, s 34 and CPR, r 31.17.

stances[74] and where such a course will not occasion injustice to the party who gave disclosure.[75] The court will be concerned to protect the privacy of the person who produced the document or to whom the document relates. A different attitude is taken to disclosure to, and use by, prosecuting authorities of material obtained under compulsion.[76] A court may itself instigate disclosure to the appropriate public authorities (including professional bodies) of tax evasion or other unlawful conduct when satisfied that it is in the public interest to do so.[76a]

(3) Where the person who disclosed the document and the person to whom the document belongs consent.[77] Neither of these persons is necessarily the subject of the information and if neither is interested in keeping the information confidential the subject must rely on the court exercising its discretion to restrict or prohibit use of the document if it contains sensitive personal information.[78]

The provisions of CPR, r 31.22(1) relate only to the obligations of the parties in relation to disclosed documents but they impact on the position of non-parties in so far as a party who is at liberty to 'use' a disclosed document, may make it available to a non-party (in the absence of a special order under CPR, r 31.22(2)).[79]

Family court proceedings[80]

17.17 In children cases documents filed with the court are prevented by the Family Proceedings Rules 1991[81] from being used outside the family proceedings without the leave of a family court judge.[82] This rule follows a long-established practice of confidentiality in children proceedings that derives from the wardship jurisdiction.[83] Confidentiality attaches to all aspects of the proceedings, the

---

[74] *Chase v NGN Ltd* [2002] EWHC 1101, paras 12–19. The strictness with which courts approach the leave question is illustrated by *Bourns Inc v Raychem Corp* [1999] 3 All ER 154, a patent case decided before the CPR came into force. Leave was refused to use documents outside the taxation proceedings in which they had been disclosed, including the main proceedings on appeal. As the documents were subject to LPP, permission was also refused to use the documents in American litigation involving the same parties even though in the US privilege would be deemed to have been waived.

[75] *Crest Homes Plc v Marks* [1987] 2 All ER 1074.

[76] In *A v A* [2000] FLR 701, 718 where Charles J suggested that the fact that information is required in the public interest by prosecuting authorities was a 'special circumstance' and in *Eronat v Tabbah* [2002] EWCA Civ 950, para 19 Mance LJ said the same about assisting a foreign investigating body or court (whether or not the offence in question had a parallel in English law).

[76a] *A v A* [2000] 1 FLR 701. cp para 17.21 below. And cp *S v S* [1997] 2 FLR 774; *R v R* [1998] 1 FLR 922.

[77] CPR, r 31.22(1)(c).

[78] CPR, r 31.22(2).

[79] See para 17.23 below.

[80] M Wright, 'Disclosure of Documents in Children Cases' [1993] Family L 348.

[81] SI 1991/1247, r 4.23 headed 'confidentiality of documents'.

[82] See also Family Proceedings Courts (Children Act 1989) Rules 1991, SI 1991/1395, r 23 which prohibits documents being disclosed other than to specified persons.

[83] *Re G* [1996] 2 All ER 65, 69.

evidence of the parties,[84] the reports filed and the document disclosed.[84a] Even when children are not involved, all information about financial means (whether disclosed under compulsion or voluntarily) is protected by an implied undertaking before, during and after the proceedings.[85]

17.18 **Disclosure for use in criminal investigations and other litigation** Numerous cases deal with the exercise of the court's discretion to allow use of documents (including reports by expert witnesses) filed with the court in children proceedings for a collateral purpose.[86] The same approach is taken regardless of whether the information was obtained in the wardship jurisdiction,[87] in public law Children Act cases[88] and in private law child litigation.[89] The court attempts to balance the competing interests in disclosure and non-disclosure. Relevant factors will vary from case to case but will always include the impact of disclosure on the child[90] and the importance of maintaining confidentiality and encouraging candour.[91] Guidance given in *Re EX*[92] is in favour of the disclosure of information to the police for the purpose of a pending investigation or to a defendant in criminal proceedings.[93] In *Re D* Sir Stephen Brown P said: '[i]n relation to criminal proceedings it is clear that the wardship court should not, as it were, seek to erect a barrier which will prejudice the operation of another branch of the judicature.'[94]

17.19 There may be more reluctance to release confidential information for use in a civil action. In *Re Manda*[95] a boy of 18 and an ex-ward of court was permitted to use confidential evidence (including a consultant paediatrician's suspicions of child abuse) to pursue an action for negligence and trespass against a health authority. Balcombe LJ warned: 'if social workers and others in a like position believe that the evidence they give in child proceedings will in *all* circumstances remain confidential, then the sooner they are disabused of that belief the better.'[96] In *Re*

---

[84] eg *Re D and M* [2002] EWHC 2820.
[84a] *Clibbery v Allan* [2002] EWCA Civ 45; [2002] 1 All ER 865, para 47. The rule does not apply to documents that are not held by the court in the court file (*Re G* [1996] 2 All ER 65, 72–73, cp *Re M* [2002] EWHC 2482).
[85] *Clibbery v Allan* [2002] EWCA Civ 45; [2002] 1 All ER 865, paras 72–73, 106.
[86] Cases besides those mentioned in the text and later footnotes include *Re L* [1996] 2 All ER 78; *Re V* [1999] 1 FLR 267; *A Health Authority v X* [2001] EWCA Civ 2014; [2002] 2 All ER 780.
[87] *Re Manda* [1993] 1 FLR 205.
[88] eg *Re EC* [1996] 2 FLR 725.
[89] eg *Vernon v Bosley (No 2)* [1997] 1 All ER 614, 652.
[90] *Re L* [2000] 1 FLR 913; *Re X* [2001] 2 FLR 440.
[91] *S v S* [1997] 2 FLR 774; *Re R* [2003] EWCA Civ 19, para 10.
[92] [1997] Fam 76. But see *Re D and M* [2002] EWHC 2820, para 12.
[93] eg *Re C* [1997] Fam 76; *Oxford CC v L* [1997] 1 FLR 235; *Re W* [1998] 2 FLR 135, 145.
[94] [1994] 1 FLR 346, 351.
[95] [1993] 1 All ER 733.
[96] ibid at 743 (emphasis added). Sir John Megaw (at 746) expressed concern that professionals who provided evidence in such cases under the umbrella of an express or implied promise of confidentiality might in future be less frank and co-operative. Contrast *Re R* [1998] 1 FLR 433, 435.

A. Control of Documents

X, Y and Z,[97] however, the court refused disclosure of materials used in wardship proceedings to enable a newspaper to defend a libel action brought by two paediatricians whom the newspaper had criticized for using and teaching unsound techniques in the investigation of child abuse. The court was concerned that 'doctors and others bound by constraints of professional confidence' and social workers would be discouraged from speaking openly about their views and discoveries in future cases.

Disclosure to regulatory bodies Family courts are inclined to allow disclosure of information to a public or quasi-public body that is in a position to protect vulnerable members of the public. In *A CC v W*[98] the General Medical Council, which was contemplating initiating proceedings for serious professional misconduct, applied successfully for access to documents adduced in care proceedings indicating sexual abuse by a registered medical practitioner against his daughter. In *A Health Authority v X* Thorpe LJ said that there was 'obviously a high public interest, analogous to the public interest in the due administration of criminal justice, in the proper administration of professional disciplinary hearings, particularly in the field of medicine'.[99] In *Re R*[100] a finding of sexual abuse was disclosed, on application, to the probation service who employed the abuser. **17.20**

The court may release confidential information on its own initiative. In *Re L*[101] the guardian ad litem was directed by the court in care proceedings to report to the UK Central Council for Nursing, Midwifery and Health Visiting (UKCC), the body responsible at that time for the registration of nurses, that the mother, a registered nurse, was suffering from a severe personality disorder and to disclose to the UKCC expert psychiatric evidence adduced in the proceedings. **17.21**

Access to Documentary Evidence by Non-Parties

Inspection of documents filed with the court

Both in civil and in family proceedings the court has opportunities to control public access to use of documents used in the proceedings after they are over. By CPR, r 5.4(2)(c), the court must give permission for a non-party to search for, inspect and take a copy of any document held on the court file other than a claim **17.22**

---

[97] [1992] 1 FLR 8, 96–97.
[98] [1997] 1 FLR 574. See also *Re A* [1998] 2 FLR 641.
[99] [2001] EWCA Civ 2014; [2002] 2 All ER 780, para 19. The applicant in this case was a health authority that wished to see medical records that were produced to the court or generated forensically in the course of care proceedings in order to determine whether a GP practice had complied with its conditions of service. Evidence of non-compliance was likely to result in disciplinary proceedings against non-complying doctors. cp *Dooley v Law Society* (Ch D, 13 December 2001) transcript p 11.
[100] [1998] 1 FLR 433.
[101] [2000] 1 FLR 913. cp *Woolgar v Chief Constable of Sussex and UKCC* [1999] 3 All ER 604, 615.

form which has been served or a judgment or order made in public.[102] Inspection of the court file without leave, knowing that leave is required, is a contempt of court.[103] Access to documents filed or lodged in family proceedings similarly requires leave of the court.[104] This does not apply to the parties. If they have originals or copies of documents on the court files that are not the subject of an implied undertaking they can disclose them to third parties without committing a contempt of court.[105] The point of CPR, r 5.4(2)(c) and its Family Proceedings Rules equivalent, r 10.20(3) is to make it more difficult for a stranger 'going to the court office and inspecting or taking a copy of any document other than a decree or order made in open court' and 'thus assists the parties . . . in controlling the degree to which the proceedings receive wider publicity'.[106]

Use of documents

17.23 CPR, r 31.22(2) enables the court to make an order restricting or prohibiting further 'use'[107] of documents disclosed in proceedings, even if read to or by the court. Should such an order be in force and the document nonetheless reach a third party by accident or theft, a third party who uses the document aware of the order commits a contempt of court.[108]

17.24 The factors to be considered when deciding whether to make an order are detailed in *Lilly Icos Ltd v Pfizer Ltd*.[109] Buxton LJ said that the court must start from the premise that there must be very good reasons for departing from the normal rule of publicity. Account must be taken of the limited or central role of the document in the trial, any 'chilling' effect of an order upon the interests of third parties, the specific reasons why the applicant would be damaged by the publication and whether the trial would be held in secret or witness statements or skeletons be adduced in closed form without the order.[110]

Witness statements

17.25 A witness statement by a professional that has been used as evidence in chief is open to inspection unless the court directs to the contrary during the trial.[111] Under CPR, r 32.13(2), (3) the professional (like any witness) may apply to the

---

[102] Anyone willing to pay the prescribed fee can inspect and copy the claim and judgment.
[103] *Dobson v Hastings* [1992] 2 All ER 94.
[104] Family Proceedings Rules 1991, SI 1991/1247, r 10.20(3). See also Family Proceedings Rules 1991, r 4.23 which applies to proceedings under the Children Act 1989.
[105] *Clibbery v Allan* [2001] 2 FCR 577.
[106] per Munby J, *Clibbery v Allan* [2001] 2 FCR 577, para 81.
[107] The judgment in *Lilly Icos Ltd v Pfizer Ltd* [2002] EWCA Civ 2; [2002] 1 All ER 842, para 5 implies that use includes disclosure.
[108] ibid, para 5.
[109] ibid.
[110] ibid, para 25.
[111] CPR, r 32.13(1).

B. Restricting Publicity

court for a direction to withhold the statement from public inspection. The grounds for a direction are: the interests of justice, the public interest, 'the nature of any expert medical evidence in the statement', 'the nature of any confidential information (including information relating to personal financial matters) in the statement' and 'the need to protect the interests of any child or patient'.[112] The court has the option of allowing an edited version of the statement to be inspected.[113] The witness statement of a professional that has been served but not been put in evidence, or has been put in evidence in proceedings held in private, may be used only for the purpose of the proceedings in which it was served unless the professional or the court consents otherwise.[114]

B. Restricting Publicity

Open Justice

Effect of disclosure of confidential information to a court

17.26 Subject to constraints of space, normally anyone can attend a trial, be it civil[115] or criminal, and the media is at liberty to publish a fair and accurate account for the benefit of those unable to attend in person.[116] Confidential information revealed in open court loses its confidentiality whether or not members of the public are present in the courtroom or the evidence is reported.[117]

> [T]he administration of justice in this country is a matter of public interest, and to be conducted (again as a general rule) in public, and, consequently, . . . there can be nothing privileged or confidential which passes in open court.[118]

17.27 The confidentiality of a document can be lost even without the document being read out in court.[119] In proceedings to which the public are admitted it is enough that:

---

[112] CPR, r 32.13(2), (3). Any witness—not just professionals—can make an application.
[113] CPR, r 32.13(4).
[114] CPR, r 32.12.
[115] CPR, r 39.2(1), CPR PD 39, para 1.2.
[116] Contempt of Court Act 1981, s 4(1).
[117] *Marcel v Commissioner of Police of the Metropolis* [1992] 1 All ER 72, 81; *Bunn v BBC* [1998] 3 All ER 552, 557. See also CPR, rr 31.22(1)(a), 32.12 (2)(c).
[118] per Stirling J, *Goldstone v Williams Deacon & Co* [1899] 1 Ch 47, 52.
[119] The public has no automatic access to a document that is read out or referred to in court. To see a document filed with the court requires the court's leave (see para 17.22 above). This is readily granted (*Gio Personal Investment Services Ltd v Liverpool and London Steamship Protection and Indemnity Association Ltd* [1999] 1 WLR 984) except in family proceedings (Family Proceedings Rules 1991, r 10.20(1), (3)). Witness statements used in lieu of oral evidence in civil proceedings are freely available to the public for inspection and copying (CPR, r 32.13(1) and see para 17.25 above). A member of the public is probably entitled to access to documents attached to the witness statement: *Gio Personal Investment Services Ltd v Liverpool and London Steamship Protection and Indemnity Association Ltd* [1999] 1 WLR 984, 901.

(1) the document has been filed with the court and a material part read out in court;[120] or
(2) counsel drew the judge's attention to the document during the hearing and it was then silently read by the judge;[121] or
(3) the document was read by the judge before coming into court and was referred to in court by judge or counsel (even indirectly by reference to a skeleton argument which is incorporated in submissions in open court);[122] or
(4) the document contains material that the judge read and on which he based his decision.[123]

The party claiming that a document put before the court did not enter the public domain has the burden of proving this.[124] If parts of a document are irrelevant, those parts can be covered up to prevent entry into the public domain and loss of confidentiality.[125]

Rationale for open justice

17.28 There are solid grounds for requiring justice to be administered in public. In *R v Legal Aid Board, ex p Kaim Todner*[126] Lord Woolf MR listed deterrence of inappropriate courtroom behaviour; maintaining public confidence in the administration of justice, demonstrating the impartiality of justice and discouraging uninformed and inaccurate criticism of judicial proceedings. Openness has many further benefits: it encourages consistent judging, may result in the availability of further evidence, through the fear of exposure discourages exaggerated testimony, deters anti-social conduct by members of the public who see criminals brought to justice and adds to the criminal's punishment by subjecting him to public humiliation.

17.29 But open justice comes at a price, especially where confidential personal client information is made public. There is the general though fairly minimal risk that in future potential clients will be deterred from disclosing secrets to—or even consulting—professionals.[127] There is the immediate risk in some cases of harm (in the broadest sense of that term) to a litigant or witness. This is particularly undesirable when that person falls into a vulnerable category, for example, a child.

---

[120] *Smithkline Beecham Biologicals SA v Connaught Laboratories Inc* [1999] 4 All ER 498, 508.
[121] ibid.
[122] *Derby v Weldon (No 2)*, The Times, 20 October 1988, approved in *SmithKline Beecham Biologicals SA v Connaught Laboratories Inc* [1999] 4 All ER 498, 509.
[123] *Smithkline Beecham Biologicals SA v Connaught Laboratories Inc* [1999] 4 All ER 498, 509–510. See further R Taylor, 'Open justice and subsequent disclosure' (1999) 149 NLJ 1203.
[124] *Barings Plc v Coopers & Lybrand* (2000) 150 NLJ 681.
[125] cp *Capital Corporate Finance Group Ltd v Bankers Trust Co* [1995] 1 WLR 172, 176. See also *McIvor v Southern Health & Social Services Board* [1978] 2 All ER 625, 628.
[126] [1998] 3 All ER 541, 550.
[127] *Birmingham Post & Mail Ltd v Birmingham City Council* (1993) 17 BMLR 116, 121. cp para 1.46 above.

B. Restricting Publicity

English law offers a number of procedural devices for reducing an immediate risk. All involve, to greater or lesser extent, interference with the principle of open justice and therefore their availability is subject to stringent conditions.

Hearing Evidence in Private

Excluding the public

A hearing 'in chambers'

When a trial requires disclosure of confidential personal information which has not yet entered the public domain, a litigant may apply to have the case dealt with in private to preserve his privacy. Prior to the CPR 1998 there were two categories of private hearing: those heard in chambers[128] and those heard in secret. Courts sat in chambers generally as a matter of administrative convenience or of custom. A chambers hearing is private in the sense that members of the public and press are not given admission as of right but 'if requested, permission should be granted to attend when and to the extent that this is practical'.[129] Ordinarily, if proceedings are in chambers, it is permitted to report the evidence, both oral and affidavit, that was presented.[130]

17.30

A hearing 'in secret'

Hearings, whether in chambers or in an ordinary courtroom, may take place in secret (in camera).[131] A secret hearing is one from which all but the trial participants are excluded and later publication of the proceedings is prohibited.[132] The power to hold a secret hearing may be derived either from the court's inherent power[133] or from legislation. Children proceedings in the High Court and county courts,[134] wardship hearings[135] and medical treatment applications in the High Court[136] are automatically heard in chambers *and* in secret. The Matrimonial Causes Act 1973[137] provides that evidence of sexual capacity shall be held in

17.31

---

[128] Proceedings in chambers tend to be less formal; they may be held in an ordinary room. Solicitors have a right to be heard when proceedings are conducted in chambers. See further J Jaconelli, *Open Justice* (Oxford: 2002) 76.

[129] per Lord Woolf, *Hodgson v Imperial Tobacco* [1998] 2 All ER 673, 687. See also, Law Commission report 8, *Report on the Powers of Appeal Courts to Sit in Private and the Restrictions upon Publicity in Domestic Proceedings* (Cmnd 3149, 1966) 5. If neither party publicizes the proceedings, privacy may be protected.

[130] See para 17.44 below.

[131] *Trustor AB v Smallbone* [2000] 1 All ER 811.

[132] *Clibbery v Allan* [2002] EWCA Civ 45; [2002] 1 All ER 865, para 19.

[133] *R v Lewes Prison (Governor), ex p Doyle* [1917] 2 KB 254, 271.

[134] *Clibbery v Allan* [2002] EWCA Civ 45; [2002] 1 All ER 865, paras 47–48. See also Family Proceedings Rules 1991, r 4.16(7); *Re P-B* [1997] 1 All ER 58; *A and B and C and D v Times Newspapers Ltd and Express Newspapers Ltd* [2002] EWHC 2444.

[135] *Re F (A Minor)* [1977] 1 All ER 114, 122, 125.

[136] *F v West Berkshire Health Authority* [1989] 2 All ER 545, 569.

[137] s 48(2). See also Adoption Act 1976, s 64.

camera in proceedings for the nullification of a marriage unless the judge thinks that in the interests of justice the evidence should be heard in open court. Magistrates' courts may be closed to the public in the interests of the administration of justice or public decency when indecent evidence is received.[138] Closing proceedings to the public, even if it is just while a particular witness testifies, is not something judges do lightly. Exclusion of the public must be objectively justified.[139] In criminal trials in the Crown Court advance notice must be given of the intention to hold proceedings in secret and publicized by the court[140] to give the media an opportunity to object. It is now common for judges to hear representations from the media in other proceedings.[141]

A hearing 'in private' (CPR Pt 39)

17.32 There is a presumption under the CPR that proceedings will take place in public.[142] This allows both attendance and access to any judgment delivered or order made.[143] CPR, r 39.2(3) states that a hearing, or any part of it:

may be in private if...
(a) publicity would defeat the object of the hearing; ...
(c) it involves confidential information (including information relating to personal financial matters) and publicity would damage that confidentiality[144]
(d) a private hearing is necessary to protect the interests of any child[145] or patient
...
(g) the court considers this to be necessary, in the interests of justice.[146]

These rules enable the court to respect the private life of witnesses, litigants and third parties about whom confidential personal information has to be disclosed to the court.

17.33 There is no definition of 'private'. In *Clibbery v Allan*[147] Dame Butler-Sloss said that 'in private' means 'in chambers'. Proceedings to which the public are not admitted and which cannot be reported are hearings 'in secret'.[148] On its face, this

---

[138] Magistrates' Courts Act 1980, 69(4).
[139] *Clibbery v Allan* [2002] EWCA Civ 45; [2002] 1 All ER 865 para 16.
[140] Crown Court Rules 1982, SI 1982/1109, r 24A.
[141] A Nicol, G Millar, A Sharland, *Media Law and Human Rights* (London: 2001) 123.
[142] CPR, r 39.2(1). The CPR do not regulate family proceedings in the High Court. These are governed by the Family Proceedings Rules where there is no presumption that the hearing is public: *Clibbery v Allan* [2002] EWCA Civ 45; [2002] 1 All ER 865, paras 50, 124.
[143] CPR, Pt 39 PD, para 1.11.
[144] CPR, r 39.2(3)(c) should be read in conjunction with the relevant PD, para 1.5 which lists ten categories of proceedings which, in the first instance, should be listed to be heard in private.
[145] It has long been customary for cases concerned with the welfare and upbringing of children to be heard in chambers: *Re M* [1990] 1 All ER 205, 208. See also Family Proceedings Rules 1991, r 4.16(7).
[146] r 39.2(3).
[147] [2002] EWCA Civ 45; [2002] 1 All ER 865, para 18.
[148] ibid, para 20.

B. Restricting Publicity

is not quite consistent with what Lord Woolf had to say about Part 39 in *R v Bow County Court, ex p Pelling*. He identified three types of hearing:

> First of all there are hearings in open court. Secondly, there are hearings in the judge's room or chambers to which the public have access. Thirdly, there are hearings in court or in the judge's room or chambers which are in private. If the hearing is a public hearing in chambers there may be a limit on the number of members of the public who can attend and the judge deals with this as appropriate as a matter of discretion.[149]

This equates a private hearing with one that takes place 'in secret'[150] but the Practice Direction shows that a private hearing is not normally to be understood either as a hearing in chambers in the traditional sense[151] or a secret hearing, but a new hybrid: a hearing for which non-parties need leave of the judge to attend and to receive a copy of the judgment or order.[152] In most circumstances this will be as good as a hearing in secret. In *Dooley v Law Society*[153] an application by a solicitor to discharge a notice of intervention in relation to his practice by the Law Society was, at the solicitor's request, held in chambers (ie in private) in order to protect clients who were allegedly involved in possible dishonesty and to avoid breaches of legal professional privilege. This enabled Neuberger J to exclude press and public. But subsequently he held that the Law Society could use the transcript without leave of the court in disciplinary proceedings against the solicitor because the proceedings were in chambers (ie in private) but not in secret.[154]

---

[149] [1999] 4 All ER 751, 758. See also at 760 where Lord Woolf again appears to assume for the purpose of setting out when a litigant in person is entitled to be accompanied by a McKenzie friend that a hearing in private is one that is held in secret.

[150] In *Dooley v Law Society* (Ch D, 13 December 2001) Neuberger J said that 'in private' can mean in chambers or in secret.

[151] A judge considering an application to sit in private is directed to take into account the requirement of an open hearing contained in Art 6(1) by CPR, PD 39, para 1.4A. This in itself is an indication that a private hearing is not the kind of hearing in chambers to which Lord Woolf referred in *Hodgson v Imperial Tobacco Ltd* [1998] 2 All ER 673, 687, namely a hearing to which a member of the public should be admitted if practicable and which can be reported so long as this causes no substantial prejudice to the administration of justice.

[152] 'If the court or judge's room in which the proceedings are taking place has a sign on the door indicating that the proceedings are private, members of the public who are not parties to the proceedings will not be admitted unless the court permits' (CPR, Pt 39 PD, para 1.09); 'Where there is no such sign on the door of the court or judge's room, members of the public will be admitted where practicable' (CPR, Pt 39 PD, para 1.10); 'When a judgment is given or an order is made in private, if any member of the public who is not a party to the proceedings seeks a transcript of the judgment or a copy of the order, he must seek the leave of the judge who gave the judgment or made the order' (CPR, Pt 39 PD, para 1.12).

[153] (Ch D, 13 December 2001.)

[154] Neuberger J doubted that he had jurisdiction to sit in secret to prevent disclosure of the proceedings. However in *H (A Healthcare Worker) v Associated Newspapers Ltd* [2002] EWCA Civ 195; [2002] EMLR 23, para 43 Kennedy LJ held that a judge sitting in private had an implied power to forbid the reporting of information presented in a hearing conducted in private.

Impact of the European Convention on Human Rights

17.34 At common law prior to 1999 it was not permitted to hold a hearing in secret to preserve privacy[155] or because this is what all the parties wanted. It had to be shown that 'a public hearing is likely to lead directly or indirectly to a denial of justice'.[156] In the Human Rights Act 1998 (HRA) era the starting point is still the principle of open justice,[157] which is enshrined in Article 6(1), but the grounds for departing from that principle have been enlarged. The Article 6 right is subject to exceptions: 'the press and public may be excluded from all or part of the trial in the interest of morals, public order or national security in a democratic society, where the interests of juveniles or the protection of the private life of the parties so require, or to the extent strictly necessary in the opinion of the court in special circumstances where publicity would prejudice the interests of justice.'[158] This change underpins CPR, r 39.2(3)(c) and (d) which allow a private hearing in civil proceedings governed by the CPR to protect the confidentiality of information (whether or not in issue) or the interests of a child. The argument that r 39.2(2)(c) is ultra vires the rule-makers' powers was rejected in *R (on the application of Pelling) v Bow County Court*.[159]

17.35 At least[160] two other Convention rights may bear on whether proceedings should be open or closed: Article 8(1), which requires respect to be shown for private life, and Article 10, which protects freedom of expression and therefore potentially reinforces the open justice principle. The relevance of Article 10(1) lies in the possibility that it, unlike Article 6(1) which benefits only the litigants,[161] may confer a right on the public and the media to be present during a judicial hearing. Harris, O'Boyle and Warwick,[162] however, comment that the 'Strasbourg authorities have

---

[155] *Scott v Scott* [1913] AC 417, 439.

[156] per Lord Donaldson, *R v Chief Registrar of Friendly Societies, ex p New Cross Building Society* [1984] 2 All ER 27, 31. The main reasons for holding a criminal trial in secret were either the protection of national security or someone's identity, eg *X v Y* [1988] 2 All ER 648. See also Crown Court Rules 1982, r 24A(1), (2). It was recognized in *ex p Guardian Newspapers Ltd* [1999] 1 WLR 2130, 2148 that there might be other reasons for holding proceedings in secret.

[157] *Clibbery v Allan* [2002] EWCA Civ 45; [2002] 1 All ER 865, paras 47–48.

[158] Interference with the right to a public hearing on any of these grounds will have to be necessary and proportionate: see para 3.19 above.

[159] [2001] EWCA Civ 122.

[160] Art 2 would be relevant if the witness is at risk of reprisals if identified.

[161] As Art 6(1) is intended to benefit the litigants, they can waive the right to a public hearing, so long as this does 'not run counter to any important public interest': *Hakansson v Sweden* (1990) 13 EHRR 1, para 66.

[162] *Law of the European Convention on Human Rights* (London: 1995) 379. In *Leander v Sweden* (1987) 9 EHRR 433, para 74, the ECtHR held that Art 10 'basically prohibits a Government from restricting a person from receiving information that others wish or may be willing to impart to him'. On the other hand, in the US the Supreme Court has held that the First Amendment contains a right of public access to criminal trials and possibly also civil trials: *Richmond Newspapers v Virginia* 448 US 555 (1980). In *R (on the application of Pelling) v Bow County Court* [2001] UKHRR 165, para 40 the Divisional Court dismissed the *Richmond* case as inconsistent with Arts 6 and 10 which allow parties to waive publicity.

B. Restricting Publicity

not been receptive to the argument that Article 10 protects *access* to information on which to base an opinion or otherwise to exercise Article 10 freedoms more effectively'.

In the event that Article 8(1) is engaged, that right will have to be weighed against the Article 6(1) right of litigants to a public trial should a litigant object to secrecy.[163] Mostly, opposition to a closed hearing will come from the media. Whatever the source of objection, the privacy interests of the child are likely to be treated as paramount:[164] '[i]t is widely recognized in European jurisprudence that the balance in children cases is in favour of confidentiality.'[165]

17.36

When medical evidence of extreme sensitivity such as sexual incapacity or infection with the HIV virus is presented to a court, the balance is also likely to come down on the side of privacy. In *Z v Finland*[166] the European Court of Human Rights (ECtHR) would not have upheld a court order that compelled the applicant's doctors to give evidence of her HIV status in criminal proceedings against her husband had the questioning taken place in open court.

17.37

> The interference with the applicant's private and family life which the contested orders entailed was thus subject to important limitations and was accompanied by effective and adequate safeguards against abuse.[167]

It is noteworthy that none of the express qualifications to Article 6(1) applied in *Z v Finland*: a public hearing did not prejudice the administration of justice,[168] there was no concern about morality, public order and national security and the privacy qualification did not apply because the wife, an adult, was not a litigant.

Anonymity Orders

Persons who are not parties

Witnesses

Courts have a discretion to allow a witness to give evidence anonymously.[169] The procedure to be followed in making an application for anonymity is laid down in *R v Bedfordshire Coroner, ex p Local Sunday Newspapers Ltd*.[170] The HRA has had a twofold effect:

17.38

---

[163] cp *Clibbery v Allan* [2001] 2 FLR 819, para 140. See also para 3.24 above.
[164] cp *Re Z* (Fam Div, 13 October 2000).
[165] *Clibbery v Allan* [2002] EWCA Civ 45; [2002] 1 All ER 865, para 82 citing *B v UK* [2001] 2 FLR 261. cp *A and B and C and D v Times Newspapers Ltd and Express Newspapers Ltd* [2002] EWHC 2444, paras 9–10.
[166] (1998) 25 EHRR 371. *Scott v Scott* [1913] AC 417 (annulment proceedings involving evidence of impotence) would probably be heard in private today.
[167] ibid, para 103.
[168] As it might be if there was danger to the safety of a witness: *X v UK* 2 Digest 452 (1977).
[169] CPR, r 39.2(4). In proceedings not covered by these rules the power to make such an order is inherent in the judge's power to control proceedings.
[170] (2000) 164 JP 283.

(1) it has reversed the original common law rule[171] that privacy is not a valid reason for witness anonymity by its incorporation of Article 8 into domestic law;[172]

(2) it has imposed a requirement that measures be taken to prevent any unfairness to the parties arising from such an order, especially the defence in criminal proceedings.[173]

17.39 In *Z v Finland*[174] the ECtHR found that Article 8(1) had been breached when an appellate court had published a judgment that named a witness (the wife of the accused) whom the judgment disclosed was infected with the HIV virus. Pecuniary damages amounting to £12,500 were awarded. The ECtHR's concern was not with the possible frustration of justice which before 1999 was the only acceptable reason in English law for an anonymity order,[175] but with the effect on the private and family life of the witness and the deterrent effect on members of the public seeking diagnosis or treatment for AIDS.[176] If anonymity for a witness is opposed, the court cannot make an anonymity order without taking into account the right to freedom of expression of the opposing party.[177]

Non-witnesses

17.40 Initially Z had refused to give evidence at her husband's trial and because of this her doctors were compelled to give evidence about her HIV seropositive status, this being a matter relevant to the charge of attempted manslaughter against her husband.[178] It is implicit in the ECtHR's judgment that the wife's identity would have had to have been concealed whether or not she had become a witness.[179] Therefore now in English law there may be circumstances in which a court must conceal the identity of non-witnesses to protect their privacy. One circumstance in which this might apply is if a professional were to be called to give evidence about medical research involving identifiable individuals. Indeed, in *Z v Finland*

---

[171] *R v Westminster City Council, ex p Castelli* (1995) 30 BMLR 123, 128.
[172] *Z v Finland* (12998) 25 EHRR 371 (discussed in main text).
[173] The judge must know who the witness is and, in criminal cases, counsel must be able to observe the demeanour of the witness during questioning and have questions put to the witnesses: *Doorson v Netherlands* (1996) 22 EHRR 330. Guidelines promulgated by the Court of Appeal in *R v Taylor* [1995] Crim LR 253 which allow a criminal conviction to be based solely on the evidence of anonymous creditworthy witnesses appear to be incompatible with Art 6(1): R Costigan and P Thomas, 'Anonymous Witnesses' (2000) 51 Northern Ireland LQ 326, 348 et seq.
[174] (1998) 25 EHRR 371.
[175] *R v Evesham Justices, ex p McDonagh* (1988) 87 Cr App R 28, 35; *Re D* (1997) 45 BMLR 191, 198. The usual pre-HRA reason for concealment was the risk of reprisals.
[176] (1998) 25 EHRR 371, para 96.
[177] CPR, r 39.2(4) must be interpreted in this way to be Convention-compliant.
[178] The husband had raped a number of women, allegedly aware at the time that by doing so he exposed them to the risk of getting AIDs.
[179] She agreed to give evidence because her doctors had been compelled to tell the court the material evidence that related to her. There was therefore no point in her continuing to exercise her right not to give evidence in a case concerning her husband.

the doctors compelled to give evidence included one who had interviewed the wife for research purposes.[180]

Restraining soliciting of information

A court may impose an order forbidding information from being solicited (usually by a media organization) about someone whose identity the court decides needs to be protected from publicity.[181] An order was obtained forbidding until further order the soliciting by any person of any information relating to the Maltese Siamese twins, Jodie and Mary, that was not already in the public domain.[182] The court also enjoined publication of the name or address of any witness who gave evidence (save for the names of three doctors) in a manner calculated to lead to the identification of any place the twins were being cared for or treated. In a case in which the sperm of the husband of a woman receiving fertility treatment was mixed up with that of a man of another race whose wife was also receiving fertility treatment at the same clinic, Dame Butler-Sloss said that the court had a duty to protect the private lives of the two couples and the mixed race twins born to the white couple and prevent them from becoming victims of intrusive and distressing publicity in a situation that was not of their making.[183] Accordingly, injunctions were granted to prevent them from being identified or approached, identification of the clinic and the NHS trust area responsible for the clinic.[184] 17.41

Parties

To avoid an unjustifiable invasion of the claimant's right to respect for private life, a court may conceal the claimant's identity by the use of a pseudonym.[185] Sometimes this requires the identity of an opponent[186] (and even the name of the claimant's solicitor)[187] to be concealed as well. Naming the claimant who has been 17.42

---

[180] (1998) 25 EHRR 371, para 30.
[181] *H (A Healthcare Worker) v Associated Newspapers Ltd* [2002] EWCA Civ 195; [2002] EMLR 23, para 61. cp *Kelly v BBC* [2002] 1 All ER 323, 358.
[182] *Central Manchester Health Care NHS Trust v Michaelangelo Attard* (18 June 2001, varied 25 August 2001).
[183] *X NHS Trust v A* (Fam Div, 31 July 2002).
[184] See also *Cumbria CC v X*, The Times, 25 June 1990. The restriction on naming the clinic and NHS trust area was subsequently lifted: *Leeds Teaching Hospitals NHS Trust v A* (QB, 4 November 2002).
[185] eg *A v National Blood Authority* [2001] 3 All ER 289 (an action by 114 recipients of blood transfusions who had been infected with hepatitis C); *R (on the application of F) v Oxfordshire NHS Trust* [2001] EWHC Admin 535 (challenge to a decision taken in respect of a person detained under the Mental Health Act 1983, name suppressed under CPR r 39.2). Applicants to the ECtHR frequently claim anonymity and do not require an order of the court to do so.
[186] eg *H (A Healthcare Worker) v Associated Newspapers Ltd* [2002] EWCA Civ 195; [2002] 3 WLR 542 (applicant a professional with HIV infection, opponent his employer); *B v NHS Hospital Trust* [2002] EWHC 429; [2002] 2 All ER 449 (application by paralysed patient for declaration that continued connection to life-support machine an unlawful trespass).
[187] *A v B plc and C ('Flitcroft')* [2002] EWCA Civ 337; [2002] 3 WLR 542.

awarded an injunction against a professional, interceptor or stranger to restrain publication of confidential personal information could nullify the injunction. In a civil action governed by the CPR the court has authority under CPR, r 39.2(4) to 'order that the identity of any party . . . must not be disclosed if it considers non-disclosure necessary in order to protect the interests of that party . . .'.[188]

17.43 Concealing the identity of a party may be necessary to protect the privacy of a third party (whether or not a witness).[189] For example, where the victim and perpetrator of an offence are related. If there is no specific rule of court or legislative provision that allows this, the judge can draw on his inherent power to control the proceedings to do whatever is necessary.[190] As in all cases restricting publicity, account has to be taken of any opposing party's freedom of expression rights.

Reporting Restrictions

Proceedings held in private

17.44 It is not automatically unlawful or a contempt of court to report what happened during proceedings held in chambers or in private[191] or even what happened in proceedings held in secret.[192] Publication has to be prohibited by legislation[193] or forbidden by a court with power to ban reporting[194] or calculated to interfere with the due administration of justice.[195]

17.45 The Administration of Justice Act 1960, s.12 provides that certain cases that are routinely heard in private and in secret[196] may not be reported without leave. This category includes wardship cases, proceedings brought under the Children Act 1989 and other hearings that relate wholly or mainly to the maintenance or upbringing of a minor.[197] Without leave, it is a contempt of court to knowingly[198]

---

[188] In *H (A Healthcare Worker) v Associated Newspapers Ltd* [2002] EWCA Civ 195; [2002] EMLR 23, para 18 the Court of Appeal held that an order to suppress the identity of the claimant for the benefit of the defendant could not be made under CPR, r 39.2(4). It allowed the order under CPR, 39.2(3)(a) and (c) on the basis that implicit in the power to order the court to be closed lay a power to conceal the identity of a party to achieve the same objective.

[189] eg *R (on the application of Stevens) v Plymouth City Council* [2002] EWCA Civ 388; [2002] 1 FLR 1177.

[190] *H (A Healthcare Worker) v Associated Newspapers Ltd* [2002] EWCA Civ 195; [2002] EMLR 23, para 43.

[191] *Dooley v Law Society* (Ch D, 13 December 2001); *Clibbery v Allan* [2002] EWCA Civ 45; [2002] 1 All ER 865, para 17.

[192] *Att-Gen v Leveller Magazine* [1979] 1 All ER 745, 751, 760–761.

[193] eg Judicial Proceedings (Regulations of Reports) Act 1926, s 1 (see para 17.47 below).

[194] eg by an injunction or an order made under Contempt of Court Act 1981, s 11 (see para 17.49 below).

[195] *Att-Gen v Leveller Magazine* [1979] 1 All ER 745, 751, 761.

[196] See para 17.31 above.

[197] For details see D Burrows, *Evidence in Family Proceedings* (Bristol: 1999) 202 et seq. See also *Cleveland CC v F* [1995] 2 All ER 236, 239–240. See also Adoption Act 2002 s 101.

[198] On the need for mens rea see *Re F* [1977] 1 All ER 114, 122, 131, 137.

B. Restricting Publicity

disclose information disclosed in these proceedings (including the names of the parties) for *any* purpose.[199] The embargo extends to statements of evidence and confidential reports and accounts of interviews submitted to the court.[200] Proceedings heard in private under CPR, r 39.2(3) cannot be reported if the judge exercises an inherent power to forbid disclosure of information.[201] Third parties who know of and ignore the order will be in contempt of court.

Proceedings in open court

Inherent power to prevent publicity

An inherent power allows a civil court: **17.46**

(1) to restrain publication of information made available because of proceedings that would pre-empt the decision of the Court if disclosed or to protect the identity of someone involved in the proceedings;[202]
(2) in extraordinary circumstances,[203] to prevent the media disclosing the comings and goings of parties and witnesses *outside* premises where a trial is proceeding in secret.[204]

In the absence of any specific power to control publicity, the inherent power enables the court to protect the identity of an applicant for an injunction to restrain disclosure of confidential personal information or to prevent reporting of the presence at the trial of a professional—say an AIDS expert—the very mention of whose attendance might infringe the privacy of someone connected with the case.

Statutory reporting restrictions[205]

A miscellany of statutory provisions allows the courts to restrain reporting of evidence given in open and a fortiori in closed proceedings. Of particular interest to health professionals will be the Judicial Proceedings (Regulation of Reports) Act 1926 which makes publication of 'indecent matter' or medical details calculated to injure public morals unlawful.[206] Judicial views about what constitutes **17.47**

---

[199] Administration of Justice Act 1960, s 12(1)(a).
[200] *Re F (A Minor)* [1977] 1 All ER 114. See also para 17.17 above.
[201] *H (A Healthcare Worker) v Associated Newspapers Ltd* [2002] EWCA Civ 195; [2002] EMLR 23, para 43.
[202] *Re P-B* [1997] 1 All ER 58, 61; *H (A Healthcare Worker) v Associated Newspapers Ltd* [2002] EWCA Civ 195; [2002] EMLR 23, para 43.
[203] Normally, the media may identify witnesses who are not the subject of an anonymity order even if not permitted to discover or report what they say in the witness box: *X v Dempster* [1999] 1 FLR 894.
[204] *Re G* [1999] 1 FLR 409.
[205] P Carey, *Media Law* (2nd edn, London: 1999) 155–165.
[206] s 1(1)(a). The restriction can be enforced by a criminal prosecution or by injunction at the instigation of an individual injured or threatened with injury by unlawful publication: *Argyll v Argyll* [1967] 1 Ch 302, 338 et seq. Section 1(2) specifies that only a proprietor, editor, master printer or publisher can be convicted pursuant to s 1.

'indecent matter' have no doubt changed drastically since 1926. In proceedings for dissolution of marriage and certain other family proceedings the Act also makes it unlawful to publish a line-by-line account of evidence.[207]

17.48 A broader power to restrict reporting is found in the Contempt of Court Act 1981. Section 4(2) allows the publication of a report of proceedings, or any part of proceedings, to be *postponed* where 'necessary for avoiding a substantial risk of prejudice to the administration of justice in those proceedings, or in any other proceedings, pending or imminent'.[208] On 8 May 1996 Curtis J imposed a s 4(2) order without limitation of time forbidding identification of Dr B, a psychiatrist, who had given evidence during the trial of Brett Tyler for the sex-murder of a 9-year-old boy.[209] That the order was made pursuant to s 4(2) is surprising since the section does not confer power to impose an indefinite ban.[210]

17.49 Orders permanently banning identification of parties or witnesses are normally made under Contempt of Court Act 1981, s 11.[211] This section allows a court to prohibit publication of 'a name or other matter' that has been lawfully withheld from the public during the proceedings.[212] It is a precondition to an order under the section that the administration of justice or some other public interest is endangered by disclosure.[213]

European Convention on Human Rights

Interference with Article 10

17.50 At one time disclosure to the media of confidential documents read out in open court constituted a contempt of court.[214] The ECtHR ruled this to be a violation of the Article 10 right to freedom of expression in *Harman v UK*.[215] Since reporting restrictions impinge on the freedom of expression of the parties,[216] journalists

---

[207] Judicial Proceedings (Regulation of Reports) Act 1926, s 1(1)(b). A 'concise statement of the charges, defences and countercharges in support of which evidence has been given' is allowed.

[208] This provision was considered in *R v Beck, ex p Daily Telegraph* [1993] 2 All ER 177. See also, T Ingman, *The English Legal Process* (7th edn, London: 1998) 143 et seq.

[209] According to 'Naming of psychiatrist banned', Media Lawyer, September 1996, 12 the doctor, who had given evidence about the defendant's attendance at a group therapy session, was 'anxious about confidentiality in his continuing occupation'.

[210] Anyone aggrieved by an order may appeal to the Court of Appeal under the Criminal Justice Act 1988, s 159 but in this case this appears not to have happened.

[211] *R v Westminster City Council, ex p Castelli* (1995) 30 BMLR 123. An injunction may occasionally be a possibility, eg *Re S* [2003] EWHC 254 [Fam] (exercise of the court's inherent jurisdiction to protect a child subject to the High Court's 'care' jurisdiction).

[212] s 11. Information disclosed by a professional about a client in open court could not be the subject of a s 11 order.

[213] *Birmingham Post and Mail Ltd v Birmingham City Council* [1993] 17 BMLR 118, 121.

[214] *Harman v Secretary of State for the Home Department* [1983] 1 AC 280.

[215] (1984) DR 38, 53.

[216] *B v UK* [2001] FCR 221.

B. Restricting Publicity

and media organizations,[217] any restriction imposed must be justifiable. This may be because the interference is necessary for one of the reasons mentioned in Article 10(2) and is proportionate to the end being pursued[217a] or because protection of some other Convention right outweighs the Article 10 right to freedom of expression.[218] A s 11 order that lasts longer than absolutely necessary would fail the test of proportionality.[218a]

Conflict between Article 8 and Articles 10 and 6

Reporting of personal information deployed in litigation may unjustifiably compromise an individual's Article 8 right to respect for private life and where this is the case the courts as public authorities may have to consider reporting restrictions.[219] In *Z v Finland*[220] the ECtHR found that Article 8(1) would be violated if a judicial decision were implemented that the transcripts of evidence given by the applicant's doctors and her medical records should become accessible to the public after ten years. When Article 8(1) is engaged, a balance must be struck between the private and public interest in preserving an individual's privacy and the private and public interest in enabling a party who wishes to do so to publicize the proceedings. A balance must also be struck between the public interest in maintaining the privacy of proceedings to enable justice to be done or the protection of an individual's privacy and the public interest in the publicity of proceedings to ensure public confidence in the administration of justice. Each case must be considered on its own merits but two important factors will be the sensitivity of the information[221] and whether it concerns a child.[222] 'It is widely recognized in European jurisprudence that the balance in children cases is in favour of confidentiality.'[223]

17.51

---

[217] *R v Secretary of State for Health, ex p Wagstaff* [2001] 1 WLR 292, 671.
[217a] See para 3.19 above.
[218] See para 3.26 et seq above.
[218a] cp *Birmingham Post and Mail Ltd v Birmingham City Council* [1993] 17 BMLR 118, a pre-HRA case in which a s 11 order was found unsatisfactory at common law because of excessive duration.
[219] HRA, s 6(1).
[220] (1988) 25 EHRR 371.
[221] *Z v Finland* (1998) 25 EHRR 371; *Clibbery v Allan* [2001] 2 FLR 819. The Court of Appeal [2002] EWCA Civ 45; [2002] 1 All ER 865, did not disagree with Munby J's handling of the balancing issue.
[222] *B v UK* [2001] 2 FCR 221.
[223] per Butler-Sloss P, *Clibbery v Allan* [2002] EWCA Civ 45; [2002] 1 All ER 865, para 82. But see *Re S* [2003] EWHC 254 (Fam) where reporting restrictions were thought unlikely to be effective to protect the child and the public interest in press reports of the trial of the child's mother for murder was considerable.

Part V

RELATED MATTERS

18

DATA PROTECTION AND FREEDOM OF INFORMATION

A. Data Protection Act 1998	18.01	Enforcement of the Data Protection Principles	18.47
Introduction	18.01		
First Data Protection Principle	18.08	B. Freedom of Information	18.51
Second Data Protection Principle	18.29	The Freedom of Information Act 2000	18.51
Other Data Protection Principles	18.34	Requests for Personal Information	18.53
Exemptions	18.37		

A. Data Protection Act 1998[1]

Introduction

The Data Protection Act 1998 (DPA), which implements EU Directive (EC) 95/46,[2] regulates almost all aspects of activity by a professional in relation to the storage, use and disclosure of personal information contained in a client's records.[3] It is important at the outset to appreciate two points. The first is that although the DPA gives the client access rights,[4] the client derives no property rights from the data protection regime. The second is that although the EU Directive was designed to promote an individual's right to informational privacy[5] (along with removing obstacles to the free flow of information within the

18.01

---

[1] R Jay and A Hamilton, *Data Protection Law and Practice* (London: 1999). For an examination of how the Act applies in universities see the JISC Data Protection Code of Practice for the HE and FE Sectors produced by Hull University at http://www.jisc.ac.uk/pub00/dp_code.html#664.

[2] This draws inspiration from the OECD's *Guidelines Governing the Protection of Privacy and Trans-Border Flow of Personal Data* (1980) and the Council of Europe's *Convention for the Protection of Individuals with Regard to Automatic Processing of Personal Data* (1981).

[3] The DPA goes beyond the EU Directive in that it regulates the processing of data that is not subject to EU law. On the question whether a member State can provide a more extensive protection for personal data or give it a wider scope than the Directive see *Bodil Lindqvist v Kammaraklagan* [2002] Celex No 601C0101 (advocate general). A decision of the ECJ is awaited.

[4] See ch 19.

[5] Art 1(1) gives as the Directive's objective to 'protect the fundamental rights and freedoms of natural persons, and in particular their right of privacy with respect to the processing of personal data'. See also Recitals 10 and 11.

Chapter 18: Data Protection and Freedom of Information

European Union) what it and the Data Protection Act 1998 protect is *data*, rather than information.[6]

18.02 Two things distinguish personal data from personal information:[7]

(1) Information is built from data; data is information in latent form.[8] Clark explains:

> 'Information' is data which is pertinent to a particular decision, and hence data becomes information only in particular contexts. Such a distinction goes to the very heart of the important concept of 'relevance'. Most data protection regulation should therefore be concerned with 'data', although it may be appropriate to phrase some requirements in terms of 'information', in particular those relating to use and disclosure.[9]

(2) Personal data is by definition in a record. The DPA does not seek to control the disclosure of information from memory[10] or regulate visual or aural surveillance unless the fruits of the surveillance are reduced to a form capable of 'processing'. Even the coverage of personal data is not total: the definition of personal data does not include every kind of record[11] and anything recorded for domestic purposes falls outside the Act.[12]

Notification

18.03 In order to be in a position to be able to collect and use personal data lawfully,[13] the professional, or, if the professional is employed, the professional's employer,[14] must (in the absence of a relevant exemption)[15]

(1) have notified details[16] of intended processing to the Information Commissioner for inclusion in the on-line register of data protection notifications he maintains[17] and

---

[6] Contrast the Freedom of Information Act 2000 (see para 18.51 below) which is concerned with data *and* information.

[7] This distinction is ignored in the use of headings in the FOIA (see eg s 40).

[8] 'Information can . . . be conceived of as "data" that has been "processed" in some way': P Roth, 'What is "Personal Information"?' (2002) 20 NZULR 40, 51.

[9] R Clark, 'The OECD Data Protection Guidelines: A Template for Evaluating Information Privacy Law and Proposals for Information Privacy Law', available at http://www.anu.edu.au/people/Roger.Clarke/DV/PaperOECD.html>

[10] Should the recipient of the information disclosed from memory use it to create a record of the type to which the DPA applies, the DPA will bite at that point.

[11] DPA, s 1(1); see para 18.06 below. From 2005 it will cover almost all records of public authorities.

[12] DPA, s 36.

[13] DPA, s 17(1).

[14] If the employer is registered, an employed professional who holds some personal data needed for her work at home will not have to register separately.

[15] Manual data (DPA, s 17(2)) is exempted from the notification requirement.

[16] Requirements are laid down in DPA, s 16(1): Name and address of data controller, personal data being processed, categories of data subjects, purposes of processing, description of recipients of processed data, destination of overseas transfers. Notification rules are contained in the Data Protection (Notification and Notification Fees) Regulations 2000, SI 2000/188.

[17] Sch 1, Pt II, para 5.

A. Data Protection Act 1998

(2) abide by all the requirements of the DPA.

Failure to notify, where required to do so, is a strict liability criminal offence punishable by a potentially unlimited fine.[18] The other obligations imposed by the Act apply whether or not the professional has complied with the notification procedure. Those obligations, other than subject access rights (SARs), that are of particular relevance to professionals are summarized in this chapter. SARs are dealt with in chapter 19.[19]

The scope of data protection

Forms of data

The data to which the DPA applies falls into various overlapping categories[20] **18.04**

(1) Health records, that is, 'information relating to the physical or mental health or condition of an individual' made by or for 'a health professional in connection with the care of that individual'.[21]
(2) Educational records, that is, information about a pupil made by, or for, a teacher or governing body at a local education authority school or special school based on information from that pupil, the pupil's parent, a teacher or other school employee 'other than information which is processed by a teacher solely for the teacher's own use'.[22]
(3) Public records, that is, local authority housing and social services records.[23]
(4) 'Personal data',[24] that is, data that relates to any[25] 'living individual'[26] (the data subject), who can be identified:
   (a) from that data itself; or
   (b) from the data in association with other data[27] already in the possession

---

[18] DPA, s 21. If trial takes place in the Crown Court. The maximum sentence on summary conviction is a fine not exceeding £5,000: DPA, s 60(2). Failure to notify the Commissioner of changes to registered details is also a criminal offence, though not one of strict liability: s 21(2), (3).
[19] See para 19.21 below.
[20] The first three categories are referred to collectively as 'accessible record[s]': DPA, s 68.
[21] DPA, s 68(2). Health professionals are defined in s 69. They include doctors, dentists, pharmaceutical chemists, nurses and clinical psychologists.
[22] DPA, Sch 11, para 2.
[23] DPA, s 68, Sch 12.
[24] DPA, s 1(1). Manual unstructured personal data held by public authorities (s 1(1)(e)) is exempted from most of the data protection principles (s 33A) and is therefore not included in the analysis.
[25] He need not be a UK citizen or resident: IC, *Data Protection Act 1998 – Legal Guidance* 2.4.
[26] This excludes data about companies and associations who are legal persons but not individuals and deceased persons and their estates.
[27] G Laurie, *Genetic Privacy* (Cambridge: 2002) 253 suggests that genetic data of one client may be 'personal data' of all family members because they can all be identified by it: 'Dr G might test X for colorectal cancer adenomatous polyposis—a dominant disorder that reveals clear patterns of disease within families. If Dr G is also the family doctor for X's siblings and children, does Dr G now hold "personal data" on those other family members?'.

of,[28] or likely to come into the possession of,[29] the person with responsibility for making decisions about the data (the data controller).[30]

and includes, as well as facts about an individual, expressions of opinion and intention with respect to an individual.[31]

18.05 Some potential fallacies need dispelling:

(1) 'Personal data' does not have to be about a single person;[32] it may be about a group of people such as a team.
(2) 'Personal data' need not be about an individual's private life;[33] the earnings of the sole proprietor of a business are personal data.[34]
(3) An individual does not have to be named to be identifiable.[35]
(4) 'Personal data' does not have to be confidential (even information in a public record is subject to the DPA)[36] and the data (or some of it) can be false.[37]
(5) Data that has been stripped of personal identifiers so that one individual cannot be distinguished from another is not 'personal data'[38]—the Information Commissioner, however, maintains that coded data (sometimes known as pseudonymized data) is personal data if the decoding key remains in existence (whether or not the data controller has any intention to link the two data sets) and that the process of anonymization is subject to data protection law.[39]
(6) 'Personal data' includes sound and visual data[40] that is stored in a manner that attracts the operation of the DPA,[41] for example, digitally stored photographs.

---

[28] Possession, in the opinion of the Information Commissioner, does not have to involve physical control; a data controller is deemed to be in the possession of data where an external processor has contracted to process the data for the data controller. See IC, *Data Protection Act 1998—Legal Guidance* 2.2.4.

[29] This provision has provoked unease about data controllers: how are they to know what information is likely to come into their possession?

[30] See para 18.11 below.

[31] DPA, s 1.

[32] IC, *Data Protection Act 1998—Legal Guidance* 2.2.1. A joint bank account is given as an example.

[33] IC, *Data Protection Act 1998—Legal Guidance* 2.2.1.

[34] cp *Niemetz v Germany* (1992) 16 EHRR 97.

[35] IC *Data Protection Act 1998—Legal Guidance* 2.2.3. If it is possible to single out an individual from others for the purpose of taking decisions or action in relation to that individual, the individual is someone who has been identified. See also para 1.05 above.

[36] eg *R v Rees* (CA, 20 October 2000) para 22; *R (on the application of Robertson) v Wakefield Metropolitan Council* [2001] EWHC Admin 915; [2002] 2 WLR 889, (electoral roll).

[37] The data subject has a right to seek rectification, erasure and destruction: DPA, s 14.

[38] The EU Directive expressly excludes anonymized data in recital 26.

[39] IC, *Data Protection Act 1998—Legal Guidance* 2.2.5. and para 18,08 above. See also, J Strobl, 'Data Protection Legislation: Interpretation and Barriers to Research' (2000) 321 British Medical J 890; N Wildish and M Turle, 'Anonymous data–inside or outside data protection law?' *Privacy Laws & Business UK Newsletter* May 2002 pp 21–22.

[40] Directive (EC) 95/46, preamble, para 15.

[41] See para 18.06 below.

A. Data Protection Act 1998

Forms of data storage

Whereas all health, educational and public records are caught by the DPA,[42] other records containing personal data are not subject to the DPA unless automated (for example, a computer database)[43] or organized and accessed manually in a 'relevant filing system'.[44] 'A relevant filing system' means 'any set of information' that is 'structured, either by reference to individuals or by reference to criteria relating to individuals, in such a way that specific information relating to a particular individual is readily accessible'.[45] The definition is complex but the general idea is clear enough: the data must be part of a filing system that is indexed either by reference to named individuals, for example, a card file with client surnames sorted alphabetically, or indexed by reference to criteria relating to individuals such that information about specific individuals can be easily extracted. The Information Commissioner suggests that data is 'readily accessible' if in the course of day-to-day operations in the data controller's organization the information can be located by a straightforward search.[46] The EU Directive makes it clear that storage of the data set may be geographically dispersed.[47] Thus a collection of student records dispersed amongst members of a university faculty is a relevant filing system. A file that is not part of a filing system is not caught by the DPA.[48] Nor are files organized chronologically.[49] Ironically, an individual's personal information may be subject to the DPA if he engages a professional who maintains a proper filing system but may not be if he engages one who does not use a computer and does not keep any other properly organized records.[50]

18.06

An amendment in the Freedom of Information Act means that from 2005 almost[51] all unstructured personal data held by a public authority will be subject

18.07

---

[42] DPA, s 68.

[43] Defined in DPA, s 1(1)(a)–(b) as 'processed by means of equipment operating automatically in response to instructions given for that purpose'.

[44] DPA, s 1(1)(c). For a detailed analysis of what this entails see H Barnard, 'Data Protection Act 1998—manual data' (2002) 152 NLJ 925. The DPA does not address the question of cross-referencing of manual with computerized records.

[45] Directive (EC) 95/46 does not mention structuring 'by reference to individuals or by reference to criteria relating to individuals'. Article 2(c) defines 'personal data filing system' as 'any structured set of personal data which are accessible according to specific criteria, whether centralized, decentralized or dispersed on a functional or geographical basis'. The access criteria were selected by the UK Government.

[46] IC, *Data Protection Act 1998—Legal Guidance* 2.1.1.

[47] Art 2(c) speaks of personal data that is 'centralized, decentralized or dispersed on a functional or geographical basis'.

[48] J Maxeiner, 'Freedom of Information and the EU Data Protection Directive' (1995) 48 Federal Communications LJ 93, 100–101 citing Common Position, Statements for Entry in the Minutes, 4730/95.

[49] *Hansard*, HL vol 587, col. 467 (16 March 1998) (Lord Williams).

[50] cp M Tugendhat and I Christie (eds), *The Law of Privacy and the Media* (Oxford: 2002) para 4.06. Of course, for some professions, failure to maintain proper records is a disciplinary matter.

[51] Certain Crown and armed services personnel matters are excepted.

to the DPA.[52] For others the DPA makes transitional arrangements that exempt the contents of structured manual files held prior to 24 October 1998 from having to comply with many of the data protection principles until 24 October 2007.[53]

First Data Protection Principle

Personal data

Processing the data

18.08 The parts of the DPA of most concern to professionals will be the first and second data protection principles which are part of a scheme to make the processing of personal data as transparent as possible to the data subject. The first data protection principle states that

> [p]ersonal data shall be processed fairly and lawfully and, in particular shall not be processed unless . . . at least one of the conditions in Schedule 2 is met.[54]

This principle must be obeyed on every occasion that personal data is processed. 'Processing' covers almost anything that can be done to data from collection to destruction including holding, using and disclosing.[55] There is no difference between disclosing the information internally within the organization for which the data controller works and to an outsider. It is arguable that processing includes authentication of personal data that has been leaked to the press[56] if the data has to be consulted to be verified.[57] It has been suggested judicially that processing does not include the act of anonymizing data,[58] a view not shared by the Information Commissioner who takes the view that data is not beyond the reach of the Act until the process of anonymization is complete.[59]

---

[52] This change will enlarge SARs where public authorities are concerned (see para 19.21 below) but manual unstructured personal data held by public authorities (DPA, s 1(1)(e)) will be exempted from most of the data protection principles (DPA, s 33A).

[53] Sch 8, para 14. There is complete exemption from the second, third, fourth and fifth data protection principles and s 14(1)–(3) and partial exemption from the first data protection principle.

[54] DPA, Sch 1, Pt I, para 1.

[55] '"[P]rocessing" in relation to information or data, means . . . carrying out any operation or set of operations on the information or data including— . . . (c) disclosure of the information or data by transmission, dissemination or otherwise making available . . .': DPA, s 1.

[56] *Lord Ashcroft v Att-Gen* [2002] EWHC 1122, QB, paras 31–32.

[57] DPA, s 1(b).

[58] *R v Department of Health, ex p Source Informatics Ltd* [2000] 1 All ER 786, 798–799. Lord Lester, who appeared for the General Medical Council, submitted that Directive (EC) 95/46 no more applies to the process of anonymizing data than to the use or disclosure of anonymous data (which falls outside the definition of 'personal data') and Simon Brown LJ was inclined to agree.

[59] IC, *Data Protection Act 1998—Legal Guidance* 2.2.5. It is to be noted that 'processing' is defined in s (1)(1) as meaning '*any* operation . . . on the information including . . . (b) retrieval, consultation or use of the information or data' (italics added). The Commissioner's view is shared by A Grubb, 'Breach of Confidence Anonymised Information' (2000) 8 Medical L Rev 115, 118. But if the process of anonymization involves no third party disclosure, where is the need for data protection? The data subject is not prejudiced but the data controller may be put to disproportionate effort.

A. Data Protection Act 1998

Lawful processing of personal data

The first data protection principle lays down three cumulative[60] requirements: **18.09**

(1) legality,
(2) fairness, and
(3) compliance with one of the conditions specified in Sch 2[61] and, for sensitive personal data, Sch 3.[62]

Legality is established by reference to the general law: processing must not be contrary to the common law or any enactment (including the Human Rights Act (HRA)). Disclosure of personal data that breaches an equitable[63] or contractual[64] obligation of confidentiality automatically contravenes the first data protection principle.[65] Processing may be in breach of this principle even though the professional complies with at least one of the Sch 2 (and where applicable, Sch 3) processing conditions. These conditions do not legitimize the disclosure or use of personal information; they are an additional hurdle to the use or disclosure of personal information.

Fair processing of personal data

What is fair processing?   Fair processing and lawful processing are independent   **18.10**
requirements. It is no answer to a complaint that data was processed unfairly that it was processed lawfully and with the client's consent. The client will not have consented to the data being processed unfairly. Fairness is not defined. The Data Protection Tribunal (now the Information Tribunal) has said that '[f]airness . . . requires us to weigh up the interests of data subjects and data users'.[66] The Information Commissioner's view, however, is that the data subject's interests are paramount.[67] Guidance on what fair processing involves is set out in Sch 1, Pt II (the fair processing code).[68] Compliance with the fair processing code does not of itself ensure fair processing,[69] but raises this presumption. Data obtained under an enactment[70] must be treated as having been fairly obtained.[71]

---

[60] *Campbell v MGN Ltd* [2002] EWHC 499; [2002] EMLR 30, paras 102, 119.
[61] See para 18.18 below.
[62] See para 18.25 below.
[63] See ch 5.
[64] See ch 4.
[65] *Campbell v MGN Ltd* [2002] EWHC 499; [2002] EMLR 30, paras 106, 119.
[66] *British Gas Trading Ltd v Data Protection Registrar* [1997–98] Info TLR 393.
[67] IC, *Data Protection Act 1998—Legal Guidance* 3.1.7: 'in assessing fairness, the first and paramount consideration must be given to the consequences of the processing to the interests of the data subject.'
[68] paras 1–4.
[69] IC, *Data Protection Act 1998—Legal Guidance* 3.1.7.
[70] It makes no difference whether the disclosure was compulsory or discretionary.
[71] DPA, Sch 1, Pt II, para 1(2).

18.11 **Information requirements prior to collection of the data** The client must be informed prior to collection of the data of:

(1) the identity of the 'data controller'. This is the person or persons who 'determines' the purposes for which, and the manner in which, the personal data is to be processed.[72] The data controller may be a natural person,[73] a legal entity[74] or an unincorporated body.[75] For self-employed professionals the data controller will be the professional. With employed professionals there are many possibilities. Should the professional be a data controller, she may share this role with others in the same organization or with the employer. Every person who can determine the purposes for which and manner in which any of the client's personal data is processed will be a data controller vis-à-vis the client.

(2) The purpose or purposes of the processing. Did Parliament intend the data subject to be separately notified of purposes set out in the on-line register? The wording of the DPA suggests not[76] but the Information Commissioner requires more effective communication of processing purpose(s) to the data subject[77] and, given the broad register entries,[78] this seems justified.

(3) Any further information, having regard to the specific circumstances in which the data is or is to be processed, that is 'necessary' to enable the processing to be fair.[79] In considering whether disclosure of further information is necessary, the Information Commissioner advises that the data controller consider:

   (a) whether the client is likely to understand the announced processing purposes,

---

[72] DPA, s 1(1). The Information Commissioner regards the power to determine the purpose of processing as the primary requirement; decisions about the manner of processing may be delegated: IC, *Data Protection Act 1998—Legal Guidance* 2.5. On the question of who is a 'data controller' see *P v Wozencroft* [2002] EWHC 1724, Fam Div, where counsel drew attention to the use of the present tense of the verb (ie 'determines'). An interceptor can be a data controller: cp *Douglas v Hello! Ltd (No 2)* [2003] EWCA Civ 139, para 45.

[73] DPA does not usually apply to a professional based outside the UK: DPA, s 5; *Douglas v Hello! Ltd* [2002] EWHC 2560.

[74] Local authorities, for example, are the data controllers of social work records and NHS trusts of hospital records.

[75] cp Council of Europe, *Convention for the Protection of Individuals with regard to the Automatic Processing of Personal Data* (28 January 1981) Art 2(d) defines a 'controller of the file' as 'the natural or legal person, public authority, agency or any other body who is competent according to the national law to decide what should be the purpose of the automated data file, which categories of personal data should be stored and which operations should be applied to them'.

[76] See Sch 1, Part II, para 5(b).

[77] I C, *Data Protection Act 1998—Legal Guidance*, para 3.2(b).

[78] See para 18.30 below.

[79] Sch 1, Part II, para 2(3)(c), (d).

A. Data Protection Act 1998

> (b) the likely consequences of such processing, and
>
> (c) whether particular disclosures can reasonably be anticipated.[80]
>
> The Information Tribunal and Information Commissioner are in agreement that an individual must be informed of non-obvious purposes for which information is processed at the point of collection.[81] Given the sensitivity of medical data, the Commissioner recommends telling the patient of any foreseeable disclosures of that kind of data.[82] The Commissioner says that data subjects must be told whether use or disclosure of data is mandatory or optional.[83] In the context of health care, this means distinguishing between essential and non-essential disclosures. The optional (non-essential) category includes: disclosures to social workers, hospital chaplains and the media; disclosures for the purposes of teaching and clinical trials.

Fair processing information can be given to the client orally (by telephone, for example) or in writing. In the case of health data, acceptable methods of giving written notice 'include a standard information leaflet, information provided face to face in the course of a consultation, information included with an appointment letter . . . or letter sent to a patient's home'.[84] A poster in the surgery or waiting room or a notice in a local newspaper which is not backed up by any other communication is unlikely to be sufficient. **18.12**

Information requirements after collection of the data   When a new use of data is identified *after* the data has been collected, this must be brought to the client's attention before the processing for that purpose occurs except where the processing is for a purpose (such as the detection or prevention of crime)[85] which is exempt from the fair processing requirement. **18.13**

> The fact that processing when undertaken could be used for a registered purpose does not . . . render the processing fair when it is established it was not in fact carried out for a purpose to which a data subject had agreed. For example, if a data user obtained information from a data subject for one agreed purpose and then later

---

[80] IC, *Data Protection Act 1998—Legal Guidance* 3.1.7.3. A very different view is taken by D Bainbridge and G Pearce, 'Tilting at Windmills—Has the New Data Protection Law Failed to make a Significant Contribution to Rights of Privacy?' (2000) 2 J of Information, L and Technology, available at http://elj.warwick.ac.uk/jilt/00-2/bainbridge.html. It is their opinion that only the most limited information needs to be provided.

[81] *Innovations (Mail Order) Ltd v Data Protection Registrar* (29 September 1993) para 30; *Linguaphone Institute Ltd v Data Protection Registrar* (DA/94 31/49/1, 14 July 1995) para 14; *British Gas Trading Ltd v Data Protection Registrar* [1997–98] Info TLR 393. See also DoH, *Working Together to Safeguard Children* (London: 1999) Appendix, available from http://www.doh.gov.uk.

[82] *Draft Guidance on the Use and Disclosure of Medical Data* (May 2001) para 13.

[83] IC, *Use and Disclosure of Health Data* (May 2002) 7, 18.

[84] ibid at 8.

[85] See para 18.44 below.

deliberately processed the personal data derived from the information for a purpose he knew would not be agreed it would in most circumstances be likely to amount to unfair processing and a breach of the first data protection principle.[86]

18.14 The notification obligation applies to use of medical data for medical research. Although medical research is exempt from the second data protection principle[87] and may be undertaken without patient consent,[88] it is not exempt from the fair processing requirement of the first data protection principle.[89]

18.15 Should a professional hold personal data that concerns a third party (say a relative) as well as the client, fairness may require the professional to notify both the client and the third party before processing the data for a new purpose[90] unless informing the third party would involve disproportionate effort.[91]

18.16 Significance of the method of obtaining The first paragraph of the fair processing code states that in deciding whether processing is fair regard is to be had to the method by which the data was obtained including whether any person from whom the data was obtained was deceived or misled about the purpose for which it was to be processed.[92] In *Campbell v MGN Ltd* [93]Morland J held that surreptitious photographing of Campbell as she left a Narcotics Anonymous meeting breached the fair processing code. The Court of Appeal[94] held that the 'processing' fell within the DPA, s 32 exemption for journalism but agreed that readers might find the covert photography offensive.[95]

18.17 Personal data not supplied by a third party The information requirements of the fair processing code apply to information about a client obtained from a source other than from the client. Part II of the first Schedule,[96] however, allows the data controller to disregard the fair processing code where the data was obtained from a third party or generated by the data controller and

---

[86] *British Gas Trading Ltd v Data Protection Registrar* [1997–98] Info TLR 393.
[87] See para 18.42 below.
[88] Consent is not required by the DPA (see para 18.25 below). Disclosure and use is likely to be lawful at common law without consent (see paras 13.51–13.52 above). If there is a relevant order, s 60 of the Health and Social Care Act 2001, s 60 (see para 13.53 above) will in any event obviate the need for consent at common law.
[89] The Information Commissioner wrote in a letter to The Times on 22 May 2001 that although personal data may be used for the purposes of medical research without the patient's explicit consent it is still necessary that 'patients are given a clear explanation of the purposes for which it is intended to use their data'.
[90] *Data Protection Act 1998—Legal Guidance* 3.1.7.4.
[91] See para 18.17 below
[92] DPA, Sch 1, Pt II, para 1(1).
[93] [2002] EWHC 499, [2002] EMLR 30, para 103.
[94] [2002] EWCA Civ 1373.
[95] Ibid, para 54. cp *R v Loveridge* [2001] 2 Cr App R 29, para 30.
[96] Sch 1, Pt II, para 3(2).

A. Data Protection Act 1998

(1) recording or disclosing the data is necessary for compliance with a non-contractual legal obligation *or*

(2) compliance would involve 'disproportionate effort' (a question of fact)[97] *and* there is no unfairness.

The Secretary of State has by statutory instrument[98] prescribed further conditions which must be met before the information requirements may be ignored. In both situation (1) and (2), the data controller must still provide the relevant information to any individual who requests it in writing.[99] In situation (2), if no request is received, the data controller must keep a record of the reasons why compliance involves 'disproportionate effort'.[100] There is no need to rely on the disproportionate effort exception if the client has been provided with the fair processing information by the data controller's third party source.[101]

'Conditions' permitting processing of personal data

Consent   Schedule 2 sets out 'conditions' that permit the processing of personal data. The first is consent.[102] Given that data protection is designed to protect the individual's informational privacy, it is logical to allow data to be processed with the data subject's consent. What it is that constitutes consent is considered in chapter 13. If the data controller relies on consent to process personal data and that consent is withdrawn for any reason or none, processing (including data retention) ceases to be lawful unless some alternative processing condition is satisfied. The multitude of alternative processing conditions means that it will rarely be possible for the client to prevent processing by refusing or withdrawing consent.[103]   18.18

'Conditions' not involving consent   Processing without consent is permitted by the DPA[104] when 'necessary' for any one of a number of reasons: 18.19

(1) for the performance of the client's contractual or prospective contractual obligations;[105]

---

[97] *Data Protection Act 1998—An Introduction*, ch 3. Relevant factors include cost, time difficulty and the effect on the client. The EU Directive 95/46EC, Art 11 confines 'disproportionate effort' primarily to processing for historical and scientific research purposes.
[98] Data Protection (Conditions under Paragraph 3 of Part II of Sch 1) Order 2000, SI 2000/185.
[99] ibid, r 4. The 'in writing' requirement is satisfied by a notice transmitted by electronic means.
[100] ibid, r 5.
[101] *Guidance on the Use and Disclosure of Health Data* (May 2002) p 9.
[102] Sch 2, para 1.
[103] D Bainbridge and G Pearce, 'Tilting at Windmills—Has the New Data Protection Law failed to make a Significant Contribution to Rights of Privacy?' (2000) 2 J of Information, L and Technology, para 3.4.
[104] Consent may still be required by the common law duty of confidence.
[105] DPA, Sch 2, para 2(a)–(b).

(2) in order to comply with the data controller's non-contractual legal obligations;[106]

(3) to protect the client's 'vital interests';[107]

(4) for the administration of justice;[108]

(5) for the exercise of statutory functions;[109]

(6) for exercise of Crown, ministerial or governmental functions[110] or the exercise of any other functions of a public nature exercised in the public interest;[111]

(7) to pursue the 'legitimate interests' of the data controller or a third party to whom the information is disclosed 'except where the processing is unwarranted in any particular case by reason of prejudice to the rights and freedoms or legitimate interests of [the client]'.[112]

18.20 **Problematic points** There is scope for argument about the parameters of some of the non-consensual processing 'conditions' as they apply to professional–client relationships:

(1) What is meant by 'vital interests'? For instance, are the 'vital interests' of a patient engaged when identifiable personal data is disclosed by a doctor to enable fraud by others to be detected?[113] The Information Commissioner's opinion is that 'vital interests' are restricted to 'matters of life or death, for example, the disclosure of a data subject's medical history to a hospital casualty department treating the data subject after a serious road accident'.[114] This view can be traced back to recital 31 of the EU Directive which says that processing is lawful when carried out 'to protect an interest which is essential for the data subject's life'. But, arguably, something may be, practically speaking,

---

[106] DPA,Sch 2, para 3. This prevents a conflict between a statutory obligation to make disclosure, eg Medicine Act 1983, s 35A and the DPA if the client explicitly refuses to allow the disclosure.

[107] DPA Sch 2, para 4. This exemption is important if the client is incompetent to consent, though the exemption will be of very limited assistance if the courts adopt the very narrow view of the Information Commissioner that the term 'vital interests' means matters of life and death: see para 18.20 below.

[108] DPA, Sch 2, para 5(a). This dispenses with client consent when a court requires information.

[109] DPA, Sch 2, para 5(b). This allows a great deal of information sharing within the public sector.

[110] DPA, Sch 2, para 5(c).

[111] DPA, Sch 2, para 5(d). In *Campbell v MGN* [2002] EWHC 499; [2002] EMLR 30, para 110 Morland J said that 'the commercial publication of newspapers is not the exercise of a function of a public nature'.

[112] DPA, Sch 2, para 6. It is on the basis of this condition that schools are allowed to publish their examination results to the media: Data Protection Commissioner, *Compliance Advice, Disclosure of Examination Results by Schools to the Media* (2001).

[113] M Chester, 'Practice Points' (2001) 98 LS Gaz 50.

[114] *Data Protection Act 1998—An Introduction* 3.1.1.

A. Data Protection Act 1998

essential to an individual's well-being (for example, removing a disfiguring birthmark or harelip) without being a matter of life and death.[115]

(2) When is processing without consent 'necessary'? In the Information Commissioner's opinion the data controller must be able to show 'that it would not be possible to achieve [the purpose being pursued] with a reasonable degree of ease' without processing personal, as opposed to anonymous, data.[116] In guidance on the *Use and Disclosure of Health Data*[117] the Information Commissioner states that in considering whether processing is 'necessary', the data controller must consider objectively whether the purpose for which the data is processed 'can be achieved only by the processing of personal data' and whether the 'processing is proportionate to the aim pursued'.

(3) What are the 'legitimate interests' of the professional and the client and what constitutes 'unwarranted' prejudice to the latter's rights and freedoms and legitimate interests? The Secretary of State has statutory authority to specify what these are but has not done so.[118] Legitimate interests includes all Convention rights including freedom of expression (Article 10) and respect for private life (Article 8). Oliver points out that the provision introduces a proportionality test weighted in favour of the data controller which contrasts with the Directive which forbids 'processing . . . if the data controller's legitimate interests are, "overridden by the interests or fundamental rights and freedoms of the data subject" '.[119] Both the doctrine of indirect effect and the HRA may require the DPA condition to be interpreted in a more even-handed way.

Data protection and discretionary disclosures Finding a DPA gateway for the lawful discretionary disclosures described in chapters 11 and 12 is not always straightforward. Take voluntary disclosures with statutory authority.[120] Condition 3 ('compliance with any legal obligation to which the controller is subject') is inapplicable.[121] A professional operating in the public sector may be able to rely on condition 5 (exercise of a statutory functions)[122] or 6 (functions of a public nature

18.21

---

[115] Even disclosure of suspicions of child abuse might not qualify as a matter of 'life or death'.
[116] IC, *Use and Disclosure of Health Data* (May 2002) 4.
[117] ibid.
[118] DPA, Sch 2, para 6(2).
[119] H Oliver, 'Email and Internet Monitoring in the Workplace: Information Privacy and Contracting Out' (2002) 31 Industrial LJ 321, 346.
[120] See para 12.14 above.
[121] DPA Sch 2, para 3.
[122] '[F]or the exercise of any functions conferred on any person by or under any enactment': Sch 2, para 5(b).

exercised in the public interest)[123] but a professional in private practice probably has to fall back on the open-ended condition 7: 'processing is necessary for the purposes of legitimate interests pursued by the data controller or by the third party or parties to whom the data are disclosed.'[124] As already explained, this has a proportionality requirement.[125]

18.22 For professionals operating in the private sector, pinpointing the condition that justifies disclosure that a client/patient threatens the physical safety of a third party[126] without the client's consent is problematic.[127] It is difficult to invoke the compliance with a legal obligation ground (condition 2) because there is usually no public law duty to expose iniquity[128] and a private law duty to disclose confidential information to prevent serious harm to a third party along *Tarasoff*[129] lines has not been recognized in English law.[130] In order to satisfy Sch 2 the professional will have to show either that disclosure involves 'the exercise of functions of a public nature . . . in the public interest' (condition 6) or a legitimate interests justification (condition 7).[131] The interests that count in the latter case are those of the disclosing party and the recipient of the information who may not be the person at risk. If the recipient is not the person at risk, condition 7 will restrict disclosure to an individual or body with a legitimate interest in receiving and acting on the information. The voluntary self-interest disclosures described in chapter 12 must satisfy the condition 7 proportionality test[132] in order to comply with the DPA.

Sensitive personal data

Definition

18.23 The DPA creates a special category of 'sensitive personal data'. In the EU Directive data in this special this special category is described as data 'which are capable by their nature of infringing fundamental freedoms or privacy'.[133] For the purposes of the DPA[134] sensitive data about a client is data about *his*:

---

[123] '[F]or the exercise of any functions of the Crown, a Minister of the Crown of a government department' or 'for the exercise of any other function of a public nature exercised in the public interest by any person': Sch 2, para 5 (c) and (d).
[124] DPA, Sch 2, para 6(1).
[125] Interference with the rights and freedoms of the client must not be 'unwarranted'.
[126] See ch 11.
[127] DPA, s 29 recognizes exemptions for the processing of personal data for the purposes of the prevention or detection of crime (see para 18.44 below) but not from the conditions laid down in Schs 2 and 3.
[128] See paras 20.01–20.05 below.
[129] *Tarasoff v Regents of University of California* 551 P 2d 334 (1976): see paras 20.07 et seq.
[130] See para 20.09 below.
[131] DPA, Sch 2, para 6. See para 18.19 above.
[132] See para 18.20 above. But the DPA, s 35 exemption may apply: see para 18.38 below.
[133] Art 33.
[134] DPA, s 2.

- racial or ethnic origin;
- political opinions;
- 'religious beliefs or other beliefs of a similar nature';[135]
- trade union membership;
- physical or mental health or condition;[136]
- sex life;
- criminality, alleged or proven;[137]
- criminal proceedings, their disposal and sentencing.

Details of efforts to overcome drug addiction by attending self-help drug therapy meetings are within this sensitive data category.[138] The client's financial, tax and business affairs generally are not. Information about his upbringing and education are not sensitive personal data except to the extent that they disclose *his* criminality,[139] religious beliefs or are inextricably tied up with his medical data. A person's home or work address is not normally sensitive personal data, but in some circumstances it can be, for example, inclusion of an individual's name in a list of donors to a political organization.[140] Many professionals (especially lawyers) handle sensitive and non-sensitive personal data about the same client and the conditions which they must meet when personal data is released without the client's consent will depend upon the kind of data involved. 18.24

Conditions for processing sensitive personal data

To comply with the first data protection principle, use or disclosure of sensitive personal data by a professional must be lawful and fair, satisfy one of the conditions in Sch 2 for processing personal data[141] and, *additionally*,[142] meet one of the conditions laid down in Sch 3, namely: 18.25

(1) *explicit*[143] consent from the client (*not* implied[144] consent);[145]

---

[135] DPA, s 2(c). Directive (EC) 95/46 prohibits the processing of data revealing 'religious or philosophical beliefs'. This should be taken into account when interpreting 'beliefs of a similar nature'.

[136] No distinction is made between data relating to mental health and minor physical injuries. Note overlap with definition of health record: para 18.04 above.

[137] *Lord Ashcroft v Att-Gen* [2002] EWHC 1122, QB, para 30.

[138] *Campbell v MGN Ltd* [2002] EWHC 499; [2002] EMLR 30, para 87.

[139] Thus information that the client was sexually abused in his youth is not in law sensitive personal information except to the extent that this information impinges on his mental or physical health even though the client may regard the information as particularly sensitive.

[140] This might constitute information about the individual's political opinions. Likewise, inclusion of name and address in a list of subscribers to a gay magazine would be information about the individual's sexual orientation.

[141] See paras 18.18–18.19 above.

[142] DPA, Sch 1, para 1(b).

[143] See para 13.02 above.

[144] Implied consent, because it involves an inference, is not explicit consent. For an analysis of implied consent see para 13.34 above.

[145] Sch 3, para 1.

Chapter 18: Data Protection and Freedom of Information

(2) information contained in the data has been made public as a result of steps 'deliberately taken' by the client;[146]

(3) be carried out in the course of the legitimate activities of a charitable body;[147]

(4) be 'necessary' for one of the following:
   (a) employment law obligations;[148]
   (b) to protect the vital interests of the client or another person *and* consent cannot be given by the client or has been unreasonably withheld by the client or the professional cannot reasonably be expected to obtain the client's consent;[149]
   (c) to exercise legal rights;[150]
   (d) to administer justice;[151]
   (e) to carry out a ministerial, Crown or statutory function;[152]
   (f) to enable a 'health professional'[153] or a person who owes an equivalent duty of confidentiality to process information for 'medical purposes' (defined as including preventative medicine, medical diagnosis, medical research, provision of care and treatment, management of heath care services);[154]
   (g) racial or ethnic monitoring for equal opportunities purposes.[155]

18.26 The second condition is similar to the public domain defence to an action for breach of confidence.[156] Tugendhat argues that something can be '*manifestly* made public by the data subject' (the terminology used in the EU Directive)[157] without being 'made public as a result of steps *deliberately* taken by the data subject' (the language of the DPA) and vice versa.[158] From this he deduces that the DPA has removed a public

---

[146] Sch 3, para 5.
[147] Sch 3, para 4. There are further conditions set out in the paragraph.
[148] Sch 3, para 2.
[149] Sch 3, para 3. For data protection purposes this enables inter alia a doctor to disclose to a patient's sexual partner that the patient is HIV seropositive if the patient refuses to do so; likewise, it allows the doctor to disclose medical information about a patient who is unconscious or mentally incapacitated. It does not dispense with the need for a lawful basis for breaching an equitable/contractual obligation of confidentiality. Notice that while Sch 2, para 4 allows disclosure without consent to protect the vital interests of the client, Sch 3 allows disclosure without consent to protect the vital interests of the client or 'another person'.
[150] Further details are set out in Sch 3, para 6.
[151] Sch 3, para 7(1)(a).
[152] Sch 3, para 7(1)(b), (c).
[153] Defined in s 68. The definition includes registered doctors, dentists, opticians, pharmaceutical chemists, nurses, health visitors, midwives, osteopaths, chiropractors, clinical psychologists and speech therapists.
[154] Sch 3, para 8.
[155] Sch 3, para 9.
[156] See paras 5.09 et seq and 5.59.
[157] Directive (EC) 95/46 Art 8(2)(e) (italics added). The Directive may reflect the Latin 'manifesto' meaning clearly or palpably. According to Art 29 DP Working Party, Opinion 3/99 (3 May 1999) 4, 11, data made public by the data subject does not lose its protection ipso facto and for ever.
[158] DPA, Sch 3, para 5 (italics added).

A. Data Protection Act 1998

domain defence that the Directive intended should be available.[159] Whether or not this is right, the data protection publicity defence is a narrower defence than the English public domain defence and inconsistent with the Press Complaints Commission's Privacy Code[160] which the courts must consider in media and literature cases.[161] In the event of information in the data being put into the public domain by a third party, disclosure of the information by the professional will be a breach of the DPA regardless of whether it is a breach of confidence.[162]

Additional conditions for processing sensitive data without explicit consent have been added by the Data Protection (Processing of Sensitive Personal Data) Order 2000. These include processing which is in the '*substantial* public interest'[163] *and* necessary for any one of the following purposes: 18.27

(1) the prevention or detection of any unlawful act in circumstances where obtaining explicit consent might prejudice that purpose;[164]
(2) in relation to dishonesty, malpractice, seriously improper conduct or unfitness or incompetence or the mismanagement of services by any body;[165]
(3) 'disclosure'[166] for artistic, journalistic or literary purposes of information about the commission or alleged commission of an unlawful act that involves dishonesty, malpractice or other seriously improper conduct by a person or raises a question of fitness or competence and the data controller believes on reasonable grounds[167] that the publication is in the public interest;[168]
(4) to discharge any function which is designed for the provision of confidential counselling, advice support or any other service;[169]
(5) research whose object is not to support decisions with respect to particular individuals.[170]

---

[159] M Tugendhat, 'The Data Protection Act 1998 and the Media' [2000] Yearbook of Copyright and Media Law 115, 124; M Tugendhat and I Christie (eds), *The Law of Privacy and the Media* (Oxford: 2002) para 5.39.
[160] The Code requires the Commission to have regard to the extent to which material has, or is about to, become available to the public.
[161] HRA, s 12(4).
[162] But see paras 4.10 and 5.14 above.
[163] Italics added.
[164] Data Protection (Processing of Sensitive Personal Data) Order 2000, SI 2000/417, Sch, para 1.
[165] ibid, para 2.
[166] Does it matter that information was disclosed to a newspaper that decided not to run the story? See M Tugendhat and I Christie (eds), *The Law of Privacy and the Media* (Oxford:, 2002) para 588.
[167] *Campbell v MGN Ltd* [2002] EWHC 499; [2002] EMLR 30, para 118.
[168] Data Protection (Processing of Sensitive Personal Data) Order 2000, Sch, para 3. Considered in *Campbell v MGN Ltd* [2002] EWHC 499; [2002] EMLR 30, paras 115 et seq where all the conditions of the paragraph were held to be cumulative.
[169] Data Protection (Processing of Sensitive Personal Data) Order 2000, Sch, para 4.
[170] ibid, para 9.

Chapter 18: Data Protection and Freedom of Information

Other grounds are that the processing is:

(6) for the purpose of carrying on an insurance business or for certain pension purposes and is information about specified relatives;[171]
(7) to monitor equal opportunities;[172]
(8) in furtherance of legitimate political purposes;[173]
(9) necessary for the exercise of any functions conferred on a constable by any rule of law.[174]

Interface with the Human Rights Act 1998

18.28 Disclosure of sensitive personal information without client consent inevitably breaches the client's right to respect for private life. Being able to point to a foundation in the general law for the disclosure and compliance with a prescribed condition in DPA, Schs 2 and 3 does not necessarily make the processing lawful for the purposes of the first data protection principle. If the professional works for a public authority, and possibly even if she does not, the disclosure must not contravene the HRA.[175] To achieve compliance, disclosure of confidential information about the client without the client's consent must be for one of the aims listed in Article 8(2), be proportionate to that aim and necessary for a pressing social reason.[176]

Second Data Protection Principle

Processing purposes

18.29 The second data protection principle provides:

> [p]ersonal data shall be obtained only for one or more specified and lawful purposes, and shall not be further processed in any manner incompatible with that purpose or those purposes.

The purposes will have been specified either:

(1) on the general notification that appears on the Information Commissioner's on-line register of data protection notifications;[177] or
(2) to the client at the time the data was collected.[178]

---

[171] Data Protection (Processing of Sensitive Personal Data) Order 2000, Sch, para 5. See also para 6.
[172] ibid, para 7. Sch 3, para 9 only covers equal opportunities monitoring of persons of different racial and ethnic backgrounds.
[173] ibid, para 8.
[174] ibid, para 10. Considered in *R v Chief Constables of C and D, ex p A* [2001] 2 FCR 431.
[175] See paras 3.04 et seq.
[176] See para 3.19 above.
[177] DPA, Sch 1, Pt II, para 5; see para 18.03 above.
[178] DPA, Sch 1, Pt II, paras 2–4. Fair processing may require this option to be used: para 18.11 above.

A. Data Protection Act 1998

The purposes that appear on the on-line register tend to be rather broad, for example, 'delivery of healthcare' (in the case of a hospital or a GP practice) or 'staff, agent and contractor administration; advertising, marketing, public relations, general advice services; accounts and records; education; student and staff support services; research' (in the case of a university).[179] Whether such uninformative generalizations comply with the second data protection principle has not been tested. Breaches of the second data protection principle occur when a data controller processes data (or discloses data to a third party who intends to process the data) for a purpose that is incompatible with announced data processing purposes.[180] **18.30**

Compatible and incompatible processing

Meaning of 'incompatible'

There is an ambiguity in the second data protection principle. 'Incompatible' could mean either: **18.31**

(1) a purpose that is inconsistent with the notified purposes;[181] or
(2) a purpose that will not have been anticipated by the data subject.

For example, if the purpose notified to the client for collecting health data is 'medical treatment', processing the data collected for the purpose of fraud detection involves processing it for an unanticipated purpose but not an inconsistent one.[182] To give the word 'incompatible' its literal meaning of 'inconsistent', however, runs contrary to the spirit of the EU Directive and the fair processing code which are intended to make the processing of personal data transparent to the data subject. Therefore, amongst data protection cognoscenti the second data protection principle is understood to allow processing for the original data collection purpose or some *kindred* purpose.[183]

When a Cambridge college was asked by someone writing a biography about the writer Kingsley Amis to disclose the names and addresses of all those who had read English in the college under Kingsley's direction so that the writer could contact them, the college correctly turned down the request because this was not a purpose kindred to any purpose for which the information had been collected. For the same reason a school cannot disclose the names and addresses of its former pupils to the organizers of a school reunion. Had the college been asked for records about Kingsley Amis and not his students the second data protection **18.32**

---

[179] These are actual examples taken from the register.
[180] DPA, Sch 1, Pt I and Pt II, para 5. cp *Association of Chief Police Officers Data Protection Code of Practice* (November 2001) para 6.
[181] DPA, s 33(2) could be said to lend support to this interpretation.
[182] The broader the purposes of collection of which the Information Commissioner was notified, the less likely that a disclosure will be incompatible with those purposes.
[183] cp I Lloyd, *The Data Protection Act 1998* (London: 1998) 61.

principle would have been no obstacle. This is not only because Amis was dead[184] when the request was received but also because the DPA provides that processing of data for statistical, historical or other research purposes is not incompatible with the purposes for which the data was obtained.[185]

Permitted disclosures for incompatible purposes

18.33 Disclosure for an incompatible purpose does not contravene the second data protection principle if the client is notified of the intention to process the data for an incompatible purpose and consents.[186] When a professional disregards a common law duty of confidence to comply with a statutory disclosure obligation[187] or discloses information on the grounds of self-interest[188] or to further an overriding public interest,[189] the purpose of the disclosure may be incompatible with the purposes for which the information was collected. In the likely event that the client withholds consent, disclosure will nevertheless not breach the DPA if there is a relevant exemption to the second data protection principle. Non-disclosure exemptions include disclosures 'required' by an enactment, rule of law or court order[190] and disclosures for the purposes of crime detection or prevention and the collection of taxes where failure to disclose would be likely to prejudice these objectives.[191] Voluntary data-sharing between public sector agencies for an incompatible purpose may be prevented because of the absence of a generalized non-disclosure exemption for public interest breaches of confidence.[192] These cannot be described as 'required' by law.

Other Data Protection Principles

Third to seventh data protection principles[193]

18.34 There are eight data protection principles in all. The first two have been discussed. The remainder are:

- personal data must be adequate, relevant, up-to-date, not excessive in relation to the processes for which data is processed (third principle);
- personal data shall be accurate and kept up-to-date (fourth principle);

---

[184] See para 18.04 above.
[185] DPA, s 33(2). See para 18.42 below.
[186] The Information Commissioner takes the view that consent at this stage must normally be express or explicit: IC, *Use and Disclosure of Health Data* (May 2002) 19.
[187] See ch 10.
[188] See paras 12.23 et seq.
[189] See ch 11.
[190] DPA, s 35(1).
[191] DPA, s 29.
[192] It is a defence to a criminal prosecution under DPA, s 55(1) (see para 6.56 above), however, that the disclosing was justified as being in the public interest.
[193] For more details see IC, *Data Protection Act 1998—Legal Guidance* 3.3–3.7.

A. Data Protection Act 1998

- personal data is not to be kept longer than actually necessary (fifth principle);[194]
- personal data shall be processed in accordance with the rights of the data subject (sixth principle);[195]
- security measures must be adopted proportionate to the sensitivity of the data, the state of technology and the cost of the measures (seventh principle);[195a]
- trans-border data flows (eighth principle, see below).

Eighth principle: trans-border data flows[196]

18.35 The eighth data protection principle prohibits the 'transfer'[197] of personal data to a country outside the European Economic Area (EU Member States, Iceland, Lichtenstein, Norway) unless that country has an 'adequate' level of data protection. The adequacy of a country's data protection laws is determined by all the surrounding circumstances: the nature of the data, its country of origin and final destination, the purposes for which and period during which the data is intended to be processed and the laws, international obligations, professional rules and security obligations in the country in question.[198] The European Commission has officially decided[199] that Hungary, Switzerland and Canada have adequate levels of protection and has negotiated 'safe harbor' privacy principles with the United States.[200]

18.36 There are various circumstances under which client data may be lawfully transferred to countries where the data protection regime is not adequate[201] including any one of the following:

(1) the client has given consent;[202]
(2) transfer is necessary

---

[194] Professionals would be wise to keep client data at least until the expiration of limitation periods (see para 9.01 above) for actions in tort, contract and breach of confidence in equity. Data can be retained for archival purposes.
[195] Rights of data subjects to have access to their personal data, to have the data corrected or erased and to prevent use of data which may cause damage or distress are dealt with in ch 19.
[195a] See paras 6.35–6.36 above.
[196] IC, *Data Protection Act 1998—Legal Guidance* 3.8. See also C Kuner, *European Data Law and Online Business* (Oxford: 2003) ch 4.
[197] A distinction must be drawn between transfer and transit, that is, the passage of personal data through a country without being processed there. Personal data is not transferred from the UK to a country with an unacceptable level of data protection in contravention of the eighth data protection principle by passing through there 'en route' to a recipient in a country with an acceptable level of data protection.
[198] DPA, Sch 1, para 13.
[199] DPA, Sch 1, para 15.
[200] An overview and details of the Safe Harbor framework are posted on the US Department of Commerce website at http://www.exports.gov/safeharbor/sh_documents.html. Under Federal Trade Commissions Act, s 5 breach of the principles by an organization that has publicly committed itself to apply the principles might be considered deceptive and actionable by the Federal Trade Commission.
[201] DPA, Sch 1, para 14.   [202] DPA, Sch 4, para 1.

(a) to satisfy the client's contractual obligations or a contract for the client's benefit;[203]
(b) to protect the vital interests of the client;[204]
(c) 'for reasons of substantial public interest';[205]
(d) for establishing, exercising or defending legal rights;[206]

(3) where the data is exported under a contract which contains standard contractual clauses for the protection of the data as approved in Directive (EC) 2001/497;[207]

(4) if the Information Commissioner determines that in the particular case the data enjoys adequate protection.[208]

Exemptions[209]

18.37 There are a number of exemptions in the DPA that relieve the professional of complying with all, some, or some part of the data protection principles. All the exemptions must be construed so far as is possible in a way that is compatible with Article 8 of the European Convention on Human Rights.[210] This means that the processing must be necessary in a democratic society and proportionate to one of the aims set out in Article 8(2).[211]

Section 35 (statutory authority and legal purposes)

18.38 By s 35, a disclosure is exempt from the non-disclosure provisions[212] when disclosure of confidential client information is:

(1) 'required'[213] by statute, common law or the order of a court;[214] *or*
(2) 'necessary' for:
    (a) the purposes of legal proceedings or prospective legal proceedings;[215] or
    (b) obtaining legal advice;[216] or
    (c) establishing, exercising or defending legal rights.[217]

---

[203] DPA, Sch 4, paras 2,3.
[204] DPA, Sch 4, para 6.
[205] DPA, Sch 4, para 4.
[206] DPA, Sch 4, para 5.
[207] See also DPA, Sch 4, para 8.
[208] DPA, Sch 4, para 9.
[209] For exemptions to subject access rights see paras 19.28 et seq.
[210] See HRA, s 3.
[211] See para 3.19 above.
[212] That is the data protection principles, apart from the seventh principle (security), and compliance with Sch 2 (conditions for processing personal data) and 3 (conditions for processing sensitive personal data), to the extent that they are inconsistent with the disclosure in question: DPA, s 27.
[213] cp para 18.33 above.
[214] s 35(1) which was applied in *Guyer v Walton* [2001] STC (SCD) 75. Sch 7, para 10 contains an additional exemption from the subject information provisions (see s 27) for data that is subject to LPP.
[215] s 35(2)(a).
[216] s 35(2)(b).
[217] s 35(2).

A. Data Protection Act 1998

The first exemption renders any statute-backed or court-ordered demand for disclosure with which the professional has to comply data protection-compliant. The remaining exemptions make disclosures that are lawful but not compelled by law data protection-compliant *provided* disclosure enables the professional or the recipient third party to bring or defend a legal action, consult a lawyer for other purposes, or, by non-litigious means, to assert a legal right, enforce a legal duty or exercise a legal power. This will exempt the bulk of disclosures motivated by self-interest that are mentioned in chapter 12.[218]

Section 32 (journalism, literature, art)

Section 32 seeks to balance data protection with freedom of expression by exempting data processed for the 'special purposes'[219] of journalism, literature and art from all but the seventh (duty to keep data secure) data protection principle and from most data subject rights.[220] One consequence is to prevent wealthy individuals obtaining gagging injunctions against newspapers immediately before publication. The s 32 exemption may be of interest to professionals and clients if client data finds its way into the hands of the media[221] or if a client gets wind of the fact that a professional or a third party intends to publish a book that contains confidential information about him sourced from records generated by the professional relationship.[222] The conditions for the exemption to apply are that

18.39

(1) the personal data is used or disclosed *solely* for special purposes;[223] *and*
(2) 24 hours immediately before the relevant time, there had been no prior publication of the material by the data controller;[224] *and*
(3) the processing 'is undertaken with a view to . . . publication';[225] *and*
(4) the data controller reasonably believes that,
   (a) 'having regard . . . to the special importance of the public interest in freedom of expression', publication would be in the public interest;[226] *and*
   (b) in all the circumstances, compliance with data protection principles or data subject rights is incompatible with the special purposes.[227]

---

[218] See paras 12.23 et seq. It would not cover the disclosure that happened in *Sunderland v Barclays Bank Ltd* (1938) 5 LDAB 163.
[219] See DPA, s 3.
[220] SAR (s 7); right to prevent processing likely to cause damage or distress (s 10); rights in relation to automated decision-taking (s 12); right to rectification, blocking, erasure and destruction (ss 14(1)–(3)).
[221] Doubtless it was s 32 that prevented Theakston from relying on the DPA to prevent the newspaper publishing the details of his visit to a brothel in *Theakston v MGN Ltd* [2002] EWHC 137; [2002] EMLR 22.
[222] s 32(1)(a) speaks of processing '*any* journalistic, literary or artistic material by *any* person' with a view to publication (italics added).
[223] DPA, s 32(1).
[224] DPA, s 32(4)(b).
[225] DPA, s 32(1).
[226] DPA, s 32(1)(b).
[227] DPA, s 32(1)(c). See eg *Campbell v MGN Ltd* [2002] EWCA Civ 1373, para 137.

So long as all four conditions are satisfied, the special purposes exemption can be relied upon both before and after publication.[228] Where computer processing of data is followed by publication in hard copy, publication of the hard copy is to be treated as part of the processing operation and within the scope of the exemption.[229]

18.40 In deciding on the reasonableness of a media organization's belief that publication is in the public interest, regard 'may' be had to what any relevant media code of practice has to say about privacy.[230] Only a belief that publication is in the public interest is necessary; there is no need for publication to be in the public interest. However, in practice this will be a factor because in assessing the reasonableness of the belief that publication is in the public interest the court will have to take account of Article 8 (right to respect for private life). Interference with this right has to be necessary and proportionate.[231] It is hard to argue that a disclosure that is believed to be, but is not in fact, in the public interest is necessary. The court must also have regard to Article 10 (freedom of expression).[232]

18.41 In response to media lobbying there is a procedure by which proceedings under the DPA[233] against a data controller may be stayed.[234] The procedure for removing the stay is complex and unlikely to be of concern to a professional.[235]

Section 33 (research purposes)

18.42 Personal data used in research is often collected for some quite different purpose.

> In order to successfully conduct their research, cardiologists evaluating the effectiveness of different drugs, historians studying the involvement of certain persons in a particular political development, sociologists analyzing the role of welfare agencies, and criminologists investigating the family background of juvenile delinquents

---

[228] *Campbell v MGN Ltd* [2002] EWCA Civ 1373, para 121.
[229] ibid, paras 107, 130.
[230] DPA, s 35(3). The code must be one that appears in a schedule to the Data Protection (Designated Codes of Practice) (No 2) Order 2000 (SI 2000/1864). For the print media the relevant code is the PCC's Code of Practice (see para 9.10 above), for radio the Radio Authority's Radio Code, for BBC television the Producer's Guidelines and for other television the BSC's Code on Fairness and Privacy (see para 9.17 above) and the ITC's Programme Code (see para 9.21 above).
[231] See para 3.19 above.
[232] The need to take account of Art 10 is reiterated in HRA, s 12.
[233] Those that may be relevant are s 7(9) (enforcing subject access in a court); s 10(4) (preventing processing likely to cause damage or distress); and s 13 (compensation for breach of statutory duty).
[234] s 32(4).
[235] The Information Commissioner must make a determination under s 45 that the sole reason for the processing is not the special purposes or that previously unpublished personal data is not being processed with a view to publication. The Commissioner can require information about the processing (s 44), but, except in urgent cases (s 44(6)), provision of the information can be delayed until a right of appeal to the Information Tribunal has been exhausted (ss 44(5), 48(1)).

A. Data Protection Act 1998

must have access to a substantial amount of data provided by the persons concerned in a different context and for clearly different reasons.[236]

To avoid stultifying research, s 33 contains an exemption from the second (incompatible purposes)[237] and the fifth (out-dated information) data protection principles and s 7 (data subject access)[238] for personal data that is processed 'for research purposes' (a phrase that is undefined except that it includes statistical or historical purposes).[239] All the other data protection rules continue to apply. In particular, disclosure must be fair and have a lawful basis (consent,[240] public interest[241] or statutory authority[242]). The s 33 exemption becomes available when three conditions are met:

(1) the processing is conducted in a way that is not likely to cause substantial damage or distress to the client;[243] *and*
(2) the information is not to be processed in order to support decisions with respect to particular individuals;[244] *and*
(3) the results of the processing are not to be disclosed (in books, articles, reports, dissertations, etc.) in a form which allows identification of the client[245] or for non-research purposes.[246]

It is irrelevant that the data was originally obtained under statutory compulsion.

Since the fair processing code of the first data protection applies,[247] the client must be notified of the intention to process his data for research if research is a non-obvious processing purpose[248]—unless the disproportionate effort notification

18.43

---

[236] S Simitis, 'Data Protection Law and The European Union's Directive: The Challenge for the United States: From the Market to the Polis: The EU Directive on the Protection of Personal Data' (1995) 80 Iowa L Rev 445, 457.
[237] Thus personal data obtained for a non-research purpose (for example, health data collected during treatment) can be processed for a research purpose of which the client was not previously advised without seeking client consent.
[238] See para 19.21 below.
[239] s 33(1).
[240] Query: if consent is relied upon and is withdrawn, may the researcher continue to process data that has been received already? Perhaps the answer is that the data must be destroyed (processing includes holding data), but the results of research done during the period of consent can be retained. This assumes that there is no public interest or statutory authority to process the data without consent. If there is, then withdrawal of consent will not matter.
[241] See para 13.51 above.
[242] eg Health and Social Care Act 2001 (See paras 13.51–13.52 above).
[243] DPA, s 33(1)(b).
[244] DPA, s 33(1)(a). This does not prevent the research data having some effect on individuals so long as they have not been targeted in the research.
[245] DPA, s 33(4)(b).
[246] DPA, s 33(5)(a). Except that disclosure to the client or his agent or at the client's request is allowed.
[247] See para 8.11 above.
[248] IC, *Data Protection Act 1998—Legal Guidance* 5.7 and see para 18.14 above.

exemption applies.[249] The processing of *sensitive* personal data must comply with the conditions set out in Sch 3[250] or the Data Protection (Processing of Sensitive Personal Data) Order 2000. The latter allows for sensitive data processing which 'is in the substantial public interest and is necessary for research purposes and does not support measures with respect to the particular data subject except with their specific consent nor cause or be likely to cause substantial damage and distress'.[251] As the seventh data protection principle (data security) has to be satisfied, it is advisable to anonymize the data to as great an extent as possible to increase the security of the processing. Care must be taken to comply with the eighth data protection principle if personal data is exported overseas.[252] For countries outside the European Economic Area the only safe option may be to obtain the data subject's explicit consent unless the data has been stripped of personal identifiers.

Sections 28, 29, 31 (national security, regulatory activity, crime and tax)

18.44 Further exemptions are found in

- Section 28 which, where necessary, exempts the data protection principles to safeguard national security.[253]
- Section 31 which allows disclosure without explanation to the client if this is necessary to protect members of the public from 'dishonesty, malpractice or other seriously improper conduct by or the unfitness or incompetence of, persons authorized to carry on any profession or activity'.[254]
- Section 29 which partially disables the first data protection principle except the obligation to comply with the processing conditions in Schs 2 (non-sensitive personal data)[255] and 3 (sensitive personal data)[256] and exempts the non-disclosure provisions[257] to the extent that compliance 'would be likely to prejudice'[258] the following processing purposes:

---

[249] DPA, Sch 1, Pt II, para 3(2): see para 18.17 above. Reasons for believing that disproportionate effort is required should be noted in case they are challenged.

[250] See para 18.25 above. There is an exemption for processing of personal data for medical research purposes (DPA, Sch 3, para 8).

[251] r 9

[252] See para 18.35 above.

[253] A certificate signed by a Minister is conclusive evidence of the fact, subject to an appeal to the Information Tribunal by any person directly affected by the issuing of the certificate: DPA, s 28(2), (4).

[254] DPA, s 31(2).

[255] See paras 18.18–18.19 above.

[256] See para 18.25 above.

[257] DPA, s 29(3).

[258] Mere possibility of prejudice will not do: *Equifax Europe Ltd v Data Protection Registrar* Data Protection Tribunal (June 1991) DA/9025/49/7. The Association of Chief Police Officers' code of practice advises police officers to accompany any request for disclosure of personal data under the s 29 exemption with an explanation that the data requested is necessary for an investigation. ACPO and representatives of the ISP industry have worked out a standard form for the police to use which is available at http://www.linx.net/misc/ dpa28-3form.html.

—'prevention or detection of crime';[259] *or*
—'apprehension or prosecution of offenders'; *or*
—'assessment or collection of any tax or duty or of any imposition of a similar nature'.

Removal of the obligation to process personal data where it is likely to be prejudicial enables the data controller to report suspicions of money laundering or drug trafficking by a client without informing the client.[260]

The fact that s 29 allows a data controller to disregard some elements of the data protection regime does not imply that the data controller is under a legal compulsion to divulge information to the police or any other executive agency that satisfies the conditions laid down in s 29. Compulsory disclosure requires additional statutory authority.[261] Data may be disclosed under s 29 without a specific request for the information if s 29(3) is satisfied and there is a basis in law (such as the public interest[262]) for the disclosure.

Freedom of Information Act exemptions

The Freedom of Information Act 2000 amends the DPA to exempt manual unstructured personal data held by public authorities[263] from the first, second, third, fifth, seventh and eighth data protection principles and much of the sixth principle and disapplies a variety of other provisions.[264]

18.45

18.46

Enforcement of the Data Protection Principles

Any person 'who is, or believes himself to be, directly affected by any processing of personal data' by a professional may apply to the Information Commissioner for an assessment of the lawfulness of the processing.[265] The applicant does not have to be the data subject. This has implications for the processing of genetic data which is shared by blood relatives. The Information Commissioner cannot respond to an application unless it is actually being processed. This is probably because the DPA (probably by oversight) makes no provision for situations in which processing is threatened but has not yet occurred.[266]

18.47

---

[259] cp *R v Chief Constables of C and D, ex p A* [2001] 2 FCR 431.
[260] See para 10.20 above.
[261] See chs 10 and 14. For example, to obtain disclosure from an ISP for the purposes of investigating a crime, the police can rely on Regulation of Investigatory Powers Act 2000, s 22 (4); see para 14.102 above.
[262] See ch 11.
[263] DPA, s 1(1)(e).
[264] DPA, s 33A (not in force).
[265] DPA, s 42(1). The Information Commissioner can intervene on her own initiative.
[266] One solution in these circumstances is to exercise the right to require the data controller not to begin processing data and, if this does not work, apply to a court for a compliance order: see para 8.26 above. Another possibility is to persuade the Information Commissioner to exercise her power under s 43(1)(b) to require information on her own initiative.

18.48 Once satisfied of the client's identity, and on being supplied with information by which to identify the processing, the Commissioner must carry out an appropriate assessment.[267] The Information Commissioner may serve an 'information notice' on the professional (or whoever is the data controller).[268] No enactment or rule of law prohibiting or restricting the disclosure of information will excuse the furnishing of the information to the Commissioner[269] except legal professional privilege (LPP).[270] If the Commissioner finds that the data controller has contravened, or is contravening, the data protection principles, the Commissioner will try to resolve the matter informally. If this fails the Commissioner may issue an enforcement notice[271] which may require remedial action to be taken and/or the processing to be stopped.

18.49 The data controller can appeal an enforcement notice to the independent Information (formerly Data Protection) Tribunal.[272] The burden is on the Information Commissioner to establish that his decision should be upheld.[273] The Tribunal can summon and hear witnesses and argument or make a determination without a hearing.[274] A data controller who continues to contravene the DPA after dismissal of an appeal commits a criminal offence which is punishable by a potentially unlimited fine.[275] Equipment used for the processing can be forfeited, erased or destroyed.[276] It is a defence to show that due diligence was exercised to comply with the enforcement notice.[277] There is a right of appeal from the decision of the Tribunal to the High Court on a point of law.[278]

---

[267] DPA, s 42(2). In deciding what is appropriate the Commissioner may have regard to the extent to which the request raises a matter of substance, any delay in making the request and whether the applicant has SARs in respect of the personal data (s 43(3)).

[268] DPA, s 43(1).

[269] DPA, s 58. The Information Commissioner has powers of entry, search and seizure: see para 14.69 above.

[270] DPA, s 43(6)–(7). In the light of the House of Lord's decision in *R v Special Commissioner, ex p Morgan Grenfell & Co* [2002] UKHL 21; [2002] 2 WLR 1299 the limitation of LPP to communications with respect to obligations, liabilities and rights under the DPA is likely to be ineffective.

[271] DPA, s 40. The DPA does not require the Information Commissioner to take enforcement action on every occasion that a breach of the Act occurs. An enforcement order is unlikely to be issued for a one-off error. The compliance advice relating to the Child Support Agency states: '[w]here a failure arises as a result of weaknesses in a data controller's practices and procedures, the Commissioner attempts to make effective use of her limited resources by concentrating on ensuring that the data controller follows best practice and is able to comply with the Principles in the future. Where a breach has resulted as a consequence of human error or a single failure to comply with procedures, there is little further action that she can take.' See http://www.dataprotection.gov.uk.

[272] DPA, s 48. This has a legally qualified chair and a representative of the interests of data controllers and data subjects.

[273] Data Protection Tribunal (Enforcement Appeals) Rules 2000, SI 2000/189, r 22.

[274] ibid.

[275] If trial takes place in the Crown Court: DPA, s 60(2).

[276] DPA, s 60(4).

[277] DPA, s 47(3).

[278] DPA, s 49(6)(a)

18.50 Whether or not the Commissioner becomes involved, the client may bring a civil action in the High Court or a county court[279] against a data controller who has breached the DPA for compensation for damage caused by the breach and for linked distress.[280] The client also has the option of serving a notice on the data controller requiring the data controller to cease, or not to begin, the processing of personal data on the grounds that it is causing, or is likely to cause, substantial and unwarranted damage or distress.[281] When the DPA 1984 was in force it was the Information Commissioner's practice to use publicity as an additional sanction by publishing details of investigations into data protection breaches by named parties on the Commission's website and in the annual report to Parliament. Since the DPA 1988 forbids disclosure of information about identifiable individuals or businesses obtained by or furnished to the Commissioner for the purposes of the Act without consent except where the information is available to the public from other sources or disclosure is necessary in the public interest,[282] the naming and shaming of those in breach of the DPA has been discontinued.

B. Freedom of Information

The Freedom of Information Act 2000[283]

18.51 The DPA is complimented by the Freedom of Information Act 2000 (FIOA). Under the FOIA (which is not yet in force)[284] 'any person' (including a company) has a right on application:

(1) to be told in writing whether a 'public authority' holds information on a given subject and, if it does,
(2) to have the information communicated.[285]

'Information' means 'information recorded in any form'.[286] A consultation paper explained that this 'includes paper records and information recorded electronically, or by any other technological means. The records may be structured or unstructured, and the information may be recorded in any number of different

---

[279] DPA, s 15(1).
[280] DPA, s 13; see para 4.49 above.
[281] DPA, s 10(1); see para 8.26 above.
[282] DPA, s 59.
[283] S Palmer, 'Freedom of Information: The New Proposals' in J Beatson and Y Cripps (eds), *Freedom of Expression and Freedom of Information: Essays in Honour of Sir David Williams* (Oxford: 2000) 249; J Wadham, J Griffiths and B Rigby, *Freedom of Information Act 2000* (London: 2001); J. MacDonald & C. Jones (eds), *The Law of Freedom of Information* (Oxford: 2003).
[284] The date specified for right of access to information comes into force is 30 November 2005 unless the Secretary of State appoints an earlier date. This right is expected to be brought into force in January 2005: *Hansard*, HL vol 628, cols 457–458 (13 November 2001).
[285] FOIA, s 1.
[286] FOIA, s 84.

forms, styles, media and location.'[287] It does not include information in records that have been destroyed before the application was received. The Act makes it a criminal offence to destroy, erase, deface or conceal a record once a request for the information has been made with the intention of preventing its disclosure.[288] The public authority may charge a handling fee[289] and ask for assistance from the applicant to identify and locate requested information.[290] It is not obliged to comply with a request where the cost of doing so is disproportionate[291] or if the request is vexatious or repeated.[292] Disclosure is not normally required for information that is to be published anyway[293] or is reasonably accessible to the public by other means.[294] The FOIA is supported by a Code of Practice issued under s 45 of the Act.[295]

18.52 Public authorities are defined and listed in Sch 1. Local authorities, NHS bodies such as hospitals, GP practices, dentists, pharmacists and opticians, maintained schools, further and higher education corporations and universities fall within the remit of the FOIA. There is provision for further authorities to be added.[296] Once the FIOA provisions have been brought into force they apply to information no matter when or how acquired. Every public authority must have a 'publication scheme' that meets with the approval of the Information Commissioner to make its documents available to the public.[297]

Requests for Personal Information

Subject access rights

18.53 Where a client seeks personal information about himself he must use the subject access provisions of the DPA which are outlined in chapter 19.[298] The FOIA extends the client's data SAR and the right to have inaccurate records corrected under the DPA to all personal information held about the client by the public authority.[299] Public authorities must not only (like all data controllers) give access to computer data and structured manual files,[300] but also (unlike all data con-

---

[287] LCD, *Freedom of Information: Consultation on Draft Legislation* (Cm 4355, 1999) Pt II, para 22, available at http://www.lcd.gov.uk/foi/dexplan1.htm.
[288] FOIA, s 77. The penalty is a fine.
[289] FOIA, s 9.　　[290] FOIA, s 1(3).
[291] FOIA, s 12.　　[292] FOIA, s 14.
[293] FOIA, s 20.　　[294] FOIA, s 21.
[295] The Code of Practice on the Discharge of the Functions of Public Authorities under the Freedom of Information Act is available at http://www.lcd.gov.uk/foi/codepafunc.htm.
[296] FOIA, ss.4, 5.
[297] FOIA, s 19.
[298] See para 19.21 below. The applicant is not required to specify the legislation on which he intends to rely. A data subject access application incorrectly made under the FOIA can thus be dealt with as an application for access under the DPA.
[299] FOIA, ss. 68, 69.
[300] See para 18.06 above.

B. Freedom of Information

trollers) unstructured manual files, provided the request 'describes the information requested'.[301] A public authority is under a statutory duty to provide advice and assistance to the applicant,[302] but even so, this requirement may hinder access to unstructured files.

Requests for personal information about third parties

Kinds of exemptions

Public authorities retain a great deal of personal information in their files, including some sourced under compulsion from professionals. Clients should not worry unduly about records that are less than 30 years old; public authorities can rely on a large number of exemptions to refuse information. The exemptions are divided into two categories: the absolute and the qualified. Absolute exemptions apply on a class basis and irrespective of the prejudice disclosure might cause. Court records and documents served in litigation[303] and information gathered for criminal investigations and proceedings[304] and for other investigations and proceedings by public authorities using confidential sources[305] are absolutely exempt. No matter how harmless, nothing need be shown. The duty to confirm or deny the existence of information does not arise in relation to these specific categories of information either.[306] Qualified exemptions allow information to be withheld if disclosure would be prejudicial to the public interest. 18.54

Enforcement

If disclosure is refused, the reason and the relevant exemption must generally be stated.[307] An appeal lies to the Information Commissioner[308] who can issue an enforcement order.[309] If this is disobeyed it may result in the data controller being found in contempt of court.[310] For records held by government departments and any public authority designated by the Secretary of State, the Commissioner's decision is subject to a ministerial veto that cannot be appealed.[311] 18.55

There is no civil right of action in respect of any failure to comply with any duty that the Act imposes.[312] 18.56

---

[301] FOIA, s 8(1)(c).
[302] FOIA, s 16. See also the draft Code of Practice, para 8, which requires the public authority to help the applicant to describe the information.
[303] FOIA, s 32.
[304] FOIA, s 30(1).
[305] FOIA, s 30(2).
[306] FOIA, ss 30(3), 32(3).
[307] FOIA, s 17.
[308] FOIA, s 50.
[309] FOIA, s 52.
[310] FOIA, s 54.
[311] FOIA, s 53.
[312] FOIA, s 56(1).

Exemptions for personal information

18.57 Under the FOIA regime the following kinds of personal information need not be disclosed. Information whose disclosure:

(1) contravenes any of the eight data protection principles found in the DPA[313] or would do so if that Act applied to manual data;[314] *or*

(2) contravenes DPA, s 10[315] (right to prevent processing likely to cause damage or distress); *or*

(3) the individual to whom the personal information relates himself has no SAR to the information because of an exemption in DPA Pt IV[316] (for example, on grounds of national security or crime prevention);[317]

(4) would constitute a breach of confidence actionable by any person at the date of the request;[318] *or*

(5) would breach LPP in legal proceedings;[319] *or*

(6) would be likely to endanger the physical or mental health or safety of any individual;[320] *or*

(7) would be likely to prejudice law enforcement;[321] *or*

(8) is prohibited by law.[322]

An exemption is an absolute one if the reason is (1), (4),[323] (6) or (8). If the reason for the exemption is (2), (3), (5)[324] or (7) the exemption is qualified and the public authority must disclose the data unless, in all the circumstances of the case, the public interest in non-disclosure outweighs the public interest in disclosure.[325] This ensures that each request is considered on its merits.[326]

Protecting the interests of the data subject

18.58 Disclosure of personal information may affect a third party's legal rights such as the right to respect for private and family life (Article 8). The Code of Practice provides that where 'the consent of the third party would enable a disclosure to be

---

[313] FOIA, s 40 (2)–(3).
[314] Personal information to which the DPA does not apply because it is contained in unstructured manual files and policy files is required by the FOIA to be treated as if the DPA did apply.
[315] FOIA, s 40(2)–(3).
[316] FOIA, s 40(4).
[317] See para 18.44 above.
[318] FOIA, s 41. The Draft Code of Practice (para 30) discourages public authorities from too readily accepting information in confidence.
[319] FOIA, s 42. For a discussion of legal professional privilege see ch 16.
[320] FOIA, s 38.
[321] FOIA, s 31.
[322] FOIA, s 44.
[323] The s 2 public interest disclosure test does not apply because a public interest defence to an action for breach of confidence already exists, as to which see ch 11.
[324] Although the duty is not absolute, the duty to confirm or deny is excluded.
[325] FOIA, s 2(1)(b), 2(2)(b). The duty to confirm or deny does not arise in relation to (2) or (3): DPA, s 40(5).
[326] *Hansard*, HL, col. 831 (22 November 2000).

B. Freedom of Information

made an authority should consult that party prior to reaching a decision unless it is clear ... that the consent would not be forthcoming'.[327] Consultation is recommended even where an affected party has no legal rights unless this would involve disproportionate costs or is unnecessary because the public authority does not intend to disclose the information on some other legitimate ground.[328]

Information about the dead

The situation is rather different if the applicant wants information about someone who is dead. Information about the dead is not protected by the DPA[329] and may not be actionable as a breach of confidence.[330] This removes many of the possible exemptions under the FOIA. In its treatment of the dead, the FOIA differs markedly from its Irish and Australian counterparts which accord much the same protection to personal data about the dead as the living.[331] Release by NASA of the tape of the last conversation of the astronauts on the final flight of the Challenger space shuttle was blocked by a US court because disclosure under the US Freedom of Information Act would have invaded the privacy of the families of the dead astronauts.[332] In England there are no specific statutory grounds on which a public authority could refuse disclosure in a similar circumstance.[333]

18.59

Historical records

The FOIA modifies existing rules about access to historical records. Under the FOIA, once a document containing personal information becomes a historical record (that is a public record retained beyond 30 years)[333a] the exemptions for LPP, court records and information held for the purpose of a criminal investigation cease.[334] Access to information in historical records covered by surviving non-absolute exemptions cannot be refused without the public authority first consulting the Lord Chancellor.[335] The decision to refuse access will have to take account of the Convention right of freedom of expression (Article 10) and of

18.60

---

[327] Draft Code of Practice, para 21.
[328] ibid, para 22.
[329] See para 18.04 above.
[330] It is problematic whether a breach of confidence is actionable if the confider is dead: see paras 4.16 and 5.46 above. As to whether LPP can protect information about a dead client see para 16.29 above.
[331] Freedom of Information Act 1982, s 41(1); Freedom of Information Act 1997, s 28.
[332] *New York Times Co v National Aeronautics and Space Administration* 920 F 2d 1002, 1009–1010 (1990).
[333] Disclosure could contravene Art 8 and therefore HRA, s 6.
[333a] FOIA, s 62(1).
[334] FOIA, s 63(1). By Public Records Act 1958, s 5(2) where inspection of the records would involve 'a breach of good faith' by the holder of the record, access may be restricted. It is on this basis that NHS medical records are currently withheld after 30 years. Section 5(2) is, however, to be repealed by the FOIA by November 2005 at the latest.
[335] FOIA, s 65.

respect for private and family life (Article 8). Until the FOIA comes into force (on 1 January 2005) the Lord Chancellor and the appropriate Minister will continue to have a wide discretionary power to refuse disclosure. Under guidelines formulated in 1993 disclosure can be refused if it would cause 'substantial distress' or danger to people affected by disclosure, or their descendants.[336] Any exercise of this discretion must take into account Articles 8 and 10. In view of the importance attached by the courts to the right of freedom of expression,[337] it is doubtful whether distress to descendants is a legitimate ground for withholding personal information about someone who is dead.

---

[336] *Open Government* (Cm 2290, 1993).
[337] See paras 3.17 and 3.29 above.

19

DISCLOSURE TO THE CLIENT

A. Client's Right to See Own Records	19.03	C. Records and Information Relating to Minors	19.72
Common Law Rights	19.03	Access to Records	19.72
Client's Statutory Rights of Access to Records	19.21	Right to Information	19.83
B. Client's Right to Information	19.58	D. Records and Information of Incompetent Adult	19.114
Fiduciary-Professionals	19.58	E. Requiring Disclosure to Third Parties	19.116
Disclosure by Professionals Not Owing Fiduciary Duties	19.64		

The client has an obvious human desire to know everything that the professional knows about him and why the professional took decisions affecting him.[1] But the client's need to know what the professional knows runs deeper than this. Without knowing what information the professional holds, the client cannot ensure that what the professional has recorded is accurate. The client may consent to the release of personal information to potential employers, banks and building societies, insurers, immigration officials and others that is misleading or plain wrong.[2] The European Court of Human Rights (ECtHR) accepts that storage and use of information coupled with refusal to allow an opportunity to refute it amounts to a prima facie interference with Article 8.[3] Equally importantly, personal autonomy is limited if access to information is arbitrarily refused. How can a person make autonomous decisions with respect to his life if he is ignorant of important facts about himself?[4] To adapt an example that Feldman gives, if a doctor does not tell her patient the true nature of his medical condition, the patient may be prevented from making informed decisions about whether to marry, to have

19.01

---

[1] cp *Doody v Secretary of State* [1993] 3 All ER 92, 98.
[2] D Feldman, *Civil Liberties and Human Rights in England and Wales* (2nd edn, Oxford: 2002) 516.
[3] *Leander v Sweden* (1987) 9 EHRR 433; *Rotaru v Romania* Application 28341/95, 8 BHRC 449, para 46.
[4] cp Human Genetics Commission, *Inside Information* (May 2002) para 3.2; M Wynia and D Cummins, 'Shared Expectations for Protection of Identifiable Health Care Information' (2001) 16 J of General Internal Medicine 100, 106.

children, to travel or to take out a mortgage. Also the revelations that he decides to make about his state of health to his friends, family, employers and social services will be unintentionally incomplete.[5]

19.02 This chapter examines the legal rights of the client to have access to his personal records and to be given personal information when the information is not wanted for litigation.[6] Topics covered include:

(1) the right of the client to inspect and copy the professional's records;
(2) ownership of the records;
(3) the client's right to information about himself and his affairs;
(4) parental rights to information about, and access to, records of a child and, also, the right to veto disclosure of information by the professional to the child;
(5) the client's right to have the professional disclose information to a third party.

A. Client's Right to See Own Records

Common Law Rights

Proprietary right

Ownership of the physical record

19.03 The client is entitled to any physical record that is the client's property unless the professional (or the professional's employer) has a lien against the item as security for unpaid professional fees.[7] The physical record will belong to the client if:

(1) it was provided by the client;
(2) it was specially obtained for, and paid for, by the client;[8]
(3) in generating the record the professional acted as the client's agent.[9]

Otherwise the record will belong either to the professional or the professional's employer.[10] The professional's or employer's property interest is subject to:

---

[5] D Feldman, *Civil Liberties and Human Rights in England and Wales* (2nd edn, Oxford: 2002) 515.
[6] In a litigation situation all professionals can be compelled to provide the client or his lawyer with relevant documentation and information. See chs 14 and 15.
[7] *Ex p Cobeldick* (1883) 12 QBD 149. cp *Harrison v Festus Timothy* [1998] 2 CL 1. A solicitor who terminates a retainer may be compelled to deliver up papers required for litigation even though he has a lien over them for unpaid fees: *Gamlen Chemical Co (UK) Ltd v Rochem Ltd* [1980] 1 All ER 1049. cp Case Note: 16579, NZ Privacy Commissioner (November 2001) available at http://www.privacy.org.nz
[8] *Breen v Williams* (1996) 1 ALR 259, 270.
[9] ibid.
[10] *R v Mid Glamorgan Family Health Services* [1995] 1 All ER 357, 363.

A. Client's Right to See Own Records

(1) the client's common law and statutory rights of access;[11] and
(2) the client's right that confidentiality be maintained.[12]

Ownership of personal information

19.04 The personal information, which is the client's real concern, cannot be owned.[13] The only property rights in information that exist in English law are intellectual property rights. In the eyes of the law information is infinitely divisible without loss to anyone. '[T]here can be no proprietorship in information as information because once imparted by one person to another, it belongs equally to them both.'[14] If the judges were to change this, it is not a foregone conclusion that they would follow popular opinion and hold that personal information about a client belongs to the client.[15] Ownership of information about the client that only a professional applying expertise could have discovered (for example, knowledge of the presence of an internal tumour) might be vested in the professional. In *London School Board v Northcroft*[16] the claimant demanded memoranda that contained building measurements made by quantity surveyors whom the claimant had employed. A L Smith J said:

> Now I would like to know how it can be said that what I call the private memoranda which were made by Messrs Northcroft for the purpose of framing that which ultimately became the property of the plaintiffs, namely the bill of quantities, ever became the property of the plaintiffs. The paper belonged to Messrs. Northcroft, the ink belonged to Messrs. Northcroft, and the brains that put the calculations on paper belonged to Messrs. Northcroft; and I want to know how the document which came into existence ever became the property of the plaintiffs.

Professional acting as agent of the client

19.05 **General position** The ownership of documents in an agency relationship is as stated by MacKinnon LJ in *Leicestershire CC v Farada*:[17]

> If an agent brings into existence certain documents while in the employment of his principal, they are the principal's documents and the principal can claim that the agent should hand them over.

19.06 Even though a client–professional relationship may not be one of agency, the professional may occasionally act as the client's agent. When this happens, documents generated by the professional belong to the client.[18] In *Chantry Martin v*

---

[11] Discussed later in this chapter.
[12] *Re Axelrod* (1994) 119 DLR (4th) 37 and see chs 4 and 5.
[13] See paras 7.31 and 6.70 above.
[14] per Dawson and Toohey, *Breen v Williams* (1996) 138 DLR 259, 271, and 264, 288, 301–302. See also *Boardman v Phipps* [1967] 2 AC 46, 102, 127–128, cf 107.
[15] See paras 2.28 above.
[16] (1889) 2 Hudson's BC 4th edn, 147.
[17] [1941] 2 All ER 483, 487.
[18] [1953] 2 QB 286, 294.

Martin[19] the court held that an accountant's correspondence with the Inland Revenue for the purpose of settling a client company's tax liability was the property of the company because in conducting that correspondence the accountant operated as the client company's agent.

19.07 Solicitors The solicitor-client relationship is generally one of agency.[20] In the absence of a lien,[21] the client is entitled to documents brought into existence for the client's purposes.[22] When a solicitor's retainer is terminated and another solicitor instructed, the file will be passed to the new solicitor once the invoice has been settled.[23] The client will not be entitled to every document generated in the relationship: the solicitor owns attendance notes and working papers[24] and letters from the client.[25]

> Entries of attendance, tape recordings of conversations, etc, inter-office memoranda partner to partner, partner to staff, entries in diaries, office journals and books of account belong to the solicitor.[26]

The client has no right to these or to copies 'unless the access is obtained under some statutory provision dealing with solicitors and clients or under a discovery process'.[27]

Professional not acting in the capacity of agent

19.08 Doctors Generally the doctor–patient relationship is not one of agency.[28] Except for pathology reports, X-rays and any other items that the private patient

---

[19] D Nicolson and J Webb, *Professional Legal Ethics* (Oxford: 1999) 132.

[20] In *Re Garcia* 78 BR 68 (1987) the court ordered an attorney to hand over to the client's opponent files subject to a lien because otherwise future litigants might try to avoid discovery of documents by passing them to attorneys and then refusing to pay the attorneys' fees. The court also suggested that a lien could not be used to deny documents that a client needs to defend a criminal charge. If there is an effective lien, at common law the client is not entitled to the documents, copies or inspection but the statutory right of access under the DPA cannot be refused (DPA, s 27(5)).

[21] *Ex p Horsfall* (1827) 108 ER 820; *Howard v Gunn* (1863) 55 ER 181.

[22] *Wallace Bogan & Co v Cove* [1997] IRLR 453, 455.

[23] *R v Special Commissioner, ex p Morgan Grenfell & Co Ltd* [2002] UKHL 21; [2002] 2 WLR 1299, paras 19, 24. See also *Chantrey Martin v Martin* [1953] 2 QB 286, 293. In *Wentworth v de Montfort* (1988) 15 NSWLR 348, 355–356 it was said that a document made for the benefit of both the client and the solicitor but chargeable to the client belongs to the client but that the solicitor is entitled to retain a copy.

[24] *Re Thomson* (1855) 52 ER 714; *Re Wheatcroft* (1877) 6 Ch D 97.

[25] per Rice JA, *McInerney v MacDonald* (1990) 66 DLR (4th) 736, 738. Similarly, an accountant will 'own . . . working papers, draft accounts, copies of schedules and audit papers, notes and calculations': *Re Hay and Institute of Chartered Accountants of Alberta* (1988) 54 DLR (4th) 26, 29.

[26] per Young J, *Zeus Chemical Products Pty Ltd v Jaybee Design and Marketing Pty Ltd* (NSW, 1998), 532 citing *Cordery on Solicitors* (7th edn, London: 1981) 100.

[27] *Breen v Williams* (1996) 138 ALR 259, 266, 270, 280.

[28] ibid at 270. The fact that they are left in the charge of a doctor or hospital does not affect their ownership.

A. Client's Right to See Own Records

has paid for[29] and anything intended to be patient-held, medical records are not the patient's property.[30] They are, for private patients, the property of the doctor or the clinic where the client was seen[31] and for NHS patients the relevant NHS institution[32] and therefore ultimately the Secretary of State.

When a doctor who owns medical files dies, the ownership of the files passes to her personal representative.[33] In *Re Axelrod*[34] the Court of Appeal for Ontario decided that a dentist in private practice could pledge the practice files and patient list to obtain credit so long as the confidentiality interest of the patients in the contents of their files was preserved by the creditor when realizing its security. In the event of insolvency, confidentiality could be maintained by the dentist writing to patients to inform them that a new dentist was taking over and that their files would be turned over to the new dentist unless other instructions were received from them. Patients who wanted to change to another dental practice were to be invited to collect their records. Because dental records contain 'sensitive personal data',[35] in England the explicit[36] consent of the patient to the transfer of the records from dentist to dentist would be required. 19.09

Other professionals Records prepared or acquired by a self-employed professional acting in the services of a client in a non-agency capacity are owned by the professional.[37] 19.10

> In a professional relationship, the object to be achieved will ordinarily be the supply of expert advice . . . [or] the preparation and delivery of skilled plans . . . or the like. The client is concerned with the achievement of that purpose rather than with what the professional does in achieving it. In such a case the purpose of the contract is not the creation of such documents; the documents have come into existence only because the professional has, in the particular circumstances, deemed it expedient to create them in order to achieve the true purpose of the contract. . . . In such cases, the documents created by the professional in the course of preparing to give the advice or to furnish the plans will ordinarily remain the property of the professional.[38]

---

[29] *R v Mid Glamorgan Family Health Services, ex p Martin* [1995] 1 All ER 356, 363; *Breen v Williams* (1996) 1 ALR 259, 270.
[30] *Health Services for Men v D'Souza* [1999] NSWSC 969.
[31] The judgment in *R v Mid Glamorgan Family Health Services Authority, ex p Martin* [1995] 1 WLR 110, 116 proceeded on the footing that the medical records were the legal property of the health authority. See further J McHale, 'The general practitioner and confidentiality' in C Dowrick and L Frith (eds), *General Practice and Ethics* (London, 1999) 73.
[32] *Estate of Finkle* (1977) 395 NYS 2d 343, 344–345 cited by Gummow J in *Breen v Williams* (1996) 138 ALR 359, 300.
[33] 20 OR (3d) 133.
[34] See para 18.23 above.
[35] See para 18.25 above.
[36] *Leicestershire CC v Faraday* [1941] 2 All ER 483, 487. Of course, the parties can change this arrangement contractually.
[37] per Mahoney J, *Breen v Williams* (1994) 35 NSWLR 522.
[38] If the record is owned by the employer this does not mean that the employer is entitled to access to confidential information in the record: see para 21.03 below.

If the professional is in employment, the records sometimes belong to the professional and sometimes to the employer. Ownership will depend on whether the records were for the professional's own information or intended to form part of the employer's records.[39]

Contractual right

The general position

19.11   When the relationship between professional and client is contractual, the contract may give the client a right of access to, or ownership of, the records. If there is no express provision, a court is unlikely to imply either term unless the relationship is one of agency.[40]

Doctors

19.12   In *Breen v Williams*, a decision of the High Court of Australia, Brennan CJ was ready to contemplate an implied term in the contract between a doctor and patient that gave the patient a right to *information* in the patient's medical record when '(1) refusal to make the disclosure requested might prejudice the general health of the patient (2) the request for disclosure is reasonable having regard to all the circumstances and (3) reasonable reward for the service of disclosure is tendered or assured' but this did not mean that the client had an implied contractual right to inspect and copy his medical record. 'Where that duty can be performed without giving the patient access to the doctor's records, there is no foundation for implying any obligation to give that access.'[41] The rest of the High Court did not foresee any circumstance in which an implied contractual right of access to medical records might exist.[42]

19.13   In England access to medical records by a patient being treated within the NHS could not be based on an implied contractual term because there is no contractual relationship.[43]

Equitable right

Professionals in a fiduciary relationship

19.14   When the professional–client relationship is a fiduciary one (as all agency relationships are), the client has a right of access to documents belonging to the

---

[39] See paras 19.05 and 19.14.
[40] (1996) 138 ALR 259, 263.
[41] ibid at 272, 297–298. Contrast *McInerney v MacDonald* (1992) 93 DLR (4th) 415.
[42] *Pfizer Corp v Minister of Health* [1965] AC 512.
[43] cp *O'Rourke v Darbyshire* [1920] AC 581, 626. As regards the fiduciary nature of the solicitor–client relationship see *Sidaway v Bethlem Royal Hospital* [1984] 1 All ER 1018, 1032.

professional that concern the client's affairs.[44] In *Wentworth v De Montfort*[45] the New South Wales Supreme Court concluded that a solicitor's trust account records of his dealings with a client's money, his financial records concerning a client and the solicitor's trust account bank statements were the property of the solicitor, but that the client had a right to inspect them and to be provided, if asked for, with copies.[46] Of course, this would be at the client's expense.[47]

Doctors

In English law the doctor–patient relationship is not a fiduciary one,[48] even though the doctor does have certain obligations of a fiduciary nature. These are to protect the confidentiality of client information[49] and not to use undue influence to obtain gifts.[50] The position of the Supreme Court of Canada is quite the opposite. In *McInerney v MacDonald*[51] it held that the doctor–patient relationship imposes a fiduciary duty on the doctor to provide the patient with reasonable access to examine and copy the patient's own medical records in their entirety on payment of a legitimate fee so long as disclosure would not be seriously detrimental to the patient or likely to harm a third party. In *Breen v Williams*[52] the High Court of Australia refused to follow *McInerney v MacDonald*.

19.15

Innominate right

R v Mid Glamorgan Family Health Services, ex p Martin

In *R v Mid Glamorgan Family Health Services, ex p Martin*[53] the Court of Appeal assumed that a patient has a non-contractual right of access to medical records (whether NHS or private)[54] that are not covered by a statutory access scheme.[55] According to Sir Roger Parker the circumstances under which the right of access arises are 'infinitely various, and it is neither desirable nor possible for this or any

19.16

---

[44] (1988) NSWLR 348.
[45] *Re Thomson* (1855) 52 ER 714.
[46] ibid. Cp *Re Hay and Institute of Chartered Accountants of Alberta* (1988) 54 DLR (4th) 26, 29.
[47] *Sidaway v Bethlem Royal Hospital Governors* [1985] 1 All ER 643, 651, HL.
[48] *W v Egdell* [1990] 1 All ER 835 and see generally ch 5.
[49] *Sidaway v Bethlem Royal Hospital* [1984] 1 All ER 1018, 1032, CA; see para 5.80 above.
[50] (1992) 93 DLR (4th) 415, 424. cp *Emmett v Eastern Dispensary and Casualty Hospital* 396 F 2d 931 (1967); *Cannell v Medical Surgical Clinic* 315 NE 2d 278 (1974).
[51] (1996) 138 ALR 259. The view was taken that the doctor has a fiduciary duty of loyalty but that it is proscriptive not prescriptive, ie the doctor must avoid conflicts of interest and unauthorized benefits but has no duty to take the positive step of allowing access to records. In so far as the High Court applied duties of loyalty to the doctor, it may go beyond the current English position (see paras 5.80–5.83 above) though *Sidaway v Bethlem Royal Hospital* [1984] 1 All ER 1018, 1031–1032, CA could be read as forbidding the doctor from profiting from the patient.
[52] [1995] 1 All ER 356, 365.
[53] ibid, 363.
[54] cp WHO, *Declaration on the Promotion of Patients' Rights in Europe* (Amsterdam: 1994) para 4.4. Contrast *Boyle v Glasgow Royal Infirmary and Associated Hospitals* 1969 SC 72, 82.
[55] [1995] 1 All ER 356, 362.

court to attempt to set out the scope of the duty to afford access or, its obverse, the scope of the patient's right to demand access. Each case must depend on its own facts.'[56] No attempt was made to explain the legal source of the access right.[57] It may be that non-disclosure is as unconscionable in the eyes of equity[58] as is disclosure without authority.[59]

19.17 The right of access, whatever its jurisprudential origins, is capable of qualification. The respondents, two health authorities, had offered sight of the records to the applicant's medical advisers but had refused the applicant access on therapeutic grounds. This decision was upheld by the Court of Appeal.[60]

> [A] doctor, likewise a health authority as the owner of a patient's medical records, may deny the patient access to them if it is in his best interests to do so, for example if their disclosure would be detrimental to his health.[61]

It was stressed that a doctor may not arbitrarily refuse a patient access to his records.

> [T]he doctor's general duty . . . is to act at all times in the best interests of the patient. Those interests would usually require that a patient's medical records should not be disclosed to third parties; conversely, that they should usually, for example, be handed on by one doctor to the next or made available to the patient's legal advisers if they are reasonably required for the purposes of legal proceedings in which he is involved.[62]

19.18 Martin turned to Strasbourg for help but his application was held inadmissible.[63] The Commission considered that the offer of disclosure to Martin's medical advisers struck a fair balance between the authorities' legitimate aim, which was to protect Martin's mental health, and the applicant's desire for access to records covering significant incidents in his life. The interference with Article 8(1) created by the refusal to allow Martin to see his medical records was therefore justified.

Gaskin v UK

19.19 In applying to the Commission Martin had relied upon the decision in *Gaskin v UK*.[64] In that case refusal to allow the applicant access to his childhood case records unless those who had compiled them (medical practitioners, schoolteachers, probation officers, social workers and health visitors) consented to the disclosure was

---

[56] J Davies, 'Patient's Rights of Access to their Health Records' (1996) 2 Medical L Intl 189.
[57] cp R Magnusson, 'A Triumph for Medical Paternalism: *Breen v Williams*, Fiduciaries and Patient Access to Medical Records' [1995] Tort L J 12.
[58] *Stephens v Avery* [1988] 2 WLR 1280, 1286; see para 5.03 above.
[59] The decision has been criticized on the grounds that there was insufficient evidence for this conclusion: [1994] Medical L Rev 353, 356; D Freeman, 'Common Law Access to Medical Records' (1996) 59 MLR 101, 109.
[60] per Nourse LJ, [1995] 1 All ER 356, 363.
[61] ibid.
[62] (1996) 21 EHHR CD 113; 4 EHRLR 442.
[63] (1989) 12 EHRR 36. See now also *MG v UK* Application 39393/98, 24 September 2002.
[64] cp *Re X* [2001] 2 FLR 440, para 34.

A. Client's Right to See Own Records

successfully challenged. The Strasbourg Court held that in some circumstances a positive obligation to allow access to information arises under the Article 8 right to respect for private and family life. In *Gaskin* the records were an essential source of knowledge about the applicant's childhood and formative years and therefore denial of access was an interference with Article 8(1).[65] Although respect for the confidentiality of the records promoted the effective operation of the child care system and to that extent it was a legitimate aim, the court considered that the interference was disproportionate because there was no procedure for an independent authority to review the decision to refuse Gaskin access to inspect the records.

It is difficult to assess the implications of *Gaskin* for professional records generally.[66] In *Russo v Nugent Care Society*[67] the claimant was refused access to documents that had been created before and shortly after her adoption. The claimant's Article 8 rights were held not to be infringed by this refusal. Scott Baker J said that *Gaskin* was no authority for the proposition that a person had a general right of access to personal data and that *Gaskin* was a decision 'dependant upon the facts of that case'. Even if Article 8 applies, the right of access may be subject to safeguards and restrictions that strike a fair balance between the general interest of the community and the interests of the individual.[68] It is to be noted that in *Gaskin* the applicant was not held to have an entitlement to the data, only to have his request submitted to independent review. **19.20**

Client's Statutory Rights of Access to Records

Data Protection Act 1998

Subject access rights

Policy and nature The policy behind Data Protection Act 1998 (DPA) s 7 is to make transparent to the individual who is processing personal data about him and why.[69] Upon written request, proof of identity[70] and payment of a prescribed fee,[71] the DPA entitles the client[72] to be informed by a professional, or the data **19.21**

---

[65] In *M v UK* Application 39393/98, 24 September 2002, para 29, a distinction was drawn between the records of a child and those of an adult.
[66] [2001] EWHC Admin 566; [2002] 1 FLR 1, para 60. Many of the documents had emanated from third parties.
[67] *Gaskin v UK* (1990) 12 EHRR 36, 47. cp *Botta v Italy* (1998) 26 EHRR 241, para 33.
[68] Without this knowledge exercise of personal autonomy is inhibited: German Federal Constitutional Court, Census Decision, (1984) 5 Human Rights Law J 94, 100.
[69] DPA, s 7(3).
[70] DPA, s 7(2); Data Protection (Subject Access) (Fees and Miscellaneous Provisions) Regulations 2000, SI 2000/191.
[71] The client may apply through an agent. The professional should require evidence of the agent's identity and authority to make the application on behalf of the client before providing access.
[72] If the professional is self-employed it will be the professional. If the professional is employed it may be either the professional or someone else in the organization in which the professional is employed: see para 18.11 above.

Chapter 19: Disclosure to the Client

controller in the organization employing the professional,[73] whether 'personal data'[74] of which the client is the data subject is being or has been 'processed'[75] by or on behalf of the professional/data controller.[76] While no reasons have to be given for the inquiry, the client may be asked to provide information reasonably needed to enable the data to be located.[77] The professional/data controller has 40 days (or 15 school days for education records)[78] to satisfy the request.

Scope

19.22 Subject access rights (SARs) apply to all automated personal data (including e-mail) and all personal data in structured manual files (as defined in the DPA).[79] Exceptionally, there is a right of access to data in unstructured health records[80] social work records[81] and the educational records of schools in the public sector.[82] Maintaining dual records—one version for the client and another for the use of the professional—is illegal. Files have to be disclosed no matter how damaging to the professional. Thus the Department of Trade had to disclose records that described the applicant as a 'prat' and an 'out-and-out nutter'.[83]

19.23 When amendments introduced by the Freedom of Information Act 2000 come into force SARs will be extended to all unstructured manual files held by public authorities. An amendment to the DPA[84] provides that a public authority is not obliged to allow subject access in relation to any unstructured personal data unless the request contains a description of the data, and that even if it does, the public authority can refuse to deal with the request on grounds of cost.

Specific rights

19.24 If the client receives the answer that personal data about the client is being processed (this includes being held),[85] the client is entitled to a description of that

---

[73] See para 18.04 above.
[74] See para 18.08 above.
[75] DPA, s 7(1)(a). This right was equated with 'inspection' under the CPR in *P v Wozencroft* [2002] EWHC 1724, Fam Div.
[76] DPA, s 7(3).
[77] DPA, s 7 (3); Data Protection (Subject Access) (Fees and Miscellaneous Provisions) Regulations 2000, SI 200/191, reg 5.
[78] See para 18.06 above. The access right extends to data cross-referenced or linked to the file.
[79] DPA, s 68(1)(a). This includes X-rays which are also to be treated as 'data' for the purposes of s 1: *Hubble v Peterborough Hospitals NHS Trust* (21 March 2001).
[80] DPA, s 68(1) (c).
[81] DPA, s 68(1)(b).
[82] G Maguire and P Church, 'Enforcement of the Data Protection Act 1998: compliance at all costs?' (2002) 152 NLJ 147, 148.
[83] s 9A(2), (3).
[84] DPA, s 7(1)(a) and see para 18.08 above.
[85] DPA, s 7 (1)(b)(i),(ii).

A. Client's Right to See Own Records

data and told why it is being processed[86] and to whom it has been, or may be, disclosed.[87] The client has the further rights:

- unless this would involve 'disproportionate effort'[88] or be impossible, to a copy[89] in an intelligible[90] and permanent form of all or any part,[91] of the personal data as it was at the time of the request (apart from deletions or amendments that would have been made irrespective of the request);[92]
- to be given any information available about the source of data that is not exempt;[93] and
- if expressly sought,[94] to be informed of the logic of any process of automated decision-making applied to the data which significantly affects the client.[95]

There is no cut-off date for subject access to personal data. Octogenarians can ask to see their school and university records, if they have been retained. Since this may be very inconvenient and there is no compulsion to retain personal data before an access request is received, the data protection regime (consistently with the fifth data protection principle)[96] creates an incentive to weed out personal data that is no longer needed.

No conditional access

A professional who is worried about non-comprehension or miscomprehension of data by the client can offer to organize disclosure in the presence of a suitably qualified person but cannot make access conditional on the client agreeing to such an arrangement. Access cannot be refused because of non-payment of professional fees.[97]

19.25

---

[86] DPA, s 7 (1)(b)(iii).
[87] Not to be confused with disproportionate cost which is not a good ground to refuse data: *Hubble v Peterborough Hospitals NHS Trust* (21 March 2001) (requiring supply of copies of X-rays).
[88] DPA, s 8(2).
[89] This is intended to prevent information being disclosed in encrypted form: X-rays are 'intelligible' for the purposes of this requirement: *Hubble v Peterborough Hospitals NHS Trust* (21 March 2001).
[90] This was intended to prevent information from being disclosed in encrypted form. X-rays have been held to be 'intelligible' for the purposes of the intelligibility requirement: *Hubble v Peterborough Hospitals NHS Trust* (21 March 2001).
[91] DPA, s 7 (7).
[92] DPA, s 8(6). It is an offence under Freedom of Information Act 2000, s 77(1) for any person to alter, deface, erase or destroy records with the intention of defeating a subject access request that has been made to a public authority under DPA, s 7.
[93] DPA, s 7(1)(c), (8). The professional is not obliged to disclose the identity of the source where this is an individual: see para 19.32 below.
[94] Data Protection (Subject Access) (Fees and Miscellaneous Provisions) Regulations 2000, SI 2000/191, reg 2.
[95] DPA, s 7(1)(d).
[96] See para 18.34 above.
[97] DPA, s 27(5).

Relationship to other law

19.26 The client's right of access takes priority over legislation and rules of law prohibiting or restricting the disclosure, or authorizing the withholding, of information[98] other than:

(1) enactments listed in the Data Protection (Miscellaneous Subject Access Exemptions) Order 2000;[99]
(2) court orders prohibiting access;
(3) later legislation overriding the DPA.

Sanctions

19.27 A professional who fails to supply information legitimately requested under s 7 contravenes the sixth data protection principle which requires personal data to be processed in accordance with the rights of data subjects.[100] The client may complain to the Information Commissioner who can serve an enforcement notice[101] or seek an order for disclosure from a court.[102] The court in its discretion may order the professional to comply and award compensation for any damage suffered as a result of the initial failure to do so.[103] Damages are recoverable for distress so long as other damage has been suffered.[104] If the complaint relates to the denial of access to an NHS health record, it will be possible to invoke the NHS complaints procedure[105] before resorting to the Information Commissioner or a court.

Exemptions to the subject access rights

19.28 The DPA and ancillary legislation contain many exemptions to SARs. The professional who withholds information from a client under one of these is not obliged to identify the withheld information or even inform the client that anything has been kept back.

19.29 **Repeat requests** Grounds of exemption include that the professional has complied with an identical or similar request by the client and a reasonable time has not elapsed since the last request.[105a] What is a reasonable lapse of time depends on 'the nature of the data, the purpose for which the data are processed and the frequency with which the data are altered'.[106]

---

[98] ibid.
[99] SI 2000/419. Those are concerned with adoption records and reports and parental order records and reports under Human Fertilization and Embryology Act 1990, s 20.
[100] DPA, Sch 1, Part I.
[101] DPA, s 40(1). See also paras 18.48–18.49 above.
[102] DPA, s 7(9). Both High Court and county court have jurisdiction: DPA, s 15.
[103] DPA, s 13. See also para 18.50 above.
[104] DPA, s 13(2)(a).
[105] See para 9.05 above.
[105a] DPA, s 8(3).
[106] DPA, s 8(4).

A. Client's Right to See Own Records

Excluded matter DPA, Part IV lists categories of excluded information. These include: data processed for the purposes of national security,[107] crime prevention or taxation,[108] regulatory activity,[109] research,[110] asserting legal rights,[111] disclosure under compulsion of law[112] and disclosure for the special purposes of journalism, and artistic and literary expression.[113]

19.30

A ministerial certificate is conclusive evidence that data is being processed for national security purposes and is on this ground exempt from the requirements of s 7, subject to an appeal to the Information Tribunal by a person 'directly affected' by the issuing of the certificate.[114] In an important first ruling, the Information Tribunal[115] held that the Minister had acted ultra vires in issuing a certificate that enabled the Security Service (MI5) to adopt a blanket policy of neither confirming nor denying whether an applicant's personal data was held without regard to whether national security might be prejudiced by a positive response. This was because the Human Rights Act 1998 (HRA) requires the Secretary of State's certificate to be proportionate to the right to respect for private life. Article 8 is engaged because knowledge as to whether files are held is a precondition to the applicant exercising his Article 8 right to access and refute information.[116] The message of this decision, as relevant to professionals as to MI5, is that any decision to refuse access must satisfy tests of prejudice and proportionality.

19.31

Data relating to third parties A client has no right to data that relates to an identifiable[117] third party[118] (including information about who provided the personal data in the requested record).[119] Those parts of the data relating to the client that the professional is unable to disclose without revealing information relating to a third party may be withheld[120] (though there is no obligation to do so). The information *must* be disclosed notwithstanding that it contains information about a third party if:

19.32

---

[107] DPA, s 28; see para 18.44 above.
[108] DPA, s 29; see para 18.44 above.
[109] DPA, s 31; see para 18.44 above.
[110] DPA, s 33; see para 18.42 above.
[111] DPA, s 35(2); see para 18.38 above.
[112] DPA, s 35(1); see para 18.38 above.
[113] DPA, s 32; see para 18.39 above.
[114] DPA s 28(2), (4). Under s 28(5), if the Tribunal finds, applying principles of judicial review, that the Minister did not have reasonable grounds for issuing the certificate, the Tribunal can quash the certificate.
[115] *Norman Baker MP v Secretary of State for the Home Department* (Information Tribunal (National Security Appeals), 1 October 2001). The judgment is available on the Lord Chancellor's website at http://www.lcd.gov.uk.
[116] para 67.
[117] DPA, s 8(7). Predicting whether the client is likely to identify the third party because of special knowledge may prove extremely difficult for the professional.
[118] DPA, s 7(4).
[119] DPA, s 7(5).
[120] DPA, s 7(4). eg disclosure that A has a genetic condition may disclose that B, a relative, has that condition.

Chapter 19: Disclosure to the Client

(1) the third party consents;[121] or

(2) the information is contained in a health record and the third party is a health professional[122] who compiled or contributed to the record or was involved in the care of the client;[123] *or*

(3) the third party is employed in education or something ancillary or is a social or probation worker in the public sector—provided no serious harm to that person's physical or mental health or condition is likely to be caused by disclosure;[124] *or*

(4) it is reasonable in all the circumstances to comply with the request without the third party's consent.[125]

The professional is never excused from disclosing information that can be provided without revealing information about other individuals,[126] if necessary by deleting or masking their names and other identifiers.

19.33 In determining whether it is reasonable to supply information without third party consent (which by implication includes deciding whether consent has been unreasonably refused) the professional/data controller must take into account:

- any duty of confidentiality owed to the third party;
- steps taken to secure consent;
- the third party's capacity to consent; and
- the express refusal of consent by the third party.[127]

The fact that the third party already knows the third party information is likely to be relevant.[128] That the third party is dead or that the records concern events long ago may also be relevant.

19.34 Should disclosure be refused because a relevant third party has not consented, the client may complain to the Information Commissioner or appeal to the courts.[129]

---

[121] DPA, s 7(4)(a).

[122] Health professionals are defined by DPA, s 69 as registered medical practitioners, dentists, opticians, pharmacists, nurses, midwives, health visitors, clinical psychologists, child psychotherapists, osteopaths, chiropractors, chiropodists, dieticians, occupational therapists, physiotherapists, radiographers, speech therapists, music and art therapists, orthoptists, prosthetists, medical laboratory technicians and scientists who head health service departments. Health professionals do not include alternative health practitioners and psychotherapists unless they fall into one of the named categories. The category does not include students.

[123] Data Protection (Subject Access Modification) (Health) Order 2000, SI 2000/413, r 8(a).

[124] Data Protection (Subject Access Modification) (Education) Order 2000, SI 2000/414, r 7 (1)(a).

[125] DPA, s 7(4)(b).

[126] DPA, s 7(5).

[127] DPA, s 7(6).

[128] Office of the Information Commissioner, *Introduction to the Data Protection Act* version 2, 'Subject Access Rights and Third Party Information' 4, available from http://www.dataprotection.gov.uk.

[129] DPA, ss 7 (a), 15 and 40.

A. Client's Right to See Own Records

Conversely, the third party has on specified grounds a right of appeal to a court if his refusal of consent is overridden.[130]

Confidential references The client has no right to require a data controller[131] to show him a confidential written[132] reference 'given or to be given by the data controller' in connection with the client's existing or prospective education, employment, training or appointment to any office or the provision of services to the client. This is because of an exemption in Sch 7.[133] The exemption neither defines 'reference' nor gives any indication of whether it applies to internal documents such as a report about the suitability of an employee for promotion or the quality of a student's academic research.[134]   **19.35**

Schedule 7 is treated by the Information Commissioner as dealing exclusively with the disclosure obligation of the data controller responsible for giving the reference although it might be argued that a reference remains 'a reference given . . . in confidence by the data controller'[135] after it has been received. If it is an internal reference, the document may not have passed into the hands of another data controller. The advice of the Information Commissioner is that the normal SAR set out in s 7 applies to the reference once in the hands of the recipient data controller. This means that the recipient must disclose the reference in response to an application by the client with or without the professional's consent 'although the recipient is entitled to take steps to protect the identity of third parties such as the author of the reference'.[136] But with many references the point   **19.36**

---

[130] On the grounds that disclosure is likely to cause serious harm to his physical or mental health or condition. SI 2000/415 reg 7, SI 2000/413 reg 8, SI 2000/414 reg 7.

[131] The professional who wrote the reference may or may not be the 'data controller' (see para 18.11 above). If she is not: (1) she is not covered by the exemption, but (2) the client has no enforceable SAR against her under DPA, s 7.

[132] Telephone references are not subject to the DPA if no record is made of the conversation. If the recipient makes a record the DPA applies even if the professional gives the reference entirely from memory.

[133] DPA, Sch 7, para 1. If the author of the reference has kept notes about the subject of the reference or has written a confidential report about that person which is held in a computer or in a structured manual file these will have to be disclosed.

[134] See para 19.71 below where *R v University of Cambridge, ex p Persaud* [2001] ELR 64 is discussed. The reference in para 1(a) to 'education' *and* 'prospective education' indicates that the Sch is not concerned exclusively with acceptance onto an academic programme. The courts have adopted a hands off approach to questions of academic judgement. Query: how does one distinguish pure academic judgement (which need not be disclosed and cannot be challenged except on procedural grounds) from the provision of a reference when an opinion is sought about whether a student should be allowed to proceed with research?

[135] This argument is not precluded by the use of the indefinite article ('a' or 'any') rather than the definite article ('the').

[136] Employment Code of Practice (Draft) on the use of personal data in employer/employee relationships, para 4.3, available from http://www.dataprotection.gov.uk. By DPA, s 7(4) information relating to a third party (including information identifying a source: s 7(5)) can be withheld unless the third party had consented or it is reasonable in the circumstances to identify that person without consent (see para 19.32 above). If the identity of the author of the reference is known and there

of concern is not the identity of the author, which is often known, but the contents. If the identity of the referee is known Sch 7 provides no protection.

19.37 If the Information Commissioner's interpretation is correct, it reverses the law that applied before the DPA came into force with regard to references written in confidence. Parliament was not told that this was the effect of the DPA and there was no consultation with educational institutions or employer organizations about such an important change to the law. Disclosure of the reference by the recipient, of course, depends on the reference having been retained as part of a relevant manual filing system or in automated equipment.[137] There is no obligation to file or retain a reference and for external candidates who fail to get the job to which they aspired or fail to be accepted by an educational institution to which they applied there is little likelihood of reading the reference since the normal practice is to destroy the references of discarded candidates.[138] Only if an identical reference is received and retained by another institution will the data subject discover what the referee said.[139]

19.38 Is the Information Commissioner right in this approach? In evaluating the Information Commissioner's interpretation of s 7(4) and the Sch 7 exemption, the following points need to be considered:

(1) The Government White Paper that preceded the DPA stated that 'the Government believes that it may be necessary to provide exemptions for employment and academic references provided in confidence'.[140] The implication of this is that the reference is not to be seen by the subject of the reference.

(2) Had it been intended that the subject of the reference be given access to the reference after receipt by another data controller, Parliament would surely have spelled out SARs to internal references which involve only one data controller.

(3) Widespread exercise of SARs with respect to educational and employer references could undermine the reference system by discouraging frank references. The US Family Educational Rights and Privacy Act 1974 gives students a right to inspect and review confidential references unless this right is waived in advance. The overwhelming majority of students waive this right because

---

is no information about any third party in the reference, it is unlikely that the Information Commissioner would approve the withholding of any part of the reference. If the identity of the author of the reference is unknown, an obligation of confidentiality is a relevant consideration.

[137] DPA, s 1.
[138] But once the Freedom of Information Act is in force, by s 77(1) it will be an offence for a public authority to destroy the reference once a SAR is received.
[139] UCAS applicants who fail to be accepted by their university of choice but are accepted by another university may find this.
[140] *Data Protection: the Government's Proposals* (1997) para 3.22, available at http://www.lcd.gov.uk/ccpd/datap1.htm.

A. Client's Right to See Own Records

they know that the recipient will place much more weight on a private letter of recommendation than one to which they have access.[141] It is true that in the law of libel employment references are privileged, it being recognized that it is in the public interest 'for a particular recipient to receive frank and uninhibited communication of particular information from a particular source'[142] but it is not only fear of litigation that deters candour in references.[143]

(4) There is the risk of the data subject who obtains access attempting to influence subsequent references from the same source.

(5) The recipient of a reference marked confidential owes an equitable obligation of confidentiality to its author.[144] Should the recipient decide to disclose the reference, the recipient will be processing data and, if the data is held in electronic format or in a relevant manual file, this must be done in accordance with the provisions of the DPA, including the first data protection principle. This requires data to be processed lawfully under the general law as well as in terms of the data protection principles found in the DPA.[145] It is normally unlawful (that is, a breach of confidence) to disclose a reference that is the subject of an equitable obligation of confidentiality to the subject of that reference without the consent of the author.[146] DPA, s 27(5) allows the DPA, s 7 SAR to override the equitable obligation of confidentiality but abrogation is subject to the exemptions provided in Part IV.[147] These include the exemption for confidential references in Sch 7.[148]

Medical data A 'health professional'[149] may refuse the client access to medical data (including mental health data) in her control on the grounds that this 'would be likely to cause serious harm to the physical or mental health or condition of [the patient]'.[150] Distressing facts should not be withheld from a patient who could cope with the information with appropriate counselling.[151] Access may be refused if disclosure involves a risk of serious harm to the physical or mental health

19.39

---

[141] Privacy Sub-Committee of the Law Reform Commission of Hong Kong, *Civil Liability for Invasion of Privacy* (1999) 71.
[142] per Lord Nicholls, *Reynolds v Times Newspapers Ltd* [1999] 4 All ER 609, 616.
[143] cp *R v University of Cambridge, ex p Persaud* [2001] ELR 64, para 23.
[144] Even without an express statement that the reference is confidential, the circumstances may indicate that the reference was intended to be confidential. For the requirements of such a duty see chs 5 and 6.
[145] See para 18.09 above.
[146] Neither the public domain nor the public interest defences will apply.
[147] DPA, s 27(5) commences: 'Except as provided by this part . . .'.
[148] See ibid, s 37.
[149] See para 19.32 n122 above.
[150] Data Protection (Subject Access Modification) (Health) Order 2000, SI 2000/413, r 5(1) made pursuant to DPA, s 30(1). cp Access to Medical Reports Act 1988, s 7(1). There is no requirement to obtain a medical opinion about the potential harmful effects of disclosure.
[151] Circular LAC (87) 10 which explains the corresponding provision in the Data Protection (Subject Access Modification) (Health) Order 1987, SI 1987/1903 (made under Data Protection

or condition of a third party. If a patient is refused access to medical records, it has been suggested that the health professional should say that there is no data to which the client is entitled to avoid distressing the client.[152]

19.40 There is no right of access to fertilization and embryology information.[153]

19.41 **Social work data** The right of access to the social work records of a local authority, a local education authority, a Health and Social Services Board or Trust or probation committee is limited to a right to be informed that data is being processed if:

(1) disclosure would invade a third party's right of privacy (other than a 'relevant person')[154] such as a social worker or guardian ad litem; or
(2) would be likely to prejudice the carrying out of social work by causing serious harm to the physical or mental health or condition of the client or any other person.[155]

There is no right to information contained in adoption and parental order records and reports.[156]

19.42 **Data supplied to a court** There is no right of subject access to a report or information supplied to a court for the purposes of health, wardship or childcare proceedings if the information may be in whole or in part withheld by the court.[157]

19.43 **Education data** 'Personal data consisting of information recorded by candidates during an academic, professional or other examination' (in other words, examination scripts) are exempt from the subject access provisions[158] and data subjects are not entitled to know their examination mark in advance of the general release of results.[159] Once the results of an examination have been published, the marks

---

Act 1984, s 29) says in para 9 that 'serious harm' was a reference to 'a minority who are unstable or have little insight' who 'may exceptionally need to be protected permanently from certain damaging revelations about themselves'.

[152] P Parsloe, 'The Unintended Impact of Computers on Social Work Practice' in R Cnaan and P Parsloe (eds), *The Impact of Information Technology on Social Work Practice* (New York: Haworth Press, 1989) 176.

[153] Data Protection (Miscellaneous Subject Access Exemptions) Order 2000, SI 2000/419. The Human Fertilisation and Embryology Act 1990 provides an alternative access procedure to some information.

[154] Data Protection (Subject Access Modification) (Social Work) Order 2000, SI 2000/415, r 7(2).

[155] ibid r 5.

[156] Data Protection (Miscellaneous Subject Access Exemptions) Order 2000, SI 2000 419; Data Protection (Miscellaneous Subject Access Exemptions) (Amendment) Order 2000, SI 2000/ 1865.

[157] Data Protection (Subject Access Modification) (Health) Order 2000, SI 2000/413, r 4; Data Protection (Subject Access Modification) (Social Work) Order 2000, SI 2000/415, r 4; Data Protection (Subject Access Modification) (Education) Order 2000, SI 2000/414, r 4.

[158] DPA, Sch 7, para 9. This does not mean that they must be withheld.

[159] If there is a delay of more than 40 days before the results are announced, the candidate is entitled to be informed of his mark as recorded on the date of the request but the mark need only be supplied (a) within five months of the request, or (b) within 40 days of the announcement of the results, whichever is the earlier: DPA, Sch 7, paras 8(2), (3).

A. Client's Right to See Own Records

awarded and examiners' comments (including in a University context those of external examiners) must, on request, be released.[160] Examination Board minutes in which an identifiable student is discussed must be disclosed unless this cannot be done without also disclosing personal information about another candidate.[161]

19.44 The right of access to an 'educational record'[162] is confined to pupils and ex-pupils of special schools and schools funded by a local education authority;[163] private schools are exempt. The access right applies to information produced by teachers (other than information kept by teachers solely for personal use)[164] and information emanating from the pupil, the pupil's parents, education welfare officers and employees of the local education authority.[165] Information obtained from others, for example, a local police liaison officer, need not be disclosed. The record holder is entitled to withhold an educational record to the extent to which access would be likely to cause serious harm to the physical or mental health or condition of the pupil or any other person.[166]

19.45 Separate provision is made in the Education (Pupil Information) (England) Regulations 2000[167] for a pupil who has left, or proposes to leave, school to be supplied with a school leaver's report by the head teacher. There is no SAR to statements and records of the special educational needs of children.[168]

19.46 **Self-incrimination and legal professional privilege** The professional need not satisfy a SAR request if this would expose the professional to the risk of a criminal prosecution other than under the DPA.[169]

19.47 Data is exempt from SARs if the data consists of information for which legal professional privilege could be claimed in legal proceedings.[170] The legality of an organization circulating information internally with the predominant object of avoiding SARs by issuing it in the form of confidential legal advice to employees from the organization's legal department or from an outside solicitor has not been tested by a court.

---

[160] See DPA, Sch 7, para 8. As regards examiners' comments, see Sch 7, para 8(1). To make sense of comments (DPA, s 8 (2)) some parts of the script may have to be disclosed or an explanation provided.
[161] See para 19.32 above.
[162] '[A]ny record of information processed by or on behalf of the governing body of, or a teacher at, any school . . .': DPA, Sch 11.
[163] DPA, Sch 11, para 3.
[164] DPA, Sch 11, para 2.
[165] DPA, Sch 11, para 4.
[166] Data Protection (Subject Access Modification) (Education) Order 2000, SI 2000/414, r 5.
[167] SI 2000/297, reg 9.
[168] Data Protection (Miscellaneous Subject Access Exemptions) Order 2000, SI 2000/419.
[169] DPA, Sch 7, para 11(1).
[170] DPA, Sch 7, para 10; see ch 16.

Chapter 19: Disclosure to the Client

Additional rights

19.48 The DPA confers a number of additional rights on clients. Of particular interest to professionals will be the client's rights:

(1) To have inaccurate or misleading factual data and opinions based on the inaccurate or misleading data rectified, blocked, erased or destroyed and to have third parties with whom the erroneous data was shared notified of the error.[171] Alternatively, where the professional has taken reasonable steps to ensure accuracy, to have a supplementary statement of the 'true' facts added to the record.[172] If the professional refuses, the client can complain to the Information Commissioner[173] or apply to a court.[174] Difficult questions may arise when allegations of sexual abuse or non-accidental injury to a child are recorded in medical or social work files and there has been no finding of abuse.[175] Likewise when there is an allegation of sexual assault involving an adult and no prosecution. The court's power to order rectification is discretionary. In *P v Wozencroft*[176] Wilson J refused to allow s 14 to be used as a vehicle to enable an expert's report to be challenged after litigation had been concluded when the claimant had failed to avail himself of the opportunity to cross-examine the expert during the litigation.

(2) To require the professional to cease or not begin processing personal data for a specified purpose or in a specified manner about the client on the ground that for specified reasons[177] this is likely to cause 'substantial' and 'unwarranted'[178] damage or distress to the client or another person.[179] The right does not exist if processing is done for any of the first four Sch 2 conditions.[180] If the data controller thinks the cessation request unjustified, reasons must be given.[181] If these reasons are unacceptable to the applicant, the matter can be taken before a court.[182]

---

[171] DPA, s 14.
[172] DPA, Sch 1, Pt II, para 7.
[173] DPA, s 40(3).
[174] DPA, s 14. The powers of the court, which are extensive and complex, are considered in R Jay and A Hamilton, *Data Protection Law and Practice* (London: 1999) 12–15.
[175] A Pack, '"We'd like to know a little bit about you for our files"—The Data Protection Act 1998' [2000] Family L 759.
[176] [2002] EWHC 1724, Fam Div.
[177] Data Protection Directive (EC) 95/46 Art 14 requires a 'justified objection' involving 'compelling legitimate grounds' from the data subject to the continued processing of personal data about the data subject.
[178] Assessing whether damage or distress is 'unwarranted' will require the application of a proportionality test.
[179] DPA, s 10(1). Normally processing that complies with the first data protection principle's fairness code ought not to cause substantial damage or distress. Section 10(1) might prevent publication of test or examination results of students in a format that allows the students to be identified.
[180] DPA, s 10(2)
[181] DPA, s 10(3)(b).
[182] DPA, s 10(4).

A. Client's Right to See Own Records

(3) To invoke the Information Commissioner's assessment powers.[183]

Access to Medical Reports Act 1988

This Act gives a patient access rights to a 'medical report'[184] prepared for an actual or potential employer or insurer[185] by a registered medical practitioner 'who is or has been responsible for the clinical care' of the patient. It does this by requiring the employer or insurer (the applicant) to notify the patient in writing that he proposes to apply for a report and of the patient's rights.[186] The patient may notify the applicant in writing that he wishes to see the report before it is supplied and, if he does, the applicant must inform the doctor of this in writing.[187] The doctor, for her part, must, on receiving the notification, withhold the report until the patient has been given access, corrections requested by the patient have been dealt with and the patient has consented to the report being forwarded.[188] A copy of the report must be retained by the doctor for at least six months during which period the patient is entitled to access.[189] **19.49**

The Act gives no right of access to a report by a medical practitioner who does not have, and has never had, a doctor–patient relationship with the applicant, for example a doctor acting solely for an insurer.[190] Whether an occupational health professional is covered by the Act will depend upon the extent of her responsibilities, if any, toward the employee. **19.50**

It has not been decided whether the Act covers oral reports. Section 1 confers on the patient a right of access 'to *any* medical report relating to the individual'[191] and the definition of 'medical report' in s 2 is general but provisions dealing with amendment rights and retention of a copy of the report assume that the report is in writing.[192] **19.51**

Under the Act the patient has the following rights: **19.52**

(1) to be notified of the application and to withhold consent to it;[193]

---

[183] DPA, s 42; see para 18.47 above.
[184] That is a report 'relating to the physical or mental health of the individual': s 2.
[185] Reports for other purposes should be accessible under the DPA.
[186] Access to Medical Reports Act 1988, s 3; see para 19.52 below.
[187] Access to Medical Reports Act 1988, s 4. No independent duty is placed on the doctor to check whether the applicant wants to see the report before it is supplied. Therefore, if the applicant neglects his duty to notify the doctor that the patient wants advance access, the report may be supplied without the patient's having had an opportunity to see the report and ask for corrections.
[188] Access to Medical Reports Act 1988, ss 4, 5.
[189] ibid, s 6.
[190] See para 1.28 above.
[191] See also the long title which says that the Act aims at allowing individuals access to reports about themselves provided by medical practitioners for employment and insurance purposes. This purpose would be undermined if the medical practitioner could supply an oral report that by-passed the Act.
[192] Access to Medical Reports Act 1988, ss 5(2), 6.
[193] ibid, s 3(1).

Chapter 19: Disclosure to the Client

(2) before the report is sent, to see the report;[194]
(3) to seek an amendment of inaccuracies in the report and, if the doctor refuses to make the corrections, to have a statement attached disputing the information;[195]
(4) after being given access, to stop the report from being sent;[196]
(5) to see the report at any time within six months after its supply;[197]
(6) the right to be informed of his rights.[198]

Enforcement of the rights is by resort to a county court.[199] A doctor who ignores the patient's rights can be reported to the General Medical Council (GMC) for unprofessional conduct and the patient may be entitled to compensation for breach of statutory duty.[199a]

19.53 There are several exemptions to the access provisions:

(1) The medical practitioner is not obliged to give the patient access to any part of the medical report whose disclosure would in the practitioner's opinion be likely to cause serious harm to the physical or mental health of the patient or another person or which would indicate the intentions of the medical practitioner in respect of the patient.[200]
(2) There is no right of access to any part of a medical report that would be likely to reveal information about a third person or the identity of a third person who supplied the practitioner with information about the patient, unless the third party consents or is a health professional.[201] No obligation is placed on the medical practitioner to seek the consent of the third party.

The patient must be notified if his application is refused for one of these reasons.[202]

Access to Health Records Act 1990

19.54 This Act was introduced to give a patient, whether NHS or private, a right, subject to certain exceptions,[203] to be given a copy of the whole or a part of a man-

---

[194] Access to Medical Reports Act 1988, s 4. No charge may be made for allowing the client to inspect the report but a 'reasonable fee' can be levied for a copy.
[195] ibid, s 5(2)
[196] ibid, s 5(1).
[197] ibid, s 6(2).
[198] ibid, s 3(2).
[199] ibid, s 8
[199a] See para 4.50 above.
[200] Access to Medical Reports Act 1988, s 7(1). cp para 19.39 above.
[201] ibid, s 7(2). cp para 19.32 above.
[202] ibid, s 7(3)(a). Contrast para 19.39 above.
[203] Those parts of a health record likely to cause serious physical or mental harm to any individual (Access to Health Records Act 1990, s 5(1)(a)(i)) or those which would reveal information provided by, or relating to an identifiable third party (s 5(1)(a)(ii)) (other than a health professional) who had not consented to the disclosure (s 5(1)(b)).

A. Client's Right to See Own Records

ually held 'health record'[204] made after 1 November 1991[205] in connection with the care of the patient by a 'health professional' (defined as in the DPA).[206] The patient access rights under this Act have been superseded by those contained in the DPA[207] except in so far as the 1990 Act permits access by the deceased's personal representative[208] and by someone who may have a claim arising out of the patient's death.[209] The rights of access of the latter are restricted to those parts that are relevant.[210]

19.55 Where there is a right of access under the 1990 Act, if the patient provided the information or underwent the investigation on the understanding that it would not be revealed to anyone or to the particular applicant seeking the information (for example, an insurance company), access must be refused unless ordered by a court.[211] In addition, the right of access can be denied if, in the opinion of the record holder, disclosure would (1) cause serious harm to the physical or mental health of any other person, or (2) would identify a third person who has not consented to being identified and is not a health professional involved in the care of the patient.[212]

19.56 An applicant who is dissatisfied with the way an access request is handled can make a complaint through the NHS complaints procedure or, as a last resort, apply to a county court.[213]

Health and Social Care Act 2001

19.57 Section 60 (2)(a) allows the Secretary of State to make regulations requiring communications between clinicians to be copied lawfully to the patient-subjects of the correspondence.

---

[204] A record of information relating to the physical or mental health of the patient: Access to Health Records Act 1990, s 1(1).
[205] There is no right of access to information recorded before November 1991 unless the information is needed to make sense of information recorded after November 1991: Access to Health Records Act 1990, s 5(1)(b), (2).
[206] See Access to Health Records Act 1990, s 2.
[207] DPA Sch 16, Pt I.
[208] Access to Health Records Act 1990, s 3(1)(f).
[209] ibid, s 3(1)(f)
[210] ibid, s 5(4).
[211] ibid, s 5(3). See also s 4(3): 'access shall not be given . . . if the record includes a note, made at the patient's request, that he did not wish access to be given on such an application.'
[212] ibid, s 5(1). Cp para 19.53 above.
[213] ibid, s 8.

B. Client's Right to Information

Fiduciary-Professionals

The obligation to disclose information

19.58 It is well settled that in the paradigm professional fiduciary relationship of solicitor and client, the solicitor has a legal duty to disclose to a mentally competent client information about the client's affairs that comes to the solicitor's knowledge[214]

> Clients are entitled to expect that solicitors will exert themselves single-mindedly in their interests and to make available any knowledge which they have which is material to the client's interests.[215]

This is subject to the exception that the information is not information as to which the solicitor owes another client an obligation of confidentiality.[216] In *Hilton v Barker, Booth & Eastwood*[217] Parker LJ suggested that a term in a solicitor's retainer that confidential information obtained from another client in another transaction should be disclosed without the informed consent of the other client would offend against public policy.

19.59 As a prophylactic measure, the solicitor must disclose any personal interest in a transaction. Should the solicitor act for another party to the transaction (lender and purchaser or vendor and purchaser, for example, in a conveyance) the client must be told.[218] Disclosure enables the client to make an informed choice about whether to go elsewhere for legal representation.[219] A solicitor who acts for both parties to a transaction cannot withhold information imparted by one party from the other or give information to only one client.[220] Similarly, where several persons retain a solicitor jointly, the joint clients must be given the same information.[221]

---

[214] *Moody v Cox* [1917] 2 Ch 71, 83; *Jacks v Davis* [1980] 6 WWR 11, 16.

[215] per Bryne J, *Marron v J Chatham Duant Pty Ltd* (Vic SC 13 November 1998). See also *Re A Firm of Solicitors* [1992] 1 All ER 253, 262.

[216] The duty of confidentiality overrides the disclosure duty: *Daniels v Clifford Chance* (28 April 1989); cp *Kelly v Cooper* [1993] AC 205. Query: if a solicitor is instructed by B in a matter about which she has relevant public domain information but which she cannot disclose to B because of equitable and contractual obligations to A (see paras 4.10, 5.14 above), how can that solicitor continue to act for B if some other solicitor could discover and communicate the relevant information to B? cp *Spector v Ageda* [1971] 3 All ER 417, 440.

[217] [2002] EWCA Civ 723, para 47.

[218] Joint representation is allowed if all the parties consent if their interests diverge but are not in direct conflict. cp Law Society's *Guide to Professional Conduct of Solicitors* (8th edn, London: Law Society, 1999) para 15.03.

[219] *Clark Boyce v Mouat* [1993] 4 All ER 268, 275; *Haira v Burbery Mortgage Finance & Savings Ltd* [1995] 3 NZLR 396, 405.

[220] *Mortgage Express Ltd v Bowerman & Partners* [1996] 2 All ER 836.

[221] *Re Konigsberg* [1989] 3 All ER 289; *Clark Boyce v Mouat* [1993] 4 All ER 268, 275; *Farrow Mortgage Services Pty Ltd v Webb* (1996) 39 NSWLR 601, 608. And see para 16.16 above.

B. Client's Right to Information

19.60 The knowledge that must be disclosed to the client is that of the individual solicitor handling the client's affairs and, semble, if that solicitor is employed, the partner for whom she works. The knowledge of all those who work for or are a partner in a large firm of solicitors is not imputed to the retained solicitor.

> The solicitors in the present case comprised 107 partners at the last count. It seems to me impracticable and even absurd to say that they are under a duty to reveal to each client, and use for his benefit, any knowledge possessed by any one of their partners or staff.[222]

Scope of the disclosure obligation

19.61 The solicitor's disclosure obligation is a limited one. Its extent is determined by materiality and the terms of the retainer.[223] In *McMaster v Byrne*[224] Lord Cohen recommended that materiality be judged by 'the natural reaction of the reasonable man'. A solicitor advising a mortgagee must satisfy the mortgagee's express disclosure instructions and, unless contrary to the express terms of the retainer,[225] pass on information that a reasonably competent solicitor would conclude was material to some aspect of the work she was doing.

> A client cannot expect a solicitor to undertake work he has not asked him to do, and will not wish to pay him for such work. But if in the course of doing the work he is instructed to do the solicitor comes into possession of information which is not confidential and which is clearly of potential significance to the client, I think that the client would reasonably expect the solicitor to pass it on and feel understandably aggrieved if he did not.[226]

In *Bristol and West Building Society v Baden, Barnes Groves and Co,* Chadwick J suggested that the phrase 'in the course of doing the work he is instructed to do' reflected an important and significant qualification to the solicitor's duty to disclose information[227] but this was doubted in *Hilton v Barker Booth & Eastwood*.[228]

---

[222] per Staughton LJ, *Re A Firm of Solicitors* [1992] 1 All ER 253, 265. See further H Vans, *Lawyers' Liabilities* (London: 2002) 53–54.
[223] *Halifax Mortgage Services v Secretary of State* [1998] PNLR 616, 632.
[224] [1952] 1 All ER 1362, 1367.
[225] eg *National Home Loans Corp plc v Giffen, Couch and Archer* [1997] 3 All ER 808.
[226] per Sir Thomas Bingham MR, *Mortgage Express Ltd v Bowman* [1996] 2 All ER 836, 842. Although this case does not deal with personal information it is probably relevant to personal information.
[227] 'A solicitor is obliged to disclose information which comes into his possession in the course of doing the work which the lender has instructed him to do; but he is not obliged to disclose information which has come into his possession independently of any work which the lender has instructed him to do—including for example information which has come into his possession as a result of earlier transactions in which he has been retained by the borrower. To impose on a solicitor the obligation to inform the [lender] everything that he knows—including matters which he knows as a result of acting for the borrower in the past which might affect the lending decision . . . would in my view be oppressive and unrealistic.' [2000] Lloyd's Rep PN 788, 791. See also *Omega Trust Co Ltd v Wright Son and Peppe* [1998] PNLR 337, 348; *Nationwide Building Society v Balmer Radmore* [1999] Lloyd's Rep PN 241.
[228] [2002] EWCA Civ 723, paras 23, 48.

'I should have thought that it was the obligation of the solicitor to advise ... of any non-confidential matter relevant to the intended transaction of which he already knew.'[229] It has been held that information that strongly suggests fraud or some other serious crime must be disclosed even if acquired in an unconnected transaction.[230]

Consequences of failing to disclose material facts

19.62 Failure to disclose material facts to the client is actionable as a breach of contract[231] or as the tort of negligence.[232] If the omission is intentional it may be a breach of fiduciary duty. In *McKaskell v Benseman* clients had instructed a solicitor about a dispute with their neighbours. The neighbours' solicitor wrote a letter containing a gratuitously offensive remark about the clients to the solicitor who chose not to inform them of this to avoid making an inflammatory situation between neighbours worse. The neighbours' solicitor on request sent a substitute letter from which the offensive passage had been excised and the original letter was destroyed. When the clients learned of the offensive letter they brought an action against their solicitor for breach of fiduciary duty. Giving judgment for the clients, Jeffries J decided that the letter was not 'a trifling and insignificant detail' that could be legitimately held back and said:

> *The fiduciary must, in dealing with those to whom he owes such an obligation reveal fully all circumstances that might affect their affairs, and is thus under a duty of disclosure not imposed on others.* For whatever reasons, and notwithstanding the perceived detrimental consequences to the [claimants], the solicitors still were obliged to disclose to them the letter no matter what the consequences. . . . Lawyers, as well as other professional men, as part of their practice have to convey not infrequently to clients unwelcome, bad, and even at times, devastating information. The greatest care should always be taken on the occasion of such communication, but, nevertheless, it must be done. . . . This decision is reached in a climate whereby clients and patients of professional people have rights that must be recognized, and it may be because of that environment the proceedings have been brought. Twenty, or even 15 years ago the right to know and to be placed in a position to make an informed decision, and if necessary informed consent, about one's life were not as sharply developed as they now are. Professional men had greater scope to make decisions for people, which in a different milieu might have been acceptable even if done sometimes without knowledge or consent. Society has changed, and so must the law keep itself abreast of those changes.[233]

---

[229] per Sir Robert Morritt, *Hilton v Barker Booth & Eastwood* [2002] EWCA Civ 723, para 23.
[230] *Nationwide Building Society v Balmer Radmore* [1999] Lloyd's Rep PN 241.
[231] *Groom v Crocker* [1938] 2 All ER 394, 413.
[232] In *Groom v Crocker* [1938] 2 All ER 394 Scrutton LJ said that no action against a solicitor lay in tort except where there is fraud. This is no longer so: *Midland Bank Trust Co Ltd v Hett, Stubbs and Kemp (A Firm)* [1978] 3 All ER 571; *White v Jones* [1995] 1 All ER 691, 703.
[233] [1989] 3 NZLR 75, 87–88 (italics added).

B. Client's Right to Information

Solicitor's ethical disclosure obligations

19.63 Solicitors have an ethical as well as legal duties to keep their clients informed.[234] Law Society guidance recognizes exceptions where disclosure would be unlawful or an abuse of another lawyer's privilege over documents.[235] The Law Society's guidance further states that the duty to disclose material information may be excluded on therapeutic grounds where disclosure might harm the client's physical or mental state. Therapeutic privilege is recognized for doctors.[236] There is no firm legal authority that solicitors can avail themselves of a similar privilege but that they can is probable.[237] When in family proceedings a solicitor is instructed directly by a child whom she thinks would be damaged by being given material information, the solicitor can apply to a court for a non-disclosure direction.[238]

Disclosure by Professionals Not Owing Fiduciary Duties

The general position

19.64 Most professionals do not have a legal relationship of trust and confidence with their clients. The category that does not include doctors and other health professionals.[239] In *Western Home Counties Developments Ltd v Stone, Toms and Partners* O'Connor LJ rejected the claimant's contention that the defendant architects had breached a fiduciary obligation by their failure to disclose information.

> I reject the submission that [the architects] were in a fiduciary relationship with [the claimant]. They were under no separate duty to pass on information; their acts and obligations are to be judged by the ordinary standards applicable to professional men. That is the test which the judge applied and I can find no grounds for disturbing his conclusion that [the architects] were not guilty of negligence . . .[240]

---

[234] Law Society, *The Guide to the Professional Conduct of Solicitors* (8th edn, London: 1999) 331, 16.06. cp Solicitors' Practice (Costs Information and Client Care) Amendment Rule 1999, r 15; Solicitors' Cost Information and Client Care Code 1999. For a highly critical analysis of the guidance on disclosure see D Nicolson and J Webb, *Professional Legal Ethics* (Oxford: 1999) 138. No rules have been formulated with respect to barristers presumably because the solicitor is the main point of contact with the client.

[235] *The Guide to the Professional Conduct of Solicitors* (8th edn, London: 1999) 332, 16.06, para 6. Query: is there a disclosure obligation when the opponent's solicitor accidentally discloses privileged materials during pre-trial disclosure if these probably cannot be used in the litigation (see paras 6.108 et seq above)?

[236] See para 19.68 below.

[237] In litigation disclosure can be limited to the client's legal advisers: see paras 17.02 and 17.04 above. The privilege claimed by the Law Society for solicitors is comparable to that contained in Data Protection (Subject Access Modification) (Social Work) Order 2000, SI 2000/415, r 5.

[238] cp *Re M* [1994] 1 FLR 760.

[239] See paras 5.80 amd 19.15 above.

[240] (CA, 19 March 1984.)

Chapter 19: Disclosure to the Client

To avoid breaching a tortious duty of care *at the very least* [241] the professional must meet accepted standards of disclosure in her own profession.[242] If the professional–client relationship is a contractual one, express or implied[243] promises of disclosure must be satisfied. Any statutory provision requiring the client to be given information about himself must also be complied with. There are, for example, health and safety at work regulations that require medical information to be given to workers.[244]

Doctors[245]

19.65 A doctor must provide the patient with information about the nature and risk of prospective treatment. If she does not, the patient is injured by the treatment and would not have agreed to the procedure had proper disclosure been made, the doctor will be liable in negligence.[246] The law about what the patient must be told is still evolving.[247] In the context of diagnosis and treatment McNair J said in *Bolam v Friern Hospital Management Committee*:

> A doctor is not guilty of negligence if he has acted in accordance with a practice accepted as proper by a responsible body of medical men skilled in that particular art . . . merely because there is a body of opinion that takes a contrary view.[248]

This 'reasonable practitioner' test was applied by the House of Lords in *Sidaway v Bethlem Royal Hospital Governors*[249] to a decision not to warn a patient of a very

---

[241] While there is a marked (but waning) tendency to defer to accepted practice amongst doctors in establishing standards of reasonable conduct (see *Bolam v Friern Hospital Management Committee* [1957] 2 All ER 118 and main text below), the courts are less inclined to defer to accepted standards in other professions. In *Johnson v Bingley* [1997] PNLR 392, a negligence case involving a solicitor, B Hytner sitting as a Deputy High Court Judge said: '[the *Bolam*] test arose out of an action for medical negligence. Such actions are, in my view, *sui generis*; it is difficult to envisage circumstances in which a practice followed by a substantial number of skilled and experienced surgeons would be held to be a negligent one, albeit that a greater number of surgeons follow a different practice. However, such is not the case in industrial accidents—see: *Morris v West Hartlepool Steam Navigation Co Ltd* [1956] 1 All ER 385, nor in solicitor's negligence cases.' See also para 3.47 above.

[242] An action in negligence will not, however, succeed unless tangible injury can be traced by the client to the breach of the disclosure obligation. cp para 19.65 below.

[243] Two important considerations would be whether an obligation to disclose information is necessary to give efficacy to the contract and what is customary in the particular profession. cp para 4.05 above.

[244] D Kloss, *Occupational Health Law* (3rd edn, Oxford: 1988) 78–79.

[245] For the most recent DoH guidance see *Reference Guide to Consent for Examination or Treatment* (2001) paras 5.1–5.6 where the case law and GMC guidelines are summarized.

[246] For the patient, establishing a causal link between the failure to warn, or to warn adequately, of the risks and the injury suffered may be difficult: *Chester v Afshar* [2002] EWCA Civ 724, [2002] 3 All ER 552.

[247] HGC, *Inside Information* (May 2002) para 3.9. For a recently published detailed analysis of the cases see J Mason, R McCall Smith and G Laurie, *Law and Medical Ethics* (6th edn, London: Butterworths, 2002) 354 et seq.

[248] *Bolam v Friern Hospital Management Committee* [1957] 2 All ER 118.

[249] [1985] 1 All ER 643, 652. See also *Gold v Haringey Health Authority* [1987] 2 All ER 888.

B. Client's Right to Information

small risk of very serious injury. The doctor was exonerated of negligent failure to inform because he had done what a substantial body of responsible medical opinion would have done in the circumstances.[250]

The courts have begun a retreat from the *Bolam* test in cases involving allegations of negligent diagnosis and treatment. If a medical practice cannot withstand logical analysis it is no answer that it is approved by a respected body of medical opinion.[251] In cases of allegedly negligent disclosure, an approach that is more respectful of patient autonomy[252] is also emerging.[253] The standard by which the doctor is judged is shifting from what a reasonable doctor would do to what a reasonable patient might expect.[254] The HRA should cement this trend because the Article 8 right to 'respect for private life is plainly engaged'.[255]   **19.66**

In *Pearce v United Bristol Healthcare NHS Trust*[256] Lord Woolf said the patient must normally be informed of any significant (not necessarily life-threatening) risk which would affect the judgment of a reasonable patient regardless of customary professional practice.[257] If a risk is insignificant, the doctor must still give an honest answer to an inquisitive patient who asks about it. The latest GMC guidance states   **19.67**

> You must respond honestly to any questions the patient raises and, as far as possible, answer as fully as the patient wishes.... Some patients may want to know whether any of the risks or benefits of treatment are affected by the choice of institution or doctor providing the care. You must answer such questions as fully, accurately and objectively as possible.[258]

---

[250] The GMC's guidance on providing information to patients is some evidence of professional practice. cp *Airedale NHS Trust v Bland* [1993] 1 All ER 821, 872. The guidance in *Seeking patients' consent: the ethical considerations* (London: 2000) 3 is very general and therefore unhelpful for specific cases.

[251] *Bolitho v City and Hackney Health Authority* [1997] 4 All ER 771, 770; *Calver v Westwood Veterinary Group* [2001] Lloyd's Rep Med 20.

[252] *Chester v Afshar* [2002] EWCA Civ 724; [2002] 3 All ER 552, para 47.

[253] A Plomer, 'Medical Research, Consent and the European Convention on Human Rights and Biomedicine' in A Garwood-Gowers, J Tingle and T Lewis (eds), *Healthcare Law: The Impact of the Human Rights Act 1998* (London: 2001) 321. cp *Sidaway v Bethlem Royal Hospital Governors* [1985] 1 All ER 643, 663.

[254] L Skene and R Smallwood, 'Informed consent: lessons from Australia' (2002) 324 British Medical J 39 referring to *Smith v Tunbridge Wells Health Authority* [1994] MLR 334 and *Pearce v United Bristol Healthcare NHS Trust* (1998) 48 BMLR 118. See also DoH, *Reference Guide to Consent for Examination or Treatment* (2001) para 5, available at http://www.doh.gov.uk/consent/refguide.pdf. The shift in these cases toward the reasonable patient perspective is viewed with caution by J Montgomery, *Health Care Law* (2nd edn, Oxford: 2002) 242 et seq.

[255] S Sedley, 'Information as a Human Right' in J Beatson and Y Cripps (eds), *Freedom of Expression and Freedom of Information: Essays in Honour of Sir David Williams* (Oxford: 2000) 248.

[256] (1998) 48 BMLR 118.

[257] This is similar to the test adopted by the High Court of Australia in *Rogers v Whitaker* (1992) 175 CLR 479, 490. Note the distinction between (1) diagnosis and treatment, and (2) provision of information to the patient.

[258] GMC, *Seeking patients' consent: the ethical considerations* (2000) 6.

A patient's signature on a hospital consent form does not prevent the patient later complaining that the doctor negligently failed to provide adequate information. Skene and Millwood argue that this is so '[e]ven if the form states that the patient acknowledges that he or she has been fully informed and given the opportunity to ask questions'.[259]

Information that does not have to be disclosed

19.68 The GMC does not require doctors to disclose information where 'disclosure of some relevant information would cause the patient serious harm'.[260] This is supported by case law and legislation.[261] It is not a breach of Article 8 to keep medical information from a patient which it would be harmful for the patient to know.[262] The GMC's guidance about seeking consent does not allow doctors to withhold information for fear of upsetting the patient or because the patient might decide to refuse treatment.[263] Serious harm means just that. If relatives ask that information be withheld from the patient, GMC guidelines instruct the doctor to seek the views of the patient.[264]

19.69 A doctor has no legal obligation to disclose information to the patient that is not material to the patient's diagnosis and treatment but might be of interest to the patient—unless, of course, a contract says otherwise. There is, therefore, no obligation on a doctor to tell a patient that the police have made inquiries about him.

19.70 In an emergency[265] a doctor can give treatment without giving the patient information and without obtaining the patient's consent. This is justified by a principle of necessity.[266]

---

[259] L Skene and S Millwood, '"Informed Consent" to Medical Procedures: The Current Law in Australia, Doctors' Knowledge of the Law and their practices in Informing Patients' in L Shotton (ed), *Health Care Law and Ethics* (Katoomba: 1997) 78.
[260] GMC, *Seeking patients' consent: the ethical considerations* (London: 2000) 6–7.
[261] *Sidaway v Bethlem Royal Hospital Governors* [1985] 1 All ER 643; *Rogers v Whitaker* (1992) 175 CLR 479, 486, 490, but see 494; *R (on the appication of Wooder) v Feggetter* [2002] EWCA Civ 554; [2002] 3 WLR 591, para 30; Data Protection (Subject Access Modification) (Health) Order 2000, SI 2000/413, r 5(1). cp Mental Health Review Tribunal Rules 1983, SI 1983/942, r 12(2); Access to Medical Reports Act 1988, s 7(1).
[262] *Martin v UK* (1996) 21 EHRR CD 112, 115.
[263] cp *Battersby v Tottman* (1985) 37 SASR 524.
[264] GMC, *Seeking patients' consent: the ethical considerations* (London: 2000) 7.
[265] The courts have not had occasion to define what constitutes an emergency. Does it extend beyond life-threatening situations?
[266] J Mason, R McCall Smith and G Laurie, *Medical Ethics* (6th edn, London: Butterworths, 2002) 312 et seq. See also para 13.11 above.

B. Client's Right to Information

Higher education

19.71 In some circumstances, for example higher education, non-disclosure of personal information to a client may raise a public law issue of procedural fairness[267] which can be raised in a public law action.[268] In *R v University of Cambridge, ex p Persaud* the applicant challenged the refusal of the University to disclose to her reports by her academic supervisor and a senior academic[269] about her PhD research before removing her name from the register of graduate students. Maurice Kay J said:

> There are sound and obvious reasons why reports to those who have to make academic judgments . . . should remain confidential thus enabling the reporters to express themselves frankly in the knowledge that what they have to say will not be made available to the subjects of the reports.[270]

Although the Court of Appeal subsequently disagreed with the judge's conclusion that the University of Cambridge had acted fairly, it approved of this aspect of the judgment. Chadwick LJ said:

> I would accept that there is no principle of fairness which requires, as a general rule, that a person should be entitled to challenge, or make representations with a view to changing, a purely academic judgment on his or her work or potential. But each case must be examined on its own facts. On a true analysis, this case is not . . . a challenge to academic judgment.[271]

The University of Cambridge's unfairness was found to lie in its refusal to disclose to her the identity of the senior academic who had reviewed the viability of her PhD research project so that she could raise any concerns that she might have about his impartiality and expertise and in not warning her that her project was no longer regarded as having the potential to merit the award of a PhD so that she could make representations on this point.

---

[267] Where a public law requirement of procedural fairness applies, its contents in any particular case 'depends on the character of the decision making body, the nature of the decision which it has to make and the regulatory framework (if any) within which it is required to operate', per Chadwick LJ, *R v University of Cambridge, ex p Persaud* [2001] EWCA Civ 534; [2001] ELR 480, para 33.
[268] All public law remedies are discretionary.
[269] The relationship between the senior academic and the PhD student is not a professional–client relationship within the definition adopted in ch 1.
[270] *R v University of Cambridge, ex p Persaud* [2001] ELR 64, QB, para 23.
[271] [2001] EWCA Civ. 534; [2001] ELR 480, para 41.

C. Records and Information Relating to Minors

Access to Records

Data Protection Act 1998

The competent child

19.72 There is no minimum age for the exercise of subject access rights under DPA, s 7;[272] a competent child may apply for access to his own records without parental consent. The Information Commissioner's legal advice to data controllers is that they must 'judge whether the child understands the nature of the request. If the child understands, he or she is entitled to exercise the right'.[273] The Access to Health Records Act 1990, which the DPA has substantially replaced, allowed a person with parental responsibility to apply for access to medical records on behalf of a child,[274] but if the child was sufficiently mature to make the application the child's consent to the parental application was required.[275] This is not replicated in the DPA. The Data Protection (Subject Access Modification) (Health) Order 2000 allows a child to expressly forbid disclosure of his medical record to a person who has parental responsibility for him.[276] This is not exactly the same as requiring the professional to obtain consent from a *Gillick* competent[277] child every time a parent applies to see his medical records, but this interpretation is widely placed on the provision.[278]

The incompetent child

19.73 **Voluntary disclosure**   SARs are irrelevant if a professional agrees voluntarily to disclose information about a child to the parent. No breach of confidence is involved because the professional can act on a parent's proxy consent. This still leaves the problem of finding a condition for processing the data under Sch 2[279] and (in the case of sensitive personal data) Sch 3 to the DPA.[280] This cannot be the consent of the data subject[281] unless proxy consent is consent for this purpose because the data subject (the child) lacks the capacity to consent.[282] Accepting

---

[272] See para 19.21 above.
[273] IC, *Data Protection Act 1998—legal guidance* 4.1.6.
[274] Access to Health Records Act 1990, s 3(1)(c).
[275] ibid, s 4(2)(a).
[276] SI 2000/413, r 5(3)(c). Is this right restricted to the *Gillick* competent minor?
[277] See para 13.13 above.
[278] Department of Health, *Data Protection Guidance to Social Services* (March 2000) para 5.9 and the *Draft DPA Code of Practice for Social Services* (1999) para 11.4, available at http://www.interface-associates.ltd.uk/SSIMG/docs/DPA_CoPSS/copss.htm.
[279] See paras 18.18 et seq.
[280] See para 18.25 above.
[281] DPA, Sch 2, para 1; Sch 3, para 1.
[282] DPA, Sch 3, para 3 envisages situations in which consent is given on behalf of the data subject, but presumably that means by someone who is competent to consent.

C. Records and Information Relating to Minors

proxy consent involves reading 'the data subject'[283] as 'the data subject or the person with parental responsibility for the data subject'. For non-sensitive personal data this can be avoided by the parent claiming that disclosure was necessary to pursue the parent's own legitimate interests.[284] If the personal data is sensitive data, the parent might argue that is 'necessary for the purposes of . . . exercising . . . legal [ie parental] rights'[285] or for exercising functions conferred under an enactment.[286] In matters of life and death, the parent can rely on the condition that processing is necessary 'to protect the vital interests of the data subject or another person in a case where . . . consent cannot be given by or on behalf of the data subject'.[287]

Exercise of subject access rights DPA, s 7 entitles 'an individual' to be informed by the data controller whether personal data 'of which that individual is the data subject'[288] is being processed, to be given details of the processing and to have communicated 'to him'[289] 'the information constituting any personal data of which the individual is the data subject'. The assumption is always that the applicant is the data subject which in this instance is the child. Stern argues that s 7 can be construed in two ways: (1) that only a competent data subject can access records, or (2) that records may be requested by anyone but only the data subject (the child) may receive them.[290]

19.74

Neither interpretation makes sense. The first interpretation means that a parent has no right of access to the records of an incompetent child. Arguably, this is an unjustifiable interference with the parent's Article 8 right to respect for family life. The second interpretation is illogical and cannot have been intended by Parliament. Just imagine if the data subject were six months old! The Information Commissioner's Legal Guidance says that 'if the child does not understand the nature of the request' the parent 'is entitled to make the request on behalf of the child *and to receive the response*'.[291] The best way forward is for the words 'an individual' to be interpreted as meaning 'an individual or the person with parental responsibility for that individual'. To a large extent the issue is academic because a responsible professional is only going to resist access to a child's records by a

19.75

---

[283] DPA, Sch 2, para 1; Schedule 3 para 1.
[284] DPA, Sch 2, para 6.
[285] DPA, Sch 3, para 6(c).
[286] DPA, Sch 3, para 7(b) relying on Children Act 1989, ss 2, 3.
[287] DPA, Sch 3, para 3; *Data Protection Act 1998—legal guidance* 3.1.1. On the interpretation of 'vital interests' see para 18.20 above.
[288] DPA, s 7(1)(a).
[289] DPA, s 7(1)(c).
[290] K Stern, 'Confidentiality and Medical Records' in A Grubb (ed.), *Principles of Medical Law* (4th cumulative supplement, Oxford: 2001) 104.
[291] *Data Protection Act 1998—legal guidance* 4.1.6. See also DoH, *Data Protection Guidance to Social Services* (March 2000) para 5.9.

parent if she thinks that disclosure is against the child's best interests. If the court agrees with this assessment it will find a way of denying the parent SARs.[292]

Exceptions to parental access

19.76 The parent should be refused access to a child's records under the DPA

(1) if any of the DPA exemptions applies;[293]
(2) in the case of an educational record,[294] to information about the child's exposure to abuse where this would not be in the child's best interests, or where access would be likely to cause serious harm to the physical or mental health of the child or a third party;[295]
(3) in the case of a health or social work record, if information was provided by the child in the expectation that it would not be disclosed to the parent, if the child expressly indicates that the information should not be disclosed to the parent, or if parental access would cause serious harm to the physical or mental health of the child;[296]
(4) if the child is dead;[297]
(5) to certain court reports.[298]

19.77 Apart from these specific statutory exceptions which are based either on legislation or precedent, it seems likely that a court would allow any professional to withhold access to information when there is a risk that disclosure will be seriously detrimental to the child's health or welfare.[299] Disclosure of the child's address when disclosure carries a significant risk of kidnapping might be an example.

---

[292] cp para 19.77 below.
[293] See paras 19.28 et seq above. Grounds of exemption include identification of a third party who supplied information or, in the case of health and social work records, risk of serious harm to the physical or mental health or condition of the child.
[294] See Education (Pupil Information) (England) Regulations 2000, SI 2000/297.
[295] Data Protection (Subject Access Modification) (Education) Order 2000, SI 2000/414, r 7. Reports about child abuse may be made available to the child's parents at a child protection conference: Dfes, Circular 10/95 *Protecting Children from Abuse: The Role of the Education Service,* esp para 28. See also para 19.89 below.
[296] Data Protection (Subject Access Modification) (Health) Order 2000, SI 2000/413, r 5; Data Protection (Subject Access Modification) (Social Work) Order 2000, SI 2000/415, r 5. See para 19.89 below.
[297] *R (on the application of Addinell) v Sheffield City Council* [2001] ACD 61. The DPA applies to living individuals only.
[298] See para 19.42 above.
[299] cp *R (on the application of Stevens) v Plymouth City Council* [2002] EWCA Civ 388; [2002] 1 FLR 1177, paras 30, 49. The *Draft Code of Practice on the Data Protection Act and Personal Information for the Social Services* (1999) para 11.4 states that 'where the child has insufficient intellectual capacity to give informed consent, staff will provide parents . . . as much information as they judge to be consonant with the welfare of the child and will not result in severe harm to the child or any third party'. The Draft Code is available at: http://www.interfaceassociates.ltd.uk/SSIMG/-docs/DPA_CoPSS/copss.htm.

C. Records and Information Relating to Minors

19.78 If one parent seeks access to a child's records, there is no statutory obligation to inform the other though this is sometimes done if the parents are separated.[300] A natural father without parental responsibility for the child has no right of access to the child's non-educational records without a specific issue[301] order from a court.

Educational records

19.79 Under the Education (Pupil Information) (England) Regulations 2000 a 'parent' of a pupil under the age of 18 who is attending a maintained school has a right to see the pupil's official educational record unless this right has been removed by a court order.[302] A parent is defined in Education Act 1996, s 576 to include all natural parents, any person who has parental responsibility for a minor and any person who, although not a natural parent, has care of a minor such as a foster parent. In some situations there will be numerous persons with parental rights of access to the child's records. For example, the grandparents with whom the child is living and the child's natural parents.[303]

19.80 The head teacher must disclose the education record, and if requested, supply a copy, within 15 days of receiving a written request.[304] An educational record is defined as being any record of information about a pupil which is processed by or on behalf of the governing body or a teacher, other than information processed by a teacher solely for the teacher's own use.[305] It should contain results of school tests, school reports and copies of correspondence concerning the pupil.

19.81 The head teacher must not supply material:

(1) whose disclosure would be likely to cause serious harm to the physical or mental health or condition of the pupil or someone else;[306]
(2) concerning exposure to child abuse when this is not in the child's best interests;[307]
(3) which might reveal information about someone other than the pupil to which the request relates (including the identity of sources other than the access applicant).[308]

---

[300] BMA, *Consent, Rights and Choices in Health Care for Children and Young Persons* (London: 2000) 84.
[301] Children Act 1989, s 8(1).
[302] SI 2000/297. A parent's right to information may be restricted by a prohibited steps order issued under Children Act 1989, s 8(1).
[303] DfEE, *Schools, 'Parents' and 'Parental Responsibility'* (June 2000).
[304] Education (Pupil Information) (England) Regulations 2000, SI 2000/297, r 5. Inspection is to be allowed free of charge. A charge, not exceeding the actual cost of supply, may be made for a copy.
[305] ibid, r 3(1).
[306] ibid, r 3(1). See also para 19.76 above.
[307] Education (Pupil Information) (England) Regulations 2000, SI 2000/297. See also para 19.76 above.
[308] DPA s 7(4) as modified by Data Protection (Subject Access Modification) (Education) Order 2000, SI 2000/414, r 7. See para 19.32 above.

19.82 A pupil under the age of 18 is unable to prevent his parents exercising their statutory right of access to the educational record. Though the regulation does not say so, the parent's right of access to the educational record must cease on the pupil's eighteenth birthday.[309] It would be impossible to defend non-consensual disclosure of the record to the parent of a mentally competent pupil over 18 if challenged as being an infringement of Article 8. Significantly, the Education (Pupil Information) (England) Regulations 2000 do not cover further education colleges.

Right to Information

Parents

School information

19.83 By the Education (Pupil Information) (England) Regulations 2000 the head teacher of a maintained school has to make available to a parent[310] of every pupil under 18[311] before the end of the summer term of each school year free of charge[312] a written report of the pupil's educational achievements.[313] The regulations specify that the report must provide information about the pupil's general progress, the pupil's progress in all subjects and activities studied, the pupil's attendance record and the results of any public examinations taken.[314] The head teacher has a discretion to include more information and to issue more than one report a year.[315] The obligation of the school does not end with the report. Parents must be notified of arrangements to discuss its contents with a teacher. There is no duty to supply a parent with a report about a pupil who is an adult[316] and no report is sent to a parent about a pupil who is above compulsory schooling age[317] and is proposing to leave school or has left.[318] Instead the pupil is provided with a school leaver's report setting out his educational achievements.[319]

---

[309] Under previous regulations the parent did not have access to the education record once the pupil attained 18. The DfEE says that the new regulations were not intended to change this. But see Education (Pupil Information) England Regulations 2000, SI 2000/297, r 6(2)(a) which gives the head teacher a discretion to send a report to the parents of a pupil over the age of 18 in 'special circumstances'.

[310] As defined in Education Act 1996, s 576 and discussed above in the main text.

[311] Except those attending nursery school.

[312] Education (Pupil Information) (England) (Amendment) Regulations 2001, SI 2001/1212, r 4.

[313] ibid, r 6(1), (2)(b). A commitment to provide parents with information about their child's progress at least once a year is included in the *Parent's Charter* (1991).

[314] Education (Pupil Information) (England) Regulations 2000, SI 2000/297, Sch 1.

[315] ibid, r 6(7).

[316] ibid, r 6(2)(a).

[317] A pupil ceases to be of compulsory school age on the last Friday in June in the school year in which the pupil attains the age of 16.

[318] Education (Pupil Information) (England) Regulations 2000, SI 2000/297, r 6(3).

[319] ibid, r 9.

C. Records and Information Relating to Minors

General

Apart from the statutory right to receive school reports, what rights do parents have to information about their children? Whether a natural parent or not, anyone who has parental responsibility[320] for a child has a right to be included in decisions about the child's upbringing and, consequently, must be legally entitled to receive information needed for this purpose. The DPA is no obstacle to disclosure of non-sensitive personal information about the child, whatever the child's age, because the parent has a legitimate interest in the information.[321]

19.84

Normally a professional does not have to provide information about a child to a natural parent who does not have parental responsibility for the child. Unusually, because the broad definition of parent in Education Act 1996, s 576 includes natural parents and carers, schools must share information with a natural parent without legal responsibility for the child unless a court order disallows this.[322] A natural parent without parental authority has a right to be consulted by a local authority about decisions taken in relation to the child where a local authority is accommodating the child.[323] It follows that social workers must provide the relevant information.

19.85

Practical problems about the disclosure of information by a professional to a parent about a child tend to arise when:

19.86

- the professional thinks that it is not in the child's best interests to release information to a parent; *or*
- the child does not want information to be given to a parent.

Withholding information from parents

The best interests of the child The legal and natural parent's right to information about a child is subject to the principle that the child's welfare is the paramount concern:[324]

19.87

---

[320] Parental responsibility is defined in Children Act 1989, s 3 to mean the rights, duties, powers, responsibilities and authority which by law are vested in a parent in relation to a child and the child's property. Parental responsibility for a child vests automatically in the mother (s 2) and, if she is married, her husband. Parental responsibility can be withdrawn by a court. The natural father of a child may acquire parental responsibility by various means (s 4). Someone who is not a natural parent may obtain parental responsibility by adoption, guardianship, a residence order or being named in an emergency protection order. A number of people may have parental responsibility for a child as may a local authority. The Adoption and Children Act 2002, s 111, which is not yet in force, amends the law regarding acquisition of parental responsibility by unmarried fathers. For a step-parent see s 112.

[321] Sch 2, para 6. For sensitive personal data see para 19.73 above.

[322] DfEE guidance, 'Schools, "parents" and "parental responsibility"' (June 2000) para 12, available from http://www.fnf.org.uk/dfee.htm.

[323] Children Act 1989, s 22(4). See further A Bainham, *Children: The Modern Law* (2nd edn, Bristol: 1998) 159.

[324] cp Access to Health Records Act 1990, s 4(2).

> Once the rule of the parents' absolute authority over minor children is abandoned, the solution to the problem . . . can no longer be found by referring to rigid parental rights at any particular age. The solution depends on a judgment of what is best for the welfare of the particular child.[325]

If a child reveals sexual abuse or neglect by a parent, disclosing the allegation to the parents may endanger the child. In these and other circumstances in which disclosure is not in the child's best interests (physically or psychologically) a doctor[326] can withhold information from the parent.[327] If the parent invokes Article 8(1), the professional can argue that non-disclosure is necessary for 'the protection of health and morals' and 'the protection of the rights and freedoms of others'.[328]

19.88 Predicting the circumstances in which a court would hold that disclosure is not in the child's best interests is fraught with difficulty. Suppose that genetic testing of a child shows unexpectedly that the child's legal father is not the natural father. Should this information be suppressed?[329] There is on-going debate as to whether a child should be told a genetic test outcome such as that he has the gene for a debilitating late onset genetic disorder, and whether the parents have the right to this information if the child, when old enough to choose, might not wish to know.[330]

19.89 It is probable that any discretion that a health professional has to withhold information is shared with all professionals.[331] It makes no sense to allow a school

---

[325] per Lord Fraser, *Gillick v West Norfolk and Wisbech Area Health Authority* [1985] 3 All ER 402, 412. See also *Re Z* [1995] 4 All ER 961, 984–985. The jurisprudence on the ECHR also puts the welfare of the child ahead of the interests of the parents. On this point see the judgment of Thorpe LJ, *Payne v Payne* [2001] 1 FLR 1052, para 38; *Re C* [2002] NI Fam 14, para 2 citing *Sahin v Germany* [2002] 1 FLR 119.

[326] cp *Re DH* [1994] FLR 679 where Wall J said that there were circumstances in which a doctor could carry out covert video surveillance without parental consent if abuse was suspected. GMC, *Seeking patient's consent: the ethical considerations* (London: 2000) 14 sets out criteria by which to decide what is in the best interests of a patient who lacks capacity to decide.

[327] Data Protection (Subject Access Modification) (Education) Order 2000, SI 2000/414, r 5(2) and Data Protection (Subject Access Modification) (Health) Order 2000, SI 2000/413, r 5(1) offer statutory analogies. See also *TP v UK* (2002) 34 EHRR 2, para 80.

[328] Art 8(2): see para 3.19 above.

[329] A Lucassen and M Parker, 'Revealing false paternity: some ethical considerations' (2001) 357 (9261) The Lancet 1033. They note that in 1994 the Committee on Assessing Genetic Risks in the Institute of Medicine in the US recommended that only the woman should be informed of a finding of false paternity to avoid genetic testing disrupting families. Query: what if failure to disclose will have an adverse effect on the father's future reproductive choices?

[330] 'A milestone in genetics: A nightmare for privacy', *Privacy Laws and Business International Newsletter*, May 2001.

[331] This is implicitly acknowledged in the latest Dfee guidance that covers disclosure of underage sexual activity by pupils to teachers: *Sex and Relationship Education Guidance* (July 2000) 0116/2000, para 7.2, available from http://www.dfee.gov.uk. Parents are not permitted to have access to an education record in so far as it discloses exposure to child abuse: Data Protection (Subject Access Modification) (Education) Order 2000, SI 2000/414, r 5. cp *R (on the application of Stevens) v Plymouth City Council* [2002] EWCA Civ 388; [2002] 1 FLR 1177, paras 30, 49.

C. Records and Information Relating to Minors

nurse or doctor to keep a female pupil's under-age sexual activity from the parents if she thinks that the parents might harm the girl if they found out but deny the girl's teacher the same discretion to withhold information. The discretion to suppress information in the child's best interests is additional to the statutory right to withhold access under DPA, s 7 to health, education and social work records where access is likely to cause serious harm to the child[332] or, in the case of health and social work records, where the child had provided information on the understanding that it would not be made known to the parents and has not expressly consented to disclosure.[333] It is possible that professionals may have a *duty* to withhold information about a child from a parent if disclosure carries a real risk of serious harm to the child.[334]

Remedies if information is wrongly withheld   What can the parent do if a professional refuses to divulge information about a minor to which the parent believes he is entitled? A specific issue order under the Children Act 1989[335] might be the solution but the information would have to relate to an aspect of parental responsibility for the child. It would, for example, do so if the application were designed to compel a social worker to divulge the whereabouts of a run-away child. It would then fall to the court to decide whether it was in the child's best interests for the parent to be informed of the child's whereabouts. If the information does not concern parental responsibility the options are to try to invoke the inherent jurisdiction of the High Court or to seek a disclosure order in wardship proceedings. The former would put the whole of the child's life under the court's control.   19.90

In *R (on the application of Addinell) v Sheffield City Council*[336] a father challenged the decision of Sheffield City Council not to give him access to the social service records of his son who, while in local authority care, had died aged about 17. The court rejected the father's argument that the right to respect for family life guaranteed under Article 8(1) of the European Convention on Human Rights (ECHR) imposed a positive obligation on the state through legislation, or failing that, the common law to allow him access to information about his son. Sullivan J pointed out that Article 8(1) gave his dead son a right to privacy too. *Gaskin v UK*[337] was distinguished as being about 'an individual who had been in care [and] was seeking *his own records* so that he could better understand *his own*   19.91

---

[332] See para 19.76 above.
[333] Data Protection (Subject Access Modification) (Health) Order 2000, SI 2000/413, r 5(2); Data Protection (Subject Access Modification) (Social Work) Order 2000, SI 2000/414, r 5(2); see para 19.76 above.
[334] cp *R v Registrar General, ex p Smith* [1990] 2 All ER 170, 174 where the Registrar General's statutory duty to provide a person with information to enable him to obtain a birth certificate was subject on public policy grounds to a duty to withhold the information where providing it would give risk to a real risk of serious danger to a member of the public.
[335] s 8(1).
[336] [2000] ACD 61.
[337] (1989) 12 EHRR 36; see para 19.19 above.

circumstances'.[338] Whether or not the *Sheffield City Council* Case was rightly decided,[339] it is not of universal application.

19.92 In *TP v UK* a video of an interview by a psychiatrist of a child of 4 who was suspected of having been sexually abused was kept from the child's mother on the grounds of medical confidentiality even though the woman's boyfriend, the prime suspect, had been shown the video. The ECtHR said that it was '... essential that a parent be placed in a position where he or she may obtain access to information which is relied on by the authorities in taking measures of protective care' save 'where disclosure of a child's statements may place that child at risk'.[340] Further, the state's positive obligation 'to protect the interests of the family required the information to be made available to the parent concerned, even in the absence of any request by the parent. If there were doubts as to whether this posed a risk to the welfare of the child'[341] the matter should be submitted to a court to resolve. The *TP* and *Sheffield City Council* decisions together suggest that any right that a natural parent may have to information from a public authority about a child deriving from Article 8(1) depends upon many factors including the age of the child, the reason that the information is wanted[342] and the consequences for the child.

Ability of child to veto disclosure to parents

19.93 Can a child who receives professional help, stop the professional from disclosing this fact to the parents or stop the professional passing on to the parents information acquired in the child–professional relationship? In other words, has the child vis-à-vis its parent(s) any rights of confidentiality?

> A teenage girl fell off her bike and is admitted to hospital with a head injury. Her parents ask what reason she gave for the accident. Should the doctor tell the parents that she has been drinking despite the child's insistence that they not be told?[343]

Medical confidentiality and minors[344]

19.94 The cases and literature on the issue of confidentiality and minors are almost exclusively concerned with the doctor–patient relationship.[345] That a doctor owes

---

[338] per Sullivan J, ibid, para 12 (italics added).
[339] cp GMC advice mentioned in para 19.97 below regarding information about the death of a child.
[340] *TM v UK* (2002) 34 EHRR 2, para 80.
[341] ibid, para 82.
[342] cp *R (on the application of Stevens) v Plymouth City Council* [2002] EWCA Civ 388; [2002] 1 FLR 1177, para 46.
[343] P Jeffreys, 'Consent to medical Treatment', 11 July 2001, available at http://www.elderabuse.org.uk/documents/mencapconference/jeffreys%20presentation.ppt.
[344] J Montgomery, *Health Care Law* (2nd edn, Oxford: 2002) 308–311.
[345] For comments on disclosure of abuse by a solicitor see A Cleland, 'Dilemmas posed by young clients' (1998) 43 J of the L Society of Scotland 27, 28 and for disclosure of under-age sexual activity by a teacher see N Harris (ed), *Children, Sex Education and the Law* (London: 1996) particularly the essays by Bridgeman (ch 3) and Thomson (ch 6).

an obligation of confidentiality to a child-patient[346]—even to a brain-damaged severely handicapped baby—is not in any doubt.[347] Capacity on the part of the client to enter into the professional relationship and to understand confidentiality as a concept[348] are not necessary for an obligation of confidentiality to arise. 'The duty of confidence may arise in equity independently of a transaction or relationship between parties.'[349]

The mature child: disclosing medical information A competent child is one who is able to understand fully what is involved in a proposed course of action.[350] The competent child can consent to the disclosure of confidential information[351] but it does not necessarily follow that the child can veto disclosure of information to a parent. It is impossible to say whether or not the competent child has a power of veto because the judiciary has not spoken with one voice. The only thing one can be absolutely confident about is that when doctor and competent child agree that it is for the best that the parents should *not* be informed, the doctor can lawfully withhold information from the parent.   **19.95**

The leading authority, and cause of the confusion, is *Gillick v West Norfolk and Wisbech Area Health Authority*.[352] In this case the House of Lords was asked to consider Department of Health guidelines that permitted a doctor to give contraceptive advice to a girl under 16 without the knowledge of the girl's parents. A majority[353] of Law Lords held those guidelines were lawful but different reasons were given. Lord Fraser was of the opinion that if a child was competent the doctor had neither a legal duty to disclose information to the parents nor to withhold it.[354] The doctor had to do whatever was in the child's best interests.[355] Lord Scarman, on the other hand, was of the opinion that parents lose the right to determine whether or not a young person receives medical treatment, and with it   **19.96**

---

[346] BMA, *Consent, Rights and Choices in Health Care for Children and Young People* (London: 2000) 79–80.

[347] *Re C (A Minor)(Wardship: Medical Treatment)(No2)* [1989] 2 All ER 791; *Re Z (A Minor) (Identification Restrictions on Publication)* [1995] 4 All ER 961, 979; *Venables v NGN* [2001] 1 All ER 908, para 103.

[348] Children grasp the concept of confidentiality somewhere between the ages of 12 and 15 years: D Joseph and J Onek, 'Confidentiality in psychiatry' in S Block, P Chodoff and S Green (eds), *Psychiatric Ethics* (3rd edn, New York: 1999) 126.

[349] per Butler-Sloss P, *Venables v NGN* [2001] 1 All ER 908, para 81. See also ch 6.

[350] *Gillick v West Norfolk and Wisbech Area Health Authority* [1985] 3 All ER 402, 423.

[351] See paras 13.13 et seq.

[352] [1985] 3 All ER 402.

[353] The main majority judgments were delivered by Lord Fraser and by Lord Scarman. Lord Bridge, [1985] 3 All ER 402, 428 agreed with the reasons of both.

[354] In 1971 the GMC dismissed a charge against a family doctor who revealed to the father of his 16-year-old patient that she had been prescribed an oral contraceptive by a family planning organization: The Times, 6, 8 March 1971.

[355] [1985] 3 All ER 402, 413. This could be rationalized as an application of the public interest exception (see ch 11) to confidentiality: cp I Kennedy and A Grubb, *Medical Law* (3rd edn, London: 2000) 1079.

any right to the disclosure of confidential information, when the child has sufficient maturity to make up his own mind.[356] This age will vary from child to child.

19.97 Consistent with Lord Scarman's view, but not Lord Fraser's, the British Medical Association's (BMA's) advice to doctors in *Confidentiality and People under Sixteen*[357] is that mature children can forbid disclosure of confidential information to parents[358] unless silence puts someone else at risk. Guidance to pharmacists by the Royal Pharmaceutical Society states that pharmacists should not normally disclose information about medicines supplied to teenage children to their parents.[359] The GMC, however, requires doctors to explain to parents the reasons for, and circumstances of, the death of a child under 16.[360]

19.98 Judges in later cases have dissociated themselves from Lord Scarman's views,[361] but these cases have involved life-threatening situations and the issue has been one of consent to treatment not to disclosure of information.[362] Current Department of Health rules (which are not binding in law) assume that a health professional will normally keep the fact of, and contents of, a consultation with a competent child confidential if the child does not want the parents to be told.[363] Research shows that if young people are not confident about confidentiality they are unwilling to share some health concerns with doctors.[364] This is particularly so with respect to contraception, pregnancy, sexually transmitted diseases and substance and drug abuse. A Scottish fatal accident inquiry in 1998 into the death of a 14-year-old girl from an overdose of an antidepressant drug concluded that the decision of her doctor to abide by her refusal to allow her parents to be told that she had been prescribed the drug had been correct.[365] The BMA says that in 'all cases involving young people, health professionals should try to persuade them to allow their parents to be informed'.[366]

---

[356] [1985] 3 All ER 402, 417–418, 423–424.
[357] Available on the BMA's website at http://web.bma.org.uk.
[358] This was the assumption underpinning Access to Health Records Act 1990, ss 4(2)(a) and 5(3).
[359] *Standards of Professional Performance*, Part 2, C, available from http://www.rpsgb.org.uk/.
[360] BMA, *Consent, Rights and Choices in Health Care for Children and Young People* (London: 2000) 81.
[361] *Re R (A Minor)* [1991] 4 All ER 177, 185; *Re W (A Minor)* [1992] 4 All ER 627, 633.
[362] See para 13.16 above.
[363] DoH, *The Protection and Use of Patient Information*, HSG (96) 18 (1996) para 4.10.
[364] T Cheng et al, 'Confidentiality in health care: a survey of knowledge, perceptions, and attitudes among high school students' (1993) 29 J of the American Medical Association 1404; BMA, *Consent, Rights and Choices in Health Care for Children and Young Persons* (London: 2000) 80, 218.
[365] For further information about the case of Emma Hendry see J Mason, R McCall Smith and G Laurie, *Law and Medical Ethics* (6th edn, London: 2002) 255.
[366] BMA, *Consent, Rights and Choices in Health Care for Children and Young Persons* (London: 2000) 82.

C. Records and Information Relating to Minors

The immature child: disclosing medical information Their Lordships in *Gillick v West Norfolk and Wisbech Area Health Authority* were agreed that a child who is not competent cannot prevent the disclosure by a professional of information to a parent which the doctor considers to be in the child's best interests to disclose. Following the decision the GMC advised doctors that children who are not competent to consent to medical treatment cannot be guaranteed confidentiality.[367] This does not mean that parents can insist on being told everything.[368] The right to be kept informed is at best a prima facie right: information can be withheld if disclosure is against the child's best interests.[369] The BMA says that if contraception is refused to a child because of lack of understanding of what is involved, the doctor should keep the request secret unless there are 'very convincing reasons to the contrary'.[370] A risk of exploitation or abuse is a possible reason for overriding the objections of the child.[371]

19.99

A doctor who does decide to disclose information to parents against the child's wishes should, according to Lord Fraser, first 'seek to persuade [the child] to agree to the doctor's informing the parents'.[372] This is a requirement in the latest GMC guidelines,[373] and with good reason. 'To breach confidentiality without informing the patient and in contradiction of patient refusal may irreparably damage the trust between the doctor and patient.'[374] In rare cases discussing disclosure with the child might itself cause serious harm to the child and when this is so this step can be dispensed with.[375]

19.100

The mature child: disclosing non-health related information How should a social worker respond if, for example, a mature young person who has run away from home asks that his whereabouts be kept from his parents? There is certainly no duty to give the information to the parents. Is it unlawful to do so without the

19.101

---

[367] A Grubb and D Pearl, 'Medicine, Health, the Family and the Law' [1986] Family L 227, 240. Contrast J Montgomery, *Health Care Law* (Oxford: 1997) 301–304.
[368] cp Access to Health Records Act 1990, s 4(2)(b).
[369] See paras 19.87–19.88 above.
[370] BMA, *Consent, Rights and Choices in Health Care for Children and Young People* (London: 2000) 84. Lord Scarman suggested extra-judicially (L Scarman, 'Law and Medical Practice' in P Byrne (ed), *Medicine in Contemporary Society* (Oxford: 1987) 138) that if an immature child asked for contraceptive treatment and the doctor refused to take her on as a patient, 'the duty of confidence is there and the law would not, I think require the doctor to break that confidence' to tell the parents that she had sought her out for contraception.
[371] cp para 12.11 above.
[372] [1985] 3 All ER 402, 413.
[373] GMC, *Confidentiality: Protecting and Providing Information* (London: 2000) para 38: '[i]f such patients ask you not to disclose information to a third party, you should try to persuade them to allow an appropriate person to be involved in the consultation. If they refuse and you are convinced it is essential, in their medical interests, you may disclose relevant information to an appropriate person or authority. In such cases you must tell the patient before disclosing any information.'
[374] BMA *Confidentiality and people under 16*, available from http://web.bma.org.uk.
[375] BMA, *Consent, Rights and Choices in Health Care for Children and Young People* (London: 2000) 218.

minor's consent? It seems sensible to follow the rule that applies to health information: probable lawful disclosure if the professional is of the opinion that disclosure is in the young person's best interests, whatever the young person might think.[376] This criterion would ordinarily be satisfied when the information affects something within the parent's decision-making responsibilities[376a] and disclosure entails no danger to the child. A factor that might need to be borne in mind in some cases is that once the parents have the information they cannot be prevented from disseminating it without a court order.[377]

Children

19.102 How much can children find out about themselves from professionals? Many scenarios may be imagined in which a parent may wish to veto the disclosure of information to a child by a professional:

- The child might wish to find a parent who is separated or divorced from the one with whom the child is living or to discover the whereabouts of grandparents who are estranged from that parent.
- An adopted child, who is aware that he is adopted, may want to trace his birth parents.
- A child who is seriously ill may want to know the full details of his condition which may be terminal.

May the professional give the child information if a parent objects? Does the professional have a duty to answer the questions of a '*Gillick* competent'[378] child?

Data Protection Act 1998

19.103 There is no common law authority that children, even mature children, have a right *as children* to information about themselves.[379] However, under the DPA children who understand the nature of the request can use the subject access provisions in the DPA to obtain access to the records that a professional holds about them.[380] In addition to being given a copy of the record, the DPA entitles a minor to be given details of the purposes for which the data is processed, the sources of the data (if known) and the individuals or organizations to which the data may have been disclosed.[381] The Act makes no mention of a parental right of consultation or veto. Medical and social work data may be withheld because of potential

---

[376] See para 19.95 et seq.
[376a] cp R Toulson and C Phipps, *Confidentiality* (London: 1996) 153–154.
[377] As in *Re Z* [1996] 1 FLR 191.
[378] See para 13.13 above.
[379] cp *MG v UK* Application 39393/98, 24 September 2002, para 29.
[380] DPA, s 7. See para 19.70 above.
[381] See paras 19.21 and 19.24 above.

C. Records and Information Relating to Minors

harm to the child.[382] In other cases, if the data controller thinks disclosure would be harmful to the child and the child is under 16, a decision is likely to be taken that the child lacks the maturity to handle the information and is, therefore, not competent to make the subject access request.[383]

19.104 The DPA expressly states that in Scotland a person under the age of 16 years shall be taken to have the capacity to exercise any right under the Act 'where he has a general understanding of what it means to exercise that right' and that 'a person of twelve years of age or more shall be presumed to be of sufficient age and maturity to have such understanding'.[384] Since there is no reason to think that the maturation process proceeds at a different pace in England, this would seem to be a sensible rule to apply in England and Wales too and explains the Information Commissioner's legal guidance that 'by the age of 12 a child can be expected to have sufficient maturity to understand the nature of the request'.[385] This does not rule out the possibility that a child younger than 12 may have sufficient maturity to exercise SARs. The Information Commissioner's compliance advice on access to education records states that the DPA gives 'all school students regardless of age, the right of access to their school pupil records'.[386]

Pedigree information

19.105 An adopted child who knows[387] or suspects that he is adopted and wants to investigate his biological origins is currently barred by law from obtaining a copy of his original birth certificate until he attains adulthood.[388] The recently passed Adoption and Children Act 2002, when in force, will allow information about birth parents to be provided to someone under 18 if the adoption agency considers that disclosure is appropriate.[389] A professional who knows the identity of the birth parents and, ignoring the legislative procedures, discloses the information to the child, could very possibly be sued for breach of confidence by the birth parents on the basis that this was obviously restricted information.[390]

19.106 A child conceived by a donated gamete or embryo (AID) has fewer information rights as an adult than an adopted child but greater rights as a child. Should that child wish to marry, she may ask the Human Fertilization and Embryology

---

[382] See paras 19.39 and 19.41 above.
[383] cp *Gillick v West Norfolk and Wisbech Area Health Authority* [1985] 3 All ER 402, 413, 423.
[384] DPA, s 66.
[385] IC, *Data Protection Act 1998 – Legal Guidance* 4.1.6.
[386] http://www.dataprotection.co.uk.
[387] Parents have no legal obligation to tell their child that either or both are not the biological parent(s). A high percentage of adopted children are told of their adoption but those conceived by AID are usually not told about the manner of their conception.
[388] Adoption Act 1976, s 51. The adopted child must also wait until he is 18 to take advantage of the Adoption Contact Register which has existed since 1991 (Adoption Act 1976, s 51A).
[389] Adoption and Children Act 2002, s 62.
[390] See ch 6. cp *Humphers v First Interstate Bank of Oregon* 696 P 2d 527 (1985).

Authority (HFEA) whether the prospective spouse is a relative.[391] Anyone who is 18 years of age or older is entitled to be told by the HFEA whether he was born as the result of infertility treatment using donated gametes or embryos and to be provided by the HFEA with such further information as regulations require.[392] No one but the HFEA can give out this information and no identifying information about the donor may be provided without the order of a court.[393]

Medical information

19.107 At the age of 16 a child can consent to medical treatment.[394] With this right must go the right to obtain details of the condition and the proposed medical treatment. Below the age of 16, the doctor has a discretion to provide medical treatment without parental knowledge and involvement if the child is *Gillick* competent.[395] This must mean that the doctor can give the child information without parental consent. It is likely that this applies even if the parent knows about, and has approved, the treatment since the child is usually able to access his medical records under the DPA anyway.[396]

19.108 If the doctor thinks that disclosure of medical information would harm a child (whatever his age) information may be withheld.[397] Health professionals normally defer to the views of the parents about the effect of disclosure on a child—especially when the issue is whether to tell a child that he has a life-threatening or terminal illness.[398] US studies estimate that 25 per cent of the children in the US diagnosed with HIV/AIDS are unaware of their condition. Children as old as 15 years have not been told.[399] Withholding this information from teenage children has drawbacks.[400] A child who is unaware of the seriousness of his illness

---

[391] Human Fertilization and Embryology Act 1990, s 31(6).
[392] ibid, s 31(3). There are at present no regulations. The DoH has put out a consultation paper about whether identifying information should be provided about the donor: 'Providing Information about Gamete or Embryo Donors' (2002), available at http://www.doh.gov.uk/gametedonors/index.htm. For a discussion of the issues see E Blyth, 'Donor assisted conception and donor off-spring rights to genetic information' (1998) 6 Intl J of Children's Rights 237; E Blyth, 'Sharing Genetic Origins Information' (2000) 14 Children and Society 11.
[393] Human Fertilization and Embryology Act 1990, ss 33(5), 34, 35; DPA, s 35A.
[394] Family Law Reform Act 1969, s 8(1); see para 13.12 above.
[395] See para 13.13 above.
[396] See para 19.72 above.
[397] 'The solution depends on a judgment of what is best for the welfare of the particular child', per Lord Fraser, *Gillick v West Norfolk and Wisbech Area Health Authority* [1985] 3 All ER 402, 412. cp Data Protection (Subject Access Modification) (Health) Order 2000, SI 2000/413, r 5(1) and see para 19.68 above.
[398] J van Straaten, 'The Minor's Limited Right to Confidential Health Care and the Inverse of Confidentiality: A Parent's Decision Not to Disclose Illness Status to a Minor Child' (2000) 20 Children's Legal Rights J 46, 49–50.
[399] ibid at 50.
[400] The American Academy of Pediatrics strongly encourages disclosure of HIV status to children of school age and says that physicians have an ethical obligation to provide full disclosure to adolescent patients: 'Disclosure of Illness Status to Children and Adolescents with HIV Infection' (1999) 103 Pediatrics 164, 165.

C. Records and Information Relating to Minors

might not take medication conscientiously or co-operate with treatment. If the child is HIV and sexually active, there is a risk that a third party might become infected.

Other information

19.109 If a child is '*Gillick* competent',[401] disclosure of information to the child by a professional without parental approval should, absent legislation forbidding disclosure, be lawful if the professional is satisfied that disclosure is in the child's best interests. For younger children, parents probably have the power to veto disclosure. This type of situation seems to fall into the class Butler-Sloss P spoke of in *Re C* when she said that 'a space in which parental decisions are final, undoubtedly exists'.[402]

19.110 In relation to information about legal proceedings and rights, it is worth noting that the European Convention on the Exercise of Children's Rights[403] contains the following provision in Article 3:

> A child considered by internal law as having sufficient understanding, in the case of proceedings before a judicial authority affecting him or her, shall be granted, and shall be entitled to request, the following rights:
>
> a. to receive all relevant information;
> b. to be consulted and express his or her views;
> c. to be informed of the possible consequences of compliance with these views and the possible consequences of any decision.

Convention arguments

19.111 Since Article 8 of the ECHR applies to a minor,[404] if a '*Gillick* competent'[405] child requests information about himself and is denied it by a professional *solely*[406] because the parent does not want the information disclosed to the child, the child might have a human rights grievance. There is no general right of access to personal information,[407] nevertheless respect for private and family life imposes positive obligations on the state (of which the court is a branch) to facilitate the individual's access to information inter alia about identity,[408] childhood and early development[409] and arguably about the whereabouts of blood relatives with

---

[401] See para 13.13 above.
[402] [1999] 2 FLR 1004, 1021.
[403] Strasbourg, 25 January 1996, available at http://conventions.coe.int/treaty/en/Treaties/Html/160.htm.
[404] See para 13.18 above. The adopted child's welfare is the paramount consideration: Adoption and Children Act 2002, s 62(6)(a).
[405] See para 13.13 above.
[406] This means that the professional is not convinced that withholding the information is in the child's best interests.
[407] *Gaskin v UK* (1989) 12 EHRR 36, para 37.
[408] *Milulic v Croatia* Application 53176/99, para 54.
[409] *Gaskin v UK* (1989) 12 EHRR 36, para 49. *MG v UK* Application 39393/98, 24 September 2002, para 29.

whom the individual has an established relationship[410] and the state of the individual's health.[411]

19.112 It is hard to believe that the ECtHR would find that delaying access to information about birth parents until the age of 18 violates the Convention.[412] In *Gaskin*[413] the Commission's opinion stressed that the applicant was an adult implying that as a child Gaskin might not have had a right to see his case records.[414] The position of the AID child is different from the adopted child. Even as an adult the legislation denies him identifying information about the donor. But here the absence of consensus amongst Member States on the question whether AID offspring should be given this information[415] will probably defeat a complaint.[416] Non-identifying information is another matter. Article 8 is engaged when both identifying and non-identifying information is sought; the absence of arrangements to provide non-identifying information that would enable an AID offspring to increase his understanding of his identity could be a breach of Article 8,[417] but not necessarily before the child has attained adulthood. A balance has to be achieved with the other considerations mentioned in Article 8(2).[418]

Strangers

19.113 In the absence of a statutory right, a stranger has no entitlement to confidential personal information about a child and disclosure of such information to a stranger by a professional, absent compelling public interest grounds,[419] is unlawful. The BMA is concerned about confidential health information being disclosed by teachers to

---

[410] The extent of the positive obligations of the state in respect of Art 8 is uncertain: *X, Y & Z v UK* (1997) 24 EHRR 143, para 41.

[411] cp *McGinley v UK* (1998) 27 EHRR 1, paras 99–101; *Martin v UK* (1996) 21 EHHR CD 113, 4 EHRLR 442. Once the child has attained the age of 16 parents can no longer veto disclosure of information because of the Family Law Reform Act 1969, s 8(1). Information can be withheld by health professionals on therapeutic grounds. See para 19.68 above.

[412] See G Van Beuren, 'Children's Access to Adoption Records' (1995) 58 MLR 37, 45. The child might object that blood relatives (eg grandparents) might be dead by the time he attains adulthood.

[413] (1989) 11 EHRR 402, para 100; see para 19.19 above.

[414] See also *MG v UK* Application 39393/98, 24 September 2002, para 29. J Fontin, 'Rights Brought Home for Children' (1999) 62 MLR 350, 358 comments that in *Nielson v Denmark* (1989) 11 EHRR 175 the ECtHR showed no inclination to protect the wishes of a child (in that case against being deprived of liberty (Art 5) on the authority of a parent). U Kilkelly, *The Child and the European Convention on Human Rights* (Aldershot: 1999) 120, however, points out that the decision is not recent and conflicts with the principles of the 1989 UN Convention whose standards are now almost universally accepted. The child was also relatively young at 12 years of age.

[415] *X, Y & Z v UK* (1997) 24 EHRR 143, para 44.

[416] See further U Kilkelly, *The Child and the European Convention on Human Rights* (Aldershot: 1999) 101–102. *Odièvre v France* Application 42326/98 13 February 2003.

[417] *Rose v Secretary of State for Health* [2002] EWHC 1593, para 46.

[418] ibid, para 47.

[419] See ch 11.

school inspectors without the consent of pupils or parents[420] and with school nurses being put under pressure, or even a contractual obligation, to report consultations to the head teacher.[421] Schools sometimes try to verify that a pupil was truthful in giving a visit to the GP or a dentist as an excuse for not attending school. The BMA says that to confirm or deny the visit (without appropriate consent) is a breach of medical confidentiality.[422] In child protection inquiries, health professionals may be approached to disclose the health records of all the children in a family without the consent of the children or a parent. It is unlawful for these records to be handed over, or health information to be provided, unless the public interest defence applies.[423]

D. Records and Information of Incompetent Adult

19.114 An application pursuant to DPA, s 7 for access to the records that a professional holds by a mentally handicapped or mentally ill person should be treated in the same way as that of any other adult if the applicant is competent.[424] The DPA makes no provision for access on behalf of an adult who is not and the common law does not confer authority on anyone else to apply for the information.[425] A person acting within the terms of a registered Enduring Power of Attorney or under Court of Protection authority[426] can request access on behalf of an adult who lacks the capacity to manage his own property and affairs.[427] There is some doubt about whether the former extends to medical and welfare records.[428]

19.115 When a third party applies for access to a professional's record on behalf of a mentally incapacitated person, the professional should not disclose information in a social work or health record:

(a) provided by the data subject in the expectation that it would not be disclosed to the person making the request;

---

[420] BMA, *Consent, Rights and Choices in Health Care for Children and Young People* (London: 2000) 219.
[421] ibid at 217.
[422] ibid at 220.
[423] See ch 11.
[424] As DoH, *Data Protection Act 1998 Guidance to Social Services* (March 2000) para 5.11 advises, mental disorder does not equate with mental incapacity. The mentally ill are not disbarred from seeking access to information from a professional. An assessment of competence must be made that is issue-specific: cp *Re C* [1994] 1 All ER 819, 823; *Masterman-Lister v Brutton & Co* [2002] EWCA Civ 1889.
[425] *R (on the application of Stevens) v Plymouth City Council* [2002] EWCA Civ 388; [2002] 1 FLR 1177, para 18. Cp *F v West Berkshire Health Authority* [1989] 2 All ER 545, 551 where Lord Brandon said that no one could consent to medical treatment on behalf of a mentally incapacitated person.
[426] cp *Willsher v UK* (1997) EHRR CD 188, 190; SI 2000/415 reg 5 (4)(c). On the jurisdiction of the Court of Protection which turns on the interpretation of the word 'affairs' in the Mental Health Act 1983, s 95 see *Re W (EEM)* [1971] Ch 123, 143.
[427] *Data Protection Act 1998—Guidance to Social Services* (March 2000) para 5.11.
[428] See para 12.09 above.

(b) obtained as a result of any examination or investigation to which the data subject consented in the expectation that the information would not be so disclosed; or

(c) which the data subject has expressly indicated should not be so disclosed.[429]

E. Requiring Disclosure to Third Parties

19.116 Professionals may be asked by clients to disclose information to third parties. Doctors receive many requests from patients in connection with insurance and prospective employment. Medical reports for these two purposes are regulated by the Access to Medical Reports Act 1988.[430] When the professional–client relationship is contractual, failure to relay information at the client's request to a third party may be a breach of contract and, whether or not there is a contract, non-compliance with a request to supply information may be actionable in negligence if the inaction causes the client tangible injury.[431]

19.117 It is important that information supplied at the client's request to third parties is accurate. A failure on this front may attract liability in negligence.[432] An action for breach of contract (where there is a contract) is another possibility.

> I can see no reason why a solicitor should not be under a duty to his client to exercise due care and skill when making statements to third parties, so that if he fails in that duty and his client suffers damage in consequence, he may be liable to his client in damages.[433]

If the failure involves a breach of the DPA the client may be entitled to be compensated for the damage without proof of negligence.[434]

---

[429] Data Protection (Subject Access Modification) (Social Work) Order 2000, SI 2000/415, r 5(3); Data Protection (Subject Access Modification) (Health) Order 2000, SI 2000/413, r 5(3). Similarly, information about child abuse in an education record is exempt from disclosure if this would not be in the best interests of the data subject: Data Protection (Subject Access Modification) (Education) Order 2000, SI 2000/414, r 5(2).

[430] See para 19. 49 above.

[431] J Finch (ed), *Speller's Law Relating to Hospitals* (7th edn, London: 1994) 392.

[432] cp *Spring v Guardian Assurance* [1994] 3 All ER 129; *Turner v Royal Bank of Scotland* [2001] EWCA Civ 64; [2001] 1 All ER (Comm) 1057. Were a client to sue a professional for providing inaccurate information, there may be issues of policy, foreseeability, causation and remoteness of damage. The same applies if the third party who relied upon the inaccurate information were to sue the professional.

[433] per Lord Goff, *Spring v Guardian Assurance plc* [1994] 3 All ER 129, 146.

[434] See para 4.49 above.

20

DUTY TO WARN THIRD PARTIES

A. Public Law Duty	20.01	Child and Elder Abuse	20.23
When a Public Law Duty to Warn Might Arise	20.04	Risk of HIV Infection	20.28
		Genetic Conditions	20.37
Impact of the Human Rights Act 1998	20.05	Risk of Non-Violent Crime or Fraud	20.40
B. Private Law Duty	20.06		
Risk of Bodily Harm	20.07		

A. Public Law Duty

20.01 A professional who honestly believes that a client poses a serious threat to the physical well-being of an unsuspecting third party is justified in English law in disclosing this to an appropriate person,[1] notwithstanding that the information is confidential. So much is clear from the Court of Appeal's decision in *W v Egdell*[2] in favour of a psychiatrist sued by his patient for breach of contract and confidence for making known to the authorities the violent tendencies of the patient.[3] This case happened to involve a doctor, but it has been argued in a previous chapter that the same exception to confidentiality applies to all professionals.[4] In *R v Kennedy*, for example, it was a probation officer who took advantage of the exception.[5]

20.02 When *W v Egdell* was heard at first instance in the High Court, Scott J went further. He said that a doctor 'owes a duty not only to his patient but also a duty to the public. His duty to the public would require him . . . to place before the proper authorities the result of his examination if, in his opinion, the public interest so required. This would be so . . . whether or not the patient instructed him not to

---

[1] As to who that might be see para 11.63 above.
[2] [1990] 1 All ER 835.
[3] cp *Simonsen v Swenson* 177 NW 831 (1920) where a doctor who warned the owner of a hotel that a guest was probably suffering from a contagious disease after the patient refused to leave the hotel was held not liable.
[4] See paras 11.12, 11.24–11.25 above.
[5] *R v Kennedy* (CA, 30 April 1998).

do so'.[6] A similar duty to warn the public is mentioned in Shaw LJ's judgment in *Schering Chemicals v Falkman Ltd*:

> If the subject matter is something which is inimical to the public interest or threatens individual safety, a person in possession of the knowledge of that subject matter cannot be obliged to conceal it although he acquired that knowledge in confidence. In some situations it may be his duty to reveal what he knows.[7]

And in *R v Harrison* Rougier J said that a prison chaplain would have been 'in breach of his duty if he had not alerted the authorities'[8] to a spine-chilling announcement by a remand prisoner that he intended to pursue a career of murder having got such a buzz out of attacking and killing a man.

20.03 Exactly what kind of duty are these judges talking about? Only someone performing a public law function can be under an enforceable public law duty, and since this was not true of any of the people said to owe a duty to warn in these cases, that duty must have been an ethical one. Scott J may have had in mind that failure by a doctor to disclose information about a serious risk to public safety might constitute professional misconduct.[9]

When a Public Law Duty to Warn Might Arise

20.04 There are circumstances in which a public law duty may be owed to disclose information about the dangers presented by one individual to another.[10] In *R v Devon CC, ex p L*[11] the High Court held that social workers were under a duty to inform two mothers and a grandmother that a man who, in turn, lived with each of them was a child abuser if this was their reasonably held belief. The court based the duty upon the local authority's statutory duty under Child Care Act 1980, s 1 to promote the welfare of children. This duty has been restated in the Children Act

---

[6] [1989] 1 All ER 1089, 1104. In the Court of Appeal's judgments there is no mention of a disclosure duty.

[7] *Schering Chemicals v Falkman Ltd* [1981] 2 All ER 321, 337 (italics added).

[8] (CA, 10 July 2000.) See also *Duncan v Medical Practitioners Disciplinary Committee* [1986] 1 NZLR 513, 521.

[9] GMC, *Confidentiality: Protecting and Providing Information* (London: 2000) para 36. The GMC seems to be the only self-regulating English profession to mandate disclosure of a risk of physical injury to a third party. In *Re R* [1993] 4 All ER 702, 705 Thorpe J said that the legal representatives of the parties in Children Act proceedings had a duty (presumably as officers of the court) to disclose information relevant to the welfare of a child even if contrary to the interests of the client and within the scope of legal professional privilege. See also *Re DH* [1994] 1 FLR 679 where Wall J said that this applied to family proceedings generally. Non-observance of this duty could attract disciplinary measures. In 1981 the NSW Bar Council decided that a barrister had a professional duty to inform the judge and his opponent, and to advise the police, of a threat by a client to shoot her children if she lost custody of them: Y Ross, *Ethics in Law in Australia* (Sydney: 2001) 366 citing NSW Bar Association *Annual Report* (1981) 12.

[10] In *G v G* [1990] 1 FLR 395, 399 the Court of Appeal said that a court which became aware that a child was at risk of abuse had a duty to alert the relevant welfare services.

[11] [1991] 2 FLR 541.

A. Public Law Duty

1989.[12] To fulfil the duty effectively social services may need the help of other public agencies. Under Children Act 1989, s 47(9) any local authority, or education or housing authority, any health authority or NHS trust, and anyone else whom the Secretary of State or National Authority of Wales authorizes, has a duty to assist a local authority inquiry about a child who is suspected of suffering, or is likely to suffer, significant harm by providing relevant information unless it would be unreasonable in all the circumstances of the case to lend assistance.[13] However, failure to provide this information is not actionable as a private law breach of statutory duty.[14]

Impact of the Human Rights Act 1998

The Human Rights Act 1998 (HRA) has had a twofold impact on the issue of a public law duty. First, when a public law duty to warn exists, it must be exercised in a manner that is compatible with the HRA.[15] Any disclosure that interferes with the client's right to respect for private life (Article 8(1)) must be in accordance with law, proportionate to a legitimate aim and fulfil a pressing social need.[16] Secondly, one or more of the adopted Convention rights may compel recognition of a public (or even a private)[17] law duty to warn.[18] The prime candidate here is Article 2 which states that '[e]veryone's right to life shall be protected by law'. Article 2 gives rise to positive obligations on the part of the state to take steps to safeguard the lives of those within its jurisdiction;[19] obligations that extend beyond the provision of effective criminal laws.[20] In *LCB v UK* the European Court of Human Rights (ECtHR) held that Article 2 could require a state to warn a member of the armed forces that his exposure to nuclear radiation could put the life of his future child at risk if this appeared likely at the time.[21] Given this background, an English court

20.05

---

[12] s 17(1). See also Sch 2, Pt 1, para 4(1).
[13] Children Act 1989, s 47(10). See further para 10.11 above. There is also a statutory duty under s 27 on such bodies to comply with a request by a local authority to assist it in carrying out its functions under Children Act 1989, Pt III provided the request does not prejudice the discharge of their own duties and obligations and is compatible with their statutory or other duties and obligations.
[14] *X v Bedfordshire CC* [1995] 2 AC 633, 747.
[15] s 6(1).
[16] *Re V* [1999] 1 FLR 267, 273; *R v Local Authority and Police Authority in the Midlands, ex p LM* [2000] 1 FLR 612; *C (R on the application of?) v LB Waltham Forest* [2002] EWHC 2007, paras 52–54. See also V Smith, 'Disclosing Child Abuse Suspicions—A Public Authority Dilemma' [2000] Family L 910.
[17] See para 20.16 below.
[18] The HRA might provide a springboard for arguing that a lawyer is under a duty to warn of threats by a client against a judge, a subject raised in para 15.35 above.
[19] Art 1 of the Convention on which the state's positive obligation is founded has not been incorporated into domestic law by the HRA but by HRA, s 2 a domestic court determining a question which has arisen in connetion with a Convention right must take into account relevant judgments of the ECtHR. These judgments recognize that the state has positive obligations in respect of certain Convention articles (cp para 3.06 above).
[20] *Osman v UK* (1998) 5 BHRC 293, para 115.
[21] (1999) 27 EHRR 212.

might be persuaded that Article 2 imposes on a public authority a duty to warn a known individual for whom the authority's client poses 'a real and immediate risk to life'[22] and also that the court, as a public authority itself, is required to reach such a conclusion by HRA, s 6(1).[23] In *Venables v NGN Ltd* Butler-Sloss P said: '[t]here is a positive duty on the court as a public authority to take steps to protect individuals from the criminal acts of others.'[24] This allowed the court in that case to impose an injunction on the media (including media organizations that were not parties to the litigation) to prevent publication of the new names, addresses and appearances of the two applicants because of the real possibility of significant harm from revenge attacks if this information were to become public.[25] Although Article 2 is absolute, positive obligations are not.[26] The burden of giving a warning must be considered, but an obligation to warn an identifiable individual would not impose a disproportionate burden. A similar duty to warn might arise under Article 3 which guarantees freedom from torture, inhuman or degrading treatment or punishment, including that administered by a private individual,[27] or even Article 8 which under respect for private life protects physical and psychological integrity.[28] Once the existence of a right is established, a public authority that fails to give an appropriate warning about the risks posed by a client could be sued under HRA, s 7.[29] It is not necessary for the claimant to show that 'but for' the omission to warn or protect the claimant would have avoided harm; merely that the failure to act 'had a significant influence on the course of events' and that a warning 'judged reasonably' might have been 'expected to avoid or at least minimise the risk or the damage suffered'.[30]

B. Private Law Duty

20.06 If a professional has no public law duty to warn of the dangerousness of a client, she may still have a private law duty to speak out. In the absence of statutory authority, this duty, if it exists at all, must arise under the law of negligence.

---

[22] *Osman v UK* (1998) 5 BHRC 293, para 116. In this case, the ECtHR decided that the police neither knew nor ought to have known that the life of a member of the Osman family was in danger and therefore no obligation to protect arose. cp *LCB v UK* (1998) 27 EHRR 212, para 40.
[23] See paras 3.05–3.07 above.
[24] [2001] 1 All ER 908, para 99. Cp para 83.
[25] *Venables v NGN Ltd* [2001] 1 All ER 908, para 94. This test was derived from child abuse cases.
[26] *R (on the application of Pretty) v DPP* [2001] UKHL 61; [2002] 1 AC 8000, para 90.
[27] *A v UK* (1998) 27 EHRR 611, para 22; *Z v UK* (2002) 34 EHRR 3, para 73.
[28] *X v Netherlands* (1985) 8 EHRR 235; *Botta v Italy* (1998) 26 EHRR 241, para 32.
[29] See para 4.45 above.
[30] *E v UK* Application 33218/96, 26 November 2002, paras 99–100.

B. Private Law Duty

Risk of Bodily Harm

The *Tarasoff* case[31]

The jurisprudential genesis of the duty to warn of potential harm is *Tarasoff v Regents of the University of California*.[32] The Tarasoffs were the parents of a young woman who was brutally murdered by Poddar, a graduate student at the University of California Berkley, who felt rejected by their daughter. Poddar had been an out-patient at the University's student health centre where he had informed a clinical psychologist treating him that he planned to murder Ms Tarasoff when she returned from a trip to Brazil. This threat was taken seriously. The psychologist, who knew of his patient's violent tendencies and that he had bought a gun consulted with colleagues, attempted to have his patient institutionalized and contacted the campus police who briefly detained Poddar before releasing him because he appeared rational. But no one warned Ms Tarasoff or anyone likely to apprise her of the danger she was in.[33] **20.07**

The Supreme Court of California initially held that when a mental health therapist determines that his patient presents a serious danger of violence to another he has a duty to warn the would-be victim.[34] In a second ruling,[35] after a rehearing, the court modified its decision by holding that a therapist has a duty to take reasonable steps to protect a third party against foreseeable danger from a patient. This duty could be discharged in a number of ways, depending on the circumstances, including informing either the intended victim of the threat or others likely to pass the information on to the victim or by notifying the police of the danger. Whether on the facts of this case a warning to Ms Tarasoff was required (in addition to the warning to the police that was given) was not decided.[36] **20.08**

Tarasoff in England and Wales

A relationship of sufficient proximity

The consensus of academic opinion is that *Tarasoff* would not be followed in England.[37] No English precedent imposes a duty on a professional to warn a third **20.09**

---

[31] The articles on this case and its progeny are legion. A good starting point is R Slovenko, *Psychotherapy and Confidentiality* (Springfield, Illinois: 1998) ch 2. See also E Kermani, *Handbook of Psychiatry and Law* (Chicago: 1989) 32 et seq.
[32] 529 P 2d 553, 554 (1974) (*Tarasoff I*) vacated at 551 P 2d 334 (1976) (*Tarasoff II*).
[33] Which, since she was away, meant giving the warning to her parents.
[34] *Tarasoff v Regents of the University of California* 529 P 2d 553, 554 (1974).
[35] 551 P 2d 334, 340, 345–346 (1976).
[36] This was because the case was an appeal from the University's demurrer. When the case went back to court for this determination the University settled out of court.
[37] P Moodie and M Wright, 'Confidentiality, Codes and Courts: An Examination of the Significance of Professional Guidelines on Medical Ethics in Determining the Legal Limits of Confidentiality' (2000) 29 Anglo-American L Rev 39, 50. cp Australian Law Reform Commission, DP 14, *Privacy and Personal Information* (Sydney: 1980) para 113; D Madden, *Medicine, Ethics & the*

party that a client has threatened to harm the third party. In fact it is unusual for the common law to oblige A to go to the aid of B when A has caused, or threatens, no harm to B.

> The common law imposes no prima facie general duty to rescue, safeguard or warn another from or of reasonably foreseeable loss or injury or to take reasonable care to ensure that another does not sustain such loss or injury.[38]

A duty of care requires a special relationship between victim and defendant that is sufficiently proximate. Proximity is not a simple question of geography or foreseeability.[39] The competing moral claims of the parties to compensation and protection from undue burden of legal responsibility have also to be balanced.[39a] In nonfeasance cases in which there has been a finding of proximity one of the following factors has been present:[40] the defendant created or increased the danger to the claimant;[41] or the defendant controlled the agent of harm;[42] or the claimant justifiably relied upon the defendant exercising a statutory power to protect the claimant from harm;[43] or the defendant voluntarily assumed responsibility for the claimant's protection.[44]

20.10 In *Tarasoff* these proximity-creating factors were absent.[45] Nothing in the judgments suggests that Ms Tarasoff so much as knew that Poddar was seeing a therapist. The Californian Supreme Court alluded in *Tarasoff I* to the control that a therapist exercises over a patient[46] but because Poddar was not in custody the therapist had no physical or legal hold over him.[47] Commentators argue that without

---

Law (Dublin: 2002) 99–101. Tentative support for *Tarasoff* has been expressed by courts in some common law jurisdictions. See *Tanner v Norys* [1980] 4 WWR 33; *Wenden v Trikha* (1991) 116 AR (2d) 80; *R v Lowe* (SC Vic, 1996, LEXIS 1330) 63; *Smith v Jones* (1999) 169 DLR (4th) 385, 406.

[38] per Deane J, *Sutherland Shire Council v Heyman* (1985) 157 CLR 424, 502. See further K Williams, 'Medical Samaritans: Is there a Duty to Treat?' (2001) 21 OJLS 393.

[39] *Hill v Chief Constable West Yorkshire* [1988] 2 All ER 238, 243.

[39a] *HJ Van de Wetering v Capital Coast Health Ltd* (NZ HC, 19 May 2000) 9.

[40] J Logie, 'Affirmative Action in the Law of Tort: The Case of the Duty to Warn' [1989] CLJ 115; J Stapleton, 'Duty of Care Factors: a Selection from the Judicial Menus' in P Cane and J Stapleton (eds), *The Law of Obligations* (Oxford: 1998) 60 and N Gray and J Edelman, 'Developing the law of omissions: a common law duty to rescue?' (1998) Tort LJ 18.

[41] *Hill v Chief Constable of West Yorkshire* [1988] 2 All ER 238, 242 explaining *Home Office v Dorset Yacht Co Ltd* [1970] 2 All ER 294. Cp *Capital and Counties plc v Hampshire CC* [1997] 2 All ER 865.

[42] *Home Office v Dorset Yacht* [1970] 2 All ER 294, 328.

[43] *Sutherland Shire Council v Heyman* (1985) 157 CLR 424, 502. cp *Caparo Industries v Dickman* [1990] 1 All ER 568.

[44] cp *Goodwill v British Pregnancy Advisory Service* [1996] 2 All ER 161, 163, 169; *Phelps v Hillingdon LBC* [2000] 4 All ER 504, 518 where assumption of responsibility was said to be objectively determined.

[45] R MacKay 'Dangerous Patients: Third Party Safety and Psychiatrist's Duties—Walking the Tarasoff Tightrope' 30. (1990) Medicine Science & the L 52; M. Jones, 'Medical confidentiality and the public interest' (1990) 6 Professional Negligence 16; A Abadee, 'The Medical Duty of Confidentiality and Prospective Duty of Disclosure: Can they Co-exist?' (1995) 3 J of L and Medicine 75, 84.

[46] *Tarasoff v Regents of the University of California* 529 P 2d 553, 558 (1974).

[47] cp *Nasser v Parker* 455 SE 2d 502, 506 (1995).

involuntary detention there can be no genuine control over a patient.[48] The one possible proximity-creating factor in *Tarasoff* was the therapist's failure to carry through Poddar's hospitalization. The abortive attempt may have increased the risk to Ms Tarasoff because it deterred Poddar from seeking further treatment which, had it continued, might have averted the tragedy.[49] But this argument was not relied upon in *Tarasoff II* where the court said that a duty to a third party could derive from the therapist's special relationship to the patient. The rationale for the court's decision was a policy one: although there is a public interest in confidential communications between therapist and patient, this 'must yield to the extent to which disclosure is essential to avert danger to others. The protection privilege ends where the public peril begins.'[50]

> In this risk-infested society, we can hardly tolerate the further exposure to danger that would result from a concealed knowledge of the therapist that his patient was lethal. If the exercise of reasonable care to protect the threatened victim requires the therapist to warn the endangered party or those who can reasonably be expected to notify him, we see no sufficient interest that would protect and justify concealment.[51]

Miers[52] controversially argues that proximity may arise from the ability of the professional to identify the claimant as a person endangered by the client.[53] For this he relies upon *Osman v Ferguson*,[54] an action against the police for failure to protect a father and son from a stalker, a deranged former teacher who was infatuated with Osman junior. It is true that in interlocutory appeal proceedings McCowan LJ said that it was arguable that the boy and his family had a special relationship with the police because the police knew that the schoolteacher posed a distinctive risk to them.[55] There are several reasons, however, for thinking that Miers attaches too much importance to this. First, what is arguable may not be accepted. Secondly, ensuring public safety is the raison d'être of the police, it is not the raison d'être of a professional.[56] That the police have a duty to protect those they know to be at risk of harm does not mean that a psychiatrist (or any other professional) is under a similar duty. Thirdly, there was present in *Osman* a more

20.11

---

[48] D Mendelson and G Mendelson, 'Tarasoff down under: the psychiatrist's duty to warn in Australia' [1991] J of Psychiatry & Law 33, 49. See also R MacKay, 'Dangerous Patients: Third Party Safety and Psychiatrist's Duties—Walking the Tarasoff Tightrope' 30. (1990) Medicine Science & the L 52, 56.
[49] *Tarasoff v Regents of the University of California* 529 P 2d 553, 554, 559 (1974).
[50] per Tobriner J, *Tarasoff v Regents of the University of California* 551 P 2d 334, 347 (1976).
[51] ibid.
[52] D Miers, 'Liability for Injuries Caused by Violent Patients' [1996] J of Personal Injury L 314, 316.
[53] He writes specifically about a psychiatrist whose patient has expressed violent intentions toward a third party.
[54] [1993] 4 All ER 344.
[55] ibid, at 350.
[56] All the authorities discussed by the Court of Appeal in *Osman* involved the police.

orthodox proximity-creating factor: the police had told the claimant's father (who was fatally shot by the stalker) that they knew who was harrassing the family and that he 'should not worry for his own safety or that of his family'.[57] In saying this the police invited the family to rely upon them for protection.

Policy

20.12 Though there may have been no proximity on the facts of *Tarasoff,* proximity may not always be lacking in actions by those who claim not to have received a warning from a mental health professional when they should have done. The victim may be a known relative of the client or another client or the professional may have done something to increase the risk of harm to the victim[58] or the victim may have been encouraged to rely on the professional or the professional may have acquiesced to such reliance.[59]

20.13 Before a duty of care, and by extension, a duty to warn, will be imposed by an English court, the court must be satisfied of more than proximity between victim and defendant and that harm to the victim was reasonably foreseeable. The court must also be satisfied that it is fair, just and reasonable to impose a duty of care.[60] In *Osman*[61] the Court of Appeal found that the police owed the claimants no duty of care in spite of accepting that there might be a 'special relationship'. The reason was the court's conception of public policy.[62]

20.14 There are powerful policy arguments against recognition of a *Tarasoff* legal duty which have persuaded some (admittedly only a small minority)[63] of the US courts that the *Tarasoff* approach is wrong. A major concern is the impact of the decision on medical confidentiality. The dissenting judge in *Tarasoff* feared that a duty to warn

> will cripple the use and effectiveness of psychiatry: many people, potentially violent—yet susceptible to treatment—will be deterred from seeking it; those seeking aid will be inhibited from making the self-revelation necessary to effective treatment; finally, requiring the psychiatrist to violate the patient's trust by forcing

---

[57] [1993] 4 All ER 344, 347.
[58] eg *Re Goebel* 703 NE 2d 1045 (1998) where the lawyer made it more likely that the client would find and murder the victim by revealing part of the victim's address to the murderer.
[59] cp *Al-Kandari v J R Brown & Co* [1988] 1 All ER 833, 839.
[60] *Caparo Industries plc v Dickman* [1990] 1 All ER 568, 573–574; see para 4.21 above.
[61] [1993] 4 All ER 344.
[62] The ECtHR in *Osman v UK* (1998) 5 BHRC 293 found that Art 6 had been contravened by the decision to strike out the action before trial because it amounted to a restriction on the right of access to the courts. This decision, from which the ECtHR resiled in *Z v UK* (2002) 34 EHRR 3, prevented courts from striking out negligence actions on the grounds that it would not be fair, just and reasonable to impose a duty of care at the interlocutory stage when the full facts were not before the court.
[63] *Boynton v Burglass* 590 So 2d 446 (1992); *Nasser v Parker* 455 SE 2d 502, 506 (1995); *Thapar v Zezulka* 994 SW 2d 635 (1999) declined to recognize a Tarasoff-type duty.

B. Private Law Duty

the doctor to disseminate confidential statements will destroy the interpersonal relationship by which treatment is effected.[64]

Deterring individuals from seeking treatment that may cure them disadvantages their potential victims as well as the individuals themselves.

Additional arguments against a duty are: the difficulty of accurately predicting violence,[65] the possibility that informing on the patient might increase the risk of violence to the patient,[66] the probability that where the professional genuinely believes that a third party's life is put at serious risk by the client, the professional will rely on the public interest exception to breach confidentiality anyway,[67] the adequacy of existing mechanisms for holding mental health professionals accountable[68] and the danger, if there is a duty to warn or to protect, of defensive warnings[69] and overuse of compulsory detention.[70] In *Van De Wetering v Capital Coast Health Ltd*[71] Master Thomson of the New Zealand High Court held that a hospital had no duty to take active steps to protect members of the public from a psychiatric patient whom the hospital ought to have known was dangerous and who eventually shot and killed four people and wounded a fifth. 20.15

A responsible clinician has to be able to focus exclusively on the best interests of the patient. It would impose an intolerable burden on a clinician to be under the

---

[64] per Clark J, *Tarasoff v Regents of the University of California* 551 P 2d 334, 360 (1976).
[65] *Tarasoff v Regents of the University of California* 551 P 2d 334, 344, 354, 360–361(1976). See also F Farnham and D James, '"Dangerousness" and dangerous law' (2001) 358 (9297) The Lancet 1926; M Backstrom, 'Unveiling the Truth when it Matters Most: Implementing the Tarasoff Duty to California's Attorneys' (1999) 73 Southern California L Rev 139, 159.
[66] 'The Duty to Protect Third Parties and Negligent Release' in B Weiner and R Wettstein (eds), *Legal Issues in Mental Health Care* (New York: 1993) 245. The patient might be goaded into action particularly if paid a visit by the police; alternatively, the patient might become violent toward the mental health professional by whom he feels betrayed.
[67] When John Masterton told a psychiatrist at the Maudsley Hospital, South London, that he was having fantasies of killing Harriet Harman MP, the psychiatrist straightaway telephoned Ms Harman to warn her because she and her colleagues thought that there was a genuine risk of violence: The Times, 14 September 1999, 5. cp *W v Egdell* [1990] 1 All ER 835; *R v Crozier* (1991) 8 BMLR 128; *R v Kennedy* (CA, 30 April 1998). As a matter of law, disclosure on public interest grounds is discretionary: see para 11.01 above.
[68] 'As for increasing the accountability of psychiatrists and health authorities, given long-established complaints procedures, the recent rash of inquiries and intense media interest, it is perhaps doubtful that an extension of tortious duties would have any significant effect': F Morris and G Adshead, 'The liability of psychiatrists for the violent acts of their patients' (1997) 147 NLJ 558.
[69] cp *Palmer v Tees Health Authority* [1998] 45 BMLR 88. After *Tarasoff* there was a big increase in the number of reports by psychiatrists to police of threats of violence by patients: V Mangalmurti, 'Psychotherapists' fear of Tarasoff: all in the mind?' (1994) 22 J of Psychiatry and Law 37. Not all of these were probably justified. It was Tobriner J's opinion in *Tarasoff II* 551 P 2d 334, 346 (1976) that the 'risk that unnecessary warnings may be given is a reasonable price to pay for the lives of possible victims that may be saved'.
[70] *Tarasoff v Regents of the University of California* 551 P 2d 334, 361–362 (1976). See also 'The Duty to Protect Third Parties and Negligent Release' in B Weiner and R Wettstein (eds), *Legal Issues in Mental Health Care* (New York: 1993) 242.
[71] (NZ HC 19 May 2000.)

constant threat or legal responsibility for the conduct of his/her patients. Otherwise, and plainly contrary to public policy, the clinician will inevitably sublimate or deprioritise the patient's best interests in favour of cautious self-protection. That would be particularly so when the clinician has no right to control the patient's behaviour, other than by obtaining a compulsory treatment order.[72]

When the professional is an employee of the NHS the diversion of resources from patient care to litigation may be an additional concern.[73] A final point is that a warning is only valuable if countermeasures can be taken to mitigate the risk of harm; situations may arise where effective countermeasures are not available.

The limits of *Tarasoff*

20.16 Most English comments about *Tarasoff* were written before the HRA came into force. Has the HRA changed anything? Possibly the obligation of the courts, as public authorities, to develop the law of tort so that it is compatible with Convention rights,[74] including the right to life,[75] freedom from degrading treatment and the right to respect for private life, which extends to a right to physical integrity,[76] may have swung the balance in favour of imposing upon mental health professionals an obligation to give a warning of 'the existence of a real and immediate risk' of violence to a third party from the criminal acts of a patient of which they were aware or ought to have been aware.[77] The burden on the professional of a warning is likely to be modest. The main drawback of the warning is that it infringes the patient's privacy. Nevertheless, where there is a real and immediate risk of serious injury to another, a court might decide that a duty to warn the third party of his danger represents a fair balance between everyone's interests: those of the professional, the patient, the potential victim and society. The duty to warn, were it to exist, would need to be confined to situations in which the professional

---

[72] ibid at 16.
[73] D Miers, 'Liability for Injuries Caused by Violent Patients' [1996] J of Personal Injury L 314, 321–322. However, *Tarasoff*-style actions in the US are relatively rare. B Markesinis and S Deakin, *Tort Law* (4th edn, Oxford: 1999) 283 are scathing of this argument which, they say, 'strikes at the heart of medical negligence litigation. . . . Is it really being suggested that otherwise justified actions against doctors and NHS Trusts should fail because they are expensive?'
[74] See para 3.05 above.
[75] cp *Tucker v News Media Ownership Ltd* [1986] 2 NZLR 716, 734.
[76] See para 20.05 above.
[77] The test derives from *Osman v UK* (1998) 5 BHRC 293, para 116. J Wright, *Tort Law and Human Rights* (Oxford: 2001) 129, having surveyed the Strasbourg jurisprudence relevant to the question whether Art 8 imposes a positive obligation on the UK to impose a legal duty to rescue, is of the opinion that 'the pre-eminence accorded the protection of physical integrity under Art 8' makes it 'arguable . . . that an obligation to rescue/warn on the part of private actors may be inferred from the general thrust of the jurisprudence. If a duty to rescue is cast in terms that the individual need only act to the extent that he/she is not exposed to personal danger the fair balance that needs to be struck between the interests of the individual and the wider community will be met. There is no case directly on point, but this is not surprising given that the United Kingdom is exceptional in failing to impose such an obligation upon individuals, either through criminal or civil law.'

B. Private Law Duty

has a public interest defence to an action for breach of confidence.[78] Otherwise the professional might escape liability to the victim only to incur liability in contract or in equity to the client.

Other limitations on liability are likely. A duty to warn an intended adult victim who is already alive to the danger makes no sense.[79] Most US jurisdictions that recognize a *Tarasoff* duty have, either by judicial fiat or legislation,[80] limited that duty to situations involving: 20.17

(1) an explicit verbal threat[81]
(2) of serious bodily harm,[82]
(3) to a named or readily identifiable third party,[83] and
(4) a clear and imminent danger.

Thus in *Little v All Phoenix South Community Health Center*[84] the Court of Appeals of Arizona threw out a lawsuit by a psychiatric patient's wife who was stabbed by the patient. The patient had told those caring for him that he was having 'stupid thoughts' of armed robbery, murder, arson and suicide. The court said that such vague statements did not require any specific person to be warned that the patient was dangerous.

One can confidently predict that if English law recognizes a duty to warn or protect at all, that duty will only be owed to someone readily identifiable[85] because otherwise the duty would get out of hand. In *Palmer v Tees Health Authority* Gage J said that for the defendant Health Authority to owe a duty of care to a claimant who was injured by the wrongdoing of a psychiatric patient, the claimant must be someone 'who came into a special or exceptional or distinctive category of risk 20.18

---

[78] See ch 11.
[79] cp *Hawkins v King County* 602 P 2d 361, 365 (1979).
[80] See P Appelbaum et al, 'Statutory approaches to limiting psychiatrists' liability for their patients' violent acts' (1989) 146 American J of Psychiatry 821; 'The Duty to Protect Third Parties and Negligent Release' in B Weiner and R Wettstein (eds), *Legal Issues in Mental Health Care* (New York: 1993) 247.
[81] But see *Jablonski by Pahls v US* 712 F 2d 391, 398 (1983); *Jones v Smith* (1999) 169 DLR (4th) 385, 406.
[82] But in *Peck v Counseling Service of Addison County* the *Tarasoff* duty was extended by the Vermont Supreme Court to include threats of arson on that theory that '[a]rson is a violent act and represents a lethal threat to human beings who may be in the vicinity of the conflagration'. per Hill J, 499 A 2d 422, 424 (1985).
[83] The leading case in favour of this restriction is *Thompson v County of Alameda* 614 P 2d 728 (1980) and see *Brady v Hopper* 570 F Supp 1333 Contrast *Lipari v Sears, Roebuck & Co* 497 F Supp 185 (1980). cp *Wenden v Trikha* (1991) 116 AR (2d) 80. There is no duty to warn others if the patient threatens suicide: *Bellah v Greenson* 73 Cal App (3d) 911 (1977).
[84] 919 P 2d 1368 (1995).
[85] cp *Osman v UK* (1998) 5 BHRC 293, para 116. In *W v Egdell* [1990] 1 All ER 835 there was no readily identifiable victim but the question was the legality of a breach of confidentiality, not the existence of a duty to warn.

from the activities of the third party'.[86] Gage J's judgment was upheld on appeal[87] and followed in *W v S CC*[88] where the Court of Appeal held that a lack of proximity meant that the Council was under no duty to warn the claimants' mothers that they lived in the vicinity of a 13-year-old boy with propensities toward sexual abuse of young children. Sir Martin Nourse said:

> [T]he claimants in this case did not come into a special or exceptional or distinctive category of risk. They were simply members of a wide category of members of the general public. The defendants did not know of any friendship or association between [the abuser] and any of the claimants. . . . Even if the defendants had been under some duty to warn others, it is not shown that they were under a duty to warn the claimants' mothers any more than the mothers of all other young children living within 75 yards of X Court or beyond.

The difficulties that the Council would have faced, given the fact that the abuser was not in Council care, had it been under a duty, were also stressed:

> When one asks what is suggested that the claimant [sic] could and should have done, it amounts to the proposition that the mere charges made against [the abuser] and their nature or, after 3rd September 1993, the fact of two convictions for indecent assault, should have led to the local authority contacting all neighbours, or at least all neighbours who might have families or children with them or visiting them, in the immediate neighbourhood with a view presumably to drawing their attention to [the abuser]; alternatively, it amounts to the proposition that they should have provided 24-hour accompaniment for [the abuser], or at least day-time accompaniment. Those propositions seem to me very remarkable in their consequences. One can envisage that they could and would give rise to very substantial objection and difficulties if they were accepted as potential legal duties.

Tarasoff and professionals who are not mental health specialists

20.19 *Tarasoff* involved a mental health professional. How far does its reach extend? Social workers,[89] GPs, counsellors, clergy,[90] teachers, probation officers,[91] nurses and lawyers[92] all from time to time hear clients threaten violence. If mental health

---

[86] [1998] 45 BMLR 88, 101. Cp *Hill v Chief Constable West Yorkshire* [1988] 2 All ER 238, 243. But see *Kines Estate v Lychuk* (1998) 123 Man R (2d) 151, para 7.
[87] *Palmer v Tees Health Authority* [1999] Lloyd's Rep Med 351.
[88] [2001] EWCA Civ 691.
[89] The Australian Law Reform Commission in *Report on Privacy* (Sydney: 1993) para 951 gives the example of a recipient of welfare who, during an interview, threatened to kill the person who had informed the authorities that he was living with a woman who was employed. Shortly afterwards the threat was carried out.
[90] In *Neufang v Aetna Casualty & Surety Co* (No 81-08118-CSs Fla Cir Ct, Broward County) an unreported 1981 case filed in Florida a wife was shot one day after her husband began marital counselling with a clergyman. The wife, relying in *Tarasoff*, sued the clergyman for failing to warn her of her husband's violent propensities. The case was dismissed.
[91] eg *R v Kennedy* (CA, 30 April 1998).
[92] L Levin, 'Testing the Radical Experiment: A Study of Lawyer Response to Clients Who Intend to Harm Others' (1994) 47 Rutgers L Rev 81; G Lewis, 'Client threats' (1983) 57 Law Institute J 847.

professionals have a duty to warn someone appropriate of the risk of a client causing another serious physical injury, do some, or all, of these other categories of professional also have a duty to deliver a similar warning?

Policy

Lawyers and other professionals who are not mental health professionals   20.20
There are obvious problems in imposing a reporting requirement on people who are not mental health professionals. The problem is acute if the client makes no explicit threats,[93] but even if he does, the professional is not trained to assess their sincerity. An Alberta code of ethics for the legal profession which mandates disclosure of prospective crimes of violence by a client states that the lawyer 'must first assess whether it is reasonable to assume that the client will carry out the expressed intention'.[94] How is a lawyer to know whether or not the red-faced client who waves his fist at the mere mention of the judge's name and says he will 'shoot the bastard' is simply venting his anger when mental health professionals have so much difficulty predicting violence? When asked to apply the *Tarasoff* duty to an attorney in *Hawkins v King County*, the Washington Court of Appeals declined to do so, accepting the position advanced by amicus 'that the obligation to warn, when confidentiality would be compromised to the client's detriment, must be permissive at most, unless it appears beyond a reasonable doubt that the client has formed a firm intention to inflict serious personal injuries on an unknowing third person'.[95] It seems in any event most unlikely that an English court, if it endorsed a *Tarasoff*-style duty at all, would apply that duty to lawyers given the importance the courts attach to legal professional privilege[96] and the practical difficulties of observing a duty to warn without over-reporting.[97] Moreover, a common law duty to warn would encourage lawyers to warn clients against disclosing planned wrongdoing to them which would not be in the public interest.[98] Given that a professional already has a *discretion* to disclose a serious risk of violence to a third party, the case for imposing on most classes of professional a *duty* to warn either the would-be victim or the authorities is not convincing.

Teachers   Schoolteachers may be a special case. Proximity and policy both point   20.21
to an obligation to warn and protect a child who is known to be, or can reasonably

---

[93] eg *W v S CC* [2001] EWCA Civ 691. The Court of Appeal thought that the Council had no reason to foresee that the abuser, himself a boy of 13, whom a court had allowed bail, would re-offend.

[94] *Code of Professional Conduct*, ch 7, r 8(c), commentary, available from http://www.lawsocietyalberta.com. A number of Canadian jurisdictions mandate disclosure in these circumstances: see para 11.14 above.

[95] 602 P 2d 361, 365 (1979).

[96] See para 16.25 above.

[97] For the case for imposing an *ethical* duty on lawyers to give a warning see A Dodek, 'Doing Our Duty: The Case for a Duty of Disclosure to Prevent Death or Serious Harm' (2001) 50 University of New Brunswick LJ 21.

[98] See para 1.47 above.

be foreseen to be, at risk of harm when on school property or off school premises in the charge of a teacher. The law says that a 'teacher owes a duty of care for the physical safety of a child attending school under the charge of that teacher'.[99] Whether the danger is from a member of staff, a stranger or another child should not matter. The courts have held that on rare occasions a school might be in breach of duty for failing to take steps within its power to combat the harmful behaviour of one pupil towards another outside school.[100] Whether or not a school has a legal duty to protect a child from being harmed outside the school gates before or after school, it is not unreasonable to expect the school to warn an unwary child, or the child's parents, of such a danger (if known to the school) so that they can take defensive measures. The vulnerability of children, their quasi-paternal relationship with their teachers and the simplicity of a warning, justifies a duty and not merely a discretion to act proactively. There is some precedent for this in the government guidance[101] that requires teachers to report suspicions of child abuse occurring outside the school.[102]

Other requirements for liability

20.22 For civil liability to follow the omission of a warning, a professional must not only owe the claimant a duty, but breach that duty. If a responsible body of professional opinion would have advised against a warning preferring instead to counsel the client against violence, it may be difficult to prove a breach of duty.[103] Establishing a causal connection between breach of duty and the particular injury suffered may present further difficulties. The court must be persuaded that a warning would have put a stop to the violence. Sadly, this is not always the case. An Australian lawyer who did inform the police and the court that his client had threatened to kill other litigants acted in vain.[104]

Child and Elder Abuse

20.23 Many common law jurisdictions, though thus far not England and Wales, have enacted legislation compelling professionals such as doctors, social workers, dentists, teachers and nurses to report suspected physical, sexual or psychological

---

[99] per Lord Clyde, *Phelps v Hillingdon LBC* [2000] 4 All ER 504, 532. For a similar Government pronouncement see Dfes, Circular 10/95 *Protecting Children from Abuse: The Role of the Education Service*, Introduction, para 4: 'schools and colleges have a pastoral responsibility towards their pupils and should recognise that pupils have a fundamental right to be protected from harm. Children cannot learn effectively unless they feel secure. Every school and college should, therefore, develop a child protection policy which reflects its statutory duties and pastoral responsibilities.'
[100] *Bradford-Smart v West Sussex CC* [2002] EWCA Civ 7; [2002] 1 FCR 425, paras 34, 36.
[101] There was talk of making this a statutory duty: Guardian, 29 June 2002.
[102] Dfes, Circular 10/95 *Protecting Children from Abuse: The Role of the Education Service* esp paras 14, 27.
[103] See para 19.65 above. Courts are more deferential to medical opinion than prevailing standards in some other professions (see para 19.64 above).
[104] G Lewis, 'Client threats' (1983) 58 Law Institute J 847.

B. Private Law Duty

violence against a child with or without the victim's consent.[105] Some US states and Canadian provinces also mandate reporting of abuse of the elderly.[106] Elderly people are known to be reluctant to self-report abuse[107] because of feelings of powerlessness, fear of retaliation, shame and—particularly—anxiety that it may lead to institutionalization.[108] Might the law of negligence be developed to fill the lacuna in English law? An affirmative answer depends, in the first instance, upon judicial willingness to impose a duty to warn.[109]

A relationship of sufficient proximity

A tortious duty demands a relationship of sufficient proximity.[110] Establishing this proximity may be problematic when the client is not the person being abused but, for example, a member of the victim's family[111] or even the abuser himself. In *JAW v Roberts*[112] a professional counselling a couple for their marital difficulties discovered that their foster-son was being abused by his foster-father and did not report this to the authorities. The Indiana Court of Appeals held that because no special relationship existed between counsellor and victim, the counsellor owed the victim no duty to report the abuse. Typically, however, the victim is the client and when this is the case proximity is not an issue. For example:

20.24

- A pregnant 15-year-old patient reveals to her doctor that the father of the baby is her stepfather.[113]
- An elderly widow who lives with her daughter confides to a social worker that her daughter deliberately spills scalding tea over her.

In these scenarios the duty battleground will be policy.

---

[105] There is a mandatory reporting law for child abuse in all US states, in all Canadian jurisdictions except Yukon and in most Australian states: W Renke, 'The Mandatory Reporting of Child Abuse under the Child Welfare Act' (1999) 7 Health LJ 91, nn 6, 9, 10. For the Canadian law see R Bessner, *The Duty to Report Child Abuse* available at: http://canada.justice.gc.ca/ps/yj/rp/doc/Paper106.rtf; and M McCallum, 'Mandatory Child Abuse Reporting and Confidentiality in the Lawyer–Client Relationship' (2001) 50 University of New Brunswick LJ 263. A mandatory reporting law was debated in New Zealand in 1994: J Yates, 'Mandatory Reporting of Child Abuse and the Public/Private Distinction' (1994) 7 Auckland L Rev 781.

[106] E Welfel et al, 'Mandated Reporting of Abuse/Maltreatment of Older Adults: A Primer for Counselors' (2000) J of Counseling and Development 284.

[107] This takes various forms: infliction of physical injury, neglect, inappropriate medication, financial exploitation.

[108] H Astbury et al, 'The impact of domestic violence on individuals' (2000) 173 Medical J of Austrlia 427.

[109] Liability would further depend on establishing a breach of the duty, causation and damage that is not too remote. Cp para 20.22 above

[110] See para 20.09 above.

[111] In *R v C* (1993) 14 Cr App R (S) 562 a woman receiving counselling for childhood sexual abuse told the therapist that a younger member of the family might still be being abused by her abuser. The therapist reported this to the police and the abuser was prosecuted.

[112] 627 NE 2d 802 (1994).

[113] Anon, 'An Ethical Debate: Child protection: medical responsibilities' (1996) 313 British Medical J 671.

Policy

Children

20.25 A strong case can be made for a duty to warn an organization such as the NSPCC, the police or social services that a child is, or is suspected of being, at risk of abuse.[114] Abuse tends to be repeated, therefore unless the child has ceased to have contact with the abuser there is usually a high risk of repetition. In *Gillick v West Norfolk and Wisbech Area Health Authority* Eveleigh LJ commented that there 'is no law of confidentiality which would command silence when the welfare of the child is concerned'.[115] Children are physically and emotionally vulnerable and society has a duty, recognized by Parliament in the Children Act 1989,[116] to protect them if their parents do not. Professionals employed by a health authority, local education authority or social services department may already be required by their terms of employment to report suspected child abuse.[117] This duty may be reinforced by government guidance or an ethical code. For example, teachers 'have a professional responsibility to share relevant information about the protection of children with other professionals, particularly investigative agencies'.[118] Department of Health guidance states that 'any person who has knowledge of, or a suspicion that a child is suffering significant harm, should refer their concern to one or more of the agencies with statutory duties and/or powers to investigate or intervene'.[119] The General Medical Council (GMC) guidance on confidentiality says that a doctor who believes that a child is the victim of neglect or physical, sexual or emotional abuse 'should give information promptly to an appropriate responsible person or statutory authority' if she believes that disclosure is in the patient's best interests.[120] The doctor must be prepared to justify non-disclosure.[121] Continuing or threatened child abuse is one of the few circumstances in which the Law Society allows a lawyer to breach an obligation of

---

[114] W Renke, 'The Mandatory Reporting of Child Abuse under the Child Welfare Act' (1999) 7 Health LJ 91, 99–107. A common law duty to warn has been recognized in the US: *Golden Spread Council, Inc v Atkins* 926 SW 2d 287, 291 (1996).

[115] [1985] 1 All ER 533, 559.

[116] A local authority is required by s 47 to investigate cases where it is suspected that a child is suffering or is likely to suffer 'significant harm'.

[117] P Jenkins, *Counselling, Psychotherapy and the Law* (London: 1997) 134; D Daniels and P Jenkins, *Therapy with Children* (London: 2000) 86–88. Such persons may also be subject to Children Act 1989, s 47(9) which, depending upon how it is interpreted, may place them under a duty to breach confidentiality in order to assist a local authority with inquiries into suspected cases of child abuse: see para 10.11 above.

[118] DfEE Circular 10/95 *Protecting Children From Abuse: the Role of the Education Service* para 27.

[119] *Working Together Under the Children Act 1989* (1991) para 5.11.1. See also *Protection and Use of Patient Information* HSG (96) 18 (1996) para 4.11

[120] GMC, *Confidentiality: Protecting and Providing Information* (June 2000) para 39.

[121] On the earlier versions of the guidance see 'An Ethical Debate: Child protection: medical responsibilities' (1996) 313 British Medical J 671.

B. Private Law Duty

confidentiality to a client. The Law Society, however, stops short of imposing a duty to report the abuse.[122]

If as a consequence of a professional failing to notify the authorities that a child is at risk of continued abuse by a particular person, a child in a relationship of proximity with a professional remains vulnerable to, and is in fact abused by that person, the opportunity should exist to sue the professional in negligence. From the professional's standpoint, a duty to report child abuse is no bad thing. It increases the chances of the professional relationship surviving the reporting of the abuse because the decision to act can be represented to the child and the child's parents as having been forced upon the professional by law.

The elderly

It is much less likely that a duty, whether statutory or tortious, will be imposed upon professionals who come into contact with the elderly to report elder abuse be it physical, sexual, psychological, financial or neglect if the victim is frail but competent and does not want to complain.[123] To make reporting of elder abuse mandatory regardless of the wishes of the victim is an infringement of the victim's dignity and autonomy[124] and likely also to infringe the victim's Article 8 right to respect for private life. The Law Society does not envisage non-consensual disclosure under any circumstances. It advises solicitors that if an adult client has suffered abuse the solicitor should suggest 'where the client, or the solicitor on the client's behalf, go for help' but that the solicitor 'is absolutely bound by the duty of confidentiality to the client'.[125] Should an adult victim of abuse be incompetent (whether elderly or not) the case for mandatory reporting is very much stronger. It is hard to see reasons for distinguishing between those lacking competence through age and those lacking it through mental incapacity. They are both equally deserving of protection.

20.26

20.27

---

[122] When the client is the abuser or another adult or an immature child the decision whether or not to disclose is left to the discretion of the solicitor who must be guided by the public interest and be prepared to justify the disclosure or non-disclosure, if called upon to do so, to a court or disciplinary tribunal: Law Society, *The Guidance to the Professional Conduct of Solicitors* (7th edn, London: 1996), Annex 16A, 294. If the client is a '*Gillick* competent' minor (see para 13.13 above) the Law Society's advice is not to reveal the abuse to a third party without the client's consent except when the solicitor 'knows or strongly suspects that younger siblings are being abused or where the child is in fear of his or her life or of serious injury' (at 297). This advice is not repeated in the most recent edition of the Law Society *Guidance*.

[123] The 'No Secrets' (2001) guidance from the DoH on the protection of vulnerable adults points out that disclosure of abuse of an elderly person may be justifiable on public interest grounds (para 5.8). An example given is of a situation where other vulnerable persons are also at risk of harm (para 5.6). On this ground the guidance advises against giving assurances of absolute confidentiality (para 5.6). See http://www.doh.gov.uk/pub/docs/doh/nosecrets.pdf.

[124] Conceded by J Jones and M Lupton, 'Liability in Delict for Failure to Report Family Violence' (1999) 116 South African LJ 371 who argue for a duty to warn.

[125] R White, 'Confidentiality and Privilege: Child Abuse and Child Abduction' (1992) 1 Child Abuse Rev 60, 61. This sets out the Law Society guidance. Compare and contrast the approach of the court in *Howell-Smith v Price* (CA, 26 April 1996) discussed in paras 12.03–12.04 above.

Risk of HIV Infection

Background to US law

20.28 A majority of US jurisdictions have held that once a doctor has diagnosed a contagious or infectious illness such as tuberculosis the treating doctor has a duty to warn members of the patient's family at risk of infection of the nature of the disease and how to avoid it.[126] One court has even imposed a duty to warn relatives of a foreseeable risk of contracting a non-contagious disease from an environment shared with the patient.[127] A study in 1998 at two US hospitals found that four out of every ten persons who were HIV seropositive did not advise their sexual partners of their HIV status and almost two-thirds of the defaulters did not always use a condom.[128] Such high risk behaviour has fuelled debate as to whether a doctor (or any other professional)[129] has an analogous duty to inform past and present sexual and needle-sharing partners of an HIV patient of that patient's condition[130] if the patient refuses to do so.[131]

20.29 Most writers admit that disclosure in an HIV/AIDs case is not on all fours with disclosure of a contagious disease.[132] On the one hand the danger of the complaint spreading is less because AIDS is not caught by casual contact, on the other the great stigma attached to this disease means that there is a much greater danger that sufferers will not agree to reveal the diagnosis. Relatively few US cases[133] address

---

[126] T Bateman, Annotation, 'Liability of doctor or other health practitioner to third party contracting contagious disease from doctor's patient', 3 ALR 5th 370 (1992). The doctor's duty to prevent transmission of contagious diseases was recognized before the *Tarasoff* duty to which it is very similar.

[127] *Bradshaw v Daniel* 854 SW 2d 865 (1993) noted [1994] Medical L Rev 237.

[128] 'Sex Partners Often Silent About HIV', New York Times, 9 February 1998, A10.

[129] The question has been posed whether an attorney would have a duty to disclose a client's HIV status to the woman with whom he lives: D Cooper, 'The Ethical Rules Lack Ethics: Tort Liability when a Lawyer Fails to Warn a Third Party of a Client's Threat to Cause Serious Physical Harm or Death' (2000) 36 Idaho L Rev 479, 504, 521.

[130] There may also be a duty to warn those charged with the care of the patient's health who might be at risk of infection.

[131] Some of the US literature is summarized in A Harding et al, 'Confidentiality Limits with Clients who Have HIV: A review of Ethical and Legal Guidelines and Professional Practices' (1993) 71 J of Counseling and Development 297. See also M Neave, 'AIDS—Confidentiality and the Duty to Warn' (1987) U of Tasmania L Rev 1, 23–31; A Grubb and D Pearl, *Blood Testing, AIDS and DNA Profiling, Law and Policy* (Bristol: 1990) 52–55; J Sestito, 'The Duty to Warn Third Parties and AIDS in Canada' (1996) Health L in Canada 83. The question whether the doctor should give a warning if she does not believe the patient's promise to tell is even more problematic.

[132] The situation is unlike *Tarasoff v Regents of the University of California* 551 P 2d 334, 361–362 (1976) in so far as there is no specific or immediate threat of serious injury or death to a third party. In fact there is no risk at all to the partner, if the partner was infected before the patient was discovered to be HIV seropositive. Even if the partner is infection-free, the danger from the patient is a passive one. This has not stopped American writers speculating about the application of the *Tarasoff* duty in AIDS cases: D Casswell, 'Disclosure by a Physician of Aids-Related Patient Information: An Ethical and Legal Dilemma' (1989) 68 Canadian Bar Rev 224, 235 et seq.

[133] A health organization was enjoined from divulging the results of a patient's HIV test to his former wife, who had tested negative in an HIV test, in *Doe v Prime Health/ Kansas City AIDS Litigation Reporter* 1641 (1988). See also *Garcia v Santa Rosa Health Care Corp* 925 SW 2d 372 (1996).

The US legal position

Duty to warn the patient of the risk of infection to others

The leading US legal decision is *Reisner v Regents of the University of California*.[135] In this case an infected sexual partner sued a doctor for failing to inform the patient or her parents until after the patient was diagnosed with AIDS five years later that at the age of 12 she had received HIV infected blood during surgical procedure, a fact of which the doctor had been made aware the day after his patient had received the contaminated blood. The court said that this omission prevented the girl, her parents or both from warning the defendant of her condition. The doctor did not know the defendant, or even that he existed, but the court reasoned that he should have realized that as the girl matured the likelihood would grow that she would engage in sexual activity with someone.[136]

20.30

A quite different view was taken in *Prasesel v Johnson*[137] of the failure of a doctor to warn a patient suffering from epilepsy that he should not drive. The patient suffered a seizure at the wheel of his car, struck another vehicle and killed the driver. The Supreme Court of Texas ruled that the patient's physicians were not in breach of a duty owed to the deceased because 'the benefit of warning an epileptic not to drive is incremental but the consequences of imposing a duty are great'.[138] The court's explanation was that the patient might not have heeded the warning and, knowing that he was an epileptic, must have had at least some inkling of the risks attached to driving a car.

20.31

---

[134] J Gates and B Arons, *Privacy and Confidentiality in Mental Health Care* (Baltimore, 2000) 163.
[135] 37 Cal Rptr 2d 518 (1995).
[136] 37 Cal Rptr 2d 518, 521 (1995).
[137] 967 SW 2d 391 (1998). Contrast: *Gooden v Tips* 651 SW 2d 364 (1983) where a doctor was held to owe a third party a duty to warn the patient not to drive after prescribing Quaalude to a patient with a history of drug abuse; *Myers v Quesenberry* 144 Ca App 3d 888 (1983) where doctors were held to owe a third party a duty to warn a patient with an uncontrolled diabetic condition not to drive; *Spillane v Wasserman* (1992) 37 ACWS (3d) 412 where an accident caused by the defendant's epilepsy caused the death of a cyclist and the court held that the defendant's doctors should have warned the defendant not to drive a heavy goods vehicle.
[138] per Owen J 967 SW 2d 391, 397 (1998). English courts may be more inclined to impose a private law duty to report to the authorities unfitness to drive because of the GMC reporting guidelines: *Confidentiality: Protecting and Providing Information* (London: 2000) para 37.

Duty to warn a third party at risk of infection

20.32 The court's opinion in *Reisner* strongly implies that the doctor's duty to the defendant did not extend beyond informing the patient, her parents or both of her HIV status and the risk of infection of a sexual partner.[139] In the circumstances of that case, imposing a duty on the doctor to warn the patient's sexual partner(s) would have been unrealistic. The doctor had no way of discovering, other than by constant surveillance, whom his patient dated during the remainder of her life. In a similar Canadian case, a doctor who failed to warn a patient that he had received contaminated blood during a blood transfusion whilst undergoing cardiac surgery was held liable to the man's wife when she became infected with AIDS.[140] The court, having concluded that the deceased would have told his wife of the HIV risk if he had been told, declined to decide whether the defendant owed the wife an independent duty.

The position in English law

Duty to warn a third party at risk of infection

20.33 **Relationship of sufficient proximity** In England an action in negligence founded on the failure of a doctor to warn a third party either directly or via the infected patient of the risk of contracting HIV through unprotected sexual intercourse with the patient would founder unless the court were prepared to find a special relationship of proximity between doctor and claimant.[141] If the claimant is (1) the patient's wife or long-term partner, and (2) also the doctor's patient[142] it is probable there would be sufficient proximity for a duty. The absence of (2) might not be fatal if the doctor were aware of the sexual relationship. In *Goodwill v British Pregnancy Authority Service*[143] the Court of Appeal held that no special relationship existed between a health service provider and the sexual partner of a patient who had relied upon the provider's negligent advice about fertility after a vasectomy. Emphasis was placed on the fact that the claimant was not the patient's sexual partner at the time the advice was given but one of an unpredictable class of possible future sexual partners.[144] It seems to have been accepted that had the

---

[139] 'Once the physician warns the patient of the risk to others and advises the patient how to prevent the spread of the disease, the physician has fulfilled his duty—and no more (but no less) is required', per Vogel J, 37 Cal Rptr 2d 518, 523 (1995).

[140] *Pittman v Bain* (1994) 112 DLR (4th) 257. See also *DiMarco v Lynch Homes—Chester County Inc* 583 A 2d 422, 424–425 (1990) a hepatitis B case in which the patient was given erroneous advice with the result that her sexual partner became infected with hepatitis B and *BT v Oei* [1999] NSWSC 1082 in which a doctor was held liable to a woman who contracted HIV from her husband because the doctor failed to have the husband tested for HIV in circumstances where a competent doctor would have done so.

[141] See para 20.09 above.

[142] cp *C v D* [1925] 1 DLR 734, 738.

[143] [1996] 2 All ER 161.

[144] ibid at 169, 170.

B. Private Law Duty

claimant been the patient's wife at the time of the vasectomy the doctor would have owed her a duty.[145]

Policy A duty in tort law depends upon the court's perception of public policy as well as proximity.[146] In discussing policy one needs to distinguish the duty to warn a third party directly from the duty to warn a third party via the patient. A duty to warn a third party directly conflicts with the doctor's duty of confidentiality to the patient. In HIV/AIDS cases preserving medical confidentiality is recognized to be vitally important. There is a considerable risk that if confidentiality cannot be guaranteed persons will be deterred from seeking HIV testing or, when they seek help, of being completely candid about their sexual practices.[147] This risk must be viewed against the background that voluntary testing and counselling is considered to offer the best hope of stopping the spread of AIDS.[148] In the long run, a legal duty to warn sexual partners at risk of infection without patient consent may compromise more lives than it saves if the duty leads a significant number of infected persons to delay or avoid testing. 'The fact that a particular disclosure of a patient's dangerousness could have saved the life of a particular third party should not obscure the fact that a general rule requiring disclosure may in fact lead to the deaths of more individuals. If such costs are involved, a rule providing for such disclosure is not the sort that prudent men and women ought to adopt.'[149] The possibility that the duty may have this effect (testing the theory empirically is difficult), makes it improbable that English courts will impose upon a doctor a legally enforceable duty to notify a patient's partner directly of the patient's diagnosis—even if the claimant and patient share a doctor. This is the more so because the GMC leaves a warning to the discretion of the doctor.[150] International guidelines too treat disclosure without patient consent as procedure of last resort in an extreme case.[151]

20.34

Duty to warn the patient

Confidentiality is not an obstacle to the imposition of a duty on the doctor along *Reisner* lines. The GMC rules of ethics oblige doctors to explain to patients

20.35

---

[145] ibid at 161, 167, 170. The Court of Appeal envisages only a duty to a sexual partner who is married to the patient. In confining the duty to a married partner the court can be seen either as 'exalting an unheeded morality over reality' (per Larsen J, *Di Marco v Lynch Homes—Chester County Inc* 583 A 2d 422, 425 (1990)) or sensibly restricting 'the scope of liability to a manageable, predictable class' (per Levine J, *Miller v Rivard* 585 NYS 2d 523, 527 (1992)).

[146] Proximity and policy, in practice, are not totally separate issues. Policy informs findings about proximity.

[147] M Neave, 'AIDS—Confidentiality and the Duty to Warn' (1987) U Tasmania L Rev 1, 3–4; A Vedder, 'HIV/AIDS and the Point and Scope of Medical Confidentiality' in R Bennett and C Erin (eds), *HIV and AIDS: Testing, Screening and Confidentiality* (Oxford: 1999) ch 9; J Gates and B Arons, *Privacy and Confidentiality in Mental Health Care* (Baltimore: 2000) 163. See also *X v Y* [1988] 2 All ER 648, 653.

[148] *X v Y* [1988] 2 All ER 648, 653, 654.

[149] H Engelhardt, *The Foundations of Bioethics* (New York: 1986) 299.

[150] See para 11.58 above.

[151] ibid.

suffering from a serious communicable disease (including HIV/AIDS) the nature of their illness and ways of protecting others from infection.[152] A common law duty to a non-patient to inform the patient of his HIV status and how to guard against its transmission would be in keeping with this ethical obligation. The New South Wales Supreme Court was persuaded in *BT v Oei*[153] that there were no public policy objections to imposing such a duty and proximity was found in the reasonable foreseeability of harm to BT who was the patient's girlfriend and later his wife. The Court of Appeal's decision in *Goodwill v British Pregnancy Authority Service* probably precludes liability if the sexual partner was unknown to the doctor.[154]

Causation

20.36 Should a doctor owe a duty to a third party to inform the patient that he is HIV seropositive, proving causation may be problematic.[155] The claimant would have to show that the infection occurred after the patient's HIV status was, or should have been, discovered by the doctor and that the agent of infection was the patient. This could be difficult for a claimant with several sexual partners or a claimant who had regularly had sexual intercourse with the patient over many years.[156] Further, if the claimant has knowing and willingly engaged in high-risk sexual behaviour[157] with the patient, a court might treat this as the effective cause of infection.[158]

Genetic Conditions

Duty to warn blood relatives and sexual partners

20.37 There has been speculation,[159] and in America some case law, about whether a professional whose patient has a genetic flaw that has familial implications has a common law duty to inform:

---

[152] GMC, *Serious Communicable Diseases Guidance to Doctors* (October 1997), available from http://www.gmc-uk.org/.
[153] [1999] NSWSC 1082. For an analysis of this case see B Hocking and S Muirhead, 'Warning, warning, warning—all doctors!' (2000) 16 Professional Negligence 31.
[154] See para 20.33 above. cp commentary [1997] Medical L Rev 255.
[155] The issues are discussed by R Paterson, 'AIDS, HIV Testing and Medical Confidentiality' (1991) 7 Otago L Rev 379, 400–404.
[156] M Jones, 'Medical confidentiality and the public interest' (1990) 6 Professional Negligence 16, 22. But see *Pittman Estate v Bain* (1994) 112 DLR (4th) 257 and *BT v Oei* [1999] NSWSC 1082. The claimant in *Oei* overcame the first obstacle (the second did not apply) and the claimant in *Pittman* overcame both.
[157] Unprotected casual intercourse, especially between men.
[158] In *Goodwill v Pregnancy Service* [1996] 2 All ER 161, 170, Thorpe LJ said that the claimant had a responsibility to protect herself against unwanted conception and to take independent advice. However, in *BT v Oei* [1999] NSWSC 1082 the claimant succeeded even though she at times ignored her doctor's advice about the danger of contracting hepatitis B (from which her partner also suffered) through unprotected sexual intercourse.
[159] C NgWena and R Chadwick, 'Genetic Diagnostic Information and the Duty of Confidentiality: Ethics and Law' (1993)1 Medical L Intl 73; G Laurie, Obligations arising from genetic information—negligence and the protection of familial interests (1999) 11 Child & Family L Q 109; D Bell and B Bennett, 'Genetic Secrets and the Family' [2001] Medical L Rev 130, 149.

B. Private Law Duty

(1) the patient's spouse if the information might affect the spouse's reproductive choices; and

(2) blood relatives who may be predisposed to the same defect or whose reproductive choices might be affected by the information.

The British Medical Association (BMA),[160] the Nuffield Council on Bioethics[161] and the House of Commons Science and Technology Committee[162] are all against imposing a general legal duty to warn relatives if the patient objects. And experience shows that some patients do object.[163] In the face of this unanimous opposition, it is unlikely that if a relationship of proximity exists an English court would hold a health care professional under a *duty* to override the wishes of the patient to warn those personally 'at risk'[164] or whose offspring might be. This is not to say that if a doctor knows that her patient, A, has a debilitating genetic condition, she should avoid taking the precautionary measures that a competent physician would take to protect B, another patient and a relative of A's, who is at risk of developing the same condition. If A objects to disclosure, every effort would need to be made to avoid alerting B to A's diagnosis, or to minimize the extent of disclosure if this proves impossible, but the need to protect patient A's medical confidentiality cannot justify offering B suboptimum medical care.[165]

20.38

Duty to warn patient of risk to blood relatives

Whether an English court could be persuaded , as one US court has been,[166] to support a more limited duty to warn the patient that his relatives are at risk of a genetic condition depends, as always in novel duty situations, upon whether the court is satisfied that a duty is in the public interest and that there is a relationship of proximity, in this instance between the doctor and the relatives. When the

20.39

---

[160] BMA, *Human Genetics: Choice and Responsibility* (Oxford: 1998) 71.
[161] *Genetic Screening Ethical Issues* (London: 1993) para 5.29.
[162] House of Commons Science and Technology Committee, *Human Genetics: The Science and Its Consequences* (1995) para 228.
[163] C NgWena and R Chadwick, 'Genetic Diagnostic Information and the Duty of Confidentiality: Ethics and Law' (1993)1 Medical L Intl 73, 79. One reason may be that the results incidentally disclose non-paternity.
[164] Contrast *Pate v Threlkel* 661 So 2d 278 (1995).
[165] cp G Laurie, *Genetic Privacy* (Cambridge: 2002) 270–271. He uses the example of a health care professional who is aware of a genetic disorder in a family through testing one member, who is faced with the dilemma of whether to offer a pre-natal test to another member of the family, also a patient, who is pregnant. His conclusion is that 'in the straightforward case of a highly penetrant monogenic disorder it is strongly arguable that a health care professional would owe a duty to a pregnant patient' to carry out the pre-natal tests.
[166] *Pate v Threlkel* 661 So 2d 278 (1995). For a discussion of this case and *Safer v Estate of Pack* 677 A 2d 1188 (1996) where a duty to warn relatives directly was recognized see C Parker, 'Camping Trips and Family Trees: Must Tennessee Physicians Warn their Patients' Relatives of Genetic Risks' (1998) 65 Tennessee L Rev 585; J Burnett, 'A Physician's Duty to Warn a Patient's Relatives of a Patient's Genetically Inheritable Disease' (1999) 36 Houston L Rev 559.

relatives are closely related to the patient, and in particular where the relatives are also patients of the doctor, the case for a duty is a strong one. Bell and Bennett write that 'in the case where the family member is a patient of the same doctor, it is arguable that the person is relying on the doctor to prevent injury to them by providing proper care and treatment, and that in appropriate cases this would include the provision of information obtained from another family member of a genetic condition which is treatable'.[167] Medical confidentiality is not an issue and the only policy reasons for rejecting the duty are the danger of the patient disclosing the information for malicious motives or in an inept manner and a conflict of interests between the patient and the relatives. For instance, it may not be in the patient's best interests to know all about the condition and its implications for relatives if the patient himself cannot be successfully treated.[168]

Risk of Non-Violent Crime or Fraud[169]

20.40 Suppose that a professional, say an accountant or lawyer, has discovered that a client is committing, or is about to commit, fraud or a crime that involves no risk of serious bodily harm or death to another. If there is no relevant statutory disclosure obligation[170] and she says nothing to the victim, the police or any other public body is she in breach of a duty of care to the victim?

20.41 In a commercial transaction in which the third party is legally represented, the answer is generally no.[171]

> The duty of a solicitor who is not a party to, but knows of, a fraud upon the opposite party in a commercial transaction where all parties have, and rely upon, their own solicitors, is . . . not to himself misrepresent the transaction.[172]

The judicial reluctance to impose a duty of care in nonfeasance situations[173] is reinforced when the harm to the claimant is financial by a reluctance to allow recovery for pure economic loss.[174]

---

[167] D Bell and B Bennett, 'Genetic Secrets and the Family' [2001] Medical L Rev 130, 150.
[168] G Laurie, *Genetic Privacy* (Cambridge: 2002) 268.
[169] A McCall Smith, 'The Duty to Rescue and the Common law' in M Menlowe and A McCall Smith (eds), *The Duty to Rescue* (Aldershot: 1993) 83.
[170] The money laundering and terrorist legislation is discussed in ch 10. Solicitors have a statutory duty imposed by Solicitors Act 1974, s 34 to submit an annual report prepared by an accountant to the Law Society. In *Law Society v KPMG Peat Marwick* [2000] 4 All ER 540 the Court of Appeal upheld a decision of Scott V-C that accountants employed by a firm of solicitors to prepare their annual report owed the Law Society a duty to prepare the report with reasonable care. A substantial fraud should have been discovered and disclosed.
[171] cp *Banque Financiere de la Cite v Westgate Insurance* [1990] 2 All ER 947.
[172] per Dennis Lane J, *Seaway Trust Co v Markle* (1991) 47 CPC (2d) 258.
[173] See para 20.09 above.
[174] *Yuen Kun Keu v Att-Gen of Hong Kong* [1990] 1 WLR 821, 827.

B. Private Law Duty

> [A]s a general rule, apart from cases of assumption of responsibility arising under the principle in *Hedley Byrne & Co Ltd v Heller & Partners Ltd* no action will lie in respect of such loss in the tort of negligence.[175]

There are two exceptions to the general position. The first is where the professional has given an undertaking to the victim upon which the victim has relied.[176] The second applies to accountants employed to audit company accounts.[177] Confidential personal information is not likely to be involved.

---

[175] per Lord Goff, *White v Jones* [1995] 1 All ER 691, 699.
[176] *Allied Finance and Investments Ltd v Haddow & Co* [1983] NZLR 22; cp *Al-Kandari v J R Brown & Co* [1988] 1 All ER 833, 839.
[177] If the auditor discovers large-scale fraud or other irregularities by a senior employee of the company and the auditor suspects the management may be involved or is turning a blind eye to what is going on, the auditor may have a duty 'to report directly to a third party [such as the Department of Trade and Industry or even the police] without the knowledge or consent of the management. . . . Among the relevant considerations would be the extent to which the fraud or other irregularity is likely to result in material gain or loss for any person or is likely to affect a large number of persons and the extent to which the non-disclosure of the fraud or other irregularity is likely to enable it to be repeated with impunity', per Kennedy LJ, *Sasea Finance Ltd v KPMG* [2000] 1 BCLC 989, 993.

21

THE EMPLOYED PROFESSIONAL AND PARTNERSHIPS

A. Disclosure to the Employer	21.02	European Convention on Human Rights, Article 10	21.29
Employer Access to Confidential Client Information	21.02	C. Employer's Responsibilities for Employee's Disclosures	21.31
B. Disclosure Outside the Workplace	21.17	Civil Liability for Breach of Confidence by an Employee	21.31
The Professional's Obligation of Confidentiality to the Employer	21.17	D. Partnerships	21.37
Whistleblowing	21.23		

This chapter looks at the complications for confidentiality in professional–client relationships created by the fact that the professional is an employee. It concludes with a brief comment about the liability of a partnership for unauthorized disclosures by a partner. **21.01**

A. Disclosure to the Employer

Employer Access to Confidential Client Information

Professionals who are obliged to keep confidential client information from the employer

With so many professionals employed in public and private sector organizations rather than self-employed, it is important to establish the extent to which an employer is entitled to have access to the confidential information that a professional has about her clients. **21.02**

The employer may own the paper on which personal information about the client is recorded and the filing cabinet in which the records are stored, but this does not give the employer a right to know their contents.[1] There is a clear distinction **21.03**

---

[1] cp *Guidance on Ethics for Occupational Physicians* (5th edn, London: 1999) para 2.44. 'Confidential information may be recorded on physical property which belongs to A but which is in the posession of B, [sic] the circumstances may show that an obligation of confidence in respect of

between ownership of records and a right of access to the information in them. In the absence of legislation, a court order or a public interest ground for the disclosure,[2] an employed professional must not reveal information about the client to the employer without the client's consent, express or implied, if the relationship between professional and client is one in which the client can reasonably expect an unqualified obligation of confidentiality from the professional in respect of the information. The position is the same whether the information is held in a record or in the professional's memory.

Occupational health professionals[3]

21.04 It was explained in chapter 1 that when the occupational health professional conducts a pre-employment health check the effective client is the employer and the examinee is owed only the most minimal confidentiality obligations.[4] The point here is to consider the confidentiality obligations of the occupational health professional toward an employee with whom she has established a therapeutic relationship. The leading legal authority is *Dunn v British Coal Corporation*, an action by a miner against his employer for damages for injuries sustained at work. The Court of Appeal accepted that neither the employer nor the employer's lawyers were entitled to see the claimant's occupational health records without the claimant's consent.

> [T]he employer's solicitors took the view, correctly in my opinion, that although these records had been compiled by their own servant or agent the employee was entitled to claim that as between him and the doctor they were confidential.[5]

To avoid unfairness to the employer, the court ordered that the action be stayed unless the claimant consented to the employer being given sight of the records.[6] Department of Health guidance on AIDS/HIV infected health care workers[6a] states that occupational health practitioners are 'obliged ethically and professionally not to release notes or information without the consent of the individual'.[7]

---

the information is nevertheless owed by B to C. A's right to demand return of the property should not alter this.' *Gore v Scales* (Ch D, 14 November 2002) para 84, per Kevin Garnet QC.

[2] See ch 11.
[3] S Cox, 'Medical confidentiality: A guide for HR and line managers on the duties of the OH department' [2000] (Mar/April) OCR 32.
[4] See para 1.29 above.
[5] per Stuart-Smith LJ, [1993] ICR 591, para 7.
[6] See para 14.09 above.
[6a] *AIDS/HIV Infected Health Care Workers: Guidance on the Management of Infected Health Care Workers and Patient Notification* (1999).
[7] F Bennion, *Professional Ethics* (London:, 1969) recounts the experience of the director of the student health service at University College Aberystwyth who was dismissed for refusing to supply details of pregnancies among women students. The doctor was later reinstated under pressure from the BMA.

A. Disclosure to the Employer

21.05 The Faculty of Occupational Medicine of the Royal College of Physicians (FOM) explains in its guidance that normally:

> the informed written consent of the individual is required before access to clinical information may be granted to others, whoever they may be and whether professionally qualified or not, e.g. solicitors, insurers, managers, trade union representatives, HSE staff, etc.[8]

Some occupational health departments have an agreement with the employer that acknowledges the exclusive right of the occupational physician and nurse to access clinical medical records.[9] The Information Commissioner's draft code of practice on the use of personal data in employer/employee relationships endorses the standards of the FOM.[10] It states that the first and second data protection principles[11] require that employees be clearly told the extent to which the occupational health professional is obligated to the employer to disclose information and that explicit consent must be obtained to this processing.[12] Disclosures should not include clinical details. Thus an occupational health professional assessing an employee's fitness for work, sickness absence and other health/work matters for the employer should not divulge the medication that the employee is taking and the treatment received.[13]

21.06 The legal and ethical rules about confidentiality do not, despite the seeming illogicality involved, prevent knowledge of a disability known to the occupational health department from being imputed to the employer in disability discrimination proceedings.[14] Kloss comments: '[i]n no other area of medicine is a third party deemed to be in possession of confidential information which the doctor holding the information is ethically constrained from revealing to him without the consent of the patient.'[15]

21.07 The occupational health professional, like any other professional, must disclose information in response to a court order and to the extent required by statute and may do so where there is an overriding public interest in disclosure[16] whether or

---

[8] *Guidance on Ethics for Occupational Physicians* (5th edn, London: 1999) para 2.5.
[9] D Kloss, *Occupational Health Law* (3rd edn, Oxford: 1998) 56.
[10] *Guidance on Ethics for Occupational Physicians* (5th edn, London: 1999).
[11] Discussed in ch 18.
[12] para 3.7, available from http://www.dataprotection.gov.uk.
[13] Guidance from the BMA, *Confidentiality and disclosure of health information* (London: 1999) and the FOM are both clear about this. Nevertheless, a survey for the Occupational Health Rev in 1998 found that 64% of occupational physicians had come under occasional or frequent pressure from non-medical colleagues to break this principle: 62 OHR 19.
[14] *Code of Practice for the Elimination of Discrimination in the Field of Employment against Disabled Persons or Persons who have had a Disability* (1996) para 4.62.
[15] D Kloss, 'Pre-Employment Health Screening' in M Freeman and A Lewis (eds), *Law and Medicine* (Oxford: 2000) 466–467.
[16] See ch 11.

not an employee to whom an obligation of confidentiality is owed consents. An occupational health physician would be justified in informing an employer that an employee is suffering from a condition that is putting the lives of fellow employees at serious risk.[17]

Other professionals

21.08 The obligation to withhold information from the employer does not just apply to occupational health practitioners. The GMC's guidance states that whenever doctors assume contractual obligations to disclose information about a client to a third party, the doctor must first obtain 'written consent to the disclosure from the patient or a person properly authorised to act on the patient's behalf' and 'only information relevant to the request for disclosure' may be disclosed.[18] The Law Society's *Employed Solicitors Code 1990*[19] provides in para 1(e) that 'where an employed solicitor is acting for a person other than the employer . . . any information disclosed to the solicitor by the client is confidential and cannot be disclosed to the employer without the express consent of the client'.

Professionals who are obliged to disclose confidential client information to the employer

Schoolteachers

21.09 Some professionals have contractual obligations to reveal confidential personal information about clients to an employer. Teachers belong in this category. By the terms and conditions of their employment, teachers must work 'under the reasonable direction of the headteacher'.[20] Teachers are expected to report suspicions of child abuse (including allegations of abuse by teachers).[21] Departmental guidance requires this.[22] The obligation to pass on information about abuse and possibly other information restricts the teacher's capacity to promise confidentiality to pupils.[23] If a promise is inadvertently given that cannot be kept the teacher has a

---

[17] *Guidance on Ethics for Occupational Physicians* (5th edn, London: 1999) paras 2.8, 7.15; J Tamin, 'Medical Confidentiality' (1998) 72 Occupational Health Rev 29, 30.
[18] GMC, *Confidentiality: Protecting and Providing Information* (June 2000) para 34.
[19] http://www.guide-on-line.lawsociety.org.uk/.
[20] School Teachers' Pay and Conditions Document 2002, available at http://www.askatl.org.uk/payandconditions/pay/teachers/paynews/040902.htm, para 64.1.1.
[21] See para 2.24 above.
[22] Dfes circular 10/95, *Protecting Children from Abuse: The Role of the Education Service*; Dfes, *Sex and Relationship Education Guidance* 0116/2000, available at http://www.dfee.gov.uk/circulars/dfeepub/jul00/030700/confi.htm.
[23] Dfes, circular 10/95, *Protecting Children from Abuse: The Role of the Education Service* esp para 14: '[i]f a child confides in a member of staff and requests that the information is kept secret, it is important that the member of staff tells the child sensitively that he or she has a responsibility to refer cases of alleged abuse to the appropriate agencies for the child's own sake. Within that context, the child should . . . be assured that the matter will be disclosed only to people who need to know about it.'

A. Disclosure to the Employer

dilemma. If she suppresses the information she will be in breach of her contract of employment, if she passes on the information, subject to any public interest defence,[24] she can (in theory) be sued by the pupil for breach of confidence: compliance with the terms of a contract of employment is no defence.[25]

Social workers

Public sector social workers are another category of professionals who must avoid unqualified promises of confidentiality. Legally binding guidance issued under the Local Authority Social Services Act 1970, s 7 envisages disclosure of confidential information provided by or about social work clients **21.10**

(1) 'to social services staff directly involved in a case and their line-managers';
(2) 'to anyone else who cares for one of their clients, for example a voluntary body or foster carers, where the information is, or is likely to be, needed for the purposes of that care',[26]
(3) to senior management for quality audit and planning,
(4) to social services students and trainees; and
(5) if necessary to enable the authority to discharge its statutory functions, to other departments of the authority and other organizations.[27]

Social workers in the voluntary sector may have a contractual obligation to divulge information to a line-manager.

The practice in social work is to include a discussion about confidentiality and its parameters on first contact with the client. The client may be asked to sign an acknowledgement that information will normally be shared with appropriate parties.[28] When dealing with young persons and children, social workers are told to ensure that the client understands why the information is needed and that 'whilst the intention is not to make copies of [the] form, there might be occasions where the local authority is requested to make the information available to other professionals. Although confidentiality will be respected as far as possible, it cannot always be guaranteed.'[29] The local authority must ensure that anyone who has access to personal information is made aware that the information is confidential.[30] **21.11**

---

[24] See ch 11.
[25] Law Commission Report 110, *Breach of Confidence* (Cmnd 8388, 1981) para 4.56.
[26] DoH, 'Social Care Policy', para 6.15, available at http://www.doh.gov.uk/scg/datap.htm.
[27] ibid, para 6.18.
[28] Mental Health Special Interest Group, 'Response to the Green Paper: Reform of the Mental Health Act 1983', consultation point T, available at http://www.basw.co.uk/mhsig/papers/-mhareview.htm.
[29] DoH, *Looking After Children: Assessing Outcomes in Child Care. Revisions to Planning and Review Forms* (2000).
[30] 'Social Care Policy', para 6.21.

Chapter 21: *The Employed Professional and Partnerships*

Military, prison and police doctors

21.12 Doctors employed as police surgeons[31] or working in prisons[32] or in the armed forces are another group with obligations of disclosure to their employer that may override confidentiality to the patient. The guidelines on confidentiality for police surgeons make it clear that the detainee or victim must be warned before being examined that the police surgeon has a duty to pass to the police information relevant to a police investigation. Consent must be obtained to the conduct of the examination on this basis. Information that is not germane to the case but provided solely in a therapeutic context is subject to the same obligation of confidentiality that applies in a 'normal' doctor–patient relationship. If the police request information about the medical examination that is not included in the forensic report, the consent of the patient should be obtained before the information is released to the police or prosecuting authorities unless 'exceptionally, disclosure can be justified by the potential for serious harm to others or a likely miscarriage of justice'.[33]

21.13 Doctors working in prisons may have cause to breach medical confidentiality in more circumstances than regular GPs. The prison doctor has a contractual duty to maintain the security of the prison[34] which may oblige disclosure of information to the prison authorities about illicit drug taking or other activity that threatens law and order in the prison. Where the information exposes a risk of serious injury to a third party, disclosure would in any case be justified as being in the public interest.[35] The Working Group on Doctors Working in Prisons[36] has recommended that guidance be issued on the best way for prison doctors to cope with ethical difficulties.[37] These include breaches of medical confidentiality in order to expose maltreatment of prisoners. The BMA has criticized the belief of some prison governors, discipline officers and prison officials that 'by the nature of

---

[31] The police surgeon, also known as a forensic medical examiner or forensic physician, is a self-employed, independent individual appointed (usually by contract) by the police to provide 'medical care and, when required, forensic assessment of prisoners and suspects in police custody, complainants . . . [injured] police officers and attend scenes of death to pronounce life extinct'. The results of the forensic examination may ultimately be used in evidence in court: J Howitt and M Stark, *The Role of the Independent Forensic Physician* (London: 1999).

[32] On the special problems confronting the prison doctor see the BMA's *Background Paper on the Proposed World Medical Association Statement on Health Care for Prisoners and Other Detainees*, available from http://www.wma.net.

[33] BMA, *The Medical Profession and Human Rights* (London: 2001) 137. See also, 'Revised interim guidelines on confidentiality for police surgeons in England, Wales and Northern Ireland' (1998), available from http://www.bma.org.uk.

[34] BMA On-line ethics, available from http://www.bma.org.uk.

[35] See para 11.21 above. cp *R v Kennedy* (CA, 30 April 1998).

[36] DoH, HM Prison Service, *Report of the Working Group on Doctors Working in Prisons* (December 2001) para 6.18, available from http://www.doh.gov.uk.

[37] For an account of these difficulties see 'Prison Doctors' in BMA, *The Medical Profession and Human Rights* (London: 2001).

A. Disclosure to the Employer

their position, they are entitled to unimpeded access to all the information in a prisoner's health records'.[38] The prison doctor's duty is to maintain confidentiality to the greatest extent possible in a prison context.[39] The BMA agrees with the European Committee for the Prevention of Torture that 'all medical examinations should be conducted out of the hearing and sight of prison officers unless the doctor concerned requests otherwise'.[40] US constitutional law is a useful comparative source on the obligations of prisons and prison doctors. In US law an individual has a constitutional right to privacy under the Fourteenth Amendment that protects the individual's interest is the confidentiality of his medical information.[41] This right is not lost upon incarceration. However, a prisoner does not enjoy a right of privacy in his medical information to the same extent as a free citizen. His 'constitutional right is subject to substantial restrictions and limitations in order for correctional officials to achieve legitimate correctional goals and maintain institutional security. Specifically an inmate's constitutional right may be curtailed by a policy or regulation that is shown to be 'reasonably related to legitimate penological interests'.[42]

'[T]he military physician must accept a different set of obligations than the non-military physician, in particular, to place the military's interests above both the patient's and the physician's interests'.[43] Military doctors must report confidential patient information to the commanding officer, with or without patient consent, when the security, health, safety or welfare of the unit or the patient is at serious risk. A recent rule change has removed the obligation to inform the commanding officer of the homosexual orientation of patients when there is no such risk.[44]

21.14

---

[38] BMA, *The Medical Profession and Human Rights* (London: 2001) 110.

[39] cp The Council of Europe, Committee of Ministers, Recommendation R (93) 6 on the prison and criminological aspects of the control of transmissible diseases (1993) para 8 which states that '[i]nformation about the health of prisoners is confidential. The doctor may only provide such information to the other members of the medical team, and exceptionally to the prison management, as is strictly necessary for the treatment and care of the prisoner or to examine the health of the prisoners and staff. . . . Disclosure of information should follow the same principles as those applied in the general community.' See also Council of Europe, Committee of Ministers, Recommendation R(98) 7 (1998) paras 13, 18.

[40] BMA, *The Medical Profession and Human Rights* (London: 2001) 111.

[41] *Whalen v Roe* 429 US 589, 599 (1977).

[42] *Doe v Delie* 257 F 3d 309, 317 (2001). This case involved a former inmate who was HIV-seropositive who was told by medical staff that his infection would be kept confidential. Because of certain prison practices (an 'open door' examination room policy, the disclosure of his medical condition to corrections officer escorts and the loud announcement of the names of his medications by a nurse in the presence of other inmates) his condition was not kept confidential and for this he sued the prison.

[43] T Beauchamp and J Childress, *Principles of Biomedical Ethics* (New York: 2001) 316. The emphasis is rather different in J Mason, R McCall Smith and G Laurie, *Law and Medical Ethics* (6th edn, London: 2002) 256, who describe the doctor–patient relationship as being as in civilian practice 'with the proviso that the doctor's duty to society is accentuated when this is formulated as a duty to a fighting unit'.

[44] *Armed Forces First Special Report* (2001), Memorandum Submitted by Ministry of Defence, Appendix 3 to the Minutes of Evidence, available from http://www.parliament.the-stationery-office.co.uk.

Probation officers

21.15 Probation officers are in a position similar to prison doctors. They must not put the confidentiality interests of clients ahead of those of the security of the prison and the safety of the public.[45]

Obligations of a general practitioner to make disclosures to a health authority

21.16 GPs operating within the NHS are bound by the Terms of Service for Doctors[46] set out in Sch 2 to the National Health Service (General Medical Services) Regulations 1992. Paragraph 36 of these terms states that '[a] doctor shall send the records relating to the Health Authority—(a) as soon as possible, at the request of the Health Authority'.[47] These terms do not confer on a health authority an unqualified right to demand confidential medical records. The case[48] which decided this was brought by an anonymous health authority against an anonymous GP practice as a result of facts that had emerged in care proceedings. The Health Authority, wishing to consider the extent that Dr X and his partners had complied with their terms of service, asked to inspect copies of the GP records of 17 named patients and ex-patients. The doctor did everything he could to obtain the consent of the patients to the disclosure but failed to do so in two cases. He refused to hand over these records without an order of a court. Munby J ruled that there was a compelling public interest to allow the Health Authority to see patient records that were reasonably required to enable the Health Authority to exercise its responsibilities under the National Health Service Act 1977. Since disclosure of medical records to a health authority was an interference with a patient's right to respect for private life under Article 8 the disclosure had to satisfy the usual Convention criteria of 'necessity' and 'proportionality' and was conditional on there being efficient and adequate safeguards against abuse.[49] Further disclosure of the information was forbidden without leave of the court except to a medical discipline committee or the NHS Tribunal or the GMC who would be subject to an obligation to take effective and adequate safeguards against abuse. The Health Authority's appeal from the decision that disclosure was conditional on a court order to which express conditions could be attached was dismissed.[50] Thorpe LJ accepted the submission for the respondent that the conflict between the private/public interest in the confidentiality of medical records and some other public interest was a matter for a judge.[51] Munby J had been right to say:

---

[45] See *R v Kennedy* (CA, 30 April 1998).
[46] As amended by the National Health Service (General Medical Services) Amendment (No 4) Regulations 2000, SI 2000/2383.
[47] para 36(6).
[48] *A Health Authority v X* [2001] Lloyd's Rep Med 349.
[49] ibid, para 71.
[50] *A Health Authority v X* [2001] EWCA Civ 2014, [2002] 2 All ER 780.
[51] ibid, para 25.

B. Disclosure Outside the Workplace

Dr X's ultimate obligation is to comply with whatever order the court may make. But prior to that point being reached his duty, like that of any other professional or other person who owes a duty of confidentiality to his patient or client, is to assert that confidentiality in answer to any claim by a third party for disclosure and to put before the court every argument that can properly be put against disclosure.[52]

B. Disclosure Outside the Workplace

The Professional's Obligation of Confidentiality to the Employer[53]

During the period of employment[54]

The law draws a sharp distinction between disclosure of confidential information by an employee during and after the period of employment. A contract of employment contains an implied duty of fidelity to serve the employer faithfully.[55] This prohibits the employee during the employment from disclosing or using confidential information acquired through the work for an unauthorized purpose.[56] For example, in *Thornley v ARA Ltd*[57] an employee who disclosed confidential research findings about Tornado aircraft to the press believing this to be in the public interest was held by the Employment Appeal Tribunal to have breached an implied term of his contract of employment. Some employees who make unauthorized disclosure will be in breach of an express confidentiality clause in the contract of employment.[58] Whether the duty not to disclose confidential information is express or implied, its breach renders the professional liable to be sued by the employer in contract[59] and, subject to the observance of disciplinary procedures, summary dismissal for misconduct.[60] An employee who discloses confidential

21.17

---

[52] *A Health Authority v X* [2001] Lloyd's Rep Med 349, para 9.
[53] A Stewart, 'Confidentiality and the Employment Relationship' (1988) 1 Australian J of Labour L 1.
[54] cp para 6.38 above. R Dean, *The Law of Trade Secrets and Personal Information* (2nd edn, Sydney 2002) [4.35] et seq.
[55] *Hivac v Park Royal Scientific Instruments Ltd* [1946] Ch 169, 174. For further details see I Smith and G Thomas, *Industrial Law* (7th edn, London: 2000) 133. The duty of fidelity probably derives from the more general duty of mutual trust and confidence that was recognized in *Malik v BCCI SA* [1997] 3 All ER to exist between an employer and employee.
[56] *Initial Services Ltd v Putterill* [1967] 3 All ER 145, 148; *Att-Gen v Guardian Newspaper (No 2)* [1988] 3 All ER 545, 571. See also R Scott, 'Developments in the Law of Confidentiality' [1990] Denning LJ 77, 79.
[57] (EAT 669/76, 11 May 1977.)
[58] See para 4.04 above.
[59] For the general principles governing an action in contract for breach of confidence see ch 4. The officer who investigated the Moors' murders was sued by his employer for breach of confidence when he published a book incorporating Myra Hyndley's confession: G Robertson and A Nicol, *Robertson and Nicol on Media Law* (4th edn, London: 2002) 237.
[60] B Napier, 'Confidentiality and Labour Law' in L Clarke (ed), *Confidentiality and the Law* (London: 1990) 110–111, 120–121.

personal information about clients in return for money may additionally commit an offence under the Prevention of Corruption Act 1906 and, if employed in the public sector, also under the Public Bodies Corrupt Practices Act 1889.[61] The disclosure could involve various other crimes including offences under the Data Protection Act 1998,[62] the Computer Misuse Act 1990[63] and the Theft Act 1968.[64]

21.18 An action in contract against the professional by the employer for breach of an express or implied obligation of confidentiality will fail if the employee is able to rely on a defence of disclosure in the public interest.[65] A clause in the contract of employment ousting the defence would be unenforceable as contrary to policy.[66] A defence of public interest would not necessarily make dismissal of the employee unfair.[67] Dismissal would be unfair if the disclosure was a qualifying disclosure under the terms of the Public Disclosure Act 1998.[68]

After the termination of employment[69]

21.19 After the termination of the employment, an ex-employee is under a continuing equitable obligation[70] not to divulge the employer's trade secrets subject to any public interest defence.[71] Trade secrets have to be distinguished from confidential information that once learned becomes part of the employee's expertise. So long as the employment continues, the professional must not use or disclose this information except for the benefit of the employer, but when the employment has ended she is entitled to use it in her own business or in the service of some other employer.[72] Confidential information in this category includes the identity of the employer's clients. After leaving the employment, the professional may approach them and offer her services.[73] However, the professional must not make or copy a list of the employer's clients or deliberately memorize such a list with the intention of soliciting her former employer's clients after resigning from her position.[74]

---

[61] See para 6.75 above.
[62] See paras 6.56 above and 21.22 below.
[63] See para 6.60 above.
[64] See para 6.68 above.
[65] See ch 11.
[66] See para 11.04 above. cp ERA, s 43J.
[67] L Vickers, *Freedom of Speech and Employment* (Oxford: 2002) 188–190. But see *Fitzpatrick v Road Transport Industry Training Board* (26 January 1977) cited by Y Cripps, *The Legal Implications of Disclosure in the Public Interest* (2nd edn, London: 1994) 318 n 27.
[68] See para 21.25 below.
[69] cp para 6.39 above.
[70] The obligation may also exist as an implied contractual duty: *Initial Services Ltd v Putterill* [1967] 3 All ER 145, 148, 150.
[71] *Lion Laboratories Ltd v Evans* [1984] 2 All ER 417.
[72] *Faccenda Chicken Ltd v Fowler* [1986] 1 All ER 617, 625–626; *Dranez Anstalt v Hayek* [2002] 1 BCLC 693.
[73] *Wallace Bogan & Co v Cove* [1997] IRLR 453.
[74] *Faccenda Chicken Ltd v Fowler* [1986] 1 All ER 617, 625; *Roger Bullivant Ltd v Ellis* [1987] IRLR 491.

B. Disclosure Outside the Workplace

Trade secrets, the category of information that is so confidential that the professional cannot lawfully use it after termination of the employment,[75] tends to be chemical formulae and specialized manufacturing processes. Whether the information is strictly speaking a trade secret or not,[76] there can be no conceivable justification for allowing the professional to disclose or exploit confidential personal information concerning the affairs of the clients of the former employer unless they choose to remain clients of the professional after termination of her employment.[77] This is not a situation where it can be said that the former employer could and should have protected the information by an express covenant[78] for if the information is disclosed those who will suffer most are likely to be the employer's clients who are innocent parties.[79] The hallmarks of a trade secret are: information of obvious sensitivity and confidentiality, restricted access, isolation from other information and instructions that the information is strictly confidential.[80] These are also the badge of confidential client information.

21.20

The professional's contract of employment may contain an express covenant prohibiting the employed professional, on leaving the employment, from disclosing confidential information.[81] The expressly assumed obligation can be wider than the equitable obligation of confidentiality including, for example, a ban on contacting the former employer's clients. A confidentiality clause cannot prohibit a public interest disclosure.[82]

21.21

Unlawful disclosure

The Data Protection Act 1998 (DPA) creates a number of criminal offences. It is an offence for a person, without the consent of the data controller, to knowingly

21.22

---

[75] *Faccenda Chicken Ltd v Fowler* [1986] 1 All ER 617, 626.

[76] 'In our judgment the information will only be protected if it can properly be classed as a trade secret or *as material which, while not properly to be described as a trade secret, is in all the circumstances of such a highly confidential nature as to require the same protection as a trade secret eo nominee,*' per Neill LJ, [1986] 1 All ER 617, 626 (italics added).

[77] cp *Campbell v Frisbee* [2002] EWHC 328; [2002] EMLR 31, para 21; *Koch Shippping Inc v Richards Butler* [2002] EWCA Civ 1280; see para 6.39 above. Query: would equity intervene to prevent disclosure of information by an ex-employee if that information has entered the public domain? There may still be reasons for insisting on silence: see para 5.14 above. But see *Att-Gen v Blake* [1996] 3 All ER 903, 907, 909 where loss of confidentiality was treated by counsel for the Crown and the judge as extinguishing the equitable obligation of the former intelligence officer to the Crown.

[78] *AT Poeton (Gloucester Plating) Ltd v Horton* [2000] ICR 1208.

[79] It was suggested in *Faccenda Chicken Ltd v Fowler* [1986] 1 All ER 617, 626 that mere confidential information cannot be protected by an express covenant. If this is right, and some doubt that it is (see *Balston Ltd v Headline Filters Ltd* [1987] FSR 330, 347) this is a strong argument for treating confidential client information as a trade secret because confidential client information is just the type of information that employers must be able to protect.

[80] [1986] 1 All ER 617, 626–627.

[81] *Att-Gen v Blake* [2000] 4 All ER 385, 390.

[82] See para 11.04 above.

or recklessly obtain or disclose personal data or to procure the disclosure to another person of the information.[83] An employed professional who discloses information about a client or former client without the authority of the employer, whether or not still working for the employer, could be prosecuted for this offence. No offence is committed if the disclosure was required or authorized by law or was necessary to prevent or detect crime or the professional acted in the reasonable belief that she had a legal right to disclose the data or that the employer would have consented if the employer had known or that in the particular circumstances her action was justified as being in the public interest.[84]

Whistleblowing[85]

Public Interest Disclosure Act 1998

21.23 The disclosure of information by an employee which she reasonably regards as evidence of malpractice in the workplace is known as 'whistleblowing'.[86] Traditionally regarded as a vice,[87] whistleblowing has come to be seen in a more favourable light. So much so that in 1998 the Public Interest Disclosure Act[88] was passed to protect 'workers' who make 'qualifying disclosures'. The 1998 Act supplements the public interest defence to a contractual action for breach of confidence by safeguarding the employee who discloses confidential information on public interest grounds against other forms of reprisal such as dismissal, loss of benefits, transfer and demotion. Express contractual promises of confidentiality that purport to override the protection are void.[89]

Protection given by the Public Interest Disclosure Act[90]

21.24 Regardless of length of service,[91] a 'worker' who is subjected to 'detriment' falling short of dismissal at the hands of an employer as a result[92] of making a protected disclosure may seek compensation, including an amount for mental distress,[93]

---

[83] DPA, s 55.
[84] DPA s 55(2).
[85] J Bowers, J Lewis and J Mitchell, *Whistleblowing: the New Law* (London: 1999); Y Cripps, 'The Public Interest Disclosure Act 1998' in J Beatson and Y Cripps, *Freedom of Expression and Freedom of Information* (Oxford: 2000) ch 17.
[86] S Vernon, 'Legal aspects of whistleblowing in the social services' in G Hunt (ed), *Whistleblowing in the Social Services* (London: 1998) 222.
[87] ibid at 223.
[88] This amends the ERA.
[89] ERA, s 43J.
[90] On the limitations of the protection offered see J Gobert and M Punch, 'Whistleblowers, the Public Interest and the Public Interest Disclosure Act 1998' (2000) 63 MLR 25, 48–49.
[91] ERA, s 108(3)(ff).
[92] Whistleblowing must be the principle cause of the detriment: *Aspinall v MSI Mech Forge Ltd* EAT/891/01, 5 July 2002.
[93] Employment Protection Act 1996, s 49 does not mention compensation for mental distress, but it has been held that when action short of dismissal is taken against an employee for trade union reasons compensation may reflect distress: *Brassington v Cauldron Wholesale Ltd* [1977] IRLR 479.

B. Disclosure Outside the Workplace

from an employment tribunal.[94] Outright dismissal is automatically an unfair dismissal[95] for the purposes of Employment Rights Act 1996 (ERA), s 100. Apart from the basic award (calculated according to length of service), the dismissed employee is entitled to a 'compensatory award'[96] reflecting what is 'just and equitable in the circumstances'. The usual upper limit to compensation for unfair dismissal does not apply.[97] The term 'worker'[98] is broadly defined and covers most public and private sector employed professionals including agency workers and medical and dental personnel working within the NHS. It does not cover self-employed professionals and voluntary workers.

Qualifying disclosures

To be a qualifying disclosure the subject matter of the disclosure must concern (in the past, present or future) one of the following:[99] **21.25**

- a criminal offence;
- breach of a legal obligation;[100]
- a miscarriage of justice;
- the endangering of the health or safety of an individual;
- damage to the environment; or
- a cover-up of any of these matters.

No link between the worker's employment and the subject matter of the disclosure is necessary and the malpractice need not be in the United Kingdom.[101] The Act distinguishes between four categories of information recipient:

- the whistleblower's superior or employer;[102]
- a Minister of the Crown (relevant when the employer was appointed by a Minister);[103]
- a prescribed external person (the regulator or agency with responsibility for supervising the employer);[104] and
- unspecified outsiders[105] (including the police, the media and members of Parliament).

---

[94] ERA, s 48(1A). The burden of showing that any detriment was justified rests with the employer: ERA, s 48(2).
[95] Employment Protection Act 1996, s 103A. Full details must be given of the disclosure in the pleadings: *Sim v Manchester Action on Health* (2001) EAT/0085/01.
[96] Employment Protection Act 1996, s 123.
[97] Public Interest Disclosure (Compensation) Regulations 1999, SI 1999/1548, reg 3.
[98] ERA, s 43K(1).
[99] This includes a contractual obligation: *Parkins v Sodexho Ltd* [2002] IRLR 109.
[100] ERA, s 43B.
[101] ERA, s 43B(2).
[102] ERA, s 43C.
[103] ERA, s 43E.
[104] ERA, s 43F. Prescribed persons are identified in the Public Interest Disclosure (Prescribed Persons) Order 1999, SI 1999/1549.
[105] ERA, s 43G.

The Act is drafted so as to encourage disclosure to the first three categories of recipient, with internal reporting the first preference. For disclosures to persons or organizations in the fourth category stringent conditions must be satisfied. From the standpoint of the employee, the most favourable conditions apply when disclosure concerns some 'exceptionally serious failure'[106] such as child abuse, criminal activity or the release of a dangerous psychiatric patient into the community. Here disclosure to an unspecified outsider is a protected disclosure provided:[107]

(1) the worker acted:
  (a) in good faith, and *not* for purposes of personal gain;[108] and
  (b) in the reasonable belief that the information and allegation are substantially true;[109] and
  (c) in the reasonable belief that the disclosure 'tends to show' something that qualifies as a protected disclosure.
(2) disclosure does not involve commission of a criminal offence;[110]
(3) in the circumstances of the case, it is reasonable to make the disclosure,[111] particular regard being had to the identity of the person to whom the disclosure is made.[112]

21.26 Judging by the case law on the public interest defence to breach of confidence[113] and the specific reference to the identity of the person to whom disclosure is made as a relevant factor, disclosure to an outsider is more likely to be seen as reasonable if made to someone in a position to take remedial action, such as the police, than if made to the media. It is also probable that a whistleblower will be expected to raise her concerns internally before going to an unspecified outsider if the employer has an effective procedure for dealing with the employee's concerns. If the disclosure is *not* of an exceptionally serious matter one of a number of specified reasons for not raising the matter internally[114] *must* be satisfied in addition to the conditions that apply to disclosure of an exceptionally serious matter.[115] These are:

---

[106] ERA, s 43H.
[107] ERA, s 43H(1).
[108] In this respect the ERA is stricter than the common law public interest defence: see para 11.61 above and para 21.27 below. The burden of providing bad faith rests with the employer. It is possible that the bad faith exception infringes Art 10.
[109] In this respect the ERA may also be stricter than the common law public interest defence rule: see para 11.60 above.
[110] ERA, s 43B(3). A conviction is unlikely to be necessary. The condition is a barrier to whistleblowing for those working for public authorities who are subject to a statutory restriction on disclosing confidential information, as to which see para 3.43 above. It may be necessary to imply a public-interest exception to legislation restricting disclosure to avoid infringing Art 10.
[111] ERA, s 43H(1)(e).
[112] ERA, s 43H(2).
[113] See ch 11.
[114] ERA, s 43G(2).
[115] ERA, s 43G.

B. Disclosure Outside the Workplace

- the worker reasonably believes that she will be subject to detriment by the employer if she makes a disclosure to the employer; *or*
- she reasonably believes that it is likely that evidence relating to the relevant failure will be concealed or destroyed if disclosure is made to the employer; *or*
- she has previously made a disclosure of substantially the same information to the employer or to a prescribed regulator.[116]

In determining the reasonableness of a disclosure regard is to be had to a number of factors[117] including the seriousness of the malpractice, whether it is continuing or likely to recur and 'whether the disclosure is made in breach of a duty of confidentiality owed by the employer to any other person'.[118]

The public interest defence and lawful whistleblowing compared

21.27 The protection offered by the legislation in cases of external disclosure, whether or not the matter disclosed is 'exceptionally serious', is considerably less generous than the public interest defence to an action for breach of confidence or contract developed by the courts.[119] First, motive matters. When the public interest defence is claimed the court is not interested in whether the disclosing party acted for personal gain or out of altruism.[120] Secondly, while all the qualifying kinds of disclosure would probably constitute good reasons for relying on the public interest defence,[121] the converse is not true: disclosure of serious financial mismanagement in a nationalized industry which might justify a public interest disclosure or exposure of false publicity, a ground recognized in *Woodward v Hutchins* as justifying disclosure in the public interest,[122] would not fit within any of the statutory criteria unless breach of a legal obligation were involved.

Obtaining legal advice before making a disclosure

21.28 Such is the convoluted structure of the Public Interest Disclosure Act that the employed professional may want to take legal advice before making a disclosure. Disclosures of qualifying information are allowed unconditionally in the course of obtaining legal advice.[123] The lawyer is forbidden to disclose the information further except on the instructions of the whistleblower whose disclosure it then becomes.[124]

---

[116] See Public Interest Disclosure (Prescribed Persons) Order 1999, SI 1999/1549.
[117] ERA, s 43G.
[118] ERA, s 43G(3)(d).
[119] See ch 11.
[120] See para 11.61 above.
[121] The disclosure which occurred in *Lion Laboratories Ltd v Evans* [1984] 2 All ER 417 could, for instance, be represented as an attempt to avert a miscarriage of justice.
[122] [1977] 1 WLR 760, 764. See para 11.10 above. Query: whether the disclosure in this case was disproportionate and therefore an interference with the Art 8 right to respect for private life.
[123] ERA, s 43D.
[124] ERA, s 43B(4). This prevents the lawyer from making the information public and claiming that it is a protected disclosure. The public interest in encouraging candour within the lawyer–client relationship is given priority over the public interest in the public disclosure of the information.

European Convention on Human Rights, Article 10[125]

21.29 Article 10, which guarantees freedom of expression, may offer whistleblowers some protection against reprisals, particularly to those working in the public sector.[126] A New Zealand council employee dismissed for criticizing council policy at a public meeting was permitted to invoke a provision similar to article 10(1) in the New Zealand Bill of Rights[127] before an employment court.[128] In *Vogt v Germany*[129] the European Court of Human Rights decided that dismissal of a schoolteacher because of the expression of political views was prima facie a breach of Article 10.

21.30 There are two reasons why a whistle-blowing professional may derive little assistance from Article 10. First, a prima facie breach of Article 10(1) may be justified.[130] Secondly, the confidentiality of personal information concerning a client will be protected by Article 8 of the European Convention on Human Rights.[131] This right to respect for private life must be balanced against the professional's freedom of expression. Freedom of expression may not triumph.[132]

C. Employer's Responsibilities for Employee's Disclosures

Civil Liability for Breach of Confidence by an Employee

21.31 An employer such as an NHS trust is vicariously liable for the wrongful acts and omissions of an employed professional committed in the course of her employment.[133] A client who suffers a breach of confidentiality at the hands of an employed professional may therefore be able to sue not only the professional who

---

[125] J Bowers, J Lewis and J Mitchell, *Whistleblowing: The New Law* (London: 1999) ch 13.
[126] HRA s 6(1) prohibits a 'public authority' from acting in a way that is incompatible with an adopted Convention right. Those working in the private sector could benefit from Art 10 to the extent that an employment tribunal, as a public authority, must take the Convention into account when adjudicating on an employment dispute: see para 3.05 above.
[127] s 14 guarantees a 'right to freedom of expression including the freedom to seek, receive, and impart information and opinions of any kind in any form'.
[128] *Lowe v Tararua District Council* (27 June 1994). Although the employee made the disclosure at a public meeting at which she was present in an official capacity this does not appear to have had a bearing on the availability of s 14 as a defence. Contrast *Hobbs v North Shore City Council* [1992] 1 ERNZ 32.
[129] (1995) 21 EHRR 205. On the significance of this case see L Vickers, 'Whistleblowing in the public sector and the ECHR' [1997] PL 595.
[130] *Grigoriades v Greece* (1997) 27 EHRR 464, para 45.
[131] See para 3.03 above.
[132] See para 3.29 above.
[133] Once the employee has ceased to be employed, the employer cannot be held vicariously responsible for a breach of the obligation of confidentiality by the employee. In order to pin any liability onto the employer negligence on the employer's part would have to be established (see para 21.35 below).

C. Employer's Responsibilities for Employee's Disclosures

is to blame but also her employer who may be free of blame. Since confidentiality is something that it is ultimately the employer's duty to provide, the employer can be held liable whether the professional is employed under a contract of service or a contract of services.[134]

21.32 Traditionally the employer had no liability for the intentional acts of an employee done during working time unless the acts were either authorized by the employer[135] or were an unauthorized or wrongful mode of doing something that was authorized.[136] This seemly ruled out vicarious responsibility in tort and equity for the knowing disclosure of information when the disclosure was not done with the intention of benefiting the employer[137] and even more so if the breach of confidentiality contravened rules laid down by the employer. Negligent disclosure of confidential information by the employed professional was another matter. This could result in vicarious liability if the disclosure was a wrongful or unauthorized mode of performing an authorized task or direct liability for employing someone unsuitable.

21.33 The decision of the House of Lords in *Lister v Hesley Hall Ltd*[138] to hold an employer vicariously liable for the sexual abuse of a child in its care at a boarding school has radically altered the law of vicarious liability. The courts no longer have a problem with holding an employer liable for the intentional wrongdoing of an employee provided that there is a 'close and direct' connection between what the employee was employed to do and the wrongful act.[139]

> [I]t is no answer to say that the employee was guilty of intentional wrongdoing, or that his act was not merely tortious but criminal, or that he was acting exclusively for his own benefit, or that he was acting contrary to express instructions, or that his conduct was the very negation of his employer's duty.[140]

But their Lordships said that to satisfy the 'close and direct' test the employee must do 'more than make the most of an opportunity presented by the fact of his employment'.[141] Of the case at hand, Lord Steyn said: '[t]he question is whether

---

[134] cp *Cassidy v Ministry of Health* [1951] 1 All ER 574. Under a contract of services the employer can say what is to be done, under a contract of service the employer can also direct how it is to be done.

[135] If a breach of confidence occurs at the instigation of the employer, this is personal not vicarious liability. The employer is directly responsible for the wrong committed by his agent, the employee.

[136] R Heuston and R Buckley (eds), *Salmond and Heuston on the Law of Torts* (21st edn, London: 1996) 443.

[137] *Armagas Ltd v Mudogas SA* [1986] 2 All ER 385, 392. See also *Hornsby v Clark Kenneth Leventhal* [1998] PNLR 635, 645.

[138] *Lister v Hesley Hall Ltd* [2001] UKHL 22; 2001] 2 All ER 769.

[139] ibid, paras 24, 48. For a case in which vicarious liability was found on this basis see *Healys v Mishcon de Reya* [2002] EWHC 2480, para 35 (newly recruited solicitor took client files from the firm in which he had previously worked without the consent of the clients or the former employer and was permitted to work on them by his new employer).

[140] per Lord Millett, ibid, para 79.

[141] per Lord Millett, ibid, para 79. See also Lord Clyde, paras 45, 50.

the warden's torts were so closely connected with the employment that it would be fair and just to hold the employers vicariously liable. On the facts of the case the answer is yes. After all, the sexual abuse was inextricably interwoven with the carrying out by the warden of his duties . . .'.[142] Lord Millett said that the warden had 'abused the special position in which the school had placed him to enable it to discharge its own responsibilities, with the result that the assaults were committed by the very employee to whom the school had entrusted the care of the boys'.[143]

21.34 In *Balfron Trustees Ltd v Russell, Jones & Walker*[144] in which it was alleged that an employed solicitor knowingly assisted a breach of trust, Laddie J said that the starting point is to identify the duty of the employer to the claimant. If the employer delegated performance of a duty owed to the claimant to the employee and the employee failed to carry out the employer's instructions, whatever the employee did is to be treated as falling within the scope of employment vis-à-vis the claimant even though the employee's act was so heinous that it could not reasonably be said to form part of his obligations vis-à-vis the employer.

21.35 If this type of reasoning is applied to an unauthorized disclosure of confidential information by an employed professional, it may be possible to pin liability on the employer for the unlawful disclosure. An NHS trust, for example, has a duty to treat patients and to safeguard the confidentiality of information about that treatment. Both duties are of necessity delegated to employees. If a doctor or nurse involved in the treatment of a patient were to abuse the patient's medical confidentiality, the abuse, although expressly prohibited by Department of Health guidance,[145] would still fall within the scope of the employed professional's employment vis-à-vis the patient and the NHS would be liable for the breach of confidence.[146] The NHS might not be liable if a hospital porter or window cleaner entered a manager's office without permission and finding on the desk there the medical file of a famous person stole it. On these facts there is no close connection between the employment and the crime. The employment provides the temporal and spatial opportunity to commit the theft but the crime is not inextricably interwoven with carrying out the only duties delegated to the employee: portering or window-cleaning. The NHS trust might be held directly liable in negligence for insufficiently supervising its employees or failing to keep patient data securely to prevent unauthorized access. When an employed professional working in the private sector breaches a client's confidence there is an additional possibility of

---

[142] *Lister v Hesley Hall Ltd* [2001] UKHL 22, para 28.
[143] ibid, para 82.
[144] (HC, 9 July 2001) para 33.
[145] DoH, *The Protection and Use of Patient Information* HSG(96) 18 (1996), a summary of which appears at http://www.doh.gov.uk/confiden/cgmsum.htm.
[146] An employer who is responsible for the torts and crimes of an employee is surely responsible also for the employee's equitable wrongs.

D. Partnerships

suing the employer for breach of an implied contractual promise of confidentiality.[147]

Breach of confidence by the employee of a self-employed professional

21.36 The principles outlined above govern the vicarious liability of a self-employed professional for a breach of confidence by her employee.

D. Partnerships

21.37 When professionals form a partnership each partner is an agent for all other partners; an act by one partner is the act of the other members.[148] Therefore each partner assumes an obligation to keep information about all the clients of the partnership confidential and to use information about the clients for the purposes of the partnership. The courts, however, no longer treat all partners as having the knowledge of any one of them when an issue of candour towards the client arises[149] or impute the knowledge of one to all where an effective Chinese wall has been constructed.[150]

21.38 If a professional leaves the partnership, she is subject to the same obligation of confidentiality as an ex-employee:[151] she may solicit former clients whose names or whereabouts she carries in her head but she may not remove confidential records to enable her to contact the partnership's clients.[152]

21.39 If a professional who belongs to a partnership breaches an equitable or contractual obligation of confidentiality to a client of the partnership, the partners may be jointly and severally liable for the consequences.[153] The test of vicarious liability is whether the partner's wrongful conduct was so closely connected with acts that the partner was authorized to undertake that it can be fairly regarded as having been done in the ordinary course of the partnership's business.[154] The court must make a value judgment in each case having regard to all the circumstances and any relevant precedents.[155]

---

[147] See para 4.05 above.
[148] *R v O'Halloran, ex p Hamer* [1913] VLR 116.
[149] See para 19.60 above.
[150] See paras 6.92 et seq above.
[151] See para 21.19 above. See also comments in *Rakusen v Ellis, Munday and Clarke* [1912] 1 Ch 831.
[152] *Gore v Scales* (Ch D, 14 November 2002).
[153] Partnership Act 1890, ss 9, 10.
[154] *Dubai Aluminium Co Ltd v Salaam* [2002] UKHL 48, paras 23, 43, 124, 129. This is the test also for determining an employer's vicarious liability for the wrongful acts of an employee: see para 21.33 above.
[155] ibid, para 26. There are at present no precedents. *Hamlyn v Johnston & Co* [1903] 1 KB 81, 85 is a reverse of the situations this book addresses: a partner in a firm obtained confidential information about a rival's activities for the firm's benefit. The means used (bribery of an employee) was unlawful and the firm was made to compensate the rival for its losses.

BIBLIOGRAPHY

Books

Alberstat, T, T Cassels, E Overs (eds), *T Crone: Law and the Media* (Oxford: Focal Press, 2002).
Alldridge, P, *Money Laundering Law* (Oxford: Hart, 2003).
Allen, A, *Uneasy Access: Privacy for Women in a Free Society* (Totowa, NJ: Rowman & Littlefield, 1988).
Andrews, N, *Principles of Civil Procedure* (London: Sweet & Maxwell, 1994).
Archbold, Criminal Pleading, Evidence and Practice (London: Sweet & Maxwell, 1997).
Arnull, A, A Dashwood, M Ross and D Wyatt, *Wyatt & Dashwood's European Union Law* (4th edn, London: Sweet & Maxwell, 2000).
Auburn, J, *Legal Professional Privilege* (Oxford: Hart Publishing, 2000).
Bainbridge, D, *Data Protection Law* (London: CLT Professional Publishing, 2000).
Bainham, A, *Children: The Modern Law* (2nd edn, Bristol: Family Law, 1998).
Baker, P and P St J Langan, *Snell's Equity* (29th edn, London: Sweet & Maxwell, 1990).
Bar Council, *Code of Conduct of the Bar of England and Wales* (7th edn, London: Bar Council, 1999).
Baughen, S, Professionals and Fiduciaries: Perils and Pitfalls (Saffron Walden: Gostick Hall Publications, 2002).
Beatson, J, *Anson's Law of Contract* (27th edn, Oxford: OUP, 1998).
Beauchamp, T and J Childress, *Principles of Biomedical Ethics* (5th edn, Oxford: OUP, 2001).
Beltrami, J, *A Deadly Innocence* (Edinburgh: Mainstream, 1989).
Bennett, C, *Regulating Privacy* (Ithaca: Cornell U Press, 1992).
Bennett, R, and C, Errin, *HIV and AIDS: testing, screening and confidentiality* (Oxford: OUP, 2001).
Bennion, F, *Professional Ethics* (London: Charles Knight & Co, 1969).
Birks, P, *Privacy and Loyalty* (Oxford: Clarendon Press, 1997).
Blackstone's Commentaries (13th edn, 1796).
Blume, P, *Protection of Informational Privacy* (Copenhagen: Djof, 2002).
BMA, *Assessment of Mental Capacity* (London: BMA, 1995).
—— *Confidentiality and disclosure of health information* (London: BMA, 1999).
—— *Consent, Rights and Choices in Health Care for Children and Young Persons* (London: BMA, 2000).
—— *Human Genetics—Choice and Responsibility* (Oxford: OUP, 1998).
—— *Medical Ethics Today* (London: BMJ Publishing, 1993).

Bibliography

BMA, *Philosophy and Practice of Medical Ethics* (London: BMA, 1988).

—— *The Medical Profession and Human Rights* (London: Zed, 2001).

Bok, S, *Secrets: The Ethics of Concealment and Revelation* (Oxford: OUP, 1984).

Bollas, C and D Sundelson, *The New Informants* (London: Karnac, 1996).

Bond, T, *Confidentiality: Counselling and the Law* (3rd edn, Rugby: British Association for Counselling, 1999).

Boon, A and J Levin, *The Ethics and Conduct of Lawyers* (Oxford: Hart, 1999).

Bosworth-Davies, R and G Saltmarsh, *Money Laundering* (London: Chapman & Hall, 1994).

Bowers, J, J Lewis and J Mitchell, *Whistleblowing: the New Law* (London: Sweet & Maxwell, 1999).

Brazier, M (ed), *Clerk & Lindsell on Torts* (17th edn, London: Sweet & Maxwell, 1995).

—— *Medicine, Patients and the Law* (2nd edn, London: Penguin, 1992).

Brearley, K, *Employment Covenants and Confidential Information: law, practice and technique* (2nd edn, London: Butterworths, 1999).

British Association for Counselling, *Code of Ethics and Practice for Counsellors* (Rugby: British Association for Counselling, 1997).

Burrows, A, *Remedies for Torts and Breach of Contract* (2nd edn, London: Butterworths, 1994).

Burrows, D, *Evidence in Family Proceedings* (Bristol: Family Law, 1999).

Butler, I and H Williamson, *Children Speak: Children, Trauma and Social Work* (London: Longman, 1994).

Callahan, J, *Ethical Issues in Professional Life* (Oxford: OUP 1988).

Cambridge Health Informatics Ltd, *Gaining Patient Consent to Disclosure* (on-line publication http:www.doh.gov.uk/ipu/confiden/gpcd.).

Carey, P, *Media Law* (2nd edn, London: Sweet & Maxwell, 1999).

—— *Data Protection in the United Kingdom* (London: Blackstone Press, 2000).

Cate, F, *Privacy in the Information Age* (Washington: Brookings Institution Press, 1997).

Cavoukian, A and D Tapscott, *Who Knows: Safeguarding your privacy in a networked world* (New York: McGraw-Hill, 1997).

Clarke, L, *Confidentiality and the Law* (London: Lloyds of London, 1990).

Clayton, R and H Tomlinson, *The Law of Human Rights* (Oxford: OUP, 2000).

Coleman, A, *The Legal Protection of Trade Secrets* (London: Sweet & Maxwell, 1992).

Cooley, *Cooley on Torts* (2nd edn, 1888).

Cordery on Solicitors (9th edn, London: Butterworths, 1995).

Cornish, W, *Intellectual Property* (4th edn, London: Sweet & Maxwell, 1999).

Cranston, R (ed), *Legal Ethics and Professional Responsibility* (Oxford: Clarendon Press, 1995).

Cresswell, P et al (eds), *Encyclopaedia of Banking Law* (London: Butterworths, 1998).

Cretney, S and D Lush, *Enduring Powers of Attorney* (4th edn, Bristol: Jordans, 1996).

Cripps, Y, *The Legal Implications of Disclosure in the Public Interest* (2nd edn, London: Sweet & Maxwell, 1994).

Daniel, S, *Confidentiality and Young People* (Leicester: Centre for Social Action, De Montfort U, 1997).

Daniels, D and P Jenkins, *Therapy with Children* (London: SAGE, 2000).

Bibliography

Davies, G, *Copyright and the Public Interest* (2nd edn, London: Sweet & Maxwell, 2002).
Davies, M, *The Essential Social Worker* (3rd edn, Aldershot: Arena, 1994).
Dean, R, *The Law of Trade Secrets and Personal Secrets* (2nd edn, Sydney: LBC, 2002).
DeCew, J, *In Pursuit of Privacy* (Ithaca: Cornell UP, 1997).
Dennis, I, *The Law of Evidence* (London: Sweet & Maxwell, 1999).
Desiatnik, R, *Legal Professional Privilege in Australia* (St Leonards: Prospect Media, 2000).
Dickson, D, *Confidentiality and Privacy in Social Work* (New York: The Free Press 1998).
Eicke, T and D Scorey, *Human Rights Damages: Principles and Practice* (London: Sweet & Maxwell, 2001).
Engelhardt, H, *The Foundations of Bioethics* (New York: OUP, 1986).
Epp, J, *Building on the Decade of Disclosure in Criminal Procedure* (London: Cavendish, 2001).
Etzioni, A, *The Limits of Privacy* (New York: Basic Books, 1999).
Evans, H, *Lawyers' Liabilities* (2nd edn, London: Sweet & Maxwell, 2002).
Faculty of Occupational Medicine, *Guidance on Ethics for Occupational Physicians* (5th edn, London: Royal College of Physicians, 1999).
Feldman, D, *Civil Liberties and Human Rights in England and Wales* (2nd edn, Oxford: OUP, 2002).
Fennell, P, *The All England Reports Annual Review 2000* (London: Butterworths, 2001).
Fenwick, H, *Civil Liberties* (2nd edn, London: Cavendish, 1998).
Finch, J (ed), *Speller's Law Relating to Hospitals* (7th edn, London: Chapman & Hall, 1994).
Finn, P, *Fiduciary Obligations* (Sydney: Law Book Co, 1977).
Forston, R, *Misuse of Drugs and Drug Trafficking Offences* (4th edn, London: Sweet & Maxwell, 2002).
Fortin, J, *Children's Rights and the Developing Law* (London: Butterworths, 1998).
Foster, C, T Wynn and N Ainley, *Disclosure and Confidentiality: A Practitioner's Guide* (London: FT Law & Tax, 1996).
—— and N Peacock, *Clinical Confidentiality* (London: Monitor, 2000).
Foster, C, and Peacock, N, *Clinical Confidentiality* (Sudbury, Suffolk: Monitor Press, 2000).
Fridman, G, *The Law of Agency* (7th edn, London: Butterworths, 1996).
—— *Restitution* (2nd edn, Toronto: Carswell, 1992).
Gates, J and B Arons, *Privacy and Confidentiality in Mental Health Care* (Baltimore: Paul H Brookes, 2000).
Gibson, D, *Aspects of Privacy Law* (Toronto: Butterworths, 1980).
Glover, J, *Commercial Equity Fiduciary Relationships* (Sydney: Butterworths, 1995).
GMC, *Confidentiality* (London: GMC, 1995).
—— *Confidentiality: Protecting and Providing Information* (London: GMC, 2000).
—— *Seeking patients' consent: the ethical considerations* (London: GMC, 2000).
Goff and Jones, *The Law of Restitution*, ed G Jones (5th edn, London: Sweet & Maxwell, 1998).
Griew, E, *The Theft Acts* (7th edn, London: Sweet & Maxwell, 1995).
Griffiths-Baker, J, *Serving Two Masters: Conflicts of Interest in the Modern Law Firm* (Oxford: Hart, 2002).

Bibliography

Grubb, A, *The Law of Tort* (London: Butterworths, 2001).

—— and D Pearl, *Blood Testing, AIDS and DNA Profiling, Law and Policy* (Bristol: Family Law, 1990).

Gunderson, M, D Mayo and F Rhame, *Aids: Testing and Privacy* (Salt Lake City: U of Utah Press, 1989).

Gurry, F, *Breach of Confidence* (Oxford: Clarendon Press, 1984).

Harris, B, *The Law and Practice of Disciplinary and Regulatory Proceedings* (2nd edn, Chichester: Barry Rose, 1999).

Harris, D, M O'Boyle and C Warbrick, *Law of the European Convention on Human Rights* (London: Butterworths, 1995).

—— D Campbell and R Halson, *Remedies in Contract and Tort* (2nd edn, London: Butterworths, 2002).

Harris, N, *Professional Codes of Conduct in the United Kingdom: A Directory* (London: Mansell, 1989).

—— (ed), *Children, Sex Education and the Law* (London: National Children's Bureau, 1996).

Hedges, A, *Confidentiality: The Public View* (London: Stationery Office, 1996).

Herschman, D and A MacFarlane, *Children Law and Practice* (Bristol: Jordan, 1995).

Heuston, R and R Buckley, *Salmond and Heuston on the Law of Torts* (21st edn, London: Sweet & Maxwell, 1996).

Hockton, A, *The Law of Consent to Medical Treatment* (London: Sweet & Maxwell, 2002).

Hollander, C, and Salzedo, S, *Conflicts of Interest and Chinese Walls* (London: Sweet & Maxwell, 2000).

Howard, M, *Phipson on Evidence* (15th edn, London: Sweet & Maxwell, 2000).

Howitt, J and M Stark, *The Role of the Independent Forensic Physician* (London: Association of Police Surgeons, 1999).

Hughes, G, *Data Protection in Australia* (Melbourne: Law Book Co, 1991).

Hutchings, C and S Thomas, *PPA Privacy Handbook* (London: Charles Russell, 2001).

Ingman, T, *The English Legal Process* (7th edn, London, 1998).

Inness, J, *Privacy, Intimacy and Isolation* (New York: OUP, 1992).

Jaconelli, J, *Open Justice* (Oxford: OUP, 2002).

James, M, *Privacy and human rights: an international and comparative study, with special reference to developments in information technology* (Aldershot: Dartmouth, 1994).

Jay, R and A Hamilton, *Data Protection Law and Practice* (London: Sweet & Maxwell, 1999).

Jayawickrama, N, *The Judicial Application of Human Rights Law* (Cambridge: CUP, 2002).

Jenkins, P, *Counselling, Psychotherapy and the Law* (London: SAGE, 1997).

—— (ed), *Legal Issues in Counselling and Psychotherapy* (London: SAGE, 2002).

Johnstone, P and R Jones, *Investigations and Enforcement* (London: Butterworths, 2001).

Jones, G (ed), Goff and Jones, *The Law of Restitution* (6th edn, Sweet & Maxwell, 2000).

Jones, M, *Medical Negligence* (London: Sweet & Maxwell, 1996).

Kaye, P, *English Law of Torts* (Chichester: Barry Rose, 1996).

Keeton, W (ed), *Prosser and Keeton on The Law of Torts* (5th edn, St Paul: West, 1984).

Kennedy, L, *A Presumption of innocence: The Amazing Case of Patrick Meehan* (London: Gollancz, 1996).

Bibliography

Kennedy, W L and A Grubb, *Medical Law* (3rd edn, London: Butterworths, 2000).
Kermani, E, *Handbook of Psychiatry and Law* (Chicago: Year Book Medical Publishers, 1989).
Kerridge, I, M Lowe and J McPhee, *Ethics and Law for the Health Professional* (North Sydney: Social Science Press, 1998).
Kilkelly, U, *The Child and the European Convention on Human Rights* (Aldershot: Ashgate/Dartmouth, 1999).
Kirk, D and A Woodcock, *Serious fraud: investigation and trial* (London: Butterworths, 1997).
Kloss, D, *Occupational Health Law* (3rd edn, Oxford: Blackwell, 1988).
Kultgen, J, *Ethics and Professionalism* (Philadelphia: U of Pennsylvania Press, 1988).
Kuner C, *European Data Privacy Law and Online Business* (Oxford: OUP, 2003).
Laurie, G, *Genetic Privacy* (Cambridge: CUP, 2002).
Law Society, *The Guide to the Professional Conduct of Solicitors* (8th edn, London: Law Society, 1999) (http://www.guide-on-line.lawsociety.org.uk/).
Ligertwood, A, *Australian Evidence* (3rd edn, Sydney: Butterworths, 1998).
Lloyd, I, *The Data Protection Act 1998* (London: Butterworths, 1998).
Lund, T, *A Guide to the Professional Conduct and Etiquette of Solicitors* (London: Law Society, 1960).
MacDonald, J and C Jones (eds), *The Law of Freedom of Information* (Oxford: OUP, 2003)
McGee, A, *Limitation Periods* (2nd edn, London: Sweet & Maxwell, 1994).
McHale, J, *Medical Confidentiality and Legal Privilege* (London: Routledge, 1993).
McLean, D, *International Co-operation in Civil and Criminal Matters* (Oxford: OUP, 2002).
Madden, D, *Medicine, Ethics and the Law* (Dublin: Butterworths, 2002).
Manes, R, and Silver, M, *Solicitor–Client Privilege in Canada* (Toronto: Butterworths, 1993).
—— *The Law of Confidential Communications in Canada* (Toronto: Butterworths, 1996).
Markesinis, B, *A Comparative Introduction to the German Law of Torts* (3rd edn, Oxford: Clarendon, 1994).
—— *Protecting Privacy* (Oxford: OUP, 1999).
—— and S Deakin, *Tort Law* (4th edn, Oxford: Clarendon, 1999).
Mason, J, R McCall Smith and G Laurie, *Law and Medical Ethics* (London: Butterworths, 1999).
Matthews, P and H Malek, *Disclosure* (London: Sweet & Maxwell, 2000).
Meagher, P, W Gummow and J Lehane, *Equity, Doctrine and Remedies* (3rd edn, Sydney: Butterworths, 1992).
Milmo, P and W Rogers (eds), *Gatley on Libel and Slander* (9th edn, London: Sweet & Maxwell, 1998).
Mizell, L, *Invasion of Privacy* (New York: Berkley Books, 1998).
Montgomery, J, *Health Care Law* (2nd edn, Oxford: Clarendon Press, 2001).
Moore, B, *Privacy* (New York: M E Sharpe, 1984).
Moore, W and G Rosenblum, *The Professions: Roles and Rules* (New York: Russell Sage Foundation, 1970).
Mulcahy, L (ed), *Human Rights and Civil Practice* (London: Sweet & Maxwell, 2001).
Mullany, N and P Handford, *Tort Liability for Psychiatric Damage* (London: Sweet & Maxwell, 1993).

Bibliography

Murphy, P (ed), *Blackstone's Criminal Practice 2001* (11th edn, London: Blackstone, 2001).

——— *Evidence* (7th edn, London: Blackstone, 2000).

Murray, C and L Harris, *Mutual Assistance in Criminal Matters* (London: Sweet & Maxwell, 2000).

Nakajima, C, and Sheffield, E, *Conflicts of Interest and Chinese Walls* (London: Butterworths, 2002).

Neate, F, *Banking Secrecy: Financial Privacy and Related Restrictions* (London: Oyez Publishing, 1980).

Nicol, A, G Millar and A Sharland, *Media Law and Human Rights* (London: Blackstone, 2001).

Nicolson, D and J Webb, *Professional Legal Ethics* (Oxford: OUP, 1999).

Nuffield Council on Bioethics, *Genetic Screening: Ethical Issues* (London: Nuffield Council on Bioethics, 1993).

Oakley, A, *Constructive Trusts* (3rd edn, London: Sweet & Maxwell, 1997).

O'Dair, R, *Legal Ethics: Text and Materials* (London: Butterworths, 2001).

Ogilvie, M, *Canadian Banking Law* (Toronto: Carswell, 1991).

O'Neill, O, *Autonomy and Trust in Bioethics* (Cambridge: CUP, 2002).

Ontario Law Reform Commission, *Report on Genetic Testing* (Toronto: Ontario Law Reform Commission, 1996).

Oyen, E, and Beckford, J, *Confidentiality: theory and practice: the social functions of confidentiality* (London: Sage, 1982).

Parkinson, P, *The Principles of Equity* (Sydney: LBC, 1996).

Passmore, C, *Privilege* (Birmingham: CLT Professional Training, 1998).

Percy, R and C Walton (eds), *Charlesworth & Percy on Negligence* (9th edn, London: Sweet & Maxwell, 1997).

Perri 6, *The Future of Privacy*, vol. 1 (London: Demos, 1998).

Proulx, M and D Layton, *Ethics and Canadian Criminal Law* (Toronto: Irwin Law, 2001).

Randall, F, and Downie, R, *Palliative Care Ethics* (2nd edn, Oxford: 1999).

Rankin, W, *Confidentiality and the Clergy* (Harrisburg: Morehouse Publishing, 1990).

Reid, B, *Confidentiality and the Law* (London: Waterlow, 1986).

Robertson, G, *The Justice Game* (London: Chatto & Windus, 1999).

——— and A Nicol, *Media Law* (4th edn, London: Sweet & Maxwell, 2002).

Rogers, W (ed), *Winfield & Jolowicz on Tort* (15th edn, London: Sweet & Maxwell, 1998).

Ross, S, *Ethics in Law* (Sydney: Butterworths, 1998).

Ross, Y, *Ethics in Law in Australia* (Sydney: Butterworths, 2001).

Rotenberg, M, *The Privacy Law Sourcebook 2000* (Washington DC: Electronic Privacy Information Center, 2000).

Rothstein, M, *Genetic Secrets: Protecting Privacy and Confidentiality in the Genetic Era* (New Haven: Yale, 1997).

Royal College of Psychiatrists, *Good Psychiatric Practice: Confidentiality* (London: Royal College of Psychiatrists, 2000).

Sack, R, *Sack on Defamation* (3rd edn, New York: PLI Press, 2002).

Schoeman, F (ed), *Philosophical Dimensions of Privacy: An Anthology* (Cambridge: CUP, 1984).

Bibliography

Seneviratne, M, *The Legal Profession: Regulation and the Consumer* (London: Sweet & Maxwell, 1999).

Seneviratne, M, *Ombudsmen: Public Services and Administrative Justice* (London: Sweet & Maxwell 2002).

Shorts, E and C De Than, *Civil Liberties* (London: Sweet & Maxwell, 1998).

Slovenko, R, *Psychotherapy and Confidentiality* (Springfield, Illinois: Charles C Thomas, 1998).

Smith, A, *Property Offences* (London: Sweet & Maxwell, 1994).

Smith, I and G Thomas, *Industrial Law* (7th edn, London: Butterworths, 2000).

Smith, J, *The Law of Theft* (8th edn, London: Butterworths, 1997).

Stauch, M et al, *Sourcebook on Medical Law* (London: Cavendish, 1998).

Stone, J and J Matthews, *Complementary Medicine and the Law* (Oxford: OUP, 1996).

Stone, R, *Entry, Search and Seizure* (3rd edn, London: Sweet & Maxwell, 1997).

Stone, S and R Liebman, *Testimonial Privileges* (1st edn, Colorado Springs: Shepard's, 1983).

—— and R Taylor, *Testimonial Privileges* (2nd edn, Colorado Springs: Shepard's, 1993).

Strong, JW (ed), *McCormick on Evidence* (5th edn, St Paul: West, 1999).

Swenson, L, *Psychology and Law for the Helping Professions* (2nd edn, Pacific Grove: Brooks/Cole, 1997).

Tapper, C (ed), *Cross & Tapper on Evidence* (8th edn, London: Butterworths, 1995).

Thomas, T, *Privacy and Social Services* (Aldershot: Arena, 1995).

Tomlinson, H (ed), *Privacy and the Media: The Developing Law* (London: 2002).

Toulson, R and C Phipps, *Confidentiality* (London: Sweet & Maxwell, 1996).

Trindade, F and P Cane, *The Law of Torts in Australia* (Melbourne: OUP, 1985).

Tugendhat, M and I Christie, *The Law of Privacy and the Media* (Oxford: OUP, 2002).

Turkington, R and A Allen, *Privacy Law: Cases and Materials* (St Paul: West Group, 1999).

Vickers, L, *Freedom of Speech and Employment* (Oxford: OUP, 2002).

Wacks, R, *Personal Information, Privacy and the Law* (Oxford: Clarendon Press, 1989).

—— *Personal Information* (Oxford: Oxford University Press, 1993).

—— *Privacy and Press Freedom* (London: Blackstone, 1995).

Wadham, J, J Griffiths and B Rigby, *Freedom of Information Act 2000* (London: Blackstone, 2001).

Wagner DeCew, J, *In Pursuit of Privacy* (Ithaca: Cornell U Press, 1997).

Walker, C, *The Anti-Terrorism Legislation* (Oxford: OUP, 2002).

Warne, D and N Elliott (eds), *Banking Litigation* (London: Sweet & Maxwell, 1999).

Watson, B, *Litigation Liabilities* (Bembridge: Palladian Law Publishing, 2002).

Webb, D, *Ethics: Professional Responsibility and the Lawyer* (Wellington: Butterworths, 2000).

Weiner, B and R Wettstein, *Legal Issues in Mental Health Care* (New York: Plenum Press, 1993).

Weir, T, *Tort Law* (Oxford: OUP, 2002).

Westin, A, *Computers, Health Records and Citizen Rights* (Washington DC: National Bureau of Standards, 1976).

—— *Privacy and Freedom* (London: Bodley Head, 1967).

Wheat, K (ed), *Recovering Damages for Psychiatric Injury* (2nd edn, Oxford: OUP, 2002).

Wigmore, J, *Evidence in Trials at Common Law* (Boston: McNaughten Rev, 1961).
Wilkin, S, *The Law of Waiver, Variation and Estoppel* (2nd edn, Oxford: OUP 2002).
Wraith, R and G Lamb, *Public Inquiries as an Instrument of Government* (London: George Allen & Unwin, 1971).
Wright, J, *Tort Law and Human Rights* (Oxford: Hart, 2001).
Young J, (ed), *Privacy* (Chichester: Wiley, 1978).

Articles in books

Airaksinen, T, 'Professional Ethics' in R Chadwick (ed), *Encyclopedia of Applied Ethics* (California: Academic Press, 1998).

Aitken, G and M Spencer, 'Confidentiality—Medical Records' in M Powers and N Harris (eds), *Clinical Negligence* (3rd edn, London: Butterworths, 2000).

Bagshaw, R, 'Obstacles on the Path to Privacy Torts' in P Birks (ed), *Privacy and Loyalty* (Oxford: Clarendon, 1997).

Bainham, A, 'Sex education: a family lawyer's perspective' in N Harris (ed), *Children, Sex Education and the Law* (London: National Children's Bureau, 1996).

Barendt, E, 'Media intrusion: the case for legislation' in D Tambini and C Heyward, *Rules by Recluses?* (London: IPPR, 2002).

Barendt, E, 'Privacy as a Constitutional Right and Value' in P Birks (ed), *Privacy and Loyalty* (Oxford: Clarendon Press, 1997).

—— 'Media intrusion: the case for legislation' in D Tambini and C Heyward (eds), *Ruled by Recluses?* (London: IPPR, 2002).

Bayles, M, 'The Professions' in J Callahan (ed), *Ethical Issues in Professional Life* (Oxford: OUP, 1988).

Bleich, J, 'Clergy Privilege and Conscientious Objection to the Privilege' in R O'Dair and A Lewis, *Law and Religion* (Oxford: OUP, 2001).

Brindle, M and G Dehn, 'Confidence, Public Interest, the Lawyer' in R Cranston (ed), *Legal Ethics and Professional Responsibility* (Oxford: Clarendon Press, 1995).

Byrne, E, 'Privacy' in R Chadwick (ed), *Encyclopedia of Applied Ethics* (California: Academic Press, 1998).

Cain, P, 'The Limits of Confidentiality in Healthcare' in C Cordess (ed), *Confidentiality and Mental Health* (London: Jessica Kingsley, 2001).

Capron, A, 'Genetics and Insurance: Access and Using Private Information' in E Paul, F Miller, J Paul (eds) *The Right to Privacy* (Cambridge: CUP, 2000).

Cavoukian, A, 'The Promise of Privacy-Enhancing Technologies: Applications in Health Information Networks' in C Bennett and R Grant (eds), *Visions of Privacy: Policy Choices for the Digital Age* (Toronto: U of Toronto Press, 1999).

Cooper, J, 'Horizontality: The Application of Human Rights Standards in Private Disputes' in R English and P Havers (eds), *Human Rights and the Common Law* (Oxford: Hart, 2000).

Cordess, C, 'Confidentiality and Contemporary Practice' in C Cordess (ed), *Confidentiality and Mental Health* (London: Jessica Kingsley, 2001).

Cranston, R, 'Legal Ethics and Professional Responsibility' in R Cranston (ed), *Legal Ethics and Professional Responsibility* (Oxford: Clarendon Press, 1995).

Bibliography

DeCew, J, 'The Priority of Privacy for Medical Information' in E Paul, F Miller, J Paul (eds.) *The Right to Privacy* (Cambridge: CUP, 2000).

Dubs, Lord, 'The Broadcasting Standards Commission and privacy complaints' in D Tambini and C Heyward (eds), *Ruled by Recluses?* (London: IPPR, 2002).

English, R, 'Confidentiality and Defamation' in R English and P Havers (eds), *Human Rights and the Common Law* (Oxford: Hart, 2000).

Feldman, D, 'Privacy-related Rights: Their Social Value' in P Birks (ed), *Privacy and Loyalty* (Oxford: Clarendon Press, 1997).

—— 'Information and Privacy' in J Beatson and Y Cripps (eds), *Freedom of Expression and Freedom of Information: Essays in Honour of Sir David Williams* (Oxford: OUP, 2000).

Ferriter, M and M Butwell, 'Confidentiality and Research in Mental Health' in C Cordess (ed), *Confidentiality and Mental Health* (London: Jessica Kingsley, 2001).

Garwood-Gowers, A, 'Time for Competent Minors to have the same right of self-determination as competent adults with respect to medical intervention?' in A Garwood-Gowers, J Tingle and T Lewis (eds), *Healthcare: The Impact of the Human Rights Act 1998* (London: Cavendish, 2001).

Gutheil, T, 'Ethics and forensic psychiatry' in S Bloch, P Chodoff and S Green (eds), *Psychiatric Ethics* (3rd edn, Oxford: OUP, 1999).

Hurwitz, B, 'Informed consent for access to medical records for health services research' in L Doyal and J Tobias (eds), *Informed Consent in Medical Research* (London: BMJ Books, 2001).

Joseph, D and J Onek, 'Confidentiality in psychiatry' in S Bloch, P Chodoff and S Green (eds), *Psychiatric Ethics* (3rd edn, Oxford: OUP, 1999).

Jowell, J and J Cooper, 'Introduction: Defining Human Rights Principles' in J Jowell and J Cooper (eds), *Understanding Human Rights Principles* (Oxford: Hart, 2001).

Kaul, A, 'Confidentiality in Dual Responsibility Settings' in C Cordess (ed), *Confidentiality and Mental Health* (London: Jessica Kingsley, 2001).

Kennedy, I, 'The Fiduciary Relationship and its Application to Doctors and Patients' in P Birks (ed), *Wrongs and Remedies in the Twenty-first century* (Oxford: Clarendon Press, 1996).

Kloss, D, 'Pre-Employment Health Screening' in M Freeman and A Lewis, *Law and Medicine* (Oxford: OUP, 2000).

Levi, M, 'Covert Policing and the Investigation of Organized Fraud: The English Experience in International Context' in C Fijnaut and G Marx (eds), *Police Surveillance in Comparative Perspective* (The Hague: Kluwer Law Intl, 1995).

McCall Smith, A, 'The Duty to Rescue and the Common Law' in M Menlowe and A McCall Smith (eds), *The Duty to Rescue* (Aldershot: Dartmouth, 1993).

McHale, J, 'The general practitioner and confidentiality' in C Dowrick and L Frith (eds), *General Practice and Ethics* (London: Routledge, 1999).

Mulcahy, A, 'Consumer Protection and Advertising' in L Mulcahy (ed), *Human Rights and Civil Practice* (London: Sweet & Maxwell, 2001).

Napier, B, Confidentiality and Labour Law' in L Clarke (ed), *Confidentiality and the Law* (London: Lloyd's of London, 1990).

Oakley, J, 'The Morality of Breaching Confidentiality to Protect Others' in L Shotton (ed), *Health Care, Law and Ethics* (Katoomba, NSW: Social Science Press, 1997).

Bibliography

Palmer, N and P Kohler, 'Information as Property' in N Palmer and E McKendrick, *Interests in Goods* (London: Lloyd's of London Press, 1993).

Palmer, S, 'Freedom of Information: The New Proposals' in J Beatson and Y Cripps (eds), *Freedom of Expression and Freedom of Information: Essays in Honour of Sir David Williams* (Oxford: OUP, 2000).

Parent, W, 'Privacy, Morality and the Law' in J Callahan (ed), *Ethical Issues in Professional Life* (New York: OUP, 1988).

Parsloe, P, 'The Unintended Impact of Computers on Social Work Practice' in R Cnaan and P Parsloe (eds), *The Impact of Information Technology on Social Work Practice* (New York: Haworth Press, 1989).

Peacock, N, 'Human Rights and Clinical Guidelines' in J Tingle and C Foster (eds), *Clinical Guidelines: Law, Policy and Practice* (London: Cavendish, 2002).

Plomer, A, 'Medical Research, Consent and the European Convention on Human Rights and Biomedicine' in A Garwood-Gowers, J Tingle and T Lewis, *Healthcare: The Impact of the Human Rights Act 1998* (London: Cavendish, 2001).

Pritchard, J, 'Codes of Ethics' in R Chadwick (ed), *Encyclopedia of Applied Ethics* (California: Academic Press, 1998).

Robinson, W, 'Privacy and the Appropriation of Identity' in G Collste (ed), *Ethics and Information Technology* (Delhi: New Academic Publishers, 1998).

Samuels, A, 'Confidence and Privilege and the Lawyer' in J Young (ed), *Privacy* (Chichester: Wiley, 1978).

Scarman, L, 'Law and Medical Practice' in P Byrne (ed), *Medicine in Contemporary Society* (London: King Edward's Hospital Fund for London, 1987).

Scott, R, 'Confidentiality' in J Beatson and Y Cripps (eds), *Freedom of Expression and Freedom of Information: Essays in Honour of Sir David Williams* (Oxford: OUP, 2000).

Sedley, S, 'Information as a Human Right' in J Beatson and Y Cripps (eds), *Freedom of Expression and Freedom of Information: Essays in Honour of Sir David Williams* (Oxford: OUP, 2000).

Skene, L and S Millwood, 'Informed Consent to Medical Procedures: the Current Law in Australia, Doctors' Knowledge of the Law and their Practices in Informing Patients' in L Shotton (ed), *Health Care, Law and Ethics* (Katoomba, NSW: Social Science Press, 1997).

Stapleton, J, 'Duty of Care Factors: a Selection from the Judicial Menus' in P Canc and J Stapleton (eds), *The Law of Obligations* (Oxford: Clarendon Press, 1998).

Stern, K, 'Confidentiality and Medical Records' in A Grubb (ed), *Principles of Medical Law* (4th cumulative supplement, Oxford: OUP, 2001).

Todd, S, 'Protection of Privacy' in N Mullany (ed), *Torts in the Nineties* (North Ryde: LBC, 1997).

Tugendhat, M, 'Privacy and Celebrity' in E Barendt and A Firth (eds), *Yearbook of Copyright and Media Law 2001/2002* (Oxford: Clarendon Press, 2002).

Vedder, A, 'HIV/AIDS and the Point and Scope of Medical Confidentiality' in R Bennett and C Erin, *HIV and AIDS: Testing, Screening and Confidentiality* (Oxford: OUP, 1999).

—— 'Medical Data, New Information Technologies, and the Need for Normative Principles Other than Privacy Rules' in M Freeman and A Lewis, *Law and Medicine* (Oxford: OUP, 2000).

Velecky, L, 'The Concept of Privacy' in J Young (ed), *Privacy* (Chichester: Wiley, 1978).

Vernon, S, 'Legal aspects of whistleblowing in the social services' in G Hunt (ed), *Whistleblowing in the Social Services* (London: Arnold, 1998).

Walters, L, 'Ethical Aspects of Medical Confidentiality' in T Beauchamp and L Walters (eds), *Contemporary Issues in Bioethics* (California: Dickenson Pub Co, 1978).

Williams, K and J, 'Vulnerable Adults—Confidentiality and Inter-Disciplinary Working' in A Garwood-Gowers, J Tingle and T Lewis, *Healthcare: The Impact of the Human Rights Act 1998* (London: Cavendish, 2001).

Williams, N, 'Four Questions of Privilege: The Litigation Aspect of Legal Professional Privilege' in I Scott (ed), *International Perspectives on Civil Justice* (London: Sweet & Maxwell, 1990).

Woolf, 'The Human Rights Act 1998 and Remedies' in M Andenas and M Fairgrieve, *Judicial Review in International Perspective* II (The Hague: Kluwer Law Intl, 2000).

Zuckerman, A, 'Privilege and public interest' in C Tapper (ed), *Crime, Proof and Punishment: essays in memory of Sir Rupert Cross* (London: Butterworths, 1981).

Journal articles

Abadee, A, 'The Medical Duty of Confidentiality and Prospective Duty of Disclosure: Can they Co-exist?' (1995) 3 J of L and Medicine 75.

Aitken, L, 'Developments in Equitable Compensation: Opportunity or Danger?' (1993) 67 Australian LJ 596.

Akdeniz, Y, N Taylor and C Walker, 'Regulation of Investigatory Powers Act 2000 (1): BigBrother.gov.uk: State surveillance in the age of information and rights' [2001] Crim LR 73.

Alexander, V, 'The Corporate Attorney–Client Privilege: A Study of the Participants' (1989) St John's L Rev 191.

Andrews, N, 'The Influence of Equity Upon the Doctrine of Legal Professional Privilege' (1989) 105 LQR 608.

Anon, 'An Ethical Debate: Child protection: medical responsibilities' (1996) 313 British Medical J 671.

Appelbaum, P et al, 'Statutory approaches to limiting psychiatrists' liability for their patients' violent acts' (1989) 146 American J of Psychiatry 821.

Astbury, H et al, 'The impact of domestic violence on individuals' (2000) 173 Medical J of Australia 427.

Auburn, J, 'Implied Waiver and Adverse Inferences' (1999) 115 LQR 590.

Avary, J, 'Privilege, Confidence and Illegally Obtained Evidence' (1977) 15 Osgoode Hall LJ 456.

Backstrom, M, 'Unveiling the Truth when it Matters Most: Implementing the Tarasoff Duty to California's Attorneys' (1999) 73 Southern California L Rev 139.

Bainbridge, D and G Pearce, 'Tilting at Windmills—Has the New Data Protection Law Failed to make a Significant Contribution to Rights of Privacy?' (2000) 2 J of Information, L and Technology.

Baker, P, 'Taxation and the European Convention on Human Rights' [2000] BTR 211.

Balen, P, 'Access to Health Records' [2002] JPIL 405.

Bibliography

Ball, S and J Connolly, 'Requiring School Attendance: A Little Used Sentencing Power' [1999] Crim LR 183.

Barendt, E, 'Privacy and the Press' [1995] 1 Media & Entertainment L 27.

Barnard, H, 'Data Protection Act 1998—manual data' (2002) 152 NLJ 925.

Bell, D and B Bennett, 'Genetic Secrets and the Family' [2001] Medical L Rev 130.

Benn, S, 'The Protection and Limitation of Privacy' (1978) 52 Australian LJ 686.

Berryman, J, 'Injunctions—The Ability to Bind Non-Parties' (2002) 81 Canadian Bar Rev 207.

Beyleveld, D and E Histed, 'Betrayal of Confidence in the Court of Appeal' (2000) 4 Medical L Intl 277.

Binning, P, 'In Safe Hands? Striking the balance between Privacy and Security' [2002] EHRLR 737. Birkinshaw, P, 'Freedom of Information' (1990) 140 NLJ 1637.

Blom-Cooper, L and L Pruitt, 'Privacy, Jurisprudence of the Press Complaints Commission' (1994) 23 Anglo-American L Rev 133.

Bloustein, E, 'Privacy as an Aspect of Human Dignity: An Answer to Dean Prosser' (1964) 39 New York U L Rev 962.

Blyth, E, 'Donor assisted conception and donor off-spring rights to genetic information' (1998) 6 Intl J of Children's Rights 237.

—— 'Sharing Genetic Origins Information' (2000) 14 Children and Society 11.

Bogaert, W, '"The Unwanted Gaze: The Destruction of Privacy in America" by J Rosen' (2000) 10 Boston U Public Interest LJ 196.

Bohlman, E, 'Privacy in the Age of Information' (2002) J of Information, L and Technology 2.

Bolton Research Group, 'Patients' knowledge and expectations of confidentiality in primary health care' (2000) British J of General Practice 901.

Brahams, D, 'IVF Legislation: Error Causes Confidentiality Trap' (1991) 338 Lancet 1449.

Brasse, G, 'The Confidentiality of a Child's Instructions' [1996] Family L 733.

Brazier, M and C Bridge, 'Coercion or Caring: Analysing Adolescent Autonomy' (1996) 16 LS 84.

Brocker, L, 'Sacred Secrets: The Clergy–Penitent Privilege Finds its Way into the News' (1996) 57 Oregon State Bar 15.

Broomekamp, B, 'The Human Rights Act 1998 in Comparison with the Protection of Privacy and Personality in Germany' in [2000] Yearbook of Media and Copyright L 66.

Brown, A, 'Money Laundering: A European and U.K. Perspective' [1997] 8 J of Intl Banking L 307.

Brown, B, 'Powers to combat serious fraud: the Inland Revenue Consultative Paper' [2000] BTR 61.

Brown, P, 'Cancer Registries Fear Imminent Collapse' (2000) 321 British Medical J 849.

Brown, R, 'Crime and Computers' (1983) 7 Criminal LJ 68.

Burden, K and P Gregoire, 'Client Communication by E-Mail' (1999) 15 Computer L & Security R 311.

Burnett, J, 'A Physician's Duty to Warn a Patient's Relatives of a Patient's Genetically Inheritable Disease' (1999) 36 Houston L Rev 559.

Burrows, D, 'Privilege and Disclosure after Re L' (1996) 140 SJ 560.

Calcutt, D, 'Freedom of the Press, Freedom from the Press' [1994] Denning LJ 1.

Bibliography

Cameron, E, 'Confidentiality in HIV/AIDS: Some Reflections on India and South Africa' (2001) 1 Oxford U Commonwealth LJ 35.

Capper, D, 'Damages for breach of the equitable duty of confidence' [1994] 14 LS 313.

Carss-Frisk, M, 'Public Authorities: The Developing Definition' [2002] European Human Rights L Rev 319.

Cartwright, J, 'Remoteness of Damage in Contract and Tort' [1996] CLJ 488.

Carty, H, 'Intentional Violation of Economic Interests: The Limits of Common Law Liability' (1988) 104 LQR 250.

Cassidy, J, 'Proceeds of Crime—Finally Enacted' (2002) 6 Tax LJ 55.

Casswell, D, 'Disclosure by a Physician of AIDS-Related Patient Information: An Ethical and Legal Dilemma' (1989) 68 Canadian Bar Rev 224.

Cheng, T et al, 'Confidentiality in health care: a survey of knowledge, perceptions, and attitudes among high school students' (1993) 29 J of the American Medical Association 1404.

Chester, M, 'The patient's perspective on medical privacy' (2000) 18/5 British J of Healthcare Computing & Information Management 20.

—— 'Practice Points' (2001) 98 LS Gaz 50.

Clarke, L, 'Breach of Confidence and the Employment Relationship' (2002) 31 Industrial LJ 353.

Clarke, P, 'Damages in Contract for Mental Distress' (1978) 52 Australian LJ 626.

Clayton, R, 'Developing Principles for Human Rights' [2002] European Human Rights L Rev 175.

Cleland, A, 'Dilemmas posed by young clients' (1998) 43 J of the L Society of Scotland 27.

Coad, J, 'Harassment by the Media' [2002] Entertainment L Rev 18.

Cohen, K, 'Some Legal Issues in Counselling and Psychotherapy' (1992) 20 British J of Guidance and Counselling 10.

Cole, W, 'Religious Confidentiality and the Reporting of Child Abuse' (1987) 21 Columbia J of L and Social Problems 1.

Collingridge, M, S Miller and W Bowles, 'Privacy and Confidentiality in Social Work' (2001) 54(2) Australian Social Work 3.

Cooper, D, 'The Ethical Rules Lack Ethics: Tort Liability when a Lawyer Fails to Warn a Third Party of a Client's Threat to Cause Serious Physical Harm or Death' (2000) 36 Idaho L Rev 479.

Cooter, R and B Freedman, 'The Fiduciary Relationship: Its Economic Character and Legal Consequences' (1991) 66 New York U L Rev 1045.

Corker, D, 'Third party disclosure' (1999) 149 NLJ 1006.

—— 'The CPIA Disclosure Regime: PII and Third Party Disclosure' (2000) 40 Medicine, Science & the L 116.

—— 'Legal privilege hangs in balance' (2002) 99 LS Gaz 10.

Costigan, R and P Thomas, 'Anonymous Witnesses' (2000) 51 Northern Ireland LQ 326.

Cox, S, 'Medical confidentiality: A guide for HR and line managers on the duties of the OH department' [2000] (Mar/April) OCR 32.

Craig, J, 'Invasion of Privacy and Charter Values' (1997) 42 McGill LJ 355.

—— and Nolte, N, 'Privacy and Free Speech in Germany and Canada: Lessons for an English Privacy Tort' [1998] European Human Rights L Rev 162.

Cripps, Y, 'Disclosure in the Public Interest: The Predicament of the Public Sector Employee' [1983] PL 600.

Cripps, Y, 'The public interest defence to the action for breach of confidence and the Law Commission's proposals on disclosure in the public interest' (1984) 4 OJLS 361.

—— 'Judicial Proceedings and Refusals to Disclose the Identity of Sources of Information' [1984] CLJ 266.

—— 'New Statutory Duties of Disclosure for Auditors in the Regulated Financial Sector' (1996) 112 LQR 667.

Cross, J, 'Trade Secrets, Confidential Information, and the Criminal Law' (1991) 36 McGill LJ 525.

D'Amato, 'Comment: Professor Posner's Lecture on Privacy' (1978) 12 Georgia L Rev 497.

Davies, J, 'Patient's Rights of Access to their Health Records' (1996) 2 Medical L Intl 189.

Davies, P, 'Computer Misuse' (1995) 145 NLJ 1776.

Dawson, J, 'Compelled Production of Medical Records' [1998] McGill LJ 25.

Dickens, B, 'Legal Protection of Psychiatric Confidentiality' (1978) 1 Intl J of L and Psychiatry 255.

Dixon, J, 'Privacy, secrecy and confidentiality in the family proceedings' (2002) 32 Family L 353.

Dodek, A, 'Doing Our Duty: The Case for a Duty of Disclosure to Prevent Death or Serious Harm' (2001) 50 University of New Brunswick LJ 21.

Doyal, L, 'Human Need and the Right of Patients to Privacy' (1997) 14 J of Contemporary Health Law and Policy 1.

Doyle, L, 'Informed consent in medical research' (1997) 314 British Medical J 1107.

Dunkel, Y, 'Medical Privacy Rights in Anonymous Data: Discussion of Rights in the United Kingdom and the United States in the Light of the Source Informatics Cases' (2001) Loyola of Los Angeles Intl & Comparative L Rev 41.

Edgar, H and H Sandomire, 'Medical Privacy Issues in the Age of AIDS: Legislative Options' (1990) 16 American J of L and Medicine 157.

Editorial, 'Angered patients and the medical profession' (1999) 170 Medical J of Australia 576.

Edwards, K, 'Accountants' Duty of Secrecy and Care' (1960) 110 LJ 714.

Elks, L, 'Disclosure by local authorities: An examination of the Criminal Appeal Act 1995' [2000] J of Local Government L 32.

Elliott, M, 'Privacy, confidentiality and horizontality: the case of the celebrity wedding photographs' (2001) 60 Camb LJ 231.

Elwood, J, 'Outing, Privacy and the First Amendment' (1992) 102 Yale LJ 747, 760–762.

Enonchong, N, 'Breach of Contract and Damages for Mental Distress' [1996] OJLS 617.

Epp, J, 'Production of confidential records held by a third party via witness summons in sexual offence proceedings' (1997) 1 Intl J of Evidence & Proof 122.

Evans, K, 'Of Privacy and Prostitutes' (2002) 20 NZLR 71.

Evans, S, 'Defending Discretionary Remedialism' (2001) 23 Sydney L Rev 463.

Fairgrieve, D, 'The Human Rights Act 1998, Damages and Tort Law' [2001] PL 695.

Farnham, F and D James, '"Dangerousness" and dangerous law' (2001) 358 (9297) The Lancet 1926.

Bibliography

Feldman, D, 'Access to Clients' Documents after the Police and Criminal Evidence Act 1984' [1985] Professional Negligence 24.

—— 'Press Freedom and Police Access to Journalistic Material' [1995] 1 Yearbook of Media and Entertainment L 3.

Fenwick, H, 'Covert Surveillance under the Regulation of Investigatory Powers Act 2000, Part II' [2001] J of Criminal L 521.

—— and G Phillipson, 'Confidence and Privacy: A Re-Examination' (1996) 55 CLJ 447.

Finn, P, 'Professionals and Confidentiality' (1992) 14 Sydney L Rev 317.

Flanagan, W, 'Genetic Data and Medical Confidentiality' (1995) 3 Health LJ 269.

Flannigan, R, 'Fiduciary Regulation of Sexual Exploitation' (2000) 79 Canadian Bar Rev 301.

Fogl, R, 'Sex, Laws and Videotape: The Ambit of Solicitor–Client Privilege in Canadian Criminal Law as Illuminated in *R v Murray*' (2001) 50 University of New Brunswick LJ 187.

Folk, F, 'Two Exceptions to a Lawyer's Duty of Confidentiality: Defence of Reputation and Pursuit of Fees' (2000) 58 Advocate (Vancouver) 33.

Fontin, J, 'Rights Brought Home for Children' (1999) 62 MLR 350.

Forrai, G, 'Confidential Information—A General Survey' (1968–71) 6 Sydney L Rev 382.

France, E, 'Privacy, data protection and freedom of information' (2000) 2 Interactive Marketing 11.

Freeman, D, 'Common Law Access to Medical Records' (1996) 59 MLR 101.

Fridman, G, 'Interference with Trade or Business' (1993) 1 Tort L Rev 19.

Fried, C, 'Privacy' (1968) 77 Yale LJ 475.

Friedman, D, 'Privacy and Technology' (2000) 17 Social Philosophy and Policy 186.

Friend, D, 'Too High a Price for Truth: The Exception to the Attorney–Client Privilege for Contemplated Crimes and Frauds' (1986) 64 North Carolina L Rev 443.

Gavison, R, 'Privacy and the Limits of Law' (1980) 89 Yale LJ 421.

Gelman, S, 'Client access to agency records: a comparative analysis' (1991) 34 Intl Social Work 191.

Gewirth, A, 'Confidentiality in Child-Welfare Practice' (2001) 75 Social Service Rev 479.

Ghent, J, 'Waiver or Loss of Right of Privacy' 57 ALR 3d 16 (1974).

Gibbons, S, 'Subsequent Use of Documents Obtained Through Disclosure in Civil Proceedings—The "Purpose of the Proceedings" Test' (2001) 20 Civil Justice Q 303.

Giles, S, 'Promises Betrayed; Breaches of Confidence as a Remedy for Invasions of Privacy' (1995) 43 Buffalo L Rev 1.

Giliker, P, 'A "new" head of damages: damages for mental distress in the English law of torts' [2001] LS 19.

Glover, J, 'Is breach of confidence a fiduciary wrong? Preserving the reach of judge-made law' [2001] LS 594.

Goldsmith, M and K Balmforth, 'The Electronic Surveillance of Privileged Communications: A Conflict of Doctrines' (1991) 64 Southern California L Rev 903.

Gostin, L, 'Health Information Privacy' (1995) 80 Cornell L Rev 451.

Gray, N and J Edelman, 'Developing the law of omissions: a common law duty to rescue?' (1998) Tort LJ 18.

Gronow, M, 'Restitution for Breach of Confidence' (1996) 10 Intellectual Property J 219.

Gronow, M, 'Restitution for Breach of Confidence' (1996) 10 Intellectual Property J 219.
—— 'Damages for Breach of Confidence' (1994) 2 Australian Intellectual Property J 95.
Grubb, A, 'The Doctor as Fiduciary' [1994] CLP 311.
—— 'Breach of Confidence Anonymised Information' (2000) 8 Medical L Rev 115.
—— and D Pearl, 'Medicine, Health, the Family and the Law' [1986] Family L 227.
Hamilton, I and J Wilson, 'Representation of Children in Private Law Proceedings Under the Children Act 1989' (1998) 8 Representing Children 32.
Hammond, R, 'Theft of Information' (1984) 100 LQR 252.
Hapwood, V, 'Guidelines in medical practice: the legal issues' (1998) Cephalalgia Suppl 21, 57.
Harding, A et al, 'Confidentiality Limits with Clients who Have HIV: A review of Ethical and Legal Guidelines and Professional Practices' (1993) 71 J of Counseling and Development 297.
Hartmann, C, 'The emergence of a statutory right to privacy tort in England' [1995] 6 J of Media L and Practice 10.
Hazard, G, 'An Historical Perspective on the Attorney–Client Privilege' (1978) 66 California L Rev 1061.
Hebenton, B and T Thomas, 'The Police and Social Services Departments in England and Wales: the exchange of personal information' [1992] J of Social Welfare & Family Law 114.
Hocking, B and S Muirhead, 'Warning, warning, warning—all doctors!' (2000) 16 Professional Negligence 31.
Hohfeld, W, 'Some Fundamental Legal Conceptions as Applied in Legal Reasoning' (1913) 23 Yale LJ 16.
Hooley, R, 'Banker's references and the bank's duty of confidentiality: when practice does not make perfect' (2002) 59 Camb LJ 21.
Howarth, D, 'Privacy, Confidentiality and the Cult of Celebrity' [2002] Camb LJ 264.
Hutchinson, A, 'Sex, lawyers and videotapes—A Canadian blockbuster' (2000) 150 NLJ 1008.
Hyam, H, 'Disclosure of confidential information' (2002) 152 NLJ 1129.
Jagim, R et al, 'Mental Health Professionals' Attitudes Toward Confidentiality, Privilege and Third-Party Disclosure' (1978) Professional Psychology 458.
Jenkins, P, 'Terrorism and the law' (2001) 12 Counselling & Psychotherapy J 42.
Jensen, D, 'Punitive Damages for Breach of Fiduciary Obligation' (1996) 19 U of Queensland LJ 125.
Jones, G, 'Breach of confidence—after Spycatcher' (1989) 42 Current Legal Problems 49.
Jones, G, 'Restitution of Benefits Obtained in Breach of Another's Confidence' (1970) 86 LQR 463.
Jones, J and M Lupton, 'Liability in Delict for Failure to Report Family Violence' (1999) 116 South African LJ 371.
Jones, M, 'Medical confidentiality and the public interest' (1990) 6 Professional Negligence 16.
JRL, 'Privileged Communications, Part 1, Communications with Spiritual Advisers' (1958) 13 Northern Ireland LQ 160.

Bibliography

—— 'Privileged Communications, Part 3, Doctor and Patient' (1958) 13 Northern Ireland LQ 284.

Julie, R, 'High-Tech Surveillance tools and the Fourth Amendment: Reasonable Expectations of Privacy in the Technological Age' (2000) 37 American Criminal L Rev 127.

Katz, J, 'Sex, Lies, Videotapes and Telephone Conversations: The Common Law of Privacy from a New Zealand Perspective' [1995] 1 EIPR 6.

Kerrison, S and A Pollock, 'Complaints as Accountability? The Case of Health Care in the United Kingdom' [2001] PL 115.

Kingston, M, 'Case closed by "dead man walking?"' (2000) 150 NLJ 705.

Kirby, M, 'Privacy in Cyberspace' (1998) 21 U of New South Wales LJ 323.

Klinck, D, '"Things of Confidence": Loyalty, Secrecy and Fiduciary Obligation' (1990) 54 Saskatchewan L Rev 73.

Knerr, C and J Carroll, 'Confidentiality and Criminological Research: The Evolving Body of Law' (1978) 69 J of Criminal L and Criminology 311.

Knoppers, B et al, 'Professional Disclosure of Familial Genetic Information' (1998) 62 American J of Human Genetics 474.

Koewn, J, 'The Ashes of AIDS and the Phoenix of Informed Consent' (1989) 52 MLR 790.

Koomen, K, 'Breach of confidence and the public interest defence: is it in the public interest?' (1994) 10 Queensland University of Technology LJ 56.

Koroway, E, 'Confidentiality in the Law of Evidence' (1978) 16 Osgoode Hall LJ 260.

Kottow, M, 'Medical Confidentiality: An Intransigent and Absolute Obligation' (1986) 12 J of Medical Ethics 117.

Laidlaw, H, 'Solicitor–Client Privilege: To Disclose or Not to Disclose . . . Remains the Question, Even after Death' (1995) Estates Trust J 56.

Laster, D, 'Commonalities Between Breach of Confidence and Privacy' (1990) 14 New Zealand Universities L Rev 144.

—— 'Breaches of Confidence and Privacy by Misuse of Personal Information' (1989) 7 Otago LR 31

Laurie, G, 'Challenging Medico Legal Norms' (2001) 22 J of Legal Medicine 1.

—— 'Obligations arising from genetic information—negligence and the protection of familial interests' (1999) 11 Child and Family LQ 109.

Leach, P, 'The Security Service Bill' (1996) 146 NLJ 224.

Leigh, I and L Lustgarten, 'Making Rights Real: The Courts, Remedies and the Human Rights Act' [1999] CLJ 509.

Leng, T, 'Protecting confidential client information' (2000) 16 Professional Negligence 103.

Lesser, H and Z Pickup, 'Law Ethics and Confidentiality' (1990) 17 J of L and Soc 17.

Lester, A and D Pannick, 'The impact of the Human Rights Act on private law: the knight's move' (2000) 116 LQR 380.

—— 'Breaches of Confidence and Privacy by Misuse of Personal Information' (1989) 7 Otago LR 31.

Levi, M, 'Taking financial sources to the cleaners' (1995) 145 NLJ 26.

Levin, L, 'Testing the Radical Experiment: A Study of Lawyer Response to Clients who Intend to Harm Others' (1994) 47 Rutgers L Rev 81.

Lewis, G, 'Client threats' (1983) 57 L Institute J 847.
Loder, R, 'When Silence Screams' (1996) 29 Loyola of Los Angeles L Rev 1785.
Logie, J, 'Affirmative Action in the Law of Tort: The Case of the Duty to Warn' [1989] CLJ 115.
Loscalzo, T, 'Cell phones and client confidentiality' (2001) 37 Trial 19.
Lucassen, N, and M Parker, 'Revealing false paternity: some ethical considerations' (2001) 357 (9261) The Lancet 1033.
McCallum, M, "Mandatory Child Abuse Reporting and Confidentiality in the Lawyer–Client Relationship' (2001) 50 University of New Brunswick LJ 263.
McDonagh, M, 'FOI and confidentiality of commercial information [2001] Public Law 256.
McEwan, J, 'The Uncertain Status of Privilege in Children Act Cases: Re L' (1997) 1 Intl J of Evidence & Proof 80.
MacKay, R, 'Dangerous Patient: Third Party Safety and Psychiatrists' Duties—Walking the Tarasoff Tightrope' (1990) 30 Medicine, Science and Law 52.
McSherry, B, 'Confidentiality of Psychiatric and Psychological Communications: The Public Interest Exception' (2001) 8 Psychiatry, Psychology and L 12.
McVea, H, '"Heard it Through the Grapevine": Chinese Walls and Former Client Confidentiality in Law Firms' (2000) 59 Camb LJ 370.
Magnusson, R, 'Recovery for Mental Distress in Tort, with Special Reference to Harmful Words and Statements' (1994) 2 Tort LJ 145.
—— 'A Triumph for Medical Paternalism: *Breen v Williams*, Fiduciaries and Patient Access to Medical Records' [1995] Tort LJ 12.
Maguire, G and P Church, 'Enforcement of the Data Protection Act 1998: compliance at all costs?' (2002) 152 NLJ 147.
Mahendra, B, 'Medical disclosure and confidentiality' (2001) 151 NLJ 10.
—— 'Clarifying confidentiality' (2002) 152 NLJ 1585.
Mahoney, R, 'Evidence' [2001] NZLR 85.
—— 'Reforming Litigation Privilege' [2002] Common L World Rev 66.
Maixner, A, 'Confidentiality of Health Information Postmortem' (2001) 125 Archives of Pathology & Laboratory Medicine 1189.
Mangalmurti, V, 'Psychotherapists' fear of Tarasoff: all in the mind?' (1994) 22 J of Psychiatry and L 37.
Matthews, P, 'Breach of confidence and legal privilege' [1981] 1 LS 77.
Maxeiner, J, 'Freedom of Information and the EU Protection Directive' (1995) 48 Federal Communications LJ 93.
Mendelson, D and G Mendelson, 'Tarasoff down under: the psychiatrist's duty to warn in Australia' [1991] J of Psychiatry & L 33.
Michael, J, 'Open Justice: Publicity and the Judicial Process' [1993] CLP 190.
Michalik, P, 'The availability of compensatory and exemplary damages in equity: A Note on the Aquaculture decision' (1991) 21 Victoria U of Wellington L Rev 391.
—— 'Doctors' Fiduciary Duties' (1998) 6 J of L and Medicine 168.
Miers, D, 'Liability for Injuries Caused by Violent Patients' [1996] J of Personal Injury L 314.
Mintz, J, 'The Remains of Privacy's Disclosure Tort: an Exploration of the Private Domain' (1996) 55 Maryland L Rev 425.

Bibliography

Mirfield, P, 'Regulation of Investigatory Powers Act 2000 (2): Evidential Aspects' [2001] Crim LR 91.

Mithani, A, 'Disclosure in bankruptcy—the extent to which a trustee in bankruptcy is entitled to obtain documents from a bankrupt's former solicitor' (1994) 92(2) LS Gaz 20.

Montgomery, J, 'Confidentiality in the modernized NHS: the challenge of data protection' [1999] Bulletin of Medical Ethics 18.

Moodie, P and M Wright, 'Confidentiality, Codes and Courts: An Examination of the Significance of Professional Guidelines on Medical Ethics in Determining the Legal Limits of Confidentiality' (2000) 29 Anglo-American L Rev 39.

Moodie, P, and Wright, M, 'Confidentiality, codes and courts: an examination of the significance of professional guidelines on medical ethics in determining the legal limits of confidentiality' (2000) 29 Anglo-American LR 39.

Moore, N, 'Limits to Attorney–Client Confidentiality: a "Philosophically Informed" and Comparative Approach to Legal and Medical Ethics' (1985–86) 36 Case Western Reserve L Rev 177.

Moore, P and M Wright, 'Confidentiality, Codes and Courts' (2000) 29 Anglo-American L Rev 39.

Moreham, N, '*Douglas and others v Hello! Ltd*—the Protection of Privacy in English Private Law' (2001) 64 MLR 767.

Morris, F and G Adshead, 'The liability of psychiatrists for the violent acts of their patients' (1997) 147 NLJ 558.

Moscarino, G and M Shumaker, 'Beating the Shell Game: Bank Secrecy Laws and Their Impact on Civil Recovery in International Fraud Actions' (1997) 18 Comp L 177.

Mullender, R, 'Privacy, Paedophilia and the European Convention on Human Rights: A Deontological Approach' [1998] PL 384.

Munro, E, 'Empowering looked-after children' (2001) 6 Child and Family Social Work 129.

Murphy, G, 'The Innocence at Stake Test and Legal Professional Privilege: A Logical Progression for the Law . . . But Not in England' [2001] Crim LR 728.

Naismith, S, 'Photographs, Privacy and Freedom of Expression' [1996] European Human Rights L Rev 150.

Neave, M, 'AIDS—Confidentiality and the Duty to Warn (1987) U of Tasmania L Rev 1.

—— and M Weinberg, 'The Nature and Function of Equities' (1978) 6 U of Tasmania L Rev 115.

Newbold, A, 'Safeguarding client information' (1988) 85 LS Gaz 10.

—— 'The Crime/Fraud Exception to Legal Professional Privilege' (1990) 53 MLR 472.

Ngwena, C and R Chadwick, 'Genetic Diagnostic Information and the Duty of Confidentiality: Ethics and Law' (1993) 1 Medical L Intl 73.

Nokes, G, 'Professional Privilege' (1950) 66 LQR 88.

Norrie, K, 'Medical Confidentiality' (1988) 36 Forensic Science Intl 143.

Note, 'Functional Overlap between the Lawyer and other Professionals: Its Implications for the Privileged Communications Doctrine' (1962) 71 Yale LJ 1226.

Note, 'Developments—Privileged Communications' (1985) 98 Harvard L Rev 1501.

Oliver, H, 'Email and Internet Monitoring in the Workplace: Information Privacy and Contracting Out' (2002) 31 Industrial LJ 321.

Ormerod, D, 'Confidentiality in children cases' (1995) 7 Child and Family LQ 1.

—— 'ECHR and the Exclusion of Evidence: Trial Remedies for Article 8 Breaches?' [2003] Crim LR 61.

Ormrod, J and L Ambrose, 'Confidential communications—public opinion' (1999) 8 J of Mental Health 413.

Oyen, E, 'Trend Report: The Social Functions of Confidentiality' (1982) 30 Current Sociology 1.

Pack, A, '"We'd like to know a little bit about you for our files"—The Data Protection Act 1998' [2000] Family L 759.

Parker, C, 'Camping Trips and Family Trees: Must Tennessee Physicians Warn their Patients' Relatives of Genetic Risks' (1998) 65 Tennessee L Rev 585.

Parsons, D, 'The meaning of "public interest"' (2001) 6 Communications L 191.

Paterson, R, 'AIDS, HIV Testing and Medical Confidentiality' (1991) 7 Otago L Rev 379.

Paton-Simpson, E, 'Private Circles and Public Squares: Invasion of Privacy by the Publication of "Private Facts"' (1998) 61 MLR 318.

—— 'Privacy and the Reasonable Paranoid: The Protection of Privacy in Public Places' (2000) 50 U of Toronto LJ 305.

Pattenden, R, 'Expert Opinion Evidence Based on Hearsay' [1982] Crim LR 85.

—— 'Self-incrimination and the threat of prosecution under foreign law: *Brannigan v Davison*' (1998) 2 Intl J of Evidence & Proof 44.

—— 'Litigation privilege and expert opinion evidence' (2000) 4 Intl J of Evidence & Proof 213.

Patterson, R, 'Legal Ethics and the Lawyer's Duty of Loyalty' (1980) 29 Emory LJ 909.

Peiris, G, 'Medical Professional Privilege in Commonwealth Law' (1984) 33 Intl and Comparative LQ 301.

Phillipson, G and H Fenwick, 'Breach of Confidence as a Privacy Remedy in the Human Rights Act Era' (2000) 63 MLR 660.

Pinker, R, 'Human Rights and self-regulation of the press' (1999) 4 Communications L 51.

—— 'Press freedom and press regulation—current trends in their European context' (2002) 7 Communications Law 102.

Pizer, J, 'The public interest exception to the breach of confidence action: are the lights about to change?' (1994) 20 Monash University LR 67.

—— 'Press freedom and press regulation—current trends in their European context' (2002) 7 Communications L 102.

Plowden, P, 'Right to Privacy' [2001] J of Civil Liberties 57.

Powers, M, 'A Cognitive Access Definition of Privacy' (1996) 15 L and Philosophy 369.

Prosser, W, 'Privacy' (1960) 48 California L Rev 383.

Pugh-Thomas, A, 'Who is your client?' (1997) SJ 44.

Rachels, J, 'Why Privacy is Important' [1975] 4 Philosophy and Public Affairs 323.

Reid, A and N Ryder, 'For Whose Eyes Only? A Critique of the United Kingdom's Regulation of Investigatory Powers Act 2000 (2001) 10 Information and Communications Technology L 179.

Renke, W, 'The Mandatory Reporting of Child Abuse under the Child Welfare Act' (1999) 7 Health LJ 91.

Reynolds, F, 'Apparent Authority' [1994] JBL 144.
Rhodes, K, 'Open Court Proceedings and Privacy Law' (1996) 74 Texas L Rev 881.
Richardson, M, 'Breach of confidence, surreptitiously or accidently obtained information and privacy: theory versus law' (1994) 19 Melbourne U L Rev 673.
Richardson, M, 'Whither Breach of Confidence: A Right of Privacy for Australia?' (2002) 26 Melbourne ULR 381.
Ricketson, S, 'Confidential Information—A New Property Interest?' (1978) 11 Melbourne ULR 223.
Riley, A, 'Saunders and the Power to Obtain Information in Community and United Kingdom Competition Law' (2000) 25 ELR 264.
Rind, D et al, 'Maintaining the Confidentiality of Medical Records Shared over the Internet and the World Wide Web' (1997) 127 Annals of Internal Medicine 138.
Ritchie, A, 'Discovery Against Non Parties' [1996] J of Personal Injury L 339.
Rix, K, 'Privilege and the prison inmate medical record' (2000) 11 J of Forensic Psychiatry 654.
Roback, H, 'Effects of Confidentiality Limitations on the Psychotherapeutic Process' (1995) 4 J of Psychotherapy Practice and Research 185.
Roth, P, 'What is "Personal Information?"' (2002) 20 NZULR 40.
Rowe, J, 'The Terrorism Act 2000' [2001] Crim LR 527.
Saltzburg, S, 'Privileges and Professionals: Lawyers and Psychiatrists' (1980) 66 Virginia L Rev 597.
Savulescu, J and L Skene, 'Who has the Right to Access Medical Information from a Deceased Person? Ethical and Legal Perspectives' (2000) 8 J of L and Medicine 81.
Schonsheck, J, 'Privacy and Discrete "Social Spheres"' (1997) 7 Ethics & Behavior 221.
Schuman, D et al, 'The Privilege Study (Part III): Psychotherapist–Patient Communications in Canada' (1986) 9 Intl J of Law and Psychiatry 393.
Scott, R, 'Developments in the Law of Confidentiality' [1990] Denning LJ 77.
—— 'Procedures at Inquiries—The Duty to Be Fair' (1995) 111 LQR 596.
—— 'The Use of Public Interest Immunity Claims in Criminal Cases' [1995] 2 Web J of Current Legal Issues 1.
Sestito, J, 'The Duty to Warn Third Parties and AIDS in Canada' (1996) Health L in Canada 83.
Shah, R, 'Private lives—the government's ability to make information about individuals the property of the public' (1994) 91 LS Gaz 28.
Shils, E, 'Privacy: Its Constitutional Vicissitudes' (1966) 31 L and Contemporary Problems 281.
Shirvington, V, 'Ethics: Tossed on stormy ethical Cs: conundrums for 2000' (2000) 38 (1) L Society J 36.
Sim, D, 'The Right to Solitude in the US and Singapore: A Call for a Fundamental Reordering' (2002) 22 Loyola of Los Angeles Entertainment L Rev 443.
Simitis, S, 'Data Protection Law and The European Union's Directive: The Challenge for the United States: From the Market to the Polis: The EU Directive on the Protection of Personal Data' (1995) 80 Iowa L Rev 445.
Simon, Lord, 'Evidence Excluded by Considerations of State Interest' [1955] CLJ 62.
Simon, W, 'Ethical Discretion in Lawyering' (1988) 101 Harvard L Rev 1083.

Skene, L and R Smallwood, 'Informed consent: lessons from Australia' (2002) 324 British Medical J 39.
Smith, A, 'The Idea of Deception' [1982] Crim LR 721.
Smith, R, 'Publishing information about patients' (1995) 311 British Medical J 1240.
Smith, V, 'Disclosing Child Abuse Suspicions—A Public Authority Dilemma' [2000] Family L 910.
Stewart, A, 'Confidentiality and the Employment Relationship' (1988) 1 Australian J of Labour L 1.
—— and M Chesterman, 'Confidential Material: The Position of the Media' (1992) 14 Adelaide L Rev 1.
Stobbs, M, 'Ethical Issues Facing the Bar' (1998) 1 Legal Ethics 27.
Stone, R, 'PACE: Special Procedures and Legal Privilege' [1988] Crim LR 498.
—— 'Usual and Ostensible Authority—One Concept or Two' [1993] JBL 325.
Strobl, J, 'Data Protection Legislation: Interpretation and Barriers to Research' (2000) 321 British Medical J 890.
Stuckey, J, 'The equitable action for breach of confidence: Is information ever property?' (1981) 9 Sydney LR 402.
Stuckey, J, 'When, If at All, Does a Third Party Innocently Implicated in Another's Breach of Confidence Become Liable to the Discloser?' (1981) 4 U of New South Wales LJ 80.
Sugar, S, 'Banking on dispute resolution' (2001) 145 SJ 338.
Swain, R, 'Ethical codes, confidentiality and the law' (1996) 17 Irish J of Psychology 95.
Tamin, J, 'Medical Confidentiality' (1998) 72 Occupational Health Rev 29.
Tapper, C, ' "Computer Crime": Scotch Mist?' [1987] Crim LR 4.
—— 'Prosecution and Privilege' (1996) 1 Intl J of Evidence & Proof 5.
Temkin, J, 'Digging the Dirt: Disclosure of Records of Sexual Assault Cases' [2002] 61 CLJ 126.
Tettenborn, A, 'Breach of Confidence, Secrecy and the Public Domain' (1982) 11 Anglo-American LR 273.
Thick, A and D Chun, 'Depositing old documents' (1992) 89(30) LS Gaz 21.
Thomas, T, 'Employment Screening and the Criminal Records Bureau' (2002) 31 Industrial LJ 55.
Thomson, M, 'Privacy before and after the Human Rights Act' [2001] 6 Communications L 180.
Townsend-Smith, R, 'Harassment as a Tort in England and American Law: The Boundaries of Wilkinson v Downton' (1995) 24 Anglo-American L Rev 299.
Trindade, F, 'The Intentional Infliction of Purely Mental Distress' (1986) 8 OJLS 219.
Tugendhat, M, 'The Data Protection Act 1998 and the Media' [2000] Yearbook of Copyright and Media L 115.
—— 'Privacy and celebrity' (2001) 37 Amicus Curiae 3.
Tunkel, V, 'Lawyers and their Waste Products' (2000) 150 NLJ 384.
Tur, R, 'Confidentiality and Accountability' (1992) 1 Griffith L Rev 73.
—— 'Medical Confidentiality and Disclosure: Moral Conscience and Legal Constraints' (1998) 15 J of Applied Philosophy 15.

Vaines, P, 'Taxing Matters' (2002) 152 NLJ 787.

Van Beuren, G, 'Children's Access to Adoption Records' (1995) 58 MLR 37.

Van Straaten, J, 'The Minor's Limited Right to Confidential Health Care and the Inverse of Confidentiality: A Parent's Decision Not to Disclose Illness Status to a Minor Child' (2000) 20 Children's Legal Rights J 46.

Vaver, D, 'Keeping Secrets, Civilly Speaking' (1991–92) 13 Advocates' Quarterly 334.

Verity, C and A Nicoll, 'Consent, confidentiality and the threat to public health surveillance' (2002) 324 British Medical J 1210.

Vickers, L, 'Whistleblowing in the public sector and the ECHR' [1997] PL 595.

Vickery, A, 'Breach of Confidence: An Emerging Tort (1982) 82 Columbia LR 1426.

Vine, A, 'Is the Paramountcy Principle Compatible with Article 8?' [2000] Family Law 826.

Wacks, R, 'Breach of Confidence and the Protection of Privacy' [1977] NLJ 328.

—— 'The Poverty of "Privacy"' (1980) 96 LQR 73.

Wadsley, J, 'Money Laundering: Professionals as Policemen' [1994] Conveyancer and Property Lawyer 275.

Walters, J, 'Revenue Raids' [1998] RTR 213.

—— 'Information: Compliance v Confidentiality' (2001) 3 Corporate Tax Rev 161.

Warren, S and L Brandeis, 'The Right to Privacy' (1890) 4 Harvard L Rev 193.

Watson, B, 'Disclosure of Computerized Health Care Information: Provider Privacy Rights Under Supply Side Competition' (1981–82) 7 American J of L and Medicine 281.

Watson, F, 'Overstepping boundaries' (1999) Professional Social Work, September, 14.

Watson, G and F Au, 'Solicitor–Client Privilege and Litigation Privilege in Civil Litigation' (1998) 77 Canadian Bar Rev 315.

Watson, S, 'Keeping Secrets that Harm Others: Medical Standards Illuminate Lawyer's Dilemma' (1992) 71 Nebraska L Rev 1123.

Wei, G, 'Surreptitious taking of confidential information' (1992) 12 LS 302.

Weiner, M and D Shuman, 'Privilege—a comparative study' (1985) J of Psychiatry and L 373.

Welfel, E et al, 'Mandated Reporting of Abuse/Maltreatment of Older Adults: A Primer for Counselors' (2000) J of Counseling and Development 284.

Wheat, K, 'Lawyers, Confidentiality and Public and Private Interests' (2000) 1 Legal Ethics 184.

Wheeldon, S, 'Reflections on the concept of "property" with particular reference to breach of confidence' (1997) 8 Auckland ULR 353.

White, R, 'Confidentiality and Privilege: Child Abuse and Child Abduction' (1992) 1 Child Abuse Rev 60.

Wildish, N, and Turle, M, 'Anonymous data—inside or outside data protection law?' Privacy Laws and Business UK Newsletter, May 2002, p 20.

Williams, C, 'The Effect of Domestic Money-Laundering Countermeasures on the Banker's Duty of Confidentiality' (1998) 13 Banking & Finance L Rev 25.

Williams, G, '"On the QT and very Hush Hush": A Proposal to extend California's Constitutional right to Privacy to Protect Public Figures from Publication of Confidential Personal Information' (1999) 19 Loyola of Los Angeles Entertainment L Rev 337.

Williams, K, 'Medical Samaritans: Is there a Duty to Treat?' (2001) 21 OJLS 393.

Williams, N, 'Four Questions of Privilege: the Litigation Aspect of Legal Professional Privilege' (1990) 9 CJQ 139.

Winfield, P, 'Privacy' (1931) 47 LQR 23.

Wright, M, 'Disclosure of Documents in Children Cases' [1993] Family L 348.

Wynia, M and D Cummins, 'Shared Expectations for Protection of Identifiable Health Care Information' (2001) 16 J of General Internal Medicine 100.

Yates, J, 'Mandatory Reporting of Child Abuse and the Public/Private Distinction' (1994) 7 Auckland L Rev 781.

Young, A, 'Judicial Sovereignty and the Human Rights Act 1998' [2002] CLJ 53.

Zacharias, F, 'Rethinking Confidentiality' (1989) 74 Iowa L Rev 351.

—— 'Specificity in Professional Responsibility Codes' (1993) 69 Notre Dame L Rev 223.

—— 'Harmonizing Privilege and Confidentiality' (1999) 43 South Texas L Rev 69.

Zimmerman, D, 'Requiem for a Heavyweight: A Farewell to Warren and Brandeis's Privacy Tort' (1983) 68 Cornell L Rev 291.

Zuckerman, A, 'The Weakness of the PACE Special Procedure for Protecting Confidential Material' [1990] Crim LR 473.

—— 'Confidentiality and Fraud' (1991) 107 LQR 380.

—— 'More About Confidentiality and Fraud' (1992) 108 LQR 380.

—— 'Public Interest Immunity—A Matter of Prime Judicial Responsibility' (1994) 57 MLR 703.

—— 'Legal Professional Privilege—The Cost of Absolutism' (1996) 113 LQR 535.

INDEX

abortion 3.42, 13.09
abroad, proceedings
  civil litigation 14.133–14.136
  criminal proceedings
    investigations 14.138
    trials 14.137
access privacy 1.14
  meaning 1.14
accidental disclosure 6.01, 6.89–6.111
  admissibility of material in proceedings
      6.95–6.97
    civil proceedings 6.99–6.100
    confidential information 6.95
    criminal proceedings 6.101, 6.102
    privileged information 6.96, 6.97
    secondary evidence 6.98
  breach of confidence 6.103–6.111
    confidential information 6.111
    criminal proceedings, communication
        required for 6.106, 6.107
    discovery of leak before information used
        6.103–6.111
    pre-trial disclosure 6.108–6.110
    use of communication in civil proceedings
        6.103
  Chinese walls 6.94
  conflicts of interest 6.92–6.94
  criminal proceedings, exclusion from 6.101,
      6.102
  examples 6.89
  police 6.102
  pre-trial disclosure 6.108–6.110
  prevention 6.94
  professional's liability 6.90–6.94
    unconscious use 6.90, 6.91
  secondary evidence, admissibility 6.98
  solicitors 6.92, 6.93, 6.94
  unconscious use 6.90, 6.91
  voluntary act, unintended consequence of
      6.89
account monitoring order 14.18
account of profits 8.71–8.73
accountants 1.25
  breach of confidence 5.27
  breach of fiduciary duty 5.65
  coercive statutory disclosure 10.03
  conflicts of interest 6.93

  financial wrongdoing, prevention and exposure
      of 11.31
  money laundering 10.25
  privilege 16.42
  public interest defence 11.31
  self-interest, disclosure motivated by 12.30
adoption records
  access 19.105
  breach of confidence 5.49, 5.50
adultery
  defamation 4.35
adverse drug reactions 13.52
advice
  public interest, before disclosure in 11.69
  whistleblowing, before 21.28
advocates *see also* barristers
  privilege 16.42
agency
  breach of fiduciary duty 5.66
  consent 13.39
  disclosure to the client 19.05–19.07
    generally 19.07
    solicitors 19.07
  ownership of documents 19.05–19.07
  partnerships 21.37
  solicitors 19.07
aggravated damages 8.66–8.68
  mental distress 8.67
AID, children conceived by 19.106, 19.112
AIDS *see* HIV/AIDS
American Cyanamid **principles** 8.09
  balance of convenience 8.17
  breach of confidence 8.10
  HRA 1998, s 12 and 8.15, 8.16
anonymity
  breach of confidence 5.32–5.38, 13.50
  Data Protection Act 1998 1.05, 18.05, 18.08
  health information 13.50
  orders 17.38–17.43
    non-parties 17.38–17.41
    non-witnesses 17.40
    soliciting information, restraining 17.41
    witnesses 17.38, 17.39
  privacy 1.14
art
  Data Protection Act 1998 18.39–18.41
  dealers, money laundering by 10.25

Index

assault 6.82
assessment powers
  information Commissioner 18.39, 19.48
associational privacy 1.14
attentional privacy 1.14
auditors
  money laundering 10.25
  privilege 16.42
Australia
  breach of fiduciary duty 5.80, 5.83
  breach of statutory duty 4.51
  privilege 16.43, 16.44
authorship
  false attribution, action for 5.51
automated-decision making 19.24
autopsy records 5.47

banking 1.25
  banker's books 14.04, 14.10, 14.57
  breach of confidence 5.27
  coercive statutory disclosure 10.03, 10.04, 10.06
  defence, acquisition of information by 14.132
  duration of obligation of confidentiality 4.14
  financial wrongdoing, prevention and exposure of 11.29
  investigation of offences 14.57
  Jack Report 10.03
  money laundering 10.25
  pre-trial disclosure 14.04, 14.10
  privilege 16.42
  public interest defence
    detection of completed crimes 11.32
    financial wrongdoing, prevention and exposure of 11.29
    self-interest, disclosure motivated by 12.32
bankruptcy *see also* **insolvency professionals** 5.55
barristers 1.25
  breach of confidence 5.29
  breach of contract 4.02
  codes of ethics 11.16
  contract
    intentional disclosure 4.02
  counsel to counsel disclosure in criminal litigation 17.07
  iniquity, disclosure of 11.16
  intentional disclosure
    contract 4.02
    public interest defence 11.16
  warn, duty to 20.19, 20.20
best interests of client, disclosure in 12.02–12.13
  autonomy of client 12.06, 12.07
  children 12.11–12.13
    ground for disclosure 12.11

    legal professional privilege 12.12, 12.13
    sexual abuse 12.11
  competent adult 12.02–12.08
    autonomy of client 12.06, 12.07
    consultation 12.02–12.05
    emergencies 12.08
    mental illness 12.03, 12.04
  consultation
    competent adult 12.02–12.05
    mental illness 12.03, 12.04
  emergencies 12.08
  incompetent adult 12.09, 12.10
    Court of Protection 12.09
    mental illness 12.10
    power of attorney 12.09
    proxy authorization 12.09
  legal professional privilege 12.12, 12.13
  mental illness 12.03, 12.04, 12.10
  sexual abuse 12.11
blackmail 6.82
blocking
  inaccurate or misleading data 19.48
blood samples
  breach of confidence 5.29
  dead person 13.09
  legal professional privilege, and 15.27, 16.22
  relatives, disclosure of results to 13.60
bodily samples
  breach of confidence 5.29
bona fide purchaser for value defence
  breach of confidence 7.31, 7.32
breach of confidence 5.02–5.63
  absolute, confidentiality cannot be 1.54, 1.55
  abuse of confidence 5.31
  accidental disclosure 6.103–6.111
    confidential information 6.111
    criminal proceedings, communication required for 6.106, 6.107
    discovery of leak before information used 6.103–6.111
    pre-trial disclosure 6.108–6.110
    use of communication in civil proceedings 6.103
  accountants 5.27
  American Cyanamid principles 8.10
  anonymous information 5.32–5.38, 7.34
  authentication of information 5.63
  bankers 5.27
  barristers 5.29
  basis 5.02, 5.03
  blood samples 5.29
  bodily samples 5.29
  bona fide purchaser for value defence 7.31, 7.32
  breach of fiduciary duty, overlap with 5.68–5.79

Index

breach of confidence (*cont.*):
  broadcasters 5.14
  cessation of obligation 5.44, 5.45
  claimant 5.43
  co-existence of contractual and equitable obligations 5.28
  compelled disclosure, use of information from 10.36
  confidential impartation of information 5.06, 5.24–5.27
    accountants 5.27
    bankers 5.27
    doctors 5.27
    established professional relationships of confidentiality 5.27
    health professional 5.27
    lawyers 5.27
    pharmacists 5.26
    policy 5.27
    priests 5.27
    relationship of trust 5.24, 5.25
    social workers 5.27
    stockbrokers 5.27
    tests 5.24–5.26
  constructive trusts 8.78, 8.79
  contract, relationship to 5.04, 5.28
  criminal records 5.18–5.22
  damages 5.41, 8.37–8.41
  death of client 5.46–5.54
    adoption records 5.49, 5.50
    autopsy records 5.47
    crime reconstructions 5.51
    doctors 5.53, 5.54
    European Convention on Human Rights 5.52
    legislative analogies 5.51
    need for confidentiality after 5.46, 5.47
    offensiveness of disclosure 5.47
    post-mortem legal protection 5.48
    United States 5.47
  detriment 5.06, 5.40, 5.41, 5.42, 6.26
  development 5.02, 5.03
  direct proof 5.39
  disclosure of information 5.29, 5.39
  doctors 5.27, 5.53, 5.54
  employees 5.28, 5.30, 21.18
  false information 1.21, 6.13
  goal of action 5.79
  good faith basis 5.03
  health professional 5.27
  historical development 5.02, 5.03
  HIV/AIDS 1.40, 5.04
  inadvertent disclosure 5.78
  inference, proof by 5.39
  injunctions 6.02, 8.10
  intangible loss 5.41
  intentional disclosure 4.60
  interception
    see also interceptor *below*
    professional v employee 6.41
  interceptor 6.02–6.25
    change of direction in law 6.05–6.08
    determining whether information in confidential/private 6.19–6.23
    detriment caused by unauthorized disclosure 6.26
    elements of action 6.03
    information capable of being private 6.17, 6.18
    informational privacy, breach of 6.10–6.13
    insistence on relationship of trust 6.04
    media privacy codes 6.21
    privileged communications, interception of 6.09
    public figures 6.22, 6.23
    public policy 6.20
    rationale of action 6.02
    reasonable expectation of privacy 6.14–6.25
    without disclosure, interception 6.27, 6.28
  issues in law, facing 2.34
  justification 1.54–1.57
    absolute, confidentiality cannot be 1.54, 1.55
    obligatory versus discretionary disclosure 1.56, 1.57
  lawyers 5.27, 16.11
  legal, professional privilege, overlap 11.77–11.80
  legitimate interest 5.41
  loss suffered 5.40
  marital confidences 5.04
  Megarry test 5.06, 5.07
  mental distress 4.60, 8.51, 8.57–8.59
  monetary awards 5.41, 8.37–8.41, 8.57–8.59
  naming client 5.29
  origins 5.02
  overlap with breach of fiduciary duty 5.68–5.79
  partnerships 21.37–21.39
  personal nature of obligation 5.43
  pharmacists 5.26, 5.32, 5.38
  policy 5.79, 8.53, 8.54
  pre-HRA 1998 5.04
  priests 5.27
  proving 5.39
  public domain, information in 5.09–5.22, 7.33, 17.27, 18.26
    approach of courts 5.11
    Article 8, impact of 5.13
    authentication of information 5.63
    codes of ethics 5.15

breach of confidence (*cont.*):
public domain, information in
   commercial information 5.14
   criminal records 5.18
   defendant responsible for putting information into public domain 5.60
   determination 5.10
   general rule 5.59–5.63
   generally accessible information 5.12
   meaning 5.09
   mixed information 5.09
   obviously private information 5.23
   open court, information disclosed in 5.18, 17.27
   passing out of public domain, information 5.16, 5.17
   press freedom 5.22
   private life, respect for 5.13
   professionals 5.14, 5.15
   substantial number of people 5.11
public figures 6.22–6.25
quality of confidence 5.06, 5.08–5.23
   public domain, information in 5.09–5.22
   trivial character, information of 5.08
reasonable expectation of privacy 6.14–6.25
relationship of trust 5.23, 5.25–5.27, 6.03, 6.04, 6.13, 7.26
relatives, information provided by 5.29
remedies 8.78, 8.79
research, information used for 5.29, 5.35, 13.53
reservation of rights 5.30
sensitive information 5.29
sexual matters 5.04
social workers 5.27
solicitors 6.94
stockbrokers 5.27
strangers 7.25–7.30
   anonymous information 7.34
   bona fide purchaser for value defence 7.31, 7.32
   client v stranger 7.25–7.27
   defences 7.31–7.34
   liability of stranger 7.27
   professional v stranger 7.29, 7.30
   public domain, information in 7.33
   traditional position 7.25
surgeons 5.44
tacit consent 5.39
termination of professional relationship 5.44, 5.45
third party 7.20–7.34
   accessory liability of innocent third party 7.22
   anonymous information 7.34
   bona fide purchaser for value defence 7.31, 7.32
   client v third party 7.20–7.22
   defences 7.31–7.34
   injunctions 7.23, 7.24
   public domain, information in 7.33
tort 4.60
trade secrets 5.04, 5.29, 6.91
trivial information 5.08
troubled conscience test 5.32, 5.33
unauthorized disclosure or use 5.28–5.42
   abuse of confidence 5.31
   admission of professional relationship 5.29
   anonymous information 5.32–5.38
   barristers 5.29
   blood samples 5.29
   bodily samples 5.29
   candour, ensuring 5.29
   co-existence of contractual and equitable obligations 5.28
   conscience 5.38
   employees 5.28, 5.30
   identification 5.32–5.36
   naming client 5.29
   non-identifying information 5.32, 5.33, 5.34
   not breaching obligation of confidentiality, disclosures 5.31
   personal observation of private events 5.29
   pharmacists 5.32, 5.38
   policies and purposes of law 5.29
   privacy of client, protecting 5.29, 5.34
   purposes for which not intended, disclosure of information for 5.29
   relatives, information provided by 5.29
   research, information used for 5.29, 5.35
   reservation of rights 5.30
   scope of obligation of confidentiality 5.29, 5.30
   sensitive information 5.29
   supplied by client, disclosure of information 5.29
   third parties, disclosure or use of information obtained from 5.29
unauthorized disclosure or use 5.28–5.42
   trade secrets 5.29
   troubled conscience test 5.32, 5.33
   unconscionable disclosure or use 5.31
   use of information 5.29
unconscionable disclosure or use 5.31
use of information 5.29
breach of contract *see also* contract
barristers 4.02
inducing, third party 7.37, 7.43
interception
   employed, disclosure while 6.38
   media, disclosure to 6.40
   professional v employee 6.38–6.40

Index

breach of contract (*cont.*):
  interception
    public interest defence 6.38
    termination of employment, disclosure after 6.39
  media, disclosure to 6.40
  public interest defence 6.38
breach of fiduciary duty 5.64–5.83
  accountants 5.65
  agency 5.66
  Australia 5.80, 5.83
  breach of confidence, overlap with 5.68–5.79
  Canada 5.81
  commercially valuable information 5.80, 5.82
  confidentiality as aspect of fiduciary duty 5.67–5.73
  constructive trusts 8.76, 8.77
  criminal records 5.76
  damages 8.36
  doctors 5.80, 5.81
  duration of duty of loyalty 5.77
  election, right of 5.71–5.73
  fiduciary 5.64–5.66
  goal of action 5.79
  inadvertent disclosure 5.78
  loyalty, duty of 5.67
  monetary awards 8.36
  overlap with breach of confidence 5.68–5.79
  personal information 5.80–5.83
  rationale for fiduciary duties 5.65
  solicitors 5.65, 6.94
  stockbrokers 5.65
  strangers 7.35
  termination of fiduciary relationship 5.77
  third parties 7.35
breach of statutory duty 4.45–4.52
  Australia 4.51
  Data Protection Act 1998 4.49, 6.35, 6.36
  doctors 4.51
  Human Rights Act 1998 4.45–4.48
    cause of action 4.45
    effect of disclosure 4.46
    public authority 4.47, 4.48
  interception
    client v interceptor 6.30
    client v professional 6.35, 6.36
  mental distress 4.52
  no express cause of action, statutory non-disclosure provisions with 4.50, 4.51
  strangers 7.43
  third party 7.43
  United States 4.51
British Banking Association Banking Code
  duration of obligation of confidentiality 4.14

broadcasters
  breach of confidence 5.14
  public domain, information in 5.14
Broadcasting Standards Commission 9.17–9.20
  abolition 9.20
  adjudications 9.17
  Code 3.08, 9.17
  complaints 9.18
  hearings 9.17
  material not broadcast 9.19
  membership 9.17
  powers 9.17, 9.18
burden of proof
  interim injunctions 8.15, 8.16
burglary 6.82

Calcutt Committee 9.15, 9.16
Caldicott Committee 3.48
Caldicott guardian 2.28
Canada
  breach of fiduciary duty 5.81
  doctors 1.04, 19.15
  elder abuse 20.23
  privilege 16.43
  public figures 6.22
cancer registries 13.53
capacity
  children 13.12–13.21
  consent 13.08–13.21
    adults 13.08–13.11
    authority to consent 13.09
    emergencies 13.11
    power of attorney 13.11
    unlawful disclosure 13.08
change of employment
  professionals 5.55–5.59
child abuse *see also* children
  best interests of client, disclosure in 12.11
  college counsellors, reporting by 2.23
  inaccurate or misleading data 19.48
  investigations 3.48
  sexual 12.11
  unfounded 19.48
  warn, duty to 20.23–20.26
    policy 20.25, 20.26
    proximity 20.24
children *see also* minors
  abuse *see* child abuse
  AID, conceived by 19.106, 19.112
  best interests of client, disclosure in 12.11–12.13
    ground for disclosure 12.11
    sexual abuse 12.11
  consent
    ability of child to consent 13.13–13.15
    ability of parent to consent 13.16–13.19

765

Index

children (*cont.*):
consent
assessment of maturity 13.13
below the age of 16 13.13–13.15, 13.20
between ages 16 and 18 13.12
emergency medical treatment 13.16
family proceedings 13.14
genetic testing 13.15
Human Rights Act 1998 13.18
legislative precedents 13.17
mature children under 16 13.13–13.19
medical records, access to 13.17
policy 13.19
preventing parental consent 13.21
seriousness of decision 13.15
special education needs, children of 13.14, 13.17, 13.56
tender years, children of 13.20, 13.21
documents, control of 17.05, 17.06
educational records, access to 19.79–19.82
emergencies 13.16
Human Rights Act 1998 13.18
legal professional privilege 12.12, 12.13
medical confidentiality 19.95–19.98
immature child 19.99, 19.100
mature child 19.95–19.98
missing 10.02, 10.19, 19.101
parents, refusal of information about offspring 19.87–19.98
pedigree information 19.105, 19.106
private and family life, respect for 13.18, 19.111
reporting restrictions 17.45, 17.51
rights 2.29
sexual abuse
see child abuse
special education needs, children of 13.14, 13.17, 13.56
subject access rights 19.72–19.75
Chinese walls 6.94
civil litigation *see also* litigation
abroad, proceedings 14.133–14.136
accidental disclosure, admissibility of material in proceedings 6.99–6.100
documents, control of 17.14–17.19
interception *see* interception
clergy
Article 9, and 3.16
conciliation privilege 11.20
physical evidence of a crime, handing over 11.39, 11.40
privilege 16.42
public interest defence 11.39, 11.40
search warrants 14.23
warn, duty to 20.19

clients
attitudes to confidentiality 2.26–2.28
best interests of client, disclosure in 12.02–12.23
see also best interests of client, disclosure in
confidentiality
autonomy, aids to 1.36
harmful consequences 1.39–1.43
human dignity, respect for 1.37, 1.38
value of 1.36–1.43
defined 1.27–1.28
disclosure to *see* disclosure to the client
engagement of professional by 1.27
examinees, distinguished from 1.28–1.29
giving information to 2.34, 19.58–19.71
mental illness 12.03
payment 1.27
professionals and 1.23–1.32
coded data
Data Protection Act 1998 18.05
codes
broadcasting 3.08
ethics 1.26, 2.22
see also Codes of ethics
human rights and duty to consider 3.08
codes of ethics 3.46–3.47
barristers 11.16
compelled disclosures 10.01
confidentiality 1.26, 3.47
counsellors 11.20
disciplinary proceedings 3.47
doctors 3.47
doctors
public interest defence 11.18
EU versions 3.47
General Medical Council 3.47
genetic information 11.54
informed consent 13.32
international versions 3.47
Law Society 3.47, 11.15
legal requirements, compliance with 3.47
legal significance 3.47
negligence 3.47
Nursing and Midwifery Council 3.47, 11.17
observations 3.47
pharmacists 11.17
psychologists 11.18
public domain, information in 5.15
public interest defence 11.14–11.20
barristers 11.16
counsellors 11.20
doctors 11.18
nurses 11.17
pharmacists 11.17
social workers 11.19
solicitors 11.15

Index

codes of ethics (*cont.*):
  purpose 3.46
  social workers 11.19
  solicitors 3.47
    public interest disclosure 11.15
coercive statutory disclosure 10.02–10.23 *see also* compelled disclosures
  accountants 10.03
  banking 10.03, 10.04, 10.06
  children 10.02
  confidentiality 10.04–10.12
    banking 10.04, 10.06
    dentists 10.07
    doctors 10.06
    excusing non-disclosure 10.12
    HRA 1998, impact of 10.08–10.10
    pre-HRA 1998 position 10.06
    reasonable excuse for non-disclosure 10.11, 10.12
    statutory protection 10.04, 10.05
  dentists 10.07
  doctors 10.03, 10.06
  European Convention on Human Rights
    Article 6 10.15
    Article 8 10.13, 10.14
  foreign law 10.23
  HRA 1998, impact of 10.08–10.10
  legal professional privilege 10.13–10.21
    Article 6 10.15
    Article 8 10.13, 10.14
    data protection 10.20
    family proceedings 10.14
    making disclosure 10.16
    missing child 10.19
    money laundering 10.17, 10.18
    national security 10.20
    notifying client 10.17–10.21
    police request not to notify client 10.21
    prisoners 10.14
    subject access rights 10.20
    terrorism 10.13
  missing child 10.19
  money laundering 10.02
  national security 10.20
  nature of 10.02
  non-disclosure, consequences of 10.22
  probation officers 10.03
  reasonable excuse for non-disclosure 10.11, 10.12
  road traffic offences 10.06
  social workers 10.02
  solicitors 10.02, 10.03
  terrorism 10.02, 10.13
  use of information
    breach of confidence 10.36
    collateral purposes 10.34–10.40

  covert means, information obtained by 10.38
  criminal prosecutions 10.34
  express statutory restriction 10.35
  implied statutory restriction 10.35
  public interest, disclosure in 10.40
  public law duty 10.39
  volunteered information 10.37
Commission for Health Improvement
  death of client 5.51
companies
  confidentiality 1.18
compelled disclosures 3.33–3.40
  codes of ethics 10.01
  coercive statutory disclosure *see* coercive statutory disclosure
  compliance 10.01
  covert means, use of information obtained by 10.38
  data-sharing 3.40
  defamation 10.01
  discrimination 3.38
  effect on professional confidentiality 3.39
  entry powers 3.37
  forms of compulsion 3.34–3.38
    entry powers 3.37
    oral examination 3.38
    orders to produce documents or information 3.35
    reporting requirements 3.36
  investigatory powers 3.33
  orders to produce documents or information 3.35
  personal information 3.33
  reporting requirements 3.36
  statutory disclosure *see* coercive statutory disclosure
  use of information
    breach of confidence 10.36
    collateral purposes 10.35–10.40
    covert means, information obtained by 10.38
    criminal prosecutions 10.34
    express statutory restrictions 10.35
    implied statutory restrictions 10.35
    public interest disclosure 10.40
    public law duty 10.39
    volunteered information 10.37
competence to consent *see* capacity, consent
complaints procedures 9.05
compulsory disclosure *see* coercive statutory disclosure; compelled disclosures; money laundering
computers
  employee misuse of information 2.08
  employees, misuse of computer information by 2.07

767

Index

computers (*cont.*):
  forgery offences 6.74
  hacking 2.06, 2.07, 6.62
  internet 2.05
  modification of contents of computer system 6.63
  scanning 2.07
  security 2.05–2.10
  software bugs 2.07
  technological changes 2.04–2.10
  unauthorized access 6.28
    accessories 6.62
    Computer Misuse Act 1990 s 1 6.60–6.62
    forms of access 6.61
    function, performance of 6.62
    further offence, commission of 6.63
    hackers 6.62
    intent 6.62
    modification of contents of computer system 6.63
    unauthorized purpose, access for 6.61
  viruses 2.07
conciliation privilege 16.07
conduct
  consent 13.34, 13.35
confidence, breach of *see* breach of confidence
confidential information
  accidental disclosure 6.111
  admissibility of material in proceedings 6.95
  criminal offences 6.54, 6.55
  defence, acquisition of information by 14.126
  property rights, as 5.02, 6.70, 7.31, 19.04
  publicity restriction 17.26, 17.27
  theft 6.70, 6.71
confidentiality
  absolute, confidentiality cannot be 1.54, 1.55
  breach *see* breach of confidence
  clients, value to 1.36–1.43
    autonomy, aids to 1.36
    harmful consequences 1.39–1.43
    human dignity, respect for 1.37, 1.38
  codes of ethics 3.47
  coercive statutory disclosure 10.04–10.12
    banking 10.04, 10.06
    dentists 10.07
    doctors 10.06
    excusing non-disclosure 10.12
    HRA 1998, impact of 10.08–10.10
    reasonable excuse for non-disclosure 10.11, 10.12
    road traffic offences 10.06
    statutory protection 10.04, 10.05
  companies 1.18
  compelled disclosures 3.33–3.40
    see also compelled disclosures
  data-sharing 2.18, 2.19

  defamation and 1.1
  definition 1.16, 1.17
  developments in law 1.20
  discrimination, role in preventing 1.41
  doctors 1.17
  ethics 1.16–1.18
  examinee, duty owed to 1.29–1.31
  exceptions 2.34
  existence of obligation 2.34
  false information 1.16
  function of obligation 1.21, 1.35–1.53
  issue 1.17
  justification 1.35–1.53
  law, in 1.19–1.22, 5.02–5.63
  legislation 3.33–3.45
    compelled disclosures 3.33–3.40
    see also compelled disclosures
  malpractice, shielding 1.53, 1.54
  presuppositions 1.06
  privacy and 1.06, 1.44
  professionals, value to 1.53
  public attitudes 2.26–2.28
  scope of obligation 2.34
  society, value to 1.44–1.52
    candour argument 1.46–1.52
    ethical argument 1.46–1.48
    privacy and democracy 1.44
    unreserved candour argument 1.46–1.52
    vulnerable, protection of 1.45
  surrender of privacy 1.17
  third party, obligation towards 1.20
  trade secrets 1.18
  true information 1.16, 1.21
  trust 1.06
  vulnerable, protection of 1.45
conflicts of interest
  accidental disclosure 6.92–6.94
  accountants 6.93
  solicitors 6.92, 6.93
consent
  abortion 13.09
  absence of penalty-free choice 13.24, 13.25
  agency 13.39
  audience 13.60
  authority 13.09
    capacity 13.08–13.21
      see also capacity, consent
    adults 13.08–13.11
    authority to consent 13.09
    children 13.12–13.21
      see also children *below*
    emergencies 13.11
    lacking 13.11
    legal capacity 13.10, 13.11
    mental capacity 13.10, 13.11
    power of attorney 13.11

Index

consent (*cont.*):
  authority
    Scotland 13.11
    unlawful disclosure 13.08
  children 13.12–13.21
    see also under disclosure to client
    ability of child to consent 13.13–13.15
    ability of parent to consent 13.16–13.19
    assessment of maturity 13.13
    between ages 16 and 18 13.12
    emergency medical treatment 13.16
    family proceedings 13.14
    genetic testing 13.15
    Human Rights Act 1998 13.18
    legislative precedents 13.17
    mature children under 16 13.13–13.19
    medical records, access to 13.17
    parental consent 13.16–13.19
    policy 13.19
    preventing parental consent 13.21
    seriousness of decision 13.15
    special education needs, children of 13.14, 13.17
    tender years, children of 13.20, 13.21
  collateral use 13.61
  colleagues, consultation with 13.43, 13.44
  compelled by law, consent 13.23
  conditions 13.62
  conduct 13.34, 13.35
  copyright 13.01
  data protection 13.01
    implied 13.37
  Data Protection Act 1998
    First Data Protection Principle 18.18
    informed consent 13.30–13.32
  detail, amount of 13.59
  doctors 13.45
  duration 13.05–13.07
  effect 13.01
  emergencies 13.11
  emergency medical treatment 13.16
  explicit consent 13.02, 13.03
  express 13.02–13.33
    active affirmation 13.02
    audience 13.60
    capacity to consent 13.08–13.21
    collateral use 13.61
    detail, amount of 13.59
    duration of consent 13.05–13.07
    explicit consent 13.02, 13.03
    extent of disclosure 13.59
    falsification 13.02, 13.04
    forms 13.02–13.04
    implied consent, giving rise to issues of 13.59
    informed consent 13.28–13.33
    lapse 13.06, 13.07
    parameters 13.59–13.62
    reality of consent 13.22–13.27
    retraction 13.05
  falsification 13.02, 13.04
  Family Division 13.11, 13.16, 13.19
  freely given consent 13.22
  genetic testing 13.15
  health care 13.49–13.54
    anonymized data 13.50
  health care
    secondary purposes, disclosure of 13.49–13.54
  implied 13.34–13.62
    agency 13.39
    collateral use 13.61
    colleagues, consultation with 13.43, 13.44
    conduct 13.34, 13.35
    data protection 13.37
    detail, amount of 13.59
    doctors 13.45
    drug reactions, adverse 13.52
    health care 13.49–13.54
    meaning 13.34, 13.35
    medical information 13.41, 13.42
    medical purposes 13.54
    parameters 13.59–13.62
    primary purposes, disclosure for 13.34–13.45
    publications 13.55
    relatives, disclosure to 13.57, 13.58
    secondary purposes, disclosure for 13.38, 13.46–13.58
    silence 13.36, 13.37
    support staff, disclosure to 13.45
    training, research and management purposes 13.48
  infertility treatment 13.08
  informed consent 13.28–13.33
    codes of ethics 13.32
    common law 13.28
    contractual obligations 13.33
    Data Protection Act 1998 13.30–13.32
    disclosure to client 19.01
    infertility treatment 13.29
  lapse 13.06, 13.07
  libel 13.01
  medical records 13.09, 13.41, 13.42
  outside jurisdiction, information 13.23
  parameters 13.59–13.62
  power of attorney 13.11
  psychological pressure 13.26
  reality 13.22–13.27
    absence of penalty-free choice 13.24, 13.25
    compelled by law, consent 13.23
    divining genuine consent 13.27

Index

consent (*cont.*):
  reality
    freely given consent 13.22
    outside jurisdiction, information 13.23
    penalty-free choice 13.24, 13.25
    psychological pressure 13.26
    undue influence 13.22
  relatives, disclosure to 13.57, 13.58
  retraction 13.05
  Scotland 13.11
  silence 13.36, 13.37
  solicitors 13.40
  special education needs 13.14, 13.17, 13.56
  support staff, disclosure to 13.45
  training, research and management purposes 13.48
  undue influence 13.22
conspiracy
  advantages of action 4.43
  commercial interests, interference with 4.44
  corruption 6.76
  criminal offences
    corruption, to commit 6.76
    defraud, conspiracy to 6.77–6.81
    interceptor, prosecuting 6.76–6.81
    stranger, prosecuting a 6.84, 9.85
  defraud, to 6.77–6.81
  disadvantages of action 4.44
  elements 4.43
  forms 4.43
  interception
    client v interceptor 6.29
    professional v employee 6.43
  motive 4.44
  pecuniary losses 4.44
  simple 4.43
  strangers 7.43
  third party 7.39, 7.43
  unlawful means 4.43
constructive trusts 8.76–8.79
  breach of confidence 8.78, 8.79
  breach of fiduciary duty 8.76, 8.77
contempt of court
  media 7.12–7.15
  reporting restricted to prevent prejudicing administration of justice 17.48
contraceptive advice
  teachers, from 2.24
contract
  barristers 4.02
  co-existence of contractual and equitable obligations 5.28
  compelled disclosures 10.01
  equitable damages 8.33, 8.34
  intentional disclosure 4.02–4.18
    basics 4.02, 4.03

intentional disclosure
  breach of obligation 4.18
  clergy 4.02
  codes of ethics 4.05
  confidentiality as a contractual term 4.04, 4.05
  consideration 4.02
  death of client 4.16, 4.17
  direct observation 4.09
  doctors 4.08, 4.11
  duration of obligation of confidentiality 4.14–4.17
  existence of contract 4.02
  extent of duty of confidentiality 4.06–4.11
  health professionals 4.02
  implied terms 4.05, 4.12, 4.13
  known already, information 4.10, 4.11
  non-disclosure clauses 4.04
  obligation of confidentiality 4.04, 4.05
  oral contracts 4.05
  public domain, information in 4.10, 4.11
  public interest 4.12
  repudiation of contract 4.15
  social workers 4.02
  teachers 4.02
  termination of professional-client relationship 4.14
  third parties, information from 4.07, 4.08
  trivial information 4.06
mental distress 8.46–8.49
monetary awards 8.28
  equitable damages 8.33, 8.34
peace and enjoyment, contracts to provide 8.47
privity 4.03
repudiation 4.15
social workers, intentional disclosure by 4.02
termination of professional-client relationship 4.14
conversion
  interceptor 6.50, 6.51
  stranger 7.42
  third party 7.42
copyright
  consent 13.01
  diaries 5.85
  drawings 5.85
  duration 5.84
  intentional disclosure 5.84–5.87
    disclosure 5.86, 5.87
    judicial proceedings 5.87
    nature of copyright 5.84
    photographs 5.85, 5.86
  interception
    client v interceptor 6.31
    professional v employee 6.45

Index

copyright (cont.):
  interception
    professional v interceptor 6.53
  knowing sale of infringing material 6.82
  monetary awards 8.29
  nature 5.84
  original work 5.84
  ownership 5.85
  photographs 5.85
  property right, as 5.84
  public interest defence 11.82, 11.83
  strangers 7.43, 7.44
  third party 7.43, 7.44
  unconscious infringement 6.91
corporations
  secrecy 1.12
corruption
  conspiracy 6.76
  criminal offences 6.75, 6.76
Council of Europe 3.52
counsel *see* barristers
counsellors
  codes of ethics 11.20
  conciliation privilege 16.07
  iniquity, disclosure of 11.19
  public interest defence 11.20
  warn, duty to 20.19
Court of Protection 12.09, 13.11
covert means
  use of information obtained by 10.38
covert surveillance 14.70–14.122
  admissibility of fruits of surveillance 14.76, 14.77
  arrangements, surveillance 14.102–14.104
  collateral intrusion 14.70
  collateral use of documents 17.11
  communications data 14.102–14.105
    arrangements, surveillance 14.402–14.404
    multiple illegality of arrangements possible 14.105
  data content interception warrants 14.92–14.95
  directed 14.119–14.122
    authorization 14.120, 14.121
    definition 14.119
    European Convention on Human Rights 14.122
    grounds 14.119
    police 14.120
    procedures 14.119
  entry, covert
    interference with property 14.79–14.81
    Police Act 1997 14.72–14.75
    secret intelligence services 14.79–14.81
  European Convention on Human Rights 14.122

  Human Rights Act 1998 14.71
  importance 14.70
  interception of communications 14.88–14.101
    data content interception warrants 14.92–14.95
    lawful interception under RIPA 14.90, 14.91
    legally privileged and confidential material 14.96–14.98
    private networks 14.89
    secrecy of interception 14.99–14.101
  interference with property
    entry, covert 14.79–14.81
    secret intelligence services 14.79–14.81
  intrusive surveillance 14.106–14.118
    admissibility of fruits in evidence 14.118
    business premises 14.108
    Code of Practice 14.113, 14.114
    confidential communications 14.115–14.117
    consistently providing information of same quality 14.107
    content of communication 14.109
    definition 14.106–14.109
    grounds 14.110–14.113
    hotels 14.108
    legally privileged communications 14.114–14.117
    location of surveillance 14.108
    long-distance equipment 14.107
    necessity 14.113
    office premises 14.108
    police cells 14.108
    prisons 14.108
    procedures 14.110–14.113
    proportionality 14.112
    residential premises 14.108
  lawyers 14.70
  Police Act 1997 14.72–14.77
    dual approval 14.73–14.75
    dwellings 14.73
    entry, covert 14.72–14.75
    interference with property 14.72–14.75
    legally privileged material 14.74
  Regulation of Investigatory Powers Act 2000 14.83–14.87
    regulated forms of surveillance 14.83–14.85
    sanctions 14.86, 14.87
  secret intelligence services 14.78–14.82
    entry, covert 14.79–14.81
    interference with property 14.79–14.81
  uses 14.70
crime reconstructions 5.51
Criminal Assets Recovery Authority 14.18

Index

Criminal Cases Review Commission 3.40
criminal offences
  assault 6.82
  blackmail 6.82
  burglary 6.82
  computer access, unauthorized 6.60–6.63
  Computer Misuse Act 1990 6.60–6.63
  confidential information and 6.54, 6.55
  conspiracy
    corruption, to commit 6.76
    defraud, to 6.77–6.81
    interceptor, prosecuting 6.76–6.81
    stranger, prosecuting a 6.84, 9.85
  copyright, knowing sale of infringing material 6.82
  corruption 6.75, 6.76
  data protection 6.56–6.59
  Data Protection Act 1998 21.22
  deception 6.73, 6.74
  defence, acquisition of information by 14.123–14.132
    confidential material 14.126
    investigating authorities, material held by 14.124
    public interest immunity 14.127
    third parties, material held by 14.125
    unused police material 14.124, 14.125
    used police material 14.123
  defraud, conspiracy to 6.77–6.81
  electricity abstraction 6.72
  forgery 6.74
  Freedom of Information Act 2000 18.51
  genetic information 6.83
  government 14.54, 14.55
  information as property 6.55
  intentional damage to property 6.82
  interception of communications
    Regulation of Investigatory Powers Act 2000 6.64–6.66
    Wireless Telegraphy Act 1949 6.67, 6.86
  libel, criminal 6.87
  proceeds of crime 14.53
  property, damage to 6.82
  property offences 6.55
  prosecution 14.19–14.132 *see also* police
    acquisition of confidential information by prosecution 14.19–14.69
    banking 14.57
    covert surveillance *see* covert surveillance
    espionage 14.55
    excluded material *see* excluded material
    financial services 14.56
    government information, confidential 14.54
    proceedings of crime 14.53
    search warrants 14.19–14.35
      see also search warrants
  seizure 14.35–14.40
  Serious Fraud Office 14.52
  special procedure material *see* special procedure material
  tax investigations 14.62–14.68
    see also tax investigations
  voluntary disclosure in public interest 14.41, 14.42
  public interest, commission in 6.88
  recklessly damaging property 6.82
  Regulation of Investigatory Powers Act 2000 6.64–6.66
    consent to prosecution from DPP 6.66
    penalties 6.66
    private telecommunications system, intercepting communication on course of transmission through 6.65
    public postal service or public telecommunications system, interception of communication in course of transmission through 6.64, 7.43
  search warrants 14.19–14.35 *see also* search warrants
  strangers, prosecuting 6.84–6.87
    accessories 6.84
    conspiracy 6.84, 9.85
    theft 6.85
  theft 6.68–6.74
    borrowing 6.69
    confidential information 6.70, 6.71
    deception 6.73, 6.74
    definition 6.68
    electricity abstraction 6.72
    exam papers 6.70
    intention to permanently deprive 6.68, 6.70
    strangers, prosecuting 6.84
  use of compulsory disclosed information for prosecution of 10.34
  Wireless Telegraphy Act 1949 6.67, 6.86
criminal records *see also* criminal offences; previous convictions
  breach of confidence 5.18
  breach of fiduciary duty 5.76
  Human Rights Act 1998 and disclosure of 5.21
  intentional disclosure 4.11
  public domain, information in 5.18
Crown Prosecution Service
  collateral use of documents 17.09
customer information order 14.18
Customs and Excise
  tax investigations 14.68

damages *see also* monetary awards
  aggravated 8.66–8.68

Index

damages *see also* monetary awards (*cont.*):
  breach of confidence 5.41, 8.37–8.41
  breach of fiduciary duty 8.36
  equity 8.33–8.39
    contract 8.33, 8.34
    exclusively equitable interest, interference with 8.35–8.41
    tort 8.33, 8.34
  exemplary damages 8.69–8.70
  heads of damage 8.42–8.65
    mental distress 8.46–8.59
      see also mental distress
    privacy, loss of 8.64, 8.65
    reputation, injury to 8.60–8.63
    tangible injury 8.42–8.45
  Human Rights Act 1998 8.30–8.32
  injury 8.42–8.45
  mental distress 8.46–8.59
    see also mental distress
  reputation, injury to 8.60–8.63
  tangible injury 8.42–8.45
data
  content interception warrants 14.92–14.95
  information distinguished 1.03, 18.02
  protection *see* data protection; Data Protection Act 1998
data controller 18.11
data protection
  Act of 1998 *see* Data Protection Act 1998
  compliance order 8.26, 8.27
  consent 13.01
    implied 13.37
    informed consent 13.30–13.32
  criminal offences 6.56–6.59
  informed consent 13.30–13.32
  pre-trial disclosure 14.04
Data Protection Act 1998 18.01–18.50 *see also* data protection
  anonymized data 18.08
  art 18.39–18.41
  background 18.01
  breach of statutory duty 4.49
  categories of data 18.04, 18.05
  chronological files 18.06
  coded data 18.05
  consent
    disclosure 3.41
    First Data Protection Principle 18.18
  crime 18.44, 18.45
  criminal offences 21.22
  data controller 18.11
  data processor 6.36
  dead, information about 18.59
  death of client 5.51
  educational records 18.04
  enforcement of Data Protection Principles 18.47–18.50
  exemptions 18.37–18.46
    art 18.39–18.41
    construction 18.37
    crime 18.44, 18.45
    effect 18.37
    Freedom of Information Act 2000 exemptions 18.46
    journalism 18.39–18.41
    legal purposes 18.38
    literature 18.39–18.41
    media 18.39–18.41
    national security 18.44, 18.45
    public interest, publication in 18.40
    regulatory activity 18.44, 18.45
    research purposes 18.42, 18.43
    special purposes 18.39–18.41
    statutory authority 18.38
    taxation 18.44, 18.45
  fair and lawful processing 18.08–18.28
    see also First Data Protection Principle *below*
  First Data Protection Principle 18.08–18.28
    after collection of data, information required 18.13–18.15
    anonymized data 18.08
    conditions 18.09, 18.18–18.22
    consent 18.18
    data controller 18.11
    discretionary disclosures 18.21, 18.22
    fair processing 18.10–18.17
    fairness 18.09
    further information 18.11
    health records 18.12
    lawful processing of personal data 18.09
    legality 18.09
    legitimate interests of professional 18.19, 18.20
    medical records 18.12
    medical research 18.14
    method of obtaining 18.16
    necessary processing 18.19, 18.20
    non-consensual processing 18.19, 18.20
    oral notice 18.12
    personal data 18.09–18.19
    prior to collection of data, information requirements 18.11, 18.12
    processing the data 18.08
    public interest and self-interest disclosures 18.22
    purpose/s of processing 18.11
    requirements 18.09
    sensitive personal data 18.09, 18.23–18.28
    third parties 18.15, 18.17
    vital interests, protection of 18.19, 18.20
    without consent, processing 18.19, 18.20

773

Index

Data Protection Act 1998 (*cont.*):
  forms
    data 18.04, 18.05
    data storage 18.06, 18.07
  geographically dispersed data 18.06
  health records 18.04
    First Data Protection Principle 18.12
  information and data distinguished 18.02
  journalists 18.39–18.41
  lawful purposes 18.29–18.33
    see also Second Data Protection Principle *below*
  literature 18.39–18.41
  media 18.39–18.41
  medical records 18.04
    First Data Protection Principle 18.12
  medical research 18.14
  national security 18.44, 18.45
  notification 18.03–18.07
    failure 18.03
  personal data
    examples 18.05
    fair and lawful processing 18.08–18.28
      see also First Data Protection Principle *above*
    group of people 18.05
    meaning 18.04, 18.05
    sound data 18.05
    unstructured 18.07
    visual data 18.05
  policy 19.21
  principles
    enforcement 18.47–18.50
    First Data Protection Principle 18.08–18.28
    Second Data Protection Principle 18.29–18.33
    Third Data Protection Principle 18.34
    Fourth Data Protection Principle 18.34
    Fifth Data Protection Principle 18.34, 18.34
    Sixth Data Protection Principle 18.34
    Seventh Data Protection Principle 18.34
    Eighth Data Protection Principle 18.34, 18.35–18.36
  pseudonymized data 18.05
  public interest defence 18.40
  public records 18.04
  readily accessible data 18.06
  regulatory activity 18.44, 18.45
  relevant filing system 18.06, 18.07
  restriction of disclosure under 3.41
  rights 3.41
  SARs *see* subject access rights
  scope 18.04–18.07
  Second Data Protection Principle 18.29–18.33
    breaches 18.30
    compatible processing 18.31, 18.32
    incompatible processing 18.31–18.33
    permitted disclosures for incompatible purposes 18.33
    processing purposes 18.29, 18.30
  sensitive personal data
    additional conditions 18.25–18.27
    conditions for processing 18.25–18.27
    definition 18.23, 18.24
    deliberately taken steps by client 18.25, 18.26
    examples 18.24
    explicit consent 18.25
    First Data Protection Principle 18.09, 18.23–18.28
    grounds 18.27
    Human Rights Act 1998 18.28
    public domain defence 18.26
    purposes of processing 18.27
    substantial public interest 18.27
  sound data 18.05
  stay of proceedings 18.41
  storage, data 18.06, 18.07
  subject access rights *see* subject access rights
  taxation 18.44, 18.45
  trans-border data flows 18.35, 18.36
  unlawful disclosure 21.22
  unstructured personal data 18.07
  visual data 18.05
data-sharing 2.14–2.20
  benefits 2.14
  compelled disclosures 3.40
  confidentiality 2.18, 2.19
  European Convention on Human Rights 2.17
  initiatives 2.15
  introduction 2.14
  meaning 2.14
  multi-disciplinary partnerships 2.20
  privacy 2.17
    duration 5.16–5.19
  public sector organizations 2.15, 2.16
  rationale 2.15
  statutory gateways 2.16
  teams, professional 2.19
death
  client *see* death of client
  Data Protection Act 1998 18.59
  Freedom of Information Act 2000 18.59
  professionals 5.55–5.58
death of client
  autopsy records 5.47
  breach of confidence 5.46–5.54

death of client (*cont.*):
  breach of confidence
    adoption records 5.49, 5.50
    autopsy records 5.47
    crime reconstructions 5.51
    doctors 5.53, 5.54
    European Convention on Human Rights 5.51
    HIV infected care workers 5.51
    legislative analogies 5.51
    need for confidentiality after 5.46, 5.47
    offensiveness of disclosure 5.47
    post-mortem legal protection 5.48
    public records 5.51
    soft law 5.51
    survivors, interest of 5.47
    United States 5.47
  certificates, death 5.51
  Commission for Health Improvement 5.51
  crime reconstructions 5.51
  Data Protection Act 1998 5.51
  electronic communications 5.51
  European Convention on Human Rights 5.52
  HIV infected care workers 5.51
  intentional disclosure 4.16, 4.17
  legal advice privilege 16.29
  public records 5.51
  survival of obligation of confidence 4.16, 4.17
deceit
  interception 6.52
deception 6.73, 6.74
decisional privacy 1.14
defamation 1.21, 4.34–4.40
  absolute privilege 4.39
  adultery 4.35
  breach of confidence, statement originating in 4.38
  compelled disclosures 10.01
  confidentiality and 1.1
  defences 4.36–4.39
  disciplinary proceedings 4.39
  disease 4.35
  doctors 4.40
  elements 4.34
  fair comment 4.36
  improper disclosure of personal information 4.35–4.40
  innuendo 4.34
  interception
    client v interceptor 6.29
  judicial proceedings, statements made during 4.39
  justification 4.36
  libel 4.35
  malice 4.36, 4.37, 4.39, 4.40
  meaning of defamatory information 4.34

  mental distress 4.35, 8.50
  offence, imputations of commission of 4.35
  open court, information disclosed in 5.18
  personal information 4.34
  previous convictions 5.18
  public interest 4.36, 4.39
  purpose of tort 4.34
  qualified privilege 4.36
  reputation 4.35
  self-interest, disclosure motivated by 12.37
  special damage 4.35
  spent convictions 4.36
  third party 7.38
  unsuitability as action 4.35
  untrue statements 4.36
defence, acquisition of information by 14.123–14.132
  bank accounts 14.132
  confidential information 14.126
  court-enforced disclosure 14.129–14.131
    bank accounts 14.132
  professional, material held by 14.128–14.132
  public interest immunity 14.127
  third parties, material held by 14.125
  unused police material 14.124
  used police material 14.123
  voluntary disclosure 14.128
defences
  compelled *see* coercive statutory disclosure; compelled disclosures; money laundering
  consent *see* consent; waiver
  defamation 4.36–4.39
  money laundering 10.33
  public interest *see* public interest defence
  voluntary disclosure *see* best interests of client, disclosure in; self-interest, disclosure in; voluntary disclosure
defraud, conspiracy to 6.77–6.81
delivery up 8.74, 8.75
dentists 1.25
  coercive statutory disclosure 10.07
destruction
  inaccurate or misleading data 19.48
  items 8.74, 8.75
diaries
  copyright 5.85
directed surveillance 14.119–14.122
disciplinary proceedings
  alternative to litigation 9.07
  codes of ethics 3.47
  defamation 4.39
  lawyers, against
    common law 12.24–12.26
    Law Society guidelines 12.23
    self-interest, disclosure in 12.23–12.25

Index

disciplinary proceedings (*cont.*):
  solicitors
    common law 12.24
    Law Society guidance 12.23
    self-interest, disclosure in 12.23–12.25
disclosure
  accidental *see* accidental disclosure
  barring, legislation 3.41–3.45
  best interests of clients, disclosure in 12.02–12.13
    see also best interests of client, disclosure in
  client, to *see* disclosure to the client
  compelled *see* coercive statutory disclosure; compelled disclosures; money laundering
  compelled disclosures 3.33–3.40
    see also compelled disclosures
  employer, to 21.02–21.06
    see also employer
  incompetent adult 19.114, 19.115
  minors 19.72–19.113
    see also minors
  multi-layered legal protection 3.44
  non-disclosure 3.41–3.45
  pre-trial *see* pre-trial disclosure
  self-interest, disclosure motivated by 12.23–12.41
    see also self-interest, disclosure in
  statutory authority 12.14–12.22
  subject of information, to 3.45
  unintentional *see* accidental disclosure; interception; interceptor
  voluntary
    best interests of clients, disclosure in 12.02–12.13
      see also best interests of client, disclosure in
    self-interest, disclosure motivated by 12.23–12.41
      see also self-interest, disclosure in
    statutory authority 12.14–12.22
  whistleblowing *see* whistleblowing
disclosure to the client 19.01–19.117
  Access to Medical Reports Act 1988 19.49–19.53
  agency 19.05–19.07
    generally 19.06, 19.07
    solicitors 19.07
  arbitrary refusal 19.01
  childhood case records 19.19, 19.20
  doctors 19.08, 19.09, 19.12, 19.15, 19.65–19.70
  educational records 19.79–19.82
  equitable right to see own records 19.14, 19.15
  higher education 19.71
  inaccurate or misleading data 19.48
  incompetent adult 19.114, 19.115
  informed consent 19.01
  medical records 19.01, 19.08, 19.09, 19.12, 19.13, 19.15, 19.16–19.18
    Access to Health Records Act 1990 19.54–19.57
    Access to Medical Reports Act 1988 19.49–19.53
    Health and Social Care Act 2001 19.57
  minors 19.72–19.113
    see also consent
    access to records 19.72–19.82
    best interests of child 19.87–19.89
    child abuse 19.92
    competent child 19.72
    DPA 1998 19.72–19.75, 19.103, 19.104
    educational records 19.79–19.82
    European Convention on Human Rights 19.111, 19.112
    exceptions to parental access 19.76–19.78
    genetic testing 19.88
    incompetent child 19.73–19.75
    legal proceedings 19.110
    medical confidentiality 19.94–19.100, 19.107, 19.108
    non-health related information 19.101
    objections by parent to disclosure 19.102
    pedigree information 19.105, 19.106
    remedies for wrongfully withholding information 19.90–19.92
    right to information 19.83–19.113
    social work records 19.101
    subject access rights 19.72–19.75
    vetoing disclosure 19.93
    withholding information from parents 19.87–19.92
  need to know, client's 19.01
  own records 19.03–19.57
    childhood case records 19.19, 19.20
    common law 19.03–19.10
    contractual right 19.11–19.13
    doctors 19.08, 19.09, 19.12, 19.15
    equitable right 19.14, 19.15
    Gaskin v UK 19.19, 19.20
    innominate right 19.16–19.18
    medical records 19.08, 19.09, 19.12, 19.13, 19.15, 19.16–19.18
    non-agency relationships 19.08–19.10
    ownership of physical record 19.03
    personal information, ownership 19.04
    unpaid fees 19.03
  ownership of physical record 19.03
  personal autonomy 19.01
  rationale 19.01
  right to information 19.58–19.71

Index

disclosure to the client (*cont.*):
  right to information
    doctors 19.65–19.70
    fiduciary-professionals 19.58–19.63
    higher education 19.71
    non-fiduciary professionals 19.64–19.71
  social work records 19.101
  statutory access rights
    Access to Health Records Act 1990
      19.54–19.57
    Access to Medical Reports Act 1988
      19.49–19.53
    Data Protection Act 1998 19.21–19.47
    see also subject access rights
    Health and Social Care Act 2001 19.57
    inaccurate or misleading data 19.48
  subject access rights 19.21–19.47
    see also subject access rights
  third parties, disclosure to 19.116, 19.117
  unpaid fees 19.03
discovery proceedings 7.03–7.19
  contempt of court 7.12–7.15
  ECHR, Article 10 7.16–7.18
  freedom of expression 7.16–7.18
  identity, discovering
    innocent stranger 7.05–7.08
    third party 7.05–7.08
    wrongdoer 7.04
  identity of wrongdoer, discovering 7.04
  innocent facilitators, against 7.04–7.08
    innocent stranger, discovering identity of
      7.05–7.08
    third party, discovering identity of
      7.05–7.08
    wrongdoer, discovering identity of 7.04
  media sources 7.12–7.18
    contempt of court 7.12–7.15
    delivery up of property disclosing leak 7.19
    ECHR, Article 10 7.16–7.18
    presumption against disclosure 7.15
  parameters of jurisdiction 7.10
  procedural points 7.11
  third party
    identity, discovering 7.05–7.08
  types of action 7.03
  wrongdoer, application against 7.03, 7.09
discrimination
  compelled disclosures 3.38
  confidentiality, role of 1.41
disease
  breach of statutory duty 4.51
  defamation 4.35
diseases
  doctors reporting 3.36
disloyalty
  interception 6.02–6.88

  see also interception; interceptor
dismissal
  whistleblowing 21.24
disqualification
  professionals 5.55
distress, intentional infliction of 4.29–4.33
  elements 4.29, 4.30
  interception
    client v interceptor 6.29
  mental distress 4.33
  personal information, intentional disclosure of
    4.31, 4.32
  presence of claimant 4.32
  truth of information 4.32
DNA screening 2.02
doctors *see also* medical records
  blood samples, unauthorized use or disclosure
    of 5.29
  breach of confidence 5.27, 5.53, 5.54
  breach of fiduciary duty 5.80, 5.81
  breach of statutory duty 4.51
  Canada 1.04, 19.15
  codes of ethics 3.47
    public interest defence 11.18
  coercive statutory disclosure 10.03, 10.06
  compelled disclosures 3.35
  confidentiality 1.17
  consent 13.45
  death of patient, non-consensual disclosure
    after 5.53, 5.54
  defamation 4.40
  detection of completed crimes 11.33, 11.35
  disclosure to the client 19.08, 19.09, 19.12,
    19.13, 19.15, 19.65–19.70
  diseases, reporting 3.36
  employers, disclosure to 21.08, 21.12–21.14
  examinee-professional relationship 1.29–1.31
  gifts to 19.15
  health authority, disclosures by GPs to 21.16
  Health Service Commissioner, provision of
    information to 10.03
  iniquity, disclosure of 11.18
  intentional disclosure
    contract 4.08, 4.11
  limits of obligation of confidentiality 4.13
  malice 4.40
  military 21.12, 21.14
  officious bystander test 4.13
  personal information 1.04
  police 21.12
  prescribing, information about 1.4
  prison 21.12, 21.13
  privilege 16.42
  production of documents 3.35
  property of patient, obtaining 5.80
  public interest defence 11.66

doctors (*cont.*):
  public interest defence
    codes of ethics 11.18
    detection of completed crimes 11.33, 11.35
    drug reactions, adverse 13.52
    prevention of harm to the person 11.21–11.23
    secondary purposes, disclosure for 13.51, 13.52
  publications, disclosure in 13.55
  reporting requirements 3.36
  search warrants 14.23
  self-interest, disclosure motivated by 12.30, 12.31, 12.32, 12.33
  undue influence 19.15
  warn, duty to 20.19
documents, control of 17.02–17.25
  collateral use of documents 17.09–17.21
    Civil Procedure Rules 1998 17.16
    civil proceedings 17.14–17.19
    criminal investigation, information gathered for 17.09–17.13
    defence, subsequent use by 17.12, 17.13
    family court proceedings 17.17–17.21
    regulatory bodies, disclosure to 17.20, 17.21
    surveillance, use of material for 17.11
  counsel to counsel disclosure in criminal litigation 17.07
  criminal proceedings 17.07
  limiting inspection 17.02–17.08
    Article 6 ECHR 17.08
    children, protection of 17.05, 17.06
    criminal proceedings 17.07
    enforcement 17.03
    procedure 17.02
    reasons 17.02
    therapeutic privilege 17.04
  reasons 17.02
  therapeutic privilege 17.04
drawings
  copyright 5.85
drug reactions, adverse 13.52
drug trafficking
  Criminal Assets Recovery Authority 14.18
  money laundering 10.24, 10.25
drugs
  police investigations 14.51
  production order 14.51
duty to warn *see* warn, duty to

e-mails
  interception 6.34
  negligence 6.34
education *see also* educational records
  contraceptive advice to pupils 2.24

  higher 19.71
  school records 3.40
  sex education 2.24
  special educational needs 3.42
  Youth Court powers 3.40
educational records *see also* education
  Data Protection Act 1998 18.04
  disclosure to the client 19.79–19.82
  examination marks 19.43
  minors, access by 19.79–19.82
  parental access 19.83–19.93
    withholding information 19.87–19.89
  private schools 19.44
  school leaver's report 19.45
  source of information in 19.44
  subject access rights 19.22, 19.43–19.45
elder abuse
  Canada 20.23
  warn, duty to 20.23, 20.27
electricity abstraction 6.72
embryology information 19.40
emergencies
  best interests of client, disclosure in 12.08
  children 13.16
  consent 13.11, 13.16
  medical 13.16, 19.70
  medical records 12.08, 13.17
  parental consent where medical emergency 13.16
  voluntary disclosure 12.08
employees
  breach of confidence 5.28, 5.30, 21.18
    employer's liability for 21.31–21.36
  criminal offences *see* criminal offences
  guidelines 2.22, 2.23
  interception 6.32–6.47
    breach of confidence 6.41
    breach of contract 6.38–6.40
    breach of statutory duty 6.35, 6.37
    conspiracy 6.43
    conversion 6.42, 6.43
    corrupt employees 6337
    identifying employee 6.46, 6.47
    medical records 6.47
    negligence 6.32–6.34
  misuse of computer information by 2.07
  money laundering 10.27
  professionals as 2.21–2.24
  prosecuting disloyal employees 6.54–6.83
    see also criminal offences
  public interest disclosures *see* whistleblowing
  whistleblowing *see* whistleblowing
employer
  breach of confidence by employee, liability for 21.31–21.36
  disclosure to 21.02–21.16

Index

employer (*cont.*):
  disclosure to
    confidential client information
      21.02–21.16
    doctors 21.08
    general practitioners 21.16
    military doctors 21.12, 21.14
    occupational health professionals
      21.04–21.07
    ownership of paper and filing system
      21.03
    police doctors 21.12
    prison doctors 21.12, 21.13
    probation officers 21.15
    social workers 21.10, 21.11
    solicitors 21.08
    teachers 21.09
  doctors, disclosure by 21.08
  military doctors, disclosure by 21.12, 21.14
  occupational health professionals
    21.04–21.07
  outside workplace, disclosures 21.17–21.30
    during period of employment 21.17, 21.18
    termination of employment 21.19–21.21
    unlawful disclosure 21.22
  police doctors, disclosure by 21.12
  prison doctors, disclosure by 21.12, 21.13
  probation officers, disclosure by 21.15
  social workers, disclosure by 21.10, 21.11
  solicitors, disclosure by 21.08
  teachers, disclosure by 21.09
entry powers
  compelled disclosures 3.37
  Health and Safety officials 3.37
  inspections 3.37
equity
  account of profits 8.71–8.73
  breach of confidence 5.02–5.63
    see also breach of confidence
  breach of fiduciary duty 5.64–5.83
    see also breach of fiduciary duty
  co-existence of contractual and equitable obligations 5.28
  damages 8.33–8.39
    contract 8.33, 8.34
    exclusively equitable interest, interference with 8.35–8.41
    tort 8.33, 8.34
  intentional disclosure 5.02–5.83
    breach of confidence 5.02–5.63
      see also breach of confidence
    breach of fiduciary duty 5.64–5.83
      see also breach of fiduciary duty
  loyalty, duty of 5.67
  mental distress 8.51, 8.52

erasure
  inaccurate or misleading data 19.48
espionage
  investigations 14.55
  search warrants 14.55
estate agents
  money laundering 10.25
ethics
  codes 1.26, 2.22
    see also codes of ethics
  confidentiality 1.16–1.18
  written code 1.26
European Convention on Human Rights 3.02
    see also Human Rights Act 1998
  breach of confidence 5.52
  coercive statutory disclosure
    Article 6 10.15
    Article 8 10.13, 10.14
  conflicting Convention rights
    Articles 8 and 10, conflict between 3.29–3.32
    proportionality 3.26–3.32
  covert surveillance 14.122
  data-sharing 2.17
  death of client 5.52
  directed surveillance 14.122
  domestic law, impact on 3.55
  expression, freedom of *see* freedom of expression
  fair hearing, right to 3.10–3.15
    interference with 3.23
  interference with 3.19–3.25
    expression, freedom of 3.19–3.23
    fair trial, right to 3.23
    lawyers, communications with 3.25
    private and family life, respect for 3.19–3.23
    proportionality 3.20–3.22
    public hearing, right to 3.24
  justified interference with 3.19–3.25
  lawyers, communications with 3.25
  life, right to 3.16
  minors, access to information by 19.111, 19.112
  privacy 1.07
  private and family life, respect for *see* private and family life, respect for
  proportionality 3.20–3.22
    conflicting Convention rights 3.26–3.32
  public hearing, interference with right to 3.24
  religion, freedom of 3.16
  reporting restrictions 17.50, 17.51
  torture or inhuman or degrading treatment, right to protection from 3.16
  whistleblowing 21.29, 21.30
European Union 3.52

Index

examination papers 6.70
examinee
 professional, duties owed by 1.29–1.32
 service to 1.29
excluded material
 production order 14.25–14.28
 public interest defence 14.41, 14.42
 search warrants 14.21, 14.23, 14.24, 14.29
  opposing application 14.30–14.32
 warning client 14.43, 14.44
exemplary damages 8.69–8.70
expert witnesses 15.24–15.30
 confidentiality of reports 15.24
expression, freedom of 3.17, 3.18
 interference with 3.19–3.23

fair hearing, right to 3.10–3.15
 interference with 3.23
 lawyers, communications with 3.10–3.12
 litigation, information relevant to 3.13
 open court principle 3.13
 private and family life, relationship with right to respect for 3.14 3.15
false image, correcting 11.10
family proceedings
 children's consent to disclosure of information 13.14
 coercive statutory disclosure 10.14
 collateral use of documents 17.17–17.21
 consent to disclosure 13.14
 legal professional privilege 10.14
 pre-trial disclosure 14.04
 prohibited steps order 13.21
fee recovery
 self-interest, disclosure motivated by 12.34–12.36
  lawyers 12.35, 12.36
  non-lawyers 12.34
fees
 handling fee under FOIA 2000 18.51
 recovery *see* fee recovery
 subject access rights 19.21
 unpaid 19.03, 19.25
feminists 1.34
fertilization information 140
fiduciary
 disclosure to the client 19.58–19.63
 duty, breach of *see* breach of fiduciary duty
financial services
 investigations 14.56
food poisoning 3.36
foreign law
 coercive statutory disclosure 10.23
forgery
 criminal offences 6.74

fraud
 conspiracy to defraud 6.77–6.81
 insurance 11.30
 social security 11.30
 warn, duty to 20.40, 20.41
freedom of expression 3.17, 3.18
 discovery proceedings 7.16–7.18
 interference 3.19–3.23
 media 5.22, 7.16–7.18, 17.50, 17.51
 reporting restrictions 17.50, 17.51
 whistleblowing 21.29, 21.30
Freedom of Information Act 2000
 Code of Practice 18.51, 18.58
 commencement 18.51
 criminal offences 18.51
 Data Protection Act 1998 exemptions 18.46
 death 18.59
 destruction of information before commencement 18.51
 forms of records 18.51
 handling fee 18.51
 historical records 18.50
 information 18.51
 public authorities 18.51, 18.52
 publication scheme 18.52
 recorded in any form, information 18.51
 rights 18.51
 structured records 18.51
 subject access rights 18.53
 third parties 18.54–18.58
  enforcement 18.55, 18.56
  kinds of exemption 18.54
  personal information exemptions 18.57
  protecting interests of data subject 18.58
 unstructured records 18.51

General Medical Council
 codes of ethics 3.47
  obligation of confidentiality 6.32
 public interest defence 11.18
 research purposes, use of patient information for 11.45
genetic information 6.83, 11.53–11.59
 BMA advice 11.54, 11.56
 codes of ethics 11.54
 consent to tests 13.15, 13.41
 disclosure in public interest 11.56
 minors 19.88
 public interest defence 11.53–11.59
 warn, duty to 20.37–20.39
  blood relatives 20.37, 20.38
  patient of risk to blood relatives, warning 20.39
  sexual partners 20.37, 20.38
government
 confidential information 14.54, 14.55

Index

hacking, computers 2.06, 2.07, 6.62
harassment
  Protection from Harassment Act 1997
    7.40–7.41
    civil action 7.40
    disclosure of personal information,
      application to 7.41
Health and Safety officials
  entry powers 3.37
health records *see* medical records
healthcare professionals *see also* doctors; nurses; pharmacists
  breach of confidence 5.27
  public interest defence 11.17, 11.18
higher education
  disclosure to the client 19.71
historical records
  Freedom of Information Act 2000 18.50
HIV/AIDS
  breach of confidence 5.04
  breach of confidentiality 1.40
  care workers 5.51
  consent to blood sample for testing 13.41
  partner notification 11.58
  prisoners 11.59
  public interest defence 11.58, 11.59
  recklessly infecting others 11.59
  United States law 20.28–20.32
  warn, duty to 20.28–20.36
    causation 20.36
    English law 20.33–20.36
    patient, warning 20.35
    policy 20.34
    proximity 20.33
    United States law 20.28–20.32
human dignity
  respect for 1.37, 1.38
human rights 3.02–3.32
  Act of 1998 *see* Human Rights Act 1998
  duty to consider privacy codes 3.08
  European Convention on Human Rights *see* European Convention on Human Rights
  expression, freedom of 3.17, 3.18
    interference with 3.19–3.23
  fair hearing, right to 3.10–3.15
  injunctions 8.07
  interpretative obligation 3.04
  legal assistance, right to 3.10
  legal professional privilege 3.10
  life, right to 3.16
  private and family life, respect for 3.03
    public domain, information in 5.13
  proportionality 3.20–3.22
  religion, freedom of 3.16

  torture or inhuman or degrading treatment, right to protection from 3.16
Human Rights Act 1998 3.02 *see also* European Convention on Human Rights; human rights
  breach of statutory duty 4.45–4.48
    cause of action 4.45
    effect of disclosure 4.46
    public authority 4.47, 4.48
  children 13.18
  codes, requirement to take into account 9.09
  coercive statutory disclosure, impact on 10.08–10.10
  covert surveillance 14.71
  criminal record, disclosure of 5.21
  damages 8.30–8.32
  hybrid public authorities 4.47
  impact 3.04–3.09
  indirect horizontal effect 3.05–3.09
  interim injunctions 8.11–8.25
    American Cyanamid and 8.15, 8.16
    media cases 8.13
    'particular regard' for freedom of expression 8.14
    prior notice 8.12
    protection of freedom of expression 8.11
    summary of relevant factors 8.25
    Woolf guidelines 8.18–8.24
  interpretative obligation 3.04
  legal professional privilege 16.09
  media freedom 5.22
  mental distress 8.55, 8.56
  non-disclosure 16.02
  privilege 16.48–16.51
  proportionality 11.13
  public authorities
    damages recovered from 8.30–8.32
    liability 3.09
    meaning 4.47, 4.48
    status of courts 3.05–3.07
  public domain, information in 5.20–5.22
  public interest defence 11.13
  warn, duty to 20.05

immigration 14.69
imprisonment
  professionals 5.55
inaccurate or misleading data
  blocking 19.48
  child abuse 19.48
  destruction 19.48
  disclosure to the client 19.48
  erasure 19.48
  rectification 19.48
  true facts 19.48

Index

inadvertent disclosure *see also* accidental disclosure
  breach of confidence 5.78
  breach of fiduciary duty 5.78
  causes 2.25
  methods 2.25
  personal information 2.25
incompetent adult
  best interests of client, disclosure in 12.09, 12.10
    Court of Protection 12.09, 13.11
    mental illness 12.10
    power of attorney 12.09
    proxy authorisation 12.09
  capacity to consent 13.10–13.11
  subject access 19.114, 19.115
Independent Television Commission 3.08, 9.20, 9.21–9.23
  abolition 9.20
  formal warnings 9.23
  Programme Code 9.21, 9.22
  sanctions 9.23
  serious or persistent breaches 9.23
inducing breach of contract
  strangers 7.43
  third party 7.37, 7.43
infertility treatment 13.08
  child's access to records 19.106
  informed consent 13.29
  pre-trial disclosure 14.04
information
  data distinguished 1.03, 18.02
  data protection *see* data protection
  Freedom of Information Act 2000 18.51
  increased recording and storage 2.02, 2.03
  personal *see* personal information
  property, as 6.55
  sensitive *see* sensitive information
  storage, increased 2.02, 2.03
Information Commissioner
  assessment powers 18.39, 19.48
  codes of practice 3.50
  guidance 3.50, 3.51
  investigative powers 14.69
  roles 3.50
informational privacy *see also* data protection
  meaning 1.14
informed consent 13.28–13.33
  codes of ethics 13.32
  common law 13.28
  contractual obligations 13.33
  data protection 13.30–13.32
  disclosure to the client 19.01
  infertility treatment 13.29
  statutory requirements 13.29–13.32
    infertility treatment 13.29

informer
  journalist, relationship with 1.32
injunctions 8.02–8.25
  American Cyanamid principles 8.09, 8.10
  availability 8.02
  breach of confidence 6.02, 8.10
  damages substituted for 8.06
  definition 8.02
  duration 8.06
  HRA, s 12 8.11–8.25
    American Cyanamid 8.15, 8.16
    balance of convenience 8.17
    burden of proof 8.15, 8.16
    media cases 8.13
    'particular regard' to freedom of expression 8.14
    prior notice 8.12
    protection of freedom of expression 8.11
  human rights 8.07
  interim 8.08–8.25
    American Cyanamid principles 8.09, 8.10
    breach of confidence 8.10
    general principles 8.08–8.10
    HRA, s 12 8.11–8.25
    refusal 8.10
    status quo, maintenance of 8.08
  judicial discretion 8.07
  lifting 8.06
  media cases 8.13
  permanent
    availability 8.02
    definition of injunction 8.02
    duration 8.06
    general principles 8.02
    judicial discretion 8.07
    public domain, information in 8.04
    quia timet injunctions 8.03
    refusal 8.07
    unavailability 8.04–8.07
  preventing wrongdoer from benefiting from wrong 8.05
  public domain, information in 8.04
  quia timet 8.03
  refusal 8.07, 8.10
  summary of relevant factors 8.25
  unavailability 8.04–8.07
  Woolf guidelines 8.18–8.24
injurious falsehood 1.21, 4.41, 4.42
injury
  damages 8.42–8.45
Inland Revenue
  production notices 3.35
inquiries 15.49–15.56
  compelling evidence from professional 15.51, 15.52
  media access 15.54–15.56

Index

inquiries (*cont.*):
  non-statutory 15.53
  procedure 15.49
  public access 15.54
  purpose 15.49
  Tribunal of Inquiries (Evidence) Act 1921
    15.50
insolvency
  legal professional privilege and 10.13
  public authority disclosure of confidential
    information to court 15.38–15.40
inspections
  entry powers 3.37
insurance company
  solicitors 10.03
insurance fraud
  public interest defence 11.30
insurers
  medical records 13.59
intellectual property
  search orders 14.15
intentional disclosure
  breach of confidence 4.60
  breach of statutory duty 4.45–4.52
    see also breach of statutory duty
  conspiracy 4.43, 4.44
  contract 4.02–4.18
    barristers 4.02
    basics 4.02, 4.03
    breach of obligation 4.18
    codes of ethics 4.05
    confidentiality as a contractual term 4.04,
      4.05
    consideration 4.02
    death of client 4.16, 4.17
    direct observation 4.09
    doctors 4.08, 4.11
    duration of obligation of confidentiality
      4.14–4.17
    existence of contract 4.02
    extent of duty of confidentiality 4.06–4.11
    health professionals 4.02
    implied terms 4.05, 4.12, 4.13
    known already, information 4.10, 4.11
    limits of confidentiality 4.12, 4.13
    non-disclosure clauses 4.04
    oral contracts 4.05
    privity of contract 4.03
    public domain, information in 4.10, 4.11
    public interest 4.12
    repudiation of contract 4.15
    teachers 4.02
    termination of professional-client
      relationship 4.14
    third parties, information from 4.07, 4.08
    trivial information 4.06

copyright 5.84–5.87
  judicial proceedings 5.87
  nature of copyright 5.84
  photographs 5.85, 5.86
criminal records 4.11
death of client 4.16, 4.17
defamation 4.34–4.40
  see also defamation
distress, intentional infliction of 4.29–4.33
  elements 4.29, 4.30
  mental distress 4.33
  personal information, intentional disclosure
    of 4.31, 4.32
  presence of claimant 4.32
  truth of information 4.32
doctors
  contract 4.08, 4.11
equity 5.02–5.83
  breach of confidence 5.02–5.63
    see also breach of confidence
  breach of fiduciary duty 5.64–5.83
    see also breach of fiduciary duty
injurious falsehood 4.41, 4.42
known already, information 4.10, 4.11
limits of confidentiality 4.12, 4.13
medical history 4.11
negligence 4.20–4.28
  additional requirements for liability 4.27
  breach of duty of care 4.27
  causation 4.27
  duty of care 4.21, 4.22
  forseeability of harm 4.21, 4.22, 4.24,
    4.25
  liability 4.21
  policy arguments for duty 4.26
  proximity 4.22, 4.23
  relevance 4.20–4.22
  remoteness 4.21, 4.28
  special relationship 4.21
obligation of confidentiality
  contract 4.04, 4.05
public domain, information in 4.10, 4.11
  see also public domain, information in
repudiation of contract 4.15
teachers
  contract 4.02
tort 4.19–4.60
  breach of statutory duty 4.45–4.52
    see also breach of statutory duty
  conspiracy 4.43–4.44
  defamation 4.34–4.40
    see also defamation
  distress, intentional infliction of 4.29–4.33
  generally 4.19
  infringement of privacy 4.53–4.59
  injurious falsehood 4.41, 4.42

Index

intentional disclosure (*cont.*):
  tort
    negligence 4.20–4.28
    see also negligence
  trivial information
    contract 4.06
intentional infliction of distress *see* distress, intentional infliction of
interception 6.01, 6.02–6.88 *see also* covert surveillance; interceptor
  breach of confidence 6.02–6.25
    change of direction in law 6.05–6.08
    determining whether information in confidential/private 6.19–6.23
    detriment caused by unauthorized disclosure 6.26
    elements of action 6.03
    information capable of being private 6.17, 6.18
    informational privacy, breach of 6.10–6.12
    insistence on relationship of trust 6.04
    media privacy codes 6.21
    privileged communications, interception of 6.09
    professional v employee 6.41
    public figures 6.22–6.25
    public policy 6.20
    rationale of action 6.02
    reasonable expectation of privacy 6.14–6.25
    relationship of trust 6.03, 6.04
    without disclosure, interception 6.27, 6.28
  breach of contract
    employed, disclosure while 6.38
    media, disclosure to 6.40
    professional v employee 6.38–6.40
    public interest defence 6.38
    termination of employment, disclosure after 6.39
  breach of statutory duty
    client v interceptor 6.30
    client v professional 6.35, 6.36
  civil actions
    client v interceptor 6.02–6.31
    client v professional 6.32–6.37
    professional v employee 6.38–6.47
    professional v interceptor 6.48–6.53
  client v interceptor 6.02–6.31
    breach of confidence 6.02–6.25
      see also under breach of confidence
    breach of statutory duty 6.30
    conspiracy 6.29
    copyright 6.31
    defamation 6.29
    informational privacy, breach of 6.10–6.13
    intentional infliction of distress 6.29

    malicious falsehood 6.29
    tort claims 6.29
  client v professional 6.32–6.37
    breach of statutory duty 6.35, 6.36
    corrupt employee 6.37
    e-mails 6.34
  client v professional
    negligence 6.32–6.34, 6.37
    not employee, interception by person who is 6.32–6.34
  conspiracy
    client v interceptor 6.29
    professional v employee 6.43
    professional v interceptor 6.48, 6.49
  conversion
    professional v employee 6.42
    professional v interceptor 6.50, 6.51
  copyright
    client v interceptor 6.31
    professional v employee 6.45
    professional v interceptor 6.53
  criminal offences *see* criminal offences
  criminal prosecutions 6.54–6.88
    interceptor 6.54–6.83
  deceit 6.52
  defamation
    client v interceptor 6.29
  disloyalty 6.02–6.88
  e-mails 6.34
  employee, corrupt 6.37
  intentional infliction of distress
    client v interceptor 6.29
  malicious falsehood
    client v interceptor 6.29
  negligence
    client v professional 6.32–6.34, 6.37
  private and family life, respect for 6.28
  professional v employee 6.38–6.47
    breach of confidence 6.41
    breach of contract 6.38–6.40
    conspiracy 6.43
    conversion 6.42
    copyright 6.45
    criminal offences *see* criminal offences
    identifying employee 6.46, 6.47
    prosecution of disloyal employees 6.54–6.83
      see also criminal offences
    tort 6.42–6.44
    trespass 6.44
  professional v interceptor 6.48–6.52
    conspiracy 6.48, 6.49
    conversion 6.50, 6.51
    copyright 6.53
    deceit 6.52
    interference with trade 6.48, 6.49
    tort 6.48–6.52

Index

interception (*cont.*):
  public figures
    breach of confidence 6.22, 6.23
  tort
    client v interceptor 6.29
    conspiracy 6.29, 6.43
    conversion 6.42
    defamation 6.29
    distress, intentional infliction of 6.29
    malicious falsehood 6.29
    professional v employee 6.42–6.44
    professional v interceptor 6.48–6.52
    trespass 6.44
  trespass
    professional v employee 6.44
interceptor 1.34 *see also* interception
  breach of confidence 6.02–6.29
    change of direction in law 6.05–6.08
    determining whether information is
      confidential/private 6.19–6.23
    detriment caused by unauthorized disclosure
      6.26
    elements of action 6.03
    information capable of being private 6.17,
      6.18
    informational privacy, breach of 6.10–6.13
    insistence on relationship of trust 6.04
    privileged communications, interception of
      6.09
    public figures 6.22, 6.23
    public policy 6.20
    rationale of action 6.02
    reasonable expectation of privacy
      6.14–6.25
    relationship of trust 6.03, 6.04
    without disclosure, interception 6.27,
      6.28
  breach of statutory duty 6.30
  conspiracy 6.29
  conversion 6.50, 6.51
  copyright 6.31
  criminal offences 6.54–6.83
    see also criminal offences
  defamation 6.29
  distress, intentional infliction of 6.29
  informational privacy, breach of 6.10–6.12
  malicious falsehood 6.29
  meaning 1.33
  privileged communications, interception of
    6.09
  professional, claim by 6.48–6.53
    conspiracy 6.48, 6.49
    conversion 6.50, 6.51
    interference with trade 6.48, 6.49
    tort 6.48–6.52
    trespass 6.50, 6.51

prosecuting 6.54–6.83
  see also criminal offences
public policy
  breach of confidence 6.20
  trespass 6.50, 6.51
interceptors
  public interest defence 11.75, 11.76
interference with contractual relations
  third party 7.36
interim injunctions 8.08–8.25
  American Cyanamid principles 8.09
    balance of convenience 8.17
    breach of confidence cases 8.10
    HRA 1998, s 12 8.15, 8.16
  balance of convenience 8.17
  burden of proof 8.15, 8.16
  general principles 8.08–8.10
  HRA 1998, s 12 8.11–8.25
    American Cyanamid cases 8.15, 8.16
    balance of convenience 8.17
    burden of proof 8.15, 8.16
    media cases 8.13
    'particular regard' for freedom of expression
      8.14
    prior notice 8.12
    protection of freedom of expression 8.11
    summary of relevant factors 8.25
    Woolf guidelines 8.18–8.24
  media 8.13
  refusal 8.10
  status quo, maintenance of 8.08
  Woolf guidelines 8.18–8.24
international dimension 3.52–3.55
  Council of Europe 3.52
  domestic impact of supranational and
    international instruments 3.53, 3.54
  European Union 3.52
  Organisation for Economic Co-operation and
    Development (OECD) 3.52, 3.53
  'soft law' 3.53
  supranational instruments 3.52
  United Nations 3.52, 3.53
internet 2.05
intimacy
  meaning 1.14
  privacy 1.14
intrusive surveillance 14.106–14.118

Jack report 10.03
journalists *see also* media
  Data Protection Act 1998 18.39–18.41
  informer, relationship with 1.32
  privilege 16.42
judicial proceedings
  defamation and statements made during
    4.39

Index

laches 9.01
laundering *see* money laundering
law
  issues confronting 2.34, 2.35
  society and 2.01
Law Commission
  mental distress 8.50
Law Society
  codes of ethics 3.47
lawyer–client privilege 16.16 *see also* legal advice privilege
lawyers
  breach of confidence 5.27
  human rights and communications with 3.10–3.12, 3.25
legal advice privilege 16.16–16.19 *see also* legal professional privilege
  confidentiality 16.18
  death of client 16.29
  derivative materials 16.22
  detection of completed crimes 11.38
  duration 16.28, 16.29
  innocence at stake, when 16.25–16.27
  litigation privilege 16.16, 16.20, 16.21
  location of advice 16.18
  meaning 16.16
  non-adversarial proceedings 16.41
  non-lawyer professionals 16.19
  professional capacity 16.17
  scope 16.22–16.27
  what is not protected 16.23, 16.24
legal professional privilege 16.08–16.15 *see also* legal advice privilege; litigation privilege
  abuse 16.15
  best interests of client, disclosure in 12.12, 12.13
  children 12.12, 12.13
  circumventing 16.10
  coercive statutory disclosure 10.13–10.21
    Article 6 10.15
    Article 8 10.13, 10.14
    data protection 10.20
    family proceedings 10.14
    making disclosure 10.16
    missing child 10.19
    money laundering 10.17, 10.18
    national security 10.20
    notifying client 10.17–10.21
    police request not to notify client 10.21
    prisoners 10.14
    subject access rights 10.20
    terrorism 10.13
  common law rationale 16.08
  conflict with legal professional privilege 11.77–11.80
  duration 16.28, 16.29
  evidential nature 16.10, 16.11
  evidential rule 1.22
  family proceedings
    coercive statutory disclosure 10.14
  human rights 3.10
  Human Rights Act 1998 16.09
  judicial proceedings 16.10, 16.11
  loss 16.31–16.41
    iniquity 16.35–16.37
    waiver 16.31–16.34
  missing child 10.19
  money laundering 10.17, 10.18, 10.30, 10.31
  nature 16.10–16.15
  necessary implication, limitation by 16.13, 16.14
  non-adversarial proceedings 16.39–16.41
  non-judicial contexts 16.11–16.14
  origins 16.08–16.09
  outside adjudication, no relevance 16.11
  prisoners 10.14
  rationale 16.08
  search warrants 14.23
  seizure 14.37–14.40
  statutory limitation 16.14
  subject access rights 10.20, 19.47
  tax collection 16.13, 16.15
  waiver
    express waiver 16.31–16.33
    imputed 16.34
libel 4.35 *see also* defamation
  consent 13.01
  criminal 6.87
  mental distress 8.49
licensed conveyancers
  privilege 16.42
licensing 1.26
life, right to 3.16
limitation period 9.01
literature
  Data Protection Act 1998 18.39–18.41
litigation
  abroad
    civil proceedings 14.133–14.136
    criminal proceedings 14.137, 14.138
  advantages 9.02
  alternatives 9.04–9.23
    advantages 9.04
    Broadcasting Standards Commission 9.17–9.20
    complaints procedures 9.05
    disciplinary proceedings 9.07
    Independent Television Commission 9.21–9.23
    media regulatory bodies 9.08–9.23

Index

litigation *(cont.)*:
alternatives
Office of Communications (OFCOM) 9.20
ombudsmen 9.06
Press Complaints Commission *see* Press Complaints Commission
concurrent liability 9.01
control of documents 17.02–17.25
costs 9.03
Criminal Assets Recovery Authority 14.18
disadvantages 9.03
factors affecting 9.01
limitation period 9.01
pre-trial disclosure *see* pre-trial disclosure
privacy in 9.03
privacy, protection of 17.01–17.51
  access to documents by non-parties 17.22–17.25
  collateral use of documents 17.09–17.21
  control of documents 17.02–17.25
  see also documents, control of
  inspection of documents filed with court 17.22
  limiting inspection of documents 17.02–17.08
  restriction of publicity *see* publicity restriction
  withholding information from a party 17.02–17.08
  witness statements 17.25
private hearings 17.30–17.37
  chambers, hearing in 17.30
  CPR Pt 39 17.32, 17.33
  European Convention on Human Rights 17.34
  secret hearings 17.31
publicity *see* publicity restriction
reporting restrictions 17.44–17.51
restriction of publicity *see* publicity restriction
search orders 14.15–14.17
  applicant 14.16
  contents 14.16
  documents in support 14.17
  effect 14.16
  intellectual property 14.15
  purpose 14.15
  requirements for grant 14.17
selection of cause of action 9.01
litigation privilege 16.16 *see also* legal advice privilege; legal professional privilege
non-adversarial proceedings 16.39, 16.40
loyalty, duty of 5.67

magistrates' court
search warrants 14.19–14.35
see also search warrants
malice
defamation 4.36, 4.37, 4.39
doctors 4.40
injurious falsehood 4.41
malicious falsehood
interception
  client v interceptor 6.29
malpractice
confidentiality shielding 1.53, 1.54
management
consent to disclosure for purposes of 13.48
marital confidences
breach of confidence 5.04
market research
pharmacists, sale of information by 5.32
media
Broadcasting Standards Commission 9.17–9.20
contempt of court 7.12–7.15
Data Protection Act 1998 18.39–18.41
discovery of sources 7.12–7.18
  Contempt of Court Act 1981, s 10 7.12–7.15
freedom of expression 5.22, 7.16–7.18, 17.50, 17.51
Independent Television Commission 9.21–9.23
interception and disclosure of information to 6.40
interim injunctions 8.13
Office of Communications (OFCOM) 9.20
Press Complaints Commission *see* Press Complaints Commission
privacy codes 6.21
public interest, disclosure of matters in 11.73, 11.74
regulatory bodies 9.08–9.23
  Broadcasting Standards Commission 9.17–9.20
  Independent Television Commission 9.21–9.23
  Office of Communications (OFCOM) 9.20
  Press Complaints Commission *see* Press Complaints Commission
  reform 9.20
reporting restrictions *see* reporting restrictions
sources
  delivery up of property disclosing leak 7.19
  discovery 7.19
medical practitioners *see* doctors

Index

medical records *see also* doctors
  Access to Health Records Act 1990
    19.54–19.57
  Access to Medical Reports Act 1988
    19.49–19.53
  consent 13.09, 13.17, 13.41, 13.42
  consent of child for access to 13.17
  Data Protection Act 1998 18.04
    First Data Protection Principle 18.12
  disclosure to the client 19.01, 19.08, 19.09,
    19.12, 19.13, 19.15, 19.16–19.18
    Access to Health Records Act 1990
      19.54–19.57
    Access to Medical Reports Act 1988
      19.49–19.53
    Health and Social Care Act 2001 19.57
  emergencies 12.08, 13.17
  equitable right to see 19.15
  Health and Social Care Act 2001 19.57
  insurers 13.59
  minors, access by 19.94–19.100, 19.107,
    19.108
  ownership 19.08, 19.09
  pre-trial disclosure 14.04, 14.09
  research purposes, disclosure for 11.45
  serious harm, access causing 19.39
  subject access rights 19.39
  subpoena duces tecum 15.03
  tribunals 15.48
  unauthorized disclosure 6.47
medical research
  consent to disclosure for purposes of 13.48
  Data Protection Act 1998 18.14
  disclosure of information by doctors 11.45
  General Medical Council 11.45
  pharmacists, sale of information by 5.32,
    11.44
mental distress 4.33, 8.46–8.59, 9.01
  aggravated damages 8.67
  breach of confidence 4.60, 8.51, 8.57–8.59
  breach of statutory duty 4.52
  contract 8.46–8.49
  defamation 4.35, 8.50
  equity 8.51, 8.52
  feigning distress, client 8.53, 8.54
  forms of distress 8.46
  general rule 8.49
  Human Rights Act 1998 8.55, 8.56
  intentional torts 8.50
  Law Commission 8.50
  libel 8.49
  meaning 8.46
  negligence 8.50
  peace and enjoyment, contracts to provide 8.47
  physical effects 8.48
  physical inconvenience 8.47
  restitutionary damages 8.48
  tort 8.48–8.50
mental health
  disclosure of problems 1.40
  professionals' duty to warn 20.07–20.20
  warn, duty to 20.07–20.20
mental illness
  best interests of client, disclosure in 12.03,
    12.04, 12.10
microfilm technology 2.04
military doctors, disclosure by 21.12, 21.14
ministerial certificates 19.31
ministers of religion 1.25
minors *see also* children
  access to records 19.72–19.82
    see also disclosure to the client *below*
    competent child 19.72
    Data Protection Act 19.72–19.75
    incompetent child 19.73–19.75
    medical confidentiality 19.94–19.100,
      19.107, 19.108
  AID, conceived by 19.106, 19.112
  disclosure to the client 19.72–19.113
    access to records 19.72–19.82
    best interests of child 19.87–19.89
    child abuse 19.92
    competent child 19.72
    DPA 1998 19.72–19.75, 19.103, 19.104
    educational records 19.79–19.82
    European Convention on Human Rights
      19.111, 19.112
    exceptions to parental access 19.76–19.78
    genetic testing 19.88
    incompetent child 19.73–19.75
    legal proceedings 19.110
    medical confidentiality 19.94–19.100,
      19.107, 19.108
    objections by parent to disclosure 19.102
    pedigree information 19.105, 19.106
    remedies for wrongfully withholding
      information 19.90–19.92
    social work records 19.101
    vetoing disclosure 19.93
    withholding information from parents
      19.87–19.92
  educational records, access to 19.79–19.82
  genetic testing 19.88
  medical confidentiality 19.94–19.100,
    19.107, 19.108
    immature children 19.99, 19.100
    mature child 19.95–19.98
    mature children 19.95–19.98
  pedigree information 19.105, 19.106
  private and family life, respect for 19.111
  right to information 19.83–19.113
  subject access rights 19.72–19.75

Index

misconduct
professionals 5.55
mislead court, duty not to
criminal record of client 15.34
knowingly giving false evidence 15.31, 15.32
unwittingly giving false information 15.33
missing child
coercive statutory disclosure 10.19
legal professional privilege 10.19
monetary awards 8.69–8.70 *see also* damages
aggravated damages 8.66–8.68
breach of confidence 5.41, 8.37–8.41, 8.57–8.59
breach of copyright 8.29
breach of fiduciary duty 8.36
causes of action
  breach of copyright 8.29
  contract 8.28
  equity, damages in 8.33–8.39
  HRA 1998, recovery of damages from public authority under 8.30–8.32
  tort 8.28
contract 8.28
equitable damages 8.33, 8.34
copyright 8.29
equity, damages in 8.33–8.39
  breach of confidence 8.37–8.41
  breach of fiduciary duty 8.36
  contract 8.33, 8.34
  tort 8.33, 8.34
exemplary damages 8.69, 8.70
HRA 1998, recovery of damages from public authority under 8.30–8.32
privacy, loss of 8.64, 8.65
reputation, injury to 8.60–8.63
tort 8.28
money laundering 10.02, 10.24–10.33
accountants 10.25
art dealers 10.25
assisting the money laundering of the proceeds of crime 10.32
auditors 10.25
banking 10.25
criminal conduct 10.25
defences 10.33
drug trafficking 10.24, 10.25
employees 10.27
estate agents 10.25
legal professional privilege 10.17, 10.18, 10.30, 10.31
notifying client of disclosure 10.17, 10.18
real estate agents 10.25
reasonable suspicion 10.28, 10.29
related offences 10.32
reporting obligations 10.25–10.31
  criminal conduct 10.25

drug trafficking 10.25
employees 10.27
immunity from suit 10.26
legal professional privilege 10.30, 10.31
reporting obligations
  professionals in regulated sector 10.24, 10.25
  reasonable suspicion 10.28, 10.29
  terrorism 10.25
solicitors 10.25
statutory regimes 10.24
tax advisers 10.25
terrorism 10.24, 10.25
tipping off offences 10.17, 10.18
money-laundering
reporting 3.36, 3.37

National Confidentiality and Security Advisory Body 3.48
National Health Service
Caldicott Committee 3.48
protocols 3.48
'soft law' 3.48
national security
coercive statutory disclosure 10.20
Data Protection Act 1998 18.44, 18.45
ministerial certificates 19.31
subject access rights 19.30, 19.31
natural person
meaning 1.02
need-to-know 12.01
negligence
codes of ethics 3.47
compelled disclosures 10.01
duty of care 4.21
e-mails 6.34
forseeability of harm 4.21, 4.22, 4.24, 4.25
intentional disclosure 4.20–4.28
  additional requirements for liability 4.27
  breach of duty of care 4.27
  causation 4.27
  duty of care 4.21, 4.22
  forseeability of harm 4.21, 4.22, 4.24, 4.25
  liability 4.21
  policy arguments for duty 4.26
  proximity 4.22, 4.23
  relevance 4.20–4.22
  remoteness 4.21, 4.28
  special relationship 4.21
interception
  client v professional 6.32–6.34, 6.37
liability 4.21
mental distress 8.50
policy arguments for duty 4.26
proximity 4.22, 4.23
warn, duty to *see* warn, duty to

Index

New Zealand
  privilege 16.43
non-disclosure
  conciliation privilege 16.07
  generally 16.01
  Human Rights Act 1998 16.02
  legal advice privilege *see* legal advice privilege
  legal professional privilege *see* legal professional privilege
  privilege *see* conciliation privilege; legal advice privilege; legal professional privilege; privilege; public interest immunity
  self-incrimination, privilege against 16.06
  statutory inadmissibility 16.02–16.04
    compulsion, information obtained under 16.03, 16.04
    Human Rights Act 1998 16.02
non-sensitive information
  meaning 1.02
  personal information 1.02
Norwich Pharmacal jurisdiction 14.03 *see also* discovery proceedings
nurses 1.25
  iniquity, disclosure of 11.17
  public interest defence
    codes of ethics 11.17
    detection of completed crimes 11.36
  warn, duty to 20.19
Nursing and Midwifery Council
  codes of ethics 3.47, 11.17
  public interest defence 11.17

occupational health practitioners
  disclosure to employer 21.04–21.07
  reporting 3.36
offences *see* criminal offences
Office of Communications (OFCOM) 9.20
official secrets 1.12, 3.38, 14.54
ombudsmen 9.06
open court principle 3.13
open justice 17.26–17.29
oral examination 3.38
Organisation for Economic Co-operation and Development (OECD) 3.52, 3.53
ownership
  agency relationships 19.06–19.08
  medical records 19.08, 19.09
  personal information 19.04
  physical record 19.03
  self-employed professionals, records of 19.10

partnerships 21.37–21.39
patent agents
  privilege 16.42
pathology reports 19.08
patient records
  attitudes to disclosure of 2.28
  technology 2.04
PCC *see* Press Complaints Commission
peace and enjoyment, contracts to provide 8.47
pedigree information 19.105, 19.106
personal information 1.01–1.05
  about individual, information 1.04, 1.05
  attitudes of public to disclosure of 2.27, 2.28
  black market 2.13
  breach of fiduciary duty 5.80–5.83
  definition 1.02, 1.03
  disclosure to client 19.04
  doctors 1.04
  existence, manner of 1.03
  identifiable, who is 1.05
  inadvertent disclosure 2.25
  individual, information about 1.02
  intentional disclosure causing distress 4.31, 4.32
  legal definition 1.03
  natural person 1.02
  non-sensitive information 1.02
  ownership 19.04
  prescribing doctor 1.04
  public trust in protection of 2.30, 2.31
  sensitive information 1.02
  small group, information about 1.04
  work communications 1.04
pharmacists 1.25, 11.17
  breach of confidence 5.26, 5.32, 5.38
  codes of ethics 11.17
  customer records, transfer of 5.56
  market research, sale of information for purposes of 5.32, 11.44
  public interest defence 11.17, 11.44
  stock-taking 5.38
photographs
  copyright 5.85
physical or bodily privacy
  meaning 1.14, 1.15
physical record
  ownership 19.03
physicians 1.25 *see also* doctors
police
  accidental disclosure 6.102
  drugs investigations 14.51
  excluded materials *see* excluded materials
  investigatory powers, regulation of 3.33
  malpractice 6.102
  Police and Criminal Evidence Act 1984 3.33
  powers
    production orders *see* production orders
    search warrants *see* search warrants
    terrorism 14.46–14.50
  proceeds of crime 14.53
  production orders *see* production orders

Index

police (*cont.*):
  search warrants *see* search warrants
  seizure 14.35–14.40
  special procedure materials *see* special procedure materials
  surveillance by 3.33
  terrorism investigations 14.46–14.50
    account monitoring 14.50
    definition of investigations 14.46
    search and seizure 14.46–14.49
police doctors, disclosure by 21.12
power of attorney 12.09
  consent 13.11
Press Complaints Commission
  anticipated breaches 9.16
  Calcutt Committee 9.15, 9.16
  challenging adjudication 9.15
  Code 3.08, 9.10
    adjudication 9.09
    anticipated breaches 9.15
    HRA 1998, impact of 9.09
    ratification 9.09
  conciliation 9.08
  constitution 9.08
  formal adjudication 9.08
    challenging 9.15
    Code of Practice 9.09
    printing 9.08, 9.16
  inconsistency 9.16
  membership 9.08
  powers 9.08, 9.09
  privacy
    adjudications 9.11, 9.12
    breach of code 9.13
    code 9.10
    complaints 9.11
  public interest 9.15
  shortcomings 9.14–9.16
  stop publication, no power to 9.16
pre-trial disclosure
  accidental disclosure 6.108–6.110
  banking 14.04, 14.10
  bars to orders for 14.05, 14.06
  Civil Procedure Rules 14.05, 14.06, 14.08, 14.11, 14.14
  client but not professional is litigant 14.08–14.12
    banking 14.10
    Civil Procedure Rules 14.08, 14.11
    medical records 14.09
  compulsory 14.02–14.14
    banking 14.04, 14.10
    bars to orders for 14.05, 14.06
    Civil Procedure Rules 14.05, 14.06, 14.08, 14.11
    client but not professional is litigant 14.08–14.12
    confidential documents 14.07
    data protection 14.04
    family proceedings 14.04
    infertility treatment 14.04
    legislation requiring disclosure 14.04
    'likely to support' case 14.06
    medical records 14.04, 14.09
    necessary disclosure 14.05, 14.06
    neither professional not client is litigant 14.02–14.07
    Norwich Pharmacal jurisdiction 14.03
    privileged documents 14.05
    proportionality 14.06, 14.07
    public interest immunity 14.05
  confidential documents 14.07
  data protection 14.04
  family proceedings 14.04
  infertility treatment 14.04
  legislation requiring 14.04
  'likely to support' case 14.06
  medical records 14.04, 14.09
  necessary disclosure 14.05, 14.06
  neither professional nor client is litigant 14.02–14.07
    banking 14.04
    Civil Procedure Rules 14.04
  neither professional not client is litigant
    confidential documents 14.07
    data protection 14.04
    family proceedings 14.04
    infertility treatment 14.04
    medical records 14.04
    necessary disclosure 14.05, 14.06
    Norwich Pharmacal jurisdiction 14.03
    privileged documents 14.05
    proportionality 14.06, 14.07
    public interest immunity 14.05
  Norwich Pharmacal jurisdiction 14.03
  privileged documents 14.05
  professional, litigation against 14.13, 14.14
  proportionality 14.06, 14.07
  public interest immunity 14.05
previous convictions *see also* **criminal records**
  defamation 5.18
priests
  breach of confidence 5.27
prison
  chaplain, public interest defence of 11.25
  doctors 21.12, 21.13
prisoners
  coercive statutory disclosure 10.14
  HIV/AIDS 11.59
  legal professional privilege 10.14

791

Index

privacy *see also* private and family life, respect for
   access privacy 1.14
   anonymity 1.14
   aspects 1.14
   associational 1.14
   attentional 1.14
   attitude of public to 2.30
   autonomy 1.36
   communications 1.14
   confidentiality and 1.06, 1.44
   control definition 1.09, 1.10
   data-sharing 2.17
   decisional 1.14
   definition 1.07–1.11
   democracy 1.44
   dignity, protection of 1.12
   European Convention on Human Rights 1.07
   forms 1.14, 1.15
   informational privacy 1.14
   infringing right 1.11
   intimacy 1.14
   meaning 1.06
   personality, protection of 1.12
   philosophical perspective 1.07
   physical or bodily privacy 1.14, 1.15
   presuppositions 1.06
   proprietary 1.14
   relational 1.14
   right to 1.07
   'right to be left alone' 1.11
   secrecy 1.12, 1.13
   self, notion of 1.09
   social privacy 1.13
   sociological perspective 1.08
   spatial 1.14, 1.15
   territorial 1.14
   trust 1.06
   uses of term 1.08
   value 1.44
   Warren-Brandeis formulation 1.11
private and family life, respect for 3.03
   children 13.18, 19.111
   interception 6.28
   interference with 3.19–3.22
   minors 19.111
   public interest defence 11.06
   reporting restrictions 17.51
   whistleblowing 21.30
private hearings 17.30–17.37
   chambers, hearing in 17.30
   CPR Pt 39 17.32, 17.33
   European Convention on Human Rights 17.34
   secret, hearing in 17.31
privilege
   absolute right 1.22
   accountants 16.42
   advocates 16.42
   application of rule 1.22
   auditors 16.42
   Australia 16.43, 16.44
   bankers 16.42
   Canada 16.43
   categories 16.05
   clergy 16.42
   common law 16.05
   definition 16.05
   doctors 16.42
   Human Rights Act 1998 16.48–16.51
   iniquity
     legal professional privilege 16.35–16.37
     other privileges 16.38
   journalists 16.42
   lawyer-client privilege 16.16
   legal advice privilege 16.16–16.19
     confidentiality 16.18
     death of client 16.29
     derivative materials 16.22
     duration 16.28, 16.29
     innocence at stake, when 16.25–16.27
     lawyer-client privilege 16.16
     litigation privilege 16.16, 16.20, 16.21
     location of advice 16.18
     meaning 16.16
     non-lawyer professionals 16.19
     professional capacity 16.17
     scope 16.22–16.27
     what is not protected 16.23, 16.24
   legal professional *see* legal professional privilege
   licensed conveyancers 16.42
   litigation privilege 16.16
   litigators 16.42
   meaning 1.22
   New Zealand 16.43
   non-lawyers
     Australia 16.43, 16.44
     Canada 16.43
     common law jurisdictions 16.43
     English law 16.42, 16.45–16.47
     Human Rights Act 1998 16.48–16.51
     New Zealand 16.43
     United States 16.43
   operation 1.22
   patent agents 16.42
   principal privileges 16.05
   probate practitioners 16.42
   public interest defence 11.77–11.80
   public interest immunity *see* public interest immunity
   self-incrimination, privilege against 16.06
   trade mark agents 16.42
   United States 16.05, 16.43
   waiver 16.38

Index

privity of contract 4.03
probate practitioners
 privilege 16.42
probation 3.42
probation officers
 coercive statutory disclosure 10.03
 conciliation privilege 16.07
 employers, disclosure to 21.15
 search warrants 14.23
 warn, duty to 20.19
proceeds of crime 14.53
production of documents
 doctors 3.35
 Inland Revenue 3.35
production order 14.18
 drugs 14.51
 excluded material 14.25–14.28
  opposing order 14.30–14.32
  requirements of order 14.33, 14.34
 requirements of order 14.33, 14.34
 special procedure material 14.25–14.28
  opposing order 14.30–14.32
  requirements of order 14.33, 14.34
professionals *see also individual professions* e.g. accountants; dentists; doctors etc.
 attitudes to confidentiality 2.32, 2.33
 bankruptcy 5.55
 Bennion 1.23, 1.24
 change of employment 5.55–5.59
 characteristics 1.23, 1.24
 clients and 1.23–1.32
 codes of practice 2.22
 death 5.55–5.58
 definition 1.23
 discontinuance of activities 5.55–5.58
 disqualification 5.55
 employed 2.21–2.24
 employees 1.26
 examinee, duties owed to 1.29–1.32
 examples 1.25
 imprisonment 5.55
 meaning 1.23, 1.24
 misconduct 5.55
 non-professionals distinguished 1.26
 public sector 5.55
 retirement 5.55–5.59
 sale of business 5.55
 third parties 1.33
 trust on 2.31
 value of confidentiality to 1.53
 workplace pressures 2.25
prohibited steps order 13.21
property
 copyright as 5.84
 damage to 6.82
 doctors obtaining 5.80

information as 6.55
 intellectual 14.15
 interference with 14.79–14.81
 recklessly damaging 6.82
 search orders 14.15
proportionality
 European Convention on Human Rights 3.20–3.22
 conflicting Convention rights 3.26–3.32
proprietary privacy
 meaning 1.14
pseudonymized data
 Data Protection Act 1998 18.05
psychiatrists 1.25
 public interest defence 11.21
psychologists 1.25
 iniquity, disclosure of 11.18
 public interest defence 11.18, 11.67
psychotherapists
 prevention of harm to the person 11.24
 public interest defence 11.24
public authority
 Human Rights Act 1998 4.47, 4.48
 liability 3.09
public domain, information in
 breach of confidence 5.09–5.22
  approach of courts 5.11
  Article 8, impact of 5.13
  authentication of information 5.63
  codes of ethics 5.15
  commercial information 5.14
  criminal records 5.18
  defendant responsible for putting information into public domain 5.60
  determination 5.10
  general rule 5.59–5.63
  generally accessible information 5.12
  meaning 5.09
  mixed information 5.09
  open court, information disclosed in 5.18
  passing out of public domain, information 5.16, 5.17
  private life, respect for 5.13
  professionals 5.14, 5.15
  substantial number of people 5.11
 broadcasters 5.14
 codes of ethics 5.15
 commercial information 5.14
 criminal records 5.18
 determination 5.10
 duration 5.16–5.19
 generally accessible information 5.12
 Human Rights Act 1998 5.20–5.22
 injunctions 8.04
 mixed information 5.09
 open court, information disclosed in 5.18

Index

public domain, information in (*cont.*):
  passing out of public domain, information 5.16, 5.17
  private life, respect for 5.13
  professionals 5.14, 5.15
  substantial number of people 5.11
public figures
  breach of confidence 6.22–6.25
  Canada 6.22
  expectation of privacy 6.22, 6.24, 6.25
  interception
    breach of confidence 6.22–6.25
  involuntary 6.23
  meaning 6.22
  not of own doing, notoriety 6.23
  reasonable expectation of privacy 6.22, 6.24, 6.25
  United States 6.22, 6.23, 6.25
public hearing, interference with right to 3.24
public interest defence 11.01–11.83
  accountants 11.31
  advice before making disclosure 11.69
  alerting client
    ethical obligation 11.70
    legal obligation 11.71
  banking
    detection of completed crimes 11.32
    financial wrongdoing, prevention and exposure of 11.29
  barristers 11.16
  breach of contract 6.38
  cancer registries 13.53
  cause of action to which applies 11.02
  clergy 11.39, 11.40
  client, alerting
    ethics 11.70
    law 11.71
  codes of ethics 11.14–11.20
    barristers 11.16
    counsellors 11.20
    doctors 11.18
    nurses 11.17
    pharmacists 11.17
    psychologists 11.18
    social workers 11.19
    solicitors 11.15
  compelled disclosures 10.40
  copyright 11.82, 11.83
  counsellors 11.20
  Data Protection Act 1998 18.40
  detection of completed crimes 11.32–11.38
    banking 11.32
    doctors 11.33, 11.35
  detection of completed crimes
    non-lawyers 11.32–11.37
    nurses 11.36
    police 11.32
    social workers 11.34
    solicitors 11.38
  discretionary disclosure 11.01, 11.08
  doctors 11.66
    codes of ethics 11.18
    detection of completed crimes 11.33, 11.35
    drug reactions, adverse 13.52
    prevention of harm to the person 11.21–11.23
    research purposes, disclosure of information for 11.45
    secondary purposes, disclosure for 13.51, 13.52
  drug reactions, adverse 13.52
  excluded material 14.41, 14.42
  existence of obligation of confidentiality 11.07
  false image, correcting 11.10
  financial rewards 11.61
  financial wrongdoing, prevention and exposure of 11.26–11.31
    accountants 11.31
    banking 11.29
    human rights 11.30
    insurance fraud 11.30
    other professionals 11.28–11.31
    public funds, protection of 11.30
    social security fraud 11.30
    solicitors 11.26, 11.27
  future retention and use of information 11.68
  General Medical Council 11.18
  genetic information *see* genetic information
  healthcare professionals 11.17, 11.18
  HIV/AIDS 11.58, 11.59
  how much disclosed 11.66–11.68
  HRA 1998 11.13, 11.46
  illegally acquired information 11.75, 11.76
  improper motive 11.61
  iniquity, disclosure of 11.09–11.38
    balancing interests 11.11, 11.12
    barristers 11.16
    codes of ethics 11.14–11.20
    counsellors 11.20
    doctors 11.18
    false image, correcting 11.10
    healthcare professionals 11.17, 11.18
    HRA 1998 11.13
    meaning of iniquity 11.09
    nurses 11.17
    pharmacists 11.17
    professionals, disclosure by 11.11–11.13
    proportionality 11.13
    solicitors 11.15
  insurance fraud 11.30
  interceptors 11.75, 11.76
  justification 11.81

Index

public interest defence (*cont.*):
  limiting principle, whether 11.07, 11.08
  manner of disclosure 11.62–11.65
  meaning 11.03–11.06
  media 11.73, 11.74
  medical purposes 13.54
  mental state of professional 11.60, 11.61
  minor offences 11.25
  motive of professional 11.61
  nature 11.03–11.06
  nurses 11.17
    codes of ethics 11.17
    detection of completed crimes 11.36
  Nursing and Midwifery Council 11.17
  overriding obligation of confidentiality 11.08
  pharmacists 11.17
  physical evidence, incriminating 11.39, 11.40
    solicitors 11.39, 11.40
  predicting 11.06
  prevention of harm to the person
    balancing interests 11.23
    doctors 11.21–11.23
    European Convention on Human Rights 11.23, 11.25
    minor offences 11.25
    prison chaplain 11.25
    psychiatrists 11.21
    psychotherapists 11.24
    solicitors 11.24, 11.25
  prison chaplain 11.25
  private life, respect for 11.06
  privilege 11.77–11.80
  psychiatrists 11.21
  psychologists 11.18, 11.67
  psychotherapists 11.24
  public good 11.03, 11.04
  recipients 11.62–11.65
  research purposes, patient information used for 11.45
  responsible authorities, disclosure to 11.63
  scope of duty of confidentiality 11.07
  social security fraud 11.30
  social workers 11.19
    codes of ethics 11.19
    detection of completed crimes 11.34
  solicitors
    codes of ethics 11.15, 11.38
    detection of completed crimes 11.38
    financial wrongdoing, prevention and exposure of 11.26, 11.27
  solicitors
    physical evidence, incriminating 11.39, 11.40
    prevention of harm to the person 11.24, 11.25

  special procedure material 14.41, 14.42
  strangers 11.75, 11.76
  telephone tapping 11.75
  third parties 11.72–11.76
    protection 11.49–11.52
  tort 11.81
  vagueness 11.05, 11.06
  whistleblowing compared 21.27
  without iniquity, disclosure 11.41–11.52
    balancing interests 11.41, 11.42
    Human Rights Act 1998 11.46
    indirect benefit to client 11.43
    legal confidentiality 11.47, 11.48
    medical confidentiality 11.44, 11.45
    research purposes, patient information used for 11.45
    third party protection 11.49–11.52
public interest disclosures *see* whistleblowing
public interest immunity 16.52–16.64
  balancing operation 16.62
  civil proceedings 16.61, 16.62
  class claims
    contents claims distinguished 16.56
    judicial attitude 16.58
    survival 16.57
  contents claims 16.56
  court decision 16.55
  criminal proceedings 16.63, 16.64
  defence, acquisition of information by 14.127
  effect 16.52
  establish, what professionals must 16.60
  general principles 16.52–16.55
  pre-trial disclosure 14.05
  prima facie immune classes 16.59
public records
  death of client 5.51
publications, disclosure in 13.55
publicity restriction 17.26–17.51
  anonymity orders 17.38–17.43
    non-parties 17.38–17.41
    non-witnesses 17.40
    parties 17.42, 17.43
    soliciting information, restraining 17.41
    witnesses 17.38, 17.39
  defamation 5.18
  disclosure of confidential information to court 17.26, 17.27
  open justice 17.26–17.29
    disclosure of confidential information to court 17.26, 17.27
    rationale 17.28, 17.29
  private hearings 17.30–17.37
    chambers, hearing in 17.30
    CPR Pt 39 17.32, 17.33
    secret, hearing in 17.31
  reporting restrictions 17.44–17.51

publicity restriction (*cont.*):
  reporting restrictions
    children 17.45
    European Convention on Human Rights
      17.50, 17.51
    freedom of expression 17.50, 17.51
    indecent matter 17.47
    medical details 17.47
    open court, proceedings in 17.46–17.49
    permanent orders 17.49
    prejudicing administration of justice 17.48
    private and family life, respect for 17.51
    private proceedings 17.44, 17.45
    statutory reporting restrictions
      17.47–17.49
pupils
  contraceptive advice from teachers 2.24

***quia timet* injunctions** 8.03 *see also* injunctions

real estate agents
  money laundering 10.25
references
  subject access rights 19.35–19.39
Regulation of Investigatory Powers Act 2000
  covert surveillance
    regulated forms of surveillance
      14.83–14.85
    sanctions 14.86, 14.87
  criminal offences 6.64–6.66
    consent to prosecution from DPP 6.66
    penalties 6.66
    private telecommunications system,
      intercepting communication on course
      of transmission through 6.65, 7.43
    public postal service or public telecommuni-
      cations system, interception of com-
      munication in course of transmission
      through 6.64
relational privacy
  meaning 1.14
relatives
  consent to disclosure to 13.57, 13.58
    European Convention on Human Rights
      17.34
  information provided by 5.29
religion, freedom of 3.16
remedies
  account of profits 8.71–8.73
  after-the-event
    account of profits 8.71–8.73
    breach of confidence 8.78, 8.79
  after-the-event
    constructive trusts 8.76, 8.77
    damages *see* damages
    delivery up 8.74, 8.75
    destruction of items 8.74, 8.75
    monetary awards *see* damages; monetary awards
  breach of confidence 8.78, 8.79
  constructive trusts 8.76–8.79
  damages *see* damages
  data protection compliance order 8.26, 8.27
  delivery up 8.74, 8.75
  destruction of items 8.74, 8.75
  injunctions *see* injunctions; interim injunctions
  monetary awards *see* damages; monetary
    awards
  prior restraint
    data protection compliance order 8.26,
      8.27
    injunctions *see* injunctions; interim injunc-
      tions
reporting
  compelled disclosures 3.36
  doctors 3.36
  food poisoning 3.36
  money-laundering 3.36, 3.37
  occupational health practitioners 3.36
  restrictions *see* reporting restrictions
  terrorism 3.36
reporting restrictions 17.44–17.51
  children 17.45, 17.51
  European Convention on Human Rights
    17.50, 17.51
  freedom of expression 17.50, 17.51
  indecent matter 17.47
  medical details 17.47
  open court, proceedings in 17.46–17.49
    inherent power to prevent publicity 17.46
    statutory reporting restrictions
      17.47–17.49
  permanent 17.49
  prejudicing administration of justice 17.48
  private and family life, respect for 17.51
  private proceedings 17.44, 17.45
repudiation of contract
  intentional disclosure 4.15
reputation, injury to 8.60–8.63
research
  breach of confidence where information used
    for 5.29, 5.35
  consent to disclosure for purposes of 13.48
  Data Protection Act 1998 exemption 18.42,
    18.43
retirement
  professionals 5.55–5.59
road traffic offences
  coercive statutory disclosure 10.06

sale of business
  professionals 5.55
SARs *see* subject access rights

Index

scanning 2.07, 2.09
school teachers *see* teachers
Scotland
  consent 13.11
search and seizure warrant 14.18
search orders 14.15–14.17 *see also* seizure
  applicant 14.16
  contents 14.16
  documents in support 14.17
  effect 14.16
  intellectual property 14.15
  purpose 14.15
  requirements for grant 14.17
search warrants 14.19–14.35, 14.61
  clergy 14.23
  conditions 14.19, 14.20
  doctors 14.23
  espionage 14.55
  excluded material 14.21, 14.23, 14.24, 14.29
    opposing application 14.30–14.32
  financial services investigations 14.56
  legal professional privilege 14.23
  legally privileged material 14.22, 14.23, 14.24
  opposing application 14.30–14.32
  probation officers 14.23
  proceeds of crime 14.53
  serious arrestable offence 14.19
  social workers 14.23
  special procedure material 14.21, 14.23, 14.29
    opposing application 14.30–14.32
  tax investigations 14.65–14.67
  teachers 14.23
secrecy
  corporations 1.12
  intentional concealment 1.13
  meaning 1.12
  privacy 1.12, 1.13
  public sphere 1.12
secret, hearing in 17.31
secret intelligence services
  covert surveillance 14.78–14.82
seizure
  drugs investigations 14.51
  legal professional privilege 14.37–14.40
  legally privileged material 14.37, 14.38
  police 14.35–14.40
  powers 14.35–14.40, 14.61
  tax investigations 14.65–14.67
self-defence *see* self-interest, disclosure motivated by
self-employment 1.26
self-incrimination
  privilege against 16.06
  subject access rights 19.46

self-interest, disclosure motivated by 12.23–12.41
  accountants 12.30
  affirmative breach of confidentiality
    defamation 12.37
    disputes 12.37–12.38
    extent of disclosure 12.39, 12.40
    fee recovery 12.34–12.36
    springboard doctrine 12.37, 12.38
    withdrawal of services 12.41
  banking 12.32
  civil actions against lawyers 12.27–12.29
  defamation 12.37
  defensive breach of confidentiality 12.23–12.29
  disciplinary action against lawyers 12.23–12.26
    Law Society guidance 12.23
  doctors 12.30, 12.31, 12.32, 12.33
  fee recovery 12.34–12.36
    lawyers 12.35, 12.36
    non-lawyers 12.34
  implied waiver 12.33
  non-lawyers, proceedings against 12.30–12.33
  springboard doctrine 12.37, 12.38
  withdrawal of services 12.41
self-regulation 1.26
sensitive information *see also* sensitive personal data
  breach of confidence 5.29
  meaning 1.02
  personal information 1.02
  purpose for which information used 1.02
sensitive personal data
  conditions for processing 18.25–18.27
    additional conditions 18.25–18.27
    deliberately taken steps by client 18.25
    explicit consent 18.25
  Data Protection Act 1998
    additional conditions 18.25–18.27
    conditions for processing 18.25–18.27
    definition 18.23, 18.24
    deliberately taken steps by client 18.25, 18.26
    examples 18.24
    explicit consent 18.25
    First Data Protection Principle 18.09, 18.23–18.28
    grounds 18.27
    Human Rights Act 1998 18.28
    public domain defence 18.26
    purposes of processing 18.27
    substantial public interest 18.27
  definition 18.23, 18.24
  examples 18.24

Index

Serious Fraud Office 14.52, 14.58–14.60
  collateral use of documents 17.09
  establishment 14.58
  failure to comply with request 14.60
  restrictions on powers 14.59, 14.60
sexual abuse
  best interests of client, disclosure in 12.11
  children 12.11
sexual conduct
  breach of confidence 5.04
sexual orientation
  breach of confidence 5.04
sexually transmitted diseases 3.42
  consent to disclose 13.04
silence
  consent 13.36, 13.37
social privacy 1.13
social security fraud
  public interest defence 11.30
social services 3.48
  'soft law' 3.48, 3.49
social work records *see also* social workers
  disclosure to the client 19.101
  parental access 19.101
  subject access rights 19.22, 19.41
social workers 1.25 *see also* social work records
  codes of ethics 11.19
  coercive statutory disclosure 10.02
  conciliation privilege 16.07
  employer, disclosure to 21.10, 21.11
  iniquity, disclosure of 11.19
  intentional disclosure
    contract 4.02
  public interest defence
    codes of ethics 11.19
    detection of completed crimes 11.34
  search warrants 14.23
  warn, duty to 20.19
'soft law' 3.48–3.51
  examples 3.48
  Information Commissioner's guidance 3.50, 3.51
  international dimension 3.53
  legal status 3.49
  National Health Service 3.48
  public sector guidance 3.48, 3.49
  social services 3.48, 3.49
software bugs 2.07
solicitors 1.25
  accidental disclosure 6.92, 6.93, 6.94
  agency 19.07
  breach of confidence 6.94
  breach of fiduciary duty 5.65, 6.94
  Chinese walls 6.94
  civil claims against 12.27–12.29
  codes of ethics 3.47

  coercive statutory disclosure 10.02, 10.03
  conflicts of interest 6.92, 6.93
  consent 13.40
  destruction of client file 5.56
  detection of completed crimes 11.38
  disciplinary proceedings
    common law 12.24
    Law Society guidance 12.23
    self-interest, disclosure in 12.23–12.25
  employers, disclosure to 21.08
  financial wrongdoing, prevention and exposure of 11.26, 11.27
  iniquity, disclosure of 11.15
  insurance company 10.03
  legal advice privilege *see* legal advice privilege
  money laundering 10.25
  physical evidence of a crime, handing over 11.39, 11.40
  prevention of harm to the person 11.24
  public interest defence
    codes of ethics 11.15
    detection of completed crimes 11.38
    financial wrongdoing, prevention and exposure of 11.26, 11.27
    physical evidence, incriminating 11.39, 11.40
    prevention of harm to the person 11.24, 11.25
  retention of papers by 5.56
  self-interest, disclosure in
    civil claims 12.27–12.29
    disciplinary proceedings 12.23–12.25
  terms of engagement 5.56
  therapeutic privilege 17.04
  transfer of client file 5.56
  warn, duty to 20.19, 20.20
sound data
  Data Protection Act 1998 18.05
spatial privacy
  meaning 1.14, 1.15
special education needs, children with 3.42, 13.14, 13.17, 19.45
special procedure material
  production order 14.25–14.28
  public interest defence 14.41, 14.42
  search warrants 14.21, 14.23, 14.29
    opposing application 14.30–14.32
  warning client 14.43, 14.44
spent convictions
  defamation 4.36
springboard doctrine 12.37, 12.38
statutory authority
  voluntary disclosure 12.14–12.22
    Anti-terrorism, Crime and Security Act 2001 12.18–12.22
    Crime and Disorder Act 1998 12.15–12.17
    generally 12.14

Index

stockbrokers 1.25
  breach of fiduciary duty 5.65
strangers 1.33
  breach of confidence 7.25–7.30
    client v stranger 7.25–7.27
    defences 7.31–7.34
    liability of stranger 7.27
    professional v stranger 7.29, 7.30
    traditional position 7.25
  breach of fiduciary duty 7.35
  breach of statutory duty 7.43
  conspiracy 7.43
  conversion 7.42
  copyright 7.43, 7.44
  inducing breach of contract 7.43
  public interest defence 11.75, 11.76
  tort 7.36–7.43
subject access rights 3.45, 10.20, 18.53, 19.21–19.47
  application 19.21
  automated-decision making 19.24
  children 19.72–19.75
  conditional access, no 19.25
  confidential references 19.35–19.38
  court, data supplied to 19.42
  court orders prohibiting 19.26
  damaging files 19.22
  Data Protection Act 1998 3.45, 19.21–19.47
  date 19.24
  disproportionate effort 19.24
  dual records 19.22
  educational records 19.22, 19.43–19.45
  embryology information 19.40
  excluded matter 19.30, 19.31
  exemptions 19.28–19.47
    confidential references 19.35–19.38
    court, data supplied to 19.42
    educational records 19.43–19.45
    embryology information 19.40
    excluded matter 19.30, 19.31
    fertilization information 19.40
    legal professional privilege 19.47
    medical data 19.39
    national security 19.30, 19.31
    references 19.35–19.39
    repeat requests 19.29
  exemptions
    self-incrimination 19.46
    social work records 19.41
    third parties 19.32–19.34
  failure to supply 19.27
  fees 19.21
  fertilization information 19.40
  impossibility 19.24
  legal professional privilege 19.47
  legislation overriding DPA 19.26
  medical data 19.39
  minors 19.72–19.75
  miscomprehension 19.25
  national security 19.30, 19.31
  nature 19.21
  non-comprehension 19.25
  policy 19.21
  references 19.35–19.39
  relationship to other law 19.26
  repeat requests 19.29
  request 19.21
  sanctions 19.27
  scope 19.22, 19.23
  self-incrimination 19.46
  social work records 19.22, 19.41
  special education needs, children with 19.45
  specific rights 19.24
  third parties 19.32–19.34
  unpaid fees 19.25
  unstructured health records 19.22
  unstructured manual files 19.23
subpoena duces tecum 15.02, 15.03
  setting aside 15.05–15.07
support staff
  disclosure to 13.45
surgeons 1.25
  breach of confidence 5.44
surveillance
  covert *see* covert surveillance
  devices 2.09
  police, by 3.33

tax advisers
  money laundering 10.25
tax investigations 14.62–14.68
  advance notice of application for production 14.63
  compliance with order for production 14.64
  Customs and Excise 14.68
  production procedure 14.62, 14.63
  search of premises 14.65
  seizure powers 14.65
  Special Compliance Office 14.62
taxation
  Data Protection Act 1998 18.44, 18.45
teachers 1.25
  contraceptive advice to pupils 2.24
  employer, disclosure to 21.09
  intentional disclosure
    contract 4.02
  warn, duty to 20.19, 20.21
technology
  bugging 2.10
  change in 2.01–2.33
  computers 2.04–2.10
  hacking, computer 2.06, 2.07

Index

technology (cont.):
  interception of data 2.06–2.10
  microfilm 2.04
  networked computers 2.06
  new 2.04–2.10
  patient records 2.04
  recording of information, increased 2.02, 2.03
  scanning 2.07, 2.09
  security 2.05–2.10
  software bugs 2.07
  surveillance devices 2.09
  telephone tapping 2.09
  viruses 2.07
telephone tapping 2.09 *see also* covert surveillance
  public interest defence 11.75
territorial privacy
  meaning 1.14
terrorism
  coercive statutory disclosure 10.02, 10.13
  money laundering 10.24, 10.25
  police investigations 14.46–14.50
    definition of investigation 14.46
    search and seizure 14.46–14.49
  reporting 3.36
  search, police power of 14.46–14.49
  seizure, police power of 14.46–14.49
  tipping off offences 10.17
theft 6.68–6.74
  confidential information 6.70, 6.71
  criminal offences
    strangers, prosecuting 6.84
  deception 6.73, 6.74
  definition 6.68
    borrowing 6.69
  electricity abstraction 6.72
  examination papers 6.70
  intention to permanently deprive 6.68, 6.70
  strangers, prosecuting 6.85
therapeutic privilege 17.04
third parties
  breach of confidence 7.20–7.34
    accessory liability of innocent third party 7.22
    anonymous information 7.34
  breach of confidence
    bona fide purchaser for value defence 7.31, 7.32
    client v third party 7.20–7.22
    defences 7.31–7.34
    injunctions 7.23, 7.24
    public domain, information in 7.33
  breach of fiduciary duty 7.35
  breach of statutory duty 7.43
  client v third party
    breach of confidence 7.20–7.22

  breach of fiduciary duty 7.35
  tort 7.36–7.39
  conspiracy 7.39, 7.43
  conversion 7.42
  copyright 7.43, 7.44
  defamation 7.38
  duty to warn *see* warn, duty to
  engagement of professional by 1.28
  Freedom of Information Act 2000 18.54–18.58
    enforcement 18.55, 18.56
    kinds of exemption 18.54
    personal information exemptions 18.57
    protecting interests of data subject 18.58
  inducement of breach of contract 7.43
  inducing breach of contract 7.37
  interception of communications 7.43
  interference with contractual relations 7.36
  meaning 1.33, 7.20
  'need to know' information 2.11
  pressure for disclosure to 2.11–2.20
  professional v third party 7.42, 7.43
  Protection from Harassment Act 1997 7.40–7.41
  subject access rights to data relating to 19.32–19.34
  tort 7.36–7.43
    client v third party 7.36–7.39
    conspiracy 7.39, 7.43
    conversion 7.42
    defamation 7.38
    inducement of breach of contract 7.43
    inducing breach of equitable obligation 7.37
    interference with contractual relations 7.36
  warn, duty to *see* warn, duty to
tort
  breach of confidence 4.60
  breach of statutory duty 4.45–4.52
    see also breach of statutory duty
  compelled disclosures 10.01
  conspiracy 6.29, 6.42
  conversion 6.42
  deceit 6.52
  distress, intentional infliction of 4.29–4.33
    elements 4.29, 4.30
    mental distress 4.33
    personal information 4.31, 4.32
    presence of claimant 4.32
    truth of information 4.32
  infringement of privacy 4.53–4.59
    characteristics 4.53
    failed bills and proposals 4.58
    HRA 1998 4.59
    pre-HRA English law 4.57
    United States 4.54–4.56

Index

tort (*cont.*):
  injurious falsehood 4.41, 4.42
  intentional disclosure 4.19–4.60
    breach of confidence 4.60
    breach of statutory duty 4.45–4.52
      see also breach of statutory duty
    conspiracy 4.43–4.44
    defamation 4.34–4.40
      see also defamation
    distress, intentional infliction of 4.29–4.33
    infringement of privacy 4.53–4.59
    injurious falsehood 4.41, 4.42
    negligence 4.20–4.28
      see also negligence
  interception
    client v interceptor 6.29
    conspiracy 6.29, 6.42, 6.48, 6.49
    conversion 6.42, 6.44, 6.50, 6.51
    deceit 6.52
    defamation 6.29
    distress, intentional infliction of 6.29
    interference with trade 6.48, 6.49
    malicious falsehood 6.29
    professional v interceptor 6.48–6.52
    trespass 6.44, 6.50, 6.51
  malicious falsehood 6.29
  mental distress 8.48–8.50
  monetary awards 8.28
  negligence *see* negligence
  public interest defence 11.81
  strangers 7.36–7.43
  third party 7.36–7.43
  trespass 6.44, 6.50, 6.51
tracing 7.02–7.19
  discovery proceedings *see* discovery proceedings
  generally 7.01
  meaning 7.02
  problem of 7.02
trade mark agents
  privilege 16.42
trade secrets
  breach of confidence 5.04, 5.29, 6.91
  confidentiality 1.18
training
  consent to disclosure for purposes of 13.48
trans-border data flows 18.35, 18.36
trespass 6.44
  interceptor 6.50, 6.51
trials *see also* publicity restriction
  attitude of courts 15.15
  documentary evidence 15.02–15.12
    civil proceedings 15.02, 15.03
    criminal proceedings 15.04
    handling confidential documents 15.10, 15.11

  obtaining confidential documents for trial 15.02–15.12
  setting aside summons/subpoena 15.05–15.07
  significance of confidential information 15.08, 15.09
  subpoena duces tecum 15.02, 15.03
  summons 15.01, 15.02
  unfairly obtained documents 15.12
  witness summons 15.02, 15.05–15.07
  expert witnesses 15.24–15.30
    calling opponent's expert to give evidence 15.25–15.30
    confidentiality of reports 15.24
  handling confidential documents 15.10, 15.11
    unlawfully obtained documents 15.12
  judicial discretion 15.15–15.21
    attitude of courts 15.15, 15.16
  mislead court, duty not to 14.31–14.35
    criminal record of client 15.34
    knowingly giving false evidence 15.31, 15.32
    security of court/members 15.35
    unwittingly giving false evidence 15.33
  oral evidence 14.13–14.30
    attitude of courts 15.15, 15.16
    civil proceedings 15.17
    consequences of disclosure 15.22, 15.23
    criminal proceedings 15.18, 15.19
    judicial discretion 15.15–15.21
    obligation to disclose confidential personal information 15.13, 15.14
    procedure 15.20, 15.21
  pre-trial disclosure *see* pre-trial disclosure
  public authority disclosure of confidential
    general position 15.36, 15.37
    information to court 14.36–14.40
    insolvency 15.38–15.40
  security of court/members 15.35
  setting aside summons/subpoena 15.05–15.07
  subpoena duces tecum 15.02, 15.03
    setting aside 15.05–15.07
  unfairly obtained documents 15.12
  unlawfully obtained documents 15.12
  witness summons 15.02
    setting aside 15.05–15.07
tribunals 15.41–15.48
  medical reports 15.48
  oral evidence by professional of confidential matters 15.44
  pre-hearing disclosure by professional of confidential matters 15.41–15.43
  protection of confidential personal information 15.45–15.47
  safeguards 15.48

Index

trivial information
  breach of confidence 5.08
  intentional disclosure
    contract 4.06
trusts
  constructive 8.76–8.79

undue influence
  consent 13.22
  doctors 19.15
unfair dismissal
  whistleblowing 21.24
unintentional disclosure 6.01–6.111
  accidental disclosure *see* accidental disclosure
  interception *see* interception; interceptor
United States
  breach of statutory duty 4.51
  HIV/AIDS, duty to warn of 20.28–20.32
  infringement of privacy 4.54–4.56
  privilege 16.05, 16.43
  public figures 6.22, 6.23, 6.25
  waiver 13.01, 13.64
university lecturers 1.25
unpaid fees
  disclosure to the client and 19.03
  subject access rights 19.25

venereal disease 3.42
viruses
  computers 2.07
visual data
  Data Protection Act 1998 18.05
voluntary disclosure
  best interests of clients, disclosure in 12.02–12.13
    see also best interests of client, disclosure in
  emergencies 12.08
  self-interest, disclosure motivated by 12.23–12.41
    see also self-interest, disclosure in
  statutory authority 12.14
  statutory authority
    Anti-terrorism, Crime and Security Act 2001 12.18–12.22
    Crime and Disorder Act 1998 12.15–12.17
    generally 12.14
vulnerable, protection of
  confidentiality 1.45

waiver 13.63–13.67
  emergence of defence of 13.01
  English cases 13.63–13.67
  legal professional privilege
    express waiver 16.31–16.33
    imputed 16.34
  prerequisites 13.67

press intrusion 13.66
previous disclosures 13.63
privilege 16.38
public domain 13.64, 13.65
tolerance of disclosure by others 13.63
United States 13.01, 13.64
voluntary conduct 13.63
warn, duty to 20.01–20.41
  AIDS/HIV 20.28–20.36
  barristers 20.19, 20.20
  breach of duty 20.22
  causation 20.22
    HIV/AIDS 20.36
  child abuse 20.23–20.26
    policy 20.25, 20.26
    proximity 20.24
  clergy 20.19
  counsellors 20.19
  doctors 20.19
  elder abuse 20.23, 20.27
  fraud 20.40, 20.41
  genetic information 20.37–20.39
    blood relatives 20.37, 20.38
    patient of risk to blood relatives, warning 20.39
    sexual partners 20.37, 20.38
  HIV/AIDS 20.28–20.36
    causation 20.36
    English law 20.33–20.36
    patient, warning 20.35
    policy 20.34
    proximity 20.33
    United States law 20.28–20.32
  HRA 1998 20.05
  liability 20.22
  mental health professionals 20.07–20.20
  non-violent crime 20.40, 20.41
  nurses 20.19
  policy 20.20, 20.21
    HIV/AIDS 20.34
    risk of bodily harm 20.12–20.15
  private law duty 20.06–20.41
    risk of bodily harm 20.07–20.22
  probation officers 20.19
  proximity requirement 20.09–20.11, 20.33
  public law duty 20.01–20.05
    circumstances 20.04
    HRA 1998 20.05
  risk of bodily harm 20.07–20.22
    policy 20.12–20.15
    sufficient proximity 20.09–20.11
    Tarasoff case 20.07–20.20
  social workers 20.19
  solicitors 20.19, 20.20
  Tarasoff case 20.07–20.20
  teachers 20.19, 20.21

Index

warrant
  data interception 14.92–14.95
  search 14.19–14.35
  see also search warrants
whistleblowing 21.23–21.30
  advice 21.28
  attitudes to 21.23
  categories of information recipient 21.25
  detriment 21.24
  dismissal 21.24
  European Convention on Human Rights 21.29, 21.30
  freedom of expression 21.29, 21.30
  legal advice before 21.28
  meaning 21.23
  overriding protection 21.23
  private and family life, respect for 21.30
  protection of workers 21.23, 21.24–21.26
  public interest defence compared 21.27
  qualifying disclosures 21.24, 21.25
  reasonableness of disclosure 21.26
  recipient of information 21.25, 21.26
  unfair dismissal 21.24
  workers 21.24
witness statements 17.25
witness summons 15.02
  setting aside 15.05–15.07
Woolf guidelines 8.18–8.24

x-rays 19.08